D0212345

Practical Business Math Procedures

The McGraw-Hill/Irwin Series in Operations and Decision Sciences

Supply Chain Management

Benton
Purchasing and Supply Chain Management
Second Edition

Burt, Petcavage, and Pinkerton
Supply Management
Eighth Edition

Bowersox, Closs, and Cooper
Supply Chain Logistics Management
Fourth Edition

Johnson, Leenders, and Flynn
Purchasing and Supply Management
Fourteenth Edition

Simchi-Levi, Kaminsky, and Simchi-Levi
Designing and Managing the Supply Chain: Concepts, Strategies, Case Studies
Third Edition

Project Management

Brown and Hyer
Managing Projects: A Team-Based Approach
Second Edition

Larson and Gray
Project Management: The Managerial Process
Fifth Edition

Service Operations Management

Fitzsimmons and Fitzsimmons
Service Management: Operations, Strategy, Information Technology
Seventh Edition

Management Science

Hillier and Hillier
Introduction to Management Science: A Modeling and Case Studies Approach with Spreadsheets
Fourth Edition

Stevenson and Ozgur
Introduction to Management Science with Spreadsheets
First Edition

Manufacturing Control Systems

Jacobs, Berry, Whybark, and Vollmann
Manufacturing Planning & Control for Supply Chain Management
Sixth Edition

Business Research Methods

Cooper-Schindler
Business Research Methods
Eleventh Edition

Business Forecasting

Wilson, Keating, and John Galt Solutions, Inc.
Business Forecasting
Sixth Edition

Linear Statistics and Regression

Kutner, Nachtsheim, and Neter
Applied Linear Regression Models
Fourth Edition

Business Systems Dynamics

Sterman
Business Dynamics: Systems Thinking and Modeling for a Complex World
First Edition

Operations Management

Cachon and Terwiesch
Matching Supply with Demand: An Introduction to Operations Management
Third Edition

Finch
Interactive Models for Operations and Supply Chain Management
First Edition

Jacobs and Chase
Operations and Supply Chain Management: The Core
Third Edition

Jacobs and Chase
Operations and Supply Chain Management
Fourteenth Edition

Jacobs and Whybark
Why ERP? A Primer on SAP Implementation
First Edition

Schroeder, Goldstein, and Rungtusanatham
Operations Management in the Supply Chain: Decisions and Cases
Sixth Edition

Stevenson
Operations Management
Eleventh Edition

Swink, Melnyk, Cooper, and Hartley
Managing Operations across the Supply Chain
First Edition

Product Design

Ulrich and Eppinger
Product Design and Development
Fifth Edition

Business Math

Slater/Wittry
Practical Business Math Procedures
Twelfth Edition

Slater/Wittry
Practical Business Math Procedures, Brief Edition
Eleventh Edition

Slater/Wittry
Math for Business and Finance: An Algebraic Approach
First Edition

Business Statistics

Bowerman, O'Connell, Murphree, and Orris
Essentials of Business Statistics
Fourth Edition

Bowerman, O'Connell, and Murphree
Business Statistics in Practice
Sixth Edition

Doane and Seward
Applied Statistics in Business and Economics
Fourth Edition

Jaggia and Kelly
Business Statistics: Communicating with Numbers
First Edition

Lind, Marchal, and Wathen
Basic Statistics for Business and Economics
Eighth Edition

Lind, Marchal, and Wathen
Statistical Techniques in Business and Economics
Fifteenth Edition

Practical Business Math Procedures

Twelfth Edition

JEFFREY SLATER

North Shore Community College
Danvers, Massachusetts

SHARON M. WITTRY

Pikes Peak Community College
Colorado Springs, Colorado

Mc Graw Hill Education

PRACTICAL BUSINESS MATH PROCEDURES, TWELFTH EDITION

Published by McGraw-Hill Education, 2 Penn Plaza, New York, NY 10121. Copyright © 2017 by McGraw-Hill Education. All rights reserved. Printed in the United States of America. Previous editions © 2014, 2011, 2008, and 2006. No part of this publication may be reproduced or distributed in any form or by any means, or stored in a database or retrieval system, without the prior written consent of McGraw-Hill Education, including, but not limited to, in any network or other electronic storage or transmission, or broadcast for distance learning.

Some ancillaries, including electronic and print components, may not be available to customers outside the United States.

This book is printed on acid-free paper.

6 7 8 9 LWI 21 20 19

ISBN 978-1-259-54055-4 (student edition)
MHID 1-259-54055-3 (student edition)

ISBN 978-1-259-65738-2 (teacher's edition)
MHID 1-259-65738-8 (teacher's edition)

Senior Vice President, Products & Markets: *Kurt L. Strand*
Vice President, General Manager, Products & Markets: *Marty Lange*
Vice President, Content Design & Delivery: *Kimberly Meriwether David*
Managing Director: *James Heine*
Brand Manager: *Dolly Womack*
Director, Product Development: *Rose Koos*
Lead Product Developer: *Michele Janicek*
Product Developer: *Christina Holt*
Marketing Manager: *Lynn Breithaupt*
Director of Digital Content Development: *Douglas Ruby*
Digital Product Analyst: *Kevin Shanahan*
Director, Content Design & Delivery: *Linda Avenarius*
Program Manager: *Mark Christianson*
Content Project Managers: *Kathryn D. Wright, Bruce Gin, and Karen Jozefowicz*
Buyer: *Sandy Ludovissy*
Design: *Matt Diamond*
Content Licensing Specialists: *Beth Thole and Melissa Leick*
Cover Image: *© Mark Dierker*
Compositor: *Aptara, Inc.*
Printer: *LSC Communications*

All credits appearing on page or at the end of the book are considered to be an extension of the copyright page.

Library of Congress Cataloging-in-Publication Data

Names: Slater, Jeffrey, 1947- author. | Wittry, Sharon M.
Title: Practical business math procedures/Jeffrey Slater, Sharon M. Wittry.
Description: Twelfth edition. | New York, NY: McGraw-Hill Education, [2017]
Identifiers: LCCN 2015037740 | ISBN 9781259540554 (alk. paper) | ISBN 1259540553 (alk. paper)
Subjects: LCSH: Business mathematics—Problems, exercises, etc.
Classification: LCC HF5694 .S57 2017 | DDC 650.01/513—dc23 LC record available at
http://lccn.loc.gov/2015037740

The Internet addresses listed in the text were accurate at the time of publication. The inclusion of a website does not indicate an endorsement by the authors or McGraw-Hill Education, and McGraw-Hill Education does not guarantee the accuracy of the information presented at these sites.

www.mhhe.com

Dedication

To Bernie Boy … My best Golden Doodle.
To Shelley … My best Friend.
Love, Jeff

To my lovely daughters, Tiffani and
Mallori, I could not be more proud of
you both.
Love you, Mom

Note to Students

ROADMAP TO SUCCESS

How to use this book and the Total Slater/Wittry Learning System.

Step 1: **Each chapter is broken down into Learning Units. Read and master one Learning Unit at a time.**

How do I know whether I understand it?

- Try the Practice Quiz. All the worked-out solutions are provided. If you still have questions, watch the authors on YouTube, in Connect, or through the instructor and work each problem out.

- For more practice, try the Extra Practice Quiz. Worked-out solutions are in Appendix B.

Once you feel confident with the subject matter, go on to the next Learning Unit in the chapter.

Step 2: **Review the Interactive Chapter Organizer at the end of the chapter.**

How do I know if I understand it?

- The third column, "You try it," gives you the chance to do additional practice.

Step 3: **Do assigned problems at the end of the chapter (or Appendix A). These may include discussion questions, drill, word problems, challenge problems, video cases, as well as projects from Surf to Save and Kiplinger's magazine.**

Can I check my homework?

- Appendix C has check figures for all the odd-numbered problems.

Step 4: **Take the Summary Practice Test.**

Can I check my progress?

- Appendix C has check figures for all problems.

What do I do if I do not match check figures?

- Review the video tutorial on YouTube, in Connect, or through the instructor—the authors work out each problem.

To aid you in studying the book, we have developed the following color code:

Blue: Movement, cancellations, steps to solve, arrows, blueprints

Purple and yellow: Formulas and steps

Green: Tables and forms

Red: Key items we are solving for

If you have difficulty with any text examples, pay special attention to the red and the blue. These will help remind you of what you are looking for as well as what the procedures are.

FEATURES

The following are the features students have told us have helped them the most.

Blueprint Aid Boxes

For the first eight chapters (not in Chapter 4), blueprint aid boxes are available to help you map out a plan to solve a word problem. We know the harder thing to do in solving word problems is often figuring out where to start. Use the blueprint as a model to get started.

Business Math Handbook

This reference guide contains all the tables found in the text. It makes homework, exams, etc., easier to deal with than flipping back and forth through the text.

Interactive Chapter Organizer

At the end of each chapter is a quick reference guide called the Interactive Chapter Organizer, in which key points, formulas, and examples are provided. A list of vocabulary terms is also included, as well as Check Figures for Extra Practice Quizzes. A column called "You try it" gives you a chance to do additional practice. And solutions are provided in Appendix B. (A complete glossary is found at the end of the text.) Think of the Interactive Chapter Organizer as your set of notes and use it as a reference when doing homework problems and reviewing before exams.

*For **extra help** from your authors—Sharon and Jeff—see the videos in Connect.*

These videos are also available on YouTube!

Additionally, a series of author-created tutorial videos are available on YouTube, in Connect, or through your instructor. The videos cover all of the Learning Unit Practice Quizzes and Summary Practice Tests.

Video Cases

There are six video cases applying business math concepts to real companies such as Six Flags, Subaru of Indiana Automotive, Noodles & Company, Buycostume.com, and DHL. You can watch these videos in Connect. Some background case information and assignment problems incorporating information on the companies are included at the end of Chapters 6, 7, 8, 13, 16, and 19.

Surf to Save

At the end of each chapter you will find word problems with links to sites and publications. These problems give you a chance to apply the theory provided in the chapter to the real world. Put your math skills to work.

Group Activity: Personal Finance, a Kiplinger Approach

In each chapter you can debate a business math issue based on a *Kiplinger's Personal Finance* magazine article. This is great for critical thinking, as well as improving your writing skills.

Spreadsheet Templates

Excel® templates are available for selected end-of-chapter problems. You can run these templates as-is or enter your own data. The templates also include an interest table feature that enables you to input any percentage rate and any terms. The program then generates table values for you.

Cumulative Reviews

At the end of Chapters 3, 8, and 13 are word problems that test your retention of business math concepts and procedures. Check figures for *all* cumulative review problems are in Appendix C.

Vocabulary

Each chapter opener includes a Vocabulary Preview covering the key terms in the chapter. The Interactive Chapter Organizer also includes the terms. There's also a glossary at the end of the text.

Acknowledgments

Academic Experts, Contributors

Dawn P. Addington

Tom Bilyeu

James P. DeMeuse

Joe Hanson

Deborah Layton

Lynda L. Mattes

Joseph M. Nicassio

Jo Ann Rawley

Karen Ruedinger

Kelly Russell

Marge Sunderland

Mary Frey

Jason Tanner

Patrick Cunningham

Paul Tomko

Peter VanderWeyst

Company/Applications

Chapter 1

Facebook—*Problem solving*

Google—*Reading and writing numbers*

Walmart—*Rounding numbers*

Neiman Marcus—*Adding and subtracting numbers*

Chapter 2

Mobile Manufacturers—*Introduction*

M&M's/Mars—*Fractions and multiplication*

Chapter 3

Johnny Rockets—*Introduction*

Microsoft Surface—*Decimal applications*

Toyota—*Multiplication and division shortcuts for decimals*

Chapter 4

Umpqua Bank; Starbucks—*Introduction*

MasterCard; American Express—*Checking account*

Morgan Chase; Citigroup; Bank of America—*Bank reconciliation*

Chapter 5

Mattel—*Unknowns*

Stop and Shop Supermarket—*Equations*

Chapter 6

Revlon Inc.—*Introduction*

Proctor & Gamble—*Percent increase and decrease*

Chapter 7

Staples; Google—*Introduction*

Michael's—*Discounts*

Amazon; United Parcel Service—*Shipping*

Chapter 8

Gap—*Markup on cost and selling price*

Chapter 9

Levi Strauss—*Introduction*

McDonald's—*Gross pay*

Internal Revenue Service—*Circular E*

Chapter 10

Twitter—*Introduction*

Chapter 11

Treasury Department—*Treasury bills*

Chapter 12

LearnVest—*Introduction*

Chapter 13

Social Security Administration—*Introduction*

Dunkin' Donuts—*Compounding*

Chapter 14

Santander—*Introduction*

Federal Trade Commission—*Installments*

Citibank; MasterCard—*Finance Charge*

Chapter 15

Pentagon Federal Credit Union—*Mortgages*

Chapter 16

J. Crew Group Inc.—*Introduction*

Hertz—*Sarbanes-Oxley Act*

Microsoft; Oracle—*Booking revenue*

YUM Corp.—*Financial statement*

Kroger; Costco; Safeway—*Cost of goods sold*

Chapter 17

Big Lots—*Depreciation*

American Airlines—*ACRS*

Chapter 18

Sears—*Introduction*

Apple; McGraw-Hill—*Inventory turnover*

Whole Foods; Kroger; Safeway; Sprouts; Walmart—*Inventory turnover*

Chapter 19

Caton Auto—*Introduction*

Tax Foundation—*Sales Tax*

Chapter 20

Target; Neiman Marcus Group—*Cyberattacks*

Chapter 21

Skechers USA; Foot Locker—*Introduction*

Wendy's; Burger King; Domino's—*Price/earnings ratio*

Berkshire Hathaway—*Dividends*

American Funds—*Mutual funds*

Chapter 22

U.S. Census Bureau—*Median*

Dow Jones & Co.—*Circle graphs*

Contents

Practical Business Math Procedures

CHAPTER 1

Whole Numbers: How to Dissect and Solve Word Problems

© Everett Collection Inc./Alamy

'Gangnam' Re-Styles YouTube

BY MIKE AYERS

Since his breakout hit "Gangnam Style" made its debut in July 2012, it has become the most watched video on YouTube to date, scoring more than 2.1 billion views. While this feat is staggering in itself, **Google** posted a nugget on its YouTube Google+ page Monday about this accomplishment, saying that the video had been viewed so many times Google needed to "upgrade" the video site's back end.

When YouTube was designed, it was never expected for a video to exceed 2,147,483,647 views because of how the counter software was originally coded. "It's like a car odometer," says YouTube spokesperson Matt McLernon. "Once it rolls over the last nine, it resets." He said the company expected two billion would be enough. It wasn't.

Exactly how did Google know they were in need of an upgrade?

A few months ago, site technicians noticed the view count for "Gangnam Style" would eventually hit that number and require a behind-the-scenes tweak. If they didn't do anything, in this case, the number would have remained static in the video's counter, but YouTube would continue to keep an accurate count of views in a separate location. Google updated the entire site's counter software, making it so a video can now register more than 9 quintillion views—or 9,223,372,036,854,775,808.

YouTube and Google marked the occasion with a special counter on the "Gangnam Style"

page. A cursor hovering over the counter spins through the view count in the way a mileage counter on a car would.

Along with being a catchy song—it was still in the top five of YouTube songs streamed this past summer—Psy's YouTube channel has bumped his other tracks into stratospheric numbers as well. Earlier this year, he released a collaboration with Snoop Dogg called "Hangover," which has been viewed more than 162 million times since June 8.

"This is what happens when the whole world can play something at the same time," Mr. McLernon said. "And when one video brings you to a channel, you often go and watch other videos."

Reprinted by permission of The Wall Street Journal, copyright 2014 Dow Jones & Company, Inc. All rights reserved worldwide.

LEARNING UNIT OBJECTIVES

LU 1–1: Reading, Writing, and Rounding Whole Numbers

1. Use place values to read and write numeric and verbal whole numbers.
2. Round whole numbers to the indicated position.
3. Use blueprint aid for dissecting and solving a word problem.

LU 1–2: Adding and Subtracting Whole Numbers

1. Add whole numbers; check and estimate addition computations.
2. Subtract whole numbers; check and estimate subtraction computations.

LU 1–3: Multiplying and Dividing Whole Numbers

1. Multiply whole numbers; check and estimate multiplication computations.
2. Divide whole numbers; check and estimate division computations.

VOCABULARY PREVIEW

Here are key terms in this chapter. After completing the chapter, if you know the term, place a checkmark in the box. If you don't know the term, look it up and put the page number where it can be found.

Addends ☐ Decimal point ☐ Decimal system ☐ Difference ☐ Dividend ☐ Divisor ☐ Minuend ☐
Multiplicand ☐ Multiplier ☐ Partial products ☐ Partial quotient ☐ Product ☐ Quotient ☐ Remainder ☐
Rounding all the way ☐ Subtrahend ☐ Sum ☐ Whole number ☐

GLOBAL

The *Wall Street Journal* clip "For Facebook Video Ads," shows a video ad on Facebook costs about 1 million dollars *per day*.

People of all ages make personal business decisions based on the answers to number questions. Numbers also determine most of the business decisions of companies. For example, go to the website of a company such as Nike and note the importance of numbers in the company's business decision-making process.

The *Wall Street Journal* clipping "Top 10 Countries" shows that nearly 1 million workers work for Nike in 477 factories worldwide.

For Facebook Video Ads, $1 Million Is Just the Start

BY REED ALBERGOTTI

A video ad on Facebook will cost advertisers about $1 million a day, but the social network won't accept a check from just anyone.

Reprinted by permission of *The Wall Street Journal,* copyright 2014 Dow Jones & Company, Inc. All rights reserved worldwide.

Top 10 Countries by Number of Workers	Factories	Workers
1. Vietnam	65	312,667
2. China	195	249,665
3. Indonesia	40	168,167
4. Sri Lanka	23	32,224
5. Thailand	35	31,163
6. India	25	28,195
7. Brazil	55	22,592
8. Bangladesh	4	21,567
9. Mexico	25	18,525
10. Honduras	10	17,252

Source: *The Wall Street Journal,* 4/22/14.

Nike has to use numbers to see:

1. If sales goals are met.
2. If inventory outages are minimized.
3. How much should be spent on new-product development.
4. How to improve production facilities to achieve lower unit costs and better quality control.

Your study of numbers begins with a review of basic computation skills that focuses on speed and accuracy. You may think, "But I can use my calculator." Even if your instructor allows you to use a calculator, you still must know the basic computation skills. You need these skills to know what to calculate, how to interpret your calculations, how to make estimates to recognize errors you made in using your calculator, and how to make calculations when you do not have a calculator.

The United States' numbering system is the **decimal system** or *base 10 system.* Your calculator gives the 10 single-digit numbers of the decimal system—0, 1, 2, 3, 4, 5, 6, 7, 8, and 9. The center of the decimal system is the **decimal point.** When you have a number with a decimal point, the numbers to the left of the decimal point are **whole numbers** and the numbers to the right of the decimal point are decimal numbers (discussed in Chapter 3). When you have a number *without* a decimal, the number is a whole number and the decimal is assumed to be after the number.

This chapter discusses reading, writing, and rounding whole numbers; adding and subtracting whole numbers; and multiplying and dividing whole numbers.

Learning Unit 1–1: Reading, Writing, and Rounding Whole Numbers

Wow! Did you know that back in 2012 over 144 billion e-mails were sent daily worldwide? In this unit, we will see how to read, write, and round whole numbers.

Now let's begin our study of whole numbers.

144,000,000,000

**Daily worldwide
e-mail traffic
in 2012**

Source: *The Wall Street Journal.*

GLOBAL

Reading and Writing Numeric and Verbal Whole Numbers

The decimal system is a *place-value system* based on the powers of 10. Any whole number can be written with the 10 digits of the decimal system because the position, or placement, of the digits in a number gives the value of the digits.

To determine the value of each digit in a number, we use a place-value chart (Figure 1.1) that divides numbers into named groups of three digits, with each group separated by a comma. To separate a number into groups, you begin with the last digit in the number and insert commas every three digits, moving from right to left. This divides the number into the named groups (units, thousands, millions, billions, trillions) shown in the place-value chart. Within each group, you have a ones, tens, and hundreds place. Keep in mind that the leftmost group may have fewer than three digits.

In Figure 1.1, the numeric number 1,605,743,891,412 illustrates place values. When you study the place-value chart, you can see that the value of each place in the chart is 10 times the value of the place to the right. We can illustrate this by analyzing the last four digits in the number 1,605,743,891,412 :

$$1,412 = (1 \times 1,000) + (4 \times 100) + (1 \times 10) + (2 \times 1)$$

So we can also say, for example, that in the number 745, the "7" means seven hundred (700); in the number 75, the "7" means 7 tens (70).

To read and write a numeric number in verbal form, you begin at the left and read each group of three digits as if it were alone, adding the group name at the end (except the last units group and groups of all zeros). Using the place-value chart in Figure 1.1, the number 1,605,743,891,412 is read as one trillion, six hundred five billion, seven hundred forty-three million, eight hundred ninety-one thousand, four hundred twelve. You do not read zeros. They fill vacant spaces as placeholders so that you can correctly state the number values. Also, the numbers twenty-one to ninety-nine must have a hyphen. Note in the *Wall Street Journal* clip "Literal Translations" how place value is identified in different languages. And

Literal translations

Here is what some numbers are called in different languages. Several languages other than English more clearly identify the place value of the numbers.

Language	27	17
English	'twenty'-'seven'	'seventeen'
Chinese	'two'-'ten'-'seven'	'ten'-'seven'
Japanese	'two'-'ten'-'seven'	'ten'-'seven'
Turkish	'twenty'-'seven'	'ten'-'seven'

Source: *The Wall Street Journal, 9/11/14.*

FIGURE 1.1

Whole number place-value chart

Whole Number Groups

	Trillions				Billions				Millions				Thousands				Units			
Hundred trillions	Ten trillions	Trillions	Comma	Hundred billions	Ten billions	Billions	Comma	Hundred millions	Ten millions	Millions	Comma	Hundred thousands	Ten thousands	Thousands	Comma	Hundreds	Tens	Ones (units)	Decimal Point
		1	,	6	0	5	,	7	4	3	,	8	9	1	,	4	1	2	.

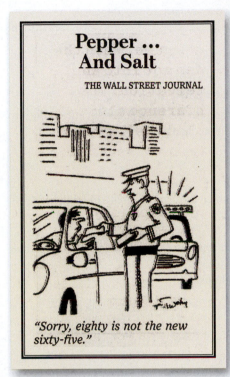

Pepper ... And Salt

THE WALL STREET JOURNAL

"Sorry, eighty is not the new sixty-five."

From *The Wall Street Journal*, permission Cartoon Features Syndicate.

Google and Advertisers Follow You to the Mall

BY ALISTAIR BARR

Retailers have long struggled to determine whether online ads fuel sales in bricks-and-mortar stores. Now, **Google** Inc. is testing a way to solve that puzzle.

A pilot program begun by the Internet company is helping about six advertisers match the anonymous tracking cookies on users' computers to in-store sales information collected by data providers like **Acxiom** Corp. and **DataLogix Holdings** Inc., according to people familiar with the test.

Reprinted by permission of *The Wall Street Journal*, copyright 2014 Dow Jones & Company, Inc. All rights reserved worldwide.

most important, when you read or write whole numbers in verbal form, do not use the word *and*. In the decimal system, *and* indicates the decimal, which we discuss in Chapter 3.

By reversing this process of changing a numeric number to a verbal number, you can use the place-value chart to change a verbal number to a numeric number. Remember that you must keep track of the place value of each digit. The place values of the digits in a number determine its total value.

Before we look at how to round whole numbers, we should look at how to convert a number indicating parts of a whole number to a whole number. We will use the following *Wall Street Journal* clip about Google as an example.

Google has ad revenue of 50.5 billion dollars. This amount is 50 billion plus 500 million of an additional billion. The following steps explain how to convert decimal numbers into a regular whole number:

CONVERTING PARTS OF A MILLION, BILLION, TRILLION, ETC., TO A REGULAR WHOLE NUMBER

Step 1. Drop the decimal point and insert a comma.

Step 2. Add zeros so the leftmost digit ends in the word name of the amount you want to convert. Be sure to add commas as needed.

EXAMPLE Convert 2.1 million to a regular whole number.

Step 1. 2.1 million
↓
2,1   Change the decimal point to a comma.
↓↓ ↓↓↓
Step 2. 2,100,000   Add zeros and commas so the whole number indicates million.

LO 2

Rounding Whole Numbers

Many of the whole numbers you read and hear are rounded numbers. Government statistics are usually rounded numbers. The financial reports of companies also use rounded numbers. All rounded numbers are *approximate* numbers. The more rounding you do, the more you approximate the number.

Rounded whole numbers are used for many reasons. With rounded whole numbers you can quickly estimate arithmetic results, check actual computations, report numbers that change quickly such as population numbers, and make numbers easier to read and remember.

Numbers can be rounded to any identified digit place value, including the first digit of a number (rounding all the way). To round whole numbers, use the following three steps:

ROUNDING WHOLE NUMBERS

Step 1. Identify the place value of the digit you want to round.

Step 2. If the digit to the right of the identified digit in Step 1 is 5 or more, increase the identified digit by 1 (round up). If the digit to the right is less than 5, do not change the identified digit.

Step 3. Change all digits to the right of the rounded identified digit to zeros.

EXAMPLE 1   Round 9,362 to the nearest hundred.

Step 1.   9,362   The digit 3 is in the hundreds place value.

Step 2.   The digit to the right of 3 is 5 or more (6). Thus, 3, the identified digit in Step 1, is now rounded to 4. You change the identified digit only if the digit to the right is 5 or more.

9,462

Step 3.   9,400   Change digits 6 and 2 to zeros, since these digits are to the right of 4, the rounded number.

By rounding 9,362 to the nearest hundred, you can see that 9,362 is closer to 9,400 than to 9,300.

Next, we show you how to round to the nearest thousand.

EXAMPLE 2   Round 67,951 to the nearest thousand.

Step 1.   67,951   The digit 7 is in the thousands place value.

Step 2.   The digit to the right of 7 is 5 or more (9). Thus, 7, the identified digit in Step 1, is now rounded to 8.

68,951

Step 3.   68,000   Change digits 9, 5, and 1 to zeros, since these digits are to the right of 8, the rounded number.

By rounding 67,951 to the nearest thousand, you can see that 67,951 is closer to 68,000 than to 67,000.

Now let's look at **rounding all the way.** To round a number all the way, you round to the first digit of the number (the leftmost digit) and have only one nonzero digit remaining in the number.

EXAMPLE 3   Round 7,843 all the way.

Step 1.   7,843   Identified leftmost digit is 7.

Step 2.   Digit to the right of 7 is greater than 5, so 7 becomes 8.

8,843

Step 3.   8,000   Change all other digits to zeros.

Rounding 7,843 all the way gives 8,000.

Remember that rounding a digit to a specific place value depends on the degree of accuracy you want in your estimate. For example, in the *Wall Street Journal* article "Wal-Mart Fights Back in China," 9.8 million rounded all the way would be 10 million. Note the digit to the right of the identified digit is 5 or greater so the identified digit (9) is rounded up to 10.

Wal-Mart Fights Back In China

By Laurie Burkitt
And Shelly Banjo

Over the past three years, Chinese authorities have fined Wal-Mart Stores Inc. $9.8 million, sanctioning the retailer for using misleading pricing, selling poor-quality products and even peddling donkey meat that turned out to be fox.

Reprinted by permission of *The Wall Street Journal*, copyright 2014 Dow Jones & Company, Inc. All rights reserved worldwide.

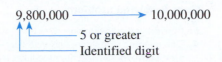

```
9,800,000  ──────►  10,000,000
        ▲ ▲
        │ └── 5 or greater
        └──── Identified digit
```

Before concluding this unit, let's look at how to dissect and solve a word problem.

How to Dissect and Solve a Word Problem

As a student, your author found solving word problems difficult. Not knowing where to begin after reading the word problem caused the difficulty. Today, students still struggle with word problems as they try to decide where to begin.

Solving word problems involves *organization* and *persistence*. Recall how persistent you were when you learned to ride a two-wheel bike. Do you remember the feeling of success you experienced when you rode the bike without help? Apply this persistence to word problems. Do not be discouraged. Each person learns at a different speed. Your goal must be to FINISH THE RACE and experience the success of solving word problems with ease.

To be organized in solving word problems, you need a plan of action that tells you where to begin—a blueprint aid. Like a builder, you will refer to this blueprint aid constantly until you know the procedure. The blueprint aid for dissecting and solving a word problem appears below. Note that the blueprint aid serves an important function—**it decreases your math anxiety.**
Remember to RTDQ2: Read the darn question and then read it again before trying to solve it.

LO 3

Blueprint Aid for Dissecting and Solving a Word Problem

	The facts	Solving for?	Steps to take	Key points
BLUEPRINT				

© Roberts Publishing Services

Now let's study this blueprint aid. The first two columns require that you *read* the word problem slowly. Think of the third column as the basic information you must know or calculate before solving the word problem. Often this column contains formulas that provide the foundation for the step-by-step problem solution. The last column reinforces the key points you should remember.

It's time now to try your skill at using the blueprint aid for dissecting and solving a word problem.

The Word Problem On the 100th anniversary of Tootsie Roll Industries, the company reported sharply increased sales and profits. Sales reached one hundred ninety-four million dollars and a record profit of twenty-two million, five hundred fifty-six thousand dollars. The company president requested that you round the sales and profit figures all the way.

Study the following blueprint aid and note how we filled in the columns with the information in the word problem. You will find the organization of the blueprint aid most helpful. Be persistent! You *can* dissect and solve word problems! When you are finished with the word problem, make sure the answer seems reasonable.

	The facts	Solving for?	Steps to take	Key points
BLUEPRINT	*Sales:* One hundred ninety-four million dollars. *Profit:* Twenty-two million, five hundred fifty-six thousand dollars.	Sales and profit rounded all the way.	Express each verbal form in numeric form. Identify leftmost digit in each number.	Rounding all the way means only the leftmost digit will remain. All other digits become zeros.

MONEY tips

Do not carry your Social Security card in your wallet. Keep it and other important documents in a safe deposit box or fireproof container. Shred any document that contains personal information, such as anything with your Social Security number on it, old bank statements, applications for loans, and so on.

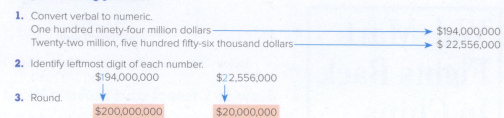

Steps to solving problem

1. Convert verbal to numeric.

One hundred ninety-four million dollars ⟶ $194,000,000

Twenty-two million, five hundred fifty-six thousand dollars ⟶ $ 22,556,000

2. Identify leftmost digit of each number.

$194,000,000 $22,556,000

3. Round. $200,000,000 $20,000,000

Note that in the final answer, $200,000,000 and $20,000,000 have only one nonzero digit.

Remember that you cannot round numbers expressed in verbal form. You must convert these numbers to numeric form.

Now you should see the importance of the information in the third column of the blueprint aid. When you complete your blueprint aids for word problems, do not be concerned if the order of the information in your boxes does not follow the order given in the text boxes. Often you can dissect a word problem in more than one way.

Your first Practice Quiz follows. Be sure to study the paragraph that introduces the Practice Quiz.

LU 1–1   PRACTICE QUIZ

Complete this Practice Quiz to see how you are doing.

At the end of each learning unit, you can check your progress with a Practice Quiz. If you had difficulty understanding the unit, the Practice Quiz will help identify your area of weakness. Work the problems on scrap paper. Check your answers with the worked-out solutions that follow the quiz. Ask your instructor about specific assignments and the videos available in Connect for each unit Practice Quiz.

1. Write in verbal form:

    a. 7,948   **b.** 48,775   **c.** 814,410,335,414

2. Round the following numbers as indicated:

Nearest ten	Nearest hundred	Nearest thousand	Rounded all the way
a. 92	**b.** 745	**c.** 8,341	**d.** 4,752

3. Kellogg's reported its sales as five million, one hundred eighty-one thousand dollars. The company earned a profit of five hundred two thousand dollars. What would the sales and profit be if each number were rounded all the way? (*Hint:* You might want to draw the blueprint aid since we show it in the solution.)

*For **extra help** from your authors—Sharon and Jeff—see the videos in Connect.*

These videos are also available on YouTube!

✓ Solutions

1. **a.** Seven thousand, nine hundred forty-eight

    b. Forty-eight thousand, seven hundred seventy-five

    c. Eight hundred fourteen billion, four hundred ten million, three hundred thirty-five thousand, four hundred fourteen

2. **a.** 90   **b.** 700   **c.** 8,000   **d.** 5,000

3. Kellogg's sales and profit:

BLUEPRINT	The facts	Solving for?	Steps to take	Key points
	Sales: Five million, one hundred eighty-one thousand dollars. *Profit:* Five hundred two thousand dollars.	Sales and profit rounded all the way.	Express each verbal form in numeric form. Identify leftmost digit in each number.	Rounding all the way means only the leftmost digit will remain. All other digits become zeros.

Steps to solving problem

1. Convert verbal to numeric.

   Five million, one hundred eighty-one thousand ——————————————→ $5,181,000
   Five hundred two thousand ——————————————————————————→ $ 502,000

2. Identify leftmost digit of each number.
   $5,181,000 $502,000

3. Round.
   $5,000,000 $500,000

LU 1–1a   EXTRA PRACTICE QUIZ WITH WORKED-OUT SOLUTIONS

Need more practice? Try this **Extra Practice Quiz** (check figures in the Interactive Chapter Organizer). Worked-out Solutions can be found in Appendix B.

1. Write in verbal form:
   a. 8,682   **b.** 56,295   **c.** 732,310,444,888
2. Round the following numbers as indicated:

Nearest ten	Nearest hundred	Nearest thousand	Rounded all the way
a. 43	**b.** 654	**c.** 7,328	**d.** 5,980

3. Kellogg's reported its sales as three million, two hundred ninety-one thousand dollars. The company earned a profit of four hundred five thousand dollars. What would the sales and profit be if each number were rounded all the way?

Learning Unit 1–2: Adding and Subtracting Whole Numbers

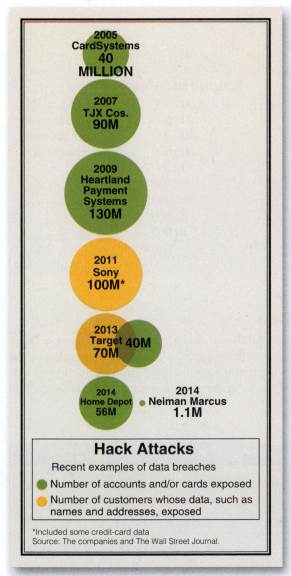

2005
CardSystems
40
MILLION

2007
TJX Cos.
90M

2009
Heartland
Payment
Systems
130M

2011
Sony
100M*

2013
Target 40M
70M

2014
Home Depot
56M

2014
● **Neiman Marcus**
1.1M

Hack Attacks

Recent examples of data breaches

● Number of accounts and/or cards exposed

● Number of customers whose data, such as names and addresses, exposed

*Included some credit-card data
Source: The companies and The Wall Street Journal.

Source: *The Wall Street Journal*, 2/24/14.

LO 1 We hear in the news that because of data breaches credit cards have sometimes been compromised. This means new credit cards need to be issued. Note in the *Wall Street Journal* "Hack Attacks" the difference in the costly breaches between TJX and Heartland.

Heartland	$130,000,000
TJX	− 90,000,000
	$ 40,000,000

This unit teaches you how to manually add and subtract whole numbers. When you least expect it, you will catch yourself automatically using this skill.

Addition of Whole Numbers

To add whole numbers, you unite two or more numbers called **addends** to make one number called a **sum,** *total,* or *amount.* The numbers are arranged in a column according to their place values—units above units, tens above tens, and so on. Then, you add the columns of numbers from top to bottom. To check the result, you re-add the columns from bottom to top. This procedure is illustrated in the steps that follow.

ADDING WHOLE NUMBERS

Step 1. Align the numbers to be added in columns according to their place values, beginning with the units place at the right and moving to the left.

Step 2. Add the units column. Write the sum below the column. If the sum is more than 9, write the units digit and carry the tens digit.

Step 3. Moving to the left, repeat Step 2 until all place values are added.

EXAMPLE

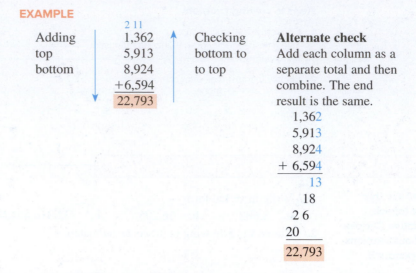

	2 11			
Adding	1,362	↑	Checking	**Alternate check**
top	5,913		bottom to	Add each column as a
bottom	8,924		to top	separate total and then
	+6,594			combine. The end
	22,793			result is the same.

```
    1,362
    5,913
    8,924
 +  6,594
       13
       18
      2 6
     20
    22,793
```

How to Quickly Estimate Addition by Rounding All the Way   In Learning Unit 1–1, you learned that rounding whole numbers all the way gives quick arithmetic estimates. Using the following *Wall Street Journal* clipping about defective airbags, note how you can round each number all the way and the total will not be rounded all the way. Remember that rounding all the way does not replace actual computations, but it is helpful in making quick commonsense decisions.

GLOBAL

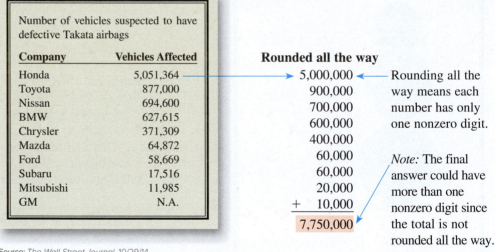

Number of vehicles suspected to have defective Takata airbags

Company	Vehicles Affected		Rounded all the way	
Honda	5,051,364	→	5,000,000	← Rounding all the
Toyota	877,000		900,000	way means each
Nissan	694,600		700,000	number has only
BMW	627,615		600,000	one nonzero digit.
Chrysler	371,309		400,000	
Mazda	64,872		60,000	*Note:* The final
Ford	58,669		60,000	answer could have
Subaru	17,516		60,000	more than one
Mitsubishi	11,985		20,000	nonzero digit since
GM	N.A.		+ 10,000	the total is not
			7,750,000	rounded all the way.

Source: *The Wall Street Journal*, 10/29/14.

Subtraction of Whole Numbers

LO 2

Subtraction is the opposite of addition. Addition unites numbers; subtraction takes one number away from another number. In subtraction, the top (largest) number is the **minuend.** The number you subtract from the minuend is the **subtrahend,** which gives you the **difference** between the minuend and the subtrahend. The steps for subtracting whole numbers follow.

SUBTRACTING WHOLE NUMBERS

Step 1.   Align the minuend and subtrahend according to their place values.

Step 2.   Begin the subtraction with the units digits. Write the difference below the column. If the units digit in the minuend is smaller than the units digit in the subtrahend, borrow 1 from the tens digit in the minuend. One tens digit is 10 units.

Step 3.   Moving to the left, repeat Step 2 until all place values in the subtrahend are subtracted.

© David R. Frazier Photolibrary, Inc.

EXAMPLE   The previous *Wall Street Journal* clipping about airbags illustrates the subtraction of whole numbers:

What is the difference in the number of vehicles affected between Subaru and Mitsubishi? As shown below you can use subtraction to arrive at the 5,531 difference.

$$
\begin{array}{r}
17,516 \\
-11,985 \\
\hline
5,531
\end{array}
$$
← Minuend (larger number)
← Subtrahend
← Difference

Check
$$
\begin{array}{r}
5,531 \\
+11,985 \\
\hline
17,516
\end{array}
$$

In subtraction, borrowing from the column at the left is often necessary. Remember that 1 ten = 10 units, 1 hundred = 10 tens, and 1 thousand = 10 hundreds.

In the tens column in the example above, 8 cannot be subtracted from 1 so we borrow from the hundreds column, resulting in 11 less 8 equals 3. In the hundreds column, we cannot subtract 9 from 4 so we borrow 10 hundreds from the thousands column leaving 14 hundreds. 14 less 9 equals 5.

Checking subtraction requires adding the difference (5,531) to the subtrahend (11,985) to arrive at the minuend (17,516).

How to Dissect and Solve a Word Problem

Accurate subtraction is important in many business operations. In Chapter 4 we discuss the importance of keeping accurate subtraction in your checkbook balance. Now let's check your progress by dissecting and solving a word problem.

The Word Problem   Hershey's produced 25 million Kisses in one day. The same day, the company shipped 4 million to Japan, 3 million to France, and 6 million throughout the United States. At the end of that day, what is the company's total inventory of Kisses? What is the inventory balance if you round the number all the way?

MONEY tips

Be vigilant about sharing personal information. Change passwords often and do not share them.

	The facts	Solving for?	Steps to take	Key points
BLUEPRINT	*Produced:* 25 million. *Shipped:* Japan, 4 million; France, 3 million; United States, 6 million.	Total Kisses left in inventory. Inventory balance rounded all the way.	Total Kisses produced − Total Kisses shipped = Total Kisses left in inventory.	Minuend − Subtrahend = Difference. Rounding all the way means rounding to last digit on the left.

Steps to solving problem

1. Calculate the total Kisses shipped.

$$
\begin{array}{r}
4,000,000 \\
3,000,000 \\
+\ 6,000,000 \\
\hline
13,000,000
\end{array}
$$

2. Calculate the total Kisses left in inventory.

$$
\begin{array}{r}
25,000,000 \\
-13,000,000 \\
\hline
12,000,000
\end{array}
$$

3. Rounding all the way.

Identified digit is 1. Digit to right of 1 is 2, which is less than 5. *Answer:* 10,000,000 .

The Practice Quiz that follows will tell you how you are progressing in your study of Chapter 1.

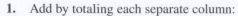

LU 1–2   PRACTICE QUIZ

Complete this **Practice Quiz** to see how you are doing.

1. Add by totaling each separate column:

   8,974
   6,439
   + 6,941

2. Estimate by rounding all the way (do not round the total of estimate) and then do the actual computation:

   4,241
   8,794
   + 3,872

3. Subtract and check your answer:

   9,876
   − 4,967

4. Jackson Manufacturing Company projected its year 2013 furniture sales at $900,000. During 2013, Jackson earned $510,000 in sales from major clients and $369,100 in sales from the remainder of its clients. What is the amount by which Jackson over- or underestimated its sales? Use the blueprint aid, since the answer will show the completed blueprint aid.

*For **extra help** from your authors–Sharon and Jeff–see the videos in Connect.*

These videos are also available on YouTube!

✓ Solutions

1.		2. **Estimate**	**Actual**	3.	**Check**
	14			8 18 6 16	
	14	4,000	4,241	9,876 ◄──	4,909
	2 2	9,000	8,794	− 4,967	+ 4,967
	20	+ 4,000	+ 3,872	4,909	9,876
	22,354	**17,000**	**16,907**		

4. Jackson Manufacturing Company over- or underestimated sales:

	The facts	Solving for?	Steps to take	Key points
BLUEPRINT	*Projected 2013 sales:* $900,000. *Major clients:* $510,000. *Other clients:* $369,100.	How much were sales over- or underestimated?	Total projected sales − Total actual sales = Over- or underestimated sales.	Projected sales (minuend) − Actual sales (subtrahend) = Difference.

Steps to solving problem

1. Calculate total actual sales.

   $ 510,000
   + 369,100
   $ 879,100

2. Calculate overestimated or underestimated sales.

   $900,000
   − 879,100
   $ 20,900 (overestimated)

LU 1–2a   EXTRA PRACTICE QUIZ WITH WORKED-OUT SOLUTIONS

Need more practice? Try this **Extra Practice Quiz** (check figures in the Interactive Chapter Organizer. Worked-out Solutions can be found in Appendix B.

1. Add by totaling each separate column:

   9,853
   7,394
   +8,843

2. Estimate by rounding all the way (do not round the total of estimate) and then do the actual computation:

   3,482
   6,981
   +5,490

3. Subtract and check your answer:

   9,787
   −5,968

4. Jackson Manufacturing Company projected its year 2013 furniture sales at $878,000. During 2013, Jackson earned $492,900 in sales from major clients and $342,000 in sales from the remainder of its clients. What is the amount by which Jackson over- or underestimated its sales?

Learning Unit 1–3: Multiplying and Dividing Whole Numbers

LO 1

The *Wall Street Journal* clip in the margin reveals that $16 billion fraud loss occurred in 2013. If the $16 billion figure were for 4 quarters the fraud would be $4 billion per quarter. If you divide $16 billion by 4 quarters you would get $4,000,000,000.

This unit will sharpen your skills in two important arithmetic operations—multiplication and division. These two operations frequently result in knowledgeable business decisions.

Multiplication of Whole Numbers—Shortcut to Addition

From calculating the cost of fraud for 4 quarters you know that multiplication is a *shortcut to addition*:

$4,000,000,000 \times 4 = $16,000,000,000

or

$4,000,000,000 + $4,000,000,000 + $4,000,000,000 + $4,000,000,000 = $16,000,000,000

Before learning the steps used to multiply whole numbers with two or more digits, you must learn some multiplication terminology.

Note in the following example that the top number (number we want to multiply) is the **multiplicand.** The bottom number (number doing the multiplying) is the **multiplier.** The final number (answer) is the **product.** The numbers between the multiplier and the product are **partial products.** Also note how we positioned the partial product 2090. This number is the result of multiplying 418 by 50 (the 5 is in the tens position). On each line in the partial products, we placed the first digit directly below the digit we used in the multiplication process.

EXAMPLE

	418	←	Top number (multiplicand)
	× 52	←	Bottom number (multiplier)
Partial products	836		
	2090		
	21,736	←	Product answer

$2 \times 418 = 836$
$50 \times 418 = + 20,900$
$21,736$

Fraud losses on bank and credit card accounts in 2013: **$16 billion**

Source: *The Wall Street Journal*, 9/5/14.

Pepper ... And Salt

THE WALL STREET JOURNAL

25
×37

"No, Jason, you can't call tech support."

From *The Wall Street Journal*, permission Cartoon Features Syndicate.

We can now give the following steps for multiplying whole numbers with two or more digits:

MULTIPLYING WHOLE NUMBERS WITH TWO OR MORE DIGITS

Step 1.   Align the multiplicand (top number) and multiplier (bottom number) at the right. Usually, you should make the smaller number the multiplier.

Step 2.   Begin by multiplying the right digit of the multiplier with the right digit of the multiplicand. Keep multiplying as you move left through the multiplicand. Your first partial product aligns at the right with the multiplicand and multiplier.

Step 3.   Move left through the multiplier and continue multiplying the multiplicand. Your partial product right digit or first digit is placed directly below the digit in the multiplier that you used to multiply.

Step 4.   Continue Steps 2 and 3 until you have completed your multiplication process. Then add the partial products to get the final product.

Checking and Estimating Multiplication   We can check the multiplication process by reversing the multiplicand and multiplier and then multiplying. Let's first estimate 52×418 by rounding all the way.

EXAMPLE

$$
\begin{array}{r}
50 \leftarrow \quad 52 \\
\times\ 400 \leftarrow \times\ 418 \\
\hline
20{,}000 \qquad 416 \\
52 \\
20\ 8 \\
\hline
21{,}736
\end{array}
$$

By estimating before actually working the problem, we know our answer should be about 20,000. When we multiply 52 by 418, we get the same answer as when we multiply 418×52—and the answer is about 20,000. Remember, if we had not rounded all the way, our estimate would have been closer. If we had used a calculator, the rounded estimate would have helped us check the calculator's answer. Our commonsense estimate tells us our answer is near 20,000—not 200,000.

Before you study the division of whole numbers, you should know (1) the multiplication shortcut with numbers ending in zeros and (2) how to multiply a whole number by a power of 10.

MULTIPLICATION SHORTCUT WITH NUMBERS ENDING IN ZEROS

Step 1.   When zeros are at the end of the multiplicand or the multiplier, or both, disregard the zeros and multiply.

Step 2.   Count the number of zeros in the multiplicand and multiplier.

Step 3.   Attach the number of zeros counted in Step 2 to your answer.

EXAMPLE

$$
\begin{array}{r}
65{,}000 \\
\times\ 420 \\
\hline
\end{array}
\qquad
\begin{array}{r}
65 \\
\times\ 42 \\
\hline
1\ 30 \\
26\ 0 \\
\hline
27{,}300{,}000
\end{array}
\qquad
\begin{array}{r}
3 \text{ zeros} \\
+\ 1 \text{ zero} \\
\hline
4 \text{ zeros}
\end{array}
$$

No need to multiply rows of zeros

$$
\begin{array}{r}
65{,}000 \\
\times\qquad 420 \\
\hline
00\ 000 \\
1\ 300\ 00 \\
26\ 000\ 0 \\
\hline
27{,}300{,}000
\end{array}
$$

MULTIPLYING A WHOLE NUMBER BY A POWER OF 10
Step 1. Count the number of zeros in the power of 10 (a whole number that begins with 1 and ends in one or more zeros such as 10, 100, 1,000, and so on).
Step 2. Attach that number of zeros to the right side of the other whole number to obtain the answer. Insert comma(s) as needed every three digits, moving from right to left.

EXAMPLE 99 × 10   = 99<u>0</u>   = 990   ← Add 1 zero
99 × 100 = 9,9<u>00</u> = 9,900   ← Add 2 zeros
99 × 1,000 = 99,<u>000</u> = 99,000 ← Add 3 zeros

When a zero is in the center of the multiplier, you can do the following:

EXAMPLE

$$\begin{array}{r} 658 \\ \times\ 403 \\ \hline 1\ 974 \\ 263\ 2\square \\ \hline 265,174 \end{array}$$

$$\begin{array}{r} 3 \times 658 =\quad 1,974 \\ 400 \times 658 = +\ 263,200 \\ \hline 265,174 \end{array}$$

Division of Whole Numbers

Division is the reverse of multiplication and a time-saving shortcut related to subtraction. For example, in the introduction of this learning unit you determined that fraud for 4 quarters resulted in \$4,000,000,000 loss per quarter. You multiplied \$4,000,000,000 × 4 to get \$16,000,000,000. Since division is the reverse of multiplication you can also say that \$16,000,000,000 ÷ 4 = \$4,000,000,000.

Division can be indicated by the common symbols ÷ and ⌐, or by the bar — in a fraction and the forward slant / between two numbers, which means the first number is divided by the second number. Division asks how many times one number (**divisor**) is contained in another number (**dividend**). The answer, or result, is the **quotient.** When the divisor (number used to divide) doesn't divide evenly into the dividend (number we are dividing), the result is a **partial quotient,** with the leftover amount the **remainder** (expressed as fractions in later chapters). The following example illustrates *even division* (this is also an example of *long division* because the divisor has more than one digit).

EXAMPLE

$$\begin{array}{r} 18 \leftarrow \text{Quotient} \\ \text{Divisor} \longrightarrow 15\overline{)270} \leftarrow \text{Dividend} \\ \underline{15} \\ 120 \\ \underline{120} \end{array}$$

This example divides 15 into 27 once with 12 remaining. The 0 in the dividend is brought down to 12. Dividing 120 by 15 equals 8 with no remainder; that is, even division. The following example illustrates *uneven division with a remainder* (this is also an example of *short division* because the divisor has only one digit).

EXAMPLE

$$\begin{array}{r} 24\ \text{R1} \leftarrow \text{Remainder} \\ 7\overline{)169} \\ \underline{14} \\ 29 \\ \underline{28} \\ 1 \end{array}$$

Check
(7 × 24) + 1 = 169
Divisor × Quotient + Remainder = Dividend

Note how doing the check gives you assurance that your calculation is correct. When the divisor has one digit (short division) as in this example, you can often calculate the division mentally as illustrated in the following examples:

EXAMPLES

$$\begin{array}{r} 108 \\ 8\overline{)864} \end{array} \qquad \begin{array}{r} 16\ \text{R6} \\ 7\overline{)118} \end{array}$$

Next, let's look at the value of estimating division.

Estimating Division   Before actually working a division problem, estimate the quotient by rounding. This estimate helps you check the answer. The example that follows is rounded all the way. After you make an estimate, work the problem and check your answer by multiplication.

EXAMPLE

$$\begin{array}{r} 36 \text{ R}111 \\ 138\overline{)5,079} \\ 4\ 14 \\ \hline 939 \\ 828 \\ \hline 111 \end{array}$$

Estimate

$$\begin{array}{r} 50 \\ 100\overline{)5,000} \end{array}$$

Check

$$\begin{array}{r} 138 \\ \times\ 36 \\ \hline 828 \\ 4\ 14 \\ \hline 4,968 \\ +\ 111 \quad \longleftarrow \text{ Add remainder} \\ \hline 5,079 \end{array}$$

Now let's turn our attention to division shortcuts with zeros.

Division Shortcuts with Zeros   The steps that follow show a shortcut that you can use when you divide numbers with zeros.

DIVISION SHORTCUT WITH NUMBERS ENDING IN ZEROS

Step 1.   When the dividend and divisor have ending zeros, count the number of ending zeros in the divisor.

Step 2.   Drop the same number of zeros in the dividend as in the divisor, counting from right to left.

Note the following examples of division shortcuts with numbers ending in zeros. Since two of the symbols used for division are ÷ and $\overline{)}$, our first examples show the zero shortcut method with the ÷ symbol.

EXAMPLES

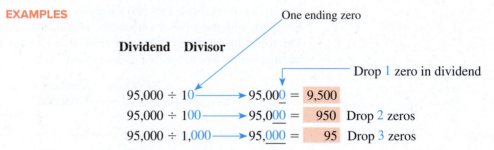

$$95,000 \div 10 \longrightarrow 95,00\underline{0} = \boxed{9,500}$$
$$95,000 \div 100 \longrightarrow 95,0\underline{00} = \boxed{950} \quad \text{Drop 2 zeros}$$
$$95,000 \div 1,000 \longrightarrow 95,\underline{000} = \boxed{95} \quad \text{Drop 3 zeros}$$

One ending zero

Drop 1 zero in dividend

In a long division problem with the $\overline{)}$ symbol, you again count the number of ending zeros in the divisor. Then drop the same number of ending zeros in the dividend and divide as usual.

EXAMPLE $6,5\underline{00}\overline{)88,0\underline{00}}$ $\longleftarrow$ Drop 2 zeros

$$65\overline{)880}$$ $\longleftarrow$

$$\begin{array}{r} 13 \text{ R}35 \\ 65\overline{)880} \\ 65 \\ \hline 230 \\ 195 \\ \hline 35 \end{array}$$

You are now ready to practice what you learned by dissecting and solving a word problem.

How to Dissect and Solve a Word Problem

The blueprint aid presented in LU 1-1(3) will be your guide to dissecting and solving the following word problem.

The Word Problem   Dunkin' Donuts sells to four different companies a total of $3,500 worth of doughnuts per week. What is the total annual sales to these companies? What is the yearly sales per company? (Assume each company buys the same amount.) Check your answer to show how multiplication and division are related.

MONEY tips

College *is* worth it! College graduates earn substantially more money each year than high school graduates *and* that wage premium is increasing steadily—almost twice as much. Stay in school.

	The facts	Solving for?	Steps to take	Key points
BLUEPRINT	*Sales per week:* $3,500. *Companies:* 4.	Total annual sales to all four companies. Yearly sales per company.	Sales per week × Weeks in year (52) = Total annual sales. Total annual sales ÷ Total companies = Yearly sales per company.	Division is the reverse of multiplication.

Steps to solving problem

1. Calculate total annual sales. $3,500 × 52 weeks = $182,000

2. Calculate yearly sales per company. $182,000 ÷ 4 = $45,500

Check

$45,500 × 4 = $182,000

It's time again to check your progress with a Practice Quiz.

LU 1–3   PRACTICE QUIZ

Complete this Practice Quiz to see how you are doing.

1. Estimate the actual problem by rounding all the way, work the actual problem, and check:

   Actual   Estimate   Check

   3,894
   × 18

2. Multiply by shortcut method: 3. Multiply by shortcut method:
   77,000   95 × 10,000
   × 1,800

4. Divide by rounding all the way, complete the actual calculation, and check, showing remainder as a whole number.

   26)5,325

5. Divide by shortcut method:

   4,000)96,000

6. Assume General Motors produces 960 Chevrolets each workday (Monday through Friday). If the cost to produce each car is $6,500, what is General Motors' total cost for the year? Check your answer.

*For **extra help** from your authors—Sharon and Jeff—see the videos in Connect.*

These videos are also available on YouTube!

✓ Solutions

1. **Estimate**   **Actual**   **Check**
   4,000   3,894   8 × 3,894 =   31,152
   × 20   × 18   10 × 3,894 = + 38,940
   80,000   31 152   70,092
                             38 94
                             70,092

2. 77 × 18 = 1,386 + 5 zeros = 138,600,000   3. 95 + 4 zeros = 950,000

4. **Rounding**   **Actual**   **Check**
         166 R20   204 R21   26 × 204 = 5,304
   30)5,000   26)5,325   +   21
      3 0   5 2   5,325
      2 00   125
      1 80   104
        200   21
        180
         20

5. Drop 3 zeros = $\dfrac{24}{4\overline{)96}}$

6. General Motors' total cost per year:

	The facts	Solving for?	Steps to take	Key points
BLUEPRINT	*Cars produced each workday:* 960. *Workweek:* 5 days. *Cost per car:* $6,500.	Total cost per year.	Cars produced per week × 52 = Total cars produced per year. Total cars produced per year × Total cost per car = Total cost per year.	Whenever possible, use multiplication and division shortcuts with zeros. Multiplication can be checked by division.

Steps to solving problem

1. Calculate total cars produced per week.

5 × 960 = 4,800 cars produced per week

2. Calculate total cars produced per year.

4,800 cars × 52 weeks = 249,600 total cars produced per year

3. Calculate total cost per year.

249,600 cars × $6,500 = $1,622,400,000 (multiply 2,496 × 65 and add zeros)

Check

$1,622,400,000 ÷ 249,600 = $6,500 (drop 2 zeros before dividing)

LU 1–3a   EXTRA PRACTICE QUIZ WITH WORKED-OUT SOLUTIONS

Need more practice? Try this Extra Practice Quiz (check figures in the Interactive Chapter Organizer). Worked-out Solutions can be found in Appendix B.

1. Estimate the actual problem by rounding all the way, work the actual problem, and check:

Actual   **Estimate**   **Check**

$$\begin{array}{r} 4,938 \\ \times \quad 19 \\ \hline \end{array}$$

2. Multiply by shortcut method:

$$\begin{array}{r} 86,000 \\ \times \ 1,900 \\ \hline \end{array}$$

3. Multiply by shortcut method:

86 × 10,000

4. Divide by rounding all the way, complete the actual calculation, and check, showing remainder as a whole number.

$26\overline{)6,394}$

5. Divide by the shortcut method:

$3,000\overline{)99,000}$

6. Assume General Motors produces 850 Chevrolets each workday (Monday through Friday). If the cost to produce each car is $7,000, what is General Motors' total cost for the year? Check your answer.

INTERACTIVE CHAPTER ORGANIZER

Topic/Procedure/Formula	Examples	You try it*
Reading and writing numeric and verbal whole numbers Placement of digits in a number gives the value of the digits (Figure 1.1). Commas separate every three digits, moving from right to left. Begin at left to read and write number in verbal form. Do not read zeros or use *and*. Hyphenate numbers twenty-one to ninety-nine. Reverse procedure to change verbal number to numeric.	462 → Four hundred sixty-two 6,741 → Six thousand, seven hundred forty-one	**Write in verbal form** 571 → 7,943 →
Rounding whole numbers 1. Identify place value of the digit to be rounded. 2. If digit to the right is 5 or more, round up; if less than 5, do not change. 3. Change all digits to the right of rounded identified digit to zeros.	643 to nearest ten 4 in tens place value 3 is not 5 or more Thus, 643 rounds to 640 .	**Round to nearest ten** 691
Rounding all the way Round to first digit of number. One nonzero digit remains. In estimating, you round each number of the problem to one nonzero digit. The final answer is not rounded.	468,451 → 500,000 The 5 is the only nonzero digit remaining.	**Round all the way** 429,685 →
Adding whole numbers 1. Align numbers at the right. 2. Add units column. If sum is more than 9, carry tens digit. 3. Moving left, repeat Step 2 until all place values are added. Add from top to bottom. Check by adding bottom to top or adding each column separately and combining.	$\begin{array}{r}1\\65\\+\ 47\\\hline 112\end{array}$ $\begin{array}{r}12\\+10\\\hline 112\end{array}$ Checking sum of each digit	**Add** 76 +38
Subtracting whole numbers 1. Align minuend and subtrahend at the right. 2. Subtract units digits. If necessary, borrow 1 from tens digit in minuend. 3. Moving left, repeat Step 2 until all place values are subtracted. Minuend less subtrahend equals difference.	**Check** $\begin{array}{r}5\ 18\\6\cancel{8}5\\-492\\\hline 193\end{array}$ $\begin{array}{r}193\\+492\\\hline 685\end{array}$	**Subtract** 629 −134
Multiplying whole numbers 1. Align multiplicand and multiplier at the right. 2. Begin at the right and keep multiplying as you move to the left. First partial product aligns at the right with multiplicand and multiplier. 3. Move left through multiplier and continue multiplying multiplicand. Partial product right digit or first digit is placed directly below digit in multiplier. 4. Continue Steps 2 and 3 until multiplication is complete. Add partial products to get final product. **Shortcuts:** (a) When multiplicand or multiplier, or both, end in zeros, disregard zeros and multiply; attach same number of zeros to answer. If zero is in center of multiplier, no need to show row of zeros. (b) If multiplying by power of 10, attach same number of zeros to whole number multiplied.	$\begin{array}{r}223\\\times\ 32\\\hline 446\\6\ 69\\\hline 7,136\end{array}$ a. $\begin{array}{r}48,000\\\times\quad 40\end{array}$ $\begin{array}{r}48\\4\\\hline 1,920,000\end{array}$ 3 zeros + 1 zero ← 4 zeros $\begin{array}{r}524\\\times\ 206\\\hline 3\ 144\\104\ 8\\\hline 107,944\end{array}$ b. 14 × 10 = 140 (attach 1 zero) 14 × 1,000 = 14,000 (attach 3 zeros)	**Multiply** 491 × 28 **Multiply by shortcut** 13 × 10 = 13 × 1,000 =

(continues)

INTERACTIVE CHAPTER ORGANIZER

Topic/Procedure/Formula	Examples	You try it*
Dividing whole numbers **1.** When divisor is divided into the dividend, the remainder is less than divisor. **2.** Drop zeros from dividend right to left by number of zeros found in the divisor. Even division has no remainder; uneven division has a remainder; divisor with one digit is short division; and divisor with more than one digit is long division.	**1.** $\begin{array}{r} 5\ R6 \\ 14\overline{)76} \\ 70 \\ \hline 6 \end{array}$ **2.** $5{,}000 \div 100 = 50 \div 1 = 50$ $5{,}000 \div 1{,}000 = 5 \div 1 = 5$	**Divide** **1.** $16\overline{)95}$ **Divide by shortcut** **2.** $4{,}000 \div 100$ $4{,}000 \div 1{,}000$

KEY TERMS	Addends Decimal point Decimal system Difference Dividend Divisor	Minuend Multiplicand Multiplier Partial products Partial quotient Product	Quotient Remainder Rounding all the way Subtrahend Sum Whole number

Check Figures for Extra Practice Quizzes. (Worked-out Solutions are in Appendix B.)	LU 1–1a **1.** a. Eight thousand, six hundred eighty-two; b. Fifty-six thousand, two hundred ninety-five; c. Seven hundred thirty-two billion, three hundred ten million, four hundred forty-four thousand, eight hundred eighty-eight **2.** a. 40; b. 700; c. 7,000; d. 6,000 **3.** $3,000,000; $400,000	LU 1–2a **1.** 26,090 **2.** 15,000; 15,953 **3.** 3,819 **4.** $43,100 (over)	LU 1–3a **1.** 100,000; 93,822 **2.** 163,400,000 **3.** 860,000 **4.** 245 R24 **5.** 33 **6.** $1,547,000,000

*Worked-out solutions are in Appendix B.

Critical Thinking Discussion Questions with Chapter Concept Check

1. List the four steps of the decision-making process. Do you think all companies should be required to follow these steps? Give an example.

2. Explain the three steps used to round whole numbers. Pick a whole number and explain why it should not be rounded.

3. How do you check subtraction? If you were to attend a movie, explain how you might use the subtraction check method.

4. Explain how you can check multiplication. If you visit a local supermarket, how could you show multiplication as a shortcut to addition?

5. Explain how division is the reverse of multiplication. Using the supermarket example, explain how division is a time-saving shortcut related to subtraction.

6. Chapter Concept Check. Using all the math you learned in Chapter 1, calculate the difference in cost and calories from dining at Subway versus McDonald's. Go online or visit these stores in your area to find current food prices.

END-OF-CHAPTER PROBLEMS

Check figures for odd-numbered problems in Appendix C.   Name _____   Date _____

DRILL PROBLEMS

Add the following: *LU 1-2(1)*

1–1. $\begin{array}{r} 68 \\ +\ 14 \end{array}$	**1–2.** $\begin{array}{r} 850 \\ +\ 670 \end{array}$	**1–3.** $\begin{array}{r} 77 \\ +\ 77 \end{array}$	**1–4.** $\begin{array}{r} 88 \\ +\ 75 \end{array}$

1–5. $\begin{array}{r} 6{,}251 \\ +\ 7{,}329 \end{array}$ **1–6.** $\begin{array}{r} 59{,}481 \\ 51{,}411 \\ +\ 70{,}821 \end{array}$ **1–7.** $\begin{array}{r} 78{,}159 \\ 15{,}850 \\ +\ 19{,}681 \end{array}$

Subtract the following: *LU 1-2(2)*

1–8. $\begin{array}{r} 68 \\ -\ 19 \end{array}$ **1–9.** $\begin{array}{r} 80 \\ -42 \end{array}$ **1–10.** $\begin{array}{r} 287 \\ -\ 199 \end{array}$

1–11. $\begin{array}{r} 9{,}000 \\ -5{,}400 \end{array}$ **1–12.** $\begin{array}{r} 9{,}800 \\ -8{,}900 \end{array}$ **1–13.** $\begin{array}{r} 1{,}622 \\ -\ 548 \end{array}$

Multiply the following: *LU 1-3(1)*

1–14. $\begin{array}{r} 50 \\ \times\ 6 \end{array}$ **1–15.** $\begin{array}{r} 510 \\ \times\ 61 \end{array}$ **1–16.** $\begin{array}{r} 800 \\ \times\ 200 \end{array}$

1–17. $\begin{array}{r} 677 \\ \times\ 503 \end{array}$ **1–18.** $\begin{array}{r} 309 \\ \times\ 850 \end{array}$ **1–19.** $\begin{array}{r} 450 \\ \times\ 280 \end{array}$

Divide the following by short division: *LU 1-3(2)*

1–20. $4\overline{)1{,}600}$ **1–21.** $9\overline{)810}$ **1–22.** $4\overline{)164}$

Divide the following by long division. Show work and remainder. *LU 1-3(2)*

1–23. $6\overline{)520}$ **1–24.** $62\overline{)8{,}915}$

Add the following without rearranging: *LU 1-2(1)*

1–25. $95 + 310$ **1–26.** $1{,}055 + 88$

1–27. $666 + 950$ **1–28.** $1{,}011 + 17$

1–29. Add the following and check by totaling each column individually without carrying numbers: *LU 1-2(1)*

Check

```
  8,539
  6,842
+ 9,495
```

Estimate the following by rounding all the way and then do actual addition: *LU 1-1(2), LU 1-2(1)*

	Actual	**Estimate**		**Actual**	**Estimate**
1–30.	7,700 9,286 + 3,900		**1–31.**	6,980 3,190 + 7,819	

Subtract the following without rearranging: *LU 1-2(2)*

1–32.   190 − 66

1–33.   950 − 870

1–34.   Subtract the following and check answer: *LU 1-2(2)*

```
  591,001
− 375,956
```

Multiply the following horizontally: *LU 1-3(1)*

1–35.   19 × 7

1–36.   84 × 8

1–37.   27 × 8

1–38.   19 × 5

Divide the following and check by multiplication: *LU 1-2(2)*

1–39.   45)876   **Check**

1–40.   46)1,950   **Check**

Complete the following: *LU 1-2(2)*

1–41.
```
  9,200
− 1,510

−   700
```

1–42.
```
  3,000,000
−   769,459

−    68,541
```

1–43.   Estimate the following problem by rounding all the way and then do the actual multiplication: *LU 1-1(2), LU 1-3(1)*

Actual   **Estimate**
```
  870
× 81
```

Divide the following by the shortcut method: *LU 1-3(2)*

1–44.   1,000)950,000

1–45.   100)70,000

1–46. Estimate actual problem by rounding all the way and do actual division: *LU 1-1(2), LU 1-3(2)*

Actual   **Estimate**

$$695\overline{)8,950}$$

WORD PROBLEMS

1–47. *The Wall Street Journal* reported that the cost for lightbulbs over a 10-year period at a local Walmart parking lot in Kansas would be $248,134 if standard lightbulbs were used. If LED lightbulbs were used over the same period, the total cost would be $220,396. What would Walmart save by using LED bulbs? *LU 1-2(2)*

1–48. An education can be the key to higher earnings. In a U.S. Census Bureau study, high school graduates earned $30,400 per year. Associate's degree graduates averaged $38,200 per year. Bachelor's degree graduates averaged $52,200 per year. Assuming a 50-year work-life, calculate the lifetime earnings for a high school graduate, associate's degree graduate, and bachelor's degree graduate. What's the lifetime income difference between a high school and associate's degree? What about the lifetime difference between a high school and bachelor's degree? *LU 1-3(1), LU 1-2(2)*

1–49. Assume season-ticket prices in the lower bowl for the Buffalo Bills will rise from $480 for a 10-game package to $600. Fans sitting in the best seats in the upper deck will pay an increase from $440 to $540. Don Manning plans to purchase two season tickets for either lower bowl or upper deck. **(a)** How much more will two tickets cost for lower bowl? **(b)** How much more will two tickets cost for upper deck? **(c)** What will be his total cost for a 10-game package for lower bowl? **(d)** What will be his total cost for a 10-game package for upper deck? *LU 1-2(2), LU 1-3(1)*

1–50. Some ticket prices for *Lion King* on Broadway were $70, $95, $200, and $250. For a family of four, estimate the cost of the $95 tickets by rounding all the way and then do the actual multiplication: *LU 1-1(2), LU 1-3(1)*

1–51. Walt Disney World Resort and United Vacations got together to create a special deal. The air-inclusive package features accommodations for three nights at Disney's All-Star Resort, hotel taxes, and a four-day unlimited Magic Pass. Prices are $609 per person traveling from Washington, DC, and $764 per person traveling from Los Angeles. **(a)** What would be the cost for a family of four leaving from Washington, DC? **(b)** What would be the cost for a family of four leaving from Los Angeles? **(c)** How much more will it cost the family from Los Angeles? *LU 1-3(1)*

1–52. NTB Tires bought 910 tires from its manufacturer for $36 per tire. What is the total cost of NTB's purchase? If the store can sell all the tires at $65 each, what will be the store's gross profit, or the difference between its sales and costs (Sales − Costs = Gross profit)? *LU 1-3(1), LU 1-2(2)*

1–53. What was the total average number of visits for these websites? *LU 1-2(1), LU 1-3(2)*

Website	Average daily unique visitors
1. Orbitz.com	1,527,000
2. Mypoints.com	1,356,000
3. Americangreetings.com	745,000
4. Bizrate.com	503,000
5. Half.com	397,000

1–54. Yahoo! Health reported in November 2014 that 6 out of 10 adults in the United States are obese or overweight. Research has shown coffee has several health-related benefits. One such benefit is an antioxidant, chlorogenic acid (CGA), that may help protect against several obesity-related diseases. During a 15-week study, if 67 mice did not gain weight during the test period and an additional 48 demonstrated insulin resistance, how many mice were positively affected by the injection of the CGA solution? *LU 1-2(1)*

1–55. A report from the Center for Science in the Public Interest—a consumer group based in Washington, DC—released a study listing calories of various ice cream treats sold by six of the largest ice cream companies. The worst treat tested by the group was 1,270 total calories. People need roughly 2,200 to 2,500 calories per day. Using a daily average, how many additional calories should a person consume after eating ice cream? *LU 1-2(1), LU 1-3(2)*

1–56. At Rose State College, Alison Wells received the following grades in her online accounting class: 90, 65, 85, 80, 75, and 90. Alison's instructor, Professor Clark, said he would drop the lowest grade. What is Alison's average? *LU 1-2(1)*

1–57. The Bureau of Transportation's list of the 10 most expensive U.S. airports and their average fares is given below. Please use this list to answer the questions that follow. *LU 1-2(1, 2)*

1. Houston, TX	$477
2. Huntsville, AL	473
3. Newark, NJ	470
4. Cincinnati, OH	466
5. Washington, DC	465
6. Charleston, SC	460
7. Memphis, TN	449
8. Knoxville, TN	449
9. Dallas–Fort Worth, TX	431
10. Madison, WI	429

a. What is the total of all the fares?

b. What would the total be if all the fares were rounded all the way?

c. How much does the actual number differ from the rounded estimate?

1–58. Ron Alf, owner of Alf's Moving Company, bought a new truck. On Ron's first trip, he drove 1,200 miles and used 80 gallons of gas. How many miles per gallon did Ron get from his new truck? On Ron's second trip, he drove 840 miles and used 60 gallons. What is the difference in miles per gallon between Ron's first trip and his second trip? *LU 1-3(2)*

1–59. In December 2014, the night train from Berlin to Paris was canceled because of the attractiveness of low-cost alternatives. A midweek journey from Berlin to Paris by night train (four bunks to a room) costs 70 euros and takes 12 hours. A two-hour flight with one piece of checked luggage costs 55 euros. What is the difference between the fares in euros? *LU 1-2(2)*

1–60. Assume BarnesandNoble.com has 289 business math texts in inventory. During one month, the online bookstore ordered and received 1,855 texts; it also sold 1,222 on the web. What is the bookstore's inventory at the end of the month? If each text costs $59, what is the end-of-month inventory cost? *LU 1-2(1), LU 1-2(2)*

1–61. Assume Cabot Company produced 2,115,000 cans of paint in August. Cabot sold 2,011,000 of these cans. If each can cost $18, what were Cabot's ending inventory of paint cans and its total ending inventory cost? *LU 1-2(2), LU 1-3(1)*

1–62. A local community college has 20 faculty members in the business department, 40 in psychology, 26 in English, and 140 in all other departments. What is the total number of faculty at this college? If each faculty member advises 25 students, how many students attend the local college? *LU 1-2(1), LU 1-3(1)*

1–63. Hometown Buffet had 90 customers on Sunday, 70 on Monday, 65 on Tuesday, and a total of 310 on Wednesday to Saturday. How many customers did Hometown Buffet serve during the week? If each customer spends $9, what were the total sales for the week? *LU 1-2(1), LU 1-3(1)*

If Hometown Buffet had the same sales each week, what were the sales for the year?

1–64. A local travel agency projected its year 2015 sales at $880,000. During 2015, the agency earned $482,900 sales from its major clients and $116,500 sales from the remainder of its clients. How much did the agency overestimate its sales? *LU 1-2(2)*

1–65. Ryan Seary works at US Airways and earned $71,000 last year before tax deductions. From Ryan's total earnings, his company subtracted $1,388 for federal income taxes, $4,402 for Social Security, and $1,030 for Medicare taxes. What was Ryan's actual, or net, pay for the year? *LU 1-2(1, 2)*

1–66. CompareCards.com announced in January 2015 credit card offers with no interest payments for 18 months through 2016. If 11 credit card companies make this offer and 25,652 people are approved, on average how many new customers does each credit card company gain? *LU 1-3(2)*

1–67. Roger Company produces beach balls and operates three shifts. Roger produces 5,000 balls per shift on shifts 1 and 2. On shift 3, the company can produce 6 times as many balls as on shift 1. Assume a 5-day workweek. How many beach balls does Roger produce per week and per year? *LU 1-2(1), LU 1-3(1)*

1–68. Assume 6,000 children go to Disneyland today. How much additional revenue will Disneyland receive if it raises the cost of admission from $31 to $41? *LU 1-2(1), LU 1-3(1)*

1–69. Moe Brink has a $900 balance in his checkbook. During the week, Moe wrote the following checks: rent, $350; telephone, $44; food, $160; and entertaining, $60. Moe also made a $1,200 deposit. What is Moe's new checkbook balance? *LU 1-2(1, 2)*

1–70. A local Sports Authority store, an athletic sports shop, bought and sold the following merchandise: *LU 1-2(1, 2)*

	Cost	Selling price
Tennis rackets	$2,900	$ 3,999
Tennis balls	70	210
Bowling balls	1,050	2,950
Sneakers	+ 8,105	+14,888

What was the total cost of the merchandise bought by Sports Authority? If the shop sold all its merchandise, what were the sales and the resulting gross profit (Sales − Costs = Gross profit)?

1–71. Rich Engel, the bookkeeper for Engel's Real Estate, and his manager are concerned about the company's telephone bills. *eXcel* Last year the company's average monthly phone bill was $32. Rich's manager asked him for an average of this year's phone bills. Rich's records show the following: *LU 1-2(1), LU 1-3(2)*

January	$ 34	July	$ 28
February	60	August	23
March	20	September	29
April	25	October	25
May	30	November	22
June	59	December	41

What is the average of this year's phone bills? Did Rich and his manager have a justifiable concern?

1–72. On Monday, a local True Value Hardware sold 15 paint brushes at $3 each, six wrenches at $5 each, seven bags of grass *eXcel* seed at $3 each, four lawn mowers at $119 each, and 28 cans of paint at $8 each. What were True Value's total dollar sales on Monday? *LU 1-2(1), LU 1-3(1)*

1–73. While redecorating, Lee Owens went to Carpet World and bought 150 square yards of commercial carpet. The total cost of the carpet was $6,000. How much did Lee pay per square yard? *LU 1-3(2)*

1–74. Washington Construction built 12 ranch houses for $115,000 each. From the sale of these houses, Washington received *eXcel* $1,980,000. How much gross profit (Sales − Costs = Gross profit) did Washington make on the houses? *LU 1-2(2), LU 1-3(1, 2)*

The four partners of Washington Construction split all profits equally. How much will each partner receive?

CHALLENGE PROBLEMS

1–75. A mall in Lexington has 18 stores. The following is a breakdown of what each store pays for rent per month. The rent is based on square footage.

5 department/computer stores	$1,250	2 bakeries	$ 500
5 restaurants	860	2 drugstores	820
3 bookstores	750	1 supermarket	1,450

Calculate the total rent that these stores pay annually. What would the answer be if it were rounded all the way? How much more each year do the drugstores pay in rent compared to the bakeries? *LU 1-2(2), LU 1-3(1)*

1–76. Paula Sanchez is trying to determine her 2015 finances. Paula's actual 2014 finances were as follows: *LU 1-1, LU 1-2, LU 1-3*

2014				
Income:		Assets:		
Gross income	$69,000	Checking account	$ 1,950	
Interest income	450	Savings account	8,950	
Total	$69,450	Automobile	1,800	
Expenses:		Personal property	14,000	
Living	$24,500	Total	$26,700	
Insurance premium	350	Liabilities:		
Taxes	14,800	Note to bank	4,500	
Medical	585	Net worth	$22,200	($26,700 − $4,500)
Investment	4,000			
Total	$44,235			

Net worth = Assets − Liabilities
(own)   (owe)

Paula believes her gross income will double in 2015 but her interest income will decrease $150. She plans to reduce her 2015 living expenses by one-half. Paula's insurance company wrote a letter announcing that her insurance premiums would triple in 2015. Her accountant estimates her taxes will decrease $250 and her medical costs will increase $410. Paula also hopes to cut her investments expenses by one-fourth. Paula's accountant projects that her savings and checking accounts will each double in value. On January 2, 2015, Paula sold her automobile and began to use public transportation. Paula forecasts that her personal property will decrease by one-seventh. She has sent her bank a $375 check to reduce her bank note. Could you give Paula an updated list of her 2015 finances? If you round all the way each 2014 and 2015 asset and liability, what will be the difference in Paula's net worth?

SUMMARY PRACTICE TEST

Do you need help? The videos in Connect have step-by-step worked-out solutions. These videos are also available on YouTube!

1. Translate the following verbal forms to numbers and add.   *LU 1-1(1), LU 1-2(1)*

   a. Four thousand, eight hundred thirty-nine

   b. Seven million, twelve

   c. Twelve thousand, three hundred ninety-two

2. Express the following number in verbal form.   *LU 1-1(1)*

   9,622,364

3. Round the following numbers.   *LU 1-1(2)*

Nearest ten	Nearest hundred	Nearest thousand	Round all the way
a. 68	b. 888	c. 8,325	d. 14,821

4. Estimate the following actual problem by rounding all the way, work the actual problem, and check by adding each column of digits separately.   *LU 1-1(2), LU 1-2(1)*

Actual	Estimate	Check
1,886		
9,411		
+ 6,395		

5. Estimate the following actual problem by rounding all the way and then do the actual multiplication.   *LU 1-1(2), LU 1-3(1)*

Actual	Estimate
8,843	
× 906	

6. Multiply the following by the shortcut method.   *LU 1-3(1)*

   829,412 × 1,000

7. Divide the following and check the answer by multiplication.   *LU 1-3(1, 2)*

   Check

   39)‾14,800

8. Divide the following by the shortcut method.   *LU 1-3(2)*

   6,000 ÷ 60

9. Ling Wong bought a $299 iPod that was reduced to $205. Ling gave the clerk three $100 bills. What change will Ling receive?   *LU 1-2(2)*

10. Sam Song plans to buy a $16,000 Ford Focus with an interest charge of $4,000. Sam figures he can afford a monthly payment of $400. If Sam must pay 40 equal monthly payments, can he afford the Ford Focus?   *LU 1-2(1), LU 1-3(2)*

11. Lester Hal has the oil tank at his business filled 20 times per year. The tank has a capacity of 200 gallons. Assume **(a)** the price of oil fuel is $3 per gallon and **(b)** the tank is completely empty each time Lester has it filled. What is Lester's average monthly oil bill? Complete the following blueprint aid for dissecting and solving the word problem.   *LU 1-3(1, 2)*

	The facts	Solving for?	Steps to take	Key points
BLUEPRINT				

Steps to solving problem

SURF TO SAVE

Earning and spending money 🔍

PROBLEM 1
Textbook budget

Working with a budget of $1,000 visit http://www.amazon.com/ and search for the textbooks you are using for your classes this term. Round prices to the nearest dollar and ignore sales tax and delivery charges. Will your budgeted amount of $1,000 be enough to purchase all of your books? If so, how much money do you have left? If not, how much more money do you need?

Discussion Questions

1. What are the pros and cons of having a budget?
2. Should college students, who are traditionally low wage earners, still utilize a budget? Why?

PROBLEM 2
Budget expenses for a trip

Imagine you are planning a 4-night stay, Monday through Thursday, in New York City. Go to http://www.hertz.com to find the daily rate for the car you'd like. Then, go to http://www2.choicehotels.com to choose a hotel and determine the nightly room rate. Calculate your total cost for the car and lodging, ignoring taxes and rounding rates to the nearest dollar.

Discussion Questions

1. Using your existing salary, how would you budget for this trip to ensure you have the appropriate funds? Be specific.
2. What types of expenses might you incur once you are on this trip?

PROBLEM 3
Determine wage breakdowns

Visit http://www.bls.gov/oes/current/oes_nat.htm#11-0000 and select an occupational category that is within the area you would like to pursue. Using the annual mean wage column, what will your earnings be per month, per week, per day, and per hour, assuming a 40-hour workweek?

Discussion Questions

1. What determines the level of pay associated with each of these occupational categories?
2. What are some ways in which you could increase your pay over the course of your career?

PROBLEM 4
How much reading can you afford?

Go to http://www.amazon.com. Search for the list of "Top 100 books." If you have $100 to spend, how many of the Top 100 books could you buy if you started with the number one book and worked your way down the list? Ignore shipping and handling and taxes.

Discussion Questions

1. If you owned an e-reader, how many more e-books could you purchase with the same $100?
2. Based on your current salary, how many hours must you work to afford spending this $100 on books?

MOBILE APPS ✕

MathPad 4 (Clay Cat Designs) Focuses on solving word problems through addition, subtraction, division, and multiplication.

Basic Math (Explorer Technologies) Uses repetition of problems to build up basic math skills.

A KIPLINGER APPROACH

By Kaitlin Pitsker, From *Kiplinger's Personal Finance*, May 2015.

■ MORE STUDENTS MIGHT GET HELP WITH TUITION.

■ EDUCATION

FREE COMMUNITY COLLEGE FOR ALL?

It would require a lot of money and student mentorship programs.

COMMUNITY COLLEGE HAS long been an affordable alternative to a four-year degree. So when President Obama recently announced a plan to offer two years of community college at no cost to students, Americans' ears perked up. Some states and cities already pick up the tab for select students, and these programs offer clues about what a federal program might look like.

States that help cover college costs for eligible students include Georgia, New Jersey and Tennessee; cities include Chicago, Pittsburgh and Syracuse, N.Y. The programs vary, but most limit funding based on family income and kick in after federal and state aid is exhausted. Many programs require students to earn good grades—in high school, while enrolled at the community college, or both.

For such programs to work, they need sufficient financial backing, quality controls and tools to help students perform well, says Thomas Bailey, director of the Community College Research Center at Columbia University. For example, Tennessee's program, which launches this year and is open to all in-state residents, includes a mentorship program to help students graduate.

But funding can be a problem. To save money, New Jersey scaled back its program in 2009 to cover fewer students. A plan on the drawing board in Michigan would cover tuition at the state's participating community colleges and public universities, but it would require students to pay a portion of their future earnings to finance the program.

With a $60 billion price tag over 10 years and a Republican-led Congress, Obama's plan is unlikely to be approved anytime soon. But students can explore other low-cost options for furthering their education or boosting their careers by earning nondegree credentials—for example, at computer-coding boot camps or by enrolling in certificate programs sponsored by community colleges and companies such as Microsoft. **KAITLIN PITSKER**

EXCERPT FROM
The Kiplinger Letter

FUN AND GAMES AT THE OFFICE

Some employers actually want workers to play computer games on the job. Games reward staffers for boosting sales, soliciting customer feedback and more. Some have leader boards to foster what employers hope will be friendly competition. Others help employees track progress in meeting wellness or fitness goals. Well-designed games lure workers with the fun of online fantasy sports. (www.kiplingerbiz.com/ahead/games)

■ THE BUZZ

TAKE THE DISCOUNT (OR NOT)

Move over, Sunday coupons: Retailers dangle discounts in other ways these days. But to get the deals, you have to give something in return. Here's our take on when the trade-off is worth it.

Become an e-mail subscriber. Worth it, but wait until you're buying a big-ticket item, says online shopping expert Michelle Madhok. You get a discount of, say, 10% or more, but the coupon is good only once, and only for a limited time.

Connect on social media. Worth it for retailers where you shop frequently. By "liking" stores on Facebook or following them on Twitter, you get early access to sales or special discounts. The same goes for downloading a store's mobile app. For example, Gilt.com, a flash-sale Web site, runs mobile-only sales.

Get a store credit card. Not worth it, especially if you carry a balance. The average interest rate for retail cards is 23%, compared with 15% on general-purpose cards. The interest you pay will quickly wipe out the discount of 15% or more you get when you open the card. Instead, use sites such as GiftCardGranny.com to find discounted store gift cards. The savings can be as much as 20% or more. **CAROLYN BIGDA**

RANA FAURE/GETTY IMAGES

BUSINESS MATH ISSUE

Sixty billion dollars to fund free community college is way too expensive.

1. List the key points of the article and information to support your position.
2. Write a group defense of your position using math calculations to support your view.

Classroom Notes

CHAPTER 2

Fractions

© moodboard/Superstock

Talk To Me

The number of mobile-phone users world-wide is expected to exceed five billion by 2017, with more than half of those living and working in the Asia-Pacific region.

2013 TOTAL 4.31 billion

2017 TOTAL 5.10 billion

- ● Asia-Pacific
- ● Middle East and Africa
- ● Europe
- ● Latin America
- ● North America

Source: eMarketer

Source: *The Wall Street Journal*, 7/8/14.

LU 2–1: Types of Fractions and Conversion Procedures

1. Recognize the three types of fractions.
2. Convert improper fractions to whole or mixed numbers and mixed numbers to improper fractions.
3. Convert fractions to lowest and highest terms.

LU 2–2: Adding and Subtracting Fractions

1. Add like and unlike fractions.
2. Find the least common denominator by inspection and prime numbers.
3. Subtract like and unlike fractions.
4. Add and subtract mixed numbers with the same or different denominators.

LU 2–3: Multiplying and Dividing Fractions

1. Multiply and divide proper fractions and mixed numbers.
2. Use the cancellation method in the multiplication and division of fractions.

VOCABULARY PREVIEW

Here are key terms in this chapter. After completing the chapter, if you know the term, place a checkmark in the box. If you don't know the term, look it up and put the page number where it can be found.

Cancellation ☐ Common denominator ☐ Denominator ☐ Equivalent ☐ Fraction ☐ Greatest common divisor ☐ Higher terms ☐ Improper fraction ☐ Least common denominator (LCD) ☐ Like fractions ☐ Lowest terms ☐ Mixed numbers ☐ Numerator ☐ Prime numbers ☐ Proper fraction ☐ Reciprocal ☐ Unlike fractions ☐

Reprinted by permission of *The Wall Street Journal*, copyright 2012 Dow Jones & Company, Inc. All rights reserved worldwide.

Market Divided Over Fractions

By Andrew Ackerman and Telis Demos

For some stock prices, the new math might look a lot like the old math: Regulators are thinking about bringing back the fraction.

The move would at least partly undo an 11-year-old rule that replaced fractions of a dollar in stock prices, like 1/8 and 1/16, with pennies. The idea of that change was to trim investors' trading costs: One-cent increments can lead to narrower gaps between the prices at which brokers buy and sell shares—potentially reducing their opportunity to shave off profits.

The *Wall Street Journal* clipping "Market Divided Over Fractions" illustrates the use of a fraction. From the clipping you learn that regulators are thinking of bringing back fractions like $\frac{1}{8}$ and $\frac{1}{16}$ to trade stocks.

Now let's look at Milk Chocolate M&M'S® candies as another example of using fractions.

As you know, M&M'S® candies come in different colors. Do you know how many of each color are in a bag of M&M'S®? If you go to the M&M'S website, you learn that a typical bag of M&M'S® contains approximately 17 brown, 11 yellow, 11 red, and 5 each of orange, blue, and green M&M'S®.[1]

The 1.69-ounce bag of M&M'S® shown on the next page contains 55 M&M'S®. In this bag, you will find the following colors:

18 yellow	9 blue	6 brown
10 red	7 orange	5 green

The number of yellow candies in a bag might suggest that yellow is the favorite color of many people. Since this is a business math text, however, let's look at the 55 M&M'S® in terms of fractional arithmetic.

[1] Off 1 due to rounding.

55 pieces in the bag

© Food Tree Images/Alamy

Of the 55 M&M'S® in the 1.69-ounce bag, 5 of these M&M'S® are green, so we can say that 5 parts of 55 represent green candies. We could also say that 1 out of 11 M&M'S® is green. Are you confused?

For many people, fractions are difficult. If you are one of these people, this chapter is for you. First you will review the types of fractions and the fraction conversion procedures. Then you will gain a clear understanding of the addition, subtraction, multiplication, and division of fractions.

Learning Unit 2–1: Types of Fractions and Conversion Procedures

LO 1

This chapter explains the parts of whole numbers called **fractions.** With fractions you can divide any object or unit—a whole—into a definite number of equal parts. For example, the bag of 55 M&M'S® described above contains 6 brown candies. If you eat only the brown M&M'S®, you have eaten 6 parts of 55, or 6 parts of the whole bag of M&M'S®. We can express this in the following fraction:

© Amazing Images/Alamy

6 is the **numerator,** or top of the fraction. The numerator describes the number of equal parts of the whole bag that you ate.

$$\frac{6}{55}$$

55 is the **denominator,** or bottom of the fraction. The denominator gives the total number of equal parts in the bag of M&M'S®.

Before reviewing the arithmetic operations of fractions, you must recognize the three types of fractions described in this unit. You must also know how to convert fractions to a workable form.

Types of Fractions

In the *Wall Street Journal* clipping, "Market Divided Over Fractions," we saw $\frac{1}{8}$ and $\frac{1}{16}$, which are proper fractions.

PROPER FRACTIONS
A **proper fraction** has a value less than 1; its numerator is smaller than its denominator.

EXAMPLES $\frac{1}{4}, \frac{1}{2}, \frac{1}{10}, \frac{1}{12}, \frac{1}{3}, \frac{4}{7}, \frac{2}{3}, \frac{9}{10}, \frac{12}{13}, \frac{18}{55}, \frac{499}{1,000}, \frac{501}{1,000}$

FOXTROT by Bill Amend

FOXTROT © 2014 Bill Amend. Reprinted with permission of ANDREWS MCMEEL SYNDICATION. All rights reserved.

IMPROPER FRACTIONS

An **improper fraction** has a value equal to or greater than 1; its numerator is equal to or greater than its denominator.

EXAMPLES $\dfrac{14}{14}, \dfrac{7}{6}, \dfrac{15}{14}, \dfrac{22}{19}$

MIXED NUMBERS

A **mixed number** is the sum of a whole number greater than zero and a proper fraction.

EXAMPLES $5\dfrac{1}{6}, 5\dfrac{9}{10}, 8\dfrac{7}{8}, 33\dfrac{5}{6}, 139\dfrac{9}{11}$

Conversion Procedures

In Chapter 1 we worked with two of the division symbols ($\div$ and $\overline{)}\,$). The horizontal line (or the diagonal) that separates the numerator and the denominator of a fraction also indicates division. The numerator, like the dividend, is the number we are dividing into. The denominator, like the divisor, is the number we use to divide. Then, referring to the 6 brown M&M's® in the bag of 55 M&M's® $\left(\dfrac{6}{55}\right)$ shown at the beginning of this unit, we can say that we are dividing 55 into 6, or 6 is divided by 55. Also, in the fraction $\dfrac{3}{4}$, we can say that we are dividing 4 into 3, or 3 is divided by 4. *Remember "The top dog gets the hat" when converting proper fractions to decimals. For example, in the fraction $\frac{3}{4}$, the 3 is the top dog. The division sign is the hat. Put the hat over the 3 and divide: $4\overline{)3} = .75$.*

Working with the smaller numbers of simple fractions such as $\frac{3}{4}$ is easier, so we often convert fractions to their simplest terms. In this unit we show how to convert improper fractions to whole or mixed numbers, mixed numbers to improper fractions, and fractions to lowest and highest terms.

Converting Improper Fractions to Whole or Mixed Numbers
Business situations often make it necessary to change an improper fraction to a whole number or mixed number. You can use the following steps to make this conversion:

CONVERTING IMPROPER FRACTIONS TO WHOLE OR MIXED NUMBERS

LO 2

Step 1. Divide the numerator of the improper fraction by the denominator.

Step 2. **a.** If you have no remainder, the quotient is a whole number.

b. If you have a remainder, the whole number part of the mixed number is the quotient. The remainder is placed over the old denominator as the proper fraction of the mixed number.

EXAMPLES

$$\frac{15}{15} = 1 \qquad \frac{16}{5} = 3\frac{1}{5} \qquad 5\overline{)16} \begin{array}{c} 3\text{ R1} \\ \hline \end{array}$$

$$\begin{array}{r} \underline{15} \\ 1 \end{array}$$

Converting Mixed Numbers to Improper Fractions By reversing the procedure of converting improper fractions to mixed numbers, we can change mixed numbers to improper fractions.

CONVERTING MIXED NUMBERS TO IMPROPER FRACTIONS

Step 1. Multiply the denominator of the fraction by the whole number.

Step 2. Add the product from Step 1 to the numerator of the old fraction.

Step 3. Place the total from Step 2 over the denominator of the old fraction to get the improper fraction.

EXAMPLE $6\frac{1}{8} = \frac{(8 \times 6) + 1}{8} = \frac{49}{8}$ Note that the denominator stays the same.

Converting (Reducing) Fractions to Lowest Terms When solving fraction problems, you always reduce the fractions to their lowest terms. This reduction does not change the value of the fraction. For example, in the bag of M&M'S®, 5 out of 55 were green. The fraction for this is $\frac{5}{55}$. If you divide the top and bottom of the fraction by 5, you have reduced the fraction to $\frac{1}{11}$ without changing its value. Remember, we said in the chapter introduction that 1 out of 11 M&M'S® in the bag of 55 M&M'S® represents green candies. Now you know why this is true.

To reduce a fraction to its lowest terms, begin by inspecting the fraction, looking for the largest whole number that will divide into both the numerator and the denominator without leaving a remainder. This whole number is the **greatest common divisor,** which cannot be zero. When you find this largest whole number, you have reached the point where the fraction is reduced to its **lowest terms.** At this point, no number (except 1) can divide evenly into both parts of the fraction.

REDUCING FRACTIONS TO LOWEST TERMS BY INSPECTION

LO 3

Step 1. By inspection, find the largest whole number (greatest common divisor) that will divide evenly into the numerator and denominator (does not change the fraction value).

Step 2. Divide the numerator and denominator by the greatest common divisor. Now you have reduced the fraction to its lowest terms, since no number (except 1) can divide evenly into the numerator and denominator.

EXAMPLE $\frac{24}{30} = \frac{24 \div 6}{30 \div 6} = \frac{4}{5}$

Using inspection, you can see that the number 6 in the above example is the greatest common divisor. When you have large numbers, the greatest common divisor is not so obvious. For large numbers, you can use the following step approach to find the greatest common divisor:

STEP APPROACH FOR FINDING GREATEST COMMON DIVISOR

Step 1. Divide the smaller number (numerator) of the fraction into the larger number (denominator).

Step 2. Divide the remainder of Step 1 into the divisor of Step 1.

Step 3. Divide the remainder of Step 2 into the divisor of Step 2. Continue this division process until the remainder is a 0, which means the last divisor is the greatest common divisor.

EXAMPLE

	Step 1	**Step 2**	
$\dfrac{24}{30}$	$24\overline{)30}$ $\dfrac{1}{}$ $\dfrac{24}{6}$	$6\overline{)24}$ $\dfrac{4}{}$ $\dfrac{24}{0}$	$\dfrac{24 \div 6}{30 \div 6} = \dfrac{4}{5}$

Reducing a fraction by inspection is to some extent a trial-and-error method. Sometimes you are not sure what number you should divide into the top (numerator) and bottom (denominator) of the fraction. The following reference table on divisibility tests will be helpful. Note that to reduce a fraction to lowest terms might result in more than one division.

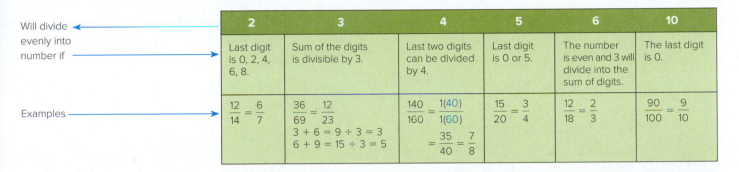

	2	**3**	**4**	**5**	**6**	**10**
Will divide evenly into number if	Last digit is 0, 2, 4, 6, 8.	Sum of the digits is divisible by 3.	Last two digits can be divided by 4.	Last digit is 0 or 5.	The number is even and 3 will divide into the sum of digits.	The last digit is 0.
Examples	$\dfrac{12}{14} = \dfrac{6}{7}$	$\dfrac{36}{69} = \dfrac{12}{23}$ $3 + 6 = 9 \div 3 = 3$ $6 + 9 = 15 \div 3 = 5$	$\dfrac{140}{160} = \dfrac{1(40)}{1(60)}$ $= \dfrac{35}{40} = \dfrac{7}{8}$	$\dfrac{15}{20} = \dfrac{3}{4}$	$\dfrac{12}{18} = \dfrac{2}{3}$	$\dfrac{90}{100} = \dfrac{9}{10}$

Converting (Raising) Fractions to Higher Terms   Later, when you add and subtract fractions, you will see that sometimes fractions must be raised to **higher terms.** Recall that when you reduced fractions to their lowest terms, you looked for the largest whole number (greatest common divisor) that would divide evenly into both the numerator and the denominator. When you raise fractions to higher terms, you do the opposite and multiply the numerator and the denominator by the same whole number. For example, if you want to raise the fraction $\frac{1}{4}$, you can multiply the numerator and denominator by 2.

EXAMPLE $\dfrac{1}{4} \times \dfrac{2}{2} = \dfrac{2}{8}$

The fractions $\frac{1}{4}$ and $\frac{2}{8}$ are **equivalent** in value. By converting $\frac{1}{4}$ to $\frac{2}{8}$, you only divided it into more parts.

Let's suppose that you have eaten $\frac{4}{7}$ of a pizza. You decide that instead of expressing the amount you have eaten in 7ths, you want to express it in 28ths. How would you do this?

To find the new numerator when you know the new denominator (28), use the steps that follow.

MONEY tips

Visit ethnic grocery stores for great buys on avocados, mangoes, limes, red onions, and other fruits and vegetables. Prices tend to be much cheaper.

> **RAISING FRACTIONS TO HIGHER TERMS WHEN DENOMINATOR IS KNOWN**
>
> **Step 1.** Divide the *new* denominator by the *old* denominator to get the common number that raises the fraction to higher terms.
>
> **Step 2.** Multiply the common number from Step 1 by the old numerator and place it as the new numerator over the new denominator.

EXAMPLE $\dfrac{4}{7} = \dfrac{?}{28}$

Step 1. Divide 28 by 7 = 4.

Step 2. Multiply 4 by the numerator 4 = 16.
Result:

$$\dfrac{4}{7} = \dfrac{16}{28} \qquad \left(\textit{Note: This is the same as multiplying } \dfrac{4}{7} \times \dfrac{4}{4}.\right)$$

Note that $\frac{4}{7}$ and $\frac{16}{28}$ are equivalent in value, yet they are different fractions.

Now try the following Practice Quiz to check your understanding of this unit.

LU 2–1   PRACTICE QUIZ

Complete this **Practice Quiz** to see how you are doing.

1. Identify the type of fraction—proper, improper, or mixed:

    a. $\dfrac{4}{5}$ b. $\dfrac{6}{5}$ c. $19\dfrac{1}{5}$ d. $\dfrac{20}{20}$

2. Convert to a mixed number:

    $\dfrac{160}{9}$

3. Convert the mixed number to an improper fraction:

    $9\dfrac{5}{8}$

4. Find the greatest common divisor by the step approach and reduce to lowest terms:

    a. $\dfrac{24}{40}$ b. $\dfrac{91}{156}$

5. Convert to higher terms:

    a. $\dfrac{14}{20} = \dfrac{}{200}$ b. $\dfrac{8}{10} = \dfrac{}{60}$

For **extra help** from your authors–Sharon and Jeff–see the videos in Connect.

These videos are also available on YouTube!

✓ Solutions

1. a. Proper
    b. Improper
    c. Mixed
    d. Improper

2.
$$17\frac{7}{9}$$
$$9\overline{)160}$$
$$\underline{9}$$
$$70$$
$$\underline{63}$$
$$7$$

3.
$$\frac{(9 \times 8) + 5}{8} = \boxed{\frac{77}{8}}$$

4. a.
$$\overset{1}{24\overline{)40}} \quad \overset{1}{16\overline{)24}} \quad \overset{2}{\boxed{8}\,\overline{)16}}$$
$$\underline{24} \qquad \underline{16} \qquad \underline{16}$$
$$16 \qquad\ \ 8 \qquad\quad 0$$

    $\boxed{8}$ is greatest common divisor.

$$\frac{24 \div 8}{40 \div 8} = \boxed{\frac{3}{5}}$$

    b.
$$\overset{1}{91\overline{)156}} \quad \overset{1}{65\overline{)91}} \quad \overset{2}{26\overline{)65}} \quad \overset{2}{\boxed{13}\,\overline{)26}}$$
$$\underline{91} \qquad \underline{65} \qquad \underline{52} \qquad \underline{26}$$
$$65 \qquad 26 \qquad 13 \qquad\ 0$$

    $\boxed{13}$ is greatest common divisor.

$$\frac{91 \div 13}{156 \div 13} = \boxed{\frac{7}{12}}$$

5. a.
$$\overset{10}{20\overline{)200}}$$
$10 \times 14 = 140$
$$\frac{14}{20} = \frac{\boxed{140}}{200}$$

    b.
$$\overset{6}{10\overline{)60}}$$
$6 \times 8 = 48$
$$\frac{8}{10} = \frac{\boxed{48}}{60}$$

LU 2–1a   EXTRA PRACTICE QUIZ WITH WORKED-OUT SOLUTIONS

Need more practice? Try this **Extra Practice Quiz** (check figures in the Interactive Chapter Organizer). Worked-out Solutions can be found in Appendix B.

1. Identify the type of fraction—proper, improper, or mixed:

    a. $\dfrac{2}{5}$ b. $\dfrac{7}{6}$ c. $18\dfrac{1}{3}$ d. $\dfrac{40}{40}$

2. Convert to a mixed number (do not reduce):

    $\dfrac{155}{7}$

3. Convert the mixed number to an improper fraction:

$$8\frac{7}{9}$$

4. Find the greatest common divisor by the step approach and reduce to lowest terms:

   a. $\frac{42}{70}$ **b.** $\frac{96}{182}$

5. Convert to higher terms:

   a. $\frac{16}{30} = \frac{}{300}$ **b.** $\frac{9}{20} = \frac{}{60}$

Learning Unit 2–2: Adding and Subtracting Fractions

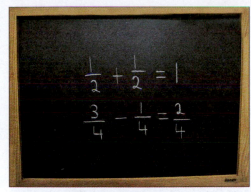

© Roberts Publishing Services

More teachers are using online video-sharing sites that are modeled after Google Inc.'s YouTube. As you can see in the video screenshot provided, these fractions can be added because the fractions have the same denominator. These are called *like fractions.*

In this unit you learn how to add and subtract fractions with the same denominators (**like fractions**) and fractions with different denominators (**unlike fractions**). We have also included how to add and subtract mixed numbers.

Addition of Fractions

When you add two or more quantities, they must have the same name or be of the same denomination. You cannot add 6 quarts and 3 pints unless you change the denomination of one or both quantities. You must either make the quarts into pints or the pints into quarts. The same principle also applies to fractions. That is, to add two or more fractions, they must have a **common denominator.**

Adding Like Fractions   In our video-sharing clipping at the beginning of this unit we stated that because the fractions had the same denominator, or a common denominator, they were *like fractions.* Adding like fractions is similar to adding whole numbers.

> **ADDING LIKE FRACTIONS**
>
> **Step 1.** Add the numerators and place the total over the original denominator.
>
> **Step 2.** If the total of your numerators is the same as your original denominator, convert your answer to a whole number; if the total is larger than your original denominator, convert your answer to a mixed number.

EXAMPLE $\frac{1}{7} + \frac{4}{7} = \frac{5}{7}$

The denominator, 7, shows the number of pieces into which some whole was divided. The two numerators, 1 and 4, tell how many of the pieces you have. So if you add 1 and 4, you get 5, or $\frac{5}{7}$.

Adding Unlike Fractions   Since you cannot add *unlike fractions* because their denominators are not the same, you must change the unlike fractions to *like fractions*—fractions with the same denominators. To do this, find a denominator that is common to all the fractions you want to add. Then look for the **least common denominator (LCD).**[2] The LCD is the smallest nonzero whole number into which all denominators will divide evenly. You can find the LCD by inspection or with prime numbers.

Finding the Least Common Denominator (LCD) by Inspection   The example that follows shows you how to use inspection to find an LCD (this will make all the denominators the same).

EXAMPLE $\frac{3}{7} + \frac{5}{21}$

Inspection of these two fractions shows that the smallest number into which denominators 7 and 21 divide evenly is 21. Thus, 21 is the LCD.

[2]Often referred to as the *lowest common denominator.*

You may know that 21 is the LCD of $\frac{3}{7} + \frac{5}{21}$, but you cannot add these two fractions until you change the denominator of $\frac{3}{7}$ to 21. You do this by building (raising) the equivalent of $\frac{3}{7}$, as explained in Learning Unit 2–1. You can use the following steps to find the LCD by inspection:

Step 1.   Divide the new denominator (21) by the old denominator (7): $21 \div 7 = 3$.

Step 2.   Multiply the 3 in Step 1 by the old numerator (3): $3 \times 3 = 9$. The new numerator is 9.

Result:

$$\frac{3}{7} = \frac{9}{21}$$

Now that the denominators are the same, you add the numerators.

$$\frac{9}{21} + \frac{5}{21} = \frac{14}{21} = \frac{2}{3}$$

Note that $\frac{14}{21}$ is reduced to its lowest terms $\frac{2}{3}$. Always reduce your answer to its lowest terms.

You are now ready for the following general steps for adding proper fractions with different denominators. These steps also apply to the following discussion on finding LCD by prime numbers.

> ### ADDING UNLIKE FRACTIONS
>
> **Step 1.**   Find the LCD.
>
> **Step 2.**   Change each fraction to a like fraction with the LCD.
>
> **Step 3.**   Add the numerators and place the total over the LCD.
>
> **Step 4.**   If necessary, reduce the answer to lowest terms.

Finding the Least Common Denominator (LCD) by Prime Numbers   When you cannot determine the LCD by inspection, you can use the prime number method. First you must understand prime numbers.

> ### PRIME NUMBERS
>
> A **prime number** is a whole number greater than 1 that is only divisible by itself and 1. The number 1 is not a prime number.

FRAZZ © 2010 Jef Mallett. Dist. By ANDREWS MCMEEL SYNDICATION. Reprinted with permission. All rights reserved.

EXAMPLES   2, 3, 5, 7, 11, 13, 17, 19, 23, 29, 31, 37, 41, 43

Note that the number 4 is not a prime number. Not only can you divide 4 by 1 and by 4, but you can also divide 4 by 2. A whole number that is greater than 1 and is only divisible by itself and 1 has become a source of interest to some people.

EXAMPLE $\dfrac{1}{3} + \dfrac{1}{8} + \dfrac{1}{9} + \dfrac{1}{12}$

Step 1. Copy the denominators and arrange them in a separate row.

$$3 \quad 8 \quad 9 \quad 12$$

Step 2. Divide the denominators in Step 1 by prime numbers. Start with the smallest number that will divide into at least two of the denominators. Bring down any number that is not divisible. Keep in mind that the lowest prime number is 2.

$$\dfrac{2\;/\;3 \quad 8 \quad 9 \quad 12}{3 \quad 4 \quad 9 \quad 6}$$

Note: The 3 and 9 were brought down, since they were not divisible by 2.

Step 3. Continue Step 2 until no prime number will divide evenly into at least two numbers.

Note: The 3 is used, since 2 can no longer divide evenly into at least two numbers.

$$\begin{array}{r} 2\;/\;3 \quad 8 \quad 9 \quad 12 \\ 2\;/\;3 \quad 4 \quad 9 \quad 6 \\ 3\;/\;3 \quad 2 \quad 9 \quad 3 \\ \hline 1 \quad 2 \quad 3 \quad 1 \end{array}$$

Step 4. To find the LCD, multiply all the numbers in the divisors (2, 2, 3) and in the last row (1, 2, 3, 1).

$$\boxed{2 \times 2 \times 3} \times \boxed{1 \times 2 \times 3 \times 1} = \boxed{72} \; \text{(LCD)}$$

$$\text{Divisors} \quad \times \quad \text{Last row}$$

Step 5. Raise each fraction so that each denominator will be 72 and then add fractions.

$$\boxed{\dfrac{1}{3} = \dfrac{?}{72}} \quad \boxed{\begin{array}{l} 72 \div 3 = 24 \\ 24 \times 1 = 24 \end{array}}$$

$$\dfrac{24}{72} + \dfrac{9}{72} + \dfrac{8}{72} + \dfrac{6}{72} = \dfrac{47}{72}$$

$$\boxed{\dfrac{1}{8} = \dfrac{?}{72}} \quad \boxed{\begin{array}{l} 72 \div 8 = 9 \\ 9 \times 1 = 9 \end{array}}$$

The above five steps used for finding LCD with prime numbers are summarized as follows:

FINDING LCD FOR TWO OR MORE FRACTIONS

Step 1. Copy the denominators and arrange them in a separate row.

Step 2. Divide the denominators by the smallest prime number that will divide evenly into at least two numbers.

Step 3. Continue until no prime number divides evenly into at least two numbers.

Step 4. Multiply all the numbers in divisors and last row to find the LCD.

Step 5. Raise all fractions so each has a common denominator and then complete the computation.

Adding Mixed Numbers

The following steps will show you how to add mixed numbers:

ADDING MIXED NUMBERS

Step 1. Add the fractions (remember that fractions need common denominators, as in the previous section).

Step 2. Add the whole numbers.

Step 3. Combine the totals of Steps 1 and 2. Be sure you do not have an improper fraction in your final answer. Convert the improper fraction to a whole or mixed number. Add the whole numbers resulting from the improper fraction conversion to the total whole numbers of Step 2. If necessary, reduce the answer to lowest terms.

Using prime numbers to find LCD of example

$$2 \,\underline{/\,20\ \ 5\ \ 4}$$
$$2 \,\underline{/\,10\ \ 5\ \ 2}$$
$$5 \,\underline{/\ \ 5\ \ 5\ \ 1}$$
$$\ \ 1\ \ \ 1\ \ \ 1$$

$2 \times 2 \times 5 = 20$ LCD

EXAMPLE

$$
\begin{array}{r}
4\dfrac{7}{20} \\[6pt]
6\dfrac{3}{5} \\[6pt]
+\ 7\dfrac{1}{4} \\ \hline
\end{array}
\qquad
\begin{array}{r}
4\dfrac{7}{20} \\[6pt]
6\dfrac{12}{20} \\[6pt]
+\ 7\dfrac{5}{20} \\ \hline
\end{array}
$$

$$\dfrac{3}{5} = \dfrac{?}{20}$$

$$20 \div 5 = 4$$
$$\times\ 3$$
$$\overline{\ \ 12\ \ }$$

Step 1 → $\dfrac{24}{20} = 1\dfrac{4}{20}$

Step 2 $+\ 17$
Step 3 $= 18\dfrac{4}{20} = 18\dfrac{1}{5}$

Subtraction of Fractions

The subtraction of fractions is similar to the addition of fractions. This section explains how to subtract like and unlike fractions and how to subtract mixed numbers.

Subtracting Like Fractions   To subtract like fractions, use the steps that follow.

LO 3

SUBTRACTING LIKE FRACTIONS
Step 1. Subtract the numerators and place the answer over the common denominator.
Step 2. If necessary, reduce the answer to lowest terms.

EXAMPLE $\dfrac{9}{10} - \dfrac{1}{10} = \dfrac{8 \div 2}{10 \div 2} = \dfrac{4}{5}$

 **Step 1**   **Step 2**

Subtracting Unlike Fractions   Now let's learn the steps for subtracting unlike fractions.

SUBTRACTING UNLIKE FRACTIONS
Step 1. Find the LCD.
Step 2. Raise the fraction to its equivalent value.
Step 3. Subtract the numerators and place the answer over the LCD.
Step 4. If necessary, reduce the answer to lowest terms.

EXAMPLE

$$
\begin{array}{r}
\dfrac{5}{8} \\[6pt]
-\ \dfrac{2}{64} \\ \hline
\end{array}
\qquad
\begin{array}{r}
\dfrac{40}{64} \\[6pt]
-\ \dfrac{2}{64} \\ \hline
\dfrac{38}{64} = \dfrac{19}{32}
\end{array}
$$

By inspection, we see that LCD is 64.
Thus $64 \div 8 = 8 \times 5 = 40$.

Subtracting Mixed Numbers   When you subtract whole numbers, sometimes borrowing is not necessary. At other times, you must borrow. The same is true of subtracting mixed numbers.

LO 4

SUBTRACTING MIXED NUMBERS	
When Borrowing Is Not Necessary	*When Borrowing Is Necessary*
Step 1. Subtract fractions, making sure to find the LCD.	**Step 1.** Make sure the fractions have the LCD.
Step 2. Subtract whole numbers.	**Step 2.** Borrow from the whole number of the minuend (top number).
Step 3. Reduce the fraction(s) to lowest terms.	**Step 3.** Subtract the whole numbers and fractions.
	Step 4. Reduce the fraction(s) to lowest terms.

EXAMPLE   Where borrowing is not necessary: Find LCD of 2 and 8. LCD is 8.

$$6\frac{1}{2}$$

$$-\frac{3}{8}$$

$$6\frac{4}{8}$$

$$-\frac{3}{8}$$

$$6\frac{1}{8}$$

EXAMPLE   Where borrowing is necessary:

$$3\frac{1}{2} = \qquad 3\frac{2}{4} = \qquad 2\frac{6}{4}\;\left(\frac{4}{4}+\frac{2}{4}\right)$$

$$-1\frac{3}{4} = \qquad -1\frac{3}{4} \qquad -1\frac{3}{4}$$

$$\text{LCD is } 4. \qquad\qquad\qquad 1\frac{3}{4}$$

Since $\frac{3}{4}$ is larger than $\frac{2}{4}$, we must borrow 1 from the 3. This is the same as borrowing $\frac{4}{4}$. A fraction with the same numerator and denominator represents a whole. When we add $\frac{4}{4}+\frac{2}{4}$, we get $\frac{6}{4}$. Note how we subtracted the whole number and fractions, being sure to reduce the final answer if necessary.

© Ariel Skelley/Blend Images/Corbis

How to Dissect and Solve a Word Problem

Let's now look at how to dissect and solve a word problem involving fractions.

The Word Problem   Albertsons grocery store has $550\frac{1}{4}$ total square feet of floor space. Albertsons' meat department occupies $115\frac{1}{2}$ square feet, and its deli department occupies $145\frac{7}{8}$ square feet. If the remainder of the floor space is for groceries, what square footage remains for groceries?

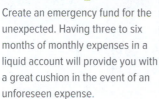

MONEY tips

Create an emergency fund for the unexpected. Having three to six months of monthly expenses in a liquid account will provide you with a great cushion in the event of an unforeseen expense.

	The facts	Solving for?	Steps to take	Key points
BLUEPRINT	*Total square footage:* $550\frac{1}{4}$ sq. ft. *Meat department:* $115\frac{1}{2}$ sq. ft. *Deli department:* $145\frac{7}{8}$ sq. ft.	Total square footage for groceries.	Total floor space − Total meat and deli floor space = Total grocery floor space.	Denominators must be the same before adding or subtracting fractions. $\frac{8}{8}=1$ Never leave improper fraction as final answer.

Steps to solving problem

1. Calculate total square footage of the meat and deli departments.

$$
\begin{array}{lrcr}
\text{Meat:} & 115\frac{1}{2} & = & 115\frac{4}{8} \\[2mm]
\text{Deli:} & +145\frac{7}{8} & = & +145\frac{7}{8} \\[2mm]
\hline
& & & 260\frac{11}{8} = 261\frac{3}{8} \text{ sq. ft.}
\end{array}
$$

2. Calculate total grocery square footage.

Check

$$
\begin{array}{rcccl}
550\frac{1}{4} & = & 550\frac{2}{8} & = & 549\frac{10}{8} \\[2mm]
-261\frac{3}{8} & = & -261\frac{3}{8} & = & -261\frac{3}{8}\;\left(\frac{2}{8}+\frac{8}{8}\right) \\[2mm]
\hline
& & & & 288\frac{7}{8} \text{ sq. ft.}
\end{array}
$$

$$261\frac{3}{8}$$
$$+288\frac{7}{8}$$
$$549\frac{10}{8} = 550\frac{2}{8} = 550\frac{1}{4}\text{ sq. ft.}$$

Note how the above blueprint aid helped to gather the facts and identify what we were looking for. To find the total square footage for groceries, we first had to sum the areas for meat and deli. Then we could subtract these areas from the total square footage. Also note that in Step 1 above, we didn't leave the answer as an improper fraction. In Step 2, we borrowed from the 550 so that we could complete the subtraction.

It's your turn to check your progress with a Practice Quiz.

LU 2–2 **PRACTICE QUIZ**

Complete this **Practice Quiz** to see how you are doing.

1. Find LCD by the division of prime numbers:
   12, 9, 6, 4

2. Add and reduce to lowest terms if needed:

   a. $\dfrac{3}{40} + \dfrac{2}{5}$ b. $2\dfrac{3}{4} + 6\dfrac{1}{20}$

3. Subtract and reduce to lowest terms if needed:

   a. $\dfrac{6}{7} - \dfrac{1}{4}$ b. $8\dfrac{1}{4} - 3\dfrac{9}{28}$ c. $4 - 1\dfrac{3}{4}$

4. Computerland has $660\frac{1}{4}$ total square feet of floor space. Three departments occupy this floor space: hardware, $201\frac{1}{8}$ square feet; software, $242\frac{1}{4}$ square feet; and customer service, _____ square feet. What is the total square footage of the customer service area? You might want to try a blueprint aid, since the solution will show a completed blueprint aid.

*For **extra help** from your authors–Sharon and Jeff–see the videos in Connect.*

These videos are also available on YouTube!

✓ Solutions

1.
   $$
   \begin{array}{c|cccc}
   2 & 12 & 9 & 6 & 4 \\
   2 & 6 & 9 & 3 & 2 \\
   3 & 3 & 9 & 3 & 1 \\
   \hline
     & 1 & 3 & 1 & 1
   \end{array}
   $$
   LCD $= 2 \times 2 \times 3 \times 1 \times 3 \times 1 \times 1 = \boxed{36}$

2. a. $\dfrac{3}{40} + \dfrac{2}{5} = \dfrac{3}{40} + \dfrac{16}{40} = \boxed{\dfrac{19}{40}}$

   $\left(\begin{array}{c} \dfrac{2}{5} = \dfrac{?}{40} \\ 40 \div 5 = 8 \times 2 = 16 \end{array} \right)$

   b.
   $$
   \begin{array}{r}
   2\frac{3}{4} \\
   + 6\frac{1}{20} \\
   \hline
   \end{array}
   \qquad
   \begin{array}{r}
   2\frac{15}{20} \\
   + 6\frac{1}{20} \\
   \hline
   8\frac{16}{20} = \boxed{8\frac{4}{5}}
   \end{array}
   $$

   $\dfrac{3}{4} = \dfrac{?}{20}$

   $20 \div 4 = 5 \times 3 = 15$

3. a.
   $$
   \begin{array}{r}
   \frac{6}{7} = \frac{24}{28} \\
   - \frac{1}{4} = - \frac{7}{28} \\
   \hline
   \boxed{\frac{17}{28}}
   \end{array}
   $$

   b.
   $$
   \begin{array}{r}
   8\frac{1}{4} = 8\frac{7}{28} = 7\frac{35}{28} \\
   -3\frac{9}{28} = -3\frac{9}{28} = -3\frac{9}{28} \\
   \hline
   4\frac{26}{28} = \boxed{4\frac{13}{14}}
   \end{array}
   $$

   $\left(\dfrac{28}{28} + \dfrac{7}{28} \right)$

   c.
   $$
   \begin{array}{r}
   3\frac{4}{4} \\
   - 1\frac{3}{4} \\
   \hline
   \boxed{2\frac{1}{4}}
   \end{array}
   $$
   Note how we showed the 4 as $3\frac{4}{4}$.

4. Computerland's total square footage for customer service:

	The facts	Solving for?	Steps to take	Key points
BLUEPRINT	*Total square footage:* $660\frac{1}{4}$ sq. ft. *Hardware:* $201\frac{1}{8}$ sq. ft. *Software:* $242\frac{1}{4}$ sq. ft.	Total square footage for for customer service.	Total floor space − Total hardware and software floor space = Total customer service floor space.	Denominators must be the same before adding or subtracting fractions.

Steps to solving problem

1. Calculate the total square footage of hardware and software.

$$201\frac{1}{8} = \quad 201\frac{1}{8} \text{ (hardware)}$$
$$+\ 242\frac{1}{4} = +\ 242\frac{2}{8} \text{ (software)}$$
$$443\frac{3}{8}$$

2. Calculate the total square footage for customer service.

$$660\frac{1}{4} = \quad 660\frac{2}{8} = 659\frac{10}{8} \text{ (total square footage)}$$
$$-443\frac{3}{8} = -443\frac{3}{8} = -443\frac{3}{8} \text{ (hardware plus software)}$$
$$216\frac{7}{8} \text{ sq. ft. (customer service)}$$

LU 2–2a	**EXTRA PRACTICE QUIZ WITH WORKED-OUT SOLUTIONS**

Need more practice? Try this **Extra Practice Quiz** (check figures in the Interactive Chapter Organizer). Worked-out Solutions can be found in Appendix B.

1. Find the LCD by the division of prime numbers:
   10, 15, 9, 4

2. Add and reduce to lowest terms if needed:

   a. $\dfrac{2}{25} + \dfrac{3}{5}$ **b.** $3\dfrac{3}{8} + 6\dfrac{1}{32}$

3. Subtract and reduce to lowest terms if needed:

   a. $\dfrac{5}{6} - \dfrac{1}{3}$ **b.** $9\dfrac{1}{8} - 3\dfrac{7}{32}$ **c.** $6 - 1\dfrac{2}{5}$

4. Computerland has $985\frac{1}{4}$ total square feet of floor space. Three departments occupy this floor space: hardware, $209\frac{1}{8}$ square feet; software, $382\frac{1}{4}$ square feet; and customer service, _____ square feet. What is the total square footage of the customer service area?

Learning Unit 2–3: Multiplying and Dividing Fractions

The following recipe for Coconutty "M&M'S"® Brand Brownies makes 16 brownies. What would you need if you wanted to triple the recipe and make 48 brownies?

© Roberts Publishing Services

Coconutty "M&M'S"® Brand Brownies

6 squares (1 ounce each) semi-sweet chocolate
½ cup (1 stick) butter
¾ cup granulated sugar
2 large eggs
1 tablespoon vegetable oil
1 teaspoon vanilla extract
1¼ cups all-purpose flour
3 tablespoons unsweetened cocoa powder
1 teaspoon baking powder
½ teaspoon salt
1½ cups "M&M'S"® Brand MINIS Chocolate
     Candies, divided

Adapted from Mars, Inc.

Preheat oven to 350°F. Grease 8 × 8 × 2-inch pan; set aside. In small saucepan combine chocolate, butter, and sugar over low heat; stir constantly until smooth. Remove from heat; let cool. In bowl beat eggs, oil, and vanilla; stir in chocolate mixture until blended. Stir in flour, cocoa powder, baking powder, and salt. Stir in 1 cup "M&M's"® Brand MINIS Chocolate

Candies. Spread batter in prepared pan. Bake 35 to 40 minutes or until toothpick inserted in center comes out clean. Cool. Prepare a coconut topping. Spread over brownies; sprinkle with $\frac{1}{2}$ cup "M&M's"® Brand MINIS Chocolate Candies.

In this unit you learn how to multiply and divide fractions.

LO 2

Multiplication of Fractions

Multiplying fractions is easier than adding and subtracting fractions because you do not have to find a common denominator. This section explains the multiplication of proper fractions and the multiplication of mixed numbers.

MULTIPLYING PROPER FRACTIONS[3]
Step 1. Multiply the numerators and the denominators.
Step 2. Reduce the answer to lowest terms or use the cancellation method.

First let's look at an example that results in an answer that we do not have to reduce.

EXAMPLE $\dfrac{1}{7} \times \dfrac{5}{8} = \boxed{\dfrac{5}{56}}$

In the next example, note how we reduce the answer to lowest terms.

EXAMPLE $\dfrac{5}{1} \times \dfrac{1}{6} \times \dfrac{4}{7} = \dfrac{20}{42} = \boxed{\dfrac{10}{21}}$ Keep in mind $\dfrac{5}{1}$ is equal to 5.

We can reduce $\frac{20}{42}$ by the step approach as follows:

$$\begin{array}{r} 2 \\ 20\overline{)42} \\ 40 \\ \overline{2} \end{array} \qquad \begin{array}{r} 10 \\ 2\overline{)20} \\ 20 \\ \overline{0} \end{array}$$

We could also have found the greatest common divisor by inspection.

$$\dfrac{20 \div 2}{42 \div 2} = \boxed{\dfrac{10}{21}}$$

As an alternative to reducing fractions to lowest terms, we can use the **cancellation** technique. Let's work the previous example using this technique.

EXAMPLE $\dfrac{5}{1} \times \dfrac{1}{\overset{}{\underset{3}{6}}} \times \dfrac{\overset{2}{\cancel{4}}}{7} = \boxed{\dfrac{10}{21}}$ 2 divides evenly into 4 twice and into 6 three times.

Note that when we cancel numbers, we are reducing the answer before multiplying. We know that multiplying or dividing both numerator and denominator by the same number gives an equivalent fraction. So we can divide both numerator and denominator by any number that divides them both evenly. It doesn't matter which we divide first. Note that this division reduces $\frac{10}{21}$ to its lowest terms.

Multiplying Mixed Numbers   The following steps explain how to multiply mixed numbers:

MULTIPLYING MIXED NUMBERS
Step 1. Convert the mixed numbers to improper fractions.
Step 2. Multiply the numerators and denominators.
Step 3. Reduce the answer to lowest terms or use the cancellation method.

EXAMPLE $2\dfrac{1}{3} \times 1\dfrac{1}{2} = \dfrac{7}{\underset{1}{\cancel{3}}} \times \dfrac{\overset{1}{\cancel{3}}}{2} = \dfrac{7}{2} = \boxed{3\dfrac{1}{2}}$

      Step 1 **Step 2** **Step 3**

---

[3]You would follow the same procedure to multiply improper fractions.

Division of Fractions

When you studied whole numbers in Chapter 1, you saw how multiplication can be checked by division. The multiplication of fractions can also be checked by division, as you will see in this section on dividing proper fractions and mixed numbers.

Dividing Proper Fractions   The division of proper fractions introduces a new term—the **reciprocal.** To use reciprocals, we must first recognize which fraction in the problem is the divisor—the fraction that we divide by. Let's assume the problem we are to solve is $\frac{1}{8} \div \frac{2}{3}$. We read this problem as "$\frac{1}{8}$ divided by $\frac{2}{3}$." The divisor is the fraction after the division sign (or the second fraction). The steps that follow show how the divisor becomes a reciprocal.

FRAZZ © 2013 Jef Mallett. Dist. By ANDREWS MCMEEL SYNDICATION. Reprinted with permission. All rights reserved.

DIVIDING PROPER FRACTIONS
Step 1.   Invert (turn upside down) the divisor (the second fraction). The inverted number is the *reciprocal.*
Step 2.   Multiply the fractions.
Step 3.   Reduce the answer to lowest terms or use the cancellation method.

Do you know why the inverted fraction number is a reciprocal? Reciprocals are two numbers that when multiplied give a product of 1. For example, 2 (which is the same as $\frac{2}{1}$) and $\frac{1}{2}$ are reciprocals because multiplying them gives 1.

EXAMPLE $\frac{1}{8} \div \frac{2}{3}$ $\frac{1}{8} \times \frac{3}{2} = \boxed{\frac{3}{16}}$

Dividing Mixed Numbers   Now you are ready to divide mixed numbers by using improper fractions.

DIVIDING MIXED NUMBERS
Step 1.   Convert all mixed numbers to improper fractions.
Step 2.   Invert the divisor (take its reciprocal) and multiply. If your final answer is an improper fraction, reduce it to lowest terms. You can do this by finding the greatest common divisor or by using the cancellation technique.

EXAMPLE $8\frac{3}{4} \div 2\frac{5}{6}$

Step 1. $\frac{35}{4} \div \frac{17}{6}$

Step 2. $\frac{35}{\cancel{4}_2} \times \frac{\cancel{6}^3}{17} = \frac{105}{34} = \boxed{3\frac{3}{34}}$ Here we used the cancellation technique.

How to Dissect and Solve a Word Problem

The Word Problem   Jamie ordered $5\frac{1}{2}$ cords of oak. The cost of each cord is $150. He also ordered $2\frac{1}{4}$ cords of maple at $120 per cord. Jamie's neighbor, Al, said that he would share the wood and pay him $\frac{1}{5}$ of the total cost. How much did Jamie receive from Al?

Note how we filled in the blueprint aid columns. We first had to find the total cost of all the wood before we could find Al's share—$\frac{1}{5}$ of the total cost.

MONEY tips

Make good buying decisions. Do not spend more money than you make. In fact, remember to pay yourself first by putting away money each paycheck for your retirement—even $10 each paycheck adds up.

	The facts	Solving for?	Steps to take	Key points
BLUEPRINT	Cords ordered: $5\frac{1}{2}$ at $150 per cord; $2\frac{1}{4}$ at $120 per cord. Al's cost share: $\frac{1}{5}$ the total cost.	What will Al pay Jamie?	Total cost of wood × $\frac{1}{5}$ = Al's cost.	Convert mixed numbers to improper fractions when multiplying. Cancellation is an alternative to reducing fractions.

Steps to solving problem

1. Calculate the cost of oak.

$$5\frac{1}{2} \times \$150 = \frac{11}{2} \times \overset{\$75}{\cancel{\$150}} = \$825$$
$$\phantom{5\frac{1}{2} \times \$150 = \frac{11}{\underset{1}{2}}}$$

2. Calculate the cost of maple.

$$2\frac{1}{4} \times \$120 = \frac{9}{\underset{1}{\cancel{4}}} \times \overset{\$30}{\cancel{\$120}} = \$270$$

$$\overline{\$1,095}\ \text{(total cost of wood)}$$

3. What Al pays.

$$\frac{1}{\underset{1}{\cancel{5}}} \times \overset{\$219}{\cancel{\$1,095}} = \boxed{\$219}$$

You should now be ready to test your knowledge of the final unit in the chapter.

LU 2–3 | **PRACTICE QUIZ**

Complete this Practice Quiz to see how you are doing.

*For **extra help** from your authors–Sharon and Jeff–see the videos in Connect.*

These videos are also available on YouTube!

1. Multiply (use cancellation technique):

   a. $\dfrac{4}{8} \times \dfrac{4}{6}$ b. $35 \times \dfrac{4}{7}$

2. Multiply (do not use canceling; reduce by finding the greatest common divisor):

   $\dfrac{14}{15} \times \dfrac{7}{10}$

3. Complete the following. Reduce to lowest terms as needed.

   a. $\dfrac{1}{9} \div \dfrac{5}{6}$ b. $\dfrac{51}{5} \div \dfrac{5}{9}$

4. Jill Estes bought a mobile home that was $8\frac{1}{8}$ times as expensive as the home her brother bought. Jill's brother paid $16,000 for his mobile home. What is the cost of Jill's new home?

✓ Solutions

1. a. $\dfrac{\cancel{4}}{\underset{2}{\cancel{8}}} \times \dfrac{\cancel{4}}{\cancel{6}} = \dfrac{1}{3}$ b. $\overset{5}{\cancel{35}} \times \dfrac{4}{\cancel{7}} = \boxed{20}$

2. $\dfrac{14}{15} \times \dfrac{7}{10} = \dfrac{98 \div 2}{150 \div 2} = \boxed{\dfrac{49}{75}}$

   $98\overline{)150}$ $52\overline{)98}$ $46\overline{)52}$ $6\overline{)46}$ $4\overline{)6}$ $2\overline{)4}$

   $\underline{98}$ $\underline{52}$ $\underline{46}$ $\underline{42}$ $\underline{4}$ $\underline{4}$

   52 46 6 4 2 0

3. a. $\dfrac{1}{9} \times \dfrac{6}{5} = \dfrac{6 \div 3}{45 \div 3} = \boxed{\dfrac{2}{15}}$ b. $\dfrac{51}{5} \times \dfrac{9}{5} = \dfrac{459}{25} = \boxed{18\dfrac{9}{25}}$

4. Total cost of Jill's new home:

	The facts	Solving for?	Steps to take	Key points
BLUEPRINT	Jill's mobile home: $8\frac{1}{8}$ as expensive as her brother's. Brother paid: $16,000.	Total cost of Jill's new home.	$8\frac{1}{8}$ × Total cost of Jill's brother's mobile home = Total cost of Jill's new home.	Canceling is an alternative to reducing.

Steps to solving problem

1. Convert $8\frac{1}{8}$ to a mixed number. $\dfrac{65}{8}$

2. Calculate the total cost of Jill's home. $\dfrac{65}{\underset{1}{\cancel{8}}} \times \overset{\$2,000}{\cancel{\$16,000}} = \boxed{\$130,000}$

LU 2–3α   **EXTRA PRACTICE QUIZ WITH WORKED-OUT SOLUTIONS**

Need more practice? Try this Extra Practice Quiz (check figures in the Interactive Chapter Organizer). Worked-out Solutions can be found in Appendix B.

1. Multiply (use cancellation technique):

   a. $\dfrac{6}{8} \times \dfrac{3}{6}$ b. $42 \times \dfrac{1}{7}$

2. Multiply (do not use canceling; reduce by finding the greatest common divisor):

   $\dfrac{13}{117} \times \dfrac{9}{5}$

3. Complete the following. Reduce to lowest terms as needed.

   a. $\dfrac{1}{8} \div \dfrac{4}{5}$ b. $\dfrac{61}{6} \div \dfrac{6}{7}$

4. Jill Estes bought a mobile home that was $10\frac{1}{8}$ times as expensive as the home her brother bought. Jill's brother paid $10,000 for his mobile home. What is the cost of Jill's new home?

INTERACTIVE CHAPTER ORGANIZER

Topic/Procedure/Formula	Example	You try it*
Types of fractions *Proper:* Value less than 1; numerator smaller than denominator. *Improper:* Value equal to or greater than 1; numerator equal to or greater than denominator. *Mixed:* Sum of whole number greater than zero and a proper fraction.	$\dfrac{3}{5}, \dfrac{7}{9}, \dfrac{8}{15}$ $\dfrac{14}{14}, \dfrac{19}{18}$ $6\dfrac{3}{8}, 9\dfrac{8}{9}$	**Identify type of fraction** $\dfrac{3}{10}, \dfrac{9}{8}, 1\dfrac{4}{5}$
Fraction conversions *Improper to whole or mixed:* Divide numerator by denominator; place remainder over old denominator. *Mixed to improper:* $\dfrac{\text{Whole number} \times \text{Denominator} + \text{Numerator}}{\text{Old denominator}}$	$\dfrac{17}{4} = 4\dfrac{1}{4}$ $4\dfrac{1}{8} = \dfrac{32+1}{8} = \dfrac{33}{8}$	**Convert to mixed number** $\dfrac{18}{7}$ **Convert to improper fraction** $5\dfrac{1}{7}$
Reducing fractions to lowest terms 1. Divide numerator and denominator by largest possible divisor (does not change fraction value). 2. When reduced to lowest terms, no number (except 1) will divide evenly into both numerator and denominator.	$\dfrac{18 \div 2}{46 \div 2} = \dfrac{9}{23}$	**Reduce to lowest terms** $\dfrac{16}{24}$
Step approach for finding greatest common denominator 1. Divide smaller number of fraction into larger number. 2. Divide remainder into divisor of Step 1. Continue this process until no remainder results. 3. The last divisor used is the greatest common divisor.	$\dfrac{15}{65} \longrightarrow 15\overline{)65}\overset{4}{}\quad 5\overline{)15}\overset{3}{}$ $\dfrac{60}{5}\dfrac{15}{0}$ **5** is greatest common divisor.	**Find greatest common denominator** $\dfrac{20}{50}$
Raising fractions to higher terms Multiply numerator and denominator by same number. Does not change fraction value.	$\dfrac{15}{41} = \dfrac{?}{410}$ $410 \div 41 = 10 \times 15 = \boxed{150}$	**Raise to higher terms** $\dfrac{16}{31} = \dfrac{?}{310}$

(continues)

INTERACTIVE CHAPTER ORGANIZER

Topic/Procedure/Formula	Examples	You try it*
Adding and subtracting like and unlike fractions When denominators are the same (like fractions), add (or subtract) numerators, place total over original denominator, and reduce to lowest terms. When denominators are different (unlike fractions), change them to like fractions by finding LCD using inspection or prime numbers. Then add (or subtract) the numerators, place total over LCD, and reduce to lowest terms.	$\frac{4}{9} + \frac{1}{9} = \boxed{\frac{5}{9}}$ $\frac{4}{9} - \frac{1}{9} = \frac{3}{9} = \boxed{\frac{1}{3}}$ $\frac{4}{5} + \frac{2}{7} = \frac{28}{35} + \frac{10}{35} = \frac{38}{35} = \boxed{1\frac{3}{35}}$	**Add** $\frac{3}{7} + \frac{2}{7}$ **Subtract** $\frac{5}{7} - \frac{2}{7}$ **Add** $\frac{5}{8} + \frac{3}{40}$
Prime numbers Whole numbers larger than 1 that are only divisible by itself and 1.	2, 3, 5, 7, 11	**List the next two prime numbers after 11**
LCD by prime numbers 1. Copy denominators and arrange them in a separate row. 2. Divide denominators by smallest prime number that will divide evenly into at least two numbers. 3. Continue until no prime number divides evenly into at least two numbers. 4. Multiply all the numbers in the divisors and last row to find LCD. 5. Raise fractions so each has a common denominator and complete computation.	$\frac{1}{3} + \frac{1}{6} + \frac{1}{8} + \frac{1}{12} + \frac{1}{9}$ 2 $\overline{\big)\,3\quad6\quad8\quad12\quad9}$ 2 $\overline{\big)\,3\quad3\quad4\quad6\quad9}$ 3 $\overline{\big)\,3\quad3\quad2\quad3\quad9}$ $\quad\;1\quad1\quad2\quad1\quad3$ $2 \times 2 \times 3 \times 1 \times 1 \times 2 \times 1 \times 3 = \boxed{72}$	**Find LCD** $\frac{1}{2} + \frac{1}{4} + \frac{1}{5}$
Adding mixed numbers 1. Add fractions. 2. Add whole numbers. 3. Combine totals of Steps 1 and 2. If denominators are different, a common denominator must be found. Answer cannot be left as improper fraction.	$1\frac{4}{7} + 1\frac{3}{7}$ Step 1: $\frac{4}{7} + \frac{3}{7} = \frac{7}{7}$ Step 2: $1 + 1 = 2$ Step 3: $2\frac{7}{7} = \boxed{3}$	**Add mixed numbers** $2\frac{1}{4} + 3\frac{3}{4}$
Subtracting mixed numbers 1. Subtract fractions. 2. If necessary, borrow from whole numbers. 3. Subtract whole numbers and fractions if borrowing was necessary. 4. Reduce fractions to lowest terms. If denominators are different, a common denominator must be found.	$12\frac{2}{5} - 7\frac{3}{5}$ $11\frac{7}{5} - 7\frac{3}{5}$ $= 4\frac{4}{5}$ Due to borrowing $\frac{5}{5}$ from number 12 $\frac{5}{5} + \frac{2}{5} = \frac{7}{5}$ The whole number is now 11.	**Subtract mixed numbers** $11\frac{1}{3}$ $-2\frac{2}{3}$
Multiplying proper fractions 1. Multiply numerators and denominators. 2. Reduce answer to lowest terms or use cancellation method.	$\frac{4}{7} \times \frac{7}{9} = \boxed{\frac{4}{9}}$	**Multiply and reduce** $\frac{4}{5} \times \frac{25}{26}$
Multiplying mixed numbers 1. Convert mixed numbers to improper fractions. 2. Multiply numerators and denominators. 3. Reduce answer to lowest terms or use cancellation method.	$1\frac{1}{8} \times 2\frac{5}{8}$ $\frac{9}{8} \times \frac{21}{8} = \frac{189}{64} = \boxed{2\frac{61}{64}}$	**Multiply and reduce** $2\frac{1}{4} \times 3\frac{1}{4}$

(continues)

INTERACTIVE CHAPTER ORGANIZER

Topic/Procedure/Formula	Examples	You try it*
Dividing proper fractions 1. Invert divisor. 2. Multiply. 3. Reduce answer to lowest terms or use cancellation method.	$\dfrac{1}{4} \div \dfrac{1}{8} = \dfrac{1}{\underset{1}{\cancel{4}}} \times \dfrac{\overset{2}{\cancel{8}}}{1} = 2$	**Divide** $\dfrac{1}{8} \div \dfrac{1}{4}$
Dividing mixed numbers 1. Convert mixed numbers to improper fractions. 2. Invert divisor and multiply. If final answer is an improper fraction, reduce to lowest terms by finding greatest common divisor or using the cancellation method.	$1\dfrac{1}{2} \div 1\dfrac{5}{8} = \dfrac{3}{2} \div \dfrac{13}{8}$ $= \dfrac{3}{\underset{1}{\cancel{2}}} \times \dfrac{\overset{4}{\cancel{8}}}{13}$ $= \dfrac{12}{13}$	**Divide mixed numbers** $3\dfrac{1}{4} \div 1\dfrac{4}{5}$

KEY TERMS	Cancellation Common denominator Denominator Equivalent Fraction Greatest common divisor	Higher terms Improper fraction Least common denominator (LCD) Like fractions Lowest terms	Mixed numbers Numerator Prime numbers Proper fraction Reciprocal Unlike fractions

Check Figures for Extra Practice Quizzes. (Worked-out Solutions are in Appendix B.)	LU 2–1a 1. a. P b. I c. M d. I 2. $22\dfrac{1}{7}$ 3. $\dfrac{79}{9}$ 4. a. 14; $\dfrac{3}{5}$ b. 2; $\dfrac{48}{91}$ 5. a. 160 b. 27	LU 2–2a 1. 180 2. a. $\dfrac{17}{25}$ b. $9\dfrac{13}{32}$ 3. a. $\dfrac{1}{2}$ b. $5\dfrac{29}{32}$ c. $4\dfrac{3}{5}$ 4. $393\dfrac{7}{8}$ sq. ft.	LU 2–3a 1. a. $\dfrac{3}{8}$ b. 6 2. 117; $\dfrac{1}{5}$ 3. a. $\dfrac{5}{32}$ b. $11\dfrac{31}{36}$ 4. $101,250

*Worked-out solutions are in Appendix B.

Critical Thinking Discussion Questions with Chapter Concept Check

1. What are the steps to convert improper fractions to whole or mixed numbers? Give an example of how you could use this conversion procedure when you eat at Pizza Hut.

2. What are the steps to convert mixed numbers to improper fractions? Show how you could use this conversion procedure when you order doughnuts at Dunkin' Donuts.

3. What is the greatest common divisor? How could you use the greatest common divisor to write an advertisement showing that 35 out of 60 people prefer MCI to AT&T?

4. Explain the step approach for finding the greatest common divisor. How could you use the MCI–AT&T example in question 3 to illustrate the step approach?

5. Explain the steps of adding or subtracting unlike fractions. Using a ruler, measure the heights of two different-size cans of food and show how to calculate the difference in height.

6. What is a prime number? Using the two cans in question 5, show how you could use prime numbers to calculate the LCD.

7. Explain the steps for multiplying proper fractions and mixed numbers. Assume you went to Staples (a stationery superstore). Give an example showing the multiplying of proper fractions and mixed numbers.

8. **Chapter Concept Check.** Using all the information you have learned about fractions, search the web to find out how many cars are produced in the United States in a year and what fractional part represents cars produced by foreign-owned firms. Finally, present calculations using fractions.

Classroom Notes

END-OF-CHAPTER PROBLEMS   **connect** (plus+)

Check figures for odd-numbered problems in Appendix C.   Name _____ Date _____

DRILL PROBLEMS

Identify the following types of fractions: *LU 2-1(1)*

2–1. $\dfrac{3}{8}$ **2–2.** $\dfrac{7}{6}$ **2–3.** $\dfrac{25}{13}$

Convert the following to mixed numbers: *LU 2-1(2)*

2–4. $\dfrac{91}{10}$ **2–5.** $\dfrac{921}{15}$

Convert the following to improper fractions: *LU 2-1(2)*

2–6. $8\dfrac{7}{8}$ **2–7.** $19\dfrac{2}{3}$

Reduce the following to the lowest terms. Show how to calculate the greatest common divisor by the step approach.   *LU 2-1(3)*

2–8. $\dfrac{16}{38}$ **2–9.** $\dfrac{44}{52}$

Convert the following to higher terms: *LU 2-1(3)*

2–10. $\dfrac{9}{10} = \dfrac{}{70}$

Determine the LCD of the following (a) by inspection and (b) by division of prime numbers: *LU 2-2(2)*

2–11. $\dfrac{3}{4}, \dfrac{7}{12}, \dfrac{5}{6}, \dfrac{1}{5}$ **Check**

      Inspection

2–12. $\dfrac{5}{6}, \dfrac{7}{18}, \dfrac{5}{9}, \dfrac{2}{72}$ **Check**

      Inspection

2–13. $\dfrac{1}{4}, \dfrac{3}{32}, \dfrac{5}{48}, \dfrac{1}{8}$ **Check**

      Inspection

Add the following and reduce to lowest terms: *LU 2-2(1), LU 2-1(3)*

2–14. $\dfrac{3}{9} + \dfrac{3}{9}$ **2–15.** $\dfrac{3}{7} + \dfrac{4}{21}$

2–16. $6\dfrac{1}{8} + 4\dfrac{3}{8}$ **2–17.** $6\dfrac{3}{8} + 9\dfrac{1}{24}$

2–18. $9\dfrac{9}{10} + 6\dfrac{7}{10}$

Subtract the following and reduce to lowest terms: *LU 2-2(3), LU 2-1(3)*

2–19. $\dfrac{11}{12} - \dfrac{1}{12}$

2–20. $14\dfrac{3}{8} - 10\dfrac{5}{8}$

2–21. $12\dfrac{1}{9} - 4\dfrac{2}{3}$

Multiply the following and reduce to lowest terms. Do not use the cancellation technique for these problems.   *LU 2-3(1), LU 2-1(3)*

2–22. $17 \times \dfrac{4}{2}$

2–23. $\dfrac{5}{6} \times \dfrac{3}{8}$

2–24. $8\dfrac{7}{8} \times 64$

Multiply the following. Use the cancellation technique.   *LU 2-3(1), LU 2-1(2)*

2–25. $\dfrac{4}{10} \times \dfrac{30}{60} \times \dfrac{6}{10}$

2–26. $3\dfrac{3}{4} \times \dfrac{8}{9} \times 4\dfrac{9}{12}$

Divide the following and reduce to lowest terms. Use the cancellation technique as needed.   *LU 2-3(2), LU 2-1(2)*

2–27. $\dfrac{12}{9} \div 4$

2–28. $18 \div \dfrac{1}{5}$

2–29. $4\dfrac{2}{3} \div 12$

2–30. $3\dfrac{5}{6} \div 3\dfrac{1}{2}$

WORD PROBLEMS

2–31. Michael Wittry has been investing in his Roth IRA retirement account for 20 years. Two years ago, his account was worth $215,658. After losing $\frac{1}{3}$ of its original value, it then gained $\frac{1}{2}$ of its new value back. What is the current value of his Roth IRA?   *LU 2-3(1)*

2–32. Delta pays Pete Rose $180 per day to work in the maintenance department at the airport. Pete became ill on Monday and went home after $\frac{1}{6}$ of a day. What did he earn on Monday? Assume no work, no pay.   *LU 2-3(1)*

2–33. Energy.gov stated by the end of 2013, the United States' wind power capacity provided enough electricity to power nearly 16 million homes annually—more than the total number of homes in the state of California. If only $\frac{1}{4}$ of the capacity were used, how many homes were powered?   *LU 2-3(1)*

2–34. Joy Wigens, who works at Putnam Investments, received a check for $1,600. She deposited $\frac{1}{4}$ of the check in her Citibank account. How much money does Joy have left after the deposit?   *LU 2-3(1)*

2–35. Lee Jenkins worked the following hours as a manager for a local Pizza Hut: $14\frac{1}{4}$, $5\frac{1}{4}$, $8\frac{1}{2}$, and $7\frac{1}{4}$. How many total hours did Lee work?   *LU 2-2(1)*

2–36. Lester bought a piece of property in Vail, Colorado. The sides of the land measure $115\frac{1}{2}$ feet, $66\frac{1}{4}$ feet, $106\frac{1}{8}$ feet, and $110\frac{1}{4}$ feet. Lester wants to know the perimeter (sum of all sides) of his property. Can you calculate the perimeter for Lester?   *LU 2-2(1)*

2–37. Tiffani Lind got her new weekly course schedule from Roxbury Community College in Boston. Following are her classes and their length: Business Math, $2\frac{1}{2}$ hours; Introduction to Business, $1\frac{1}{2}$ hours; Microeconomics, $1\frac{1}{2}$ hours; Spanish, $2\frac{1}{4}$ hours; Marketing, $1\frac{1}{4}$ hours; and Business Statistics, $1\frac{3}{4}$ hours. How long will she be in class each week?   *LU 2-2(1)*

2–38. Seventy-seven million people were born between 1946 and 1964. The U.S. Census classifies this group of individuals as baby boomers. It is said that today and every day for the next 18 years, 10,000 baby boomers will reach 65. If $\frac{1}{4}$ of the 65 and older age group uses e-mail, $\frac{1}{5}$ obtains the news from the Internet, and $\frac{1}{6}$ searches the Internet, find the LCD and determine total technology usage for this age group as a fraction.   *LU 2-2(1, 2)*

2–39. At a local Walmart store, a Coke dispenser held $19\frac{1}{4}$ gallons of soda. During working hours, $12\frac{3}{4}$ gallons were dispensed. How many gallons of Coke remain?   *LU 2-2(2, 3)*

2–40. *The Wall Street Journal* reported the biggest music comeback in 2014 was vinyl records. Nearly 8 million vinyl records were sold in 2014, mostly to younger markets. If there were 15 vinyl record factories pressing records in the United States in 2014, and only $\frac{2}{3}$ remain operational in 2015, how many factories closed down?   *LU 2-3(1)*

2–41. A local garden center charges $250 per cord of wood. If Logan Grace orders $3\frac{1}{2}$ cords, what will the total cost be?   *LU 2-3(1)*

2–42. A local Target store bought 90 pizzas at Pizza Hut for its holiday party. Each guest ate $\frac{1}{6}$ of a pizza and there was no pizza left over. How many guests did Target have for the party?   *LU 2-3(1)*

2–43. Marc, Steven, and Daniel entered into a Subway sandwich shop partnership. Marc owns $\frac{1}{9}$ of the shop and Steven owns $\frac{1}{4}$. What part does Daniel own?   *LU 2-2(1, 2)*

2–44. Lionel Sullivan works for Burger King. He is paid time and one-half for Sundays. If Lionel works on Sunday for 6 hours at a regular pay of $8 per hour, what does he earn on Sunday?   *LU 2-3(1)*

2–45. Michael Mann's 2015 hit movie *Blackhat* had an early screening for 200 security specialists including those from Google, Facebook, Apple, Tesla, Twitter, Square, and Cisco. The response was positive. If $\frac{19}{20}$ of the specialists deemed the scenes were 95% plausible, how many specialists rejected them?   *LU 2-3(1)*

2–46. A trip to the White Mountains of New Hampshire from Boston will take you $2\frac{3}{4}$ hours. Assume you have traveled $\frac{1}{11}$ of the way. How much longer will the trip take?   *LU 2-3(1, 2)*

*e**X**cel*

2–47. Andy, who loves to cook, makes apple cobbler for his family. The recipe (serves 6) calls for $1\frac{1}{2}$ pounds of apples, $3\frac{1}{4}$ cups of flour, $\frac{1}{4}$ cup of margarine, $2\frac{3}{8}$ cups of sugar, and 2 teaspoons of cinnamon. Since guests are coming, Andy wants to make a cobbler that will serve 15 (or increase the recipe $2\frac{1}{2}$ times). How much of each ingredient should Andy use?   *LU 2-3(1, 2)*

*e**X**cel*

2–48. Mobil allocates $1{,}692\frac{3}{4}$ gallons of gas per month to Jerry's Service Station. The first week, Jerry sold $275\frac{1}{2}$ gallons; second week, $280\frac{1}{4}$ gallons; and third week, $189\frac{1}{8}$ gallons. If Jerry sells $582\frac{1}{2}$ gallons in the fourth week, how close is Jerry to selling his allocation?   *LU 2-2(4)*

2–49. A marketing class at North Shore Community College conducted a viewer preference survey. The survey showed that $\frac{5}{6}$ of the people surveyed preferred Apple's iPhone over the Blackberry. Assume 2,400 responded to the survey. How many favored using a Blackberry?   *LU 2-3(1, 2)*

2–50. The price of a used Toyota LandCruiser has increased to $1\frac{1}{4}$ times its earlier price. If the original price of the LandCruiser was \$30,000, what is the new price?   *LU 2-3(1, 2)*

2–51. Tempco Corporation has a machine that produces $12\frac{1}{2}$ baseball gloves each hour. In the last 2 days, the machine has run for a total of 22 hours. How many baseball gloves has Tempco produced?   *LU 2-3(2)*

2–52. Alicia, an employee of Dunkin' Donuts, receives $23\frac{1}{4}$ days per year of vacation time. So far this year she has taken $3\frac{1}{8}$ days in January, $5\frac{1}{2}$ days in May, $6\frac{1}{4}$ days in July, and $4\frac{1}{4}$ days in September. How many more days of vacation does Alicia have left?   *LU 2-2(1, 2, 3)*

2–53. A Hamilton multitouch watch was originally priced at \$600. At a closing of the Alpha Omega Jewelry Shop, the watch is being reduced by $\frac{1}{4}$. What is the new selling price?   *LU 2-3(1)*

*e**X**cel*

2–54. Shelly Van Doren hired a contractor to refinish her kitchen. The contractor said the job would take $49\frac{1}{2}$ hours. To date, the contractor has worked the following hours:

Monday	$4\frac{1}{4}$
Tuesday	$9\frac{1}{8}$
Wednesday	$4\frac{1}{4}$
Thursday	$3\frac{1}{2}$
Friday	$10\frac{5}{8}$

How much longer should the job take to be completed?   *LU 2-2(4)*

2–55. An issue of *Taunton's Fine Woodworking* included plans for a hall stand. The total height of the stand is $81\frac{1}{2}$ inches. If the base is $36\frac{5}{16}$ inches, how tall is the upper portion of the stand?   *LU 2-2(4)*

2–56. Albertsons grocery planned a big sale on apples and received 750 crates from the wholesale market. Albertsons will bag these apples in plastic. Each plastic bag holds $\frac{1}{9}$ of a crate. If Albertsons has no loss to perishables, how many bags of apples can be prepared?   *LU 2-3(1)*

2–57. Frank Puleo bought 6,625 acres of land in ski country. He plans to subdivide the land into parcels of $13\frac{1}{4}$ acres each. Each parcel will sell for $125,000. How many parcels of land will Frank develop? If Frank sells all the parcels, what will be his total sales?   *LU 2-3(1)*

If Frank sells $\frac{3}{5}$ of the parcels in the first year, what will be his total sales for the year?

2–58. A local Papa Gino's conducted a food survey. The survey showed that $\frac{1}{9}$ of the people surveyed preferred eating pasta to hamburger. If 5,400 responded to the survey, how many actually favored hamburger?   *LU 2-3(1)*

2–59. Tamara, Jose, and Milton entered into a partnership that sells men's clothing on the web. Tamara owns $\frac{3}{8}$ of the company and Jose owns $\frac{1}{4}$. What part does Milton own?   *LU 2-2(1, 3)*

2–60. *Quilters Newsletter Magazine* gave instructions on making a quilt. The quilt required $4\frac{1}{2}$ yards of white-on-white print, 2 yards blue check, $\frac{1}{2}$ yard blue-and-white stripe, $2\frac{3}{4}$ yards blue scraps, $\frac{3}{4}$ yard yellow scraps, and $4\frac{7}{8}$ yards lining. How many total yards are needed?   *LU 2-2(1, 2)*

2–61. A trailer carrying supplies for a Krispy Kreme from Virginia to New York will take $3\frac{1}{4}$ hours. If the truck traveled $\frac{1}{5}$ of the way, how much longer will the trip take?   *LU 2-3(1, 2)*

2–62. Land Rover has increased the price of a FreeLander by $\frac{1}{5}$ from the original price. The original price of the FreeLander was $30,000. What is the new price? *LU 2-3(1, 2)*

CHALLENGE PROBLEMS

2–63. *Woodsmith* magazine gave instructions on how to build a pine cupboard. Lumber will be needed for two shelves $10\frac{1}{4}$ inches long, two base sides $12\frac{1}{2}$ inches long, and two door stiles $29\frac{1}{8}$ inches long. Your lumber comes in 6 foot lengths. **(a)** How many feet of lumber will you need? **(b)** If you want $\frac{1}{2}$ a board left over, is this possible with two boards? *LU 2-2(1, 2, 3, 4)*

2–64. Jack MacLean has entered into a real estate development partnership with Bill Lyons and June Reese. Bill owns $\frac{1}{4}$ of the partnership, while June has a $\frac{1}{5}$ interest. The partners will divide all profits on the basis of their fractional ownership. The partnership bought 900 acres of land and plans to subdivide each lot into $2\frac{1}{4}$ acres. Homes in the area have been selling for $240,000. By time of completion, Jack estimates the price of each home will increase by $\frac{1}{3}$ of the current value. The partners sent a survey to 12,000 potential customers to see whether they should heat the homes with oil or gas. One-fourth of the customers responded by indicating a 5-to-1 preference for oil. From the results of the survey, Jack now plans to install a 270-gallon oil tank at each home. He estimates that each home will need five fills per year. The current price of home heating fuel is $1 per gallon. The partnership estimates its profit per home will be $\frac{1}{8}$ the selling price of each home. From the above, please calculate the following: *LU 2-1(1, 2, 3), LU 2-2(1, 2, 3, 4), LU 2-3(1, 2)*

a. Number of homes to be built.

b. Selling price of each home.

c. Number of people responding to survey.

d. Number of people desiring oil.

e. Average monthly cost per house to heat using oil.

f. Amount of profit Jack will receive from the sale of homes.

SUMMARY PRACTICE TEST

Do you need help? The videos in Connect have step-by-step worked-out solutions. These videos are also available on YouTube!

Identify the following types of fractions. *LU 2-1(1)*

1. $5\frac{1}{8}$

2. $\frac{2}{7}$

3. $\frac{20}{19}$

4. Convert the following to a mixed number. *LU 2-1(2)*

$\frac{163}{9}$

5. Convert the following to an improper fraction. *LU 2-1(2)*

$8\frac{1}{8}$

6. Calculate the greatest common divisor of the following by the step approach and reduce to lowest terms. *LU 2-2(1, 2)*

$\frac{63}{90}$

7. Convert the following to higher terms. *LU 2-1(3)*

$\frac{16}{94} = \frac{?}{376}$

8. Find the LCD of the following by using prime numbers. Show your work. *LU 2-2(2)*

$\frac{1}{8} + \frac{1}{3} + \frac{1}{2} + \frac{1}{12}$

9. Subtract the following. *LU 2-2(4)*

$15\frac{4}{5}$

$-8\frac{19}{20}$

Complete the following using the cancellation technique. *LU 2-3(1, 2)*

10. $\frac{3}{4} \times \frac{2}{4} \times \frac{6}{9}$

11. $7\frac{1}{9} \times \frac{6}{7}$

12. $\frac{3}{7} \div 6$

13. A trip to Washington from Boston will take you $5\frac{3}{4}$ hours. If you have traveled $\frac{1}{3}$ of the way, how much longer will the trip take? *LU 2-3(1)*

14. Quiznos produces 640 rolls per hour. If the oven runs $12\frac{1}{4}$ hours, how many rolls will the machine produce? *LU 2-3(1, 2)*

15. A taste-testing survey of Zing Farms showed that $\frac{2}{3}$ of the people surveyed preferred the taste of veggie burgers to regular burgers. If 90,000 people were in the survey, how many favored veggie burgers? How many chose regular burgers? *LU 2-3(1)*

16. Jim Janes, an employee of Enterprise Co., worked $9\frac{1}{4}$ hours on Monday, $4\frac{1}{2}$ hours on Tuesday, $9\frac{1}{4}$ hours on Wednesday, $7\frac{1}{2}$ hours on Thursday, and 9 hours on Friday. How many total hours did Jim work during the week? *LU 2-2(1, 2)*

17. JCPenney offered a $\frac{1}{3}$ rebate on its $39 hair dryer. Joan bought a JCPenney hair dryer. What did Joan pay after the rebate? *LU 2-3(1)*

SURF TO SAVE

Can you afford to eat? 🔍

PROBLEM 1
Avoid fees

Go to http://money.usnews.com/money/personal-finance/articles/2012/08/10/10-annoying-bankfeesand-how-to-avoid-them and read "10 Annoying Bank Fees—and How to Avoid Them." Determine which of these fees is the most costly to the account holder.

Discussion Questions

1. Why do banks charge fees?
2. What types of fees does your bank charge? How do these fees have an impact on how you use your account?

PROBLEM 2
Cook up a winner!

Go to http://www.campbellsoup.com. Search for the recipe called "Festive Chicken."

1 tsp. onion powder; 1/2 tsp. paprika; 1/4 tsp. garlic powder; 1/4 tsp. pepper; 2 lb. chicken parts, skin removed; 1 can (10 3/4 oz.) Campbell's Cream of Mushroom soup OR 98% Fat Free Cream of Mushroom soup; 1/3 cup buttermilk; 1 small red pepper, chopped; 4 green onions, sliced; chopped fresh parsley

The recipe makes 4 servings. If you needed 20 servings for a company outing, how much of each ingredient would you need?

Discussion Questions

1. How much would it cost you to make 20 servings?
2. Would it be less expensive for you to purchase five pizzas to share?

PROBLEM 3
What is your grocery budget?

Visit http://www.walmart.com/cp/Grocery/976759 to find the prices for 20 grocery items that you normally buy within a 1-week time frame. What is the total cost for these items? Determine the fraction of your weekly income needed to cover this expenditure. Now expand this expenditure for the entire month and year. Based on the monthly and yearly expense, determine the fraction of your earnings that would be needed to make these purchases.

Discussion Questions

1. Do you prefer to buy name brand or store brand items? Why?
2. Assume your salary will increase by 1/3 of your current earnings. Would it affect which groceries you would purchase?

PROBLEM 4
Saving for a rainy day

Visit http://www.tradingeconomics.com/united-states/personal-savings to see the rate of savings in the United States. Using your current or expected salary upon completion of your educational pursuits, how would these savings rates be reflected in your personal situation?

Discussion Questions

1. If you saved 1/10 of your current or projected income for 1 year, how much would you have?
2. If you continued, how much would you have after 10 years of saving? What are the pros and cons of establishing and following a savings goal?

MOBILE APPS ❌

Everyday Mathematics Equivalent Fractions (McGraw-Hill School Education Group) Offers a quick and easy approach to understand concepts related to fractions.

Fraction Calculator Plus Free (Digitalchemy, LLC) (PCB Enterprises) Assists in the addition, subtraction, multiplication, and division of fractions.

A KIPLINGER APPROACH

By Patricia Mertz Esswein, From *Kiplinger's Personal Finance*, December 2013.

■ **LOWDOWN**

What You Need To Know About Tech Warranties

Extended coverage could pay off if your phone, laptop or tablet meets with an accident. **BY PATRICIA MERTZ ESSWEIN**

1. The dog ate my smart phone. In a recent survey of 1,000 parents, half said their kids had damaged a laptop, tablet or smart phone. Pets do their share of mischief, too. Plus, plenty of responsible adults drop a phone or laptop and crack the screen. So if you're buying a mobile device this holiday season, purchasing an extended warranty or service contract that covers what the industry calls accidental damage from handling (ADH) could be a smart move. It will cover repair or replacement of your device due to mishaps that manufacturers' warranties typically exclude.

2. Do your homework. Even if you intend to buy your tech gift at the mall, comparison-shop warranties on the Web, including the sites of retailers where you think you might buy the item and companies that sell warranties directly to consumers. Among the latter are Square Trade .com, ElectronicWarranty .com and Safeware.com, all

of which are rated A or A+ by the Better Business Bureau. Find out the terms and conditions of extended coverage: deductibles, limitations (such as the number of damage incidents covered) and exemptions.

3. Take your time. An extended warranty, even with beefed-up protection, typically costs 10% to 20% of the product's retail price, according to the Service Contract Industry Council. You're likely to get a hard sell at checkout because extended warranties generate a lot of profit for retailers—as much as 50% of what you pay for them. You can generally buy an extended warranty within 30 or 90 days of the purchase date. So if you're not sure you want the coverage, just say no at the time of purchase.

4. It pays to shop. Best Buy will charge you $180 for two years of extended coverage with ADH on an iPad, more than one-third of the

$499 purchase price. You'll pay no deductibles, and there's no limit on the number of incidents covered, but you're entitled to only one free replacement. Apple's own AppleCare+ for iPad costs $99; it covers two incidents of accidental damage, each with a $49 service fee (deductible). The best deal: SquareTrade's two-year coverage with no deductible. It also costs $99 but covers unlimited incidents, up to the amount you paid for your device.

5. Convenience counts. Most extended-service warranties require you to take your device to a local authorized service provider or ship it to a more distant service depot. SquareTrade allows you to choose your service

provider. For example, you can get repairs at a local Apple "Genius Bar" or an independent repair shop. You can also send your device to SquareTrade's own service depot (the repair and shipping will be free). If you take your device to an Apple store or repair shop, you'll pay out of pocket and submit a receipt for reimbursement.

6. And to play it safe... First of all, file your sales invoice and any paperwork regarding product claims. Register the extended warranty so there will be no hassle when you need repairs. And get a case for your phone or tablet. For example, for an iPad you can buy the OtterBox Defender Series case with screen protector and stand for $60 on Amazon.com. ■

OWEN DAVEY

BUSINESS MATH ISSUE

With technology changing so fast, taking out a tech warranty is a poor financial choice.

1. List the key points of the article and information to support your position.
2. Write a group defense of your position using math calculations to support your view.

CHAPTER 3

Decimals

© Bernd Obermann/Ovoworks/Getty Images

Order's Up

Ingredient costs for a Johnny Rockets Single burger rise sharply by the time they reach Nigeria.

MENU PRICE

$5.49 HOBOKEN, N.J.

$14 LAGOS, NIGERIA

U.S. WHOLESALE PRICES PER KILOGRAM

NIGERIA COSTS PER KILOGRAM

Tomato
$3.45

$10.73

Cheddar Cheese
$4.12

$13.88

Ground Beef
$4.17

$7.57*

Iceberg Lettuce
$2.16

$10.09

*Beef is from local cattle.

Sources: USDA (U.S. wholesale prices); Johnny Rockets (retail prices, Nigeria costs)

Note: Illustration doesn' include all ingredients.

Research by Drew Hinshaw

Graphic by Alberto Cervantes/ The Wall Street Journal

Reprinted by permission of *The Wall Street Journal*, copyright 2013 Dow Jones & Company, Inc. All rights reserved worldwide.

LU 3–1: Rounding Decimals; Fraction and Decimal Conversions

1. Explain the place values of whole numbers and decimals; round decimals.
2. Convert decimal fractions to decimals, proper fractions to decimals, mixed numbers to decimals, and pure and mixed decimals to decimal fractions.

LU 3–2: Adding, Subtracting, Multiplying, and Dividing Decimals

1. Add, subtract, multiply, and divide decimals.
2. Complete decimal applications in foreign currency.
3. Multiply and divide decimals by shortcut methods.

VOCABULARY PREVIEW

Here are key terms in this chapter. After completing the chapter, if you know the term, place a checkmark in the box. If you don't know the term, look it up and put the page number where it can be found.

Decimal ☐ Decimal fraction ☐ Decimal point ☐ Mixed decimal ☐ Pure decimal ☐ Repeating decimal ☐ Rounding decimals ☐

Spill Spending

Under Thursday's ruling BP faces up to $18 billion in Clean Water Act penalties.

Amount BP has spent/set aside, in billions	
Litigation and settlement costs	$25.87
Spill response costs	$14.30
Clean Water Act penalties	$ 3.51
Environmental costs	$ 3.03
Other Costs	$ 1.94
	$48.65
Recoveries	($ 5.68)
TOTAL	**$42.97**

BP so far had set aside $3.5 billion.

Source: the company   Data as second quarter 2014.   The Wall Street Journal

Source: *The Wall Street Journal,* 9/5/14.

Oil spills in the Gulf of Mexico have cost BP millions of dollars. The *Wall Street Journal* article shows the specific costs BP has set aside or spent so far in the cleanup. Just for litigation and spill response costs, the total is:

$25.87 million
+14.30 million
$40.17 million

Chapter 2 introduced the 1.69-ounce bag of M&M'S® shown in Table 3.1. In Table 3.1, the six colors in the 1.69-ounce bag of M&M'S® are given in fractions and their values expressed in decimal equivalents that are rounded to the nearest hundredths.

This chapter is divided into two learning units. The first unit discusses rounding decimals, converting fractions to decimals, and converting decimals to fractions. The second unit shows you how to add, subtract, multiply, and divide decimals, along with some shortcuts for multiplying and dividing decimals. Added to this unit is a global application of decimals dealing with foreign exchange rates. One of the most common uses of decimals occurs when we spend dollars and cents, which is a *decimal number.*

A **decimal** is a decimal number with digits to the right of a *decimal point,* indicating that decimals, like fractions, are parts of a whole that are less than one. Thus, we can interchange the terms *decimals* and *decimal numbers.* Remembering this will avoid confusion between the terms *decimal, decimal number,* and *decimal point.*

Learning Unit 3–1: Rounding Decimals; Fraction and Decimal Conversions

In Chapter 1 we stated that the **decimal point** is the center of the decimal numbering system. So far we have studied the whole numbers to the left of the decimal point and the parts of whole numbers called fractions. We also learned that the position of the digits in a whole number gives the place values of the digits (Figure 1.1). Now we will study the position (place

TABLE   3.1

Analyzing a bag of M&M'S®

LO 1

© Acorn 1/Alamy

Color*	Fraction	Decimal
Yellow	$\frac{18}{55}$	.33
Red	$\frac{10}{55}$	.18
Blue	$\frac{9}{55}$	.16
Orange	$\frac{7}{55}$	.13
Brown	$\frac{6}{55}$	.11
Green	$\frac{5}{55}$	.09
Total	$\frac{55}{55} = 1$	1.00

*The color ratios currently given are a sample used for educational purposes. They do not represent the manufacturer's color ratios.

values) of the digits to the right of the decimal point (Figure 3.1). Note that the words to the right of the decimal point end in *ths*.

You should understand why the decimal point is the center of the decimal system. If you move a digit to the left of the decimal point by place (ones, tens, and so on), *you increase its value 10 times for each place (power of 10).* If you move a digit to the right of the decimal point by place (tenths, hundredths, and so on), *you decrease its value 10 times for each place.*

EXAMPLES $.06 ←—————— The 6 is in the hundred*ths* place value.

1.527 ——————→ The 5 is in the ten*ths* place value.

2.8394 ——————→ The 4 is in the ten thousand*ths* place value.

.33 ——————→ The thirty-three hundred*ths* represents the yellow M&M'S® in our M&M'S® bag of 55 M&M'S®.

1.69 oz. ——————→ The one ounce and sixty-nine hundred*ths* of another ounce is the weight of our bag of M&M'S®.

Do you recall from Chapter 1 how you used a place-value chart to read or write whole numbers in verbal form? To read or write decimal numbers, you read or write the

FIGURE   3.1

Decimal place-value chart

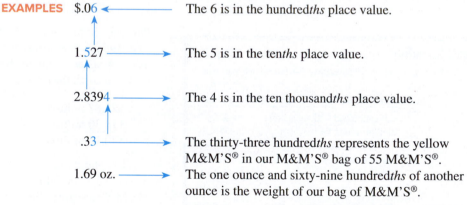

Thousands	Hundreds	Tens	Ones (units)	Decimal point (and)	Tenths	Hundredths	Thousandths	Ten thousandths	Hundred thousandths
1,000	100	10	1	and	$\frac{1}{10}$	$\frac{1}{100}$	$\frac{1}{1,000}$	$\frac{1}{10,000}$	$\frac{1}{100,000}$

decimal number as if it were a whole number. Then you use the name of the decimal place of the last digit as given in Figure 3.1. For example, you would read or write the decimal .0796 as seven hundred ninety-six ten thousandths (the last digit, 6, is in the ten thousandths place).

To read a decimal with four or fewer whole numbers, you can also refer to Figure 3.1. For larger whole numbers, refer to the whole number place-value chart in Chapter 1 (Figure 1.1). For example, from Figure 3.1 you would read the number 126.2864 as one hundred twenty-six and two thousand eight hundred sixty-four ten thousandths. *Remember to read the decimal point as* "and."

Now let's round decimals. Rounding decimals is similar to the rounding of whole numbers that you learned in Chapter 1.

Rounding Decimals

From Table 3.1, you know that the 1.69-ounce bag of M&M's® introduced in Chapter 2 contained $\frac{18}{55}$, or .33, yellow M&M's®. The .33 was rounded to the nearest hundredth. **Rounding decimals** involves the following steps:

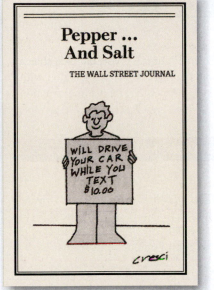

Pepper ...
And Salt

THE WALL STREET JOURNAL

WILL DRIVE
YOUR CAR
WHILE YOU
TEXT
$10.00

cresci

From *The Wall Street Journal*, permission Cartoon Features Syndicate.

ROUNDING DECIMALS TO A SPECIFIED PLACE VALUE
Step 1. Identify the place value of the digit you want to round.
Step 2. If the digit to the right of the identified digit in Step 1 is 5 or more, increase the identified digit by 1. If the digit to the right is less than 5, do not change the identified digit.
Step 3. Drop all digits to the right of the identified digit.

Let's practice rounding by using the $\frac{18}{55}$ yellow M&M's® that we rounded to .33 in Table 3.1. Before we rounded $\frac{18}{55}$ to .33, the number we rounded was .32727. This is an example of a **repeating decimal** since the 27 repeats itself.

EXAMPLE   Round .3272727 to the nearest hundredth.

Step 1.   .3272727   The identified digit is 2, which is in the hundredths place (two places to the right of the decimal point).

Step 2.   The digit to the right of 2 is more than 5 (7). Thus, 2, the identified digit in Step 1, is changed to 3.

.3372727

Step 3.   .33   Drop all other digits to the right of the identified digit 3.

We could also round the .3272727 M&M'S® to the nearest tenth or thousandth as follows:

	Tenth	**or**	**Thousandth**
.3272727 →	.3	.3272727 →	.327

OTHER EXAMPLES

Round to nearest dollar:	$166.39	→	$166
Round to nearest cent:	$1,196.885	→	$1,196.89
Round to nearest hundredth:	$38.563	→	$38.56
Round to nearest thousandth:	$1,432.9981	→	$1,432.998

The rules for rounding can differ with the situation in which rounding is used. For example, have you ever bought one item from a supermarket produce department that was marked "3 for $1" and noticed what the cashier charged you? One item marked "3 for $1" would not cost you $33\frac{1}{3}$ cents rounded to 33 cents. You will pay 34 cents. Many retail stores round to the next cent even if the digit following the identified digit is less than $\frac{1}{2}$ of a penny. In this text we round on the concept of 5 or more.

LO 2

Fraction and Decimal Conversions

In business operations we must frequently convert fractions to decimal numbers and decimal numbers to fractions. This section begins by discussing three types of fraction-to-decimal conversions. Then we discuss converting pure and mixed decimals to decimal fractions.

FRAZZ © 2014 Jef Mallett. Dist. By ANDREWS MCMEEL SYNDICATION. Reprinted with permission. All rights reserved.

Converting Decimal Fractions to Decimals   From Figure 3.1 you can see that a **decimal fraction** (expressed in the digits to the right of the decimal point) is a fraction with a denominator that has a power of 10, such as $\frac{1}{10}$, $\frac{17}{100}$, and $\frac{23}{1,000}$. To convert a decimal fraction to a decimal, follow these steps:

CONVERTING DECIMAL FRACTIONS TO DECIMALS
Step 1. Count the number of zeros in the denominator.
Step 2. Place the numerator of the decimal fraction to the right of the decimal point the same number of places as you have zeros in the denominator. (The number of zeros in the denominator gives the number of digits your decimal has to the right of the decimal point.) Do not go over the total number of denominator zeros.

Now let's change $\frac{3}{10}$ and its higher multiples of 10 to decimals.

EXAMPLES

Verbal form	Decimal fraction	Decimal[1]	Number of decimal places to right of decimal point
a. Three tenths	$\frac{3}{10}$	.3	1
b. Three hundredths	$\frac{3}{100}$	.03	2
c. Three thousandths	$\frac{3}{1,000}$	.003	3
d. Three ten thousandths	$\frac{3}{10,000}$	.0003	4

© Don Farrall/Getty Images

Note how we show the different values of the decimal fractions above in decimals. The zeros after the decimal point and before the number 3 indicate these values. If you add zeros after the number 3, you do not change the value. Thus, the numbers .3 , .30 , and .300 have the same value. So 3 tenths of a pizza, 30 hundredths of a pizza, and 300 thousandths of a pizza are the same total amount of pizza. The first pizza is sliced into 10 pieces. The second pizza is sliced into 100 pieces. The third pizza is sliced into 1,000 pieces. Also, we don't need to place a zero to the left of the decimal point.

Converting Proper Fractions to Decimals   Recall from Chapter 2 that proper fractions are fractions with a value less than 1. That is, the numerator of the fraction is smaller than its denominator. How can we convert these proper fractions to decimals? Since proper fractions are a form of division, it is possible to convert proper fractions to decimals by carrying out the division.

[1]From .3 to .0003, the values get smaller and smaller, but if you go from .3 to .3000, the values remain the same.

> ### CONVERTING PROPER FRACTIONS TO DECIMALS
>
> **Step 1.** Divide the numerator of the fraction by its denominator. (If necessary, add a decimal point and zeros to the number in the numerator.)
>
> **Step 2.** Round as necessary.

EXAMPLES

$$\frac{3}{4} = 4\overline{)3.00} \quad \begin{array}{r} .75 \\ \underline{2\,8} \\ 20 \\ \underline{20} \end{array}$$

$$\frac{3}{8} = 8\overline{)3.000} \quad \begin{array}{r} .375 \\ \underline{2\,4} \\ 60 \\ \underline{56} \\ 40 \\ \underline{40} \end{array}$$

$$\frac{1}{3} = 3\overline{)1.000} \quad \begin{array}{r} .333 \\ \underline{9} \\ 10 \\ \underline{9} \\ 10 \\ \underline{9} \\ 1 \end{array}$$

Note that in the last example $\frac{1}{3}$, the 3 in the quotient keeps repeating itself (never ends). The short bar over the last 3 means that the number endlessly repeats.

Converting Mixed Numbers to Decimals

A mixed number, you will recall from Chapter 2, is the sum of a whole number greater than zero and a proper fraction. To convert mixed numbers to decimals, use the following steps:

> ### CONVERTING MIXED NUMBERS TO DECIMALS
>
> **Step 1.** Convert the fractional part of the mixed number to a decimal (as illustrated in the previous section).
>
> **Step 2.** Add the converted fractional part to the whole number.

EXAMPLE

$$8\frac{2}{5} = \textbf{(Step 1)} \quad 5\overline{)2.0} \quad \begin{array}{r} .4 \\ \underline{2\,0} \end{array} \qquad \textbf{(Step 2)} = \begin{array}{r} 8.00 \\ +\ .40 \\ \hline 8.40 \end{array}$$

Now that we have converted fractions to decimals, let's convert decimals to fractions.

Converting Pure and Mixed Decimals to Decimal Fractions
A **pure decimal** has no whole number(s) to the left of the decimal point (.43, .458, and so on). A **mixed decimal** is a combination of a whole number and a decimal. An example of a mixed decimal follows.

EXAMPLE   737.592 = Seven hundred thirty-seven and five hundred ninety-two thousandths

Note the following conversion steps for converting pure and mixed decimals to decimal fractions:

> ### CONVERTING PURE AND MIXED DECIMALS TO DECIMAL FRACTIONS
>
> **Step 1.** Place the digits to the right of the decimal point in the numerator of the fraction. Omit the decimal point. (For a decimal fraction with a fractional part, see examples **c** and **d** below.)
>
> **Step 2.** Put a 1 in the denominator of the fraction.
>
> **Step 3.** Count the number of digits to the right of the decimal point. Add the same number of zeros to the denominator of the fraction. For mixed decimals, add the fraction to the whole number.

	EXAMPLES	Step 1	Step 2	Places	Step 3
	a. .3	$\dfrac{3}{}$	$\dfrac{3}{1}$	1	$\dfrac{3}{10}$
	b. .24	$\dfrac{24}{}$	$\dfrac{24}{1}$	2	$\dfrac{24}{100}$
	c. $.24\dfrac{1}{2}$	$\dfrac{245}{}$	$\dfrac{245}{1}$	3	$\dfrac{245}{1,000}$

If desired, you can reduce the fractions in Step 3.

Before completing Step 1 in example **c**, we must remove the fractional part, convert it to a decimal ($\frac{1}{2}$ = .5), and multiply it by .01 (.5 × .01 = .005). We use .01 because the 4 of .24 is in the hundredths place. Then we add .005 + .24 = .245 (three places to right of the decimal) and complete Steps 1, 2, and 3.

	d. $.07\dfrac{1}{4}$	$\dfrac{725}{}$	$\dfrac{725}{1}$	4	$\dfrac{725}{10,000}$

In example **d**, be sure to convert $\frac{1}{4}$ to .25 and multiply by .01. This gives .0025. Then add .0025 to .07, which is .0725 (four places), and complete Steps 1, 2, and 3.

	e. 17.45	$\dfrac{45}{}$	$\dfrac{45}{1}$	2	$\dfrac{45}{100} = 17\dfrac{45}{100}$

Example **e** is a mixed decimal. Since we substitute *and* for the decimal point, we read this mixed decimal as seventeen and forty-five hundredths. Note that after we converted the .45 of the mixed decimal to a fraction, we added it to the whole number 17.

The Practice Quiz that follows will help you check your understanding of this unit.

MONEY tips

Set up automatic payments for the minimum payment due on your debt and eliminate late fees. Create an alert with your smartphone or computer for each bill. Pay more than the minimum whenever possible.

LU 3–1 | PRACTICE QUIZ

Complete this **Practice Quiz** to see how you are doing.

Write the following as a decimal number.

1. Four hundred eight thousandths

Name the place position of the identified digit:

2. 6.8241 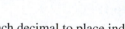 **3.** 9.3942

Round each decimal to place indicated:

		Tenth	**Thousandth**
4.	.62768	**a.**	**b.**
5.	.68341	**a.**	**b.**

Convert the following to decimals:

6. $\dfrac{9}{10,000}$ **7.** $\dfrac{14}{100,000}$

Convert the following to decimal fractions (do not reduce):

8. .819   **9.** 16.93   **10.** $.05\dfrac{1}{4}$

Convert the following fractions to decimals and round answer to nearest hundredth:

11. $\dfrac{1}{6}$ **12.** $\dfrac{3}{8}$ **13.** $12\dfrac{1}{8}$

*For **extra help** from your authors—Sharon and Jeff—see the videos in Connect.*

These videos are also available on YouTube!

✓ Solutions

1. .408 (3 places to right of decimal)

2. Hundredths   **3.** Thousandths

4. a. .6 (identified digit 6—digit to right less than 5)   **b.** .628 (identified digit 7—digit to right greater than 5)

5. a. .7 (identified digit 6—digit to right greater than 5)   **b.** .683 (identified digit 3—digit to right less than 5)

6. .0009 (4 places)   **7.** .00014 (5 places)

8. $\dfrac{819}{1,000}$ $\left(\dfrac{819}{1 + 3 \text{ zeros}}\right)$ **9.** $16\dfrac{93}{100}$

10. $\dfrac{525}{10,000}$ $\left(\dfrac{525}{\underset{1 + 4 \text{ zeros}}{}} \quad \dfrac{1}{4} \times .01 = .0025 + .05 = .0525 \right)$

11. $.16666 = \boxed{.17}$ **12.** $.375 = \boxed{.38}$ **13.** $12.125 = \boxed{12.13}$

LU 3–1a	**EXTRA PRACTICE QUIZ WITH WORKED-OUT SOLUTIONS**

Need more practice? Try this Extra Practice Quiz (check figures in the Interactive Chapter Organizer). Worked-out Solutions can be found in Appendix B.

Write the following as a decimal number:
1. Three hundred nine thousandths

Name the place position of the identified digit:
2. 7.9324 **3.** 8.3682

Round each decimal to place indicated:

	Tenth	Thousandth
4. .84361	**a.**	**b.**
5. .87938	**a.**	**b.**

Convert the following to decimals:

6. $\dfrac{8}{10,000}$ **7.** $\dfrac{16}{100,000}$

Convert the following to decimal fractions (do not reduce):

8. .938 **9.** 17.95 **10.** $.03\dfrac{1}{4}$

Convert the following fractions to decimals and round answer to nearest hundredth:

11. $\dfrac{1}{8}$ **12.** $\dfrac{4}{7}$ **13.** $13\dfrac{1}{9}$

Learning Unit 3–2: Adding, Subtracting, Multiplying, and Dividing Decimals

GLOBAL

The *Wall Street Journal* clip in the chapter opener uses decimals while showing the difference in menu prices of a Johnny Rockets hamburger of $8.51 between Hoboken, NJ, and Lagos, Nigeria.

$$\begin{array}{r} \$14.00 \\ -\,5.49 \\ \hline \$\ 8.51 \end{array}$$

This learning unit shows you how to add, subtract, multiply, and divide decimals. You also make calculations involving decimals, including decimals used in foreign currency.

Pluggers have been cloud computing for years.

Addition and Subtraction of Decimals

Since you know how to add and subtract whole numbers, to add and subtract decimal numbers you have only to learn about the placement of the decimals. The following steps will help you:

ADDING AND SUBTRACTING DECIMALS

Step 1. Vertically write the numbers so that the decimal points align. You can place additional zeros to the right of the decimal point if needed without changing the value of the number.

Step 2. Add or subtract the digits starting with the right column and moving to the left.

Step 3. Align the decimal point in the answer with the above decimal points.

EXAMPLES   Add $4 + 7.3 + 36.139 + .0007 + 8.22$.

Whole number to the right of the last digit is assumed to have a decimal. →

$$
\begin{array}{r}
4.0000 \\
7.3000 \\
36.1390 \\
.0007 \\
8.2200 \\
\hline
55.6597
\end{array}
$$

Extra zeros have been added to make calculation easier.

Subtract $45.3 - 15.273$.

$$
\begin{array}{r}
^{2\,9\,10}\\
45.3\cancel{0}\cancel{0}\cancel{0} \\
-15.273 \\
\hline
30.027
\end{array}
$$

Subtract $7 - 6.9$.

$$
\begin{array}{r}
^{6\ 10}\\
\cancel{7}.\cancel{0} \\
-6.9 \\
\hline
.1
\end{array}
$$

Multiplication of Decimals

The multiplication of decimal numbers is similar to the multiplication of whole numbers except for the additional step of placing the decimal in the answer (product). The steps that follow simplify this procedure.

MULTIPLYING DECIMALS

Step 1. Multiply the numbers as whole numbers, ignoring the decimal points.

Step 2. Count and total the number of decimal places in the multiplier and multiplicand.

Step 3. Starting at the right in the product, count to the left the number of decimal places totaled in Step 2. Place the decimal point so that the product has the same number of decimal places as totaled in Step 2. If the total number of places is greater than the places in the product, insert zeros in front of the product.

EXAMPLES

Step 1 →

$$
\begin{array}{r}
8.52 \\
\times\ 6.7 \\
\hline
5\,964 \\
51\,12 \\
\hline
57.084
\end{array}
$$

(2 decimal places)
(1 decimal place) ← Step 2

Step 3 →

$$
\begin{array}{r}
2.36 \\
\times\ .016 \\
\hline
1416 \\
236 \\
\hline
.03776
\end{array}
$$

(2 places)
(3 places)

Need to add zero

Division of Decimals

If the divisor in your decimal division problem is a whole number, first place the decimal point in the quotient directly above the decimal point in the dividend. Then divide as usual. If the divisor has a decimal point, complete the steps that follow.

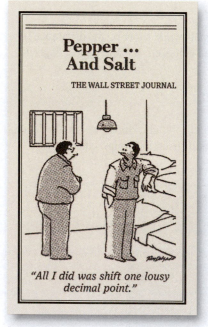

Pepper ... And Salt

THE WALL STREET JOURNAL

"All I did was shift one lousy decimal point."

From *The Wall Street Journal*, permission Cartoon Features Syndicate.

DIVIDING DECIMALS

Step 1. Make the divisor a whole number by moving the decimal point to the right.

Step 2. Move the decimal point in the dividend to the right the same number of places that you moved the decimal point in the divisor (Step 1). If there are not enough places, add zeros to the right of the dividend.

Step 3. Place the decimal point in the quotient above the new decimal point in the dividend. Divide as usual.

EXAMPLE

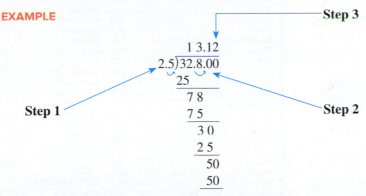

Step 3

$$
\begin{array}{r}
1\,3.12 \\
2.5\overline{\smash{)}\,32.8.00} \\
25 \\
\hline
7\,8 \\
7\,5 \\
\hline
3\,0 \\
2\,5 \\
\hline
50 \\
50 \\
\hline
\end{array}
$$

Step 1

Step 2

Stop a moment and study the above example. Note that the quotient does not change when we multiply the divisor and the dividend by the same number. This is why we can move the decimal point in division problems and always divide by a whole number.

Decimal Applications in Foreign Currency

LO 2

GLOBAL

EXAMPLE

Hanna Lind, who lives in Canada, wanted to buy a new Microsoft Surface 3. She went on eBay and found that the cost would be $600 in U.S. dollars. Wanting to know how much this would cost in Canadian dollars, Hanna consulted the following *Wall Street Journal*'s currency table and found that a Canadian dollar was worth $.8817 in U.S. dollars. Therefore, for each Canadian dollar it would cost $1.1341 to buy a U.S. good.

Using this information, Hanna completed the following calculation to determine what a Surface would cost her:

$600   × $1.1341   = $680.46
(cost of the Surface in   (cost of the Surface
U.S. dollars)   in Canadian dollars)

To check her findings, Hanna did the following calculation:

$680.46   × $.8817   = $599.96 (off due to rounding)
(cost of the Surface in   (what the Canadian dollar   (U.S. selling price)
Canadian dollars)   is worth against the
                     U.S. dollar)

© Oleksiy Maksymenko Photography/Alamy

GLOBAL

Reprinted by permission of *The Wall Street Journal*, copyright 2014
Dow Jones & Company, Inc. All rights reserved worldwide.

Currencies & Commodities | WSJ.com/fx

Currencies

U.S.-dollar foreign-exchange rates in late New York trading

Country/currency	in US$	per US$	US$ vs. YTD chg (%)	Country/currency	in US$	per US$	US$ vs. YTD chg (%)
Americas				**Europe**			
Argentina peso	.1172	8.5319	30.9	**Czech Rep.** koruna	.04519	22.126	11.3
Brazil real	.3906	2.5602	8.4	**Denmark** krone	.1676	5.9673	9.9
Canada dollar	.8817	1.1341	6.8	**Euro area** euro	1.2470	.8019	10.2
Chile peso	.001632	612.60	16.5	**Hungary** forint	.004073	245.53	13.6
Colombia peso	.0004414	2265.50	17.4	**Norway** krone	.1441	6.9396	14.3
Ecuador US dollar	1	1	unch	**Poland** zloty	.2986	3.3490	10.8
Mexico peso	.0715	13.9876	7.3	**Russia** ruble	.01956	51.116	55.3
Peru new sol	.3418	2.926	4.4	**Sweden** krona	.1344	7.4381	15.5
Uruguay peso	.04243	23.5680	11.2	**Switzerland** franc	1.0367	.9646	8.0
Venezuela b. fuerte	.157480	6.3500	unch	1-mos forward	1.0371	.9642	7.4
				3-mos forward	1.0377	.9636	7.4
Asia-Pacific				6-mos forward	1.0391	.9624	7.4
Australian dollar	.8489	1.1780	5.0	**Turkey** lira	.4514	2.2152	3.1
1-mos forward	.8470	1.1807	4.8	**UK pound**	1.5729	.6358	5.3
3-mos forward	.8434	1.1856	4.8	1-mos forward	1.5727	.6359	5.0
6-mos forward	.8379	1.1934	4.9	3-mos forward	1.5720	.6361	5.0
China yuan	.1625	6.1532	1.6	6-mos forward	1.5707	.6367	5.0
Hong Kong dollar	.1289	7.7556	unch				
India rupee	.01615	61.910	0.1	**Middle East/Africa**			
Indonesia rupiah	.0000813	12295	1.1	**Bahrain** dinar	2.6517	.3771	unch
Japan yen	.008446	118.40	12.4	**Egypt** pound	.1399	7.1505	2.8
1-mos forward	.008451	118.32	11.0	**Israel** shekel	.2549	3.9239	13.1
3-mos forward	.008455	118.27	11.0	**Jordan** dinar	1.4187	.7049	−0.4
6-mos forward	.008464	118.15	11.0	**Kuwait** dinar	3.4362	.2910	3.0
Malaysia ringgit	.2919	3.4263	4.4	**Lebanon** pound	.0006612	1512.45	0.5
New Zealand dollar	.7866	1.2713	4.5	**Saudi Arabia** riyal	.2664	3.7536	0.1
Pakistan rupee	.00982	101.855	−3.3	**South Africa** rand	.0910	10.9912	4.8
Philippines peso	.0223	44.841	1.0	**UAE** dirham	.2722	3.6732	unch
Singapore dollar	.7653	1.3066	3.5				
South Korea won	.0009010	1109.90	5.1			Close	Net Chg %ChgYTD %Chg
Taiwan dollar	.03212	31.135	4.0				
Thailand baht	.03050	32.790	0.2	**WSJ Dollar Index**		80.79	−0.10 −0.12 9.46
Vietnam dong	.00004674	21395	1.2				

Sources: ICAP plc., WSJ Market Data Group

LO 3

Multiplication and Division Shortcuts for Decimals

The shortcut steps that follow show how to solve multiplication and division problems quickly involving multiples of 10 (10, 100, 1,000, 10,000, etc.).

SHORTCUTS FOR MULTIPLES OF 10

Multiplication

Step 1. Count the zeros in the multiplier.

Step 2. Move the decimal point in the multiplicand the same number of places to the right as you have zeros in the multiplier.

Division

Step 1. Count the zeros in the divisor.

Step 2. Move the decimal point in the dividend the same number of places to the left as you have zeros in the divisor.

In multiplication, the answers are *larger* than the original number.

EXAMPLE If Toyota spends $60,000 for magazine advertising, what is the total value if it spends this same amount for 10 years? What would be the total cost?

$$\$60{,}000 \times 10 = \boxed{\$600{,}000}$$ (1 place to the right)

OTHER EXAMPLES
$$6.89 \times 10 = \boxed{68.9}$$ (1 place to the right)

$$6.89 \times 100 = \boxed{689.}$$ (2 places to the right)

$$6.89 \times 1{,}000 = \boxed{6{,}890.}$$ (3 places to the right)

© philipus/Alamy

In division, the answers are *smaller* than the original number.

EXAMPLES	$6.89 \div 10 = .689$	(1 place to the left)
	$6.89 \div 100 = .0689$	(2 places to the left)
	$6.89 \div 1,000 = .00689$	(3 places to the left)
	$6.89 \div 10,000 = .000689$	(4 places to the left)

Next, let's dissect and solve a word problem.

How to Dissect and Solve a Word Problem

The Word Problem May O'Mally went to Sears to buy wall-to-wall carpet. She needs 101.3 square yards for downstairs, 16.3 square yards for the upstairs bedrooms, and 6.2 square yards for the halls. The carpet cost $14.55 per square yard. The padding cost $3.25 per square yard. Sears quoted an installation charge of $6.25 per square yard. What was May O'Mally's total cost?

By completing the following blueprint aid, we will slowly dissect this word problem. Note that before solving the problem, we gather the facts, identify what we are solving for, and list the steps that must be completed before finding the final answer, along with any key points we should remember. Let's go to it!

MONEY tips

Formula for Financial Success: Reduce Spending + Decrease Debt + Increase Savings (Investing) = Healthy Net Worth

	The facts	Solving for?	Steps to take	Key points
BLUEPRINT	*Carpet needed:* 101.3 sq. yd.; 16.3 sq. yd.; 6.2 sq. yd. *Costs:* Carpet, $14.55 per sq. yd.; padding, $3.25 per sq. yd.; installation, $6.25 per sq. yd.	Total cost of carpet, padding, and installation.	Total square yards × Cost per square yard = Total cost.	Align decimals. Round answer to nearest cent.

Steps to solving problem

1. Calculate the total number of square yards.

        101.3
         16.3
          6.2
        123.8 square yards

2. Calculate the total cost per square yard.

        $14.55
         3.25
         6.25
        $24.05

3. Calculate the total cost of carpet, padding, and installation.
        $123.8 \times \$24.05 = \$2,977.39$

It's time to check your progress.

LU 3–2   **PRACTICE QUIZ**

Complete this **Practice Quiz** to see how you are doing.

1. Rearrange vertically and add:
14, .642, 9.34, 15.87321

2. Rearrange and subtract:
28.1549 − .885

3. Multiply and round the answer to the nearest tenth:
28.53×17.4

4. Divide and round to the nearest hundredth:
$2,182 \div 2.83$

Complete by the shortcut method:

5. 14.28 × 100   **6.** 9,680 ÷ 1,000   **7.** 9,812 ÷ 10,000

8. Could you help Mel decide which product is the "better buy"?

  Dog food A: $9.01 for 64 ounces   **Dog food B:** $7.95 for 50 ounces

Round to the nearest cent as needed:

9. At Avis Rent-A-Car, the cost per day to rent a medium-size car is $39.99 plus 29 cents per mile. What will it cost to rent this car for 2 days if you drive 602.3 miles? Since the solution shows a completed blueprint, you might use a blueprint also.

10. A trip to Mexico cost 6,000 pesos. What would this be in U.S. dollars? Check your answer.

*For **extra help** from your authors–Sharon and Jeff–see the videos in Connect.*

These videos are also available on YouTube!

✓ Solutions

1.   14.00000
          .64200
         9.34000
        15.87321
      39.85521

2.
    7 10 14 14
    2̶8̶.1̶5̶4̶9
    − .8850
    27.2699

3.   28.53
         × 17.4
          11 412
         199 71
         285 3
        ─────── = **496.4**
        496.422

4.   771.024 = 771.02
        2.83)218200.000
              1981
              ────
              2010
              1981
              ────
               290
               283
               ───
                7 00
                5 66
                ────
                1 340
                1 132

5. 14.28 = **1,428**   **6.** 9,680 = **9.680**   **7.** 9,812 = **9.812**

8. A: $9.01 ÷ 64 = **$.14**   **B:** $7.95 ÷ 50 = **$.16**   Buy A.

9. Avis Rent-A-Car total rental charge:

	The facts	Solving for?	Steps to take	Key points
BLUEPRINT	Cost per day, $39.99. 29 cents per mile. Drove 602.3 miles. 2-day rental.	Total rental charge.	Total cost for 2 days' rental + Total cost of driving = Total rental charge.	In multiplication, count the number of decimal places. Starting from right to left in the product, insert decimal in appropriate place. Round to nearest cent.

Steps to solving problem

1. Calculate total cost for 2 days' rental. $39.99 × 2 = $79.98

2. Calculate the total cost of driving. $.29 × 602.3 = $174.667 = $174.67

3. Calculate the total rental charge.
            $ 79.98
           + 174.67
           ─────────
           $254.65

10. 6,000 × $.0715 = **$429**

  Check $429 × 13.9876 = 6,000.68 pesos due to rounding

LU 3-2a — EXTRA PRACTICE QUIZ WITH WORKED-OUT SOLUTIONS

Need more practice? Try this **Extra Practice Quiz** (check figures in the Interactive Chapter Organizer). Worked-out Solutions can be found in Appendix B.

1. Rearrange vertically and add:
   16, .831, 9.85, 17.8321

2. Rearrange and subtract:
   29.5832 − .998

3. Multiply and round the answer to the nearest tenth:
   29.64 × 18.2

4. Divide and round to the nearest hundredth:
   3,824 ÷ 4.94

Complete by the shortcut method:

5. 17.48 × 100
6. 8,432 ÷ 1,000
7. 9,643 ÷ 10,000

8. Could you help Mel decide which product is the "better buy"?
   Dog food A: $8.88 for 64 ounces   **Dog food B:** $7.25 for 50 ounces

Round to the nearest cent as needed:

9. At Avis Rent-A-Car, the cost per day to rent a medium-size car is $29.99 plus 22 cents per mile. What will it cost to rent this car for 2 days if you drive 709.8 miles?

10. A trip to Mexico costs 7,000 pesos. What would this be in U.S. dollars? Check your answer.

INTERACTIVE CHAPTER ORGANIZER

Topic/Procedure/Formula	Examples	You try it*
Identifying place value $10, 1, \frac{1}{10}, \frac{1}{100}, \frac{1}{1,000}$, etc.	.439 in thousandths place value	**Identify place value** .8256
Rounding decimals 1. Identify place value of digit you want to round. 2. If digit to right of identified digit in Step 1 is 5 or more, increase identified digit by 1; if less than 5, do not change identified digit. 3. Drop all digits to right of identified digit.	.875 rounded to nearest tenth = .9 ↖ Identified digit	**Round to nearest tenth** .841
Converting decimal fractions to decimals 1. Decimal fraction has a denominator with multiples of 10. Count number of zeros in denominator. 2. Zeros show how many places are in the decimal.	$\frac{8}{1,000} = .008$ $\frac{6}{10,000} = .0006$	**Convert to decimal** $\frac{9}{1,000}$ $\frac{3}{10,000}$
Converting proper fractions to decimals 1. Divide numerator of fraction by its denominator. 2. Round as necessary.	$\frac{1}{3}$ (to nearest tenth) = .3	**Convert to decimal (to nearest tenth)** $\frac{1}{7}$
Converting mixed numbers to decimals 1. Convert fractional part of the mixed number to a decimal. 2. Add converted fractional part to whole number.	$6\frac{1}{4}$ $\frac{1}{4} = .25 + 6 = 6.25$	**Convert to decimal** $5\frac{4}{5}$
Converting pure and mixed decimals to decimal fractions 1. Place digits to right of decimal point in numerator of fraction. 2. Put 1 in denominator. 3. Add zeros to denominator, depending on decimal places of original number. For mixed decimals, add fraction to whole number.	.984 (3 places) 1. $\frac{984}{}$ 2. $\frac{984}{1}$ 3. $\frac{984}{1,000}$	**Convert to fraction** .865

(continues)

INTERACTIVE CHAPTER ORGANIZER

Topic/Procedure/Formula	Examples	You try it*

Adding and subtracting decimals
1. Vertically write and align numbers on decimal points.
2. Add or subtract digits, starting with right column and moving to the left.
3. Align decimal point in answer with above decimal points.
	Add 1.3 + 2 + .4
	1.3
	2.0
	.4
	3.7
	
	Subtract 5 − 3.9 4 10
	               5̸.0̸
	              −3.9
	                   1.1
		Add
		1.7 + 3 + .8
		
		Subtract
		6 − 4.1

Multiplying decimals
1. Multiply numbers, ignoring decimal points.
2. Count and total number of decimal places in multiplier and multiplicand.
3. Starting at right in the product, count to the left the number of decimal places totaled in Step 2. Insert decimal point. If number of places greater than space in answer, add zeros.
	2.48 (2 places)
	× .018 (3 places)
	   1 984
	   2 48
	  .04464
		Multiply
		  3.49
		× .015

Dividing a decimal by a whole number
1. Place decimal point in quotient directly above the decimal point in dividend.
2. Divide as usual.
	1.1
	42)46.2
	  42
	   42
	   42
		Divide (to nearest tenth)
		33)49.5

Dividing if the divisor is a decimal
1. Make divisor a whole number by moving decimal point to the right.
2. Move decimal point in dividend to the right the same number of places as in Step 1.
3. Place decimal point in quotient above decimal point in dividend. Divide as usual.
	14.3
	2.9)41.39
	  29
	  123
	  116
	   79
	   58
	   21
		Divide (to nearest tenth)
		3.2)1.48

Shortcuts on multiplication and division of decimals When multiplying by 10, 100, 1,000, and so on, move decimal point in multiplicand the same number of places to the right as you have zeros in multiplier. For division, move decimal point to the left.	4.85 × 100 = 485 4.85 ÷ 100 = .0485	**Multiply by shortcut** 6.92 × 100 **Divide by shortcut** 6.92 ÷ 100

KEY TERMS	Decimal Decimal fraction Decimal point	Mixed decimal Pure decimal Repeating decimal	Rounding decimals

| **Check Figures for Extra Practice Quizzes. (Worked-out Solutions are in Appendix B.)** | LU 3–1a
1. .309
2. Hundredths
3. Ten-thousandths
4. a. .8
    b. .844
5. a. .9
    b. .879
6. .0008
7. .00016
     8. $\frac{938}{1,000}$
     9. $17\frac{95}{100}$
   10. $\frac{325}{10,000}$
11. .13
12. .57
13. 13.11 | LU 3–2a
1. 44.5131   **6.** 8.432
2. 28.5852   **7.** .9643
3. 539.4   **8.** Buy A $.14
4. 774.09   **9.** $216.14
5. 1,748   **10.** $500.50 |

Note: For how to dissect and solve a word problem, see Learning Unit 3-2.

*Worked-out solutions are in Appendix B.

Critical Thinking Discussion Questions with Chapter Concept Check

1. What are the steps for rounding decimals? Federal income tax forms allow the taxpayer to round each amount to the nearest dollar. Do you agree with this?

2. Explain how to convert fractions to decimals. If 1 out of 20 people buys a Land Rover, how could you write an advertisement in decimals?

3. Explain why .07, .70, and .700 are not equal. Assume you take a family trip to Disney World that covers 500 miles. Show that $\frac{8}{10}$ of the trip, or .8 of the trip, represents 400 miles.

4. Explain the steps in the addition or subtraction of decimals. Visit a car dealership and find the difference between two sticker prices. Be sure to check each sticker price for accuracy. Should you always pay the sticker price?

5. **Chapter Concept Check.** Visit a publisher's website and calculate the difference between the prices for a printed text and an e-book. Estimate what you think the profit is to the publisher based on your research.

Classroom Notes

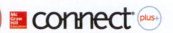
Check figures for odd-numbered problems in Appendix C. Name _____ Date _____

DRILL PROBLEMS

Identify the place value for the following: *LU 3-1(1)*

3–1. 9.4758   **3–2.** 543.2163

Round the following as indicated: *LU 3-1(1)*

	Tenth	**Hundredth**	**Thousandth**
3–3. .7391			
3–4. 6.8629			
3–5. 5.8312			
3–6. 6.8415			
3–7. 6.5555			
3–8. 75.9913			

Round the following to the nearest cent: *LU 3-1(1)*

3–9. $4,822.775   **3–10.** $4,892.046

Convert the following types of decimal fractions to decimals (round to nearest hundredth as needed): *LU 3-1(2)*

3–11. $\dfrac{8}{100}$ **3–12.** $\dfrac{3}{10}$ **3–13.** $\dfrac{61}{1,000}$ **3–14.** $\dfrac{610}{1,000}$

3–15. $\dfrac{91}{100}$ **3–16.** $\dfrac{979}{1,000}$ **3–17.** $16\dfrac{61}{100}$

Convert the following decimals to fractions. Do not reduce to lowest terms. *LU 3-1(2)*

3–18. .9   **3–19.** .71   **3–20.** .009   **3–21.** .0125

3–22. .609   **3–23.** .825   **3–24.** .9999   **3–25.** .7065

Convert the following to mixed numbers. Do not reduce to the lowest terms. *LU 3-1(2)*

3–26. 7.1   **3–27.** 28.48   **3–28.** 6.025

Write the decimal equivalent of the following: *LU 3-1(2)*

3–29. Five thousandths   **3–30.** Three hundred three and two hundredths

3–31. Eighty-five ten thousandths   **3–32.** Seven hundred seventy-five thousandths

Rearrange the following and add: *LU 3-2(1)*

3–33. .115, 10.8318, 4.7, 802.4811   **3–34.** .005, 2,002.181, 795.41, 14.0, .184

Rearrange the following and subtract: *LU 3-2(1)*

3–35. 9.2 − 5.8   **3–36.** 7 − 2.0815   **3–37.** 3.4 − 1.08

Estimate by rounding all the way and multiply the following (do not round final answer): *LU 3-2(1)*

3–38. 6.24 × 3.9   **3–39.** .413 × 3.07
       Estimate   **Estimate**

3–40. 675 × 1.92   **3–41.** 4.9 × .825
       Estimate   **Estimate**

Divide the following and round to the nearest hundredth: *LU 3-2(1)*

3–42. .8931 ÷ 3

3–43. 29.432 ÷ .0012

3–44. .0065 ÷ .07

3–45. 7,742.1 ÷ 48

3–46. 8.95 ÷ 1.18

3–47. 2,600 ÷ .381

Convert the following to decimals and round to the nearest hundredth: *LU 3-1(2)*

3–48. $\dfrac{1}{8}$ **3–49.** $\dfrac{1}{25}$ **3–50.** $\dfrac{5}{6}$ **3–51.** $\dfrac{5}{8}$

Complete these multiplications and divisions by the shortcut method (do not do any written calculations):   *LU 3-2(3)*

3–52. 96.7 ÷ 10

3–53. 258.5 ÷ 100

3–54. 8.51 × 1,000

3–55. .86 ÷ 100

3–56. 9.015 × 100

3–57. 48.6 × 10

3–58. 750 × 10

3–59. 3,950 ÷ 1,000

3–60. 8.45 ÷ 10

3–61. 7.9132 × 1,000

WORD PROBLEMS

As needed, round answers to the nearest cent.

3–62. A Chevy Volt costs $29,000 in the United States. Using the exchange rate given in the WSJ's Currencies & Commodities table earlier in this chapter, what would it cost in Canada? Check your answer.   *LU 3-2(2)*

3–63. Dustin Pedroia got 7 hits out of 12 at bats. What was his batting average to the nearest thousandths place?   *LU 3-1(2)*

3–64. Pete Ross read in a *Wall Street Journal* article that the cost of parts and labor to make an Apple iPhone 4S were as follows: *LU 3-2(1)*

Display	$37.00	Wireless	$23.54
Memory	$28.30	Camera	$17.60
Labor	$ 8.00	Additional items	$81.56

Assuming Pete pays $649 for an iPhone 4S, how much profit does the iPhone generate?

3–65. At the Party Store, Joan Lee purchased 21.50 yards of ribbon. Each yard cost 91 cents. What was the total cost of the ribbon? Round to the nearest cent.   *LU 3-2(1)*

3–66. Douglas Noel went to Home Depot and bought four doors at $42.99 each and six bags of fertilizer at $8.99 per bag. What was the total cost to Douglas? If Douglas had $300 in his pocket, what does he have left to spend?   *LU 3-2(1)*

3–67. The stock of Intel has a high of $30.25 today. It closed at $28.85. How much did the stock drop from its high?   *LU 3-2(1)*

3–68. Pete is traveling by car to a computer convention in San Diego. His company will reimburse him $.48 per mile. If Pete travels 210.5 miles, how much will Pete receive from his company?   *LU 3-2(1)*

3–69. Mark Ogara rented a truck from Avis Rent-A-Car for the weekend (2 days). The base rental price was $29.95 per day plus $14\frac{1}{2}$ cents per mile. Mark drove 410.85 miles. How much does Mark owe?   *LU 3-2(1)*

3–70. Nursing home costs are on the rise as consumeraffairs.com reports in its quarterly newsletter. The average cost is around $192 a day with an average length of stay of 2.5 years. Calculate the cost of the average nursing home stay. *LU 3-2(1)*

3–71. Bob Ross bought a smartphone on the web for $89.99. He saw the same smartphone in the mall for $118.99. How much did Bob save by buying on the web? *LU 3-2(1)*

3–72. Russell is preparing the daily bank deposit for his coffee shop. Before the deposit, the coffee shop had a checking account balance of $3,185.66. The deposit contains the following checks:

No. 1	$ 99.50	No. 3	$8.75
No. 2	110.35	No. 4	6.83

Russell included $820.55 in currency with the deposit. What is the coffee shop's new balance, assuming Russell writes no new checks? *LU 3-2(1)*

3–73. According to worldpopulationstatistics.com, if the population in India increased .75% in 2014 to 1,261,527,930.25, it **eXcel** would make up 17.5% of the world's population. If the population in China increased 2.7% in 2014 to 1,390,510,630.116, making up 19.3% of the world, how much more did China grow than India in 2014 in numbers? *LU 3-2(1)*

3–74. Randi went to Lowe's to buy wall-to-wall carpeting. She needs 110.8 square yards for downstairs, 31.8 square yards for the halls, and 161.9 square yards for the bedrooms upstairs. Randi chose a shag carpet that costs $14.99 per square yard. She ordered foam padding at $3.10 per square yard. The carpet installers quoted Randi a labor charge of $3.75 per square yard. What will the total job cost Randi? *LU 3-2(1)*

3–75. Paul Rey bought four new Dunlop tires at Goodyear for $95.99 per tire. Goodyear charged $3.05 per tire for mounting, $2.95 per tire for valve stems, and $3.80 per tire for balancing. If Paul paid no sales tax, what was his total cost for the four tires? *LU 3-2(1)*

3–76. Shelly is shopping for laundry detergent, mustard, and canned tuna. She is trying to decide which of two products is the **eXcel** better buy. Using the following information, can you help Shelly? *LU 3-2(1)*

Laundry detergent A	**Mustard A**	**Canned tuna A**
$2.00 for 37 ounces	$.88 for 6 ounces	$1.09 for 6 ounces

Laundry detergent B	**Mustard B**	**Canned tuna B**
$2.37 for 38 ounces	$1.61 for $12\frac{1}{2}$ ounces	$1.29 for $8\frac{3}{4}$ ounces

3–77. Roger bought season tickets for weekend professional basketball games. The cost was $945.60. The season package **eXcel** included 36 home games. What is the average price of the tickets per game? Round to the nearest cent. Marcelo, Roger's friend, offered to buy four of the tickets from Roger. What is the total amount Roger should receive? *LU 3-2(1)*

3–78. A nurse was to give each of her patients a 1.32-unit dosage of a prescribed drug. The total remaining units of the drug at the hospital pharmacy were 53.12. The nurse has 38 patients. Will there be enough dosages for all her patients? *LU 3-2(1)*

3–79. Jill Horn went to Japan and bought an animation cel of Spongebob. The price was 25,000 yen. Using the WSJ's Currencies & Commodities table shown earlier in the chapter, what is the price in U.S. dollars? Check your answer. *LU 3-2(2)*

3–80. Facebook Newsroom stated Facebook had 1 million users in 2004. In January 2014, it had 1.23 billion monthly active users. What has the Facebook users' growth been since 2004? *LU 3-2(1)*

3–81. Reuters reported in January 2015 consumer confidence is the strongest it has been since 2007 based on growing optimism about the jobs market and the overall economy. The Conference Board issued a 102.9 rating for January 2015 compared to 93.1 in December 2014. How much has the rating increased? *LU 3-2(1)*

3–82. Morris Katz bought four new tires at Goodyear for $95.49 per tire. Goodyear also charged Morris $2.50 per tire for mounting, $2.40 per tire for valve stems, and $3.95 per tire for balancing. Assume no tax. What was Morris's total cost for the four tires? *LU 3-2(1)*

3–83. The *Denver Post* reported that Xcel Energy is revising customer charges for monthly residential electric bills and gas bills. Electric bills will increase $3.32. Gas bills will decrease $1.74 a month. **(a)** What is the resulting new monthly increase for the entire bill? **(b)** If Xcel serves 2,350 homes, how much additional revenue would Xcel receive each month? *LU 3-2(1)*

3–84. Steven is traveling to an auto show by car. His company will reimburse him $.29 per mile. If Steven travels 890.5 miles, how much will he receive from his company? *LU 3-2(1)*

3–85. Gracie went to Home Depot to buy wall-to-wall carpeting for her house. She needs 104.8 square yards for downstairs, 17.4 square yards for halls, and 165.8 square yards for the upstairs bedrooms. Gracie chose a shag carpet that costs $13.95 per square yard. She ordered foam padding at $2.75 per square yard. The installers quoted Gracie a labor cost of $5.75 per square yard in installation. What will the total job cost Gracie? *LU 3-2(1)*

CHALLENGE PROBLEMS

3–86. Fred and Winnie O'Callahan have put themselves on a very strict budget. Their goal at the end of the year is to buy a car
eXcel for $14,000 in cash. Their budget includes the following per dollar:

> $.40 food and lodging
> .20 entertainment
> .10 educational

Fred earns $2,000 per month and Winnie earns $2,500 per month. After 1 year will Fred and Winnie have enough cash to buy the car? *LU 3-2(1)*

3–87. Jill and Frank decided to take a long weekend in New York. City Hotel has a special getaway weekend for $79.95. The price is per person per night, based on double occupancy. The hotel has a minimum two-night stay. For this price, Jill and Frank will receive $50 credit toward their dinners at City's Skylight Restaurant. Also included in the package is a $3.99 credit per person toward breakfast for two each morning.

Since Jill and Frank do not own a car, they plan to rent a car. The car rental agency charges $19.95 a day with an additional charge of $.22 a mile and $1.19 per gallon of gas used. The gas tank holds 24 gallons.

From the following facts, calculate the total expenses of Jill and Frank (round all answers to nearest hundredth or cent as appropriate). Assume no taxes.   *LU 3-2(1)*

Car rental (2 days):		Dinner cost at Skylight	$182.12
Beginning odometer reading	4,820	Breakfast for two:	
Ending odometer reading	4,940	Morning No. 1	24.17
Beginning gas tank: $\frac{3}{4}$ full		Morning No. 2	26.88
Gas tank on return: $\frac{1}{2}$ full		Hotel room	79.95
Tank holds 24 gallons			

 ## SUMMARY PRACTICE TEST

Do you need help? The videos in Connect have step-by-step worked-out solutions. These videos are also available on YouTube!

1. Add the following by translating the verbal form to the decimal equivalent.   *LU 3-1(1), LU 3-2(1)*

Three hundred thirty-eight and seven hundred five thousandths
Nineteen and fifty-nine hundredths
Five and four thousandths
Seventy-five hundredths
Four hundred three and eight tenths

Convert the following decimal fractions to decimals.   *LU 3-1(2)*

2. $\dfrac{7}{10}$

3. $\dfrac{7}{100}$

4. $\dfrac{7}{1,000}$

Convert the following to proper fractions or mixed numbers. Do not reduce to the lowest terms.   *LU 3-1(2)*

5. .9

6. 6.97

7. .685

Convert the following fractions to decimals (or mixed decimals) and round to the nearest hundredth as needed.   *LU 3-1(2)*

8. $\dfrac{2}{7}$

9. $\dfrac{1}{8}$

10. $4\dfrac{4}{7}$

11. $\dfrac{1}{13}$

12. Rearrange the following decimals and add. *LU 3-2(1)*

    5.93,   11.862,   284.0382,   88.44

13. Subtract the following and round to the nearest tenth. *LU 3-2(1)*

    13.111 − 3.872

14. Multiply the following and round to the nearest hundredth. *LU 3-2(1)*

    7.4821 × 15.861

15. Divide the following and round to the nearest hundredth. *LU 3-2(1)*

    203,942 ÷ 5.88

Complete the following by the shortcut method. *LU 3-2(3)*

16. 62.94 × 1,000

17. 8,322,249.821 × 100

18. The average pay of employees is $795.88 per week. Lee earns $820.44 per week. How much is Lee's pay over the average? *LU 3-2(1)*

19. Lowes reimburses Ron $.49 per mile. Ron submitted a travel log for a total of 1,910.81 miles. How much will Lowes reimburse Ron? Round to the nearest cent. *LU 3-2(1)*

20. Lee Chin bought two new car tires from Michelin for $182.11 per tire. Michelin also charged Lee $3.99 per tire for mounting, $2.50 per tire for valve stems, and $4.10 per tire for balancing. What is Lee's final bill? *LU 3-2(1)*

21. Could you help Judy decide which of the following products is cheaper per ounce? *LU 3-2(1)*

    Canned fruit A   **Canned fruit B**

    $.37 for 3 ounces $.58 for $3\frac{3}{4}$ ounces

22. Paula Smith bought a computer tablet for 350 euros. Using the WSJ's Currencies & Commodities table shown earlier in the chapter, what is this price in U.S. dollars? *LU 3-2(2)*

23. Google stock traded at a high of $522.00 and closed at $518.55. How much did the stock fall from its high? *LU 3-2(1)*

SURF TO SAVE

How far does your money go? 🔍

 PROBLEM 1
Get ready for your new job

Go to http://www.officemax.com. Choose an expensive pen, briefcase, and portfolio. If you were to order all three of these items for your new job, how much would they cost before taxes? (Assume shipping on your order is free.) Assuming your sales tax is 6%, how much would you pay in sales tax on this purchase? Note: Expensive pens are found under "Fine & Better" pens in the pen section. Searching for "Briefcase" is the easiest way to find briefcases at the site.

Discussion Questions

1. What other expenses will you most likely incur as you start your new career?
2. How will these expenses impact the starting salary you will need to earn?

 PROBLEM 2
Dollars and euros

Go to http://www.oanda.com/convertered/classic. If you converted US$5,000 to euros on January 1, 2015, what was the value represented in euros? If you convert these euros back to U.S. dollars at *today's* exchange rate, how much money would you have? Answers will vary.

Discussion Questions

1. How did these amounts change based on the date of the conversion?
2. What does this tell you about the state of the economy in the U.S. versus the European Union?

 PROBLEM 3
Online stock trading

Using a search engine of your choice, search for "online stock trading." Based on your search results, determine which company offers the highest and lowest cost per online trade. What is the difference between the highest and lowest cost?

Discussion Questions

1. If you were to begin trading stocks online, would the lowest cost per trade be the key determining factor in choosing an online broker? Why or why not?
2. Assume you made three online trades per month for an entire year. What is the difference in total yearly cost between the highest and lowest cost broker based on this level of online trading?

 PROBLEM 4
Mind over matter

Airlines charge almost $200 if a suitcase weighs more than 50 pounds. The skycap tells you your suitcase weighs 22 kilograms. You think that each kilogram is equal to 2.2 pounds. Do you owe additional fees for an overweight suitcase? Use the converter at http://www.metric-conversions.org/weight/kilograms-to-pounds.htm to verify your answer.

Discussion Questions

1. Why do you think airlines charge for overweight baggage and additional baggage?
2. Do these fees impact which airline you fly?

MOBILE APPS ✖

Equations with Decimals (YourTeacher.com) Provides a tutorial on decimals.

Fractions to Decimal and vice versa (Essence Computing) Assists in the conversion of fractions to their decimal equivalents and vice versa.

PERSONAL FINANCE

A KIPLINGER APPROACH

By Lisa Gerstner, From *Kiplinger's Personal Finance*, August 2013.

●● WHEN DEBIT WINS

For many, the ability to control cash flow with a debit card trumps any extra benefits a credit card provides. When the money you have in the bank is gone, you stop spending. That's why Heather Mumaw of Arlington, Va., makes nearly all of her purchases using a debit card. She puts one or two charges a month on her credit card—usually larger purchases, such as plane tickets, as well as reimbursed work expenses—to maintain a positive credit history. Many people use a debit card for spending on essentials that they don't want to finance, such as groceries, utilities and gas.

Although traditional debit card rewards programs have faded, you could benefit from new incentives. Bank of America customers enrolled in BankAmeriDeals can get cash back on certain purchases when they use their debit cards—for example, a $2 credit for a purchase at Panera Bread. With Chase's Disney Visa debit card, you can get discounts on some Disney purchases and access to a "Character Meet 'N' Greet" at Walt Disney World and Disneyland resorts.

If you have a rewards checking account, you may have a good reason to use a debit card several times per month: earning a bigger yield. Miller has Community Financial Services Bank's Kasasa Cash checking account, which pays 3.05% on balances of up to $20,000. To get that rate, he must make 12 monthly transactions with his debit card, enroll in online banking, receive e-statements, and have one monthly direct deposit or electronic transfer. (Look for top-yielding rewards checking accounts at www.depositaccounts.com.)

One downside: You could end up paying overdraft fees—which run an average of $31—if you're enrolled in an overdraft-protection plan and spend beyond your checking-account balance. You can opt out of overdraft protection, meaning your card will be declined at the register if you try to spend more than you have in the bank.

PLASTIC PERKS

Credit cards
- Best protection against fraud and merchant disputes.
- No-interest grace period.
- Builds credit history.
- Rewards, such as cash back and plane tickets, on some cards.
- Perks such as travel insurance, concierge services and purchase protection.

Debit cards
- Spending limited to bank-account balance.
- No need to make payments.
- No worries about interest charges.
- May qualify you for higher-yield rewards checking.
- Discounts or credits for certain types of purchases.

Prepaid debit cards
- No risk of overdrawing your account with most cards.
- Features similar to a checking account on many cards: direct deposit of paychecks, ATM access, online bill-paying.
- Convenient for parents who want to transfer money to kids.
- Easier to acquire with poor credit.

A small percentage of checking accounts also charge 35 cents to $1.50 each time you enter a PIN to make a debit card purchase.

●● PREPAID: A NEW CONTENDER

As prepaid debit cards become more popular, it's worth asking whether one deserves a slot in your wallet. In a survey by the National Foundation for Credit Counseling and the Network Branded Prepaid Card Association, 81% of those who use a prepaid card regularly said they felt more in control of their money with a prepaid card than with a debit card tied to a checking account.

When it comes to fees, a free checking account that reimburses out-of-network ATM charges beats a prepaid card (with most prepaid cards, you pay the bank's ATM fee). But if managing money has been a problem for you, you might save on overdraft fees with a prepaid card. Most of them don't let you spend more than is loaded on the card. And if your checking account hits you with other types of fees, a prepaid card might be less pricey. Javelin Strategy & Research found that bank prepaid cards cost consumers an average of $6.89 a month in fees, while basic checking accounts charged an average of $8.84 a month.

One prepaid card worth checking out is the low-fee Bluebird card from American Express and Walmart. It allows you to add up to four subaccounts—handy for parents who want to load money onto their kids' cards. The primary cardholder can control daily spending limits and ATM access on the subaccounts and receive e-mail alerts about activity. The Bluebird card also recently added check-writing and introduced Federal Deposit Insurance Corp. coverage against bank failure—a feature lacking on some prepaid cards. Both the Bluebird and the American Express Prepaid cards offer purchase protection, roadside assistance and travel-emergency services. ■

BUSINESS MATH ISSUE

Prepaid cards are no cheaper than debit cards.

1. List the key points of the article and information to support your position.
2. Write a group defense of your position using math calculations to support your view.

A Word Problem Approach—Chapters 1, 2, 3

1. The top rate at the Waldorf Towers Hotel in New York is $754. The top rate at the Ritz Carlton in Boston is $730. If John spends 9 days at one of these hotels, how much can he save if he stays at the Ritz?   *LU 1-2(2), LU 1-3(1)*

2. Robert Half Placement Agency was rated best by 4 to 1 in an independent national survey. If 250,000 responded to the survey, how many rated Robert Half the best?   *LU 2-3(1)*

3. Of the 63.2 million people who watch professional football, only $\frac{1}{5}$ watch the commercials. How many viewers do not watch the commercials?   *LU 2-3(1)*

4. AT&T advertised a 500-minute prepaid domestic calling card for $25. Diamante sells a 500-minute prepaid domestic calling card for $12.25. Assuming Bill Splat needs two 500-minute cards, how much could he save by buying Diamante's?   *LU 3-2(1)*

5. A square foot of rental space in New York City, Boston, and Providence costs as follows: New York City, $6.25; Boston, $5.75; and Providence, $3.75. If Hewlett Packard wants to rent 112,500 square feet of space, what will Hewlett Packard save by renting in Providence rather than Boston?   *LU 3-2(1)*

6. American Airlines has a frequent-flier program. Coupon brokers who buy and sell these awards pay between 1 and $1\frac{1}{2}$ cents for each mile earned. Fred Dietrich earned a 50,000-mile award (worth two free tickets to any city). If Fred decided to sell his award to a coupon broker, approximately how much would he receive?   *LU 3-2(1)*

7. Lillie Wong bought four new Firestone tires at $82.99 each. Firestone also charged $2.80 per tire for mounting, $1.95 per tire for valves, and $3.15 per tire for balancing. Lillie turned her four old tires in to Firestone, which charged $1.50 per tire to dispose of them. What was Lillie's final bill?   *LU 3-2(1)*

8. Tootsie Roll Industries bought Charms Company for $65 million. Some analysts believe that in 4 years the purchase price could rise to three times as much. If the analysts are right, how much did Tootsie Roll save by purchasing Charms immediately?   *LU 1-3(1)*

9. Today the average business traveler will spend $47.73 a day on food. The breakdown is dinner, $22.26; lunch, $10.73; breakfast, $6.53; tips, $6.23; and tax, $1.98. If Clarence Donato, an executive for Kroger, spends only .33 of the average, what is Clarence's total cost for food for the day? If Clarence wanted to spend $\frac{1}{3}$ more than the average on the next day, what would be his total cost on the second day? Round to the nearest cent.   *LU 2-3(1), LU 3-2(1)*

Be sure you use the fractional equivalent in calculating $.3\overline{3}$.

CHAPTER 4

Banking

© Stewart Cohen/Getty Images

Bank To-Do List: Make a Deposit, Grab a Brew, Maybe Strike a Pose

BY CHARLES PASSY

Forget free toasters—think beer and yoga.

Those extras are among the draws being used by banks to lure customers to branches in an age when checks can be deposited with a smartphone picture and mortgage applications filled out online.

An **Umpqua Bank** branch in Portland, Oregon, drew a crowd of 150 last fall with an Oktoberfest-style celebration, replete with pretzels, beer and a strolling accordionist. Such events are part of a larger slate of community events and programs—from yoga classes to dog fairs—that Umpqua offers in its 200-plus branches. The idea is simple: The more reasons a bank gives customers—or just as important, potential customers—to visit a branch, the more likely the bank will grab a piece of their business. "You take the chore" of going to the bank "and turn it into a pleasant experience," says Eve Callahan, an Umpqua spokeswoman.

Technologies, a software and analytics company that works with financial institutions. "Banks have not cracked the other channels as a means to cross-sell," he says.

The new approach is similar to the **Starbucks** model. In some instances, it can be as basic as providing free coffee and Wi-Fi—or, in the case of TD Bank, free coin-counting at "Penny Arcade" machines. Other banks are opening up their spaces for community meetings, or hosting their own classes and seminars.

Reprinted by permission of The Wall Street Journal, copyright 2013 Dow Jones & Company, Inc. All rights reserved worldwide.

**Pepper ...
And Salt**

THE WALL STREET JOURNAL

From The Wall Street Journal, permission Cartoon Features Syndicate.

"That's banking for you. If we make money, nobody loves us. If we lose money, everybody hates us."

LU 4–1: The Checking Account

1. Define and state the purpose of signature cards, checks, deposit slips, check stubs, check registers, and endorsements.
2. Correctly prepare deposit slips and write checks.

LU 4–2: Bank Statement and Reconciliation Process; Latest Trends in Mobile Banking

1. Explain trends in the banking industry.
2. Define and state the purpose of the bank statement.
3. Complete a check register and a bank reconciliation.
4. Explain the trends in mobile banking.

VOCABULARY PREVIEW

Here are key terms in this chapter. After completing the chapter, if you know the term, place a checkmark in the box. If you don't know the term, look it up and put the page number where it can be found.

Automatic teller machine (ATM) ☐ Bank reconciliation ☐ Bank statement ☐ Banking apps ☐ Blank endorsement ☐ Check ☐ Check register ☐ Check stub ☐ Credit memo (CM) ☐ Debit card ☐ Debit memo (DM) ☐ Deposit slip ☐ Deposits in transit ☐ Draft ☐ Drawee ☐ Drawer ☐ Electronic funds transfer (EFT) ☐ Endorse ☐ Full endorsement ☐ Mobile banking ☐ Nonsufficient funds (NSF) ☐ Outstanding checks ☐ Overdrafts ☐ Payee ☐ Restrictive endorsement ☐ Signature card ☐

The *Wall Street Journal* clip "Bank To-Do List" in the chapter opener shows how technology has changed how banks are marketing themselves. In this chapter we will look at how to do banking transactions manually, followed by a look at the latest trends in banking.

An important fixture in today's banking is the **automatic teller machine (ATM).** The ability to get instant cash is a convenience many bank customers enjoy.

The effect of using an ATM card is the same as using a **debit card**—both transactions result in money being immediately deducted from your checking account balance. As a result, debit cards have been called enhanced ATM cards or *check cards.* Often banks charge fees for these card transactions. The frequent complaints of bank customers have made many banks offer their ATMs as a free service, especially if customers use an ATM in the same network as their bank. Some banks charge fees for using another bank's ATM.

Remember that the use of debit cards involves planning. As *check cards,* you must be aware of your bank balance every time you use a debit card. Also, if you use a credit card instead of a debit card, you can only be held responsible for $50 of illegal charges; and during the time the credit card company investigates the illegal charges, they are removed from your account. However, with a debit card, this legal limit only applies if you report your card lost or stolen within two business days. The *Wall Street Journal* clip shows the impact Apple Pay has on banks. Banks do not want customers to switch.

This chapter begins with a discussion of the checking account. You will follow Molly Kate as she opens a checking account for Gracie's Natural Superstore and performs her banking transactions. Pay special attention to the procedure used by Gracie's to reconcile its checking account and bank statement. This information will help you reconcile your checkbook records with the bank's record of your account. The chapter concludes by discussing the latest technology trends in banking.

Apple Pay

Hundreds of financial institutions are jumping onto **Apple** Inc.'s new mobile-payment system, hoping to keep a tight grip on customers who might otherwise be tempted to switch banks if their current debit and credit cards can't be used with the newest iPhone.

The scramble began as soon as Apple announced the new Apple Pay service last month, say industry executives. In its initial announcement, Apple included the nation's largest banks, as well as credit-card networks **Visa** Inc., **MasterCard** Inc. and **American Express** Co. But the new service came as a surprise to many smaller lenders, tapping a merchant application on the phone.

The payment service is available on Apple's new iPhone 6 and its forthcoming digital watch.

In addition to massive card issuers like **J.P. Morgan Chase &** Co. and **Bank of America** Corp., Apple Pay also will be offered by lenders ranging from regional banks **Regions Financial** Corp. in Birmingham, Ala. and **BB&T** Corp. in Winston-Salem, N.C., to smaller institutions such as

'We are fighting for the hearts, minds and eyeballs of members.'

Reprinted by permission of *The Wall Street Journal,* copyright 2014 Dow Jones & Company, Inc. All rights reserved worldwide.

Learning Unit 4–1: The Checking Account

 LO 1

With an increase in mobile banking some have predicted the end of paper checks. Note in the *Wall Street Journal* clip "Bitcoin" more than half of businesses today still pay with paper checks. In LU 4–2, we will look at how to pay with smartphones. A **check** or **draft** is a written order instructing a bank, credit union, or savings and loan institution to pay a designated amount of your money on deposit to a person or an organization. Checking accounts are offered to individuals and businesses. Note that the business checking account usually receives more services than the personal checking account but may come with additional fees.

Most small businesses depend on a checking account for efficient record keeping. In this learning unit you will follow the checking account procedures of a newly organized small business. You can use many of these procedures in your personal check writing. You will also learn about e-checks.

Bitcoin? Firms Still Cling To Writing Paper Checks

BY VIPAL MONGA

On Saturdays around 7 a.m., before he goes to the gym, Ken Goldman sits on the couch with his laptop and pays household bills online. It takes about five to 10 minutes.

CFO JOURNAL On weekdays, however, he goes to work at **Black Duck Software** Inc., an international consulting firm with $50 million in sales. Twice a month, a staff accountant comes to his office with a stack of about 50 checks and it takes Mr. Goldman about half an hour to sign them all with a pen.

"In this day and age it doesn't make sense," said Mr. Goldman, the 200-employee company's chief financial officer. "It's like sending a letter when there's email."

A growing number of consumers don't hesitate to buy a cup of coffee using an iPhone, bid for a dress on eBay and pay for it via PayPal, or purchase a sofa on OverStock.com with virtual bitcoins. But for American businesses, the old-fashioned paper check remains the preferred payment method.

Reprinted by permission of *The Wall Street Journal*, copyright 2014 Dow Jones & Company, Inc. All rights reserved worldwide.

Opening the Checking Account

Molly Kate, treasurer of Gracie's Natural Superstore, went to Ipswich Bank to open a business checking account. The bank manager gave Molly a **signature card.** The signature card contained space for the company's name and address, references, type of account, and the signature(s) of the person(s) authorized to sign checks. If necessary, the bank will use the signature card to verify that Molly signed the checks. Some companies authorize more than one person to sign checks or require more than one signature on a check.

Molly then lists on a **deposit slip** (or deposit ticket) the checks and/or cash she is depositing in her company's business account. The bank gave Molly a temporary checkbook to use until the company's printed checks arrived. Molly also will receive *preprinted* checking account deposit slips like the one shown in Figure 4.1. Since the deposit slips are in duplicate, Molly can keep a record of her deposit. Note that the increased use of making deposits at ATM machines has made it more convenient for people to make their deposits.

FIGURE 4.1   Deposit slip

DEPOSIT TICKET		
Gracie's Natural Superstore	CASH	
80 Garfield St.	LIST CHECK SINGLY	
Bartlet, NH 01835	53-7058	1,800 00
	53-7058	200 00
DATE March 4 20 15		
DEPOSITS MAY NOT BE AVAILABLE FOR IMMEDIATE WITHDRAWAL		
	TOTAL FROM OTHER SIDE	
	TOTAL ITEMS TOTAL	2,000 00

USE OTHER SIDE FOR ADDITIONAL LISTING ◄ ENTER TOTAL HERE

BE SURE EACH ITEM IS PROPERLY ENDORSED.

IPSWICH BANK
ipswichbank.com

A211370587A 88190662

CHECKS AND OTHER ITEMS ARE RECIEVED FOR DEPOSIT SUBJECT TO THE PROVISIONS OF THE UNIFORM COMMERCIAL CODE OR ANY APPLICABLE COLLECTION AGREEMENT.

Preprinted numbers in magnetic ink identify bank number, routing and sorting of the check, and Gracie's Natural Superstore account number

The 53-7058 is taken from the upper right corner of the check from the top part of the fraction. This number is known as the American Bankers Association transit number. The 53 identifies the city or state where the bank is located and the 7058 identifies the bank.

FIGURE 4.2   The structure of a check

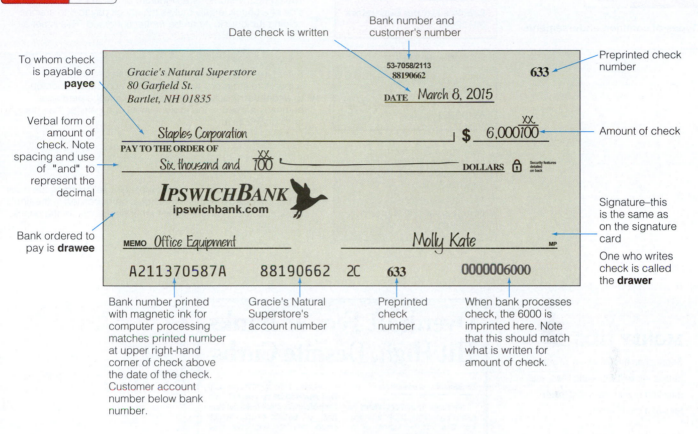

To whom check
is payable or
payee

Verbal form of
amount of
check. Note
spacing and use
of "and" to
represent the
decimal

Bank ordered to
pay is **drawee**

Date check is written

Bank number and
customer's number

Preprinted check
number

Amount of check

Signature–this
is the same as
on the signature
card

One who writes
check is called
the **drawer**

Bank number printed
with magnetic ink for
computer processing
matches printed number
at upper right-hand
corner of check above
the date of the check.
Customer account
number below bank
number.

Gracie's Natural
Superstore's
account number

Preprinted
check
number

When bank processes
check, the 6000 is
imprinted here. Note
that this should match
what is written for
amount of check.

Writing business checks is similar to writing personal checks. Before writing any checks, however, you must understand the structure of a check and know how to write a check. Carefully study Figure 4.2. Note that the verbal amount written in the check should match the figure amount. If these two amounts are different, by law the bank uses the verbal amount. Also, note the bank imprint on the bottom right section of the check. When processing the check, the bank imprints the check's amount. This makes it easy to detect bank errors.

LO 2

Using the Checking Account

Once the check is written, the writer must keep a record of the check. Knowing the amount of your written checks and the amount in the bank should help you avoid writing a bad check. Business checkbooks usually include attached **check stubs** to keep track of written checks. The sample check stub in the margin shows the information that the check writer will want to record. Some companies use a **check register** to keep their check records instead of check stubs. Figure 4.6 later in the chapter shows a check register with a ✓ column that is often used in balancing the checkbook with the bank statement (Learning Unit 4–2).

Gracie's Natural Superstore has had a busy week, and Molly must deposit its checks in the company's checking account. However, before she can do this, Molly must **endorse,** or sign, the back left side of the checks. Figure 4.3 explains the three types of check endorsements: **blank endorsement, full endorsement,** and **restrictive endorsement.** These endorsements transfer Gracie's ownership to the bank, which collects the money from the person or company issuing the check. Federal Reserve regulation limits all endorsements to the top $1\frac{1}{2}$ inches of the trailing edge on the back left side of the check.

After the bank receives Molly's deposit slip, shown in Figure 4.1, it increases (or credits) Gracie's account by $2,000. Often Molly leaves the deposit in a locked bag in a night depository. Then the bank credits (increases) Gracie's account when it processes the deposit on the next working day.

In the following *Wall Street Journal* clip "Overdraft Fees" banks are trying to increase profits by charging higher overdraft fees. Later in the chapter we will look at online banking and the decrease in check writing.

Check Stub

It should be completed before the check is written.

No. 633	$ 6000 XX/100	
March 8	20 15	
To Staples Corp.		
For Other Furniture		
	DOLLARS	CENTS
BALANCE	14,416	24
AMT. DEPOSITED		
TOTAL	14,416	24
AMT. THIS CHECK	6,000	00
BALANCE FORWARD	8,416	24

FIGURE 4.3

Types of common endorsements

A. Blank Endorsement

Gracie's Natural Superstore 88190662

The company stamp or a signature alone on the back left side of a check legally makes the check payable to anyone holding the check. It can be *further* endorsed. This is not a safe type of endorsement.

B. Full Endorsement

Pay to the order of Ipswich Bank **Gracie's Natural Superstore** 88190662

Safer type of endorsement since Gracie's Natural Superstore indicates the name of the company or person to whom the check is to be payable. Only the person or company named in the endorsement can transfer the check to someone else.

C. Restrictive Endorsement

Pay to the order of Ipswich Bank For deposit only **Gracie's Natural Superstore** 88190662

Safest endorsement for businesses. Gracie's stamps the back of the check so that this check must be deposited in the firm's bank account. This limits any further negotiation of the check.

MONEY tips

Conduct an annual check of your bank's interest rates and fees. You may find higher rates and lower fees at a credit union.

Overdraft Fees at Banks Hit High, Despite Curbs

BY ANNAMARIA ANDRIOTIS

Squeezed by falling revenue on deposit accounts, banks are turning to a familiar source of income: overdraft fees.

Nearly four years after regulators tried to curb the fees, banks are lifting them to new heights. The median fee for withdrawing more from a checking account than a customer has on deposit increased to an estimated $30 in 2013—a record—up from $29 in 2012 and $26 in 2009, based on a survey of 2,890 banks and credit unions by Moebs Services Inc., an economic-research firm in Lake Bluff, Ill.

"Banks have a revenue gap that needs to be recouped," said Greg McBride, chief financial analyst at Bankrate.com, which tracks overdraft fees and other charges.

Banks' fee revenue from checking, savings and other deposit accounts has been sliding since several regulations took effect. The Federal Reserve in 2010 stopped banks from automatically charging customers overdraft fees on debit-card and automated-teller-machine transactions.

Reprinted by permission of *The Wall Street Journal*, copyright 2014 Dow Jones & Company, Inc. All rights reserved worldwide.

Let's check your understanding of this unit.

LU 4–1 **PRACTICE QUIZ**

Complete this Practice Quiz to see how you are doing.

Complete the following check and check stub for Long Company. Note the $9,500.60 balance brought forward on check stub No. 113. You must make a $690.60 deposit on May 3. Sign the check for Roland Small.

Date	Check no.	Amount	Payable to	For
June 5, 2015	113	$83.76	Angel Corporation	Rent

No. _113_	$ _____	
_____ 20 ___		
To _____		
For _____		

	DOLLARS	CENTS
BALANCE	9,500	60
AMT. DEPOSITED		
TOTAL		
AMT. THIS CHECK		
BALANCE FORWARD		

Long Company
22 Aster Rd.
Salem, MA 01970

No. 113

PAY TO THE ORDER OF _____ _____ 20 ____   5-13/110

$ _____

_____ **DOLLARS**

IPSWICHBANK
ipswichbank.com

MEMO _____

A011000138A   14 0380 113

*For **extra help** from your authors–Sharon and Jeff–see the videos in Connect.*

These videos are also available on YouTube!

✓ **Solution**

No. _113_	$ _83.76_		
June 5	20 _15_		
To _Angel Corp._			
For _Rent_			
		DOLLARS	**CENTS**
BALANCE		9,500	60
AMT. DEPOSITED		690	60
TOTAL		10,191	20
AMT. THIS CHECK		83	76
BALANCE FORWARD		10,107	44

Long Company
22 Aster Rd.
Salem, MA 01970

No. 113

PAY TO THE ORDER OF _Angel Corporation_   June 5 20 _15_   5-13/110 $ _83 76/100_

Eighty-three and _76/100_ _____ DOLLARS

IpswichBank
ipswichbank.com

Roland Small

MEMO _Rent_

A011000138A   14 0380 113

LU 4–1a   **EXTRA PRACTICE QUIZ WITH WORKED-OUT SOLUTIONS**

Need more practice? Try this Extra Practice Quiz (check figures in the Interactive Chapter Organizer). Worked-out Solutions can be found in Appendix B.

Complete the following check and stub for Long Company. Note the $10,800.80 balance brought forward on check stub No. 113. You must make an $812.88 deposit on May 3. Sign the check for Roland Small.

Date	**Check no.**	**Amount**	**Payable to**	**For**
June 8, 2015	113	$79.88	Lowe Corp.	Advertising

No. _113_	$ _____		
	20 _____		
To _____			
For _____			
		DOLLARS	**CENTS**
BALANCE		10,800	80
AMT. DEPOSITED			
TOTAL			
AMT. THIS CHECK			
BALANCE FORWARD			

Long Company
22 Aster Rd.
Salem, MA 01970

No. 113

PAY TO THE ORDER OF _____   20 ____   5-13/110 $ _____

_____ DOLLARS

IpswichBank
ipswichbank.com

MEMO_____

A011000138A   14 0380 113

Learning Unit 4–2: Bank Statement and Reconciliation Process; Latest Trends in Mobile Banking

LO 1

Trends in Banking Industry

Today more and more people are using smartphone apps from lenders to do their banking transactions. In the *Wall Street Journal* clip "More Ways to Use Smartphones," we see the latest trend in **mobile banking.** Also, note the other *Wall Street Journal* clip, "Checks and Balances," which shows the cost of banking online only versus traditional banking.

Be vigilant in safeguarding business and personal information to bank safely electronically. The rest of this learning unit is divided into two sections: (1) bank statement and reconciliation process, and (2) latest trends in mobile banking. The bank statement discussion will teach you why it was important for Gracie's Natural Superstore to reconcile its checkbook balance with the balance reported on its bank statement. Note that you can also use this reconciliation process in reconciling your personal checking account to avoid the expensive error of an overdrawn account.

Reprinted by permission of *The Wall Street Journal,* copyright 2013 Dow Jones & Company, Inc. All rights reserved worldwide.

Banks are now testing smartphone apps to replace the use of ATM cards.

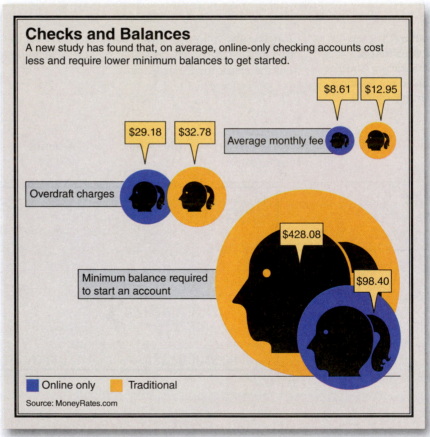

Source: *The Wall Street Journal,* 9/6/14.

Bank Statement and Reconciliation Process

Each month, Ipswich Bank sends Gracie's Natural Superstore a **bank statement** (Figure 4.4). We are interested in the following:

1. Beginning bank balance.
2. Total of all the account increases. Each time the bank increases the account amount, it *credits* the account.
3. Total of all account decreases. Each time the bank decreases the account amount, it *debits* the account.
4. Final ending balance.

FIGURE   4.4

Bank statement

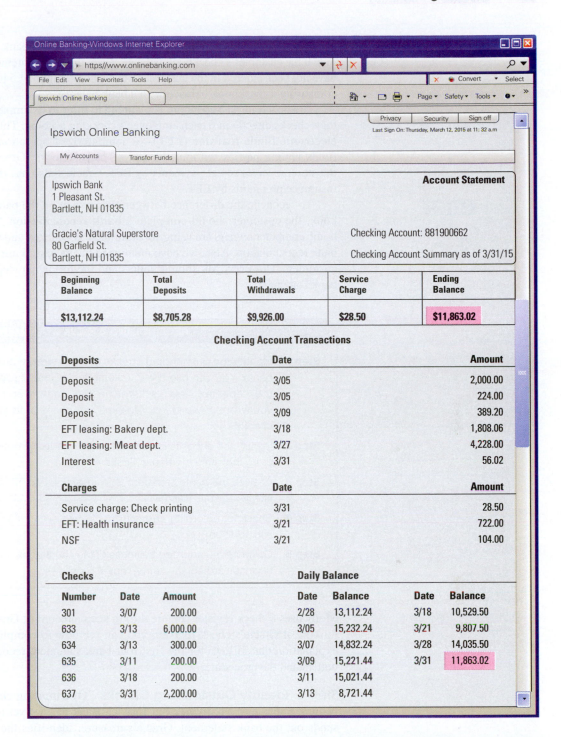

FIGURE   4.5

Reconciling checkbook with
bank statement

Checkbook balance		Bank balance
+ EFT (electronic funds transfer)	– NSF check	+ Deposits in transit
+ Interest earned	– Online fees	– Outstanding checks
+ Notes collected^	– Automatic payments*	± Bank errors
+ Credit memo		
+ Direct deposits	– Overdrafts†	
– ATM withdrawals	– Service charges	
– Automatic withdrawals	– Stop payments‡	
– Debit memo	± Book errors§	

^Notes (money) collected by a financial institution on behalf of a customer.

*Preauthorized payments for utility bills, mortgage payments, insurance, etc.

†**Overdrafts** occur when the customer has no overdraft protection and a check bounces back to the company or person who received the check because the customer has written a check without enough money in the bank to pay for it.

‡A stop payment is issued when the writer of the check does not want the receiver to cash the check.

§If a $60 check is recorded at $50, the checkbook balance must be decreased by $10.

Due to differences in timing, the bank balance on the bank statement frequently does not match the customer's checkbook balance. Also, the bank statement can show transactions that have not been entered in the customer's checkbook. Figure 4.5 tells you what to look for when comparing a checkbook balance with a bank balance.

Gracie's Natural Superstore is planning to offer to its employees the option of depositing their checks directly into each employee's checking account. This is accomplished through the **electronic funds transfer (EFT)**—a computerized operation that electronically transfers funds among parties without the use of paper checks. Gracie's, which sublets space in the store, receives rental payments by EFT. Gracie's also has the bank pay the store's health insurance premiums by EFT.

LO 3

To reconcile the difference between the amount on the bank statement and in the checkbook, the customer should complete a **bank reconciliation.** Today, many companies and home computer owners are using software such as Quicken and QuickBooks to complete their bank reconciliation. Also, we have mentioned the increased use of **banking apps** available to customers. However, you should understand the following steps for manually reconciling a bank statement.

RECONCILING A BANK STATEMENT
Step 1. Identify the outstanding checks (checks written but not yet processed by the bank). You can use the ✓ column in the check register (Figure 4.6) to check the canceled checks listed in the bank statement against the checks you wrote in the check register. The unchecked checks are the outstanding checks.
Step 2. Identify the deposits in transit (deposits made but not yet processed by the bank), using the same method in Step 1.
Step 3. Analyze the bank statement for transactions not recorded in the check stubs or check registers (like EFT).
Step 4. Check for recording errors in checks written, in deposits made, or in subtraction and addition.
Step 5. Compare the adjusted balances of the checkbook and the bank statement. If the balances are not the same, repeat Steps 1–4.

Molly uses a check register (Figure 4.6) to keep a record of Gracie's checks and deposits. By looking at Gracie's check register, you can see how to complete Steps 1 and 2 above. The explanation that follows for the first four bank statement reconciliation steps will help you understand the procedure.

Step 1. Identify Outstanding Checks   **Outstanding checks** are checks that Gracie's Natural Superstore has written but Ipswich Bank has not yet recorded for payment when it sends out the bank statement. Gracie's treasurer identifies the following checks written on 3/31 as outstanding:

No. 638	$572.00
No. 639	638.94
No. 640	166.00
No. 641	406.28
No. 642	917.06

Step 2. Identify Deposits in Transit   **Deposits in transit** are deposits that did not reach Ipswich Bank by the time the bank prepared the bank statement. The March 30 deposit of $3,383.26 did not reach Ipswich Bank by the bank statement date. You can see this by comparing the company's bank statement with its check register.

Step 3. Analyze Bank Statement for Transactions Not Recorded in Check Stubs or Check Register   The bank statement of Gracie's Natural Superstore (Figure 4.4) begins with the deposits, or increases, made to Gracie's bank account. Increases to accounts are

FIGURE   4.6

FIGURE   4.6

Gracie's Natural Superstore
check register

NUMBER	DATE 2015	DESCRIPTION OF TRANSACTION	PAYMENT/DEBIT (−)		√	FEE (IF ANY) (−)	DEPOSIT/CREDIT (+)		BALANCE $ 12,912 24	
	3/04	Deposit	$			$	$ 2,000	00	+ 2,000	00
									14,912	24
	3/04	Deposit					224	00	+ 224	00
									15,136	24
633	3/08	Staples Company	6,000	00	✓				− 6,000	00
									9,136	24
634	3/09	Health Foods Inc.	1,020	00	✓				− 1,020	00
									8,116	24
	3/09	Deposit					389	20	+ 389	20
									8,505	44
635	3/10	Liberty Insurance	200	00	✓				− 200	00
									8,305	44
636	3/18	Ryan Press	200	00	✓				− 200	00
									8,105	44
637	3/29	Logan Advertising	2,200	00	✓				− 2,200	00
									5,905	44
	3/30	Deposit					3,383	26	+ 3,383	26
									9,288	70
638	3/31	Sears Roebuck	572	00					− 572	00
									8,716	70
639	3/31	Flynn Company	638	94					− 638	94
									8,077	76
640	3/31	Lynn's Farm	166	00					− 166	00
									7,911	76
641	3/31	Ron's Wholesale	406	28					− 406	28
									7,505	48
642	3/31	Grocery Natural, Inc.	917	06					− 917	06
									$6,588	42

RECORD ALL CHARGES OR CREDITS THAT AFFECT YOUR ACCOUNT

REMEMBER TO RECORD AUTOMATIC PAYMENTS/DEPOSITS ON DATE AUTHORIZED.

known as credits. These are the result of a **credit memo (CM)**. Gracie's received the following increases or credits in March:

1. *EFT leasing:* $1,808.06 and $4,228.00.
   Each month the bakery and meat departments pay for space they lease in the store.
2. *Interest credited:* $56.02.
   Gracie's has a checking account that pays interest; the account has earned $56.02.

When Gracie's has charges against its bank account, the bank decreases, or debits, Gracie's account for these charges. Banks usually inform customers of a debit transaction by a **debit memo (DM)**. The following items will result in debits to Gracie's account:

1. *Service charge:* $28.50.
   The bank charged $28.50 for printing Gracie's checks.
2. *EFT payment:* $722.
   The bank made a health insurance payment for Gracie's.
3. *NSF check:* $104.
   One of Gracie's customers wrote Gracie's a check for $104. Gracie's deposited the check, but the check bounced for **nonsufficient funds (NSF)**. Thus, Gracie's has $104 less than it figured.

Step 4. Check for Recording Errors   The treasurer of Gracie's Natural Superstore, Molly Kate, recorded check No. 634 for the wrong amount—$1,020 (see the check register). The bank statement showed that check No. 634 cleared for $300. To reconcile Gracie's checkbook balance with the bank balance, Gracie's must add $720 to its checkbook balance. Neglecting to record a deposit also results in an error in the company's checkbook balance. As you can see, reconciling the bank's balance with a checkbook balance is a necessary part of business and personal finance.

Step 5. Completing the Bank Reconciliation   Now we can complete the bank reconciliation on the back side of the bank statement as shown in Figure 4.7. This form is usually on the back of a bank statement. If necessary, however, the person reconciling the bank statement can construct a bank reconciliation form similar to Figure 4.8.

FIGURE   **4.7**

Reconciliation process

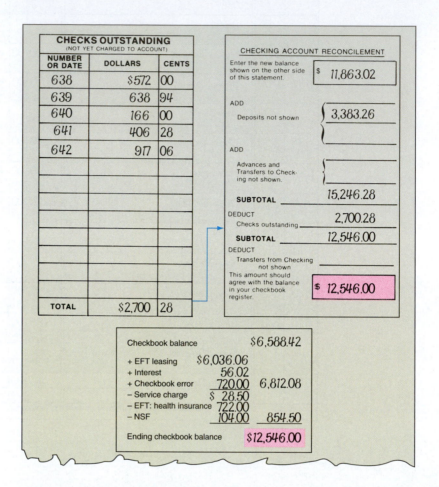

FIGURE   **4.8**

Bank reconciliation

GRACIE'S NATURAL SUPERSTORE
Bank Reconciliation as of March 31, 2015

Checkbook balance			Bank balance		
Gracie's checkbook balance		$6,588.42	Bank balance		$11,863.02
Add:			Add:		
EFT leasing: Bakery dept.	$1,808.06		Deposit in transit, 3/30		3,383.26
EFT leasing: Meat dept.	4,228.00				$15,246.28
Interest	56.02				
Error: Overstated check No. 634	720.00	$ 6,812.08			
		$13,400.50			
Deduct:			Deduct:		
Service charge	$ 28.50		Outstanding checks:		
NSF check	104.00		No. 638	$572.00	
EFT health insurance payment	722.00	854.50	No. 639	638.94	
			No. 640	166.00	
			No. 641	406.28	
			No. 642	917.06	2,700.28
Reconciled balance		$12,546.00	Reconciled balance		$12,546.00

MONEY tips

Always review your monthly bank statement to ensure there are no errors. The earlier you catch an error, the easier it is to remedy.

LO 4

Trends in Mobile Banking

The *Wall Street Journal* clip on mobile banking raises many questions about trends in mobile banking.

Mobile Finance

Financial dinosaurs haven't gone extinct. They have just gotten bigger.

Two decades ago, Bill Gates described banks as "dinosaurs" that would be bypassed by innovative technology. Yet since then banks have survived challenges from personal-finance software, early virtual banks and the Internet.

Now, there again is talk about banking being disrupted. Money is pouring into financial technology startups. The initial public offerings of **Lending-Club** and **On Deck Capital** were wildly successful.

The introduction of Apple Pay appears to be on the way to making mobile payments mainstream. A recent Capital IQ report declared 2015 will be the year mobile-payment technology "finally achieves widespread acceptance."

Have we finally reached the extinction event for banking dinosaurs? Not by a long shot. One of the lessons of recent years is that the dinosaur metaphor is inapt for banks. They

have proved more resilient than other businesses swamped by technology.

Branching Out

Share of bank customers surveyed who would consider a bank with no branch locations.

Ages 18 to 34   39%

35 to 55   29%

55 and over   16%

Source: Accenture   The Wall Street Journal

Because banks control the payment system, they are like the underlying terrain on which all the other economic animals run. Disruption tends to occur over them, not through them. That is likely to be the case again for big banks. Smaller, regional ones may be overwhelmed.

Take Apple Pay or PayPal. Both essentially operate on top

of incumbent banking and credit-card systems. No matter how successful Apple Pay is, customers will still need to link it to credit cards or bank accounts. LendingClub, too, is dependent on banks: 87% of its net revenue in 2013 came from banks that originate its loans.

As mobile banking becomes more widespread, banks with the largest, most robust networks will benefit. Banks that can afford to invest in technology will be rewarded. And those with the biggest customer bases will be able to drive the best bargains with newcomers like Apple Pay. **J.P. Morgan Chase, Citigroup,** and **Bank of America** already are far along as early adopters of mobile technology.

What's more, the biggest banks have capital markets and advisory businesses that make them less dependent on the ordinary banking business whose margins may be squeezed by new technology competitors.

Reprinted by permission of *The Wall Street Journal,* copyright 2015 Dow Jones & Company, Inc. All rights reserved worldwide.

LU 4–2   PRACTICE QUIZ

Complete this Practice Quiz to see how you are doing.

Rosa Garcia received her February 3, 2015, bank statement showing a balance of $212.80. Rosa's checkbook has a balance of $929.15. The bank statement showed that Rosa had an ATM fee of $12.00 and a deposited check returned fee of $20.00. Rosa earned interest of $1.05. She had three outstanding checks: No. 300, $18.20; No. 302, $38.40; and No. 303, $68.12. A deposit for $810.12 was not on her bank statement. Prepare Rosa Garcia's bank reconciliation.

*For **extra help** from your authors—Sharon and Jeff—see the videos in Connect.*

These videos are also available on YouTube!

✓ Solution

ROSA GARCIA					
Bank Reconciliation as of February 3, 2015					
Checkbook balance			**Bank balance**		
Rosa's checkbook balance		$ 929.15	Bank balance		$ 212.80
Add:			Add:		
Interest		1.05	Deposit in transit		810.12
		$930.20			$1,022.92
Deduct:			Deduct:		
Deposited check returned fee	$20.00		Outstanding checks:		
			No. 300	$18.20	
ATM	12.00	32.00	No. 302	38.40	
			No. 303	68.12	124.72
Reconciled balance		$898.20	Reconciled balance		$ 898.20

LU 4–2a EXTRA PRACTICE QUIZ WITH WORKED-OUT SOLUTIONS

Need more practice? Try this Extra Practice Quiz (check figures in the Interactive Chapter Organizer). Worked-out Solutions can be found in Appendix B.

Earl Miller received his March 8, 2015, bank statement, which had a $300.10 balance. Earl's checkbook has a $1,200.10 balance. The bank statement showed a $15.00 ATM fee and a $30.00 deposited check returned fee. Earl earned $24.06 interest. He had three outstanding checks: No. 300, $22.88; No. 302, $15.90; and No. 303, $282.66. A deposit for $1,200.50 was not on his bank statement. Prepare Earl's bank reconciliation.

INTERACTIVE CHAPTER ORGANIZER

Topic/Procedure/Formula	Examples	You try it*
Types of endorsements *Blank:* Not safe; can be further endorsed. *Full:* Only person or company named in endorsement can transfer check to someone else. *Restrictive:* Check must be deposited. Limits any further negotiation of the check.	Jones Co. 21-333-9 Pay to the order of Regan Bank Jones Co. 21-333-9 Pay to the order of Regan Bank. For deposit only. Jones Co. 21-333-9	**Write a sample of a blank, full, and restrictive endorsement.** Use Pete Co. Acct. # 24-111-9

Bank reconciliation
 	
Checkbook balance
+ EFT (electronic funds transfer)
+ Interest earned
+ Notes collected
+ Direct deposits
− ATM withdrawals
− NSF check
− Online fees
− Automatic withdrawals
− Overdrafts
− Service charges
− Stop payments
± Book errors (see note, below)
CM—adds to balance
DM—deducts from balance
 	
Bank balance
+ Deposits in transit
− Outstanding checks
± Bank errors
	Checkbook balance
	Balance $800
	  − NSF 40
	           $760
	  − Service charge 4
	           $756
	
	Bank balance
	Balance $ 632
	  + Deposits in transit 416
	          $1,048
	  − Outstanding checks 292
	        $ 756
		Calculate ending checkbook balance
		1. Beg. checkbook bal.: $300
		2. NSF: $50
		3. Deposit in transit: $100
		4. Outstanding check: $60
		5. ATM service charge: $20

KEY TERMS	Automatic teller machine (ATM) Bank reconciliation Bank statement Banking apps Blank endorsement Check Check register Check stub	Debit card Debit memo (DM) Deposit slip Deposits in transit Draft Drawee Drawer Electronic funds transfer (EFT) Endorse	Full endorsement Mobile banking Nonsufficient funds (NSF) Outstanding checks Overdrafts Payee Restrictive endorsement Signature card
Check Figures for Extra Practice Quizzes. (Worked-out Solutions are in Appendix B.)	LU 4–1a Ending Balance Forward $11,533.80	LU 4–2a Reconciled Balance $1,179.16

Note: If a $60 check is recorded as $50, we must decrease checkbook balance by $10.

*Worked-out solutions are in Appendix B.

Critical Thinking Discussion Questions with Chapter Concept Check

1. Explain the structure of a check. The trend in bank statements is not to return the canceled checks. Do you think this is fair?

2. List the three types of endorsements. Endorsements are limited to the top $1\frac{1}{2}$ inches of the trailing edge on the back left side of your check. Why do you think the Federal Reserve made this regulation?

3. List the steps in reconciling a bank statement. Today, many banks charge a monthly fee for certain types of checking accounts. Do you think all checking accounts should be free? Please explain.

4. What are some of the trends in mobile banking? Will we become a cashless society in which all transactions are made with some type of credit card?

5. What do you think of the government's intervention in trying to bail out banks? Should banks be allowed to fail?

6. **Chapter Concept Check.** Create your own company and provide needed data to prepare a bank reconciliation. Then go to a bank website and explain how you would use the bank's app versus the manual system of banking.

Classroom Notes

Check figures for odd-numbered problems in Appendix C.   Name _____   Date _____

DRILL PROBLEMS

4–1. Fill out the check register that follows with this information for July 2015:   *LU 4-1(1)*

July	7	Check No. 959	AT+T	$143.50
	15	Check No. 960	Staples	66.10
	19	Deposit		800.00
	20	Check No. 961	West Electric	451.88
	24	Check No. 962	Bank of America	319.24
	29	Deposit		400.30

		RECORD ALL CHARGES OR CREDITS THAT AFFECT YOUR ACCOUNT					BALANCE	
NUMBER	DATE 2015	DESCRIPTION OF TRANSACTION	PAYMENT/DEBIT (−)	√	FEE (IF ANY) (−)	DEPOSIT/CREDIT (+)	$ 4,500	75
			$		$	$		

4–2. November 1, 2015, Payroll.com, an Internet company, has a $10,481.88 checkbook balance. Record the following transactions for Payroll.com by completing the two checks and check stubs provided. Sign the checks Garth Scholten, controller.   *LU 4-1(2)*

a. November 8, 2015, deposited $688.10

b. November 8, check No. 190 payable to Staples for office supplies—$766.88

c. November 15, check No. 191 payable to Best Buy for computer equipment—$3,815.99.

4–3. Using the check register in Problem 4–1 and the following bank statement, prepare a bank reconciliation for Lee.com. *LU 4-2(3)*

BANK STATEMENT			
Date	Checks	Deposits	Balance
7/1 balance			$4,500.75
7/18	$143.50		4,357.25
7/19		$800.00	5,157.25
7/26	319.24		4,838.01
7/30	15.00 SC		4,823.01

WORD PROBLEMS

4–4. The World Bank forecasts growth of world trade to be 3%, up from 2.6% in 2014. This change has caused Galapagos
eXcel Islands Resort to analyze its current financial situation, beginning with reconciling its accounts. Galapagos Islands Resort received its bank statement showing a balance of $8,788. Its checkbook balance is $15,252. Deposits in transit are $3,450 and $6,521. There is a service charge of $45 and interest earned of $3. Notes collected total $1,575. Outstanding checks are No. 1021 for $1,260 and No. 1022 for $714. All numbers are in U.S. dollars. Help Galapagos Islands Resort reconcile its balances. *LU 4-2(3)*

4–5. The U.S. Chamber of Commerce provides a free monthly bank reconciliation template at business.uschamber.com/tools/bankre_m.asp. Annie Moats just received her bank statement notice online. She wants to reconcile her checking account with her bank statement and has chosen to reconcile her accounts manually. Her checkbook shows a balance of $698. Her bank statement reflects a balance of $1,348. Checks outstanding are No. 2146, $25; No. 2148, $58; No. 2152, $198; and No. 2153, $464. Deposits in transit are $100 and $50. There is a $15 service charge and $5 ATM charge in addition to notes collected of $50 and $25. Reconcile Annie's balances.   *LU 4-2(3)*

4–6. A local bank began charging $2.50 each month for returning canceled checks. The bank also has an $8.00 "maintenance" fee if a checking account slips below $750. Donna Sands likes to have copies of her canceled checks for preparing her income tax returns. She has received her bank statement with a balance of $535.85. Donna received $2.68 in interest and has been charged for the canceled checks and the maintenance fee. The following checks were outstanding: No. 94, $121.16; No. 96, $106.30; No. 98, $210.12; and No. 99, $64.84. A deposit of $765.69 was not recorded on Donna's bank statement. Her checkbook shows a balance of $806.94. Prepare Donna's bank reconciliation.   *LU 4-2(3)*

4–7. Ben Luna received his bank statement with a $27.04 fee for a bounced check (NSF). He has an $815.75 monthly mortgage
eXcel payment paid through his bank. There was also a $3.00 teller fee and a check printing fee of $3.50. His ATM card fee
was $6.40. There was also a $530.50 deposit in transit. The bank shows a balance of $119.17. The bank paid Ben $1.23
in interest. Ben's checkbook shows a balance of $1,395.28. Check No. 234 for $80.30 and check No. 235 for $28.55 were
outstanding. Prepare Ben's bank reconciliation.   *LU 4-2(3)*

4–8. Kameron Gibson's bank statement showed a balance of $717.72. Kameron's checkbook had a balance of $209.50. Check
No. 104 for $110.07 and check No. 105 for $15.55 were outstanding. A $620.50 deposit was not on the statement. He has
his payroll check electronically deposited to his checking account—the payroll check was for $1,025.10. There was also
a $4 teller fee and an $18 service charge. Prepare Kameron Gibson's bank reconciliation.   *LU 4-2(3)*

4–9. Banks are finding more ways to charge fees, such as a $25 overdraft fee. Sue McVickers has an account in Fayetteville;
eXcel she has received her bank statement with this $25 charge. Also, she was charged a $6.50 service fee; however, the good
news is she earned $5.15 interest. Her bank statement's balance was $315.65, but it did not show the $1,215.15 deposit
she had made. Sue's checkbook balance shows $604.30. The following checks have not cleared: No. 250, $603.15; No.
253, $218.90; and No. 254, $130.80. Prepare Sue's bank reconciliation.   *LU 4-2(3)*

4–10. Carol Stokke receives her April 6 bank statement showing a balance of $859.75; her checkbook balance is $954.25. The bank statement shows an ATM charge of $25.00, NSF fee of $27.00, earned interest of $2.75, and Carol's $630.15 refund check, which was processed by the IRS and deposited to her account. Carol has two checks that have not cleared—No. 115 for $521.15 and No. 116 for $205.50. There is also a deposit in transit for $1,402.05. Prepare Carol's bank reconciliation.   *LU 4-2(3)*

4–11. Lowell Bank reported the following checking account fees: $2 to see a real-live teller, $20 to process a bounced check, and $1 to $3 if you need an original check to prove you paid a bill or made a charitable contribution. This past month you had to transact business through a teller six times—a total $12 cost to you. Your bank statement shows a $305.33 balance; your checkbook shows a $1,009.76 balance. You received $1.10 in interest. An $801.15 deposit was not recorded on your statement. The following checks were outstanding: No. 413, $28.30; No. 414, $18.60; and No. 418, $60.72. Prepare your bank reconciliation.   *LU 4-2(3)*

4–12. According to the January 26, 2015, *Portland Business Journal,* Jim Houser, a Portland auto specialist, landed a key Small Business Administration appointment. Help Jim reconcile Remington's Auto Clinic's checkbook and bank balance according to the following: bank statement balance, $18,769; checkbook balance, $22,385,015; interest earned, $3,948; deposits in transit, $100,656 and $22,375,000; ATM card fees, $150; outstanding checks—No. 10189, $55,678; No. 10192, $15,287; No. 10193, $22,350; and No. 10194, $12,297.   *LU 4-2(3)*

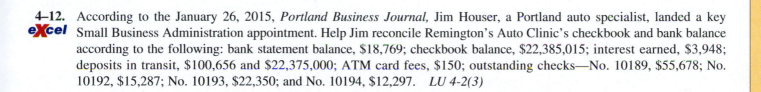

4–13. Identity Theft Resource Center (ITRC) provides consumer and victim support, public education, and advice. Marlena's grandmother is concerned her identity has been stolen. Help Marlena reconcile her grandmother's checkbook and bank statement. The checkbook reflects a balance of $1,245. The bank statement shows a balance of $207. Notes collected were $100 and $210. The bank charged a $25 service fee. Outstanding checks were No. 255, $985; No. 261, $233; and No. 262, $105. There is a deposit in transit of $2,646. Has the account been compromised?   *LU 4-2(2)*

CHALLENGE PROBLEMS

4–14. Carolyn Crosswell, who banks in New Jersey, wants to balance her checkbook, which shows a balance of $985.20. The bank shows a balance of $1,430.33. The following transactions occurred: $135.20 automatic withdrawal to the gas company, $6.50 ATM fee, $8.00 service fee, and $1,030.05 direct deposit from the IRS. Carolyn used her debit card five times and was charged 45 cents for each transaction; she was also charged $3.50 for check printing. A $931.08 deposit was not shown on her bank statement. The following checks were outstanding: No. 235, $158.20; No. 237, $184.13; No. 238, $118.12; and No. 239, $38.83. Carolyn received $2.33 interest. Prepare Carolyn's bank reconciliation.   *LU 4-2(3)*

4–15. Melissa Jackson, bookkeeper for Kinko Company, cannot prepare a bank reconciliation. From the following facts, can you help her complete the June 30, 2015, reconciliation? The bank statement showed a $2,955.82 balance. Melissa's checkbook showed a $3,301.82 balance. Melissa placed a $510.19 deposit in the bank's night depository on June 30. The deposit did not appear on the bank statement. The bank included two DMs and one CM with the returned checks: $690.65 DM for NSF check, $8.50 DM for service charges, and $400.00 CM (less $10 collection fee) for collecting a $400.00 non-interest-bearing note. Check No. 811 for $110.94 and check No. 912 for $82.50, both written and recorded on June 28, were not with the returned checks. The bookkeeper had correctly written check No. 884, $1,000, for a new cash register, but she recorded the check as $1,069. The May bank reconciliation showed check No. 748 for $210.90 and check No. 710 for $195.80 outstanding on April 30. The June bank statement included check No. 710 but not check No. 748.   *LU 4-2(3)*

 ## SUMMARY PRACTICE TEST

Do you need help? The videos in Connect have step-by-step worked-out solutions. These videos are also available on YouTube!

1. Walgreens has a $12,925.55 beginning checkbook balance. Record the following transactions in the check stubs provided. *LU 4-1(2)*
   a. November 4, 2015, check No. 180 payable to Ace Medical Corporation, $1,700.88 for drugs.
   b. $5,250 deposit—November 24.
   c. November 24, 2015, check No. 181 payable to John's Wholesale, $825.55 merchandise.

No. _____ $ _____			No. _____ $ _____		
_____ 20 _____			_____ 20 _____		
To _____			To _____		
For _____			For _____		
	DOLLARS	CENTS		DOLLARS	CENTS
BALANCE			BALANCE		
AMT. DEPOSITED			AMT. DEPOSITED		
TOTAL			TOTAL		
AMT. THIS CHECK			AMT. THIS CHECK		
BALANCE FORWARD			BALANCE FORWARD		

2. On April 1, 2015, Lester Company received a bank statement that showed a balance of $8,950. Lester showed an $8,000 checking account balance. The bank did not return check No. 115 for $750 or check No. 118 for $370. A $900 deposit made on March 31 was in transit. The bank charged Lester $20 for check printing and $250 for NSF checks. The bank also collected a $1,400 note for Lester. Lester forgot to record a $400 withdrawal at the ATM. Prepare a bank reconciliation. *LU 4-2(3)*

3. Felix Babic banks at Role Federal Bank. Today he received his March 31, 2015, bank statement showing a $762.80 balance. Felix's checkbook shows a balance of $799.80. The following checks have not cleared the bank: No. 140, $130.55; No. 149, $66.80; and No. 161, $102.90. Felix made an $820.15 deposit that is not shown on the bank statement. He has his $617.30 monthly mortgage payment paid through the bank. His $1,100.20 IRS refund check was mailed to his bank. Prepare Felix Babic's bank reconciliation. *LU 4-2(3)*

4. On June 30, 2015, Wally Company's bank statement showed a $7,500.10 bank balance. Wally has a beginning checkbook balance of $9,800.00. The bank statement also showed that it collected a $1,200.50 note for the company. A $4,500.10 June 30 deposit was in transit. Check No. 119 for $650.20 and check No. 130 for $381.50 are outstanding. Wally's bank charges $.40 cents per check. This month, 80 checks were processed. Prepare a reconciled statement. *LU 4-2(3)*

SURF TO SAVE

Choosing and maintaining a bank account

PROBLEM 1
Bank costs

Go to http://www.bankrate.com/brm/rate/bank_home.asp. Select "Local" and "Interest checking" under the "Find a Checking Account" section. Then, select "Traditional" in the city and state near where you live. Which account requires the highest average minimum balance to avoid monthly service fees? Which account requires the lowest average minimum balance to avoid monthly service fees? Which account would you select for your personal checking account from this list?

Discussion Questions

1. What are the most important criteria for you in selecting a checking account? Why?

2. Discuss the pros and cons of using a local versus an Internet-based checking account.

PROBLEM 2
Checkbook vs. bank statement balance

Go to http://googolplex.cuna.org/12433/cnote/article.php?doc_id=2502. Use the Checking/Debit Account Calculator and "Go Figure" based on the following: your register balance, $525.89; interest earnings, $1.23; bank fees, $8.99; statement balance, $698.00; deposits in transit, $150.00; withdrawals in transit, $250.00.

Discussion Questions

1. Based on the difference you found in the adjusted balances, where would you begin to look to determine what is causing this discrepancy?

2. How could this tool be useful for your own checking account?

PROBLEM 3
Mobile banking

Visit http://www.banking.com/2013/05/13/pros-and-cons-of-mobile-only-banking/#.VPXt0XzF_ao and read the article "Mobile Only Banking: The Pros & Cons for Financial Institutions." What are the pros and cons to mobile banking customers?

Discussion Questions

1. Do you feel comfortable with mobile banking? Why or why not?

2. In the future, will we see more or less mobile banking? Why?

PROBLEM 4
How much money do you have?

Go to http://www.capitalone.com/financial-education/money-basics/balancing-budget/balance-your-checkbook/ and read the article "Balancing and Budgeting—Balancing Your Checkbook." Calculate your checkbook balance for the month if you started out with $621.00 and wrote four checks for $108.95, $100.00, $49.20, and $349.26 and made three deposits of $100.00, $55.00, and $200.00.

Discussion Questions

1. Do you maintain an up-to-date checkbook balance? Why or why not?

2. What are some potential problems you could encounter if your checkbook balance is not kept up to date?

MOBILE APPS

Checkbook (Appxy) Helps track purchases and balance a check register.

Pocket Expense (Appxy) Tracks finances on multiple devices and analyzes spending with a variety of reporting functions.

PERSONAL FINANCE

A KIPLINGER APPROACH

From *Kiplinger's Personal Finance*, February 2015.

SAVINGS ACCOUNTS

EMERGENCY FUNDS: GE Capital Bank Online Savings and MySavingsDirect MySavings (tie). Neither account has a minimum-balance requirement, and each pays 1.05% in interest. The banks won't charge you transaction fees to move money into or out of the accounts (but check with any other banks involved in the transfer about their fees). Plus, there are no inactivity fees if your account sits untouched for a while, although funds in accounts left idle for years may eventually be turned over to your state's government.

BIG BALANCES: UFB Direct Savings. If you have $25,000 or more in the account, the full balance earns 1.25% (a balance of less than $25,000 earns 0.20%). There's no minimum-balance require-ment and no inactivity fee. After you make your first deposit, UFB Direct doesn't initiate transfers into or out of its savings accounts with other banks, so check whether other institutions that you use as a funding source charge fees for transfers.

SAVING FOR A GOAL: Barclays Dream Account. If you're saving for, say, a big vacation or a down payment on a home, consider this account. It pays a respectable 1.05% interest rate and has no minimum-balance requirement. It also offers the opportunity to earn a few more bucks in interest each year: Every time you make a deposit into the account for six consecutive months, you'll get a 2.5% bonus on the interest earned during that period. And if you make no withdrawals for six months, you earn an additional 2.5% bonus on interest earned. You can't deposit more than $1,000 per month in a sin-gle account, but you can have up to three accounts.

CERTIFICATES OF DEPOSIT: Nationwide. The insurance giant's online banking arm consistently provides relatively healthy interest rates across the board on cer-tificates of deposit, which require a $500 minimum deposit. With a deposit of less than $100,000, you'll earn 1.14% on a one-year CD, 1.33% on a two-year CD and 1.45% on a three-year CD (other maturities are available); depos-its of $100,000 or more earn 0.05 per-centage point more. Early-withdrawal penalties are reasonable: 90 days' in-terest on the amount withdrawn from a one-year CD and 180 days' interest for a two- or three-year CD.

A DO-IT-ALL BANK

Ally offers a range of accounts with low fees and competitive interest rates, making it an attractive choice if you want to do all your banking under one virtual roof. The Interest Checking ac-count, yielding 0.60% on balances of $15,000 or more and 0.10% on smaller balances, requires no minimum bal-ance. Plus, Ally reimburses all fees that other banks charge customers to use their ATMs domestically. The overdraft fee is $9 per item, with a max-imum of one fee per day, but having money transferred from a linked ac-count is free.

With a 0.99% rate and no minimum-balance requirement, Ally's Online Savings account competes with other top-yielding accounts. The money market deposit account (no minimum balance) has a smaller yield of 0.85%, but it comes with a debit card and checks. And Ally's certificates of de-posit have competitive rates (1.05% on a one-year CD) and no minimum-deposit requirement. Early-withdrawal fees are below average, ranging from 60 to 150 days' worth of interest. The No Penalty CD, with no early-with-drawal fee, has a lower yield (0.87% for an 11-month term). ∎

At a Glance

FIND THE ONLINE CHECKING ACCOUNT THAT SUITS YOU BEST

None of these accounts charges a monthly maintenance fee or requires that you keep a minimum balance. Interest rates and fees are as of early February.

Checking account	Minimum deposit to open	Reimburses ATM fees	Overdraft policy	Pays interest	Mobile deposit	Free bill pay
Ally Interest	No	Unlimited	$9 per day; free transfer from linked account	0.1% for balances up to $10,000; 0.6% on larger balances	Yes	Yes
Bank of Internet USA	$100	Unlimited	Free transfer from linked account	Tiered rates up to 1.25%	Yes	Yes
Bank5 Connect	$10	Up to $15 per billing cycle	$15 per item; free transfer from linked account	0.76% with minimum balance of $100	Yes	Yes
Capital One 360	No	No	You pay interest on line of credit	0.2% up to $50,000; 0.75% up to $100,000	Yes	Yes
Evantage	$1	Up to $25 a month	$25 per item; free transfer from linked account	1.5% on balances up to $10,000; 0.5% on larger balances	No	10 payments a month

SOURCES: Online banks

BUSINESS MATH ISSUE

If a customer uses online checking, then the bank should not charge a fee for overdraft protection.

1. List the key points of the article and information to support your position.
2. Write a group defense of your position using math calculations to support your view.

CHAPTER 5

Solving for the Unknown A How-to Approach for Solving Equations

© The McGraw-Hill Companies, Inc./John Flournoy, photographer

Pepper ... And Salt

THE WALL STREET JOURNAL

"Looks like the two party system did start with a big bang."

From *The Wall Street Journal*, permission Cartoon Features Syndicate.

New Credit Scores to Ease Access to Loans

BY ANNAMARIA ANDRIOTIS

A change in how the most widely used credit score in the U.S. is tallied will likely make it easier for tens of millions of Americans to get loans.

Fair Isaac Corp. said Thursday that it will stop including in its FICO credit-score calculations any record of a consumer failing to pay a bill if the bill has been paid or settled with a collection agency. The San Jose, Calif., company also will give less weight to unpaid medical bills that are with a collection agency.

The moves follow months of discussions with lenders and the Consumer Financial Protection Bureau aimed at boosting lend-ing without creating more credit risk. Since the recession, many lenders have approved only the best borrowers, usually those with few or no blemishes on their credit report.

The changes are expected to boost consumer lending, especially among borrowers shut out of the market or charged high interest rates because of their low scores. "It expands banks' ability to make loans for people who might not have qualified and to offer a lower price [for others]," said Nessa Feddis, senior vice president of consumer protection and payments at the American Bankers Association, a trade group.

Reprinted by permission of *The Wall Street Journal*, copyright 2014 Dow Jones & Company, Inc.

LU 5–1: Solving Equations for the Unknown

1. Explain the basic procedures used to solve equations for the unknown.
2. List the five rules and the mechanical steps used to solve for the unknown in seven situations; know how to check the answers.

LU 5–2: Solving Word Problems for the Unknown

1. List the steps for solving word problems.
2. Complete blueprint aids to solve word problems; check the solutions.

VOCABULARY PREVIEW

Here are key terms in this chapter. After completing the chapter, if you know the term, place a checkmark in the box. If you don't know the term, look it up and put the page number where it can be found.

Constants ☐ Equation ☐ Expression ☐ Formula ☐ Knowns ☐ Unknown ☐ Variables ☐

Do children want to play with traditional or digital games? Mattel thinks it has the winning formula. The following *Wall Street Journal* clip shows how Mattel is merging traditional and digital together.

Learning Unit 5–1 explains how you can solve for unknowns in equations. In Learning Unit 5–2 you learn how to solve for unknowns in word problems. When you complete these learning units, you will not have to memorize as many formulas to solve business and personal math applications. The *Wall Street Journal* chapter opener clip, "New Credit Scores to Ease Access to Loans," discusses how a new formula is being used for calculating credit scores. With the increasing use of computer software, a basic working knowledge of solving for the unknown has become necessary.

Traditional Toys Add Apps To Keep Up With Smartphones

By Anne Marie Chaker

Can toys and apps play nicely together?

Several big toy brands think they finally have the right formula for mixing digital play with tangible toys. They have arrived at this point after years of struggling to devise new versions of traditional toys that will appeal to young children as much as a tablet or smartphone.

Mattel Inc. says it has a winner with Barbie Fashion Design Maker, for ages 6 and up. Girls design Barbie-size fashions on a computer or tablet and print them out on sticker-backed fabric. The $50 kit, now hitting stores, comes with eight sheets of printer-friendly fabric, which girls mold to the Barbie. They can upload photos (a cat's face, a tennis racket) using the app or downloadable software and embellish Barbie's clothes with the images. And they can create a portfolio for storing and displaying the creations.

Reprinted by permission of *The Wall Street Journal*, copyright 2014 Dow Jones & Company, Inc. All rights reserved worldwide.

Learning Unit 5–1: Solving Equations for the Unknown

The following Rose Smith letter is based on a true story. Note how Rose states that the blueprint aids, the lesson on repetition, and the chapter organizers were important factors in the successful completion of her business math course.

Rose Smith
15 Locust Street
Lynn, MA 01915

Dear Professor Slater,

Thank you for helping me get through your Business Math class. When I first started, my math anxiety level was real high. I felt I had no head for numbers. When you told us we would be covering the chapter on solving equations, I'll never forget how I started to shake. I started to panic. I felt I could never solve a word problem. I thought I was having an algebra attack.

Now that it's over (90 on the chapter on unknowns), I'd like to tell you what worked for me so you might pass this on to other students. It was your blueprint aids. Drawing boxes helped me to think things out. They were a <u>tool</u> that helped me more clearly understand how to dissect each word problem. They didn't solve the problem for me, but gave me the direction I needed. <u>Repetition</u> was the key to my success. At first I got them all wrong but after the third time, things started to click. I felt more confident. Your chapter organizers at the end of the chapter were great. Thanks for your patience – your repetition breeds success – now students are asking me to help them solve a word problem. Can you believe it!

Best,

Rose

Rose Smith

Many of you are familiar with the terms *variables* and *constants*. If you are planning to prepare for your retirement by saving only what you can afford each year, your saving is a *variable;* if you plan to save the same amount each year, your saving is a *constant*. Now you can also say that you cannot buy clothes by size because of the many variables involved. This unit explains the importance of mathematical variables and constants when solving equations.

Basic Equation-Solving Procedures

Do you know the difference between a mathematical expression, equation, and formula? A mathematical **expression** is a meaningful combination of numbers and letters called *terms*.

PLUGGERS by Gary Brookins

Email: pluggermail@aol.com

Thanks to
Loren Loop
Creswell,
Oregon

SO, GRAMPS, DO WE DIVIDE OR MULTIPLY THE INTEGER?

Write to: Pluggers
P. O. Box 29347
Henrico, VA
23242

You're a plugger if your 9-year-old grandchild asks for help with homework and you have no clue what it's about.

© 2014 Tribune Content Agency, LLC; Brookins Art, LLC

Operational signs (such as $+$ or $-$) within the expression connect the terms to show a relationship between them. For example, $6 + 2$ and $6A - 4A$ are mathematical expressions. An **equation** is a mathematical statement with an equals sign showing that a mathematical expression on the left equals the mathematical expression on the right. An equation has an equals sign; an expression does not have an equals sign. A **formula** is an equation that expresses in symbols a general fact, rule, or principle. Formulas are shortcuts for expressing a word concept. For example, in Chapter 10 you will learn that the formula for simple interest is Interest (I) = Principal (P) × Rate (R) × Time (T). This means that when you see $I = P \times R \times T$, you recognize the simple interest formula. Now let's study basic equations.

As a mathematical statement of equality, equations show that two numbers or groups of numbers are equal. For example, $6 + 4 = 10$ shows the equality of an equation. Equations also use letters as symbols that represent one or more numbers. These symbols, usually a letter of the alphabet, are **variables** that stand for a number. We can use a variable even though we may not know what it represents. For example, $A + 2 = 6$. The variable A represents the number or **unknown** (4 in this example) for which we are solving. We distinguish variables from numbers, which have a fixed value. Numbers such as 3 or -7 are **constants** or **knowns,** whereas A and $3A$ (this means 3 times the variable A) are variables. So we can now say that variables and constants are *terms of mathematical expressions.*

Usually in solving for the unknown, we place variable(s) on the left side of the equation and constants on the right. The following rules for variables and constants are important.

VARIABLES AND CONSTANTS RULES

1. If no number is in front of a letter, it is a 1: $B = 1B$; $C = 1C$.
2. If no sign is in front of a letter or number, it is a +: $C = +C$; $4 = +4$.

You should be aware that in solving equations, the meaning of the symbols +, −, ×, and ÷ has not changed. However, some variations occur. For example, you can also write $A \times B$ (A times B) as $A \cdot B$, $A(B)$, or AB. Also, A divided by B is the same as A/B. Remember that to solve an equation, you must find a number that can replace the unknown in the equation and make it a true statement. Now let's take a moment to look at how we can change verbal statements into variables.

Assume Dick Hersh, an employee of Nike, is 50 years old. Let's assign Dick Hersh's changing age to the symbol A. The symbol A is a variable.

Verbal statement	Variable A (age)
Dick's age 8 years ago	$A - 8$
Dick's age 8 years from today	$A + 8$
Four times Dick's age	$4A$
One-fifth Dick's age	$A/5$

FIGURE 5.1

Equality in equations

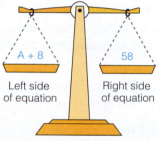

Left side of equation   Right side of equation

Dick's age in 8 years will equal 58.

To visualize how equations work, think of the old-fashioned balancing scale shown in Figure 5.1. The pole of the scale is the equals sign. The two sides of the equation are the two pans of the scale. In the left pan or left side of the equation, we have $A + 8$; in the right pan or right side of the equation, we have 58. To solve for the unknown (Dick's present age), we isolate or place the unknown (variable) on the left side and the numbers on the right. We will do this soon. For now, remember that to keep an equation (or scale) in balance, we must perform mathematical operations (addition, subtraction, multiplication, and division) to *both* sides of the equation.

SOLVING FOR THE UNKNOWN RULE

Whatever you do to one side of an equation, you must do to the other side.

How to Solve for Unknowns in Equations

LO 2

This section presents seven drill situations and the rules that will guide you in solving for unknowns in these situations. We begin with two basic rules—the opposite process rule and the equation equality rule.

FRAZZ © 2014 Jef Mallett. Dist. By ANDREWS MCMEEL SYNDICATION. Reprinted with permission. All rights reserved.

OPPOSITE PROCESS RULE

If an equation indicates a process such as addition, subtraction, multiplication, or division, solve for the unknown or variable by using the opposite process. For example, if the equation process is addition, solve for the unknown by using subtraction.

EQUATION EQUALITY RULE

You can add the same quantity or number to both sides of the equation and subtract the same quantity or number from both sides of the equation without affecting the equality of the equation. You can also divide or multiply both sides of the equation by the same quantity or number *(except zero)* without affecting the equality of the equation.

   To check your answer(s), substitute your answer(s) for the letter(s) in the equation. The sum of the left side should equal the sum of the right side.

Drill Situation 1: Subtracting Same Number from Both Sides of Equation

Example	**Mechanical steps**	**Explanation**
$A + 8 = 58$	$\begin{aligned} A + 8 &= 58 \\ -8 \quad &\;\; -8 \\ \hline A \quad &= 50 \end{aligned}$	8 is subtracted from *both* sides of equation to isolate variable A on the left.
Dick's age A plus 8 equals 58.		**Check**
		$50 + 8 = 58$
		$58 = 58$

Note: Since the equation process used *addition,* we use the opposite process rule and solve for variable A with *subtraction.* We also use the equation equality rule when we subtract the same quantity from both sides of the equation.

Drill Situation 2: Adding Same Number to Both Sides of Equation

Example	**Mechanical steps**	**Explanation**
$B - 50 = 80$	$\begin{aligned} B - 50 &= 80 \\ +50 \quad &\;\; +50 \\ \hline B \quad &= 130 \end{aligned}$	50 is added to *both* sides to isolate variable B on the left.
Some number B less 50 equals 80.		**Check**
		$130 - 50 = 80$
		$80 = 80$

Note: Since the equation process used *subtraction,* we use the opposite process rule and solve for variable B with *addition.* We also use the equation equality rule when we add the same quantity to both sides of the equation.

Drill Situation 3: Dividing Both Sides of Equation by Same Number

Example	**Mechanical steps**	**Explanation**
$7G = 35$	$7G = 35$	By dividing both sides by 7, G equals 5.
Some number G times 7 equals 35.	$\dfrac{7G}{7} = \dfrac{35}{7}$	**Check**
	$G = 5$	$7(5) = 35$
		$35 = 35$

Note: Since the equation process used *multiplication,* we use the opposite process rule and solve for variable G with *division.* We also use the equation equality rule when we divide both sides of the equation by the same quantity.

Drill Situation 4: Multiplying Both Sides of Equation by Same Number

Example	**Mechanical steps**	**Explanation**
$\dfrac{V}{5} = 70$	$\dfrac{V}{5} = 70$	By multiplying both sides by 5, V is equal to 350.
Some number V divided by 5 equals 70.	$5\left(\dfrac{V}{5}\right) = 70(5)$	**Check**
	$V = 350$	$\dfrac{350}{5} = 70$
		$70 = 70$

Note: Since the equation process used *division,* we use the opposite process rule and solve for variable *V* with *multiplication.* We also use the equation equality rule when we multiply both sides of the equation by the same quantity.

Drill Situation 5: Equation That Uses Subtraction and Multiplication to Solve for Unknown

MULTIPLE PROCESSES RULE
When solving for an unknown that involves more than one process, do the addition and subtraction before the multiplication and division.

Example	**Mechanical steps**	**Explanation**
$\dfrac{H}{4} + 2 = 5$	$\dfrac{H}{4} + 2 = 5$	1. Move constant to right side by subtracting 2 from both sides.
When we divide unknown *H* by 4 and add the result to 2, the answer is 5.	$\begin{aligned} \dfrac{H}{4} + 2 &= 5 \\ -2 & -2 \\ \hline \dfrac{H}{4} &= 3 \end{aligned}$	2. To isolate *H*, which is divided by 4, we do the opposite process and multiply 4 times *both* sides of the equation.
	$\cancel{4}\left(\dfrac{H}{\cancel{4}}\right) = 4(3)$	
	$H = \boxed{12}$	

Check

$$\dfrac{12}{4} + 2 = 5$$
$$3 + 2 = 5$$
$$5 = 5$$

Drill Situation 6: Using Parentheses in Solving for Unknown

PARENTHESES RULE
When equations contain parentheses (which indicate grouping together), you solve for the unknown by first multiplying each item inside the parentheses by the number or letter just outside the parentheses. Then you continue to solve for the unknown with the opposite process used in the equation. Do the additions and subtractions first; then the multiplications and divisions.

Example	**Mechanical steps**	**Explanation**
$5(P - 4) = 20$	$5(P - 4) = 20$	1. Parentheses tell us that everything inside parentheses is multiplied by 5. Multiply 5 by *P* and 5 by −4.
The unknown *P* less 4, multiplied by 5 equals 20.	$\begin{aligned} 5P - 20 &= 20 \\ +20 & +20 \\ \hline \dfrac{\cancel{5}P}{\cancel{5}} &= \dfrac{40}{5} \\ P &= \boxed{8} \end{aligned}$	2. Add 20 to both sides to isolate 5*P* on left.
		3. To remove 5 in front of *P*, divide both sides by 5 to result in *P* equals 8.

Check

$$5(8 - 4) = 20$$
$$5(4) = 20$$
$$20 = 20$$

MONEY tips

Negotiate. Over 9 out of 10 customers who ask for a discount on items such as electronics, appliances, furniture, and medical bills receive one. Just ask. You could be saving money.

Drill Situation 7: Combining Like Unknowns

LIKE UNKNOWNS RULE

To solve equations with like unknowns, you first combine the unknowns and then solve with the opposite process used in the equation.

Example	Mechanical steps	Explanation
$4A + A = 20$	$4A + A = 20$ $\dfrac{\cancel{5}A}{\cancel{5}} = \dfrac{20}{5}$ $A = 4$	To solve this equation: $4A + 1A = 5A$. Thus, $5A = 20$. To solve for A, divide both sides by 5, leaving A equals 4.

Check

$4(4) + 4 = 20$
$20 = 20$

Always, always, always do a logic check on your answer. Reread the word problem to see if your answer makes sense. If it does, move on. If it does not, review your strategy for solving the problem and make any needed adjustments.

Before you go to Learning Unit 5–2, let's check your understanding of this unit.

LU 5–1 | **PRACTICE QUIZ**

Complete this Practice Quiz to see how you are doing.

1. Write equations for the following (use the letter Q as the variable). Do not solve for the unknown.
   a. Nine less than one-half a number is fourteen.
   b. Eight times the sum of a number and thirty-one is fifty.
   c. Ten decreased by twice a number is two.
   d. Eight times a number less two equals twenty-one.
   e. The sum of four times a number and two is fifteen.
   f. If twice a number is decreased by eight, the difference is four.

2. Solve the following:
   a. $B + 24 = 60$
   b. $D + 3D = 240$
   c. $12B = 144$
   d. $\dfrac{B}{6} = 50$
   e. $\dfrac{B}{4} + 4 = 16$
   f. $3(B - 8) = 18$

*For **extra help** from your authors—Sharon and Jeff—see the videos in Connect.*

These videos are also available on YouTube!

✓ Solutions

1. a. $\dfrac{1}{2}Q - 9 = 14$
   b. $8(Q + 31) = 50$
   c. $10 - 2Q = 2$
   d. $8Q - 2 = 21$
   e. $4Q + 2 = 15$
   f. $2Q - 8 = 4$

2. a. $B + 24 = 60$
      $\underline{-24 \quad -24}$
      $B \quad = \quad \boxed{36}$

   b. $\dfrac{\cancel{4}D}{\cancel{4}} = \dfrac{240}{4}$
      $D = \boxed{60}$

   c. $\dfrac{\cancel{12}B}{\cancel{12}} = \dfrac{144}{12}$
      $B = \boxed{12}$

   d. $\cancel{6}\left(\dfrac{B}{\cancel{6}}\right) = 50(6)$
      $B = \boxed{300}$

   e. $\dfrac{B}{4} + 4 = \quad 16$
      $\underline{\phantom{\dfrac{B}{4}}-4 \quad -4}$
      $\dfrac{B}{4} = \quad 12$
      $\cancel{4}\left(\dfrac{B}{\cancel{4}}\right) = 12(4)$
      $B = \boxed{48}$

   f. $3(B - 8) = \quad 18$
      $3B - 24 = \quad 18$
      $\underline{+24 \quad +24}$
      $\dfrac{\cancel{3}B}{\cancel{3}} = \dfrac{42}{3}$
      $B = \boxed{14}$

Need more practice? Try this **Extra Practice Quiz** (check figures in the Interactive Chapter Organizer). Worked-out Solutions can be found in Appendix B.

1. Write equations for the following (use the letter Q as the variable). Do not solve for the unknown.
   a. Eight less than one-half a number is sixteen.
   b. Twelve times the sum of a number and forty-one is 1,200.
   c. Seven decreased by twice a number is one.
   d. Four times a number less two equals twenty-four.
   e. The sum of three times a number and three is nineteen.
   f. If twice a number is decreased by six, the difference is five.

2. Solve the following:
   a. $B + 14 = 70$
   b. $D + 4D = 250$
   c. $11B = 121$
   d. $\dfrac{B}{8} = 90$
   e. $\dfrac{B}{2} + 2 = 250$
   f. $3(B - 6) = 18$

Learning Unit 5–2: Solving Word Problems for the Unknown

When you buy a candy bar such as a Snickers, you should turn the candy bar over and carefully read the ingredients and calories contained on the back of the candy bar wrapper. For example, on the back of the Snickers wrapper you will read that there are "170 calories per piece." You could misread this to mean that the entire Snickers bar has 170 calories. However, look closer and you will see that the Snickers bar is divided into three pieces, so if you eat the entire bar, instead of consuming 170 calories, you will consume 510 calories. Making errors like this could result in a weight gain that you cannot explain.

© McGraw-Hill Education. Mark Dierker, photographer

$$\frac{1}{3}S = 170 \text{ calories}$$

$$3\left(\frac{1}{3}S\right) = 170 \times 3$$

$$S = \boxed{510} \text{ calories per bar}$$

In this unit, we use blueprint aids in six different situations to help you solve for unknowns. Be patient and *persistent*. Remember that the more problems you work, the easier the process becomes. Do not panic! Repetition is the key. Study the five steps that follow. They will help you solve for unknowns in word problems.

SOLVING WORD PROBLEMS FOR UNKNOWNS
Step 1. Carefully read the entire problem. You may have to read it several times.
Step 2. Ask yourself: What is the problem looking for?
Step 3. When you are sure what the problem is asking, let a variable represent the unknown. If the problem has more than one unknown, represent the second unknown in terms of the same variable. For example, if the problem has two unknowns, Y is one unknown. The second unknown is $4Y$—4 times the first unknown.
Step 4. Visualize the relationship between unknowns and variables. Then set up an equation to solve for unknown(s).
Step 5. Check your result to see if it is accurate.

The next clip from *The Wall Street Journal*, "How to Ace That Test," may also help you in the process of solving word problems.

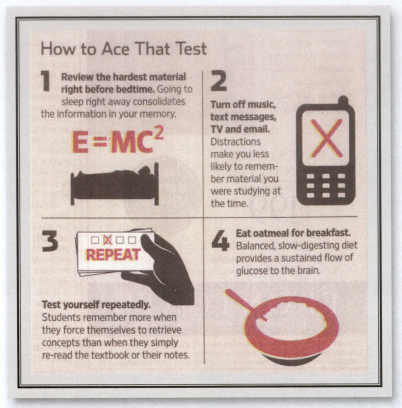

Reprinted by permission of *The Wall Street Journal,* copyright 2011 Dow Jones & Company, Inc. All rights reserved worldwide.

Word Problem Situation 1: Number Problems Today on sale at a local Stop and Shop supermarket, the price of a 1-pound can of Maxwell House coffee is $9.99. This is a $2 savings. What was the original price of the can of coffee?

© Roberts Publishing Services

LO 2

BLUEPRINT	Unknown(s)	Variable(s)	Relationship*
	Original price of Maxwell House	P	$P - \$2 =$ New price

Mechanical steps

$$P - 2 = \$9.99$$
$$\underline{+2 \quad +2}$$
$$P \quad = \quad \$11.99$$

*This column will help you visualize the equation before setting up the actual equation.

Explanation

The original price less $2 = $9.99. Note that we added $2 to both sides to isolate P on the left. Remember, $IP = P$.

Check

$11.99 − 2 = $9.99
$9.99 = $9.99

Word Problem Situation 2: Finding the Whole When Part Is Known A local Burger King budgets $\frac{1}{8}$ of its monthly profits on salaries. Salaries for the month were $12,000. What were Burger King's monthly profits?

BLUEPRINT	Unknown(s)	Variable(s)	Relationship
	Monthly profits	P	$\frac{1}{8}P$ Salaries = $12,000

Mechanical steps

$$\frac{1}{8}P = \$12,000$$

$$8\left(\frac{P}{8}\right) = \$12,000(8)$$

$$P = \boxed{\$96,000}$$

Explanation

$\frac{1}{8}P$ represents Burger King's monthly salaries. Since the equation used division, we solve for P by multiplying both sides by 8.

Check

$\frac{1}{8}($96,000) = $12,000$
$12,000 = $12,000

Word Problem Situation 3: Difference Problems ICM Company sold 4 times as many computers as Ring Company. The difference in their sales is 27. How many computers of each company were sold?

BLUEPRINT	Unknown(s)	Variable(s)	Relationship
	ICM	$4C$	$4C$
	Ring	C	$-C$ 27

Note: If problem has two unknowns, assign the variable to smaller item or one who sells less. Then assign the other unknown using the same variable. *Use the same letter.*

Mechanical steps

$$4C - C = 27$$

$$\frac{3C}{3} = \frac{27}{3}$$

$$C = \boxed{9}$$

Ring = $\boxed{9}$ computers
ICM = 4(9)
= $\boxed{36}$ computers

Explanation

The variables replace the names ICM and Ring. We assigned Ring the variable C, since it sold fewer computers. We assigned ICM $4C$, since it sold 4 times as many computers.

Check

36 computers
−9
27 computers

Word Problem Situation 4: Calculating Unit Sales Together Barry Sullivan and Mitch Ryan sold a total of 300 homes for Regis Realty. Barry sold 9 times as many homes as Mitch. How many did each sell?

BLUEPRINT	Unknown(s)	Variable(s)	Relationship
	Homes sold:		
	B. Sullivan	$9H$	$9H$
	M. Ryan	H^*	$+H$ 300 homes

*Assign H to Ryan since he sold less.

Mechanical steps

$$9H + H = 300$$

$$\frac{10H}{10} = \frac{300}{10}$$

$$H = \boxed{30}$$

Ryan: $\boxed{30}$ homes
Sullivan: 9(30) = $\boxed{270}$ homes

Explanation

We assigned Mitch H, since he sold fewer homes. We assigned Barry $9H$, since he sold 9 times as many homes. Together Barry and Mitch sold 300 homes.

Check

30 + 270 = 300

Word Problem Situation 5: Calculating Unit and Dollar Sales (Cost per Unit) When Total Units Are Not Given Andy sold watches ($9) and alarm clocks ($5) at a flea market. Total sales were $287. People bought 4 times as many watches as alarm clocks. How many of each did Andy sell? What were the total dollar sales of each?

	Unknown(s)	Variable(s)	Price	Relationship
BLUEPRINT	*Unit sales:*			
	Watches	4C	$9	36C
	Clocks	C	5	+ 5C
				$287 total sales

Mechanical steps

$$36C + 5C = 287$$
$$\frac{41C}{41} = \frac{287}{41}$$
$$C = \boxed{7}$$

$\boxed{7}$ clocks

$4(7) = \boxed{28}$ watches

Explanation

Number of watches times $9 sales price plus number of alarm clocks times $5 sales price equals $287 total sales.

Check

$$7(\$5) + 28(\$9) = \$287$$
$$\$35 + \$252 = \$287$$
$$\$287 = \$287$$

Word Problem Situation 6: Calculating Unit and Dollar Sales (Cost per Unit) When Total Units Are Given Andy sold watches ($9) and alarm clocks ($5) at a flea market. Total sales for 35 watches and alarm clocks were $287. How many of each did Andy sell? What were the total dollar sales of each?

MONEY tips

Go green. Recycle plastics, paper, cardboard, glass, steel, aluminum cans and foil, plastic bags, motor oil, tires, batteries, computer printers, compost, household cleaners, and so on. Reduce the volume of packaging you require by using a canvas bag. Do your part to help solve the unknown environmental challenges of the future.

	Unknown(s)	Variable(s)	Price	Relationship
BLUEPRINT	*Unit sales:*			
	Watches	W*	$9	9W
	Clocks	35 − W	5	+ 5(35 − W)
				$287 total sales

*The more expensive item is assigned to the variable first only for this situation to make the mechanical steps easier to complete.

Mechanical steps

$$9W + 5(35 - W) = 287$$
$$9W + 175 - 5W = 287$$
$$4W + 175 = 287$$
$$\underline{-175 \qquad -175}$$
$$\frac{4W}{4} = \frac{112}{4}$$
$$W = \boxed{28}$$

Watches = $\boxed{28}$

Clocks = 35 − 28 = $\boxed{7}$

Explanation

Number of watches (*W*) times price per watch plus number of alarm clocks times price per alarm clock equals $287. Total units given was 35.

Check

$$28(\$9) + 7(\$5) = \$287$$
$$\$252 + \$35 = \$287$$
$$\$287 = \$287$$

Why did we use 35 − W? Assume we had 35 pizzas (some cheese, others meatball). If I said that I ate all the meatball pizzas (5), how many cheese pizzas are left? Thirty? Right, you subtract 5 from 35. Think of 35 − W as meaning one number.

Note in Word Problem Situations 5 and 6 that the situation is the same. In Word Problem Situation 5, we were not given total units sold (but we were told which sold better). In Word Problem Situation 6, we were given total units sold, but we did not know which sold better.

Now try these six types of word problems in the Practice Quiz. Be sure to complete blueprint aids and the mechanical steps for solving the unknown(s).

LU 5–2 **PRACTICE QUIZ**

Complete this **Practice Quiz** to see how you are doing.

Situations

1. An L. L. Bean sweater was reduced $30. The sale price was $90. What was the original price?
2. Kelly Doyle budgets $\frac{1}{8}$ of her yearly salary for entertainment. Kelly's total entertainment bill for the year is $6,500. What is Kelly's yearly salary?
3. Micro Knowledge sells 5 times as many computers as Morse Electronics. The difference in sales between the two stores is 20 computers. How many computers did each store sell?

4. Susie and Cara sell stoves at Elliott's Appliances. Together they sold 180 stoves in January. Susie sold 5 times as many stoves as Cara. How many stoves did each sell?
5. Pasquale's Pizza sells meatball pizzas ($6) and cheese pizzas ($5). In March, Pasquale's total sales were $1,600. People bought 2 times as many cheese pizzas as meatball pizzas. How many of each did Pasquale's sell? What were the total dollar sales of each?
6. Pasquale's Pizza sells meatball pizzas ($6) and cheese pizzas ($5). In March, Pasquale's sold 300 pizzas for $1,600. How many of each did Pasquale's sell? What was the dollar sales price of each?

*For **extra help** from your authors—Sharon and Jeff—see the videos in Connect.*

These videos are also available on YouTube!

✓ Solutions

1.

BLUEPRINT	Unknown(s)	Variable(s)	Relationship
	Original price	P*	P − $30 = Sale price Sale price = $90

*p = Original price.

Mechanical steps

$$P - \$30 = \$90$$
$$\underline{+ 30 \quad + 30}$$
$$P \quad = \quad \boxed{\$120}$$

2.

BLUEPRINT	Unknown(s)	Variable(s)	Relationship
	Yearly salary	S*	$\frac{1}{8}S$ Entertainment = $6,500

*S = Salary.

Mechanical steps

$$\frac{1}{8}S = \$6,500$$
$$8\left(\frac{S}{8}\right) = \$6,500(8)$$
$$S = \boxed{\$52,000}$$

3.

BLUEPRINT	Unknown(s)	Variable(s)	Relationship
	Micro	5C*	5C
	Morse	C	− C 20 computers

*C = Computers.

Mechanical steps

$$5C - C = 20$$
$$\frac{4C}{4} = \frac{20}{4}$$
$$C = \boxed{5} \text{ (Morse)}$$
$$5C = \boxed{25} \text{ (Micro)}$$

4.

BLUEPRINT	Unknown(s)	Variable(s)	Relationship
	Stoves sold:		
	Susie	5S*	5S
	Cara	S	+ S 180 stoves

*S = Stoves.

Mechanical steps

$$5S + S = 180$$
$$\frac{6S}{6} = \frac{180}{6}$$
$$S = \boxed{30} \text{ (Cara)}$$
$$5S = \boxed{150} \text{ (Susie)}$$

5.

BLUEPRINT	Unknown(s)	Variable(s)	Price	Relationship
	Meatball	M	$6	6M
	Cheese	2M	5	+ 10M $1,600 total sales

Mechanical steps

$$6M + 10M = 1,600$$
$$\frac{16M}{16} = \frac{1,600}{16}$$
$$M = \boxed{100} \text{ (meatball)}$$
$$2M = \boxed{200} \text{ (cheese)}$$

Check

$$(100 \times \$6) + (200 \times \$5) = \$1,600$$
$$\$600 + \$1,000 = \$1,600$$
$$\$1,600 = \$1,600$$

6.

BLUEPRINT	Unknown(s)	Variable(s)	Price	Relationship
	Unit sales:			
	Meatball	*M**	$6	6*M*
	Cheese	300 − *M*	5	+ 5(300 − *M*)
				$1,600 total sales

*We assign the variable to the most expensive item to make the mechanical steps easier to complete.

Mechanical steps

$$6M + 5(300 - M) = 1{,}600$$
$$6M + 1{,}500 - 5M = 1{,}600$$
$$M + 1{,}500 = 1{,}600$$
$$\underline{-1{,}500 \qquad -1{,}500}$$
$$M = 100$$

Meatball = 100

Cheese = 300 − 100 = 200

Check

$$100(\$6) + 200(\$5) = \$600 + \$1{,}000$$
$$= \$1{,}600$$

LU 5–2a   EXTRA PRACTICE QUIZ WITH WORKED-OUT SOLUTIONS

Need more practice? Try this **Extra Practice Quiz** (check figures in the Interactive Chapter Organizer). Worked-out Solutions can be found in Appendix B.

Situations

1. An L. L. Bean sweater was reduced $50. The sale price was $140. What was the original price?

2. Kelly Doyle budgets $\frac{1}{7}$ of her yearly salary for entertainment. Kelly's total entertainment bill for the year is $7,000. What is Kelly's yearly salary?

3. Micro Knowledge sells 8 times as many computers as Morse Electronics. The difference in sales between the two stores is 49 computers. How many computers did each store sell?

4. Susie and Cara sell stoves at Elliott's Appliances. Together they sold 360 stoves in January. Susie sold 2 times as many stoves as Cara. How many stoves did each sell?

5. Pasquale's Pizza sells meatball pizzas ($7) and cheese pizzas ($6). In March, Pasquale's total sales were $1,800. People bought 3 times as many cheese pizzas as meatball pizzas. How many of each did Pasquale's sell? What were the total dollar sales of each?

6. Pasquale's Pizza sells meatball pizzas ($7) and cheese pizzas ($6). In March, Pasquale's sold 288 pizzas for $1,800. What was the dollar sales price of each?

INTERACTIVE CHAPTER ORGANIZER

Solving for unknowns from basic equations	Mechanical steps to solve unknowns	Key point(s)	You try it*
Situation 1: Subtracting same number from both sides of equation	$D + 10 = 12$ $\underline{-10 \qquad -10}$ $D = 2$	Subtract 10 from both sides of equation to isolate variable *D* on the left. Since equation used addition, we solve by using opposite process—subtraction.	**Solve** $E + 15 = 14$
Situation 2: Adding same number to both sides of equation	$L - 24 = 40$ $\underline{+24 \qquad +24}$ $L = 64$	Add 24 to both sides to isolate unknown *L* on left. We solve by using opposite process of subtraction—addition.	**Solve** $B - 40 = 80$
Situation 3: Dividing both sides of equation by same number	$6B = 24$ $\dfrac{\cancel{6}B}{\cancel{6}} = \dfrac{24}{\cancel{6}}$ $B = 4$	To isolate *B* on the left, divide both sides of the equation by 6. Thus, the 6 on the left cancels—leaving *B* equal to 4. Since equation used multiplication, we solve unknown by using opposite process—division.	**Solve** $5C = 75$

(continues)

INTERACTIVE CHAPTER ORGANIZER

Solving for unknowns from basic equations	Mechanical steps to solve unknowns	Key point(s)	You try it*
Situation 4: Multiplying both sides of equation by same number	$$\frac{R}{3} = 15$$ $$3\left(\frac{R}{3}\right) = 15(3)$$ $$R = \boxed{45}$$	To remove denominator, multiply both sides of the equation by 3—the 3 on the left side cancels, leaving R equal to 45. Since equation used division, we solve unknown by using opposite process—multiplication.	**Solve** $$\frac{A}{6} = 60$$
Situation 5: Equation that uses subtraction and multiplication to solve for unknown	$$\frac{B}{3} + 6 = 13$$ $$\underline{\quad -6 \quad -6\quad}$$ $$\frac{B}{3} = 7$$ $$3\left(\frac{B}{3}\right) = 7(3)$$ $$B = \boxed{21}$$	1. Move constant 6 to right side by subtracting 6 from both sides. 2. Isolate B on left by multiplying both sides by 3.	**Solve** $$\frac{C}{4} + 10 = 17$$
Situation 6: Using parentheses in solving for unknown	$$6(A - 5) = 12$$ $$6A - 30 = 12$$ $$\underline{\quad +30 \quad +30\quad}$$ $$\frac{6A}{6} = \frac{42}{6}$$ $$A = \boxed{7}$$	Parentheses indicate multiplication. Multiply 6 times A and 6 times -5. Result is $6A - 30$ on left side of the equation. Now add 30 to both sides to isolate $6A$ on left. To remove 6 in front of A, divide both sides by 6, to result in A equal to 7. Note that when deleting parentheses, we did not have to multiply the right side.	**Solve** $$7(B - 10) = 35$$
Situation 7: Combining like unknowns	$$6A + 2A = 64$$ $$\frac{8A}{8} = \frac{64}{8}$$ $$A = \boxed{8}$$	$6A + 2A$ combine to $8A$. To solve for A, we divide both sides by 8.	**Solve** $$5B + 3B = 17$$

Solving for unknowns from word problems	Blueprint aid	Mechanical steps to solve unknown with check	You try it*
Situation 1: Number problems **U.S. Air reduced its airfare to California by $60. The sale price was $95. What was the original price?**	**BLUEPRINT** 	Unknown(s)	Variable(s)	Relationship
Original price	P	P − $60 = Sale price Sale price = $95		$$P - \$60 = \$\,95$$ $$\underline{\quad +60 \qquad +60\quad}$$ $$P = \boxed{\$155}$$ **Check** $$\$155 - \$60 = \$95$$ $$\$95 = \$95$$	**Solve** U.S. Air reduced its airfare to California by $53. The sale price was $110. What was the original price?
Situation 2: Finding the whole when part is known **K. McCarthy spends $\frac{1}{8}$ of her budget for school. What is the total budget if school costs $5,000?**	**BLUEPRINT** 	Unknown(s)	Variable(s)	Relationship
Total budget	B	⅛B School = $5,000		$$\frac{1}{8}B = \$5,000$$ $$8\left(\frac{B}{8}\right) = \$5,000(8)$$ $$B = \boxed{\$40,000}$$ **Check** $$\frac{1}{8}(\$40,000) = \$5,000$$ $$\$5,000 = \$5,000$$	**Solve** K. McCarthy spends $\frac{1}{7}$ of her budget for school. What is the total budget if school costs $6,000?

(continues)

INTERACTIVE CHAPTER ORGANIZER

Solving for unknowns from word problems	Blueprint aid	Mechanical steps to solve unknown with check	You try it*
Situation 3: Difference problems Moe sold 8 times as many suitcases as Bill. The difference in their sales is 280 suitcases. How many suitcases did each sell?	BLUEPRINT | Unknown(s)	Variable(s)	Relationship | |---|---|---| | *Suitcases sold:* Moe Bill | 8S S | 8S − S 280 suitcases |	$8S - S = 280$ $\dfrac{7S}{7} = \dfrac{280}{7}$ $S = 40$ (Bill) $8(40) = 320$ (Moe) **Check** $320 - 40 = 280$ $280 = 280$	**Solve** Moe sold 9 times as many suitcases as Bill. The difference in their sales is 640 suitcases. How many suitcases did each sell?
Situation 4: Calculating unit sales Moe sold 8 times as many suitcases as Bill. Together they sold a total of 360. How many did each sell?	BLUEPRINT | Unknown(s)	Variable(s)	Relationship | |---|---|---| | *Suitcases sold:* Moe Bill | 8S S | 8S + S 360 suitcases |	$8S + S = 360$ $\dfrac{9S}{9} = \dfrac{360}{9}$ $S = 40$ (Bill) $8(40) = 320$ (Moe) **Check** $320 + 40 = 360$ $360 = 360$	**Solve** Moe sold 9 times as many suitcases as Bill. Together they sold a total of 640. How many did each sell?
Situation 5: Calculating unit and dollar sales (cost per unit) when *total units not given* Blue Furniture Company ordered sleepers ($300) and nonsleepers ($200) that cost $8,000. Blue expects sleepers to out-sell nonsleepers 2 to 1. How many units of each were ordered? What were dollar costs of each?	BLUEPRINT | Unknown(s)	Variable(s)	Price	Relationship | |---|---|---|---| | Sleepers Nonsleepers | 2N N | $300 200 | 600N + 200N $8,000 total cost |	$600N + 200N = 8,000$ $\dfrac{800N}{800} = \dfrac{8,000}{800}$ $N = 10$ (nonsleepers) $2N = 20$ (sleepers) **Check** $10 \times \$200 = \$2,000$ $20 \times \$300 = \underline{\ 6,000}$ $= \$8,000$	**Solve** Blue Furniture Company ordered sleepers ($400) and nonsleepers ($300) that cost $15,000. Blue expects sleepers to outsell nonsleepers 3 to 1. How many units of each were ordered? What were dollar costs of each?
Situation 6: Calculating unit and dollar sales (cost per unit) when *total units given* Blue Furniture Company ordered 30 sofas (sleepers and nonsleepers) that cost $8,000. The wholesale unit cost was $300 for the sleepers and $200 for the nonsleepers. How many units of each were ordered? What were dollar costs of each?	BLUEPRINT | Unknown(s)	Variable(s)	Price	Relationship | |---|---|---|---| | *Unit costs* Sleepers Nonsleepers | S 30 − S | $300 200 | 300S +200(30 − S) $8,000 total cost | *Note:* When the total units are given, the higher-priced item (sleepers) is assigned to the variable first. This makes the mechanical steps easier to complete.	$\begin{aligned}300S + 200(30-S) &= 8,000\\ 300S + 6,000 - 200S &= 8,000\\ 100S + 6,000 &= 8,000\\ -6,000 && -6,000\\ \dfrac{100S}{100} &= \dfrac{2,000}{100}\\ S &= 20\\ \text{Nonsleepers} = 30 - 20 &= 10\end{aligned}$ **Check** $20(\$300) + 10(\$200) = \$8,000$ $\$6,000 + \$2,000 = \$8,000$ $\$8,000 = \$8,000$	**Solve** Blue Furniture Company ordered 40 sofas (sleepers and nonsleepers) that cost $15,000. The wholesale unit cost was $400 for the sleepers and $300 for the nonsleepers. How many units of each were ordered? What were dollar costs of each?

KEY TERMS	Constants Equation Expression	Formula Knowns Unknown	Variables

Check Figures for Extra Practice Quizzes. (Worked-out Solutions are in Appendix B.)

LU 5–1a
1. a. $Q/2 - 8 = 16$ b. $12(Q + 41) = 1,200$
   c. $7 - 2Q = 1$ d. $4Q - 2 = 24$
   e. $3Q + 3 = 19$ f. $2Q - 6 = 5$
2. a. 56   b. 50   c. 11
   d. 720   e. 496   f. 12

LU 5–2a
1. $P = \$190$
2. $S = \$49,000$
3. Morse 7; Micro 56
4. Cara 120; Susie 240
5. Meatball 72; cheese 216; Meatball = $504; cheese = $1,296
6. Meatball $504; cheese $1,296

*Worked-out solutions are in Appendix B.

Critical Thinking Discussion Questions with Chapter Concept Check

1. Explain the difference between a variable and a constant. What would you consider your monthly car payment—a variable or a constant?

2. How does the opposite process rule help solve for the variable in an equation? If a Mercedes costs 3 times as much as a Saab, how could the opposite process rule be used? The selling price of the Mercedes is $60,000.

3. What is the difference between Word Problem Situations 5 and 6 in Learning Unit 5–2? Show why the more expensive item in Word Problem Situation 6 is assigned to the variable first.

4. **Chapter Concept Check.** Go to a weight-loss website and create several equations on how to lose weight. Be sure to create a word problem and specify the steps you need to take to solve this weight-loss problem.

Classroom Notes

END-OF-CHAPTER PROBLEMS   connect plus+

Check figures for odd-numbered problems in Appendix C.   Name _____   Date _____

DRILL PROBLEMS (First of Three Sets)

Solve the unknown from the following equations: *LU 5-1(2)*

5–1. $X - 20 = 210$ **5–2.** $A + 64 = 98$ **5–3.** $Q + 100 = 400$ **5–4.** $Q - 60 = 850$

5–5. $5Y = 75$ **5–6.** $\dfrac{P}{6} = 92$ **5–7.** $8Y = 96$ **5–8.** $\dfrac{N}{16} = 5$

5–9. $4(P - 9) = 64$ **5–10.** $3(P - 3) = 27$

WORD PROBLEMS (First of Three Sets)

5–11. Lee and Fred are elementary school teachers. Fred works for a charter school in Pacific Palisades, California, where class size reduction is a goal for 2013. Lee works for a noncharter school where funds do not allow for class size reduction policies. Lee's fifth-grade class has 1.4 times as many students as Fred's. If there are a total of 60 students, how many students does Fred's class have? How many students does Lee's class have?   *LU 5-2(2)*

5–12. A car that originally cost $3,668 in 1955 is valued today at $62,125 if in excellent condition, which is $1\frac{3}{4}$ times as much as
eXcel a car in very nice condition—if you can find an owner willing to part with one for any price. What would be the value of the car in very nice condition?   *LU 5-2(2)*

5–13. Jessica and Josh are selling Entertainment Books to raise money for the art room at their school. One book sells for $15. Jessica received the prize for selling the most books in the school. Jessica sold 15 times more books than Josh. Together they sold 256 books. How many did each one of them sell?   *LU 5-2(1)*

5–14. Nanda Yueh and Lane Zuriff sell homes for ERA Realty. Over the past 6 months they sold 120 homes. Nanda sold 3 times
eXcel as many homes as Lane. How many homes did each sell?   *LU 5-2(2)*

5–15. Dots sells T-shirts ($2) and shorts ($4). In April, total sales were $600. People bought 4 times as many T-shirts as shorts. How many T-shirts and shorts did Dots sell? Check your answer. *LU 5-2(2)*

5–16. Dots sells a total of 250 T-shirts ($2) and shorts ($4). In April, total sales were $600. How many T-shirts and shorts did Dots sell? Check your answer. *Hint:* Let S = Shorts. *LU 5-2(2)*

DRILL PROBLEMS (Second of Three Sets)

Solve the unknown from the following equations: *LU 5-1(2)*

5–17. $7B = 490$

5–18. $7(A - 5) = 63$

5–19. $\dfrac{N}{9} = 7$

5–20. $18(C - 3) = 162$

5–21. $9Y - 10 = 53$

5–22. $7B + 5 = 26$

WORD PROBLEMS (Second of Three Sets)

5–23. On a flight from Boston to San Diego, American reduced its Internet price by $190.00. The new sale price was $420.99. What was the original price? *LU 5-2(2)*

5–24. Jill, an employee at Old Navy, budgets $\frac{1}{5}$ of her yearly salary for clothing. Jill's total clothing bill for the year is $8,000. What is her yearly salary? *LU 5-2(2)*

5–25. Bill's Roast Beef sells 5 times as many sandwiches as Pete's Deli. The difference between their sales is 360 sandwiches. e**X**cel How many sandwiches did each sell? *LU 5-2(2)*

5–26. The count of discouraged unemployed workers rose to 503,000, $2\frac{1}{2}$ times as many as in the previous year. How many discouraged unemployed workers were there in the previous year?   *LU 5-2(2)*

5–27. A local Computer City sells batteries ($3) and small boxes of pens ($5). In August, total sales were $960. Customers bought 5 times as many batteries as boxes of pens. How many of each did Computer City sell? Check your answer.   *LU 5-2(2)*

5–28. Staples sells boxes of pens ($10) and rubber bands ($4). Leona ordered a total of 24 cartons for $210. How many boxes of each did Leona order? Check your answer. *Hint:* Let P = Pens.   *LU 5-2(2)*

DRILL PROBLEMS (Third of Three Sets)

Solve the unknown from the following equations: *LU 5-1(2)*

5–29. $A + 90 - 15 = 210$

5–30. $5Y + 15(Y + 1) = 35$

5–31. $3M + 20 = 2M + 80$

5–32. $20(C - 50) = 19{,}000$

WORD PROBLEMS (Third of Three Sets)

5–33. If Colorado Springs, Colorado, has 1.2 times as many days of sunshine as Boston, Massachusetts, how many days of sunshine does each city have if there are a total of 464 days of sunshine between the two in a year? (Round to the nearest day.)   *LU 5-2(2)*

5–34. Ben and Jerry's sells 4 times more ice cream cones ($3) than shakes ($8). If last month's sales totaled $4,800, how many of each were sold? Check your answer.   *LU 5-2(1)*

5–35. Ivy Corporation gave 84 people a bonus. If Ivy had given 2 more people bonuses, Ivy would have rewarded $\frac{2}{3}$ of the workforce. How large is Ivy's workforce?   *LU 5-2(2)*

5–36. Jim Murray and Phyllis Lowe received a total of $50,000 from a deceased relative's estate. They decided to put $10,000 in a trust for their nephew and divide the remainder. Phyllis received $\frac{3}{4}$ of the remainder; Jim received $\frac{1}{4}$. How much did Jim and Phyllis receive?   *LU 5-2(2)*

5–37. The first shift of GME Corporation produced $1\frac{1}{2}$ times as many lanterns as the second shift. GME produced 5,600 lanterns in November. How many lanterns did GME produce on each shift?   *LU 5-2(2)*

5–38. Levi Jeans Company at the Silverthorne, Colorado, outlet store sells bootcut jeans for $40 and straight leg jeans for $60. If customers bought 5 times more bootcut than straight leg jeans and last month's sales totaled $6,500, how many of each type of jeans were sold? Check your answer.   *LU 5-2(2)*

5–39. Ace Hardware sells boxes of wrenches ($100) and hammers ($300). Howard ordered 40 boxes of wrenches and hammers for $8,400. How many boxes of each are in the order? Check your answer.   *LU 5-2(2)*

5–40. The Susan Hansen Group in St. George, Utah, sells $16,000,000 of single-family homes and townhomes a year. If single-family homes, with an average selling price of $250,000, sell 3.5 times more often than townhomes, with an average selling price of $190,000, how many of each are sold? (Round to nearest whole.)   *LU 5-2(2)*

5–41. Want to donate to a better cause? Consider micro-lending. Micro-lending is a process where you lend directly to entrepreneurs in developing countries. You can lend starting at $25. Kiva.org boasts a 99% repayment rate. The average loan to an entrepreneur is $388.44 and the average loan amount is $261.14. With a total amount loaned of $283,697,150, how many people are lending money if the average number of loans per lender is 8? (Round final answer to nearest whole lender.)   *LU 5-2(2)*

CHALLENGE PROBLEMS

5–42. Myron Corporation is sponsoring a walking race at its company outing. Leona Jackson and Sam Peterson love to walk. Leona walks at the rate of 5 miles per hour. Sam walks at the rate of 6 miles per hour. Assume they start walking from the same place and walk in a straight line. Sam starts $\frac{1}{2}$ hour after Leona. Answer the questions that follow. *Hint:* Distance = Rate × Time.   *LU 5-2(2)*

a. How long will it take Sam to meet Leona?

b. How many miles would each have walked?

c. Assume Leona and Sam meet in Lonetown Station where two buses leave along parallel routes in opposite directions. The bus traveling east has a 60 mph speed. The bus traveling west has a 40 mph speed. In how many hours will the buses be 600 miles apart?

5–43. Bessy has 6 times as much money as Bob, but when each earns $6, Bessy will have 3 times as much money as Bob. How much does each have before and after earning the $6? *LU 5-2(2)*

SUMMARY PRACTICE TEST

Do you need help? The videos in Connect have step-by-step worked-out solutions. These videos are also available on YouTube!

1. Delta reduced its round-trip ticket price from Portland to Boston by $140. The sale price was $401.90. What was the original price? *LU 5-2(2)*

2. David Role is an employee of Google. He budgets $\frac{1}{7}$ of his salary for clothing. If David's total clothing for the year is $12,000, what is his yearly salary? *LU 5-2(2)*

3. A local Best Buy sells 8 times as many iPods as Sears. The difference between their sales is 490 iPods. How many iPods did each sell? *LU 5-2(2)*

4. Working at Staples, Jill Reese and Abby Lee sold a total of 1,200 calculators. Jill sold 5 times as many calculators as Abby. How many did each sell? *LU 5-2(2)*

5. Target sells sets of pots ($30) and dishes ($20) at the local store. On the July 4 weekend, Target's total sales were $2,600. People bought 6 times as many pots as dishes. How many of each did Target sell? Check your answer. *LU 5-2(2)*

6. A local Dominos sold a total of 1,600 small pizzas ($9) and pasta dinners ($13) during the Super Bowl. How many of each did Dominos sell if total sales were $15,600? Check your answer. *LU 5-2(2)*

SURF TO SAVE

How can you solve the world's problems? 🔍

PROBLEM 1
I'm going to Disney World!

You are planning a family trip to a Disney Theme Park of your choice and have a budget of $1,250 to spend on park admissions for your family of 4 adults. Using https://disneyworld.disney.go.com/tickets/ how would you allocate your budgeted amount of $1,250 among the ticket choices?

Discussion Questions

1. Do you feel a budget of $1,250 for theme park tickets is reasonable for your group of 4? Why or why not?

2. How much money would you budget for meals and other expenses on this trip?

PROBLEM 2
More people, more debt

Go to http://www.census.gov/main/www/popclock.html to find the U.S. population. Then, go to http://www.brillig.com/debt_clock to find the U.S. national debt. Use these data to determine the U.S. government's debt per person. Compare this with the number quoted on the debt clock site.

Discussion Questions

1. What do you feel is fueling the growth in the U.S. population?

2. Do you think the national debt will continue to rise? Why?

PROBLEM 3
Fueling your travels

Go to http://www.fuelcostcalculator.com. Find the average cost of fuel for your state. If the vehicle you drive averages 25 miles per gallon, what would it cost for you to travel 1,500 miles for your summer vacation?

Discussion Questions

1. Based on rising fuel prices, should you consider an electric or hybrid car for your next purchase? Why?

2. How would the price of driving to your destination compare to other forms of travel (i.e., air, train, bus, etc.)? Which would be your preferred method of travel for your vacation?

PROBLEM 4
A stock price you'll "like"

Go to http://www.nasdaq.com/ and find the current stock price for Facebook, Inc. (FB). Assuming you want to purchase a total of 150 shares, what would these shares cost in total?

Discussion Questions

1. What do you feel determines the price of this particular stock?

2. Do you believe the price of Facebook stock will increase or decrease in the future? Why?

MOBILE APPS ❌

Equation Genius (Meow Dev) Assists in solving for unknown values.

Word Problems, Math (honeHead) Solving for the unknown using over 250 questions and showing the step-by-step approach for solving the problem.

A KIPLINGER APPROACH

By Jessica L. Anderson, From *Kiplinger's Personal Finance*, October 2014.

JESSICA ANDERSON > Drive Time

Cash Out Your Lease

A contract is a contract, right? You sign on the dotted line and agree to certain terms. With a lease, you agree to pay *x* amount for, say, 36 months, and at the end of the lease term you can either buy the vehicle or turn it in.

But there's a third option listed in your contract, although it's unlikely any dealer will mention it: You can sell your leased car yourself before the end of the lease.

A colleague at *Kiplinger's,* Manny Schiffres, recently did this. He had five months left on his leased Lexus ES 350 when he decided he didn't need the car anymore and wanted out of the contract. Rather than putting up with the hassle of selling the car to a private party, he sold it to CarMax, which handled the paperwork and paid off the leasing company. He saved about $3,000 on the remaining payments and insurance.

You could walk away from your lease with a check in your hand if your vehicle is worth more than the purchase price written into the lease. Used-car values have shot up in the past few years. Plus, the residual value—what the car is assumed to be worth at the end of the lease term—is rarely spot-on.

Take the money and run. Some dealers are beating customers to the punch, contacting lessees to offer a sweet deal on a new leased vehicle. In leasing lingo, this is called a pull-ahead program. The offer may include waiving your last few payments and end-of-lease fees. The new monthly payments might even be lower than what you are paying now. It sounds great, but don't take the bait—at least not yet. The fact that they are reaching out to lessees means they want your car and they are confident they can turn around and sell it for a profit, says Tarry Shebesta, president of Lease Compare.com.

You may be able to pull the profit out of the car yourself, but you'll need to know what your vehicle is worth. Look at a site that lists used-car values, such as Kelley Blue Book (www.kbb.com), NADA Guides (www.nadaguides.com) or Edmunds.com, for the dealer retail price. Then call your leasing company and find out what your current payoff amount is, including the remaining payments, the cost to buy the car and the termination fee (a few hundred dollars).

When your payoff is less than what the car is worth, it makes sense to sell it. A dealer or CarMax can appraise the car, contact the leasing company for the payoff quote and write you a check for the difference. If you'd rather try your hand at boosting your profit by selling the car to an individual, LeaseCompare.com will handle the paperwork for $495 so the title transfers directly to the new owner and sales tax is paid only once. Otherwise, you'd pay tax to purchase the car from the leasing company, and the person who buys your car would pay tax to register the car (dealer-to-dealer transfers don't incur sales tax).

If you wait until the end of the lease and turn the car in, be prepared to pay some fees. You'll pay a disposition fee of $200 to $500 to cover the cost for the leasing company to clean up the car, prepare it for sale and handle the paperwork. If you've gone over the mileage allotment, you'll pay about 20 cents per extra mile.

If the car has a few scratches, you probably won't be charged for excess wear and tear. But get anything more serious fixed before you turn the car in. It will likely be cheaper to pay for the fixes yourself than to be billed for the damage later.

Don't dismiss the option of buying the car at the end of the lease and keeping it, even if comparable vehicles are selling for less than the lease's purchase price. You'll pay a purchase option fee of $200 to $500, but the peace of mind of knowing the car's history may be worth the extra cost. ■

ASK JESSICA A QUESTION AT JANDERSON@KIPLINGER.COM, OR FOLLOW HER ON FACEBOOK OR TWITTER AT JANDERSONDRIVES.

> " **You could walk away with a check if your vehicle is worth more than the purchase price written into the lease.**"

LISE METZGER

BUSINESS MATH ISSUE

A lease means that your payment is constant and not variable.

1. List the key points of the article and information to support your position.
2. Write a group defense of your position using math calculations to support your view.

Percents and Their Applications

DILBERT © 2013 Scott Adams. Used By permission of ANDREWS MCMEEL SYNDICATION. All rights reserved.

© Brand X Pictures/Getty Images

In selected countries...

A sampling of countries that rank among highest in percentage of individuals using Internet (2013 figures)

Rank & Country	Percentage
1. Iceland	96.
2. Norway	95.
3. Netherlands	94.
4. Bahrain	90.0
5. U.K.	89.8%
6. United Arb Emirates	88.0%
7. Switzerland	86.7%
8. Japan	86.3%
9. South Korea	84.8%
10. U.S.	84.2%
11. Germany	84.0%
12. Australia	83.0%

Source: *The Wall Street Journal*, 7/8/14.

Going Undercover

- Many Internet users, feeling privacy laws don't adequately protect them, are looking for ways to protect themselves.

68%
of Internet users say that current laws are not sufficient in protecting people's privacy online.

86%
of Internet users have taken steps online to remove or cover up their digital footprints.

- Percentage of Internet users who say they have taken the following steps.

Step	Percentage
Cleared cookies and browser history	64%
Deleted/edited something they posted	41%
Set their browser to disable or turn off cookies	41%
Not used a website because it asked for their real name	36%
Used a temporary username/email address	26%
Posted comments without revealing who they were	25%
Asked someone to remove something posted about them	21%
Used a public computer to browse anonymously	18%
Used fake name/untraceable username	18%
Ecrypted their communications	14%
Used service that allows them to browse anonymously	14%
Gave inaccurate information about themselves	13%

Source: *The Wall Street Journal*, 3/24/14.

LU 6–1: Conversions

1. Convert decimals to percents (including rounding percents), percents to decimals, and fractions to percents.
2. Convert percents to fractions.

LU 6–2: Application of Percents—Portion Formula

1. List and define the key elements of the portion formula.
2. Solve for one unknown of the portion formula when the other two key elements are given.
3. Calculate the rate of percent increases and decreases.

VOCABULARY PREVIEW

Here are key terms in this chapter. After completing the chapter, if you know the term, place a checkmark in the box. If you don't know the term, look it up and put the page number where it can be found.

Base ☐ Percent decrease ☐ Percent increase ☐ Percents ☐ Portion ☐ Rate ☐

GLOBAL

The following *Wall Street Journal* clip, "Revlon to Exit China," illustrates the use of percents to show relationships between numbers. For example, China has represented 2% of Revlon's sales. Now Revlon plans to exit China as well as reduce its workforce by 15%. The *Wall Street Journal* chapter openers state 86% of internet users are cautious about their internet usage, and Iceland has the highest percentage of people using the internet at 96.6%.

To understand percents, you should first understand the conversion relationship between decimals, percents, and fractions as explained in Learning Unit 6–1. Then, in Learning Unit 6–2, you will be ready to apply percents to personal and business events.

Revlon to Exit China

BY EVERDEEN MASON

Revlon Inc. plans to exit its struggling operations in China and cut more than 15% of its workforce, in the first major action taken by the cosmetics company's new chief executive.

Revlon, which sells products under its namesake and Almay brands, has reported weak demand in China, which accounts for about 2% of its total sales.

A spokesman said Revlon decided to exit China after it "made a holistic assessment" of operational costs versus opportunities in the market.

Reprinted by permission of *The Wall Street Journal*, copyright 2014 Dow Jones & Company, Inc. All rights reserved worldwide.

Learning Unit 6–1: Conversions

 LO 1

When we described parts of a whole in previous chapters, we used fractions and decimals. Percents also describe parts of a whole. The word *percent* means per 100. The percent symbol (%) indicates hundredths (division by 100). **Percents** are the result of expressing numbers as part of 100.

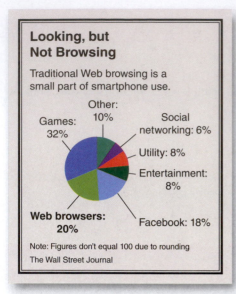

Looking, but Not Browsing

Traditional Web browsing is a small part of smartphone use.

Games: 32%
Other: 10%
Social networking: 6%
Utility: 8%
Entertainment: 8%
Facebook: 18%
Web browsers: 20%

Note: Figures don't equal 100 due to rounding
The Wall Street Journal

Source: *The Wall Street Journal*, 3/10/14.

© Hero/Corbis/Glow Images

Percents can provide some revealing information. The *Wall Street Journal* clipping "Looking but Not Browsing" in the margin shows that 18% of smartphone users are on Facebook, which means 18 users out of 100.

Let's return to the M&M's® example from earlier chapters. In Table 6.1, we use our bag of 55 M&M's® to show how fractions, decimals, and percents can refer to the same parts of a whole. For example, the bag of 55 M&M'S® contains 18 yellow M&M's®. As you can see in Table 6.1, the 18 candies in the bag of 55 can be expressed as a fraction ($\frac{18}{55}$), decimal (.33), and percent (32.73%). If you visit the M&M'S® website, you will see that the standard is 11 yellow M&M'S®. The clipping (below) "What Colors Come in Your Bag?" shows an M&M'S® Milk Chocolate Candies Color Chart.

In this unit we discuss converting decimals to percents (including rounding percents), percents to decimals, fractions to percents, and percents to fractions. You will see when you study converting fractions to percents why you should first learn how to convert decimals to percents.

Pepper ... And Salt

THE WALL STREET JOURNAL

COFFEE

"It's pricey because it's 100% pre-Columbian."

From *The Wall Street Journal*, permission Cartoon Features Syndicate.

What Colors Come In Your Bag?

10%	5.5
10%	5.5
10%	5.5
30%	16.5
20%	11
20%	11

| TABLE | 6.1 | Analyzing a bag of M&M'S® |

Color	Fraction	Decimal (hundredth)	Percent (hundredth)
Yellow	$\frac{18}{55}$	.33	32.73%
Red	$\frac{10}{55}$	.18	18.18
Blue	$\frac{9}{55}$	.16	16.36
Orange	$\frac{7}{55}$	.13	12.73
Brown	$\frac{6}{55}$	.11	10.91
Green	$\frac{5}{55}$	.09	9.09
Total	$\frac{55}{55} = 1$	1.00	100.00%

Information adapted from http://us.mms.com/us/about/products/milkchocolate/

Converting Decimals to Percents

The *Wall Street Journal* clip "Looking but Not Browsing" (above) shows 32% of users play games on smartphones. If the clipping had stated the 32% as a decimal (.32), could you give its equivalent in percent? The decimal .32 in decimal fraction is $\frac{32}{100}$. As you know, percents are the result of expressing numbers as part of 100, so 32% = $\frac{32}{100}$. You can now conclude that .32 = $\frac{32}{100}$ = 32%.

The steps for converting decimals to percents are as follows:

CONVERTING DECIMALS TO PERCENTS
Step 1. Move the decimal point two places to the right. You are multiplying by 100. If necessary, add zeros. This rule is also used for whole numbers and mixed decimals.
Step 2. Add a percent symbol at the end of the number.

EXAMPLES

$.49 = .49. = \boxed{49\%}$ $.8 = .80. = \boxed{80\%}$ $8 = 8.00. = \boxed{800\%}$

Add 1 zero to make two places.   Add 2 zeros to make two places.

$.425 = .42.5 = \boxed{42.5\%}$ $.007 = .00.7 = \boxed{.7\%}$ $2.51 = 2.51. = \boxed{251\%}$

Caution: One percent means 1 out of every 100. Since .7% is less than 1%, it means $\frac{7}{10}$ of 1%—a very small amount. Less than 1% is less than .01. To show a number less than 1%, you must use more than two decimal places and add 2 zeros. Example: .7% = .007.

Use "D2P" to help you remember how to change a decimal to a percent. "D" stands for "decimal," "2" tells you to move the decimal two places, and "P" stands for "percent." Since P is to the right of D in D2P, we move the decimal two places to the right and add a percent sign:
$.159 = 15.9\%$

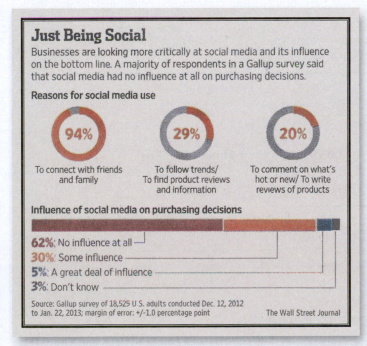

Rounding Percents

When necessary, percents should be rounded. Rounding percents is similar to rounding whole numbers. Use the following steps to round percents:

ROUNDING PERCENTS
Step 1. When you convert from a fraction or decimal, be sure your answer is in percent before rounding.
Step 2. Identify the specific digit. If the digit to the right of the identified digit is 5 or greater, round up the identified digit.
Step 3. Delete digits to the right of the identified digit.

For example, Table 6.1 shows that the 18 yellow M&M'S® rounded to the nearest hundredth percent is 32.73% of the bag of 55 M&M'S®. Let's look at how we arrived at this figure.

When using a calculator, you press 18 ÷ 55 %. This allows you to go right to percent, avoiding the decimal step.

Step 1. $\frac{18}{55} = .3272727 = 32.72727\%$ Note that the number is in percent! Identify the hundredth percent digit.

Step 2. $\phantom{\frac{18}{55}} 32.73727\%$ Digit to the right of the identified digit is greater than 5, so the identified digit is increased by 1.

Step 3. $\phantom{\frac{18}{55}} \boxed{32.73\%}$ Delete digits to the right of the identified digit.

Just Being Social
Businesses are looking more critically at social media and its influence on the bottom line. A majority of respondents in a Gallup survey said that social media had no influence at all on purchasing decisions.

Reasons for social media use

94% — To connect with friends and family

29% — To follow trends/ To find product reviews and information

20% — To comment on what's hot or new/ To write reviews of products

Influence of social media on purchasing decisions

62%: No influence at all
30%: Some influence
5%: A great deal of influence
3%: Don't know

Source: Gallup survey of 18,525 U.S. adults conducted Dec. 12, 2012 to Jan. 22, 2013; margin of error: +/-1.0 percentage point   The Wall Street Journal

Reprinted by permission of *The Wall Street Journal,* copyright 2013 Dow Jones & Company, Inc. All rights reserved worldwide.

Converting Percents to Decimals

Note in the *Wall Street Journal* clip "Just Being Social" that 94% of people surveyed use social media to connect to family and friends.

The *Wall Street Journal* clipping "Just Being Social" shows businesses are interested in how people use social media.

To convert percents to decimals, you reverse the process used to convert decimals to percents. In our earlier discussion on converting decimals to percents, we asked if the 32% in the "Looking but Not Browsing" clipping had been in decimal and not percent, could you convert the decimal to the 32%? Once again, the definition of percent states that $32\% = \frac{32}{100}$. The fraction $\frac{32}{100}$ can be written in decimal form as .32. You can conclude that $32\% = \frac{32}{100} = .32$. Now you can see this procedure in the following conversion steps:

> **CONVERTING PERCENTS TO DECIMALS**
>
> **Step 1.** Drop the percent symbol.
>
> **Step 2.** Move the decimal point two places to the left. You are dividing by 100. If necessary, add zeros.

Remember our D2P trick for converting decimals to percents? Well good news! It works in reverse for converting percents to decimals. Because we are changing a percent to a decimal, read D2P from right to left, that is, P2D. Start by removing the percent sign and then move the decimal two places to the left because P is to the left of D in P2D.

$$15.9\% = 15.9 = .159$$

EXAMPLES

Note that when a percent is less than 1%, the decimal conversion has at least two leading zeros before the number .004.

$.4\% = .00.4 = \boxed{.004}$ $2\% = .02. = \boxed{.02}$ $.83\% = .00.83 = \boxed{.0083}$

Add 2 zeros to
make two places.

Add 1 zero to
make two places.

Add 2 zeros to
make two places.

$49\% = .49. = \boxed{.49}$ $54.5\% = .54.5 = \boxed{.545}$ $824.4\% = 8.24.4 = \boxed{8.244}$

Note the example .83% comes from the *Wall Street Journal* clip in the margin, "CD Yields Hold Steady."

Now we must explain how to change fractional percents such as $\frac{1}{5}\%$ to a decimal. Remember that fractional percents are values less than 1%. For example, $\frac{1}{5}\%$ is $\frac{1}{5}$ of 1%. Fractional percents can appear singly or in combination with whole numbers. To convert them to decimals, use the following steps:

> **CONVERTING FRACTIONAL PERCENTS TO DECIMALS**
>
> **Step 1.** Convert a single fractional percent to its decimal equivalent by dividing the numerator by the denominator. If necessary, round the answer.
>
> **Step 2.** If a fractional percent is combined with a whole number (mixed fractional percent), convert the fractional percent first. Then combine the whole number and the fractional percent.
>
> **Step 3.** Drop the percent symbol; move the decimal point two places to the left (this divides the number by 100).

EXAMPLES

$\frac{1}{5}\% = .20\% = .00.20 = \boxed{.0020}$ Think of $7\frac{3}{4}\%$ as

$\frac{1}{4}\% = .25\% = .00.25 = \boxed{.0025}$ $7\% = \quad .07$

$7\frac{3}{4}\% = 7.75\% = .07.75 = \boxed{.0775}$ $+\frac{3}{4}\% = + .0075$

$6\frac{1}{2}\% = 6.5\% = .06.5 = \boxed{.065}$ $7\frac{3}{4}\% = \quad .0775$

Converting Fractions to Percents

When fractions have denominators of 100, the numerator becomes the percent. Other fractions must be first converted to decimals; then the decimals are converted to percents.

CD Yields Hold Steady

Yields on certificates of deposit were mostly unchanged in the latest week.

The average yield on six-month "jumbo" CDs, which typically require deposits of $95,000 or more, remained unchanged at 0.15% from the week earlier, according to Bankrate.com. The yield on five-year jumbos, however, fell to 0.83% from 0.84% the week earlier.

The average yields on small-denomination "savings" CDs remained mostly unchanged in the latest week. The average six-month CD yield was unchanged at 0.14% from the week earlier, said Bankrate.com. The average two-year yield also remained unchanged, at 0.38% from the week earlier. The average five-year yield, however, fell to 0.81% from 0.82% the week earlier.

Reprinted by permission of *The Wall Street Journal*, copyright 2015 Dow Jones & Company, Inc. All rights reserved worldwide.

CONVERTING FRACTIONS TO PERCENTS

Step 1. Divide the numerator by the denominator to convert the fraction to a decimal.

Step 2. Move the decimal point two places to the right; add the percent symbol.

EXAMPLES

$$\frac{3}{4} = .75 = .75 = \boxed{75\%} \qquad \frac{1}{5} = .20 = .20 = \boxed{20\%} \qquad \frac{1}{20} = .05 = .05 = \boxed{5\%}$$

LO 2

Converting Percents to Fractions

Using the definition of percent, you can write any percent as a fraction whose denominator is 100. Thus, when we convert a percent to a fraction, we drop the percent symbol and write the number over 100, which is the same as multiplying the number by $\frac{1}{100}$. This method of multiplying by $\frac{1}{100}$ is also used for fractional percents.

CONVERTING A WHOLE PERCENT (OR A FRACTIONAL PERCENT) TO A FRACTION

Step 1. Drop the percent symbol.

Step 2. Multiply the number by $\frac{1}{100}$.

Step 3. Reduce to lowest terms.

EXAMPLES

$$76\% = 76 \times \frac{1}{100} = \frac{76}{100} = \boxed{\frac{19}{25}} \qquad \frac{1}{8}\% = \frac{1}{8} \times \frac{1}{100} = \boxed{\frac{1}{800}}$$

$$156\% = 156 \times \frac{1}{100} = \frac{156}{100} = 1\frac{56}{100} = \boxed{1\frac{14}{25}}$$

Sometimes a percent contains a whole number and a fraction such as $12\frac{1}{2}\%$ or 22.5%. Extra steps are needed to write a mixed or decimal percent as a simplified fraction.

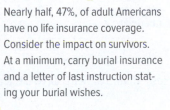

MONEY tips

Nearly half, 47%, of adult Americans have no life insurance coverage. Consider the impact on survivors. At a minimum, carry burial insurance and a letter of last instruction stating your burial wishes.

CONVERTING A MIXED OR DECIMAL PERCENT TO A FRACTION

Step 1. Drop the percent symbol.

Step 2. Change the mixed percent to an improper fraction.

Step 3. Multiply the number by $\frac{1}{100}$.

Step 4. Reduce to lowest terms.

Note: If you have a mixed or decimal percent, change the decimal portion to its fractional equivalent and continue with Steps 1 to 4.

EXAMPLES $$12\frac{1}{2}\% = \frac{25}{2} \times \frac{1}{100} = \frac{25}{200} = \boxed{\frac{1}{8}}$$

$$12.5\% = 12\frac{1}{2}\% = \frac{25}{2} \times \frac{1}{100} = \frac{25}{200} = \boxed{\frac{1}{8}}$$

$$22.5\% = 22\frac{1}{2}\% = \frac{45}{2} \times \frac{1}{100} = \frac{45}{200} = \boxed{\frac{9}{40}}$$

It's time to check your understanding of Learning Unit 6–1.

LU 6–1   PRACTICE QUIZ

Complete this **Practice Quiz** to see how you are doing.

Convert to percents (round to the nearest tenth percent as needed):

1. .6666 _____
2. .832 _____
3. .004 _____
4. 8.94444 _____

Convert to decimals (remember, decimals representing less than 1% will have at least 2 leading zeros before the number):

5. $\frac{1}{4}\%$ _____
6. $6\frac{3}{4}\%$ _____
7. 87% _____
8. 810.9% _____

Convert to percents (round to the nearest hundredth percent):

9. $\frac{1}{7}$ _____
10. $\frac{2}{9}$ _____

Convert to fractions (remember, if it is a mixed number, first convert to an improper fraction):

11. 19% _____
12. $71\frac{1}{2}\%$ _____
13. 130% _____
14. $\frac{1}{2}\%$ _____
15. 19.9% _____

*For **extra help** from your authors–Sharon and Jeff–see the videos in Connect.*

These videos are also available on YouTube!

✓ Solutions

1. $.66.66 = \boxed{66.7\%}$
2. $.83.2 = \boxed{83.2\%}$
3. $.00.4 = \boxed{.4\%}$
4. $8.94.444 = \boxed{894.4\%}$
5. $\frac{1}{4}\% = .25\% = \boxed{.0025}$
6. $6\frac{3}{4}\% = 6.75\% = \boxed{.0675}$
7. $87\% = .87. = \boxed{.87}$
8. $810.9\% = 8.10.9 = \boxed{8.109}$
9. $\frac{1}{7} = .14.285 = \boxed{14.29\%}$
10. $\frac{2}{9} = .22.2\bar{2} = \boxed{22.22\%}$
11. $19\% = 19 \times \frac{1}{100} = \boxed{\frac{19}{100}}$
12. $71\frac{1}{2}\% = \frac{143}{2} \times \frac{1}{100} = \boxed{\frac{143}{200}}$
13. $130\% = 130 \times \frac{1}{100} = \frac{130}{100} = 1\frac{30}{100} = \boxed{1\frac{3}{10}}$
14. $\frac{1}{2}\% = \frac{1}{2} \times \frac{1}{100} = \boxed{\frac{1}{200}}$
15. $19\frac{9}{10}\% = \frac{199}{10} \times \frac{1}{100} = \boxed{\frac{199}{1,000}}$

LU 6–1a   EXTRA PRACTICE QUIZ WITH WORKED-OUT SOLUTIONS

Need more practice? Try this **Extra Practice Quiz** (check figures in the Interactive Chapter Organizer). Worked-out Solutions can be found in Appendix B.

Convert to percents (round to the nearest tenth percent as needed):

1. .4444
2. .782
3. .006
4. 7.93333

Convert to decimals (remember, decimals representing less than 1% will have at least 2 leading zeros before the number):

5. $\frac{1}{5}\%$
6. $7\frac{4}{5}\%$
7. 92%
8. 765.8%

Convert to percents (round to the nearest hundredth percent):

9. $\frac{1}{3}$
10. $\frac{3}{7}$

Convert to fractions (remember, if it is a mixed number, first convert to an improper fraction):

11. 17%
12. $82\frac{1}{4}\%$
13. 150%
14. $\frac{1}{4}\%$
15. 17.8%

Learning Unit 6-2: Application of Percents—Portion Formula

The bag of M&M'S® we have been studying contains Milk Chocolate M&M'S®. M&M/Mars also makes Peanut M&M'S® and some other types of M&M'S®. To study the application of percents to problems involving M&M'S®, we make two key assumptions:

1. Total sales of Milk Chocolate M&M'S®, Peanut M&M'S®, and other M&M'S® chocolate candies are $400,000.

2. Eighty percent of M&M'S® sales are Milk Chocolate M&M'S®. This leaves the Peanut and other M&M'S® chocolate candies with 20% of sales (100% − 80%).

80% M&M'S® Milk Chocolate M&M'S®		20% M&M'S® Peanut and other chocolate candies		100% Total sales ($400,000)
	+		=	

Before we begin, you must understand the meaning of three terms—*base, rate,* and *portion.* These terms are the key elements in solving percent problems.

*   **Base (B).** The **base** is the beginning whole quantity or value (100%) with which you will compare some other quantity or value. Often the problems give the base after the word *of.* For example, the whole (total) sales of M&M'S®—Milk Chocolate M&M'S, Peanut, and other M&M'S® chocolate candies—are $400,000.

*   **Rate (R).** The **rate** is a percent, decimal, or fraction that indicates the part of the base that you must calculate. The percent symbol often helps you identify the rate. For example, Milk Chocolate M&M'S® currently account for 80% of sales. So the rate is 80%. Remember that 80% is also $\frac{4}{5}$, or .80.

*   **Portion (P).** The **portion** is the amount or part that results from the base multiplied by the rate. For example, total sales of M&M'S® are $400,000 (base); $400,000 times .80 (rate) equals $320,000 (portion), or the sales of Milk Chocolate M&M'S®. *A key point to remember is that portion is a number and not a percent. In fact, the portion can be larger than the base if the rate is greater than 100%.*

Solving Percents with the Portion Formula

In problems involving portion, base, and rate, we give two of these elements. You must find the third element. Remember the following key formula:

$$\text{Portion } (P) = \text{Base } (B) \times \text{Rate } (R)$$

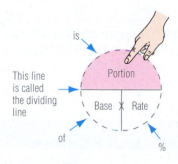

To help you solve for the portion, base, and rate, this unit shows pie charts. The shaded area in each pie chart indicates the element that you must solve for. For example, since we shaded *portion* in the pie chart at the left, you must solve for portion. To use the pie charts, put your finger on the shaded area (in this case portion). The formula that remains tells you what to do. So in the pie chart at the left, you solve the problem by multiplying base by the rate. Note the circle around the pie chart is broken since we want to emphasize that portion can be larger than base if rate is greater than 100%. The horizontal line in the pie chart is called the dividing line, and we will use it when we solve for base or rate.

The following example summarizes the concept of base, rate, and portion. Assume that you received a small bonus check of $100. This is a gross amount—your company did not withhold any taxes. You will have to pay 20% in taxes.

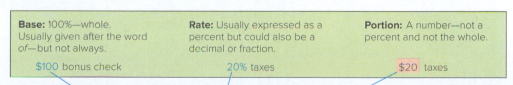

Base: 100%—whole. Usually given after the word *of*—but not always.	**Rate:** Usually expressed as a percent but could also be a decimal or fraction.	**Portion:** A number—not a percent and not the whole.
$100 bonus check	20% taxes	$20 taxes

First decide what you are looking for. You want to know how much you must pay in taxes—the portion. How do you get the portion? From the portion formula Portion (P) = Base (B) × Rate (R), you know that you must multiply the base ($100) by the rate (20%). When you do this, you get $100 × .20 = $20. So you must pay $20 in taxes.

Let's try our first word problem by taking a closer look at the M&M'S® example to see how we arrived at the $320,000 sales of Milk Chocolate M&M'S® given earlier. We will be using blueprint aids to help dissect and solve each word problem.

Solving for Portion

The Word Problem Sales of Milk Chocolate M&M'S® are 80% of the total M&M'S® sales. Total M&M'S® sales are $400,000. What are the sales of Milk Chocolate M&M'S®?

	The facts	Solving for?	Steps to take	Key points
BLUEPRINT	*Milk Chocolate M&M'S® sales:* 80%. *Total M&M'S® sales:* $400,000.	Sales of Milk Chocolate M&M'S®.	Identify key elements. *Base:* $400,000. *Rate:* .80. *Portion:* ? Portion = Base × Rate.	Amount or part of beginning Portion (?) Base × Rate ($400,000) (.80) Beginning whole quantity (often after "of") Percent symbol or word (here we put into decimal) Portion and rate must relate to same piece of base.

Steps to solving problem

1. Set up the formula.   Portion = Base × Rate

2. Calculate portion (sales of Milk $P = \$400,000 \times .80$
 Chocolate M&M'S®). $P = \$320,000$

In the first column of the blueprint aid, we gather the facts. In the second column, we state that we are looking for sales of Milk Chocolate M&M'S®. In the third column, we identify each key element and the formula needed to solve the problem. Review the pie chart in the fourth column. *The portion and rate must relate to the same piece of the base.* In this word problem, we can see from the solution below the blueprint aid that sales of Milk Chocolate M&M'S® are $320,000. The $320,000 does indeed represent 80% of the base. Note here that the portion ($320,000) is less than the base of $400,000 since the rate is less than 100%.

Now let's work another word problem that solves for the portion.

The Word Problem Sales of Milk Chocolate M&M'S® are 80% of the total M&M'S® sales. Total M&M'S® sales are $400,000. What are the sales of Peanut and other M&M'S® chocolate candies?

	The facts	Solving for?	Steps to take	Key points
BLUEPRINT	*Milk Chocolate M&M'S® sales:* 80%. *Total M&M'S® sales:* $400,000.	Sales of Peanut and other M&M'S® chocolate candies.	Identify key elements. *Base:* $400,000. *Rate:* .20 (100% − 80%). *Portion:* ? Portion = Base × Rate.	If 80% of sales are Milk Chocolate M&M'S, then 20% are Peanut and other M&M'S® chocolate candies. Portion (?) Base × Rate ($400,000) (.20) Portion and rate must relate to same piece of base.

Steps to solving problem

1. Set up the formula.   Portion = Base × Rate

2. Calculate portion (sale of Peanut and other $P = \$400,000 \times .20$
   M&M'S® chocolate candies). $P = \$80,000$

    In the previous blueprint aid, *note that we must use a rate that agrees with the portion so the portion and rate refer to the same piece of the base.* Thus, if 80% of sales are Milk Chocolate M&M'S®, 20% must be Peanut and other M&M'S® chocolate candies (100% − 80% = 20%). So we use a rate of .20.

    In Step 2, we multiplied $400,000 × .20 to get a portion of $80,000. This portion represents the part of the sales that were *not* Milk Chocolate M&M'S®. Note that the rate of .20 and the portion of $80,000 relate to the same piece of the base—$80,000 is 20% of $400,000. Also note that the portion ($80,000) is less than the base ($400,000) since the rate is less than 100%.

    Take a moment to review the two blueprint aids in this section. Be sure you understand why the rate in the first blueprint aid was 80% and the rate in the second blueprint aid was 20%.

Solving for Rate

The Word Problem Sales of Milk Chocolate M&M'S® are $320,000. Total M&M'S® sales are $400,000. What is the percent of Milk Chocolate M&M'S® sales compared to total M&M'S® sales?

	The facts	Solving for?	Steps to take	Key points
BLUEPRINT	*Milk Chocolate M&M'S® sales:* $320,000. *Total M&M'S® sales:* $400,000.	Percent of Milk Chocolate M&M'S® sales to total M&M'S® sales.	Identify key elements. *Base:* $400,000. *Rate:* ? *Portion:* $320,000 $\text{Rate} = \dfrac{\text{Portion}}{\text{Base}}$	Since portion is less than base, the rate must be less than 100% Portion ($320,000) Base ($400,000) × Rate (?) Portion and rate must relate to the same piece of base.

Steps to solving problem

1. Set up the formula. $\text{Rate} = \dfrac{\text{Portion}}{\text{Base}}$

2. Calculate rate (percent of Milk $R = \dfrac{\$320,000}{\$400,000}$
   Chocolate M&M'S® sales). $R = 80\%$

    Note that in this word problem, the rate of 80% and the portion of $320,000 refer to the same piece of the base.

The Word Problem Sales of Milk Chocolate M&M'S® are $320,000. Total sales of Milk Chocolate M&M'S, Peanut, and other M&M'S® chocolate candies are $400,000. What percent of Peanut and other M&M'S® chocolate candies are sold compared to total M&M'S® sales?

	The facts	Solving for?	Steps to take	Key points
BLUEPRINT	*Milk Chocolate M&M'S® sales: $320,000.* *Total M&M'S® sales: $400,000.*	Percent of Peanut and other M&M'S® chocolate candies sales compared to total M&M'S® sales.	Identify key elements. *Base:* $400,000. *Rate:* ? *Portion:* $80,000 ($400,000 − $320,000). $\text{Rate} = \dfrac{\text{Portion}}{\text{Base}}$	Represents sales of Peanut and other M&M'S® chocolate candies ↓ Portion ($80,000) / Base × Rate ($400,000) (?) When portion becomes $80,000, the portion and rate now relate to same piece of base.

Steps to solving problem

1. Set up the formula. $\qquad\qquad \text{Rate} = \dfrac{\text{Portion}}{\text{Base}}$

2. Calculate rate. $\qquad\qquad R = \dfrac{\$80,000}{\$400,000}$ ($400,000 − $320,000)

$\qquad\qquad\qquad\qquad\qquad R = \boxed{20\%}$

The word problem asks for the rate of candy sales that are *not* Milk Chocolate M&M'S. Thus, $400,000 of total candy sales less sales of Milk Chocolate M&M'S® ($320,000) allows us to arrive at sales of Peanut and other M&M'S® chocolate candies ($80,000). The $80,000 portion represents 20% of total candy sales. The $80,000 portion and 20% rate refer to the same piece of the $400,000 base. Compare this blueprint aid with the blueprint aid for the previous word problem. Ask yourself why in the previous word problem the rate was 80% and in this word problem the rate is 20%. In both word problems, the portion was less than the base since the rate was less than 100%.

Now we go on to calculate the base. Remember to read the word problem carefully so that you match the rate and portion to the same piece of the base.

Solving for Base

The Word Problem Sales of Peanut and other M&M'S® chocolate candies are 20% of total M&M'S® sales. Sales of Milk Chocolate M&M'S® are $320,000. What are the total sales of all M&M'S®?

	The facts	Solving for?	Steps to take	Key points
BLUEPRINT	*Peanut and other M&M'S® chocolate candies sales: 20%.* *Milk Chocolate M&M'S® sales: $320,000.*	Total M&M'S® sales.	Identify key elements. *Base:* ? *Rate:* .80 (100% − 20%) *Portion:* $320,000 $\text{Base} = \dfrac{\text{Portion}}{\text{Rate}}$	Portion ($320,000) / Base × Rate (?) (.80) (100% − 20%) Portion ($320,000) and rate (.80) do relate to the same piece of base.

Steps to solving problem

1. Set up the formula. $\qquad\qquad \text{Base} = \dfrac{\text{Portion}}{\text{Rate}}$

2. Calculate the base. $\qquad\qquad B = \dfrac{\$320,000}{.80} \longleftarrow$ $320,000 is 80% of base

$\qquad\qquad\qquad\qquad\qquad B = \boxed{\$400,000}$

Note that we could not use 20% for the rate. The $320,000 of Milk Chocolate M&M'S® represents 80% (100% − 20%) of the total sales of M&M'S®. We use 80% so that the portion and rate refer to same piece of the base. Remember that the portion ($320,000) is less than the base ($400,000) since the rate is less than 100%.

Calculating Percent Increases and Decreases

LO 3

The following *Wall Street Journal* clipping shows Procter & Gamble is keeping the price of Tide at $11.99 but reducing the number of loads the new product washes from 60 to only 48 loads. Let's calculate the cost per load (rounded to nearest cent) before and after the load change:

Before

$$\frac{\$11.99}{60 \text{ loads}} = \$.20 \text{ per load}$$

After

$$\frac{\$11.99}{48 \text{ loads}} = \$.25 \text{ per load}$$

Using this clipping, let's look at how to calculate percent increases and decreases.

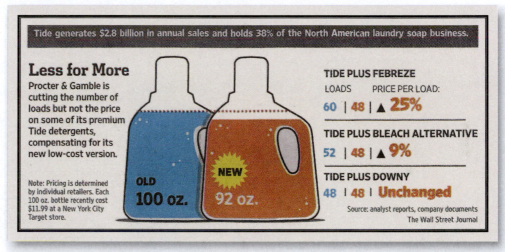

Reprinted by permission of *The Wall Street Journal*, copyright 2014 Dow Jones & Company, Inc. All rights reserved worldwide.

The Tide Example: Rate of Percent Increase in Price per Load

Assume: per load cost increase from $.20 to $.25

$$\text{Rate} = \frac{\text{Portion}}{\text{Base}} \quad \begin{array}{l} \longleftarrow \text{Difference between old and new price per load} \\ \longleftarrow \text{Old price per load} \end{array}$$

$$R = \frac{\$.05}{\$.20} \qquad (\$.25 - \$.20)$$

$$R = \boxed{25\%} \text{ increase}$$

Let's prove the 25% with a pie chart.

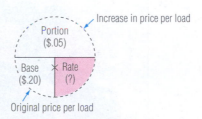

The formula for calculating **percent increase** is as follows:

Percent increase

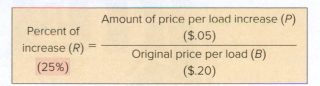

Percent of increase (R) (25%)	=	Amount of price per load increase (P) ($.05)
		Original price per load (B) ($.20)

Now let's look at how to calculate the math for a decrease in price per load for Tide.

The Tide Example: Rate of Percent Decrease

Assume: Price of $11.99 but loads increase from 60 to 70. The first step is to calculate the price per load (rounded to nearest cent) before and after:

Before

$$\frac{\$11.99}{60} = \$.20 \text{ per load}$$

After

$$\frac{\$11.99}{70} = \$.17 \text{ per load}$$

$$\text{Rate} = \frac{\text{Portion}}{\text{Base}} \longleftarrow \text{Difference between old and new price per load} \\ \longleftarrow \text{Old price per load}$$

$$R = \frac{\$.03}{\$.20} \qquad (\$.20 - \$.17 = \$.03)$$

$$R = \boxed{15\%} \text{ decrease}$$

Let's prove the 15% with a pie chart.

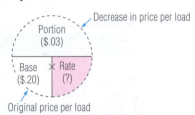

The formula for calculating **percent decrease** is as follows:

Percent decrease

$$\text{Percent of decrease } (R) = \frac{\text{Amount of price per load decrease } (P)}{\text{Original price per load } (B)}$$
$$\text{(15\%)} = \frac{(\$.03)}{(\$.20)}$$

In conclusion, the following steps can be used to calculate percent increases and decreases:

CALCULATING PERCENT INCREASES AND DECREASES

Step 1. Find the difference between amounts (such as sales).

Step 2. Divide Step 1 by the original amount (the base): $R = P \div B$. Be sure to express your answer in percent.

Before concluding this chapter, we will show how to calculate a percent increase and decrease using M&M'S® (Figure 6.1).

FIGURE 6.1

Bag of 18.40-ounce M&M'S®

© Acorn 1/Alamy

Additional Examples Using M&M'S

The Word Problem Sheila Leary went to her local supermarket and bought the bag of M&M'S® shown in Figure 6.1 (p. 154). The bag gave its weight as 18.40 ounces, which was 15% more than a regular 1-pound bag of M&M'S®. Sheila, who is a careful shopper, wanted to check and see if she was actually getting a 15% increase. Let's help Sheila dissect and solve this problem.

	The facts	Solving for?	Steps to take	Key points
BLUEPRINT	*New bag of M&M'S®:* 18.40 oz. 15% increase in weight. *Original bag of M&M'S®:* 16 oz. (1 lb.)	Checking percent increase of 15%.	Identify key elements. *Base:* 16 oz. *Rate:* ? *Portion:* 2.40 oz. $\left(\begin{array}{c} 18.40 \text{ oz.} \\ -16.00 \\ \hline 2.40 \text{ oz.} \end{array}\right)$ $\text{Rate} = \dfrac{\text{Portion}}{\text{Base}}$	Difference between base and new weight Portion (2.40 oz.) Base × Rate (16 oz.) (?) Original amount sold

Steps to solving problem

1. Set up the formula. $\text{Rate} = \dfrac{\text{Portion}}{\text{Base}}$

2. Calculate the rate. $R = \dfrac{2.40 \text{ oz.}}{16.00 \text{ oz.}}$ ← Difference between base and new weight.
 ← Old weight equals 100%.

   $R = 15\% \text{ increase}$

The new weight of the bag of M&M'S® is really 115% of the old weight:

$$\begin{array}{rcl} 16.00 \text{ oz.} & = & 100\% \\ +\ 2.40 & = & +\ 15 \\ \hline 18.40 \text{ oz.} & = & 115\% = 1.15 \end{array}$$

We can check this by looking at the following pie chart:

Portion = Base × Rate
18.40 oz. = 16 oz. × 1.15

Portion (18.40 oz.)
 Base × Rate (16 oz.) (1.15)
 100%

Why is the portion greater than the base? Remember that the portion can be larger than the base only if the rate is greater than 100%. Note how the portion and rate relate to the same piece of the base—18.40 oz. is 115% of the base (16 oz.).

Let's see what could happen if M&M/Mars has an increase in its price of sugar. This is an additional example to reinforce the concept of percent decrease.

The Word Problem The increase in the price of sugar caused the M&M/Mars company to decrease the weight of each 1-pound bag of M&M'S® to 12 ounces. What is the rate of percent decrease?

	The facts	Solving for?	Steps to take	Key points
BLUEPRINT	*16-oz. bag of M&M'S®:* reduced to 12 oz.	Rate of percent decrease.	Identify key elements. *Base:* 16 oz. *Rate:* ? *Portion:* 4 oz. (16 oz. − 12 oz.) $\text{Rate} = \dfrac{\text{Portion}}{\text{Base}}$	Amount of decrease Portion (4 oz.) Base × Rate (16 oz.) (?) Old base 100%

MONEY tips

When planning for retirement, a rule of thumb is that you will need 70% of your preretirement pay to live comfortably. This number assumes your house is paid off and you are in good health. Automating your savings can be a huge factor in helping you reach your goals. So, begin planning early in life and start saving for a financially sound retirement.

Steps to solving problem

1. Set up the formula.

$$\text{Rate} = \frac{\text{Portion}}{\text{Base}}$$

2. Calculate the rate.

$$R = \frac{4 \text{ oz.}}{16.00 \text{ oz.}}$$

$$R = 25\% \text{ decrease}$$

The new weight of the bag of M&M'S® is 75% of the old weight:

$$
\begin{array}{rcl}
16 \text{ oz.} & = & 100\% \\
-\ 4 & & -\ 25 \\
\hline
12 \text{ oz.} & = & 75\%
\end{array}
$$

We can check this by looking at the following pie chart:

$$\text{Portion} = \text{Base} \times \text{Rate}$$

$$12 \text{ oz.} = 16 \text{ oz.} \times .75$$

Note that the portion is smaller than the base because the rate is less than 100%. Also note how the portion and rate relate to the same piece of the base—12 ounces is 75% of the base (16 oz.).

After your study of Learning Unit 6–2, you should be ready for the Practice Quiz.

LU 6–2   PRACTICE QUIZ

Complete this **Practice Quiz** to see how you are doing.

Solve for portion:

1. 38% of 900.
2. 60% of $9,000.

Solve for rate (round to the nearest tenth percent as needed):

3. 430 is _____% of 5,000.
4. 200 is _____% of 700.

Solve for base (round to the nearest tenth as needed):

5. 55 is 40% of _____.
6. 900 is $4\frac{1}{2}$% of _____.

Solve the following (blueprint aids are shown in the solution; you might want to try some on scrap paper):

7. Five out of 25 students in Professor Ford's class received an A grade. What percent of the class *did not* receive the A grade?

8. Abby Biernet has yet to receive 60% of her lobster order. Abby received 80 lobsters to date. What was her original order?

9. Assume in 2014 Dunkin' Donuts Company had $300,000 in doughnut sales. In 2015, sales were up 40%. What are Dunkin' Donuts sales for 2015?

10. The price of an Apple computer dropped from $1,600 to $1,200. What was the percent decrease?

11. In 1982, a ticket to the Boston Celtics cost $14. In 2015, a ticket cost $50. What is the percent increase to the nearest hundredth percent?

For **extra help** from your authors—Sharon and Jeff—see the videos in Connect.

These videos are also available on YouTube!

✓ **Solutions**

1. $342 = 900 \times .38$

$(P) = (B) \times (R)$

2. $\$5,400 = \$9,000 \times .60$

$(P) = (B) \times (R)$

3. $\dfrac{(P)430}{(B)5,000} = .086 = 8.6\% \ (R)$

4. $\dfrac{(P)200}{(B)700} = .2857 = 28.6\% \ (R)$

5. $\dfrac{(P)55}{(R).40} = 137.5 \ (B)$

6. $\dfrac{(P)900}{(R).045} = 20,000 \ (B)$

7. Percent of Professor Ford's class that did not receive an A grade:

	The facts	Solving for?	Steps to take	Key points
BLUEPRINT	5 As. 25 in class.	Percent that did not receive A.	Identify key elements. *Base:* 25 *Rate:* ? *Portion:* 20 (25 − 5) $\text{Rate} = \dfrac{\text{Portion}}{\text{Base}}$	Portion (20) Base × Rate (25) (?) The whole Portion and rate must relate to same piece of base.

Steps to solving problem

1. Set up the formula. $\text{Rate} = \dfrac{\text{Portion}}{\text{Base}}$

2. Calculate the base rate. $R = \dfrac{20}{25}$

$R = 80\%$

8. Abby Biernet's original order:

	The facts	Solving for?	Steps to take	Key points
BLUEPRINT	60% of the order not in. 80 lobsters received.	Total order of lobsters.	Identify key elements. *Base:* ? *Rate:* .40 (100% − 60%) *Portion:* 80 $\text{Base} = \dfrac{\text{Portion}}{\text{Rate}}$	Portion (80) Base × Rate (?) (.40) 80 lobsters represent 40% of the order Portion and rate must relate to same piece of base.

Steps to solving problem

1. Set up the formula. $\text{Base} = \dfrac{\text{Portion}}{\text{Rate}}$

2. Calculate the base rate. $B = \dfrac{80}{.40}$ ← 80 lobsters is 40% of base.

$B = 200 \text{ lobsters}$

9. Dunkin' Donuts Company sales for 2015:

	The facts	Solving for?	Steps to take	Key points
BLUEPRINT	*2014:* $300,000 sales. *2015:* Sales up 40% from 2014.	Sales for 2015.	Identify key elements. *Base:* $300,000. *Rate:* 1.40. Old year 100% New year + 40 140% *Portion:* ? Portion = Base × Rate.	2015 sales Portion (?) Base × Rate ($300,000) (1.40) 2014 sales When rate is greater than 100%, portion will be larger than base.

Steps to solving problem

1. Set up the formula.   Portion = Base × Rate

2. Calculate the portion. $P = \$300{,}000 \times 1.40$

                                  $P = \$420{,}000$

10. Percent decrease in Apple computer price:

	The facts	Solving for?	Steps to take	Key points
BLUEPRINT	Apple computer was $1,600; now, $1,200.	Percent decrease in price.	Identify key elements. *Base:* $1,600. *Rate:* ? *Portion:* $400 ($1,600 − $1,200). Rate = $\dfrac{\text{Portion}}{\text{Base}}$	Difference in price Portion ($400) Base ($1,600) × Rate (?) Original price

Steps to solving problem

1. Set up the formula.   Rate = $\dfrac{\text{Portion}}{\text{Base}}$

2. Calculate the rate. $R = \dfrac{\$400}{\$1{,}600}$

                              $R = 25\%$

11. Percent increase in Boston Celtics ticket:

© Jim Davis/The Boston Globe via Getty Images

	The facts	Solving for?	Steps to take	Key points
BLUEPRINT	$14 ticket (old). $50 ticket (new).	Percent increase in price.	Identify key elements. *Base:* $14 *Rate:* ? *Portion:* $36 ($50 − $14) Rate = $\dfrac{\text{Portion}}{\text{Base}}$	Difference in price Portion ($36) Base ($14) × Rate (?) Original price When portion is greater than base, rate will be greater than 100%.

Steps to solving problem

1. Set up the formula.   Rate = $\dfrac{\text{Portion}}{\text{Base}}$

2. Calculate the rate. $R = \dfrac{\$36}{\$14}$

                $R = 2.5714 = 257.14\%$

(continues)

LU 6–2a	EXTRA PRACTICE QUIZ WITH WORKED-OUT SOLUTIONS

Need more practice? Try this Extra Practice Quiz (check figures in the Interactive Chapter Organizer). Worked-out Solutions can be found in Appendix B.

Solve for portion:

1. 42% of 1,200

2. 7% of $8,000

Solve for rate (round to nearest tenth percent as needed):

3. 510 is _____% of 6,000.

4. 400 is _____% of 900.

Solve for base (round to the nearest tenth as needed):

5. 30 is 60% of _____.

6. 1,200 is $3\frac{1}{2}$% of _____.

7. Ten out of 25 students in Professor Ford's class received an A grade. What percent of the class did not receive the A grade?

8. Abby Biernet has yet to receive 70% of her lobster order. Abby received 90 lobsters to date. What was her original order?

9. A local Dunkin' Donuts Company had $400,000 in doughnut sales in 2013. In 2014, sales were up 35%. What are Dunkin' Donuts sales for 2014?

10. The price of an Apple computer dropped from $1,800 to $1,000. What was the percent decrease? (Round to the nearest hundredth percent.)

11. In 1982, a ticket to the Boston Celtics cost $14. In 2013, a ticket cost $75. What is the percent increase to the nearest hundredth percent?

INTERACTIVE CHAPTER ORGANIZER

Topic/Procedure/Formula	Examples	You try it*
Converting decimals to percents **1.** Move decimal point two places to right. If necessary, add zeros. This rule is also used for whole numbers and mixed decimals. **2.** Add a percent symbol at end of number.	.81 = .81. = 81% .008 = .00.8 = .8% 4.15 = 4.15. = 415%	**Convert to percent** .92 .009 5.46
Rounding percents **1.** Answer must be in percent before rounding. **2.** Identify specific digit. If digit to right is 5 or greater, round up. **3.** Delete digits to right of identified digit.	Round to the nearest hundredth percent. $\frac{3}{7}$ = .4285714 = 42.85714 = 42.86%	**Round to the nearest hundredth percent** $\frac{2}{9}$
Converting percents to decimals **1.** Drop percent symbol. **2.** Move decimal point two places to left. If necessary, add zeros. For fractional percents: **1.** Convert to decimal by dividing numerator by denominator. If necessary, round answer. **2.** If a mixed fractional percent, convert fractional percent first. Then combine whole number and fractional percent. **3.** Drop percent symbol; move decimal point two places to left.	.89% = .0089 95% = .95 195% = 1.95 $8\frac{3}{4}$% = 8.75% = .0875 $\frac{1}{4}$% = .25% = .0025 $\frac{1}{5}$% = .20% = .0020	**Convert to decimal** .78% 96% 246% $7\frac{3}{4}$% $\frac{3}{4}$% $\frac{1}{2}$%

INTERACTIVE CHAPTER ORGANIZER

Topic/Procedure/Formula	Examples	You try it*
Converting fractions to percents 1. Divide numerator by denominator. 2. Move decimal point two places to right; add percent symbol.	$\frac{4}{5} = .80 = 80\%$	**Convert to percent** $\frac{3}{5}$
Converting percents to fractions Whole percent (or fractional percent) to a fraction: 1. Drop percent symbol. 2. Multiply number by $\frac{1}{100}$. 3. Reduce to lowest terms. Mixed or decimal percent to a fraction: 1. Drop percent symbol. 2. Change mixed percent to an improper fraction. 3. Multiply number by $\frac{1}{100}$. 4. Reduce to lowest terms. If you have a mixed or decimal percent, change decimal portion to fractional equivalent and continue with Steps 1 to 4.	$64\% \longrightarrow 64 \times \frac{1}{100} = \frac{64}{100} = \frac{16}{25}$ $\frac{1}{4}\% \longrightarrow \frac{1}{4} \times \frac{1}{100} = \frac{1}{400}$ $119\% \longrightarrow 119 \times \frac{1}{100} = \frac{119}{100} = 1\frac{19}{100}$ $16\frac{1}{4}\% \longrightarrow \frac{65}{4} \times \frac{1}{100} = \frac{65}{400} = \frac{13}{80}$ $16.25\% \longrightarrow 16\frac{1}{4}\% = \frac{65}{4} \times \frac{1}{100}$ $= \frac{65}{400} = \frac{13}{80}$	**Convert to fractions** 74% $\frac{1}{5}\%$ 121% $17\frac{1}{5}\%$ 17.75%
Solving for portion "is" Portion (?) Base ($1,000) × Rate (.10) "of" "%"	10% of Mel's paycheck of $1,000 goes for food. What portion is deducted for food? $\$100 = \$1,000 \times .10$ *Note:* If question was what amount does not go for food, the portion would have been: $\$900 = \$1,000 \times .90$ (100% − 10% = 90%)	**Find portion** Base $2,000 Rate 80%
Solving for rate Portion ($100) Base ($1,000) × Rate (?)	Assume Mel spends $100 for food from his $1,000 paycheck. What percent of his paycheck is spent on food? $\frac{\$100}{\$1,000} = .10 = 10\%$ *Note:* Portion is less than base since rate is less than 100%.	**Find rate** Base $2,000 Portion $500
Solving for base Portion ($100) Base (?) × Rate (.10)	Assume Mel spends $100 for food, which is 10% of his paycheck. What is Mel's total paycheck? $\frac{\$100}{.10} = \$1,000$	**Find base** Rate 20% Portion $200

(continues)

INTERACTIVE CHAPTER ORGANIZER

Topic/Procedure/Formula	Examples	You try it*
Calculating percent increases and decreases	Stereo, $2,000 original price. Stereo, $2,500 new price.	**Find percent increase** Old price $500 New price $600

Amount of decrease or increase

Portion

Base × Rate (?)

Original price

$$\frac{\$500}{\$2,000} = .25 = \boxed{25\%} \text{ increase}$$

Check
$2,000 × 1.25 = $2,500
Note: Portion is greater than base since rate is greater than 100%.

Portion ($2,500)

Base × Rate ($2,000) (1.25)

KEY TERMS	Base	Percent increase	Portion
	Percent decrease	Percents	Rate

Check Figures for Extra Practice Quizzes. (Worked-out Solutions are in Appendix B.)	LU 6–1a		LU 6–2a	
	1. 44.4%	**8.** 7.658	**1.** 504	**7.** 60%
	2. 78.2%	**9.** 33.33%	**2.** 560	**8.** 300
	3. .6%	**10.** 42.86%	**3.** 8.5%	**9.** $540,000
	4. 793.3%	**11.** $\frac{17}{100}$	**4.** 44.4%	**10.** 44.44%
	5. .0020	**12.** $\frac{329}{400}$	**5.** 50	**11.** 435.71%
	6. .0780	**13.** $1\frac{1}{2}$	**6.** 34,285.7	
	7. .92	**14.** $\frac{1}{400}$		
		15. $\frac{89}{500}$		

Note: For how to dissect and solve a word problem, see learning unit 6-2.

*Worked-out solutions are in Appendix B.

Critical Thinking Discussion Questions with Chapter Concept Check

1. In converting from a percent to a decimal, when will you have at least 2 leading zeros before the whole number? Explain this concept, assuming you have 100 bills of $1.

2. Explain the steps in rounding percents. Count the number of students who are sitting in the back half of the room as a percent of the total class. Round your answer to the nearest hundredth percent. Could you have rounded to the nearest whole percent without changing the accuracy of the answer?

3. Define portion, rate, and base. Create an example using Walt Disney World to show when the portion could be larger than the base. Why must the rate be greater than 100% for this to happen?

4. How do we solve for portion, rate, and base? Create an example using Apple computer sales to show that the portion and rate do relate to the same piece of the base.

5. Explain how to calculate percent decreases or increases. Many years ago, comic books cost 10 cents a copy. Visit a bookshop or newsstand. Select a new comic book and explain the price increase in percent compared to the 10-cent comic. How important is the rounding process in your final answer?

6. **Chapter Concept Check.** Go to the Google or Facebook site and find out how many people the company employs. Assuming a 10% increase in employment this year, calculate the total number of new employees by the end of the year, and identify the base rate and portion. If, in the following year, the 10% increase in employment fell by 5%, what would the total number of current employees be?

Classroom Notes

END-OF-CHAPTER PROBLEMS

Check figures for odd-numbered problems in Appendix C.   Name _____   Date _____

DRILL PROBLEMS

Convert the following decimals to percents: *LU 6-1(1)*

6–1. .96   **6–2.** .259   **6–3.** .4

6–4. 8.00   **6–5.** 3.561   **6–6.** 6.006

Convert the following percents to decimals: *LU 6-1(1)*

6–7. 4%   **6–8.** 14%   **6–9.** $64\frac{3}{10}\%$

6–10. 75.9%   **6–11.** 119%   **6–12.** 89%

Convert the following fractions to percents (round to the nearest tenth percent as needed):   *LU 6-1(1)*

6–13. $\frac{1}{12}$ **6–14.** $\frac{1}{400}$

6–15. $\frac{7}{8}$ **6–16.** $\frac{11}{12}$

Convert the following percents to fractions and reduce to the lowest terms: *LU 6-1(2)*

6–17. 4%   **6–18.** $18\frac{1}{2}\%$

6–19. $31\frac{2}{3}\%$ **6–20.** $61\frac{1}{2}\%$

6–21. 6.75%   **6–22.** 182%

Solve for the portion (round to the nearest hundredth as needed):   *LU 6-2(2)*

6–23. 7% of 150   **6–24.** 125% of 4,320   **6–25.** 25% of 410
eXcel   eXcel   eXcel

6–26. 119% of 128.9   **6–27.** 17.4% of 900   **6–28.** 11.2% of 85
eXcel   eXcel   eXcel

6–29. $12\frac{1}{2}\%$ of 919   **6–30.** 45% of 300

6–31. 18% of 90   **6–32.** 30% of 2,000

Solve for the base (round to the nearest hundredth as needed):   *LU 6-2(2)*

6–33. 170 is 120% of _____   **6–34.** 36 is .75% of _____

6–35. 50 is .5% of _____   **6–36.** 10,800 is 90% of _____

6–37. 800 is $4\frac{1}{2}\%$ of _____

Solve for rate (round to the nearest tenth percent as needed):   *LU 6-2(2)*

6–38. _____ of 80 is 50   **6–39.** _____ of 85 is 92

6–40. _____ of 250 is 65   **6–41.** 110 is _____ of 100

6–42. .09 is _____ of 2.25   **6–43.** 16 is _____ of 4

Solve the following problems. Be sure to show your work. Round to the nearest hundredth or hundredth percent as needed: *LU 6-2(2)*

6–44. What is 180% of 310?

6–45. 66% of 90 is what?

6–46. 40% of what number is 20?

6–47. 770 is 70% of what number?

6–48. 4 is what percent of 90?

6–49. What percent of 150 is 60?

Complete the following table: *LU 6-2(3)*

Product	Selling price 2013	Selling price 2014	Amount of decrease or increase	Percent change (to nearest hundredth percent as needed)
6–50. Apple iPad	$650	$500		
6–51. Smartphone	$100	$120		

WORD PROBLEMS (First of Four Sets)

6–52. At a local Dunkin' Donuts, a survey showed that out of 1,200 customers eating lunch, 240 ordered coffee with their meal.
e**X**cel What percent of customers ordered coffee?   *LU 6-2(2)*

6–53. What percent of customers in Problem 6–52 did not order coffee?   *LU 6-2(2)*
e**X**cel

6–54. In January 2015, the price of gas was on average $2.05 per gallon. This was $1.20 cheaper than a year before. What is the price decrease? Round to the nearest hundredth percent.   *LU 6-2(3)*

6–55. Wally Chin, the owner of an ExxonMobil station, bought a used Ford pickup truck, paying $2,000 as a down payment. He still owes 80% of the selling price. What was the selling price of the truck?   *LU 6-2(2)*

6–56. Maria Fay bought four Dunlop tires at a local Goodyear store. The salesperson told her that her mileage would increase by 8%. Before this purchase, Maria was getting 24 mpg. What should her mileage be with the new tires to the nearest hundredth? *LU 6-2(2)*

6–57. The Social Security Administration announced the following rates to explain what percent of your Social Security benefits you will receive based on how old you are when you start receiving Social Security benefits.

eXcel

Age	Percent of benefit
62	75
63	80
64	86.7
65	93.3
66	100

Assume Shelley Kate decides to take her Social Security at age 63. What amount of Social Security money will she receive each month, assuming she is entitled to $800 per month? *LU 6-2(2)*

6–58. Assume that in the year 2015, 800,000 people attended the Christmas Eve celebration at Walt Disney World. In 2016, attendance for the Christmas Eve celebration is expected to increase by 35%. What is the total number of people expected at Walt Disney World for this event? *LU 6-2(2)*

eXcel

6–59. Pete Smith found in his attic a Woody Woodpecker watch in its original box. It had a price tag on it for $4.50. The watch was made in 1949. Pete brought the watch to an antiques dealer and sold it for $35. What was the percent of increase in price? Round to the nearest hundredth percent. *LU 6-2(3)*

6–60. Christie's Auction sold a painting for $24,500. It charges all buyers a 15% premium of the final bid price. How much did the bidder pay Christie's? *LU 6-2(2)*

WORD PROBLEMS (Second of Four Sets)

6–61. Out of 9,000 college students surveyed, 540 responded that they do not eat breakfast. What percent of the students do not eat breakfast? *LU 6-2(2)*

6–62. What percent of college students in Problem 6–61 eat breakfast?   *LU 6-2(2)*

6–63. *Bloomberg Business* reports that in 2014 Jim Tananbaum, CEO of Foresite Capital, celebrated his 50th birthday at Burning Man, the annual arts festival attracting 60,000 people to the Black Rock Desert in Nevada. He invited 120 guests at $16,500 per person. What percent of total attendees did Jim invite?   *LU 6-2(2)*

6–64. Rainfall for January in Fiji averages 12″ according to *World Travel Guide*. This year it rained 5% less. How many inches (to the nearest tenth) did it rain this year?   *LU 6-2(2)*

6–65. Jim and Alice Lange, employees at Walmart, have put themselves on a strict budget. Their goal at year's end is to buy a boat for $15,000 in cash. Their budget includes the following:

   40% food and lodging   20% entertainment   10% educational

Jim earns $1,900 per month and Alice earns $2,400 per month. After 1 year, will Alice and Jim have enough cash to buy the boat?   *LU 6-2(2)*

6–66. Uscourts.gov reports there were 936,795 bankruptcy filings in 2014. If there were 310,061 Chapter 13 filings, what percent of filings were not Chapter 13? Round to the nearest whole percent.   *LU 6-2(2)*

6–67. The Museum of Science in Boston estimated that 64% of all visitors came from within the state. On Saturday, 2,500 people attended the museum. How many attended the museum from out of state?   *LU 6-2(2)*

6–68. Staples pays George Nagovsky an annual salary of $36,000. Today, George's boss informs him that he will receive a $4,600 raise. What percent of George's old salary is the $4,600 raise? Round to the nearest tenth percent.   *LU 6-2(2)*

6–69. In 2014, a local Dairy Queen had $550,000 in sales. In 2015, Dairy Queen's sales were up 35%. What were Dairy Queen's sales in 2015?   *LU 6-2(2)*

6–70. Blue Valley College has 600 female students. This is 60% of the total student body. How many students attend Blue Valley College?   *LU 6-2(2)*

6–71. Dr. Grossman was reviewing his total accounts receivable. This month, credit customers paid $44,000, which represented 20% of all receivables (what customers owe) due. What was Dr. Grossman's total accounts receivable?   *LU 6-2(2)*

6–72. Massachusetts has a 5% sales tax. Timothy bought a Toro lawn mower and paid $20 sales tax. What was the cost of the lawn mower before the tax?   *LU 6-2(2)*

6–73. The price of an antique doll increased from $600 to $800. What was the percent of increase? Round to the nearest tenth percent.   *LU 6-2(3)*

6–74. A local Barnes and Noble bookstore ordered 80 marketing books but received 60 books. What percent of the order was missing?   *LU 6-2(2)*

WORD PROBLEMS (Third of Four Sets)

6–75. RealtyTrac reported that the number of foreclosures filed in 2014 in the United States was 1,117,426 down from a high of 2,871,891 properties in 2010. What is the percent decrease in foreclosures (to the nearest tenth percent)?   *LU 6-2(2)*

6–76. Due to increased mailing costs, the new rate will cost publishers $50 million; this is 12.5% more than they paid the previous year. How much did it cost publishers last year? Round to the nearest hundreds. *LU 6-2(2)*

6–77. Jim Goodman, an employee at Walgreens, earned $45,900 in 2015, an increase of 17.5% over the previous year. What were Jim's earnings in 2014? Round to the nearest cent. *LU 6-2(2)*

6–78. If the number of mortgage applications declined by 7% to 1,625,415, what had been the previous year's number of applications? *LU 6-2(2)*

6–79. In 2015, the price of a business math text rose to $150. This is 8% more than the 2014 price. What was the old selling price? Round to the nearest cent. *LU 6-2(2)*

6–80. Web Consultants, Inc., pays Alice Rose an annual salary of $48,000. Today, Alice's boss informs her that she will receive a $6,400 raise. What percent of Alice's old salary is the $6,400 raise? Round to the nearest tenth percent. *LU 6-2(2)*

6–81. Earl Miller, a lawyer, charges Lee's Plumbing, his client, 25% of what he can collect for Lee from customers whose accounts are past due. The attorney also charges, in addition to the 25%, a flat fee of $50 per customer. This month, Earl collected $7,000 from three of Lee's past-due customers. What is the total fee due to Earl? *LU 6-2(2)*

6–82. A local Petco ordered 100 dog calendars but received 60. What percent of the order was missing? *LU 6-2(2)*

6–83. Ray's Video uses MasterCard. MasterCard charges $2\frac{1}{2}$% on net deposits (credit slips less returns). Ray's made a net deposit of $4,100 for charge sales. How much did MasterCard charge Ray's? *LU 6-2(2)*

6–84. Internetlivestats.com reported in February 2015 around 40% of the world population has an Internet connection today. If there are 3,061,707,850 users, what is the world population? *LU 6-2(2)*

WORD PROBLEMS (Fourth of Four Sets)

6–85. Chevrolet raised the base price of its Volt by $1,200 to $33,500. What was the percent increase? Round to the nearest tenth percent. *LU 6-2(2)*

6–86. The sales tax rate is 8%. If Jim bought a new Buick and paid a sales tax of $1,920, what was the cost of the Buick before the tax? *LU 6-2(2)*

6–87. Puthina Unge bought a new Dell computer system on sale for $1,800. It was advertised as 30% off the regular price. What was the original price of the computer? Round to the nearest dollar. *LU 6-2(2)*

6–88. John O'Sullivan has just completed his first year in business. His records show that he spent the following in advertising:

Internet $600   Radio $650   Yellow Pages $700   Local flyers $400

What percent of John's advertising was spent on the Yellow Pages? Round to the nearest hundredth percent. *LU 6-2(2)*

6–89. Jay Miller sold his ski house at Attitash Mountain in New Hampshire for $35,000. This sale represented a loss of 15% off the original price. What was the original price Jay paid for the ski house? Round your answer to the nearest dollar. *LU 6-2(2)*

6–90. Out of 4,000 colleges surveyed, 60% reported that SAT scores were not used as a high consideration in viewing their applications. How many schools view the SAT as important in screening applicants? *LU 6-2(2)*

6–91. If refinishing your basement at a cost of $45,404 would add $18,270 to the resale value of your home, what percent of your cost is recouped? Round to the nearest percent.   *LU 6-2(2)*

6–92. A major airline laid off 4,000 pilots and flight attendants. If this was a 12.5% reduction in the workforce, what was the size of the workforce after the layoffs?   *LU 6-2(2)*

6–93. Assume 450,000 people line up on the streets to see the Macy's Thanksgiving Parade in 2014. If attendance is expected to increase 30%, what will be the number of people lined up on the street to see the 2015 parade?   *LU 6-2(2)*

CHALLENGE PROBLEMS

6–94. Each Tuesday, Ryan Airlines reduces its one-way ticket from Fort Wayne to Chicago from $125 to $40. To receive this special $40 price, the customer must buy a round-trip ticket. Ryan has a nonrefundable 25% penalty fare for cancellation; it estimates that about nine-tenths of 1% will cancel their reservations. The airline also estimates this special price will cause a passenger traffic increase from 400 to 900. Ryan expects revenue for the year to be 55.4% higher than the previous year. Last year, Ryan's sales were $482,000. To receive the special rate, Janice Miller bought two round-trip tickets. On other airlines, Janice has paid $100 round trip (with no cancellation penalty). Calculate the following: *LU 6-2(2)*

a. Percent discount Ryan is offering.

b. Percent passenger travel will increase.

c. Sales for new year.
d. Janice's loss if she cancels one round-trip flight.
e. Approximately how many more cancellations can Ryan Airlines expect (after Janice's cancellation)?

6–95. A local Dunkin' Donuts shop reported that its sales have increased exactly 22% per year for the last 2 years. This year's sales were $82,500. What were Dunkin' Donuts' sales 2 years ago? Round each year's sales to the nearest dollar.   *LU 6-2(2)*

 SUMMARY PRACTICE TEST

Do you need help? The videos in Connect have step-by-step worked-out solutions. These videos are also available on YouTube!

Convert the following decimals to percents.   *LU 6-1(1)*

1. .921   **2.** .4   **3.** 15.88   **4.** 8.00

Convert the following percents to decimals.   *LU 6-1(1)*

5. 42%   **6.** 7.98%   **7.** 400%   **8.** $\frac{1}{4}$%

Convert the following fractions to percents. Round to the nearest tenth percent. *LU 6-1(1)*

9. $\dfrac{1}{6}$

10. $\dfrac{1}{3}$

Convert the following percents to fractions and reduce to the lowest terms as needed. *LU 6-1(2)*

11. $19\dfrac{3}{8}\%$

12. 6.2%

Solve the following problems for portion, base, or rate:

13. An Arby's franchise has a net income before taxes of $900,000. The company's treasurer estimates that 40% of the company's net income will go to federal and state taxes. How much will the Arby's franchise have left? *LU 6-2(2)*

14. Domino's projects a year-end net income of $699,000. The net income represents 30% of its annual sales. What are Domino's projected annual sales? *LU 6-2(2)*

15. Target ordered 400 iPods. When Target received the order, 100 iPods were missing. What percent of the order did Target receive? *LU 6-2(2)*

16. Matthew Song, an employee at Putnam Investments, receives an annual salary of $120,000. Today his boss informed him that he would receive a $3,200 raise. What percent of his old salary is the $3,200 raise? Round to the nearest hundredth percent. *LU 6-2(2)*

17. The price of a Delta airline ticket from Los Angeles to Boston increased to $440. This is a 15% increase. What was the old fare? Round to the nearest cent. *LU 6-2(2)*

18. Scupper Grace earns a gross pay of $900 per week at Office Depot. Scupper's payroll deductions are 29%. What is Scupper's take-home pay? *LU 6-2(2)*

19. Mia Wong is reviewing the total accounts receivable of Wong's department store. Credit customers paid $90,000 this month. This represents 60% of all receivables due. What is Mia's total accounts receivable? *LU 6-2(2)*

In a constantly changing business environment, new product and service development can invigorate a company, improve market share, and ensure desired financial performance. Six Flags, with its "Go Big! Go Six Flags" motto, knows it must regularly add new rides and upgrade existing ones in its theme parks to remain on top.

Located in Grand Prairie, Texas, Six Flags first opened in 1961 and grew to become the largest regional theme park system in the world. Central to this growth was the constant development of new and record-setting theme park rides, following a well-defined process of product development. Consider the Kingda Ka roller coaster that opened in May 2005 at the Six Flags Great Adventure & Wild Safari in Jackson, New Jersey. This is the largest of the Six Flags parks, and Kingda Ka is the tallest and fastest coaster in North America.

Getting to the May 2005 ride opening required significant planning and a coordinated effort. Six Flags' new product development process ensures both. It guides and choreographs the hundreds of tasks involved in building a roller coaster, from preparing the foundation to erecting the steel frame to installing the hydraulic system that allows for speeds of 128 mph to fitting out the cars.

Six Flags relies on several key documents to control and monitor all resources, including raw materials, equipment, and the people involved in the construction of the ride. The Statement of Work (SOW) is a written statement that describes the work to be done and includes a preliminary project schedule and completion dates. The SOW details project milestones, key completion events, and budget parameters. The Work Breakdown Structure (WBS) defines the hierarchy of tasks, subtasks, and work packages and is key to managing the logistics of the project. The project Gantt chart illustrates the project schedule and helps identify the critical path within the project. The critical path represents the longest chain of tasks in terms of time to complete. If there is a delay in any step in the critical path, the whole project can be delayed.

The Kingda Ka ride had a 15-month project schedule of which 9 to 10 months were actual construction time. The coaster took 16 months to complete and came in 10% over budget. Success in new product development requires careful planning, well-defined milestones, teamwork, and flexibility to respond to unforeseen changes. The successful Kingda Ka ride was no exception.

PROBLEM 1

As stated in the case, the original project schedule for the Kingda Ka coaster was 15 months but the project actually took 16 months to complete. What was the percent increase over the original scheduled completion time? Round your answer to the nearest percent.

PROBLEM 2

Review the video case to identify the timing of key steps in the construction of the Kingda Ka, including start of conceptual planning, start of foundation construction, start of steel erection, and completion of the project. What percent of the actual total project time had elapsed by the time foundation construction began? By the time steel erection began? Round answers to the nearest percent.

PROBLEM 3

The project Gantt chart shown in the video indicated that 145 days were planned for site preparation, 119 days for foundations, and 133 for steel erection. What was the percentage of time needed for each of these three steps assuming 397 days were needed in total? Round answers to the nearest percent.

PROBLEM 4

The Kindga Ka is currently the tallest steel roller coaster, at 456 feet high. The second tallest is the Top Thrill Dragster at Cedar Point in Sandusky, Ohio, at 420 feet. How much taller is the Kingda Ka in both feet and percentage (*to the nearest tenth percent*)?

PROBLEM 5

If Six Flags wanted to build a roller coaster that was 5% taller than the Kingda Ka, how tall would the coaster need to be? Round answer to the nearest foot.

PROBLEM 6

Six Flags rates its rides as mild, moderate, or max. The Six Flags Great Adventure park where the Kingda Ka ride is located has a total of 49 rides. Of these, 12 have a max rating, 8 have a moderate rating, and the remainder are rated mild. Express each of the ride types as a fraction and then determine the percentage each comprises of the total. Reduce fractions to the lowest possible terms and round percentages to the nearest percent.

PROBLEM 7

The Kingda Ka ride covers 3,118 feet of track. The Green Lantern, a new ride at the same park, has ¾ mile of track. Which ride is longer and by what percent? Round answer to the nearest percent.

PROBLEM 8

As the case states, the Kingda Ka ride reaches speeds of 128 mph due to its hydraulic system. The Green Lantern ride is designed to reach speeds of 63 mph. What percent increase would be needed for the Green Lantern ride to match the speed attained on the Kingda Ka? Round answer to the nearest tenth percent.

Class Discussion In any project, project managers must balance three key variables—time, cost, and quality. Typically one variable is most critical in a project and should problems arise, the other two may be sacrificed to achieve the one that is key to the project's success. Discuss how these three variables were managed in the Kingda Ka project.

SURF TO SAVE

Need help with money and investing? 🔍

PROBLEM 1
All-in-one and one for all

Assume you want to buy an all-in-one printer/ scanner/copier/fax machine. Go to www.staples.com and choose an all-in-one machine to meet your needs. How much does it cost? If your state charged 7% sales tax, what would be the amount of the tax on this purchase?

Discussion Questions

1. Is the all-in-one machine less expensive than purchasing separate machines for all of these tasks?

2. When might it be a better option to buy individual machines versus an all-in-one? Why?

PROBLEM 3
Buy low, sell high

Go to http://finance.yahoo.com/q/hp?s=GE to view the historical stock prices for General Electric Company (GE). Compare the price of the stock from today versus the price 1 year ago today. (Use the closing price.) What was the percent change in the stock price?

Discussion Questions

1. Assuming you had purchased 500 shares of this stock 1 year ago today, what is the value of your increase/decrease?

2. Based on the current value of your 500 shares, do you feel this is a wise investment for you? Why or why not?

PROBLEM 2
Earning the minimum

Go to http://www.dol.gov/whd/minwage/chart.htm to view the historical changes made to the federal minimum wage. Compare the last 3 changes to the federal minimum wage and determine the percentage change between each.

Discussion Questions

1. Do you feel the federal minimum wage should be increased? Why?

2. Assume the current federal minimum wage was increased by 5%. How would this impact someone who works 20 hours per week?

PROBLEM 4
On the move, will my money follow?

Assume your employer is relocating to another state. You can keep your current job and salary if you move. Go to http://cgi.money.cnn.com/tools/costofliving/ costofliving.html, enter your current state and city, a new destination state and city, and your current yearly salary. Click on "Get result". Based on the calculation, what is the percent increase or decrease of your salary? Is this move worth your while financially?

Discussion Questions

1. Other than income, what factors would influence your decision to move to another state?

2. What factors help explain the change in income between the two locations you selected?

MOBILE APPS

PercentDiff (Shaolo LLC) Calculates percentage change or percentage for given numbers.

Easy Percentage Calculator (RedVok Software) Calculates percentages easily.

PERSONAL FINANCE

A KIPLINGER APPROACH

By Susannah Snider, From *Kiplinger's Personal Finance*, September 2013.

COLLEGE »

A Crash Course in Money Management

Give students the tools they need to master their finances. **BY SUSANNAH SNIDER**

WHEN IT COMES TO BANK accounts, the cost of newbie mistakes adds up fast. For example, overdraft charges, at about $35 a pop, can quickly put your freshman in the hole. But parents can help students make smart choices about overdraft programs, plus steer them to accounts that don't charge maintenance or low-balance fees. You can also help them set up text alerts so they don't miss a payment or overdraw. "The experience of banking wisely is something you can learn in college without paying for the course," says Richard Barrington, of MoneyRates.com.

Checking. Free checking is quickly becoming ancient history, but some banks still waive fees for students. **U.S. BANK** and **CITIBANK** offer free student checking and allow free out-of-network ATM withdrawals (though U.S. Bank limits them to four per month, and outside banks may charge their own ATM fees). **BANK OF AMERICA** also offers free checking. After graduation these banks funnel you into non-student accounts. Other banks waive fees if you, for

example, maintain a minimum balance or make one direct deposit each month.

Overdraft charges are a big drain on young-adult accounts. If you opt in and use your debit card or go to the ATM without cash in your account to cover the transaction, the bank fronts you the money—but you pay a stiff penalty. Many banks let you link a checking account to savings as a backup, typically for a fee of about $10 per transfer if you overdraw. Or you can simply choose to let the transaction be declined. Embarrassment at the register can be a powerful motivator to improve balance tracking.

Savings. Online banks usually offer better interest rates than the big brick-and-mortar banks. **BARCLAYS** online bank recently offered 0.9% on savings with no minimum balance or fees,

and **ALLY BANK** paid 0.84% with no minimum or fees. If self-control is an issue, try stashing money in a separate bank. Otherwise, "it's too easy to click a button and move your money from savings to checking," says Erin Baehr, of Baehr Family Financial.

Credit. Make a judgment call on credit cards. Having one can help students improve their credit score, learn to manage debt and pay for emergencies. But a debit card is better for spendthrifts and those perfecting money skills. Plus, the feds have made it tough for applicants younger than 21 years old to qualify, requiring that they have an income or enlist a co-signer. If you co-sign, you may be stuck holding the bill or sacrificing your credit rating if your student can't pay.

If a credit card is right, look for one targeted to students. The **BANKAMERICARD CREDIT CARD FOR STUDENTS** carries no annual fee. Applicants younger than 21 must demonstrate the ability to pay based on income, such as earnings from summer or part-time jobs, or apply with a co-signer. ■

STUDENT-FRIENDLY APPS

ATMs. Using an out-of-network ATM will ding you more than $4, on average, according to a Bankrate.com survey. Dodge the fee with MasterCard's **ATM HUNTER**. Plug in your address or let the GPS pinpoint your location. You'll see a list of nearby ATMs and their affiliated banks. Free for iPhone, Android and Windows Phone.

Budgeting. The **LEARNVEST** app syncs with LearnVest's Money Center to help you track spending, save for goals and find financial tips. It's known for being geared toward women, but guys can use it, too. Free for iPhone.

Saving. Automate saving with **SAVED PLUS.** The app funnels a percentage of each purchase from a checking account into a savings account. Specify a goal, such as building an emergency fund or paying off a loan, plus the percentage of spending to set aside. Free for iPhone and Android.

TOM STEWART/CORBIS

BUSINESS MATH ISSUE

.9% or .84% on savings is way too low in today's marketplace.

1. List the key points of the article and information to support your position.
2. Write a group defense of your position using math calculations to support your view.

CHAPTER 7

Discounts: Trade and Cash

© Kevin Schafer/Getty Images

When Staples Offers Items for a Penny, New York Buys Kleenex by the Pound

* * *

Offices Order Products 'Up the Yin-Yang'; The 200 Cans of Dust-Off Nobody Wants

By Mark Maremont

Staples Inc. made the State of New York quite a promise: Buy your office supplies from us, and we'll sell you a bunch of things for a penny apiece. This unleashed a rush on the retailer as government offices and qualifying organizations across the state gobbled up the one-cent items.

A Brooklyn charity benefiting disabled people ordered 240,000 boxes of facial tissue and 48,000 rolls of paper towels, according to documents obtained in a public-records request. Rome, N.Y., wanted 100,000 CD-Rs. A State Department of Motor Vehicles office ordered 8,000 rolls of packaging tape.

© D. Hurst/Alamy

"We ordered things we didn't even need," said Nancy Sitone, manager of office services at United Cerebral Palsy Association of Greater Suffolk Inc. "I have some products up the yin-yang."

Staples was named New York's official office-supplies vendor in May 2013. Besides state agencies, those able to order under the contract include city halls, schools, police departments and many charities.

To win the three-year contract, Staples agreed to sell 219 popular items at a penny apiece. It hoped to turn a profit from thousands of other items that weren't on sale.

Reprinted by permission of *The Wall Street Journal*, copyright 2014 Dow Jones & Company, Inc. All rights reserved worldwide.

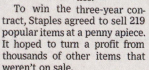

STONE SOUP © 2013 Jan Eliot. Reprinted with permission of ANDREWS MCMEEL SYNDICATION. All rights reserved.

LU 7–1: Trade Discounts—Single and Chain (Includes Discussion of Freight)

1. Calculate single trade discounts with formulas and complements.
2. Explain the freight terms *FOB shipping point* and *FOB destination*.
3. Find list price when net price and trade discount rate are known.
4. Calculate chain discounts with the net price equivalent rate and single equivalent discount rate.

LU 7–2: Cash Discounts, Credit Terms, and Partial Payments

1. List and explain typical discount periods and credit periods that a business may offer.
2. Calculate outstanding balance for partial payments.

VOCABULARY PREVIEW

Here are key terms in this chapter. After completing the chapter, if you know the term, place a checkmark in the box. If you don't know the term, look it up and put the page number where it can be found.

Cash discount ☐ Chain discounts ☐ Complement ☐ Credit period ☐ Discount period ☐ Due dates ☐ End of credit period ☐ End of month (EOM) ☐ FOB destination ☐ FOB shipping point ☐ Freight terms ☐ Invoice ☐ List price ☐ Net price ☐ Net price equivalent rate ☐ Ordinary dating ☐ Receipt of goods (ROG) ☐ Series discounts ☐ Single equivalent discount rate ☐ Single trade discount ☐ Terms of the sale ☐ Trade discount ☐ Trade discount amount ☐ Trade discount rate ☐

Do you think it was due to a misunderstanding that executives from Google used discounted fuel from the federal government for their private planes? The following *Wall Street Journal* article discusses this situation.

Google Execs Got Discount On Jet Fuel, NASA Says

BY MARK MAREMONT

Top **Google** Inc. executives saved millions of dollars by flying their private jet fleet on discounted fuel purchased from the federal government that they weren't entitled to buy, according to a new inspector general review released Wednesday.

Reprinted by permission of *The Wall Street Journal*, copyright 2013 Dow Jones & Company, Inc. All rights reserved worldwide.

This chapter discusses two types of discounts taken by retailers—trade and cash. A **trade discount** is a reduction off the original selling price (list price) of an item and is not related to early payment. A **cash discount** is the result of an early payment based on the terms of the sale.

Learning Unit 7–1: Trade Discounts—Single and Chain (Includes Discussion of Freight)

LO 1

The merchandise sold by retailers is bought from manufacturers and wholesalers who sell only to retailers and not to customers. These manufacturers and wholesalers offer retailer discounts so retailers can resell the merchandise at a profit. The discounts are off the manufacturers' and wholesalers' **list price** (suggested retail price), and the amount of discount that retailers receive off the list price is the **trade discount amount.** The below website of The Krazy Coupon Lady shows how consumers can get digital coupons. Keep in mind that retailers can track customer purchases and preferences. The smartphone is a great tool customers can use to find discounts and retailers can use to gather marketing data.

© iPhone/Alamy

When you make a purchase, the retailer (seller) gives you a purchase **invoice.** Invoices are important business documents that help sellers keep track of sales transactions and buyers keep track of purchase transactions. North Shore Community College Bookstore is a retail seller of textbooks to students. The bookstore usually purchases its textbooks directly from publishers. Figure 7.1 shows a sample of what a textbook invoice from McGraw-Hill Higher Education to the North Shore Community College Bookstore might look like. Note that the trade discount amount is given in percent. This is the **trade discount rate,** which is a percent off the list

price that retailers can deduct. The following formula for calculating a trade discount amount gives the numbers from the Figure 7.1 invoice in parentheses:

TRADE DISCOUNT AMOUNT FORMULA
Trade discount amount = List price × Trade discount rate
($2,887.50)   ($11,550)   (25%)

The price that the retailer (bookstore) pays the manufacturer (publisher) or wholesaler is the **net price.** In the chapter opener, the *Wall Street Journal* clipping shows how Staples won New York's office supply business with an amazing net price offer. The following formula for calculating the net price gives the numbers from the Figure 7.1 invoice in parentheses:

NET PRICE FORMULA					
Net price	=	List price	−	Trade discount amount
($8,662.50)		($11,550)		($2,887.50)

FIGURE 7.1

Bookstore invoice showing a trade discount

Invoice No.: 5582

McGraw-Hill Higher Education
1333 Burr Ridge Parkway
Burr Ridge, Illinois 60527

Date: July 8, 2016
Ship: Two-day UPS
Terms: 2/10, n/30

Sold to: North Shore Community College Bookstore
1 Ferncroft Road
Danvers, MA 01923

Description	Unit list price	Total amount
50 Financial Management—Block/Hirt	$195	$9,750.00
10 Introduction to Business—Nichols	180	1,800.00
	Total List Price	11,550.00
	Less: Trade Discount 25%	2,887.50
	Net Price	8,662.50
	Plus: Prepaid Shipping Charge	+125.00
	Total Invoice Amount	$8,787.50

© The McGraw-Hill Companies, Inc./John Flournoy, photographer

Frequently, manufacturers and wholesalers issue catalogs to retailers containing list prices of the seller's merchandise and the available trade discounts. To reduce printing costs when prices change, these sellers usually update the catalogs with new *discount sheets.* The discount sheet also gives the seller the flexibility of offering different trade discounts to different classes of retailers. For example, some retailers buy in quantity and service the products. They may receive a larger discount than the retailer who wants the manufacturer to service the products. Sellers may also give discounts to meet a competitor's price, to attract new retailers, and to reward the retailers who buy product-line products. Sometimes the ability of the retailer to negotiate with the seller determines the trade discount amount.

Retailers cannot take trade discounts on freight, returned goods, sales tax, and so on. Trade discounts may be single discounts or a chain of discounts. Before we discuss single trade discounts, let's study freight terms.

Freight Terms

The most common **freight terms** are *FOB shipping point* and *FOB destination.* These terms determine how the freight will be paid. The key words in the terms are *shipping point* and *destination.*

FOB shipping point means free on board at shipping point; that is, the buyer pays the freight cost of getting the goods to the place of business.

For example, assume that IBM in San Diego bought goods from Argo Suppliers in Boston. Argo ships the goods FOB Boston by plane. IBM takes title to the goods when the aircraft in Boston receives the goods, so IBM pays the freight from Boston to San Diego. Frequently, the seller (Argo) prepays the freight and adds the amount to the buyer's (IBM) invoice. When paying the invoice, the buyer takes the cash discount off the net price and adds the freight cost. FOB shipping point can be illustrated as follows:

FOB shipping point (Boston)

Boston

San Diego

Argo Suppliers
(IBM takes title here)

Buyer pays the freight

IBM
(Buyer pays the freight costs)

FOB destination means the seller pays the freight cost until it reaches the buyer's place of business. If Argo ships its goods to IBM FOB destination or FOB San Diego, the title to the goods remains with Argo. Then it is Argo's responsibility to pay the freight from Boston to IBM's place of business in San Diego. FOB destination can be illustrated as follows:

FOB destination (San Diego)

Boston

Argo Suppliers
(Has title)

Seller pays the freight

IBM
(Gets title on arrival of goods)

The following *Wall Street Journal* clippings show some new trends in shipping. Amazon wants to deliver packages by drone. UPS wants to cut down on theft of packages left on doorsteps by providing pickup locations for customers who do not want to wait at home.

GLOBAL

Amazon Makes Request To FAA to Test Drones

By Jack Nicas

Amazon.com Inc. formally requested permission from the Federal Aviation Administration to start testing drones, an important step toward the online retail giant's goal to use the devices to deliver packages.

Amazon first unveiled the plans in December, dubbing the proposed service Amazon Prime Air and saying drones would eventually be able to deliver small packages to customers in less than 30 minutes. In its petition to the FAA, posted Thursday, Amazon said it is now on its eighth- and ninth-generation drone prototypes, including some that can travel more than 50 miles an hour and carry five-pound packages, which would cover 86% of products it sells.

Reprinted by permission of *The Wall Street Journal*, copyright 2014 Dow Jones & Company, Inc. All rights reserved worldwide.

UPS Has a New Plan: Pick-Up at the Cleaners

By Laura Stevens

United Parcel Service Inc. on Wednesday said it is launching a service that will boost e-commerce profitability by cutting down on delivery stops, allowing customers to pick up their packages at dry cleaners, convenience stores and pharmacies.

Called "Access Point," it is designed for people who work, as well as those who live in big cities, where packages left on doorsteps could be stolen. UPS customers will no longer have to stay at home to sign for a package.

of those living in an urban area said it would be convenient to have items shipped to a local retailer when they aren't home to receive it themselves.

"The folks that live in cities -- if they're not home and they don't have a doorman, they can't get a package. So they browse online and shop in stores," says Alan Gershenhorn, chief commercial officer at UPS. "Now they'll be able to browse online and shop online."

Reprinted by permission of *The Wall Street Journal*, copyright 2014 Dow Jones & Company, Inc. All rights reserved worldwide.

Now you are ready for the discussion on single trade discounts.

Single Trade Discount

In the introduction to this unit, we showed how to use the trade discount amount formula and the net price formula to calculate the McGraw-Hill Higher Education textbook sale to the North Shore Community College Bookstore. Since McGraw-Hill Higher Education gave the bookstore only one trade discount, it is a **single trade discount.** In the following word problem, we use the formulas to solve another example of a single trade discount. Again, we will use a blueprint aid to help dissect and solve the word problem.

The Word Problem The list price of a Macintosh computer is $2,700. The manufacturer offers dealers a 40% trade discount. What are the trade discount amount and the net price?

	The facts	Solving for?	Steps to take	Key points
BLUEPRINT	List price: $2,700. Trade discount rate: 40%.	Trade discount amount. Net price.	Trade discount amount = List price × Trade discount rate. Net price = List price − Trade discount amount.	Trade discount amount Portion (?) Base × Rate ($2,700) (.40) List price Trade discount rate

Steps to solving problem

1. Calculate the trade discount amount. $2,700 × .40 = $1,080

2. Calculate the net price. $2,700 − $1,080 = $1,620

Now let's learn how to check the dealers' net price of $1,620 with an alternate procedure using a complement.

How to Calculate the Net Price Using Complement of Trade Discount Rate

The **complement** of a trade discount rate is the difference between the discount rate and 100%. The following steps show you how to use the complement of a trade discount rate:

> **CALCULATING NET PRICE USING COMPLEMENT OF TRADE DISCOUNT RATE**
>
> **Step 1.** To find the complement, subtract the single discount rate from 100%.
>
> **Step 2.** Multiply the list price times the complement (from Step 1).

Think of a complement of any given percent (decimal) as the result of subtracting the percent from 100%.

Step 1.   100%
             − 40 ← Trade discount rate
             ─────
              60% or .60

Portion (?) Base × Rate ($2,700) (.60) List price

The complement means that we are spending 60 cents per dollar because we save 40 cents per dollar. Since we planned to spend $2,700, we multiply .60 by $2,700 to get a net price of $1,620.

Step 2. $1,620 = $2,700 × .60

Note how the portion ($1,620) and rate (.60) relate to the same piece of the base ($2,700). The portion ($1,620) is smaller than the base, since the rate is less than 100%.

Be aware that some people prefer to use the trade discount amount formula and the net price formula to find the net price. Other people prefer to use the complement of the trade discount rate to find the net price. The result is always the same.

LO 3

Finding List Price When You Know Net Price and Trade Discount Rate The following formula has many useful applications:

> ### CALCULATING LIST PRICE WHEN NET PRICE AND TRADE DISCOUNT RATE ARE KNOWN
>
> $$\text{List price} = \frac{\text{Net price}}{\text{Complement of trade discount rate}}$$

Next, let's see how to dissect and solve a word problem calculating list price.

The Word Problem A Macintosh computer has a $1,620 net price and a 40% trade discount. What is its list price?

	The facts	Solving for?	Steps to take	Key points
BLUEPRINT	Net price: $1,620. Trade discount rate: 40%.	List price.	List price = $\dfrac{\text{Net price}}{\text{Complement of trade discount rate}}$	Net price — Portion ($1,620); Base (?) × Rate (.60); List price; 100% − 40%

Steps to solving problem

1. Calculate the complement of the trade discount.

$$\begin{array}{r} 100\% \\ -\ 40 \\ \hline 60\% = .60 \end{array}$$

2. Calculate the list price.

$$\frac{\$1,620}{.60} = \boxed{\$2,700}$$

Note that the portion ($1,620) and rate (.60) relate to the same piece of the base.

Let's return to the McGraw-Hill Higher Education invoice in Figure 7.1 and calculate the list price using the formula for finding list price when the net price and trade discount rate are known. The net price of the textbooks is $8,662.50. The complement of the trade discount rate is $100\% - 25\% = 75\% = .75$. Dividing the net price $8,662.50 by the complement .75 equals $11,550, the list price shown in the McGraw-Hill Higher Education invoice. We can show this as follows:

$$\frac{\$8,662.50}{.75} = \$11,550, \text{ the list price}$$

Chain Discounts

LO 4

Frequently, manufacturers want greater flexibility in setting trade discounts for different classes of customers, seasonal trends, promotional activities, and so on. To gain this flexibility, some sellers give **chain** or **series discounts**—trade discounts in a series of two or more successive discounts.

Sellers list chain discounts as a group, for example, 20/15/10. Let's look at how Mick Company arrives at the net price of office equipment with a 20/15/10 chain discount.

EXAMPLE The list price of the office equipment is $15,000. The chain discount is 20/15/10. The long way to calculate the net price is as follows:

Step 1	Step 2	Step 3	Step 4
$15,000	$15,000	$12,000	$10,200
× .20	− 3,000	− 1,800	− 1,020
$ 3,000	$12,000	$10,200	$ 9,180 net price
	× .15	× .10	
	$ 1,800	$ 1,020	

Note how we multiply the percent (in decimal) times the new balance after we subtract the previous trade discount amount. *Never add the 20/15/10 together.* For example, in Step 3, we change the last discount, 10%, to decimal form and multiply times $10,200. Remember that each percent is multiplied by a successively *smaller* base. You could write the 20/15/10 discount rate in any order and still arrive at the same net price. Thus, you would get the $9,180 net price if the discount were 10/15/20 or 15/20/10. However, sellers usually give the larger discounts first. *Never try to shorten this step process by adding the discounts.* Your net price will be incorrect because, when done properly, each percent is calculated on a different base.

Net Price Equivalent Rate   In the example above, you could also find the $9,180 net price with the **net price equivalent rate**—a shortcut method. Let's see how to use this rate to calculate net price.

CALCULATING NET PRICE USING NET PRICE EQUIVALENT RATE

Step 1. Subtract each chain discount rate from 100% (find the complement) and convert each percent to a decimal.

Step 2. Multiply the decimals. Do not round off decimals, since this number is the net price equivalent rate.

Step 3. Multiply the list price times the net price equivalent rate (Step 2).

The following word problem with its blueprint aid illustrates how to use the net price equivalent rate method.

The Word Problem   The list price of office equipment is $15,000. The chain discount is 20/15/10. What is the net price?

	The facts	Solving for?	Steps to take	Key points
BLUEPRINT	List price: $15,000. Chain discount: 20/15/10.	Net price.	Net price equivalent rate. Net price = List price × Net price equivalent rate.	Do not round net price equivalent rate.

Steps to solving problem

1. Calculate the complement of each rate and convert each percent to a decimal.

100%	100%	100%
− 20	− 15	− 10
80%	85%	90%
↓	↓	↓
.8	.85	.9

2. Calculate the net price equivalent rate. (Do not round.)

.8 × .85 × .9 = .612   Net price equivalent rate. For each $1, you are spending about 61 cents.

3. Calculate the net price (actual cost to buyer).

$15,000 × .612 = $9,180

Next we see how to calculate the trade discount amount with a simpler method. In the previous word problem, we could calculate the trade discount amount as follows:

$15,000 ← List price
− 9,180 ← Net price
$ 5,820 ← Trade discount amount

MONEY tips

Double-check invoices. On average 9 out of 10 invoices contain an error.

Single Equivalent Discount Rate You can use another method to find the trade discount by using the **single equivalent discount rate.**

CALCULATING TRADE DISCOUNT AMOUNT USING SINGLE EQUIVALENT DISCOUNT RATE	
Step 1.	Subtract the net price equivalent rate from 1. This is the single equivalent discount rate.
Step 2.	Multiply the list price times the single equivalent discount rate. This is the trade discount amount.

Let's now do the calculations.

Step 1.   1.000 ← If you are using a calculator, just press 1.
            − .612
             .388 ← This is the single equivalent discount rate.

Step 2. $15,000 × .388 = $5,820 → This is the trade discount amount.

Remember that when we use the net price equivalent rate, the buyer of the office equipment pays $.612 on each $1 of list price. Now with the single equivalent discount rate, we can say that the buyer saves $.388 on each $1 of list price. The .388 is the single equivalent discount rate for the 20/15/10 chain discount. Note how we use the .388 single equivalent discount rate as if it were the only discount.

Knowing the terminology for what you pay and what you save is an important step in understanding how to calculate net price and trade discount amounts. The pie charts show the terminology relating to each.

It's time to try the Practice Quiz.

LU 7–1 | **PRACTICE QUIZ**

Complete this Practice Quiz to see how you are doing.[1]

1. The list price of a dining room set with a 40% trade discount is $12,000. What are the trade discount amount and net price? (Use the complement method for net price.)
2. The net price of a video system with a 30% trade discount is $1,400. What is the list price?
3. Lamps Outlet bought a shipment of lamps from a wholesaler. The total list price was $12,000 with a 5/10/25 chain discount. Calculate the net price and trade discount amount. (Use the net price equivalent rate and single equivalent discount rate in your calculation.)

✓ **Solutions**

1. Dining room set trade discount amount and net price:

*For **extra help** from your authors—Sharon and Jeff—see the videos in Connect.*

These videos are also available on YouTube!

BLUEPRINT	The facts	Solving for?	Steps to take	Key points
	List price: $12,000. *Trade discount rate:* 40%.	Trade discount amount. Net price.	Trade discount amount = List price × Trade discount rate. Net price = List price × Complement of trade discount rate.	Trade discount amount — Portion (?) — Base × Rate ($12,000) (.40) — List price — Trade discount rate

---

[1]For all three problems we will show blueprint aids. You might want to draw them on scrap paper.

Steps to solving problem

1. Calculate the trade discount. $12,000 × .40 = $4,800 Trade discount amount

2. Calculate the net price. $12,000 × .60 = $7,200 (100% − 40% = 60%)

2. Video system list price:

	The facts	Solving for?	Steps to take	Key points
BLUEPRINT	Net price: $1,400. Trade discount rate: 30%.	List price.	List price = $$\frac{Net\ price}{Complement\ of\ trade\ discount}$$	Net price Portion ($1,400) Base × Rate (?) (.70) List price 100% −30%

Steps to solving problem

1. Calculate the complement of trade discount.   100%
                                                       − 30
                                                       ‾‾‾‾‾
                                                       70% = .70

2. Calculate the list price. $$\frac{\$1,400}{.70} = \$2,000$$

3. Lamps Outlet's net price and trade discount amount:

	The facts	Solving for?	Steps to take	Key points
BLUEPRINT	List price: $12,000. Chain discount: 5/10/25.	Net price. Trade discount amount.	Net price = List price × Net price equivalent rate. Trade discount amount = List price × Single equivalent discount rate.	Do not round off net price equivalent rate or single equivalent discount rate.

Steps to solving problem

1. Calculate the complement of each chain discount.

100%	100%	100%
− 5	− 10	− 25
95%	90%	75%

2. Calculate the net price equivalent rate.   .95 × .90 × .75 = .64125

3. Calculate the net price. $12,000 × .64125 = $7,695

4. Calculate the single equivalent discount rate.   1.00000
                                                     − .64125
                                                     ‾‾‾‾‾‾‾
                                                      .35875

5. Calculate the trade discount amount. $12,000 × .35875 = $4,305

LU 7–1a   **EXTRA PRACTICE QUIZ WITH WORKED-OUT SOLUTIONS**

Need more practice? Try this **Extra Practice Quiz** (check figures in the Interactive Chapter Organizer). Worked-out Solutions can be found in Appendix B.

1. The list price of a dining room set with a 30% trade discount is $16,000. What are the trade discount amount and net price? (Use the complement method for net price.)

2. The net price of a video system with a 20% trade discount is $400. What is the list price?

3. Lamps Outlet bought a shipment of lamps from a wholesaler. The total list price was $14,000 with a 4/8/20 chain discount. Calculate the net price and trade discount amount. (Use the net price equivalent rate and single equivalent discount rate in your calculation.)

Learning Unit 7–2: Cash Discounts, Credit Terms, and Partial Payments

LO 1

To introduce this learning unit, we will use the New Hampshire Propane Company invoice that follows. The invoice shows that if you pay your bill early, you will receive a 19-cent discount. Every penny counts.

© Ingram Publishing

New Hampshire Propane Company

Date	Description	Qty.	Price	Total
	Previous Balance			**$0.00**
06/24/16	PROPANE	3.60	$3.40	$12.24

Invoice No. 004433L	**Totals this invoice:** $12.24
	AMOUNT DUE: $12.24
Invoice Date 6/26/16	**Prompt Pay Discount: $0.19**
	Net Amount Due if RECEIVED by 07/10/16: $12.05
Due Date 7/26/16	

Now let's study cash discounts.

Cash Discounts

In the New Hampshire Propane Company invoice, we receive a cash discount of 19 cents. This amount is determined by the **terms of the sale,** which can include the credit period, cash discount, discount period, and freight terms.

Buyers can often benefit from buying on credit. The time period that sellers give buyers to pay their invoices is the **credit period.** Frequently, buyers can sell the goods bought during this credit period. Then, at the end of the credit period, buyers can pay sellers with the funds from the sales of the goods. When buyers can do this, they can use the consumer's money to pay the invoice instead of their money.

Sellers can also offer a cash discount, or reduction from the invoice price, if buyers pay the invoice within a specified time. This time period is the **discount period,** which is part of the total credit period. Sellers offer this cash discount because they can use the dollars to better advantage sooner than later. Buyers who are not short of cash like cash discounts because the goods will cost them less and, as a result, provide an opportunity for larger profits.

A cash discount is for prompt payment. A trade discount is not.

Trade discounts should be taken before cash discounts.

Remember that buyers do not take cash discounts on freight, returned goods, sales tax, and trade discounts. Buyers take cash discounts on the *net price* of the invoice. Before we discuss how to calculate cash discounts, let's look at some aids that will help you calculate credit **due dates** and **end of credit periods.**

Aids in Calculating Credit Due Dates Sellers usually give credit for 30, 60, or 90 days. Not all months of the year have 30 days. So you must count the credit days from the date of the invoice. The trick is to remember the number of days in each month. You can choose one of the following three options to help you do this.

Option 1: Days-in-a-Month Rule You may already know this rule. Remember that every 4 years is a leap year.

Years divisible by 4 are leap years. Leap years occur in 2012 and 2016.

> Thirty days has September, April, June, and November; all the rest have 31 except February has 28, and 29 in leap years.

Option 2: Knuckle Months Some people like to use the knuckles on their hands to remember which months have 30 or 31 days. Note in the following diagram that each knuckle represents a month with 31 days. The short months are in between the knuckles.

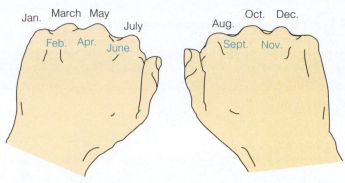

31 days: Jan., March, May, July, Aug., Oct., Dec.

A financial calculator can calculate maturity date, the number of days between dates and loan date.

Option 3: Days-in-a-Year Calendar The days-in-a-year calendar (excluding leap year) is another tool to help you calculate dates for discount and credit periods (Table 7.1). For example, let's use Table 7.1 to calculate 90 days from August 12.

EXAMPLE By Table 7.1: August 12 = 224 days
$$\begin{array}{r} 224 \\ +\ 90 \\ \hline 314 \end{array} \text{ days}$$

Search for day 314 in Table 7.1. You will find that day 314 is November 10. In this example, we stayed within the same year. Now let's try an example in which we overlap from year to year.

When using the days-in-a-year calendar, always put the number of days in the numerator and 365 (366 in leap years or 360 for ordinary interest) as the denominator.

EXAMPLE What date is 80 days after December 5?

Table 7.1 shows that December 5 is 339 days from the beginning of the year. Subtracting 339 from 365 (the end of the year) tells us that we have used up 26 days by the end of the year. This leaves 54 days in the new year. Go back in the table and start with the beginning of the year and search for 54 (80 − 26) days. The 54th day is February 23.

By table

365	days in year
− 339	days until December 5
26	days used in year

80	days from December 5
− 26	days used in year
54	days in new year or February 23

Without use of table

December	31
− December	5
	26
+ 31	days in January
	57
+ 23	due date (February 23)
80	total days

When you know how to calculate credit due dates, you can understand the common business terms sellers offer buyers involving discounts and credit periods. Remember that discount and credit terms vary from one seller to another.

Common Credit Terms Offered by Sellers

The common credit terms sellers offer buyers include *ordinary dating, receipt of goods (ROG),* and *end of month (EOM).* In this section we examine these credit terms. To determine the due dates, we used the exact days-in-a-year calendar (Table 7.1).

Ordinary Dating Today, businesses frequently use the **ordinary dating** method. It gives the buyer a cash discount period that begins with the invoice date. The credit terms of two common ordinary dating methods are 2/10, n/30 and 2/10, 1/15, n/30.

| TABLE | 7.1 | Exact days-in-a-year calendar (excluding leap year)* |

Day of month	31 Jan.	28 Feb.	31 Mar.	30 Apr.	31 May	30 June	31 July	31 Aug.	30 Sept.	31 Oct.	30 Nov.	31 Dec.
1	1	32	60	91	121	152	182	213	244	274	305	335
2	2	33	61	92	122	153	183	214	245	275	306	336
3	3	34	62	93	123	154	184	215	246	276	307	337
4	4	35	63	94	124	155	185	216	247	277	308	338
5	5	36	64	95	125	156	186	217	248	278	309	339
6	6	37	65	96	126	157	187	218	249	279	310	340
7	7	38	66	97	127	158	188	219	250	280	311	341
8	8	39	67	98	128	159	189	220	251	281	312	342
9	9	40	68	99	129	160	190	221	252	282	313	343
10	10	41	69	100	130	161	191	222	253	283	314	344
11	11	42	70	101	131	162	192	223	254	284	315	345
12	12	43	71	102	132	163	193	224	255	285	316	346
13	13	44	72	103	133	164	194	225	256	286	317	347
14	14	45	73	104	134	165	195	226	257	287	318	348
15	15	46	74	105	135	166	196	227	258	288	319	349
16	16	47	75	106	136	167	197	228	259	289	320	350
17	17	48	76	107	137	168	198	229	260	290	321	351
18	18	49	77	108	138	169	199	230	261	291	322	352
19	19	50	78	109	139	170	200	231	262	292	323	353
20	20	51	79	110	140	171	201	232	263	293	324	354
21	21	52	80	111	141	172	202	233	264	294	325	355
22	22	53	81	112	142	173	203	234	265	295	326	356
23	23	54	82	113	143	174	204	235	266	296	327	357
24	24	55	83	114	144	175	205	236	267	297	328	358
25	25	56	84	115	145	176	206	237	268	298	329	359
26	26	57	85	116	146	177	207	238	269	299	330	360
27	27	58	86	117	147	178	208	239	270	300	331	361
28	28	59	87	118	148	179	209	240	271	301	332	362
29	29	—	88	119	149	180	210	241	272	302	333	363
30	30	—	89	120	150	181	211	242	273	303	334	364
31	31	—	90	—	151	—	212	243	—	304	—	365

*Often referred to as a Julian calendar.

2/10, n/30 Ordinary Dating Method The 2/10, n/30 is read as "two ten, net thirty." Buyers can take a 2% cash discount off the gross amount of the invoice if they pay the bill within 10 days from the invoice date. If buyers miss the discount period, the net amount—without a discount—is due between day 11 and day 30. *Freight, returned goods, sales tax, and trade discounts must be subtracted from the gross before calculating a cash discount.*

EXAMPLE $400 invoice dated July 5: terms 2/10, n/30; no freight; paid on July 11.

Step 1. Calculate end of 2% discount period:

July 5 date of invoice

+ 10 days

July 15 end of 2% discount period

Step 2. Calculate end of credit period:

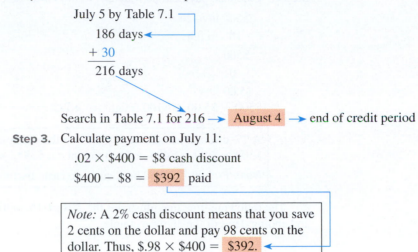

July 5 by Table 7.1

186 days

+ 30

216 days

Search in Table 7.1 for 216 → August 4 → end of credit period

Step 3. Calculate payment on July 11:

.02 × $400 = $8 cash discount

$400 − $8 = $392 paid

> *Note:* A 2% cash discount means that you save 2 cents on the dollar and pay 98 cents on the dollar. Thus, $.98 × $400 = $392.

The following time line illustrates the 2/10, n/30 ordinary dating method beginning and ending dates of the above example:

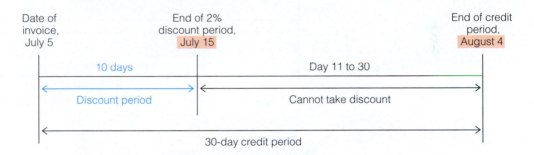

Date of invoice, July 5 — End of 2% discount period, July 15 — End of credit period, August 4

10 days | Day 11 to 30

Discount period | Cannot take discount

30-day credit period

2/10, 1/15, n/30 Ordinary Dating Method The 2/10, 1/15, n/30 is read "two ten, one fifteen, net thirty." The seller will give buyers a 2% (2 cents on the dollar) cash discount if they pay within 10 days of the invoice date. If buyers pay between day 11 and day 15 from the date of the invoice, they can save 1 cent on the dollar. If buyers do not pay on day 15, the net or full amount is due 30 days from the invoice date.

EXAMPLE $600 invoice dated May 8; $100 of freight included in invoice price; paid on May 22. Terms 2/10, 1/15, n/30.

Step 1. Calculate the end of the 2% discount period:

May   8 date of invoice

+ 10 days

May 18 end of 2% discount period

Step 2. Calculate end of 1% discount period:

May 18 end of 2% discount period

+   5 days

May 23 end of 1% discount period

Step 3. Calculate end of credit period:

May 8 by Table 7.1

128 days

+ 30

158 days

Search in Table 7.1 for 158 → June 7 → end of credit period

Step 4. Calculate payment on May 22 (14 days after date of invoice):

$600 invoice
-100 freight
$500
$\times$ .01
$5.00
$500 - $5.00 + $100 freight = $595

> A 1% discount means we pay $.99 on the dollar or
> $500 $\times$ $.99 = $495 + $100 freight = $595.
>
> *Note:* Freight is added back since no cash discount is taken on freight.

The following time line illustrates the 2/10, 1/15, n/30 ordinary dating method beginning and ending dates of the above example:

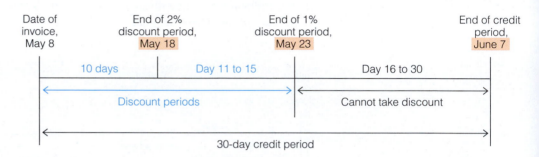

Receipt of Goods (ROG)

3/10, n/30 ROG With the **receipt of goods (ROG),** the cash discount period begins when buyer receives goods, *not* the invoice date. Industry often uses the ROG terms when buyers cannot expect delivery until a long time after they place the order. Buyers can take a 3% discount within 10 days *after* receipt of goods. The full amount is due between day 11 and day 30 if the cash discount period is missed.

EXAMPLE $900 invoice dated May 9; no freight or returned goods; the goods were received on July 8; terms 3/10, n/30 ROG; payment made on July 20.

Step 1.   Calculate the end of the 3% discount period:

July   8 date goods arrive
$+$ 10 days
July 18 end of 3% discount period

Step 2.   Calculate the end of the credit period:

July 8 by Table 7.1
189 days
$+$ 30
219 days

Search in Table 7.1 for 219 → August 7 → end of credit period

Step 3.   Calculate payment on July 20:

Missed discount period and paid net or full amount of $900.

The following time line illustrates 3/10, n/30 ROG beginning and ending dates of the above example:

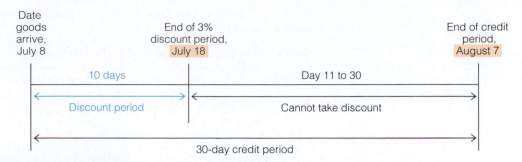

Date goods arrive, July 8		End of 3% discount period, July 18		End of credit period, August 7
	10 days		Day 11 to 30	
	← Discount period →		Cannot take discount	
←		30-day credit period		→

© Purestock/SuperStock

End of Month (EOM)[2]   In this section we look at invoices involving **end of month (EOM)** terms. If an invoice is dated the *25th or earlier* of a month, we follow one set of rules. If an invoice is dated after the 25th of the month, a new set of rules is followed. Let's look at each situation.

Invoice Dated 25th or Earlier in Month, 1/10 EOM   If sellers date an invoice on the 25th or earlier in the month, buyers can take the cash discount if they pay the invoice by the first 10 days of the month following the sale (next month). If buyers miss the discount period, the full amount is due within 20 days after the end of the discount period.

EXAMPLE $600 invoice dated July 6; no freight or returns; terms 1/10 EOM; paid on August 8.

Step 1.   Calculate the end of the 1% discount period:

　　　August 10 ←─────────────────────

　　　　　　　　　　　　First 10 days of month following sale.

Step 2.   Calculate the end of the credit period:

　　　August 10
　　　+ 20 days
　　　August 30 → Credit period is 20 days after discount period.

Step 3.   Calculate payment on August 8:

　　　.99 × $600 = $594

　　The following time line illustrates the beginning and ending dates of the EOM invoice of the previous example:

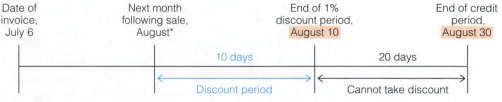

Date of invoice, July 6	Next month following sale, August*	End of 1% discount period, August 10	End of credit period, August 30
		10 days	20 days
		← Discount period →	← Cannot take discount →

*Even though the discount period begins with the next month following the sale, if buyers wish, they can pay before the discount period (date of invoice until the discount period).

Invoice Dated after 25th of Month, 2/10 EOM   When sellers sell goods *after* the 25th of the month, buyers gain an additional month. The cash discount period ends on the 10th day of the second month that follows the sale. Why? This occurs because the seller guarantees the 15 days' credit of the buyer. If a buyer bought goods on August 29, September 10 would be only 12 days. So the buyer gets the extra month.

[2]Sometimes the Latin term *proximo* is used. Other variations of EOM exist, but the key point is that the seller guarantees the buyer 15 days' credit. We assume a 30-day month.

EXAMPLE $800 invoice dated April 29; no freight or returned goods; terms 2/10 EOM; payment made on June 18.

Step 1. Calculate the end of the 2% discount period: ┐

June 10 ◄───────────────┘   First 10 days of second month following sale

Step 2. Calculate the end of the credit period: ──┐

June 10

$\underline{+\ 20}$ days

June 30 ◄─────────────── Credit period is 20 days after discount period.

Step 3. Calculate the payment on June 18:

No discount; $800 paid.

The following time line illustrates the beginning and ending dates of the EOM invoice of the above example:

Date of invoice, April 29	2nd month following sale, June*	End of 2% discount period, June 10	End of credit period, June 30
		10 days	20 days
		◄─── Discount period ───►	◄─ Cannot take discount ─►

*Even though the discount period begins with the second month following the sale, if buyers wish, they can pay before the discount date (date of invoice until the discount period).

Solving a Word Problem with Trade and Cash Discount

Now that we have studied trade and cash discounts, let's look at a combination that involves both a trade and a cash discount.

The Word Problem Hardy Company sent Regan Corporation an invoice for office equipment with a $10,000 list price. Hardy dated the invoice July 29 with terms of 2/10 EOM (end of month). Regan receives a 30% trade discount and paid the invoice on September 6. Since terms were FOB destination, Regan paid no freight charge. What was the cost of office equipment for Regan?

	The facts	Solving for?	Steps to take	Key points
BLUEPRINT	List price: $10,000. Trade discount rate: 30%. Terms: 2/10 EOM. Invoice date: 7/29. Date paid: 9/6.	Cost of office equipment.	Net price = List price × Complement of trade discount rate. After 25th of month for EOM. Discount period is 1st 10 days of second month that follows sale.	Trade discounts are deducted before cash discounts are taken. Cash discounts are not taken on freight or returns.

Steps to solving problem

1. Calculate the net price.

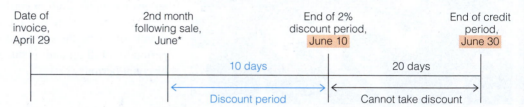

$10,000 × .70 = $7,000   100%
        − 30% (trade discount)

2. Calculate the discount period.   Sale: 7/29 Month 1: Aug. Month 2: Sept 10 ──► Paid on Sept. 6—is entitled to 2% off.

3. Calculate the cost of office equipment.

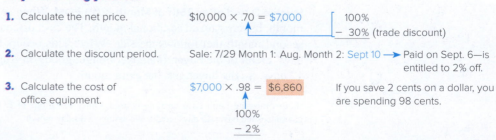

$7,000 × .98 = $6,860   If you save 2 cents on a dollar, you are spending 98 cents.

100%

− 2%

LO 2

MONEY tips

The formula for determining your credit score is roughly: 35% from your payment history (may include library fines and parking tickets); 30% determined by your debt to available credit ratio; 15% on the length of your credit history—the fewer and older the accounts, the better; 10% based on how many recent accounts were opened along with the number of inquiries made by lenders on your credit report; and, finally, 10% for the types of credit used.

Partial Payments

Often buyers cannot pay the entire invoice before the end of the discount period. To calculate partial payments and outstanding balance, use the following steps:

CALCULATING PARTIAL PAYMENTS AND OUTSTANDING BALANCE

Step 1. Calculate the complement of a discount rate.

Step 2. Divide partial payments by the complement of a discount rate (Step 1). This gives the amount credited.

Step 3. Subtract Step 2 from the total owed. This is the outstanding balance.

EXAMPLE   Molly McGrady owed $400. Molly's terms were 2/10, n/30. Within 10 days, Molly sent a check for $80. The actual credit the buyer gave Molly is as follows:

Step 1. $100\% - 2\% = 98\% \rightarrow .98$

Step 2. $\dfrac{\$80}{.98} = \$81.63$ $\qquad\qquad$ $\dfrac{\$80}{1 - .02}$ ← Discount rate

Step 3. $400.00

$\qquad$ $\underline{- \ 81.63}$ partial payment—although sent in $80

$\qquad$ $\boxed{\$318.37}$ outstanding balance

Note: We do not multiply $.02 \times \$80$ because the seller did not base the original discount on $80. When Molly makes a payment within the 10-day discount period, 98 cents pays each $1 she owes. Before buyers take discounts on partial payments, they must have permission from the seller. Not all states allow partial payments.

You have completed another unit. Let's check your progress.

LU 7–2 | **PRACTICE QUIZ**

Complete this **Practice Quiz** to see how you are doing.

Complete the following table:

	Date of invoice	Date goods received	Terms	Last day* of discount period	End of credit period
1.	July 6		2/10, n/30		
2.	February 19	June 9	3/10, n/30 ROG		
3.	May 9		4/10, 1/30, n/60		
4.	May 12		2/10 EOM		
5.	May 29		2/10 EOM		

*If more than one discount, assume date of last discount.

6. Metro Corporation sent Vasko Corporation an invoice for equipment with an $8,000 list price. Metro dated the invoice May 26. Terms were 2/10 EOM. Vasko receives a 20% trade discount and paid the invoice on July 3. What was the cost of equipment for Vasko? (A blueprint aid will be in the solution to help dissect this problem.)

7. Complete amount to be credited and balance outstanding:

Amount of invoice: $600
Terms: 2/10, 1/15, n/30
Date of invoice: September 30
Paid October 3: $400

*For **extra help** from your authors—Sharon and Jeff—see the videos in Connect.*

These videos are also available on YouTube!

✓ Solutions

1. End of discount period: July 6 + 10 days = July 16
End of credit period: By Table 7.1, July 6 =   187 days
                                             + 30 days
                                             217 → search ⟶ Aug. 5

2. End of discount period: June 9 + 10 days = July 19
End of credit period: By Table 7.1, June 9 =   160 days
                                             + 30 days
                                             190 → search ⟶ July 9

3. End of discount period: By Table 7.1, May 9 =   129 days
                                                     + 30 days
                                                     159 → search ⟶ June 8

End of credit period: By Table 7.1, May 9 =   129 days
                                            + 60 days
                                            189 → search ⟶ July 8

4. End of discount period: June 10
End of credit period: June 10 + 20 = June 30

5. End of discount period: July 10
End of credit period: July 10 + 20 = July 30

6. Vasko Corporation's cost of equipment:

	The facts	Solving for?	Steps to take	Key points
BLUEPRINT	List price: $8,000. Trade discount rate: 20%. Terms: 2/10 EOM. Invoice date: 5/26. Date paid: 7/3.	Cost of equipment.	Net price = List price × Complement of trade discount rate. EOM before 25th: Discount period is 1st 10 days of month that follows sale.	Trade discounts are deducted before cash discounts are taken. Cash discounts are not taken on freight or returns.

Steps to solving problem

1. Calculate the net price. $8,000 × .80 = $6,400   ⌐ 100%
                                                                                      └ − 20%
2. Calculate the discount period.   Until July 10
3. Calculate the cost of office equipment. $6,400 × .98 = $6,272

$$\left(\begin{array}{c}100\% \\ - 2\%\end{array}\right)$$

7. $\dfrac{\$400}{.98} = \$408.16$, amount credited.

$600 − $408.16 = $191.84, balance outstanding.

LU 7–2a   **EXTRA PRACTICE QUIZ WITH WORKED-OUT SOLUTIONS**

Need more practice? Try this Extra Practice Quiz (check figures in the Interactive Chapter Organizer). Worked-out Solutions can be found in Appendix B.

Complete the following table:

	Date of invoice	Date goods received	Terms	Last day of discount period*	End of credit period
1.	July 8		2/10, n/30		
2.	February 24	June 12	3/10, n/30 ROG		
3.	May 12		4/10, 1/30, n/60		
4.	April 14		2/10 EOM		
5.	April 27		2/10 EOM		

*If more than one discount, assume date of last discount.

6. Metro Corporation sent Vasko Corporation an invoice for equipment with a $9,000 list price. Metro dated the invoice June 29. Terms were 2/10 EOM. Vasko receives a 30% trade discount and paid the invoice on August 9. What was the cost of equipment for Vasko?

7. Complete amount to be credited and balance outstanding:

Amount of invoice: $700
Terms: 2/10, 1/15, n/30
Date of invoice: September 28
Paid October 3: $600

INTERACTIVE CHAPTER ORGANIZER

Topic/Procedure/Formula	Examples	You try it*
Trade discount amount $\text{Trade discount amount} = \text{List price} \times \text{Trade discount rate}$	$600 list price 30% trade discount rate Trade discount amount = $600 × .30 = $180	**Calculate trade discount amount** $700 list price 20% trade discount

Calculating net price
 	
 $\text{Net price} = \text{List price} - \text{Trade discount amount}$
 or
 $\text{List price} \times \text{Complement of trade discount price}$
	$600 list price
	 30% trade discount rate
	 Net price = $600 × .70 = $420
	   1.00
	  − .30
	   .70
		Calculate net price
		 $700 list price
		 20% trade discount

Freight FOB shipping point—buyer pays freight. FOB destination—seller pays freight.	Moose Company of New York sells equipment to Agee Company of Oregon. Terms of shipping are FOB New York. Agee pays cost of freight since terms are FOB shipping point.	**Calculate freight** If a buyer in Boston buys equipment with shipping terms of FOB destination, who will pay cost of freight?
Calculating list price when net price and trade discount rate are known $\text{List price} = \dfrac{\text{Net price}}{\text{Complement of trade discount rate}}$	40% trade discount rate Net price, $120 $\dfrac{\$120}{.60} = \$200$ list price (1.00 − .40)	**Calculate list price** 60% trade discount rate Net price, $240
Chain discounts Successively lower base.	5/10 on a $100 list item $ 100 $ 95 × .05 × .10 $ 5.00 $9.50 (running balance) $95.00 − 9.50 $85.50 net price	**Calculate net price** 6/8 on $200 list item

(continues)

INTERACTIVE CHAPTER ORGANIZER

Topic/Procedure/Formula	Examples	You try it*
Net price equivalent rate $\dfrac{\text{Actual cost}}{\text{to buyer}} = \dfrac{\text{List}}{\text{price}} \times \dfrac{\text{Net price}}{\text{equivalent rate}}$ Take complement of each chain discount and multiply—do not round. $\dfrac{\text{Trade discount}}{\text{amount}} = \dfrac{\text{List}}{\text{price}} - \dfrac{\text{Actual cost}}{\text{to buyer}}$	Given: 5/10 on $1,000 list price Take complement: .95 × .90 = .855 　　　　　　　　　　　(net price equivalent) $1,000 × .855 = **$855** 　　　　　　　　(actual cost or net price) 　　　　$1,000 　　− 　855 　　**$ 145**　trade discount amount	**Calculate net price equivalent rate, net price, and trade discount amount** 6/8 on $2,000 list
Single equivalent discount rate $\dfrac{\text{Trade discount}}{\text{amount}} = \dfrac{\text{List}}{\text{price}} \times \dfrac{1 - \text{Net price}}{\text{equivalent rate}}$	See preceding example for facts: 1 − .855 = .145 .145 × $1,000 = **$145**	**From the above You Try It, calculate single equivalent discount**
Cash discounts Cash discounts, due to prompt payment, are not taken on freight, returns, etc.	Gross　　$1,000 (includes freight) Freight　　$25　　　Terms 2/10, n/30 Returns　　$25　　Purchased: Sept. 9; 　　　　　　　　　　　paid Sept. 15 　Cash discount = $950 × .02 = **$19**	**Calculate cash discount** Gross　$2,000 (includes freight) Freight　　$40　　Terms 2/10, n/30 Returns　　$40　Purchased: Sept. 2; 　　　　　　　　　　paid Sept. 8
Calculating due dates *Option 1:* Thirty days has September, April, June, and November; all the rest have 31 except February has 28, and 29 in leap years. *Option 2:* Knuckles—31-day month; in between knuckles are short months. *Option 3:* Days-in-a-year table.	Invoice $500 on March 5; terms 2/10, n/30　　　　　　March　5 *End of discount*　　　　　　　+ 10 *period:*　　　　→　　**March 15** *End of credit*　　March 5 = 64 days *period by*　　　　　　　　+ 30 *Table 7.1:*　　　→　　94 days 　　Search in Table 7.1　**April 4**	**Calculate end of discount and end of credit periods** Invoice $600 on April 2; terms 2/10, n/30
Common terms of sale **a. Ordinary dating** Discount period begins from date of invoice. Credit period ends 20 days from the end of the discount period unless otherwise stipulated; example, 2/10, n/60—the credit period ends 50 days from end of discount period.	Invoice $600 (freight of $100 included in price) dated March 8; payment on March 16; 3/10, n/30.　March　8 *End of discount*　　　　　　　+ 10 *period:*　　　→　　**March 18** *End of credit*　March 8 =　67 days *period by*　　　　　　　　+ 30 *Table 7.1:*　　　→　　97 days 　　Search in Table 7.1　**April 7** *If paid on March 16:* .97 × $500 = $485 　　　　　　+ 100　freight 　　　　　　**$585**	**Calculate amount paid** Invoice $700 (freight of $100 included in price) dated May 7; payment May 15; 2/10, n/30

(continues)

INTERACTIVE CHAPTER ORGANIZER

Topic/Procedure/Formula	Examples	You try it*
b. Receipt of goods (ROG) Discount period begins when goods are received. Credit period ends 20 days from end of discount period.	4/10, n/30, ROG. $600 invoice; no freight; dated August 5; goods received October 2, payment made October 20. October 2 *End of discount* + 10 *period:* ⟶ October 12 *End of* October 2 = 275 *credit period* + 30 *by Table 7.1:* ⟶ 305 ↓ Search in Table 7.1 November 1 *Payment on October 20:* No discount, pay $600	**Calculate amount paid** 3/10, n/30, ROG. $700 invoice; no freight; dated September 6; goods received September 20; payment made October 15.
c. End of month (EOM) On or before 25th of the month, discount period is 10 days after month following sale. After 25th of the month, an additional month is gained.	$1,000 invoice dated May 12; no freight or returns; terms 2/10 EOM. *End of discount period* ⟶ June 10 *End of credit period* ⟶ June 30	**Calculate end of discount and end of credit periods** $2,000 invoice dated October 11; terms 2/10 EOM
Partial payments $\text{Amount credited} = \dfrac{\text{Partial payment}}{1 - \text{Discount rate}}$	$200 invoice; terms 2/10, n/30; dated March 2; paid $100 on March 5. $\dfrac{\$100}{1 - .02} = \dfrac{\$100}{.98} = \$102.04$	**Calculate amount credited** $400 invoice; terms 2/10, n/30; dated May 4; paid $300 on May 7.

KEY TERMS	Cash discount Chain discounts Complement Credit period Discount period Due dates End of credit period End of month (EOM) FOB destination	FOB shipping point Freight terms Invoice List price Net price Net price equivalent rate Ordinary dating Receipt of goods (ROG) Series discounts	Single equivalent discount rate Single trade discount Terms of the sale Trade discount Trade discount amount Trade discount rate

Check Figures for Extra Practice Quizzes. (Worked-out Solutions are in Appendix B.)	LU 7–1a **1.** $4,800 TD; $11,200 NP **2.** $500 **3.** $9,891.84 NP; TD $4,108.16	LU 7–2a **1.** July 18; Aug. 7 **2.** June 22; July 12 **3.** June 11; July 11 **4.** May 10; May 30 **5.** June 10; June 30 **6.** $6,174 **7.** a. $612.24 b. $87.76

*Worked-out solutions are in Appendix B.

Critical Thinking Discussion Questions with Chapter Concept Check

1. What is the net price? June Long bought a jacket from a catalog company. She took her trade discount off the original price plus freight. What is wrong with June's approach? Who would benefit from June's approach—the buyer or the seller?

2. How do you calculate the list price when the net price and trade discount rate are known? A publisher tells the bookstore its net price of a book along with a suggested trade discount of 20%. The bookstore uses a 25% discount rate. Is this ethical when textbook prices are rising?

3. If Jordan Furniture ships furniture FOB shipping point, what does that mean? Does this mean you get a cash discount?

4. What are the steps to calculate the net price equivalent rate? Why is the net price equivalent rate *not* rounded?

5. What are the steps to calculate the single equivalent discount rate? Is this rate off the list or net price? Explain why this calculation of a single equivalent discount rate may not always be needed.

6. What is the difference between a discount and credit period? Are all cash discounts taken before trade discounts? Do you agree or disagree? Why?

7. Explain the following credit terms of sale:

   a. 2/10, n/30.

   b. 3/10, n/30 ROG.

   c. 1/10 EOM (on or before 25th of month).

   d. 1/10 EOM (after 25th of month).

8. Explain how to calculate a partial payment. Whom does a partial payment favor—the buyer or the seller?

9. **Chapter Concept Check.** Search Facebook to find out what customer discounts companies offer to Facebook users. Be sure to talk about shipping charges and trade and cash discounts. What kind of savings can you find?

END-OF-CHAPTER PROBLEMS

Check figures for odd-numbered problems in Appendix C.   Name _____   Date _____

DRILL PROBLEMS

For all problems, round your final answer to the nearest cent. Do not round net price equivalent rates or single equivalent discount rates.

Complete the following: *LU 7-1(4)*

	Item	List price	Chain discount	Net price equivalent rate (in decimals)	Single equivalent discount rate (in decimals)	Trade discount	Net price
7–1.	Apple iPad	$799	3/1				
7–2.	Samsung Blu-Ray player	$199	8/4/3				
7–3.	Canon document scanner	$269	7/3/1				

Complete the following: *LU 7-1(4)*

	Item	List price	Chain discount	Net price	Trade discount
7–4.	Trotter treadmill	$3,000	9/4		
7–5.	Maytag dishwasher	$450	8/5/6		
7–6.	Sony digital camera	$320	3/5/9		
7–7.	Land Rover roofrack	$1,850	12/9/6		

7–8. Which of the following companies, A or B, gives a higher discount? Use the single equivalent discount rate to make your choice (convert your equivalent rate to the nearest hundredth percent).

eXcel

Company A	Company B
8/10/15/3	10/6/16/5

Complete the following: *LU 7-2(1)*

	Invoice	Date goods are received	Terms	Last day* of discount period	Final day bill is due (end of credit period)
7–9.	June 18		1/10, n/30		
7–10.	Nov. 27		2/10 EOM		
7–11.	May 15	June 5	3/10, n/30, ROG		
7–12.	April 10		2/10, 1/30, n/60		
7–13.	June 12		3/10 EOM		
7–14.	Jan. 10	Feb. 3 (no leap year)	4/10, n/30, ROG		

*If more than one discount, assume date of last discount.

Complete the following by calculating the cash discount and net amount paid: *LU 7-2(1)*

	Gross amount of invoice (freight charge already included)	Freight charge	Date of invoice	Terms of invoice	Date of payment	Cash discount	Net amount paid
7–15.	$7,000	$100	4/8	2/10, n/60	4/15		
7–16.	$600	None	8/1	3/10, 2/15, n/30	8/13		
7–17.	$200	None	11/13	1/10 EOM	12/3		
7–18.	$500	$100	11/29	1/10 EOM	1/4		

Complete the following: *LU 7-2(2)*

	Amount of invoice	Terms	Invoice date	Actual partial payment made	Date of partial payment	Amount of payment to be credited	Balance outstanding
7–19.	$700	2/10, n/60	5/6	$400	5/15		
7–20.	$600	4/10, n/60	7/5	$400	7/14		

WORD PROBLEMS (Round to Nearest Cent as Needed)

7–21. The list price of a smartphone is $299. A local Samsung dealer receives a trade discount of 20%. Find the trade discount amount and the net price. *LU 7-1(1)*

7–22. A model NASCAR race car lists for $79.99 with a trade discount of 40%. What is the net price of the car? *LU 7-1(1)*

eXcel

7–23. Lucky you! You went to couponcabin.com and found a 20% off coupon to your significant other's favorite store. Armed with that coupon, you went to the store only to find a storewide sale offering 10% off everything in the store. In addition, your credit card has a special offer that allows you to save 10% if you use your credit card for all purchases that day. Using your credit card, what will you pay before tax for the $155 gift you found? Use the single equivalent discount to calculate how much you save and then calculate your final price. *LU 7-1(4)*

7–24. Levin Furniture buys a living room set with a $4,000 list price and a 55% trade discount. Freight (FOB shipping point) of $50 is not part of the list price. What is the delivered price (including freight) of the living room set, assuming a cash discount of 2/10, n/30, ROG? The invoice had an April 8 date. Levin received the goods on April 19 and paid the invoice on April 25. *LU 7-1(1, 2)*

7–25. A manufacturer of skateboards offered a 5/2/1 chain discount to many customers. Bob's Sporting Goods ordered 20 skateboards for a total $625 list price. What was the net price of the skateboards? What was the trade discount amount? *LU 7-1(4)*

7–26. Home Depot wants to buy a new line of fertilizers. Manufacturer A offers a 21/13 chain discount. Manufacturer B offers a 26/8 chain discount. Both manufacturers have the same list price. What manufacturer should Home Depot buy from? *LU 7-1(4)*

eXcel

7–27. Maplewood Supply received a $5,250 invoice dated 4/15/16. The $5,250 included $250 freight. Terms were 4/10, 3/30, n/60. **(a)** If Maplewood pays the invoice on April 27, what will it pay? **(b)** If Maplewood pays the invoice on May 21, what will it pay? *LU 7-2(1)*

7–28. A local Sports Authority ordered 50 pairs of tennis shoes from Nike Corporation. The shoes were priced at $85 for each pair with the following terms: 4/10, 2/30, n/60. The invoice was dated October 15. Sports Authority sent in a payment on October 28. What should have been the amount of the check? *LU 7-2(1)*

eXcel

7–29. Macy of New York sold LeeCo. of Chicago office equipment with a $6,000 list price. Sale terms were 3/10, n/30 FOB New York. Macy agreed to prepay the $30 freight. LeeCo. pays the invoice within the discount period. What does LeeCo. pay Macy? *LU 7-2(2)*

eXcel

7–30. Royal Furniture bought a sofa for $800. The sofa had a $1,400 list price. What was the trade discount rate Royal received? Round to the nearest hundredth percent. *LU 7-2(1)*

7–31. The Consumer Electronics Show (CES) reports that the HP Spectre laptop computer starts at $999.99 for a base configuration. The model displayed at its recent show costs $1,399, $100 more than the comparable 13-inch Apple MacBook Air. If Computers-R-Us buys the HP Spectre at the show with 3/15, net 30 terms on August 22, how much does it need to pay on September 5? *LU 7-2(1)*

7–32. Bally Manufacturing sent Intel Corporation an invoice for machinery with a $14,000 list price. Bally dated the invoice July 23 with 2/10 EOM terms. Intel receives a 40% trade discount. Intel pays the invoice on August 5. What does Intel pay Bally? *LU 7-2(1)*

7–33. On August 1, Intel Corporation (Problem 7–32) returns $100 of the machinery due to defects. What does Intel pay Bally on August 5? Round to nearest cent. *LU 7-2(1)*

7–34. Stacy's Dress Shop received a $1,050 invoice dated July 8 with 2/10, 1/15, n/60 terms. On July 22, Stacy's sent a $242 partial payment. What credit should Stacy's receive? What is Stacy's outstanding balance? *LU 7-2(2)*

7–35. On March 11, Jangles Corporation received a $20,000 invoice dated March 8. Cash discount terms were 4/10, n/30. On March 15, Jangles sent an $8,000 partial payment. What credit should Jangles receive? What is Jangles' outstanding balance? *LU 7-2(2)*

7–36. A 2015 Porsche Macan Turbo starts at a consumer price of $72,300. If a dealership can purchase 10 with a 15/10/5 chain discount, what is the net price for the dealership? *LU 7-1(4)*

7–37. A local Barnes and Noble paid a $79.99 net price for each calculus textbook. The publisher offered a 20% trade discount. What was the publisher's list price? *LU 7-2(3)*

7–38. Rocky Mountain Chocolate Factory (RMCF) founder and president Frank Crail employs 220 people in 361 outlets in the United States, Canada, United Arab Emirates, Japan, South Korea, and Saudi Arabia. If RMCF purchases 20 kilograms of premium dark chocolate at $16.25 per kilo, what is the net price with a 10/5 chain discount? Round to the nearest cent. *LU 7-1(1)*

7–39. Vail Ski Shop received a $1,201 invoice dated July 8 with 2/10, 1/15, n/60 terms. On July 22, Vail sent a $485 partial payment. What credit should Vail receive? What is Vail's outstanding balance? *LU 7-2(2)*

7–40. True Value received an invoice dated 4/15/16. The invoice had a $5,500 balance that included $300 freight. Terms were 4/10, 3/30, n/60. True Value pays the invoice on April 29. What amount does True Value pay? *LU 7-1(1, 2)*

7–41. Baker's Financial Planners purchased seven new computers for $850 each. It received a 15% discount because it purchased more than five and an additional 6% discount because it took immediate delivery. Terms of payment were 2/10, n/30. Baker's pays the bill within the cash discount period. How much should the check be? Round to the nearest cent. *LU 7-1(4)*

7–42. On May 14, Talbots of Boston sold Forrest of Los Angeles $7,000 of fine clothes. Terms were 2/10 EOM FOB Boston. Talbots agreed to prepay the $80 freight. If Forrest pays the invoice on June 8, what will Forrest pay? If Forrest pays on June 20, what will Forrest pay? *LU 7-1(2), LU 7-2(1)*

7–43. Sam's Ski Boards.com offers 5/4/1 chain discounts to many of its customers. The Ski Hut ordered 20 ski boards with a total list price of $1,200. What is the net price of the ski boards? What was the trade discount amount? Round to the nearest cent. *LU 7-1(4)*

7–44. Majestic Manufacturing sold Jordans Furniture a living room set for an $8,500 list price with 35% trade discount. The $100 freight (FOB shipping point) was not part of the list price. Terms were 3/10, n/30 ROG. The invoice date was May 30. Jordans received the goods on July 18 and paid the invoice on July 20. What was the final price (include cost of freight) of the living room set? *LU 7-1(1, 2), LU 7-2(1)*

7–45. Boeing Truck Company received an invoice showing 8 tires at $110 each, 12 tires at $160 each, and 15 tires at $180 each. Shipping terms are FOB shipping point. Freight is $400; trade discount is 10/5; and a cash discount of 2/10, n/30 is offered. Assuming Boeing paid within the discount period, what did Boeing pay? *LU 7-1(4)*

7–46. Verizon offers to sell cellular phones listing for $99.99 with a chain discount of 15/10/5. Cellular Company offers to sell its cellular phones that list at $102.99 with a chain discount of 25/5. If Irene is to buy six phones, how much could she save if she buys from the lower-priced company? *LU 7-1(4)*

7–47. Living Ornaments is offering a special for wedding planners. Wedding flower orders totaling over $500 receive a 10% discount, over $750 a 15% discount, over $1,000 a 20% discount. All orders $1,500 and above receive a 25% discount. The delivery charge is $75 on weekdays and $125 on weekends. Terms are 2/10 EOM. WeddingsRUs placed an order for Thursday, June 1, delivery. The list price on the chosen flowers totals $848.50. Calculate the trade discount and the net price for the flowers to be delivered. How much does WeddingsRUs owe if they pay the invoice on July 10? (Round to the nearest cent.) *LU 7-2(1)*

CHALLENGE PROBLEMS

7–48. The original price of a 2015 Honda Insight to the dealer is $17,995, but the dealer will pay only $16,495 after rebate. If the dealer pays Honda within 15 days, there is a 1% cash discount. **(a)** How much is the rebate? **(b)** What percent is the rebate? Round to nearest hundredth percent. **(c)** What is the amount of the cash discount if the dealer pays within 15 days? **(d)** What is the dealer's final price? **(e)** What is the dealer's total savings? Round answer to the nearest hundredth. *LU 7-1(1), LU 7-2(1)*

7–49. On March 30, Century Television received an invoice dated March 28 from ACME Manufacturing for 50 televisions at a cost of $125 each. Century received a 10/4/2 chain discount. Shipping terms were FOB shipping point. ACME prepaid the $70 freight. Terms were 2/10 EOM. When Century received the goods, 3 sets were defective. Century returned these sets to ACME. On April 8, Century sent a $150 partial payment. Century will pay the balance on May 6. What is Century's final payment on May 6? Assume no taxes. *LU 7-1(1, 2, 4), LU 7-2(1)*

SUMMARY PRACTICE TEST (Round to the Nearest Cent as Needed)

Do you need help? The videos in Connect have step-by-step worked-out solutions. These videos are also available on YouTube!

Complete the following: *LU 7-1(1)*

	Item	List price	Single trade discount	Net price
1.	Apple iPod	$350	5%	
2.	Palm Pilot		10%	$190

Calculate the net price and trade discount (use net price equivalent rate and single equivalent discount rate) for the following: *LU 7-1(4)*

	Item	List price	Chain discount	Net price	Trade discount
3.	Sony HD flat-screen TV	$899	5/4		

4. From the following, what is the last date for each discount period and credit period?   *LU 7-1(1)*

	Date of invoice	Terms	End of discount period	End of credit period
a.	Nov. 4	2/10, n/30		
b.	Oct. 3, 2015	3/10, n/30 ROG (Goods received March 10, 2016)		
c.	May 2	2/10 EOM		
d.	Nov. 28	2/10 EOM		

5. Best Buy buys an iPod from a wholesaler with a $300 list price and a 5% trade discount. What is the trade discount amount? What is the net price of the iPod?   *LU 7-1(1)*

6. Jordan's of Boston sold Lee Company of New York computer equipment with a $7,000 list price. Sale terms were 4/10, n/30 FOB Boston. Jordan's agreed to prepay the $400 freight. Lee pays the invoice within the discount period. What does Lee pay Jordan's?   *LU 7-1(2), LU 7-2(1)*

7. Julie Ring wants to buy a new line of Tonka trucks for her shop. Manufacturer A offers a 14/8 chain discount. Manufacturer B offers a 15/7 chain discount. Both manufacturers have the same list price. Which manufacturer should Julie buy from?   *LU 7-1(4)*

8. Office.com received an $8,000 invoice dated April 10. Terms were 2/10, 1/15, n/60. On April 14, Office.com sent a $1,900 partial payment. What credit should Office.com receive? What is Office.com's outstanding balance? Round to the nearest cent.   *LU 7-2(2)*

9. Logan Company received from Furniture.com an invoice dated September 29. Terms were 1/10 EOM. List price on the invoice was $8,000 (freight not included). Logan receives an 8/7 chain discount. Freight charges are Logan's responsibility, but Furniture.com agreed to prepay the $300 freight. Logan pays the invoice on November 7. What does Logan Company pay Furniture.com?   *LU 7-1(4)*

RECYCLING AT SUBARU OF INDIANA AUTOMOTIVE

In 2002, Fuju Heavy Industries Ltd., parent company of Subaru of Indiana Automotive (SIA), challenged SIA with a goal no domestic manufacturing facility had achieved—zero landfill within 4 years. What seemed like a daunting goal was achieved in half the time by combining a comprehensive approach to identifying and eliminating waste with a powerful motivator.

Located in Lafayette, Indiana, SIA builds the Subaru Outback, Legacy, and Tribeca vehicle lines as well as the Toyota Camry in partnership with Toyota. SIA is currently the only Subaru auto assembly plant in the United States. Getting started on the zero landfill goal, SIA went about systematically identifying, weighing, and inventorying all waste in its 2.3 million-square-foot manufacturing facility, which performs integrated operations from stamping to final assembly.*

Once waste was identified, SIA made section managers responsible for the waste in their section and even went so far as to tie their bonus to waste elimination. Section managers along with their teams eagerly set out to find alternatives to the landfill.

For SIA, a key aspect of the solution included a rigorous approach to sorting waste and finding recyclers who were specifically interested in each type of waste and then only giving them that waste and nothing more. As an example, SIA sorts up to 17 different kinds of plastic. A second key component was SIA's partnership with Allegiant Global Services, which located recyclers, picked up waste line-side, and paid for all shipping charges.

For SIA's part, it invested in equipment that significantly reduced the volume and therefore cost of shipping waste. SIA compacts its cardboard, typically reducing 50–60 cubic yards of material to 2 cubic yards. Smaller bales weigh 350–400 lbs and large ones upwards of 1,000 lbs. SIA also has a bulb crusher on hand to crush fluorescent bulbs, separating the glass from the hazardous chemicals. This saves $2 per bulb to ship them to a recycler.

For its efforts, SIA was the first domestic auto plant to achieve Zero Landfill status in May 2004, the first to receive ISO 14001 certification, and the first to be officially designated a wildlife habitat. Clearly Subaru Indiana Automotive has found responsible environmental stewardship to be the right thing to do for the planet as well as for the bottom line.

Note: The following problems contain data that have been created by the author.

*Subaru of Indiana Automotive Inc. website: http://www.subaru-sia.com/Company/history/index.html.

PROBLEM 1

As the case states, Allegiant Global Services covers the cost of all shipping charges. If the terms included FOB for scraps Allegiant purchased from SIA, what would the terms specify? *Hint:* Research Allegiant's location to detail the terms fully.

PROBLEM 2

Suppose SIA sells each 350–400 lb bale of cardboard to Allegiant for $150. Further assume that SIA has 400 such bales to sell and offers a trade discount of 20% to Allegiant. What would the total trade discount be? What would the net price be? Round answers to the nearest dollar.

PROBLEM 3

If SIA offered a chain discount of 20/15/10 instead of the single discount, what would the net price equivalent rate be? Express your answer as a decimal and do not round.

PROBLEM 4

Suppose an invoice to Allegiant in the amount of $2,500 dated May 11 had the terms 2/10, 1/30, n/60. If the invoice were paid on June 1, how much would Allegiant owe SIA? Round your answer to the nearest dollar.

PROBLEM 5

If Allegiant were to pay $25,000 for recycled steel and SIA offered a 15% trade discount, what would the list price be? Round your answer to the nearest cent.

PROBLEM 6

Imagine an invoice to Allegiant in the amount of $15,250, dated September 8, that had the terms 2/10 EOM. If the invoice were paid on October 11, how much would Allegiant owe SIA? Round your answer to the nearest dollar.

PROBLEM 7

Suppose Allegiant had an invoice from SIA in the amount of $42,000, dated November 16. If the invoice had the terms 2/10, n/30 and Allegiant made a partial payment in the amount of $14,000 on November 23, what would the outstanding balance due be for the invoice? Round your answer to the nearest cent.

Class Discussion The case does not indicate whether Subaru Indiana Automotive has generated a net savings from its recycling efforts. Discuss the economics of the recycling program as you would anticipate them to be and determine whether you feel such a commitment would be warranted even if it cost SIA money to sustain the program.

SURF TO SAVE

PROBLEM 1
Free shipping!

Visit www.staples.com and search for DVD+RW media. Select enough of the DVD+RWs to equal an amount over $45 in order to qualify for free shipping. How much did you save on shipping? What is your discount percent when you receive free shipping on your order?

Discussion Questions

1. Why do online merchants require a certain minimum dollar purchase before giving free shipping?
2. What other incentives could the online merchant use to achieve the same goal?

PROBLEM 2
Early payment penalty?

Go to https://www.arvestbiz.com/calculators/calc_should_i_take_advantage_of_trade_discounts. Assume the following on a recent purchase you made for your small business: 30 days to make full payment, 15 days to make early payment, 3% trade discount, $45,000 annual invoice amount, and 6.5% loan interest rate. Based on these figures, should you take advantage of the trade discount?

Discussion Questions

1. What are the pros and cons of paying early for the buyer?
2. What are the benefits to companies in offering a trade discount?

PROBLEM 3
Software discounts

Go to http://www.amazon.com/software-for-students/b/ref=sv_sw_2?ie=UTF8&node=2649139011. Search for the best sellers in Software for Students and select a software program of interest to you that has a discount off the stated list price. What is the discount off the suggested list price in dollars as well as a percentage?

Discussion Questions

1. What are some reasons why the software manufacturer would offer such discounts on the software you selected?
2. Other than discounts, what incentives could the seller offer to give consumers a good deal?

PROBLEM 4
Money in bloom!

Go to http://ww11.1800flowers.com. Click on "Deal of the Week". Select any of the flower deals and calculate the discount percentage.

Discussion Questions

1. Why would 1-800-Flowers run promotions such as the Deal of the Week?
2. If there is a deal every week that allows you to save money on flowers, would you ever purchase from its standard flower arrangements? Why?

MOBILE APPS ✕

Calculate Discount & Sales Tax (Blue Sodium Corp) Helps calculate discounts in percentages or as dollar values.

Discount Calculator (ChuChu Train Productions) Calculates the prices of items after applying discounts to determine item cost and amount saved.

A KIPLINGER APPROACH

By Sandra Block, From *Kiplinger's Personal Finance*, November 2014.
By Lisa Gerstner, From *Kiplinger's Personal Finance*, November 2014.

■ KATHLEEN O'MALLEY STILL EXPECTS TO SAVE MONEY.

■ TRAVEL

A NEW TAX ON THE SHARING ECONOMY

Airbnb guests will now have to pay more.

KATHLEEN O'MALLEY FIRST used Airbnb in the summer of 2013, when she traveled through Washington State and British Columbia with her fiancé. After that, "we were hooked," says O'Malley of Portland, Ore. The couple used Airbnb to book a cottage in Sonoma for their honeymoon in September.

Airbnb connects budget-minded travelers with homeowners who have a room, apartment or house to rent. Soon, guests could pay more to sleep on someone's fold-out couch. In July, Airbnb began collecting 11.5% in city and county lodging taxes for bookings in Portland. Airbnb plans to expand the program to San Francisco, which charges a 14% hotel tax. From there, "we'll take the lessons we've learned and

move forward," says Airbnb spokesman Nick Papas.

The move is an attempt to forestall regulation that threatens to slow the company's growth. Other enterprises in the "sharing economy" are similarly pursuing agreements with state and local governments amid concerns about unfair advantages over more-traditional businesses. For instance, Colorado recently enacted legislation that authorizes ride-sharing services, such as Lyft and Uber, to operate in the state, provided drivers undergo background checks and obtain insurance.

O'Malley, founder of FrugalPortland.com, says occupancy taxes won't deter her from using Airbnb. It's still cheaper than a hotel, she says. **SANDRA BLOCK**

■ WHAT'S THE DEAL

HIGHER RATES ON STORE CARDS

Retailers dangle discounts, but you'll pay more to carry a balance.

AS YOU SHOP FOR HOLIDAY gifts, you may be tempted to open a store credit card and charge a big purchase—especially if the cashier dangles a discount of, say, 20% for signing up. But don't be dazzled by the discount if you're likely to carry a balance. The average annual percentage rate on credit cards from the country's largest retailers is 23.23%, according to a CreditCards.com survey. That's about two percentage points higher than in 2010 and more than eight percentage points higher than the average APR for standard credit cards. If you charge $500 on a card with a 23.23% rate and make a $20 payment every month, it will take you nearly three years to pay it off. You'll spend $190 in interest, outweighing any savings you'd capture by opening the card.

Still, a store card could make sense if you pay off the balance each billing cycle (or before an introductory 0% APR offer ends, if you are lucky enough to snag one). The same survey found that retailers are juicing up rewards, with some providing tiered bonuses that become better as you spend more. For example, a Macy's cardholder who spends up to $499 a year at the store

receives three annual mailings of discount coupons; someone who spends $1,000 or more per year at Macy's gets 12 mailings, plus other bonuses.

Credit limits on store cards tend to be lower than for general-purpose cards, says John Ganotis, founder of CreditCardInsider.com. Try to keep your spending on a card at no more than 20% to 30% of its limit to maintain your credit score. And avoid applying for several cards while you're on a shopping spree. A cluster of inquiries on your credit report as a result will send a negative signal to lenders and could damage your score. **LISA GERSTNER**

EXCERPT FROM
The Kiplinger Letter

PRIVACY TAKES CENTER STAGE

States are stepping up Internet privacy laws and policies. Most states require that consumers be notified of stolen credit card data, mailing addresses or phone numbers. In California, stolen passwords also trigger notification. Arizona and California prevent online booksellers and libraries from disclosing the books you order. Other laws make it easy to remove embarrassing details from online sites. (www.kiplinger biz.com/ahead/privacy)

SUSAN SEUBERT

BUSINESS MATH ISSUE

Store credit cards get you the highest discounts.

1. List the key points of the article and information to support your position.
2. Write a group defense of your position using math calculations to support your view.

Markups and Markdowns: Perishables and Breakeven Analysis

© Justin Sullivan/Getty Images

Pepper ... And Salt

THE WALL STREET JOURNAL

"It's not a fair fight. Online retailers know more about me than I do."

From *The Wall Street Journal*, permission Cartoon Features Syndicate.

Apple is not a participant in or sponsor of this promotion. Apple and the Apple logo are trademarks of Apple Inc. registered in the U.S. and other countries. Apply Pay is a trademark of Apple Inc.

Apple Pay Rolls Out, With Holes In System

By Daisuke Wakabayashi and Greg Bensinger

Starting Monday, **Apple** Inc. will begin its bold undertaking to add a wallet to its iPhones.

The iPhone already has pushed aside many once-independent devices, including cameras and GPS navigation systems. Now, Apple's new payment service will enable shoppers to buy items at more than 220,000 stores or inside apps using an iPhone and thumbprint.

Participants in the Apple Pay service include McDonald's, Whole Foods and Walgreen. Yet it won't be ubiquitous overnight.

Many retailers—including the nation's largest, **Wal-Mart Stores** Inc.—aren't part of Apple's network. Only a minority have machines capable of reading the near-field communication radio signal that makes Apple Pay work. And only Apple's newest phones, the iPhone 6 and iPhone 6 Plus, include the technology.

Apple has signed up the six biggest card issuers, accounting for roughly 83% of credit-card transactions, with 500 financial institutions coming by early next year.

Reprinted by permission of *The Wall Street Journal*, copyright 2014 Dow Jones & Company, Inc. All rights reserved worldwide.

LU 8–1: Markups[1] Based on Cost (100%)

1. Calculate dollar markup and percent markup on cost.
2. Calculate selling price when you know the cost and percent markup on cost.
3. Calculate cost when you know the selling price and percent markup on cost.

LU 8–2: Markups Based on Selling Price (100%)

1. Calculate dollar markup and percent markup on selling price.
2. Calculate selling price when cost and percent markup on selling price are known.
3. Calculate cost when selling price and percent markup on selling price are known.
4. Convert from percent markup on cost to percent markup on selling price and vice versa.

LU 8–3: Markdowns and Perishables

1. Calculate markdowns; compare markdowns and markups.
2. Price perishable items to cover spoilage loss.

LU 8–4: Breakeven Analysis

1. Calculate contribution margin.
2. Calculate breakeven point.

VOCABULARY PREVIEW

Here are key terms in this chapter. After completing the chapter, if you know the term, place a checkmark in the box. If you don't know the term, look it up and put the page number where it can be found.

Breakeven point ☐ **Contribution margin** ☐ **Cost** ☐ **Dollar markdown** ☐ **Dollar markup** ☐ **Fixed cost** ☐ **Gross profit** ☐ **Margin** ☐ **Markdowns** ☐ **Markup** ☐ **Net profit (net income)** ☐ **Operating expenses (overhead)** ☐ **Percent markup on cost** ☐ **Percent markup on selling price** ☐ **Perishables** ☐ **Selling price** ☐ **Variable cost** ☐

Gap Inc., which owns Gap, Banana Republic and Old Navy stores and websites, began inviting Web and mobile shoppers last year to "reserve in store." Shoppers reserve an item and a pickup location using one of the brand websites or apps. An employee picks the item from the selling floor and scans it to confirm the size and style. Shoppers receive an email or text when the order is ready.

Source: *The Wall Street Journal,* 12/9/14.

The chapter opening cartoon talks about tracking customers. Many retailers will send specific catalogues based on consumer buying habits. Now let's turn our attention to a store you may be familiar with—Gap. Note in the *Wall Street Journal* clip to the left, Gap is increasing its use of technology by allowing customers to shop online and pick up their merchandise at the store.

We will look at some of Gap's pricing options for its fleece hoody jackets. Before we study the two pricing methods available to Gap (percent markup on cost and percent markup on selling price), we must know the following terms:

- **Selling price.** The price retailers charge consumers. The total selling price of all the goods sold by a retailer (like Gap) represents the retailer's total sales.

- **Cost.** The price retailers pay to a manufacturer or supplier to bring the goods into the store.

- **Markup, margin,** or **gross profit.** These three terms refer to the difference between the cost of bringing the goods into the store and the selling price of the goods.

[1]Some texts use the term *markon* (selling price minus cost).

© The McGraw-Hill Companies, Inc./Andrew Resek, photographer

- **Operating expenses** or **overhead.** The regular expenses of doing business such as wages, rent, utilities, insurance, and advertising.

- **Net profit** or **net income.** The profit remaining after subtracting the cost of bringing the goods into the store and the operating expenses from the sale of the goods (including any returns or adjustments). In Learning Unit 8–4 we will take a closer look at the point at which costs and expenses are covered. This is called the *breakeven* point.

From these definitions, we can conclude that *markup* represents the amount that retailers must add to the cost of the goods to cover their operating expenses and make a profit.[2]

Let's assume Gap plans to sell hooded fleece jackets for $23 that cost $18.[3]

Basic selling price formula

| Selling price (S) | = | Cost (C) | + | Markup (M) |

| $23 | = | $18 | + | $5 |
| | | (price paid to bring fleece jackets into store) | | (amount in dollars to cover operating expenses and make a profit) |

In the Gap example, the markup is a dollar amount, or a **dollar markup.** Markup is also expressed in percent. When expressing markup in percent, retailers can choose a percent based on *cost* (Learning Unit 8–1) or a percent based on *selling price* (Learning Unit 8–2).

When you go out to dinner at a salad bar, you might be amazed to discover how much certain foods are marked up. For example, at one restaurant, potatoes are marked up 62.5% and shrimp are marked up 75%. Now let's look at how to calculate markup percents.

Learning Unit 8–1: Markups Based on Cost (100%)

In Chapter 6 you were introduced to the portion formula, which we used to solve percent problems. We also used the portion formula in Chapter 7 to solve problems involving trade and cash discounts. In this unit you will see how we use the basic selling price formula and the portion formula to solve percent markup situations based on cost. We will be using blueprint aids to show how to dissect and solve all word problems in this chapter.

Many manufacturers mark up goods on cost because manufacturers can get cost information more easily than sales information. Since retailers have the choice of using percent markup on cost or selling price, in this unit we assume Gap has chosen percent markup on cost. In Learning Unit 8–2 we show how Gap would determine markup if it decided to use percent markup on selling price.

Businesses that use **percent markup on cost** recognize that cost is 100%. This 100% represents the base of the portion formula. All situations in this unit use cost as 100%.

For markups based on cost, the base is always cost (C).

To calculate percent markup on cost, we will use the hooded fleece jacket sold by Gap and begin with the basic selling price formula given in the chapter introduction. When we know the dollar markup, we can use the portion formula to find the percent markup on cost.

Markup expressed in dollars:

Selling price ($23) = Cost ($18) + Markup ($5)

Markup expressed as a percent markup on cost:

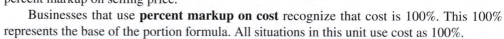

Cost	100.00%
+ Markup	+ 27.78
= Selling price	127.78%

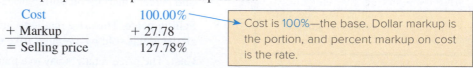

Cost is 100%—the base. Dollar markup is the portion, and percent markup on cost is the rate.

---

[2]In this chapter, we concentrate on the markup of retailers. Manufacturers and suppliers also use markup to determine selling price.

[3]These may not be actual store prices but we assume these prices in our examples.

In Situation 1 (below) we show why Gap has a 27.78% markup (dollar markup [$5] divided by cost [$18]) based on cost by presenting the hooded fleece jacket as a word problem. We solve the problem with the blueprint aid used in earlier chapters. In the second column, however, you will see footnotes after two numbers. These refer to the steps we use below the blueprint aid to solve the problem. Throughout the chapter, the numbers that we are solving for are in red. Remember that cost is the base for this unit.

LO 1

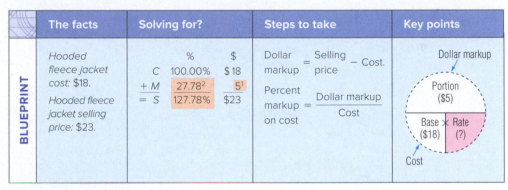

Dollar markup

Portion

Base × Rate

Cost

Percent markup on cost

Situation 1: Calculating Dollar Markup and Percent Markup on Cost

Dollar markup is calculated with the basic selling price formula $S = C + M$. When you know the cost and selling price of goods, reverse the formula to $M = S - C$. Subtract the cost from the selling price, and you have the dollar markup.

The percent markup on cost is calculated with the portion formula. For Situation 1 the *portion* (P) is the dollar markup, which you know from the selling price formula. In this unit the *rate* (R) is always the percent markup on cost and the *base* (B) is always the cost (100%). To find the percent markup on cost (R), use the portion formula $R = \frac{P}{B}$ and divide the dollar markup (P) by the cost (B). Convert your answer to a percent and round if necessary.

Now we will look at the Gap example to see how to calculate the 27.78% markup on cost.

The Word Problem The Gap pays $18 for a hooded fleece jacket, which the store plans to sell for $23. What is Gap's dollar markup? What is the percent markup on cost (rounded to the nearest hundredth percent)?

	The facts	Solving for?	Steps to take	Key points
BLUEPRINT	Hooded fleece jacket cost: $18. Hooded fleece jacket selling price: $23.	% $ C 100.00% $18 $+M$ 27.78² 5¹ $=S$ 127.78% $23	$\dfrac{\text{Dollar}}{\text{markup}} = \dfrac{\text{Selling}}{\text{price}} - \text{Cost.}$ $\dfrac{\text{Percent}}{\text{markup}}_{\text{on cost}} = \dfrac{\text{Dollar markup}}{\text{Cost}}$	Dollar markup Portion ($5) Base × Rate ($18) (?) Cost

¹Dollar markup. See Step 1, below.
²Percent markup on cost. See Step 2, below.

Steps to solving problem

1. Calculate the dollar markup.

Dollar markup = Selling price − Cost

$5 = $23 − $18

2. Calculate the percent markup on cost.

Percent markup on cost = $\dfrac{\text{Dollar markup}}{\text{Cost}}$

$= \dfrac{\$5}{\$18} = 27.78\%$

To check the percent markup on cost, you can use the basic selling price formula $S = C + M$. Convert the percent markup on cost found with the portion formula to a decimal and multiply it by the cost. This gives the dollar markup. Then add the cost and the dollar markup to get the selling price of the goods.

You could also check the cost (B) by dividing the dollar markup (P) by the percent markup on cost (R).

Check

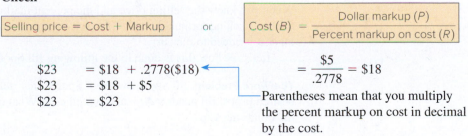

Selling price = Cost + Markup   or   Cost (B) = $\dfrac{\text{Dollar markup }(P)}{\text{Percent markup on cost }(R)}$

$23 = $18 + .2778($18)
$23 = $18 + $5
$23 = $23

$= \dfrac{\$5}{.2778} = \$18$

Parentheses mean that you multiply the percent markup on cost in decimal by the cost.

LO 2

Situation 2: Calculating Selling Price When You Know Cost and Percent Markup on Cost

When you know the cost and the percent markup on cost, you calculate the selling price with the basic selling formula $S = C + M$. Remember that when goods are marked up on cost, the cost is the base (100%). So you can say that the selling price is the cost plus the markup in dollars (percent markup on cost times cost).

Now let's look at Mel's Furniture where we calculate Mel's dollar markup and selling price.

The Word Problem Mel's Furniture bought a lamp that cost $100. To make Mel's desired profit, he needs a 65% markup on cost. What is Mel's dollar markup? What is his selling price?

BLUEPRINT	The facts	Solving for?	Steps to take	Key points
	Lamp cost: $100. Markup on cost: 65%.	% $ C 100% $100 $+ M$ 65 65^1 $= S$ 165% $165^2	Dollar markup: $S = C + M$. or $S = \text{Cost} \times \left(1 + \begin{array}{c}\text{Percent}\\\text{markup}\\\text{on cost}\end{array}\right)$	Selling price Portion (?) Base × Rate ($100) (1.65) Cost 100% +65%

^{1}Dollar markup. See Step 1, below.
^{2}Selling price. See Step 2, below.

Steps to solving problem

1. Calculate the dollar markup.
$$S = C + M$$
$$S = \$100 + .65(\$100) \longleftarrow \text{Parentheses mean you multiply the percent markup in decimal by the cost.}$$
$$S = \$100 + \boxed{\$65} \longleftarrow \text{Dollar markup}$$

2. Calculate the selling price.
$$S = \boxed{\$165}$$

You can check the selling price with the formula $P = B \times R$. You are solving for the portion (P)—the selling price. Rate (R) represents the 100% cost plus the 65% markup on cost. Since in this unit the markup is on cost, the base is the cost. Convert 165% to a decimal and multiply the cost by 1.65 to get the selling price of $165.

Check

$$\underset{(P)}{\text{Selling price}} = \underset{(B)}{\text{Cost}} \times \underset{(R)}{(1 + \text{Percent markup on cost})} = \$100 \times 1.65 = \boxed{\$165}$$

LO 3

Situation 3: Calculating Cost When You Know Selling Price and Percent Markup on Cost

When you know the selling price and the percent markup on cost, you calculate the cost with the basic selling formula $S = C + M$. Since goods are marked up on cost, the percent markup on cost is added to the cost.

Let's see how this is done in the following Jill Sport example.

The Word Problem Jill Sport, owner of Sports, Inc., sells tennis rackets for $50. To make her desired profit, Jill needs a 40% markup on cost. What do the tennis rackets cost Jill? What is the dollar markup?

	The facts	Solving for?	Steps to take	Key points
BLUEPRINT	Selling price: $50. Markup on cost: 40%.	% $ C 100% $35.71[1] + M 40 14.29[2] = S 140% $50.00	$S = C + M.$ or $Cost = \dfrac{\text{Selling price}}{\text{Percent}}$ $1 + \text{markup}$ on cost $M = S - C.$	Selling price Portion ($50) Base × Rate (?) (1.40) 100% Cost +40%

[1]Cost. See Step 1, below.

[2]Dollar markup. See Step 2, below.

Steps to solving problem

1. Calculate the cost.

$$S = C + M$$
$$\$50.00 = C + .40C \leftarrow$$ This means 40% times cost. C is
$$\frac{\$50.00}{1.40} = \frac{1.40C}{1.40}$$ the same as 1C. Adding .40C to 1C
$$\boxed{\$35.71} = C$$ gives the percent markup on cost of 1.40C in decimal.

2. Calculate the dollar markup.

$$M = S - C$$
$$M = \$50.00 - \$35.71$$
$$M = \boxed{\$14.29}$$

MONEY tips

Automate your savings. Save more money from each paycheck starting now. If you have 1% automatically taken out of your check, you will never miss it. Over time, it can add up to six figures and will help you start building a financially healthy retirement today.

You can check your cost answer with the portion formula $B = \frac{P}{R}$. Portion (P) is the selling price. Rate (R) represents the 100% cost plus the 40% markup on cost. Convert the percents to decimals and divide the portion by the rate to find the base, or cost.

Check

$$\text{Cost } (B) = \frac{\text{Selling price } (P)}{1 + \text{Percent markup on cost } (R)} = \frac{\$50.00}{1.40} = \boxed{\$35.71}$$

Now try the following Practice Quiz to check your understanding of this unit.

LU 8–1   PRACTICE QUIZ

Complete this **Practice Quiz** to see how you are doing.

Solve the following situations (markups based on cost):

1. Irene Westing bought a desk for $400 from an office supply house. She plans to sell the desk for $600. What is Irene's dollar markup? What is her percent markup on cost? Check your answer.

2. Suki Komar bought dolls for her toy store that cost $12 each. To make her desired profit, Suki must mark up each doll 35% on cost. What is the dollar markup? What is the selling price of each doll? Check your answer.

3. Jay Lyman sells calculators. His competitor sells a new calculator line for $14 each. Jay needs a 40% markup on cost to make his desired profit, and he must meet price competition. At what cost can Jay afford to bring these calculators into the store? What is the dollar markup? Check your answer.

For **extra help** from your authors–Sharon and Jeff–see the videos in Connect.

These videos are also available on YouTube!

✓ Solutions

1. Irene's dollar markup and percent markup on cost:

BLUEPRINT	The facts	Solving for?			Steps to take	Key points
	Desk cost: $400.		%	$	Dollar markup = Selling price − Cost.	Dollar markup
		C	100%	$400		Portion ($200)
	Desk selling price: $600.	+ M	50[2]	200[1]	Percent markup on cost = Dollar markup / Cost	Base × Rate ($400) (?)
		= S	150%	$600		Cost

[1]Dollar markup. See Step 1, below.
[2]Percent markup on cost. See Step 2, below.

Steps to solving problem

1. Calculate the dollar markup.

$$\text{Dollar markup} = \text{Selling price} - \text{Cost}$$
$$\$200 = \$600 - \$400$$

2. Calculate the percent markup on cost.

$$\text{Percent markup on cost} = \frac{\text{Dollar markup}}{\text{Cost}}$$
$$= \frac{\$200}{\$400} = 50\%$$

Check

Selling price = Cost + Markup **or** $\text{Cost }(B) = \dfrac{\text{Dollar markup }(P)}{\text{Percent markup on cost }(R)}$

$$\$600 = \$400 + .50(\$400)$$
$$\$600 = \$400 + \$200 \qquad\qquad = \frac{\$200}{.50} = \$400$$
$$\$600 = \$600$$

2. Dollar markup and selling price of doll:

BLUEPRINT	The facts	Solving for?			Steps to take	Key points
	Doll cost: $12 each.		%	$	Dollar markup:	Selling price
		C	100%	$12.00	S = C + M.	Portion (?)
	Markup on cost: 35%.	+ M	35	4.20[1]	or	Base × Rate ($12) (1.35)
		= S	135%	$16.20[2]	$S = \text{Cost} \times \left(1 + \begin{array}{c}\text{Percent}\\\text{markup}\\\text{on cost}\end{array}\right)$	Cost 100% +35%

[1]Dollar markup. See Step 1, below.
[2]Selling price. See Step 2, below.

Steps to solving problem

1. Calculate the dollar markup.
$$S = C + M$$
$$S = \$12.00 + .35(\$12.00)$$
$$S = \$12.00 + \boxed{\$4.20} \leftarrow \text{Dollar markup}$$

2. Calculate the selling price.
$$S = \$16.20$$

Check

$$\underset{(P)}{\text{Selling price}} = \underset{(B)}{\text{Cost}} \times (1 + \underset{(R)}{\text{Percent markup on cost}}) = \$12.00 \times 1.35 = \$16.20$$

3. Cost and dollar markup:

	The facts	Solving for?	Steps to take	Key points
BLUEPRINT	Selling price: $14. Markup on cost: 40%.	% $ C 100% $10[1] + M 40 4[2] = S 140% $14	$S = C + M.$ or $$Cost = \frac{Selling\ price}{Percent} \\ 1 + markup \\ on\ cost$$ $M = S - C.$	Selling price Portion ($14) Base × Rate (?) (1.40) Cost 100% +40%

[1]Cost. See Step 1, below.
[2]Dollar markup. See Step 2, below.

Steps to solving problem

1. Calculate the cost.

$$S = C + M$$
$$\$14 = C + .40C$$
$$\frac{\$14}{1.40} = \frac{1.40C}{1.40}$$
$$\boxed{\$10} = C$$

2. Calculate the dollar markup.

$$M = S - C$$
$$M = \$14 - \$10$$
$$M = \boxed{\$4}$$

Check

$$Cost\ (B) = \frac{Selling\ price\ (P)}{1 + Percent\ markup\ on\ cost\ (R)} = \frac{\$14}{1.40} = \$10$$

LU 8–1a   **EXTRA PRACTICE QUIZ WITH WORKED-OUT SOLUTIONS**

Need more practice? Try this Extra Practice Quiz (check figures in the Interactive Chapter Organizer). Worked-out Solutions can be found in Appendix B.

Solve the following situations (markups based on cost):

1. Irene Westing bought a desk for $800 from an office supply house. She plans to sell the desk for $1,200. What is Irene's dollar markup? What is her percent markup on cost? Check your answer.

2. Suki Komar bought dolls for her toy store that cost $14 each. To make her desired profit, Suki must mark up each doll 38% on cost. What is the dollar markup? What is the selling price of each doll? Check your answer.

3. Jay Lyman sells calculators. His competitor sells a new calculator line for $16 each. Jay needs a 42% markup on cost to make his desired profit, and he must meet price competition. At what cost can Jay afford to bring these calculators into the store? What is the dollar markup? Check your answer.

Learning Unit 8–2: Markups Based on Selling Price (100%)

Aha!

Many retailers mark up their goods on the selling price since sales information is easier to get than cost information. These retailers use retail prices in their inventory and report their expenses as a percent of sales.

For markups based on selling price, the base is always selling price (S).

Businesses that mark up their goods on selling price recognize that selling price is 100%. We begin this unit by assuming Gap has decided to use percent markup based on selling price. We repeat Gap's selling price formula expressed in dollars.

Markup expressed in dollars:

Selling price ($23) = Cost ($18) + Markup ($5)

Markup expressed as **percent markup on selling price:**

Cost	78.26%
+ Markup	+21.74
= Selling price	100.00%

> Selling price is 100%—the base. Dollar markup is the portion, and percent markup on selling price is the rate.

© David Paul Morris/Bloomberg via Getty Images

In Situation 1 (below) we show why Gap has a 21.74% markup based on selling price. In the last unit, markups were based on *cost*. In this unit, markups are based on *selling price*.

LO 1

Situation 1: Calculating Dollar Markup and Percent Markup on Selling Price

The dollar markup is calculated with the selling price formula used in Situation 1, Learning Unit 8–1: $M = S - C$. To find the percent markup on selling price, use the portion formula $R = \frac{P}{B}$, where rate (the percent markup on selling price) is found by dividing the portion (dollar markup) by the base (selling price). Note that when solving for percent markup on cost in Situation 1, Learning Unit 8–1, you divided the dollar markup by the cost.

The Word Problem The cost to Gap for a hooded fleece jacket is $18; the store then plans to sell the jacket for $23. What is Gap's dollar markup? What is its percent markup on selling price? (Round to the nearest hundredth percent.)

	The facts	Solving for?		Steps to take	Key points
BLUEPRINT	*Hooded fleece jacket cost: $18.* *Hooded fleece jacket price: $23.*	C 78.26% $+ M$ 21.74[2] $= S$ 100.00%	$18 5[1] $23	$\dfrac{\text{Dollar}}{\text{markup}} = \dfrac{\text{Selling}}{\text{price}} - \text{Cost.}$ $\dfrac{\text{Percent}}{\substack{\text{markup on}\\\text{selling price}}} = \dfrac{\text{Dollar}}{\substack{\text{markup}\\\text{Selling}\\\text{price}}}$	Dollar markup Portion ($5) Base × Rate ($23) (?) Selling price

[1]Dollar markup. See Step 1, below.

[2]Percent markup on selling price. See Step 2, below.

Steps to solving problem

1. Calculate the dollar markup.

$$\text{Dollar markup} = \text{Selling price} - \text{Cost}$$
$$\$5 = \$23 - \$18$$

2. Calculate the percent markup on selling price.

$$\dfrac{\text{Percent markup}}{\text{on selling price}} = \dfrac{\text{Dollar markup}}{\text{Selling price}}$$
$$= \dfrac{\$5}{\$23} = 21.74\%$$

You can check the percent markup on selling price with the basic selling price formula $S = C + M$. You can also use the portion formula by dividing the dollar markup (P) by the percent markup on selling price (R).

Check

Selling price = Cost + Markup	or	Selling price (B) = $\dfrac{\text{Dollar markup } (P)}{\substack{\text{Percent markup on}\\\text{selling price } (R)}}$

$23 = $18 + .2174($23)

$23 = $18 + $5

$23 = $23

$= \dfrac{\$5}{.2174} = \$23$

Parentheses mean you multiply the percent markup on selling price in decimal by the selling price.

LO 2

Situation 2: Calculating Selling Price When You Know Cost and Percent Markup on Selling Price

When you know the cost and percent markup on selling price, you calculate the selling price with the basic selling formula $S = C + M$. Remember that when goods are marked up on selling price, the selling price is the base (100%). Since you do not know the selling price, the percent markup is based on the unknown selling price. To find the dollar markup after you find the selling price, use the selling price formula $M = S - C$.

The Word Problem Mel's Furniture bought a lamp that cost $100. To make Mel's desired profit, he needs a 65% markup on selling price. What are Mel's selling price and his dollar markup?

	The facts	Solving for?	Steps to take	Key points
BLUEPRINT	Lamp cost: $100. Markup on selling price: 65%.				% $ C 35% $100.00 + M 65 185.71[2] = S 100% $285.71[1]	$S = C + M.$ or $S = \dfrac{\text{Cost}}{1 - \text{Percent markup on selling price}}$	Cost Portion ($100) Base × Rate (?) (.35) Selling price 100% −65%

[1]Selling price. See Step 1, below.
[2]Dollar markup. See Step 2, below.

Steps to solving problem

1. Calculate the selling price.

$$S = C + M$$
$$S = \$100.00 + .65S$$

$$\begin{aligned}1.00S\\-.65S\\=.35S\end{aligned}$$

$$\dfrac{-.65S}{.35S} \quad \dfrac{-.65S}{} $$
$$\dfrac{.35S}{.35} = \dfrac{\$100.00}{.35}$$
$$S = \$285.71$$

Do not multiply the .65 times $100.00. The 65% is based on selling price not cost.

2. Calculate the dollar markup.

$$M = S - C$$
$$\$185.71 = \$285.71 - \$100.00$$

You can check your selling price with the portion formula $B = \frac{P}{R}$. To find the selling price (B), divide the cost (P) by the rate (100% − Percent markup on selling price).

Check

$$\text{Selling price } (B) = \dfrac{\text{Cost } (P)}{1 - \text{Percent markup on selling price } (R)}$$

$$= \dfrac{\$100.00}{1 - .65} = \dfrac{\$100.00}{.35} = \boxed{\$285.71}$$

LO 3

Situation 3: Calculating Cost When You Know Selling Price and Percent Markup on Selling Price

When you know the selling price and the percent markup on selling price, you calculate the cost with the basic formula $S = C + M$. To find the dollar markup, multiply the markup percent by the selling price. When you have the dollar markup, subtract it from the selling price to get the cost.

The Word Problem Jill Sport, owner of Sports, Inc., sells tennis rackets for $50. To make her desired profit, Jill needs a 40% markup on the selling price. What is the dollar markup? What do the tennis rackets cost Jill?

	The facts	Solving for?	Steps to take	Key points
BLUEPRINT	Selling price: $50. Markup on selling price: 40%.				% $ C 60% $30[2] + M 40 20[1] = S 100% $50	$S = C + M.$ or $\text{Cost} = \text{Selling price} \times \left(1 - \dfrac{\text{Percent markup}}{\text{on selling price}}\right)$	Cost Portion (?) Base × Rate ($50) (.60) Selling price 100% −40%

[1]Dollar markup. See Step 1.
[2]Cost. See Step 2.

Steps to solving problem

1. Calculate the dollar markup.

$$S = C + M$$
$$\$50 = C + .40(\$50)$$

2. Calculate the cost.

$$\$50 = C + \boxed{\$20} \longleftarrow \text{Dollar markup}$$
$$\underline{-20} \qquad \underline{-20}$$
$$\boxed{\$30} = C$$

To check your cost, use the portion formula Cost (P) = Selling price (B) × (100% selling price − Percent markup on selling price) (R).

Check

$$\underset{(P)}{\text{Cost}} = \underset{(B)}{\underset{\text{price}}{\text{Selling}}} \times \left(1 - \underset{(R)}{\underset{\text{on selling price}}{\text{Percent markup}}}\right) = \$50 \times .60 = \boxed{\$30}$$

$$(1.00 - .40)$$

In Table 8.1, we compare percent markup on cost with percent markup on retail (selling price). This table is a summary of the answers we calculated from the word problems in Learning Units 8–1 and 8–2. The word problems in the units were the same except in Learning Unit 8–1, we assumed markups were on cost, while in Learning Unit 8–2, markups were on selling price. Note that in Situation 1, the dollar markup is the same $5, but the percent markup is different.

Let's now look at how to convert from percent markup on cost to percent markup on selling price and vice versa. We will use Situation 1 from Table 8.1.

LO 4

Formula for Converting Percent Markup on Cost to Percent Markup on Selling Price

To convert percent markup on cost to percent markup on selling price:

$$\frac{\text{Percent markup on cost}}{1 + \text{Percent markup on cost}}$$

$$\frac{.2778}{1 + .2778} = \boxed{21.74\%}$$

TABLE 8.1

Comparison of markup on cost versus markup on selling price

Markup based on cost—Learning Unit 8–1	Markup based on selling price—Learning Unit 8–2
Situation 1: Calculating dollar amount of markup and percent markup on cost.	*Situation 1: Calculating dollar amount of markup and percent markup on selling price.*
Hooded fleece jacket cost, $18.	Hooded fleece jacket cost, $18.
Hooded fleece jacket selling price, $23.	Hooded fleece jacket selling price, $23.
$M = S - C$	$M = S - C$
$M = \$23 - \$18 = \boxed{\$5}$ markup	$M = \$23 - \$18 = \boxed{\$5}$ markup
$M \div C = \$5 \div \$18 = 27.78\%$	$M \div S = \$5 \div \$23 = 21.74\%$
Situation 2: Calculating selling price on cost.	*Situation 2: Calculating selling price on selling price.*
Lamp cost, $100. 65% markup on cost	Lamp cost, $100. 65% markup on selling price
$S = C \times (1 + \text{Percent markup on cost})$	$S = C \div (1 - \text{Percent markup on selling price})$
$S = \$100 \times 1.65 = \boxed{\$165}$	$S = \$100.00 \div .35$
	$(100\% - 65\% = 35\% = .35)$
$(100\% + 65\% = 165\% = 1.65)$	$S = \boxed{\$285.71}$
Situation 3: Calculating cost on cost.	*Situation 3: Calculating cost on selling price.*
Tennis racket selling price, $50. 40% markup on cost	Tennis racket selling price, $50. 40% markup on selling price
$C = S \div (1 + \text{Percent markup on cost})$	$C = S \times (1 - \text{Percent markup on selling price})$
$C = \$50.00 \div 1.40$	$C = \$50 \times .60 = \boxed{\$30}$
$(100\% + 40\% = 140\% = 1.40)$	
$C = \boxed{\$35.71}$	$(100\% - 40\% = 60\% = .60)$

MONEY tips

When analyzing a job offer, make sure you include the value of the benefits. Salary alone will not let you know the value of the offer.

Formula for Converting Percent Markup on Selling Price to Percent Markup on Cost

To convert percent markup on selling price to percent markup on cost:

$$\frac{.2174}{1 - .2174} = \boxed{27.78\%}$$

Percent markup on selling price
1 − Percent markup on selling price

Key point: A 21.74% markup on selling price or a 27.78% markup on cost results in the same dollar markup of $5.

Now let's test your knowledge of Learning Unit 8–2.

LU 8–2 **PRACTICE QUIZ**

Complete this **Practice Quiz** to see how you are doing.

Solve the following situations (markups based on selling price). Note numbers 1, 2, and 3 are parallel problems to those in Practice Quiz 8–1.

1. Irene Westing bought a desk for $400 from an office supply house. She plans to sell the desk for $600. What is Irene's dollar markup? What is her percent markup on selling price (rounded to the nearest tenth percent)? Check your answer. Selling price will be slightly off due to rounding.

2. Suki Komar bought dolls for her toy store that cost $12 each. To make her desired profit, Suki must mark up each doll 35% on the selling price. What is the selling price of each doll? What is the dollar markup? Check your answer.

3. Jay Lyman sells calculators. His competitor sells a new calculator line for $14 each. Jay needs a 40% markup on the selling price to make his desired profit, and he must meet price competition. What is Jay's dollar markup? At what cost can Jay afford to bring these calculators into the store? Check your answer.

4. Dan Flow sells wrenches for $10 that cost $6. What is Dan's percent markup on cost? Round to the nearest tenth percent. What is Dan's percent markup on selling price? Check your answer.

*For **extra help** from your authors–Sharon and Jeff–see the videos in Connect.*

These videos are also available on YouTube!

✓ Solutions

1. Irene's dollar markup and percent markup on selling price:

	The facts	**Solving for?**			**Steps to take**	**Key points**
BLUEPRINT	Desk cost: $400. Desk selling price: $600.		%	$	Dollar markup = Selling price − Cost. Percent markup on selling price = Dollar markup / Selling price	Markup Portion ($200) Base ($600) × Rate (?) Selling price
		C	66.7%	$400		
		+ M	33.3²	200¹		
		= S	100%	$600		

¹Dollar markup. See Step 1, below.
²Percent markup on selling price. See Step 2, below.

Steps to solving problem

1. Calculate the dollar markup.

   Dollar markup = Selling price − Cost

   $$\boxed{\$200} = \$600 - \$400$$

2. Calculate the percent markup on selling price.

   $$\text{Percent markup on selling price} = \frac{\text{Dollar markup}}{\text{Selling price}}$$

   $$= \frac{\$200}{\$600} = \boxed{33.3\%}$$

Check

$$\frac{\text{Selling}}{\text{price}} = \text{Cost} + \text{Markup} \quad \textbf{or} \quad \text{Selling price } (B) = \frac{\text{Dollar markup } (P)}{\text{Percent markup on selling price } (R)}$$

$$\$600 = \$400 + .333(\$600)$$

$$\$600 = \$400 + \$199.80$$

$$= \frac{\$200}{.333} = \$600.60$$

$$\$600 = \$599.80 \text{ (off due to rounding)} \qquad \text{(not exactly \$600 due to rounding)}$$

2. Selling price of doll and dollar markup:

	The facts	Solving for?			Steps to take	Key points
BLUEPRINT	Doll cost: $12 each. Markup on selling price: 35%.		%	$	$S = C + M$ or $S = \dfrac{\text{Cost}}{1 - \dfrac{\text{Percent markup}}{\text{on selling price}}}$	Cost Portion ($12) Base × Rate (?) (.65) Selling price 100% −35%
		C	65%	$12.00		
		+ M	35	6.46²		
		= S	100%	$18.46¹		

¹Selling price. See Step 1, below.
²Dollar markup. See Step 2, below.

Steps to solving problem

1. Calculate the selling price.

$$S = C + M$$
$$S = \$12.00 + .35S$$
$$\underline{-.35S \qquad\qquad -.35S}$$
$$\frac{.65S}{.65} = \frac{\$12.00}{.65}$$
$$S = \boxed{\$18.46}$$

2. Calculate the dollar markup.

$$M = S - C$$
$$\boxed{\$6.46} = \$18.46 - \$12.00$$

Check

$$\text{Selling price } (B) = \frac{\text{Cost } (P)}{1 - \text{Percent markup on selling price } (R)} = \frac{\$12.00}{.65} = \boxed{\$18.46}$$

3. Dollar markup and cost:

	The facts	Solving for?			Steps to take	Key points
BLUEPRINT	Selling price: $14. Markup on selling price: 40%.		%	$	$S = C + M$ or Cost = Selling price × $\left(1 - \dfrac{\text{Percent markup}}{\text{on selling price}}\right)$	Cost Portion (?) Base × Rate ($14) (.60) Selling price 100% −40%
		C	60%	$ 8.40²		
		+ M	40	5.60¹		
		= S	100%	$14.00		

¹Dollar markup. See Step 1, below.
²Cost. See Step 2, below.

Steps to solving problem

1. Calculate the dollar markup.

$$S = C + M$$
$$\$14.00 = C + .40(\$14.00)$$

2. Calculate the cost.

$$\$14.00 = C + \boxed{\$5.60} \longleftarrow \text{Dollar markup}$$
$$\underline{-5.60 \qquad\qquad -5.60}$$
$$\boxed{\$8.40} = C$$

Check

Cost = Selling price × (1 − Percent markup on selling price) = $14.00 × .60 = $8.40
  (P)   (B)   (R)

$$(1.00 − .40)$$

4. $\text{Cost} = \dfrac{\$4}{\$6} = 66.7\%$ $\dfrac{.40}{1 - .40} = \dfrac{.40}{.60} = \dfrac{2}{3} = 66.7\%$

    $\text{Selling price} = \dfrac{\$4}{\$10} = 40\%$ $\dfrac{.667}{1 + .667} = \dfrac{.667}{1.667} = 40\%$ (due to rounding)

LU 8–2a   EXTRA PRACTICE QUIZ WITH WORKED-OUT SOLUTIONS

Need more practice? Try this Extra Practice Quiz (check figures in the Interactive Chapter Organizer). Worked-out Solutions can be found in Appendix B.

Solve the following situations (markups based on selling price).

1. Irene Westing bought a desk for $800 from an office supply house. She plans to sell the desk for $1,200. What is Irene's dollar markup? What is her percent markup on selling price (rounded to the nearest tenth percent)? Check your answer. Selling price will be slightly off due to rounding.

2. Suki Komar bought dolls for her toy store that cost $14 each. To make her desired profit, Suki must mark up each doll 38% on selling price. What is the selling price of each doll? What is the dollar markup? Check your answer.

3. Jay Lyman sells calculators. His competitor sells a new calculator line for $16 each. Jay needs a 42% markup on the selling price to make his desired profit, and he must meet price competition. What is Jay's dollar markup? At what cost can Jay afford to bring these calculators into the store? Check your answer.

4. Dan Flow sells wrenches for $12 that cost $7. What is Dan's percent markup on cost? Round to the nearest tenth percent. What is Dan's percent markup on selling price? Check your answer.

Learning Unit 8–3: Markdowns and Perishables

In the following *Wall Street Journal* clip, Dollar General reports on its new markdown strategy. Check it out.

BY ANNA PRIOR

Dollar General Corp. boosted incentives in the latest quarter to lure customers straining under a lackluster economy and to fend off increased competition from bigger retail chains.

During the latest quarter, Dollar General said it significantly increased the number of products available for between $1 and $5 and noted an increased number of markdowns, signs that indicate that the company's core low-income shoppers remain under pressure.

"Today, more than ever, given the economic environment that has lingered for quite some time, affordability has now become the focus of our core customer," Chief Executive Rick Dreiling said on the company's quarterly conference call.

Shares of Dollar General rose 3.9% to $56.41 Tuesday as the

company reiterated its full-year outlook and said sales trends began to improve in April and have continued to gain momentum.

The company also noted that it repurchased $800 million in stock in the latest quarter.

Dollar stores like Dollar Ge eral have generally benefit from bargain-hungry consume strained by a sluggish econon recovery. However, small-form dollar stores have been cuttii prices as competition for lowe income shoppers intensifies.

In addition to competitio from other dollar stores, Dolla General faces pressure fror newer entrants to the small-fc mat store market, includ **Wal-Mart Stores** Inc.'s "\ Mart Express." Meanwhile, 1 **get Corp.** has said it would gin testing a "TargetExpro format this year.

Reprinted by permission of *The Wall Street Journal*, copyright 2014 Dow Jones & Company, Inc. All rights reserved worldwide.

This learning unit focuses your attention on how to calculate markdowns. Then you will learn how a business prices perishable items that may spoil before customers buy them.

Markdowns

Markdowns are reductions from the original selling price caused by seasonal changes, special promotions, style changes, and so on. We calculate the markdown percent as follows:

$$\text{Markdown percent} = \frac{\text{Dollar markdown}}{\text{Selling price (original)}}$$

Let's look at the following Kmart example:

Dollar markdown

Portion ($7.20)

Base ($18) × Rate (?)

Original selling price

EXAMPLE Kmart marked down an $18 video to $10.80. Calculate the **dollar markdown** and the markdown percent.

$18.00 Original selling price
$-\ 10.80$ Sale price
$\ \ \$\ 7.20$ Markdown

$$\frac{\text{Dollar markdown, } \$7.20}{\text{Selling price (original), } \$18.00} = 40\%$$

Calculating a Series of Markdowns and Markups   Often the final selling price is the result of a series of markdowns (and possibly a markup in between markdowns). We calculate additional markdowns on the previous selling price. Note in the following example how we calculate markdown on selling price after we add a markup.

EXAMPLE Jones Department Store paid its supplier $400 for a TV. On January 10, Jones marked the TV up 60% on selling price. As a special promotion, Jones marked the TV down 30% on February 8 and another 20% on February 28. No one purchased the TV, so Jones marked it up 10% on March 11. What was the selling price of the TV on March 11?

January 10: Selling price = Cost + Markup

$$
\begin{aligned}
S &= \$400 + .60S \\
-.60S & \quad\quad\quad -.60S \\
\frac{.40S}{.40} &= \frac{\$400}{.40} \\
S &= \$1,000
\end{aligned}
$$

Check

$$S = \frac{\text{Cost}}{1 - \text{Percent markup on selling price}}$$

$$S = \frac{\$400}{1 - .60} = \frac{\$400}{.40} = \$1,000$$

February 8 markdown:

$$
\begin{array}{r}
100\% \\
-\ 30 \\
\hline
70\%
\end{array}
$$
→ .70 × $1,000 = $700 selling price

February 28 additional markdown:

$$
\begin{array}{r}
100\% \\
-\ 20 \\
\hline
80\%
\end{array}
$$
→ .80 × $700 = $560

March 11 additional markup:

$$
\begin{array}{r}
100\% \\
+\ 10 \\
\hline
110\%
\end{array}
$$
→ 1.10 × $560 = $616

Pricing Perishable Items

The following formula can be used to determine the price of goods that have a short shelf life such as fruit, flowers, and pastry. (We limit this discussion to obviously **perishable** items.)

To calculate the selling price of a perishable item: (1) Calculate selling price based on cost or based on selling price (total dollar sales). (2) Divide total dollar sales by the number of units available for sale (after accounting for spoilage).

$$\text{Selling price of perishables} = \frac{\text{Total dollar sales}}{\text{Number of units produced} - \text{Spoilage}}$$

MONEY tips

Do you have too much debt? Calculate your debt-to-income ratio by dividing your gross monthly income by your total monthly debt repayments. A rate close to 40% or higher should be a red flag to you to start paying off debt.

The Word Problem Audrey's Bake Shop baked 20 dozen bagels. Audrey expects 10% of the bagels to become stale and not salable. The bagels cost Audrey $1.20 per dozen. Audrey wants a 60% markup on cost. What should Audrey charge for each dozen bagels so she will make her profit? Round to the nearest cent.

BLUEPRINT	The facts	Solving for?	Steps to take	Key points
	Bagels cost: $1.20 per dozen.	Price of a dozen bagels.	Total cost.	Markup is based on cost.
	Not salable: 10%.		Total dollar markup.	
	Baked: 20 dozen.		Total selling price.	
	Markup on cost: 60%.		Bagel loss.	
			$TS = TC + TM$.	

Steps to solving problem

1. Calculate the total cost.

$TC = 20$ dozen $\times$ $1.20 = $24.00

2. Calculate the total dollar markup.

$$TS = TC + TM$$

$TS = $24.00 + .60($24.00)$

$TS = $24.00 + 14.40 ← Total dollar markup

3. Calculate the total selling price.

$TS = 38.40 ← Total selling price

4. Calculate the bagel loss.

20 dozen $\times$ .10 = 2 dozen

5. Calculate the selling price for a dozen bagels.

$$\frac{\$38.40}{18} = \$2.13 \text{ per dozen} \qquad \begin{array}{r} 20 \\ -\ 2 \end{array}$$

It's time to try the Practice Quiz.

LU 8–3 | PRACTICE QUIZ

Complete this Practice Quiz to see how you are doing.

1. Sunshine Music Shop bought a stereo for $600 and marked it up 40% on selling price. To promote customer interest, Sunshine marked the stereo down 10% for 1 week. Since business was slow, Sunshine marked the stereo down an additional 5%. After a week, Sunshine marked the stereo up 2%. What is the new selling price of the stereo to the nearest cent? What is the markdown percent based on the original selling price to the nearest hundredth percent?

2. Alvin Rose owns a fruit and vegetable stand. He knows that he cannot sell all his produce at full price. Some of his produce will be markdowns, and he will throw out some produce. Alvin must put a high enough price on the produce to cover markdowns and rotted produce and still make his desired profit. Alvin bought 300 pounds of tomatoes at 14 cents per pound. He expects a 5% spoilage and marks up tomatoes 60% on cost. What price per pound should Alvin charge for the tomatoes?

For **extra help** from your authors—Sharon and Jeff—see the videos in Connect.

These videos are also available on YouTube!

✓ Solutions

1.

$$S = C + M$$

$S = $600 + .40S$

$-.40S \qquad\qquad -.40S$

$$\frac{.60S}{.60} = \frac{\$600}{.60}$$

$S = $1,000$

Check

$$S = \frac{\text{Cost}}{1 - \text{Percent markup on selling price}}$$

$$S = \frac{\$600}{1 - .40} = \frac{\$600}{.60} = \$1,000$$

First markdown: .90 $\times$ $1,000 = $900 selling price

Second markdown: .95 $\times$ $900 = $855 selling price

Markup: 1.02 $\times$ $855 = $872.10 final selling price

$$\$1,000 - \$872.10 = \frac{\$127.90}{\$1,000} = 12.79\%$$

2. Price of tomatoes per pound:

	The facts	Solving for?	Steps to take	Key points
BLUEPRINT	300 lb. tomatoes at $.14 per pound. *Spoilage:* 5%. *Markup on cost:* 60%.	Price of tomatoes per pound.	Total cost. Total dollar markup. Total selling price. Spoilage amount. $TS = TC + TM$.	Markup is based on cost.

Steps to solving problem

1. Calculate the total cost.

$TC = 300$ lb. $\times \$.14 = \$42.00$

2. Calculate the total dollar markup.

$TS = TC + TM$

$TS = \$42.00 + .60(\$42.00)$

$TS = \$42.00 + \$25.20 \longleftarrow$ Total dollar markup

3. Calculate the total selling price.

$TS = \$67.20 \longleftarrow$ Total selling price

4. Calculate the tomato loss.

300 pounds $\times .05 = 15$ pounds spoilage

5. Calculate the selling price per pound of tomatoes.

$\dfrac{\$67.20}{285} = \boxed{\$.24}$ per pound (rounded to nearest hundredth)

$(300 - 15)$

LU 8–3a   **EXTRA PRACTICE QUIZ WITH WORKED-OUT SOLUTIONS**

Need more practice? Try this Extra Practice Quiz (check figures in the Interactive Chapter Organizer). Worked-out Solutions can be found in Appendix B.

1. Sunshine Music Shop bought a stereo for $800 and marked it up 30% on selling price. To promote customer interest, Sunshine marked the stereo down 10% for 1 week. Since business was slow, Sunshine marked the stereo down an additional 5%. After a week, Sunshine marked the stereo up 2%. What is the new selling price of the stereo to the nearest cent? What is the markdown percent based on the original selling price to the nearest hundredth percent?

2. Alvin Rose owns a fruit and vegetable stand. He knows that he cannot sell all his produce at full price. Some of his produce will be markdowns, and he will throw out some produce. Alvin must put a high enough price on the produce to cover markdowns and rotted produce and still make his desired profit. Alvin bought 500 pounds of tomatoes at 16 cents per pound. He expects a 10% spoilage and marks up tomatoes 55% on cost. What price per pound should Alvin charge for the tomatoes?

Learning Unit 8–4: Breakeven Analysis

So far in this chapter, cost is the price retailers pay to a manufacturer or supplier to bring the goods into the store. In this unit, we view costs from the perspective of manufacturers or suppliers who produce goods to sell in units, such as polo shirts, pens, calculators, lamps, and so on. These manufacturers or suppliers deal with two costs—fixed costs (*FC*) and variable costs (*VC*).

To understand how the owners of manufacturers or suppliers that produce goods per unit operate their businesses, we must understand fixed costs (*FC*), variable costs (*VC*), contribution margin (*CM*), and breakeven point (*BE*). Carefully study the following definitions of these terms:

- **Fixed costs (*FC*).** Costs that *do not change* with increases or decreases in sales; they include payments for insurance, a business license, rent, a lease, utilities, labor, and so on.

- **Variable costs (*VC*).** Costs that *do change* in response to changes in the volume of sales; they include payments for material, some labor, and so on.

- **Selling price (S).** In this unit we focus on manufacturers and suppliers who produce goods to sell in units.
- **Contribution margin (CM).** The difference between selling price (S) and variable costs (VC). This difference goes *first* to pay off total fixed costs (FC); when they are covered, *profits (or losses)* start to accumulate.
- **Breakeven point (BE).** The point at which the seller has covered all expenses and costs of a unit and has not made any profit or suffered any loss. Every unit sold after the breakeven point (BE) will bring some profit or cause a loss.

Learning Unit 8–4 is divided into two sections: calculating a contribution margin (CM) and calculating a breakeven point (BE). You will learn the importance of these two concepts and the formulas that you can use to calculate them. Study the example given for each concept to help you understand why the success of business owners depends on knowing how to use these two concepts.

LO 1

Calculating a Contribution Margin (CM)

Before we calculate the breakeven point, we must first calculate the contribution margin. The formula is as follows:

> Contribution margin (CM) = Selling price (S) − Variable cost (VC)

EXAMPLE Assume Jones Company produces pens that have a selling price (S) of $2.00 and a variable cost (VC) of $.80. We calculate the contribution margin (CM) as follows:

$$\text{Contribution margin } (CM) = \$2.00 \ (S) - \$.80 \ (VC)$$
$$CM = \boxed{\$1.20}$$

This means that for each pen sold, $1.20 goes to cover fixed costs (FC) and results in a profit. It makes sense to cover fixed costs (FC) first because the nature of an FC is that it does not change with increases or decreases in sales.

Now we are ready to see how Jones Company will reach a breakeven point (BE).

LO 2

Calculating a Breakeven Point (BE)

Sellers like Jones Company can calculate their profit or loss by using a concept called the **breakeven point (BE)**. This important point results after sellers have paid all their expenses and costs. Study the following formula and the example:

> $$\text{Breakeven point } (BE) = \frac{\text{Fixed costs } (FC)}{\text{Contribution margin } (CM)}$$

MONEY tips

Create and stick to a budget. Knowing where your money goes can help you save on unnecessary expenditures and allow you to meet your financial goals. To help you track your spending and create a budget, check out mint.com.

EXAMPLE Jones Company produces pens. The company has a fixed cost (FC) of $60,000. Each pen sells for $2.00 with a variable cost (VC) of $.80 per pen.

Fixed cost (FC)	$60,000
Selling price (S) per pen	$2.00
Variable cost (VC) per pen	$.80

$$\text{Breakeven point } (BE) = \frac{\$60,000 \ (FC)}{\$2.00 \ (S) - \$.80 \ (VC)} = \frac{\$60,000 \ (FC)}{\$1.20 \ (CM)} = \boxed{50,000 \text{ units (pens)}}$$

At 50,000 units (pens), Jones Company is just covering its costs. Each unit after 50,000 brings in a profit of $1.20 (CM).

It is time to try the Practice Quiz.

LU 8-4 **PRACTICE QUIZ**

Complete this **Practice Quiz** to see how you are doing.

*For **extra help** from your authors—Sharon and Jeff—see the videos in Connect.*

These videos are also available on YouTube!

Blue Company produces holiday gift boxes. Given the following, calculate (1) the contribution margin (*CM*) and (2) the breakeven point (*BE*) for Blue Company.

Fixed cost (*FC*)	$45,000
Selling price (*S*) per gift box	$20
Variable cost (*VC*) per gift box	$8

✓ **Solutions**

1. Contribution margin (*CM*) = $20 (*S*) − $8 (*VC*) = $12

2. Breakeven point (*BE*) = $\dfrac{\$45{,}000\,(FC)}{\$20\,(S) - \$8\,(VC)} = \dfrac{\$45{,}000\,(FC)}{\$12\,(CM)} = 3{,}750$ units (gift boxes)

LU 8-4a **EXTRA PRACTICE QUIZ WITH WORKED-OUT SOLUTIONS**

Need more practice? Try this **Extra Practice Quiz** (check figures in the Interactive Chapter Organizer). Worked-out Solutions can be found in Appendix B.

Angel Company produces car radios. Given the following, calculate (1) the contribution margin (*CM*) and (2) the breakeven point (*BE*) for Angel Company.

Fixed cost (*FC*)	$96,000
Selling price (*S*) per radio	$240
Variable cost (*VC*) per radio	$80

INTERACTIVE CHAPTER ORGANIZER

Topic/Procedure/Formula	Examples	You try it*
Markups based on cost: **Cost is 100% (base)** Selling price (*S*) = Cost (*C*) + Markup (*M*)	$400 = $300 + $100 *S* = *C* + *M*	**Calculate selling price** Cost, $400; Markup, $200
Percent markup on cost $\dfrac{\text{Dollar markup (portion)}}{\text{Cost (base)}}$ = Percent markup on cost (rate)	$\dfrac{\$100}{\$300} = \dfrac{1}{3} = 33\tfrac{1}{3}\%$	**Calculate percent markup on cost** Dollar markup, $50; Cost, $200
Cost $C = \dfrac{\text{Dollar markup}}{\text{Percent markup on cost}}$	$\dfrac{\$100}{.33} = \$303$ Off slightly due to rounding	**Calculate cost** Dollar markup, $50; Percent markup on cost, 25%
Calculating selling price *S* = *C* + *M* **Check** *S* = Cost × (1 + Percent markup on cost)	Cost, $6; percent markup on cost, 20% *S* = $6 + .20($6) **Check** *S* = $6 + $1.20 *S* = $7.20 $\boxed{\$6 \times 1.20 = \$7.20}$	**Calculate selling price** Cost, $8; Percent markup on cost, 10%
Calculating cost *S* = *C* + *M* **Check** Cost = $\dfrac{\text{Selling price}}{1 + \text{Percent markup on cost}}$	*S* = $100; *M* = 70% of cost *S* = *C* + *M* $\left(\begin{smallmatrix}\text{Remember,}\\ C = 1.00C\end{smallmatrix}\right)$ $100 = C + .70C $100 = 1.7C $\dfrac{\$100}{1.7} = C$ **Check** $58.82 = C $\boxed{\dfrac{\$100}{1 + .70} = \$58.82}$	**Calculate cost** Selling price, $200; Markup on cost, 60%

(continues)

INTERACTIVE CHAPTER ORGANIZER

Topic/Procedure/Formula	Examples	You try it*
Markups based on selling price: selling price is 100% (Base) Dollar markup = Selling price − Cost	$M = S - C$ $\$600 = \$1,000 - \$400$	**Calculate dollar markup** Cost, $2,000; Selling price, $4,500
Percent markup on selling price $\dfrac{\text{Dollar markup (portion)}}{\text{Selling price (base)}} = \dfrac{\text{Percent markup on}}{\text{selling price (rate)}}$	$\dfrac{\$600}{\$1,000} = 60\%$	**Calculate percent markup on selling price** Dollar markup, $700; Selling price, $2,800
Selling price $S = \dfrac{\text{Dollar markup}}{\text{Percent markup on selling price}}$	$\dfrac{\$600}{.60} = \$1,000$	**Calculate selling price** Dollar markup, $700; Percent markup on selling price, 50%
Calculating selling price $S = C + M$ **Check** $\text{Selling price} = \dfrac{\text{Cost}}{1 - \dfrac{\text{Percent markup}}{\text{on selling price}}}$	Cost, $400; percent markup on S, 60% $S = C + M$ $S = \$400 + .60S$ $S - .60S = \$400 + .60S - .60S$ $\dfrac{.40S}{.40} = \dfrac{\$400}{.40} \quad S = \$1,000$ **Check** → $\dfrac{\$400}{1 - .60} = \dfrac{\$400}{.40} = \$1,000$	**Calculate selling price** Cost, $800; Markup on selling price, 40%
Calculating cost $S = C + M$ **Check** $\text{Cost} = \dfrac{\text{Selling}}{\text{price}} \times \left(1 - \dfrac{\text{Percent markup}}{\text{on selling price}}\right)$	$\$1,000 = C + 60\%(\$1,000)$ $\$1,000 = C + \$600$ $\$400 = C$ **Check** → $\$1,000 \times (1 - .60)$ $\$1,000 \times .40 = \$400$	**Calculate cost** Selling price, $2,000; 70% markup on selling price
Conversion of markup percent Percent markup on cost → to → Percent markup on selling price $\dfrac{\text{Percent markup on cost}}{1 + \text{Percent markup on cost}}$ Percent markup on selling price → to → Percent markup on cost $\dfrac{\text{Percent markup on selling price}}{1 - \text{Percent markup on selling price}}$	*Round to nearest percent:* 54% markup on cost → 35% markup on selling price $\dfrac{.54}{1 + .54} = \dfrac{.54}{1.54} = 35\%$ 35% markup on selling price → 54% markup on cost $\dfrac{.35}{1 - .35} = \dfrac{.35}{.65} = 54\%$	**Calculate percent markup on selling price** Convert 47% markup on cost to markup on selling price. Round to nearest percent.
Markdowns $\text{Markdown percent} = \dfrac{\text{Dollar markdown}}{\text{Selling price (original)}}$	$40 selling price 10% markdown $\$40 \times .10 = \$4$ markdown $\dfrac{\$4}{\$40} = 10\%$	**Calculate markdown percent** Selling price, $50; Markdown, 20%
Pricing perishables 1. Calculate total cost and total selling price. 2. Calculate selling price per unit by dividing total sales in Step 1 by units expected to be sold after taking perishables into account.	50 pastries cost 20 cents each; 10 will spoil before being sold. Markup is 60% on cost. 1. $TC = 50 \times \$.20 = \$10$ $TS = TC + TM$ $TS = \$10 + .60(\$10)$ $TS = \$10 + \$6$ $TS = \$16$ 2. $\dfrac{\$16}{40 \text{ pastries}} = \$.40$ per pastry	**Calculate cost of each pastry** 30 pastries cost 30 cents each; 15 will spoil; markup is 30% on cost.

(continues)

INTERACTIVE CHAPTER ORGANIZER

Topic/Procedure/Formula	Examples	You try it*
Breakeven point (BE) $BE = \dfrac{\text{Fixed cost }(FC)}{\text{Contribution margin }(CM)}$ $\text{(Selling price, } S - \text{Variable cost, } VC)$	Fixed cost (FC) $60,000 Selling price (S) $90 Variable cost (VC) $30 $BE = \dfrac{\$60{,}000}{\$90 - \$30} = \dfrac{\$60{,}000}{\$60} = 1{,}000 \text{ units}$	**Calculate BE** Fixed cost (FC) $70,000 Selling price (S) $80 Variable cost (VC) $60

KEY TERMS			

	Breakeven point
	Contribution margin
	Cost
	Dollar markdown
	Dollar markup
	Fixed cost
	Gross profit
		Margin
		Markdowns
		Markup
		Net profit (net income)
		Operating expenses
		  (overhead)
		Percent markup on cost
			Percent markup on
			  selling price
			Perishables
			Selling price
			Variable cost

| Check Figures for Extra Practice Quizzes. (Worked-out Solutions are in Appendix B.) | LU 8–1a
1. $400; 50%
2. $5.32; $19.32
3. $11.27; $4.73 | LU 8–2a
1. $400; 33.3%
2. $22.58; $8.58
3. $6.72; $9.28
4. 71.4%; 41.7% | LU 8–3a
1. $996.69; 12.79%
2. .28 | LU 8–4a
1. $160; 600 |

*Worked-out solutions are in Appendix B.

Critical Thinking Discussion Questions with Chapter Concept Check

1. Assuming markups are based on cost, explain how the portion formula could be used to calculate cost, selling price, dollar markup, and percent markup on cost. Pick a company and explain why it would mark goods up on cost rather than on selling price.

2. Assuming markups are based on selling price, explain how the portion formula could be used to calculate cost, selling price, dollar markup, and percent markup on selling price. Pick a company and explain why it would mark up goods on selling price rather than on cost.

3. What is the formula to convert percent markup on selling price to percent markup on cost? How could you explain that a 40% markup on selling price, which is a 66.7% markup on cost, would result in the same dollar markup?

4. Explain how to calculate markdowns. Do you think stores should run 1-day-only markdown sales? Would it be better to offer the best price "all the time"?

5. Explain the five steps in calculating a selling price for perishable items. Recall a situation where you saw a store that did *not* follow the five steps. How did it sell its items?

6. Explain how Walmart uses breakeven analysis. Give an example.

7. **Chapter Concept Check.** Visit a retailer's website and find out how that retailer marks up goods and marks down specials. Present calculations based on this chapter to support your findings.

END-OF-CHAPTER PROBLEMS

Check figures for odd-numbered problems in Appendix C.   Name _____ Date _____

DRILL PROBLEMS

Assume markups in Problems 8–1 to 8–6 are based on cost. Find the dollar markup and selling price for the following problems. Round answers to the nearest cent.   *LU 8-1(1, 2)*

Item	Cost	Markup percent	Dollar markup	Selling price
8–1. iPad	$600	15%		
8–2. Burberry men's watch	$425	200%		

Solve for cost (round to the nearest cent):   *LU 8-1(3)*

8–3. Selling price of office furniture at Staples, $6,000

Percent markup on cost, 40%

Actual cost?

8–4. Selling price of lumber at Home Depot, $4,000

Percent markup on cost, 30%

Actual cost?

Complete the following: *LU 8-1(1)*

Cost	Selling price	Dollar markup	Percent markup on cost*
8–5. $15.10	$22.00	?	?
8–6. ?	?	$4.70	102.17%

*Round to the nearest hundredth percent.

Assume markups in Problems 8–7 to 8–12 are based on selling price. Find the dollar markup and cost (round answers to the nearest cent):   *LU 8-2(1, 2)*

Item	Selling price	Markup percent	Dollar markup	Cost
8–7. Sony LCD TV	$1,000	45%		
8–8. Canon scanner	$80	30%		

Solve for the selling price (round to the nearest cent):   *LU 8-2(3)*

8–9. Selling price of a complete set of pots and pans at Walmart?

40% markup on selling price

Cost, actual, $66.50

8–10. Selling price of a dining room set at Macy's?

55% markup on selling price

Cost, actual, $800

Complete the following: *LU 8-2(1)*

	Cost	Selling price	Dollar markup	Percent markup on selling price (round to nearest tenth percent)
8–11.	$14.80	$49.00	?	?
8–12.	?	?	$4	20%

By conversion of the markup formula, solve the following (round to the nearest whole percent as needed):   *LU 8-2(5)*

	Percent markup on cost	Percent markup on selling price
8–13.	12.4%	?
8–14.	?	13%

Complete the following: *LU 8-3(1, 2)*

8–15. Calculate the final selling price to the nearest cent and markdown percent to the nearest hundredth percent:

eXcel

Original selling price	First markdown	Second markdown	Markup	Final markdown
$5,000	20%	10%	12%	5%

Item	Total quantity bought	Unit cost	Total cost	Percent markup on cost	Total selling price	Percent that will spoil	Selling price per brownie
8–16. Brownies	20	$.79	?	60%	?	10%	?

Complete the following: *LU 8-4(1, 2)*

	Breakeven point	Fixed cost	Contribution margin	Selling price per unit	Variable cost per unit
8–17.		$65,000		$5.00	$1.00
8–18.		$90,000		$9.00	$4.00

WORD PROBLEMS

8–19. Bari Jay, a gown manufacturer, received an order for 600 prom dresses from China. Her cost is $35 a gown. If her markup based on selling price is 79%, what is the selling price of each gown? Round to the nearest cent.   *LU 8-2(2)*

8–20. Brian May, guitarist for Queen, does not know how to price his signature Antique Cherry Special that cost him £280 to make. He knows he wants 85% markup on cost. What price should Brian May ask for the guitar?   *LU 8-1(2)*

8–21. Cecil Green sells golf hats. He knows that most people will not pay more than $20 for a golf hat. Cecil needs a 40% markup on cost. What should Cecil pay for his golf hats? Round to the nearest cent.   *LU 8-1(4)*

8–22. Macy's was selling Calvin Klein jean shirts that were originally priced at $58.00 for $8.70. **(a)** What was the amount of the markdown? **(b)** Based on the selling price, what is the percent markdown?   *LU 8-3(1)*

8–23. Brownsville, Texas, boasts being the southernmost international seaport and the largest city in the lower Rio Grande Valley. Ben Supple, an importer in Brownsville, has just received a shipment of Peruvian opals that he is pricing for sale. He paid $150 for the shipment. If he wants a 75% markup, calculate the selling price based on selling price. Then calculate the selling price based on cost.   *LU 8-1(2), LU 8-2(2)*

8–24. Front Range Cabinet Distributors in Colorado Springs, Colorado, sells to its contractors with a 42% markup on cost. If the selling price for cabinets is $9,655, what is the cost to contractors based on cost? Round to the nearest tenth. Check your answer.   *LU 8-1(3)*

8–25. Misu Sheet, owner of the Bedspread Shop, knows his customers will pay no more than $120 for a comforter. Misu wants
eXcel a 30% markup on selling price. What is the most that Misu can pay for a comforter? *LU 8-2(4)*

8–26. Assume Misu Sheet (Problem 8–25) wants a 30% markup on cost instead of on selling price. What is Misu's cost? Round
eXcel to the nearest cent. *LU 8-1(4)*

8–27. Misu Sheet (Problem 8–25) wants to advertise the comforter as "percent markup on cost." What is the equivalent rate of
percent markup on cost compared to the 30% markup on selling price? Check your answer. Is this a wise marketing
decision? Round to the nearest hundredth percent. *LU 8-2(5)*

8–28. DeWitt Company sells a kitchen set for $475. To promote July 4, DeWitt ran the following advertisement:
eXcel
Beginning each hour up to 4 hours we will mark down the kitchen set 10%. At the end of each hour, we will mark
up the set 1%.

Assume Ingrid Swenson buys the set 1 hour 50 minutes into the sale. What will Ingrid pay? Round each calculation to
the nearest cent. What is the markdown percent? Round to the nearest hundredth percent. *LU 8-3(1)*

8–29. Angie's Bake Shop makes birthday chocolate chip cookies that cost $2 each. Angie expects that 10% of the cookies will
eXcel crack and be discarded. Angie wants a 60% markup on cost and produces 100 cookies. What should Angie price each
cookie? Round to the nearest cent. *LU 8-3(2)*

8–30. Assume that Angie (Problem 8–29) can sell the cracked cookies for $1.10 each. What should Angie price each cookie?
LU 8-3(2)

8–31. Jane Corporation produces model toy cars. Each sells for $29.99. Its variable cost per unit is $14.25. What is the breakeven point for Jane Corporation assuming it has a fixed cost of $314,800? *LU 8-4(2)*

8–32. Aunt Sally's "New Orleans Most Famous Pralines" sells pralines costing $1.10 each to make. If Aunt Sally's wants a 35% markup based on selling price and produces 45 pralines with an anticipated 15% spoilage (rounded to the nearest whole number), what should each praline be sold for? *LU 8-3(2)*

8–33. On Black Friday 2014, Amazon.com featured a Panasonic 3D Blu-Ray Player for $35 normally selling for $79. Calculate the dollar markdown and the markdown percent based on the selling price to the nearest whole percent. *LU 8-3(1)*

8–34. Working off an 18% margin, with markups based on cost, the Food Co-op Club boasts that it has 5,000 members and a 200% increase in sales. The markup is 36% based on cost. What would be its percent markup if selling price were the base? Round to the nearest hundredth percent. *LU 8-2(5)*

8–35. At a local Bed and Bath Superstore, the manager, Jill Roe, knows her customers will pay no more than $300 for a bedspread. Jill wants a 35% markup on selling price. What is the most that Jill can pay for a bedspread? *LU 8-2(4)*

8–36. Jim Abbott purchased a $60,000 RV with a 40 percent markup on selling price. **(a)** What was the amount of the dealer's markup? **(b)** What was the dealer's original cost? *LU 8-2(4)*

8–37. John's Smoothie Stand at Utah's Wasatch County's Demolition Derby sells bananas. If John bought 50 lbs. of bananas at $.23 per pound expecting 10% to spoil, how should he price his bananas to achieve 57% on selling price? *LU 8-2(4)*

8–38. Arley's Bakery makes fat-free cookies that cost $1.50 each. Arley expects 15% of the cookies to fall apart and be **eXcel** discarded. Arley wants a 45% markup on cost and produces 200 cookies. What should Arley price each cookie? Round to the nearest cent. *LU 8-3(2)*

8–39. Assume that Arley (Problem 8–38) can sell the broken cookies for $1.40 each. What should Arley price each cookie? *LU 8-3(2)*

8–40. An Apple Computer store sells computers for $1,258.60. Assuming the computers cost $10,788 per dozen, find for each computer the **(a)** dollar markup, **(b)** percent markup on cost, and **(c)** percent markup on selling price, to the nearest hundredth percent. *LU 8-1(1), LU 8-2(1)*

Prove **(b)** and **(c)** of the above problem using the equivalent formulas.

8–41. Pete Corporation produces bags of peanuts. Its fixed cost is $17,280. Each bag sells for $2.99 with a unit cost of $1.55. What is Pete's breakeven point? *LU 8-4(2)*

CHALLENGE PROBLEMS

8–42. Nissan Appliances bought two dozen camcorders at a cost of $4,788. The markup on the camcorders is 25% of the selling price. What was the original selling price of each camcorder? *LU 8-2(3)*

8–43. On July 8, 2013, Leon's Kitchen Hut bought a set of pots with a $120 list price from Lambert Manufacturing. Leon's receives a 25% trade discount. Terms of the sale were 2/10, n/30. On July 14, Leon's sent a check to Lambert for the pots. Leon's expenses are 20% of the selling price. Leon's must also make a profit of 15% of the selling price. A competitor marked down the same set of pots 30%. Assume Leon's reduces its selling price by 30%. *LU 8-2(3)*

    a. What is the sale price at Kitchen Hut?

    b. What was the operating profit or loss?

SUMMARY PRACTICE TEST

Do you need help? The videos in Connect have step-by-step worked-out solutions. These videos are also available on YouTube!

1. Sunset Co. marks up merchandise 40% on cost. A DVD player costs Sunset $90. What is Sunset's selling price? Round to the nearest cent.   *LU 8-1(2)*

2. JCPenney sells jeans for $49.50 that cost $38.00. What is the percent markup on cost? Round to the nearest hundredth percent. Check the cost.   *LU 8-1(1)*

3. Best Buy sells a flat-screen high-definition TV for $700. Best Buy marks up the TV 45% on cost. What is the cost and dollar markup of the TV?   *LU 8-1(1, 3)*

4. Sports Authority marks up New Balance sneakers $30 and sells them for $109. Markup is on cost. What are the cost and percent markup to the nearest hundredth percent?   *LU 8-1(1, 3)*

5. The Shoe Outlet bought boots for $60 and marks up the boots 55% on the selling price. What is the selling price of the boots? Round to the nearest cent.   *LU 8-2(2)*

6. Office Max sells a desk for $450 and marks up the desk 35% on the selling price. What did the desk cost Office Max? Round to the nearest cent.   *LU 8-2(4)*

7. Zales sells diamonds for $1,100 that cost $800. What is Zales's percent markup on selling price? Round to the nearest hundredth percent. Check the selling price.   *LU 8-2(1)*

8. Earl Miller, a customer of J. Crew, will pay $400 for a new jacket. J. Crew has a 60% markup on selling price. What is the most that J. Crew can pay for this jacket?   *LU 8-2(4)*

9. Home Liquidators marks up its merchandise 35% on cost. What is the company's equivalent markup on selling price? Round to the nearest tenth percent. *LU 8-2(5)*

10. The Muffin Shop makes no-fat blueberry muffins that cost $.70 each. The Muffin Shop knows that 15% of the muffins will spoil. If The Muffin Shop wants 40% markup on cost and produces 800 muffins, what should The Muffin Shop price each muffin? Round to the nearest cent. *LU 8-3(2)*

11. Angel Corporation produces calculators selling for $25.99. Its unit cost is $18.95. Assuming a fixed cost of $80,960, what is the breakeven point in units? *LU 8-4(2)*

Noodles & Company is a rapidly expanding restaurant in the "quick-casual" dining world. Close attention to detail through effective and efficient operations management is the core attribute that enables Noodles & Company to provide hot, fresh food in a timely manner. With time a scarce resource for many, Noodles & Company has found a way to satisfy the time-hungry niche market by providing high-quality food quickly.

Management spends much time analyzing business processes and functions to ensure customers receive a premium food experience. Noodles & Company plans the customers' experience from the moment they enter the restaurant to the moment they leave. Operations goals require each customer to have his or her meal within five minutes of placing an order.

Once the order is taken through the guest interaction point of purchase (30 seconds), the order is sent to the kitchen technologically. Through the division of tasks, every function of the kitchen is made as efficient as possible. The line is set up with previously portioned meats and vegetables that flow in the same flow process each dish requires. Stations have a "job aid" providing the appropriate weight and ingredients for each dish. The preheated pan is critical to throughput and operational efficiency. With the help of 30,000 BTU burners, each dish gets through the sauté line in 3.5 minutes. An additional 30 seconds is used at the garnish station and the meal is served to the customer within 5 minutes.

Just-in-time inventory maintains that only what is needed is prepared. First-in first-out (FIFO) inventory method ensures the freshest ingredients. Food preparation is conducted throughout the day to ensure freshness. Focusing on every element from entry to exit allows Noodles & Company to deliver on the company's promise of quick, fresh, customized food served in a no-tip welcoming setting.

Note: The following problems contain some data that has been created by the author.

PROBLEM 1

The video discusses the extensive planning required to meet the operational goals for serving high-quality foods quickly. The goal of 5 minutes from order-taking to serving each meal is critical to maintaining Noodles & Company's promise to the customer of high-quality food served quickly. If a meal needs to be remade due to a processing error, what percent increase is this additional 3.5 minutes?

PROBLEM 2

Noodles & Company has won numerous accolades for its unique menu offerings. In 2011 *Parents* magazine ranked the chain number 6 in its top 10 list of Best Family Restaurants. The company also earned recognition as one of America's healthiest fast-food restaurants by *Health* magazine in 2008/2009. Its CEO, Kevin Reddy, was named a Top 10 Who to Watch Executive in 2010 and 2011 by *Nation's Restaurant News*. All of this success translates to revenue growth for the chain. According to *Inc.* magazine, the company's revenues grew from $136.7 million in 2007 to $220.8 million in 2010. What was its 3-year growth? Round your answer to the nearest percent.

PROBLEM 3

In 2011, Noodles & Company had approximately 300 locations in 22 states. If it planned to grow by 12% in 2012, how many new restaurants would it open and how many locations would it then have by the end of the year if it met its target? Round answers to the nearest whole number.

PROBLEM 4

The Noodles & Company location in Ann Arbor, Michigan, sells its Japanese Pan Noodle dish for $4.49 for a small bowl and $5.59 for a regular bowl. Protein (chicken, beef, shrimp, or tofu) is available for an additional $2.35 for either size. Imagine Noodles & Company is making a 250% markup based on cost. What is the cost for a regular Japanese Pan Noodle dish with chicken? What is the dollar markup? Round answers to the nearest cent.

PROBLEM 5

In Problem 4 above, the hypothetical markup based on cost was 250%. What is the corresponding markup based on selling price? Round your answer to the nearest percent.

PROBLEM 6

Noodles & Company offers shrimp as one of its protein options. Assume that each restaurant purchases frozen shrimp in large quantities and defrosts only as much as it expects to use each day. The restaurant would likely use past daily sales to estimate how much to take out for each day's business. But even then, some amount of loss could occur because shrimp should not be refrozen. Assume further that once defrosted, shrimp can be used for up to 2 days, each portion of shrimp costs $1.80, and the company wants an 80% markup on cost. If a given location takes out enough shrimp to sell 240 portions over a 2-day period and expects that as much as 10% could go bad before selling it, how should it price each portion of shrimp to account for the possible 10% loss?

Class Discussion Given the explosive growth of the "quick-casual" dining segment with franchises such as Noodles & Company, Chipotle Mexican Grill, and Qdoba, discuss how Noodles & Company might position itself to stand out in this increasingly crowded field of options.

SURF TO SAVE

What percentage of money are you actually saving? 🔍

PROBLEM 1
Breaking even on pizza

The student business club on your campus has decided to hold a pizza fund-raiser during finals. The club plans to buy 50 pizzas from http://www.dominos.com/ and resell them in the student center. Based upon the specials advertised on the site, what will you need to charge per slice (assume 8 slices per pizza) in order to break even?

Discussion Questions

1. Since this is a fund-raiser, what would you suggest charging for each slice and, based on this, what would the net profit be to this club?

2. Why do you feel breakeven analysis is so crucial in the development of new products for businesses?

PROBLEM 2
Markups can be stressful

The bookstore at your institution has decided to purchase some stress balls to resell to students. Visit http://www.orientaltrading.com/ and search for "stress balls." Assuming the bookstore will be able to sell 2,000 of these stress balls and the markup for products of this type is 25%, what will be the final cost to the student per stress ball? How much profit, in dollars, will be made by the bookstore on this item?

Discussion Questions

1. What are the factors used to set a markup price on a particular product?

2. Why are some products marked up at a higher rate than other products?

PROBLEM 3
Save big—instantly

Go to http://www.bestbuy.com. Find a product with a rebate or instant savings. Calculate the percent markdown after rebate.

Discussion Questions

1. What are the pros and cons of rebates from the seller's perspective?

2. What are the pros and cons of rebates from the consumer's perspective?

PROBLEM 4
A picture is worth how much?

Go to www.staples.com and search for a photo printer for your home. Select one that has Total Savings details attached to it and click on "See Details" to get the original and sale price. What is the percent markdown on the original price?

Discussion Questions

1. How do the photo printers that advertise these special savings compare to those without the savings?

2. What is the seller's advantage in promoting particular photo printers using the Total Savings approach?

MOBILE APPS ✕

iMarkup (SUI Solutions) Assists in calculating markup given a particular sale price, cost, or markup percentage.

MarkUp Markdown (Dynamic Circle, Inc.) Margin calculator and sale price tool that helps determine sale price based on a given percentage off the original price.

A KIPLINGER APPROACH

By Lisa Gerstner, From *Kiplinger's Personal Finance*, June 2015.

■ **LOWDOWN**

What You Need to Know About Online Pricing

Many sites manipulate what they charge you. We tell you how to beat the system.

BY LISA GERSTNER

1. Your online profile could boost the price. Online retailers know all kinds of things about you from the electronic bread crumbs you drop, such as your IP address, and they capitalize on it using *price discrimination* or *differential pricing*. For example, a site may charge higher prices after taking note of the Web browser you're using, your location, your previous shopping habits, or your search history. Or the merchant may *steer* your search—arranging the results to guide you toward more-expensive items. If a travel site sees that you're using a MacBook Air or an iPad, say, rather than a Windows desktop, it may show you a pricier selection of hotel rooms.

2. Everybody's doing it. A recent study by Northeastern University found that several leading Web commerce sites practiced steering and price discrimination. For example, Cheap Tickets and Orbitz quoted lower prices for users who logged in than for those who didn't log in—an average of $12 a night less for about 5% of hotels. Expedia and Hotels.com steered a segment of customers toward their more-expensive hotels. Searches of Travelocity's and Home Depot's Web sites using certain mobile devices yielded different results and pricing. And Priceline changed search results based on a user's history of clicks and purchases.

3. It's legal. Although it may seem unfair, retailers aren't breaking laws when they employ differential pricing. A recent White House report notes that the idea is "to set prices based on demand, or what customers are willing to pay, rather than costs." But the report cautions that luring customers with false promises or burying significant details in the fine print can tip the scale to fraud—and that vigilance is necessary to ensure that businesses don't use data they collect online to put consumers at a disadvantage based on race, gender or religion.

4. And sometimes it works to your benefit. When a movie chain offers discounts to students, seniors and members of the military, that's price discrimination. Lower prices for members of loyalty programs fall under the same heading.

5. You can beat Web retailers at their own game. Check how a site is filtering search results, and choose the option to sort from lowest to highest price. But don't stop there. If a site offers the option to log in, check prices before you log in and again after entering your username and password. Look up prices on your personal computer as well as your smartphone and tablet. View prices on different Web browsers—say, Safari and Chrome. Run a search with "cookies" enabled (cookies provide data about your online activities to Web sites), then open a new window and turn on private, or incognito, browsing, which won't save browser history. Search again.

6. Use all the tools at your disposal. If you have a choice, compare prices on several sites and apply coupon codes. Tools such as the Honey browser add-on, Coupon Sherpa.com and Retail MeNot .com will help you find coupons. PriceGrabber.com and the InvisibleHand browser add-on can help you compare prices across sites. ■

BILL BROWN

BUSINESS MATH ISSUE

Differential pricing is a practice that should be stopped.

1. List the key points of the article and information to support your position.
2. Write a group defense of your position using math calculations to support your view.

A Word Problem Approach—Chapters 6, 7, 8

1. Assume Kellogg's produced 715,000 boxes of Corn Flakes this year. This was 110% of the annual production last year. What was last year's annual production? *LU 6-2(2)*

2. A new Sony video camera has a list price of $420. The trade discount is 10/20 with terms of 2/10, n/30. If a retailer pays the invoice within the discount period, what is the amount the retailer must pay? *LU 7-1(4), LU 7-2(1)*

3. JCPenney sells loafers with a markup of $40. If the markup is 30% on cost, what did the loafers cost JCPenney? Round to the nearest dollar. *LU 8-1(3)*

4. Aster Computers received from Ring Manufacturers an invoice dated August 28 with terms 2/10 EOM. The list price of the invoice is $3,000 (freight not included). Ring offers Aster a 9/8/2 trade chain discount. Terms of freight are FOB shipping point, but Ring prepays the $150 freight. Assume Aster pays the invoice on October 9. How much will Ring receive? *LU 7-1(4), LU 7-2(1)*

5. Runners World marks up its Nike jogging shoes 25% on selling price. The Nike shoes sell for $65. How much did the store pay for them? *LU 8-2(4)*

6. Ivan Rone sells antique sleds. He knows that the most he can get for a sled is $350. Ivan needs a 35% markup on cost. Since Ivan is going to an antiques show, he wants to know the maximum he can offer a dealer for an antique sled. *LU 8-1(3)*

7. Bonnie's Bakery bakes 60 loaves of bread for $1.10 each. Bonnie's estimates that 10% of the bread will spoil. Assume a 60% markup on cost. What is the selling price of each loaf? If Bonnie's can sell the old bread for one-half the cost, what is the selling price of each loaf? *LU 8-3(2)*

CHAPTER 9

Payroll

© The McGraw-Hill Companies, Inc./Christopher Kerrigan, photographer

Levi Reduces Orders From Cambodia

BY SUZANNE KAPNER

Levi Strauss & Co. has slashed orders from Cambodian factories amid the political unrest in the country, after a nationwide strike by garment workers to demand higher wages was quelled with a violent crackdown.

The denim maker, along with a handful of U.S. and European brands including **Gap** Inc. and **Hennes & Mauritz** AB, attended a meeting with government officials on Monday to discuss a new wage-setting mechanism.

"Levi Strauss & Co. supports the Cambodian government establishing a methodologically sound and inclusive process for determining the minimum wage to ensure stability in the industry," Levi spokeswoman Amber McCasland said. This "should lead to the announcement of a new minimum wage as soon as possible."

The company cut back its Cambodia sourcing to minimize supply-chain risk and ensure delivery, Ms. McCasland said.

The strike started on Dec. 24, as a protest against the government's offer to raise the industry's minimum wage by 19% to $95 a month. The protests ended in January after police opened fire on labor demonstrators, killing at least four people and injuring dozens more.

Reprinted by permission of *The Wall Street Journal*, copyright 2014 Dow Jones & Company, Inc. All rights reserved worldwide.

LU 9–1: Calculating Various Types of Employees' Gross Pay

1. Define, compare, and contrast weekly, biweekly, semimonthly, and monthly pay periods.
2. Calculate gross pay with overtime on the basis of time.
3. Calculate gross pay for piecework, differential pay schedule, straight commission with draw, variable commission scale, and salary plus commission.

LU 9–2: Computing Payroll Deductions for Employees' Pay; Employers' Responsibilities

1. Prepare and explain the parts of a payroll register.
2. Explain and calculate federal and state unemployment taxes.

VOCABULARY PREVIEW

Here are key terms in this chapter. After completing the chapter, if you know the term, place a checkmark in the box. If you don't know the term, look it up and put the page number where it can be found.

Biweekly ☐ Deductions ☐ Differential pay schedule ☐ Draw ☐ Employee's Withholding Allowance Certificate (W-4) ☐ Fair Labor Standards Act ☐ Federal income tax withholding (FIT) ☐ Federal Insurance Contribution Act (FICA) ☐ Federal Unemployment Tax Act (FUTA) ☐ Gross pay ☐ Medicare ☐ Monthly ☐ Net pay ☐ Overrides ☐ Overtime ☐ Payroll register ☐ Percentage method ☐ Semimonthly ☐ Social Security ☐ State income tax (SIT) ☐ State Unemployment Tax Act (SUTA) ☐ Straight commission ☐ Variable commission scale ☐ W-4 ☐ Weekly ☐

Many Face New Normal: Part-Time Pay, Full-Time Bills

By Nick Timiraos

Nearly seven million Americans are stuck in part-time jobs they don't want.

The unemployment rate has fallen sharply over the past year, but that improvement is masking a still-bleak picture for millions of workers who say they can't find full-time jobs.

Martina Morgan is deciding which bills to skip after her hours fell at an Ikea store in Renton, Wash.

In Chicago, Jessica Davis is frustrated that her schedule dwindled to 23 hours a week at a McDonald's even though her location has been hiring. "How can you not get people more hours but you hire more employees?" the 26-year-old said.

The *Wall Street Journal* clip "Many Face New Normal" talks about the difficulty of finding full-time jobs even as the economy improves.

This chapter discusses (1) the type of pay people work for, (2) how employers calculate paychecks and deductions, and (3) what employers must report and pay in taxes.

Reprinted by permission of *The Wall Street Journal*, copyright 2014 Dow Jones & Company, Inc. All rights reserved worldwide.

Learning Unit 9–1: Calculating Various Types of Employees' Gross Pay

Logan Company manufactures dolls of all shapes and sizes. These dolls are sold worldwide. We study Logan Company in this unit because of the variety of methods Logan uses to pay its employees.

Companies usually pay employees **weekly, biweekly, semimonthly,** or **monthly.** How often employers pay employees can affect how employees manage their money. Some employees prefer a weekly paycheck that spreads the inflow of money. Employees who have monthly bills may find the twice-a-month or monthly paycheck more convenient. All employees would like more money to manage.

Let's assume you earn $50,000 per year. The following table shows what you would earn each pay period. Remember that 13 weeks equals one quarter. Four quarters or 52 weeks equals a year.

Salary paid	Period (based on a year)	Earnings for period (dollars)
Weekly	52 times (once a week)	$ 961.54 ($50,000 ÷ 52)
Biweekly	26 times (every two weeks)	$1,923.08 ($50,000 ÷ 26)
Semimonthly	24 times (twice a month)	$2,083.33 ($50,000 ÷ 24)
Monthly	12 times (once a month)	$4,166.67 ($50,000 ÷ 12)

You can estimate an annual salary by doubling the full-time hourly rate and then multiplying by 1,000. Example: $15 an hour, $15 × 2 × 1,000 = $30,000. You can estimate an hourly full-time rate by dividing an annual salary by 1,000 and then dividing by 2. Example: $30,000/1,000 = $30; 30/2 = $15.

Now let's look at some pay schedule situations and examples of how Logan Company calculates its payroll for employees of different pay status.

Situation 1: Hourly Rate of Pay; Calculation of Overtime

The **Fair Labor Standards Act** sets minimum wage standards and overtime regulations for employees of companies covered by this federal law. The law provides that employees working for an hourly rate receive time-and-a-half pay for hours worked in excess of their regular 40-hour week. Many managerial people, however, are exempt from the time-and-a-half pay for all hours in excess of a 40-hour week. Other workers may also be exempt.

GLOBAL

The current federal hourly minimum wage is $7.25. Various states have passed their own minimum wages. The *Wall Street Journal* clip "On the Clock" shows states with minimum hourly wages higher than the federal rate required by law. Note that Los Angeles is planning to have a $15 minimum wage versus the $8.00 shown in the clip by 2020. *The Wall Street Journal* chapter opener "Levi Reduces Orders From Cambodia" discusses a strike by Cambodian garment workers demanding a higher minimum wage than $95 per month.

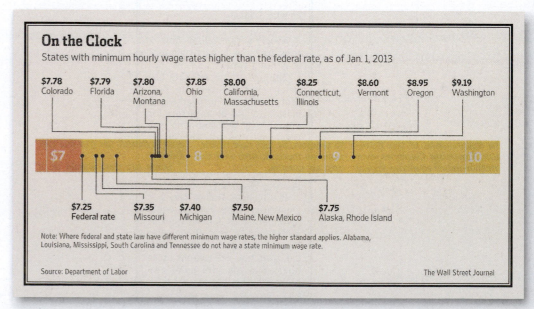

Reprinted by permission of *The Wall Street Journal,* copyright 2013 Dow Jones & Company, Inc. All rights reserved worldwide.

Now we return to our Logan Company example. Logan Company is calculating the weekly pay of Ramon Valdez who works in its manufacturing division. For the first 40 hours Ramon works, Logan calculates his **gross pay** (earnings before **deductions**) as follows:

> Gross pay = Hours employee worked × Rate per hour

Ramon works more than 40 hours in a week. For every hour over his 40 hours, Ramon must be paid an **overtime** pay of at least 1.5 times his regular pay rate. The following formula is used to determine Ramon's overtime:

> Hourly overtime pay rate = Regular hourly pay rate × 1.5

Logan Company must include Ramon's overtime pay with his regular pay. To determine Ramon's gross pay, Logan uses the following formula:

> Gross pay = Earnings for 40 hours + Earnings at time-and-a-half rate (1.5)

We are now ready to calculate Ramon's gross pay from the following data:

EXAMPLE

Employee	M	T	W	Th	F	S	Total hours	Rate per hour
Ramon Valdez	13	$8\frac{1}{2}$	10	8	$11\frac{1}{4}$	$10\frac{3}{4}$	$61\frac{1}{2}$	$9

$$61\frac{1}{2} \text{ total hours}$$
$$\underline{-40} \text{ regular hours}$$
$$21\frac{1}{2} \text{ hours overtime}^1 \qquad \text{Time-and-a-half pay: } \$9 \times 1.5 = \$13.50$$

$$\text{Gross pay} = (40 \text{ hours} \times \$9) + (21\frac{1}{2} \text{ hours} \times \$13.50)$$

$$= \qquad \$360 \qquad + \qquad \$290.25$$

$$= \boxed{\$650.25}$$

Note that the $13.50 overtime rate came out even. However, throughout the text, *if an overtime rate is greater than two decimal places, do not round it. Round only the final answer. This gives greater accuracy.*

Situation 2: Straight Piece Rate Pay

Some companies, especially manufacturers, pay workers according to how much they produce. Logan Company pays Ryan Foss for the number of dolls he produces in a week. This gives Ryan an incentive to make more money by producing more dolls. Ryan receives $.96 per doll, less any defective units. The following formula determines Ryan's gross pay:

> Gross pay = Number of units produced × Rate per unit

Companies may also pay a guaranteed hourly wage and use a piece rate as a bonus. However, Logan uses straight piece rate as wages for some of its employees.

EXAMPLE   During the last week of April, Ryan Foss produced 900 dolls. Using the above formula, Logan Company paid Ryan $864.

$$\text{Gross pay} = 900 \text{ dolls} \times \$.96$$

$$= \boxed{\$864}$$

---

[1]Some companies pay overtime for time over 8 hours in one day; Logan Company pays overtime for time over 40 hours per week.

Situation 3: Differential Pay Schedule

Some of Logan's employees can earn more than the $.96 straight piece rate for every doll they produce. Logan Company has set up a **differential pay schedule** for these employees. The company determines the rate these employees make by the amount of units the employees produce at different levels of production.

EXAMPLE Logan Company pays Abby Rogers on the basis of the following schedule:

	Units produced	Amount per unit
First 50 →	1–50	$ .50
Next 100 →	51–150	.62
Next 50 →	151–200	.75
	Over 200	1.25

Last week Abby produced 300 dolls. What is Abby's gross pay?
Logan calculated Abby's gross pay as follows:

$$(50 \times \$.50) + (100 \times \$.62) + (50 \times \$.75) + (100 \times \$1.25)$$

$$\$25 \quad + \quad \$62 \quad + \quad \$37.50 \quad + \quad \$125 \quad = \boxed{\$249.50}$$

Now we will study some of the other types of employee commission payment plans.

Situation 4: Straight Commission with Draw

Companies frequently use **straight commission** to determine the pay of salespersons. This commission is usually a certain percentage of the amount the salesperson sells. An example of one group of companies ceasing to pay commissions is the rental-car companies.

Companies such as Logan Company allow some of their salespersons to draw against their commission at the beginning of each month. A **draw** is an advance on the salesperson's commission. Logan subtracts this advance later from the employee's commission earned based on sales. When the commission does not equal the draw, the salesperson owes Logan the difference between the draw and the commission.

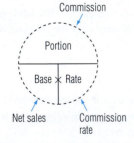

Commission

Portion

Base × Rate

Net sales   Commission rate

EXAMPLE Logan Company pays Jackie Okamoto a straight commission of 15% on her net sales (net sales are total sales less sales returns). In May, Jackie had net sales of $56,000. Logan gave Jackie a $600 draw in May. What is Jackie's gross pay?
Logan calculated Jackie's commission minus her draw as follows:

$$\$56,000 \times .15 = \$8,400$$
$$- \quad 600$$
$$\boxed{\$7,800}$$

Logan Company pays some people in the sales department on a variable commission scale. Let's look at this, assuming the employee had no draw.

Situation 5: Variable Commission Scale

A company with a **variable commission scale** uses different commission rates for different levels of net sales.

EXAMPLE Last month, Jane Ring's net sales were $160,000. What is Jane's gross pay based on the following schedule?

Up to $35,000	4%
Excess of $35,000 to $45,000	6%
Over $45,000	8%

$$\text{Gross pay} = (\$35,000 \times .04) + (\$10,000 \times .06) + (\$115,000 \times .08)$$

$$= \quad \$1,400 \quad + \quad \$600 \quad + \quad \$9,200$$

$$= \boxed{\$11,200}$$

MONEY tips

Understand the costs of credit. Do not spend money you do not currently have—especially if it is for entertainment. Avoid reaching or coming close to the maximum on your credit cards. Be careful to fully understand the terms of any credit card you use.

Situation 6: Salary Plus Commission

Logan Company pays Joe Roy a $3,000 monthly salary plus a 4% commission for sales over $20,000. Last month Joe's net sales were $50,000. Logan calculated Joe's gross monthly pay as follows:

$$\text{Gross pay} = \text{Salary} + (\text{Commission} \times \text{Sales over } \$20,000)$$
$$= \$3,000 + \quad\quad (.04 \times \$30,000)$$
$$= \$3,000 + \quad\quad\quad\quad \$1,200$$
$$= \boxed{\$4,200}$$

Before you take the Practice Quiz, you should know that many managers today receive **overrides.** These managers receive a commission based on the net sales of the people they supervise.

LU 9–1   PRACTICE QUIZ

Complete this **Practice Quiz** to see how you are doing.

1. Jill Foster worked 52 hours in one week for Delta Airlines. Jill earns $10 per hour. What is Jill's gross pay, assuming overtime is at time-and-a-half?
2. Matt Long had $180,000 in sales for the month. Matt's commission rate is 9%, and he had a $3,500 draw. What was Matt's end-of-month commission?
3. Bob Meyers receives a $1,000 monthly salary. He also receives a variable commission on net sales based on the following schedule (commission doesn't begin until Bob earns $8,000 in net sales):

$8,000–$12,000	1%	Excess of $20,000 to $40,000	5%
Excess of $12,000 to $20,000	3%	More than $40,000	8%

Assume Bob earns $40,000 net sales for the month. What is his gross pay?

For **extra help** from your authors–Sharon and Jeff–see the videos in Connect.

These videos are also available on YouTube!

✓ Solutions

1. 40 hours × $10.00 = $400.00
    12 hours × $15.00 = $180.00 ($10.00 × 1.5 = $15.00)
    $\boxed{\$580.00}$

2. $180,000 × .09 = $16,200
                    − 3,500
                    $\boxed{\$12,700}$

3. Gross pay = $1,000 + ($4,000 × .01) + ($8,000 × .03) + ($20,000 × .05)
    = $1,000 + $40 + $240 + $1,000
    = $\boxed{\$2,280}$

LU 9–1a   EXTRA PRACTICE QUIZ WITH WORKED-OUT SOLUTIONS

Need more practice? Try this **Extra Practice Quiz** (check figures in the Interactive Chapter Organizer). Worked-out Solutions can be found in Appendix B.

1. Jill Foster worked 54 hours in one week for Delta Airlines. Jill earns $12 per hour. What is Jill's gross pay, assuming overtime is at time-and-a-half?
2. Matt Long had $210,000 in sales for the month. Matt's commission rate is 8%, and he had a $4,000 draw. What was Matt's end-of-month commission?
3. Bob Myers receives a $1,200 monthly salary. He also receives a variable commission on net sales based on the following schedule (commission doesn't begin until Bob earns $9,000 in net sales).

$9,000 to $12,000	1%	Excess of $20,000 to $40,000	5%
Excess of $12,000 to $20,000	3%	More than $40,000	8%

Assume Bob earns $60,000 net sales for the month. What is his gross pay?

Learning Unit 9–2: Computing Payroll Deductions for Employees' Pay; Employers' Responsibilities

MONEY tips

Open a flexible-spending account. Eighty-five percent of employers offer them and they help you save by using pretax dollars for several expense categories.

The following *Wall Street Journal* clip, "Card Paychecks," discusses how employers cannot mandate that employees receive "card paychecks." The employer must offer choices such as paper checks, direct deposits, etc.

This unit begins by dissecting a paycheck. Then we give you an insight into the tax responsibilities of employers.

Card Paychecks Draw Warning

BY ALAN ZIBEL
AND ROBIN SIDEL

WASHINGTON—Employers can't require that workers receive paychecks on debit cards, a federal consumer regulator said Thursday, in response to concerns that companies are saddling workers with cards that carry high fees.

The Consumer Financial Protection Bureau said employers must provide other options besides paying workers on so-called payroll cards and vowed to "stop violations" of federal law. "Employees must have options when it comes to how they receive their wages," the CFPB's director, Richard Cordray, said.

The cards, which can carry fees that critics say aren't clearly disclosed, have been criticized by consumer advocates, New York's attorney general and Democrats on Capitol Hill. Payroll cards are typically aimed at people who don't have a bank account and no access to a direct-deposit program.

Reprinted by permission of *The Wall Street Journal*, copyright 2013 Dow Jones & Company, Inc. All rights reserved worldwide.

LO 1

Computing Payroll Deductions for Employees

Companies often record employee payroll information in a multicolumn form called a **payroll register.** The increased use of computers in business has made computerized registers a time-saver for many companies.

Glo Company uses a multicolumn payroll register. Below is Glo's partial payroll register showing the payroll information for JoAnn Rawley during week 49. Let's check each column to see if JoAnn's take-home pay of $1,740.72 is correct. Note how the circled letters in the register correspond to the explanations that follow.

								FICA Taxable Earnings			Deductions				
Employee name	Allow. & marital status	Cum. earn.	Sal. per week	Earnings			Cum. earn.			FICA				Health ins.	Net pay
				Reg.	Ovt.	Gross		S.S.	Med.	S.S.	Med.	FIT	SIT		
Rawley, JoAnn	M-2	117,600	2,450	2,450	—	2,450	120,050	900	2,450	55.80	35.53	370.95	147.00	100	1,740.72
	(A)	(B)	(C)	(D)			(E)	(F)	(G)	(H)	(I)	(J)	(K)	(L)	(M)

GLO COMPANY Payroll Register Week #49

Payroll Register Explanations

(A)—Allowance and marital status
(B), (C), (D)—Cumulative earnings before payroll, salaries, earnings
(E)—Cumulative earnings after payroll

When JoAnn was hired, she completed the **W-4 (Employee's Withholding Allowance Certificate)** form shown in Figure 9.1 stating that she is married and claims an allowance (exemption) of 2. Glo Company will need this information to calculate the federal income tax (J).

Before this pay period, JoAnn has earned $117,600 (48 weeks × $2,450 salary per week). Since JoAnn receives no overtime, her $2,450 salary per week represents her gross pay (pay before any deductions).

After this pay period, JoAnn has earned $120,050 ($117,600 + $2,450).

FIGURE 9.1

Employee's W-4 form

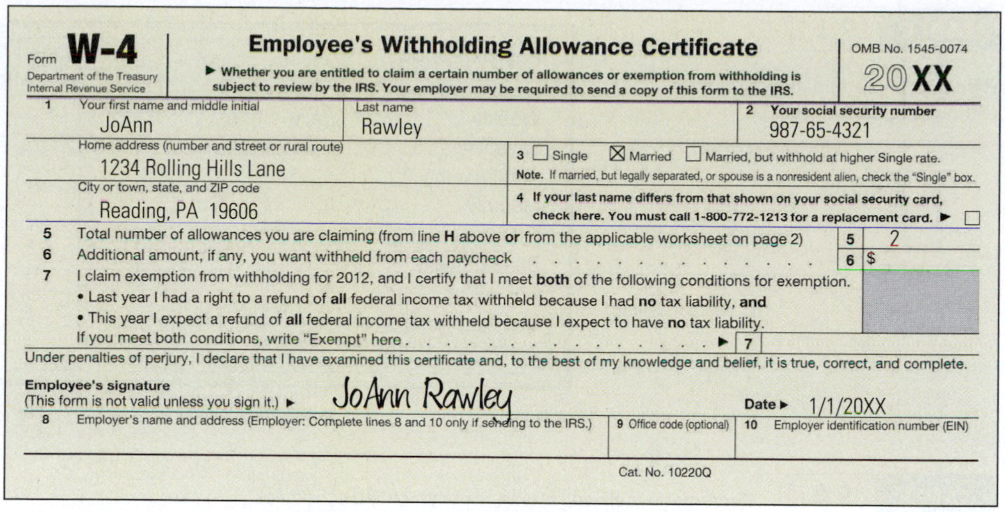

Form **W-4** Department of the Treasury Internal Revenue Service

Employee's Withholding Allowance Certificate

▶ Whether you are entitled to claim a certain number of allowances or exemption from withholding is subject to review by the IRS. Your employer may be required to send a copy of this form to the IRS.

OMB No. 1545-0074

20**XX**

1 Your first name and middle initial: JoAnn | Last name: Rawley | 2 Your social security number: 987-65-4321

Home address (number and street or rural route): 1234 Rolling Hills Lane

3 ☐ Single ☒ Married ☐ Married, but withhold at higher Single rate.

Note. If married, but legally separated, or spouse is a nonresident alien, check the "Single" box.

City or town, state, and ZIP code: Reading, PA 19606

4 If your last name differs from that shown on your social security card, check here. You must call 1-800-772-1213 for a replacement card. ▶ ☐

5 Total number of allowances you are claiming (from line H above or from the applicable worksheet on page 2) . . . 5 | 2

6 Additional amount, if any, you want withheld from each paycheck . . . 6 | $

7 I claim exemption from withholding for 2012, and I certify that I meet both of the following conditions for exemption.
- Last year I had a right to a refund of all federal income tax withheld because I had no tax liability, and
- This year I expect a refund of all federal income tax withheld because I expect to have no tax liability.

If you meet both conditions, write "Exempt" here . . . ▶ 7

Under penalties of perjury, I declare that I have examined this certificate and, to the best of my knowledge and belief, it is true, correct, and complete.

Employee's signature (This form is not valid unless you sign it.) ▶ JoAnn Rawley   Date ▶ 1/1/20XX

8 Employer's name and address (Employer: Complete lines 8 and 10 only if sending to the IRS.) | 9 Office code (optional) | 10 Employer identification number (EIN)

Cat. No. 10220Q

The **Federal Insurance Contribution Act (FICA)** funds the **Social Security** program. The program includes Old Age and Disability, Medicare, Survivor Benefits, and so on. The FICA tax requires separate reporting for Social Security and **Medicare.** We will use the following rates for Glo Company:

	Rate	Base
Social Security	6.20%	$118,500
Medicare	1.45	No base

These rates mean that JoAnn Rawley will pay Social Security taxes on the first $118,500 she earns this year. After earning $118,500, JoAnn's wages will be exempt from Social Security. Note that JoAnn will be paying Medicare taxes on all wages since Medicare has no base cutoff.

Ⓕ, Ⓖ—Taxable earnings for Social Security and Medicare

To help keep Glo's record straight, the *taxable earnings column only shows what wages will be taxed. This amount is not the tax.* For example, in week 49, only $900 of JoAnn's salary will be taxable for Social Security.

$118,500 Social Security base
− 117,600 Ⓑ
$ 900

Ⓗ—Social Security

To calculate JoAnn's Social Security tax, we multiply $900 Ⓕ by 6.2%:

$\$900 \times .062 = \$55.80$

Ⓘ—Medicare

Since Medicare has no base, JoAnn's entire weekly salary is taxed 1.45%, which is multiplied by $2,450.

$\$2{,}450 \times .0145 = \$35.53$

Ⓙ—FIT

Using the W-4 form JoAnn completed, Glo deducts **federal income tax withholding (FIT).** The more allowances an employee claims, the less money Glo deducts from the employee's paycheck. Glo uses the percentage method to calculate FIT.[2]

The Percentage Method[3] Today, since many companies do not want to store the tax tables, they use computers for their payroll. These companies use the **percentage method.** For this method we use Table 9.1 and Table 9.2 from Circular E to calculate JoAnn's FIT.

Step 1. In Table 9.1, locate the weekly withholding for one allowance. Multiply this number by 2.

$\$76.90 \times 2 = \$153.80$

[2]The *Business Math Handbook* has a sample of the wage bracket method.

[3]An alternative method is the wage bracket method shown in the *Business Math Handbook*.

TABLE	9.1

Percentage method income tax withholding allowances

Payroll Period	One Withholding Allowance
Weekly	$ 76.90
Biweekly	153.80
Semimonthly	166.70
Monthly	333.30
Quarterly	1,000.00
Semiannually	2,000.00
Annually	4,000.00
Daily or miscellaneous (each day of the payroll period)	15.40

TABLE	9.2

Percentage method income tax withholding schedules

Percentage Method Tables for Income Tax Withholding

TABLE 1—WEEKLY Payroll Period

(a) SINGLE person (including head of household)—

If the amount of wages (after subtracting withholding allowances) is: The amount of income tax to withhold is:

Not over $44 . . . . $0

Over—	But not over—		of excess over—
$44	—$222	$0.00 plus 10%	—$44
$222	—$764	$17.80 plus 15%	—$222
$764	—$1,789	$99.10 plus 25%	—$764
$1,789	—$3,685	$355.35 plus 28%	—$1,789
$3,685	—$7,958	$886.23 plus 33%	—$3,685
$7,958	—$7,990	$2,296.32 plus 35%	—$7,958
$7,990		$2,307.52 plus 39.6%	—$7,990

(b) MARRIED person—

If the amount of wages (after subtracting withholding allowances) is: The amount of income tax to withhold is:

Not over $165 . . . . $0

Over—	But not over—		of excess over—
$165	—$520	$0.00 plus 10%	—$165
$520	—$1,606	$35.50 plus 15%	—$520
$1,606	—$3,073	$198.40 plus 25%	—$1,606
$3,073	—$4,597	$565.15 plus 28%	—$3,073
$4,597	—$8,079	$991.87 plus 33%	—$4,597
$8,079	—$9,105	$2,140.93 plus 35%	—$8,079
$9,105		$2,500.03 plus 39.6%	—$9,105

TABLE 2—BIWEEKLY Payroll Period

(a) SINGLE person (including head of household)—

If the amount of wages (after subtracting withholding allowances) is: The amount of income tax to withhold is:

Not over $88 . . . . $0

Over—	But not over—		of excess over—
$88	—$443	$0.00 plus 10%	—$88
$443	—$1,529	$35.50 plus 15%	—$443
$1,529	—$3,579	$198.40 plus 25%	—$1,529
$3,579	—$7,369	$710.90 plus 28%	—$3,579
$7,369	—$15,915	$1,772.10 plus 33%	—$7,369
$15,915	—$15,981	$4,592.28 plus 35%	—$15,915
$15,981		$4,615.38 plus 39.6%	—$15,981

(b) MARRIED person—

If the amount of wages (after subtracting withholding allowances) is: The amount of income tax to withhold is:

Not over $331 . . . . $0

Over—	But not over—		of excess over—
$331	—$1,040	$0.00 plus 10%	—$331
$1,040	—$3,212	$70.90 plus 15%	—$1,040
$3,212	—$6,146	$396.70 plus 25%	—$3,212
$6,146	—$9,194	$1,130.20 plus 28%	—$6,146
$9,194	—$16,158	$1,983.64 plus 33%	—$9,194
$16,158	—$18,210	$4,281.76 plus 35%	—$16,158
$18,210		$4,999.96 plus 39.6%	—$18,210

TABLE 3—SEMIMONTHLY Payroll Period

(a) SINGLE person (including head of household)—

If the amount of wages (after subtracting withholding allowances) is: The amount of income tax to withhold is:

Not over $96 . . . . $0

Over—	But not over—		of excess over—
$96	—$480	$0.00 plus 10%	—$96
$480	—$1,656	$38.40 plus 15%	—$480
$1,656	—$3,877	$214.80 plus 25%	—$1,656
$3,877	—$7,983	$770.05 plus 28%	—$3,877
$7,983	—$17,242	$1,919.73 plus 33%	—$7,983
$17,242	—$17,313	$4,975.20 plus 35%	—$17,242
$17,313		$5,000.05 plus 39.6%	—$17,313

(b) MARRIED person—

If the amount of wages (after subtracting withholding allowances) is: The amount of income tax to withhold is:

Not over $358 . . . . $0

Over—	But not over—		of excess over—
$358	—$1,127	$0.00 plus 10%	—$358
$1,127	—$3,479	$76.90 plus 15%	—$1,127
$3,479	—$6,658	$429.70 plus 25%	—$3,479
$6,658	—$9,960	$1,224.45 plus 28%	—$6,658
$9,960	—$17,504	$2,149.01 plus 33%	—$9,960
$17,504	—$19,727	$4,638.53 plus 35%	—$17,504
$19,727		$5,416.58 plus 39.6%	—$19,727

TABLE 4—MONTHLY Payroll Period

(a) SINGLE person (including head of household)—

If the amount of wages (after subtracting withholding allowances) is: The amount of income tax to withhold is:

Not over $192 . . . . $0

Over—	But not over—		of excess over—
$192	—$960	$0.00 plus 10%	—$192
$960	—$3,313	$76.80 plus 15%	—$960
$3,313	—$7,754	$429.75 plus 25%	—$3,313
$7,754	—$15,967	$1,540.00 plus 28%	—$7,754
$15,967	—$34,483	$3,839.64 plus 33%	—$15,967
$34,483	—$34,625	$9,949.92 plus 35%	—$34,483
$34,625		$9,999.62 plus 39.6%	—$34,625

(b) MARRIED person—

If the amount of wages (after subtracting withholding allowances) is: The amount of income tax to withhold is:

Not over $717 . . . . $0

Over—	But not over—		of excess over—
$717	—$2,254	$0.00 plus 10%	—$717
$2,254	—$6,958	$153.70 plus 15%	—$2,254
$6,958	—$13,317	$859.30 plus 25%	—$6,958
$13,317	—$19,921	$2,449.05 plus 28%	—$13,317
$19,921	—$35,008	$4,298.17 plus 33%	—$19,921
$35,008	—$39,454	$9,276.88 plus 35%	—$35,008
$39,454		$10,832.98 plus 39.6%	—$39,454

Step 2. Subtract $153.80 in Step 1 from JoAnn's total pay.

$$\begin{array}{r} \$2,450.00 \\ -\ \ \ 153.80 \\ \hline \$2,296.20 \end{array}$$

Step 3. In Table 9.2, locate the married person's weekly pay table. The $2,296.20 falls between $1,606 and $3,073. The tax is $198.40 plus 25% of the excess over $1,606.

$$\begin{array}{r} \$2,296.20 \\ -\ 1,606.00 \\ \hline \$690.20 \end{array}$$

Tax $198.40 + .25($690.20)

$198.40 + $172.55 = $370.95

We assume a 6% **state income tax (SIT).**

$2,450 × .06 = $147.00

JoAnn contributes $100 per week for health insurance. JoAnn's **net pay** is her gross pay less all deductions.

$$\begin{array}{rl} \$2,450.00 & \text{gross} \\ -\ \ \ \ \ 55.80 & \text{Social Security} \\ -\ \ \ \ \ 35.53 & \text{Medicare} \\ -\ \ \ 370.95 & \text{FIT} \\ -\ \ \ 147.00 & \text{SIT} \\ -\ \ \ 100.00 & \text{health insurance} \\ \hline =\ \$1,740.72 & \text{net pay} \end{array}$$

(K)—SIT

(L)—Health insurance
(M)—Net pay

© Winston Davidian/Photodisc/Getty Images

Employers' Responsibilities

In the first section of this unit, we saw that JoAnn contributed to Social Security and Medicare. Glo Company has the legal responsibility to match her contributions. Besides matching Social Security and Medicare, Glo must pay two important taxes that employees do not have to pay—federal and state unemployment taxes.

Federal Unemployment Tax Act (FUTA) The federal government participates in a joint federal-state unemployment program to help unemployed workers. At this writing, employers pay the government a 6% **FUTA** tax on the first $7,000 paid to employees as wages during the calendar year. Any wages in excess of $7,000 per worker are exempt wages and are not taxed for FUTA. If the total cumulative amount the employer owes the government is less than $100, the employer can pay the liability yearly (end of January in the following calendar year). If the tax is greater than $100, the employer must pay it within a month after the quarter ends.

Companies involved in a state unemployment tax fund can usually take a 5.4% credit against their FUTA tax. *In reality, then, companies are paying .6% (.006) to the federal unemployment program.* In all our calculations, FUTA is .006.

EXAMPLE Assume a company had total wages of $19,000 in a calendar year. No employee earned more than $7,000 during the calendar year. The FUTA tax is .6% (6% minus the company's 5.4% credit for state unemployment tax). How much does the company pay in FUTA tax?

The company calculates its FUTA tax as follows:

$$\begin{array}{rl} & 6\% \ \text{FUTA tax} \\ -\ & 5.4\% \ \text{credit for SUTA tax} \\ \hline =\ & .6\% \ \text{tax for FUTA} \end{array}$$

.006 × $19,000 = $114 FUTA tax due to federal government

MONEY tips

The IRS has twelve items it looks for on a return that raise the chances of an audit from the average rate of 1.1%: making too much money; failing to report all taxable income; taking large charitable deductions; claiming the home office deduction; claiming rental losses; deducting business meals, travel, and entertainment; claiming 100% business use of a vehicle; writing off a loss for a hobby; running a cash business; failing to report a foreign bank account; engaging in currency transactions; and taking higher-than-average deductions.

LO 2

State Unemployment Tax Act (SUTA)   The current **SUTA** tax in many states is 5.4% on the first $7,000 the employer pays an employee. Some states offer a merit rating system that results in a lower SUTA rate for companies with a stable employment period. The federal government still allows 5.4% credit on FUTA tax to companies entitled to the lower SUTA rate. Usually states also charge companies with a poor employment record a higher SUTA rate. However, these companies cannot take any more than the 5.4% credit against the 6% federal unemployment rate.

EXAMPLE   Assume a company has total wages of $20,000 and $4,000 of the wages are exempt from SUTA. What are the company's SUTA and FUTA taxes if the company's SUTA rate is 5.8% due to a poor employment record?

The exempt wages (over $7,000 earnings per worker) are not taxed for SUTA or FUTA. So the company owes the following SUTA and FUTA taxes:

$20,000
$\underline{-\ \ \ 4,000}$ (exempt wages)
$16,000 \times .058 = $ 928 SUTA

Federal FUTA tax would then be:
$16,000 \times .006 = $ 96

You can check your progress with the following Practice Quiz.

LU 9–2 | **PRACTICE QUIZ**

Complete this Practice Quiz to see how you are doing.

*For **extra help** from your authors–Sharon and Jeff–see the videos in Connect.*

These videos are also available on YouTube!

1. Calculate Social Security taxes, Medicare taxes, and FIT for Joy Royce. Joy's company pays her a monthly salary of $9,500. She is single and claims 1 deduction. Before this payroll, Joy's cumulative earnings were $115,000. (Social Security maximum is 6.2% on $118,500, and Medicare is 1.45%.) Calculate FIT by the percentage method.

2. Jim Brewer, owner of Arrow Company, has three employees who earn $300, $700, and $900 a week. Assume a state SUTA rate of 5.1%. What will Jim pay for state and federal unemployment taxes for the first quarter?

✓ Solutions

1.   **Social Security**

    $118,500
   $\underline{-\ 115,000}$
    $\$\ \ \ 3,500 \times .062 = $ 217.00

            Medicare

            $9,500 \times .0145 = $ 137.75

   FIT
   Percentage method: $9,500.00
   $333.30 \times 1 = $ $\underline{-\ \ \ 333.30}$ (Table 9.1)
                   $9,166.70

        $7,754 to $15,967 → $1,540 plus 28% of excess over $7,754
                                               (Table 9.2)

      $9,166.70
      $\underline{-\ 7,754.00}$
        $1,412.70 \times .28 = $ $\ \ 395.56$
                      $\underline{+\ 1,540.00}$
                      $1,935.56$

2.   13 weeks $\times$ $300 = $ $\ 3,900
    13 weeks $\times$ $700 = $ 9,100 ($9,100 − $7,000) → $2,100 ⎫ Exempt wages
    13 weeks $\times$ $900 = $ $\underline{11,700}$ ($11,700 − $7,000) → $\underline{\ 4,700}$ ⎬ (not taxed for
                      $24,700 $6,800 ⎭ FUTA or SUTA)

    $24,700 − $6,800 = $17,900 taxable wages
    SUTA = .051 $\times$ $17,900 = $ 912.90
    FUTA = .006 $\times$ $17,900 = $ 107.40

                                  Note: FUTA remains at .006 whether SUTA rate is higher or lower than standard.

LU 9–2a	EXTRA PRACTICE QUIZ WITH WORKED-OUT SOLUTIONS

Need more practice? Try this Extra Practice Quiz (check figures in the Interactive Chapter Organizer). Worked-out Solutions can be found in Appendix B.

1. Calculate Social Security taxes, Medicare taxes, and FIT for Joy Royce. Joy's company pays her a monthly salary of $10,000. She is single and claims 1 deduction. Before this payroll, Joy's cumulative earnings were $118,000. (Social Security maximum is 6.2% on $118,500, and Medicare is 1.45%.) Calculate FIT by the percentage method.

2. Jim Brewer, owner of Arrow Company, has three employees who earn $200, $800, and $950 a week. Assume a state SUTA rate of 5.1%. What will Jim pay for state and federal unemployment taxes for the first quarter?

INTERACTIVE CHAPTER ORGANIZER

Topic/Procedure/Formula	Examples	You try it*
Gross pay Hours employee worked × Rate per hour	$6.50 per hour at 36 hours Gross pay = 36 × $6.50 = $234	**Calculate gross pay** $9.25 per hour; 38 hours
Overtime Gross earnings (pay) = Regular pay + Earnings at overtime rate (1½)	$6 per hour; 42 hours Gross pay = (40 × $6) + (2 × $9) = $240 + $18 = $258	**Calculate gross pay** $7 per hour; 43 hours
Straight piece rate Gross pay = Number of units produced × Rate per unit	1,185 units; rate per unit, $.89 Gross pay = 1,185 × $.89 = $1,054.65	**Calculate gross pay** 2,250 units; $.79 per unit
Differential pay schedule Rate on each item is related to the number of items produced.	1–500 at $.84; 501–1,000 at $.96; 900 units produced. Gross pay = (500 × $.84) + (400 × $.96) = $420 + $384 = $804	**Calculate gross pay** 1–600 at $.79; 601–1,000 at $.88; 900 produced
Straight commission Total sales × Commission rate Any draw would be subtracted from earnings.	$155,000 sales; 6% commission $155,000 × .06 = $9,300	**Calculate straight commission** $175,000 sales; 7% commission
Variable commission scale Sales at different levels pay different rates of commission.	Up to $5,000, 5%; $5,001 to $10,000, 8%; over $10,000, 10% Sold: $6,500 Solution: ($5,000 × .05) + ($1,500 × .08) = $250 + $120 = $370	**Calculate commission** Up to $6,000, 5%; $6,001 to $8,000, 9%; Over $8,000, 12% Sold: $12,000
Salary plus commission Regular wages (fixed) + Commissions earned	Base $400 per week + 2% on sales over $14,000 Actual sales: $16,000 $400 (base) + (.02 × $2,000) = $440	**Calculate gross pay** Base $600 per week plus 4% on sales over $16,000. Actual sales $22,000.
Payroll register Multicolumn form to record payroll. Married and paid weekly. (Table 9.2) Claims 1 allowance. FICA rates from chapter.	(see table below)	**Calculate net pay** Gross pay, $490; Married, paid weekly. Claims, one allowance. Use rates in text for Social Security, Medicare, and FIT.
FICA **Social Security Medicare** 6.2% on $118,500 (S.S.) 1.45% (Med.)	If John earns $120,000, what did he contribute for the year to Social Security and Medicare? S.S.: $118,500 × .062 = $7,347 Med.: $120,000 × .0145 = $1,740.00	**Calculate FICA** If John earns $150,000, what did he contribute to Social Security and Medicare?

Payroll register example table:

		Deductions			Net pay
Earnings		FICA			
Gross	S.S.	Med.	FIT		
1,515	93.93	21.97	173.22		1,225.88

(continues)

INTERACTIVE CHAPTER ORGANIZER

Topic/Procedure/Formula	Examples	You try it*
FIT calculation (percentage method) *Facts*: Al Doe: Married Claims: 2 Paid weekly: $1,600	$1,600.00 − 153.80 ($76.90 × 2) Table 9.1 $ 1,446.20 By Table 9.2 $1,446.20 − 520.00 $ 926.20 $35.50 + .15($926.20) $35.50 + $138.93 = $174.43	**Calculate FIT** Jim Smith, married, claims 3; Paid weekly, $1,400
State and federal unemployment Employer pays these taxes. Rates are 6% on $7,000 for federal and 5.4% for state on $7,000. 6% − 5.4% = .6% federal rate after credit. If state unemployment rate is higher than 5.4%, no additional credit is taken. If state unemployment rate is less than 5.4%, the full 5.4% credit can be taken for federal unemployment.	Cumulative pay before payroll, $6,400; this week's pay, $800. What are state and federal unemployment taxes for employer, assuming a 5.2% state unemployment rate? State → .052 × $600 = $31.20 Federal → .006 × $600 = $3.60 ($6,400 + $600 = $7,000 maximum)	**Calculate SUTA and FUTA** Cumulative pay before payroll, $6,800. This week's payroll, $9,000. State rate is 5.4%.

KEY TERMS			

	Biweekly
	Deductions
	Differential pay schedule
	Draw
	Employee's Withholding
	  Allowance Certificate (W-4)
	Fair Labor Standards Act
	Federal income tax withholding
	  (FIT)
	Federal Insurance Contribution
	  Act (FICA)
		Federal Unemployment Tax Act
		  (FUTA)
		Gross pay
		Medicare
		Monthly
		Net pay
		Overrides
		Overtime
		Payroll register
		Percentage method
		Semimonthly
			Social Security
			State income tax (SIT)
			State Unemployment Tax Act
			  (SUTA)
			Straight commission
			Variable commission scale
			W-4
			Weekly

Check Figures for Extra Practice Quizzes. (Worked-out Solutions are in Appendix B.)	LU 9–1a 1. $732 2. $12,800 3. $4,070	LU 9–2a 1. $2,075.56 2. $846.60; $99.60

*Worked-out solutions are in Appendix B.

Critical Thinking Discussion Questions with Chapter Concept Check

1. Explain the difference between biweekly and semimonthly. Explain what problems may develop if a retail store hires someone on straight commission to sell cosmetics.

2. Explain what each column of a payroll register records and how each number is calculated. Social Security tax is based on a specific rate and base; Medicare tax is based on a rate but has no base. Do you think this is fair to all taxpayers?

3. What taxes are the responsibility of the employer? How can an employer benefit from a merit-rating system for state unemployment?

4. **Chapter Concept Check.** Visit the Starbucks website to see what benefits the company provides for its employees. Be sure to discuss the responsibilities of the employee and the employer.

END-OF-CHAPTER PROBLEMS

Check figures for odd-numbered problems in Appendix C. Name _____ Date _____

DRILL PROBLEMS

Complete the following table: *LU 9-1(2)*

	Employee	M	T	W	Th	F	Hours	Rate per hour	Gross pay
9–1.	Pete Paul	11	6	9	7	6		$7.95	
9–2.	Kristina Shaw	5	9	10	8	8		$8.10	

Complete the following table (assume the overtime for each employee is a time-and-a-half rate after 40 hours): *LU 9-1(2)*

	Employee	M	T	W	Th	F	Sa	Total regular hours	Total overtime hours	Regular rate	Overtime rate	Gross earnings
9–3.	Blue	12	9	9	9	9	3			$8.00		
9–4.	Tagney	14	8	9	9	5	1			$7.60		

Calculate gross earnings: *LU 9-1(3)*

	Worker	Number of units produced	Rate per unit	Gross earnings
9–5.	Lang	480	$3.50	
9–6.	Swan	846	$ .58	

Calculate the gross earnings for each apple picker based on the following differential pay scale: *LU 9-1(3)*

1–1,000: $.03 each   1,001–1,600: $.05 each   Over 1,600: $.07 each

	Apple picker	Number of apples picked	Gross earnings
9–7.	Ryan	1,600	
9–8.	Rice	1,925	

Calculate the end-of-month commission. *LU 9-1(3)*

	Employee	Total sales	Commission rate	Draw	End-of-month commission received
9–9.	Reese	$300,000	7%	$8,000	

Ron Company has the following commission schedule:

Commission rate	Sales
2%	Up to $80,000
3.5%	Excess of $80,000 to $100,000
4%	More than $100,000

Calculate the gross earnings of Ron Company's two employees: *LU 9-1(3)*

	Employee	Total sales	Gross earnings
9–10.	Bill Moore	$ 70,000	
9–11.	Ron Ear	$155,000	

Complete the following table, given that A Publishing Company pays its salespeople a weekly salary plus a 2% commission on all net sales over $5,000 (no commission on returned goods): *LU 9-1(3)*

	Employee	Gross sales	Return	Net sales	Given quota	Commission sales	Commission rates	Total commission	Regular wage	Total wage
9–12.	Ring	$ 8,000	$ 25		$5,000		2%		$250	
eXcel										
9–13.	Porter	$12,000	$100		$5,000		2%		$250	
eXcel										

Calculate the Social Security and Medicare deductions for the following employees (assume a tax rate of 6.2% on $118,500 for Social Security and 1.45% for Medicare): *LU 9-2(1)*

	Employee	Cumulative earnings before this pay period	Pay amount this period	Social Security	Medicare
9–14.	Logan	$118,400	$3,000		
9–15.	Rouche	$112,400	$7,000		
9–16.	Cleaves	$400,000	$6,000		

Complete the following payroll register. Calculate FIT by the percentage method for this weekly period; Social Security and Medicare are the same rates as in the previous problems. No one will reach the maximum for FICA. *LU 9-2(1)*

	Employee	Marital status	Allowances claimed	Gross pay	FIT	FICA		Net pay
						S.S.	Med.	
9–17.	Mike Rice	M	2	$1,600				
9–18.	Pat Brown	M	4	$2,100				

9–19. Given the following, calculate the state (assume 5.3%) and federal unemployment taxes that the employer must pay for each of the first two quarters. The federal unemployment tax is .6% on the first $7,000. *LU 9-2(2)*

PAYROLL SUMMARY		
	Quarter 1	Quarter 2
Bill Adams	$4,000	$ 8,000
Rich Haines	8,000	14,000
Alice Smooth	3,200	3,800

WORD PROBLEMS

9–20. Lai Xiaodong, a 22-year-old college-educated man, accepted a job at Foxconn Technology (where the iPad was being produced for Apple) in Chengdu, China, for $22 a day at 12 hours a day, 6 days a week. A company perk included company housing in dorms for the 70,000 employees. It was common for 20 people to be assigned to the same three-bedroom apartment. What were Lai's hourly (rounded to the nearest cent), weekly, and annual gross pay? *LU 9-1(1)*

9–21. Rhonda Brennan found her first job after graduating from college through the classifieds of the *Miami Herald*. She was delighted when the offer came through at $18.50 per hour. She completed her W-4 stating that she is married with a child and claims an allowance of 3. Her company will pay her biweekly for 80 hours. Calculate her take-home pay for her first check. *LU 9-2(1)*

9–22. The Social Security Administration increased the taxable wage base from $117,000 to $118,500. The 6.2% tax rate is unchanged. Joe Burns earned over $120,000 each of the past two years. **(a)** What is the percent increase in the base? Round to the nearest hundredth percent. **(b)** What is Joe's increase in Social Security tax for the new year? *LU 9-2(1)*

9–23. Calculate Social Security taxes, Medicare taxes, and FIT for Jordon Barrett. He earns a monthly salary of $12,000. He is single and claims 1 deduction. Before this payroll, Barrett's cumulative earnings were $110,500. (Social Security maximum is 6.2% on $118,500 and Medicare is 1.45%.) Calculate FIT by the percentage method. *LU 9-2(1)*

9–24. Maggie Vitteta, single, works 38 hours per week at $9.00 an hour. How much is taken out for federal income tax with one withholding exemption?   *LU 9-2(1)*

9–25. Robin Hartman earns $600 per week plus 3% of sales over $6,500. Robin's sales are $14,000. How much does Robin earn?   *LU 9-1(3)*

9–26. Pat Maninen earns a gross salary of $3,000 each week. What are Pat's first week's deductions for Social Security and Medicare? Will any of Pat's wages be exempt from Social Security and Medicare for the calendar year? Assume a rate of 6.2% on $118,500 for Social Security and 1.45% for Medicare.   *LU 9-2(1)*

9–27. Richard Gaziano is a manager for Health Care, Inc. Health Care deducts Social Security, Medicare, and FIT (by percentage method) from his earnings. Assume the same Social Security and Medicare rates as in Problem 9–26. Before this payroll, Richard is $1,000 below the maximum level for Social Security earnings. Richard is married, is paid weekly, and claims 2 exemptions. What is Richard's net pay for the week if he earns $1,300?   *LU 9-2(1)*

9–28. Larren Buffett is concerned after receiving her weekly paycheck. She believes that her deductions for Social Security, Medicare, and federal income tax withholding (FIT) may be incorrect. Larren is paid a salary of $4,100 weekly. She is married, claims 3 deductions, and prior to this payroll check, has total earnings of $116,000. What are the correct deductions for Social Security, Medicare, and FIT?   *LU 9-2(2)*

9–29. Westway Company pays Suzie Chan $3,000 per week. By the end of week 52, how much did Westway deduct for Suzie's Social Security and Medicare for the year? Assume Social Security is 6.2% on $118,500 and 1.45% for Medicare. What state and federal unemployment taxes does Westway pay on Suzie's yearly salary? The state unemployment rate is 5.1%. FUTA is .8%.   *LU 9-2(1, 2)*

9–30. Sarah Jones earns $525 per week selling life insurance for Farmer's Insurance plus 5% of sales over $5,750. Sarah's sales this month (four weeks) are $20,000. How much does Sarah earn this month?   *LU 9-2(2)*

9–31. Tiffani Lind earned $1,200 during her biweekly pay period. She is married and claims 4 deductions. Her annual earnings *eXcel* to date are $52,521. Calculate her net pay. *LU 9-2(1)*

CHALLENGE PROBLEMS

9–32. The San Bernardino County Fair hires about 150 people during fair time. Their wages range from $6.75 to $8.00. California has a state income tax of 9%. Sandy Denny earns $8.00 per hour; George Barney earns $6.75 per hour. They both worked 35 hours this week. Both are married; however, Sandy claims 2 exemptions and George claims 1 exemption. Assume a rate of 6.2% on $118,500 for Social Security and 1.45% for Medicare. **(a)** What is Sandy's net pay after FIT (use the tables in the text), Social Security tax, state income tax, and Medicare have been taken out? **(b)** What is George's net pay after the same deductions? **(c)** How much more is Sandy's net pay versus George's net pay? Round to the nearest cent. *LU 9-2(1)*

9–33. Bill Rose is a salesperson for Boxes, Inc. He believes his $1,460.47 monthly paycheck is in error. Bill earns a $1,400 salary per month plus a 9.5% commission on sales over $1,500. Last month, Bill had $8,250 in sales. Bill believes his traveling expenses are 16% of his weekly gross earnings before commissions. Monthly deductions include Social Security, $126.56; Medicare, $29.60; FIT, $189.50; union dues, $25.00; and health insurance, $16.99. Calculate the following: **(a)** Bill's monthly take-home pay, and indicate the amount his check was under- or overstated, and **(b)** Bill's weekly traveling expenses. Round your final answer to the nearest dollar. *LU 9-2(1)*

SUMMARY PRACTICE TEST

Do you need help? The videos in Connect have step-by-step worked-out solutions. These videos are also available on YouTube!

1. Calculate Sam's gross pay (he is entitled to time-and-a-half).   *LU 9-1(2)*

M	T	W	Th	F	Total hours	Rate per hour	Gross pay
$9\frac{1}{4}$	$9\frac{1}{4}$	$10\frac{1}{2}$	$8\frac{1}{2}$	$11\frac{1}{2}$		\$8.00	

2. Mia Kaminsky sells shoes for Macy's. Macy's pays Mia \$12 per hour plus a 5% commission on all sales. Assume Mia works 37 hours for the week and has \$7,000 in sales. What is Mia's gross pay?   *LU 9-1(3)*

3. Lee Company pays its employees on a graduated commission scale: 6% on the first \$40,000 sales, 7% on sales from \$40,001 to \$80,000, and 13% on sales of more than \$80,000. May West, an employee of Lee, has \$230,000 in sales. What commission did May earn?   *LU 9-1(3)*

4. Matty Kim, an accountant for Vernitron, earned \$111,000 from January to June. In July, Matty earned \$20,000. Assume a tax rate of 6.2% for Social Security on \$118,500 and 1.45% on Medicare. How much are the July taxes for Social Security and Medicare?   *LU 9-2(1)*

5. Grace Kelley earns \$2,000 per week. She is married and claims 2 exemptions. What is Grace's income tax? Use the percentage method.   *LU 9-2(1)*

6. Jean Michaud pays his two employees \$900 and \$1,200 per week. Assume a state unemployment tax rate of 5.7% and a federal unemployment tax rate of .6%. What state and federal unemployment taxes will Jean pay at the end of quarter 1 and quarter 2?   *LU 9-2(2)*

SURF TO SAVE

Looking for ways to make money? 🔍

 PROBLEM 1
Selling for a living

Visit http://www.calculatorpro.com/calculator/commission-calculator/ and assume you are a salesperson working on a straight commission basis. Your sales for the month were $156,000 and are paid at a 3% commission rate. What is your commission for the month?

Discussion Questions

1. What are the pros and cons of working entirely on commission?

2. Would you be comfortable working solely on commission? Why or why not?

 PROBLEM 2
Single vs. married taxpayers

Go to http://www.paycheckcity.com/coapa/netpaycalculator.asp. Suppose you are single and earn $2,000 semimonthly. Assume it is July 1 and you have already earned $24,000. How much more federal income tax is withheld from your paycheck compared to a married person, earning the same salary, with four dependents?

Discussion Questions

1. Why do you feel the tax rates differ based on marital status?

2. Will your federal tax withholding likely increase, decrease, or stay the same over the next 10 years? Why?

 PROBLEM 3
Preparing for retirement

Go to http://www.ssa.gov/OACT/quickcalc/index.html. If you plan to retire at age 65 and currently earn $68,000 per year, determine your benefit using both today's dollars and inflated (future) dollars. What is the difference between the two values? Click to see the earnings that were used. Which number is more realistic?

Discussion Questions

1. What types of expenses do you envision having during your retirement?

2. Do you plan to work during your retirement years? Why or why not?

 PROBLEM 4
Worthy commission?

Go to http://www.nytimes.com/2011/01/30/realestate/30cov.html?pagewanted=all and read "You Don't Have to Pay It." According to the article, real estate agents' average commission rate is 6%. If a real estate agent sold five homes with an average price of $250,000 last year, what would be his/her total commission earned for the year?

Discussion Questions

1. Based on the article, what causes drops in agents' commissions?

2. Would you take on more of the tasks involved in selling your house to pay a smaller commission? Why?

MOBILE APPS ✕

Withholding Calc (3 Dogs and a Cat Software) Helps you estimate your paychecks and the impact changes to your withholdings will have on take-home pay.

Payrollguru (Payrollguru, Inc.) Assists in the calculation of paychecks, including the net pay as well as applicable taxes taken out of gross pay amounts.

A KIPLINGER APPROACH

From *Kiplinger's Personal Finance*, January 2015.

ANNUAL FORECAST ISSUE

Kiplinger's

PERSONAL FINANCE

MONEY SMART LIVING

WHERE TO INVEST IN 2015

The U.S. outshines the world, so start close to home. p28

- 8 Stocks to Buy Now ... and 5 to Sell p36
- Bonds: Don't Sweat Higher Rates p38

PLUS: Bargain Buys in Europe p31

We Test Apple Pay p58

Home Prices Keep Rising p68

SPECIAL REPORT

How to Get the Most From Social Security p48

"Stocks will continue to move up, but it will be a bumpy road."
Kristina Hooper, of Allianz Global Investors p34

JANUARY 2015

Navigating Social Security

To decide when to take benefits, you have to look at the big picture ("Social Security: The Best Path for You," Jan.). I could extract the maximum benefit from Social Security by delaying withdrawals until age 70. The downside, of course, is that I'd have to self-finance my retirement from the time I retire at 65 until I reach 70. My financial planner did a full Monte Carlo analysis, which took into account all of our family assets. It concluded that I'd realize my maximum retirement income by taking benefits at age 66.

**TIM WAKEFIELD
EAGAN, MINN.**

If you still have minor children when you collect Social Security, they are also eligible to receive benefits, and

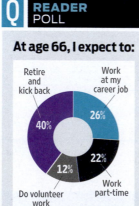

Q **READER** POLL

At age 66, I expect to:

- Retire and kick back 40%
- Work at my career job 26%
- Work part-time 22%
- Do volunteer work 12%

their benefits can add up to nearly as much as you receive. That was certainly a motivating factor for me to start collecting at 63, when my two youngest children were 13 and 11, given that their benefits would continue until they graduated from high school. I've calculated that the break-even point (when the sum of their benefits and mine starting at age 63 equals the sum of my benefits alone starting at age 70) is around age 93—assuming I live that long. And because the children's benefits have to be used for them, I'm investing their money in college savings plans.

**L.M.
BELLEVUE, WASH.**

I think Social Security should be aimed at folks who actually need it to live somewhat comfortably in old age. One way to keep the system from running out of money might be to give people who do not need the money an incentive to continue to postpone taking it after age 70. We have raised the full retirement age to 66 for people retiring now (and it will go to 67 in a few years), so the age at which you continue to qualify for deferred enhancement should rise as well.

**BETH LOKER
ROYAL OAK, MD.**

Do the math. Whether it's best to trade in your old car at the dealer or sell it yourself could depend on how much tax you'll pay on the new car ("Drive Time," Jan.). In some states with a sales tax, the value of the trade-in

FACEBOOK FEEDBACK

WOW, DID WE HEAR FROM you, both online and on social media, about our take on the economic outlook for 2015 ("Ahead," Jan.). Below are just a few of the hundreds of comments we received:

"Pulling away from the rest of the world? The last I heard, the deficit was $400 billion and the overall debt close to $18 trillion."

"Now if the 'improved U.S. economy' would only translate into decent jobs."

"Lower gas prices mean that the energy sector will soon be laying off hundreds of workers."

is deducted from the price of the new car, reducing the taxable cost of the car. I recently saved more than $1,400 in sales tax by trading in my used car.

**DICK STERN
ALLENWOOD, N.J.**

>**LETTERS TO THE EDITOR**

Letters to the editor may be edited for clarity and space, and initials will be used on request only if you include your name. Mail to Letters Editor, Kiplinger's Personal Finance, 1100 13th St., N.W., Washington, DC 20005, fax to 202-778-8976 or e-mail to feedback@kiplinger.com. Please include your name, address and daytime telephone number.

SOURCE: POLL SURVEYED 251 KIPLINGER'S READERS.

BUSINESS MATH ISSUE

By the time you plan to retire, Social Security will probably be bankrupt.

1. List the key points of the article and information to support your position.
2. Write a group defense of your position using math calculations to support your view.

Classroom Notes

CHAPTER 10

Simple Interest

Payday Loans Face New Controls

By Alan Zibel

WASHINGTON—U.S. officials are taking their first crack at writing rules for payday loans, responding to concerns that the short-term, high-rate debt can trap consumers in a cycle of borrowing they can't afford.

The Consumer Financial Protection Bureau is exploring ways to require payday lenders to make sure customers can pay back their loans, according to people familiar with the matter.

The bureau is seeking to establish the first federal regulations for the $46 billion industry, which has historically been overseen by states.

Payday loans are typically less than $500. Borrowers provide a lender with a personal check dated for the next payday or permission to debit their bank accounts two weeks later, with a finance charge added.

Consumer-advocacy groups say the loans are deceptive because borrowers often roll them over several times, racking up fees in the process. They also criticize high annual interest rates that can range from less than 200% to more than 500%, depending on the state, according to research by the Pew Charitable Trusts.

Reprinted by permission of *The Wall Street Journal*, copyright 2015 Dow Jones & Company, Inc. All rights reserved worldwide.

© Dan Kitwood/Getty Images

LU 10–1: Calculation of Simple Interest and Maturity Value

1. Calculate simple interest and maturity value for months and years.
2. Calculate simple interest and maturity value by **(a)** exact interest and **(b)** ordinary interest.

LU 10–2: Finding Unknown in Simple Interest Formula

1. Using the interest formula, calculate the unknown when the other two (principal, rate, or time) are given.

LU 10–3: U.S. Rule—Making Partial Note Payments before Due Date

1. List the steps to complete the U.S. Rule as well as calculate proper interest credits.

VOCABULARY PREVIEW

Here are key terms in this chapter. After completing the chapter, if you know the term, place a checkmark in the box. If you don't know the term, look it up and put the page number where it can be found.

Adjusted balance ☐ Banker's Rule ☐ Exact interest ☐ Interest ☐ Maturity value ☐ Ordinary interest ☐
Principal ☐ Simple interest ☐ Simple interest formula ☐ Time ☐ U.S. Rule ☐

Today social media has become popular for small businesses. (See the *Wall Street Journal* clip "Use vs. Usefulness.") Businesses use online sites for many business functions including conducting business. There are many online lending sites, too. Rates vary, so buyer beware.

In this chapter, you will study simple interest. The principles discussed apply whether you are paying interest or receiving interest. Let's begin by learning how to calculate simple interest.

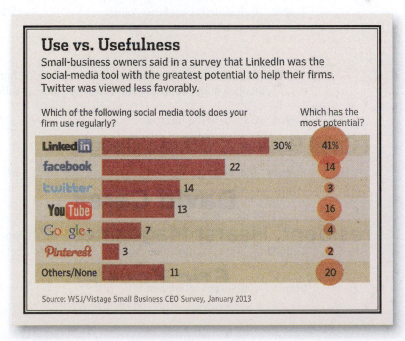

Use vs. Usefulness
Small-business owners said in a survey that LinkedIn was the social-media tool with the greatest potential to help their firms. Twitter was viewed less favorably.

Which of the following social media tools does your firm use regularly? / Which has the most potential?

	Use regularly	Most potential
Linkedin	30%	41%
facebook	22	14
twitter	14	3
YouTube	13	16
Google+	7	4
Pinterest	3	2
Others/None	11	20

Source: WSJ/Vistage Small Business CEO Survey, January 2013

Reprinted by permission of *The Wall Street Journal*, copyright 2013 Dow Jones & Company, Inc. All rights reserved worldwide.

Learning Unit 10–1: Calculation of Simple Interest and Maturity Value

Hope Slater, a young attorney, rented an office in a professional building. Since Hope recently graduated from law school, she was short of cash. To purchase office furniture for her new office, Hope went to her bank and borrowed $40,000 for 6 months at a 4% annual interest rate. **Interest** expense is the cost of borrowing money.

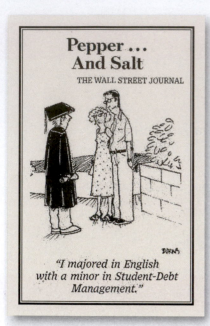

**Pepper ...
And Salt**

THE WALL STREET JOURNAL

"I majored in English
with a minor in Student-Debt
Management."

From *The Wall Street Journal*, permission Cartoon
Features Syndicate.

The original amount Hope borrowed ($40,000) is the **principal** (face value) of the loan. Hope's price for using the $40,000 is the interest rate (4%) the bank charges on a yearly basis. Since Hope is borrowing the $40,000 for 6 months, Hope's loan will have a **maturity value** of $40,800—the principal plus the interest on the loan. Thus, Hope's price for using the furniture before she can pay for it is $800 interest, which is a percent of the principal for a specific time period. To make this calculation, we use the following formula:

> Maturity value (MV) = Principal (P) + Interest (I)

$$\$40{,}800 \quad = \quad \$40{,}000 \quad + \quad \$800$$

Hope's furniture purchase introduces **simple interest**—the cost of a loan, usually for 1 year or less. Simple interest is only on the original principal or amount borrowed. Let's examine how the bank calculated Hope's $800 interest.

Simple Interest Formula

To calculate simple interest, we use the following **simple interest formula:**

> Simple interest (I) = Principal (P) × Rate (R) × Time (T)

In this formula, rate is expressed as a decimal, fraction, or percent; and time is expressed in years or a fraction of a year.

Do not round intermediate answers. Round only the final calculation.

EXAMPLE Hope Slater borrowed $40,000 for office furniture. The loan was for 6 months at an annual interest rate of 4%. What are Hope's interest and maturity value?

Using the simple interest formula, the bank determined Hope's interest as follows:

In your calculator, multiply $40,000 times .04 times 6. Divide your answer by 12. You could also use the % key—multiply $40,000 times 4% times 6 and then divide your answer by 12.

Step 1. Calculate the interest.

$$I = \$40{,}000 \underset{(P)}{\times} .04 \underset{(R)}{\times} \underset{(T)}{\frac{6}{12}}$$
$$= \$800$$

Step 2. Calculate the maturity value.

$$MV = \underset{(P)}{\$40{,}000} + \underset{(I)}{\$800}$$
$$= \$40{,}800$$

Now let's use the same example and assume Hope borrowed $40,000 for 1 year. The bank would calculate Hope's interest and maturity value as follows:

Step 1. Calculate the interest.

$$I = \$40{,}000 \underset{(P)}{\times} .04 \underset{(R)}{\times} \underset{(T)}{1 \text{ year}}$$
$$= \$1{,}600$$

Step 2. Calculate the maturity value.

$$MV = \underset{(P)}{\$40{,}000} + \underset{(I)}{\$1{,}600}$$
$$= \$41{,}600$$

Let's use the same example again and assume Hope borrowed $40,000 for 18 months. Then Hope's interest and maturity value would be calculated as follows:

Step 1. Calculate the interest.

$$I = \$40{,}000 \underset{(P)}{\times} .04 \underset{(R)}{\times} \underset{(T)}{\frac{18^{1}}{12}}$$
$$= \$2{,}400$$

Step 2. Calculate the maturity value.

$$MV = \underset{(P)}{\$40{,}000} + \underset{(I)}{\$2{,}400}$$
$$= \$42{,}400$$

Next we'll turn our attention to two common methods we can use to calculate simple interest when a loan specifies its beginning and ending dates.

---

[1]This is the same as 1.5 years.

LO 2

Two Methods for Calculating Simple Interest and Maturity Value

Method 1: Exact Interest (365 Days) The Federal Reserve banks and the federal government use the **exact interest** method. The *exact interest* is calculated by using a 365-day year. For **time,** we count the exact number of days in the month that the borrower has the loan. The day the loan is made is not counted, but the day the money is returned is counted as a full day. This method calculates interest by using the following fraction to represent time in the formula:

$$\text{Time} = \frac{\text{Exact number of days}}{365} \longleftarrow \text{Exact interest}$$

For this calculation, we use the exact days-in-a-year calendar from the *Business Math Handbook.* You learned how to use this calendar in Chapter 7.

From the *Business Math Handbook*

July 6	187th day
March 4	− 63rd day
	124 days
	(exact time of loan)

March	31
	− 4
	27
April	30
May	31
June	30
July	+ 6
	124 days

EXAMPLE On March 4, Joe Bench borrowed $50,000 at 5% interest. Interest and principal are due on July 6. What are the interest cost and the maturity value?

Step 1. Calculate the interest.

$$I = P \times R \times T$$
$$= \$50{,}000 \times .05 \times \frac{124}{365}$$
$$= \$849.32 \text{ (rounded to nearest cent)}$$

Step 2. Calculate the maturity value.

$$MV = P + I$$
$$= \$50{,}000 + \$849.32$$
$$= \$50{,}849.32$$

Method 2: Ordinary Interest (360 Days) In the **ordinary interest** method, time in the formula $I = P \times R \times T$ is equal to the following:

$$\text{Time} = \frac{\text{Exact number of days}}{360} \longleftarrow \text{Ordinary interest}$$

Since banks commonly use the ordinary interest method, it is known as the **Banker's Rule.** Banks charge a slightly higher rate of interest because they use 360 days instead of 365 in the denominator. (Here's a hint: The word *ordinary* starts with an "O" and "360" ends with a "0.") By using 360 instead of 365, the calculation is supposedly simplified. Consumer groups, however, are questioning why banks can use 360 days, since this benefits the bank and not the customer. The use of computers and calculators no longer makes the simplified calculation necessary. For example, after a court case in Oregon, banks began calculating interest on 365 days except in mortgages.

Now let's replay the Joe Bench example we used to illustrate Method 1 to see the difference in bank interest when we use Method 2.

EXAMPLE On March 4, Joe Bench borrowed $50,000 at 5% interest. Interest and principal are due on July 6. What are the interest cost and the maturity value?

Step 1. Calculate the interest.

$$I = \$50{,}000 \times .05 \times \frac{124}{360}$$
$$= \$861.11$$

Step 2. Calculate the maturity value.

$$MV = P + I$$
$$= \$50{,}000 + \$861.11$$
$$= \$50{,}861.11$$

Note: By using Method 2, the bank increases its interest by $11.79.

$$\begin{array}{r} \$861.11 \longleftarrow \text{Method 2} \\ - \ 849.32 \longleftarrow \text{Method 1} \\ \hline \$ \ 11.79 \end{array}$$

Use ordinary interest any time a problem does not specify to use exact interest.
Now you should be ready for your first Practice Quiz in this chapter.

MONEY tips

Because debit cards draw money directly from your checking account, it is critical that you protect your account. Be cautious of the ATMs you use. Any outdoor transaction is at risk if the public has access to the machine—even at gas stations. Skimming devices can easily be used to pick up your information and leave your account at risk. Never use an ATM that has been tampered with.

LU 10–1 **PRACTICE QUIZ**

Complete this **Practice Quiz** to see how you are doing.

*For **extra help** from your authors—Sharon and Jeff—see the videos in Connect.*

These videos are also available on YouTube!

Calculate simple interest (rounded to the nearest cent):

1. $14,000 at 4% for 9 months
2. $25,000 at 7% for 5 years
3. $40,000 at $10\frac{1}{2}$% for 19 months
4. On May 4, Dawn Kristal borrowed $15,000 at 8%. Dawn must pay the principal and interest on August 10. What are Dawn's simple interest and maturity value if you use the exact interest method?
5. What are Dawn Kristal's (Problem 4) simple interest and maturity value if you use the ordinary interest method?

✓ Solutions

1. $14,000 \times .04 \times \dfrac{9}{12} =$ $420

2. $25,000 \times .07 \times 5 =$ $8,750

3. $40,000 \times .105 \times \dfrac{19}{12} =$ $6,650

4.
August 10 →	222
May 4 →	− 124
	98

   $15,000 \times .08 \times \dfrac{98}{365} =$ $322.19

   $MV = $15,000 + $322.19 =$ $15,322.19

5. $15,000 \times .08 \times \dfrac{98}{360} =$ $326.67

   $MV = $15,000 + $326.67 =$ $15,326.67

LU 10–1a **EXTRA PRACTICE QUIZ WITH WORKED-OUT SOLUTIONS**

Need more practice? Try this **Extra Practice Quiz** (check figures in the Interactive Chapter Organizer). Worked-out Solutions can be found in Appendix B.

Calculate simple interest (rounded to the nearest cent):

1. $16,000 at 3% for 8 months
2. $15,000 at 6% for 6 years
3. $50,000 at 7% for 18 months
4. On May 6, Dawn Kristal borrowed $20,000 at 7%. Dawn must pay the principal and interest on August 14. What are Dawn's simple interest and maturity value if you use the exact interest method?
5. What are Dawn Kristal's (Problem 4) simple interest and maturity value if you use the ordinary interest method?

Learning Unit 10–2: Finding Unknown in Simple Interest Formula

LO 1

This unit begins with the formula used to calculate the principal of a loan. Then it explains how to find the *principal, rate,* and *time* of a simple interest loan. In all the calculations, we use 360 days and round only final answers.

Finding the Principal

EXAMPLE Tim Jarvis paid the bank $19.48 interest at 9.5% for 90 days. How much did Tim borrow using the ordinary interest method?

The following formula is used to calculate the principal of a loan:

$$\text{Principal} = \frac{\text{Interest}}{\text{Rate} \times \text{Time}}$$

Note how we illustrated this in the margin. The shaded area is what we are solving for. When solving for principal, rate, or time, you are dividing. Interest will be in the numerator, and the denominator will be the other two elements multiplied by each other.

Step 1. When using a calculator, press

Step 1. Set up the formula.

$$P = \dfrac{\$19.48}{.095 \times \dfrac{90}{360}}$$

Step 2. Multiply the denominator.

.095 times 90 divided by 360 (do not round)

Step 2. When using a calculator, press

$$P = \dfrac{\$19.48}{.02375}$$

Step 3. Divide the numerator by the result of Step 2.

$$\boxed{P = \$820.21}$$

Step 4. Check your answer.

$$\underset{(I)}{\$19.48} = \underset{(P)}{\$820.21} \times \underset{(R)}{.095} \times \underset{(T)}{\dfrac{90}{360}}$$

Finding the Rate

EXAMPLE Tim Jarvis borrowed $820.21 from a bank. Tim's interest is $19.48 for 90 days. What rate of interest did Tim pay using the ordinary interest method?

The following formula is used to calculate the rate of interest:

$$\text{Rate} = \dfrac{\text{Interest}}{\text{Principal} \times \text{Time}}$$

Step 1. Set up the formula.

$$R = \dfrac{\$19.48}{\$820.21 \times \dfrac{90}{360}}$$

Step 2. Multiply the denominator. Do not round the answer.

$$R = \dfrac{\$19.48}{\$205.0525}$$

Step 3. Divide the numerator by the result of Step 2.

$$\boxed{R = 9.5\%}$$

Step 4. Check your answer.

$$\underset{(I)}{\$19.48} = \underset{(P)}{\$820.21} \times \underset{(R)}{.095} \times \underset{(T)}{\dfrac{90}{360}}$$

MONEY tips

For each checking account you have, make certain to apply for overdraft protection to protect your account from human error and unintentional overdrafts.

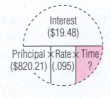

Finding the Time

EXAMPLE Tim Jarvis borrowed $820.21 from a bank. Tim's interest is $19.48 at 9.5%. How much time does Tim have to repay the loan using the ordinary interest method?

The following formula is used to calculate time:

$$\text{Time (in years)} = \dfrac{\text{Interest}}{\text{Principal} \times \text{Rate}}$$

*Time is **always** over what makes up one year:* $\dfrac{\# \text{ of days}}{360 \text{ or } 365}, \dfrac{\# \text{ of weeks}}{52},$

$$\dfrac{\# \text{ of months}}{12}, \dfrac{\# \text{ of quarters}}{4}.$$

Step 1. When using a calculator, press

820.21 × .095 M+.

Step 1. Set up the formula.

$$T = \dfrac{\$19.48}{\$820.21 \times .095}$$

Step 2. When using a calculator, press

19.48 ÷ MR =.

Step 2. Multiply the denominator. Do not round the answer.

$$T = \dfrac{\$19.48}{\$77.91995}$$

Step 3. Divide the numerator by the result of Step 2. $T = .25$ years

Step 4. Convert years to days (assume 360 days). $.25 \times 360 = $ 90 days

Aha!

Step 5. Check your answer.

$$\$19.48 = \$820.21 \times .095 \times \frac{90}{360}$$
$$\quad\;(I)\qquad\quad(P)\qquad(R)\qquad(T)$$

Whole numbers in time represent full years. No adjustment to the time calculation is needed. However, when the calculation for number of days includes a decimal, multiply the decimal by 360 or 365 as indicated, to calculate the number of days the decimal represents in a year.

EXAMPLE $T = .37$ $.37 \times 365 = 135.05 = 136$ days

When dealing with a fraction (or part) of a day, always round up to a full day even if the number being rounded is less than 5.

    Before we go on to Learning Unit 10–3, let's check your understanding of this unit.

LU 10–2   **PRACTICE QUIZ**

Complete this **Practice Quiz** to see how you are doing.

Complete the following (assume 360 days):

	Principal	Interest rate	Time (days)	Simple interest
1.	?	5%	90 days	$8,000
2.	$7,000	?	220 days	$350
3.	$1,000	8%	?	$300

*For **extra help** from your authors–Sharon and Jeff–see the videos in Connect.*

These videos are also available on YouTube!

✓ **Solutions**

1. $\dfrac{\$8,000}{.05 \times \dfrac{90}{360}} = \dfrac{\$8,000}{.0125} = $ $640,000 $P = \dfrac{I}{R \times T}$

2. $\dfrac{\$350}{\$7,000 \times \dfrac{220}{360}} = \dfrac{\$350}{\$4,277.7777} = $ 8.18% $R = \dfrac{I}{P \times T}$

(do not round)

3. $\dfrac{\$300}{\$1,000 \times .08} = \dfrac{\$300}{\$80} = 3.75 \times 360 = $ 1,350 days $T = \dfrac{I}{P \times R}$

LU 10–2a   **EXTRA PRACTICE QUIZ WITH WORKED-OUT SOLUTIONS**

Need more practice? Try this **Extra Practice Quiz** (check figures in the Interactive Chapter Organizer). Worked-out Solutions can be found in Appendix B.

Complete the following (assume 360 days):

	Principal	Interest rate	Time (days)	Simple interest
1.	?	4%	90 days	$9,000
2.	$6,000	?	180 days	$280
3.	$900	6%	?	$190

Learning Unit 10–3: U.S. Rule—Making Partial Note Payments before Due Date

LO 1

Often a person may want to pay off a debt in more than one payment before the maturity date. The **U.S. Rule** allows the borrower to receive proper interest credits. This rule states that any partial loan payment first covers any interest that has built up. The remainder of the partial payment reduces the loan principal. Courts or legal proceedings generally use the U.S. Rule. The Supreme Court originated the U.S. Rule in the case of *Story* v. *Livingston*. The *Wall Street Journal* chapter opener "Payday Loans Face New Controls" explores concerns over interest rates of more than 500%.

EXAMPLE Jeff Edsell owes $5,000 on a 4%, 90-day note. On day 50, Jeff pays $600 on the note. On day 80, Jeff makes an $800 additional payment. Assume a 360-day year. What is Jeff's adjusted balance after day 50 and after day 80? What is the ending balance due?

To calculate $600 payment on day 50:

Step 1. Calculate interest on principal from date of loan to date of first principal payment. Round to nearest cent.

$$I = P \times R \times T$$
$$I = \$5,000 \times .04 \times \frac{50}{360}$$
$$I = \$27.78$$

Step 2. Apply partial payment to interest due. Subtract remainder of payment from principal. This is the **adjusted balance** (principal).

$$
\begin{array}{r}
\$600.00 \text{ payment} \\
-\ 27.78 \text{ interest} \\
\hline
\$572.22
\end{array}
$$

$$
\begin{array}{r}
\$5,000.00 \text{ principal} \\
-\ 572.22 \\
\hline
\$4,427.78 \text{ adjusted} \\
\text{balance—} \\
\text{principal}
\end{array}
$$

To calculate $800 payment on day 80:

Step 3. Calculate interest on adjusted balance that starts from previous payment date and goes to new payment date. Then apply Step 2.

Compute interest on $4,427.78 for 30 days (80 − 50)

$$I = \$4,427.78 \times .04 \times \frac{30}{360}$$
$$I = \$14.76$$

$$
\begin{array}{r}
\$800.00 \text{ payment} \\
-\ 14.76 \text{ interest} \\
\hline
\$785.24
\end{array}
$$

$$
\begin{array}{r}
\$4,427.78 \\
-\ 785.24 \\
\hline
\$3,642.54 \text{ adjusted} \\
\text{balance}
\end{array}
$$

Step 4. At maturity, calculate interest from last partial payment. *Add* this interest to adjusted balance.

Ten days are left on note since last payment.

$$I = \$3,642.54 \times .04 \times \frac{10}{360}$$
$$I = \$4.05$$

Balance owed = $\boxed{\$3,646.59}$ $\left(\begin{array}{r} \$3,642.54 \\ +\ 4.05 \end{array}\right)$

Note that when Jeff makes two partial payments, Jeff's total interest is $46.59 ($27.78 + $14.76 + $4.05). If Jeff had repaid the entire loan after 90 days, his interest payment would have been $50—a total savings of $3.41.

Let's check your understanding of the last unit in this chapter.

© Ingram Publishing

MONEY tips

Pay off debt instead of moving it around unless you have been offered 0% interest. Be wary of companies offering to consolidate your debt into a single loan. If you do, be certain to read and understand all the terms.

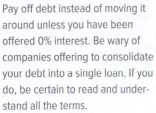

LU 10–3 **PRACTICE QUIZ**

Complete this **Practice Quiz** to see how you are doing.

Polly Flin borrowed $5,000 for 60 days at 8%. On day 10, Polly made a $600 partial payment. On day 40, Polly made a $1,900 partial payment. What is Polly's ending balance due under the U.S. Rule (assuming a 360-day year)?

For **extra help** from your authors—Sharon and Jeff—see the videos in Connect.

These videos are also available on YouTube!

✓ Solutions

$$\$5,000 \times .08 \times \frac{10}{360} = \$11.11$$

$$\begin{array}{r} \$1,900.00 \\ -\quad 29.41 \\ \hline \$1,870.59 \end{array} \qquad \begin{array}{r} \$4,411.11 \\ -\ 1,870.59 \\ \hline \$2,540.52 \end{array}$$

$$\begin{array}{r} \$600.00 \\ -\quad 11.11 \\ \hline \$588.89 \end{array} \qquad \begin{array}{r} \$5,000.00 \\ -\quad 588.89 \\ \hline \$4,411.11 \end{array}$$

$$\$2,540.52 \times .08 \times \frac{20}{360} = \$11.29$$

$$\$4,411.11 \times .08 \times \frac{30}{360} = \$29.41$$

$$\begin{array}{r} \$\quad 11.29 \\ +\ 2,540.52 \\ \hline \boxed{\$2,551.81} \end{array}$$

LU 10–3a   **EXTRA PRACTICE QUIZ WITH WORKED-OUT SOLUTION**

Need more practice? Try this Extra Practice Quiz (check figure in the Interactive Chapter Organizer). Worked-out Solution can be found in Appendix B.

Polly Flin borrowed $4,000 for 60 days at 4%. On day 15, Polly made a $700 partial payment. On day 40, Polly made a $2,000 partial payment. What is Polly's ending balance due under the U.S. Rule (assuming a 360-day year)?

INTERACTIVE CHAPTER ORGANIZER

Topic/Procedure/Formula	Examples	You try it*
Simple interest for months Interest = Principal × Rate × Time (I) (P) (R) (T)	$2,000 at 9% for 17 months $I = \$2,000 \times .09 \times \dfrac{17}{12}$ $I = \boxed{\$255}$	**Calculate simple interest** $4,000 at 3% for 18 months

Exact interest
$T = \dfrac{\text{Exact number of days}}{365}$
$I = P \times R \times T$
	$1,000 at 10% from January 5 to February 20
	$I = \$1,000 \times .10 \times \dfrac{46}{365}$
	   Feb. 20: 51 days
	   Jan. 5: − 5
	           46 days
	$I = \boxed{\$12.60}$
		Calculate exact interest
		$3,000 at 4% from January 8 to February 22

Ordinary interest (Banker's Rule) $T = \dfrac{\text{Exact number of days}}{360}$ $I = P \times R \times T$ Higher interest costs	$I = \$1,000 \times .10 \times \dfrac{46}{360}$ (51 − 5) $I = \boxed{\$12.78}$	**Calculate ordinary interest** $3,000 at 4% from January 8 to February 22
Finding unknown in simple interest formula (use 360 days) $I = P \times R \times T$	Use this example for illustrations of simple interest formula parts: $1,000 loan at 9%, 60 days $I = \$1,000 \times .09 \times \dfrac{60}{360} = \boxed{\$15}$	**Calculate interest (use 360 days)** $2,000 loan at 4%, 90 days
Finding the principal $P = \dfrac{I}{R \times T}$ $\dfrac{I}{P \times R \times T}$	$P = \dfrac{\$15}{.09 \times \dfrac{60}{360}} = \dfrac{\$15}{.015} = \boxed{\$1,000}$	**Calculate principal** *Given:* interest, $20; rate, 4%; 90 days

(continues)

INTERACTIVE CHAPTER ORGANIZER

Topic/Procedure/Formula	Examples	You try it*
Finding the rate $$R = \frac{I}{P \times T}$$	$$R = \frac{\$15}{\$1,000 \times \frac{60}{360}} = \frac{\$15}{166.66666} = .09$$ $$= \boxed{9\%}$$ *Note:* We did not round the denominator.	**Calculate rate** *Given:* interest, $20; principal, $2,000; 90 days
Finding the time $$T = \frac{I}{P \times R}$$ (in years) Multiply answer by 360 days to convert answer to days for ordinary interest.	$$T = \frac{\$15}{\$1,000 \times .09} = \frac{\$15}{\$90} = .1666666$$ $.1666666 \times 360 = 59.99 = \boxed{60 \text{ days}}$	**Calculate number of days** *Given:* principal, $2,000; rate, 4%; interest, $20
U.S. Rule (use 360 days) Calculate interest on principal from date of loan to date of first partial payment. Calculate adjusted balance by subtracting from principal the partial payment less interest cost. The process continues for future partial payments with the adjusted balance used to calculate cost of interest from last payment to present payment. Balance owed equals last adjusted balance plus interest cost from last partial payment to final due date.	12%, 120 days, $2,000 *Partial payments:* On day 40: $250 On day 60: $200 *First payment:* $$I = \$2,000 \times .12 \times \frac{40}{360}$$ $I = \$26.67$ $\begin{array}{r} \$250.00 \text{ payment} \\ - \quad 26.67 \text{ interest} \\ \hline \$223.33 \end{array}$ $\begin{array}{r} \$2,000.00 \text{ principal} \\ - \quad 223.33 \\ \hline \$1,776.67 \text{ adjusted balance} \end{array}$ *Second payment:* $$I = \$1,776.67 \times .12 \times \frac{20}{360}$$ $I = \$11.84$ $\begin{array}{r} \$200.00 \text{ payment} \\ - \quad 11.84 \text{ interest} \\ \hline \$188.16 \end{array}$ $\begin{array}{r} \$1,776.67 \\ - \quad 188.16 \\ \hline \$1,588.51 \text{ adjusted balance} \end{array}$ *60 days left:* $$\$1,588.51 \times .12 \times \frac{60}{360} = \$31.77$$ $\$1,588.51 + \$31.77 = \boxed{\$1,620.28 \text{ balance due}}$ $\begin{array}{r} \text{Total interest} = \quad \$26.67 \\ 11.84 \\ + \quad 31.77 \\ \hline \$70.28 \end{array}$	**Calculate balance due and total interest** *Given:* $4,000; 4%; 90 days *Partial payments:* On day 30: $400 On day 70: $300

(continues)

INTERACTIVE CHAPTER ORGANIZER

KEY TERMS	Adjusted balance Banker's Rule Exact interest Interest	Maturity value Ordinary interest Principal Simple interest	Simple interest formula Time U.S. Rule

Check Figures for Extra Practice Quizzes. (Worked-out Solutions are in Appendix B.)	LU 10–1a
	1. $320
	2. $5,400
	3. $5,250
	4. $20,383.56;
	   Interest = $383.56
	5. $20,388.89;
	   Interest = $388.89
		LU 10–2a
		1. $900,000
		2. 9.33%
		3. 1,267 days
			LU 10–3a
			$1,318.78

*Worked-out solutions are in Appendix B.

Critical Thinking Discussion Questions with Chapter Concept Check

1. What is the difference between exact interest and ordinary interest? With the increase of computers in banking, do you think that the ordinary interest method is a dinosaur in business today?

2. Explain how to use the portion formula to solve the unknowns in the simple interest formula. Why would rounding the answer of the denominator result in an inaccurate final answer?

3. Explain the U.S. Rule. Why in the last step of the U.S. Rule is the interest added, not subtracted?

4. Do you believe the government bailout of banks is in the best interest of the country? Defend your position.

5. **Chapter Concept Check.** Prepare calculations based on the concepts in this chapter to prove credit unions would save you money in your personal life.

END-OF-CHAPTER PROBLEMS   connect plus+

DRILL PROBLEMS

Calculate the simple interest and maturity value for the following problems. Round to the nearest cent as needed.   *LU 10-1(1)*

	Principal	Interest rate	Time	Simple interest	Maturity value
10–1.	$7,800	$4\frac{1}{4}\%$	18 mo.		
10–2.	$4,500	3%	6 mo.		
10–3.	$20,000	$6\frac{3}{4}\%$	9 mo.		

Complete the following, using ordinary interest: *LU 10-1(2)*

	Principal	Interest rate	Date borrowed	Date repaid	Exact time	Interest	Maturity value
10–4. eXcel	$1,000	8%	Mar. 8	June 9			
10–5. eXcel	$585	9%	June 5	Dec. 15			
10–6. eXcel	$1,200	12%	July 7	Jan. 10			

Complete the following, using exact interest: *LU 10-1(2)*

	Principal	Interest rate	Date borrowed	Date repaid	Exact time	Interest	Maturity value
10–7.	$1,000	8%	Mar. 8	June 9			
10–8.	$585	9%	June 5	Dec. 15			
10–9.	$1,200	12%	July 7	Jan. 10			

Solve for the missing item in the following (round to the nearest hundredth as needed):   *LU 10-2(1)*

	Principal	Interest rate	Time (months or years)	Simple interest
10–10.	$400	5%	?	$100
10–11.	?	7%	$1\frac{1}{2}$ years	$200
10–12.	$5,000	?	6 months	$300

10–13. Use the U.S. Rule to solve for total interest costs, balances, and final payments (use ordinary interest).   *LU 10-3(1)*

     Given Principal: $10,000, 8%, 240 days
               Partial payments: On 100th day, $4,000
                               On 180th day, $2,000

WORD PROBLEMS

10–14. Diane Van Os decided to buy a used snowmobile since her credit union was offering such low interest rates. She borrowed $2,700 at 3.5% on December 26, 2014, and paid it off February 21, 2016. How much did she pay in interest? (Assume ordinary interest.)   *LU 10-1(2)*

10–15. Leslie Hart borrowed $15,000 to pay for her child's education at Riverside Community College. Leslie must repay the loan at the end of 9 months in one payment with $5\frac{1}{2}$% interest. How much interest must Leslie pay? What is the maturity value?   *LU 10-1(1)*

10–16. On September 12, Jody Jansen went to Sunshine Bank to borrow $2,300 at 9% interest. Jody plans to repay the loan on e**X**cel January 27. Assume the loan is on ordinary interest. What interest will Jody owe on January 27? What is the total amount Jody must repay at maturity? *LU 10-1(2)*

10–17. Kelly O'Brien met Jody Jansen (Problem 10–16) at Sunshine Bank and suggested she consider the loan on exact interest. e**X**cel Recalculate the loan for Jody under this assumption. How much would she save in interest? *LU 10-1(2)*

10–18. On May 3, 2016, Leven Corp. negotiated a short-term loan of $685,000. The loan is due October 1, 2016, and carries a 6.86% interest rate. Use ordinary interest to calculate the interest. What is the total amount Leven would pay on the maturity date? *LU 10-1(2)*

10–19. Gordon Rosel went to his bank to find out how long it will take for $1,200 to amount to $1,650 at 8% simple interest. e**X**cel Please solve Gordon's problem. Round time in years to the nearest tenth. *LU 10-2(1)*

10–20. Lucky Champ owes $191.25 interest on a 6% loan he took out on his March 17 birthday to upgrade an oven in his Irish restaurant, Lucky's Pub and Grub. The loan is due on August 17. What is the principal (assume ordinary interest)? *LU 10-2(1)*

10–21. On April 5, 2015, Janeen Camoct took out an $8\frac{1}{2}$% loan for $20,000. The loan is due March 9, 2016. Use ordinary interest to calculate the interest. What total amount will Janeen pay on March 9, 2016? (Ignore leap year.) *LU 10-1(2)*

10–22. Sabrina Bowers took out the same loan as Janeen (Problem 10–21). Sabrina's terms, however, are exact interest. What is Sabrina's difference in interest? What will she pay on March 9, 2016? (Ignore leap year.) *LU 10-1(2)*

10–23. Max Wholesaler borrowed $2,000 on a 10%, 120-day note. After 45 days, Max paid $700 on the note. Thirty days later, Max paid an additional $630. What is the final balance due? Use the U.S. Rule to determine the total interest and ending balance due. Use ordinary interest.   *LU 10-3(1)*

10–24. Lane French had a bad credit rating and went to a local cash center. He took out a $100 loan payable in two weeks at $115. What is the percent of interest paid on this loan? Do not round denominator before dividing.   *LU 10-2(1)*

10–25. Joanne and Ed Greenwood built a new barn with an attached arena. To finance the loan, they paid $1,307 interest on $45,000 at 4.0%. What was the time, using exact interest (rounded up to the nearest day)?   *LU 10-2(1)*

10–26. On September 14, Jennifer Rick went to Park Bank to borrow $2,500 at $11\frac{3}{4}$% interest. Jennifer plans to repay the loan on January 27. Assume the loan is on ordinary interest. What interest will Jennifer owe on January 27? What is the total amount Jennifer must repay at maturity?   *LU 10-1(2)*

10–27. Steven Linden met Jennifer Rick (Problem 10–26) at Park Bank and suggested she consider the loan on exact interest. Recalculate the loan for Jennifer under this assumption.   *LU 10-1(2)*

10–28. Lance Lopes went to his bank to find out how long it will take for $1,000 to amount to $1,700 at 12% simple interest. **eXcel** Can you solve Lance's problem? Round time in years to the nearest tenth.   *LU 10-2(1)*

10–29. Andres Michael bought a new boat. He took out a loan for $24,500 at 4.5% interest for 2 years. He made a $4,500 partial payment at 2 months and another partial payment of $3,000 at 6 months. How much is due at maturity?   *LU 10-3(1)*

10–30. Shawn Bixby borrowed $17,000 on a 120-day, 12% note. After 65 days, Shawn paid $2,000 on the note. On day 89, Shawn paid an additional $4,000. What is the final balance due? Determine total interest and ending balance due by the U.S. Rule. Use ordinary interest. *LU 10-3(1)*

10–31. Carol Miller went to Europe and forgot to pay her $740 mortgage payment on her New Hampshire ski house. For her 59 days overdue on her payment, the bank charged her a penalty of $15. What was the rate of interest charged by the bank? Round to the nearest hundredth percent. (Assume 360 days.) *LU 10-2(1)*

10–32. Evander Holyfield (the champion boxer who had part of his ear bitten off by Mike Tyson) made $250 million during his boxing career but declared bankruptcy because of poor financial choices. His July interest at 15% was $155. What was Evander's principal at the beginning of August (assume 360 days)? *LU 10-2(1)*

10–33. Joey Logano won the 57th Daytona 500 in February 2015. If he paid back a $6,800 loan with $20 interest at 7.5%, what was the time of the loan (assume 360 days)? *LU 10-2(1)*

10–34. Molly Ellen, bookkeeper for Keystone Company, forgot to send in the payroll taxes due on April 15. She sent the payment
eXcel November 8. The IRS sent her a penalty charge of 8% simple interest on the unpaid taxes of $4,100. Calculate the penalty. (Remember that the government uses exact interest.) *LU 10-1(2)*

10–35. Oakwood Plowing Company purchased two new plows for the upcoming winter. In 200 days, Oakwood must make a single payment of $23,200 to pay for the plows. As of today, Oakwood has $22,500. If Oakwood puts the money in a bank today, what rate of interest will it need to pay off the plows in 200 days? (Assume 360 days.) *LU 10-2(1)*

10–36. Debbie McAdams paid 8% interest on a $12,500 loan balance. Jan Burke paid $5,000 interest on a $62,500 loan. Based on 1 year: **(a)** What was the amount of interest paid by Debbie? **(b)** What was the interest rate paid by Jan? **(c)** Debbie and Jan are both in the 28% tax bracket. Since the interest is deductible, how much would Debbie and Jan each save in taxes? *LU 10-2(1)*

10–37. Janet Foster bought a computer and printer at Computerland. The printer had a $600 list price with a $100 trade discount and 2/10, n/30 terms. The computer had a $1,600 list price with a 25% trade discount but no cash discount. On the computer, Computerland offered Janet the choice of (1) paying $50 per month for 17 months with the 18th payment paying the remainder of the balance or (2) paying 8% interest for 18 months in equal payments. *LU 10-1(2)*

    a. Assume Janet could borrow the money for the printer at 8% to take advantage of the cash discount. How much would Janet save? (Assume 360 days.)

    b. On the computer, what is the difference in the final payment between choices 1 and 2?

 SUMMARY PRACTICE TEST

Do you need help? The videos in Connect have step-by-step worked-out solutions. These videos are also available on YouTube!

1. Lorna Hall's real estate tax of $2,010.88 was due on December 14, 2015. Lorna lost her job and could not pay her tax bill until February 27, 2016. The penalty for late payment is $6\frac{1}{2}\%$ ordinary interest. *LU 10-1(1)*

    a. What is the penalty Lorna must pay?

    b. What is the total amount Lorna must pay on February 27?

2. Ann Hopkins borrowed $60,000 for her child's education. She must repay the loan at the end of 8 years in one payment with $5\frac{1}{2}\%$ interest. What is the maturity value Ann must repay? *LU 10-1(1)*

3. On May 6, Jim Ryan borrowed $14,000 from Lane Bank at $7\frac{1}{2}$% interest. Jim plans to repay the loan on March 11. Assume the loan is on ordinary interest. How much will Jim repay on March 11? *LU 10-1(2)*

4. Gail Ross met Jim Ryan (Problem 3) at Lane Bank. After talking with Jim, Gail decided she would like to consider the same loan on exact interest. Can you recalculate the loan for Gail under this assumption? *LU 10-1(2)*

5. Claire Russell is buying a car. Her November monthly interest was $210 at $7\frac{3}{4}$% interest. What is Claire's principal balance (to the nearest dollar) at the beginning of November? Use 360 days. Do not round the denominator in your calculation. *LU 10-2(1)*

6. Comet Lee borrowed $16,000 on a 6%, 90-day note. After 20 days, Comet paid $2,000 on the note. On day 50, Comet paid $4,000 on the note. What are the total interest and ending balance due by the U.S. Rule? Use ordinary interest. *LU 10-3(1)*

SURF TO SAVE

PROBLEM 1
Watching your cash

Visit http://www.thesimpledollar.com/how-i-learned-the-real-meaning-0f-six-months-same-as-cash/ and read the article concerning "same as cash deals." Assume you purchased a new home theater set for $3,000 on a "same as cash" 180-day deal. If you missed the 180-day deadline to pay off your balance and are charged 15% simple interest on the $3,000, how much do you owe?

Discussion Questions

1. What are the pros and cons to the consumer who purchases using a "same as cash" deal?
2. Why might a purchaser fail to pay off his or her balance during the "same as cash" period?

PROBLEM 2
Not free forever

Go to http://www.bestbuy.com/site/null/Credit-Cards/pcmcat102500050032.c?id=pcmcat161200050007 and select a couple of products that would put you over the $149 minimum to receive the 6-month financing offer. Estimate how much interest you would owe if you missed the 6-month deadline.

Discussion Questions

1. What are the pros and cons of "same as cash" offers for the consumer?
2. What are the pros and cons of "same as cash" offers for the seller?

PROBLEM 3
Costs of early out

Go to https://www.afbank.com/rates/cd.cfm. Find the rate for a 60-month certificate of deposit (CD). Now, navigate the site to find the penalty for early withdrawal on 60-month CDs. Calculate the penalty you would pay for early withdrawal if you initially invested $30,000.

Discussion Questions

1. Based on the penalties for early withdrawal, for what reasons would you consider taking money out early?
2. What is the value to the bank to have your money invested for a specific period of time in which you are not allowed to make withdrawals?

PROBLEM 4
Refinance or not?

Visit https://www.bankofamerica.com/auto-loans/auto-refinance-calculator.go. Assume you are thinking of refinancing your current car loan with a new 60-month loan. You still owe $15,000 on your current loan at 5% interest with a monthly payment of $350. What is the difference in your monthly payment should you decide to refinance?

Discussion Questions

1. What are the benefits to the new bank in offering deals in order to get you to refinance an existing car loan?
2. Which do you prefer: reducing the length of time or reducing the monthly payment of your loan? Why?

MOBILE APPS

Simple Loan Calculator (Clean Micro, LLC) Calculates payments based on interest rates and time period based on the amount being borrowed.

Compound Interest Calculator (Hopping Toad Software) Helps to figure interest earned as well as future values based on money invested.

A KIPLINGER APPROACH

By Sandra Block and Lisa Gerstner, From *Kiplinger's Personal Finance*, May 2015.

SELF-FUNDING

A Boomer Business

Barbara Stankowski started AMTIS, her professional services and consulting business, in 2007 with $20,000. Today the Orlando company pulls in annual revenues of more than $10 million and employs a staff of more than 100.

AMTIS provides an array of services for state and federal government agencies, including the U.S. departments of Defense, Labor, Homeland Security and Veterans Affairs. For example, the company developed new employee training for the Federal Emergency Management Agency. AMTIS also offers leadership development and coaching for executives. After a 28-year career in the Navy and several more years working in consulting and operations for two small businesses, Stankowski, now 65, felt the urge to create a business that incorporated all the elements she thought were important to a company culture. "I wanted to provide a great place for people to work, hire people who were passionate about what they do, give them the resources they needed, then share the rewards with them," she says.

The company hit some potholes on the road to becoming a flourishing business. In 2009, in the middle of the Great Recession, Stankowski had to resort to a $40,000 home-equity line of credit to cover payroll. In 2011, when annual revenues were topping $1 million, her business partner, who had provided half of the start-up money, decided to leave the company. Stankowski used the proceeds from a house she had recently sold to buy him out. Every year since, she says, AMTIS has doubled its revenues.

Two-thirds of entrepreneurs report using self-funding to start a business, according to a report from the Ewing Marion Kauffman Foundation, an entrepreneurship advocacy organization. Older entrepreneurs are especially well positioned to launch a business (and keep it afloat) with personal financial resources. Baby boomers "have networks that younger entrepreneurs don't have," says Mary Beth Izard, president of Acheve Consulting and author of *BoomerPreneurs: How Baby Boomers Can Start Their Own Business, Make Money and Enjoy Life*. If their kids are grown, she adds, their savings "aren't earmarked for their college education." The ranks of entrepreneurs older than 50 are growing: 23% of new entrepreneurs were age 55 to 64 in 2013, compared with 14% in 1996, according to a Kauffman report.

Taking advantage of federal government programs for small businesses has aided in AMTIS's growth. For example, because Stankowski has a disability related to her time in the Navy, AMTIS qualifies as a Service-Disabled Veteran-Owned Small Business. Through a mentor relationship, AMTIS and a more established company have together submitted several proposals for five-year, $100 million contracts—a prospect that could double revenues again this year, says Stankowski.

After a 28-year Navy career, Barbara Stankowski used savings to start a professional services and consulting business.

ERIKA LARSEN/REDUX

KipTip

Tap Your Assets

HOW IT WORKS: You rely on savings or home equity for start-up funds.

BEST FOR: Individuals with assets they don't have to rely on for retirement.

BIGGEST ADVANTAGES: The quickest and simplest way to fund a business—and you don't have to answer to investors or a bank.

BIGGEST DRAWBACK: Retirement savings, your home or any other assets you tap are on the line.

Patience and persistence have been key in getting AMTIS off the ground, she says. A continuing challenge is scaling the business to meet blossoming demand. For instance, if you hire new employees too soon, you won't be able to afford them—but wait too long, and you'll be understaffed. "It's a great problem to have," says Stankowski. "We just take it one bite at a time."

Stankowski draws a salary and, true to her philosophy of spreading the fruits of the company's success to her staff, has a profit-sharing program for all employees. She takes pride in presiding over a business that is not only woman-owned, but woman-run, with females filling many key positions. And she gives back to the armed services by employing veterans, whose ranks account for one-third of her staff. ∎

BUSINESS MATH ISSUE

Borrowing from a bank makes no sense if you can use your own savings.

1. List the key points of the article and information to support your position.
2. Write a group defense of your position using math calculations to support your view.

CHAPTER 11

Promissory Notes, Simple Discount Notes and the Discount Process

© The McGraw-Hill Companies, Inc./Jill Braaten, photographer

Penney Taps Credit Line

BY SERENA NG
AND KAREN TALLEY

Cash-strapped **J.C. Penney** Co. drew $850 million from a credit line to help fund its day-to-day operations, buying time for new chief executive Myron "Mike" Ullman to reverse sagging sales at the department store operator while it looks for ways to raise additional capital.

Penney on Monday said it drew down nearly half of a $1.85 billion revolving credit facility provided by its banks. The borrowed money, which is secured by inventory, credit-card receivables and other assets, will be used to pay for inventory and other costs as the chain renovates its home departments.

In February Penney got banks to increase the size of its credit facility, which matures in April 2016. But the drawdown came sooner than some analysts had expected.

"This is more cash than we thought Penney might need to get through the year and also a

bit sooner than we thought they might need it," Carol Levenson, director of research at debt analysis firm Gimme Credit, said in a note to clients. She said the move indicates that the other capital-raising options Penney is looking at could take time because "no potential equity investor was ready with a checkbook."

Often when a company draws on its revolving credit line it sends a negative message to investors that its cash running low. But in Penney's case, the company said it now has more money than it currently needs, which buys it time and financial flexibility, Ms. Levenson said.

The move "provides more than our current funding needs to ensure our continued liquidity," Chief Financial Officer Ken Hannah said. He said Penney, which has 1,100 stores, would continue to explore additional ways to raise capital with the help of its financial advisers.

Penney shares fell 1.6% to $14.39 on Monday, while its bond prices were mixed.

Bankers at **Blackstone Group LP** and **Centerview Partners** are advising J.C. Penney on its fund-raising options, which could include issuing secured loans or selling a minority stake in the company, people familiar with the matter have said.

Penney has suffered over the past year, as an overhaul planned by former Apple Inc. executive Ron Johnson went awry. Mr. Johnson left his post as CEO at Penney last week and Mr. Ullman, the company's former CEO, was reinstated.

The company's cash holdings fell 38% last year to $930 million, as sales plunged 25% and its operations consumed cash. Before Monday's move, analysts had said Penney wouldn't have enough cash to last it more than a year unless it borrowed from its credit line or raised more capital from banks or investors.

Penney will need to spend heavily to complete its home departments, the biggest of the dozens of in-store boutiques that Mr. Johnson planned for J.C.

Penney.

The $850 million in borrowings from the credit line won't be able to sustain the company for very long. Analysts from ratings firm Standard & Poor's on Monday said Penney's liquidity remains "less than adequate" given the company's "rapidly declining sales and cash flow." They said they expect meaningful changes to Penney's business over the coming months as Mr. Ullman reassesses its stores, promotions and marketing strategies.

S&P warned that additional secured borrowings on top of the revolving credit line could hurt Penney's CCC+ credit rating, which is already deep in junk territory.

It is unlikely that Penney will completely roll out Mr. Johnson's grand plan of creating myriad boutique-like shops within J.C. Penney stores, one of the main ideas in his overhaul strategy. Instead Mr. Ullman may take some components of Mr. Johnson's vision, while casting off other aspects.

Reprinted by permission of *The Wall Street Journal*, copyright 2013 Dow Jones & Company, Inc. All rights reserved worldwide.

LU 11–1: Structure of Promissory Notes; the Simple Discount Note

1. Differentiate between interest-bearing and non-interest-bearing notes.
2. Calculate bank discount and proceeds for simple discount notes.
3. Calculate and compare the interest, maturity value, proceeds, and effective rate of a simple interest note with a simple discount note.
4. Explain and calculate the effective rate for a Treasury bill.

LU 11–2: Discounting an Interest-Bearing Note before Maturity

1. Calculate the maturity value, bank discount, and proceeds of discounting an interest-bearing note before maturity.
2. Identify and complete the four steps of the discounting process.

Here are key terms in this chapter. After completing the chapter, if you know the term, place a checkmark in the box. If you don't know the term, look it up and put the page number where it can be found.

Bank discount ☐ Bank discount rate ☐ Contingent liability ☐ Discount period ☐ Discounting a note ☐
Effective rate ☐ Face value ☐ Interest-bearing note ☐ Maker ☐ Maturity date ☐ Maturity value (*MV*) ☐
Non-interest-bearing note ☐ Payee ☐ Proceeds ☐ Promissory note ☐ Simple discount note ☐
Treasury bill ☐

The *Wall Street Journal* clip "Who Supplied the Cash" reveals that only 16% of funds come from banks for launching or running a business.

This chapter begins with a discussion of the structure of promissory notes and simple discount notes. We also look at the application of discounting with Treasury bills. The chapter concludes with an explanation of how to calculate the discounting of promissory notes.

GLOBAL

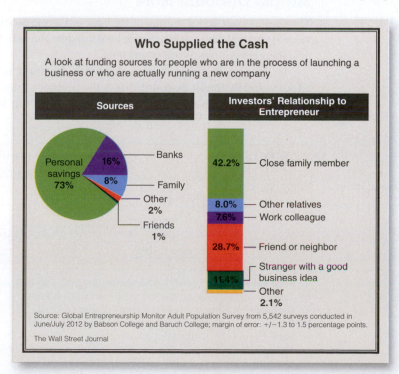

Who Supplied the Cash

A look at funding sources for people who are in the process of launching a business or who are actually running a new company

Sources

- Personal savings 73%
- Banks 16%
- Family 8%
- Other 2%
- Friends 1%

Investors' Relationship to Entrepreneur

- 42.2% — Close family member
- 8.0% — Other relatives
- 7.6% — Work colleague
- 28.7% — Friend or neighbor
- 11.4% — Stranger with a good business idea
- Other 2.1%

Source: Global Entrepreneurship Monitor Adult Population Survey from 5,542 surveys conducted in June/July 2012 by Babson College and Baruch College; margin of error: +/−1.3 to 1.5 percentage points.

The Wall Street Journal

Reprinted by permission of *The Wall Street Journal*, copyright 2013 Dow Jones & Company, Inc. All rights reserved worldwide.

Learning Unit 11–1: Structure of Promissory Notes; the Simple Discount Note

Although businesses frequently sign promissory notes, customers also sign promissory notes. For example, some student loans may require the signing of promissory notes. Appliance stores often ask customers to sign a promissory note when they buy large appliances on credit. In this unit, promissory notes usually involve interest payments.

LO 1

Structure of Promissory Notes

To borrow money, you must find a lender (a bank or a company selling goods on credit). You must also be willing to pay for the use of the money. In Chapter 10 you learned that interest is the cost of borrowing money for periods of time. Lenders charge interest as a rental fee on borrowing money.

Money lenders usually require that borrowers sign a **promissory note.** This note states that the borrower will repay a certain sum at a fixed time in the future. The note often includes the charge for the use of the money, or the rate of interest. Figure 11.1 shows a sample promissory note with its terms identified and defined. Take a moment to look at each term.

In a survey conducted by The Wall Street Journal, four percent of people had encountered promissory note scams.

In this section you will learn the difference between interest-bearing notes and non-interest-bearing notes.

Interest-Bearing versus Non-Interest-Bearing Notes   A promissory note can be interest bearing or non–interest bearing. To be interest bearing, the note must state the rate of interest. Since the promissory note in Figure 11.1 states that its interest is 9%, it is an **interest-bearing note.** When the note matures, Regal Corporation will pay back the original amount **(face value)** borrowed plus interest. The simple interest formula (also known as the interest formula) and the maturity value formula from Chapter 10 are used for this transaction.

> Interest = Face value (principal) × Rate × Time
> Maturity value = Face value (principal) + Interest

If you sign a **non-interest-bearing** promissory note for $10,000, you pay back $10,000 at maturity. The maturity value of a non-interest-bearing note is the same as its face value. Usually, non-interest-bearing notes occur for short time periods under special conditions. For example, money borrowed from a relative could be secured by a non-interest-bearing promissory note.

LO 2

Simple Discount Note

The total amount due at the end of the loan, or the **maturity value (MV),** is the sum of the face value (principal) and interest. Some banks deduct the loan interest in advance. When banks do this, the note is a **simple discount note.**

In the simple discount note, the **bank discount** is the interest that banks deduct in advance and the **bank discount rate** is the percent of interest. The amount that the borrower receives after the bank deducts its discount from the loan's maturity value is the note's

FIGURE 11.1

Interest-bearing promissory note

$10,000 **a.**   LAWTON, OKLAHOMA   *October 2, 2016* **c.**

_____ *Sixty days* **b.** _____ AFTER DATE _we_   PROMISE TO PAY TO

THE ORDER OF _____ *G.J. Equipment Company* **d.**

_____ *Ten thousand and 00/100*----------------------DOLLARS.

PAYABLE AT _____ *Able National Bank* _____

VALUE RECEIVED WITH INTEREST AT _9%_ **e.**   REGAL CORPORATION **f.**

NO. _114_   DUE *December 1, 2016*   *J.M. Moore*
                        g.   TREASURER

a. **Face value:** Amount of money borrowed—$10,000. The face value is also the principal of the note.
b. **Term:** Length of time that the money is borrowed—60 days.
c. **Date:** The date that the note is issued—October 2, 2016.
d. **Payee:** The company extending the credit—G.J. Equipment Company.
e. **Rate:** The annual rate for the cost of borrowing the money—9%.
f. **Maker:** The company issuing the note and borrowing the money—Regal Corporation.
g. **Maturity date:** The date the principal and interest rate are due—December 1, 2016.

proceeds. Sometimes we refer to simple discount notes as non-interest-bearing notes. Remember, however, that borrowers *do* pay interest on these notes.

In the example that follows, Pete Runnels has the choice of a note with a simple interest rate (Chapter 10) or a note with a simple discount rate (Chapter 11). Table 11.1 provides a summary of the calculations made in the example and gives the key points that you should remember. Now let's study the example, and then you can review Table 11.1.

We will use 360 (not 365) days for all calculations in this chapter.

EXAMPLE Pete Runnels has a choice of two different notes that both have a face value (principal) of $14,000 for 60 days. One note has a simple interest rate of 8%, while the other note has a simple discount rate of 8%. For each type of note, calculate **(a)** interest owed, **(b)** maturity value, **(c)** proceeds, and **(d)** effective rate.

LO 3

Simple interest note—Chapter 10	Simple discount note—Chapter 11
Interest	**Interest**
a. I = Face value (principal) $\times R \times T$	**a.** I = Face value (principal) $\times R \times T$
$I = \$14{,}000 \times .08 \times \dfrac{60}{360}$	$I = \$14{,}000 \times .08 \times \dfrac{60}{360}$
$I = \$186.67$	$I = \$186.67$
Maturity value	**Maturity value**
b. MV = Face value + Interest	**b.** MV = Face value
$MV = \$14{,}000 + \$186.67$	$MV = \$14{,}000$
$MV = \$14{,}186.67$	
Proceeds	**Proceeds**
c. Proceeds = Face value	**c.** Proceeds = MV − Bank discount
$= \$14{,}000$	$= \$14{,}000 - \$186.67$
	$= \$13{,}813.33$
Effective rate	**Effective rate**
d. Rate = $\dfrac{\text{Interest}}{\text{Proceeds} \times \text{Time}}$	**d.** Rate = $\dfrac{\text{Interest}}{\text{Proceeds} \times \text{Time}}$
$= \dfrac{\$186.67}{\$14{,}000 \times \dfrac{60}{360}}$	$= \dfrac{\$186.67}{\$13{,}813.33 \times \dfrac{60}{360}}$
$= 8\%$	$= 8.11\%$

Do not round intermediate answers. Round only the final calculation.

TABLE 11.1

Comparison of simple interest note and simple discount note (Calculations from the Pete Runnels example)

Simple interest note (Chapter 10)	Simple discount note (Chapter 11)
1. A promissory note for a loan with a term of usually less than 1 year. *Example:* 60 days.	**1.** A promissory note for a loan with a term of usually less than 1 year. *Example:* 60 days.
2. Paid back by one payment at maturity. Face value equals actual amount (or principal) of loan (this is not maturity value).	**2.** Paid back by one payment at maturity. Face value equals maturity value (what will be repaid).
3. Interest computed on face value or what is actually borrowed. *Example:* $186.67.	**3.** Interest computed on maturity value or what will be repaid and not on actual amount borrowed. *Example:* $186.67.
4. Maturity value = Face value + Interest. *Example:* $14,186.67.	**4.** Maturity value = Face value. *Example:* $14,000.
5. Borrower receives the face value. *Example:* $14,000.	**5.** Borrower receives proceeds = Face value − Bank discount. *Example:* $13,813.33.
6. Effective rate (true rate is same as rate stated on note). *Example:* 8%.	**6.** Effective rate is higher since interest was deducted in advance. *Example:* 8.11%.
7. Used frequently instead of the simple discount note.	**7.** Not used as much now because in 1969 congressional legislation required that the true rate of interest be revealed. Still used where legislation does not apply, such as personal loans.

Note that the interest of $186.67 is the same for the simple interest note and the simple discount note. The maturity value of the simple discount note is the same as the face value. In the simple discount note, interest is deducted in advance, so the proceeds are less than the face value. Note that the **effective rate** for a simple discount note is higher than the stated rate, since the bank calculated the rate on the face value of the note and not on what Pete received.

LO 4

Application of Discounting—Treasury Bills   When the government needs money, it sells Treasury bills. A **Treasury bill** is a loan to the federal government for 28 days (4 weeks), 91 days (13 weeks), or 1 year. Note that the *Wall Street Journal* clipping "Treasury Auctions" announces a new sale.

Treasury Auctions

The Treasury Department will auction $73 billion in debt. Details of the offerings (all with minimum denominations of $100):

◆ **Monday:** $24 billion in 13-week bills, dated Jan. 8 and maturing April 9. Cusip number is 912796FC8. Also, $24 billion in 26-week bills, dated Jan. 8 and maturing July 9. Cusip number is 912796FT1. Noncompetitive tenders must be received by 11 a.m. EST Monday and competitive tenders by 11:30 a.m.

◆ **Tuesday:** $25 billion in 52-week bills, dated Jan. 8, 2015, and maturing Jan. 7, 2016. Cusip number is 912796FP9. Noncompetitive tenders must be received by 11 a.m. Tuesday and competitive tenders by 11:30 a.m.

Reprinted by permission of *The Wall Street Journal,* copyright 2015 Dow Jones & Company, Inc. All rights reserved worldwide.

MONEY tips

Paying your rent on time can help improve your credit rating. Leaving a lease before it is up and bouncing checks to a landlord will reduce it.

Treasury bills can be bought over the phone or on the government website. The purchase price (or proceeds) of a Treasury bill is the value of the Treasury bill less the discount. For example, if you buy a $10,000, 13-week Treasury bill at 8%, you pay $9,800 since you have not yet earned your interest $\left(\$10,000 \times .08 \times \frac{13}{52} = \$200\right)$. At maturity—13 weeks—the government pays you $10,000. You calculate your effective yield (8.16% rounded to the nearest hundredth percent) as follows:

$$\frac{\$200}{(\$10,000 - \$200) \longrightarrow \$9,800 \times \dfrac{13}{52}} = \boxed{8.16\%} \text{ effective rate}$$

Now it's time to try the Practice Quiz and check your progress.

LU 11–1   **PRACTICE QUIZ**

Complete this Practice Quiz to see how you are doing.

1. Warren Ford borrowed $12,000 on a non-interest-bearing, simple discount, $9\frac{1}{2}\%$, 60-day note. Assume ordinary interest. What are **(a)** the maturity value, **(b)** the bank's discount, **(c)** Warren's proceeds, and **(d)** the effective rate to the nearest hundredth percent?

2. Jane Long buys a $10,000, 13-week Treasury bill at 6%. What is her effective rate? Round to the nearest hundredth percent.

*For **extra help** from your authors—Sharon and Jeff—see the videos in Connect.*

These videos are also available on YouTube!

✓ Solutions

1. **a.** Maturity value = Face value = $12,000

    b. Bank discount = $MV \times$ Bank discount rate $\times$ Time

    $$= \$12,000 \times .095 \times \frac{60}{360}$$

    $$= \$190$$

    c. Proceeds = MV − Bank discount

    $$= \$12,000 - \$190$$

    $$= \$11,810$$

    d. Effective rate $= \dfrac{\text{Interest}}{\text{Proceeds} \times \text{Time}}$

    $$= \frac{\$190}{\$11,810 \times \dfrac{60}{360}}$$

    $$= \$9.65\%$$

2. $\$10,000 \times .06 \times \dfrac{13}{52} = \$150$ interest $\dfrac{\$150}{\$9,850 \times \dfrac{13}{52}} = 6.09\%$

LU 11–1a   **EXTRA PRACTICE QUIZ WITH WORKED-OUT SOLUTIONS**

Need more practice? Try this Extra Practice Quiz (check figures in the Interactive Chapter Organizer). Worked-out Solutions can be found in Appendix B.

1. Warren Ford borrowed $14,000 on a non-interest-bearing, simple discount, $4\frac{1}{2}\%$, 60-day note. Assume ordinary interest. What are **(a)** the maturity value, **(b)** the bank's discount, **(c)** Warren's proceeds, and **(d)** the effective rate to the nearest hundredth percent?
2. Jane Long buys a $10,000, 13-week Treasury bill at 4%. What is her effective rate? Round to the nearest hundredth percent.

Learning Unit 11–2: Discounting an Interest-Bearing Note before Maturity

LO 1

Manufacturers frequently deliver merchandise to retail companies and do not request payment for several months. For example, Roger Company manufactures outdoor furniture that it delivers to Sears in March. Payment for the furniture is not due until September. Roger will have its money tied up in this furniture until September. So Roger requests that Sears sign promissory notes.

If Roger Company needs cash sooner than September, what can it do? Roger Company can take one of its promissory notes to the bank, assuming the company that signed the note is reliable. The bank will buy the note from Roger. Now Roger has discounted the note and has cash instead of waiting until September when Sears would have paid Roger.

Remember that when Roger Company discounts the promissory note to the bank, the company agrees to pay the note at maturity if the maker of the promissory note fails to pay the bank. The potential liability that may or may not result from discounting a note is called a **contingent liability.**

Think of **discounting a note** as a three-party arrangement. Roger Company realizes that the bank will charge for this service. The bank's charge is a **bank discount.** The actual amount Roger receives is the **proceeds** of the note. The four steps below and the formulas in the example that follows will help you understand this discounting process.

DISCOUNTING A NOTE
Step 1. Calculate the interest and maturity value.
Step 2. Calculate the discount period (time the bank holds note).
Step 3. Calculate the bank discount.
Step 4. Calculate the proceeds.

LO 2

EXAMPLE   Roger Company sold the following promissory note to the bank:

Date of note	Face value of note	Length of note	Interest rate	Bank discount rate	Date of discount
March 8	$2,000	185 days	6%	5%	August 9

What are Roger's (1) interest and maturity value (*MV*)? What are the (2) discount period and (3) bank discount? (4) What are the proceeds?

1. *Calculate Roger's interest and maturity value (MV):*

    > MV = Face value (principal) + Interest

    Interest = $2,000 \times .06 \times \dfrac{185}{360}$ ◄ Exact number of days over 360

    $ = \$61.67$

    $MV = \$2,000 + \$61.67$

    $ = \$2,061.67$

Calculating days without table:

March	31
	− 8
	23
April	30
May	31
June	30
July	31
August	9
	154

185 days—length of note
−154 days Roger held note
  31 days bank waits

2. *Calculate **discount period:***
    Determine the number of days that the bank will have to wait for the note to come due (discount period).

August 9	221 days	
March 8	− 67	
	154	days passed before note is discounted
	185 days	
	− 154	
	31	days bank waits for note to come due

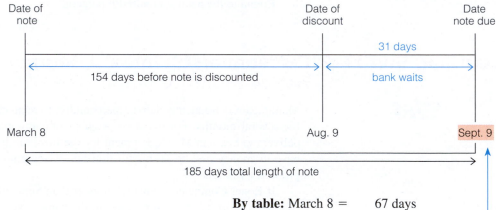

Date of note — March 8

154 days before note is discounted

Date of discount — Aug. 9

31 days — bank waits

Date note due — Sept. 9

185 days total length of note

By table: March 8 = 67 days
 + 185
 252 search in table ───

3. *Calculate bank discount (bank charge):*

    $\$2,061.67 \times .05 \times \dfrac{31}{360} = \$8.88$

> Bank discount = MV × Bank discount rate × $\dfrac{\text{Number of days bank waits for note to come due}}{360}$

MONEY tips

Protect your credit. At a minimum, review your credit report annually. Ideally, you can review your credit report for free three times per year if you stagger your free annual requests required by law from each of the three credit agencies: TransUnion, Equifax, and Experian. AnnualCreditReport.com has links to each.

4. *Calculate proceeds:*

      $2,061.67
    −   8.88
      $2,052.79

    If Roger had waited until September 9, it would have received $2,061.67. Now, on August 9, Roger received $2,000 plus $52.79 interest.

Step 1
↓
> Proceeds = MV − Bank discount (charge)
↑
Step 3

Now let's assume Roger Company received a non-interest-bearing note. Then we follow the four steps for discounting a note except the maturity value is the amount of the loan. No interest accumulates on a non-interest-bearing note. Today, many banks use simple interest instead of discounting. Also, instead of discounting notes, many companies set up *lines of credit* so that additional financing is immediately available.

The *Wall Street Journal* clipping in the chapter opener, "Penney Taps Credit Line," shows how J.C. Penney is using a credit line to fund day-to-day operations.

The Practice Quiz that follows will test your understanding of this unit.

LU 11–2 PRACTICE QUIZ

Complete this **Practice Quiz** to see how you are doing.

Date of note	Face value (principal) of note	Length of note	Interest rate	Bank discount rate	Date of discount
April 8	$35,000	160 days	11%	9%	June 8

From the above, calculate (**a**) interest and maturity value, (**b**) discount period, (**c**) bank discount, and (**d**) proceeds. Assume ordinary interest.

*For **extra help** from your authors—Sharon and Jeff—see the videos in Connect.*

These videos are also available on YouTube!

✓ Solutions

a. $I = \$35,000 \times .11 \times \dfrac{160}{360} = \boxed{\$1,711.11}$

$MV = \$35,000 + \$1,711.11 = \boxed{\$36,711.11}$

b. Discount period = 160 − 61 = 99 days

April	30		Or by table:	
	− 8		June 8	159
	22		April 8	− 98
May	+ 31			61
	53			
June	+ 8			
	61			

c. Bank discount = $\$36,711.11 \times .09 \times \dfrac{99}{360} = \boxed{\$908.60}$

d. Proceeds = $\$36,711.11 − \$908.60 = \boxed{\$35,802.51}$

LU 11–2a EXTRA PRACTICE QUIZ WITH WORKED-OUT SOLUTION

Need more practice? Try this **Extra Practice Quiz** (check figure in the Interactive Chapter Organizer). Worked-out Solution can be found in Appendix B.

From the information below, calculate (**a**) interest and maturity value, (**b**) discount period, (**c**) bank discount, and (**d**) proceeds. Assume ordinary interest.

Date of note	Face value (principal) of note	Length of note	Interest rate	Bank discount rate	Date of discount
April 10	$40,000	170 days	5%	2%	June 10

INTERACTIVE CHAPTER ORGANIZER

Topic/Procedure/Formula	Examples	You try it*
Simple discount note Bank discount = MV × Bank discount rate × Time (interest) Interest based on amount paid back and not on actual amount received.	$6,000 × .09 × $\frac{60}{360}$ = $90 Borrower receives $5,910 (the proceeds) and pays back $6,000 at maturity after 60 days. A Treasury bill is a good example of a simple discount note.	**Calculate proceeds** $4,000 note at 2% for 30 days
Effective rate $\dfrac{\text{Interest}}{\text{Proceeds} \times \text{Time}}$ ↑ What borrower receives (Face value − Discount)	*Example:* $10,000 note, discount rate 12% for 60 days. I = $10,000 × .12 × $\frac{60}{360}$ = $200 Effective rate: $\dfrac{\$200}{\$9,800 \times \frac{60}{360}}$ = $\dfrac{\$200}{\$1,633.3333}$ = 12.24% ↑ Amount borrower received	**Calculate effective rate** $15,000 note at 4% for 40 days

Discounting an interest-bearing note
1. Calculate interest and maturity value.
   I = Face value × Rate × Time
   MV = Face value + Interest
2. Calculate number of days bank will wait for note to come due (discount period).
3. Calculate bank discount (bank charge).
   $MV \times$ Bank discount rate $\times \dfrac{\text{Number of days bank waits}}{360}$
4. Calculate proceeds.
   MV − Bank discount (charge)
	Example: $1,000 note, 6%, 60 days, dated November 1 and discounted on December 1 at 8%.
	
	1. I = $1,000 × .06 × $\frac{60}{360}$ = $10
	   MV = $1,000 + $10 = $1,010
	2. 30 days
	3. $1,010 × .08 × $\frac{30}{360}$ = $6.73
	4. $1,010 − $6.73 = $1,003.27
		Calculate proceeds
		$2,000 note, 3%, 60 days, dated November 5 and discounted on December 15 at 5%

KEY TERMS	Bank discount Bank discount rate Contingent liability Discount period Discounting a note Effective rate	Face value Interest-bearing note Maker Maturity date Maturity value (*MV*) Non-interest-bearing note	Payee Proceeds Promissory note Simple discount note Treasury bill

Check Figures for Extra Practice Quizzes. (Worked-out Solutions are in Appendix B.)	LU 11–1a
	1. a. $14,000
	   b. $105
	   c. $13,895
	   d. 4.53%
	2. 4.04%
		LU 11–2a
		1. a. Int. = $944.44; $40,944.44
		   b. 109 days
		   c. $247.94
		   d. $40,696.50

*Worked-out solutions are in Appendix B.

Critical Thinking Discussion Questions with Chapter Concept Check

1. What are the differences between a simple interest note and a simple discount note? Which type of note would have a higher effective rate of interest? Why?

2. What are the four steps of the discounting process? Could the proceeds of a discounted note be less than the face value of the note?

3. What is a line of credit? What could be a disadvantage of having a large credit line?

4. Discuss the impact of a slow economy on small business borrowing.

5. **Chapter Concept Check.** Go to the Internet and determine the current status of business loans. In your answer, include concepts you learned in this chapter.

END-OF-CHAPTER PROBLEMS

connect plus+

Mc Graw Hill Education

Check figures for odd-numbered problems in Appendix C.   Name _____   Date _____

DRILL PROBLEMS

Complete the following table for these simple discount notes. Use the ordinary interest method.   *LU 11-1(2)*

	Amount due at maturity	Discount rate	Time	Bank discount	Proceeds
11–1.	$4,250	$2\frac{1}{2}\%$	190 days		
11–2.	$2,900	$6\frac{1}{4}\%$	180 days		

Calculate the discount period for the bank to wait to receive its money: *LU 11-2(1)*

	Date of note	Length of note	Date note discounted	Discount period
11–3.	April 12	45 days	May 2	
11–4.	March 7	120 days	June 8	

Solve for maturity value, discount period, bank discount, and proceeds (assume for Problems 11–5 and 11–6 a bank discount rate of 9%).   *LU 11-2(1, 2)*

	Face value (principal)	Rate of interest	Length of note	Maturity value	Date of note	Date note discounted	Discount period	Bank discount	Proceeds
11–5.	$50,000	11%	95 days		June 10	July 18			
11–6.	$25,000	9%	60 days		June 8	July 10			

11–7. Calculate the effective rate of interest (to the nearest hundredth percent) of the following Treasury bill. **eXcel   Given:** $10,000 Treasury bill, 4% for 13 weeks.   *LU 11-1(4)*

WORD PROBLEMS

Use ordinary interest as needed.

11–8. Carl Sonntag wanted to compare what proceeds he would receive with a simple interest note versus a simple discount note. Both had the same terms: $19,500 at 8% for 2 years. Compare the proceeds.   *LU 11-1(3)*

11–9. Bill Blank signed an $8,000 note at Citizen's Bank. Citizen's charges a $6\frac{1}{2}$% discount rate. If the loan is for 300 days, find **(a)** the proceeds and **(b)** the effective rate charged by the bank (to the nearest tenth percent).   *LU 11-1(3)*

11–10. You were offered the opportunity to issue either a simple interest note or a simple discount note with the following terms: $33,353 at 7% for 18 months. Based on the effective interest rate, which would you choose?   *LU 11-1(3)*

11–11. On September 5, Sheffield Company discounted at Sunshine Bank a $9,000 (maturity value), 120-day note dated June 5. Sunshine's discount rate was 9%. What proceeds did Sheffield Company receive?   *LU 11-2(1)*

11–12. The Treasury Department auctioned $21 billion in 3-month bills in denominations of $10,000 at a discount rate of 4.965%. What would be the effective rate of interest? Round your answer to the nearest hundredth percent.   *LU 11–1(4)*

11–13. There are some excellent free personal finance apps available: Mint.com, GoodBudget, Mvelopes, BillGuard, PocketExpense, HomeBudget, and Expensify. After using Mint.com, you realize you need to pay off one of your high interest loans to reduce your interest expense. You decide to discount a $5,250, 345-day note at 3% to your bank at a discount rate of 4.5% on day 210. What are your proceeds? Round each answer to the nearest cent.   *LU 11-2(1)*

11–14. Ron Prentice bought goods from Shelly Katz. On May 8, Shelly gave Ron a time extension on his bill by accepting a $3,000, 8%, 180-day note. On August 16, Shelly discounted the note at Roseville Bank at 9%. What proceeds does Shelly Katz receive? *LU 11-2(1)*

11–15. Rex Corporation accepted a $5,000, 8%, 120-day note dated August 8 from Regis Company in settlement of a past bill. On October 11, Rex discounted the note at Park Bank at 9%. What are the note's maturity value, discount period, and bank discount? What proceeds does Rex receive? *LU 11-2(1)*

11–16. On May 12, Scott Rinse accepted an $8,000, 12%, 90-day note for a time extension of a bill for goods bought by Ron Prentice. On June 12, Scott discounted the note at Able Bank at 10%. What proceeds does Scott receive? *LU 11-2(1)*

11–17. Hafers, an electrical supply company, sold $4,800 of equipment to Jim Coates Wiring, Inc. Coates signed a promissory note May 12 with 4.5% interest. The due date was August 10. Short of funds, Hafers contacted Charter One Bank on July 20; the bank agreed to take over the note at a 6.2% discount. What proceeds will Hafers receive? *LU 11-2(1)*

11–18. At www.daveramsey.com's Financial Peace University (FPU), Dave recommends Seven Baby Steps. One of these steps is "Pay off debt using the debt snowball." After graduating from FPU, Courtney Lopez-Munoz is trying to calculate the effective interest rate she is paying for a $1,789 simple discount note at $5\frac{1}{4}$% for 15 months. What rate has she been paying? Round to the nearest tenth percent. Do not round denominator calculation. *LU 11-2(1)*

11–19. Assume that 3-month Treasury bills totaling $12 billion were sold in $10,000 denominations at a discount rate of 3.605%. In addition, the Treasury Department sold 6-month bills totaling $10 billion at a discount rate of 3.55%. **(a)** What is the discount amount for 3-month bills? **(b)** What is the discount amount for 6-month bills? **(c)** What is the effective rate for 3-month bills? **(d)** What is the effective rate for 6-month bills? Round to the nearest hundredth percent. *LU 11-1(4)*

11–20. Tina Mier must pay a $2,000 furniture bill. A finance company will loan Tina $2,000 for 8 months at a 9% discount rate. The finance company told Tina that if she wants to receive exactly $2,000, she must borrow more than $2,000. The finance company gave Tina the following formula:

$$\text{What to ask for} = \frac{\text{Amount in cash to be received}}{1 - (\text{Discount} \times \text{Time of loan})}$$

Calculate Tina's loan request and the effective rate of interest to the nearest hundredth percent. *LU 11-1(3)*

 SUMMARY PRACTICE TEST

Do you need help? The videos in Connect have step-by-step worked-out solutions. These videos are also available on YouTube!

1. On December 12, Lowell Corporation accepted a $160,000, 120-day, non-interest-bearing note from Able.com. What is the maturity value of the note? *LU 11-1(1)*

2. The face value of a simple discount note is $17,000. The discount is 4% for 160 days. Calculate the following. *LU 11-1(3)*

    a. Amount of interest charged for each note.

    b. Amount borrower would receive.

    c. Amount payee would receive at maturity.

    d. Effective rate (to the nearest tenth percent).

3. On July 14, Gracie Paul accepted a $60,000, 6%, 160-day note from Mike Lang. On November 12, Gracie discounted the note at Lend Bank at 7%. What proceeds did Gracie receive? *LU 11-2(1)*

4. Lee.com accepted a $70,000, $6\frac{3}{4}$%, 120-day note on July 26. Lee discounts the note on October 28 at LB Bank at 6%. What proceeds did Lee receive? *LU 11-2(1)*

5. The owner of Lease.com signed a $60,000 note at Reese Bank. Reese charges a $7\frac{1}{4}$% discount rate. If the loan is for 210 days, find **(a)** the proceeds and **(b)** the effective rate charged by the bank (to the nearest tenth percent). *LU 11-2(1)*

6. Sam Slater buys a $10,000, 13-week Treasury bill at $5\frac{1}{2}$%. What is the effective rate? Round to the nearest hundredth percent. *LU 11-1(4)*

SURF TO SAVE

How can you make your money grow? 🔍

PROBLEM 1
T-bill tips

Go online and search for a T-bill rate calculator. Assume that you paid $9,925 for a 91-day bill with a $10,000 face value. What is the effective yield, rounded to the nearest hundredth of a percent? Calculate the ratio of the price paid to the face value in decimal format.

Discussion Questions

1. Is this a good yield for a 3-month investment? Why or why not?
2. How else could you invest this $10,000?

PROBLEM 2
Discounting simply

Visit http://www.gyplan.com/billdiscount_en.html. Assume you have borrowed $20,000 from Long Shores Bank for 90 days. Long Shores Bank has discounted your note at 12%. What are your proceeds on this note?

Discussion Questions

1. What are some reasons why businesses would need to take out such a short-term loan?
2. What are the benefits to the bank in issuing simple interest notes?

PROBLEM 3
Promissory note promises

Go to http://www.sec.state.ma.us/sct/sctprs/prsnote/promnote.pdf. After reading the document, explain how you would be able to protect yourself from fraud in the promissory note market.

Discussion Questions

1. Based on the article and the potential fraud in this area, would you invest your money this way? Why or why not?
2. What do you feel may be the root cause of fraud in this particular market?

PROBLEM 4
T-bill trends

Visit http://www.treasury.gov/resource-center/data-chart- center/interest-rates/ Pages/TextView .aspx?data=yield. Find the Daily Treasury Bill rate for a 13-week T-bill purchased on January 2 of the current year. If you purchased a $10,000 T-bill at this rate, what would be your effective rate on this T-bill?

Discussion Questions

1. What are the pros and cons to utilizing T-bills as an investment?
2. Why would the U.S. government use these T-bills to finance its operations?

MOBILE APPS ✕

Yield Curve (Business Compass LLC) Plots the yield curve for the U.S. Treasury.

Simple Interest (Business Compass LLC) Figures the amount of interest earned based on a specific rate.

A KIPLINGER APPROACH

By Sandra Block, From *Kiplinger's Personal Finance*, November 2013.

GAME PLAN

"What's the best way to lend money to a family member (and not get burned)?"

WHETHER YOU'RE LENDING money to your college-bound child or your entrepreneurial brother-in-law, treat the loan as a business transaction. That will increase the likelihood that you'll be repaid and keep the IRS at bay.

But first, think hard about whether you can afford to lend the money. "It's an investment," says Curtis Arnold, founder of CardRatings.com and coauthor of *The Complete Idiot's Guide to Person-to-Person Lending.* "You can lose the whole kit and caboodle."

Still, a direct loan is less risky than cosigning a loan, says Gerri Detweiler, director of consumer education for Credit.com. If you cosign, you're on the hook if the borrower defaults—and you may not know about it until your credit rating takes a tumble.

If a family member asks you for a loan, start by asking why he or she needs the money. A loan that would help with college tuition or the purchase of a home could improve the borrower's financial security. Similarly, a loan could help a relative recovering from a financial setback to avoid predatory lenders, Detweiler says. Conversely, lending money to a family member

who has a history of poor financial choices could enable more bad behavior. Ask the potential borrower to provide you with a copy of a credit report and score. The score probably isn't stellar, or the family member wouldn't be hitting you up for a loan. But a credit report (the prospective borrower can get one free at www.annualcreditreport .com) will give you an idea of the individual's other financial obligations.

How much to charge. If the borrower is really struggling, you may be tempted to make a no-interest loan, or charge a nominal

amount. Be aware, though, that doing so could get you into hot water with the IRS. To avoid having the transaction treated as a gift, the IRS requires that you charge at least the applicable federal rate (AFR), which is published monthly at www.irs.gov. Otherwise, the IRS could dun you for taxes on "imputed" interest income, based on the AFR when the loan was made. You're not required to charge interest if the loan is for less than $10,000, or up to $100,000 if the borrower's investment income for the year is less than $1,000.

Federal rates this year have ranged from about

0.21% to 3.28%, depending on the length of the loan. Of course, you're expected to report interest you receive as taxable income.

If you wind up forgiving the loan, you might be entangled by gift-tax rules. Gifts that exceed $14,000, including any unpaid interest, require that you file a gift-tax return and cut into your lifetime gift- and estate-tax exemptions.

Put it in writing. In addition to charging interest, drawing up a formal agreement will make it clear to the IRS that you're making a loan, not a gift. It's also a good way to ensure that everyone involved understands the terms of the loan. You can find sample promissory notes online, and Web sites such as www.bankrate.com provide tools that will calculate monthly payments.

Arnold, who has made several loans to friends and family members, uses Loan-Back (www.loanback.com), which sells a personalized loan agreement you can track online. A product that will calculate payments and provide e-mail alerts costs $29.95; a basic downloadable template (that doesn't do the math for you) is available for $14.95. **SANDRA BLOCK**

DAVE URBAN

BUSINESS MATH ISSUE

A promissory note means you are making a gift and not a loan.

1. List the key points of the article and information to support your position.
2. Write a group defense of your position using math calculations to support your view.

CHAPTER 12

Compound Interest and Present Value

© Caia Image/Glow Images

Pepper ... And Salt

THE WALL STREET JOURNAL

"If you start saving money now, you'll be able to borrow more later."

Gottschalk

From *The Wall Street Journal*, permission Cartoon Features Syndicate.

Big Benefit to an Early Start

Accumulated nest eggs at age 65 of two hypothetical investors both contribute $24,000 over time to their retirement accounts

$50/month starting at age 25

$100/month starting at age 45

$80,000
70,000
60,000
50,000
40,000
30,000
20,000
10,000
0

25   30   35   40   45   50   55   60

Note: Assumes 5% annual return (8% from market minus 3% inflation) compounded

Source: LearnVest

Source: *The Wall Street Journal*, 12/3/12.

LU 12–1: Compound Interest (Future Value)—The Big Picture

1. Compare simple interest with compound interest.
2. Calculate the compound amount and interest manually and by table lookup.
3. Explain and compute the effective rate (APY).

LU 12–2: Present Value—The Big Picture

1. Compare present value (PV) with compound interest (FV).
2. Compute present value by table lookup.
3. Check the present value answer by compounding.

VOCABULARY PREVIEW

Here are key terms in this chapter. After completing the chapter, if you know the term, place a checkmark in the box. If you don't know the term, look it up and put the page number where it can be found.

Annual percentage yield (APY) ☐ **Compound amount** ☐ **Compound interest** ☐ **Compounded annually** ☐
Compounded daily ☐ **Compounded monthly** ☐ **Compounded quarterly** ☐ **Compounded semiannually** ☐
Compounding ☐ **Effective rate** ☐ **Future value (FV)** ☐ **Nominal rate** ☐ **Number of periods** ☐
Present value (PV) ☐ **Rate for each period** ☐

Wow! The chapter opening *Wall Street Journal* clip "Big Benefit to an Early Start" shows the magic of compounding.

In this chapter we look at the power of compounding—interest paid on earned interest. Let's begin by studying Learning Unit 12–1, which shows you how to calculate compound interest.

Learning Unit 12–1: Compound Interest (Future Value)— The Big Picture

So far we have discussed only simple interest, which is interest on the principal alone. Simple interest is either paid at the end of the loan period or deducted in advance. From the chapter introduction, you know that interest can also be compounded.

Compounding involves the calculation of interest periodically over the life of the loan (or investment). After each calculation, the interest is added to the principal. Future calculations are on the adjusted principal (old principal plus interest). **Compound interest,** then, is the interest on the principal plus the interest of prior periods. **Future value (FV),** or the **compound amount,** is the final amount of the loan or investment at the end of the last period. In the beginning of this unit, do not be concerned with how to calculate compounding but try to understand the meaning of compounding.

Figure 12.1 shows how $1 will grow if it is calculated for 4 years at 8% annually. This means that the interest is calculated on the balance once a year. In Figure 12.1, we start with $1, which is the **present value (PV).** After year 1, the dollar with interest is worth $1.08. At the end of year 2, the dollar is worth $1.17. By the end of year 4, the dollar is worth $1.36 . Note how we start with the present and look to see what the dollar will be worth in the future. *Compounding goes from present value to future value.*

FIGURE **12.1**

Future value of $1 at 8% for four periods

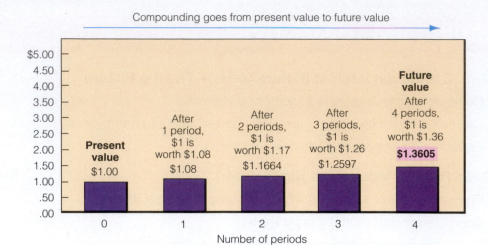

Before you learn how to calculate compound interest and compare it to simple interest, you must understand the terms that follow. These terms are also used in Chapter 13.

- **Compounded annually:** Interest calculated on the balance once a year.
- **Compounded semiannually:** Interest calculated on the balance every 6 months or every $\frac{1}{2}$ year.
- **Compounded quarterly:** Interest calculated on the balance every 3 months or every $\frac{1}{4}$ year.
- **Compounded monthly:** Interest calculated on the balance each month.
- **Compounded daily:** Interest calculated on the balance each day.
- **Number of periods:**[1] Number of years multiplied by the number of times the interest is compounded per year. For example, if you compound $1 for 4 years at 8% annually, semiannually, or quarterly, the following periods will result:

  Annually: 4 years × 1 = 4 periods
  Semiannually: 4 years × 2 = 8 periods
  Quarterly: 4 years × 4 = 16 periods

- **Rate for each period:**[2] Annual interest rate divided by the number of times the interest is compounded per year. Compounding changes the interest rate for annual, semiannual, and quarterly periods as follows:

  Annually: 8% ÷ 1 = 8%
  Semiannually: 8% ÷ 2 = 4%
  Quarterly: 8% ÷ 4 = 2%

Note that both the number of periods (4) and the rate (8%) for the annual example did not change. You will see later that rate and periods (not years) will always change unless interest is compounded yearly.

Now you are ready to learn the difference between simple interest and compound interest.

LO 1

Simple versus Compound Interest

Did you know that money invested at 6% will double in 12 years? The following *Wall Street Journal* clipping "Confused by Investing?" shows how to calculate the number of years it takes for your investment to double. Although this clip is from 2003, its information is as current today as it was then. It explains compounding and the rule of 72, so read it carefully.

---

[1]Periods are often expressed with the letter *N* or *n* for number of periods.
[2]Rate is often expressed with the letter *i* for interest.

Confused by Investing?

If there's something about your investment portfolio that doesn't seem to add up, maybe you should check your math.

Lots of folks are perplexed by the mathematics of investing, so I thought a refresher course might help. Here's a look at some key concepts:

■ **10 Plus 10 is 21**

Imagine you invest $100, which earns 10% this year and 10% next. How much have you made? If you answered 21%, go to the head of the class.

Here's how the math works. This year's 10% gain turns your $100 into $110. Next year, you also earn 10%, but you start the year with $110. Result? You earn $11, boosting your wealth to $121.

Thus, your portfolio has earned a *cumulative* 21% return over two years, but the *annualized* return is just 10%. The fact that 21% is more than double 10% can be attributed to the effect of investment compounding, the way that you earn money each year not only on your original investment, but also on earnings from prior years that you've reinvested.

■ **The Rule of 72**

To get a feel for compounding, try the rule of 72. What's that? If you divide a particular annual return into 72, you'll find out how many years it will take to double your money. Thus, at 10% a year, an investment will double in value in a tad over seven years.

Reprinted with permission of *The Wall Street Journal,* Copyright © 2003 Dow Jones & Company, Inc. All Rights Reserved Worldwide.

The following three situations of Bill Smith will clarify the difference between simple interest and compound interest.

Situation 1: Calculating Simple Interest and Maturity Value

EXAMPLE   Bill Smith deposited $80 in a savings account for 4 years at an annual interest rate of 8%. What is Bill's simple interest?

To calculate simple interest, we use the following simple interest formula:

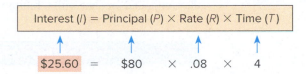

$$\text{Interest } (I) = \text{Principal } (P) \times \text{Rate } (R) \times \text{Time } (T)$$

$$\$25.60 \quad = \quad \$80 \quad \times \quad .08 \quad \times \quad 4$$

In 4 years Bill receives a total of $105.60 ($80.00 + $25.60)—principal plus simple interest.

Now let's look at the interest Bill would earn if the bank compounded Bill's interest on his savings.

Situation 2: Calculating Compound Amount and Interest without Tables[3]

You can use the following steps to calculate the compound amount and the interest manually:

CALCULATING COMPOUND AMOUNT AND INTEREST MANUALLY

Step 1.   Calculate the simple interest and add it to the principal. Use this total to figure next year's interest.

Step 2.   Repeat for the total number of periods.

Step 3.   Compound amount − Principal = Compound interest.

EXAMPLE   Bill Smith deposited $80 in a savings account for 4 years at an annual compounded rate of 8%. What are Bill's compound amount and interest?

The following shows how the compounded rate affects Bill's interest:

	Year 1	**Year 2**	**Year 3**	**Year 4**
	$80.00	$86.40	$ 93.31	$100.77
	× .08	× .08	× .08	× .08
Interest	$ 6.40	$ 6.91	$ 7.46	$ 8.06
Beginning balance	+ 80.00	+ 86.40	+ 93.31	+ 100.77
Amount at year-end	$86.40	$93.31	$100.77	$108.83

[3]For simplicity of presentation, round each calculation to the nearest cent before continuing the compounding process. The compound amount will be off by 1 cent.

Note that the beginning year 2 interest is the result of the interest of year 1 added to the principal. At the end of each interest period, we add on the period's interest. This interest becomes part of the principal we use for the calculation of the next period's interest. We can determine Bill's compound interest as follows:[4]

Compound amount	$108.83
Principal	− 80.00
Compound interest	$ 28.83 *Note:* In Situation 1 the interest was $25.60.

We could have used the following simplified process to calculate the compound amount and interest:

Year 1	Year 2	Year 3	Year 4
$80.00	$86.40	$ 93.31	$100.77
× 1.08	× 1.08	× 1.08	× 1.08
$86.40	$93.31	$100.77	$108.83 ← Future value

When using this simplification, you do not have to add the new interest to the previous balance. Remember that compounding results in higher interest than simple interest. Compounding is the *sum* of principal and interest multiplied by the interest rate we use to calculate interest for the next period. So, 1.08 above is 108%, with 100% as the base and 8% as the interest.

LO 2

Situation 3: Calculating Compound Amount by Table Lookup   To calculate the compound amount with a future value table, use the following steps:

CALCULATING COMPOUND AMOUNT BY TABLE LOOKUP

Step 1. Find the periods: Years multiplied by number of times interest is compounded in 1 year.

Step 2. Find the rate: Annual rate divided by number of times interest is compounded in 1 year.

Step 3. Go down the Period column of the table to the number of periods desired; look across the row to find the rate. At the intersection of the two columns is the table factor for the compound amount of $1.

Step 4. Multiply the table factor by the amount of the loan. This gives the compound amount.

In Situation 2, Bill deposited $80 into a savings account for 4 years at an interest rate of 8% compounded annually. Bill heard that he could calculate the compound amount and interest by using tables. In Situation 3, Bill learns how to do this. Again, Bill wants to know the value of $80 in 4 years at 8%. He begins by using Table 12.1.

Looking at Table 12.1, Bill goes down the Period column to period 4 and then across the row to the 8% column. At the intersection, Bill sees the number 1.3605. The marginal notes show how Bill arrived at the periods and rate. The 1.3605 table number means that $1 compounded at this rate will increase in value in 4 years to about $1.36. Do you recognize the $1.36? Figure 12.1 showed how $1 grew to $1.36. Since Bill wants to know the value of $80, he multiplies the dollar amount by the table factor as follows:

Four Periods

No. of times compounded in 1 year

No. of years

$$ \$80.00 \ \times \ 1.3605 \ = \ \$108.84\,^{5} $$

Principal × Table factor = Compound amount (future value)

---

[4]The formula for compounding is $A = P(1 + i)^N$, where A equals compound amount, P equals the principal, i equals interest per period, and N equals number of periods. The calculator sequence would be as follows for Bill Smith: 1 [+] .08 [y^x] 4 × 80 [=] 108.84. A Financial Calculator Guide booklet is available online that shows how to operate HP 10BII and TI BA II Plus.

[5]Off 1 cent due to rounding.

TABLE 12.1 Future value of $1 at compound interest

Period	1%	1½%	2%	3%	4%	5%	6%	7%	8%	9%	10%
1	1.0100	1.0150	1.0200	1.0300	1.0400	1.0500	1.0600	1.0700	1.0800	1.0900	1.1000
2	1.0201	1.0302	1.0404	1.0609	1.0816	1.1025	1.1236	1.1449	1.1664	1.1881	1.2100
3	1.0303	1.0457	1.0612	1.0927	1.1249	1.1576	1.1910	1.2250	1.2597	1.2950	1.3310
4	1.0406	1.0614	1.0824	1.1255	1.1699	1.2155	1.2625	1.3108	1.3605	1.4116	1.4641
5	1.0510	1.0773	1.1041	1.1593	1.2167	1.2763	1.3382	1.4026	1.4693	1.5386	1.6105
6	1.0615	1.0934	1.1262	1.1941	1.2653	1.3401	1.4185	1.5007	1.5869	1.6771	1.7716
7	1.0721	1.1098	1.1487	1.2299	1.3159	1.4071	1.5036	1.6058	1.7138	1.8280	1.9487
8	1.0829	1.1265	1.1717	1.2668	1.3686	1.4775	1.5938	1.7182	1.8509	1.9926	2.1436
9	1.0937	1.1434	1.1951	1.3048	1.4233	1.5513	1.6895	1.8385	1.9990	2.1719	2.3579
10	1.1046	1.1605	1.2190	1.3439	1.4802	1.6289	1.7908	1.9672	2.1589	2.3674	2.5937
11	1.1157	1.1780	1.2434	1.3842	1.5395	1.7103	1.8983	2.1049	2.3316	2.5804	2.8531
12	1.1268	1.1960	1.2682	1.4258	1.6010	1.7959	2.0122	2.2522	2.5182	2.8127	3.1384
13	1.1381	1.2135	1.2936	1.4685	1.6651	1.8856	2.1329	2.4098	2.7196	3.0658	3.4523
14	1.1495	1.2318	1.3195	1.5126	1.7317	1.9799	2.2609	2.5785	2.9372	3.3417	3.7975
15	1.1610	1.2502	1.3459	1.5580	1.8009	2.0789	2.3966	2.7590	3.1722	3.6425	4.1772
16	1.1726	1.2690	1.3728	1.6047	1.8730	2.1829	2.5404	2.9522	3.4259	3.9703	4.5950
17	1.1843	1.2880	1.4002	1.6528	1.9479	2.2920	2.6928	3.1588	3.7000	4.3276	5.0545
18	1.1961	1.3073	1.4282	1.7024	2.0258	2.4066	2.8543	3.3799	3.9960	4.7171	5.5599
19	1.2081	1.3270	1.4568	1.7535	2.1068	2.5270	3.0256	3.6165	4.3157	5.1417	6.1159
20	1.2202	1.3469	1.4859	1.8061	2.1911	2.6533	3.2071	3.8697	4.6610	5.6044	6.7275
21	1.2324	1.3671	1.5157	1.8603	2.2788	2.7860	3.3996	4.1406	5.0338	6.1088	7.4002
22	1.2447	1.3876	1.5460	1.9161	2.3699	2.9253	3.6035	4.4304	5.4365	6.6586	8.1403
23	1.2572	1.4084	1.5769	1.9736	2.4647	3.0715	3.8197	4.7405	5.8715	7.2579	8.9543
24	1.2697	1.4295	1.6084	2.0328	2.5633	3.2251	4.0489	5.0724	6.3412	7.9111	9.8497
25	1.2824	1.4510	1.6406	2.0938	2.6658	3.3864	4.2919	5.4274	6.8485	8.6231	10.8347
26	1.2953	1.4727	1.6734	2.1566	2.7725	3.5557	4.5494	5.8074	7.3964	9.3992	11.9182
27	1.3082	1.4948	1.7069	2.2213	2.8834	3.7335	4.8223	6.2139	7.9881	10.2451	13.1100
28	1.3213	1.5172	1.7410	2.2879	2.9987	3.9201	5.1117	6.6488	8.6271	11.1672	14.4210
29	1.3345	1.5400	1.7758	2.3566	3.1187	4.1161	5.4184	7.1143	9.3173	12.1722	15.8631
30	1.3478	1.5631	1.8114	2.4273	3.2434	4.3219	5.7435	7.6123	10.0627	13.2677	17.4494

Note: For more detailed tables, see your reference booklet, the *Business Math Handbook*.

Note all the table factors in the future value table are greater than 1. That is because investments increase in value over time due to interest being earned.

Figure 12.2 illustrates this compounding procedure. We can say that compounding is a future value (FV) since we are looking into the future. Thus,

8% Rate

8% rate = $\dfrac{8\%}{1}$ → Annual rate
                    → No. of times compounded in 1 year

$108.84 − $80.00 = $28.84 interest for 4 years at 8% compounded annually on $80.00

Now let's look at two examples that illustrate compounding more than once a year.

FIGURE 12.2

Compounding (FV)

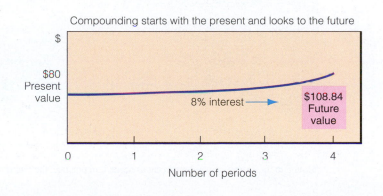

Compounding starts with the present and looks to the future

EXAMPLE   Find the interest on $6,000 at 10% compounded semiannually for 5 years. We calculate the interest as follows:

Periods = 2 × 5 years = 10 $6,000 × 1.6289 = $9,773.40

Rate = 10% ÷ 2 = 5%   − 6,000.00

10 periods, 5%, in Table 12.1 = 1.6289 (table factor) $3,773.40

                                                                    interest

EXAMPLE   Pam Donahue deposits $8,000 in her savings account that pays 6% interest compounded quarterly. What will be the balance of her account at the end of 5 years?

Periods = 4 × 5 years = 20

Rate = 6% ÷ 4 = $1\frac{1}{2}$%

20 periods, $1\frac{1}{2}$%, in Table 12.1 = 1.3469 (table factor)

$8,000 × 1.3469 = $10,775.20

Next, let's look at bank rates and how they affect interest.

LO 3

Bank Rates—Nominal versus Effective Rates (Annual Percentage Yield, or APY)

Banks often advertise their annual (nominal) interest rates and *not* their true or effective rate (annual percentage yield, or APY). This has made it difficult for investors and depositors to

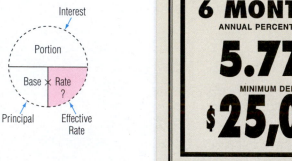

Interest

Portion

Base × Rate
?

Principal   Effective
              Rate

6 MONTH CD

ANNUAL PERCENTAGE YIELD

5.77%

MINIMUM DEPOSIT

$25,000

determine the actual rates of interest they were receiving. The Truth in Savings law forced savings institutions to reveal their actual rate of interest. The APY is defined in the Truth in Savings law as the percentage rate expressing the total amount of interest that would be received on a $100 deposit based on the annual rate and frequency of compounding for a 365-day period. As you can see from the advertisement on the left, banks now refer to the effective rate of interest as the annual percentage yield.

Let's study the rates of two banks to see which bank has the better return for the investor. Blue Bank pays 8% interest compounded quarterly on $8,000. Sun Bank offers 8% interest compounded semiannually on $8,000. The 8% rate is the **nominal rate,** or stated rate, on which the bank calculates the interest. To calculate the **effective rate (annual percentage yield,** or **APY),** however, we can use the following formula:

$$\text{Effective rate (APY)}^6 = \frac{\text{Interest for 1 year}}{\text{Principal}}$$

Now let's calculate the effective rate (APY) for Blue Bank and Sun Bank.

Note the effective rates (APY) can be seen from Table 12.1 for $1:

1.0824 ← 4 periods, 2%

1.0816 ← 2 periods, 4%

Blue, 8% compounded quarterly	Sun, 8% compounded semiannually
Periods = 4 (4 × 1)	Periods = 2 (2 × 1)
Percent = $\frac{8\%}{4}$ = 2%	Percent = $\frac{8\%}{2}$ = 4%
Principal = $8,000	Principal = $8,000
Table 12.1 lookup: 4 periods, 2%	Table 12.1 lookup: 2 periods, 4%
1.0824	1.0816
× $8,000	× $8,000
Less $8,659.20	$8,652.80
principal − 8,000.00	− 8,000.00
$ 659.20	$ 652.80
Effective rate (APY) = $\frac{\$659.20}{\$8,000}$ = .0824	$\frac{\$652.80}{\$8,000}$ = .0816
= 8.24%	= 8.16%

[6]Round to the nearest hundredth percent as needed. In practice, the rate is often rounded to the nearest thousandth.

FIGURE 12.3

Nominal and effective rates
(APY) of interest compared

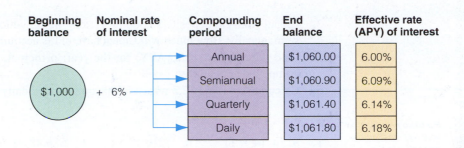

MONEY tips

Whenever possible, contribute the
maximum allowed to your retirement plan(s) to defer taxes and help
you prepare for a healthy financial
retirement. This is especially important if your employer provides a
match for your contributions.

Figure 12.3 illustrates a comparison of nominal and effective rates (APY) of interest. This comparison should make you question any advertisement of interest rates before depositing your money.

Before concluding this unit, we briefly discuss compounding interest daily.

Compounding Interest Daily

Although many banks add interest to each account quarterly, some banks pay interest that is **compounded daily,** and other banks use *continuous compounding.* Remember that continuous compounding sounds great, but in fact, it yields only a fraction of a percent more interest over a year than daily compounding. Today, computers perform these calculations.

Table 12.2 is a partial table showing what $1 will grow to in the future by daily compounded interest, 360-day basis. For example, we can calculate interest compounded daily on $900 at 6% per year for 25 years as follows:

$$\$900 \times 4.4811 = \$4{,}032.99 \text{ daily compounding}$$

TABLE 12.2   Interest on a $1 deposit compounded daily—360-day basis

Number of years	6.00%	6.50%	7.00%	7.50%	8.00%	8.50%	9.00%	9.50%	10.00%
1	1.0618	1.0672	1.0725	1.0779	1.0833	1.0887	1.0942	1.0996	1.1052
2	1.1275	1.1388	1.1503	1.1618	1.1735	1.1853	1.1972	1.2092	1.2214
3	1.1972	1.2153	1.2337	1.2523	1.2712	1.2904	1.3099	1.3297	1.3498
4	1.2712	1.2969	1.3231	1.3498	1.3771	1.4049	1.4333	1.4622	1.4917
5	1.3498	1.3840	1.4190	1.4549	1.4917	1.5295	1.5682	1.6079	1.6486
6	1.4333	1.4769	1.5219	1.5682	1.6160	1.6652	1.7159	1.7681	1.8220
7	1.5219	1.5761	1.6322	1.6904	1.7506	1.8129	1.8775	1.9443	2.0136
8	1.6160	1.6819	1.7506	1.8220	1.8963	1.9737	2.0543	2.1381	2.2253
9	1.7159	1.7949	1.8775	1.9639	2.0543	2.1488	2.2477	2.3511	2.4593
10	1.8220	1.9154	2.0136	2.1168	2.2253	2.3394	2.4593	2.5854	2.7179
15	2.4594	2.6509	2.8574	3.0799	3.3197	3.5782	3.8568	4.1571	4.4808
20	3.3198	3.6689	4.0546	4.4810	4.9522	5.4728	6.0482	6.6842	7.3870
25	4.4811	5.0777	5.7536	6.5195	7.3874	8.3708	9.4851	10.7477	12.1782
30	6.0487	7.0275	8.1645	9.4855	11.0202	12.8032	14.8747	17.2813	20.0772

Now it's time to check your progress with the following Practice Quiz.

LU 12–1   **PRACTICE QUIZ**

Complete this **Practice Quiz** to
see how you are doing.

1. Complete the following without a table (round each calculation to the nearest cent as needed):

Principal	Time	Rate of compound interest	Compounded	Number of periods to be compounded	Total amount	Total interest
$200	1 year	8%	Quarterly	a.	b.	c.

2. Solve the previous problem by using compound value (FV) in Table 12.1.

3. Lionel Rodgers deposits $6,000 in Victory Bank, which pays 3% interest compounded semiannually. How much will Lionel have in his account at the end of 8 years?

4. Find the effective rate (APY) for the year: principal, $7,000; interest rate, 12%; and compounded quarterly.

5. Calculate by Table 12.2 what $1,500 compounded daily for 5 years will grow to at 7%.

*For **extra help** from your authors—Sharon and Jeff—see the videos in Connect.*

These videos are also available on YouTube!

Check out the plastic overlays that appear at the end of Chapter 13 to review these concepts.

✓ Solutions

1. **a.** [4] (4 × 1)   **b.** [$216.48]   **c.** [$16.48] ($216.48 − $200)
    $200 × 1.02 = $204 × 1.02 = $208.08 × 1.02 = $212.24 × 1.02 = $216.48

2. $200 × 1.0824 = [$216.48] (4 periods, 2%)

3. 16 periods, $1\frac{1}{2}$%, $6,000 × 1.2690 = [$7,614]

4. 4 periods, 3%

    $$\$7,000 \times 1.1255 = \begin{array}{r} \$7,878.50 \\ -\ 7,000.00 \\ \hline \$\ 878.50 \end{array} \qquad \frac{\$878.50}{\$7,000.00} = [12.55\%]$$

5. $1,500 × 1.4190 = [$2,128.50]

LU 12–1a   **EXTRA PRACTICE QUIZ WITH WORKED-OUT SOLUTIONS**

Need more practice? Try this **Extra Practice Quiz** (check figures in the Interactive Chapter Organizer). Worked-out Solutions can be found in Appendix B.

1. Complete the following without a table (round each calculation to the nearest cent as needed):

Principal	Time	Rate of compound interest	Compounded	Number of periods to be compounded	Total amount	Total interest
$500	1 year	8%	Quarterly	a.	b.	c.

2. Solve the previous problem by using compound value (FV). See Table 12.1.

3. Lionel Rodgers deposits $7,000 in Victory Bank, which pays 4% interest compounded semiannually. How much will Lionel have in his account at the end of 8 years?

4. Find the effective rate (APY) for the year: principal, $8,000; interest rate, 6%; and compounded quarterly. Round to the nearest hundredth percent.

5. Calculate by Table 12.2 what $1,800 compounded daily for 5 years will grow to at 6%.

Learning Unit 12–2: Present Value—The Big Picture

Figure 12.1 in Learning Unit 12–1 showed how by compounding, the *future value* of $1 became $1.36. This learning unit discusses *present value*. Before we look at specific calculations involving present value, let's look at the concept of present value.

Figure 12.4 shows that if we invested 74 cents today, compounding would cause the 74 cents to grow to $1 in the future. For example, let's assume you ask this question: "If I need

FIGURE 12.4

Present value of $1 at 8% for four periods

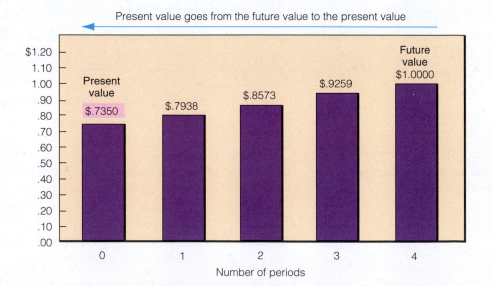

$1 in 4 years in the future, how much must I put in the bank *today* (assume an 8% annual interest)?" To answer this question, you must know the present value of that $1 today. From Figure 12.4, you can see that the present value of $1 is .7350. Remember that the $1 is only worth 74 cents if you wait 4 periods to receive it. This is one reason why so many athletes get such big contracts—much of the money is paid in later years when it is not worth as much.

LO 1

Relationship of Compounding (FV) to Present Value (PV)— The Bill Smith Example Continued

In Learning Unit 12–1, our consideration of compounding started in the *present* ($80) and looked to find the *future* amount of $108.84. Present value (PV) starts with the *future* and tries to calculate its worth in the *present* ($80). For example, in Figure 12.5, we assume Bill Smith knew that in 4 years he wanted to buy a bike that cost $108.84 (future). Bill's bank pays 8% interest compounded annually. How much money must Bill put in the bank *today* (present) to have $108.84 in 4 years? To work from the future to the present, we can use a present value (PV) table. In the next section you will learn how to use this table.

FIGURE **12.5**

Present value

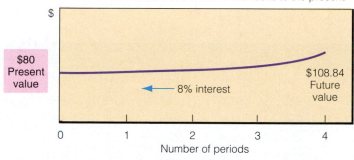

Present value starts with the future and looks to the present

LO 2

How to Use a Present Value (PV) Table[7]

To calculate present value with a present value table, use the following steps:

CALCULATING PRESENT VALUE BY TABLE LOOKUP

Step 1. Find the periods: Years multiplied by number of times interest is compounded in 1 year.

Step 2. Find the rate: Annual rate divided by number of times interest is compounded in 1 year.

Step 3. Go down the Period column of the table to the number of periods desired; look across the row to find the rate. At the intersection of the two columns is the table factor for the compound value of $1.

Step 4. Multiply the table factor times the future value. This gives the present value.

Periods

4 × 1 = 4

No. of years   No. of times compounded in 1 year

Table 12.3 is a present value (PV) table that tells you what $1 is worth today at different interest rates. To continue our Bill Smith example, go down the Period column in Table 12.3 to 4. Then go across to the 8% column. At 8% for 4 periods, we see a table factor of .7350. This means that $1 in the future is worth approximately 74 cents today. If Bill invested 74 cents today at 8% for 4 periods, Bill would have $1 in 4 years.

Since Bill knows the bike will cost $108.84 in the future, he completes the following calculation:

$108.84 × .7350 = $80.00

This means that $108.84 in today's dollars is worth $80.00. Now let's check this.

---

[7]The formula for present value is $PV = \dfrac{A}{(1 + i)^N}$, where A equals future amount (compound amount), N equals number of compounding periods, and i equals interest rate per compounding period. The calculator sequence for Bill Smith would be as follows: 1 $\boxed{+}$ .08 $\boxed{y^x}$ 4 $\boxed{=}$ $\boxed{M\,I}$ 108.84 $\boxed{\div}$ $\boxed{MR}$ $\boxed{=}$ 80.03.

LO 3

Comparing Compound Interest (FV) Table 12.1 with Present Value (PV) Table 12.3

We know from our calculations that Bill needs to invest $80 for 4 years at 8% compound interest annually to buy his bike. We can check this by going back to Table 12.1 and comparing it with Table 12.3. Let's do this now.

Compound value Table 12.1				Present value Table 12.3			
Table 12.1	Present value	Future value		**Table 12.3**	Future value	Present value	
1.3605	× ↗ $80.00	=	$108.84	.7350	× ↗ $108.84	=	$80.00
(4 per., 8%)				(4 per., 8%)			
We know the present dollar amount and find what the dollar amount is worth in the future.				We know the future dollar amount and find what the dollar amount is worth in the present.			

TABLE 12.3 Present value of $1 at end of period

Period	1%	1½%	2%	3%	4%	5%	6%	7%	8%	9%	10%
1	.9901	.9852	.9804	.9709	.9615	.9524	.9434	.9346	.9259	.9174	.9091
2	.9803	.9707	.9612	.9426	.9246	.9070	.8900	.8734	.8573	.8417	.8264
3	.9706	.9563	.9423	.9151	.8890	.8638	.8396	.8163	.7938	.7722	.7513
4	.9610	.9422	.9238	.8885	.8548	.8227	.7921	.7629	.7350	.7084	.6830
5	.9515	.9283	.9057	.8626	.8219	.7835	.7473	.7130	.6806	.6499	.6209
6	.9420	.9145	.8880	.8375	.7903	.7462	.7050	.6663	.6302	.5963	.5645
7	.9327	.9010	.8706	.8131	.7599	.7107	.6651	.6227	.5835	.5470	.5132
8	.9235	.8877	.8535	.7894	.7307	.6768	.6274	.5820	.5403	.5019	.4665
9	.9143	.8746	.8368	.7664	.7026	.6446	.5919	.5439	.5002	.4604	.4241
10	.9053	.8617	.8203	.7441	.6756	.6139	.5584	.5083	.4632	.4224	.3855
11	.8963	.8489	.8043	.7224	.6496	.5847	.5268	.4751	.4289	.3875	.3505
12	.8874	.8364	.7885	.7014	.6246	.5568	.4970	.4440	.3971	.3555	.3186
13	.8787	.8240	.7730	.6810	.6006	.5303	.4688	.4150	.3677	.3262	.2897
14	.8700	.8119	.7579	.6611	.5775	.5051	.4423	.3878	.3405	.2992	.2633
15	.8613	.7999	.7430	.6419	.5553	.4810	.4173	.3624	.3152	.2745	.2394
16	.8528	.7880	.7284	.6232	.5339	.4581	.3936	.3387	.2919	.2519	.2176
17	.8444	.7764	.7142	.6050	.5134	.4363	.3714	.3166	.2703	.2311	.1978
18	.8360	.7649	.7002	.5874	.4936	.4155	.3503	.2959	.2502	.2120	.1799
19	.8277	.7536	.6864	.5703	.4746	.3957	.3305	.2765	.2317	.1945	.1635
20	.8195	.7425	.6730	.5537	.4564	.3769	.3118	.2584	.2145	.1784	.1486
21	.8114	.7315	.6598	.5375	.4388	.3589	.2942	.2415	.1987	.1637	.1351
22	.8034	.7207	.6468	.5219	.4220	.3418	.2775	.2257	.1839	.1502	.1228
23	.7954	.7100	.6342	.5067	.4057	.3256	.2618	.2109	.1703	.1378	.1117
24	.7876	.6995	.6217	.4919	.3901	.3101	.2470	.1971	.1577	.1264	.1015
25	.7798	.6892	.6095	.4776	.3751	.2953	.2330	.1842	.1460	.1160	.0923
26	.7720	.6790	.5976	.4637	.3607	.2812	.2198	.1722	.1352	.1064	.0839
27	.7644	.6690	.5859	.4502	.3468	.2678	.2074	.1609	.1252	.0976	.0763
28	.7568	.6591	.5744	.4371	.3335	.2551	.1956	.1504	.1159	.0895	.0693
29	.7493	.6494	.5631	.4243	.3207	.2429	.1846	.1406	.1073	.0822	.0630
30	.7419	.6398	.5521	.4120	.3083	.2314	.1741	.1314	.0994	.0754	.0573
35	.7059	.5939	.5000	.3554	.2534	.1813	.1301	.0937	.0676	.0490	.0356
40	.6717	.5513	.4529	.3066	.2083	.1420	.0972	.0668	.0460	.0318	.0221

Note: For more detailed tables, see your booklet, the *Business Math Handbook.*

Note all the table factors in the present value table are less than 1. That is because money grows over time due to interest being earned so less money needs to be invested today to meet a future higher obligation.

Note that the table factor for compounding is over 1 (1.3605) and the table factor for present value is less than 1 (.7350). The compound value table starts with the present and goes to the future. The present value table starts with the future and goes to the present.

Let's look at another example before trying the Practice Quiz.

EXAMPLE   Rene Weaver needs $20,000 for college in 4 years. She can earn 8% compounded quarterly at her bank. How much must Rene deposit at the beginning of the year to have $20,000 in 4 years?

Remember that in this example the bank compounds the interest *quarterly*. Let's first determine the period and rate on a quarterly basis:

$$\text{Periods} = 4 \times 4 \text{ years} = 16 \text{ periods} \qquad \text{Rate} = \frac{8\%}{4} = 2\%$$

Now we go to Table 12.3 and find 16 under the Period column. We then move across to the 2% column and find the .7284 table factor.

$$\$20,000 \times .7284 = \boxed{\$14,568}$$

(future value)   (present value)

We illustrate this in Figure 12.6.

FIGURE 12.6

Present value

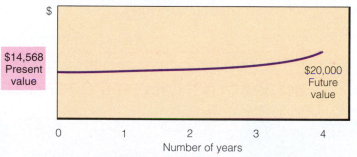

The present value is what we need **now** to have $20,000 in the future

$14,568 Present value

$20,000 Future value

Number of years

We can check the $14,568 present value by using the compound value Table 12.1:

16 periods, 2% column = 1.3728 × $14,568 = $19,998.95[8]

Let's test your understanding of this unit with the Practice Quiz.

MONEY tips

Almost 50% of full-time workers do **not** participate in their employer's retirement plan. Many companies have dollar matching programs allowing employees to receive "free" money in addition to helping reduce their taxable income. Check with your company to see what it offers.

LU 12-2   PRACTICE QUIZ

Complete this **Practice Quiz** to see how you are doing.

Use the present value Table 12.3 to complete:

Future amount desired	Length of time	Rate compounded	Table period	Rate used	PV factor	PV amount
1. $ 7,000	6 years	6% semiannually	____	____	____	____
2. $15,000	20 years	10% annually	____	____	____	____

3. Bill Blum needs $20,000 6 years from today to attend V.P.R. Tech. How much must Bill put in the bank today (12% quarterly) to reach his goal?

4. Bob Fry wants to buy his grandson a Ford Taurus in 4 years. The cost of a car will be $24,000. Assuming a bank rate of 8% compounded quarterly, how much must Bob put in the bank today?

[8]Not quite $20,000 due to rounding of table factors.

For **extra help** from your authors–Sharon and Jeff–see the videos in Connect.

These videos are also available on YouTube!

✓ **Solutions**

1. | 12 periods | (6 years × 2) | | 3% | (6% ÷ 2) | | .7014 | $4,909.80 | ($7,000 × .7014) |

2. | 20 periods | (20 years × 1) | | 10% | (10% ÷ 1) | | .1486 | $2,229.00 | ($15,000 × .1486) |

3. 6 years × 4 = 24 periods $\dfrac{12\%}{4} = 3\%$ .4919 × $20,000 = $9,838

4. 4 × 4 years = 16 periods $\dfrac{8\%}{4} = 2\%$ .7284 × $24,000 = $17,481.60

LU 12–2a   **EXTRA PRACTICE QUIZ WITH WORKED-OUT SOLUTIONS**

Need more practice? Try this **Extra Practice Quiz** (check figures in the Interactive Chapter Organizer). Worked-out Solutions can be found in Appendix B.

Use the *Business Math Handbook* to complete:

Future amount desired	Length of time	Rate compounded	Table period	Rate used	PV factor	PV amount
1. $ 9,000	7 years	$2\frac{1}{2}\%$ semiannually	___	___	___	___
2. $20,000	20 years	4% annually	___	___	___	___

3. Bill Blum needs $40,000 6 years from today to attend V.P.R. Tech. How much must Bill put in the bank today (8% quarterly) to reach his goal?

4. Bob Fry wants to buy his grandson a Ford Taurus in 4 years. The cost of a car will be $28,000. Assuming a bank rate of 4% compounded quarterly, how much must Bob put in the bank today?

INTERACTIVE CHAPTER ORGANIZER

Topic/Procedure/Formula	Examples	You try it*
Calculating compound amount without tables (future value)† Determine new amount by multiplying rate times new balance (that includes interest added on). Start in present and look to future. $\dfrac{\text{Compound}}{\text{interest}} = \dfrac{\text{Compound}}{\text{amount}} - \text{Principal}$ ⊢──Compounding──⊣ PV ⟶ FV	$100 in savings account, compounded annually for 2 years at 8%: $100 $108 × 1.08 × 1.08 $108 $116.64 (future value)	**Calculate compound amount (future value)** $200 for 2 years at 4%, compounded annually
Calculating compound amount (future value) by table lookup $\text{Periods} = \dfrac{\text{Number of times compounded per year}}{} \times \dfrac{\text{Years of loan}}{}$ $\text{Rate} = \dfrac{\text{Annual rate}}{\text{Number of times compounded per year}}$ Multiply table factor (intersection of period and rate) times amount of principal.	*Example:* $2,000 at 12% for 5 years and compounded quarterly: Periods = 4 × 5 years = 20 Rate = $\dfrac{12\%}{4}$ = 3% 20 periods, 3% = 1.8061 (table factor) $2,000 × 1.8061 = $3,612.20 (future value)	**Calculate compound amount by table lookup** $4,000 at 6% for 6 years, compounded semiannually

(continues)

INTERACTIVE CHAPTER ORGANIZER

Topic/Procedure/Formula	Examples	You try it*
Calculating effective rate (APY) Effective rate (APY) = $\dfrac{\text{Interest for 1 year}}{\text{Principal}}$ or Rate can be seen in Table 12.1 factor.	$1,000 at 10% compounded semiannually for 1 year. By Table 12.1: 2 periods, 5% 1.1025 means at end of year investor has earned 110.25% of original principal. Thus the interest is 10.25%. $1,000 × 1.1025 = $1,102.50 $\underline{\quad\quad\quad -1,000.00}$ $\quad\quad\quad\quad$ $ 102.50 $\dfrac{\$102.50}{\$1,000}$ = 10.25% effective rate (APY)	**Calculate effective rate** $4,000 at 6% for 1 year, compounded semiannually
Calculating present value (PV) by table lookup‡ Start with future and calculate worth in the present. Periods and rate computed like in compound interest. ⊢——Present value——⊣ PV ◀———————— FV Find periods and rate. Multiply table factor (intersection of period and rate) times amount of loan.	*Example:* Want $3,612.20 after 5 years with rate of 12% compounded quarterly: Periods = 4 × 5 = 20; % = 3% By Table 12.3: 20 periods, 3% = .5537 $3,612.20 × .5537 = $2,000.08 Invested today will yield desired amount in future	**Calculate present value by table lookup** Want $6,000 after 4 years with rate of 6%, compounded quarterly

KEY TERMS			
	Annual percentage yield (APY) Compound amount Compound interest Compounded annually Compounded daily	Compounded monthly Compounded quarterly Compounded semiannually Compounding Effective rate Future value (FV)	Nominal rate Number of periods Present value (PV) Rate for each period

Check Figures for Extra Practice Quizzes. (Worked-out Solutions are in Appendix B.)	LU 12–1a **1.** 4 periods; Int. = $41.22; $541.21 **2.** $541.21 **3.** $9,609.60 **4.** 6.14% **5.** $2,429.64	LU 12–2a **1.** 14 periods; $2\frac{1}{2}$%; $6,369.30 **2.** 20 periods; 4%; $9,128 **3.** $24,868 **4.** $23,878.40

*Worked-out solutions are in Appendix B.

† $A = P(1 + i)^N$.

‡ $\dfrac{A}{(1 + i)^N}$ if table not used.

Critical Thinking Discussion Questions with Chapter Concept Check

1. Explain how periods and rates are calculated in compounding problems. Compare simple interest to compound interest.

2. What are the steps to calculate the compound amount by table? Why is the compound table factor greater than $1?

3. What is the effective rate (APY)? Why can the effective rate be seen directly from the table factor?

4. Explain the difference between compounding and present value. Why is the present value table factor less than $1?

5. **Chapter Concept Check.** Create a problem using present value and compounding to show the amount you would need to put away today in a bank to have enough money to pay for a child's costs through the age of 18. Assume your own rates and periods and that the amount you put in the bank is one lump sum that will grow through compounding (without new investments).

Classroom Notes

END-OF-CHAPTER PROBLEMS **connect** plus+

Check figures for odd-numbered problems in Appendix C.   Name _____   Date _____

DRILL PROBLEMS

Complete the following without using Table 12.1 (round to the nearest cent for each calculation) and then check your answer by Table 12.1 (check will be off due to rounding). *LU 12-1(2)*

	Principal	Time (years)	Rate of compound interest	Compounded	Periods	Rate	Total amount	Total interest
12–1.	$1,250	2	4%	Semiannually				

Complete the following using compound future value Table 12.1: *LU 12-1(2)*

	Time	Principal	Rate	Compounded	Amount	Interest
12–2.	12 years	$15,000	$3\frac{1}{2}\%$	Annually		
12–3.	6 months	$15,000	6%	Semiannually		
12–4.	2 years	$15,000	8%	Quarterly		

Calculate the effective rate (APY) of interest for 1 year. *LU 12-1(3)*

12–5. Principal: $15,500
Interest rate: 12%
Compounded quarterly
Effective rate (APY):

12–6. Using Table 12.2, calculate what $700 would grow to at $6\frac{1}{2}\%$ per year compounded daily for 7 years. *LU 12-1(3)*

Complete the following using present value Table 12.3 or the present value table in the *Business Math Handbook*. *LU 12-2(2)*

	Amount desired at end of period	Length of time	Rate	Compounded	On PV Table 12.3 Period used	Rate used	PV factor used	PV of amount desired at end of period
12–7. eXcel	$6,000	8 years	3%	Semiannually				
12–8. eXcel	$8,900	4 years	6%	Monthly				
12–9. eXcel	$17,600	7 years	12%	Quarterly				

12–10. $20,000   20 years   8%   Annually

eXcel

12–11. Check your answer in Problem 12–9 by the compound value Table 12.1. The answer will be off due to rounding. *LU 12-2(3)*

WORD PROBLEMS

12–12. Sam Long anticipates he will need approximately $225,000 in 15 years to cover his 3-year-old daughter's college bills for a 4-year degree. How much would he have to invest today at an interest rate of 8 percent compounded semiannually? *LU 12-2(2)*

12–13. Lynn Ally, owner of a local Subway shop, loaned $40,000 to Pete Hall to help him open a Subway franchise. Pete plans to repay Lynn at the end of 8 years with 6% interest compounded semiannually. How much will Lynn receive at the end of 8 years? *LU 12-1(2)*

12–14. Molly Hamilton deposited $50,000 at Bank of America at 8% interest compounded quarterly. What is the effective rate (APY) to the nearest hundredth percent? *LU 12-1(3)*

12–15. Melvin Indecision has difficulty deciding whether to put his savings in Mystic Bank or Four Rivers Bank. Mystic offers **eXcel** 10% interest compounded semiannually. Four Rivers offers 8% interest compounded quarterly. Melvin has $10,000 to invest. He expects to withdraw the money at the end of 4 years. Which bank gives Melvin the better deal? Check your answer. *LU 12-1(3)*

12–16. Lee Holmes deposited $15,000 in a new savings account at 9% interest compounded semiannually. At the beginning of year 4, Lee deposits an additional $40,000 at 9% interest compounded semiannually. At the end of 6 years, what is the balance in Lee's account? *LU 12-1(2)*

12–17. Lee Wills loaned Audrey Chin $16,000 to open Snip Its Hair Salon. After 6 years, Audrey will repay Lee with 8% interest **eXcel** compounded quarterly. How much will Lee receive at the end of 6 years? *LU 12-1(2)*

12–18. Jazelle Momba wants to visit her family in Zimbabwe in 2022, which is 6 years from now. She knows that it will cost approximately $8,000 including flight costs, on-the-ground costs, and extra spending money to stay for 4 months. If she opens an account that compounds interest at 4% semiannually, how much does she need to deposit today to cover the total cost of her visit? *LU 12-1(2)*

12–19. After reviewing the CPI inflation calculator at inflationdata.com, Hanna Lind realized the importance of creating an investment plan for her future. She would need $9,691.50 in 2015 to have the same purchasing power her $7,000 (stored in a fireproof safe in her home since 2010) had when she put it there. To protect her savings against further inflation and to help her prepare for a healthy financial future, Hanna deposits her $7,000 in an investment account in 2015 earning 6% interest compounded quarterly. How much will Hanna have in her account in 2025? (Use tables in the *Business Math Handbook*.)   *LU 12-1(2)*

12–20. The International Monetary Fund is trying to raise $500 billion in 5 years for new funds to lend to developing countries. At 6% interest compounded quarterly, how much must it invest today to reach $500 billion in 5 years?   *LU 12-2(2)*

12–21. You choose to invest your $2,985 income tax refund check (rather than spend it!) in an account earning 5% compounded semiannually. How much will the account be worth in 4 years?   *LU 12-1(2, 3)*

Imagine how much you would have in your account if you did this each year!

12–22. Jim Ryan, an owner of a Burger King restaurant, assumes that his restaurant will need a new roof in 7 years. He estimates the roof will cost him $9,000 at that time. What amount should Jim invest today at 6% compounded quarterly to be able to pay for the roof? Check your answer.   *LU 12-2(2)*

12–23. Tony Ring wants to attend Northeast College. He will need $60,000 4 years from today. Assume Tony's bank pays 12% interest compounded semiannually. What must Tony deposit today so he will have $60,000 in 4 years?   *LU 12-2(2)*
eXcel

12–24. Check your answer (to the nearest dollar) in Problem 12–23 by using the compound value Table 12.1. The answer will be slightly off due to rounding.   *LU 12-1(3)*

12–25. Pete Air wants to buy a used Jeep in 5 years. He estimates the Jeep will cost $15,000. Assume Pete invests $10,000 now at 12% interest compounded semiannually. Will Pete have enough money to buy his Jeep at the end of 5 years?   *LU 12-1(2), LU 12-2(2)*

12–26. Lance Jackson deposited $5,000 at Basil Bank at 9% interest compounded daily. What is Lance's investment at the end of 4 years?   *LU 12-1(2)*

12–27. Paul Havlik promised his grandson Jamie that he would give him $6,000 8 years from today for graduating from high school. Assume money is worth 6% interest compounded semiannually. What is the present value of this $6,000? *LU 12-2(2)*

12–28. Earl Ezekiel wants to retire in San Diego when he is 65 years old. Earl is now 50. He believes he will need $300,000 to retire comfortably. To date, Earl has set aside no retirement money. Assume Earl gets 6% interest compounded semiannually. How much must Earl invest today to meet his $300,000 goal?   *LU 12-2(2)*

12–29. Jackie Rich would like to buy a $26,995 Toyota hybrid car in 4 years. Jackie wants to put the money aside now. Jackie's bank offers 8% interest compounded semiannually. How much must Jackie invest today?   *LU 12-2(2)*

12–30. Treasure Mountain International School in Park City, Utah, is a public middle school interested in raising money for next year's Sundance Film Festival. If the school raises $2,989 and invests it for 1 year at 3% interest compounded annually, what is the APY earned (round to nearest whole percent)?   *LU 12-1(2, 3)*

CHALLENGE PROBLEMS

12–31. Pete's Real Estate is currently valued at $65,000. Pete feels the value of his business will increase at a rate of 10% per year, compounded semiannually for the next 5 years. At a local fund-raiser, a competitor offered Pete $70,000 for the business. If he sells, Pete plans to invest the money at 6% compounded quarterly. What price should Pete ask? Verify your answer.   *LU 12-1(2), LU 12-2(2)*

12–32. You are the financial planner for Johnson Controls. Assume last year's profits were $700,000. The board of directors decided to forgo dividends to stockholders and retire high-interest outstanding bonds that were issued 5 years ago at a face value of $1,250,000. You have been asked to invest the profits in a bank. The board must know how much money you will need from the profits earned to retire the bonds in 10 years. Bank A pays 6% compounded quarterly, and Bank B pays $6\frac{1}{2}$% compounded annually. Which bank would you recommend, and how much of the company's profit should be placed in the bank? If you recommended that the remaining money not be distributed to stockholders but be placed in Bank B, how much would the remaining money be worth in 10 years? Use tables in the *Business Math Handbook.** Round final answer to nearest dollar.   *LU 12-1(2, 3), LU 12-2(2)*

*Check glossary for unfamiliar terms.

SUMMARY PRACTICE TEST

Do you need help? The videos in Connect have step-by-step worked-out solutions. These videos are also available on YouTube!

1. Lorna Ray, owner of a Starbucks franchise, loaned $40,000 to Lee Reese to help him open a new flower shop online. Lee plans to repay Lorna at the end of 5 years with 4% interest compounded semiannually. How much will Lorna receive at the end of 5 years? *LU 12-1(2)*

2. Joe Beary wants to attend Riverside College. Eight years from today he will need $50,000. If Joe's bank pays 6% interest compounded semiannually, what must Joe deposit today to have $50,000 in 8 years? *LU 12-2(2)*

3. Shelley Katz deposited $30,000 in a savings account at 5% interest compounded semiannually. At the beginning of year 4, Shelley deposits an additional $80,000 at 5% interest compounded semiannually. At the end of 6 years, what is the balance in Shelley's account? *LU 12-1(2)*

4. Earl Miller, owner of a Papa Gino's franchise, wants to buy a new delivery truck in 6 years. He estimates the truck will cost $30,000. If Earl invests $20,000 now at 5% interest compounded semiannually, will Earl have enough money to buy his delivery truck at the end of 6 years? *LU 12-1(2), LU 12-2(2)*

5. Minnie Rose deposited $16,000 in Street Bank at 6% interest compounded quarterly. What was the effective rate (APY)? Round to the nearest hundredth percent. *LU 12-1(2, 3)*

6. Lou Ling, owner of Lou's Lube, estimates that he will need $70,000 for new equipment in 7 years. Lou decided to put aside money today so it will be available in 7 years. Reel Bank offers Lou 6% interest compounded quarterly. How much must Lou invest to have $70,000 in 7 years? *LU 12-2(2)*

7. **eXcel** Bernie Long wants to retire to California when she is 60 years of age. Bernie is now 40. She believes that she will need $900,000 to retire comfortably. To date, Bernie has set aside no retirement money. If Bernie gets 8% compounded semiannually, how much must Bernie invest today to meet her $900,000 goal? *LU 12-2(2)*

8. Jim Jones deposited $19,000 in a savings account at 7% interest compounded daily. At the end of 6 years, what is the balance in Jim's account? *LU 12-1(2)*

SURF TO SAVE

Money investment options 🔍

PROBLEM 1
"Plant" a money tree

Go to http://www.finaid.org/calculators/compoundinterest.phtml. If you invest $1,000 for 20 years at an 8% nominal annual interest rate, how much will you earn with monthly compounding? Daily compounding? How much difference between the monthly and the daily compounding?

Discussion Questions

1. What are the pros and cons of investing your money for an extended period of time such as 20 years?

2. What is the advantage to the financial institution paying the interest on your investment while holding your investment money?

PROBLEM 2
CD investments

Visit http://www.bankrate.com/. Select one of the displayed rates on a 6-month certificate of deposit (CD). Assume you are investing $2,500 today. What will the value be at maturity?

Discussion Questions

1. Discuss the pros and cons of using CDs as an investment option.

2. Do you feel this is an appropriate investment choice for you? Why or why not?

PROBLEM 3
Doubling down!

Visit http://www.moneychimp.com/features/rule72.htm. Assuming an interest rate of 6%, how many years will it take to double your money? If you wanted to double your money in 10 years, what would be your required interest rate?

Discussion Questions

1. How does the rule of 72 assist in making investment choices?

2. What are some investments options in which you could earn at least 6%?

PROBLEM 4
You can afford your dream home

Go to http://bankrate.com/brm/calc/savecalc.asp. Suppose you want to save $25,000 for a down payment on a house and you have 10 years to save this amount. How much would you need to save monthly to achieve this goal if the interest rate is 5% compounded monthly? What happens if you can increase your interest rate to 8%?

Discussion Questions

1. How would your down payment impact the type of house you purchase?

2. How does breaking up your investment into monthly contributions assist in meeting your ultimate goals?

MOBILE APPS ✕

Compound Interest Calculator (Space Age Industries LLC) Calculates compound interest with varying amounts, duration, interest, and frequency.

InvestCalc (Fred Boratto) Figures investment values based upon present values as well as future values and what it will take to achieve these values in the future.

PERSONAL FINANCE

A KIPLINGER APPROACH

By Patricia Mertz Esswein, From *Kiplinger's Personal Finance*, March 2015.

 SUCCESS STORY

A Barber on the Cutting Edge

He offers an old-school experience with a modern, masculine twist.

PROFILE

WHO: Anthony Full, 56
WHERE: Louisville, Colo.
WHAT: Founder and owner of Rock Barbers

What prompted you to start your own business? Since 1979, I've worked in and run hair salons and barbershops. My previous job was good, but it felt routine. I'm a self-starter, and I wanted to accomplish something that I could model for my children. One of my clients shared a quote by Oliver Wendell Holmes that resonated with me: "Alas for those that never sing, but die with all their music in them!" If you have a well-thought-out idea, the risk lies in not taking it.

Why a classic American barbershop? Men always feel conspicuous in a hair salon, and barbershops are making a comeback. Rock Barbers (www.rockbarbers.com) focuses exclusively on men, and we practice old-school barbering with a modern twist. We still offer hot-towel shaves, but we'll also detail your beard and give expert haircuts. We advertise, "Dude, Get a Haircut!"

For two bits? No, the cuts are $29 and up, and the hot-towel shave is $35.

What's special about your shop? It's designed for masculine comfort. We chose substantial chairs and outfitted our stations with Kobalt toolboxes. We have flat-screen TVs, a putting green and a guitar for anyone to play. You can converse privately with your barber or join in shopwide chatter. Clients can book their appointments online.

Did you have a business plan? Absolutely. Writing one forces you to answer questions that you don't want to answer: What is my true market? What is the cost of the advertising I'd like to do? What are the tax implications of my decisions? I needed help with financial projections, so I consulted two of my clients who are accountants and another who is a CFO.

Where'd you get financing? I took a home-equity line of credit—the cheapest money going—for $150,000. The line isn't paid off yet because we've consistently reinvested profits back into the business, but we regularly make extra payments against the loan principal.

Is the shop profitable? Yes. In 2010, our first year, when it was just me, Rock Barbers grossed $50,000 in sales. Now I employ eight other barbers and four front-desk staff. The business grossed more than $400,000 in sales in 2014 and will exceed that this year.

Are you making a living? My wife is also a hairstylist and works out of our home. We combine our businesses under Rock Barbers LLC and take a combined annual salary of $50,000. That's much less than I made previously, and like all founders, I'm working eight days a week and 25 hours a day! But my business rewards me in ways other than money.

What's next? I'm launching a line of hair-care products called Rock Tools for Men in early 2015. We've earmarked about $50,000 to get it off the ground. New product lines typically get purchased by makers of existing products. So this is probably a shorter-term play if the line gets traction.

Will you ever retire? No. I'll probably reduce the days and hours that I work, but the social part is so rewarding. I'll die with my boots on. **PATRICIA MERTZ ESSWEIN**

BENJAMIN RASMUSSEN

BUSINESS MATH ISSUE

Anthony taking out an equity loan is an example of compounding his money.

1. List the key points of the article and information to support your position.
2. Write a group defense of your position using math calculations to support your view

CHAPTER 13

Annuities and Sinking Funds

© Jim McGuire/Getty Images

A Crucial Role

At every level of earnings, Social Security is a substantial source of income for retired workers. The percentage of average lifetime earnings that median first-year Social Security benefits are projected to replace, by income group:

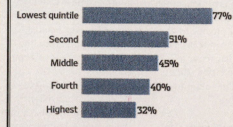

Lowest quintile **77%**
Second **51%**
Middle **45%**
Fourth **40%**
Highest **32%**

Gray and Grayer

But the 65-plus demographic is growing quickly. Population (left scale) and pct. of total (flags):

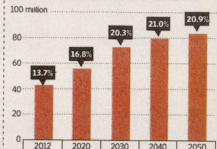

100 million

	2012	2020	2030	2040	2050
	13.7%	16.8%	20.3%	21.0%	20.9%

The Big Squeeze

The Social Security trust fund is facing shortfalls...

2010
First year that disbursements exceeded income, excluding interest on trust-fund assets

2021
First year that disbursements are projected to exceed income, including interest on trust-fund assets

2033
Year that trust-fund assets are projected to be exhausted; from this point, payroll-tax revenues will cover about 75% of currently legislated benefits

Worried Workers

And workers are concerned about the program's future. When asked how confident they are that Social Security will continue to provide benefits of at least equal value to the benefits received by retirees today, surveyed workers said:

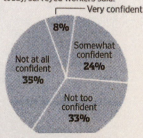

Very confident
Somewhat confident **24%**
8%
Not at all confident **35%**
Not too confident **33%**

Cloudy Outlook

When asked how big a role they expect Social Security to play in their retirement finances, surveyed workers said benefits will:

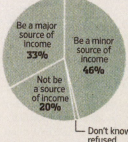

Be a major source of income **33%**
Be a minor source of income **46%**
Not be a source of income **20%**
Don't know/refused

Reprinted by permission of *The Wall Street Journal*, copyright 2014 Dow Jones & Company, Inc. All rights reserved worldwide.

LU 13–1: Annuities: Ordinary Annuity and Annuity Due (Find Future Value)

1. Differentiate between contingent annuities and annuities certain.
2. Calculate the future value of an ordinary annuity and an annuity due manually and by table lookup.

LU 13–2: Present Value of an Ordinary Annuity (Find Present Value)

1. Calculate the present value of an ordinary annuity by table lookup and manually check the calculation.
2. Compare the calculation of the present value of one lump sum versus the present value of an ordinary annuity.

LU 13–3: Sinking Funds (Find Periodic Payments)

1. Calculate the payment made at the end of each period by table lookup.
2. Check table lookup by using ordinary annuity table.

VOCABULARY PREVIEW

Here are key terms in this chapter. After completing the chapter, if you know the term, place a checkmark in the box. If you don't know the term, look it up and put the page number where it can be found.

Annuities certain ☐ Annuity ☐ Annuity due ☐ Contingent annuities ☐ Future value of an annuity ☐ Ordinary annuity ☐ Payment periods ☐ Present value of an ordinary annuity ☐ Sinking fund ☐ Term of the annuity ☐

The *Wall Street Journal* chapter opener clip about retirement and Social Security shows people are living longer and worrying more about Social Security providing enough money for retirement. Over 33% surveyed state Social Security is their major source of funds in retirement. This chapter will show you why you need to save for retirement and not rely just on Social Security. As the following clip shows, many factors—even small ones like your daily coffee spending—could affect your retirement savings.

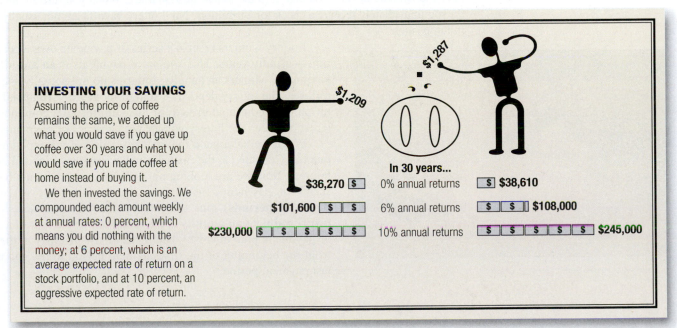

INVESTING YOUR SAVINGS
Assuming the price of coffee remains the same, we added up what you would save if you gave up coffee over 30 years and what you would save if you made coffee at home instead of buying it.

We then invested the savings. We compounded each amount weekly at annual rates: 0 percent, which means you did nothing with the money; at 6 percent, which is an average expected rate of return on a stock portfolio, and at 10 percent, an aggressive expected rate of return.

$1,209
$1,287

$36,270 $
$101,600 $ $
$230,000 $ $ $ $

In 30 years...
0% annual returns $ $38,610
6% annual returns $ $ $108,000
10% annual returns $ $ $ $ $ $245,000

Boston Sunday Globe © 2004

© The McGraw-Hill Companies, Inc./Jill Braaten, photographer

So, would you like to save $1,287? A *Boston Globe* article entitled "Cost of Living: A Cup a Day" began by explaining that each month the *Globe* runs a feature on an everyday expense to see how much it costs an average person. Since many people are coffee drinkers, the *Globe* assumed that a person drank 3 cups a day of Dunkin' Donuts coffee at the cost of $1.65 a cup. For a 5-day week, the person would spend $1,287 annually (52 weeks). If the person brewed the coffee at home, the cost of the beans per cup would be $0.10 with an annual expense of $78, saving $1,209 over the Dunkin' Donuts coffee. If a person gave up drinking coffee, the person would save $1,287.

The article continued with the discussion on "Investing Your Savings." Note how much you would have in 30 years if you invested your money in 0%, 6%, and 10% annual returns. Using the magic of compounding, if you saved $1,287 a year, your money could grow to a quarter of a million dollars.

This chapter shows how to compute compound interest that results from a *stream* of payments, or an annuity. Chapter 12 showed how to calculate compound interest on a lump-sum payment deposited at the beginning of a particular time. Knowing how to calculate interest compounding on a lump sum will make the calculation of interest compounding on annuities easier to understand.

We begin the chapter by explaining the difference between calculating the future value of an ordinary annuity and an annuity due. Then you learn how to find the present value of an ordinary annuity. The chapter ends with a discussion of sinking funds.

Learning Unit 13–1: Annuities: Ordinary Annuity and Annuity Due (Find Future Value)

Many parents of small children are concerned about being able to afford to pay for their children's college educations. Some parents deposit a lump sum in a financial institution when the child is in diapers. The interest on this sum is compounded until the child is 18, when the parents withdraw the money for college expenses. Parents could also fund their children's educations with annuities by depositing a series of payments for a certain time. The concept of annuities is the first topic in this learning unit.

Concept of an Annuity—The Big Picture

All of us would probably like to win $1 million in a state lottery. What happens when you have the winning ticket? You take it to the lottery headquarters. When you turn in the ticket, do you immediately receive a check for $1 million? No. Lottery payoffs are not usually made in lump sums.

© Buena Vista Images/Getty Images

Lottery winners receive a series of payments over a period of time—usually years. This *stream* of payments is an **annuity.** By paying the winners an annuity, lotteries do not actually spend $1 million. The lottery deposits a sum of money in a financial institution. The continual growth of this sum through compound interest provides the lottery winner with a series of payments.

When we calculated the maturity value of a lump-sum payment in Chapter 12, the maturity value was the principal and its interest. Now we are looking not at lump-sum payments but at a series of payments (usually of equal amounts over regular **payment periods**) plus the interest that accumulates. So the **future value of an annuity** is the future *dollar amount* of a series of payments plus interest.[1] The **term of the annuity** is the time from the beginning of the first payment period to the end of the last payment period.

---

[1] The term *amount of an annuity* has the same meaning as *future value of an annuity.*

FIGURE **13.1**

Future value of an annuity of $1 at 8%

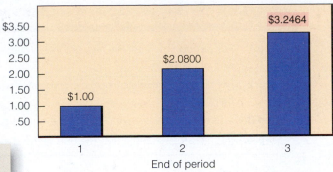

Pepper ...
And Salt

THE WALL STREET JOURNAL

"Have you heard? There's talk about raising the retirement age to 170."

From *The Wall Street Journal*, permission Cartoon Features Syndicate.

LO 1

The concept of the future value of an annuity is illustrated in Figure 13.1. Do not be concerned about the calculations (we will do them soon). Let's first focus on the big picture of annuities. In Figure 13.1 we see the following:

At end of period 1:   The $1 is still worth $1 because it was invested at the *end* of the period.

At end of period 2:   An additional $1 is invested. The $2.00 is now worth $2.08. Note the $1 from period 1 earns interest but not the $1 invested at the end of period 2.

At end of period 3:   An additional $1 is invested. The $3.00 is now worth $3.25. Remember that the last dollar invested earns no interest.

Before learning how to calculate annuities, you should understand the two classifications of annuities.

How Annuities Are Classified

Annuities have many uses in addition to lottery payoffs. Some of these uses are insurance companies' pension installments, Social Security payments, home mortgages, businesses paying off notes, bond interest, and savings for a vacation trip or college education.

Annuities are classified into two major groups: contingent annuities and annuities certain. **Contingent annuities** have no fixed number of payments but depend on an uncertain event (e.g., life insurance payments that cease when the insured dies). **Annuities certain** have a specific stated number of payments (e.g., mortgage payments on a home). Based on the time of the payment, we can divide each of these two major annuity groups into the following:

1. **Ordinary annuity**—regular deposits (payments) made at the *end* of the period. Periods could be months, quarters, years, and so on. An ordinary annuity could be salaries, stock dividends, and so on.

2. **Annuity due**—regular deposits (payments) made at the *beginning* of the period, such as rent or life insurance premiums.

The remainder of this unit shows you how to calculate and check ordinary annuities and annuities due. Remember that you are calculating the *dollar amount* of the annuity at the end of the annuity term or at the end of the last period.

LO 2

Ordinary Annuities: Money Invested at End of Period (Find Future Value)

Before we explain how to use a table that simplifies calculating ordinary annuities, let's first determine how to calculate the future value of an ordinary annuity manually.

Calculating Future Value of Ordinary Annuities Manually   Remember that an ordinary annuity invests money at the *end* of each year (period). After we calculate ordinary annuities manually, you will see that the total value of the investment comes from the *stream* of yearly investments and the buildup of interest on the current balance.

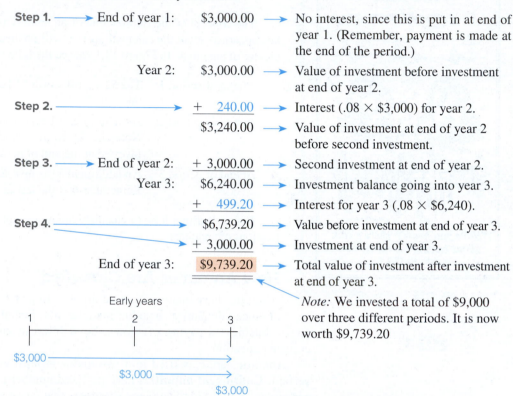

CALCULATING FUTURE VALUE OF AN ORDINARY ANNUITY MANUALLY

Step 1. For period 1, no interest calculation is necessary, since money is invested at the end of the period.

Step 2. For period 2, calculate interest on the balance and add the interest to the previous balance.

Step 3. Add the additional investment at the end of period 2 to the new balance.

Step 4. Repeat Steps 2 and 3 until the end of the desired period is reached.

EXAMPLE Find the value of an investment after 3 years for a $3,000 ordinary annuity at 8%. We calculate this manually as follows:

Step 1. ⟶ End of year 1: $3,000.00 ⟶ No interest, since this is put in at end of year 1. (Remember, payment is made at the end of the period.)

Year 2: $3,000.00 ⟶ Value of investment before investment at end of year 2.

Step 2. ⟶ + 240.00 ⟶ Interest (.08 × $3,000) for year 2.

$3,240.00 ⟶ Value of investment at end of year 2 before second investment.

Step 3. ⟶ End of year 2: + 3,000.00 ⟶ Second investment at end of year 2.

Year 3: $6,240.00 ⟶ Investment balance going into year 3.

+ 499.20 ⟶ Interest for year 3 (.08 × $6,240).

Step 4. ⟶ $6,739.20 ⟶ Value before investment at end of year 3.

+ 3,000.00 ⟶ Investment at end of year 3.

End of year 3: $9,739.20 ⟶ Total value of investment after investment at end of year 3.

Note: We invested a total of $9,000 over three different periods. It is now worth $9,739.20

When you deposit $3,000 at the end of each year at an annual rate of 8%, the total value of the annuity is $9,739.20. What we called *maturity value* in compounding is now called the *future value of the annuity*. Remember that Interest = Principal × Rate × Time, with the principal changing because of the interest payments and the additional deposits. We can make this calculation easier by using Table 13.1.

Calculating Future Value of Ordinary Annuities by Table Lookup
Use the following steps to calculate the future value of an ordinary annuity by table lookup.[2]

CALCULATING FUTURE VALUE OF AN ORDINARY ANNUITY BY TABLE LOOKUP

Step 1. Calculate the number of periods and rate per period.

Step 2. Look up the periods and rate in an ordinary annuity table. The intersection gives the table factor for the future value of $1.

Step 3. Multiply the payment each period by the table factor. This gives the future value of the annuity.

$$\frac{\text{Future value of}}{\text{ordinary annuity}} = \frac{\text{Annuity payment}}{\text{each period}} \times \frac{\text{Ordinary annuity}}{\text{table factor}}$$

[2]The formula for an ordinary annuity is $FV = PMT \times \left[\frac{(1+i)^n - 1}{i}\right]$ where FV equals future value of an ordinary annuity, PMT equals annuity payment, i equals interest, and n equals number of periods. The calculator sequence for this example is: 1 [+] .08 = [y^x] 3 [−] 1 [÷] .08 [×] 3,000 [=] 9,739.20. A *Financial Calculator Guide* is available online that shows how to operate HP 10BII and TI BA II Plus.

TABLE 13.1   Ordinary annuity table: Compound sum of an annuity of $1

Period	2%	3%	4%	5%	6%	7%	8%	9%	10%	11%	12%	13%
1	1.0000	1.0000	1.0000	1.0000	1.0000	1.0000	1.0000	1.0000	1.0000	1.0000	1.0000	1.0000
2	2.0200	2.0300	2.0400	2.0500	2.0600	2.0700	2.0800	2.0900	2.1000	2.1100	2.1200	2.1300
3	3.0604	3.0909	3.1216	3.1525	3.1836	3.2149	3.2464	3.2781	3.3100	3.3421	3.3744	3.4069
4	4.1216	4.1836	4.2465	4.3101	4.3746	4.4399	4.5061	4.5731	4.6410	4.7097	4.7793	4.8498
5	5.2040	5.3091	5.4163	5.5256	5.6371	5.7507	5.8666	5.9847	6.1051	6.2278	6.3528	6.4803
6	6.3081	6.4684	6.6330	6.8019	6.9753	7.1533	7.3359	7.5233	7.7156	7.9129	8.1152	8.3227
7	7.4343	7.6625	7.8983	8.1420	8.3938	8.6540	8.9228	9.2004	9.4872	9.7833	10.0890	10.4047
8	8.5829	8.8923	9.2142	9.5491	9.8975	10.2598	10.6366	11.0285	11.4359	11.8594	12.2997	12.7573
9	9.7546	10.1591	10.5828	11.0265	11.4913	11.9780	12.4876	13.0210	13.5795	14.1640	14.7757	15.4157
10	10.9497	11.4639	12.0061	12.5779	13.1808	13.8164	14.4866	15.1929	15.9374	16.7220	17.5487	18.4197
11	12.1687	12.8078	13.4863	14.2068	14.9716	15.7836	16.6455	17.5603	18.5312	19.5614	20.6546	21.8143
12	13.4120	14.1920	15.0258	15.9171	16.8699	17.8884	18.9771	20.1407	21.3843	22.7132	24.1331	25.6502
13	14.6803	15.6178	16.6268	17.7129	18.8821	20.1406	21.4953	22.9534	24.5227	26.2116	28.0291	29.9847
14	15.9739	17.0863	18.2919	19.5986	21.0150	22.5505	24.2149	26.0192	27.9750	30.0949	32.3926	34.8827
15	17.2934	18.5989	20.0236	21.5785	23.2759	25.1290	27.1521	29.3609	31.7725	34.4054	37.2797	40.4174
16	18.6392	20.1569	21.8245	23.6574	25.6725	27.8880	30.3243	33.0034	35.9497	39.1899	42.7533	46.6717
17	20.0120	21.7616	23.6975	25.8403	28.2128	30.8402	33.7503	36.9737	40.5447	44.5008	48.8837	53.7390
18	21.4122	23.4144	25.6454	28.1323	30.9056	33.9990	37.4503	41.3014	45.5992	50.3959	55.7497	61.7251
19	22.8405	25.1169	27.6712	30.5389	33.7599	37.3789	41.4463	46.0185	51.1591	56.9395	63.4397	70.7494
20	24.2973	26.8704	29.7781	33.0659	36.7855	40.9954	45.7620	51.1602	57.2750	64.2028	72.0524	80.9468
25	32.0302	36.4593	41.6459	47.7270	54.8644	63.2489	73.1060	84.7010	98.3471	114.4133	133.3338	155.6194
30	40.5679	47.5754	56.0849	66.4386	79.0580	94.4606	113.2833	136.3077	164.4941	199.0209	241.3327	293.1989
40	60.4017	75.4012	95.0254	120.7993	154.7616	199.6346	259.0569	337.8831	442.5928	581.8260	767.0913	1013.7030
50	84.5790	112.7968	152.6669	209.3470	290.3351	406.5277	573.7711	815.0853	1163.9090	1668.7710	2400.0180	3459.5010

Note: This is only a sampling of tables available. The *Business Math Handbook* shows tables from $\frac{1}{2}$% to 15%.

MONEY tips

Never cash out a retirement fund account until you have calculated the final cost to you. Consider paying a 10% early withdrawal penalty along with both federal and state income tax on the amount withdrawn. Determine if the withdrawal puts you in a higher tax bracket that may disqualify you from any aid (such as food stamps) you are currently receiving.

EXAMPLE   Find the value of an investment after 3 years for a $3,000 ordinary annuity at 8%.

Step 1.   Periods = 3 years × 1 = 3   Rate = $\dfrac{8\%}{\text{Annually}}$ = 8%

Step 2.   Go to Table 13.1, an ordinary annuity table. Look for 3 under the Period column. Go across to 8%. At the intersection is the table factor, 3.2464. (This was the example we showed in Figure 13.1.)

Step 3.   Multiply $3,000 × 3.2464 = $9,739.20   (the same figure we calculated manually).

Annuities Due: Money Invested at Beginning of Period (Find Future Value)

In this section we look at what the difference in the total investment would be for an annuity due. As in the previous section, we will first make the calculation manually and then use the table lookup.

Calculating Future Value of Annuities Due Manually   Use the steps that follow to calculate the future value of an annuity due manually.

CALCULATING FUTURE VALUE OF AN ANNUITY DUE MANUALLY

Step 1.   Calculate the interest on the balance for the period and add it to the previous balance.

Step 2.   Add additional investment at the *beginning* of the period to the new balance.

Step 3.   Repeat Steps 1 and 2 until the end of the desired period is reached.

Remember that in an annuity due, we deposit the money at the *beginning* of the year and gain more interest. Common sense should tell us that the *annuity due* will give a higher final value. We will use the same example that we used before.

EXAMPLE Find the value of an investment after 3 years for a $3,000 annuity due at 8%. We calculate this manually as follows:

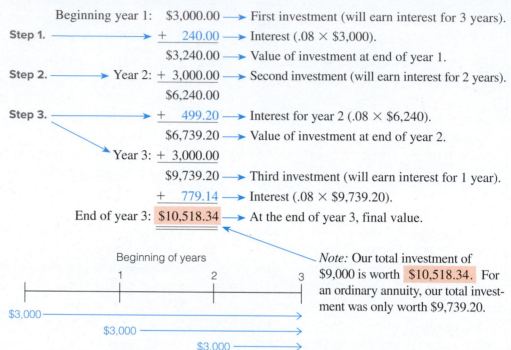

Beginning year 1: $3,000.00 ⟶ First investment (will earn interest for 3 years).
Step 1. ⟶ +   240.00 ⟶ Interest (.08 × $3,000).
  $3,240.00 ⟶ Value of investment at end of year 1.
Step 2. ⟶ Year 2: + 3,000.00 ⟶ Second investment (will earn interest for 2 years).
  $6,240.00
Step 3. ⟶ +   499.20 ⟶ Interest for year 2 (.08 × $6,240).
  $6,739.20 ⟶ Value of investment at end of year 2.
  Year 3: + 3,000.00
  $9,739.20 ⟶ Third investment (will earn interest for 1 year).
  +   779.14 ⟶ Interest (.08 × $9,739.20).
End of year 3: $10,518.34 ⟶ At the end of year 3, final value.

Beginning of years
    1   2   3

$3,000 ———————————————————⟶
    $3,000 ———————————⟶
        $3,000 ———⟶

Note: Our total investment of $9,000 is worth $10,518.34. For an ordinary annuity, our total investment was only worth $9,739.20.

Calculating Future Value of Annuities Due by Table Lookup To calculate the future value of an annuity due with a table lookup, use the steps that follow.

CALCULATING FUTURE VALUE OF AN ANNUITY DUE BY TABLE LOOKUP[3]

Step 1. Calculate the number of periods and the rate per period. Add one extra period.

Step 2. Look up in an ordinary annuity table the periods and rate. The intersection gives the table *factor* for future value of $1.

Step 3. Multiply payment each period by the table factor.

Step 4. Subtract 1 payment from Step 3.

$$\text{Future value of an annuity due} = \left(\begin{matrix} \text{Annuity} \\ \text{payment} \\ \text{each period} \end{matrix} \times \begin{matrix} \text{Ordinary*} \\ \text{annuity} \\ \text{table factor} \end{matrix} \right) - 1\,\text{Payment}$$

*Add 1 period.

Let's check the $10,518.34 by table lookup.

Step 1. Periods = 3 years × 1 =   3
                        + 1 extra
                        ―――――
                           4

Rate = $\dfrac{8\%}{\text{Annually}}$ = 8%

Step 2. Table factor, 4.5061

Step 3. $3,000 × 4.5061 = $13,518.30

Step 4.   − 3,000.00   ← Be sure to subtract 1 payment.
                        = $10,518.30   (off 4 cents due to rounding)

---

[3]The formula for an annuity due is FV = PMT × $\frac{(1 + i)^n - 1}{i}$ × (1 + i), where FV equals future value of annuity due, PMT equals annuity payment, i equals interest, and n equals number of periods. This formula is the same as that in footnote 2 except we take one more step. Multiply the future value of annuity by 1 + i since payments are made at the beginning of the period. The calculator sequence for this step is: 1 ⊞ .08 ⊜ ⊠ 9,739.20 ⊜ 10,518.34.

Note that the annuity due shows an ending value of $10,518.30, while the ending value of ordinary annuity was $9,739.20. We had a higher ending value with the annuity due because the investment took place at the beginning of each period.

Annuity payments do not have to be made yearly. They could be made semiannually, monthly, quarterly, and so on. Let's look at one more example with a different number of periods and the same rate.

Different Number of Periods and Rates   By using a different number of periods and the same rate, we will contrast an ordinary annuity with an annuity due in the following example:

EXAMPLE   Using Table 13.1, find the value of a $3,000 investment after 3 years made quarterly at 8%.

In the annuity due calculation, be sure to add one period and subtract one payment from the total value.

	Ordinary annuity	**Annuity due**	
Step 1.	Periods = 3 years × 4 = 12	Periods = 3 years × 4 = 12 + 1 = 13	**Step 1**
	Rate = 8% ÷ 4 = 2%	Rate = 8% ÷ 4 = 2%	
Step 2.	Table 13.1:	Table 13.1:	**Step 2**
	12 periods, 2% = 13.4120	13 periods, 2% = 14.6803	
Step 3.	$3,000 × 13.4120 = $40,236	$3,000 × 14.6803 = $44,040.90	**Step 3**
		− 3,000.00	**Step 4**
		$41,040.90	

Again, note that with annuity due, the total value is greater since you invest the money at the beginning of each period.

Now check your progress with the Practice Quiz.

MONEY tips

As your income increases through promotions or raises, don't immediately spend that money. Instead consider increasing your savings or retirement investment by the amount of the increase. The earlier you begin saving for retirement, the better opportunity you will have to create a healthy financial future.

LU 13–1   PRACTICE QUIZ

Complete this Practice Quiz to see how you are doing.

1. Using Table 13.1, **(a)** find the value of an investment after 4 years on an ordinary annuity of $4,000 made semiannually at 10%; and **(b)** recalculate, assuming an annuity due.

2. Wally Beaver won a lottery and will receive a check for $4,000 at the beginning of each 6 months for the next 5 years. If Wally deposits each check into an account that pays 6%, how much will he have at the end of the 5 years?

*For **extra help** from your authors–Sharon and Jeff–see the videos in Connect.*

These videos are also available on YouTube!

✓ **Solutions**

1. **a. Step 1.**   Periods = 4 years × 2 = 8   **b.** Periods = 4 years × 2   **Step 1**
            = 8 + 1 = 9
                      10% ÷ 2 = 5%   10% ÷ 2 = 5%
       Step 2.   Factor = 9.5491   Factor = 11.0265   **Step 2**
       Step 3. $4,000 × 9.5491 $4,000 × 11.0265 = $44,106   **Step 3**
            = **$38,196.40**   − 1 payment   − 4,000   **Step 4**
                                                       $40,106

2. **Step 1.**   5 years × 2 =   10 $\frac{6\%}{2} = 3\%$
                      + 1
                      11 periods
    Step 2.   Table factor, 12.8078
    Step 3. $4,000 × 12.8078 = $51,231.20
    Step 4.   − 4,000.00
                                   $47,231.20

LU 13–1a EXTRA PRACTICE QUIZ WITH WORKED-OUT SOLUTIONS

Need more practice? Try this **Extra Practice Quiz** (check figures in the Interactive Chapter Organizer). Worked-out Solutions can be found in Appendix B at end of text.

1. Using Table 13.1, **(a)** find the value of an investment after 4 years on an ordinary annuity of $5,000 made semiannually at 4%; and **(b)** recalculate, assuming an annuity due.
2. Wally Beaver won a lottery and will receive a check for $2,500 at the beginning of each 6 months for the next 6 years. If Wally deposits each check into an account that pays 6%, how much will he have at the end of the 6 years?

Learning Unit 13–2: Present Value of an Ordinary Annuity (Find Present Value)[4]

This unit begins by presenting the concept of present value of an ordinary annuity. Then you will learn how to use a table to calculate the present value of an ordinary annuity.

Concept of Present Value of an Ordinary Annuity— The Big Picture

Let's assume that we want to know how much money we need to invest *today* to receive a stream of payments for a given number of years in the future. This is called the **present value of an ordinary annuity.**

In Figure 13.2 you can see that if you wanted to withdraw $1 at the end of one period, you would have to invest 93 cents *today*. If at the end of each period for three periods you wanted to withdraw $1, you would have to put $2.58 in the bank *today* at 8% interest. (Note that we go from the future back to the present.)

FIGURE 13.2

Present value of an annuity of $1 at 8%

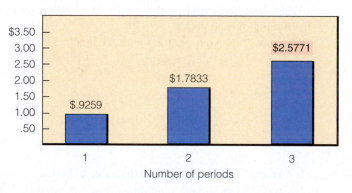

Now let's look at how we could use tables to calculate the present value of annuities and then check our answer.

LO 1

Calculating Present Value of an Ordinary Annuity by Table Lookup

Use the steps below to calculate the present value of an ordinary annuity by table lookup.[5]

CALCULATING PRESENT VALUE OF AN ORDINARY ANNUITY BY TABLE LOOKUP
Step 1. Calculate the number of periods and rate per period.
Step 2. Look up the periods and rate in the present value of an annuity table. The intersection gives the table factor for the present value of $1.
Step 3. Multiply the withdrawal for each period by the table factor. This gives the present value of an ordinary annuity.

$$\text{Present value of ordinary annuity payment} = \text{Annuity payment} \times \text{Present value of ordinary annuity table factor}$$

---

[4]For simplicity we omit a discussion of present value of annuity due that would require subtracting a period and adding a 1.

[5]The formula for the present value of an ordinary annuity is $PV = PMT \times \frac{1 - 1 \div (1 + i)^n}{i}$, where PV equals present value of annuity, PMT equals annuity payment, *i* equals interest, and *n* equals number of periods. The calculator sequence would be as follows for the John Fitch example that follows: 1 [+] .08 [yˣ] 3 [+−] [=] [M+] 1 [−] [MR] [÷] .08 [×] 8,000 [=] 20,616.78.

TABLE	13.2	Present value of an annuity of $1

Period	2%	3%	4%	5%	6%	7%	8%	9%	10%	11%	12%	13%
1	0.9804	0.9709	0.9615	0.9524	0.9434	0.9346	0.9259	0.9174	0.9091	0.9009	0.8929	0.8850
2	1.9416	1.9135	1.8861	1.8594	1.8334	1.8080	1.7833	1.7591	1.7355	1.7125	1.6901	1.6681
3	2.8839	2.8286	2.7751	2.7232	2.6730	2.6243	2.5771	2.5313	2.4869	2.4437	2.4018	2.3612
4	3.8077	3.7171	3.6299	3.5459	3.4651	3.3872	3.3121	3.2397	3.1699	3.1024	3.0373	2.9745
5	4.7134	4.5797	4.4518	4.3295	4.2124	4.1002	3.9927	3.8897	3.7908	3.6959	3.6048	3.5172
6	5.6014	5.4172	5.2421	5.0757	4.9173	4.7665	4.6229	4.4859	4.3553	4.2305	4.1114	3.9975
7	6.4720	6.2303	6.0021	5.7864	5.5824	5.3893	5.2064	5.0330	4.8684	4.7122	4.5638	4.4226
8	7.3255	7.0197	6.7327	6.4632	6.2098	5.9713	5.7466	5.5348	5.3349	5.1461	4.9676	4.7988
9	8.1622	7.7861	7.4353	7.1078	6.8017	6.5152	6.2469	5.9952	5.7590	5.5370	5.3282	5.1317
10	8.9826	8.5302	8.1109	7.7217	7.3601	7.0236	6.7101	6.4177	6.1446	5.8892	5.6502	5.4262
11	9.7868	9.2526	8.7605	8.3064	7.8869	7.4987	7.1390	6.8052	6.4951	6.2065	5.9377	5.6869
12	10.5753	9.9540	9.3851	8.8632	8.3838	7.9427	7.5361	7.1607	6.8137	6.4924	6.1944	5.9176
13	11.3483	10.6350	9.9856	9.3936	8.8527	8.3576	7.9038	7.4869	7.1034	6.7499	6.4235	6.1218
14	12.1062	11.2961	10.5631	9.8986	9.2950	8.7455	8.2442	7.7862	7.3667	6.9819	6.6282	6.3025
15	12.8492	11.9379	11.1184	10.3796	9.7122	9.1079	8.5595	8.0607	7.6061	7.1909	6.8109	6.4624
16	13.5777	12.5611	11.6523	10.8378	10.1059	9.4466	8.8514	8.3126	7.8237	7.3792	6.9740	6.6039
17	14.2918	13.1661	12.1657	11.2741	10.4773	9.7632	9.1216	8.5436	8.0216	7.5488	7.1196	6.7291
18	14.9920	13.7535	12.6593	11.6896	10.8276	10.0591	9.3719	8.7556	8.2014	7.7016	7.2497	6.8399
19	15.6784	14.3238	13.1339	12.0853	11.1581	10.3356	9.6036	8.9501	8.3649	7.8393	7.3658	6.9380
20	16.3514	14.8775	13.5903	12.4622	11.4699	10.5940	9.8181	9.1285	8.5136	7.9633	7.4694	7.0248
25	19.5234	17.4131	15.6221	14.0939	12.7834	11.6536	10.6748	9.8226	9.0770	8.4217	7.8431	7.3300
30	22.3964	19.6004	17.2920	15.3724	13.7648	12.4090	11.2578	10.2737	9.4269	8.6938	8.0552	7.4957
40	27.3554	23.1148	19.7928	17.1591	15.0463	13.3317	11.9246	10.7574	9.7790	8.9511	8.2438	7.6344
50	31.4236	25.7298	21.4822	18.2559	15.7619	13.8007	12.2335	10.9617	9.9148	9.0417	8.3045	7.6752

EXAMPLE John Fitch wants to receive an $8,000 annuity in 3 years. Interest on the annuity is 8% annually. John will make withdrawals at the end of each year. How much must John invest today to receive a stream of payments for 3 years? Use Table 13.2. Remember that interest could be earned semiannually, quarterly, and so on, as shown in the previous unit.

Step 1. 3 years × 1 = 3 periods $\dfrac{8\%}{\text{Annually}} = 8\%$

Step 2. Table factor, 2.5771 (we saw this in Figure 13.2)

Step 3. $8,000 × 2.5771 = **$20,616.80**

If John wants to withdraw $8,000 at the end of each period for 3 years, he will have to deposit $20,616.80 in the bank *today*.

$20,616.80	
+ 1,649.34	→ Interest at end of year 1 (.08 × $20,616.80)
$22,266.14	
− 8,000.00	→ First payment to John
$14,266.14	
+ 1,141.29	→ Interest at end of year 2 (.08 × $14,266.14)
$15,407.43	
− 8,000.00	→ Second payment to John
$ 7,407.43	
+ 592.59	→ Interest at end of year 3 (.08 × $7,407.43)
$ 8,000.02	
− 8,000.00	→ After end of year 3 John receives his last $8,000
.02	(off 2 cents due to rounding)

Before we leave this unit, let's work out two examples that show the relationship of Chapter 13 to Chapter 12. Use the tables in your *Business Math Handbook*.

LO 2

Lump Sum versus Annuities

EXAMPLE John Sands made deposits of $200 semiannually to Floor Bank, which pays 8% interest compounded semiannually. After 5 years, John makes no more deposits. What will be the balance in the account 6 years after the last deposit?

Step 1. Calculate amount of annuity: Table 13.1

10 periods, 4% $200 × 12.0061 = $2,401.22

Step 2. Calculate how much the final value of the annuity will grow by the compound interest table. Table 12.1

12 periods, 4% $2,401.22 × 1.6010 = $3,844.35

For John, the stream of payments grows to $2,401.22. Then this *lump sum* grows for 6 years to $3,844.35. Now let's look at a present value example.

EXAMPLE Mel Rich decided to retire in 8 years to New Mexico. What amount should Mel invest today so he will be able to withdraw $40,000 at the end of each year for 25 years *after* he retires? Assume Mel can invest money at 5% interest (compounded annually).

Step 1. Calculate the present value of the annuity: Table 13.2

25 periods, 5% $40,000 × 14.0939 = $563,756

Step 2. Find the present value of $563,756 since Mel will not retire for 8 years:

Table 12.3

8 periods, 5% (PV table) $563,756 × .6768 = $381,550.06

If Mel deposits $381,550 in year 1, it will grow to $563,756 after 8 years.

It's time to try the Practice Quiz and check your understanding of this unit.

MONEY tips

The best rates on mortgages, loans, and credit cards are offered to those with credit scores above 700. Pay your bills on time, have one long-term credit card, keep low balances or pay off balances each month, and review your credit report regularly.

LU 13–2 **PRACTICE QUIZ**

Complete this **Practice Quiz** to see how you are doing.

1. What must you invest today to receive an $18,000 annuity for 5 years semiannually at a 10% annual rate? All withdrawals will be made at the end of each period.
2. Rase High School wants to set up a scholarship fund to provide five $2,000 scholarships for the next 10 years. If money can be invested at an annual rate of 9%, how much should the scholarship committee invest today?
3. Joe Wood decided to retire in 5 years in Arizona. What amount should Joe invest today so he can withdraw $60,000 at the end of each year for 30 years after he retires? Assume Joe can invest money at 6% compounded annually.

For **extra help** from your authors–Sharon and Jeff–see the videos in Connect.

These videos are also available on YouTube!

(Use tables in *Business Math Handbook*)

✓ Solutions

1. **Step 1.** Periods = 5 years × 2 = 10; Rate = 10% ÷ 2 = 5%
   Step 2. Factor, 7.7217
   Step 3. $18,000 × 7.7217 = $138,990.60
2. **Step 1.** Periods = 10; Rate = 9%
   Step 2. Factor, 6.4177
   Step 3. $10,000 × 6.4177 = $64,177
3. **Step 1.** Calculate present value of annuity: 30 periods, 6%.
   $60,000 × 13.7648 = $825,888
   Step 2. Find present value of $825,888 for 5 years: 5 periods, 6%.
   $825,888 × .7473 = $617,186.10

LU 13–2α   **EXTRA PRACTICE QUIZ WITH WORKED-OUT SOLUTIONS**

Need more practice? Try this **Extra Practice Quiz** (check figures in the Interactive Chapter Organizer). Worked-out Solutions can be found in Appendix B at end of text.

1. What must you invest today to receive a $20,000 annuity for 5 years semiannually at a 5% annual rate? All withdrawals will be made at the end of each period.
2. Rase High School wants to set up a scholarship fund to provide five $3,000 scholarships for the next 10 years. If money can be invested at an annual rate of 4%, how much should the scholarship committee invest today?
3. Joe Wood decided to retire in 5 years in Arizona. What amount should Joe invest today so he can withdraw $80,000 at the end of each year for 30 years after he retires? Assume Joe can invest money at 3% compounded annually.

Learning Unit 13–3: Sinking Funds (Find Periodic Payments)

LO 1

A **sinking fund** is a financial arrangement that sets aside regular periodic payments of a particular amount of money. Compound interest accumulates on these payments to a specific sum at a predetermined future date. Corporations use sinking funds to discharge bonded indebtedness, to replace worn-out equipment, to purchase plant expansion, and so on.

A sinking fund is a different type of an annuity. In a sinking fund, you determine the amount of periodic payments you need to achieve a given financial goal. In the annuity, you know the amount of each payment and must determine its future value. Let's work with the following formula:

Sinking fund payment = Future value × Sinking fund table factor[6]

EXAMPLE   To retire a bond issue, Moore Company needs $60,000 in 18 years from today. The interest rate is 10% compounded annually. What payment must Moore make at the end of each year? Use Table 13.3.

TABLE   13.3

Sinking fund table based on $1

Period	2%	3%	4%	5%	6%	8%	10%
1	1.0000	1.0000	1.0000	1.0000	1.0000	1.0000	1.0000
2	0.4951	0.4926	0.4902	0.4878	0.4854	0.4808	0.4762
3	0.3268	0.3235	0.3203	0.3172	0.3141	0.3080	0.3021
4	0.2426	0.2390	0.2355	0.2320	0.2286	0.2219	0.2155
5	0.1922	0.1884	0.1846	0.1810	0.1774	0.1705	0.1638
6	0.1585	0.1546	0.1508	0.1470	0.1434	0.1363	0.1296
7	0.1345	0.1305	0.1266	0.1228	0.1191	0.1121	0.1054
8	0.1165	0.1125	0.1085	0.1047	0.1010	0.0940	0.0874
9	0.1025	0.0984	0.0945	0.0907	0.0870	0.0801	0.0736
10	0.0913	0.0872	0.0833	0.0795	0.0759	0.0690	0.0627
11	0.0822	0.0781	0.0741	0.0704	0.0668	0.0601	0.0540
12	0.0746	0.0705	0.0666	0.0628	0.0593	0.0527	0.0468
13	0.0681	0.0640	0.0601	0.0565	0.0530	0.0465	0.0408
14	0.0626	0.0585	0.0547	0.0510	0.0476	0.0413	0.0357
15	0.0578	0.0538	0.0499	0.0463	0.0430	0.0368	0.0315
16	0.0537	0.0496	0.0458	0.0423	0.0390	0.0330	0.0278
17	0.0500	0.0460	0.0422	0.0387	0.0354	0.0296	0.0247
18	0.0467	0.0427	0.0390	0.0355	0.0324	0.0267	0.0219
19	0.0438	0.0398	0.0361	0.0327	0.0296	0.0241	0.0195
20	0.0412	0.0372	0.0336	0.0302	0.0272	0.0219	0.0175
24	0.0329	0.0290	0.0256	0.0225	0.0197	0.0150	0.0113
28	0.0270	0.0233	0.0200	0.0171	0.0146	0.0105	0.0075
32	0.0226	0.0190	0.0159	0.0133	0.0110	0.0075	0.0050
36	0.0192	0.0158	0.0129	0.0104	0.0084	0.0053	0.0033
40	0.0166	0.0133	0.0105	0.0083	0.0065	0.0039	0.0023

MONEY tips

If you are trying to build credit by using a credit card, each time you make a purchase using the credit card, deduct that amount from your checking account. When your credit card bill is due, add up all your credit card deductions in your checking account. You will have enough to pay the credit card off in full.

[6]Sinking fund table is the reciprocal of the ordinary annuity table.

We begin by looking down the Period column in Table 13.3 until we come to 18. Then we go across until we reach the 10% column. The table factor is .0219.

Now we multiply $60,000 by the factor as follows:

$60,000 × .0219 = $1,314

LO 2

This states that if Moore Company pays $1,314 at the end of each period for 18 years, then $60,000 will be available to pay off the bond issue at maturity.

We can check this by using Table 13.1 (the ordinary annuity table):

$1,314 × 45.5992 = $59,917.35 (off due to rounding)

It's time to try the following Practice Quiz.

LU 13-3 | PRACTICE QUIZ

Complete this Practice Quiz to see how you are doing.

For extra help from your authors–Sharon and Jeff–see the videos in Connect.

These videos are also available on YouTube!

Today, Arrow Company issued bonds that will mature to a value of $90,000 in 10 years. Arrow's controller is planning to set up a sinking fund. Interest rates are 12% compounded semiannually. What will Arrow Company have to set aside to meet its obligation in 10 years? Check your answer. Your answer will be off due to the rounding of Table 13.3.

✓ Solution

10 years × 2 = 20 periods $\frac{12\%}{2} = 6\%$ $90,000 × .0272 = $2,448

Check $2,448 × 36.7855 = $90,050.90

LU 13-3a | EXTRA PRACTICE QUIZ WITH WORKED-OUT SOLUTION

Need more practice? Try this Extra Practice Quiz (check figure in the Interactive Chapter Organizer). Worked-out Solution can be found in Appendix B at end of text.

Today Arrow Company issued bonds that will mature to a value of $120,000 in 20 years. Arrow's controller is planning to set up a sinking fund. Interest rates are 6% compounded semiannually. What will Arrow Company have to set aside to meet its obligation in 10 years? Check your answer. Your answer will be off due to rounding of Table 13.3.

INTERACTIVE CHAPTER ORGANIZER

Topic/Procedure/Formula	Examples	You try it*
Ordinary annuities (find future value) Invest money at end of each period. Find future value at maturity. Answers question of how much money accumulates. $\frac{\text{Future value of ordinary annuity}}{} = \frac{\text{Annuity payment each period}}{} × \frac{\text{Ordinary annuity table factor}}{}$ $FV = PMT\left[\frac{(1+i)^n - 1}{i}\right]$	Use Table 13.1: 2 years, $4,000 ordinary annuity at 8% annually. Value = $4,000 × 2.0800 = $8,320 (2 periods, 8%) $FV = 4,000\left[\frac{(1+.08)^2 - 1}{.08}\right] = \$8,320$	**Calculate value of ordinary annuity** $6,000, 7% annually, 4 years

(continues)

INTERACTIVE CHAPTER ORGANIZER

Topic/Procedure/Formula	Examples	You try it*
Annuities due (find future value) Invest money at beginning of each period. Find future value at maturity. Should be higher than ordinary annuity since it is invested at beginning of each period. Use Table 13.1, but add one period and subtract one payment from answer. $$\text{Future value of an annuity due} = \left(\begin{array}{c} \text{Annuity} \\ \text{payment} \\ \text{each} \\ \text{period} \end{array} \times \begin{array}{c} \text{Ordinary}^* \\ \text{annuity} \\ \text{table} \\ \text{factor} \end{array} \right) - 1 \text{ Payment}$$ *Add 1 period. $$FV_{due} = PMT\left[\frac{(1+i)^n - 1}{i}\right](1+i)$$	*Example:* Same example as above but invest money at beginning of period. $4,000 \times 3.2464 = \begin{array}{r} \$12,985.60 \\ - \ 4,000.00 \\ \hline \$ \ 8,985.60 \end{array}$ (3 periods, 8%) $$FV_{due} = 4,000\left(\frac{(1 + .08)^2 - 1}{.08}\right)(1 + .08)$$ $$= \$8,985.60$$	**Calculate value of annuity due** $6,000, 7% annually, 4 years
Present value of an ordinary annuity (find present value) Calculate number of periods and rate per period. Use Table 13.2 to find table factor for present value of $1. Multiply withdrawal for each period by table factor to get present value of an ordinary annuity. $$\begin{array}{c} \text{Present} \\ \text{value of an} \\ \text{ordinary} \\ \text{annuity} \\ \text{payment} \end{array} = \begin{array}{c} \text{Annuity} \\ \text{payment} \end{array} \times \begin{array}{c} \text{Present} \\ \text{value of} \\ \text{ordinary} \\ \text{annuity} \\ \text{table factor} \end{array}$$ $$PV = PMT\left[\frac{1 - (1+i)^{-n}}{i}\right]$$	*Example:* Receive $10,000 for 5 years. Interest is 10% compounded annually. Table 13.2: 5 periods, 10% $$\text{What you put in today} = \begin{array}{r} 3.7908 \\ \times \ \$10,000 \\ \hline \$37,908 \end{array}$$ $$PV = 10,000\left[\frac{1 - (1 + .1)^{-5}}{.1}\right] = \$37,907.88$$	**Calculate present value of ordinary annuity** $20,000, 6 years, 4% interest compounded annually
Sinking funds (find periodic payment) Paying a particular amount of money for a set number of periodic payments to accumulate a specific sum. We know the future value and must calculate the periodic payments needed. Answer can be proved by ordinary annuity table. $$\begin{array}{c} \text{Sinking} \\ \text{fund} \\ \text{payment} \end{array} = \begin{array}{c} \text{Future} \\ \text{value} \end{array} \times \begin{array}{c} \text{Sinking} \\ \text{fund table} \\ \text{factor} \end{array}$$	*Example:* $200,000 bond to retire 15 years from now. Interest is 6% compounded annually. By Table 13.3: $200,000 \times .0430 = \$8,600$ Check by Table 13.1: $8,600 \times 23.2759 = \$200,172.74$	**Calculate periodic payment** $400,000 bond to retire 20 years from now. Interest is 5% compounded annually.

KEY TERMS	Annuities certain Annuity Annuity due Contingent annuities	Future value of an annuity Ordinary annuity Payment periods	Present value of an ordinary annuity Sinking fund Term of the annuity
Check Figures for Extra Practice Quizzes. (Worked-out Solutions are in Appendix B.)	LU 13–1a 1. a. $42,914.50 b. $43,773 2. $36,544.50	LU 13–2a 1. $175,042 2. $121,663.50 3. $1,352,584.40	LU 13–3a $1,596

*Worked-out solutions are in Appendix B.

Critical Thinking Discussion Questions with Chapter Concept Check

1. What is the difference between an ordinary annuity and an annuity due? If you were to save money in an annuity, which would you choose and why?

2. Explain how you would calculate ordinary annuities and annuities due by table lookup. Create an example to explain the meaning of a table factor from an ordinary annuity.

3. What is a present value of an ordinary annuity? Create an example showing how one of your relatives might plan for retirement by using the present value of an ordinary annuity. Would you ever have to use lump-sum payments in your calculation from Chapter 12?

4. What is a sinking fund? Why could an ordinary annuity table be used to check the sinking fund payment?

5. With the tight economy, more businesses are cutting back on matching the retirement contributions of their employees. Do you think this is ethical?

6. **Chapter Concept Check.** Create a retirement plan. Back up your retirement plan with calculations involving ordinary annuities as well as the present value of annuities.

END-OF-CHAPTER PROBLEMS

DRILL PROBLEMS

Complete the ordinary annuities for the following using tables in the *Business Math Handbook:*   *LU 13-1(2)*

	Amount of payment	Payment payable	Years	Interest rate	Value of annuity
13–1.	$4,500	Annually	10	3%	
13–2.	$12,000	Semiannually	8	7%	

Redo Problem 13–1 as an annuity due:

13–3.

Calculate the value of the following annuity due without a table. Check your results by Table 13.1 or the *Business Math Handbook* (they will be slightly off due to rounding):   *LU 13-1(2)*

	Amount of payment	Payment payable	Years	Interest rate
13–4.	$2,000	Annually	3	6%

Complete the following using Table 13.2 or the *Business Math Handbook* for the present value of an ordinary annuity: *LU 13-2(1)*

	Amount of annuity expected	Payment	Time	Interest rate	Present value (amount needed now to invest to receive annuity)
13–5.	$900	Annually	4 years	6%	
13–6.	$15,000	Quarterly	4 years	8%	

13–7.   Check Problem 13–5 without the use of Table 13.2.

Using the sinking fund Table 13.3 or the *Business Math Handbook*, complete the following: *LU 13-3(1)*

	Required amount	Frequency of payment	Length of time	Interest rate	Payment amount end of each period
13–8.	$25,000	Quarterly	6 years	8%	
13–9.	$15,000	Annually	8 years	8%	

13–10.   Check the answer in Problem 13–9 by Table 13.1.   *LU 13-3(2)*

WORD PROBLEMS (Use Tables in the *Business Math Handbook*)

13–11. John Regan, an employee at Home Depot, made deposits of $800 at the end of each year for 4 years. Interest is 4% compounded annually. What is the value of Regan's annuity at the end of 4 years?   *LU 13-1(2)*

13–12. Ed Long promised to pay his son $400 semiannually for 12 years. Assume Ed can invest his money at 6% in an ordinary annuity. How much must Ed invest today to pay his son $400 semiannually for 12 years?   *LU 13-2(1)*

13–13. Financial analysts recommend investing 15% to 20% of your annual income in your retirement fund to reach a replacement rate of 70% of your income by age 65. This recommendation increases to almost 30% if you start investing at 45 years old. Mallori Rouse is 25 years old and has started investing $3,000 at the end of each year in her retirement account. How much will her account be worth in 20 years at 8% interest compounded annually? How much will it be worth in 30 years? What about at 40 years? How much will it be worth in 50 years? Round to the nearest dollar.   *LU 13-1(2)*

13–14. After paying off a car loan or credit card, don't remove this amount from your budget. Instead, invest in your future by applying some of it to your retirement account. How much would $450 invested at the end of each quarter be worth in 10 years at 4% interest? (Use the *Business Math Handbook* tables.)   *LU 13-1(2)*

13–15. You decide to reduce the amount you spend eating out by $150 a month and invest the total saved at the end of each year in your retirement account. How much will the account be worth at 5% in 15 years?   *LU 13-1(2)*

13–16. Patricia and Joe Payne are divorced. The divorce settlement stipulated that Joe pay $525 a month for their daughter Suzanne until she turns 18 in 4 years. How much must Joe set aside today to meet the settlement? Interest is 6% a year.   *LU 13-2(1)*

13–17. Josef Company borrowed money that must be repaid in 20 years. The company wants to make sure the loan will be repaid at the end of year 20, so it invests $12,500 at the end of each year at 12% interest compounded annually. What was the amount of the original loan?   *LU 13-1(2)*

13–18. Bankrate.com reported on a shocking statistic: only 54% of workers participate in their company's retirement plan. This means that 46% do not. With such an uncertain future for Social Security, this can leave almost 1 in 2 individuals without proper income during retirement. Jill Collins, 20, decided she needs to have $250,000 in her retirement account upon retiring at 60. How much does she need to invest each year at 5% compounded annually to meet her goal? *Tip:* She is setting up a sinking fund.   *LU 13-3(1)*

13–19. Rob Herndon, an accountant with Southwest Airlines, wants to retire 50% of Southwest Airlines bonds by 2035. Calculate the payment Rob needs to make at the end of each year at 6% compounded annually to reach his goal of paying off $300,000 in 20 years.   *LU 13-1(2)*

13–20. Alice Longtree has decided to invest $400 quarterly for 4 years in an ordinary annuity at 8%. As her financial adviser, e**X**cel   calculate for Alice the total cash value of the annuity at the end of year 4.   *LU 13-1(2)*

13–21. At the beginning of each period for 10 years, Merl Agnes invests $500 semiannually at 6%. What is the cash value of this annuity due at the end of year 10?   *LU 13-1(2)*

13–22. Jeff Associates needs to repay $30,000. The company plans to set up a sinking fund that will repay the loan at the end of 8 years. Assume a 12% interest rate compounded semiannually. What must Jeff pay into the fund each period of time? Check your answer by Table 13.1.   *LU 13-3(1, 2)*

13–23. On Joe Martin's graduation from college, Joe's uncle promised him a gift of $12,000 in cash or $900 every quarter for the next 4 e**X**cel   years after graduation. If money could be invested at 8% compounded quarterly, which offer is better for Joe?   *LU 13-1(2),*
LU 13-2(1)

13–24. You are earning an average of $46,500 and will retire in 10 years. If you put 20% of your gross average income in an e**X**cel   ordinary annuity compounded at 7% annually, what will be the value of the annuity when you retire?   *LU 13-1(2)*

13–25. A local Dunkin' Donuts franchise must buy a new piece of equipment in 5 years that will cost $88,000. The company is setting up a sinking fund to finance the purchase. What will the quarterly deposit be if the fund earns 8% interest?
LU 13-3(1)

13–26. Mike Macaro is selling a piece of land. Two offers are on the table. Morton Company offered a $40,000 down payment and $35,000 a year for the next 5 years. Flynn Company offered $25,000 down and $38,000 a year for the next 5 years. If money can be invested at 8% compounded annually, which offer is better for Mike?   *LU 13-1(2)*

13–27. Al Vincent has decided to retire to Arizona in 10 years. What amount should Al invest today so that he will be able to withdraw $28,000 at the end of each year for 15 years *after* he retires? Assume he can invest the money at 8% interest compounded annually.   *LU 13-2(1)*

13–28. Victor French made deposits of $5,000 at the end of each quarter to Book Bank, which pays 8% interest compounded quarterly. After 3 years, Victor made no more deposits. What will be the balance in the account 2 years after the last deposit?   *LU 13-1(2)*

13–29. Janet Woo decided to retire to Florida in 6 years. What amount should Janet invest today so she can withdraw $50,000 at the end of each year for 20 years after she retires? Assume Janet can invest money at 6% compounded annually.   *LU 13-2(1)*

CHALLENGE PROBLEMS

13–30. Assume that you can buy a $6,000 computer system in monthly installments for 3 years. The seller charges you 12% interest compounded monthly. What is your monthly payment? Assume your first payment is due at the end of the month. Use tables in the *Business Math Handbook*.   *LU 13-2(1)*

$$\text{Monthly payment} = \frac{\text{Amount owed}}{\substack{\text{Table factor} \\ \text{for PV of annuity}}}$$

13–31. Ajax Corporation has hired Brad O'Brien as its new president. Terms included the company's agreeing to pay retirement benefits of $18,000 at the end of each semiannual period for 10 years. This will begin in 3,285 days. If the money can be invested at 8% compounded semiannually, what must the company deposit today to fulfill its obligation to Brad?   *LU 13-2(1)*

 SUMMARY PRACTICE TEST (Use Tables in the *Business Math Handbook*)

Do you need help? The videos in Connect have step-by-step worked-out solutions. These videos are also available on YouTube!

1. Lin Lowe plans to deposit $1,800 at the end of every 6 months for the next 15 years at 8% interest compounded semiannually. What is the value of Lin's annuity at the end of 15 years?   *LU 13-1(2)*

2. On Abby Ellen's graduation from law school, Abby's uncle, Bull Brady, promised her a gift of $24,000 or $2,400 every quarter for the next 4 years after graduating from law school. If the money could be invested at 6% compounded quarterly, which offer should Abby choose? *LU 13-2(1, 2)*

3. Sanka Blunck wants to receive $8,000 each year for 20 years. How much must Sanka invest today at 4% interest compounded annually? *LU 13-2(1)*

4. In 9 years, Rollo Company will have to repay a $100,000 loan. Assume a 6% interest rate compounded quarterly. How much must Rollo Company pay each period to have $100,000 at the end of 9 years? *LU 13-3(1)*

5. Lance Industries borrowed $130,000. The company plans to set up a sinking fund that will repay the loan at the end of 18 years. Assume a 6% interest rate compounded semiannually. What amount must Lance Industries pay into the fund each period? Check your answer by Table 13.1. *LU 13-3(1, 2)*

6. Joe Jan wants to receive $22,000 each year for the next 22 years. Assume a 6% interest rate compounded annually. How much must Joe invest today? *LU 13-2(1)*

7. Twice a year for 15 years, Warren Ford invested $1,700 compounded semiannually at 6% interest. What is the value of this annuity due? *LU 13-1(2)*

8. Scupper Molly invested $1,800 semiannually for 23 years at 8% interest compounded semiannually. What is the value of this annuity due? *LU 13-1(2)*

9. Nelson Collins decided to retire to Canada in 10 years. What amount should Nelson deposit so that he will be able to withdraw $80,000 at the end of each year for 25 years after he retires? Assume Nelson can invest money at 7% interest compounded annually. *LU 13-2(1)*

10. Bob Bryan made deposits of $10,000 at the end of each quarter to Lion Bank, which pays 8% interest compounded quarterly. After 9 years, Bob made no more deposits. What will be the account's balance 4 years after the last deposit? *LU 13-1(2)*

Part of Deutsche Post, the world's leading mail and logistics group, DHL maintains a presence in 220 countries and territories and generates in excess of $50 billion in annual revenues. Its 275,000 employees provide services in the following areas:

- Parcel/document express delivery services
- Freight by air, ocean, road, and rail
- Warehousing and distribution
- Supply chain solutions
- International mail solutions

Moving west across the globe, DHL's global expansion strategy was fueled by key acquisitions such as Airborne Express in the United States, which provided a much needed distribution network in North America and included an expedited shipping infrastructure on the domestic level. This acquisition propelled DHL to become a respected third player in the U.S. market, behind market leaders Federal Express and UPS.

The investment in U.S. operations enabled DHL to become equally strong in Asia, Europe, and the U.S. Its strategy for differentiation includes the three cornerstones of flexibility, responsiveness, and the human touch.

Flexibility and responsiveness are supported by an efficient regional hub system. In the U.S. DHL maintains two air/ground hubs that service five gateway locations. While the hubs service the gateways, gateways serve the DHL service centers and export to foreign destinations. This structure allows DHL to move goods efficiently with the confidence of "track 'n trace," a bar coding system that since 1986 has allowed customers to track the status of a package from the point of pickup to delivery.

The human touch refers to DHL's commitment to maintaining its own staff, rather than using subcontractors who might also provide transport services for other companies. DHL has also invested in offering "Industry Sector Solutions" essentially providing expertise in select industries such as aerospace, automotive, chemical, and consumer to name a few. The DHL brand is known for "personal commitment, proactive solutions and local strength," and key to all of this is the DHL employee.

Note: The following problems contain some data that has been created by the author.

PROBLEM 1

Assume DHL will need to replace a piece of equipment in 12 years that will cost $240,000. The company will set up a sinking fund to finance this future purchase. What amount should DHL put away quarterly if it can earn 12% interest? Round to the nearest cent. Use tables in Handbook.

PROBLEM 2

If DHL were to sell off a used aircraft and had the following two offers to consider, which one would be a better deal? How much better is the better deal? Assume 6% interest compounded annually, and down payments are not invested. Round to the nearest cent.

Offer 1: $150,000 down payment and $30,000 a year for the next 5 years.

Offer 2: $75,000 down payment and $45,000 a year for the next 5 years.

PROBLEM 3

Suppose the retirement plan for DHL salaried personnel included a $1,000 company contribution paid quarterly at the beginning of the month. Assuming these funds could be invested at 8% interest compounded quarterly, what would be the cash value at the end of 3 years? Round to the nearest cent.

PROBLEM 4

Imagine that DHL borrowed capital that needed to be repaid in 5 years. If DHL paid $150,000 at the end of each year at 10% interest compounded annually, what was the original loan amount? Round to the nearest cent.

PROBLEM 5

Assume DHL needs access to a stream of capital for the next 10 years. If DHL needs $2.5 million per year and can earn 4% interest compounded annually, how much must the company put away today to have these funds when needed? How much of DHL's capital need will come from interest earned? Round to the nearest dollar.

Class Discussion. The mail and logistics industry is a dynamic one. Consider how electronic communication might impact DHL's business. Review the DHL website for insights on how the company is responding to new forms of communication.

Class Discussion. DHL has a clear strategy for market differentiation as discussed in the video case. Research U.S. market leaders Federal Express and UPS and compare each company's strategy for differentiation.

SURF TO SAVE

PROBLEM 1
Never too early to start saving

Go to http://www.bankrate.com/brm/news/ira/20021211a.asp and read the article "Start Your Kids on the Roth Road." Suppose you open a Roth IRA for your daughter and deposit $1,000 at the end of each year to match her earned income from age 14 to age 21 (8 years). Assuming she makes no withdrawals or additions to that account after the year that she turns 21, how much will she have in the account at the end of the year that she turns 60? Assume the money in the Roth IRA account earns 8% annually on average. (*Hint:* This is like an annuity for the first 8 years and then like a savings account.)

Discussion Questions

1. What is the value in starting investments at such an early age?

2. How might having such an investment set up impact the child's future savings?

PROBLEM 2
Ready for retirement

Visit http://www.realtycalc.com/calc/forms/SinkingFund.asp and assume you would like to have $500,000 by the time you reach retirement. Assume a 5% interest rate and 20 years until retirement. What will you need to contribute monthly to achieve your goal?

Discussion Questions

1. At what age do you feel you will be ready to retire? How will this impact your savings plan for retirement?

2. How would your contributions change in the above problem if you had 30 years until retirement? What if you had 40 years?

PROBLEM 3
You're a winner

Go to http://www.straightdope.com/mailbag/mlottery.html and read the information about lotteries. Then use the "What is my future value worth today?" calculator at http://www.timevalue.com/tcalc.aspx to answer the following. If a friend won the lottery and is guaranteed payments of $100,000 for the next 30 years (total payout of $3,000,000) and long-term interest rates are at 6%, then what immediate lump-sum payment is equivalent to the 30-year payout?

Discussion Questions

1. Which would you prefer to receive, a lump sum or yearly payments for a lottery win? Why?

2. Why would the lottery organization prefer to use the payment option versus lump sum?

PROBLEM 4
Regroup, retire, and relax

Go to http://www.timevalue.com/tcalc.aspx and click "How much do I need to fund my retirement?" If you were planning to retire and can live comfortably on $3,000.00 per month for 10 years, how much money would you need to deposit now in an account earning 5% interest to be able to afford this amount? If you cut your monthly payout in half, how much would you need to deposit now?

Discussion Questions

1. How can you estimate your monthly expenses by the time you are able to retire?

2. Calculate your current monthly expenses. How might these expenses change once you reach retirement age?

MOBILE APPS ✕

FV Pro (RIEU Limited) Calculates future values, present values, interest rates, time periods, and more for annuity investments.

TimeMoney (Dalasoft Limited) Calculates the time value of money in many scenarios including annuities, loans, and sinking funds.

A KIPLINGER APPROACH

By Carolyn Bigda, From *Kiplinger's Personal Finance*, April 2015.

LOWDOWN

What You Need to Know About Funding IRAs

You can make contributions for 2014 as late as April 15. But why wait? **BY CAROLYN BIGDA**

1. TAKE IT TO THE LIMIT. Workers younger than age 50 may save up to $5,500 in a traditional IRA, a Roth or a combination of the two. If you were 50 or older at the end of last year, the ceiling is $6,500.

2. CHOOSE YOUR SIDE. You can fund a traditional or a Roth IRA, or hedge your bets by splitting your contribution. Contributions to a traditional IRA are fully tax-deductible if you don't have a workplace retirement plan; if you have an employer-provided plan, some or all of what you put away may be deductible. You don't pay taxes on your earnings inside a traditional IRA, but you will owe Uncle Sam when you make withdrawals. With a Roth, nobody gets a deduction, but you don't owe taxes on withdrawals in retirement, assuming the account has been open for at least five years. Roths have other benefits, too. You can withdraw contributions at any time free of taxes and pen-

alties. And if there's money in the account when you die, your heirs get it tax-free. With a traditional account, that legacy is subject to income taxes.

3. AND NOW FOR THE FINE PRINT. If you have a retirement plan at work, you're single and your modified adjusted gross income was $60,000 or less last year (or $96,000 or less if you're married), you still qualify for a full-fledged traditional IRA deduction. As income rises above those levels, the deduction gradually disappears. Different income limits apply for a Roth: To make even a partial deposit for 2014, your MAGI must have been less than $129,000 for singles or $191,000 for married couples.

4. DOUBLE UP YOUR SAVINGS. You usually need earned income (wages from a job, for example, but not income from investments) to put money in an IRA. But if you didn't draw a salary in 2014—say, because you

stayed at home with the kids—Uncle Sam allows you to open a so-called spousal IRA and put away up to $5,500 using your spouse's pay. (The limit is $6,500 if you're 50 or older.)

5. JUMP-START JUNIOR'S RETIREMENT. Children must earn their own money to fund an IRA, but their own money doesn't have to fund the account. If your 15-year-old daughter had a summer job in 2014, you can contribute to an IRA in her name, up to her total earnings (or the $5,500 cap, whichever is less). Go with a Roth. Your child is likely in a low tax bracket and doesn't need the up-front deduction. Fifty years from now, when her hair is turning gray, a single $5,500 contribution will have grown to more than $160,000, assuming an annualized return of 7%.

6. GOOD NEWS IF YOU'RE ON YOUR OWN. If you're self-employed—whether full-time or because you do freelance work on the side—you qualify for a simplified employee pension plan, or SEP-IRA. Contribution amounts are much larger—as much as 25% of your qualified earnings, up to a maximum of $52,000 for 2014. And if you file for an extension on your tax return, you have until October 15 to make a 2014 contribution to your SEP account. With traditional IRAs and Roths, April 15 is the last day to make a deposit for 2014, whether you file a return that day or not.

7. GET A LEG UP ON 2015. You don't have to wait until April 15, 2016, to make this year's contribution. In fact, delaying means missing out on more than a year's worth of tax-free compounding. ■

OWEN TUCKER

BUSINESS MATH ISSUE

Funding IRAs means Roth is never a good choice.

1. List the key points of the article and information to support your position.
2. Write a group defense of your position using math calculations to support your view.

A Word Problem Approach—Chapters 10, 11, 12, 13

1. Amy O'Mally graduated from high school. Her uncle promised her as a gift a check for $2,000 or $275 every quarter for 2 years. If money could be invested at 6% compounded quarterly, which offer is better for Amy? (Use the tables in the *Business Math Handbook.*)   *LU 13-2(1)*

2. Alan Angel made deposits of $400 semiannually to Sag Bank, which pays 10% interest compounded semiannually. After 4 years, Alan made no more deposits. What will be the balance in the account 3 years after the last deposit? (Use the tables in the *Business Math Handbook.*)   *LU 13-1(2)*

3. Roger Disney decides to retire to Florida in 12 years. What amount should Roger invest today so that he will be able to withdraw $30,000 at the end of each year for 20 years *after* he retires? Assume he can invest money at 8% interest compounded annually. (Use tables in the *Business Math Handbook.*)   *LU 13-2(2)*

4. On September 15, Arthur Westering borrowed $3,000 from Vermont Bank at $10\frac{1}{2}$% interest. Arthur plans to repay the loan on January 25. Assume the loan is based on exact interest. How much will Arthur totally repay?   *LU 10-1(2)*

5. Sue Cooper borrowed $6,000 on an $11\frac{3}{4}$%, 120-day note. Sue paid $300 toward the note on day 50. On day 90, Sue paid an additional $200. Using the U.S. Rule, what is Sue's adjusted balance after her first payment?   *LU 10-3(1)*

6. On November 18, Northwest Company discounted an $18,000, 12%, 120-day note dated September 8. Assume a 10% discount rate. What will be the proceeds? Use ordinary interest.   *LU 11-2(1)*

7. Alice Reed deposits $16,500 into Rye Bank, which pays 10% interest compounded semiannually. Using the appropriate table, what will Alice have in her account at the end of 6 years?   *LU 12-1(2)*

8. Peter Regan needs $90,000 5 years from today to retire in Arizona. Peter's bank pays 10% interest compounded semiannually. What will Peter have to put in the bank today to have $90,000 in 5 years?   *LU 12-2(2)*

Special Supplement

Time-Value Relationship Contents

One Lump Sum (Single Amount)

Annuity (Stream of Payments)

Compare to Exhibit 13.2 to see relationship of compounding to present value.

EXHIBIT 13.1 Compound (future value) of $.68 at 10% for 4 periods

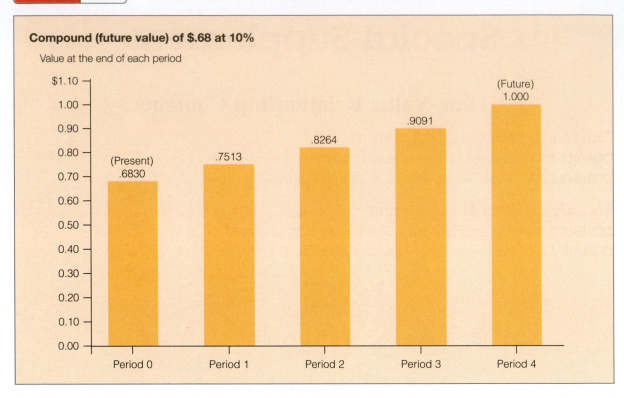

Compound (future value) of $.68 at 10%

Value at the end of each period

$.68 today will grow to $1.00 in the future.

What Exhibit 13.1 Means

If you take $.68 to a bank that pays 10%, after 4 periods you will be able to get $1.00. The $.68 is the present value, and the $1.00 is the compound value or future value. Keep in mind that the $.68 is a one lump-sum investment.

EXHIBIT **13.2** Present value of $1.00 at 10% for 4 periods

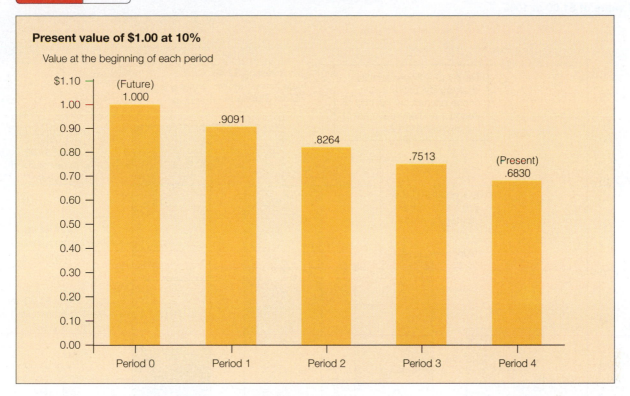

Present value of $1.00 at 10%

Value at the beginning of each period

If I need $1 in four periods, I need to invest $0.68 today.

What Exhibit 13.2 Means

If you want to receive $1.00 at the end of 4 periods at a bank paying 10%, you will have to deposit $.68 in the bank today. The longer you have to wait for your money, the less it is worth. The $1.00 is the compound or future amount, and the $.68 is the present value of a dollar that you will not receive for 4 periods.

EXHIBIT 13.3 Present value of a 4-year annuity of $1.00 at 10%

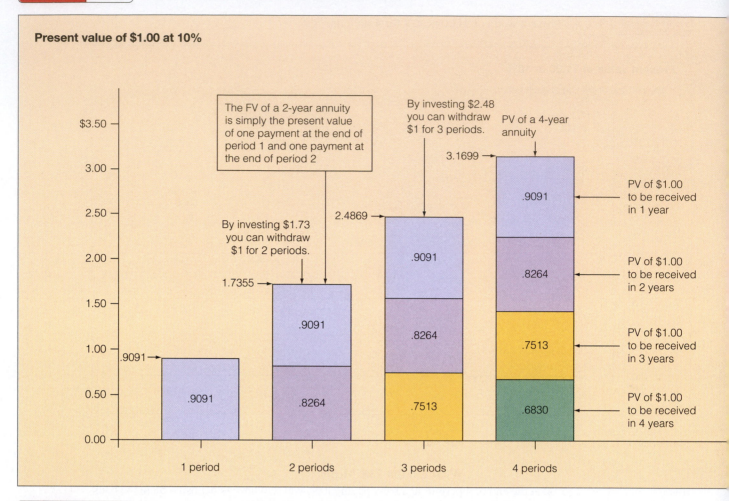

Present value of $1.00 at 10%

The FV of a 2-year annuity is simply the present value of one payment at the end of period 1 and one payment at the end of period 2

By investing $1.73 you can withdraw $1 for 2 periods.

By investing $2.48 you can withdraw $1 for 3 periods.

PV of a 4-year annuity

3.1699 →

2.4869 →

1.7355 →

.9091 →

PV of $1.00 to be received in 1 year

PV of $1.00 to be received in 2 years

PV of $1.00 to be received in 3 years

PV of $1.00 to be received in 4 years

EXHIBIT 13.4 Future value of a 4-year annuity of $1.00 at 10%

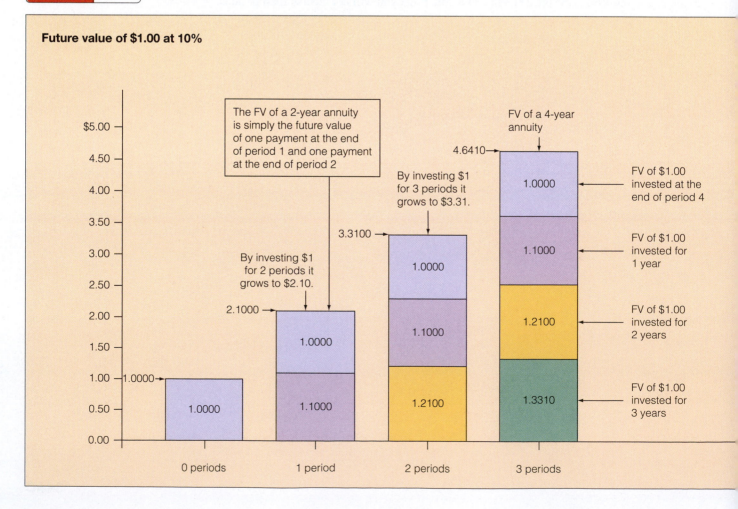

Future value of $1.00 at 10%

The FV of a 2-year annuity is simply the future value of one payment at the end of period 1 and one payment at the end of period 2

By investing $1 for 3 periods it grows to $3.31.

FV of a 4-year annuity

4.6410 →

3.3100 →

2.1000 →

1.0000 →

By investing $1 for 2 periods it grows to $2.10.

FV of $1.00 invested at the end of period 4

FV of $1.00 invested for 1 year

FV of $1.00 invested for 2 years

FV of $1.00 invested for 3 years

What Exhibit 13.3 Means*

BLUE BOX
(Top box)

Blue shows how to receive $1.00 after 1 period. You must put in $.91 today.

PURPLE BOX
(2nd box from top)

Purple shows how to receive $1.00 after 2 periods. You must put in $.83 today to get $1.00 for 2 periods. You must put in the bank today $1.74 ($.91 + $.83) to take out $1.00 for 2 periods.

YELLOW BOX
(3rd box from top)

Yellow shows how to receive $1.00 after 3 periods. You must put in $.75 today to get $1.00 for 3 periods. You also must put in the bank today $2.49 ($.91 + $.83 + $.75) to take out $1.00 for 3 periods.

GREEN BOX
(4th box from top)

Green shows how to receive $1.00 after 4 periods. You must put in $.68 today to get $1.00 for 4 periods. You also must put in the bank today $3.17 ($.91 + $.83 + $.75 + $.68) to take out $1.00 for 4 periods.

What Exhibit 13.4 Means*

BLUE BOX
(Top box)

Blue shows $1.00 invested at the end of each period. The $1.00 has no time to earn interest.

PURPLE BOX
(2nd box from top)

Purple shows the value of $1.00 after 2 periods. The $1.00 is now worth $1.10 due to compounding for 1 period.

YELLOW BOX
(3rd box from top)

Yellow shows the value of $1.00 after 3 periods. The $1.00 is now worth $1.21 due to compounding for 2 periods.

GREEN BOX
(4th box from top)

Green shows that the value of $1.00 after 4 periods is $1.33 due to compounding for 3 periods. If you put $1.00 in the bank at 10% for 4 years, the $4.00 grows to $4.64.

*From table in Handbook for 10%.

Periods	Amount of annuity	Present value of an annuity
1	1.0000	.9091
2	2.1000	1.7355
3	3.3100	2.4869
4	4.6410	3.1699

Classroom Notes

Classroom Notes

CHAPTER 14

Installment Buying

© NetPhotos/Alamy

E-Z Terms — THE 97-Month Car Loan — 8 Years to Pay

$31,032* — $460 a month**

By MIKE RAMSEY

Last month Nakisha Bishop took out a loan to buy a $23,000 Toyota Camry and pay off several thousand dollars still owed on her old car. The key to making it work: she got more than six years—75 months in all—to pay it off.

"I had a new baby on the way, and I was trying to keep my monthly payment a little bit lower to help afford child care," Ms. Bishop, a 34-year-old sheriff's deputy in Palm Beach County, Fla., said recently. She pays $480 a month for the 2013 Camry, just $5 a month more than the note on her old car. The car won't be paid off until her 1-month-old daughter is heading to first grade.

Ms. Bishop's 75-month loan illustrates two important trends rippling through the U.S. auto industry. Rising new-car prices and competition among lenders to attract borrowers is pushing loans to lengthier terms. In part, banks see the longer terms as a way to attract buyers, by keeping monthly payments under $500 a month.

The average price of a new car is now $31,000, up $3,000 in the past four years. But at the same time, the average monthly car payment edged down, to $460 from $465—the result of longer loan terms and lower interest rates.

In the final quarter of 2012, the average term of a new car note stretched out to 65 months, the longest ever, according to Experian Information Solutions Inc. Experian said that 17% of all new car loans in the past quarter were between 73 and 84 months and there were even a few as long as 97 months. Four years ago, only 11% of loans fell into this category.

Such long term loans can present consumers and lenders with heightened risk. With a six- or seven-year loan, it takes car-buyers longer to reach the point where they owe less on the car than it is worth. Having "negative equity" in a car makes it harder to trade or sell the vehicle if the owner can't make payments.

Car makers have mixed feelings about long-term loans. They allow consumers to buy more expensive—and profitable—cars. But long loans may keep some people from replacing their cars, cutting into future sales.

Few lenders were willing to *Please turn to the next page*

* The average price paid in 2012 for a new car, up $3,099 from the average price paid in 2007.

** Monthly payments were basically flat in the fourth quarter, compared with $473 in the first quarter of 2008.

Reprinted by permission of *The Wall Street Journal*, copyright 2013 Dow Jones & Company, Inc. All rights reserved worldwide.

Santander CONSUMER

Auto Loans SIMPLIFIED

Through its Drive®, RoadLoans® and Santander Auto Finance brands, Santander Consumer USA Inc. offers automotive financing through dealer partners and directly to consumers via the Internet. Our finance programs help consumers with a wide range of credit situations purchase quality vehicles.

MY ACCOUNT LOGIN 🔒
USER ID

PASSWORD

LOGIN

Forgot User ID?
Forgot Password?

CUSTOMER SUPPORT

If you have account questions or need 24/7 support, you're in the right place.

- Make a Payment
- Contact Customer Service
- Customer FAQ

OUR DEALERS

Resources to help you get your deals funded quickly and consistently.

- Become a Dealer Partner
- Dealer Extranet Login
- Dealer FAQ

Learn how a simple interest loan works and how we calculate your monthly payment by watching this short, but informative video.
Learn More About Our Loans

LU 14–1: Cost of Installment Buying

1. Calculate the amount financed, finance charge, and deferred payment.
2. Calculate the estimated APR by table lookup.
3. Calculate the monthly payment by formula and by table lookup.

LU 14–2: Revolving Charge Credit Cards

1. Calculate the finance charges on revolving charge credit card accounts.

VOCABULARY PREVIEW

Here are key terms in this chapter. After completing the chapter, if you know the term, place a checkmark in the box. If you don't know the term, look it up and put the page number where it can be found.

Amortization ☐ Amount financed ☐ Annual percentage rate (APR) ☐ Average daily balance ☐ Cash advance ☐ Credit Card Act ☐ Daily balance ☐ Deferred payment price ☐ Down payment ☐ Fair Credit and Charge Card Disclosure Act of 1988 ☐ Finance charge ☐ Installment loan ☐ Loan amortization table ☐ Open-end credit ☐ Outstanding balance ☐ Revolving charge account ☐ Truth in Lending Act ☐

The *Wall Street Journal* clip, "How to Fix a Credit-Report Error—Before It Bites Back" shows 1 out of 4 people surveyed found an error that impacted their credit report negatively. Fixing your credit report is important because it can impact the interest rate you pay and may even determine if you get offered a job.

How to Fix a Credit-Report Error—Before It Bites Back

What you don't know might hurt you.

That is a key conclusion that jumps out from a recent **Federal Trade Commission** study on errors in credit reports, those all-important records that determine whether we get credit, what interest rates we pay and sometimes whether we get a job.

In the FTC study, 262 of the 1,001 people who reviewed their credit reports spotted at least one potential "material" mistake, such as a credit-card account that wasn't theirs or a late payment that they didn't believe was late.

When the participants disputed the information with credit bureaus **Experian, Equifax** or **TransUnion**, 206 people

saw at least one credit-report change—a recognition some data was indeed wrong or couldn't be verified.

Because a credit score is generated based on information in the report, consumers can be penalized for someone else's bad behavior.

◆ An identity thief could open an account in your name or change one of your accounts to a different address and then run up debts that won't be paid. People might not learn of such accounts until debt collectors start calling.

◆ Bills that were paid might not be posted or might be posted to the wrong account, or amounts owed might be incorrect. In addition, a medical bill that your insurer was supposed to pay but didn't might linger as an unpaid debt, says Ed Mierzwinski, consumer

program director at the U.S. Public Interest Research Group, an advocacy organization based in Boston.

The lender also should be contacted and asked to fix the problem.

The credit bureaus resolve some disputes in house, but most are assigned a code that is sent to the debt holder, sometimes with a brief explanation. The debt holder then either acknowledges an error or rejects it without ever seeing supporting documentation.

Starting in June, the industry's information-exchange network will allow files to be attached so credit bureaus can send documentation to lenders, says Steve Wagner, president of Experian's North American credit-bureau operations.

Reprinted by permission of *The Wall Street Journal*, copyright 2013 Dow Jones & Company, Inc. All rights reserved worldwide.

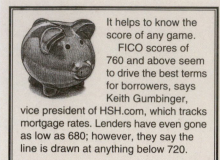

It helps to know the score of any game. FICO scores of 760 and above seem to drive the best terms for borrowers, says Keith Gumbinger, vice president of HSH.com, which tracks mortgage rates. Lenders have even gone as low as 680; however, they say the line is drawn at anything below 720.

Source: *The Wall Street Journal*, 10/17/14.

The chapter opener *Wall Street Journal* clipping shows car loans are increasing in length. This clip talks about a 97-month loan and the implications of such a long car loan.

This chapter discusses the cost of buying products via installments (closed-end credit) and revolving credit card (open-end credit). You will see in Learning Unit 14–1 that to buy a 4×4 pickup a qualified buyer must have a credit score of 720 or higher (see clip below). FICO is a measure of your credit score.

Learning Unit 14–1: Cost of Installment Buying

Installment buying, a form of *closed-end credit,* can add a substantial amount to the cost of big-ticket purchases. To illustrate this, we follow the procedure of buying a pickup truck, including the amount financed, finance charge, and deferred payment price. Then we study the effect of the Truth in Lending Act.

Amount Financed, Finance Charge, and Deferred Payment

This advertisement for the sale of a pickup truck appeared in a local paper. As you can see from this advertisement, after customers make a **down payment,** they can buy the truck with an **installment loan.** This loan is paid off with a series of equal periodic payments. These payments include both interest and principal. The payment process is called **amortization.** In the promissory notes of earlier chapters, the loan was paid off in one ending payment. Now let's look at the calculations involved in buying a pickup truck.

© Scott Olson/Getty Images

$194.38 MONTH

4X4 Pickup*
$9,345

With $300 down cash or trade for 60 months at Annual Percentage Rate of 10.5%. Amt. financed—$9,045.00. Finance chg.—$2,617.80. Total note—$11,662.80. Total deferred payment price—$11,962.80. Taxes, title, insurance additional.

*Financing is available to qualified buyers with credit scores of 720 or higher.

Checking Calculations in Pickup Advertisement

Calculating Amount Financed The **amount financed** is what you actually borrow. To calculate this amount, use the following formula:

$$\text{Amount financed} = \text{Cash price} - \text{Down payment}$$

$$\$9,045 = \$9,345 - \$300$$

Calculating Finance Charge The words **"finance charge"** in the advertisement represent the *interest* charge. The interest charge resulting in the finance charge includes the cost of credit reports, mandatory bank fees, and so on. You can use the following formula to calculate the total interest on the loan:

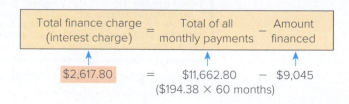

$$\begin{array}{c}\text{Total finance charge} \\ \text{(interest charge)}\end{array} = \begin{array}{c}\text{Total of all} \\ \text{monthly payments}\end{array} - \begin{array}{c}\text{Amount} \\ \text{financed}\end{array}$$

$$\$2,617.80 = \$11,662.80 - \$9,045$$
$$(\$194.38 \times 60 \text{ months})$$

Calculating Deferred Payment Price The **deferred payment price** represents the total of all monthly payments plus the down payment. The following formula is used to calculate the deferred payment price:

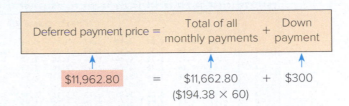

$$
\text{Deferred payment price} = \frac{\text{Total of all}}{\text{monthly payments}} + \frac{\text{Down}}{\text{payment}}
$$

$$
\$11,962.80 \quad = \quad \$11,662.80 \quad + \quad \$300
$$
$$
(\$194.38 \times 60)
$$

Truth in Lending: APR Defined and Calculated

In 1969, the Federal Reserve Board established the **Truth in Lending Act** (Regulation Z). The law doesn't regulate interest charges; its purpose is to make the consumer aware of the true cost of credit.

The Truth in Lending Act requires that creditors provide certain basic information about the actual cost of buying on credit. Before buyers sign a credit agreement, creditors must inform them in writing of the amount of the finance charge and the **annual percentage rate (APR)**. The APR represents the true or effective annual interest creditors charge. This is helpful to buyers who repay loans over different periods of time (1 month, 48 months, and so on).

To illustrate how the APR affects the interest rate, assume you borrow $100 for 1 year and pay a finance charge of $9. Your interest rate would be 9% if you waited until the end of the year to pay back the loan. Now let's say you pay off the loan and the finance charge in 12 monthly payments. Each month that you make a payment, you are losing some of the value or use of that money. So the true or effective APR is actually greater than 9%.

The APR can be calculated by formula or by tables. We will use the table method since it is more exact.

LO 2

Calculating APR Rate by Table 14.1   Note the following steps for using a table to calculate APR:

CALCULATING APR BY TABLE
Step 1. Divide the finance charge by amount financed and multiply by $100 to get the table lookup factor.
Step 2. Go to APR Table 14.1. At the left side of the table are listed the number of payments that will be made.
Step 3. When you find the number of payments you are looking for, move to the right and look for the two numbers closest to the table lookup number. This will indicate the APR.

Now let's determine the APR for the pickup truck advertisement given earlier in the chapter.

As stated in Step 1, we begin by dividing the finance charge by the amount financed and multiply by $100:

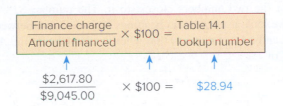

$$
\frac{\text{Finance charge}}{\text{Amount financed}} \times \$100 = \frac{\text{Table 14.1}}{\text{lookup number}}
$$

$$
\frac{\$2,617.80}{\$9,045.00} \times \$100 = \$28.94
$$

We multiply by $100, since the table is based on $100 of financing.

TABLE 14.1 Annual percentage rate table per $100

NUMBER OF PAYMENTS	ANNUAL PERCENTAGE RATE (FINANCE CHARGE PER $100 OF AMOUNT FINANCED)															
	10.00%	10.25%	10.50%	10.75%	11.00%	11.25%	11.50%	11.75%	12.00%	12.25%	12.50%	12.75%	13.00%	13.25%	13.50%	13.75%
1	0.83	0.85	0.87	0.90	0.92	0.94	0.96	0.98	1.00	1.02	1.04	1.06	1.08	1.10	1.12	1.15
2	1.25	1.28	1.31	1.35	1.38	1.41	1.44	1.47	1.50	1.53	1.57	1.60	1.63	1.66	1.69	1.72
3	1.67	1.71	1.76	1.80	1.84	1.88	1.92	1.96	2.01	2.05	2.09	2.13	2.17	2.22	2.26	2.30
4	2.09	2.14	2.20	2.25	2.30	2.35	2.41	2.46	2.51	2.57	2.62	2.67	2.72	2.78	2.83	2.88
5	2.51	2.58	2.64	2.70	2.77	2.83	2.89	2.96	3.02	3.08	3.15	3.21	3.27	3.34	3.40	3.46
6	2.94	3.01	3.08	3.16	3.23	3.31	3.38	3.45	3.53	3.60	3.68	3.75	3.83	3.90	3.97	4.05
7	3.36	3.45	3.53	3.62	3.70	3.78	3.87	3.95	4.04	4.12	4.21	4.29	4.38	4.47	4.55	4.64
8	3.79	3.88	3.98	4.07	4.17	4.26	4.36	4.46	4.55	4.65	4.74	4.84	4.94	5.03	5.13	5.22
9	4.21	4.32	4.43	4.53	4.64	4.75	4.85	4.96	5.07	5.17	5.28	5.39	5.49	5.60	5.71	5.82
10	4.64	4.76	4.88	4.99	5.11	5.23	5.35	5.46	5.58	5.70	5.82	5.94	6.05	6.17	6.29	6.41
11	5.07	5.20	5.33	5.45	5.58	5.71	5.84	5.97	6.10	6.23	6.36	6.49	6.62	6.75	6.88	7.01
12	5.50	5.64	5.78	5.92	6.06	6.20	6.34	6.48	6.62	6.76	6.90	7.04	7.18	7.32	7.46	7.60
13	5.93	6.08	6.23	6.38	6.53	6.68	6.84	6.99	7.14	7.29	7.44	7.59	7.75	7.90	8.05	8.20
14	6.36	6.52	6.69	6.85	7.01	7.17	7.34	7.50	7.66	7.82	7.99	8.15	8.31	8.48	8.64	8.81
15	6.80	6.97	7.14	7.32	7.49	7.66	7.84	8.01	8.19	8.36	8.53	8.71	8.88	9.06	9.23	9.41
16	7.23	7.41	7.60	7.78	7.97	8.15	8.34	8.53	8.71	8.90	9.08	9.27	9.46	9.64	9.83	10.02
17	7.67	7.86	8.06	8.25	8.45	8.65	8.84	9.04	9.24	9.44	9.63	9.83	10.03	10.23	10.43	10.63
18	8.10	8.31	8.52	8.73	8.93	9.14	9.35	9.56	9.77	9.98	10.19	10.40	10.61	10.82	11.03	11.24
19	8.54	8.76	8.98	9.20	9.42	9.64	9.86	10.08	10.30	10.52	10.74	10.96	11.18	11.41	11.63	11.85
20	8.98	9.21	9.44	9.67	9.90	10.13	10.37	10.60	10.83	11.06	11.30	11.53	11.76	12.00	12.23	12.46
21	9.42	9.66	9.90	10.15	10.39	10.63	10.88	11.12	11.36	11.61	11.85	12.10	12.34	12.59	12.84	13.08
22	9.86	10.12	10.37	10.62	10.88	11.13	11.39	11.64	11.90	12.16	12.41	12.67	12.93	13.19	13.44	13.70
23	10.30	10.57	10.84	11.10	11.37	11.63	11.90	12.17	12.44	12.71	12.97	13.24	13.51	13.78	14.05	14.32
24	10.75	11.02	11.30	11.58	11.86	12.14	12.42	12.70	12.98	13.26	13.54	13.82	14.10	14.38	14.66	14.95
25	11.19	11.48	11.77	12.06	12.35	12.64	12.93	13.22	13.52	13.81	14.10	14.40	14.69	14.98	15.28	15.57
26	11.64	11.94	12.24	12.54	12.85	13.15	13.45	13.75	14.06	14.36	14.67	14.97	15.28	15.59	15.89	16.20
27	12.09	12.40	12.71	13.03	13.34	13.66	13.97	14.29	14.60	14.92	15.24	15.56	15.87	16.19	16.51	16.83
28	12.53	12.86	13.18	13.51	13.84	14.16	14.49	14.82	15.15	15.48	15.81	16.14	16.47	16.80	17.13	17.46
29	12.98	13.32	13.66	14.00	14.33	14.67	15.01	15.35	15.70	16.04	16.38	16.72	17.07	17.41	17.75	18.10
30	13.43	13.78	14.13	14.48	14.83	15.19	15.54	15.89	16.24	16.60	16.95	17.31	17.66	18.02	18.38	18.74
31	13.89	14.25	14.61	14.97	15.33	15.70	16.06	16.43	16.79	17.16	17.53	17.90	18.27	18.63	19.00	19.38
32	14.34	14.71	15.09	15.46	15.84	16.21	16.59	16.97	17.35	17.73	18.11	18.49	18.87	19.25	19.63	20.02
33	14.79	15.18	15.57	15.95	16.34	16.73	17.12	17.51	17.90	18.29	18.69	19.08	19.47	19.87	20.26	20.66
34	15.25	15.65	16.05	16.44	16.85	17.25	17.65	18.05	18.46	18.86	19.27	19.67	20.08	20.49	20.90	21.31
35	15.70	16.11	16.53	16.94	17.35	17.77	18.18	18.60	19.01	19.43	19.85	20.27	20.69	21.11	21.53	21.95
36	16.16	16.58	17.01	17.43	17.86	18.29	18.71	19.14	19.57	20.00	20.43	20.87	21.30	21.73	22.17	22.60
37	16.62	17.06	17.49	17.93	18.37	18.81	19.25	19.69	20.13	20.58	21.02	21.46	21.91	22.36	22.81	23.25
38	17.08	17.53	17.98	18.43	18.88	19.33	19.78	20.24	20.69	21.15	21.61	22.07	22.52	22.99	23.45	23.91
39	17.54	18.00	18.46	18.93	19.39	19.86	20.32	20.79	21.26	21.73	22.20	22.67	23.14	23.61	24.09	24.56
40	18.00	18.48	18.95	19.43	19.90	20.38	20.86	21.34	21.82	22.30	22.79	23.27	23.76	24.25	24.73	25.22
41	18.47	18.95	19.44	19.93	20.42	20.91	21.40	21.89	22.39	22.88	23.38	23.88	24.38	24.88	25.38	25.88
42	18.93	19.43	19.93	20.43	20.93	21.44	21.94	22.45	22.96	23.47	23.98	24.49	25.00	25.51	26.03	26.55
43	19.40	19.91	20.42	20.94	21.45	21.97	22.49	23.01	23.53	24.05	24.57	25.10	25.62	26.15	26.68	27.21
44	19.86	20.39	20.91	21.44	21.97	22.50	23.03	23.57	24.10	24.64	25.17	25.71	26.25	26.79	27.33	27.88
45	20.33	20.87	21.41	21.95	22.49	23.03	23.58	24.12	24.67	25.22	25.77	26.32	26.88	27.43	27.99	28.55
46	20.80	21.35	21.90	22.46	23.01	23.57	24.13	24.69	25.25	25.81	26.37	26.94	27.51	28.08	28.65	29.22
47	21.27	21.83	22.40	22.97	23.53	24.10	24.68	25.25	25.82	26.40	26.98	27.56	28.14	28.72	29.31	29.89
48	21.74	22.32	22.90	23.48	24.06	24.64	25.23	25.81	26.40	26.99	27.58	28.18	28.77	29.37	29.97	30.57
49	22.21	22.80	23.39	23.99	24.58	25.18	25.78	26.38	26.98	27.59	28.19	28.80	29.41	30.02	30.63	31.24
50	22.69	23.29	23.89	24.50	25.11	25.72	26.33	26.95	27.56	28.18	28.80	29.42	30.04	30.67	31.29	31.92
51	23.16	23.78	24.40	25.02	25.64	26.26	26.89	27.52	28.15	28.78	29.41	30.05	30.68	31.32	31.96	32.60
52	23.64	24.27	24.90	25.53	26.17	26.81	27.45	28.09	28.73	29.38	30.02	30.67	31.32	31.98	32.63	33.29
53	24.11	24.76	25.40	26.05	26.70	27.35	28.00	28.66	29.32	29.98	30.64	31.30	31.97	32.63	33.30	33.97
54	24.59	25.25	25.91	26.57	27.23	27.90	28.56	29.23	29.91	30.58	31.25	31.93	32.61	33.29	33.98	34.66
55	25.07	25.74	26.41	27.09	27.77	28.44	29.13	29.81	30.50	31.18	31.87	32.56	33.26	33.95	34.65	35.35
56	25.55	26.23	26.92	27.61	28.30	28.99	29.69	30.39	31.09	31.79	32.49	33.20	33.91	34.62	35.33	36.04
57	26.03	26.73	27.43	28.13	28.84	29.54	30.25	30.97	31.68	32.39	33.11	33.83	34.56	35.28	36.01	36.74
58	26.51	27.23	27.94	28.66	29.37	30.10	30.82	31.55	32.27	33.00	33.74	34.47	35.21	35.95	36.69	37.43
59	27.00	27.72	28.45	29.18	29.91	30.65	31.39	32.13	32.87	33.61	34.36	35.11	35.86	36.62	37.37	38.13
60	27.48	28.22	28.96	29.71	30.45	31.20	31.96	32.71	33.47	34.23	34.99	35.75	36.52	37.29	38.06	38.83

Note: For a more detailed set of tables from 2% to 21.75%, see the reference tables in the *Business Math Handbook*.

To look up $28.94 in Table 14.1, we go down the left side of the table until we come to 60 payments (the advertisement states 60 months). Then, moving to the right, we look for $28.94 or the two numbers closest to it. The number $28.94 is between $28.22 and $28.96. So we look at the column headings and see a rate between 10.25% and 10.5%. The Truth in Lending Act requires that when creditors state the APR, it must be accurate to the nearest $\frac{1}{4}$ of 1%.[1]

[1]If we wanted an exact reading of APR when the number is not exactly in the table, we would use the process of interpolating. We do not cover this method in this course.

TABLE **14.1**   (concluded)

NUMBER OF PAYMENTS	\multicolumn{16}{c}{ANNUAL PERCENTAGE RATE}

NUMBER OF PAYMENTS	14.00%	14.25%	14.50%	14.75%	15.00%	15.25%	15.50%	15.75%	16.00%	16.25%	16.50%	16.75%	17.00%	17.25%	17.50%	17.75%
\multicolumn{17}{c}{(FINANCE CHARGE PER \$100 OF AMOUNT FINANCED)}
1	1.17	1.19	1.21	1.23	1.25	1.27	1.29	1.31	1.33	1.35	1.37	1.40	1.42	1.44	1.46	1.48
2	1.75	1.78	1.82	1.85	1.88	1.91	1.94	1.97	2.00	2.04	2.07	2.10	2.13	2.16	2.19	2.22
3	2.34	2.38	2.43	2.47	2.51	2.55	2.59	2.64	2.68	2.72	2.76	2.80	2.85	2.89	2.93	2.97
4	2.93	2.99	3.04	3.09	3.14	3.20	3.25	3.30	3.36	3.41	3.46	3.51	3.57	3.62	3.67	3.73
5	3.53	3.59	3.65	3.72	3.78	3.84	3.91	3.97	4.04	4.10	4.16	4.23	4.29	4.35	4.42	4.48
6	4.12	4.20	4.27	4.35	4.42	4.49	4.57	4.64	4.72	4.79	4.87	4.94	5.02	5.09	5.17	5.24
7	4.72	4.81	4.89	4.98	5.06	5.15	5.23	5.32	5.40	5.49	5.58	5.66	5.75	5.83	5.92	6.00
8	5.32	5.42	5.51	5.61	5.71	5.80	5.90	6.00	6.09	6.19	6.29	6.38	6.48	6.58	6.67	6.77
9	5.92	6.03	6.14	6.25	6.35	6.46	6.57	6.68	6.78	6.89	7.00	7.11	7.22	7.32	7.43	7.54
10	6.53	6.65	6.77	6.88	7.00	7.12	7.24	7.36	7.48	7.60	7.72	7.84	7.96	8.08	8.19	8.31
11	7.14	7.27	7.40	7.53	7.66	7.79	7.92	8.05	8.18	8.31	8.44	8.57	8.70	8.83	8.96	9.09
12	7.74	7.89	8.03	8.17	8.31	8.45	8.59	8.74	8.88	9.02	9.16	9.30	9.45	9.59	9.73	9.87
13	8.36	8.51	8.66	8.81	8.97	9.12	9.27	9.43	9.58	9.73	9.89	10.04	10.20	10.35	10.50	10.66
14	8.97	9.13	9.30	9.46	9.63	9.79	9.96	10.12	10.79	10.45	10.67	10.78	10.95	11.11	11.28	11.45
15	9.59	9.76	9.94	10.11	10.29	10.47	10.64	10.82	11.00	11.17	11.35	11.53	11.71	11.88	12.06	12.24
16	10.20	10.39	10.58	10.77	10.95	11.14	11.33	11.52	11.71	11.90	12.09	12.28	12.46	12.65	12.84	13.03
17	10.82	11.02	11.22	11.42	11.62	11.82	12.02	12.22	12.42	12.62	12.83	13.03	13.23	13.43	13.63	13.83
18	11.45	11.66	11.87	12.08	12.29	12.50	12.72	12.93	13.14	13.35	13.57	13.78	13.99	14.21	14.42	14.64
19	12.07	12.30	12.52	12.74	12.97	13.19	13.41	13.64	13.86	14.09	14.31	14.54	14.76	14.99	15.22	15.44
20	12.70	12.93	13.17	13.41	13.64	13.88	14.11	14.35	14.59	14.82	15.06	15.30	15.54	15.77	16.01	16.25
21	13.33	13.58	13.82	14.07	14.32	14.57	14.82	15.06	15.31	15.56	15.81	16.06	16.31	16.56	16.81	17.07
22	13.96	14.22	14.48	14.74	15.00	15.26	15.52	15.78	16.04	16.30	16.57	16.83	17.09	17.36	17.62	17.88
23	14.59	14.87	15.14	15.41	15.68	15.96	16.23	16.50	16.78	17.05	17.32	17.60	17.88	18.15	18.43	18.70
24	15.23	15.51	15.80	16.08	16.37	16.65	16.94	17.22	17.51	17.80	18.09	18.37	18.66	18.95	19.24	19.53
25	15.87	16.17	16.46	16.76	17.06	17.35	17.65	17.95	18.25	18.55	18.85	19.15	19.45	19.75	20.05	20.36
26	16.51	16.82	17.13	17.44	17.75	18.06	18.37	18.68	18.99	19.30	19.62	19.93	20.24	20.56	20.87	21.19
27	17.15	17.47	17.80	18.12	18.44	18.76	19.09	19.41	19.74	20.06	20.39	20.71	21.04	21.37	21.69	22.02
28	17.80	18.13	18.47	18.80	19.14	19.47	19.81	20.15	20.48	20.82	21.16	21.50	21.84	22.18	22.52	22.86
29	18.45	18.79	19.14	19.49	19.83	20.18	20.53	20.89	21.23	21.58	21.94	22.29	22.64	22.99	23.35	23.70
30	19.10	19.45	19.81	20.17	20.54	20.90	21.26	21.62	21.99	22.35	22.72	23.08	23.45	23.81	24.18	24.55
31	19.75	20.12	20.49	20.87	21.24	21.61	21.99	22.37	22.74	23.12	23.50	23.88	24.26	24.64	25.02	25.40
32	20.40	20.79	21.17	21.56	21.95	22.33	22.72	23.11	23.50	23.89	24.28	24.68	25.07	25.46	25.86	26.25
33	21.06	21.46	21.85	22.25	22.65	23.06	23.46	23.86	24.26	24.67	25.07	25.48	25.88	26.29	26.70	27.11
34	21.72	22.13	22.54	22.95	23.37	23.78	24.19	24.61	25.03	25.44	25.86	26.28	26.70	27.12	27.54	27.97
35	22.38	22.80	23.23	23.65	24.08	24.51	24.94	25.36	25.79	26.23	26.66	27.09	27.52	27.96	28.39	28.83
36	23.04	23.48	23.92	24.35	24.80	25.24	25.68	26.12	26.57	27.01	27.46	27.90	28.35	28.80	29.25	29.70
37	23.70	24.16	24.61	25.06	25.51	25.97	26.42	26.88	27.34	27.80	28.26	28.72	29.18	29.64	30.10	30.57
38	24.37	24.84	25.30	25.77	26.24	26.70	27.17	27.64	28.11	28.59	29.06	29.53	30.01	30.49	30.96	31.44
39	25.04	25.52	26.00	26.48	26.96	27.44	27.92	28.41	28.89	29.38	29.87	30.36	30.85	31.34	31.83	32.32
40	25.71	26.20	26.70	27.19	27.69	28.18	28.68	29.18	29.68	30.18	30.69	31.19	31.68	32.19	32.69	33.20
41	26.39	26.89	27.40	27.91	28.41	28.92	29.44	29.95	30.46	30.97	31.49	32.01	32.52	33.04	33.56	34.08
42	27.06	27.58	28.10	28.62	29.15	29.67	30.19	30.72	31.25	31.78	32.31	32.84	33.37	33.90	34.44	34.97
43	27.74	28.27	28.81	29.34	29.88	30.42	30.96	31.50	32.04	32.58	33.13	33.67	34.22	34.76	35.31	35.86
44	28.42	28.97	29.52	30.07	30.62	31.17	31.72	32.28	32.83	33.39	33.95	34.51	35.07	35.63	36.19	36.76
45	29.11	29.67	30.23	30.79	31.36	31.92	32.49	33.06	33.63	34.20	34.77	35.35	35.92	36.50	37.08	37.66
46	29.79	30.36	30.94	31.52	32.10	32.68	33.26	33.84	34.43	35.01	35.60	36.19	36.78	37.37	37.96	38.56
47	30.48	31.07	31.66	32.25	32.84	33.44	34.03	34.63	35.23	35.83	36.43	37.04	37.64	38.25	38.86	39.46
48	31.17	31.77	32.37	32.98	33.59	34.20	34.81	35.42	36.03	36.65	37.27	37.88	38.50	39.13	39.75	40.37
49	31.86	32.48	33.09	33.71	34.34	34.96	35.59	36.21	36.84	37.47	38.10	38.74	39.37	40.01	40.65	41.29
50	32.55	33.18	33.82	34.45	35.09	35.73	36.37	37.01	37.65	38.30	38.94	39.59	40.24	40.89	41.55	42.20
51	33.25	33.89	34.54	35.19	35.84	36.49	37.15	37.81	38.46	39.12	39.79	40.45	41.11	41.78	42.45	43.12
52	33.95	34.61	35.27	35.93	36.60	37.27	37.94	38.61	39.28	39.96	40.63	41.31	41.99	42.67	43.36	44.04
53	34.65	35.32	36.00	36.68	37.36	38.04	38.72	39.41	40.10	40.79	41.48	42.17	42.87	43.57	44.27	44.97
54	35.35	36.04	36.73	37.42	38.12	38.82	39.52	40.22	40.92	41.63	42.33	43.04	43.75	44.47	45.18	45.90
55	36.05	36.76	37.46	38.17	38.88	39.60	40.31	41.03	41.74	42.47	43.19	43.91	44.64	45.37	46.10	46.83
56	36.76	37.48	38.20	38.92	39.65	40.38	41.11	41.84	42.57	43.31	44.05	44.79	45.53	46.27	47.02	47.77
57	37.47	38.20	38.94	39.68	40.42	41.16	41.91	42.65	43.40	44.15	44.91	45.66	46.42	47.18	47.94	48.71
58	38.18	38.93	39.68	40.43	41.19	41.95	42.71	43.47	44.23	45.07	45.85	46.64	47.42	48.21	49.01	49.65
59	38.89	39.66	40.42	41.19	41.96	42.74	43.51	44.29	45.07	45.85	46.64	47.42	48.21	49.01	49.80	50.60
60	39.61	40.39	41.17	41.95	42.74	43.53	44.32	45.11	45.91	46.71	47.51	48.31	49.12	49.92	50.73	51.55

LO **3**

Calculating the Monthly Payment by Formula and Table 14.2

The pickup truck advertisement showed a $194.38 monthly payment. We can check this by formula and by table lookup.

By Formula

$$\frac{\text{Finance charge} + \text{Amount financed}}{\text{Number of payments of loan}} = \frac{\$2,617.80 + \$9,045}{60} = \boxed{\$194.38}$$

TABLE 14.2									

Loan amortization table (monthly payment per $1,000 to pay principal and interest on installment loan)

Terms in months	7.50%	8.00%	8.50%	9.00%	10.00%	10.50%	11.00%	11.50%	12.00%
6	$170.34	$170.58	$170.83	$171.20	$171.56	$171.81	$172.05	$172.30	$172.55
12	86.76	86.99	87.22	87.46	87.92	88.15	88.38	88.62	88.85
18	58.92	59.15	59.37	59.60	60.06	60.29	60.52	60.75	60.98
24	45.00	45.23	45.46	45.69	46.14	46.38	46.61	46.84	47.07
30	36.66	36.89	37.12	37.35	37.81	38.04	38.28	38.51	38.75
36	31.11	31.34	31.57	31.80	32.27	32.50	32.74	32.98	33.21
42	27.15	27.38	27.62	27.85	28.32	28.55	28.79	29.03	29.28
48	24.18	24.42	24.65	24.77	25.36	25.60	25.85	26.09	26.33
54	21.88	22.12	22.36	22.59	23.07	23.32	23.56	23.81	24.06
60	20.04	20.28	20.52	20.76	21.25	21.49	21.74	21.99	22.24

By Table 14.2 The **loan amortization table** (many variations of this table are available) in Table 14.2 can be used to calculate the monthly payment for the pickup truck. To calculate a monthly payment with a table, use the following steps:

MONEY tips

Control your debt. Review your credit card's year-end summary to see where your money goes.

CALCULATING MONTHLY PAYMENT BY TABLE LOOKUP

Step 1. Divide the loan amount by $1,000 (since Table 14.2 is per $1,000):

$$\frac{\$9,045}{\$1,000} = 9.045$$

Step 2. Look up the rate (10.5%) and number of months (60). At the intersection is the table factor showing the monthly payment per $1,000.

Step 3. Multiply quotient in Step 1 by the table factor in Step 2:

9.045 × $21.49 = $194.38.

Remember that this $194.38 fixed payment includes interest and the reduction of the balance of the loan. As the number of payments increases, interest payments get smaller and the reduction of the principal gets larger.[2]

Now let's check your progress with the Practice Quiz.

LU 14–1 PRACTICE QUIZ

Complete this **Practice Quiz** to see how you are doing.

© Design Pics/Don Hammond

From the partial advertisement at the right calculate the following:

1. **a.** Amount financed.
   b. Finance charge.
   c. Deferred payment price.
   d. APR by Table 14.1.
   e. Monthly payment by formula.

$288 per month	
Sale price	$14,150
Down payment	$ 1,450
Term/Number of payments	60 months

2. Jay Miller bought a New Brunswick boat for $7,500. Jay put down $1,000 and financed the balance at 10% for 60 months. What is his monthly payment? Use Table 14.2.

[2]In Chapter 15 we give an amortization schedule for home mortgages that shows how much of each fixed payment goes to interest and how much reduces the principal. This repayment schedule also gives a running balance of the loan.

TABLE   14.2   (concluded)

Terms in months	12.50%	13.00%	13.50%	14.00%	14.50%	15.00%	15.50%	16.00%
6	$172.80	$173.04	$173.29	$173.54	$173.79	$174.03	$174.28	$174.53
12	89.08	89.32	89.55	89.79	90.02	90.26	90.49	90.73
18	61.21	61.45	61.68	61.92	62.15	62.38	62.62	62.86
24	47.31	47.54	47.78	48.01	48.25	48.49	48.72	48.96
30	38.98	39.22	39.46	39.70	39.94	40.18	40.42	40.66
36	33.45	33.69	33.94	34.18	34.42	34.67	34.91	35.16
42	29.52	29.76	30.01	30.25	30.50	30.75	31.00	31.25
48	26.58	26.83	27.08	27.33	27.58	27.83	28.08	28.34
54	24.31	24.56	24.81	25.06	25.32	25.58	25.84	26.10
60	22.50	22.75	23.01	23.27	23.53	23.79	24.05	24.32

*For **extra help** from your authors–Sharon and Jeff–see the videos in Connect.*

These videos are also available on YouTube!

✓ Solutions

1. **a.** $14,150 − $1,450 = **$12,700**

    b. $17,280 ($288 × 60) − $12,700 = **$4,580**

    c. $17,280 ($288 × 60) + $1,450 = **$18,730**

    d. $\dfrac{\$4,580}{\$12,700} \times \$100 = \$36.06$; between **12.75%** and **13%**

    e. $\dfrac{\$4,580 + \$12,700}{60} = $ **$288**

2. $\dfrac{\$6,500}{\$1,000} = 6.5 \times \$21.25 = $ **$138.13** (10%, 60 months)

LU 14–1a	**EXTRA PRACTICE QUIZ WITH WORKED-OUT SOLUTIONS**

Need more practice? Try this Extra Practice Quiz (check figures in the Interactive Chapter Organizer). Worked-out Solutions can be found in Appendix B at end of text.

From the partial advertisement at the right calculate the following:

1. **a.** Amount financed.
    b. Finance charge.
    c. Deferred payment price.
    d. APR by Table 14.1.
    e. Monthly payment by formula.

$295 per month	
Sale price	$13,999
Down payment	$ 1,480
Term/Number of payments	60 months

2. Jay Miller bought a New Brunswick boat for $9,000. Jay put down $1,000 and financed the balance at 8% for 60 months. What is his monthly payment? Use Table 14.2.

Learning Unit 14–2: Revolving Charge Credit Cards

Do you owe a balance on your credit card? Let's look at how long it will take to pay off your credit card balance by making payments for the minimum amount. Study the clipping "Pay Just the Minimum, and Get Nowhere Fast."

Dustin © 2014 Steve Kelly and Jeff Parker distributed by King Features Syndicate, Inc.

Pay Just the Minimum, and Get Nowhere Fast

THE COST—IN YEARS AND DOLLARS—OF PAYING THE MINIMUM 2% OF BALANCES ON CREDIT CARDS CHARGING 17% ANNUAL INTEREST

Balance	Total Cost	Total Time
$1,000	$2,590.35	17 years, 3 months
$2,500	$7,733.49	30 years, 3 months
$5,000	$16,305.34	40 years, 2 months

SOURCE: WWW.BANKRATE.COM

Reprinted by permission of *The Wall Street Journal,* copyright 2009 Dow Jones & Company, Inc. All rights reserved worldwide.

The clipping assumes that the minimum rate on the balance of a credit card is 2%. Note that if the annual interest cost is 17%, it will take 17 years, 3 months to pay off a balance of $1,000, and the total cost will be $2,590.35. If the balance on your revolving charge credit card is more than $1,000, you can see how fast the total cost rises. If you cannot afford the total cost of paying only the minimum, it is time for you to reconsider how you use your revolving credit card. This is why when you have financial difficulties, experts often advise you first to work on getting rid of your revolving credit card debt.

Do you know why revolving credit cards are so popular? Businesses encourage customers to use credit cards because consumers tend to buy more when they can use a credit card for their purchases. Consumers find credit cards convenient to use and valuable in establishing credit. The problem is that when consumers do not pay their balance in full each month, they do not realize how expensive it is to pay only the minimum of their balance. American Express offered a card called Serve that does not allow a customer to carry a balance. It is a *prepaid* card. It allows customers to use their smartphone to transfer money and pay for their purchases.

To protect consumers, Congress passed the **Fair Credit and Charge Card Disclosure Act of 1988.** This act requires that for direct-mail application or solicitation, credit card companies must provide specific details involving all fees, grace period, calculation of finance charges, and so on. In 2009 the **Credit Card Act** was passed to provide better consumer protection in dealing with credit card companies (see the chapter opener clip).

We begin the unit by seeing how Moe's Furniture Store calculates the finance charge on Abby Jordan's previous month's credit card balance. Then we learn how to calculate the average daily balance on the partial bill of Joan Ring.

LO 1

Calculating Finance Charge on Previous Month's Balance

Abby Jordan bought a dining room set for $8,000 on credit. She has a **revolving charge account** at Moe's Furniture Store. A revolving charge account gives a buyer **open-end credit.** Abby can make as many purchases on credit as she wants until she reaches her maximum $10,000 credit limit.

Often customers do not completely pay their revolving charge accounts at the end of a billing period. When this occurs, stores add interest charges to the customers' bills. Moe's Furniture Store calculates its interest using the *unpaid balance method.* It charges $1\frac{1}{2}\%$ on the *previous month's balance,* or 18% per year. Moe's has no minimum monthly payment (many stores require $10 or $15, or a percent of the outstanding balance).

Abby has no other charges on her revolving charge account. She plans to pay $500 per month until she completely pays off her dining room set. Abby realizes that when she makes a payment, Moe's Furniture Store first applies the money toward the interest and then reduces the **outstanding balance** due. (This is the U.S. Rule we discussed in Chapter 10.) For her own information, Abby worked out the first 3-month schedule of payments, shown in Table 14.3. Note how the interest payment is the rate times the outstanding balance.

Today, most companies with credit card accounts calculate the finance charge, or interest, as a percentage of the average daily balance. Interest on credit cards can be very expensive for consumers; however, interest is a source of income for credit card companies. In the exhibit shown to the left, note the late payment warning

$20.00   **$957.19**

Payment Due Date:

01/16/2015   Payment must be received by 5:00 PM local time on the payment due date.

Late Payment Warning: If we do not receive your minimum payment by the date listed above, you may have to pay a late fee of up to $35 and your APRs may be increased up to the variable Penalty APR of 29.99%.

TABLE 14.3	Schedule of payments				
Monthly payment number	Outstanding balance due	$1\frac{1}{2}$% interest payment	Amount of monthly payment	Reduction in balance due	Outstanding balance due
1	$8,000.00	$120.00 (.015 × $8,000.00)	$500.00	$380.00 ($500.00 − $120.00)	$7,620.00 ($8,000.00 − $380.00)
2	$7,620.00	$114.30 (.015 × $7,620.00)	$500.00	$385.70 ($500.00 − $114.30)	$7,234.30 ($7,620.00 − $385.70)
3	$7,234.30	$108.51 (.015 × $7,234.30)	$500.00	$391.49 ($500.00 − $108.51)	$6,842.81 ($7,234.30 − $391.49)

issued by the credit card company. It states that a late payment could result in interest penalties close to 30%. The following is a letter I received from my credit card company when I questioned how my finance charge was calculated.

How Citibank Calculates My Finance Charge

Thank you for your recent inquiry regarding your Citi® / AAdvantage® MasterCard® account and how finance charges are calculated.

Finance charges for purchases, balance transfers, and cash advances will begin to accrue from the date the transaction is added to your balance. They will continue to accrue until payment in full is credited to your account. This means that when you make your final payment on these balances, you will be billed finance charges for the time between the date your last statement prints and the date your payment is received.

Paying your purchase balance in full each billing period by the payment due date saves you money because it allows you to take advantage of your grace period on purchases, which is not less than 20 days. You can avoid periodic finance charges on purchases (excluding balance transfers) that appear on your current billing statement if you paid the New Balance on the last statement by the payment due date on that statement and you pay your New Balance by the payment due date on your current statement. If you made a balance transfer, you may be unable to avoid periodic finance charges on new purchases, as described in the balance transfer offer.

© 2013 Tribune Content Agency, LLC; Brookins Art, LLC

Calculating Average Daily Balance   Let's look at the following steps for calculating the **average daily balance.** Remember that a **cash advance** is a cash loan from a credit card company.

CALCULATING AVERAGE DAILY BALANCE AND FINANCE CHARGE

Step 1. Calculate the daily balance or amount owed at the end of each day during the billing cycle:

$$\text{Daily balance} = \text{Previous balance} + \text{Cash advances} + \text{Purchases} - \text{Payments} - \text{Credits}$$

Step 2. When the daily balance is the same for more than 1 day, multiply it by the number of days the daily balance remained the same, or the number of days of the current balance. This gives a cumulative daily balance.

Step 3. Add the cumulative daily balances.

Step 4. Divide the sum of the cumulative daily balances by the number of days in the billing cycle.

Step 5. Finance charge = Rate per month × Average daily balance.

Step 6.* New balance = Previous balance + Cash advances + Purchases − Payments − Credits + Finance charge

Always check the number of days in the billing cycle. The cycle may not be 30 or 31 days.

Following is the partial bill of Joan Ring and an explanation of how Joan's average daily balance and finance charge were calculated. Note how we calculated each **daily balance** and then multiplied each daily balance by the number of days the balance remained the same. Take a moment to study how we arrived at 8 days. The total of the cumulative daily balances was $16,390. To get the average daily balance, we divided by the number of days in the billing cycle—30. Joan's finance charge is $1\frac{1}{2}\%$ per month on the average daily balance.

30-day billing cycle		
6/20	Billing date Previous balance	$450
6/27	Payment	$ 50 cr.
6/30	Charge: JCPenney	200
7/9	Payment	40 cr.
7/12	Cash advance	60

7 days had a balance of $450

30-day cycle − 22 (7 + 3 + 9 + 3) equals 8 days left with a balance of $620.

MONEY tips

Don't fall behind. Social media is the new method many companies are choosing to interact with their customers. Mobile technologies are used by 60% of small businesses. Apps are available to calculate retirement needs, mortgages, interest on a loan, and so much more.

	No. of days of current balance	**Current daily balance**	**Extension**
Step 1 →	7	$450	$ 3,150 ← Step 2
	3	400 ($450 − $50)	1,200
	9	600 ($400 + $200)	5,400
	3	560 ($600 − $40)	1,680
	8	620 ($560 + $60)	4,960
	30		$16,390 ← Step 3

$$\text{Average daily balance} = \frac{\$16,390}{30} = \boxed{\$546.33} \quad ← \text{Step 4}$$

Step 5 →   Finance charge = $546.33 × .015 = $8.19

Step 6 → $450 + $60 + $200 − $40 − $50 + $8.19 = $628.19

Now try the following Practice Quiz to check your understanding of this unit.

*Note: there is a shortcut to this formula. Take the last current daily balance and add the finance charge to it: $620 + $8.19 = $628.19

LU 14–2   PRACTICE QUIZ

Complete this **Practice Quiz** to see how you are doing.

1. Calculate the balance outstanding at the end of month 2 (use U.S. Rule) given the following: purchased $600 desk at the beginning of month 1; pay back $40 per month; and charge of $2\frac{1}{2}\%$ interest on unpaid balance.

2. Calculate the average daily balance and finance charge from the information that follows.

31-day billing cycle			
8/20	Billing date	Previous balance	$210
8/27	Payment		$50 cr.
8/31	Charge: Staples		30
9/5	Payment		10 cr.
9/10	Cash advance		60

Rate = 2% per month on average daily balance.

For **extra help** from your authors–Sharon and Jeff–see the videos in Connect.

These videos are also available on YouTube!

✓ **Solutions**

1.

Month	Balance due	Interest	Monthly payment	Reduction in balance	Balance outstanding
1	$600	$15.00 (.025 × $600)	$40	$25.00 ($40 − $15)	$575.00
2	$575	$14.38 (.025 × $575)	$40	$25.62	$549.38

2. Average daily balance calculated as follows:

No. of days of current balance	Current balance	Extension
7	$210	$1,470
4	160 ($210 − $50)	640
5	190 ($160 + $30)	950
5	180 ($190 − $10)	900
10	240 ($180 + $60)	2,400
31		$6,360

31 − 21 (7 + 4 + 5 + 5) ──→ 10

$$\text{Average daily balance} = \frac{\$6,360}{31} = \$205.16$$

$$\text{Finance charge} = \$4.10 \ (\$205.16 \times .02)$$

LU 14–2a   EXTRA PRACTICE QUIZ WITH WORKED-OUT SOLUTIONS

Need more practice? Try this **Extra Practice Quiz** (check figures in the Interactive Chapter Organizer). Worked-out Solutions can be found in Appendix B at end of text.

1. Calculate the balance outstanding at the end of month 2 (use U.S. Rule) given the following: purchased $300 desk at the beginning of month 1; pay back $20 per month; and charge of $1\frac{1}{4}\%$ interest on unpaid balance.

2. Calculate the average daily balance and finance charge from the following information:

31-day billing cycle			
8/21	Billing date	Previous balance	$400
8/24	Payment		$100 cr.
8/31	Charge: Staples		60
9/5	Payment		20 cr.
9/10	Cash Advance		200

Finance charge is 2% on average daily balance.

INTERACTIVE CHAPTER ORGANIZER

Topic/Procedure/Formula	Examples	You try it*
Amount financed $\dfrac{\text{Amount}}{\text{financed}} = \dfrac{\text{Cash}}{\text{price}} - \dfrac{\text{Down}}{\text{payment}}$	60 payments of $125.67 per month; cash price $5,295 with a $95 down payment Cash price $5,295 − Down payment − 95 = Amount financed $5,200	**Calculate amount financed** 60 payments of $129.99 per month; Cash price $5,400 with a $100 down payment
Total finance charge (interest) $\dfrac{\text{Total}}{\text{finance}} = \dfrac{\text{Total of}}{\text{all monthly}} - \dfrac{\text{Amount}}{\text{financed}}$ $\text{charge} \quad\quad \text{payments}$	*(continued from above)* $\dfrac{\$125.67}{\text{per month}} \times \dfrac{60}{\text{months}} = \$7,540.20$ − Amount financed − 5,200.00 = Finance charge $2,340.20	**Calculate total finance charge** *(continued from above)*
Deferred payment price $\dfrac{\text{Deferred}}{\text{payment}} = \dfrac{\text{Total of}}{\text{all monthly}} + \dfrac{\text{Down}}{\text{payment}}$ $\text{price} \quad\quad \text{payments}$	*(continued from above)* $7,540.20 + $95 = $7,635.20	**Calculate deferred payment price** *(continued from above)*
Calculating APR by Table 14.1 $\dfrac{\text{Finance charge}}{\text{Amount financed}} \times \$100 = \dfrac{\text{Table 14.1}}{\text{lookup number}}$	*(continued from above)* $\dfrac{\$2,340.20}{\$5,200.00} \times \$100 = \$45.004$ Search in Table 14.1 between 15.50% and 15.75% for 60 payments.	**Calculate APR by table** *(continued from above)*

Monthly payment
By formula:
$\dfrac{\text{Finance charge} + \text{Amount financed}}{\text{Number of payments of loan}}$
By table:
$\dfrac{\text{Loan}}{\$1,000} \times \dfrac{\text{Table}}{\text{factor}} \text{(rate, months)}$
	(continued from above)
	$\dfrac{\$2,340.20 + \$5,200.00}{60} = \$125.67$
	Given: 15.5%
	     60 months
	     $5,200 loan
	$\dfrac{\$5,200}{\$1,000} = 5.2 \times \$24.05 = \$125.06$
	    (off due to rounding of rate)
		Calculate monthly payment
		(continued from above; use 16%)

Open-end credit Monthly payment applied to interest first before reducing balance outstanding.	$4,000 purchase $250 a month payment $2\frac{1}{2}$% interest on unpaid balance $4,000 × .025 = $100 interest $250 − $100 = $150 to lower balance $4,000 − $150 = $3,850 Balance outstanding after month 1.	**Calculate balance outstanding after month 1** $5,000 purchase; $275 monthly payment; $3\frac{1}{2}$% interest on unpaid balance

Average daily balance and finance charge
 	
$\dfrac{\text{Daily}}{\text{balance}} = \dfrac{\text{Previous}}{\text{balance}} + \dfrac{\text{Cash}}{\text{advances}}$
     + Purchases − Payments
     − Credits
 	
$\dfrac{\text{Average}}{\text{daily}} = \dfrac{\text{Sum of cumulative daily balances}}{\text{Number of days in billing cycle}}$
balance
 	
$\dfrac{\text{Finance}}{\text{charge}} = \dfrac{\text{Monthly}}{\text{rate}} \times \dfrac{\text{Average}}{\text{daily}}$
balance
	30-day billing cycle; $1\frac{1}{2}$% finance charge per month
	Example: 8/21 Balance $100
	         8/29 Payment $10
	         9/12 Charge 50
	
	30-day billing cycle less the 8 and 14.
	Average daily balance equals:
	8 days × $100 = $ 800
	14 days × 90 = 1,260
	8 days × 140 = 1,120
	            $3,180 ÷ 30
	Average daily balance = $106
	Finance charge = $106 × .015 = $1.59
		Calculate daily balance and finance charge
		30-day billing cycle; $2\frac{1}{2}$% finance charge per month
		Given: 9/4 bal $200
		        9/16 payment $80
		        9/20 charge $60

(continues)

INTERACTIVE CHAPTER ORGANIZER

KEY TERMS	Amortization Amount financed Annual percentage rate (APR) Average daily balance Cash advance Credit Card Act	Daily balance Deferred payment price Down payment Fair Credit and Charge Card Disclosure Act of 1988 Finance charge	Installment loan Loan amortization table Open-end credit Outstanding balance Revolving charge account Truth in Lending Act

Check Figures for Extra Practice Quizzes. (Worked-out Solutions are in Appendix B.)	LU 14–1a
	1. a. $12,519
	   b. $5,181
	   c. $19,180
	   d. Bet. 14.50%–14.75%
	   e. $295
	2. $162.24
			LU 14–2a
			1. $267.30
			   end of month 2
			2. $410.97
			   $8.22

*Worked-out solutions are in Appendix B.

Critical Thinking Discussion Questions with Chapter Concept Check

1. Explain how to calculate the amount financed, finance charge, and APR by table lookup. Do you think the Truth in Lending Act should regulate interest charges?

2. Explain how to use the loan amortization table. Check with a person who owns a home and find out what part of each payment goes to pay interest versus the amount that reduces the loan principal.

3. What steps are used to calculate the average daily balance? Many credit card companies charge 18% annual interest. Do you think this is a justifiable rate? Defend your answer.

4. **Chapter Concept Check.** Visit the web and find information on how social networks like Facebook have had some influence on credit card companies' policies. Defend your position with the concepts learned in this chapter.

Classroom Notes

END-OF-CHAPTER PROBLEMS

connect plus+

Check figures for odd-numbered problems in Appendix C.   Name _____   Date _____

DRILL PROBLEMS

Complete the following table: *LU 14-1(1)*

	Purchase price of product	Down payment	Amount financed	Number of monthly payments	Amount of monthly payments	Total of monthly payments	Total finance charge
14–1.	Porsche Macan Turbo $73,900	$50,000		60	$518		
14–2.	Schwinn Mountain Bike $250	$100		12	$15.50		

Calculate **(a)** the amount financed, **(b)** the total finance charge, and **(c)** APR by table lookup.   *LU 14-1(1, 2)*

	Purchase price of a used car	Down payment	Number of monthly payments	Amount financed	Total of monthly payments	Total finance charge	APR
14–3.	$5,673	$1,223	48		$5,729.76		
14–4.	$4,195	$95	60		$5,944.00		

Calculate the monthly payment for Problems 14–3 and 14–4 by table lookup and formula. (Answers will not be exact due to rounding of percents in table lookup.)   *LU 14-1(3)*

14–5. **(14–3)** (Use 13% for table lookup.)

14–6. **(14–4)** (Use 15.5% for table lookup.)

14–7. Calculate the average daily balance and finance charge.   *LU 14-2(1)*

30-day billing cycle		
9/16	Billing date Previous balance	$2,000
9/19	Payment	$ 60 cr.
9/30	Charge: Home Depot	1,500
10/3	Payment	60 cr.
10/7	Cash advance	70
Finance charge is $1\frac{1}{2}$% on average daily balance		

WORD PROBLEMS

14–8. Before purchasing a used car, Cody Lind checked www.kbb.com to learn what he should offer for the used car he wanted to buy. Then he conducted a carfax.com search on the car he found to see if the car had ever been in an accident. The Carfax was clean so he purchased the used car for $14,750. He put $2,000 down and financed the rest with a 48-month, 7.5% loan. What is his monthly car payment by table lookup? *LU 14-1(1, 2)*

14–9. Troy Juth wants to purchase new dive equipment for Underwater Connection, his retail store in Colorado Springs. He was offered a $56,000 loan at 5% for 48 months. What is his monthly payment by formula? *LU 14-1(3)*

14–10. Ramon Hernandez saw the following advertisement for a used Volkswagen Bug and decided to work out the numbers to be sure the ad had no errors. Please help Ramon by calculating **(a)** the amount financed, **(b)** the finance charge, **(c)** APR by table lookup, **(d)** the monthly payment by formula, and **(e)** the monthly payment by table lookup (will be off slightly). *LU 14-1(1, 2, 3)*

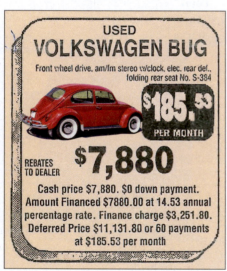

USED
VOLKSWAGEN BUG
Front wheel drive, am/fm stereo w/clock, elec. rear def.,
folding rear seat No. S-384
$185.⁵³
PER MONTH
REBATES TO DEALER **$7,880**
Cash price $7,880. $0 down payment.
Amount Financed $7880.00 at 14.53 annual
percentage rate. Finance charge $3,251.80.
Deferred Price $11,131.80 or 60 payments
at $185.53 per month

© Performance Image/Alamy

a. Amount financed:

b. Finance charge:

c. APR by table lookup:

d. Monthly payment by formula:

e. Monthly payment by table lookup (use 14.50%):

14–11. From this partial advertisement calculate: *LU 14-1(1, 2, 3)*

$95.10 per month
#43892 Used car. Cash price
$4,100. Down payment
$50. For 60 months.

a. Amount financed.

b. Finance charge.

c. Deferred payment price.

d. APR by Table 14.1.

e. Monthly payment (by formula).

14–12. If you are trying to build credit by using a credit card, each time you make a purchase with the credit card, deduct that
eXcel amount from your checking account. That way, when your credit card bill is due, you will have enough to pay the credit
card off in full. Kathy Lehner is going to start doing this. She plans on paying her credit card bill in full this month. How
much does she owe with a 12% APR and the following transactions? *LU 14-2(1)*

31-day billing cycle		
10/1	Previous balance		$1,168
10/3	Credit	$ 75 cr.	
10/12	Charge: King Soopers	152	
10/15	Payment	350 cr.	
10/25	Charge: Delta	325	
10/30	Charge: Holiday Fun	65	

14–13. Cody Lind's most recent credit card statement follows. His finance charge is 18% APR. Calculate Cody's average daily
balance, finance charge, and new balance. (Round final answers to the nearest cent.) *LU 14-2(1)*

30-day billing cycle		
9/2	Billing date	$1,200 previous balance
9/7	Payment	$ 100 cr.
9/13	Charge: Kohl's	350
9/17	Payment	200 cr.
9/28	Charge: Walmart	50

14–14. First America Bank's monthly payment charge on a 48-month, $20,000 loan is $488.26. U.S. Bank's monthly payment fee
eXcel is $497.70 for the same loan amount. What would be the APR for an auto loan for each of these banks? (Use the *Business
Math Handbook*.) *LU 14-1(1, 2)*

14–15. From the following facts, Molly Roe has requested you to calculate the average daily balance. The customer believes the average daily balance should be $877.67. Respond to the customer's concern.   *LU 14-2(1)*

28-day billing cycle			
3/18	Billing date	Previous balance	$800
3/24	Payment	$ 60 cr.	
3/29	Charge: Sears	250	
4/5	Payment	20 cr.	
4/9	Charge: Macy's	200	

14–16. Jill bought a $500 rocking chair. The terms of her revolving charge are $1\frac{1}{2}\%$ on the unpaid balance from the previous month. If she pays $100 per month, complete a schedule for the first 3 months like Table 14.3. Be sure to use the U.S. Rule.   *LU 14-2(1)*

Monthly payment number	Outstanding balance due	$1\frac{1}{2}\%$ interest payment	Amount of monthly payment	Reduction in balance due	Outstanding balance due

CHALLENGE PROBLEMS

14–17. Peg Gasperoni bought a $50,000 life insurance policy for $100 per year. Ryan Life Insurance Company sent her the following billing instructions along with a premium plan example:

"Your insurance premium notice will be mailed to you in a few days. You may pay the entire premium in full without a finance charge or you may pay the premium in installments after a down payment and the balance in monthly installments of $30. The finance charge will be added to the unpaid balance. The finance charge is based on an annual percentage rate of 15%."

If the total policy premium is:	And you put down:	The balance subject to finance charge will be:	The total number of monthly installments ($30 minimum) will be:	The monthly installment before adding the finance charge will be:	The total finance charge for all installments will be:	And the total deferred payment price will be:
$100	$30.00	$ 70.00	3	$30.00	$ 1.75	$101.75
200	50.00	150.00	5	30.00	5.67	205.67
300	75.00	225.00	8	30.00	12.84	312.84

Peg feels that the finance charge of $1.75 is in error. Who is correct? Check your answer. *LU 14-2(1)*

14–18. You have a $1,100 balance on your 15% credit card. You have lost your job and been unemployed for 6 months. You have been unable to make any payments on your balance. However, you received a tax refund and want to pay off the credit card. How much will you owe on the credit card, and how much interest will have accrued? What will be the effective rate of interest after the 6 months (to the nearest hundredth percent)? *LU 14-2(1)*

 SUMMARY PRACTICE TEST

Do you need help? The videos in Connect have step-by-step worked-out solutions. These videos are also available on YouTube!

1. Walter Lantz buys a Volvo SUV for $42,500. Walter made a down payment of $16,000 and paid $510 monthly for 60 months. What are the total amount financed and the total finance charge that Walter paid at the end of the 60 months? *LU 14-1(1)*

2. Joyce Mesnic bought an HP laptop computer at Staples for $699. Joyce made a $100 down payment and financed the balance at 10% for 12 months. What is her monthly payment? (Use the loan amortization table.) *LU 14-1(3)*

3. Lee Remick read the following partial advertisement: price, $22,500; down payment, $1,000 cash or trade; and $399.99 per month for 60 months. Calculate **(a)** the total finance charge and **(b)** the APR by Table 14.1 (use the tables in *Business Math Handbook*) to the nearest hundredth percent. *LU 14-1(1, 2)*

4. Nancy Billows bought a $7,000 desk at Furniture.com. Based on her income, Nancy could only afford to pay back $700 per month. The charge on the unpaid balance is 3%. The U.S. Rule is used in the calculation. Calculate the balance outstanding at the end of month 2. *LU 14-2(1)*

Month	Balance due	Interest	Monthly payment	Reduction in balance	Balance outstanding

5. Calculate the average daily balance and finance charge on the statement below. *LU 14-2(1)*

30-day billing cycle		
7/3	Balance	$400
7/18	Payment	100 cr.
7/27	Charge Walmart	250

Assume 2% finance charge on average daily balance.

SURF TO SAVE

The costs of paying over time 🔍

PROBLEM 1
How much car can I afford?

Go to http://www.bankrate.com. Find an auto loan rate for a 3-year loan. Then go to http://www.bankofamerica.com/vehicle_and_personal_loans/index.cfm?template=learn_calculators&context=financenter&calcid=auto05 and select your state to find the monthly payment calculator. Calculate your payments if you borrow $23,000 for 3 years at the rate you found. Suppose the auto dealer was offering a special 2.9% rate. How much could you save over the life of the loan by borrowing at the lower rate?

Discussion Questions

1. How does the interest rate you secure impact the type of car you would purchase?

2. What is the incentive to the dealer in offering such low rates on car purchases?

PROBLEM 2
Not-so-free credit

Go to http://www.bankrate.com. Follow the link to credit cards and then to "Find a Credit Card." Choose "Student Cards" from the drop-down menu to see your available options. Suppose you kept an average daily balance of $1,000 on the credit card for the entire introductory period. How much interest would you save versus the regular APR during the 0.0% introductory period? (You may assume the monthly rate is the annual rate divided by 12. If given an APR range, use the lower percentage in the range.) Suppose you continued to use the same card after the introductory period expired. How much interest would you pay over the same amount of time as the introductory period?

Discussion Questions

1. Why would banks want to offer such low rates as an introductory offer to new customers?

2. What are the pros and cons to carrying a balance on your credit card during these low introductory rate periods?

PROBLEM 3
Credit payoff

Visit http://www.bankrate.com/calculators/credit-cards/credit-card-payoff-calculator.aspx. Assume that you are carrying a $1,500 balance on your credit card with a rate of 15%. You would like to pay off this balance in 6 months. What would you need to pay monthly in order to achieve this goal?

Discussion Questions

1. What are some reasons why students carry credit card debt?

2. Do you feel most consumers understand the financial consequences of using credit card debt? Why or why not?

PROBLEM 4
Does my credit score matter?

Go to http://learn.bankofamerica.com/articles/managing-credit/ how-to-improve-your-credit-score.html to learn about how to improve your credit score.

Discussion Questions

1. How would these suggestions help your credit score?

2. Do you feel you could follow these suggestions? Why or why not?

MOBILE APPS ✕

Simple Payment Calculator (CS Software) Calculates payments for auto or home loans simply.

GooBiq Credit Card Rates (GooBiq.com) Locates current rates on a variety of credit cards including fees, credit limits, and more.

A KIPLINGER APPROACH

By Ryan Ermey, From *Kiplinger's Personal Finance*, June 2015.

FAMILY FINANCES »

Merging Your Money

For newlyweds, it makes sense to have a mix of accounts—his, hers and ours. BY RYAN ERMEY

IF YOU'RE A NEWLYWED, YOU and your spouse probably know by now what you like to do as a couple and what you like to do separately. Brunches and birthday parties? See you there. Poker nights and pedicures? See you later. But when it comes to combining your personal finances, the lines between yours, mine and ours may not be so clear.

Spending. Before you merge your credit cards, check your individual credit scores. The most common way to piggyback on a spouse's credit card is to sign on as an authorized user. But once you're authorized, the card's previous history will appear on your credit report; if the account has blemishes, your credit score will get dinged. You could also open a joint credit card. In that case, however, both spouses are responsible for the full balance of the account, so one person behaving badly will negatively affect both credit scores.

Gerri Detweiler, director of con-sumer education at Credit .com, says a common strategy is to authorize your spouse to use a card that offers favorable terms, attractive rewards and has a positive credit history, and for both spouses to maintain separate credit accounts as well. That way, she says, you can pool household purchases and work jointly toward earning airline miles or rewards points.

Many couples approach bank accounts similarly. The hybrid approach, with a joint account for shared expenses and individual ac-counts for personal spending, is a good way to go for many couples. However you choose to handle it, communication is essential. "Have these financial discussions early," says Detweiler, "while they're still money talks and not money fights."

Insurance. Assuming you've recently registered for your wedding, it should be easy to create a detailed home inventory, complete with estimated values for all of your possessions (see "3 Simple Steps," Dec. 2014). Knowing the value of your things will help you determine how much renters or homeowners coverage to buy, says Jeanne Salvatore, of the Insurance Information Institute. A typical renters policy costs $16 per month and provides $25,000 in property coverage and $300,000 to $500,000 in liability coverage. Homeowners policies usually cover personal possessions at a rate of 50% to 70% of the coverage on your home.

Getting married also gives newlyweds more choices when it comes to health insurance. If both of you have coverage at work, do a cost-benefit analysis. One spouse's employer may offer better coverage than the other's, but many employers now charge dependents a larger percentage of the cost than they impose on employees, and some businesses add a surcharge for spouses who could get coverage elsewhere.

You may be able to skip life insurance until you have kids—unless you're buying a house together and need two incomes to pay the mortgage.

Saving and investing. Make sure you have enough money socked away in an FDIC-insured bank account to cover at least six months of living expenses.

If both of you have retirement accounts through your employer, contribute enough to earn the maximum company match. After that, shift more money to the plan with better investment options and lower fees, regardless of whose plan it is. "You want to focus on what's going to give you the most bang for your buck," says Danielle Seurkamp, a certified financial planner in Cincinnati. ■

ISTOCKPHOTO.COM

BUSINESS MATH ISSUE

Once you are married, all credit cards should be in both names.

1. List the key points of the article and information to support your position.
2. Write a group defense of your position using math calculations to support your view.

Classroom Notes

CHAPTER 15

The Cost of Home Ownership

© Ryan McVay/Getty Images

Close Call

The states with the highest and lowest closing costs, according to a survey • lenders. Estimates are based on a $200,000 mortgage for a single-fami home, and a buyer with excellent credit who put 20% down. Totals wou likely be higher because some of the most variable costs are not included.

LOWEST	Lender's origination fees	Third-party fees	Total
Nevada	$1,570	$695	$2,265
Tennessee	$1,746	$620	$2,366
Missouri	$1,749	$638	$2,387
Ohio	$1,707	$685	$2,392
District of Columbia	$1,791	$612	$2,402
HIGHEST			
Texas	$2,280	$766	$3,046
Alaska	$2,195	$703	$2,897
New York	$2,109	$783	$2,892
Hawaii	$2,009	$799	$2,808
Wisconsin	$2,035	$671	$2,706

Source: Bankrate.com
Note: Does not include title insurance, title search, taxes, other government fees and escrow fees.

Source: *The Wall Street Journal*, 12/14/12.

LU 15–1: Types of Mortgages and the Monthly Mortgage Payment

1. List the types of mortgages available.
2. Utilize an amortization chart to compute monthly mortgage payments.
3. Calculate the total cost of interest over the life of a mortgage.

LU 15–2: Amortization Schedule—Breaking Down the Monthly Payment

1. Calculate and identify the interest and principal portion of each monthly payment.
2. Prepare an amortization schedule.

VOCABULARY PREVIEW

Here are key terms in this chapter. After completing the chapter, if you know the term, place a checkmark in the box. If you don't know the term, look it up and put the page number where it can be found.

Adjustable rate mortgage (ARM) ☐ Amortization schedule ☐ Amortization table ☐ Biweekly mortgage ☐ Closing costs ☐ Escrow account ☐ Fixed rate mortgage ☐ Foreclosure ☐ Graduated-payment mortgages (GPM) ☐ Home equity loan ☐ Interest-only mortgage ☐ Monthly payment ☐ Mortgages ☐ Points ☐ Reverse mortgage ☐ Short sale ☐ Subprime loans ☐

The *Wall Street Journal* chapter opener clip "Close Call" reveals that many homeowners are paying high closing costs to buy a home. If property values decrease, homeowners may have to sell their properties for less than is owed. When this happens, it is called a **short sale.**

Learning Unit 15–1: Types of Mortgages and the Monthly Mortgage Payment

Figure 15.1 lists various loan types. A type of adjustable rate mortgage called a **subprime loan** was at the root of so many foreclosures in the past few years. This type of home loan allowed buyers to have a very low interest rate—sometimes even a zero rate. This helped customers qualify for expensive homes that they would not otherwise have qualified for. Lenders offering subprimes assumed prices of homes would rise and most buyers would convert to a fixed rate before the rate was substantially adjusted upward. As we now know, prices of homes fell. Keep in mind that with low interest rates housing in 2015 has seen a rebound. The Federal Reserve is planning to slowly increase interest rates in 2016. This could have implications for the housing market.

Purchasing a home usually involves paying a large amount of interest. Note how your author was able to save $70,121.40.

Over the life of a 30-year **fixed rate mortgage** (see Figure 15.1) of $100,000, the interest would have cost $207,235. Monthly payments would have been $849.99. This would not include taxes, insurance, and so on.

Your author chose a **biweekly mortgage** (see Figure 15.1). This meant that every 2 weeks (26 times a year) the bank would receive $425. By paying every 2 weeks instead of once a month, the mortgage would be paid off in 23 years instead of 30—a $70,121.40 *savings* on interest. Why? When a payment is made every 2 weeks, the principal is reduced more quickly, which substantially reduces the interest cost.

The question facing prospective buyers concerns which type of mortgage will be best for them. Depending on how interest rates are moving when you purchase a home, you may find one type of **mortgage** to be the most advantageous for you (see Figure 15.1).

FIGURE **15.1**   Types of mortgages available

Loan types	Advantages	Disadvantages
30-year fixed rate mortgage	A predictable monthly payment.	If interest rates fall, you are locked in to higher rate unless you refinance. (Application and appraisal fees along with other closing costs will result.)
15-year fixed rate mortgage	Interest rate lower than 30-year fixed (usually $\frac{1}{4}$ to $\frac{1}{2}$ of a percent). Your equity builds up faster while interest costs are cut by more than one-half.	A larger down payment is needed. Monthly payment will be higher.
Graduated-payment mortgage (GPM)	Easier to qualify for than 30- or 15-year fixed rate. Monthly payments start low and increase over time.	May have higher APR than fixed or variable rates.
Biweekly mortgage	Shortens term loan; saves substantial amount of interest; 26 biweekly payments per year. Builds equity twice as fast.	Not good for those not seeking an early loan payoff. Extra payments per year.
Adjustable rate mortgage (ARM)	Lower rate than fixed. If rates fall, could be adjusted down without refinancing. Caps available that limit how high rate could go for each adjustment period over term of loan.	Monthly payment could rise if interest rates rise. Riskier than fixed rate mortgage in which monthly payment is stable.
Home equity loan	Cheap and reliable accessible lines of credit backed by equity in your home. Tax-deductible. Rates can be locked in. Reverse mortgages may be available to those 62 or older.	Could lose home if not paid (**foreclosure**). No annual or interest caps.
Interest-only mortgages	Borrowers pay interest but no principal in the early years (5 to 15) of the loan.	Early years build up no equity.

Reprinted by permission of *The Wall Street Journal,* copyright 2011 Dow Jones & Company, Inc. All rights reserved worldwide.

The *Wall Street Journal* clip "Downsizing" shows that interest rates (like 3.5%) for a mortgage are at record lows. The monthly payment at 6% is $2,398.20 and it drops to $1,796.18 at a 3.5% interest rate—a savings of $602.02 per month.

Have you heard that elderly people who are house-rich and cash-poor can use their home to get cash or monthly income? The Federal Housing Administration makes it possible for older homeowners to take out a **reverse mortgage** on their homes. Under reverse mortgages, senior homeowners borrow against the equity in their property, often getting fixed monthly checks. The debt is repaid only when the homeowners or their estate sells the home. The *Wall Street Journal* clip "The Fifteen-Year Mortgage" shows a new 30-year mortgage incorporating one rate change at the 15-year mark.

Reprinted by permission of *The Wall Street Journal*, copyright 2014 Dow Jones & Company, Inc. All rights reserved worldwide.

THE FIFTEEN-YEAR MORTGAGE

 Mortgage borrowers usually must decide between low rates or a long term. But one lender says you can have both.

Pentagon Federal Credit Union, the Alexandria, Va.-based credit union known as PenFed, has rolled out a 30-year amortizing mortgage that changes its rate just once, 15 years into the term of the 30-year loan. The credit union will be writing loans with the 15/15-adjustable rate mortgage up to $2 million.

PenFed says the product, launched in February, is designed to appeal to borrowers who are typically looking to refinance or purchase a second home, says Debbie Ames Naylor, executive vice president of mortgages at the federal credit union.

Now let's learn how to calculate a monthly mortgage payment and the total cost of loan interest over the life of a mortgage. We will use the following example in our discussion.

EXAMPLE   Gary bought a home for $200,000. He made a 20% down payment. The 9% mortgage is for 30 years (30 × 12 = 360 payments). What are Gary's monthly payment and total cost of interest?

LO 2

Computing the Monthly Payment for Principal and Interest

You can calculate the principal and interest of Gary's **monthly payment** using the **amortization table** shown in Table 15.1 and the following steps. (Remember that this is the same type of amortization table used in Chapter 14 for installment loans.)

 **MONEY tips**

Research the cost of different mortgages with a variety of companies before choosing one. Compare interest rates, closing costs, mortgage length (10 year, 15 year, 20 year, 30 year) and total interest for the life of each mortgage you are considering. Ensure that there is no prepayment penalty. Look into bimonthly and biweekly mortgage payments resulting in less interest paid over the life of the mortgage, too.

COMPUTING MONTHLY PAYMENT BY USING AN AMORTIZATION TABLE
Step 1. Divide the amount of the mortgage by $1,000.
Step 2. Look up the rate and term in the amortization table. At the intersection is the table factor.
Step 3. Multiply Step 1 by Step 2.

For Gary, we calculate the following:

$$\frac{\$160,000 \text{ (amount of mortgage)}}{\$1,000} = 160 \times \$8.05 \text{ (table rate)} = \$1,288$$

So $160,000 is the amount of the mortgage ($200,000 less 20%). The $8.05 is the table factor of 9% for 30 years per $1,000. Since Gary is mortgaging 160 units of $1,000, the factor of $8.05 is multiplied by 160. Remember that the $1,288 payment does not include taxes, insurance, and so on.

Calculate PITI (monthly principal, interest, taxes, and insurance): PI + (Annual property tax + Annual homeowners' insurance)/12.

EXAMPLE $1,288 + ($2,345 + $1,578)/12

$1,288 + $326.92 = $1,614.92 PITI

TABLE 15.1   Amortization table (mortgage principal and interest per $1,000)

Term in years	3½%	5%	5½%	6%	6½%	7%	7½%	8%	8½%	9%	9½%	10%	10½%	11%
										INTEREST				
10	9.89	10.61	10.86	11.11	11.36	11.62	11.88	12.14	12.40	12.67	12.94	13.22	13.50	13.78
12	8.52	9.25	9.51	9.76	10.02	10.29	10.56	10.83	11.11	11.39	11.67	11.96	12.25	12.54
15	7.15	7.91	8.18	8.44	8.72	8.99	9.28	9.56	9.85	10.15	10.45	10.75	11.06	11.37
17	6.52	7.29	7.56	7.84	8.12	8.40	8.69	8.99	9.29	9.59	9.90	10.22	10.54	10.86
20	5.80	6.60	6.88	7.17	7.46	7.76	8.06	8.37	8.68	9.00	9.33	9.66	9.99	10.33
22	5.44	6.20	6.51	6.82	7.13	7.44	7.75	8.07	8.39	8.72	9.05	9.39	9.73	10.08
25	5.01	5.85	6.15	6.45	6.76	7.07	7.39	7.72	8.06	8.40	8.74	9.09	9.45	9.81
30	4.50	5.37	5.68	6.00	6.33	6.66	7.00	7.34	7.69	8.05	8.41	8.78	9.15	9.53
35	3.99	5.05	5.38	5.71	6.05	6.39	6.75	7.11	7.47	7.84	8.22	8.60	8.99	9.37

LO 3

What Is the Total Cost of Interest?

We can use the following formula to calculate Gary's total interest cost over the life of the mortgage:

$$\begin{array}{ccc} \text{Total cost} & = & \text{Total of all} & - & \text{Amount of} \\ \text{of interest} & & \text{monthly payments} & & \text{mortgage} \end{array}$$

$$\$303{,}680 = \underset{(\$1{,}288 \times 360)}{\$463{,}680} - \$160{,}000$$

MONEY tips

Being able to afford PI (principal and interest) may be compromised when TI (taxes and insurance) is calculated. Make certain to budget for all four mortgage expenses.

Effects of Interest Rates on Monthly Payment and Total Interest Cost

Table 15.2 shows the effect that an increase in interest rates would have on Gary's monthly payment and his total cost of interest. Note that if Gary's interest rate rises to 11%, the 2% increase will result in Gary paying an additional $85,248 in total interest.

For most people, purchasing a home is a major lifetime decision. Many factors must be considered before this decision is made. Being informed about related costs and the types of available mortgages can save you thousands of dollars.

In addition to the mortgage payment, buying a home can include the following costs:

- *Closing costs:* When property passes from seller to buyer, **closing costs** may include fees for credit reports, recording costs, lawyer's fees, points, title search, and so on. A **point** is a one-time charge that is a percent of the mortgage. Two points means 2% of the mortgage. Be sure to check out the chapter opener for a table showing closing costs on the rise.

- *Escrow amount:* Usually, the lending institution, for its protection, requires that each month 1/12 of the insurance cost and 1/12 of the real estate taxes be kept in a special account called the **escrow account.** The monthly balance in this account will change depending on the cost of the insurance and taxes. Interest is paid on escrow accounts.

- *Repairs and maintenance:* This includes paint, wallpaper, landscaping, plumbing, electrical expenses, and so on.

- *PMI insurance:* When buying a house, if you do not have 20% in cash to put as a down payment lenders will require you to purchase PMI (Private Mortgage Insurance). This can be very expensive and only benefits the lender. It is important to know that as soon as 20% equity is reached in the home (determined by an appraisal), the borrower must petition to have the PMI removed. The mortgage lender will not be tracking this and you may continue to pay PMI after it is no longer required.

As you can see, the cost of owning a home can be expensive. But remember that interest costs of your monthly payment and your real estate taxes are deductible. For many, owning a home can have advantages over renting.

TABLE **15.1** (concluded)

Term in years	11½%	11¾%	12%	12½%	12¾%	13%	13½%	13¾%	14%	14½%	14¾%	15%	15½%
												INTEREST	
10	14.06	14.21	14.35	14.64	14.79	14.94	15.23	15.38	15.53	15.83	15.99	16.14	16.45
12	12.84	12.99	13.14	13.44	13.60	13.75	14.06	14.22	14.38	14.69	14.85	15.01	15.34
15	11.69	11.85	12.01	12.33	12.49	12.66	12.99	13.15	13.32	13.66	13.83	14.00	14.34
17	11.19	11.35	11.52	11.85	12.02	12.19	12.53	12.71	12.88	13.23	13.41	13.58	13.94
20	10.67	10.84	11.02	11.37	11.54	11.72	12.08	12.26	12.44	12.80	12.99	13.17	13.54
22	10.43	10.61	10.78	11.14	11.33	11.51	11.87	12.06	12.24	12.62	12.81	12.99	13.37
25	10.17	10.35	10.54	10.91	11.10	11.28	11.66	11.85	12.04	12.43	12.62	12.81	13.20
30	9.91	10.10	10.29	10.68	10.87	11.07	11.46	11.66	11.85	12.25	12.45	12.65	13.05
35	9.77	9.96	10.16	10.56	10.76	10.96	11.36	11.56	11.76	12.17	12.37	12.57	12.98

TABLE **15.2** Effect of interest rates on monthly payments

	9%	11%	Difference
Monthly payment	$1,288	$1,524.80	$236.80 per month
	(160 × $8.05)	(160 × $9.53)	
Total cost of interest	$303,680	$388,928	$85,248
	($1,288 × 360) − $160,000	($1,524.80 × 360) − $160,000	($236.80 × 360)

The following *Wall Street Journal* clip, "Adjusting the Math," shows that taking out an ARM versus a fixed rate mortgage can result in a $23,479 savings over 10 years.

Before you study Learning Unit 15–2, let's check your understanding of Learning Unit 15–1.

MONEY tips

Should you buy or rent your home? Buying actually saves you $1,743 more, on average, per year if you stay in your home for 6 years or longer. This savings results from the allowed deduction of property taxes and mortgage interest on your personal income taxes.

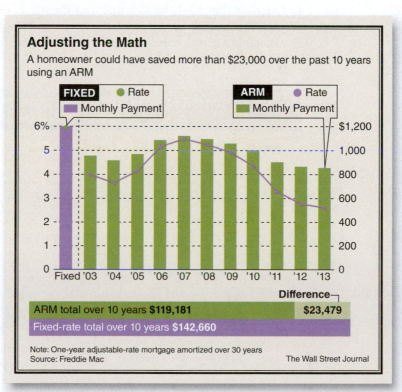

Source: *The Wall Street Journal.*

LU 15–1 PRACTICE QUIZ

Complete this **Practice Quiz** to see how you are doing.

For **extra help** from your authors–Sharon and Jeff–see the videos in Connect.

These videos are also available on YouTube!

Given: Price of home, $225,000; 20% down payment; 9% interest rate; 25-year mortgage. Solve for:

1. Monthly payment and total cost of interest over 25 years.
2. If rate fell to 8%, what would be the total decrease in interest cost over the life of the mortgage?

✓ **Solutions**

1. $225,000 − $45,000 = $180,000

$$\frac{\$180,000}{\$1,000} = 180 \times \$8.40 = \boxed{\$1,512}$$

$$\boxed{\$273,600} = \quad \$453,600 − \$180,000$$
$$(\$1,512 \times 300) \quad 25 \text{ years} \times 12 \text{ payments per year}$$

2. 8% = $1,389.60 monthly payment
 (180 × $7.72)

Total interest cost $236,880 = ($1,389.60 × 300) − $180,000

Savings $36,720 = ($273,600 − $236,880)

LU 15–1a EXTRA PRACTICE QUIZ WITH WORKED-OUT SOLUTIONS

Need more practice? Try this Extra Practice Quiz (check figures in the Interactive Chapter Organizer). Worked-out Solutions can be found in Appendix B at end of text.

Given: Price of home, $180,000; 30% down payment; 7% interest rate; 30-year mortgage. Solve for:

1. Monthly payment and total cost of interest over 30 years.
2. If rate fell to 5%, what would be the total decrease in interest cost over the life of the mortgage?

Learning Unit 15–2: Amortization Schedule—Breaking Down the Monthly Payment

LO 1

In Learning Unit 15–1, we saw that over the life of Gary's $160,000 loan, he would pay $303,680 in interest. Now let's use the following steps to determine what portion of Gary's first monthly payment reduces the principal and what portion is interest.

CALCULATING INTEREST, PRINCIPAL, AND NEW BALANCE OF MONTHLY PAYMENT

Step 1. Calculate the interest for a month (use current principal):
Interest = Principal × Rate × Time.

Step 2. Calculate the amount used to reduce the principal:
Principal reduction = Monthly payment − Interest (Step 1).

Step 3. Calculate the new principal:
Current principal − Reduction of principal (Step 2) = New principal.

Step 1. Interest (I) = Principal (P) × Rate (R) × Time (T)

$$\$1,200 \quad = \quad \$160,000 \quad \times \quad .09 \quad \times \quad \frac{1}{12}$$

Step 2. The reduction of the $160,000 principal each month is equal to the payment less interest. So we can calculate Gary's new principal balance at the end of month 1 as follows:

Monthly payment at 9% (from Table 15.1)	$1,288 (160 × $8.05)
− Interest for first month	− 1,200
= Principal reduction	$ 88

Step 3. As the years go by, the interest portion of the payment decreases and the principal portion increases.

Principal balance	$160,000
Principal reduction	− 88
Balance of principal	$159,912

Let's do month 2:

Step 1. Interest = Principal × Rate × Time

$$= \$159,912 \times .09 \times \frac{1}{12}$$

$$= \$1,199.34$$

Step 2.

$1,288.00	monthly payment
− 1,199.34	interest for month 2
$ 88.66	principal reduction

Step 3.

$159,912.00	principal balance
− 88.66	principal reduction
$159,823.34	balance of principal

Note that in month 2, interest costs drop 66 cents ($1,200.00 − $1,199.34). So in 2 months, Gary has reduced his mortgage balance by $176.66 ($88.00 + $88.66). After 2 months, Gary has paid a total interest of $2,399.34 ($1,200.00 + $1,199.34).

MONEY tips

Save money on interest by making 13 mortgage payments a year using one of the following methods:

1. Increase your monthly payment by 1/12.
2. Make one extra payment a year.
3. Pay half of your monthly payment every two weeks.

A $200,000 mortgage at 5% for 30 years will save you $32,699 on interest cost.

LO 2

Example of an Amortization Schedule

The partial **amortization schedule** given in Table 15.3 shows the breakdown of Gary's monthly payment. Note the amount that goes toward reducing the principal and toward payment of actual interest. Also note how the outstanding balance of the loan is reduced. After 7 months, Gary still owes $159,369.97. Often when you take out a mortgage loan, you receive an amortization schedule from the company that holds your mortgage.

TABLE 15.3 Partial amortization schedule

	MONTHLY PAYMENT, $1,288			
Payment number	Principal (current)	Interest	Principal reduction	Balance of principal
1	$160,000.00 $\left(\$160,000 \times .09 \times \frac{1}{12}\right)$	$1,200.00 ($1,288 − $1,200)	$88.00 ($160,000 − $88)	$159,912.00
2	$159,912.00 $\left(\$159,912 \times .09 \times \frac{1}{12}\right)$	$1,199.34 ($1,288 − $1,199.34)	$88.66 ($159,912 − $88.66)	$159,823.34
3	$159,823.34	$1,198.68	$89.32	$159,734.02
4	$159,734.02	$1,198.01	$89.99	$159,644.03
5	$159,644.03	$1,197.33	$90.67	$159,553.36
6	$159,553.36	$1,196.65	$91.35	$159,462.01
7	$159,462.01	$1,195.97*	$92.04	$159,369.97

*Off 1 cent due to rounding.

It's time to test your knowledge of Learning Unit 15–2 with a Practice Quiz.

LU 15–2 | PRACTICE QUIZ

Complete this Practice Quiz to see how you are doing.

*For **extra help** from your authors–Sharon and Jeff–see the videos in Connect.*

These videos are also available on YouTube!

$100,000 mortgage; monthly payment, $953 (100 × $9.53)

Prepare an amortization schedule for the first three periods for the following: mortgage, $100,000; 11%; 30 years.

✓ **Solution**

Payment number	Principal (current)	PORTION TO—		
		Interest	Principal reduction	Balance of principal
1	$100,000	$916.67 $\left(\$100,000 \times .11 \times \dfrac{1}{12}\right)$	$36.33 ($953.00 − $916.67)	$99,963.67 ($100,000 − $36.33)
2	$99,963.67	$916.33 $\left(\$99,963.67 \times .11 \times \dfrac{1}{12}\right)$	$36.67 ($953.00 − $916.33)	$99,927.00 ($99,963.67 − $36.67)
3	$99,927	$916.00 $\left(\$99,927 \times .11 \times \dfrac{1}{12}\right)$	$37.00 ($953.00 − $916.00)	$99,890.00 ($99,927.00 − $37.00)

LU 15–2a | EXTRA PRACTICE QUIZ WITH WORKED-OUT SOLUTION

Need more practice? Try this Extra Practice Quiz (check figures in the Interactive Chapter Organizer). Worked-out Solution can be found in Appendix B at end of text.

Prepare an amortization schedule for the first two periods for the following: mortgage, $70,000; 7%; 30 years.

INTERACTIVE CHAPTER ORGANIZER

Topic/Procedure/Formula	Examples	You try it*
Computing monthly mortgage payment Based on per $1,000 (Table 15.1): $\dfrac{\text{Amount of mortgage}}{\$1,000} \times$ Table rate	Use Table 15.1: 12% on $60,000 mortgage for 30 years. $\dfrac{\$60,000}{\$1,000} = 60 \times \$10.29$ = $617.40	**Calculate monthly payment** $70,000 mortgage at 3.5% for 30 years
Calculating total interest cost Total of all monthly payments − Amount of mortgage	Using example above: 30 years = 360 (payments) × $617.40 $222,264 − 60,000 $162,264 (mortgage interest over life of mortgage)	**Calculate total interest cost** Use the data from the problem above.

(continues)

INTERACTIVE CHAPTER ORGANIZER

Topic/Procedure/Formula	Examples	You try it*
Amortization schedule $I = P \times R \times T$ $\left(I \text{ for month} = P \times R \times \dfrac{1}{12}\right)$ $\dfrac{\text{Principal}}{\text{reduction}} = \dfrac{\text{Monthly}}{\text{payment}} - \text{Interest}$ $\dfrac{\text{New}}{\text{principal}} = \dfrac{\text{Current}}{\text{principal}} - \dfrac{\text{Reduction of}}{\text{principal}}$	Using same example: **Payment number / Portion to—** (Interest, Principal reduction, Balance of principal) 1 \$600 \$17.40 \$ 59,982.60 $\left(\$60,000 \times .12 \times \dfrac{1}{12}\right)$ $\left(\begin{array}{c}\$617.40\\-\$600.00\end{array}\right)$ $\left(\begin{array}{c}\$60,000.00\\-\$17.40\end{array}\right)$ 2 \$599.83 \$17.57 \$ 59,965.03 $\left(\$59,982.60 \times .12 \times \dfrac{1}{12}\right)$ $\left(\begin{array}{c}\$617.40\\-\$599.83\end{array}\right)$ $\left(\begin{array}{c}\$59,982.60\\-\$17.57\end{array}\right)$	**Prepare amortization for first two payments** Use the data from the problem above.

KEY TERMS	Adjustable rate mortgage (ARM) Amortization schedule Amortization table Biweekly mortgage Closing costs Escrow account	Fixed rate mortgage Foreclosure Graduated-payment mortgages (GPM) Home equity loan Interest-only mortgage Monthly payment	Mortgages Points Reverse mortgage Short sale Subprime loans

Check Figures for Extra Practice Quizzes. (Worked-out Solutions are in Appendix B.)	LU 15–1a
	1. \$839.16
	    \$176,097.60
	2. \$117,583.20
	    \$58,514.40
		LU 15–2a
		\$408.33 \$57.87 \$69,942.13
		\$408.00 \$58.20 \$69,883.93

*Worked-out solutions are in Appendix B.

Critical Thinking Discussion Questions with Chapter Concept Check

1. Explain the advantages and disadvantages of the following loan types: 30-year fixed rate, 15-year fixed rate, graduated-payment mortgage, biweekly mortgage, adjustable rate mortgage, and home equity loan. Why might a bank require a home buyer to establish an escrow account?

2. How is an amortization schedule calculated? Is there a best time to refinance a mortgage?

3. What is a point? Is paying points worth the cost?

4. Explain how rising interest rates will affect the housing market.

5. Explain a short sale.

6. Explain subprime loans and how foreclosures result.

7. **Chapter Concept Check.** Locate three mortgage options for a house you would like to buy and calculate the payment and total interest for each. Which would you choose? Why? Use concepts in the chapter to support your case.

Classroom Notes

END-OF-CHAPTER PROBLEMS connect plus+

Check figures for odd-numbered problems in Appendix C.   Name _____   Date _____

DRILL PROBLEMS

Complete the following amortization chart by using Table 15.1.   *LU 15-1(2)*

	Selling price of home	Down payment	Principal (loan)	Rate of interest	Years	Payment per $1,000	Monthly mortgage payment
15–1. eXcel	$140,000	$10,000		$3\frac{1}{2}\%$	25		
15–2. eXcel	$90,000	$5,000		$5\frac{1}{2}\%$	30		
15–3. eXcel	$190,000	$50,000		7%	35		

15–4. What is the total cost of interest in Problem 15–2?   *LU 15-1(3)*
eXcel

15–5. If the interest rate rises to 7% in Problem 15–2, what is the total cost of interest?   *LU 15-1(3)*

Complete the following: *LU 15-2(1)*

	Selling price	Down payment	Amount mortgage	Rate	Years	Monthly payment	First Payment Broken Down Into—		Balance at end of month
							Interest	Principal	
15–6.	$150,000	$30,000		7%	30				
15–7.	$225,000	$45,000		5%	15				

15–8. Bob Jones bought a new log cabin for $70,000 at 11% interest for 30 years. Prepare an amortization schedule for the first three periods.   *LU 15-2(2)*

Payment number	Portion to—		Balance of loan outstanding
	Interest	Principal	

WORD PROBLEMS

15–9. CNBC.com reported mortgage applications dropped in March 2015 due to an increase in the rate on 30-year fixed rate mortgages to an average of 4.01%. Dennis Natali wants to purchase a vacation home for $235,000 with 20% down. Calculate his monthly payment for a 20-year mortgage at 3.5%. Calculate total interest. *LU 15-1(3)*

15–10. Oprah Winfrey has closed on a 42-acre estate near Santa Barbara, California, for $50,000,000. If Oprah puts 20% down and finances at 7% for 30 years, what would her monthly payment be? *LU 15-1(2)*

15–11. Joe Levi bought a home in Arlington, Texas, for $140,000. He put down 20% and obtained a mortgage for 30 years at $5\frac{1}{2}$%.
eXcel What is Joe's monthly payment? What is the total interest cost of the loan? *LU 15-1(2, 3)*

15–12. If in Problem 15–11 the rate of interest is $7\frac{1}{2}$%, what is the difference in interest cost? *LU 15-1(3)*
eXcel

15–13. Mike Jones bought a new split-level home for $150,000 with 20% down. He decided to use Victory Bank for his mortgage. Victory was offering $13\frac{3}{4}$% for 25-year mortgages. Provide Mike with an amortization schedule for the first three periods. *LU 15-2(1, 2)*

| Payment number | Portion to— | | Balance of loan outstanding |
	Interest	Principal	

15–14. Harriet Marcus is concerned about the financing of a home. She saw a small cottage that sells for $50,000. If she puts 20% down, what will her monthly payment be at **(a)** 25 years, $11\frac{1}{2}$%; **(b)** 25 years, $12\frac{1}{2}$%; **(c)** 25 years, $13\frac{1}{2}$%; and **(d)** 25 years, 15%? What is the total cost of interest over the cost of the loan for each assumption? **(e)** What is the savings in interest cost between $11\frac{1}{2}$% and 15%? **(f)** If Harriet uses 30 years instead of 25 for both $11\frac{1}{2}$% and 15%, what is the difference in interest? *LU 15-1(2, 3)*

15–15. Mortgage Bankers Association reported the median price of a home sold in the United States in January 2015 was $199,600. Pat Radigan wants to purchase a new home for $305,500. Pat puts 20% down and will finance the remainder of the purchase. Compare the following two mortgage options he has: 10 years at 3.5% or 15 years at 5%. Calculate Pat's monthly payment as well as his total cost of interest for both the 10- and 15-year mortgage. What is the difference in interest paid between the two options (round to nearest cent in calculations)?   *LU 15-1(3)*

15–16. Daniel and Jan agreed to pay $560,000 for a four-bedroom colonial home in Waltham, Massachusetts, with a $60,000 down payment. They have a 30-year mortgage at a fixed rate of 6.00%. **(a)** How much is their monthly payment? **(b)** After the first payment, what would be the balance of the principal?   *LU 15-1(2), LU 15-2(1)*

15–17. Paying 13 mortgage payments instead of 12 per year can save you thousands in interest cost. If you had a $175,000 mortgage at 6% for 30 years, how much extra would you have to pay per year to make 13 instead of 12 mortgage payments per year? How much would you pay if you paid 1/12 of it per month?   *LU 15-1(1)*

CHALLENGE PROBLEMS

15–18. Rick Rueta purchased a $90,000 home at 9% for 30 years with a down payment of $20,000. His annual real estate tax is
eXcel $1,800 along with an annual insurance premium of $960. Rick's bank requires that his monthly payment include an escrow deposit for the tax and insurance. What is the total payment each month for Rick?   *LU 15-1(2)*

15–19. Sharon Fox decided to buy a home in Marblehead, Massachusetts, for $275,000. Her bank requires a 30% down payment. Sue Willis, an attorney, has notified Sharon that besides the 30% down payment there will be the following additional costs:

Recording of the deed	$ 30.00
A credit and appraisal report	155.00
Preparation of appropriate documents	48.00

In addition, there will be a transfer tax of 1.8% of the purchase price and a loan origination fee of 2.5% of the mortgage amount.

Assume a 30-year mortgage at a rate of 10%. *LU 15-1(2, 3)*

a. What is the initial amount of cash Sharon will need?

b. What is her monthly payment?

c. What is the total cost of interest over the life of the mortgage?

SUMMARY PRACTICE TEST

Do you need help? The videos in Connect have step-by-step worked-out solutions. These videos are also available on YouTube!

1. Pat Lavoie bought a home for $180,000 with a down payment of $10,000. Her rate of interest is 6% for 30 years. Calculate **eXcel** her **(a)** monthly payment; **(b)** first payment, broken down into interest and principal; and **(c)** balance of mortgage at the end of the month. *LU 15-1(2, 3)*

2. Jen Logan bought a home in Iowa for $110,000. She put down 20% and obtained a mortgage for 30 years at $5\frac{1}{2}\%$. What are Jen's monthly payment and total interest cost of the loan? *LU 15-1(2, 3)*

3. Christina Sanders is concerned about the financing of a home. She saw a small Cape Cod–style house that sells for $90,000. If she puts 10% down, what will her monthly payment be at **(a)** 30 years, 5%; **(b)** 30 years, $5\frac{1}{2}\%$ **(c)** 30 years, 6%; and **(d)** 30 years, $6\frac{1}{2}\%$? What is the total cost of interest over the cost of the loan for each assumption? *LU 15-1(2, 3)*

4. Loretta Scholten bought a home for $210,000 with a down payment of $30,000. Her rate of interest is 6% for 35 years. Calculate Loretta's payment per $1,000 and her monthly mortgage payment. *LU 15-1(2)*

5. Using Problem 4, calculate the total cost of interest for Loretta Scholten. *LU 15-1(3)*

SURF TO SAVE

The costs of buying a home 🔍

PROBLEM 1
15- versus 30-year loan

Go to http://www.bankrate.com/calculators/mortgages/mortgage-calculator.aspx. Suppose you can get a $90,000 loan at 8% interest and that you can make a $25,000 down payment. What would your monthly payment be on a 30-year loan? What would the monthly payment be on a 15-year loan? How much interest would you pay altogether for each loan? (Ignore property taxes and insurance in the calculations.)

Discussion Questions

1. What are the pros and cons of a 30-year versus 15-year loan?

2. Which loan period would you feel more comfortable borrowing within? Why?

PROBLEM 3
Refinancing your home

Visit https://www.wellsfargo.com/mortgage/rates/calculator/ and assume you are looking to refinance your current home loan. Your home value is $200,000 and you still owe $120,000, which will be the loan amount for this refinance.

Discussion Questions

1. If your current monthly payment is $975 on your existing 30-year loan, would you be interested in refinancing? Why or why not?

2. How much of a difference in your monthly payment amount would entice you to pursue a refinance?

PROBLEM 2
On the move

Go to http://www.interest.com/. Choose a state to which you would like to move. Using the "Find Mortgage Rate" calculator, choose a city/state on a 30-year fixed rate loan. Compare the total amount of interest you would pay to borrow $100,000 from three different lenders. Remember to include the points, or interest fees, you pay up front. For example, 2 points means a 2% fee at the start of the loan, or $100,000 × 2% = $2,000.

Discussion Questions

1. Why would researching your house costs in another state assist you in planning such a move?

2. What might explain the differences you found among lenders?

PROBLEM 4
Amortization of your loan

Using http://www.bankrate.com/calculators/mortgages/amortization-calculator.aspx calculate your amortization schedule on a $225,000 30-year home loan at a rate of 4%. Based on this amortization schedule, at what point do your monthly payments begin to apply more toward principal than interest?

Discussion Questions

1. Suppose you decided to make 1 extra normal monthly payment every April. How would this impact your payoff date?

2. What are the pros and cons of viewing a loan amortization schedule from the perspective of the buyer?

MOBILE APPS ✕

Mortgage Rates (Left Coast R&D, Inc.) Assists you in shopping for the best rates currently available.

Mortgage Calculator Plus (Appeum Inc.) Calculates fixed rate mortgages simply with the ability to run "what-if" scenarios for overpayments, loan term, loan amount, and interest rate.

A KIPLINGER APPROACH

By Patricia Mertz Esswein, From *Kiplinger's Personal Finance*, 2014.

HOME »

Reverse Mortgages With a Twist

Buy a new home in retirement without a mortgage payment. **BY PATRICIA MERTZ ESSWEIN**

CHUCK ROONEY, 75, AND HIS wife, Ellen, 71, originally set out to refinance the mortgage on their home in Decatur, Ga. But after talking with a reverse-mortgage adviser at Security 1 Lending, the couple discovered that if they took a home-equity conversion mortgage (HECM) for purchase, a type of reverse mortgage, they could downsize from their 3,600-square-foot house and buy a new home closer to family without worrying about mortgage payments.

With a traditional reverse mortgage, anyone 62 or older can tap home equity for income. An HECM for purchase is another type of reverse mortgage that helps you buy a new home. The new home must be your primary residence, but if you have the cash to make a down payment equal to about half of the home's price, you can use the proceeds from the reverse mortgage for the rest. And you can wait to sell your old home—or not sell it at all.

The Rooneys bought a 2,600-square-foot, single-story home with a golf-course view in Newnan, Ga.—minutes from the grandkids—for $235,000 in February 2014. They closed the deal with $119,000 (including closing costs) of their own money, which they withdrew from an IRA, and about $122,000 from the reverse mortgage. Because they repaid the IRA money within 60 days from the $387,500 sale price of their former home, they avoided a tax bill.

How much can you get? Lenders will determine the maximum payout, or *principal limit,* for which you'll qualify based on the price of your new home (the lesser of the purchase price or appraised value, up to $625,500), the ages of you and your spouse, and the interest rate on the loan. (To get an estimate of your principal limit and costs, use the reverse-mortgage calculator at www.mtgprofessor.com.)

■ A REVERSE MORTGAGE CAN COVER ABOUT HALF THE COST OF A NEW HOME.

Your new home must be your primary residence at least 183 days a year.

With current interest rates, the HECM for purchase will pay for roughly half of the purchase price of the home for a 62-year-old, says Shelley Giordano, of Security 1 Lending. The older the homeowner and the lower the interest rate (to a point), the more you can get. You must cover the remainder from your own funds.

If you take the maximum payout as a lump sum, you'll incur a fixed rate of interest, which ranged from 4.75% to 5.25% in late September. Or you could reserve part of your payout as a line of credit with a variable rate that was recently 2.5% to 3%. The interest tab accrues over the life of the loan, as does an annual mortgage insurance premium (1.25% of the outstanding loan balance) and any servicing fees. All are payable when the loan comes due.

At closing, you must pay the lender's origination fee and closing costs, as well as an up-front mortgage insurance premium equal to 2.5% of the home's purchase price. (If you take less than 60% of the maximum payout, the insurance premium falls to 0.5%.) You can roll those costs into the loan. You're still responsible for hazard-insurance premiums and property taxes.

When the second spouse moves, dies or sells the home, the loan must be repaid—either the mortgage balance (including accrued charges) or 95% of the current appraised value of the property, whichever is less. Options include selling the home to pay the debt, covering it out of pocket or simply handing the keys over to the lender.

Before you can shop for the best rate and costs, you must be counseled about the program (visit www.hud.gov and search for "Find an HECM Housing Counselor"). To find lenders by state, visit www.reversemortgage.org. ■

ISTOCKPHOTO.COM

BUSINESS MATH ISSUE

Reverse mortgage should not be used to buy a new home.

1. List the key points of the article and information to support your position.
2. Write a group defense of your position using math calculations to support your view.

Classroom Notes

CHAPTER 16

How to Read, Analyze, and Interpret Financial Reports

© Tim Boyle/Getty Images

Pepper ... And Salt

THE WALL STREET JOURNAL

"I followed accepted market strategies but I strayed from generally accepted accounting principles."

From *The Wall Street Journal*, permission Cartoon Features Syndicate.

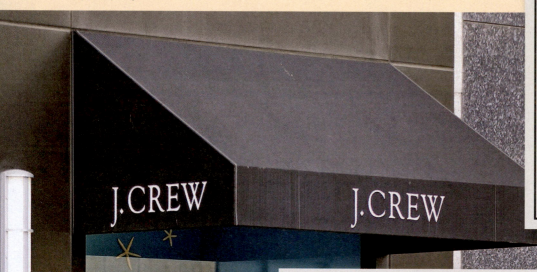

J. Crew Writes Down Its Stores

BY SUZANNE KAPNER

J. Crew Group Inc. translated retailing's historic shift toward the Web into dollars and cents on Thursday, writing down the value of its stores by more than half a billion dollars while leaving its online operations unscathed.

The move came as the apparel retailer reassessed the $3 billion price private-equity firms TPG Capital and **Leonard Green & Partners** paid for it in a 2011 buyout.

Technically, J. Crew wrote down the value of the goodwill associated with its stores by 57%, or $536 million, while leav-ing the portion assigned to its online operations unchanged. It also wrote down the value of the J. Crew brand name by $145 million.

Goodwill broadly refers to a company's intangible assets, like reputation and customer loyalty, and often reflects the premium paid for a company in an acquisition.

"It speaks to the shift in how people are shopping," said Stuart Haselden, J. Crew's chief financial officer.

"Mall traffic has been down for two years, and e-commerce has been growing across the industry," he said.

Mr. Haselden said the retailer has no plans to close stores and in fact expects to open about 20 of them under its Madewell brand next year.

The Madewell chain, which caters to young adults, has been performing better than the company's namesake J. Crew locations.

Including the write-downs, J. Crew posted a loss of $607.8 million for the quarter ended Nov. 1, compared with a profit of $35.4 million a year earlier.

Revenue for the period rose 6% to $655.2 million. Sales excluding newly opened or closed locations fell 2%, after growing 4% in the same period a year earlier.

Reprinted by permission of *The Wall Street Journal*, copyright 2014 Dow Jones & Company, Inc. All rights reserved worldwide.

LU 16–1: Balance Sheet—Report as of a Particular Date

1. Explain the purpose and the key items on the balance sheet.

2. Explain and complete vertical and horizontal analysis.

LU 16–2: Income Statement—Report for a Specific Period of Time

1. Explain the purpose and the key items on the income statement.

2. Explain and complete vertical and horizontal analysis.

LU 16–3: Trend and Ratio Analysis

1. Explain and complete a trend analysis.

2. List, explain, and calculate key financial ratios.

Here are key terms in this chapter. After completing the chapter, if you know the term, place a checkmark in the box. If you don't know the term, look it up and put the page number where it can be found.

Accounts payable ☐ Accounts receivable ☐ Acid test ☐ Asset turnover ☐ Assets ☐ Balance sheet ☐ Capital ☐ Common stock ☐ Comparative statement ☐ Corporation ☐ Cost of merchandise (goods) sold ☐ Current assets ☐ Current liabilities ☐ Current ratio ☐ Expenses ☐ Gross profit from sales ☐ Gross sales ☐ Horizontal analysis ☐ Income statement ☐ Liabilities ☐ Long-term liabilities ☐ Merchandise inventory ☐ Mortgage note payable ☐ Net income ☐ Net purchases ☐ Net sales ☐ Operating expenses ☐ Owner's equity ☐ Partnership ☐ Plant and equipment ☐ Prepaid expenses ☐ Purchase discounts ☐ Purchase returns and allowances ☐ Purchases ☐ Quick assets ☐ Quick ratio ☐ Ratio analysis ☐ Retained earnings ☐ Return on equity ☐ Revenues ☐ Salaries payable ☐ Sales (not trade) discounts ☐ Sales returns and allowances ☐ Sole proprietorship ☐ Stockholders' equity ☐ Trend analysis ☐ Vertical analysis ☐

The Sarbanes-Oxley Act (2002) was passed to ensure public companies are accurately reporting their financial statements. The following *Wall Street Journal* clip shows that errors have been found in Hertz financial statements. Hertz will have to restate its financial information as a result.

This chapter explains how to analyze two key financial reports: the *balance sheet* (shows a company's financial condition at a particular date) and the *income statement* (shows a company's profitability over a time period).[1] Business owners must understand their financial statements to avoid financial difficulties. This includes knowing how to read, analyze, and interpret financial reports.

The chapter opener clipping shows that revenues are down at J. Crew and discusses how the company is taking steps to solve this problem.

---

[1]The third key financial report is the statement of cash flows. We do not discuss this statement. For more information on the statement of cash flows, check your accounting text.

By MICHAEL CALIA

Hertz Global Holdings Inc. said it would have to restate and correct results from the past three years, according to a regulatory filing Friday that indicated more widespread accounting problems at the auto-rental company than had been thought.

Hertz, citing the results of an internal audit, said its results for 2011, most recently included in its annual report filed for 2013, "should no longer be relied upon," and that the company must restate them.

The company added that it is reviewing if the issues have had any impact on results in 2014.

"It will take time to complete this process, and previously reported information is likely to change, although the actual size of any adjustments has yet to be determined and some adjustments may offset others," the company said in its filing with the U.S. Securities and Exchange Commission.

The review "recently identified other errors related to allowances for uncollectable amounts with respect to renter obligations for damaged vehicles and restoration obligations at the end of facility leases," Hertz said.

PwC's expected shift in opinion on Hertz's internal controls shouldn't come as a surprise, given the restatement and revisions, said Charles K. Whitehead, a Cornell University professor who specializes in corporate and financial law.

Hertz shares fell about 9% on Friday after the auto-rental company said there was 'at least one material weakness' in its financial controls.

Reprinted by permission of *The Wall Street Journal,* copyright 2014 Dow Jones & Company, Inc. All rights reserved worldwide.

Learning Unit 16–1: Balance Sheet—Report as of a Particular Date

The **balance sheet** gives a financial picture of what a company is worth as of a particular date, usually at the end of a month or year. This report lists (1) how much the company owns (assets), (2) how much the company owes (liabilities), and (3) how much the owner (**owner's equity**) is worth.

Note that assets and liabilities are divided into two groups: current (*short term,* usually less than 1 year); and *long term,* usually more than 1 year. The basic formula for a balance sheet is as follows:

$$\text{Assets} - \text{Liabilities} = \text{Owner's equity}$$

Like all formulas, the items on both sides of the equals sign must balance.

By reversing the above formula, we have the following common balance sheet layout:

> Assets = Liabilities + Owner's equity

To introduce you to the balance sheet, let's assume that you collect baseball cards and decide to open a baseball card shop. As the owner of The Card Shop, your investment, or owner's equity, is called **capital.** Since your business is small, your balance sheet is short. After the first year of operation, The Card Shop balance sheet is shown as follows:

THE CARD SHOP
Balance Sheet
December 31, 2017

Report as of a particular date

Assets		Liabilities	
Cash	$ 3,000	Accounts payable	$ 2,500
Merchandise inventory (baseball cards)	4,000	**Owner's Equity**	
Equipment	3,000	E. Slott, capital	7,500
Total assets	$10,000	Total liabilities and owner's equity	$10,000

"Capital" does not mean "cash." It is the owner's investment in the company.

The heading gives the name of the company, title of the report, and date of the report. Note how the totals of both sides of the balance sheet are the same. This is true of all balance sheets.

We can take figures from the balance sheet of The Card Shop and use our first formula to determine how much the business is worth:

> Assets − Liabilities = Owner's equity (capital)

$$\$10,000 - \$2,500 = \$7,500$$

Since you are the single owner of The Card Shop, your business is a **sole proprietorship.** If a business has two or more owners, it is a **partnership.** A **corporation** has many owners or stockholders, and the equity of these owners is

© ZealPhotography/Alamy Stock Photo

called **stockholders' equity.** *Anytime you create a balance sheet, check your accuracy by adding liabilities to owner's equity. If that total equals assets, you've got it right!*

Elements of the Balance Sheet

The format and contents of all corporation balance sheets are similar. Figure 16.1 shows the balance sheet of Mool Company. As you can see, the formula Assets = Liabilities + Stockholders' equity (we have a corporation in this example) is also the framework of this balance sheet.

FIGURE 16.1   Balance sheet

Assets broken down into current assets and plant and equipment

MOOL COMPANY
Balance Sheet
December 31, 2017

Put in heading who, what, when

Liabilities broken down into current and long-term

	Assets					**Liabilities**		
a.	Current assets:				a.	Current liabilities:		
b.	Cash	$ 7,000			b.	Accounts payable	$80,000	
c.	Accounts receivable	9,000			c.	Salaries payable	12,000	
d.	Merchandise inventory	30,000		2.	d.	Total current liabilities		$ 92,000
e.	Prepaid expenses	15,000			e.	Long-term liabilities:		
1. f.	Total current assets		$ 61,000		f.	Mortgage note payable		58,000
g.	Plant and equipment:				g.	Total liabilities		$ 150,000
h.	Building (net)	$60,000				**Stockholders' Equity**		
i.	Land	84,000			a.	Common stock	$20,000	
j.	Total plant and equipment		144,000		b.	Retained earnings	35,000	
				3.	c.	Total stockholders' equity		55,000
					d.	Total liabilities and stockholders' equity		$205,000
k.	Total assets		$205,000					

Total of current assets and plant and equipment

Total is double-ruled

Total of all liabilities and stockholders' equity

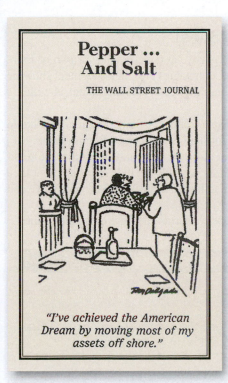

Pepper ... And Salt

THE WALL STREET JOURNAL

"I've achieved the American Dream by moving most of my assets off shore."

From *The Wall Street Journal*, permission Cartoon Features Syndicate.

To help you understand the three main balance sheet groups (assets, liabilities, and stockholders' equity) and their elements, we have labeled them in Figure 16.1. An explanation of these groups and their elements follows this paragraph. Do not try to memorize the elements. Just try to understand their meaning. Think of Figure 16.1 as a reference aid. You will find that the more you work with balance sheets, the easier it is for you to understand them.

1. **Assets:** Things of value *owned* by a company (economic resources of the company) that can be measured and expressed in monetary terms.
   a. **Current assets:** Assets that companies consume or convert to cash *within 1 year* or a normal operating cycle.
   b. **Cash:** Total cash in checking accounts, savings accounts, and on hand.
   c. **Accounts receivable:** Money *owed* to a company by customers from sales on account (buy now, pay later).
   d. **Merchandise inventory:** Cost of goods in stock for resale to customers.
   e. **Prepaid expenses:** The purchases of a company are assets until they expire (insurance or rent) or are consumed (supplies).
   f. **Total current assets:** Total of all assets that the company will consume or convert to cash within 1 year.
   g. **Plant and equipment:** Assets that will last longer than 1 year. These assets are used in the operation of the company.

    h. Building (net): The cost of the building minus the depreciation that has accumulated. Usually, balance sheets show this as "Building less accumulated depreciation." In Chapter 17 we discuss accumulated depreciation in greater detail.

    i. Land: This asset does not depreciate, but it can increase or decrease in value.

    j. Total plant and equipment: Total of building and land, including machinery and equipment.

    k. Total assets: Total of current assets and plant and equipment.

2. **Liabilities:** Debts or obligations of the company.

    a. Current liabilities: Debts or obligations of the company that are *due within 1 year.*

    b. Accounts payable: A current liability that shows the amount the company owes to creditors for services or items purchased.

    c. Salaries payable: Obligations that the company must pay within 1 year for salaries earned but unpaid.

    d. Total current liabilities: Total obligations that the company must pay within 1 year.

    e. Long-term liabilities: Debts or obligations that the company does not have to pay within 1 year.

    f. Mortgage note payable: Debt owed on a building that is a long-term liability; often the building is the collateral.

    g. Total liabilities: Total of current and long-term liabilities.

3. **Stockholders' equity (owner's equity):** The rights or interest of the stockholders to assets of a corporation. If the company is not a corporation, the term *owner's equity* is used. The word *capital* follows the owner's name under the title *Owner's Equity.*

    a. Common stock: Amount of the initial and additional investment of corporation owners by the purchase of stock.

    b. Retained earnings: The amount of corporation earnings that the company retains, not necessarily in cash form.

    c. Total stockholders' equity: Total of stock plus retained earnings.

    d. Total liabilities and stockholders' equity: Total current liabilities, long-term liabilities, stock, and retained earnings. This total represents all the claims on assets—prior and present claims of creditors, owners' residual claims, and any other claims.

Create a personal balance sheet by listing all personal assets and debts. Subtract debts from assets to calculate net worth. Do an Internet search to compare your net worth to what financial analysts recommend for your age group.

Now that you are familiar with the common balance sheet items, you are ready to analyze a balance sheet.

Vertical Analysis and the Balance Sheet

Often financial statement readers want to analyze reports that contain data for two or more successive accounting periods. To make this possible, companies present a statement showing the data from these periods side by side. As you might expect, this statement is called a **comparative statement.**

Comparative reports help illustrate changes in data. Financial statement readers should compare the percents in the reports to industry percents and the percents of competitors.

Figure 16.2 shows the comparative balance sheet of Roger Company. Note that the statement analyzes each asset as a percent of total assets for a single period. The statement then analyzes each liability and equity as a percent of total liabilities and stockholders' equity. We call this type of analysis **vertical analysis.**

The following steps use the portion formula to prepare a vertical analysis of a balance sheet.

PREPARING A VERTICAL ANALYSIS OF A BALANCE SHEET
Step 1. Divide each asset (the portion) as a percent of total assets (the base). Round as indicated.
Step 2. Round each liability and stockholders' equity (the portions) as a percent of total liabilities and stockholders' equity (the base). Round as indicated.

We can also analyze balance sheets for two or more periods by using **horizontal analysis.** Horizontal analysis compares each item in 1 year by amount, percent, or both

FIGURE **16.2**

Comparative balance sheet:
Vertical analysis

We divide each item by
the total of assets.

Portion
($8,000)

Base × Rate
($85,000)   (?)

ROGER COMPANY Comparative Balance Sheet December 31, 2016 and 2017				
	2017		**2016**	
	Amount	**Percent**	**Amount**	**Percent**
Assets				
Current assets:				
Cash	$22,000	25.88	$18,000	22.22
Accounts receivable	8,000	9.41	9,000	11.11
Merchandise inventory	9,000	10.59	7,000	8.64
Prepaid rent	4,000	4.71	5,000	6.17
Total current assets	$43,000	50.59	$39,000	48.15*
Plant and equipment:				
Building (net)	$18,000	21.18	$18,000	22.22
Land	24,000	28.24	24,000	29.63
Total plant and equipment	$42,000	49.41*	$42,000	51.85
Total assets	$85,000	100.00	$81,000	100.00
Liabilities				
Current liabilities:				
Accounts payable	$14,000	16.47	$ 8,000	9.88
Salaries payable	18,000	21.18	17,000	20.99
Total current liabilities	$32,000	37.65	$25,000	30.86*
Long-term liabilities:				
Mortgage note payable	12,000	14.12	20,000	24.69
Total liabilities	$44,000	51.76*	$45,000	55.56*
Stockholders' Equity				
Common stock	$20,000	23.53	$20,000	24.69
Retained earnings	21,000	24.71	16,000	19.75
Total stockholders' equity	$41,000	48.24	$36,000	44.44
Total liabilities and stockholders' equity	$85,000	100.00	$81,000	100.00

We divide each item by the total of
liabilities and stockholders' equity.

Portion
($20,000)

Base × Rate
($85,000)   (?)

Note: All percents are rounded to the nearest hundredth percent.

*Due to rounding.

with the same item of the previous year. Note the Abby Ellen Company horizontal analysis shown in Figure 16.3. To make a horizontal analysis, we use the portion formula and the steps that follow:

MONEY tips

Are you financially "on track"? Here is a simple calculation to help estimate what your net worth should be:

(Age × Pretax income) ÷ 10

PREPARING A HORIZONTAL ANALYSIS OF A COMPARATIVE BALANCE SHEET
Step 1. Calculate the increase or decrease (portion) in each item from the base year.
Step 2. Divide the increase or decrease in Step 1 by the old or base year.
Step 3. Round as indicated.

You can see the difference between vertical analysis and horizontal analysis by looking at the example of vertical analysis in Figure 16.2. The percent calculations in Figure 16.2 are for each item of a particular year as a percent of that year's total assets or total liabilities and stockholders' equity.

Horizontal analysis needs comparative columns because we take the difference *between* periods. In Figure 16.3, for example, the accounts receivable decreased $1,000 from 2016 to 2017.

FIGURE **16.3**

Comparative balance sheet:
Horizontal analysis

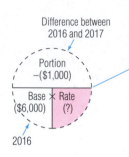

Difference between
2016 and 2017

Portion
−($1,000)

Base × Rate
($6,000)   (?)

2016

ABBY ELLEN COMPANY
Comparative Balance Sheet
December 31, 2016 and 2017

	2017	2016	INCREASE (DECREASE) Amount	INCREASE (DECREASE) Percent
Assets				
Current assets:				
Cash	$ 6,000	$ 4,000	$2,000	50.00*
Accounts receivable	5,000	6,000	(1,000)	−16.67
Merchandise inventory	9,000	4,000	5,000	125.00
Prepaid rent	5,000	7,000	(2,000)	−28.57
Total current assets	$25,000	$21,000	$4,000	19.05
Plant and equipment:				
Building (net)	$12,000	$12,000	–0–	–0–
Land	18,000	18,000	–0–	–0–
Total plant and equipment	$30,000	$30,000	–0–	–0–
Total assets	$55,000	$51,000	$4,000	7.84
Liabilities				
Current liabilities:				
Accounts payable	$ 3,200	$ 1,800	$ 1,400	77.78
Salaries payable	2,900	3,200	(300)	− 9.38
Total current liabilities	$ 6,100	$ 5,000	$1,100	22.00
Long-term liabilities:				
Mortgage note payable	17,000	15,000	2,000	13.33
Total liabilities	$23,100	$20,000	$3,100	15.50
Owner's Equity				
Abby Ellen, capital	$31,900	$31,000	$ 900	2.90
Total liabilities and owner's equity	$55,000	$51,000	$4,000	7.84

*The percents are not summed vertically in horizontal analysis.

Thus, by dividing $1,000 (amount of change) by $6,000 (base year), we see that Abby's receivables decreased 16.67% .

Let's now try the following Practice Quiz.

LU 16–1   PRACTICE QUIZ

Complete this **Practice Quiz** to see how you are doing.

1. Complete this partial comparative balance sheet by vertical analysis. Round percents to the nearest hundredth.

	2017 Amount	2017 Percent	2016 Amount	2016 Percent
Assets				
Current assets:				
a. Cash	$42,000		$40,000	
b. Accounts receivable	18,000		17,000	
c. Merchandise inventory	15,000		12,000	
d. Prepaid expenses	17,000		14,000	
	·	·	·	
	·	·	·	
	·	·	·	
Total current assets	$160,000		$150,000	

2. What is the amount of change in merchandise inventory and the percent increase?

For **extra help** from your authors–Sharon and Jeff–see the videos in Connect.

These videos are also available on YouTube!

✓ **Solutions**

		2017		2016	
1.	a. Cash	$\dfrac{\$42,000}{\$160,000} =$	26.25%	$\dfrac{\$40,000}{\$150,000} =$	26.67%
	b. Accounts receivable	$\dfrac{\$18,000}{\$160,000} =$	11.25%	$\dfrac{\$17,000}{\$150,000} =$	11.33%
	c. Merchandise inventory	$\dfrac{\$15,000}{\$160,000} =$	9.38%	$\dfrac{\$12,000}{\$150,000} =$	8.00%
	d. Prepaid expenses	$\dfrac{\$17,000}{\$160,000} =$	10.63%	$\dfrac{\$14,000}{\$150,000} =$	9.33%

2.

$$\begin{array}{r} \$15,000 \\ -\ 12,000 \\ \hline \end{array}$$

Amount = $\boxed{\$\ 3,000}$

$\text{Percent} = \dfrac{\$3,000}{\$12,000} = \boxed{25\%}$

LU 16–1a   EXTRA PRACTICE QUIZ WITH WORKED-OUT SOLUTIONS

Need more practice? Try this Extra Practice Quiz (check figures in the Interactive Chapter Organizer). Worked-out Solutions can be found in Appendix B at end of text.

1. Complete this partial comparative balance sheet by vertical analysis. Round percents to the nearest hundredth.

	2017		2016	
	Amount	Percent	Amount	Percent
Assets				
Current assets:				
a. Cash	$ 38,000		$ 35,000	
b. Accounts receivable	19,000		18,000	
c. Merchandise inventory	16,000		11,000	
d. Prepaid expenses	20,000		16,000	
.	.		.	
.	.		.	
.	.		.	
Total current assets	$180,000		$140,000	

2. What is the amount of change in merchandise inventory and the percent increase?

Learning Unit 16–2: Income Statement—Report for a Specific Period of Time

One of the most important departments in a company is its accounting department. The job of the accounting department is to determine the financial results of the company's operations. Is the company making money or losing money? The following *Wall Street Journal* clip reveals by 2017 many companies will have to speed up or slow down the rate they book revenues.

In this learning unit we look at the **income statement**—a financial report that tells how well a company is performing (its profitability or net profit) during a specific period of time (month, year, etc.). In general, the income statement reveals the inward flow of revenues (sales) against the outward or potential outward flow of costs and expenses.

LO 1

GLOBAL

Rules Alter Timetable For Booking Revenue

BY MICHAEL RAPOPORT

New rules released Wednesday will overhaul the way businesses record revenue on their books, capping a 12-year project that will affect companies ranging from software firms to auto makers to wireless providers.

The new standards, issued jointly by U.S. and global rule makers, will take effect in 2017, prompting a broad array of companies—from software giants like **Microsoft** Corp. and **Oracle** Corp. to major appliance makers—either to speed up or slow down the rate at which they book at least some of their revenue.

The rules aim to simplify and inject more uniformity into one of the most basic yardsticks of a company's performance—how well its products or services are selling.

"It's one of the most important metrics for investors in the capital markets," said Russell Golden, chairman of the Financial Accounting Standards Board, which sets accounting rules for U.S. companies and collaborated on the new rules with the global International Accounting Standards Board.

Companies were cautious in assessing the potential impact of the overhaul, but some were optimistic. "We've been waiting for it for a long time," said Ken Goldman, chief financial officer of **Black Duck Software** Inc., a provider of software and consulting services. "This levels the playing field and takes a lot of the ambiguity out of what are overly restrictive rules."

The rules are designed to replace fragmented and inconsistent standards under which companies in different industries often record their revenue differently and sometimes book a portion of it well before or after the sales that generate it.

Reprinted by permission of *The Wall Street Journal,* copyright 2014 Dow Jones & Company, Inc. All rights reserved worldwide.

The form of income statements varies depending on the company's type of business. However, the basic formula of the income statement is the same:

$$\text{Revenues} - \text{Operating expenses} = \text{Net income}$$

In a merchandising business like The Card Shop, we can expand on this formula:

Revenues (sales) ————— After any returns, allowances, or discounts
− Cost of merchandise or goods ←—— Baseball cards
= Gross profit from sales
− Operating expenses
= Net income (profit)

THE CARD SHOP Income Statement For Month Ended December 31, 2017	
Revenues (sales)	$8,000
Cost of merchandise (goods) sold	3,000
Gross profit from sales	$5,000
Operating expenses	750
Net income	$4,250

Now let's look at The Card Shop's income statement to see how much profit The Card Shop made during its first year of operation. For simplicity, we assume The Card Shop sold all the cards it bought during the year. For its first year of business, The Card Shop made a profit of $4,250.

We can now go more deeply into the income statement elements as we study the income statement of a corporation.

Elements of the Corporation Income Statement

Figure 16.4 gives the format and content of the Mool Company income statement—a corporation. The five main items of an income statement are revenues, cost of merchandise (goods) sold, gross profit on sales, operating expenses, and net income. We will follow the same pattern we used in explaining the balance sheet and define the main items and the letter-coded subitems.

1. **Revenues:** Total earned sales (cash or credit) less any sales returns and allowances or sales discounts. Note from the following *Wall Street Journal* clip that revenue for Yum is twice as large in China as in the United States.

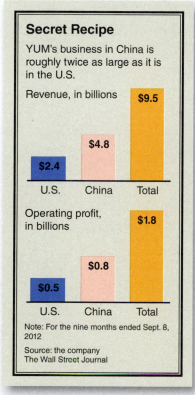

Source: *The Wall Street Journal*, 1/12/13.

a. **Gross sales:** Total earned sales before sales returns and allowances or sales discounts.

b. **Sales returns and allowances:** Reductions in price or reductions in revenue due to goods returned because of product defects, errors, and so on. When the buyer keeps the damaged goods, an allowance results.

c. **Sales (not trade) discounts:** Reductions in the selling price of goods due to early customer payment. For example, a store may give a 2% discount to a customer who pays a bill within 10 days.

d. **Net sales:** Gross sales less sales returns and allowances less sales discounts.

2. **Cost of merchandise (goods) sold:** All the costs of getting the merchandise that the company sold. The cost of all unsold merchandise (goods) will be subtracted from this item (ending inventory).

a. **Merchandise inventory, December 1, 2017:** Cost of inventory in the store that was for sale to customers at the beginning of the month.

b. **Purchases:** Cost of additional merchandise brought into the store for resale to customers.

c. **Purchase returns and allowances:** Cost of merchandise returned to the store due to damage, defects, errors, and so on. Damaged goods kept by the buyer result in a cost reduction called an *allowance*.

d. **Purchase discounts:** Savings received by the buyer for paying for merchandise before a certain date. These discounts can result in a substantial savings to a company.

e. **Cost of *net purchases*:** Cost of purchases less purchase returns and allowances less purchase discounts.

FIGURE 16.4 Income statement

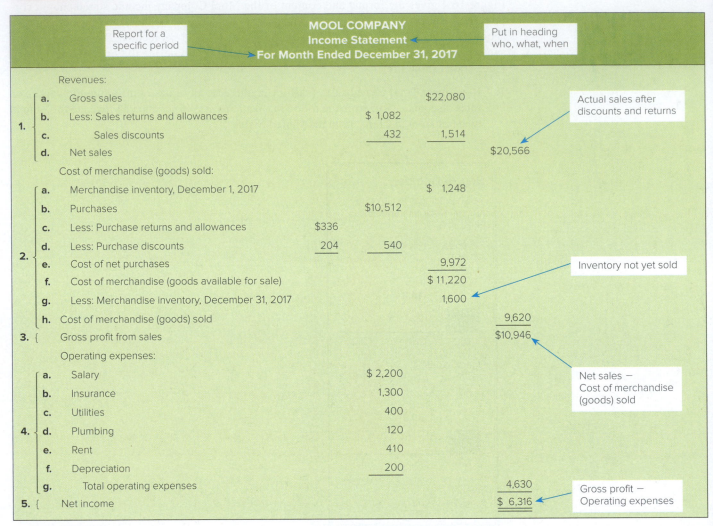

MOOL COMPANY
Income Statement
For Month Ended December 31, 2017

Report for a specific period → *Put in heading who, what, when*

		Revenues:			
1.	**a.**	Gross sales		$22,080	
	b.	Less: Sales returns and allowances	$ 1,082		
	c.	Sales discounts	432	1,514	
	d.	Net sales			$20,566

Actual sales after discounts and returns

		Cost of merchandise (goods) sold:			
2.	**a.**	Merchandise inventory, December 1, 2017		$ 1,248	
	b.	Purchases	$10,512		
	c.	Less: Purchase returns and allowances	$336		
	d.	Less: Purchase discounts	204	540	
	e.	Cost of net purchases		9,972	
	f.	Cost of merchandise (goods available for sale)		$ 11,220	
	g.	Less: Merchandise inventory, December 31, 2017		1,600	
	h.	Cost of merchandise (goods) sold			9,620

Inventory not yet sold

3. {		Gross profit from sales			$10,946

Net sales − Cost of merchandise (goods) sold

		Operating expenses:			
4. {	**a.**	Salary	$ 2,200		
	b.	Insurance	1,300		
	c.	Utilities	400		
	d.	Plumbing	120		
	e.	Rent	410		
	f.	Depreciation	200		
	g.	Total operating expenses			4,630
5. {		Net income			$ 6,316

Gross profit − Operating expenses

Note: Numbers are subtotaled from left to right.

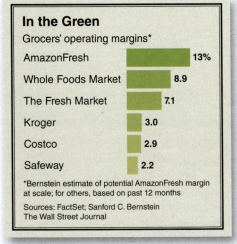

In the Green

Grocers' operating margins*

AmazonFresh	13%
Whole Foods Market	8.9
The Fresh Market	7.1
Kroger	3.0
Costco	2.9
Safeway	2.2

*Bernstein estimate of potential AmazonFresh margin at scale; for others, based on past 12 months

Sources: FactSet; Sanford C. Bernstein
The Wall Street Journal

Source: *The Wall Street Journal,* 10/28/13.

f. Cost of merchandise (goods available for sale): Sum of beginning inventory plus cost of net purchases.

g. Merchandise inventory, December 31, 2017: Cost of inventory remaining in the store to be sold.

h. Cost of merchandise (goods) sold: Beginning inventory plus net purchases less ending inventory. Note in the accompanying *Wall Street Journal* clipping the operating margin for Whole Foods Market.

3. **Gross profit from sales:** Net sales less cost of merchandise (goods) sold.

4. **Operating expenses:** Additional costs of operating the business beyond the actual cost of inventory sold.
   a.–f. Expenses: Individual expenses broken down.
   g. Total operating expenses: Total of all the individual expenses.

5. **Net income:** Gross profit less operating expenses.

Create a personal income statement: Salaries − Expenses = Savings/Investment.
 Note in the following clip how the cost of a grand latte in China is calculated.
 In the next section you will learn some formulas that companies use to calculate various items on the income statement.

GLOBAL

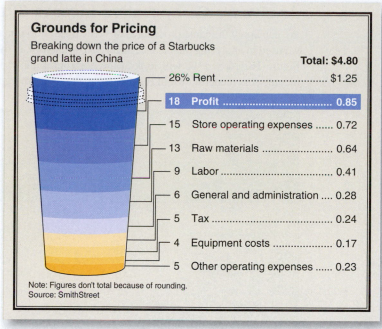

Grounds for Pricing

Breaking down the price of a Starbucks grand latte in China

Total: $4.80

— 26% Rent $1.25

— 18   Profit 0.85

— 15   Store operating expenses 0.72

— 13   Raw materials 0.64

— 9   Labor 0.41

— 6   General and administration 0.28

— 5   Tax 0.24

— 4   Equipment costs 0.17

— 5   Other operating expenses 0.23

Note: Figures don't total because of rounding.
Source: SmithStreet

Source: *The Wall Street Journal,* 10/22/13.

Calculating Net Sales, Cost of Merchandise (Goods) Sold, Gross Profit, and Net Income of an Income Statement

It is time to look closely at Figure 16.4 and see how each section is built. Use the previous vocabulary as a reference. We will study Figure 16.4 step by step.

Step 1. Calculate the net sales—what Mool earned:

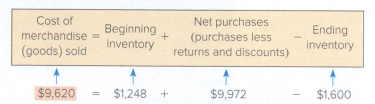

$$\text{Net sales} = \text{Gross sales} - \frac{\text{Sales returns}}{\text{and allowances}} - \text{Sales discounts}$$

$$\$20,566 = \$22,080 - \$1,082 - \$432$$

Step 2. Calculate the cost of merchandise (goods) sold:

$$\begin{matrix}\text{Cost of} \\ \text{merchandise} \\ \text{(goods) sold}\end{matrix} = \begin{matrix}\text{Beginning} \\ \text{inventory}\end{matrix} + \begin{matrix}\text{Net purchases} \\ \text{(purchases less} \\ \text{returns and discounts)}\end{matrix} - \begin{matrix}\text{Ending} \\ \text{inventory}\end{matrix}$$

$$\$9,620 = \$1,248 + \$9,972 - \$1,600$$

Step 3. Calculate the gross profit from sales—profit before operating expenses:

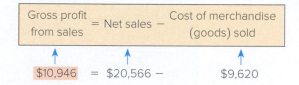

$$\begin{matrix}\text{Gross profit} \\ \text{from sales}\end{matrix} = \text{Net sales} - \begin{matrix}\text{Cost of merchandise} \\ \text{(goods) sold}\end{matrix}$$

$$\$10,946 = \$20,566 - \$9,620$$

Step 4. Calculate the net income—profit after operating expenses:

$$\text{Net income} = \text{Gross profit} - \text{Operating expenses}$$

$$\$6,316 = \$10,946 - \$4,630$$

MONEY tips

Keep a record of how much you owe and to whom you owe it. Create a plan to pay each debt off, one by one. Pay off the highest interest rate balance first.

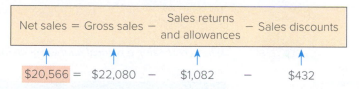

Analyzing Comparative Income Statements

We can apply the same procedures of vertical and horizontal analysis to the income statement that we used in analyzing the balance sheet. Let's first look at the vertical analysis for Royal Company, Figure 16.5. Then we will look at the horizontal analysis of Flint Company's 2016 and 2017 income statements shown in Figure 16.6. Note in the margin how numbers are calculated.

FIGURE 16.5

Vertical analysis

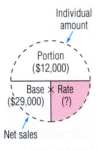

ROYAL COMPANY Comparative Income Statement For Years Ended December 31, 2016 and 2017				
	2017	**Percent of net**	**2016**	**Percent of net**
Net sales	$45,000	100.00	$29,000	100.00*
Cost of merchandise sold	19,000	42.22	12,000	41.38
Gross profit from sales	$26,000	57.78	$17,000	58.62
Operating expenses:				
Depreciation	$ 1,000	2.22	$ 500	1.72
Selling and advertising	4,200	9.33	1,600	5.52
Research	2,900	6.44	2,000	6.90
Miscellaneous	500	1.11	200	.69
Total operating expenses	$ 8,600	19.11†	$ 4,300	14.83
Income before interest and taxes	$17,400	38.67	$12,700	43.79
Interest expense	6,000	13.33	3,000	10.34
Income before taxes	$ 11,400	25.33†	$ 9,700	33.45
Provision for taxes	5,500	12.22	3,000	10.34
Net income	$ 5,900	13.11	$ 6,700	23.10†

*Net sales = 100%
†Off due to rounding.

When conducting a vertical analysis of an income statement, divide each line item by net sales.

FIGURE 16.6

Horizontal analysis

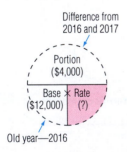

FLINT COMPANY Comparative Income Statement For Years Ended December 31, 2016 and 2017				
			INCREASE (DECREASE)	
	2017	**2016**	**Amount**	**Percent**
Sales	$90,000	$80,000	$ 10,000	
Sales returns and allowances	2,000	2,000	–0–	
Net sales	$88,000	$78,000	$ 10,000	+ 12.82
Cost of merchandise (goods) sold	45,000	40,000	5,000	+ 12.50
Gross profit from sales	$43,000	$38,000	$ 5,000	+ 13.16
Operating expenses:				
Depreciation	$ 6,000	$ 5,000	$ 1,000	+ 20.00
Selling and administrative	16,000	12,000	4,000	+ 33.33
Research	600	1,000	(400)	– 40.00
Miscellaneous	1,200	500	700	+ 140.00
Total operating expenses	$23,800	$18,500	$ 5,300	+ 28.65
Income before interest and taxes	$19,200	$19,500	$ (300)	– 1.54
Interest expense	4,000	4,000	–0–	
Income before taxes	$15,200	$15,500	$ (300)	– 1.94
Provision for taxes	3,800	4,000	(200)	– 5.00
Net income	$ 11,400	$11,500	$ (100)	– .87

The following Practice Quiz will test your understanding of this unit.

LU 16–2   PRACTICE QUIZ

Complete this **Practice Quiz** to see how you are doing.

From the following information, calculate:

a. Net sales.
b. Cost of merchandise (goods) sold.
c. Gross profit from sales.
d. Net income.

Given: Gross sales, $35,000; sales returns and allowances, $3,000; beginning inventory, $6,000; net purchases, $7,000; ending inventory, $5,500; operating expenses, $7,900.

For **extra help** from your authors—Sharon and Jeff—see the videos in Connect.

These videos are also available on YouTube!

✓ Solutions

a. $35,000 − $3,000 = $32,000 (Gross sales − Sales returns and allowances)

b. $6,000 + $7,000 − $5,500 = $7,500 (Beginning inventory + Net purchases − Ending inventory)

c. $32,000 − $7,500 = $24,500 (Net sales − Cost of merchandise sold)

d. $24,500 − $7,900 = $16,600 (Gross profit from sales − Operating expenses)

LU 16–2a   EXTRA PRACTICE QUIZ WITH WORKED-OUT SOLUTIONS

Need more practice? Try this **Extra Practice Quiz** (check figures in the Interactive Chapter Organizer). Worked-out Solutions can be found in Appendix B at end of text.

From the following information, calculate:

a. Net sales
b. Cost of merchandise (goods) sold
c. Gross profit from sales
d. Net income

Given: Gross sales, $36,000; sales returns and allowances, $2,800; beginning inventory, $5,900; net purchases, $6,800; ending inventory, $5,200; operating expenses, $8,100.

Learning Unit 16–3: Trend and Ratio Analysis

A balance sheet is like a snapshot. It reflects a company's or individual's financial position at a specific point in time. An income statement is like a video. It reflects a company's or individual's profitability over an interval of time.

Now that you understand the purpose of balance sheets and income statements, you are ready to study how experts look for various trends as they analyze the financial reports of companies. This learning unit discusses trend analysis and ratio analysis. The study of these trends is valuable to businesses, financial institutions, and consumers.

LO 1

Trend Analysis

Many tools are available to analyze financial reports. When data cover several years, we can analyze changes that occur by expressing each number as a percent of the base year. The base year is a past period of time that we use to compare sales, profits, and so on, with other years. We call this **trend analysis.**

Using the data below, we complete a trend analysis with the following steps:

MONEY tips

Check out Financial Peace University at www.daveramsey.com for some excellent personal finance training and tips.

COMPLETING A TREND ANALYSIS
Step 1. Select the base year (100%).
Step 2. Express each amount as a percent of the base year amount (rounded to the nearest whole percent).

GIVEN (BASE YEAR 2015)			
	2018	**2017**	**2016**	**2015**
Sales	$621,000	$460,000	$340,000	$420,000
Gross profit	182,000	141,000	112,000	124,000
Net income	48,000	41,000	22,000	38,000

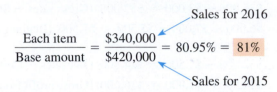

	TREND ANALYSIS			
	2018	**2017**	**2016**	**2015**
Sales	148%	110%	81%	100%
Gross profit	147	114	90	100
Net income	126	108	58	100

How to Calculate Trend Analysis

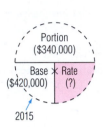

2015

$$\frac{\text{Each item}}{\text{Base amount}} = \frac{\$340,000}{\$420,000} = 80.95\% = \boxed{81\%}$$

Sales for 2016

Sales for 2015

What Trend Analysis Means Sales of 2016 were 81% of the sales of 2015. Note that you would follow the same process no matter which of the three areas you were analyzing. All categories are compared to the base year—sales, gross profit, or net income.

We now will examine **ratio analysis**—another tool companies use to analyze performance.

LO 2

MONEY tips

Keep track of the equity you have in your home. When you reach 20% or more, request to have the private mortgage insurance (PMI) removed from your mortgage. Contact your lender for details.

Ratio Analysis

A *ratio* is the relationship of one number to another. Many companies compare their ratios with those of previous years and with ratios of other companies in the industry. Companies can get ratios of the performance of other companies from their bankers, accountants, local small business centers, libraries, and newspaper articles. It is important to choose companies from similar industries when comparing ratios. For example, ratios at McDonald's will be different from ratios at Toys "R" Us. McDonald's sells more perishable products.

Percentage ratios are used by companies to determine the following:

1. How well the company manages its assets—*asset management ratios*.
2. The company's debt situation—*debt management ratios*.
3. The company's profitability picture—*profitability ratios*.

Each company must decide the true meaning of what the three types of ratios (asset management, debt management, and profitability) are saying. Table 16.1 gives a summary of the key ratios, their calculations (rounded to the nearest hundredth), and what they mean. All calculations are from Figures 16.1 and 16.4.

Now you can check your knowledge with the Practice Quiz that follows.

LU 16–3   **PRACTICE QUIZ**

Complete this **Practice Quiz** to see how you are doing.

1. Prepare a trend analysis from the following sales, assuming a base year of 2015. Round to the nearest whole percent.

	2018	**2017**	**2016**	**2015**
Sales	$29,000	$44,000	$48,000	$60,000

2. **Given:**   Total current assets (CA), $15,000; accounts receivable (AR), $6,000; total current liabilities (CL), $10,000; inventory (Inv), $4,000; net sales, $36,000; total assets, $30,000; net income (NI), $7,500.

    Calculate:
    a. Current ratio.
    b. Acid test.
    c. Average day's collection.
    d. Profit margin on sales (rounded to the nearest hundredth percent).

*For **extra help** from your authors–Sharon and Jeff–see the videos in Connect.*

These videos are also available on YouTube!

✓ **Solutions**

	2018	**2017**	**2016**	**2015**
1. Sales	48%	73%	80%	100%

$$\left(\frac{\$29,000}{\$60,000}\right) \quad \left(\frac{\$44,000}{\$60,000}\right) \quad \left(\frac{\$48,000}{\$60,000}\right)$$

2. a. $\dfrac{\text{CA}}{\text{CL}} = \dfrac{\$15,000}{\$10,000} = 1.5$

b. $\dfrac{\text{CA} - \text{Inv}}{\text{CL}} = \dfrac{\$15,000 - \$4,000}{\$10,000} = 1.1$

c. $\dfrac{\text{AR}}{\dfrac{\text{Net sales}}{360}} = \dfrac{\$6,000}{\dfrac{\$36,000}{360}} = 60 \text{ days}$

d. $\dfrac{\text{NI}}{\text{Net sales}} = \dfrac{\$7,500}{\$36,000} = 20.83\%$

TABLE 16.1   Summary of key ratios: A reference guide*

Ratio	Formula	Actual calculations	What it says	Questions that could be raised
Current ratio†	Current assets / Current liabilities (Current assets include cash, accounts receivable, and marketable securities.)	$\dfrac{\$61,000}{\$92,000} = .66{:}1$ Industry average, 2 to 1	Business has 66¢ of current assets to meet each $1 of current debt.	Not enough current assets to pay off current liabilities. Industry standard is $2 for each $1 of current debt.
Acid test (quick ratio) Top of fraction often → referred to as **quick assets**	Current assets − Inventory − Prepaid expenses / Current liabilities (Inventory and prepaid expenses are excluded because it may not be easy to convert these to cash.)	$\dfrac{\$61,000 - \$30,000 - \$15,000}{\$92,000}$ $= .17{:}1$ Industry average, 1 to 1	Business has only 17¢ to cover each $1 of current debt. This calculation excludes inventory and prepaid expenses.	Same as above but more severe.
Average day's collection	Accounts receivable / $\left(\dfrac{\text{Net sales}}{360}\right)$	$\dfrac{\$9,000}{\dfrac{\$20,566}{360}} = 158 \text{ days}$ Industry average, 90–120 days	On the average, it takes 158 days to collect accounts receivable.	Could we speed up collection since industry average is 90–120 days?
Total debt to total assets	Total liabilities / Total assets	$\dfrac{\$150,000}{\$205,000} = 73.17\%$ Industry average, 50%–70%	For each $1 of assets, the company owes 73¢ in current and long-term debt.	73% is slightly higher than industry average.
Return on equity	Net income / Stockholders' equity	$\dfrac{\$6,316}{\$55,000} = 11.48\%$ Industry average, 15%–20%	For each $1 invested by the owner, a return of 11¢ results.	Could we get a higher return on money somewhere else?
Asset turnover	Net sales / Total assets	$\dfrac{\$20,566}{\$205,000} = 10¢$ Industry average, 3¢ to 8¢	For each $1 invested in assets, it returns 10¢ in sales.	Are assets being utilized efficiently?
Profit margin on net sales	Net income / Net sales	$\dfrac{\$6,316}{\$20,566} = 30.71\%$ Industry average, 25%–40%	For each $1 of sales, company produces 31¢ in profit.	Compared to competitors, are we showing enough profits versus our increased sales?

*Inventory turnover is discussed in Chapter 18.

†For example, Wal-Mart Stores, Inc., has a current ratio of 1.51.

| LU 16–3a | EXTRA PRACTICE QUIZ WITH WORKED-OUT SOLUTIONS |

Need more practice? Try this Extra Practice Quiz (check figures in the Interactive Chapter Organizer). Worked-out Solutions can be found in Appendix B at end of text.

1. Prepare a trend analysis from the following sales, assuming a base year of 2015. Round to the nearest whole percent.

	2018	**2017**	**2016**	**2015**
Sales	$25,000	$60,000	$50,000	$70,000

2. **Given:** Total current assets (CA), $14,000; accounts receivable (AR), $5,500; total current liabilities (CL), $9,000; inventory (Inv), $3,900; net sales, $36,500; total assets, $32,000; net income (NI), $8,000. Calculate:

    a. Current ratio.
    b. Acid test.
    c. Average day's collection.
    d. Profit margin on sales (round to the nearest hundredth percent).

INTERACTIVE CHAPTER ORGANIZER

Topic/Procedure/Formula	Examples	You try it*
Balance sheet		
Vertical analysis Process of relating each figure on a financial report (down the column) to a total figure. The denominator for a balance sheet is total assets (or total liabilities + owner's equity); for an income statement it is net sales.	Current assets $ 520 `52%` Plant and equipment 480 `48` Total assets $1,000 100%	**Do vertical analysis** CA $ 400 ? P + E 600 ? Total assets $1,000 ?
Horizontal analysis Analyzing comparative financial reports shows rate and amount of change across columns item by item. (New line item amount − Old line item amount)/Old line item amount	**2017** | **2016** | **Change** | **%** Cash, $5,000 | $4,000 | $1,000 | `25%` ◄ $\left(\dfrac{\$1,000}{\$4,000}\right)$	**Do horizontal analysis** | **2017** | **2016** | **Change** | **%** Cash | $8,000 | $2,000 | ? | ?
Net sales $\dfrac{\text{Gross}}{\text{sales}} - \dfrac{\text{Sales returns}}{\text{and allowances}} - \dfrac{\text{Sales}}{\text{discounts}}$	$200 gross sales − 10 sales returns and allowances − 2 sales discounts `$ 188` net sales	**Calculate net sales** Gross sales, $400 Sales returns and allowances, $20 Sales discount, $5
Cost of merchandise (goods) sold $\dfrac{\text{Beginning}}{\text{inventory}} + \dfrac{\text{Net}}{\text{purchases}} - \dfrac{\text{Ending}}{\text{inventory}}$	$50 + $100 − $20 = `$130` Beginning inventory + Net purchases − Ending inventory = Cost of merchandise (goods) sold	**Calculate cost of merchandise sold** Beginning inventory, $50 Net purchases, $200 Ending inventory, $20
Gross profit from sales $\text{Net sales} - \dfrac{\text{Cost of merchandise}}{\text{(goods) sold}}$	$188 − $130 = `$58` gross profit from sales Net sales − Cost of merchandise (goods) sold = Gross profit from sales	**Calculate gross profit** Net sales, $400 Cost of merchandise sold, $250
Net income Gross profit − Operating expenses	$58 − $28 = `$30` Gross profit from sales − Operating expenses = Net income	**Calculate net income** Gross profit, $210 Operating expenses, $180

(continues)

INTERACTIVE CHAPTER ORGANIZER

Topic/Procedure/Formula	Examples	You try it*
Trend analysis Each number expressed as a percent of the base year. $\dfrac{\text{Each item}}{\text{Base amount}}$	**2018** **2017** **2016** Sales $200 $300 $400 ← Base year 50% 75% 100% $\left(\dfrac{\$200}{\$400}\right)$ $\left(\dfrac{\$300}{\$400}\right)$	**Prepare a trend analysis** **2018** **2017** **2016** $1,200 $800 $1,000 ← Base year
Ratios Tools to interpret items on financial reports.	Use this example for calculating the following ratios: current assets, $30,000; accounts receivable, $12,000; total current liabilities, $20,000; inventory, $6,000; prepaid expenses, $2,000; net sales, $72,000; total assets, $60,000; net income, $15,000; total liabilities, $30,000.	**Use this example for calculating the following ratios:** Current assets, $40,000; Accounts receivable, $44,000; Total current liabilities, $160,000; Inventory, $2,000; Prepaid expenses, $3,000; Net sales, $60,000; Total assets, $70,000; Net income, $16,000; Total liabilities, $180,000.
Current ratio $\dfrac{\text{Current assets}}{\text{Current liabilities}}$	$\dfrac{\$30,000}{\$20,000} = 1.5$	Use the information from the example above.
Acid test (quick ratio) Called quick assets $\dfrac{\text{Current assets} - \text{Inventory} - \text{Prepaid expenses}}{\text{Current liabilities}}$	$\dfrac{\$30,000 - \$6,000 - \$2,000}{\$20,000} = 1.1$	Use the information from the example above.
Average day's collection $\dfrac{\text{Accounts receivable}}{\left(\dfrac{\text{Net sales}}{360}\right)}$	$\dfrac{\$12,000}{\left(\dfrac{\$72,000}{360}\right)} = 60\text{ days}$	Use the information from the example above.
Total debt to total assets $\dfrac{\text{Total liabilities}}{\text{Total assets}}$	$\dfrac{\$30,000}{\$60,000} = 50\%$	Use the information from the example above.
Return on equity $\dfrac{\text{Net income}}{\text{Stockholders' equity (A} - \text{L)}}$	$\dfrac{\$15,000}{\$30,000} = 50\%$	Use the information from the example above.
Asset turnover $\dfrac{\text{Net sales}}{\text{Total assets}}$	$\dfrac{\$72,000}{\$60,000} = 1.2$	Use the information from the example above.
Profit margin on net sales $\dfrac{\text{Net income}}{\text{Net sales}}$	$\dfrac{\$15,000}{\$72,000} = .2083 = 20.83\%$	Use the information from the example above.

(continues)

INTERACTIVE CHAPTER ORGANIZER

KEY TERMS			
	Accounts payable	Horizontal analysis	Quick assets
	Accounts receivable	Income statement	Quick ratio
	Acid test	Liabilities	Ratio analysis
	Asset turnover	Long-term liabilities	Retained earnings
	Assets	Merchandise inventory	Return on equity
	Balance sheet	Mortgage note payable	Revenues
	Capital	Net income	Salaries payable
	Common stock	Net purchases	Sales (not trade) discounts
	Comparative statement	Net sales	Sales returns and
	Corporation	Operating expenses	allowances
	Cost of merchandise	Owner's equity	Sole proprietorship
	(goods) sold	Partnership	Stockholders' equity
	Current assets	Plant and equipment	Trend analysis
	Current liabilities	Prepaid expenses	Vertical analysis
	Current ratio	Purchase discounts	
	Expenses	Purchase returns and	
	Gross profit from sales	allowances	
	Gross sales	Purchases	

Check Figures for Extra Practice Quizzes. (Worked-out Solutions are in Appendix B.)	LU 16–1a	LU 16–2a	LU 16–3a
	1. a. 21.11%; 25%	**1.** a. $33,200	**1.** 36%; 86%; 71%; 100%
	b. 10.56%; 12.86%	b. $7,500	**2.** a. 1.6
	c. 8.89%; 7.86%	c. $25,700	b. 1.12
	d. 11.11%; 11.43%	d. $17,600	c. 54.2
	2. 45.45%		d. 21.92%

*Worked-out solutions are in Appendix B.

Critical Thinking Discussion Questions with Chapter Concept Check

1. What is the difference between current assets and plant and equipment? Do you think land should be allowed to depreciate?

2. What items make up stockholders' equity? Why might a person form a sole proprietorship instead of a corporation?

3. Explain the steps to complete a vertical or horizontal analysis relating to balance sheets. Why are the percents not summed vertically in horizontal analysis?

4. How do you calculate net sales, cost of merchandise (goods) sold, gross profit, and net income? Why do we need two separate figures for inventory in the cost of merchandise (goods) sold section?

5. Explain how to calculate the following: current ratios, acid test, average day's collection, total debt to assets, return on equity, asset turnover, and profit margin on net sales. How often do you think ratios should be calculated?

6. What is trend analysis? Explain how the portion formula assists in preparing a trend analysis.

7. In light of the most recent economic crises, explain how companies such as GE are trying to gain market share and increase profit margins.

8. **Chapter Concept Check.** Go online and look up the financial statement of a company that interests you to see how it is doing financially. Use ratio analysis based on concepts presented in this chapter.

END-OF-CHAPTER PROBLEMS ■ **connect** (plus+)

Check figures for odd-numbered problems in Appendix C.   Name _____   Date _____

DRILL PROBLEMS

16–1. Prepare a December 31, 2017, balance sheet for Wildland Fire Warriors like the one for The Card Shop (LU 16–1) from the following: cash, $40,000; accounts payable, $28,000; merchandise inventory, $14,000; Jim Shanel, capital, $46,000; and equipment, $20,000.   *LU 16-1(1)*

16–2. From the following, prepare a classified balance sheet for Bach Crawlers as of December 31, 2017. Ending merchandise inventory was $4,000 for the year.   *LU 16-1(1)*

Cash	$6,000	Accounts payable	$1,800
Prepaid rent	1,600	Salaries payable	1,600
Prepaid insurance	4,000	Note payable (long term)	8,000
Office equipment (net)	5,000	P. Bach, capital*	9,200

*What the owner supplies to the business. Replaces common stock and retained earnings section.

16–3. Complete a horizontal analysis for Brown Company, rounding percents to the nearest hundredth: *LU 16-1(2)*

eXcel

BROWN COMPANY Comparative Balance Sheet December 31, 2016 and 2017				
			INCREASE (DECREASE)	
	2017	**2016**	**Amount**	**Percent**
Assets				
Current assets:				
Cash	$ 15,750	$ 10,500		
Accounts receivable	18,000	13,500		
Merchandise inventory	18,750	22,500		
Prepaid advertising	54,000	45,000		
Total current assets	$106,500	$ 91,500		
Plant and equipment:				
Building (net)	$120,000	$126,000		
Land	90,000	90,000		
Total plant and equipment	$210,000	$216,000		
Total assets	$316,500	$307,500		
Liabilities				
Current liabilities:				
Accounts payable	$132,000	$120,000		
Salaries payable	22,500	18,000		
Total current liabilities	$154,500	$138,000		
Long-term liabilities:				
Mortgage note payable	99,000	87,000		
Total liabilities	$253,500	$225,000		
Owner's Equity				
J. Brown, capital	63,000	82,500		
Total liabilities and owner's equity	$316,500	$307,500		

16–4. Prepare an income statement for Hansen Realty for the year ended December 31, 2017. Beginning inventory was $1,248. Ending inventory was $1,600. *LU 16-2(1)*

Sales	$34,900
Sales returns and allowances	1,092
Sales discount	1,152
Purchases	10,512
Purchase discounts	540
Depreciation expense	115
Salary expense	5,200
Insurance expense	2,600
Utilities expense	210
Plumbing expense	250
Rent expense	180

16–5. Assume this is a partial list of financial highlights from a Best Buy annual report:

	2017	2016
	(dollars in millions)	
Net sales	$37,580	$33,075
Earnings before taxes	2,231	1,283
Net earnings	1,318	891

Complete a horizontal and vertical analysis from the above information. Round to the nearest hundredth percent. *LU 16-2(2)*

16–6. From the French Instrument Corporation second-quarter report ended 2017, do a vertical analysis for the second quarter of 2017.   *LU 16-2(2)*

FRENCH INSTRUMENT CORPORATION AND SUBSIDIARIES Consolidated Statements of Operation (Unaudited) (In thousands of dollars, except share data)			
	SECOND QUARTER		
	2017	**2016**	**Percent of net**
Net sales	$6,698	$6,951	
Cost of sales	4,089	4,462	
Gross margin	2,609	2,489	
Expenses:			
Selling, general and administrative	1,845	1,783	
Product development	175	165	
Interest expense	98	123	
Other (income), net	(172)	(99)	
Total expenses	1,946	1,972	
Income before income taxes	663	517	
Provision for income taxes	265	209	
Net income	$398	$308	
Net income per common share*	$.05	$.03	
Weighted-average number of common shares and equivalents	6,673,673	6,624,184	

*Income per common share reflects the deduction of the preferred stock dividend from net income.
'Off due to rounding.

16–7. Complete the comparative income statement and balance sheet for Logic Company, rounding percents to the nearest hundredth: *LU 16-1(2), LU 16-2(2)*

LOGIC COMPANY Comparative Income Statement For Years Ended December 31, 2016 and 2017				
			INCREASE (DECREASE)	
	2017	**2016**	**Amount**	**Percent**
Gross sales	$19,000	$15,000		
Sales returns and allowances	1,000	100		
Net sales	$18,000	$14,900		
Cost of merchandise (goods) sold	12,000	9,000		
Gross profit	$ 6,000	$ 5,900		
Operating expenses:				
Depreciation	$ 700	$ 600		
Selling and administrative	2,200	2,000		
Research	550	500		
Miscellaneous	360	300		
Total operating expenses	$ 3,810	$ 3,400		
Income before interest and taxes	$ 2,190	$ 2,500		
Interest expense	560	500		
Income before taxes	$ 1,630	$ 2,000		
Provision for taxes	640	800		
Net income	$ 990	$ 1,200		

LOGIC COMPANY Comparative Balance Sheet December 31, 2016 and 2017				
	2017		**2016**	
	Amount	**Percent**	**Amount**	**Percent**
Assets				
Current assets:				
Cash	$12,000		$ 9,000	
Accounts receivable	16,500		12,500	
Merchandise inventory	8,500		14,000	
Prepaid expenses	24,000		10,000	
Total current assets	$61,000		$45,500	
Plant and equipment:				
Building (net)	$14,500		$ 11,000	
Land	13,500		9,000	
Total plant and equipment	$28,000		$20,000	
Total assets	$89,000		$65,500	
Liabilities				
Current liabilities:				
Accounts payable	$13,000		$ 7,000	
Salaries payable	7,000		5,000	
Total current liabilities	$20,000		$12,000	
Long-term liabilities:				
Mortgage note payable	22,000		20,500	
Total liabilities	$42,000		$32,500	
Stockholders' Equity				
Common stock	$21,000		$21,000	
Retained earnings	26,000		12,000	
Total stockholders' equity	$47,000		$33,000	
Total liabilities and stockholders' equity	$89,000		$65,500	

*Off due to rounding.

From Problem 16–7, your supervisor has requested that you calculate the following ratios, rounded to the nearest hundredth:
LU 16-3(2)

	2017	2016
16–8. Current ratio.		
16–9. Acid test.		
16–10. Average day's collection.		
16–11. Asset turnover.		
16–12. Total debt to total assets.		
16–13. Net income (after tax) to the net sales.		
16–14. Return on equity (after tax).		

16–8.

16–9.

16–10.

16–11.

16–12.

16–13.

16–14.

WORD PROBLEMS

16–15. William Burris invested $100,000 in an Australian-based franchise, Rent Your Boxes, purchasing three territories in the
eXcel Washington area. After finding out the company had gone bankrupt, he rallied 10 other franchisees to join him and created a new company, Rent Our Boxes. If Rent Our Boxes had net income of $38,902 with net sales of $286,585, what was its profit margin on net sales to the nearest hundredth percent? *LU 16-3(2)*

16–16. General Motors announced a quarterly profit of $119 million for 4th quarter 2014. Below is a portion of its balance sheet. Conduct a horizontal analysis of the following line items (rounding percent to nearest hundredth): *LU 16-1(2)*

	2014 (dollars in millions)	2013 (dollars in millions)	Difference	% CHG
Cash and cash equivalents	$ 15,980	$ 15,499		
Marketable securities	9,222	16,148		
Inventories	13,642	14,324		
Goodwill	-	1,278		
Total liabilities and equity	$103,249	$144,603		

16–17. Find the following ratios for Motorola Credit Corporation's annual report: **(a)** total debt to total assets, **(b)** return on equity, **(c)** asset turnover (to nearest cent), and **(d)** profit margin on net sales. Round to the nearest hundredth percent. *LU 16-3(2)*

	(dollars in millions)
Net revenue (sales)	$ 265
Net earnings	147
Total assets	2,015
Total liabilities	1,768
Total stockholders' equity	427

16–18. Assume figures were presented for the past 5 years on merchandise sold at Chicago department and discount stores ($ million). Sales in 2016 were $3,154; in 2015, $3,414; in 2014, $3,208; in 2013, $3,152; and in 2012, $3,216. Using 2012 as the base year, complete a trend analysis. Round each percent to the nearest whole percent. *LU 16-3(1)*

16–19. Don Williams received a memo requesting that he complete a trend analysis of the following numbers using 2013 as the base year and rounding each percent to the nearest whole percent. Could you help Don with the request? *LU 16-3(1)*

	2016	2015	2014	2013
Sales	$340,000	$400,000	$420,000	$500,000
Gross profit	180,000	240,000	340,000	400,000
Net income	70,000	90,000	40,000	50,000

16–20. The French bank Société Générale reported its 2014 net income was 23,561 million euros and its operating expenses totaled 16,016 million euros. What was its gross profit? *LU 16-2(1)*

16–21. At age 32, you have assets of $275,658 and liabilities of $266,211. What is your net worth? Is this appropriate for your age? See http://money.cnn.com/tools/networth_ageincome/ and http://www.usatoday.com/story/money/personalfinance/2015/01/31/motley-fool-net-worth-age/22415229/ to determine if the net worth is adequate. *LU 16-1(1)*

16–22. On January 1, Pete Rowe bought a ski chalet for $51,000. Pete is renting the chalet for $55 per night. He estimates he can rent the chalet for 190 nights. Pete's mortgage for principal and interest is $448 per month. Real estate tax on the chalet is $500 per year.

Pete estimates that his heating bill will run $60 per month. He expects his monthly electrical bill to be $20 per month. He pays $12 per month for cable television.

What is Pete's return on the initial investment for this year? Assume rentals drop by 30% and monthly bills for heat and electricity drop by 10% each month. What would be Pete's return on initial investment? Round to the nearest tenth percent as needed. *LU 16-3(2)*

16–23. As the accountant for Tootsie Roll, you are asked to calculate the current ratio and the quick ratio for the following partial eXcel financial statement. Round to the nearest tenth. *LU 16-3(2)*

Assets		Liabilities	
Current assets:		Current liabilities:	
Cash and cash equivalents	$ 4,224,190	Notes payable to banks	$ 672,221
Investments	32,533,769	Accounts payable	7,004,075
Accounts receivable, less allowances of $748,000 and $744,000	16,206,648	Dividends payable	576,607
		Accrued liabilities	9,826,534
Inventories:		Income taxes payable	4,471,429
Finished goods and work in progress	12,650,955		
Raw materials and supplies	10,275,858		
Prepaid expenses	2,037,710		

SUMMARY PRACTICE TEST

Do you need help? The videos in Connect have step-by-step worked-out solutions. These videos are also available on YouTube!

1. Given: Gross sales, $170,000; sales returns and allowances, $9,000; beginning inventory, $8,000; net purchases, $18,000; ending inventory, $5,000; and operating expenses, $56,000. Calculate **(a)** net sales, **(b)** cost of merchandise (goods) sold, **(c)** gross profit from sales, and **(d)** net income. *LU 16-2(1)*

2. Complete the following partial comparative balance sheet by filling in the total current assets and percent column; assume no plant and equipment (round to the nearest hundredth percent as needed). *LU 16-1(2)*

	Amount	Percent	Amount	Percent
Assets				
Current assets:				
Cash	$ 9,000		$ 8,000	
Accounts receivable	5,000		7,500	
Merchandise inventory	12,000		6,900	
Prepaid expenses	7,000		8,000	
Total current assets				

*Off due to rounding.

3. Calculate the amount of increase or decrease and the percent change of each item, rounding to the nearest hundredth percent as needed. *LU 16-1(2)*

	2017	2016	Amount	Percent
Cash	$19,000	$ 8,000		
Land	70,000	30,000		
Accounts payable	21,000	10,000		

4. Complete a trend analysis for sales, rounding to the nearest whole percent and using 2015 as the base year. *LU 16-3(1)*

	2018	2017	2016	2015
Sales	$140,000	$350,000	$210,000	$190,000

5. From the following, prepare a balance sheet for True Corporation as of December 31, 2017. *LU 16-1(1)*

Building	$40,000	Mortgage note payable	$70,000
Merchandise inventory	12,000	Common stock	10,000
Cash	15,000	Retained earnings	37,000
Land	90,000	Accounts receivable	9,000
Accounts payable	50,000	Salaries payable	8,000
Prepaid rent	9,000		

6. Solve from the following facts, rounding to the nearest hundredth. *LU 16-3(2)*

Current assets	$14,000	Net sales	$40,000
Accounts receivable	$ 5,000	Total assets	$38,000
Current liabilities	$20,000	Net income	$10,100
Inventory	$ 4,000		

a. Current ratio

b. Acid test

c. Average day's collection

d. Asset turnover

e. Profit margin on sales

As a child, Jalem Getz, the CEO of BuyCostumes.com, put little thought into his Halloween costumes. Now he thinks about costumes all year long.

Jalem Getz founded online business BuyCostumes in a warehouse in the Milwaukee suburbs in 1999 taking advantage of Wisconsin's central U.S. location and cheap rent. Getz used to dislike the lack of seasons in his native California. Now, he uses the extreme seasonality of the Halloween business to turn a big profit.

The company got its start as a brick-and-mortar retail business owned by Getz and partner Jon Majdoch. While still in their early 20s, the two began operating a chain of seasonal Halloween Express franchise stores, and then branched out into a couple of lamp and home accessory shops.

In 2001, the company changed its name to BuySeasons, Inc., to reflect its new broader focus. "Rather than just focus on one season, we target consumers in different seasons," said Jalem Getz. The BuyCostumes name is still in broad use.

Being an e-tailer means not having to open a retail space for just two months of the year, or stock other items. Money saved on storefronts goes to maintaining a stock of 10,000 Halloween items—100 times what most retailers carry for the season.

"Our selection sets us apart," Getz said. "A lot of customers are looking for something unique; by having that large selection we immediately build that additional goodwill."

The key to BuySeasons' success is limiting the choice of merchandise to items that can't readily be found in neighborhood stores. That means less price competition and higher margins for BuySeasons, which has been maintaining a 47.5 percent gross margin rate on the BuyCostumes.com site.

In July 2006, Liberty Media announced plans to acquire BuySeasons Inc. for an undisclosed sum. Getz will stay on as CEO.

BuyCostumes.com is the biggest online seller of costumes. It was ranked in October 2005 in Inc. magazine as the 75th–fastest growing U.S. private firm, with revenue of $17.6 million last year and three-year growth of 1,046 percent. Sales this year are expected to hit $25 million to $28 million, according to Getz.

Other online Halloween firms also predicted double-digit growth in 2005—according to a forecast by the National Retail Federation the entire industry would have a 5% gain, leading to a record $3.3 billion in sales for the entire industry.

BuySeasons' sales reached nearly $30 million in 2005, Getz said, up from $17.6 million in 2004. The company's sales are expected to post 50% annual growth over the next three years. The company bills itself as the world's largest Internet retailer of Halloween costumes and accessories.

Note: The following problems contain some data that has been created by the author.

PROBLEM 1

BuyCostumes.com is owned by BuySeasons, Inc., which also owns the Celebrate Express websites—BirthdayExpress.com, 1stWishes.com, and CostumeExpress.com. BuySeasons, Inc., is a wholly owned subsidiary of Liberty Media Corporation (LMC) and operates within the Liberty Interactive Group. Suppose LMC has the following balance sheet information (in millions):

	Current year	Prior year
Current assets	$3,914	$ 3,542
Non–current assets		
Total assets	$7,723	$10,792
Total liabilities	$2,472	$ 5,766
Total equity		
Total liabilities and equity	$7,723	$10,792

Fill in the blanks. Round to the nearest dollar and express in millions.

PROBLEM 2

Using the data from Problem 1, create a comparative balance sheet for these two years. Round to the nearest hundredth percent.

	Current year	Prior year
Current assets	$3,914	$ 3,542
Non–current assets	$3,809	$ 7,250
Total assets	$7,723	$10,792
Total liabilities	$2,472	$ 5,766
Total equity	$5,251	$ 5,026
Total liabilities and equity	$7,723	$10,792

PROBLEM 3

Imagine that the Interactive Group at Liberty Media Corporation had the following data (all figures are in millions):

Current assets	$3,379	Net income	$ 258
Current liabilities	$7,768	Net sales	$8,305
Stockholders' equity	$5,424	Cost of goods sold	$5,332

Calculate the gross profit from sales. Express your answer in millions.

PROBLEM 4

Using the data from Problem 3, calculate the current ratio. Round to the nearest hundredth.

PROBLEM 5

Again using the data from Problem 3, calculate the return on equity. Round to the nearest hundredth.

PROBLEM 6

Again using the data from Problem 3, calculate the profit margin on net sales. Round to the nearest hundredth.

PROBLEM 7

Suppose BuyCostumes.com sales were $93 million in 2012 and were projected to increase to $97 million in 2013. What percent increase would this represent? Round to the nearest hundredth percent.

PROBLEM 8

If BuyCostumes.com had 42% of the online Halloween market and its sales were $93 million, what would be the total size of this market? Round to the nearest million.

PROBLEM 9

BuyCostumes.com currently offers a 110% guarantee. Should you find the same costume for less, BuyCostumes.com will refund 110% of the difference in purchase price. Assuming you purchased the Avengers Captain America Classic Muscle Chest child costume for $39.98 from BuyCostumes.com and then found the same costume for $32.95 with tax and shipping included at another retailer, what refund would you receive using the price guarantee? Round to the nearest dollar.

Class Discussion   With the rise in Internet shopping sites, it is becoming increasingly important for online retailers to find ways to differentiate themselves in the market. Check out BuyCostumes.com and one or two competitor sites and look for ways in which the company is setting itself apart from the competition. What ideas would you add for further differentiation in the market?

SURF TO SAVE

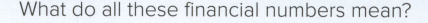

What do all these financial numbers mean? 🔍

 PROBLEM 1
Brew up some analysis!

Go to http://finance.yahoo.com/. Search for Starbucks Corporation and click on the Balance Sheet link. Prepare a vertical analysis for the 3 years of balance sheets provided.

Discussion Questions

1. What might be included as part of Starbucks' assets?

2. How does this analysis assist you in evaluating the financials of Starbucks?

 PROBLEM 3
Ratios that hit the "target"!

Go to http://finance.yahoo.com/. Search for Target Corp. and click on the Balance Sheet link. Calculate the total debt to total assets ratio for the 3 years of data provided. Are the ratios improving or deteriorating?

Discussion Questions

1. What can we learn about an organization by evaluating its debt to assets ratio?

2. What may be some of the specific debts for Target Corp.?

 PROBLEM 2
Social investing

Go to http://finance.yahoo.com/. Search for Facebook, Inc., and click on the Income Statement link. The report includes information from the 3 most recent years. Perform a horizontal analysis using the income statement data of the current year compared to the previous year.

Discussion Questions

1. What does this analysis tell you about Facebook's financial status?

2. How could you use this information in determining whether to invest in Facebook?

PROBLEM 4
What is trending?

Go to http://finance.yahoo.com/. Choose a company and view its annual financials. Print out the report and do a trend analysis of the balance sheet for the 3 years provided. Use the earliest year as the base for your calculations.

Discussion Questions

1. What does this trend analysis tell you about the company?

2. Should you perform such an analysis before investing in this company? Why or why not?

MOBILE APPS ✕

SEC Filings Express (Xamtech LLC) Analyzes real-time SEC filings.

Financial/Ratios (K Kaleeswaran) Calculates financial ratios from values contained in financial statements.

PERSONAL FINANCE

A KIPLINGER APPROACH

By Kathy Kristof, From *Kiplinger's Personal Finance*, March 2015.

The Pros and Cons of Cheap Oil

Why the 55% plunge in oil prices is roiling markets worldwide. **BY KATHY KRISTOF**

THE POSITIVES

▶ **Buoyant consumers.** With the price of a fill-up falling to its lowest level in 11 years, U.S. consumers will spend $750 less per household on gasoline this year than they did in 2014, the government estimates. That will spur consumer spending, which will lift the whole economy.

▶ **Tepid inflation.** Declining energy prices tamp down inflation, which makes it easier for the Federal Reserve to keep short-term interest rates near zero—a boon for stocks.

▶ **Business beneficiaries.** Airlines, truckers and package-delivery firms will save a fortune, given that fuel accounts for as much as 40% of their costs. Retailers, restaurants and hotels benefit directly from increased consumer spending. Banks and credit card companies also win; revenues from transaction fees go up, and consumer defaults are likely to go down.

▶ **Political pluses.** Lower oil prices hurt the economies of some energy-producing U.S. adversaries, particularly Iran, Russia and Venezuela. That could make the world a little safer.

THE NEGATIVES

▶ **Industry slump.** Falling oil prices hurt a key sector of the stock market. Since its peak last summer, the S&P Energy index has dived 21%.

▶ **Sagging economies.** Though higher supply is a major reason for oil's drop, investors worry that persistent declines are a sign of falling demand due to slowing global growth.

▶ **Job losses.** Oil at $50 a barrel could end the fracking boom and harm conventional drilling, too. Massive job losses could ensue.

▶ **Less business spending.** Nine of the nation's 20 biggest spenders on machinery and equipment are energy firms. Expect them and others to cut back on capital outlays.

▶ **Junk woes.** As oil prices have fallen, concerns about the viability of heavily indebted producers have climbed, so high-yield bonds have taken a hit.

▶ **Foreign fears.** Sinking oil hurts big energy-producing nations and raises concerns that they and their national oil companies could default on their debts. ■

ISTOCKPHOTO.COM (5)

BUSINESS MATH ISSUE

Whether oil prices go up or down, they will not really affect the income statement or balance sheet of a company.

1. List the key points of the article and information to support your position.
2. Write a group defense of your position using math calculations to support your view.

CHAPTER 17

Depreciation

© Comstock/PunchStock

Action Leaves Open the Question About Possible Tax-Filing-Season Delays

BY JOHN D. MCKINNON

WASHINGTON—The Senate voted Tuesday to extend a raft of temporary tax breaks through the rest of 2014, ending a protracted struggle that foreshadows even more difficult tax-code debates next year.

The vote was 76-16 to clear the bill that now goes to President Barack Obama, who is expected to sign it. The temporary breaks—known collectively as extenders—include more than 50 tax incentives for businesses, individuals and nonprofits.

Some are narrow, such as a write-off for teachers' classroom-supply purchases and depreciation breaks for motorsports complexes and restaurants. Others are broad, such as a deduction for state and local sales taxes and a widely used credit for business research. One popular provision allows people 70½ or older to make tax-free charitable distributions from individual retirement accounts.

But final negotiations between the Obama administration and GOP leaders broke down. Lawmakers eventually settled for the 2014-only extension.

Despite the modest nature of the final compromise, lawmakers could be helping set the stage for bigger changes next year.

The extenders have been one of the numerous problems legislators face in passing a comprehensive overhaul of the tax code. That is because their long-term cost is estimated to total almost $1 trillion during the next decade.

If lawmakers sought to make major extenders permanent as part of a tax-code overhaul, they would be under pressure to offset that cost with spending cuts or other tax increases, to keep the overhaul from boosting future deficits.

Reprinted by permission of The Wall Street Journal, copyright 2014 Dow Jones & Company, Inc. All rights reserved worldwide.

LU 17–1: Concept of Depreciation and the Straight-Line Method

1. Explain the concept and causes of depreciation.

2. Prepare a depreciation schedule and calculate partial-year depreciation.

LU 17–2: Units-of-Production Method

1. Explain how use affects the units-of-production method.

2. Prepare a depreciation schedule.

LU 17–3: Declining-Balance Method

1. Explain the importance of residual value in the depreciation schedule.

2. Prepare a depreciation schedule.

LU 17–4: Modified Accelerated Cost Recovery System (MACRS) with Introduction to ACRS (1986, 1989, 2010)

1. Explain the goals of ACRS and MACRS and their limitations.

2. Calculate depreciation using the MACRS guidelines.

VOCABULARY PREVIEW

Here are key terms in this chapter. After completing the chapter, if you know the term, place a checkmark in the box. If you don't know the term, look it up and put the page number where it can be found.

Accelerated Cost Recovery System (ACRS) ☐ Accelerated depreciation ☐ Accumulated depreciation ☐
Asset cost ☐ Book value ☐ Declining-balance method ☐ Depreciation ☐ Depreciation expense ☐
Depreciation schedule ☐ Estimated useful life ☐ General Depreciation System (GDS) ☐ Modified
Accelerated Cost Recovery System (MACRS) ☐ Residual value ☐ Salvage value ☐ Straight-line method ☐
Straight-line rate ☐ Trade-in value ☐ Units-of-production method ☐

The chapter opener clipping reports that depreciation breaks for motorsports complexes, among other tax breaks, have been extended. In Learning Units 17–1 to 17–3, we discuss methods of calculating depreciation for financial reporting. In Learning Unit 17–4, we look at how tax laws force companies to report depreciation for tax purposes. Financial reporting methods and the tax-reporting methods are both legal.

Learning Unit 17–1: Concept of Depreciation and the Straight-Line Method

Companies frequently buy assets such as equipment or buildings that will last longer than 1 year. As time passes, these assets depreciate, or lose some of their market value. The total cost of these assets cannot be shown in *1 year* as an expense of running the business. In a systematic and logical way, companies must estimate the asset cost they show as an expense of a particular period. This process is called **depreciation.** The next time you fly in a plane think how the airline will depreciate the cost of that plane over a number of years.

Remember that depreciation *does not* measure the amount of deterioration or decline in the market value of the asset. Depreciation is simply a means of recognizing that these assets are depreciating.

The depreciation process results in **depreciation expense** that involves three key factors: (1) **asset cost**—amount the company paid for the asset including freight and charges relating to the asset; (2) **estimated useful life**—number of years or time periods for which the company can use the asset; and (3) **residual value (salvage** or **trade-in value)**—expected cash value at the end of the asset's useful life.

Depreciation expense is listed on the income statement. The **accumulated depreciation** title on the balance sheet gives the amount of the asset's depreciation taken to date. Asset cost less accumulated depreciation is the asset's book value. The **book value** shows the unused amount of the asset cost that the company may depreciate in future accounting periods. At the end of the asset's life, the asset's book value is the same as its residual value—book value cannot be less than residual value.

Book value is important to a business owner because it provides a way to calculate the value of assets within a business.

Depending on the amount and timetable of an asset's depreciation, a company can increase or decrease its profit. If a company shows greater depreciation in earlier years, the company will have a lower reported profit and pay less in taxes. Thus, depreciation can be an indirect tax savings for the company.

Later in the chapter we will discuss the different methods of computing depreciation that spread the cost of an asset over specified periods of time. However, first let's look at some of the major causes of depreciation.

Causes of Depreciation

As assets, all machines have an estimated amount of usefulness simply because as companies use the assets, the assets gradually wear out. The cause of this depreciation is *physical deterioration.*

The growth of a company can also cause depreciation. Many companies begin on a small scale. As the companies grow, they often find their equipment and buildings inadequate. The use of depreciation enables these businesses to "write off" their old, inadequate equipment and buildings. *In fact, the depreciation method chosen by a company can be determined by when tax write-offs are needed most.* Companies cannot depreciate land. For example, a garbage dump can be depreciated but not the land.

Another cause of depreciation is the result of advances in technology. The computers that companies bought a few years ago may be in perfect working condition but outdated. Companies may find it necessary to replace these old computers with more sophisticated, faster, and possibly more economical machines. Thus, *product obsolescence* is a key factor contributing to depreciation.

© Kristoffer Tripplaar/Alamy

Now we are ready to begin our study of depreciation methods. The first method we will study is straight-line depreciation. It is also the most common of the three depreciation methods (straight line, units of production, and declining balance). In a survey of 600 corporations, 81% responded that they used straight-line depreciation.

Straight-Line Method

LO 2

The **straight-line method** of depreciation is used more than any other method. It tries to distribute the same amount of expense to each period of time. Most large companies, such as Gillette Corporation, Campbell's Soup, and General Mills, use the straight-line method. *Today, more than 90% of U.S. companies depreciate by straight line.* For example, let's assume Ajax Company bought equipment for $2,500. The company estimates that the equipment's period of "usefulness"—or *useful life*—will be 5 years. After 5 years the equipment will have a residual value (salvage value) of $500. The company decides to calculate its depreciation with the straight-line method and uses the following formula:

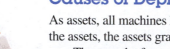

$$\frac{\text{Depreciation expense}}{\text{each year}} = \frac{\text{Cost} - \text{Residual value}}{\text{Estimated useful life in years}}$$

$$\frac{\$2,500 - \$500}{5 \text{ years}} = \$400 \text{ depreciation expense taken each year}$$

Table 17.1 gives a summary of the equipment depreciation that Ajax Company will take over the next 5 years. Companies call this summary a **depreciation schedule.** Buildings for BigLot are depreciated over 40 years while equipment is depreciated from 3 to 15 years.

TABLE **17.1**

Depreciation schedule for straight-line method

$$\frac{100\%}{\text{Number of years}} = \frac{100\%}{5} = 20\%$$

Thus, the company is depreciating the equipment at a 20% rate each year.

End of year	Depreciation cost of equipment	Depreciation expense for year	Accumulated depreciation at end of year	Book value at end of year (Cost − Depreciation at end of year)
1	$2,500	$400	$ 400	$2,100 ($2,500 − $400)
2	2,500	400	800	1,700
3	2,500	400	1,200	1,300
4	2,500	400	1,600	900
5	2,500	400	2,000	500
	↑ Cost stays the same.	↑ Depreciation expense is same each year.	↑ Accumulated depreciation increases by $400 each year.	↑ Book value is lowered by $400 until residual value of $500 is reached.

MONEY tips

Do not open several credit card accounts in a short period of time. Doing so negatively affects your credit rating if you are trying to buy or refinance a home.

Depreciation for Partial Years

If a company buys an asset before the 15th of the month, the company calculates the asset's depreciation for a full month. Companies do not take the full month's depreciation for assets bought after the 15th of the month. For example, assume Ajax Company (Table 17.1) bought the equipment on May 6. The company would calculate the depreciation for the first year as follows:

$$\frac{\$2,500 - \$500}{5\ \text{years}} = \$400 \times \frac{8}{12} = \$266.67$$

Now let's check your progress with the Practice Quiz before we look at the next depreciation method.

LU 17–1 PRACTICE QUIZ

Complete this **Practice Quiz** to see how you are doing.

1. Prepare a depreciation schedule using straight-line depreciation for the following:

Cost of truck	$16,000
Residual value	$ 1,000
Life	5 years

2. If the truck were bought on February 3, what would the depreciation expense be in the first year?

*For **extra help** from your authors—Sharon and Jeff—see the videos in Connect.*

These videos are also available on YouTube!

✓ Solutions

1.

End of year	Cost of truck	Depreciation expense for year	Accumulated depreciation at end of year	Book value at end of year (Cost − Accumulated depreciation)
1	$16,000	$3,000	$ 3,000	$13,000 ($16,000 − $3,000)
2	16,000	3,000	6,000	10,000
3	16,000	3,000	9,000	7,000
4	16,000	3,000	12,000	4,000
5	16,000	3,000	15,000	1,000 ← Note that we are down to residual value

2. $$\frac{\$16,000 - \$1,000}{5} = \$3,000 \times \frac{11}{12} = \boxed{\$2,750}$$

LU 17–1a **EXTRA PRACTICE QUIZ WITH WORKED-OUT SOLUTIONS**

Need more practice? Try this **Extra Practice Quiz** (check figures in the Interactive Chapter Organizer). Worked-out Solutions can be found in Appendix B at end of text.

1. Prepare a depreciation schedule using straight-line depreciation for the following:

Cost of truck	$20,000
Residual value	$ 2,000
Life	3 years

2. If the truck were bought on February 3, what would the depreciation expense be in the first year?

Learning Unit 17–2: Units-of-Production Method

LO 1

Unlike in the straight-line depreciation method, in the **units-of-production method** the passage of time is not used to determine an asset's depreciation amount. Instead, the company determines the asset's depreciation according to how much the company uses the asset. This use could be miles driven, tons hauled, or units that a machine produces. For example, when a company such as Ajax Company (in Learning Unit 17–1) buys equipment, the company estimates how many units the equipment can produce. Let's assume the equipment has a useful life of 4,000 units. The following formulas are used to calculate the equipment's depreciation for the units-of-production method.

MONEY tips

Unplug electronics when they are not in use. It will extend their lifespan and reduce your energy consumption.

$$\frac{\text{Depreciation}}{\text{per unit}} = \frac{\text{Cost} - \text{Residual value}}{\text{Total estimated units produced}} = \frac{\$2,500 - \$500}{4,000 \text{ units}} = \$.50 \text{ per unit}$$

$$\frac{\text{Depreciation}}{\text{amount}} = \frac{\text{Unit}}{\text{depreciation}} \times \frac{\text{Units}}{\text{produced}} = \$.50 \text{ times actual number of units}$$

Now we can complete Table 17.2. Note that the table gives the units produced each year.

LO 2

TABLE 17.2 Depreciation schedule for units-of-production method

End of year	Cost of equipment	Units produced	Depreciation expense for year	Accumulated depreciation at end of year	Book value at end of year (Cost − Accumulated depreciation)
1	$2,500	300	$ 150 (300 × $.50)	$ 150	$2,350 ($2,500 − $150)
2	2,500	400	200	350	2,150
3	2,500	600	300	650	1,850
4	2,500	2,000	1,000	1,650	850
5	2,500	700	350	2,000	500

At the end of 5 years, the equipment produced 4,000 units. If in year 5 the equipment produced 1,500 units, only 700 could be used in the calculation, or it will go below the equipment's residual value.

Units produced per year times $.50 equals depreciation expense.

Residual value of $500 is reached. (Be sure depreciation is not taken below the residual value.)

Let's check your understanding of this unit with the Practice Quiz.

LU 17–2 PRACTICE QUIZ

Complete this Practice Quiz to see how you are doing.

$$\frac{\$20,000 - \$4,000}{16,000} = \$1$$

*For **extra help** from your authors—Sharon and Jeff—see the videos in Connect.*

These videos are also available on YouTube!

From the following facts prepare a depreciation schedule:

Machine cost	$20,000
Residual value	$ 4,000

Expected to produce 16,000 units over its expected life

	2012	**2013**	**2014**	**2015**	**2016**
Units produced:	2,000	8,000	3,000	1,800	1,600

✓ **Solutions**

End of year	Cost of machine	Units produced	Depreciation expense for year	Accumulated depreciation at end of year	Book value at end of year (Cost − Accumulated depreciation)
1	$20,000	2,000	$2,000 (2,000 × $1)	$ 2,000	$18,000
2	20,000	8,000	8,000	10,000	10,000
3	20,000	3,000	3,000	13,000	7,000
4	20,000	1,800	1,800	14,800	5,200
5	20,000	1,600	1,200*	16,000	4,000

*Note that we can depreciate only 1,200 units since we cannot go below the residual value of $4,000.

LU 17–2a EXTRA PRACTICE QUIZ WITH WORKED-OUT SOLUTIONS

Need more practice? Try this Extra Practice Quiz (check figures in the Interactive Chapter Organizer). Worked-out Solutions can be found in Appendix B at end of text.

From the following facts prepare a depreciation schedule:

Machine cost	$30,000
Residual value	$ 2,000

Expected to produce 56,000 units over its expected life

	2012	**2013**	**2014**	**2015**	**2016**
Units produced	1,000	6,000	4,000	2,000	2,500

Learning Unit 17–3: Declining-Balance Method

In the declining-balance method, we cannot depreciate below the residual value.

LO 1, 2

MONEY tips

Do you have enough money? Before purchasing or adopting a pet, estimate the annual cost of caring for it to determine whether you can afford it.

The **declining-balance method** is another type of **accelerated depreciation** that takes larger amounts of depreciation expense in the earlier years of the asset. The straight-line method, you recall, estimates the life of the asset and distributes the same amount of depreciation expense to each period. To take larger amounts of depreciation expense in the asset's earlier years, the declining-balance method uses up to *twice* the **straight-line rate** in the first year of depreciation. A key point to remember is that the declining-balance method does not deduct the residual value in calculating the depreciation expense. Today, the declining-balance method is the basis of current tax depreciation.

For all problems, we will use double the straight-line rate unless we indicate otherwise. Today, the rate is often 1.5 or 1.25 times the straight-line rate. Again we use our $2,500 equipment with its estimated useful life of 5 years. As we build the depreciation schedule in Table 17.3, note the following steps:

Step 1. Rate is equal to $\frac{100\%}{5 \text{ years}} \times 2 = 40\%$.

Or another way to look at it is that the straight-line rate is $\frac{1}{5} \times 2 = \frac{2}{5} = 40\%$.

Step 2.

Depreciation expense each year	=	Book value of equipment at beginning of year	×	Depreciation rate

TABLE 17.3 Depreciation schedule for declining-balance method

End of year	Cost of equipment	Accumulated depreciation at beginning of year	Book value at beginning of year (Cost − Accumulated depreciation)	Depreciation (Book value at beginning of year × Rate)	Accumulated depreciation at end of year	Book value at end of year (Cost − Accumulated depreciation)
1	$2,500	—	$2,500	$1,000 ($2,500 × .40)	$1,000	$1,500 ($2,500 − $1,000)
2	2,500	$1,000	1,500	600 ($1,500 × .40)	1,600	900
3	2,500	1,600	900	360 ($900 × .40)	1,960	540
4	2,500	1,960	540	40	2,000	500
5	2,500	2,000	500	—	2,000	500
	↑ Original cost of $2,500 does not change. Residual value was not subtracted.	↑ Ending accumulated depreciation of 1 year becomes next year's beginning.	↑ Cost less accumulated depreciation	↑ *Note:* In year 4, only $40 is taken since we cannot depreciate below residual value of $500. In year 5, no depreciation is taken.	↑ Accumulated depreciation balance plus depreciation expense this year.	↑ Book value now equals residual value.

Step 3. We cannot depreciate the equipment below its residual value ($500). The straight-line method automatically reduced the asset's book value to the residual value. This is not true with the declining-balance method. So you must be careful when you prepare the depreciation schedule.

Now let's check your progress again with another Practice Quiz.

LU 17–3 PRACTICE QUIZ

Complete this **Practice Quiz** to see how you are doing.

*For **extra help** from your authors—Sharon and Jeff—see the videos in Connect.*

These videos are also available on YouTube!

Prepare a depreciation schedule from the following:

Cost of machine: $16,000
Rate: 40% (this is twice the straight-line rate)

Estimated life: 5 years
Residual value: $1,000

✓ **Solutions**

End of year	Cost of machine	Accumulated depreciation at beginning of year	Book value at beginning of year (Cost − Accumulated depreciation)	Depreciation (Book value at beginning of year × Rate)	Accumulated depreciation at end of year	Book value at end of year (Cost − Accumulated depreciation)
1	$16,000	$ —0—	$16,000.00	$6,400.00	$ 6,400.00	$9,600.00
2	16,000	6,400.00	9,600.00	3,840.00	10,240.00	5,760.00
3	16,000	10,240.00	5,760.00	2,304.00	12,544.00	3,456.00
4	16,000	12,544.00	3,456.00	1,382.40	13,926.40	2,073.60
5	16,000	13,926.40	2,073.60	829.44*	14,755.84	1,244.16

*Since we do not reach the residual value of $1,000, another $244.16 could have been taken as depreciation expense to bring it to the estimated residual value of $1,000.

LU 17–3a   **EXTRA PRACTICE QUIZ WITH WORKED-OUT SOLUTIONS**

Need more practice? Try this **Extra Practice Quiz** (check figures in the Interactive Chapter Organizer). Worked-out Solutions can be found in Appendix B at end of text.

Prepare a depreciation schedule for three years for the following:

Cost of machine: $31,000
Rate: 40% (this is twice the straight-line rate)

Estimated life: 5 years
Residual value: $1,000

Learning Unit 17–4: Modified Accelerated Cost Recovery System (MACRS) with Introduction to ACRS (1986, 1989, 2010)

© Kenzo Tribouillard/Getty Images

In Learning Units 17–1 to 17–3, we discussed the depreciation methods used for financial reporting. Since 1981, federal tax laws have been passed that state how depreciation must be taken for income tax purposes. Assets put in service from 1981 through 1986 fell under the federal **Accelerated Cost Recovery System (ACRS)** tax law enacted in 1981. The Tax Reform Act of 1986 established the **Modified Accelerated Cost Recovery System (MACRS)** for all property placed into service after December 31, 1986. This system, used by businesses to calculate depreciation for tax purposes based on the tax laws of 1986, 1989, and 2010, is also known as the **General Depreciation System (GDS).** For the latest updates, go to www.irs.gov/form4562. Airplanes for commercial use are usually depreciated by MACRS for 7 years or ADS (Alternative Depreciation System) for 12 years.

Depreciation for Tax Purposes Based on the Tax Reform Act of 1986 (MACRS)

Tables 17.4 and 17.5 give the classes of recovery and annual depreciation percentages that MACRS established in 1986. The key points of MACRS are:

1. It calculates depreciation for tax purposes.

2. It ignores residual value.

3. Depreciation in the first year (for personal property) is based on the assumption that the asset was purchased halfway through the year. (A new law adds a midquarter convention for all personal property if more than 40% is placed in service during the last 3 months of the taxable year.)

4. Classes 3, 5, 7, and 10 use a 200% declining-balance method for a period of years before switching to straight-line depreciation. You do not have to determine the year in which to switch since Table 17.5 builds this into the calculation.

5. Classes 15 and 20 use a 150% declining-balance method before switching to straight-line depreciation.

6. Classes 27.5 and 31.5 use straight-line depreciation.

© H. Wiesenhofer/PhotoLink/Getty Images

TABLE **17.4**

Modified Accelerated Cost Recovery System (MACRS) for assets placed in service after December 31, 1986

Class recovery period (life)	Asset types
3-year*	Racehorses more than 2 years old or any horse other than a racehorse that is more than 12 years old at the time placed into service; special tools of certain industries.
5-year*	Automobiles (not luxury); taxis; light general-purpose trucks; semiconductor manufacturing equipment; computer-based telephone central-office switching equipment; qualified technological equipment; property used in connection with research and experimentation.
7-year*	Railroad track; single-purpose agricultural (pigpens) or horticultural structures; fixtures; equipment; furniture.
10-year*	New law doesn't add any specific property under this class.
15-year†	Municipal wastewater treatment plants; telephone distribution plants and comparable equipment used for two-way exchange of voice and data communications.
20-year†	Municipal sewers.
27.5-year‡	Only residential rental property.
31.5-year‡	Only nonresidential real property.

*These classes use a 200% declining-balance method switching to the straight-line method.
†These classes use a 150% declining-balance method switching to the straight-line method.
‡These classes use a straight-line method.

Racehorses, when put in training, can be depreciated by MACRS.

| TABLE | 17.5 | Annual recovery for MACRS |

Annual recovery for MACRS

Recovery year	3-year class (200% D.B.)	5-year class (200% D.B.)	7-year class (200% D.B.)	10-year class (200% D.B.)	15-year class (150% D.B.)	20-year class (150% D.B.)
1	33.00	20.00	14.28	10.00	5.00	3.75
2	45.00	32.00	24.49	18.00	9.50	7.22
3	15.00*	19.20	17.49	14.40	8.55	6.68
4	7.00	11.52*	12.49	11.52	7.69	6.18
5		11.52	8.93*	9.22	6.93	5.71
6		5.76	8.93	7.37	6.23	5.28
7			8.93	6.55*	5.90*	4.89
8			4.46	6.55	5.90	4.52
9				6.55	5.90	4.46*
10				6.55	5.90	4.46
11				3.29	5.90	4.46
12					5.90	4.46
13					5.90	4.46
14					5.90	4.46
15					5.90	4.46
16					3.00	4.46

*Identifies when switch is made to straight line.

LO 2

EXAMPLE Using the same equipment cost of $2,500 for Ajax, prepare a depreciation schedule under MACRS assuming the equipment is a 5-year class and not part of the tax bill of 1989. Use Table 17.5. Note that percent figures from Table 17.5 have been converted to decimals.

MONEY tips

Consider refinancing your home to obtain a lower fixed interest rate. Determine whether your savings offsets the refinance costs. A rate reduction of 1.5% is generally worth the cost in the long run.

End of year	Cost	Depreciation expense	Accumulated depreciation	Book value at end of year
1	$2,500	$500 (.20 × $2,500)	$ 500	$2,000
2	2,500	800 (.32 × $2,500)	1,300	1,200
3	2,500	480 (.1920 × $2,500)	1,780	720
4	2,500	288 (.1152 × $2,500)	2,068	432
5	2,500	288 (.1152 × $2,500)	2,356	144
6	2,500	144 (.0576 × $2,500)	2,500	–0–

Check your understanding of this learning unit with the below Practice Quiz.

LU 17–4 | **PRACTICE QUIZ**

Complete this Practice Quiz to see how you are doing.

*For **extra help** from your authors—Sharon and Jeff—see the videos in Connect.*

These videos are also available on YouTube!

1. In 2015, Rancho Corporation bought semiconductor equipment for $80,000. Using MACRS, what is the depreciation expense in year 3?
2. What would depreciation be the first year for a wastewater treatment plant that cost $800,000?

✓ **Solutions**

1. $80,000 × .1920 = **$15,360**   2. $800,000 × .05 = **$40,000**

LU 17–4a	EXTRA PRACTICE QUIZ WITH WORKED-OUT SOLUTIONS

Need more practice? Try this Extra Practice Quiz (check figures in the Interactive Chapter Organizer). Worked-out Solutions can be found in Appendix B at end of text.

1. In 2015, Rancho Corporation bought semiconductor equipment for $90,000. Using MACRS, what is the depreciation expense in year 3?

2. What would depreciation be the first year for a wastewater treatment plant that cost $900,000?

INTERACTIVE CHAPTER ORGANIZER

Topic/Procedure/Formula	Examples	You try it*
Straight-line method $\text{Depreciation expense each year} = \dfrac{\text{Cost} - \text{Residual value}}{\text{Estimated useful life in years}}$ For partial years if purchased before 15th of month depreciation is taken.	Truck, $25,000; $5,000 residual value, 4-year life. $\dfrac{\text{Depreciation}}{\text{expense}} = \dfrac{\$25,000 - \$5,000}{4}$ $= \boxed{\$5,000}$ per year	**Calculate depreciation expense** Truck, $50,000; $10,000 residual value; 4-year life.
Units-of-production method $\dfrac{\text{Depreciation}}{\text{per unit}} = \dfrac{\text{Cost} - \text{Residual value}}{\text{Total estimated units produced}}$ Do not depreciate below residual value even if actual units are greater than estimate.	Machine, $5,000; estimated life in units, 900; residual value, $500. Assume first year produced 175 units. $\text{Depreciation expense} = \dfrac{\$5,000 - \$500}{900}$ $= \dfrac{\$4,500}{900}$ $= \$5$ depreciation per unit 175 units × $5 = $\boxed{\$875}$ depreciation expense	**Calculate depreciation expense** Machine, $4,000; estimated life in units, 700; residual value, $500. Assume first year produced 150 units.
Declining-balance method An accelerated method. Residual value not subtracted from cost in depreciation schedule. Do not depreciate below residual value. $\begin{aligned}\dfrac{\text{Depreciation}}{\text{expense}}\\\text{each year}\end{aligned} = \begin{aligned}\text{Book}\\\text{value of}\\\text{equipment}\\\text{at beginning}\\\text{of year}\end{aligned} \times \begin{aligned}\text{Depreciation}\\\text{rate}\end{aligned}$	Truck, $50,000; estimated life, 5 years; residual value, $10,000. $\frac{1}{5} = 20\% \times 2 = 40\%$ (assume double the straight-line rate) 	Year	Cost	Depreciation expense	Book value at end of year
---	---	---	---
1	$50,000	$20,000 ($50,000 × .40)	$30,000 ($50,000 − $20,000)
2	$50,000	$12,000 ($30,000 × .40)	$18,000 ($50,000 − $32,000)		**Calculate depreciation expense and book value for 2 years** Truck, $40,000; estimated life, 4 years; residual value, $5,000.

(continues)

INTERACTIVE CHAPTER ORGANIZER

Topic/Procedure/Formula	Examples	You try it*
MACRS/Tax Bill of 1989, 2010 After December 31, 1986, depreciation calculation is modified. Tax Act of 1989, 2010, modifies way to depreciate equipment.	Auto: $8,000, 5 years. First year, .20 × $8,000 = $1,600 depreciation expense	Auto: $7,000, 5 years. Second year = ? depreciation expense

KEY TERMS	Accelerated Cost Recovery System (ACRS) Accelerated depreciation Accumulated depreciation Asset cost Book value Declining-balance method Depreciation	Depreciation expense Depreciation schedule Estimated useful life General Depreciation System (GDS) Modified Accelerated Cost Recovery System (MACRS)	Residual value Salvage value Straight-line method Straight-line rate Trade-in value Units-of-production method

Check Figures for Extra Practice Quizzes. (Worked-out Solutions are in Appendix B.)	LU 17–1a 1. Book value EOY 3 $2,000 2. $5,500	LU 17–2a $.50; Book value EOY 5 $22,250	LU 17–3a *Depreciation expense year* 1. $12,400 2. $7,440 3. $4,464	LU 17–4a 1. $17,280 2. $45,000

*Worked-out solutions are in Appendix B.

Critical Thinking Discussion Questions with Chapter Concept Check

1. What is the difference between depreciation expense and accumulated depreciation? Why does the book value of an asset never go below the residual value?

2. Compare the straight-line method to the units-of-production method. Should both methods be based on the passage of time?

3. Why is it possible in the declining-balance method for a person to depreciate below the residual value by mistake?

4. Explain the Modified Accelerated Cost Recovery System. Do you think this system will be eliminated in the future?

5. **Chapter Concept Check.** Search the web for a car of your choice and use concepts from this chapter to provide a depreciation schedule for the car.

END-OF-CHAPTER PROBLEMS ■ connect plus+

Check figures for odd-numbered problems in Appendix C.   Name _____   Date _____

DRILL PROBLEMS

From the following facts, complete a depreciation schedule by using the straight-line method: *LU 17-1(2)*

Given Cost of Honda Accord Hybrid $32,900
Residual value $ 6,500
Estimated life   8 years

End of year	Cost of Accord	Depreciation expense for year	Accumulated depreciation at end of year	Book value at end of year
17–1.				
17–2.				
17–3.				
17–4.				
17–5.				
17–6.				
17–7.				
17–8.				

From the following facts, prepare a depreciation schedule using the declining-balance method (twice the straight-line rate): *LU 17-3(2)*

Given Chevrolet Colorado $25,000
Residual value $ 5,000
Estimated life   5 years

End of year	Cost of Chevy truck	Accumulated depreciation at beginning of year	Book value at beginning of year	Depreciation expense for year	Accumulated depreciation at end of year	Book value at end of year
17–9.						
17–10.						
17–11.						
17–12.						

For the first 2 years, calculate the depreciation expense for a $7,000 car under MACRS. This is a nonluxury car. *LU 17-4(2)*

MACRS
17–13. Year 1

MACRS
17–14. Year 2

Complete the following table given this information:

Cost of machine $94,000   Estimated units machine will produce   100,000
Residual value $ 4,000   Actual production: Year 1 Year 2
Useful life   5 years   60,000 15,000

Method	Depreciation Expense Year 1	Year 2
17–15. Straight line *LU 17-1(2)*		
17–16. Units of production *LU 17-2(2)*		
17–17. Declining balance *LU 17-3(2)*		
17–18. MACRS (5-year class) *LU 17-4(2)*		

WORD PROBLEMS

17–19. Shearer's Foods, part of the $374 billion global snack food industry, employs 3,300 people in Brewster, Ohio. If Shearer's purchased a packaging unit for $185,000 with a life expectancy of 695,000 units and a residual value of $46,000, what is the depreciation expense for year 1 if 75,000 units were produced?   *LU 17-2(2)*

17–20. Lena Horn bought a Toyota Tundra on January 1 for $30,000 with an estimated life of 5 years. The residual value of the truck
eXcel is $5,000. Assume a straight-line method of depreciation. **(a)** What will be the book value of the truck at the end of year 4?
(b) If the Tundra was bought the first year on April 12, how much depreciation would be taken the first year?   *LU 17-1(2)*

17–21. Jim Company bought a machine for $36,000 with an estimated life of 5 years. The residual value of the machine is $6,000.
eXcel Calculate **(a)** the annual depreciation and **(b)** the book value at the end of year 3. Assume straight-line depreciation.
LU 17-1(2)

17–22. Using Problem 17–21, calculate the first 2 years' depreciation, assuming the units-of-production method. This machine
eXcel is expected to produce 120,000 units. In year 1, it produced 19,000 units, and in year 2, 38,000 units.   *LU 17-2(2)*

17–23. Jim Clinnin purchased a used RV with 19,000 miles for $46,900. Originally the RV sold for $70,000 with a residual value of $20,000. After subtracting the residual value, depreciation allowance per mile was $.86. How much was Jim's purchase price over or below the book value?   *LU 17-2(1)*

17–24. Whole Foods, the world's leader in natural and organic foods, is celebrating 18 consecutive years on *Fortune*'s "100 Best Companies to Work For" list. A store opens in Houston, Texas, in April 2015 at a new Voss location. A commercial oven for $7,985 with a 5-year life and residual value of $1,100 was purchased for the store. What is the depreciation expense in year 2 for the oven? Use the straight-line method.   *LU 17-1(2)*

17–25. Perry Wiseman of Truckers Accounting Service in Omaha, Nebraska, likes to use the straight-line method. The cost of his truck was $108,000, with a useful life of 3 years and a residual value of $35,000. What would be the book value of the truck after the first year? Round your answers to the nearest dollar. *LU 17-1(2)*

17–26. If corporate headquarters for UPS in Atlanta is considering adding to its 96,000+ fleet of delivery vans, what is year 5's depreciation expense using MACRS if one van costs $78,500? *LU 17-4(2)*

CHALLENGE PROBLEMS

17–27. A delivered price (including attachments) of a crawler dozer tractor is $135,000 with a residual value of 35%. The useful life of the tractor is 7,700 hours. *LU 17-2(2)*
  a. What is the total amount of depreciation allowed?
  b. What is the amount of depreciation per hour?
  c. If the tractor is operated five days a week for an average of $7\frac{1}{4}$ hours a day, what would be the depreciation for the first year?
  d. If the hours of operation were the same each year, what would be the total number of years of useful life for the tractor? Round years to the nearest whole number.

17–28. Assume a piece of equipment was purchased July 26, 2016, at a cost of $72,000. The estimated residual value is $5,400 with a useful life of 5 years. Assume a production life of 60,000 units. Compute the depreciation for years 2016 and 2017 using **(a)** straight-line and **(b)** units-of-production (in 2016, 5,000 units were produced and in 2017, 18,000 units were produced). *LU 17-1(2), LU 17-2(2)*

 SUMMARY PRACTICE TEST

Do you need help? The videos in Connect have step-by-step worked-out solutions. These videos are also available on YouTube!

1. Leo Lucky, owner of a Pizza Hut franchise, bought a delivery truck for $30,000. The truck has an estimated life of 5 years with a residual value of $10,000. Leo wants to know which depreciation method will be the best for his truck. He asks you to prepare a depreciation schedule using the declining-balance method at twice the straight-line rate. *LU 17-3(2)*

2. Using MACRS, what is the depreciation for the first year on furniture costing $12,000? *LU 17-4(2)*

3. Abby Matthew bought a new Jeep Commander for $30,000. The Jeep Commander has a life expectancy of 5 years with a
eXcel residual value of $10,000. Prepare a depreciation schedule for the straight-line method. *LU 17-1(2)*

4. Car.com bought a Toyota for $28,000. The Toyota has a life expectancy of 10 years with a residual value of $3,000. After
eXcel 3 years, the Toyota was sold for $19,000. What was the difference between the book value and the amount received from
selling the car if Car.com used the straight-line method of depreciation? *LU 17-1(2)*

5. A machine cost $70,200; it had an estimated residual value of $6,000 and an expected life of 300,000 units. What would
be the depreciation in year 3 if 60,000 units were produced? (Round to nearest cent.) *LU 17-2(2)*

SURF TO SAVE

Purchase price versus current worth 🔍

PROBLEM 1

Computing depreciation

Go to http://www.dell.com. Find the price of a computer system that you would like to buy. Assume you bought this system for business use and the system has a residual value of $400. Compute the depreciation each year under a 5-year straight-line depreciation. Also, calculate the depreciation using MACRS (Tables 17.4 and 17.5 in the text).

Discussion Questions

1. Based on the cost of this computer system, would you keep it for more than 5 years? Why or why not?

2. Do you feel a computer system would actually be worth far less than the depreciated value you calculated? Why?

PROBLEM 2

How car values decline

Go to http://www.kbb.com. Find the price of a car you would like to buy. Assume you bought this car at that price for business use and it has a residual value of 20% of the purchase price. Compute the depreciation each year under a 5-year straight-line depreciation. Then, calculate the depreciation using MACRS (Table 17.5 in the text).

Discussion Questions

1. How does this depreciation represent the value of the car as it ages?

2. Would this depreciation impact the amount of money you would spend on a car? Why or why not?

PROBLEM 3

Calculating auto depreciation

Go to http://www.edmunds.com. Search for a target purchase price on the latest year's version of a nonluxury car. Now go to http://www.money-zine.com/Calculators/Auto-Loan-Calculators/Car-Depreciation-Calculator. Assume that you will own the car for 5 years, that its depreciation will be average, and that the car will have a residual value of 10% of the purchase price. What is the amount of the first year's depreciation? What is total depreciation over the 5 years that you own the car?

Discussion Questions

1. How does the depreciation using the online calculator compare to the depreciation using the straight-line approach?

2. What do you feel may be the difference between these two methods of computing depreciation?

PROBLEM 4

Nothing depreciates like a Deere!

Go to http://e-marketing.deere.com/ViewAllProducts.do and choose a piece of equipment. Assume a life of 5 years and an $800 residual value. Compute the depreciation for each year, using 5-year straight-line depreciation.

Discussion Questions

1. How does depreciation impact the types of purchases businesses choose to make?

2. Do you feel the depreciation on this equipment represents a fair assessment of its value over time? Why or why not?

MOBILE APPS ✕

Straight Line Depreciation (Business Compass LLC) Calculates schedules of depreciation via the straight-line method.

Depreciation (Business Compass LLC) Calculates depreciation using straight-line, production or use, sum-of-years digits, MACRS, and double-declining-balance methods.

A KIPLINGER APPROACH

By Jessica L. Anderson, From *Kiplinger's Personal Finance*, November 2014.

> **You'll find the biggest bargains on cars that buyers are steering clear of. That includes compact and midsize sedans."**

JESSICA ANDERSON > Drive Time
Expect Deals on New Models

This fall should be a very good time to buy a 2015 car or truck. Vehicle sales have heated up over the past few years, fueled by a healthier economy and low interest rates. Now automakers are fighting tooth and nail for market share. Look for cash incentives in addition to low-rate financing on more vehicles. Carmakers will also dole out dealer cash—which dealers can pass on to you.

For an even sweeter deal, shop for a 2014 model. As the new models stream into showrooms, dealers will be anxious to clear their lots. Look for average discounts to approach 10% off sticker prices by year-end. You'll find the biggest bargains on cars that buyers are steering clear of. That includes compact and midsize sedans, thanks to gas prices that were recently at their lowest levels in four years. (Buyers have been migrating to crossovers.) Lease deals are also abundant on the 2014s. For $200 or less a month, you could recently lease a Honda Accord, Hyundai Elantra, Nissan Altima or Mazda3.

A leaner, greener 2015. Among the more than 50 brand-new and redesigned models for 2015, the small-crossover segment is seeing the most action. Small crossovers meet the Goldilocks test. They're big enough to carry your family and cargo, but small enough that you won't pay an arm and a leg for gas or feel as if you're driving a truck.

And some crossovers are getting even smaller. Carmakers have been introducing subcompact crossovers, which are just a bit smaller than compacts, have lower prices and get better fuel economy. The Chevrolet Trax, Jeep Renegade and Honda HR-V—all starting at about $20,000—are among the entries for 2015 from mainstream brands. German luxury brands are also launching subcompacts—the Audi Q3 (starting at $33,425) and Mercedes-Benz GLA ($32,225)—and others are coming out with new compacts, including the Lexus

NX (about $35,000), Lincoln MKC ($33,995) and Porsche Macan ($50,895).

Luxury makes are also tweaking their entry-level sedans to tempt you to make the switch from mainstream brands. For example, Audi has reconfigured its A3, formerly available only as a hatch, as a sedan ($30,795) and Mercedes revamped the compact C-Class ($39,325).

Two midsize sedan stalwarts, the Hyundai Sonata and Toyota Camry, are redesigned for 2015, as are the Chrysler 200 and Subaru Legacy. All of these models boast enhanced suspensions for better handling, as well as better interior materials.

Have a big brood to haul? The Kia Sedona minivan gets a redesign for 2015, with "First Class" lounge seating in the second row, a 360-degree-view monitor for parking and a refrigerated glove box for cooling drinks. General Motors is overhauling its lineup of big SUVs to provide more power and 10% better fuel economy. Plus, GM has boosted legroom and enhanced ease of use of the cargo area of the Chevrolet Tahoe and Suburban and the GMC Yukon/Yukon XL.

As the industry strives to meet strict average-fuel-economy regulations that demand 54.5 miles per gallon by 2025, you'll find improved mileage, whether you're considering a vehicle with a traditional engine or an alternative powertrain. More transmissions will sport seven to nine speeds, and you'll see more turbocharging, direct injection and auto stop/start in internal combustion engines.

Sales of electric vehicles and hybrids have plateaued for now, but you'll still see more EVs in 2015: the Kia Soul EV, Volkswagen e-Golf and long-awaited Tesla Model X crossover. Volkswagen, one of the biggest sellers of diesel vehicles, is adding a new TDI engine to its Beetle, Golf, Jetta and Passat lineups, improving both power and fuel economy. ∎

ASK JESSICA A QUESTION AT JANDERSON@KIPLINGER.COM, OR FOLLOW HER ON FACEBOOK OR TWITTER AT JANDERSONDRIVES.

LISE METZGER

BUSINESS MATH ISSUE

Depreciation is not a factor when buying a vehicle.

1. List the key points of the article and information to support your position.
2. Write a group defense of your position using math calculations to support your view.

Classroom Notes

CHAPTER 18

Inventory and Overhead

© Royalty-Free/Corbis

The Music Comeback of 2014: Vinyl Records

Sales of LPs Surge 49%, but the Few, Aging Factories That Still Make Them Struggle to Keep Pace

BY NEIL SHAH

Nearly eight million old-fashioned vinyl LPs have been sold this year, up 49% from the same period last year, industry data show. Younger people, especially indie-rock fans, are buying records in greater numbers, attracted to the perceived superior sound quality of vinyl and the ritual of putting needle to groove.

But while new LPs hit stores each week, the creaky machines that press records haven't been manufactured for decades, and just one company supplies an estimated 90% of the raw vinyl that America's industry needs. As such, the nation's 15 or so still-running factories that make records face daily challenges with breakdowns and supply shortages.

Their efforts point to a problem now bedeviling a curious corner of the music industry: The record-making business is stirring to life—but it's still on its last legs.

Robert Roczynski's dozen employees work overtime at a small factory in Hamden, Conn., to make parts for U.S. record makers struggling to keep abreast of the revived interest in LPs. Mr. Roczynski's firm says orders for steel molds, which give records their flat, round shape, have tripled since 2008.

They're trying to bring the industry back, but the era has gone by," says Mr. Roczynski, 67 years old, president of Record

Products of America Inc., one of the country's few suppliers of parts for the industry.

Many producers, including the largest, **United Record Pressing** in Nashville, Tenn., are adding presses, but there has yet to be a big move by entrepreneurs to inject capital and confidence into this largely artisanal industry. Investors aren't interested in sinking serious cash into an industry that represents 2% of U.S. music sales.

Record labels are waiting months for orders that used to get filled in weeks. That is because pressing machines spit out only around 125 records an hour. To boost production, record factories are running their machines so hard—sometimes around the clock—they have to

shell out increasing sums for maintenance and repairs.

Large orders from superstars create bottlenecks, while music fans search the bins in vain for new releases by The War on Drugs, a Philadelphia indie group, or French electronic duo Daft Punk. More requests for novelty LPs—multi-colored, scented, glow-in-the-dark—gum things up further.

Nick Blandford, managing director of Secretly Group, a family of independent labels, in Bloomington, Ind., is putting in orders now to make sure his artists' LPs are in stores for next year's "Record Store Day" in April.

To get more machines, record-plant owners have been scouring the globe for mothballed presses,

snapping them up for $15,000 to $30,000, and plunking down even more to refurbish them.

Ryan Raffaelli, an assistant professor at Harvard Business School who studies what he calls "technology re-emergence," is familiar with this industrial nether-world.

Swiss mechanical watches, fountain pens and independent bookstores all re-emerged from the doldrums by reinventing themselves for consumers and then attracting investment from entrepreneurs, he says.

"The question is whether there's enough demand for vinyl *Please turn to the next page*

Reprinted by permission of The Wall Street Journal, copyright 2014 Dow Jones & Company, Inc. All rights reserved wo

LU 18–1: Assigning Costs to Ending Inventory—Specific Identification; Weighted Average; FIFO; LIFO

1. List the key assumptions of each inventory method.
2. Calculate the cost of ending inventory and cost of goods sold for each inventory method.

LU 18–2: Retail Method; Gross Profit Method; Inventory Turnover; Distribution of Overhead

1. Calculate the cost ratio and ending inventory at cost for the retail method.
2. Calculate the estimated inventory using the gross profit method.
3. Explain and calculate inventory turnover.
4. Explain overhead; allocate overhead according to floor space and sales.

VOCABULARY PREVIEW

Here are key terms in this chapter. After completing the chapter, if you know the term, place a checkmark in the box. If you don't know the term, look it up and put the page number where it can be found.

Average inventory ☐ Distribution of overhead ☐ First-in, first-out (FIFO) method ☐ GAAP ☐
Gross profit method ☐ IFRS ☐ Inventory turnover ☐ Just-in-time (JIT) inventory system ☐ Last-in,
first-out (LIFO) method ☐ Overhead expenses ☐ Periodic inventory system ☐ Perpetual inventory
system ☐ Retail method ☐ Specific identification method ☐ Weighted-average method ☐

Sears is piloting radio-frequency tags in 15 stores. Industry professionals say the technology will allow retailers to increase sales and margins by giving them a more accurate picture of the merchandise they have in stock. A Sears store manager reported that he was able to scan 400 pairs of Levi's Jeans in a few seconds and could scan all the jeans the store had in stock in 10 to 15 minutes.

Source: Suzanne Kapner, "Sears Bets Big on Technology, But at the Expense of Its Stores," *The Wall Street Journal*, 12/16/14.

The chapter opener clipping shows how difficult it is to have enough inventory for vinyl records. Note in the *Wall Street Journal* clip to the left that Sears is using new technology to control inventory. The two methods that a company can use to monitor its inventory are the *perpetual* method and the *periodic* method.

© The McGraw-Hill Companies, Inc./John Flournoy, photographer

The perpetual inventory system should be familiar to most consumers. Today, it is common for cashiers to run scanners across the product code of each item sold. These scanners read pertinent information into a computer terminal, such as the item's number, department, and price. The computer then uses the **perpetual inventory system** as it subtracts outgoing merchandise from inventory and adds incoming merchandise to inventory. However, as you probably know, the computer cannot be completely relied on to maintain an accurate count of merchandise in stock. Since some products may be stolen or lost, periodically a physical count is necessary to verify the computer count.

With the increased use of computers, many companies are changing to a perpetual inventory system of maintaining inventory records. Some small stores, however, still use the **periodic inventory system.** This system usually does not keep a running account of a store's inventory but relies only on a physical inventory count taken at least once a year. The store then uses various accounting methods to value the cost of its merchandise. In this chapter we discuss the periodic method of inventory.

You may wonder why a company should know the status of its inventory. In Chapter 16 we introduced you to the balance sheet and the income statement. Companies cannot accurately prepare these statements unless they have placed the correct value on their inventory. To do this, a company must know (1) the cost of its ending inventory (found on the balance sheet) and (2) the cost of the goods (merchandise) sold (found on the income statement).

No longer do retailers get a few seasonal deliveries; they now receive new items often, maybe even weekly, to keep their store looking fresh. Frequently, the same type of merchandise flows into a company at different costs. The value assumptions a company makes about the merchandise it sells affect the cost assigned to its ending inventory. Remember that different costs result in different levels of profit on a firm's financial reports.

This chapter begins by using the Blue Company to discuss four common methods (specific identification, weighted average, FIFO, and LIFO) that companies use to calculate the cost of ending inventory and the cost of goods sold. In these methods, the flow of costs does not always match the flow of goods. The chapter continues with a discussion of two methods of estimating ending inventory (retail and gross profit methods), inventory turnover, and the distribution of overhead.

A company must declare on its financial statements the inventory method used.

Learning Unit 18-1: Assigning Costs to Ending Inventory—Specific Identification; Weighted Average; FIFO; LIFO

LO 1, 2

Blue Company is a small artist supply store. Its beginning inventory is 40 tubes of art paint that cost $320 (at $8 a tube) to bring into the store. As shown in Figure 18.1, Blue made additional purchases in April, May, October, and December. Note that because of inflation and other competitive factors, the cost of the paint rose from $8 to $13 per tube. At the end of December, Blue had 48 unsold paint tubes. During the year, Blue had 120 paint tubes to sell. Blue wants to calculate (1) the cost of ending inventory (not sold) and (2) the cost of goods sold.

Specific Identification Method

Companies that sell high-cost items such as autos, jewelry, antiques, and so on, usually use the specific identification method.

Companies use the **specific identification method** when they can identify the original purchase cost of an item with the item. For example, Blue Company color codes its paint tubes as they come into the store. Blue can then attach a specific invoice price to each paint tube.

FIGURE 18.1

Blue Company—a case study

	Number of units purchased	Cost per unit	Total cost
Beginning inventory	40	$ 8	$ 320
First purchase (April 1)	20	9	180
Second purchase (May 1)	20	10	200
Third purchase (October 1)	20	12	240
Fourth purchase (December 1)	20	13	260
Goods (merchandise) available for sale	120		$1,200 ← Step 1
Units sold	72		
Units in ending inventory	48		

This makes the flow of goods and flow of costs the same. Then, when Blue computes its ending inventory and cost of goods sold, it can associate the actual invoice cost with each item sold and in inventory.

To help Blue calculate its inventory with the specific identification method, use the steps that follow.

CALCULATING THE SPECIFIC IDENTIFICATION METHOD

Step 1.   Calculate the cost of goods (merchandise available for sale).

Step 2.   Calculate the cost of the ending inventory.

Step 3.   Calculate the cost of goods sold (Step 1 – Step 2).

First, Blue must actually count the tubes of paint on hand. Since Blue coded these paint tubes, it can identify the tubes with their purchase cost and multiply them by this cost to arrive at a total cost of ending inventory. Let's do this now.

	Cost per unit	Total cost
20 units from April 1	$ 9	$180
20 units from October 1	12	240
8 units from December 1	13	104
Cost of ending inventory		$524 ← **Step 2**

Blue uses the following cost of goods sold formula to determine its cost of goods sold:

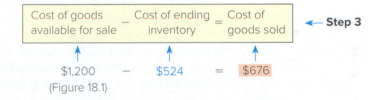

| Cost of goods available for sale | – | Cost of ending inventory | = | Cost of goods sold | ← **Step 3** |

$1,200   – $524   = $676

(Figure 18.1)

Note that the $1,200 for cost of goods available for sale comes from Figure 18.1. *Remember we are focusing our attention on Blue's purchase costs. Blue's actual selling price does not concern us here.*

Now let's look at how Blue would use the weighted-average method.

Weighted-Average Method[1]

The **weighted-average method** prices the ending inventory by using an average unit cost. Let's replay Blue Company and use the weighted-average method to find the average unit cost of its ending inventory and its cost of goods sold. Blue would use the steps that follow.

CALCULATING THE WEIGHTED-AVERAGE METHOD

Step 1.   Calculate the average unit cost.

Step 2.   Calculate the cost of the ending inventory.

Step 3.   Calculate the cost of goods sold.

---

[1]Virtually all countries permit the use of the weighted-average method.

In the table that follows, Blue makes the calculation.

	Number of units purchased	Cost per unit	Total cost
Beginning inventory	40	$ 8	$ 320
First purchase (April 1)	20	9	180
Second purchase (May 1)	20	10	200
Third purchase (October 1)	20	12	240
Fourth purchase (December 1)	20	13	260
Goods (merchandise) available for sale	120		$1,200
Units sold	72		
Units in ending inventory	48		

$$\text{Weighted-average unit cost} = \frac{\text{Total cost of goods available for sale}}{\text{Total number of units available for sale}} = \frac{\$1,200}{120 \text{ units}} = \$10 \text{ average unit cost}$$ ◄ Step 1

Average cost of ending inventory: 48 units at $10 = $480 ◄ Step 2

$$\text{Cost of goods available for sale} - \text{Cost of ending inventory} = \text{Cost of goods sold}$$

$$\$1,200 \quad - \quad \$480 \quad = \quad \$720$$ ◄ Step 3

Remember that some of the costs we used to determine the average unit cost were higher and others were lower. The weighted-average method, then, calculates an *average unit price* for goods. Companies with similar units of goods, such as rolls of wallpaper, often use the weighted-average method. Also, companies with homogeneous products such as fuels and grains may use the weighted-average method.

Now let's see how Blue Company would value its inventory with the FIFO method.

FIFO—First-In, First-Out Method

The **first-in, first-out (FIFO)** inventory valuation method assumes that the first goods (paint tubes for Blue) brought into the store are the first goods sold. Thus, FIFO assumes that each sale is from the oldest goods in inventory. FIFO also assumes that the inventory remaining in the store at the end of the period is the most recently acquired goods. This cost flow assumption may or may not hold in the actual physical flow of the goods. An example of a corporation using the FIFO method is Gillette Corporation.

Use the following steps to calculate inventory with the FIFO method.

CALCULATING THE FIFO INVENTORY

Step 1. List the units to be included in the ending inventory and their costs.

Step 2. Calculate the cost of the ending inventory.

Step 3. Calculate the cost of goods sold.

In the table that follows, we show how to calculate FIFO for Blue using the above steps.

FIFO (bottom up)	Number of units purchased	Cost per unit	Total cost
Beginning inventory	40	$ 8	$ 320
First purchase (April 1)	20	9	180
Second purchase (May 1)	20	10	200
Third purchase (October 1)	20	12	240
Fourth purchase (December 1)	20	13	260
Goods (merchandise) available for sale	120		$1,200
Units sold	72		
Units in ending inventory	48		

20 units from December 1 purchased at $13 $260

20 units from October 1 purchased at $12 ← Step 1 → 240

 8 units from May 1 purchased at $10   80

48 units result in an ending inventory cost of $580 ← Step 2

Cost of goods available for sale	−	Cost of ending inventory	=	Cost of goods sold
$1,200	−	$580	=	$620 ← Step 3

In FIFO, the cost flow of goods tends to follow the physical flow. For example, a fish market could use FIFO because it wants to sell its old inventory first. Note that during inflation, FIFO produces a higher income than other methods. So companies using FIFO during this time must pay more taxes.

We conclude this unit by using the LIFO method to value Blue Company's inventory.

LIFO—Last-In, First-Out Method

If Blue Company chooses the **last-in, first-out (LIFO)** method of inventory valuation, then the goods sold by Blue will be the last goods brought into the store. The ending inventory would consist of the old goods that Blue bought earlier.

You can calculate inventory with the LIFO method by using the steps that follow.

CALCULATING THE LIFO INVENTORY

Step 1. List the units to be included in the ending inventory and their costs.

Step 2. Calculate the cost of the ending inventory.

Step 3. Calculate the cost of goods sold.

Now we use the above steps to calculate LIFO for Blue.

LIFO (top down)	Number of units purchased	Cost per unit	Total cost
Beginning inventory	40	$ 8	$ 320
First purchase (April 1)	20	9	180
Second purchase (May 1)	20	10	200
Third purchase (October 1)	20	12	240
Fourth purchase (December 1)	20	13	260
Goods (merchandise) available for sale	120		$1,200
Units sold	72		
Units in ending inventory	48		

40 units of beginning inventory at $8 $320

8 units from April at $9   ← Step 1 →   72

48 units result in an ending inventory cost of. $392 ← Step 2

Cost of goods available for sale	−	Cost of ending inventory	=	Cost of goods sold
↑		↑		↑
$1,200	−	$392	=	$808 ← Step 3

Although LIFO doesn't always match the physical flow of goods, companies do still use it to calculate the flow of costs for products such as DVDs and computers, which have declining replacement costs. Also, during inflation, LIFO produces less income than other methods. This results in lower taxes for companies using LIFO. The following *Wall Street Journal* clip, "Balancing the Books," shows that although the LIFO method may be used inside the United States per **Generally Accepted Accounting Principles (GAAP),** the **International Financial Reporting Standards (IFRS)** do not permit companies to use this method.

GLOBAL

Balancing the Books

Accounting rulemakers are trying to move U.S. and global accounting standards closer together, but some significant differences remain.

	GAAP U.S. generally accepted accounting principles	**IFRS** International Financial Reporting Standards
NATURE OF STANDARDS	'Rules-based,' under which companies must apply detailed, bright-line rules	'Principles-based,' less-detailed rules, where companies use judgment in applying a set of guidelines
INVENTORY VALUATION	Permits 'last-in, first-out' accounting, or LIFO, which gives companies lower taxable income	Doesn't permit LIFO
DEVELOPMENT COSTS	Typically expensed against earnings every quarter	Typically capitalized on the balance sheet

Sources: American Institute of Certified Public Accountants; WSJ research

Reprinted with permission of *The Wall Street Journal*, Copyright © 2011 Dow Jones & Company, Inc. All Rights Reserved Worldwide.

Before concluding this unit, we will make a summary for the cost of ending inventory and cost of goods sold under the weighted-average, FIFO, and LIFO methods. From this summary, you can see that in times of rising prices, LIFO gives the highest cost of goods sold ($808). This results in a tax savings for Blue. The weighted-average method tends to smooth out the fluctuations between LIFO and FIFO and falls in the middle.

The key to this discussion of inventory valuation is that different costing methods produce different results. So management, investors, and potential investors should understand the different inventory costing methods and should know which method a particular company uses. For example, Fruit of the Loom, Inc., changed its inventories from LIFO to FIFO due to cost reductions.

MONEY tips

Take inventory of your assets and record all serial numbers. Save receipts as proof of purchase for high dollar items. Take a video of assets and store the file in a fireproof container offsite in the event of a loss.

Inventory method	Cost of goods available for sale	Cost of ending inventory	Cost of goods sold
Weighted average	$1,200	$480 **Step 1:** Total goods, $1,200 Total units, 120 $\frac{\$1,200}{120} = \$10$ **Step 2:** $10 \times 48 = \$480$	$1,200 - \$480 = \$720$
FIFO	$1,200	Bottom up to inventory level (48) 20 × $13 = $260 20 × $12 = 240 8 × $10 = 80 $580	$1,200 - \$580 = \$620$
LIFO	$1,200	Top down to inventory level (48) 40 × $8 = $320 8 × $9 = 72 $392	$1,200 - \$392 = \$808$

Let's check your understanding of this unit with a Practice Quiz.

LU 18–1 PRACTICE QUIZ

Complete this Practice Quiz to see how you are doing.

From the following, calculate **(a)** the cost of ending inventory and **(b)** the cost of goods sold under the assumption of (1) weighted-average method, (2) FIFO, and (3) LIFO (ending inventory shows 72 units):

	Number of books purchased for resale	Cost per unit	Total
January 1 inventory	30	$3	$ 90
March 1	50	2	100
April 1	20	4	80
November 1	60	6	360

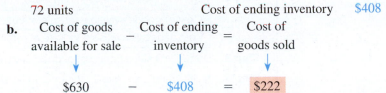

*For **extra help** from your authors—Sharon and Jeff—see the videos in Connect.*

These videos are also available on YouTube!

✓ Solutions

1. a. 72 units of ending inventory × $3.94 = $283.68 cost of ending inventory
($630 ÷ 160)

b.

$$\underset{\$630}{\text{Cost of goods available for sale}} - \underset{\$283.68}{\text{Cost of ending inventory}} = \underset{\$346.32}{\text{Cost of goods sold}}$$

2. a. 60 units from November 1 purchased at $6 $360
12 units from April 1 purchased at $4   48
72 units   Cost of ending inventory $408

b.

$$\underset{\$630}{\text{Cost of goods available for sale}} - \underset{\$408}{\text{Cost of ending inventory}} = \underset{\$222}{\text{Cost of goods sold}}$$

3. **a.**

30 units from January 1 purchased at $3		$ 90
42 units from March 1 purchased at $2		84
72	Cost of ending inventory	$174

b.

$$\underset{\text{available for sale}}{\text{Cost of goods}} - \underset{\text{inventory}}{\text{Cost of ending}} = \underset{\text{goods sold}}{\text{Cost of}}$$

$$\$630 \qquad - \qquad \$174 \qquad = \qquad \$456$$

LU 18–1a   **EXTRA PRACTICE QUIZ WITH WORKED-OUT SOLUTIONS**

Need more practice? Try this **Extra Practice Quiz** (check figures in the Interactive Chapter Organizer). Worked-out Solutions can be found in Appendix B at end of text.

From the following, calculate **(a)** the cost of ending inventory and **(b)** the cost of goods sold under the assumption of (1) weighted average, (2) FIFO, and (3) LIFO (ending inventory shows 58 units):

	Number of books purchased for resale	Cost per unit	Total
January 1 inventory	20	$4	$ 80
March 1	60	3	180
April 1	40	5	200
November 1	50	7	350

Learning Unit 18–2: Retail Method; Gross Profit Method; Inventory Turnover; Distribution of Overhead

Customers want stores to have products available for sale as soon as possible. This has led to outsourced warehouses offshore where tens of thousands of products can be stored ready to be quickly shipped to various stores.

When retailers receive their products, they go into one of their most important assets—their inventory. When the product is sold, it must be removed from inventory so it can be replaced or discontinued. Often these transactions occur electronically at the registers that customers use to pay for products. How is inventory controlled when the register of the store cannot perform the task of adding and subtracting products from inventory?

Convenience stores often try to control their inventory by taking physical inventories. This can be time-consuming and expensive. Some stores draw up monthly financial reports but do not want to spend the time or money to take a monthly physical inventory.

Many stores estimate the amount of inventory on hand. Stores may also have to estimate their inventories when they have a loss of goods due to fire, theft, flood, and the like. This unit begins with two methods of estimating the value of ending inventory—the *retail method* and the *gross profit method*.

© Alistair Berg/Digital Vision/Getty Images

Retail Method

Many companies use the **retail method** to estimate their inventory. As shown in Figure 18.2, this method does not require that a company calculate an inventory cost for each item. To calculate the $3,500 ending inventory in Figure 18.2, Green Company used the steps that follow.

LO 1

CALCULATING THE RETAIL METHOD

Step 1. Calculate the cost of goods available for sale at cost and retail: $6,300; $9,000.

Step 2. Calculate a cost ratio using the following formula:

$$\frac{\text{Cost of goods available for sale at cost}}{\text{Cost of goods available for sale at retail}} = \frac{\$6,300}{\$9,000} = .70$$

Step 3. Deduct net sales from cost of goods available for sale at retail: $9,000 − $4,000.

Step 4. Multiply the cost ratio by the ending inventory at retail: .70 × $5,000.

FIGURE **18.2**

Estimating inventory with the
retail method

	Cost	Retail	
Beginning inventory	$4,000	$6,000	
Net purchases during month	2,300	3,000	
Cost of goods available for sale **(Step 1)**	$6,300	$9,000	
Less net sales for month		4,000	**(Step 3)**
Ending inventory at retail		$5,000	
Cost ratio ($6,300 ÷ $9,000) **(Step 2)**		70%	
Ending inventory at cost (.70 × $5,000) **(Step 4)**		$3,500	

Now let's look at the gross profit method.

Gross Profit Method

To use the **gross profit method** to estimate inventory, the company must keep track of
(1) average gross profit rate, (2) net sales at retail, (3) beginning inventory, and (4) net purchases. You can use the following steps to calculate the gross profit method:

LO 2

> ### CALCULATING THE GROSS PROFIT METHOD
>
> **Step 1.** Calculate the cost of goods available for sale (Beginning inventory + Net
> purchases).
>
> **Step 2.** Multiply the net sales at retail by the complement of the gross profit rate. This is
> the estimated cost of goods sold.
>
> **Step 3.** Calculate the cost of estimated ending inventory (Step 1 − Step 2).

EXAMPLE Assume Radar Company has the following information in its records:

Gross profit on sales	30%
Beginning inventory, January 1, 2016	$20,000
Net purchases	$ 8,000
Net sales at retail for January	$12,000

If you use the gross profit method, what is the company's estimated inventory?

  The gross profit method calculates Radar's estimated cost of ending inventory at the end
of January as follows:

Goods available for sale			
Beginning inventory, January 1, 2016		$20,000	
Net purchases		8,000	
Cost of goods available for sale		$28,000	← **Step 1**
Less estimated cost of goods sold:			
Net sales at retail	$12,000		
Cost percentage (100% − 30%) **Step 2 →**	.70		
Estimated cost of goods sold		8,400	
Estimated ending inventory, January 31, 2016		$19,600	← **Step 3**

Note that the cost of goods available for sale less the estimated cost of goods sold gives the
estimated cost of ending inventory.

  Since this chapter has looked at inventory flow, let's discuss inventory turnover—a key
business ratio.

LO 3

Inventory Turnover

Apple's New Math On Textbook Pricing

McGraw-Hill Cos. normally sells high-school textbooks for $75 a pop. Now it says it will sell electronic versions of the same books, via Apple, for $15 each. How can the publisher make that work?

It's the usual answer for this kind of digital question:

"Volume," says McGraw-Hill CEO Terry McGraw.

But there's an important asterisk here, too. Normally, McGraw-Hill would sell its books directly to public schools, which would keep the texts for an average of five years.

Under Apple's new textbooks plan, though, McGraw-Hill will try something different. It will sell its books directly to each student, who will use the book for a year, then move on. They'll be able to keep the digital text, but won't be able to resell it or pass it along to another student, and McGraw-Hill anticipates that another set of students will buy new books the following year.

So Mr. McGraw figures that over five years, he'll generate the same total sales selling $15 ebooks as he would selling $75 books.

Of course, Apple will take an undisclosed cut of sales—McGraw-Hill execs wouldn't go into details, so let's assume for now that it's Apple's standard 30%—but presumably McGraw-Hill can make up some of that by forgoing the cost of print and distribution.

Reprinted by permission of *The Wall Street Journal*, copyright 2012 Dow Jones & Company, Inc. All rights reserved worldwide.

Inventory turnover is the number of times the company replaces inventory during a specific time. The *Wall Street Journal* clip "Apple's New Math On Textbook Pricing" reveals that McGraw-Hill will provide electronic versions of texts to high schools through Apple's products. Now McGraw-Hill will have fewer paper and inventory costs. Companies use the following two formulas to calculate inventory turnover:

$$\text{Inventory turnover at retail} = \frac{\text{Net sales}}{\text{Average inventory at retail}}$$

$$\text{Inventory turnover at cost} = \frac{\text{Cost of goods sold}}{\text{Average inventory at cost}}$$

Note that inventory turnover at retail is usually lower than inventory turnover at cost. This is due to theft, markdowns, spoilage, and so on. Also, retail outlets and grocery stores usually have a high turnover, but jewelry and appliance stores have a low turnover.

Now let's use an example to calculate the inventory turnover at retail and at cost.

EXAMPLE The following facts are for Abby Company, a local sporting goods store (rounded to the nearest hundredth):

Net sales	$32,000	Cost of goods sold	$22,000
Beginning inventory at retail	$11,000	Beginning inventory at cost	$ 7,500
Ending inventory at retail	$ 8,900	Ending inventory at cost	$ 5,600

With these facts, we can make the following calculations to determine **average inventory:**

$$\text{Average inventory} = \frac{\text{Beginning inventory} + \text{Ending inventory}}{2}$$

At retail: $\dfrac{\$32,000}{\dfrac{\$11,000 + \$8,900}{2}} = \dfrac{\$32,000}{\$9,950} = \boxed{3.22}$

At cost: $\dfrac{\$22,000}{\dfrac{\$7,500 + \$5,600}{2}} = \dfrac{\$22,000}{\$6,550} = \boxed{3.36}$

Healthy Premiums

Annual sales per square foot of retail space

Whole Foods	$972
Kroger	650
Safeway	564
Sprouts	564
Wal-Mart	436

Sources: FactSet; Whole Foods

Source: *The Wall Street Journal*, 2/12/14.

What Turnover Means Inventory is often a company's most expensive asset. The turnover of inventory can have important implications. Too much inventory results in the use of needed space, extra insurance coverage, and so on. A low inventory turnover could indicate customer dissatisfaction, too much tied-up capital, and possible product obsolescence. A high inventory turnover might mean insufficient amounts of inventory causing stockouts that may lead to future lost sales. If inventory is moving out quickly, perhaps the company's selling price is too low compared to that of its competitors.

In recent years the **just-in-time (JIT) inventory system** from Japan has been introduced in the United States. Under ideal conditions, manufacturers must have suppliers that will provide materials daily as the manufacturing company needs them, thus eliminating inventories. The companies that are using this system, however, have often not been able to completely eliminate the need to maintain some inventory. In the *Wall Street Journal* clip, "Healthy Premiums," notice Whole Foods generates $972 per square foot of retail space while Walmart generates only $436 per square foot.

LO 4

Distribution of Overhead

In Chapter 16 we studied the cost of goods sold and operating expenses shown on the income statement. The operating expenses included **overhead expenses**—expenses that are *not* directly associated with a specific department or product but that contribute indirectly to the running of the business. Examples of such overhead expenses are rent, taxes, and insurance.

Companies must allocate their overhead expenses to the various departments in the company. The two common methods of calculating the **distribution of overhead** are by (1) floor space (square feet) or (2) sales volume.

Calculations by Floor Space To calculate the distribution of overhead by floor space, use the steps that follow.

CALCULATING THE DISTRIBUTION OF OVERHEAD BY FLOOR SPACE

Step 1. Calculate the total square feet in all departments.

Step 2. Calculate the ratio for each department based on floor space.

Step 3. Multiply each department's floor space ratio by the total overhead.

EXAMPLE Roy Company has three departments with the following floor space:

Department A	6,000 square feet
Department B	3,000 square feet
Department C	1,000 square feet

The accountant's job is to allocate $90,000 of overhead expenses to the three departments. To allocate this overhead by floor space:

	Floor space in square feet	Ratio	
Department A	6,000	$\frac{6,000}{10,000} = 60\%$	
Department B	3,000	$\frac{3,000}{10,000} = 30\%$	← Steps 1 and 2
Department C	1,000	$\frac{1,000}{10,000} = 10\%$	
	10,000 total square feet		
Department A	.60 × $90,000 =	$54,000	
Department B	.30 × $90,000 =	27,000	← Step 3
Department C	.10 × $90,000 =	9,000	
		$90,000	

MONEY tips

Track your overhead expenses such as electricity, gas, water, sewage, etc., to determine trends. Make adjustments where needed.

Calculations by Sales To calculate the distribution of overhead by sales, use the steps that follow.

CALCULATING THE DISTRIBUTION OF OVERHEAD BY SALES
Step 1. Calculate the total sales in all departments.
Step 2. Calculate the ratio for each department based on sales.
Step 3. Multiply each department's sales ratio by the total overhead.

EXAMPLE Morse Company distributes its overhead expenses based on the sales of its departments. For example, last year Morse's overhead expenses were $60,000. Sales of its two departments were as follows, along with its ratio calculation.

Since Department A makes 80% of the sales, it is allocated 80% of the overhead expenses.

	Sales	**Ratio**	
Department A	$ 80,000	$\dfrac{\$80,000}{\$100,000} = .80$	← **Steps 1 and 2**
Department B	20,000	$\dfrac{\$20,000}{\$100,000} = .20$	
Total sales	$100,000		

These ratios are then multiplied by the overhead expense to be allocated.

Department A	.80 × $60,000 =	$48,000	
Department B	.20 × $60,000 =	12,000	← **Step 3**
		$60,000	

It's time to try another Practice Quiz.

LU 18–2 | PRACTICE QUIZ

Complete this **Practice Quiz** to see how you are doing.

1. From the following facts, calculate the cost of ending inventory using the retail method (round the cost ratio to the nearest tenth percent):

January 1—inventory at cost	$ 18,000
January 1—inventory at retail	58,000
Net purchases at cost	220,000
Net purchases at retail	376,000
Net sales at retail	364,000

2. Given the following, calculate the estimated cost of ending inventory using the gross profit method:

Gross profit on sales	40%
Beginning inventory, January 1, 2017	$27,000
Net purchases	$ 7,500
Net sales at retail for January	$15,000

3. Calculate the inventory turnover at cost and at retail from the following (round the turnover to the nearest hundredth):

Average inventory at cost	Average inventory at retail	Net sales	Cost of goods sold
$10,590	$19,180	$109,890	$60,990

4. From the following, calculate the distribution of overhead to Departments A and B based on floor space.

Amount of overhead expense to be allocated	Square footage
$70,000	10,000 Department A
	30,000 Department B

For **extra help** from your authors—Sharon and Jeff—see the videos in Connect.

These videos are also available on YouTube!

✓ Solutions

		Cost	Retail
1.	Beginning inventory	$ 18,000	$ 58,000
	Net purchases during the month	220,000	376,000
	Cost of goods available for sale	$238,000	$434,000
	Less net sales for the month		364,000
	Ending inventory at retail		$ 70,000
	Cost ratio ($238,000 ÷ $434,000)		54.8%
	Ending inventory at cost (.548 × $70,000)		$ 38,360

2. Goods available for sale

	Cost	Retail
Beginning inventory, January 1, 2017		$ 27,000
Net purchases		7,500
Cost of goods available for sale		$ 34,500
Less estimated cost of goods sold:		
Net sales at retail	$ 15,000	
Cost percentage (100% − 40%)	.60	
Estimated cost of goods sold		9,000
Estimated ending inventory, January 31, 2017		$ 25,500

3. Inventory turnover at cost $= \dfrac{\text{Cost of goods sold}}{\text{Average inventory at cost}} = \dfrac{\$60,900}{\$10,590} = 5.75$

Inventory turnover at retail $= \dfrac{\text{Net sales}}{\text{Average inventory at retail}} = \dfrac{\$109,890}{\$19,180} = 5.73$

4.

		Ratio		
Department A	10,000	$\dfrac{10,000}{40,000} = .25 \times \$70,000 =$	$17,500
Department B	30,000	$\dfrac{30,000}{40,000} = .75 \times \$70,000 =$	52,500
			$ 70,000

LU 18–2a   EXTRA PRACTICE QUIZ WITH WORKED-OUT SOLUTIONS

Need more practice? Try this **Extra Practice Quiz** (check figures in the Interactive Chapter Organizer). Worked-out Solutions can be found in Appendix B at end of text.

1. From the following, calculate the cost of ending inventory using the retail method (round the cost ratio to the nearest tenth percent):

January 1—inventory at cost	$ 19,000
January 1—inventory at retail	60,000
Net purchases at cost	265,000
Net purchases at retail	392,000
Net sales at retail	375,000

2. Given the following, calculate the estimated cost of ending inventory using the gross profit method:

Gross profit on sales	30%
Beginning inventory, January 1, 2017	$30,000
Net purchases	$ 8,000
Net sales at retail for January	$16,000

3. Calculate the inventory turnover at cost and at retail from the following (round the turnover to the nearest hundredth):

Average inventory at cost	Average inventory at retail	Net sales	Cost of goods sold
$11,200	$21,800	$129,500	$76,500

4. From the following, calculate the distribution of overhead to Departments A and B based on floor space.

Amount of overhead expense to be allocated	Square footage
$60,000	10,000 Department A
	50,000 Department B

INTERACTIVE CHAPTER ORGANIZER

Topic/Procedure/Formula	Examples	You try it*
Specific identification method Identification could be by serial number, physical description, or coding. The flow of goods and flow of costs are the same.	<table><tr><td></td><td>Cost per unit</td><td>Total cost</td></tr><tr><td>April 1, 3 units at</td><td>$7</td><td>$21</td></tr><tr><td>May 5, 4 units at</td><td>8</td><td>32</td></tr><tr><td></td><td></td><td>$53</td></tr></table> If 1 unit from each group is left, ending inventory is: $1 \times \$7 = \$7$ $+ 1 \times\ 8 = \underline{\ 8}$ $\$15$ <table><tr><td>Cost of goods available for sale</td><td>−</td><td>Cost of ending inventory</td><td>=</td><td>Cost of goods sold</td></tr><tr><td>$53</td><td>−</td><td>$15</td><td>=</td><td>$38</td></tr></table>	**Calculate ending inventory and cost of goods sold** <table><tr><td></td><td>Cost per unit</td><td>Total cost</td></tr><tr><td>May 1, 4 units at</td><td>$9</td><td></td></tr><tr><td>June 6, 3 units at</td><td>10</td><td></td></tr></table> Assume one unit from each group is left.
Weighted-average method $$\text{Weighted-average unit cost} = \frac{\text{Total cost of goods available for sale}}{\text{Total number of units available for sale}}$$	<table><tr><td></td><td>Cost per unit</td><td>Total cost</td></tr><tr><td>1/XX, 4 units at</td><td>$4</td><td>$16</td></tr><tr><td>5/XX, 2 units at</td><td>5</td><td>10</td></tr><tr><td>8/XX, 3 units at</td><td>6</td><td>18</td></tr><tr><td></td><td></td><td>$44</td></tr></table> Unit cost $= \dfrac{\$44}{9} = \$4.89$ If 5 units left, cost of ending inventory is 5 units $\times$ $4.89 = $24.45	**Calculate unit cost and cost of ending inventory** <table><tr><td></td><td>Cost per unit</td><td>Total cost</td></tr><tr><td>1/XX, 6 units at</td><td>$5</td><td>$30</td></tr><tr><td>5/XX, 4 units at</td><td>6</td><td>24</td></tr><tr><td>8/XX, 5 units at</td><td>7</td><td>35</td></tr><tr><td></td><td></td><td>$89</td></tr></table> 4 units left
FIFO—first-in, first-out method Sell old inventory first. Ending inventory is made up of last merchandise brought into store.	Using example above: 5 units left: <table><tr><td>(Last into store)</td><td>3 units at $6</td><td>$18</td></tr><tr><td></td><td>2 units at $5</td><td>10</td></tr><tr><td>Cost of ending inventory</td><td></td><td>$28</td></tr></table>	**Calculate cost of inventory by FIFO** Use weighted-average example.

(continues)

INTERACTIVE CHAPTER ORGANIZER

Topic/Procedure/Formula	Examples	You try it*
LIFO—last-in, first-out method Sell last inventory brought into store first. Ending inventory is made up of oldest merchandise in store.	Using weighted-average example: 5 units left: (First into store) 4 units at $4 $16 1 unit at $5 5 Cost of ending inventory $21	**Calculate cost of inventory by LIFO** Use weighted-average example.

Retail method
Ending inventory at cost equals:

$$\frac{\text{Cost of goods available at cost}}{\text{Cost of goods available at retail}} \times \begin{array}{c}\text{Ending}\\ \text{inventory}\\ \text{at retail}\end{array}$$

(This is cost ratio.)

	Cost	Retail
Beginning inventory	$52,000	$ 83,000
Net purchases	28,000	37,000
Cost of goods available for sale	$80,000	$120,000
Less net sales for month		80,000
Ending inventory at retail		$ 40,000

Cost ratio $= \dfrac{\$80,000}{\$120,000} = .67 = 67\%$

Rounded to nearest percent.
Ending inventory at cost, $26,800
(.67 × $40,000)

Calculate cost of ending inventory at cost and at retail

	Cost	Retail
Beginning inventory	$60,000	$80,000
Net purchases	28,000	37,000

Assume net sales of $90,000.

(Round ratio to nearest percent.)

Gross profit method

$$\begin{array}{c}\text{Beg.}\\ \text{inv.}\end{array} + \begin{array}{c}\text{Net}\\ \text{purchases}\end{array} - \begin{array}{c}\text{Estimated}\\ \text{cost of}\\ \text{goods}\\ \text{sold}\end{array} = \begin{array}{c}\text{Estimated}\\ \text{ending}\\ \text{inventory}\end{array}$$

Goods available for sale

Beginning inventory	$30,000
Net purchases	3,000
Cost of goods available for sale	$33,000
Less: Estimated cost of goods sold:	
Net sales at retail	$18,000
Cost percentage (100% − 30%)	.70
Estimated cost of goods sold	12,600
Estimated ending inventory	$ 20,400

Calculate estimated ending inventory
Given: Net sales at retail of $20,000 and a 75% gross profit.

Goods available for sale

Beginning inventory	$40,000
Net purchases	2,000

Inventory turnover at retail and at cost

$$\frac{\text{Net sales}}{\begin{array}{c}\text{Average inventory}\\ \text{at retail}\end{array}} \text{ or } \frac{\text{Cost of goods sold}}{\begin{array}{c}\text{Average inventory}\\ \text{at cost}\end{array}}$$

Inventory, January 1 at cost	$20,000
Inventory, December 31 at cost	48,000
Cost of goods sold	62,000

At cost:

$$\frac{\$62,000}{\dfrac{\$20,000 + \$48,000}{2}} = 1.82 \text{ (inventory turnover at cost)}$$

Calculate inventory turnover at cost
Jan 1 inventory at cost $40,000
Dec 31 inventory at cost $60,000
Cost of goods sold $90,000

(continues)

INTERACTIVE CHAPTER ORGANIZER

Topic/Procedure/Formula	Examples	You try it*
Distribution of overhead Based on floor space or sales volume, calculate: 1. Ratios of department floor space or sales to the total. 2. Multiply ratios by total amount of overhead to be distributed.	Total overhead to be distributed, $10,000 **Floor space** Department A 6,000 sq. ft. Department B 2,000 sq. ft. 8,000 sq. ft. Ratio A = $\frac{6,000}{8,000}$ = .75 Ratio B = $\frac{2,000}{8,000}$ = .25 Dept. A = .75 × $10,000 = $7,500 Dept. B = .25 × $10,000 = $2,500	**Calculate overhead cost to each department** Total overhead to be distributed, $30,000 **Floor space** Department A 4,000 sq. ft. Department B 6,000 sq. ft.
KEY TERMS	Average inventory Distribution of overhead First-in, first-out (FIFO) method GAAP Gross profit method IFRS	Inventory turnover Just-in-time (JIT) inventory system Last-in, first-out (LIFO) method Overhead expenses Periodic inventory system	Perpetual inventory system Retail method Specific identification method Weighted-average method
Check Figures for Extra Practice Quizzes. (Worked-out Solutions are in Appendix B.)	LU 18–1a 1. a. $276.08; b. $533.92 2. a. $390; b. $420 3. a. $194; b. $616	LU 18–2a 1. $48,356 2. $26,800 3. 6.83; 5.94 4. $10,000;$50,000

*Worked-out solutions are in Appendix B.

Critical Thinking Discussion Questions with Chapter Concept Check

1. Explain how you would calculate the cost of ending inventory and cost of goods sold for specific identification, FIFO, LIFO, and weighted-average methods. Explain why during inflation LIFO results in a tax savings for a business.

2. Explain the cost ratio in the retail method of calculating inventory. What effect will the increased use of computers have on the retail method?

3. What is inventory turnover? Explain the effect of a high inventory turnover during the Christmas shopping season.

4. How is the distribution of overhead calculated by floor space or sales? Give an example of why a store in your area cut back one department to expand another. Did it work?

5. What have you seen of levels of inventory affected by the economic crises at your local mall?

6. **Chapter Concept Check.** Search the web to find the latest techniques used by stores to control their inventory. Use all the concepts in the chapter to discuss the privacy issue as well.

Check figures for odd-numbered problems in Appendix C.   Name _____   Date _____

DRILL PROBLEMS

18–1. Using the specific identification method, calculate **(a)** the cost of ending inventory and **(b)** the cost of goods sold given the following: *LU 18-1(2)*

Date	Units purchased	Cost per unit	Ending inventory
March 1	15 Xbox's 360	$275	2 Xbox's from March
April 1	45 Xbox's 360	250	15 Xbox's from April
May 1	60 Xbox's 360	240	12 Xbox's from May

From the following, calculate the **(a)** cost of ending inventory (round the average unit cost to the nearest cent) and **(b)** cost of goods sold using the weighted-average method, FIFO, and LIFO (ending inventory shows 61 units).   *LU 18-1(2)*

	Number purchased	Cost per unit	Total
January 1 inventory	40	$4	$160
April 1	60	7	420
June 1	50	8	400
November 1	55	9	495

18–2. Weighted average:

18–3. FIFO:

18–4. LIFO:

From the following, (18–5 to 18–12) calculate the cost of ending inventory and cost of goods sold for the LIFO (18–13), FIFO (18–14), and weighted-average (18–15) methods (make sure to first find total cost to complete the table); ending inventory is 49 units: *LU 18-1(2)*

	Beginning inventory and purchases	Units	Unit cost	Total dollar cost
18–5.	Beginning inventory, January 1	5	$2.00	
18–6.	April 10	10	2.50	
18–7.	May 15	12	3.00	
18–8.	July 22	15	3.25	
18–9.	August 19	18	4.00	
18–10.	September 30	20	4.20	
18–11.	November 10	32	4.40	
18–12.	December 15	16	4.80	

18–13. LIFO:

Cost of ending inventory   Cost of goods sold

18–14. FIFO:

Cost of ending inventory   Cost of goods sold

18–15. Weighted average:

Cost of ending inventory   Cost of goods sold

18–16. From the following, calculate the cost ratio (round to the nearest hundredth percent) and the cost of ending inventory to the nearest cent under the retail method.   *LU 18-2(1)*

Net sales at retail for year	$40,000	Purchases—cost	$14,000
Beginning inventory—cost	$27,000	Purchases—retail	$19,000
Beginning inventory—retail	$49,000		

18–17. Complete the following (round answers to the nearest hundredth):   *LU 18-2(3)*

a. Average inventory at cost	b. Average inventory at retail	c. Net sales	d. Cost of goods sold	e. Inventory turnover at cost	f. Inventory turnover at retail
$14,000	$21,540	$70,000	$49,800		

Complete the following (assume $90,000 of overhead to be distributed):   *LU 18-2(4)*

	Square feet	Ratio	Amount of overhead allocated
18–18. Department A	10,000		
18–19. Department B	30,000		

18–20. Given the following, calculate the estimated cost of ending inventory using the gross profit method. *LU 18-2(2)*

| Gross profit on sales | 55% | Net purchases | $ 3,900 |
| Beginning inventory | $29,000 | Net sales at retail | $17,000 |

WORD PROBLEMS

18–21. If Exxon uses FIFO for its inventory valuation, calculate the cost of ending inventory and cost of goods sold if ending inventory is 110 barrels of crude oil. *LU 18-1(2)*

Beginning inventory and purchases	Barrels	Barrel cost	Total cost
Beginning inventory: Jan 1	125	$ 95	$11,875
March 1	50	101	5,050
June 1	65	98	6,370
September 1	75	90	6,750
December 1	50	103	5,150

18–22. Marvin Company has a beginning inventory of 12 sets of paints at a cost of $1.50 each. During the year, the store purchased 4 sets at $1.60, 6 sets at $2.20, 6 sets at $2.50, and 10 sets at $3.00. By the end of the year, 25 sets were sold. Calculate **(a)** the number of paint sets in ending inventory and **(b)** the cost of ending inventory under the LIFO, FIFO, and weighted-average methods. Round to nearest cent for the weighted average. *LU 18-1(2)*

18–23. Better Finance (previously BillFloat), based in San Francisco, California, provides leasing and credit solutions to consumers and small businesses. If Better Finance wants to distribute $45,000 worth of overhead by sales, calculate the overhead expense for each department: *LU 18-2(4)*

New customer sales (NCS)	$ 5,120,000
Current customer new sales (CCNS)	4,480,000
Current customer loan extension sales (CCLES)	3,200,000

18–24. If Comcast is upgrading its cable boxes and has 500 obsolete boxes in ending inventory, what is the cost of ending inventory using FIFO, LIFO, and the weighted-average method? *LU 18-1(2)*

Beginning inventory and purchases	Boxes	Box cost	Total cost
Beginning inventory: January 1	15,500	$15	$232,500
March 1	6,500	16	104,000
June 1	2,500	20	50,000
September 1	1,500	23	34,500
December 1	1,000	32	32,000

18–25. May's Dress Shop's inventory at cost on January 1 was $39,000. Its retail value was $59,000. During the year, May purchased additional merchandise at a cost of $195,000 with a retail value of $395,000. The net sales at retail for the year were $348,000. Calculate May's inventory at cost by the retail method. Round the cost ratio to the nearest whole percent. *LU 18-2(1)*

18–26. A sneaker outlet has made the following wholesale purchases of new running shoes: 12 pairs at $45, 18 pairs at $40, and 20 pairs at $50. An inventory taken last week indicates that 23 pairs are still in stock. Calculate the cost of this inventory by FIFO. *LU 18-1(2)*

18–27. Over the past 3 years, the gross profit rate for Jini Company was 35%. Last week a fire destroyed all Jini's inventory. Using the gross profit method, estimate the cost of inventory destroyed in the fire, given the following facts that were recorded in a fireproof safe: *LU 18-2(2)*

Beginning inventory	$ 6,000
Net purchases	64,000
Net sales at retail	49,000

18–28. Calculate cost of goods sold and ending inventory for Emergicare's bandages orders using FIFO, LIFO and average cost. There are 35 units in ending inventory. *LU 18-1(2)*

Date	Units purchased	Cost per unit	Total cost
January 1	50	$7.50	$ 375.00
April 1	45	6.75	303.75
June 1	60	6.50	390.00
September 1	55	7.00	385.00
Total	210		$1,453.75

CHALLENGE PROBLEMS

18–29. Monroe Company had a beginning inventory of 350 cans of paint at $12 each on January 1 at a cost of $4,200. During the year, the following purchases were made:

February 15	280 cans at $14.00
April 30	110 cans at $14.50
July 1	100 cans at $15.00

   Monroe marks up its goods at 40% on cost. At the end of the year, ending inventory showed 105 units remaining. Calculate the amount of sales assuming a FIFO flow of inventory. *LU 18-1(2)*

18–30. Logan Company uses a perpetual inventory system on a FIFO basis. Assuming inventory on January 1 was 800 units at $8 each, what is the cost of ending inventory at the end of October 5? *LU 18-1(2)*

Received			Sold	
Date	Quantity	Cost per unit	Date	Quantity
Apr. 15	220	$5	Mar. 8	500
Nov. 12	1,900	9	Oct. 5	200

Do you need help? The videos in Connect have step-by-step worked-out solutions. These videos are also available on YouTube!

1. Writing.com has a beginning inventory of 16 sets of pens at a cost of $2.12 each. During the year, Writing.com purchased 8 sets at $2.15, 9 sets at $2.25, 14 sets at $3.05, and 13 sets at $3.20. By the end of the year, 29 sets were sold. Calculate **(a)** the number of pen sets in stock and **(b)** the cost of ending inventory under LIFO, FIFO, and weighted-average methods.   *LU 18-1(2)*

2. Lee Company allocates overhead expenses to all departments on the basis of floor space (square feet) occupied by each department. The total overhead expenses for a recent year were $200,000. Department A occupied 8,000 square feet; Department B, 20,000 square feet; and Department C, 7,000 square feet. What is the overhead allocated to Department C? In your calculations, round to the nearest whole percent.   *LU 18-2(4)*

3. A local college bookstore has a beginning inventory costing $80,000 and an ending inventory costing $84,000. Sales for the year were $300,000. Assume the bookstore markup rate on selling price is 70%. Based on the selling price, what is the inventory turnover at cost? Round to the nearest hundredth.   *LU 18-2(3)*

4. Dollar Dress Shop's inventory at cost on January 1 was $82,800. Its retail value was $87,500. During the year, Dollar purchased additional merchandise at a cost of $300,000 with a retail value of $325,000. The net sales at retail for the year were $295,000. Calculate Dollar's inventory at cost by the retail method. Round the cost ratio to the nearest whole percent.   *LU 18-2(1)*

5. On January 1, Randy Company had an inventory costing $95,000. During January, Randy had net purchases of $118,900. Over recent years, Randy's gross profit in January has averaged 45% on sales. The company's net sales in January were $210,800. Calculate the estimated cost of ending inventory using the gross profit method.   *LU 18-2(2)*

SURF TO SAVE

The cost of carrying inventory

PROBLEM 1
"Building" worth

Visit http://finance.yahoo.com/ and search for The Home Depot, Inc. Using the financial statements provided on this site, estimate the inventory turnover ratio.

Discussion Questions

1. What does inventory turnover tell us about a company's performance?
2. Based on your analysis, would you be likely to invest in this firm? Why or why not?

PROBLEM 2
Revolving doors at Wal-Mart Stores, Inc.

Go to http://www.walmartstores.com. Follow the links to investor information and annual reports. In the most recent annual report find where Wal-Mart Stores, Inc., reports its net sales and its inventories. Use these values to estimate the inventory turnover ratio for Wal-Mart Stores.

Discussion Questions

1. How does this inventory turnover impact how Walmart orders products to sell in its stores?
2. Why do you feel Walmart is able to turn over inventory so quickly?

PROBLEM 3
Inventory turnover is on the rise!

Go to http://www.investopedia.com/articles/ 02/060502.asp and read the article. Then calculate the inventory value for the bread company mentioned in the article, assuming the company sells 300 loaves on Monday and Tuesday (and the bread isn't stale!). Use first the FIFO and then the LIFO method.

Discussion Questions

1. Why would inventory turnover be so crucial for a bread company?
2. If this were your bread company, which inventory method would you prefer (FIFO or LIFO)? Why?

PROBLEM 4
Overhead

Visit http://www.smallbizclub.com/component/k2/ item/872-why-knowing-your-overhead-cost-per-hour-is-important and read the article. Assume you operate a small business with 4 departments and a total of $75,000 in overhead expenses. Allocate overhead based on the following assumptions: department 1—250 square feet; department 2—300 square feet; department 3—450 square feet; department 4—150 square feet.

Discussion Questions

1. How does this allocation of overhead expense assist you in managing your business?
2. Why is it important to allocate overhead expense based on the square footage of departments?

MOBILE APPS

Inventory Accounting for IFRS and US GAAP (Pinfolio LLC) Calculates FIFO, LIFO, or weighted-average inventory costs.

Activity Ratios Calculator (simpaddico llc) Calculates a variety of financial ratios.

A KIPLINGER APPROACH

By Miriam Cross, From *Kiplinger's Personal Finance*, December 2014.
Kaitlin Pitsker, From *Kiplinger's Personal Finance*, December 2014.

■ ROB MULLINS PAYS EXTRA FOR FLEXIBILITY.

MATTHEW MAHON/REDUX

■ **SPENDING**

GET A RESERVATION AT THE LAST MINUTE

For a price, new tools give you an edge on snagging a hard-to-get restaurant table.

THEATERGOERS AND SPORTS fans who pay a premium can snag good seats on short notice. Now diners can do the same. A host of new tools and apps, including Resy, Table8 and Zurvu, promise for a fee to nab last-minute reservations at exclusive restaurants, such as New York's Charlie Bird and The Slanted Door in San Francisco. Other establishments are adopting a "ticketing" system, in which you hold a table by prepaying for your meal or making a deposit online. The services are rolling out in major cities, including San Francisco, New York and Chicago, with plans to expand.

When you want to eat out will determine how much you pay. It may cost nothing to reserve a table on a slow Tuesday night. But you could spend $30 for a coveted weekend slot. Why pay just to secure your seat? Rob Mullins, who books through Table8 in San Francisco, likes the ability to make last-minute plans. "We've always been treated well and given great tables," he says. "The quality of the restaurants and the flexibility is worth the extra cost."

Eateries are enthusiastic because paid services and prepaid ticketing cut down on costly no-shows. Return trips can pay off, too. "The best way for a consumer to get value is to become a regular and have a personal relationship with the restaurant," says Ryan Sutton, food critic at Eater.com.
MIRIAM CROSS

■ **WHAT'S THE DEAL**

RETAILERS RAMP UP HOLIDAY DELIVERIES

Following Amazon's lead, merchants are getting packages to you faster.

YOUR HOLIDAY PARCELS won't be arriving by drone just yet, but retailers are working to get your purchases to you more quickly and with less hassle. This holiday season, expect to see many stores ramp up and promote free buy-online, pick-up-in-store services, which reserve the item for you. Some retailers, including Williams-Sonoma and Brookstone, as well as several large mall operators, are working with Deliv, a crowdsourced delivery service that depends on local drivers using their own cars—a la Uber, the ride-sharing service. Deliv makes same-day deliveries to customers in and around certain cities for about the cost of standard shipping. And many retailers, including Macy's and Walmart, are using traditional store locations as fulfillment centers for online orders. So there's a better chance that the gift you ordered will be shipped from across town or a neighboring state, rather than from across the country.

"Everyone's playing catch-up with Amazon," says analyst Anne Zybowski, of Kantar Retail. "Amazon set an expectation with shoppers that they should be able to get free shipping and have their order in two days." Amazon also now offers same-day delivery in about a dozen cities. It has even installed lockers in retail spaces, such as 7-Elevens, to act as virtual doormen, accepting deliveries of small packages and securing them until you arrive. That's a plus for shoppers who don't want, say, their new tablet sitting on the doorstep all day.

Most retailers can't yet keep pace with same-day delivery and secure locker drop-offs, says Zybowski. But many are beefing up behind-the-scenes systems, including supply chains and inventory tracking, in an effort to get the goods to you more quickly. **KAITLIN PITSKER**

EXCERPT FROM
The Kiplinger Letter

JOB TRYOUTS FOR NEW HIRES

Expect more firms to give prospective hires a test run before a job offer to see whether they're a good fit. The idea: Bring on a candidate for a short-term project, at less pay than the regular position would entail, to see how he or she handles the work. The strategy will especially benefit small firms that face high costs associated with hiring a worker who doesn't pan out and must be replaced. (www.kiplingerbiz.com/ahead/tryout)

BUSINESS MATH ISSUE

Same day delivery is really not practical for retailers.

1. List the key points of the article and information to support your position.
2. Write a group defense of your position using math calculations to support your view.

Classroom Notes

CHAPTER 19

Sales, Excise, and Property Taxes

U.S. federal excise tax is 18.4 cents per gallon. State and other local taxes are about 30 cents per gallon.

© The McGraw-Hill Companies, Inc./Gary He, photographer

LU 19–1: Sales and Excise Taxes

1. Compute sales tax on goods sold involving trade and cash discounts and shipping charges.
2. Explain and calculate excise tax.

LU 19–2: Property Tax

1. Calculate the tax rate in decimal.
2. Convert tax rate in decimal to percent, per $100 of assessed value, per $1,000 of assessed value, and in mills.
3. Compute property tax due.

VOCABULARY PREVIEW

Here are key terms in this chapter. After completing the chapter, if you know the term, place a checkmark in the box. If you don't know the term, look it up and put the page number where it can be found.

Assessed value ☐ **Excise tax** ☐ **Mill** ☐ **Personal property** ☐ **Property tax** ☐ **Real property** ☐
Sales tax ☐ **Tax rate** ☐

The chapter opener explains that about 50 cents per gallon of gas is due to federal excise tax along with state and local taxes.

In Learning Unit 19–1 you will learn how sales taxes are calculated. Learning Unit 19–1 discusses the excise tax that is collected in addition to the sales tax. Learning Unit 19–2 explains the use of property tax.

Learning Unit 19–1: Sales and Excise Taxes

Today, many states have been raising their sales tax and excise tax.

LO 1

Sales Tax

In many cities, counties, and states, the sellers of certain goods and services collect **sales tax** and forward it to the appropriate government agency. Forty-five states have a sales tax. Of the 45 states, 28 states and the District of Columbia exempt food; 44 states and the District of Columbia exempt prescription drugs. The Tax Foundation map below shows sales tax rates by state.

Sales taxes are usually computed electronically by the new cash register systems and scanners. However, it is important to know how sellers calculate sales tax manually. The example of a car battery will show you how to manually calculate sales tax.

EXAMPLE

Selling price of a Sears battery	$32.00		Shipping charge	$3.50
Trade discount to local garage	$10.50		Sales tax	5%

Amount of
sales tax

P
($1.08)

B × R
($21.50) (.05)

$21.50 + $1.08 = $22.58
(sale)   (tax
amount)

Manual calculation

$32.00 − $10.50 = $21.50 taxable
        ×   .05
        $ 1.08 tax
      + 21.50 taxable
      + 3.50 shipping
      $26.08 total price with tax and shipping

Check

100% is base + 5% is tax = 105%
1.05 × $21.50 = $22.58
              + 3.50 shipping
              $26.08

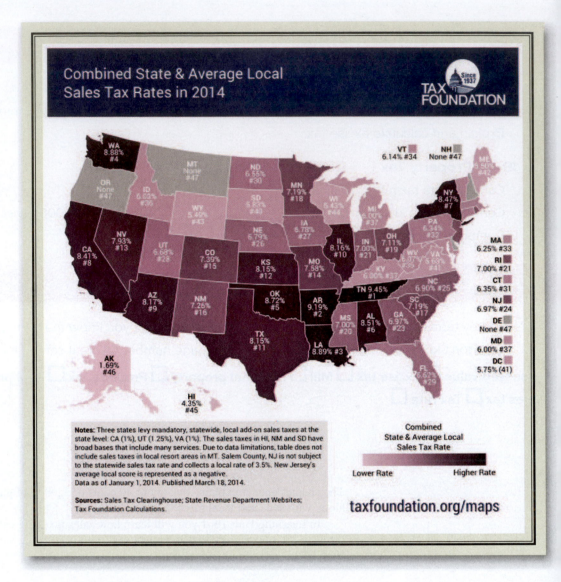

In this example, note how the trade discount is subtracted from the selling price before any cash discounts are taken. If the buyer is entitled to a 6% cash discount, it is calculated as follows:

$$.06 \times \$21.50 = \$1.29$$

Remember cash discounts are not taken on sales tax or shipping charges.

Calculating Actual Sales Managers often use the cash register to get a summary of their total sales for the day. The total sales figure includes the sales tax. So the sales tax must be deducted from the total sales. To illustrate this, let's assume the total sales for the day were $40,000, which included a 7% sales tax. What were the actual sales?

Hint: $40,000 is 107% of actual sales.

$$\text{Actual sales} = \frac{\text{Total sales}}{1 + \text{Tax rate}}$$

$$\text{Actual sales} = \frac{\$40,000}{1.07} = \$37,383.18$$

Total sales

100% sales
+ 7% tax
107% ⟶ 1.07

Thus, the store's actual sales were $37,383.18. The actual sales plus the tax equals $40,000.

Check

$37,383.18 × .07 = $ 2,616.82 sales tax
                  + 37,383.18 actual sales
                  $40,000.00 total sales including sales tax

LO 2

Excise Tax

Governments (local, federal, and state) levy **excise tax** on particular products and services. This can be a sizable source of revenue for these governments.

Consumers pay the excise tax in addition to the sales tax. The excise tax is based on a percent of the *retail* price of a product or service. This tax, which varies in different states, is imposed on luxury items or nonessentials. Examples of products or services subject to the excise tax include airline travel, telephone service, alcoholic beverages, jewelry, furs, fishing rods, tobacco products, and motor vehicles. Although excise tax is often calculated as a percent of the selling price, the tax can be stated as a fixed amount per item sold. The following example calculates excise tax as a percent of the selling price.[1]

MONEY tips

Launder your clothes in cold water and air-dry them to help combat the rising costs of energy.

EXAMPLE   On June 1, Angel Rowe bought a fur coat for a retail price of $5,000. Sales tax is 7% with an excise tax of 8%. Her total cost is as follows:

$$\begin{array}{rl} \$5,000 & \\ +\quad 350 & \text{sales tax } (.07 \times \$5,000) \\ +\quad 400 & \text{excise tax } (.08 \times \$5,000) \\ \hline \$5,750 & \end{array}$$

Let's check your progress with a Practice Quiz.

LU 19–1   PRACTICE QUIZ

Complete this **Practice Quiz** to see how you are doing.

*For **extra help** from your authors—Sharon and Jeff—see the videos in Connect.*

These videos are also available on YouTube!

From the following shopping list, calculate the total sales tax. Food items are excluded from sales tax, which is 8%.

Chicken	$6.10	Orange juice	$1.29	Shampoo	$4.10
Lettuce	$ .75	Laundry detergent	$3.65		

✓ **Solutions**

$$\begin{array}{ll} \text{Shampoo} & \$4.10 \\ \text{Laundry detergent} & +\ 3.65 \\ \hline & \$7.75 \times .08 = \boxed{\$.62} \end{array}$$

LU 19–1a   EXTRA PRACTICE QUIZ WITH WORKED-OUT SOLUTIONS

Need more practice? Try this **Extra Practice Quiz** (check figures in the Interactive Chapter Organizer). Worked-out Solutions can be found in Appendix B at end of text.

From the following shopping list, calculate the total sales tax. Food items are excluded from sales tax, which is 7%.

Chicken	$7.90	Orange juice	$1.50	Shampoo	$5.90
Lettuce	$ .85	Laundry detergent	$4.10		

Learning Unit 19–2: Property Tax

When you own property, you must pay property tax. In this unit we listen in on a conversation between a property owner and a tax assessor.

Defining Assessed Value

Bill Adams was concerned when he read in the local paper that the property tax rate had been increased. Bill knows that the revenue the town receives from the tax helps pay for fire and police protection, schools, and other public services. However, Bill wants to know how the town set the new rate and the amount of the new property tax.

---

[1]If excise tax were a stated fixed amount per item, it would have to be added to the cost of goods or services before any sales tax was taken. For example, a $100 truck tire with a $4 excise tax would be $104 before the sales tax was calculated.

Property Can Have Two Meanings

Both subject to property tax

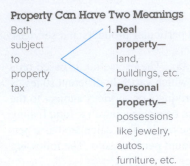

1. **Real property—** land, buildings, etc.

2. **Personal property—** possessions like jewelry, autos, furniture, etc.

Bill went to the town assessor's office to get specific details. The assessor is a local official who estimates the fair market value of a house. Before you read the summary of Bill's discussion, note the following formula:

> Assessed value = Assessment rate × Market value

Bill: What does *assessed value* mean?

Assessor: **Assessed value** is the value of the property for purposes of computing property taxes. We estimated the market value of your home at $210,000. In our town, we assess property at 30% of the market value. Thus, your home has an assessed value of $63,000 ($210,000 × .30). Usually, assessed value is rounded to the nearest dollar.

Bill: I know that the **tax rate** multiplied by my assessed value ($63,000) determines the amount of my property tax. What I would like to know is how did you set the new tax rate?

LO 1

Determining the Tax Rate

Assessor: In our town first we estimate the total amount of revenue needed to meet our budget. Then we divide the total of all assessed property into this figure to get the *tax rate*. The formula looks like this:[2]

> $$\text{Tax rate} = \frac{\text{Budget needed}}{\text{Total assessed value}}$$

Our town budget is $125,000, and we have a total assessed property value of $1,930,000. Using the formula, we have the following:

$$\frac{\$125,000}{\$1,930,000} = \$.0647668 = \boxed{.0648} \text{ tax rate per dollar}$$

Note that the rate should be rounded up to the indicated digit, *even if the digit is less than 5.* Here we rounded to the nearest ten thousandth.

LO 2

How the Tax Rate Is Expressed

Assessor: We can express the .0648 tax rate per dollar in the following forms:

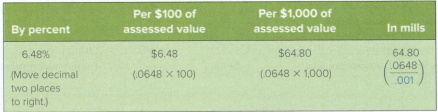

By percent	Per $100 of assessed value	Per $1,000 of assessed value	In mills
6.48%	$6.48	$64.80	64.80
(Move decimal two places to right.)	(.0648 × 100)	(.0648 × 1,000)	$\left(\frac{.0648}{.001}\right)$

MONEY tips

Review your property tax assessment annually and appeal it if it is too high. Property values have fallen dramatically in some areas leaving you at risk for paying too much for your property taxes.

A **mill** is $\frac{1}{10}$ of a cent or $\frac{1}{1,000}$ of a dollar (.001). To represent the number of mills as a tax rate per dollar, we divide the tax rate in decimal by .001. Rounding practices vary from state to state. Colorado tax bills are now rounded to the thousandth mill. An alternative to finding the rate in mills is to multiply the rate per dollar by 1,000, since a dollar has 1,000 mills. In the problems in this text, we round the mills per dollar to the nearest hundredth.

---

[2]Remember that exemptions to total assessed value include land and buildings used for educational and religious purposes and the like.

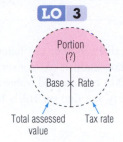

LO 3

Portion
(?)

Base × Rate

Total assessed   Tax rate
value

How to Calculate Property Tax Due[3]

Assessor: The following formula will show you how we arrive at your **property tax:**

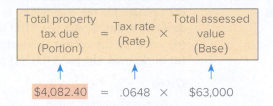

Total property tax due (Portion)	=	Tax rate (Rate)	×	Total assessed value (Base)

$4,082.40 = .0648 × $63,000

We can use the other forms of the decimal tax rate to show you how the property tax will not change even when expressed in various forms:

MONEY tips

Track the estimated value of your property using websites such as Zillow.com.

By percent	Per $100	Per $1,000	Mills
6.48% × $63,000	$\frac{\$63,000}{\$100} = 630$	$\frac{\$63,000}{\$1,000} = 63$	Property tax due
= $4,082.40	630 × $6.48	63 × $64.80	= Mills × .001 × Assessed value
	= $4,082.40	= $4,082.40	= 64.80 × .001 × $63,000
			= $4,082.40

Keep in mind you always round up when calculating the tax rate—even if the digit being rounded is less than 5.

The *Wall Street Journal* clip "How They Did It" shows how three homeowners lowered their property tax bill. If you own a home, this clip may save you money.

How They Did It
How three homeowners lowered their property-tax bill.

Homeowner:	Kelly Burns	Al Hollander	Lynne Weaver
Location:	Oak Park, Ill.	Springfield Township, N.J.	Phoenix
Assessed value before appeal:	$790,760	$605,000	$709,715
Assessed value after appeal:	$22,057.89	$550,000 in 2011 and $500,000 in 2012	$390,000
Annual property tax bill before appeal:	$370,000	$13,100	$5,597.94
Annual property tax bill after appeal:	$8,169.89	$12,000 in 2011 and $10,900 in 2012	$3,257.84
What it took to successfully appeal:	Contacted Oak Park Township assessor, who lobbied on her behalf.	Compared his assessment to neighboring homes and then hired a lawyer to argue his appeal.	Researching her neighbors' homes on the Phoenix assessor's website and going through the appeals process "half a dozen times."

Source: WSJ research

Reprinted by permission of *The Wall Street Journal,* copyright 2011 Dow Jones & Company, Inc. All rights reserved worldwide.

Now it's time to try the Practice Quiz.

[3]Some states have credits available to reduce what the homeowner actually pays. For example, 42 out of 50 states give tax breaks to people over age 65. In Alaska, the state's homestead exemption reduces the property tax of a $168,000 house from $1,512 to $253.

LU 19–2 | **PRACTICE QUIZ**

Complete this Practice Quiz to see how you are doing.

From the following facts: (1) calculate the assessed value of Bill's home; (2) calculate the tax rate for the community in decimal (to the nearest ten thousandth); (3) convert the decimal to (a) %, (b) per $100 of assessed value, (c) per $1,000 of assessed value, and (d) mills (to the nearest hundredth); and (4) calculate the property tax due on Bill's home (a) in decimal, (b) per $100, (c) per $1,000, and (d) in mills.

Given

Assessed market value	40%	Total budget needed	$ 176,000
Market value of Bill's home	$210,000	Total assessed value	$1,910,000

*For **extra help** from your authors—Sharon and Jeff—see the videos in Connect.*

These videos are also available on YouTube!

✓ **Solutions**

1. .40 × $210,000 = **$84,000**

2. $\dfrac{\$176,000}{\$1,910,000}$ = **.0922** per dollar

3. **a.** .0922 = **9.22%**

    b. .0922 × 100 = **$9.22**

    c. .0922 × 1,000 = **$92.20**

    d. $\dfrac{.0922}{.001}$ = **92.2 mills** (or .0922 × 1,000)

4. **a.** .0922 × $84,000 = **$7,744.80**

    b. $9.22 × 840 = **$7,744.80**

    c. $92.20 × 84 = **$7,744.80**

    d. 92.20 × .001 × $84,000 = **$7,744.80**

LU 19–2a | **EXTRA PRACTICE QUIZ WITH WORKED-OUT SOLUTIONS**

Need more practice? Try this Extra Practice Quiz (check figures in the Interactive Chapter Organizer). Worked-out Solutions can be found in Appendix B at end of text.

From the following facts: (1) calculate the assessed value of Bill's home; (2) calculate the tax rate for the community in decimal (to the nearest ten thousandth); (3) convert the decimal to (a) %, (b) per $100 of assessed value, (c) per $1,000 of assessed value, and (d) mills (to the nearest hundredth); and (4) calculate the property tax due on Bill's home (a) in decimal, (b) per $100, (c) per $1,000, and (d) in mills.

Given

Assessed market value	40%	Total budget needed	$ 159,000
Market value of Bill's home	$150,000	Total assessed value	$1,680,000

INTERACTIVE CHAPTER ORGANIZER

Topic/Procedure/Formula	Examples	You try it*
Sales tax Sales tax is not calculated on trade discounts. Shipping charges, etc., also are not subject to sales tax. Actual sales = $\dfrac{\text{Total sales}}{1 + \text{Tax rate}}$ Cash discounts are calculated on sale price before sales tax is added on.	Calculate sales tax: Purchased 12 bags of mulch at $59.40; 10% trade discount; 5% sales tax. $59.40 − $5.94 = $53.46 $53.46 × .05 **$2.67 sales tax** Any cash discount would be calculated on $53.46.	**Calculate sales tax** 14 bags of mulch at $62.80; 8% trade discount; 6% sales tax

(continues)

INTERACTIVE CHAPTER ORGANIZER

Topic/Procedure/Formula	Examples	You try it*
Excise tax Excise tax is calculated separately from sales tax and is an additional tax. It is based as a percent of the selling price. It could be stated as a fixed amount per item sold. In that case, the excise tax would be added to the cost of the item before any sales tax calculations. Rates for excise tax vary.	Jewelry $4,000 retail price Sales tax 7% Excise tax 10% $4,000 + 280 sales tax + 400 excise tax $4,680	**Calculate cost of jewelry** $6,000 retail price Sales tax 5% Excise tax 10%
Assessed value Assessment rate × Market value	$100,000 house; rate, 30%; $30,000 assessed value.	**Calculate assessed value** $200,000 house; rate, 40%.
Tax rate $$\frac{\text{Budget needed}}{\text{Total assessed value}} = \text{Tax rate}$$ (Round rate up to indicated digit even if less than 5.)	$$\frac{\$800,000}{\$9,200,000} = .08695 = .0870 \text{ tax rate per \$1}$$	**Calculate tax rate** Budget needed, $700,000; Total assessed value, $8,400,000. (Round up to 4 digits.)
Expressing tax rate in other forms **1.** Percent: Move decimal two places to right. Add % sign. **2.** Per $100: Multiply by 100. **3.** Per $1,000: Multiply by 1,000. **4.** Mills: Divide by .001.	**1.** .0870 = 8.7% **2.** .0870 × 100 = $8.70 **3.** .0870 × 1,000 = $87 **4.** $\dfrac{.0870}{.001}$ = 87 mills	**Using the above tax rate, calculate tax rate in:** **1.** Percent **2.** Per $100 **3.** Per $1,000 **4.** Mills
Calculating property tax $$\frac{\text{Total property}}{\text{tax due}} = \text{Tax rate} \times \frac{\text{Total assessed}}{\text{value}}$$ Various forms: **1.** Percent × Assessed value **2.** Per $100: $\dfrac{\text{Assessed value}}{\$100}$ × Rate **3.** Per $1,000: $\dfrac{\text{Assessed value}}{\$1,000}$ × Rate **4.** Mills: Mills × .001 × Assessed value	*Example:* Rate, .0870 per $1; $30,000 assessed value **1.** (.087)8.7% × $30,000 = $2,610 **2.** $\dfrac{\$30,000}{\$100}$ = 300 × $8.70 = $2,610 **3.** $\dfrac{\$30,000}{\$1,000}$ = 30 × $87 = $2,610 **4.** $\dfrac{.0870}{.001}$ = 87 mills 87 mills × .001 × $30,000 = $2,610	**Calculate property tax for various forms given:** $.0950 per $1; $40,000 assessed value

KEY TERMS	Assessed value Excise tax Mill	Personal property Property tax Real property	Sales tax Tax rate

Check Figures for Extra Practice Quizzes. (Worked-out Solutions are in Appendix B.)	LU 19–1a $.70	LU 19–2a **1.** $60,000 **2.** $.0946 **3. a.** 9.46% **b.** $9.46 **c.** 94.60 **d.** 94.6 mills **4.** $5,676 (Due to rounding, you may use .0947 and property tax would be $5,682.)

*Worked-out solutions are in Appendix B.

Critical Thinking Discussion Questions with Chapter Concept Check

1. Explain sales and excise taxes. Should all states have the same tax rate for sales tax?

2. Explain how to calculate actual sales when the sales tax was included in the sales figure. Is a sales tax necessary?

3. How is assessed value calculated? If you think your value is unfair, what could you do?

4. What is a mill? When we calculate property tax in mills, why do we use .001 in the calculation?

5. **Chapter Concept Check.** Search the web to find the latest information on taxing online sales. Do you think it is fair? Defend your position using concepts learned in this chapter.

Classroom Notes

END-OF-CHAPTER PROBLEMS

Check figures for odd-numbered problems in Appendix C.
Name _____ Date _____

DRILL PROBLEMS

Calculate the following: *LU 19-1(1, 2)*

	Retail selling price	Sales tax (6%)	Excise tax (10%)	Total price including taxes
19–1.	$750			
19–2.	$1,200			

Calculate the actual sales since the sales and sales tax were rung up together. Assume a 6% sales tax and round your answer to the nearest cent. *LU 19-1(1)*

19–3. $88,000

19–4. $26,000

Calculate the assessed value of the following pieces of property: *LU 19-2(2)*

	Assessment rate	Market value	Assessed value
19–5.	30%	$130,000	
19–6.	80%	$210,000	

Calculate the tax rate in decimal form to the nearest ten thousandth: *LU 19-2(2)*

	Required budget	Total assessed value	Tax rate per dollar
19–7.	$920,000	$39,500,000	

Complete the following:

	Tax rate per dollar	In percent	Per $100	Per $1,000	Mills
19–8.	.0956				
19–9.	.0699				

Complete the amount of property tax due to the nearest cent for each situation: *LU 19-2(3)*

	Tax rate	Assessed value	Amount of property tax due
19–10.	40 mills	$ 65,000	
19–11.	$42.50 per $1,000	105,000	
19–12.	$8.75 per $100	125,000	
19–13.	$94.10 per $1,000	180,500	

WORD PROBLEMS

19–14. Be careful when signing a work-for-hire agreement if you are a songwriter. You may lose all rights to your song in the **eXcel** copyright law world. If your song sells thousands on iTunes, you do not get to share in any of the publishing income. If you live in New Jersey and iTunes sold five of your songs for a total of $65,000, what is the tax owed at 7.0%? *LU 19-1(1)*

19–15. Don Chather bought a new Dell computer for $1,995. This included a 6% sales tax. What is the amount of sales tax and the **eXcel** selling price before the tax? *LU 19-1(1)*

19–16. Homeowners enjoy many benefits, including a federal tax deduction for state and local property taxes paid. Des Moines, Iowa, was voted one of the top 100 best places to live in 2011 by *Money* magazine. With a median home price of $100,000 and property taxes at 27.23 mills, how much does the average homeowner pay in property taxes? *LU 19-2(3)*

19–17. The median home price in Arlington, Virginia, is $577,300. If the assessment rate is 100%, what is the assessed value? *LU 19-2(2)*

19–18. Bemidji, Minnesota, needs $3,850,000 for its 2016 budget. If total assessed value of property in Bemidji is $353,211,009, **eXcel** what is the tax rate expressed as a percent, per $100, per $1,000, and in mills? *LU 19-2(2)*

19–19. Lois Clark bought a ring for $6,000. She must still pay a 5% sales tax and a 10% excise tax. The jeweler is shipping the ring, so Lois must also pay a $40 shipping charge. What is the total purchase price of Lois's ring? *LU 19-1(1, 2)*

19–20. Blunt County needs $700,000 from property tax to meet its budget. The total value of assessed property in Blunt is $110,000,000. What is the tax rate of Blunt? Round to the nearest ten thousandth. Express the rate in mills. *LU 19-2(1, 2)*

19–21. Bill Shass pays a property tax of $3,200. In his community, the tax rate is 50 mills. What is Bill's assessed value? *LU 19-2(2)*

19–22. The home of Bill Burton is assessed at $80,000. The tax rate is 18.50 mills. What is the tax on Bill's home? *LU 19-2(3)* **eXcel**

19–23. New Jersey ranks as the #1 most expensive state for property taxes. The average 2014 property tax was $8,161. If the 2016 rate is $5.99 per $100 of assessed value, how much does a homeowner owe for a property assessed at $136,500? *LU 19-2(3)*

19–24. Bill Blake pays a property tax of $2,500. In his community, the tax rate is 55 mills. What is Bill's assessed value? Round to the nearest dollar. *LU 19-2(2)*

19–25. The property tax rate for Minneapolis is $8.73 per square foot, and the Denver rate is $2.14 a square foot. If 3,500 square feet is occupied at each location, what is the difference paid in property taxes? *LU 19-2(3)*

19–26. Ginny Fieg expanded her beauty salon by increasing her space by 20%. Ginny paid property taxes of $2,800 at 22 mills. The new rate is now 24 mills. As Ginny's accountant, estimate what she may have to pay for property taxes this year. Round the final answer to the nearest dollar. In the calculation, round assessed value to the nearest dollar.   *LU 19-2(2)*

19–27. Art Neuner, an investor in real estate, bought an office condominium. The market value of the condo was $250,000 with a 70% assessment rate. Art feels that his return should be 12% per month on his investment after all expenses. The tax rate is $31.50 per $1,000. Art estimates it will cost $275 per month to cover general repairs, insurance, and so on. He pays a $140 condo fee per month. All utilities and heat are the responsibility of the tenant. Calculate the monthly rent for Art. Round your answer to the nearest dollar (at intermediate stages).   *LU 19-2(2)*

SUMMARY PRACTICE TEST

Do you need help? The videos in Connect have step-by-step worked-out solutions. These videos are also available on YouTube!

1. Carol Shan bought a new Apple iPod at Best Buy for $299. The price included a 5% sales tax. What are the sales tax and the selling price before the tax?   *LU 19-1(1)*

2. Jeff Jones bought a ring for $4,000 from Zales. He must pay a 7% sales tax and 10% excise tax. Since the jeweler is shipping the ring, Jeff must also pay a $30 shipping charge. What is the total purchase price of Jeff's ring?   *LU 19-1(1, 2)*

3. The market value of a home in Boston, Massachusetts, is $365,000. The assessment rate is 40%. What is the assessed value?   *LU 19-2(1)*

4. Jan County needs $910,000 from its property tax to meet the budget. The total value of assessed property in Jan is $180,000,000. What is Jan's tax rate? Round to the nearest ten thousandth. Express the rate in mills (to the nearest tenth).   *LU 19-2(2)*

5. The home of Nancy Billows is assessed at $250,000. The tax rate is 4.95 mills. What is the tax on Nancy's home?   *LU 19-2(3)*

6. V's Warehouse has a market value of $880,000. The property in V's area is assessed at 35% of the market value. The tax rate is $58.90 per $1,000 of assessed value. What is V's property tax?   *LU 19-2(3)*

A source of renewable energy, wind offers the opportunity for clean energy on a relatively small footprint. Wind turbines are used to create wind power by converting and capturing wind energy. Multiple wind turbines make up a wind farm.

The Meadow Lake Wind Farm in White County, Indiana, is one such farm. Phase I of the farm became operational in late 2009 and consisted of 121 wind turbines. Phase II went online in mid-2010 and Phases III and IV were added in late 2010 for a total of approximately 300 wind turbines. Future phases are planned to create one of the largest wind farms in the world. Meadow Lake Wind Farm is owned and operated by Horizon Wind Energy.

EDP Renewables North America, operating as Horizon Wind Energy in the U.S., is owned by EDP Renewables (EDPR). Headquartered in Madrid, Spain, EDPR is a leader in the renewable energy industry.

Five key factors go into developing a wind farm:

- Wind
- Transmission lines
- Land use
- Community
- Power plants

To achieve efficient wind development at competitive market prices, site assessment, access to transmission lines, and wind capacity are critical considerations. Site assessment includes an evaluation of the ground conditions for unevenness, existence of obstacles, and presence of mountains. Overall the goal is to match ideal wind capacity with minimal land impact. White County, Indiana, offered an ideal setting for a wind farm.

Once energy is generated by the turning of the wind turbines' blades, the energy flows to underground collections lines into a substation and then to another transmission line into an interconnected substation before flowing to power lines. For this reason, access to transmission lines is another critical factor in locating a wind farm.

In the case of the Meadow Lake Wind Farm, partnerships with area farmers are critical and allow for a high yield of wind energy with minimal obstacles or impact on agricultural production. Not only do local farmers benefit financially from their work with Horizon Wind Energy, but so too does the community, where significant dollars were added to the tax rolls. An unlimited resource, wind energy offers a win-win for White County and the communities served by this source of renewable and green energy.

Note: The following problems contain some data that has been created by the author.

PROBLEM 1

As indicated in the textbook, 45 states maintain a sales tax. What is the sales tax for Indiana where the Meadow Lake Wind Farm is located?

PROBLEM 2

As indicated in the video, nearly $1 billion was invested in the development of the Meadow Lake Wind Farm. Assuming 25% of those dollars were spent locally and subject to Indiana's sales tax, calculate the actual sales made locally. Round to the nearest cent.

PROBLEM 3

According to its state website (www.in.gov), Indiana maintains a 4% auto rental excise tax on vehicles weighing less than 11,000 pounds, when rented for less than 30 days. Suppose an EDP Renewables executive from its Great Lakes Regional Office in Bloomington, Illinois, rented a car to travel to the Meadow Lake Wind Farm to monitor operations. If the auto rental price for a 4-day rental was $140 before sales and excise tax, what was his total cost? (*Hint:* Assume that he returned the car with a full tank of gas and was not subject to other taxes or fees other than those noted in the question.) Round your answer to the nearest cent.

PROBLEM 4

Assume the salaries and benefits of White County government personnel amounted to $18,000,000 last year. If this represents 60% of the total county budget, what is the total budget for White County? Round to the nearest dollar.

PROBLEM 5

If the total assessed value of property in White County was $292,000,000 before the addition of the Meadow Lake Wind Farm to the tax rolls, what would the tax rate need to be to cover its budget as calculated in Problem 4? Round to the nearest hundredth.

PROBLEM 6

Now assuming that the Meadow Lake Wind Farm added $340,000,000 to the tax rolls for White County, what would the tax rate need to be to cover its budget as calculated in Problem 4? Round to the nearest hundredth.

PROBLEM 7

Based on your answers to Problems 5 and 6, by what percent did the tax rate change? Round to the nearest percent.

PROBLEM 8

Express the tax rate calculated in Problem 6 by percent, per $100, per $1,000, and in mills. Round to the nearest hundredth and nearest dollar as appropriate.

PROBLEM 9

According to www.city-data.com, the mean price (market value) of a detached house in White County in 2009 was $159,996. Assuming the county assesses property at 32% of the market value, and using the tax rate calculated in Problem 6, what would be the total property tax due for a house at this mean price? Round the assessed value to the nearest dollar and the tax due to the nearest cent.

Class Discussion   EDP first determined the ideal location for each wind turbine in White County. It then had to negotiate with each land owner to place a turbine on his property. Many of these land owners were farmers. Discuss the pros and cons these land owners likely considered when determining whether to let EDP place a turbine on their property. What decision would you have made?

SURF TO SAVE

PROBLEM 1
Taxing choices

Go to https://treas-secure.state.mi.us/ptestimator/ptestimator.asp. Suppose you buy a home in Woodhaven, Michigan, for $150,000 and its taxable value is 50% of that. The home is in Wayne County and the Woodhaven school district. How much will you pay in property taxes if you live in the home (homestead rate)? What would your taxes be if you purchased the same home in Brownstown, which is in the same county and school district?

Discussion Questions

1. What activities are supported from this property tax revenue?

2. What may cause property taxes to increase or decrease?

PROBLEM 2
The current "state" of taxing sales

Visit http://thestc.com/STrates.stm. Assume that you spend $24,750 annually on items requiring a sales tax and you live in New Jersey. How much money will you save in sales taxes if you move to New York at the state sales tax rate?

Discussion Questions

1. Why do you think some states charge higher sales tax than other states?

2. How does the issue of assessing sales tax on online purchases become complicated based on the variety of state sales tax rates?

PROBLEM 3
Paying the tax man

Go to http://www.comptroller.tn.gov/pa/paavt.asp. Suppose you live and own a business in a Tennessee city that taxes at a rate of $3.3900 per $100 of assessed value. Suppose your home is worth $150,000 and your commercial real estate property is worth $200,000. How much would you pay in property taxes annually?

Discussion Questions

1. Why would assessed values be below actual values?

2. How would the amount of property tax impact your house purchase?

PROBLEM 4
Fueling your taxes

Visit http://taxfoundation.org/blog/map-state-gasoline-tax-rates-2014, which displays gas tax rates for 2014. Find the amount of tax on gasoline in the state where you live. Suppose you purchase 1,500 gallons of fuel in a year. How much would you pay in taxes during the first quarter of the year? How much would you pay in tax for the entire year?

Discussion Questions

1. Why do you think there is such a difference in gas tax among states?

2. What are some factors that cause gas taxes to change over time?

MOBILE APPS

Sales Tax Calculator (Tardent Apps Inc.) Calculates sales tax on purchases.

Sales Tax Calculator (Arborsky LLC) Calculates sales tax on purchases.

A KIPLINGER APPROACH

By Sandra Block, From *Kiplinger's Personal Finance*, January 2015.

✳ **Family-Friendly Incentives**

TAX BREAKS FOR THE MIDDLE CLASS

IF YOU BELIEVE THAT TAX BREAKS are for millionaires and companies with offshore subsidiaries, you're probably paying too much to the IRS.

In recent years, lawmakers have enacted dozens of tax incentives targeted at middle-class families. Taking full advantage of these tax breaks is particularly important for dual-income couples because there's a good chance they'll get hit by the marriage penalty—when two individuals pay more in taxes as a married couple than they would pay if they were both single.

The tax code offers a slew of incentives for buying a home, starting a family, saving for retirement and educating your kids.

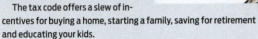

■ **Buying a home.** Once you purchase a home, you'll be eligible for an array of deductions, including mortgage interest, mortgage points and real estate taxes. If you borrow against your home—for example, by taking out a home equity line of credit—up to $100,000 in interest is deductible, no matter how you use the money.

■ **Starting a family.** The stork brings a bundle of tax breaks. The child tax credit shaves $1,000 from your tax bill, and you can claim it every year until your child turns 17. Married couples with adjusted gross income of $110,000 or less are eligible for the full credit.

You may also qualify for a tax credit that will reduce the cost of child care. If your children are younger than 13, you're eligible for a 20% to 35% credit for up to $3,000 in child-care expenses for one child or $6,000 for two or more. The percentage decreases as income increases. Eligible expenses include the cost of a nanny, preschool, before- or after-school care and summer day camp.

Another way to reduce child-care expenses is to participate in your employer's flexible spending account for dependent-care expenses. With these accounts, money is deducted from your gross salary before income, Social Security and Medicare taxes. You can contribute up to $5,000 per year.

You can't claim the child-care credit for expenses covered by a flexible spending account. In general, families that earn more than $43,000 will save more with a flexible spending account, says Laurie Ziegler, an enrolled agent in Saukville, Wis. However, even then, you may be able to use the child-care credit to offset expenses not covered by your flex account. If you paid for the care of two or more children and contributed the maximum, you can use the dependent-

care credit to cover up to an additional $1,000 in child-care costs.

■ **Saving for retirement.** Even small contributions will go a long way, especially if you take advantage of powerful tax incentives.

One of the most lucrative—and often overlooked—tax breaks is the Saver's Tax Credit. If you're married and have adjusted gross income of $59,000 or less ($29,500 or less if you're single), you can claim a credit for 10% to 50% of the amount you save, up to $2,000 for joint filers ($1,000 if you're single). Contributions to a workplace plan, such as a 401(k) or 403(b), as well as contributions to a traditional, Roth or SEP IRA, are eligible for this credit.

Families who earn too much to qualify for the Saver's Tax Credit have other options. If you're not covered by a retirement plan at work, you can deduct an IRA contribution of up to $5,500 per year for each spouse—$6,500 if you're 50 or older—no matter how much you earn. Even if you're covered by a workplace plan, you can deduct all or part of your contributions to an IRA, as long as your joint income is between $95,000 and $110,000 (or between $59,000 and $69,000 for singles).

■ **Saving and paying for college**. Contributing to a state-sponsored 529 college-savings plan while your children are young could help them avoid taking out student loans when they're old enough for college. Depending on where you live, your state may allow you to deduct a portion of your contribution on your state tax return. Withdrawals—including investment gains—for qualified college expenses are tax-free. Minimums are low: Many plans let you contribute as little as $25 a month.

The American Opportunity Credit provides a credit of up to $2,500 per student for each of the first four years of college. Middle-income and upper-middle-income families can take advantage of this tax break, which phases out between $160,000 and $180,000 for couples ($80,000 to $90,000 for singles). You can use the credit to offset the cost of tuition and related expenses, but not room and board.

Up to 40% of the credit is refundable, which means if the credit exceeds the amount you owe the IRS, you'll get a rebate. For example, suppose you owe $1,900 in federal taxes and qualify for the full credit. The nonrefundable portion of the credit will reduce your tax bill to $400, and the first $400 of the refundable portion will lower your bill to zero. You'll receive the remaining $600 as a tax refund.
SANDRA BLOCK

BUSINESS MATH ISSUE

Tax breaks are only for the wealthy.

1. List the key points of the article and information to support your position.
2. Write a group defense of your position using math calculations to support your view.

CHAPTER 20

Life, Fire, and Auto Insurance

Pajama Diaries © 2014 Terri Libenson Distributed by King Features Syndicate, Inc.

© 2009 Jupiterimages Corporation

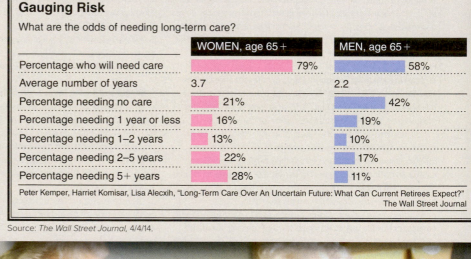

Gauging Risk

What are the odds of needing long-term care?

	WOMEN, age 65+	MEN, age 65+
Percentage who will need care	79%	58%
Average number of years	3.7	2.2
Percentage needing no care	21%	42%
Percentage needing 1 year or less	16%	19%
Percentage needing 1–2 years	13%	10%
Percentage needing 2–5 years	22%	17%
Percentage needing 5+ years	28%	11%

Peter Kemper, Harriet Komisar, Lisa Alecxih, "Long-Term Care Over An Uncertain Future: What Can Current Retirees Expect?" The Wall Street Journal

Source: *The Wall Street Journal*, 4/4/14.

LU 20–1: Life Insurance

1. Explain the types of life insurance; calculate life insurance premiums.
2. Explain and calculate cash value and other nonforfeiture options.

LU 20–2: Fire Insurance

1. Explain and calculate premiums for fire insurance of buildings and their contents.
2. Calculate refunds when the insured and the insurance company cancel fire insurance.
3. Explain and calculate insurance loss when coinsurance is not met.

LU 20–3: Auto Insurance

1. Explain and calculate the cost of auto insurance.
2. Determine the amount paid by the insurance carrier and the insured after an auto accident.

VOCABULARY PREVIEW

Here are key terms in this chapter. After completing the chapter, if you know the term, place a checkmark in the box. If you don't know the term, look it up and put the page number where it can be found.

Beneficiary ☐ Bodily injury ☐ Cash value ☐ Coinsurance ☐ Collision ☐ Comprehensive insurance ☐ Compulsory insurance ☐ Deductibles ☐ Extended term insurance ☐ Face amount ☐ Face value ☐ Fire insurance ☐ Indemnity ☐ Insured ☐ Insurer ☐ Level premium term ☐ Liability insurance ☐ No-fault insurance ☐ Nonforfeiture values ☐ Paid-up insurance ☐ Policyholder ☐ Premium ☐ Property damage ☐ Reduced paid-up insurance ☐ Short-rate table ☐ Statisticians ☐ Straight-life insurance ☐ Term insurance ☐ 20-payment life ☐ 20-year endowment ☐ Universal life ☐ Whole life ☐

Do you or a member of your family need long-term-care insurance? The chapter opener clipping "Gauging Risk" looks at your odds of needing it.

Regardless of the type of insurance you buy—life, auto, nursing home, property, or fire—be sure to read and understand the policy before you buy the insurance. It has been reported that half of the people in the United States who have property insurance have not read their policy and 60% do not understand their policy. If you do not understand your life, fire, or auto insurance policies, this chapter should answer many of your questions. We begin by studying life insurance.

Learning Unit 20–1: Life Insurance

Bob Brady owns Bob's Deli. He is 40 years of age, married, and has three children. Bob wants to know what type of life insurance protection will best meet his needs. Following is a discussion between an insurance agent, Rick Jones, and Bob.

Bob: I would like to buy a life insurance policy that will pay my wife $200,000 in the event of my death. My problem is that I do not have much cash. You know, bills, bills, bills. Can you explain some types of life insurance and their costs?

Rick: Let's begin by explaining some life insurance terminology. The **insured** is you—the **policyholder** receiving coverage. The **insurer** is the company selling the insurance policy. Your wife is the **beneficiary.** As the beneficiary, she is the person named in the policy to receive the insurance proceeds at the death of the insured (that's you, Bob). The amount stated in the policy, say, $200,000, is the **face amount** of the policy. The **premium** (determined by **statisticians** called *actuaries*) is the periodic payments you agree to make for the cost of the insurance policy. You can pay premiums annually, semiannually, quarterly, or monthly. The more frequent the payment, the higher the total cost due to increased paperwork, billing, and so on. Now we look at the different types of insurance.

LO 1

Types of Insurance

In this section Rick explains term insurance, straight life (ordinary life), 20-payment life, 20-year endowment, and universal life insurance.

Term Insurance[1]

Rick: The cheapest type of life insurance is **term insurance,** but it only provides *temporary* protection. Term insurance pays the face amount to your wife (beneficiary) only if you die within the period of the insurance (1, 5, 10 years, and so on).

For example, let's say you take out a 5-year term policy. The insurance company automatically allows you to renew the policy at increased rates until age 70. A new policy called **level premium term** may be less expensive than an annual term policy since each year for, say, 50 years, the premium will be fixed.

The policy of my company lets you convert to other insurance types without a medical examination. To determine your rates under 5-year term insurance, check this table (Table 20.1). The annual premium at 40 years per $1,000 of insurance is $3.52. We use the following steps to calculate the total yearly premium.

CALCULATING ANNUAL LIFE INSURANCE PREMIUMS
Step 1. Look up the age of the insured (for females, subtract 3 years) and the type of insurance in Table 20.1. This gives the premium cost per $1,000.
Step 2. Divide the amount of coverage by $1,000 and multiply the answer by the premium cost per $1,000.

$$\frac{\$200,000 \text{ (coverage)}}{\$1,000} = 200 \times \$3.52 = \boxed{\$704}$$

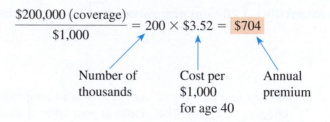

Number of thousands   Cost per $1,000 for age 40   Annual premium

Airport flight insurance is a type of term insurance.

From this formula you can see that for $704 per year for the next 5 years, we, your insurance company, offer to pay your wife $200,000 in the event of your death. At the end of the 5th year, you are not entitled to any cash from your paid premiums. If you do not renew your policy (at a higher rate) and die in the 6th year, we will not pay your wife anything. Term insurance provides protection for only a specific period of time.

Bob: Are you telling me that my premium does not build up any cash savings that you call **cash value?**

Rick: The term insurance policy does not build up cash savings. Let me show you a policy that does build up cash value. This policy is straight life.

Straight Life (Ordinary Life)

Rick: Straight-life insurance provides *permanent* protection rather than the temporary protection provided by term insurance. The insured pays the same premium each year or until

---

[1]A new term policy is available that covers policyholders until their expected retirement age.

TABLE **20.1**

Life insurance rates for males (for females, subtract 3 years from the age)[2]

Age	Five-year term	Age	Straight life	Age	Twenty-payment life	Age	Twenty-year endowment
20	1.85	20	5.90	20	8.28	20	13.85
21	1.85	21	6.13	21	8.61	21	14.35
22	1.85	22	6.35	22	8.91	22	14.92
23	1.85	23	6.60	23	9.23	23	15.54
24	1.85	24	6.85	24	9.56	24	16.05
25	1.85	25	7.13	25	9.91	25	17.55
26	1.85	26	7.43	26	10.29	26	17.66
27	1.86	27	7.75	27	10.70	27	18.33
28	1.86	28	8.08	28	11.12	28	19.12
29	1.87	29	8.46	29	11.58	29	20.00
30	1.87	30	8.85	30	12.05	30	20.90
31	1.87	31	9.27	31	12.57	31	21.88
32	1.88	32	9.71	32	13.10	32	22.89
33	1.95	33	10.20	33	13.67	33	23.98
34	2.08	34	10.71	34	14.28	34	25.13
35	2.23	35	11.26	35	14.92	35	26.35
36	2.44	36	11.84	36	15.60	36	27.64
37	2.67	37	12.46	37	16.30	37	28.97
38	2.95	38	13.12	38	17.04	38	30.38
39	3.24	39	13.81	39	17.81	39	31.84
40	3.52	40	14.54	40	18.61	40	33.36
41	3.79	41	15.30	41	19.44	41	34.94
42	4.04	42	16.11	42	20.31	42	36.59
43	4.26	43	16.96	43	21.21	43	38.29
44	4.50	44	17.86	44	22.15	44	40.09

death.[3] The premium for straight life is higher than that for term insurance because straight life provides both protection and a built-in cash savings feature. According to our table (Table 20.1), your annual premium, Bob, would be:

Face value is usually the amount paid to the beneficiary at the time of the insured's death.

$$\frac{\$200,000}{\$1,000} = 200 \times \$14.54 = \boxed{\$2,908} \text{ annual premium}$$

Bob: Compared to term, straight life is quite expensive.

Rick: Remember that term insurance has no cash value accumulating, as straight life does. Let me show you another type of insurance—20-payment life—that builds up cash value.

Twenty-Payment Life

Rick: A **20-payment life** policy is similar to straight life in that 20-payment life provides permanent protection and cash value, but you (the insured) pay premiums for only the first 20 years. After 20 years you own **paid-up insurance.** According to my table (Table 20.1), your annual premium would be:

$$\frac{\$200,000}{\$1,000} = 200 \times \$18.61 = \boxed{\$3,722} \text{ annual premium}$$

[2]The life insurance tables in this chapter show premiums for a sampling of age groups, options, and coverage available to those under 45 years of age.

[3]In the following section on nonforfeiture values, we show how a policyholder in later years can stop making payments and still be covered by using the accumulated cash value built up.

Bob: The 20-payment life policy is more expensive than straight life.

Rick: This is because you are only paying for 20 years. The shorter period of time does result in increased yearly costs. Remember that in straight life you pay premiums over your entire life. Let me show you another alternative that we call 20-year endowment.

Twenty-Year Endowment

Rick: The **20-year endowment** insurance policy is the most expensive. It is a combination of term insurance and cash value. For example, from age 40 to 60, you receive term insurance protection in that your wife would receive $200,000 should you die. At age 60, your protection *ends* and you receive the face value of the policy that equals the $200,000 cash value. Let's use my table again (Table 20.1) to see how expensive the 20-year endowment is:

$$\frac{\$200,000}{\$1,000} = 200 \times \$33.36 = \boxed{\$6,672} \text{ annual premium}$$

In summary, Bob, following is a review of the costs for the various types of insurance we have talked about:

	5-year term	Straight life	20-payment life	20-year endowment
Premium cost per year	$704	$2,908	$3,722	$6,672

Before we proceed, I have another policy that may interest you—universal life.

Universal Life Insurance

Rick: **Universal life** is basically a **whole-life** insurance plan with flexible premium schedules and death benefits. Under whole life, the premiums and death benefits are fixed. Universal has limited guarantees with greater risk on the holder of the policy. For example, if interest rates fall, the policyholder must pay higher premiums, increase the number of payments, or switch to smaller death benefits in the future.

Bob: That policy is not for me—too much risk. I'd prefer fixed premiums and death benefits.

Rick: OK, let's look at how straight life, 20-payment life, and 20-year endowment can build up cash value and provide an opportunity for insurance coverage without requiring additional premiums. We call these options **nonforfeiture values.**

Nonforfeiture Values

Rick: Except for term insurance, the other types of life insurance build up cash value as you pay premiums. These policies provide three options should you, the policyholder, ever want to cancel your policy, stop paying premiums, or collect the cash value. As shown in Figure 20.1, these options are cash value; **reduced paid-up insurance;** and **extended term insurance.**

Nonforfeiture options

Option 1: Cash value (cash surrender value)
a. Receive cash value of policy.
b. Policy is terminated.
The longer the policy has been in effect, the higher the cash value because more premiums have been paid in.

Option 2: Reduced paid-up insurance
a. Cash value buys protection without paying new premiums.
b. Face amount of policy is related to cash value buildup and age of insured. The **face amount is less than original policy.**
c. Policy continues for life (at a reduced face amount).

Option 3: Extended term insurance
a. Original face amount of policy continues for a certain period of time.
b. Length of policy depends on cash value built up and on insured's age.
c. This option results automatically if policyholder doesn't pay premiums and fails to elect another option.

For example, Bob, let's assume that at age 40 we sell you a $200,000 straight-life policy. Assume that at age 55, after the policy has been in force for 15 years, you want to stop paying premiums. From this table (Table 20.2), I can show you the options that are available.

TABLE 20.2 Nonforfeiture options based on $1,000 face value

| Years insurance policy in force | STRAIGHT LIFE | | | | 20-PAYMENT LIFE | | | | 20-YEAR ENDOWMENT | | | |
	Cash value	Amount of paid-up insurance	EXTENDED TERM Years	EXTENDED TERM Day	Cash value	Amount of paid-up insurance	EXTENDED TERM Years	EXTENDED TERM Day	Cash value	Amount of paid-up insurance	EXTENDED TERM Years	EXTENDED TERM Day
5	29	86	9	91	71	220	19	190	92	229	23	140
10	96	259	18	76	186	521	28	195	319	520	30	160
15	148	371	20	165	317	781	32	176	610	790	35	300
20	265	550	21	300	475	1,000		Life	1,000	1,000		Life

Option 1: Cash value

$$\frac{\$200,000}{\$1,000} = 200 \times \$148 = \$29,600$$

Option 2: Reduced paid-up insurance

$$\frac{\$200,000}{\$1,000} = 200 \times \$371 = \$74,200$$

Option 3: Extended term insurance

Bob could continue this $200,000 policy for 20 years and 165 days.

MONEY tips

Review your insurance policies, coverages, and deductibles annually. Consider disability, renter's, life, auto, burial, and home. Use the same insurance company for all your insurance needs to take advantage of discounts.

Insight into Health and Business Insurance Often people who interview for a new job are more concerned with the salary offered than the whole health care package such as eye care, dental care, hospital and doctor care, and so on. Be sure you know exactly what the new job offers in health insurance. For employees, company health insurance and life insurance benefits can be an important job consideration.

Some of the key types of business insurance that you may need as a business owner include fire insurance, business interruption insurance (business loss until physical damages are fixed), casualty insurance (insurance against a customer's suing your business due to an accident on company property), workers' compensation (insurance against injuries or sickness from being on the job), and group insurance (life, health, and accident). Note the

---

Cyberattacks Give Lift to Insurance

By Leslie Scism

The holiday hacker attack on **Target** Corp. was a nightmare for the retailer, but it has delivered a giant gift to insurers that sell policies covering the costs of cyberintrusions.

With vulnerability to hacking in stark relief, insurance brokers say sales of cyberinsurance have picked up sharply this year. The interest is coming from a diverse mix of customers, including public schools in Ann Arbor, Mich., which in February acquired $1 million in cyberspecific coverage for the first time, from a unit of **Zurich Insurance Group** AG.

"You hear in the news of all those things happening, and we just wanted to make sure that our employees would be covered in case of a breach," said Nancy Hoover, a school-district finance official. The district is adopting new human-resources and payroll software and was concerned its potential risk was increasing, she said. The policy's annual premium is $21,400, and it covers the cost of services to monitor credit-card accounts, among other potential expenses.

Insurers have pushed the coverage hard for a while, and this year may be an important turning point. "The Target data breach was the equivalent of 10 free Super Bowl ads," said Randy Maniloff, an insurance-industry lawyer with White & Williams.

In December, the retailer said hackers stole tens of millions of credit- and debit-card numbers in the data breach. Then, in early January, **Neiman Marcus Group** disclosed that it, too, had been victimized last year.

Just last week, another incident surfaced. The California Department of Motor Vehicles said it is investigating a potential breach of its credit-card processing systems.

Many policies cover the costs of investigations, customer notifications and credit-monitoring services, as well as legal expenses and damages from consumer lawsuits.

Reprinted by permission of *The Wall Street Journal,* copyright 2014 Dow Jones & Company, Inc. All rights reserved worldwide.

Wal-Mart Is Cutting Insurance For 30,000

Wal-Mart Stores Inc. is cutting health insurance for another 30,000 part-time workers and raising premiums for its other employees, as U.S. corporations push to contain costs in the wake of the federal health-care law.

*By Shelly Banjo,
Anna Wilde Mathews
and Theo Francis*

Autumn is typically when U.S. companies unveil changes to employee insurance plans. This is the first such enrollment period since employers could assess the full financial impact of the federal health-care overhaul, and it is a key moment as companies work to lower their spending ahead of looming taxes on the most generous plans.

Reprinted by permission of *The Wall Street Journal*, copyright 2014 Dow Jones & Company, Inc. All rights reserved worldwide.

above *Wall Street Journal* clipping "Cyberattacks Give Lift to Insurance," shows that more companies are taking out insurance against the event of a hacker attack.

Although group health insurance costs have soared recently, many companies still pay the major portion of the cost. Some companies also provide health insurance benefits for retirees. As health costs continue to rise, we can expect to see some changes in this employee benefit. Walmart is trying to contain costs it sees coming from federal health-care laws as shown in the *Wall Street Journal* clip.

Companies vary in the type of life insurance benefits they provide to their employees. This insurance can be a percent of the employee's salary with the employee naming the beneficiary; or in the case of key employees, the company can be the beneficiary.

If as an employer you need any of the types of insurance mentioned in this section, be sure to shop around for the best price. If you are in the job market, consider the benefits offered by a company as part of your salary and make your decisions accordingly.

Don't forget to subtract 3 years from a female's age when using the life insurance tables. In the next unit, we look specifically at fire insurance. Now let's check your understanding of this unit with a Practice Quiz.

LU 20–1 | PRACTICE QUIZ

Complete this Practice Quiz to see how you are doing.

1. Bill Boot, age 39, purchased a $60,000, 5-year term life insurance policy. Calculate his annual premium from Table 20.1. After 4 years, what is his cash value?
2. Ginny Katz, age 32, purchased a $78,000, straight-life policy. Calculate her annual premium. If after 10 years she wants to surrender her policy, what options and what amounts are available to her?

*For **extra help** from your authors—Sharon and Jeff—see the videos in Connect.*

These videos are also available on YouTube!

✓ Solutions

1. $\dfrac{\$60,000}{\$1,000} = 60 \times \$3.24 = \boxed{\$194.40}$ No cash value in term insurance.

2. $\dfrac{\$78,000}{\$1,000} = 78 \times \$8.46^* = \boxed{\$659.88}$

   Option 1: Cash value $78 \times \$96 = \boxed{\$7,488}$

   Option 2: Paid up $78 \times \$259 = \boxed{\$20,202}$

   Option 3: Extended term $\boxed{\text{18 years and 76 days}}$

   *For females we subtract 3 years.

LU 20–1a | EXTRA PRACTICE QUIZ WITH WORKED-OUT SOLUTIONS

Need more practice? Try this Extra Practice Quiz (check figures in the Interactive Chapter Organizer). Worked-out Solutions can be found in Appendix B at end of text.

1. Bill Boot, age 37, purchased a $70,000, 5-year term life insurance policy. Calculate his annual premium from Table 20.1. After 3 years, what is his cash value?
2. Ginny Katz, age 30, purchased a $95,000, straight-life policy. Calculate her annual premium. If after 5 years she wants to surrender her policy, what options and what amounts are available to her?

Learning Unit 20–2: Fire Insurance

LO 1

Periodically, some areas of the United States, especially California, have experienced drought followed by devastating fires. These fires spread quickly and destroy wooded areas and homes. When the fires occur, the first thought of the owners is the adequacy of their **fire insurance.** Homeowners are made more aware of the importance of fire insurance that provides for the replacement value of their home. Out-of-date fire insurance policies can result in great financial loss.

In this unit, Alice Swan meets with her insurance agent, Bob Jones, to discuss fire insurance needs for her new dress shop at 4 Park Plaza. (Alice owns the building.)

Alice: What is *extended coverage?*

Bob: Your basic fire insurance policy provides financial protection if fire or lightning damages your property. However, the extended coverage protects you from smoke, chemicals, water, or other damages that firefighters may cause to control the fire. We have many options available.

© Aaron Roeth Photography

Alice: What is the cost of a fire insurance policy?

Bob: Years ago, if you bought a policy for 2, 3, 5, or more years, reduced rates were available. Today, with rising costs of reimbursing losses from fires, most insurance companies write policies for 1 to 3 years. The cost of a 3-year policy premium is 3 times the annual premium. Because of rising insurance premiums, your total costs are cheaper if you buy one 3-year policy than three 1-year policies.

Alice: For my purpose, I will need coverage for 1 year. Before you give me the premium rates, what factors affect the cost of my premium?

Bob: In your case, you have several factors in your favor that will result in a lower premium. For example, (1) your building is brick, (2) the roof is fire-resistant, (3) the building is located next to a fire hydrant, (4) the building is in a good location (not next to a gas station) with easy access for the fire department, and (5) the goods within your store are not as flammable as, say, those of a paint store. I have a table here (Table 20.3) that gives an example of typical fire insurance rates for buildings and contents (furniture, fixtures, etc.).

TABLE 20.3

Fire insurance rates per $100 of coverage for buildings and contents

| | CLASSIFICATION OF BUILDING | | | | |
| | CLASS A | | CLASS B | | |
Rating of area	Building	Contents	Building	Contents
1	.28	.35	.41	.54
2	.33	.47	.50	.60
3	.41	.50	.61	.65

Fire insurance premium equals premium for building and premium for contents.

Let's assume your building has an insured value of $190,000 and is rated Class B, Area No. 2, and we insure your contents for $80,000. Then we calculate your total annual premium for building and contents as follows:

$$\text{Premium} = \frac{\text{Insured value}}{\$100} \times \text{Rate}$$

Building

$$\frac{\$190,000}{\$100} = 1,900 \times \$.50 = \$950$$

Contents

$$\frac{\$80,000}{\$100} = 800 \times \$.60 = \$480$$

Total premium = $950 + $480 = $1,430

For our purpose, we round all premiums to the nearest cent. In practice, the premium is rounded to the nearest dollar.

LO 2

MONEY **tips**

Make a video of the contents of your home, garage, sheds, etc., to inventory your belongings. Keep the video in a safety deposit box or fireproof box offsite. In the event of a loss, you will have a recording of your belongings. You may be amazed how much can be forgotten without documentation.

Note that when the insurance company cancels the policy, the refund ($595.83) is greater than if the insured cancels ($471.90).

Canceling Fire Insurance

Alice: What if my business fails in 7 months? Do I get back any portion of my premium when I cancel?

Bob: If the insured—that's you, Alice—cancels or wants a policy for less than 1 year, we use this **short-rate table** (Table 20.4). These rates are higher because it is more expensive to process a policy for a short time. For example, if you cancel at the end of 7 months, the premium cost is 67% of the annual premium. We would calculate your refund as follows:

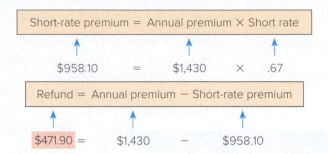

Alice: Let's say that I don't pay my premium or follow the fire codes. What happens if your insurance company cancels me?

Bob: If the insurance company cancels you, the company is *not* allowed to use the short-rate table. To calculate what part of the premium the company may keep,[4] you can prorate the premium based on the actual days that have elapsed. We can illustrate the amount of your refund by assuming you are canceled after 7 months:

For insurance company: Charge = $1,430 annual premium × $\frac{7 \text{ months elapsed}}{12}$

Charge = $834.17

For insured: Refund = $1,430 annual premium − $834.17 charge

Refund = $595.83

TABLE 20.4

Fire insurance short-rate and cancellation table

Time policy is in force	Percent of annual rate to be charged	Time policy is in force	Percent of annual rate to be charged
Days: 5	8%	Months: 5	52%
10	10	6	61
20	15	7	67
25	17	8	74
Months: 1	19	9	81
2	27	10	87
3	35	11	96
4	44	12	100

LO 3

Coinsurance

Alice: My friend tells me that I should meet the coinsurance clause. What is coinsurance?

Bob: Usually, fire does not destroy the entire property. **Coinsurance** means that you and the insurance company *share* the risk. The reason for this coinsurance clause[5] is to encourage property owners to purchase adequate coverage.

Alice: What is adequate coverage?

Bob: In the fire insurance industry, the usual rate for coinsurance is 80% of the current replacement cost. This cost equals the value to replace what was destroyed. If your insurance coverage is 80% of the current value, the insurance company will pay all damages up to the face value of the policy.

[4]Many companies use $\frac{\text{Days}}{365}$.

[5]In some states (including Wisconsin), the clause is not in effect for losses under $1,000.

Alice: Hold it, Bob! Will you please show me how this coinsurance is figured?

Bob: Yes, Alice, I'll be happy to show you how we figure coinsurance. Let's begin by looking at the following steps so you can see what amount of the insurance the company will pay.

MONEY tips

Request quotes from your insurance provider using different deductibles for each policy. Choose the one that meets your financial needs. Keep the amount of each deductible in an interest-earning account for easy access if and when it is needed.

> **CALCULATING WHAT INSURANCE COMPANY PAYS WITH COINSURANCE CLAUSE**
>
> **Step 1.** Set up a fraction. The numerator is the actual amount of the insurance carried on the property. The denominator is the amount of insurance you should be carrying on the property to meet coinsurance (80% times the replacement value).
>
> **Step 2.** Multiply the fraction by the amount of loss (up to the face value of the policy).

Although there are many types of property and homeowner's insurance policies, they usually include fire protection.

Let's assume for this example that you carry $60,000 fire insurance on property that will cost $100,000 to replace. If the coinsurance clause in your policy is 80% and you suffer a loss of $20,000, your insurance company will pay the following:

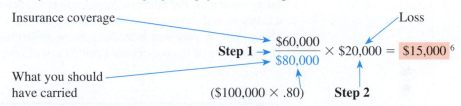

Insurance coverage ⟶   Loss

What you should have carried ⟶

$$\text{Step 1} \rightarrow \frac{\$60,000}{\$80,000} \times \$20,000 = \boxed{\$15,000} \text{ [6]}$$

($100,000 × .80)   **Step 2**

If you had had actual insurance coverage of $80,000, then the insurance company would have paid $20,000. Remember that if the coinsurance clause is met, the most an insurance company will pay is the face value of the policy.

You are now ready for the following Practice Quiz.

LU 20–2   PRACTICE QUIZ

Complete this **Practice Quiz** to see how you are doing.

1. Calculate the total annual premium of a warehouse that has an area rating of 2 with a building classification of B. The value of the warehouse is $90,000 with contents valued at $30,000.

2. If the insured in problem 1 cancels at the end of month 9, what are the costs of the premium and the refund?

3. Jones insures a building for $120,000 with an 80% coinsurance clause. The replacement value is $200,000. Assume a loss of $60,000 from fire. What will the insurance company pay? If the loss was $160,000 and coinsurance *was* met, what will the insurance company pay?

*For **extra help** from your authors—Sharon and Jeff—see the videos in Connect.*

These videos are also available on YouTube!

✓ Solutions

1. $$\frac{\$90,000}{\$100} = 900 \times \$.50 = \$450$$

    $$\frac{\$30,000}{\$100} = 300 \times \$.60 = \underline{\quad 180}$$

    $\boxed{\$630}$ ← total premium

2. $630 × .81 = \boxed{\$510.30}$ $630 − $510.30 = \boxed{\$119.70}$

3. $$\frac{\$120,000}{\$160,000} = \frac{3}{4} \times \$60,000 = \boxed{\$45,000}$$

    (.80 × $200,000) $\boxed{\$160,000}$ never more than face value

---

[6] This kind of limited insurance payment for a loss is often called an **indemnity**.

LU 20–2a   **EXTRA PRACTICE QUIZ WITH WORKED-OUT SOLUTIONS**

Need more practice? Try this Extra Practice Quiz (check figures in the Interactive Chapter Organizer). Worked-out Solutions can be found in Appendix B at end of text.

1. Calculate the total annual fire insurance premium of a warehouse that has an area rating of 3 with a building classification of A. The value of the warehouse is $80,000 with contents valued at $20,000.

2. If the insured from problem 1 cancels at the end of month 8, what are the costs of the premium and the refund?

3. Jones insures a building for $140,000 with an 80% coinsurance clause. The replacement value is $250,000. Assume a loss of $50,000 from fire. What will the insurance company pay? If the loss was $170,000 and coinsurance was met, what will the insurance company pay?

Learning Unit 20–3: Auto Insurance

If you own an auto, you have had some experience purchasing auto insurance. Often first-time auto owners do not realize that auto insurance can be a substantial expense. Insurance rates often increase when a driver is involved in an accident. Some insurance companies give reduced rates to accident-free drivers—a practice that has encouraged drivers to be more safety conscious. For example, State Farm Insurance offers a discount to drivers who maintain a safety record. An important factor in safe driving is the use of a seat belt. Make it a habit to always put on your seat belt. Note in the following *Wall Street Journal* clip, "How's My Driving?" the difference between two groups of people as to who files the most claims.

How's My Driving?

States with the biggest gap in the percentage of auto-insurance claims filed by homeowners and renters.

	% of homeowners who file claims	% of renters who file claims	Differential
Utah	11.93%	16.16%	4.23%
Oregon	14.52%	20.17%	5.65%
Maryland	15.88%	21.12%	5.25%
South Carolina	16.99%	21.34%	4.35%
Nebraska	15.17%	22.65%	7.48%

Source: Insurance.com

Source: *The Wall Street Journal*, 1/2/15.

In this unit we follow Shirley as she learns about auto insurance. Shirley, who just bought a new auto, has never purchased auto insurance. So she called her insurance agent, Bob Long, who agreed to meet her for lunch. We will listen in on their conversation.

Shirley: Bob, where do I start?

Bob: Our state has two kinds of **liability insurance,** or **compulsory insurance,** that by law you must buy (regulations and requirements vary among states). Liability insurance covers any physical damages that you inflict on others or their property. You must buy liability insurance for the following:

Liability insurance includes
1. **Bodily injury**—injury or death to people in passenger car or other cars, etc.
2. **Property damage**—injury to other people's autos, trees, buildings, hydrants, etc.

1. **Bodily injury** to others: 10/20. This means that the insurance company will pay damages to people injured or killed by your auto up to $10,000 for injury to one person per accident or a total of $20,000 for injuries to two or more people per accident.

2. **Property damage** to someone else's property: 5. The insurance company will pay up to $5,000 for damages that you have caused to the property of others.

Now we leave Shirley and Bob for a few moments as we calculate Shirley's premium for compulsory insurance.

TABLE **20.5**

Compulsory insurance (based on class of driver)

BODILY INJURY TO OTHERS		DAMAGE TO SOMEONE ELSE'S PROPERTY	
Class	**10/20**	**Class**	**5M***
10	$ 55	10	$129
17	98	17	160
18	80	18	160
20	116	20	186
Explanation of 10/20 and 5			
10		**20**	**5**
Maximum paid to one person per accident for bodily injury		Maximum paid for total bodily injury per accident	Maximum paid for property damage per accident

*M means thousands.

Calculating Premium for Compulsory Insurance[7]

Insurance companies base auto insurance rates on the territory you live in, the class of driver (class 10 is experienced driver with driver training), whether the auto is for business use, how much you drive the car, the age of the car, and the make of the car (symbol). Shirley lives in Territory 5 (suburbia). She is classified as 17 because she is an inexperienced operator licensed for less than 6 years. Her car is age 3 and symbol 4 (make of car). We use Table 20.5 to calculate Shirley's compulsory insurance. Note that the table rates in this unit are not representative of all areas of the country. In case of lawsuits, the minimum coverage may not be adequate. Some states add surcharges to the premium if the person has a poor driving record. The tables are designed to show how rates are calculated. From Table 20.5, we have the following:

> The tables we use in this unit are for Territory 5. Other tables are available for different territories.

$$
\begin{array}{rr}
\text{Bodily} & \$\ 98 \\
+\ \text{Property} & 160 \\ \hline
& \$258 \\
\end{array}
$$

Remember that the $258 premium represents minimum coverage. Assume Shirley hits two people and the courts award them $13,000 and $5,000, respectively. Shirley would be responsible for $3,000 because the insurance company would pay only up to $10,000 per person and a total of $20,000 per accident.

> Although total damages of $18,000 are less than $20,000, the insurance company pays only $15,000.

	(1)	**(2)**	
	$13,000	+ $5,000 =	$18,000
Paid by insurance company ⟶	− 10,000	− 5,000 =	− 15,000
Paid by Shirley ⟶	$ 3,000	+ $ 0 =	$ 3,000

We return to Shirley and Bob. Bob now shows Shirley how to calculate her optional insurance coverage. Remember that optional insurance coverages (Tables 20.6 to 20.10) are added to the costs in Table 20.5.

Calculating Optional Insurance Coverage

Bob: In our state, you can add optional bodily injury to the compulsory amount. If you finance your car, the lender may require specific amounts of optional insurance to protect its investment. I have two tables (Tables 20.6 and 20.7) here that we use to calculate the option of 250/500/50. This means that in an accident the insurance company will pay $250,000 per person, up to $500,000 per accident, and up to $50,000 for property damage.

[7]Some states may offer medical payment insurance (a supplement to policyholders' health and accident insurance) as well as personal injury protection against uninsured or underinsured motorists.

TABLE 20.6										
Class	15/30	20/40	20/50	25/50	25/60	50/100	100/300	250/500	500/1,000
10	27	37	40	44	47	69	94	144	187
17	37	52	58	63	69	104	146	228	298
18	33	46	50	55	60	89	124	193	251
20	41	59	65	72	78	119	168	263	344

Bodily injury

TABLE 20.7				
Class	10M	25M	50M	100M
10	132	134	135	136
17	164	166	168	169
18	164	166	168	169
20	191	193	195	197

Damage to someone else's property

Bob then explains the tables to Shirley. By studying the tables, you can see how insurance companies figure bodily injury and damage to someone else's property. Shirley is Class 17:

Bodily

250/500 = $228

Property

50M   =   + 168

$396   premium for optional bodily injury and property damage

Note: These are additional amounts to compulsory.

Collision and comprehensive are optional insurance types that pay only the insured. Note that Tables 20.8 and 20.9 are based on territory, age, and car symbol. The higher the symbol, the more expensive the car.

Shirley: Is that all I need?

Bob: No, I would recommend two more types of optional coverage: **collision** and **comprehensive.** Collision provides protection against damages to your car caused by a moving vehicle. It covers the cost of repairs less **deductibles** (amount of repair you cover first before the insurance company pays the rest) and depreciation.[8] In collision, insurance companies pay the resale or book value. So as the car gets older, after 5 or more years, it might make sense to drop the collision. The decision depends on how much risk you are willing to assume. Comprehensive covers damages resulting from theft, fire, falling objects, and so on. Now let's calculate the cost of these two types of coverage—assuming a $100 deductible for collision and a $200 deductible for comprehensive—with some more of my tables (Tables 20.8 and 20.9).

	Class	Age	Symbol	Premium	
Collision	17	3	4	$191 ($148 + $43)	Cost to
Comprehensive	17	3	4	+ 56 ($52 + $4)	reduce
				$247	deductibles

Total premium for collision and comprehensive

Shirley: Anything else?

Bob: I would also recommend that you buy towing and substitute transportation coverage. The insurance company will pay up to $25 for each tow. Under substitute transportation, the insurance company will pay you $12 a day for renting a car, up to $300 total. Again, from

---

[8]In some states, repair to glass has no deductible and many insurance companies now use a $500 deductible instead of $300.

TABLE 20.8 Collision

Classes	Age group	Symbols 1–3 $300 ded.	Symbol 4 $300 ded.	Symbol 5 $300 ded.	Symbol 6 $300 ded.	Symbol 7 $300 ded.	Symbol 8 $300 ded.	Symbol 10 $300 ded.
10–20	1	180	180	187	194	214	264	279
	2	160	160	166	172	190	233	246
	3	148	148	154	166	183	221	233
	4	136	136	142	160	176	208	221
	5	124	124	130	154	169	196	208

These classes would use all this information.

To find the premium, use the age and symbol only.

Additional cost to reduce deductible

Class	From $300 to $200	From $300 to $100
10	13	27
17	20	43
18	16	33
20	26	55

TABLE 20.9 Comprehensive

Classes	Age group	Symbols 1–3 $300 ded.	Symbol 4 $300 ded.	Symbol 5 $300 ded.	Symbol 6 $300 ded.	Symbol 7 $300 ded.	Symbol 8 $300 ded.	Symbol 10 $300 ded.
10–25	1	61	61	65	85	123	157	211
	2	55	55	58	75	108	138	185
	3	52	52	55	73	104	131	178
	4	49	49	52	70	99	124	170
	5	47	47	49	67	94	116	163

Additional cost to reduce deductible: From $300 to $200 add $4

TABLE 20.10

Transportation and towing

Substitute transportation	$16
Towing and labor	4

MONEY tips

Keep a memory card with photos of both the inside and outside of all the vehicles, structures, and property you own in a safety deposit box. Photographing VIN and serial numbers is a wise idea as well. This will help the claim process in the event of a loss.

Premiums for collision, property damage, and comprehensive are not reduced by no fault.

another table (Table 20.10), we find the additional premium for towing and substitute transportation is $20 ($16 + $4).

We leave Shirley and Bob now as we make a summary of Shirley's total auto premium in Table 20.11.

No-Fault Insurance Some states have **no-fault insurance,** a type of auto insurance that was intended to reduce premium costs on bodily injury. With no fault, one forfeits the right to sue for *small* claims involving medical expense, loss of wages, and so on. Each person collects the bodily injury from his or her insurance company no matter who is at fault. In reality, no-fault insurance has not reduced premium costs, due to large lawsuits, fraud, and operating costs of insurance companies. Many states that were once considering no fault are no longer pursuing its adoption. Note that states with no-fault insurance require the purchase of *personal-injury protection (PIP).* The most successful no-fault law seems to be in Michigan, since it has tough restrictions on the right to sue along with unlimited medical and rehabilitation benefits.

TABLE 20.11

Worksheet for calculating Shirley's auto premium

Compulsory insurance	Limits	Deductible	Premium
Bodily injury to others	$10,000 per person $20,000 per accident	None	$ 98 (Table 20.5)
Damage to someone else's property	$5,000 per accident	None	$160 (Table 20.5)
Options			
Optional bodily injury to others	$250,000 per person $500,000 per accident	None	$228 (Table 20.6)
Optional property damage	$50,000 per accident	None	$168 (Table 20.7)
Collision	Actual cash value	$100	$191 (Table 20.8) ($148 + $43)
Comprehensive	Actual cash value	$200	$ 56 (Table 20.9) ($52 + $4)
Substitute transportation	Up to $12 per day or $300 total	None	$ 16 (Table 20.10)
Towing and labor	$25 per tow	None	$ 4 (Table 20.10)
			$921 Total premium

LO 2

Calculating What the Insurance Company and the Insured Pay after an Auto Accident

When an automobile accident occurs, the insurance company pays up to the maximum of insurance coverage. The insured pays whatever is left. Because you will be financially responsible for damages not covered by your insurance, you should always get quotes from various companies for different coverage limits as well as deductibles. The cost to change to the next level of coverage may not be significant but lack of better coverage can be very costly.

Drive carefully. Tickets and accidents significantly affect the cost of your automobile insurance premiums.

Let's look at a typical example.

EXAMPLE Mario Andreety was at fault in an auto accident. He destroyed a fence and tree in a yard, causing damages of $2,500. He injured three passengers in the car he hit, which resulted in the following medical expenses: passenger 1, $25,250, passenger 2, $17,589, passenger 3, $12,567. The damage to the BMW he hit amounted to $45,888. Finally, the damage to his own vehicle came to $9,772.

a. If Mario has 15/30/10 coverage with a $500 deductible for collision and $100 deductible for comprehensive, how much will the insurance company pay? How much will Mario pay?

Insurance company pays	Mario pays
$2,500	$0 Property damage (He has $10,000 property damage.)
$15,000	$25,250 − $15,000 = $10,250 Passenger 1 (His coverage is $15,000 per person bodily injury with an accident maximum of $30,000.)
$15,000	$17,589 − $15,000 = $2,589 Passenger 2 (The $30,000 [$15,000 + $15,000] maximum bodily injury coverage has been met.)
$0 max	$12,567 − $0 = $12,567 Passenger 3 ($30,000 per accident has been reached.)
$7,500	$45,888 − $7,500 = $38,388 (His coverage is $10,000 property damage with $2,500 used.)
$9,272	$500 ($9,772 personal vehicle − $500 collision deductible)
$49,272	**$64,294**

b. If Mario has 50/100/50 with a $500 deductible for collision and $100 deductible for comprehensive, how much will the insurance company pay? How much will Mario pay?

Insurance company pays	Mario pays
$2,500	$0 Property damage
$25,250	$0 Passenger 1
$17,589	$0 Passenger 2 ($25,250 + $17,589 = $42,839)
$12,567	$0 Passenger 3 ($42,839 + $12,567 = $55,406 < $100,000)
$45,888	$0 ($2,500 + $45,888 = $48,388 < $50,000)
$9,272	$500 ($9,772 − $500)
$113,066	**$500**

Clearly, Mario would be better off paying higher premiums for better coverage. His premiums won't amount to anywhere near $64,000 a year but, after only one accident with insufficient coverage, his out-of-pocket costs could easily exceed that amount.

It's time to take your final Practice Quiz in this chapter.

LU 20–3 PRACTICE QUIZ

Complete this **Practice Quiz** to see how you are doing.

1. Calculate the annual auto premium for Mel Jones who lives in Territory 5, is a driver classified 18, and has a car with age 4 and symbol 7. His state has compulsory insurance, and Mel wants to add the following options:

   a. Bodily injury, 100/300.
   b. Damage to someone else's property, 10M.
   c. Collision, $200 deductible.
   d. Comprehensive, $200 deductible.
   e. Towing.

2. Calculate how much the insurance company and Carl Burns, the insured, pay if Carl carries 10/20/5 with $500 deductible for collision and $100 deductible for comprehensive and is at fault in an auto accident causing the following damage: $7,981, personal property; $6,454, injury to passenger 1; $4,239, injury to passenger 2; $25,250, injury to passenger 3; and $12,120 damage to Carl's car.

✓ Solutions

1. **Compulsory**

Bodily	$ 80		(Table 20.5)
Property	160		(Table 20.5)
Options			
Bodily	124		(Table 20.6)
Property	164		(Table 20.7)
Collision	192	($176 + $16)	(Table 20.8)
Comprehensive	103	($99 + $4)	(Table 20.9)
Towing	4		(Table 20.10)
Total annual premium	**$827**		

2. Carl's coverage is $10,000 per person bodily injury with an accident maximum of $20,000 bodily injury and $5,000 property damage.

Insurance company pays	Carl pays
$5,000	$2,981 Property damage
$6,454	$0 Passenger 1
$4,239	$0 Passenger 2 ($6,454 + $4,239 = $10,693)
$9,307 ($20,000 − $10,693)	$15,943 Passenger 3 ($25,250 − $9,307)
$11,620	$500
$36,620	**$19,424**

LU 20–3α	EXTRA PRACTICE QUIZ WITH WORKED-OUT SOLUTIONS

Need more practice? Try this **Extra Practice Quiz** (check figures in the Interactive Chapter Organizer). Worked-out Solutions can be found in Appendix B at end of text.

1. Calculate the annual auto premium for Mel Jones who lives in Territory 5, is a driver classified 17, and has a car with age 5 and symbol 6. His state has compulsory insurance, and Mel wants to add the following options:

   a. Bodily injury, 100/300.
   b. Damage to someone else's property, 10M.
   c. Collision, $200 deductible.
   d. Comprehensive, $200 deductible.
   e. Towing.

2. Calculate how much the insurance company and Carl Burns, the insured, pay if the insured carries 25/50/25 with $500 deductible for collision and $100 deductible for comprehensive and is at fault in an auto accident causing the following damage: $7,981, personal property; $6,454, injury to passenger 1; $4,239, injury to passenger 2; $25,250, injury to passenger 3; and $12,120 damage to Carl's car.

INTERACTIVE CHAPTER ORGANIZER

Topic/Procedure/Formula	Examples	You try it*
Life insurance Using Table 20.1, per $1,000: $$\frac{\text{Coverage desired}}{\$1,000} \times \text{Rate}$$ For females, subtract 3 years.	**Given** $80,000 of insurance desired; age 34; male. **1.** 5-year term: $$\frac{\$80,000}{\$1,000} = 80 \times \$2.08 = \boxed{\$166.40}$$ **2.** Straight life: $$\frac{\$80,000}{\$1,000} = 80 \times \$10.71 = \boxed{\$856.80}$$ **3.** 20-payment life: $$\frac{\$80,000}{\$1,000} = 80 \times \$14.28 = \boxed{\$1,142.40}$$ **4.** 20-year endowment: $$\frac{\$80,000}{\$1,000} = 80 \times \$25.13 = \boxed{\$2,010.40}$$	**Given** $90,000 of insurance desired; age 36; male. **Calculate these premiums:** 1. 5-year term 2. Straight life 3. 20-payment life 4. 20-year endowment
Nonforfeiture values **By Table 20.2** Option 1: Cash surrender value. Option 2: Reduced paid-up insurance policy continues for life at reduced face amount. Option 3: Extended term—original face policy continued for a certain period of time.	A $50,000 straight-life policy was issued to Jim Rose at age 28. At age 48 Jim wants to stop paying premiums. What are his nonforfeiture options? Option 1: $\frac{\$50,000}{\$1,000} = 50 \times \$265$ $= \boxed{\$13,250}$ Option 2: $50 \times \$550 = \boxed{\$27,500}$ Option 3: $\boxed{\text{21 years 300 days}}$	**Given** $60,000 straight-life policy issued to Ron Lee at age 30. At age 50, Ron wants to stop paying premium. **Calculate his nonforfeiture options**
Fire insurance Per $100 $$\text{Premium} = \frac{\text{Insurance value}}{\$100} \times \text{Rate}$$ Rate can be for buildings or contents.	**Given** Area 3; Class B; building insured for $90,000; contents, $30,000. Building: $\frac{\$90,000}{\$100} = 900 \times \$.61$ $= \boxed{\$549}$ Contents: $\frac{\$30,000}{\$100} = 300 \times \$.65$ $= \boxed{\$195}$ Total: $\$549 + \$195 = \boxed{\$744}$	**Calculate fire insurance premium** Area 3; Class B; insurance for $80,000; contents, $20,000.

(continues)

INTERACTIVE CHAPTER ORGANIZER

Topic/Procedure/Formula	Examples	You try it*
Canceling fire insurance—short-rate Table 20.4 (canceling by policyholder) $\dfrac{\text{Short-rate}}{\text{premium}} = \dfrac{\text{Annual}}{\text{premium}} \times \dfrac{\text{Short}}{\text{rate}}$ $\text{Refund} = \dfrac{\text{Annual}}{\text{premium}} - \dfrac{\text{Short-rate}}{\text{premium}}$ If insurance company cancels, do not use Table 20.4.	Annual premium is $400. Short rate is .35 (cancel end of 3 months). $400 × .35 = $140 Refund = $400 − $140 = $260	**Calculate refund** Annual premium is $600; insurance cancels after 4 months.
Canceling by insurance company $\text{Annual premium} \times \dfrac{\text{Months elapsed}}{12}$ (Refund is higher since company cancels.)	Using example above but insurance company cancels at end of 3 months. $400 × ¼ = $100 Refund = $400 − $100 = $300	**Calculate refund from example above if insurance company cancels**
Coinsurance Amount insurance company pays: $\dfrac{\text{Actual} \longrightarrow \text{Insurance carried (Face value)}}{\text{What coverage} \longrightarrow \text{Insurance required should have been (Rate × Replacement value)}} \times \text{Loss}$ Insurance company never pays more than the face value.	**Given** Face value, $30,000; replacement value, $50,000; coinsurance rate, 80%; loss, $10,000; insurance to meet required coinsurance, $40,000. $\dfrac{\$30,000}{\$40,000} \times \$10,000 = \$7,500$ paid by insurance company ($50,000 × .80)	**Calculate coinsurance** **Given** Face value, $40,000; replacement, $60,000; rate, 80%; loss, $9,000.

Auto insurance
Compulsory   Required insurance.
Optional   Added to cost of compulsory.
Bodily injury—pays for injury to person caused by insured.
Property damage—pays for property damage (not for insured auto).
Collision—pays for damages to insured auto.
Comprehensive—pays for damage to insured auto for fire, theft, etc.
Towing.
Substitute transportation.
	Calculate the annual premium.
	Driver class 10; compulsory 10/20/5.
	Optional
	Bodily—100/300
	Property—10M
	Collision—age 3, symbol 10, $100 deductible
	Comprehensive—$300 deductible
	
	                 ($55 + $129)
	10/20/5 $184 Table 20.5
	Bodily 94 Table 20.6
	Property 132 Table 20.7
	                 ($233 + $27)
	Collision 260 Table 20.8
	Comprehensive 178 Table 20.9
	Total premium $848
		Calculate annual premium
		Driver class 10;
		compulsory 10/20/5.
		Optional
		Bodily—100/300
		Property—10M
		Collision—age 5, symbol 8, $100 deductible
		Comprehensive—$300 deductible

KEY TERMS			
	Beneficiary Bodily injury Cash value Coinsurance Collision Comprehensive insurance Compulsory insurance Deductibles Extended term insurance Face amount Face value	Fire insurance Indemnity Insured Insurer Level premium term Liability insurance No-fault insurance Nonforfeiture values Paid-up insurance Policyholder Premium	Property damage Reduced paid-up insurance Short-rate table Statisticians Straight-life insurance Term insurance 20-payment life 20-year endowment Universal life Whole life

| Check Figures for Extra Practice Quizzes. (Worked-out Solutions are in Appendix B.) | LU 20–1a
1. $186.90; no cash value
2. $736.25
Opt. **1.** $2,755
    2. $8,170
    3. 9 years and 91 days | LU 20–2a
1. $428
2. $111.28; $316.72
3. $35,000
Never more than $170,000 | LU 20–3a
1. $817
2. $55,294; $750 |

*Worked-out solutions are in Appendix B.

Critical Thinking Discussion Questions with Chapter Concept Check

1. Compare and contrast term insurance versus whole-life insurance. At what age do you think people should take out life insurance?

2. What is meant by *nonforfeiture values?* If you take the cash value option, should it be paid in a lump sum or over a number of years?

3. How do you use a short-rate table? Explain why an insurance company gets less in premiums if it cancels a policy than if the insured cancels.

4. What is coinsurance? Do you feel that an insurance company should pay more than the face value of a policy in the event of a catastrophe?

5. Explain compulsory auto insurance, collision, and comprehensive. If your car is stolen, explain the steps you might take with your insurance company.

6. "Health insurance is not that important. It would not be worth the premiums." Please take a stand.

7. **Chapter Concept Check.** Based on concepts in the chapter, what would it cost you to set up a life insurance policy that would fit your needs?

END-OF-CHAPTER PROBLEMS connect plus+

Check figures for odd-numbered problems in Appendix C.   Name _____   Date _____

DRILL PROBLEMS

Calculate the annual premium for the following policies using Table 20.1 (for females subtract 3 years from the table).   *LU 20-1(1)*

	Amount of coverage (face value of policy)	Age and sex of insured	Type of insurance policy	Annual premium
20–1.	$100,000	39 F	Straight life	
20–2.	$200,000	42 M	20-payment life	
20–3.	$75,000	29 F	5-year term	
20–4.	$50,000	27 F	20-year endowment	

Calculate the following nonforfeiture options for Lee Chin, age 42, who purchased a $200,000 straight-life policy. At the end of year 20, Lee stopped paying premiums.   *LU 20-1(2)*

20–5.   Option 1: Cash surrender value

20–6.   Option 2: Reduced paid-up insurance

20–7.   Option 3: Extended term insurance

Calculate the total cost of a fire insurance premium (rounded to nearest cent) for a building and its contents given the following: *LU 20-2(1)*

	Rating of area	Class	Building	Contents	Total premium cost
20–8.	3	B	$90,000	$40,000	
e**X**cel					

Calculate the short-rate premium and refund of the following: *LU 20-2(2)*

	Annual premium	Canceled after	Short-rate premium	Refund
20–9.	$700	8 months by insured		
e**X**cel				
20–10.	$360	4 months by insurance company		
e**X**cel				

Complete the following: *LU 20-2(3)*

	Replacement value of property	Amount of insurance	Kind of policy	Actual fire loss	Amount insurance company will pay
20–11.	$100,000	$60,000	80% coinsurance	$22,000	
e**X**cel					
20–12.	$60,000	$40,000	80% coinsurance	$42,000	

Calculate the annual auto insurance premium for the following: *LU 20-3(1)*

20–13. Britney Sper, Territory 5
Class 17 operator
Compulsory, 10/20/5   _____

Optional

a. Bodily injury, 500/1,000   _____

b. Property damage, 25M   _____

c. Collision, $100 deductible   _____

  Age of car is 2; symbol of car is 7

d. Comprehensive, $200 deductible   _____

    Total annual premium   _____

WORD PROBLEMS

20–14. The average Roman's lifespan 2,000 years ago was 22 years. In 1900, a person was expected to live 47.3 years. In 2016, life expectancy is 79.26. If you are a 47-year-old female, what annual premium would you pay for a $200,000, 5-year term life insurance policy? What is the cash value after 3 years? *LU 20-1(1, 2)*

20–15. CBS News reported four ways to cut down on the cost of life insurance: (1) Shop around for the best rates from reputable companies, (2) improve your life expectancy by quitting smoking, etc., (3) buy life insurance when you are young, and (4) negotiate for lower premiums. Warren Kawano, age 34, was quoted $20 per month for a $100,000 term life insurance policy. Compare this to the rates in Table 20.1. *LU 20-1(1)*

20–16. Margie Rale, age 38, a well-known actress, decided to take out a limited-payment life policy. She chose this since she ex-
eXcel   pects her income to decline in future years. Margie decided to take out a 20-year payment life policy with a coverage amount of $90,000. Could you advise Margie about what her annual premium will be? If she decides to stop paying premiums after 15 years, what will be her cash value? *LU 20-1(1)*

20–17. Janette Raffa has two young children and wants to take out an additional $300,000 of 5-year term insurance. Janette is 40 years old. What will be her additional annual premium? In 3 years, what cash value will have been built up? *LU 20-1(1)*

20–18. Roger's office building has a $320,000 value, a 2 rating, and a B building classification. The contents in the building are valued at $105,000. Could you help Roger calculate his total annual premium? *LU 20-2(1)*

20–19. Abby Ellen's toy store is worth $400,000 and is insured for $200,000. Assume an 80% coinsurance clause and that a fire
eXcel   caused $190,000 damage. What is the liability of the insurance company? *LU 20-2(3)*

20–20. To an insurer, you are a statistic. Your premiums are based on your risk factors, including your credit rating. Bad credit increases the amount you pay for your premiums. Make certain to check your credit report annually for accuracy. Calculate the premium for someone in class 20 for 10/20/5. Then determine how much the premium will be for 50/100/50. What is the difference between the two? *LU 20-3(1)*

20–21. As given via the Internet, auto insurance quotes gathered online could vary from $947 to $1,558. A class 18 operator carries compulsory 10/20/5 insurance. He has the following optional coverage: bodily injury, 500/1,000; property damage, 50M; and collision, $200 deductible. His car is 1 year old, and the symbol of the car is 8. He has comprehensive insurance with a $200 deductible. Using your text, what is the total annual premium? *LU 20-3(1)*

20–22. Earl Miller insured his pizza shop for $100,000 for fire insurance at an annual rate per $100 of $.66. At the end of **eXcel** 11 months, Earl canceled the policy since his pizza shop went out of business. What was the cost of Earl's premium and his refund? *LU 20-2(2)*

20–23. Warren Ford insured his real estate office with a fire insurance policy for $95,000 at a cost of $.59 per $100. Eight months **eXcel** later the insurance company canceled his policy because of a failure to correct a fire hazard. What did Warren have to pay for the 8 months of coverage? Round to the nearest cent. *LU 20-2(2)*

20–24. If you had 10/20/5 coverage and were in a car accident causing injury to three people with injuries totaling $15,000, $9,000, and $5,000, how much would you have to pay out of pocket? If you had 50/100/50 coverage for the same scenario, how much would you have to pay out of pocket? What is the difference? *LU 20-3(1)*

20–25. Tina Grey bought a new Honda Civic and insured it with only 10/20/5 compulsory insurance. Driving up to her ski chalet one snowy evening, Tina hit a parked van and injured the couple inside. Tina's car had damage of $4,200, and the van she struck had damage of $5,500. After a lengthy court suit, the injured persons were awarded personal injury judgments of $16,000 and $7,900, respectively. What will the insurance company pay for this accident, and what is Tina's responsibility? *LU 20-3(1)*

20–26. Rusty Reft, who lives in Territory 5, carries 10/20/5 compulsory liability insurance along with optional collision that has a $300 deductible. Rusty was at fault in an accident that caused $3,600 damage to the other auto and $900 damage to his own. Also, the courts awarded $15,000 and $7,000, respectively, to the two passengers in the other car for personal injuries. How much will the insurance company pay, and what is Rusty's share of the responsibility? *LU 20-3(1)*

20–27. Marika Katz bought a new Blazer and insured it with only compulsory insurance 10/20/5. Driving up to her summer home one evening, Marika hit a parked car and injured the couple inside. Marika's car had damage of $7,500, and the car she struck had damage of $5,800. After a lengthy court suit, the couple struck were awarded personal injury judgments of $18,000 and $9,000, respectively. What will the insurance company pay for this accident, and what is Marika's responsibility? *LU 20-3(1)*

20–28. In Problem 20–27 above, what will the insurance company pay and what is Marika's responsibility if Marika has 25/50/25 coverage with $200 deductible for collision instead of 10/20/5? *LU 20-3(2)*

CHALLENGE PROBLEMS

20–29. Money.cnn.com states, "The single most important reason to own life insurance is to provide support for your dependents." Insurance4usa.com states, "Professionals suggest you have 8 to 12 times your income in life insurance." Pat and Bonnie Marsh are calculating how much life insurance they need. They have two young children with no college fund set up. Bonnie is a 35-year-old stay-at-home mom. Pat, 39, earns $68,000 per year. How much life insurance do you recommend each person have? (Note that a spouse who stays at home to raise the family generates the equivalent of a salary that needs to be taken into account. Assume Bonnie's salary is $25,000.) What will be the cost of straight-life insurance for both policies if the lowest recommended amount is used? What is the monthly premium owed? *LU 20-1(1)*

20–30. Lou Ralls insured a building and contents (area 2, class B) for $150,000. After 1 month, he canceled the policy. The next day he received a cancellation notice by the company. It stated that he was being canceled due to his previous record. How does Lou save by this insurance cancellation versus his planned cancellation? *LU 20-2(1, 2)*

SUMMARY PRACTICE TEST

Do you need help? The videos in Connect have step-by-step worked-out solutions. These videos are also available on YouTube!

1. Howard Slater, age 44, an actor, expects his income to decline in future years. He decided to take out a 20-year payment life policy with a $90,000 coverage. What will be Howard's annual premium? If he decides to stop paying premiums after 15 years, what will be his cash value? *LU 20-1(1, 2)*

2. J.C. Monahan, age 40, bought a straight-life insurance policy for $210,000. Calculate her annual premium. If after 20 years J.C. no longer pays her premiums, what nonforfeiture options will be available to her? *LU 20-1(1, 2)*

3. The property of Pote's Garage is worth $900,000. Pote has a $375,000 fire insurance policy that contains an 80% coinsurance clause. What will the insurance company pay on a fire that causes $450,000 damage? If Pote meets the coinsurance, how much will the insurance company pay? *LU 20-2(3)*

4. Lee Collins insured her pizza shop with a $90,000 fire insurance policy at a $1.10 annual rate per $100. At the end of 7 months, Lee's pizza shop went out of business so she canceled the policy. What is the cost of Lee's premium and her refund? *LU 20-2(2)*

5. Charles Prose insured his real estate office with a $300,000 fire insurance policy at $.78 annual rate per $100. Nine months later the insurance company canceled his policy because Charles failed to correct a fire hazard. What was Charles's cost for the 9-month coverage? Round to the nearest cent. *LU 20-2(2)*

6. Roger Laut, who lives in Territory 5, carries 10/20/5 compulsory liability insurance along with optional collision that has a $1,000 deductible. Roger was at fault in an accident that caused $4,800 damage to the other car and $8,800 damage to his own car. Also, the courts awarded $19,000 and $9,000, respectively, to the two passengers in the other car for personal injuries. How much does the insurance company pay, and what is Roger's share of the responsibility? *LU 20-3(1)*

SURF TO SAVE

PROBLEM 1
The cost of life insurance

Go to http://www.prudential.com. Follow the link to Products and Services—Insurance. Enter the information the site asks for and get life insurance quotes for $250,000, $500,000, $750,000, and $1,000,000 of coverage. (Use a 10-year Term Essential policy.) Does the $500,000 policy cost twice as much as the $250,000 policy? Does the $1,000,000 policy cost four times as much as the $250,000 policy? Explain your result.

Discussion Questions

1. As a college student, should you take out a life insurance policy? Why or why not?

2. How can you determine the level of life insurance coverage you should purchase?

PROBLEM 3
Protecting your car

Go to http://www.allstate.com. Get a quick quote for auto insurance in your zip code. (Use 48150 if you are taking the course outside the United States.) Find out how much it would cost to insure your car. How much would you save each year if you changed your collision and comprehensive deductibles from $250 to $1,000? What extra risks would you incur? If you had an accident and paid a $1,000 deductible, how many years would it take to make up the extra $750 you paid through lower premiums? (Assume the difference in premiums does not change.)

Discussion Questions

1. What are the pros and cons of carrying a lower deductible on your car?

2. What is the rationale behind the decision to require drivers to carry automobile insurance before they are allowed to get a driver's license?

PROBLEM 2
Paying a premium

Select 3 different companies offering a $500,000, 20-year policy that you would like to start today. Which company had the highest quote? Which company came in with the lowest quote?

Discussion Questions

1. Is price the determining factor for you in choosing which life insurance policy you would purchase? Why or why not?

2. What may be the reason for the differences in pricing among these life insurance policies?

PROBLEM 4
A smoking hot premium

Go to https://termlife.allstate.com/StartQuote.aspx? ZipKey= s068IS5rp7yIBnjrwrntCQ%3d%3d and get a life insurance quote using your own personal information for a $600,000 policy. How much does the premium quote change if you change your smoking status to a current smoker ("In the last 12 months")?

Discussion Questions

1. Why would insurance providers charge more for a policyholder who smokes versus one who doesn't smoke? Is this a fair business practice?

2. Other than smoking, what characteristics should increase or decrease your life insurance policy costs?

MOBILE APPS ✕

Life Happens Needs Calculator (LIFE Foundation) Helps determine the level of life insurance protection needed based upon the unique characteristics of the user.

Insurance Saver (Mobile Web Solutions) Organizes all insurance policy information in one location.

A KIPLINGER APPROACH

By the editors of *Kiplinger's Personal Finance*, From *Kiplinger's Personal Finance*, July 2014.

3 SIMPLE STEPS — Reshop Your Car Insurance

STEP 1

Dig out your current policy to see how much you pay every six months, as well as the limits and cost of each coverage. Also have your vehicle identification number (VIN), current mileage and as much information as possible about recent claims or moving violations. You may not find a better rate if you've had an accident or a moving violation within the past three to five years.

STEP 2

Go to CarInsurance.com and enter your information (with the same coverage your policy currently provides). In most states, you'll get immediate quotes online from several insurers, such as Esurance, 21st Century and The Hartford. Also get quotes directly from the largest insurers: Allstate, Geico, Progressive and State Farm. If you'd rather have an independent agent shop for you, go to Trusted Choice.com.

STEP 3

At www.naic.org/cis, check the closed complaint records for your insurer and the two or three companies with the best quotes. Finding the complaint ratio can be a hassle, but you don't want to risk headaches if you have a claim. As long as the ratio is close to the national median (which is 1.00), you're good to go. Call your insurer and explain that you've found a better rate. If it won't lower your premium, make the switch to the company with the lowest rates and fewest complaints.

THE PAYOFF — You can save hundreds of dollars on your premium.

BUSINESS MATH ISSUE

Basically all insurance companies' rates are the same.

1. List the key points of the article and information to support your position.
2. Write a group defense of your position using math calculations to support your view.

CHAPTER 21

Stocks, Bonds, and Mutual Funds

© Spencer Platt/Getty Images

Pepper ...
And Salt

THE WALL STREET JOURNAL

"When Daddy comes home, tell
him you still love him despite
his stupid trades in emerging
markets."

From *The Wall Street Journal*, permission Cartoon Features Syndicate.

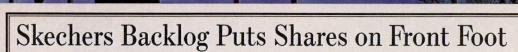

Skechers Backlog Puts Shares on Front Foot

Skechers USA may be following the cardinal rule of financial guidance: underpromise and overdeliver.

The shoe company has been expanding quickly. This has been driven by international expansion, the popularity of its new styles of casual sneakers and its push into performance footwear, endorsed by the likes of Boston Marathon winner Meb Keflezighi. Skechers saw double-digit percentage growth in its domestic and international wholesale businesses in the third quarter of 2014 as same-store sales at company-owned outlets climbed 11%.

When it reported those results in September, Skechers said it remained comfortable with analysts' consensus for sales growth in the fourth quarter of 19%. But it may be being too modest.

Skechers's reported merchandise backlog appears to be a relatively good indicator of sales growth in the following quarter. During its July results call, Skechers said its backlog had increased in the "mid-high" 20% range from the previous year. The company's third-quarter sales rose 31%. Similarly, during its April call, Skechers said its backlog had increased more than 35%. It went on to report second-quarter sales growth of 37%.

In September, Skechers said its backlog had risen in the third quarter by more than 50%. Considering the close relationship of backlog and sales growth in prior periods, an expectation of 19% fourth-quarter growth seems low.

Granted, backlog hasn't always been an exact indicator.

During its results call for the last quarter of 2013, Skechers said its backlog had risen 30%, year over year. But first-quarter 2014 results saw sales rise 21%. Still, that nine-percentage-point gap is far narrower than the 31-plus percentage points that separate Skechers's backlog growth last quarter and analysts' sales-growth estimates for the current one.

Skechers' stock trades at 16 times forward earnings, a premium to **Foot Locker**'s 14.6 times and a discount to **Nike** at 24.4 times. But Skechers's earnings estimates should rise if revenue expectations prove too low. Moreover, the company has net cash of $321 million, which could potentially be returned to shareholders down the line. For investors, Skechers could be a good fit.

—*Miriam Gottfried*

Reprinted by permission of *The Wall Street Journal*, copyright 2015 Dow Jones & Company, Inc. All rights reserved worldwide.

LU 21–1: Stocks

1. Read, calculate, and explain stock quotations.
2. Calculate dividends of preferred and common stocks; calculate return on investment.

LU 21–2: Bonds

1. Read, calculate, and explain bond quotations.
2. Compare bond yields to bond premiums and discounts.

LU 21–3: Mutual Funds

1. Explain and calculate net asset value and mutual fund commissions.
2. Read and explain mutual fund quotations.

VOCABULARY PREVIEW

Here are key terms in this chapter. After completing the chapter, if you know the term, place a checkmark in the box. If you don't know the term, look it up and put the page number where it can be found.

Bond yield ☐ **Bonds** ☐ **Cash dividend** ☐ **Common stocks** ☐ **Cumulative preferred stock** ☐ **Discount** ☐ **Dividends** ☐ **Dividends in arrears** ☐ **Earnings per share (EPS)** ☐ **Mutual fund** ☐ **Net asset value (NAV)** ☐ **Odd lot** ☐ **PE ratio** ☐ **Preferred stock** ☐ **Premium** ☐ **Price-earnings ratio** ☐ **Round lot** ☐ **Stock certificate** ☐ **Stock yield** ☐ **Stockbrokers** ☐ **Stockholders** ☐ **Stocks** ☐

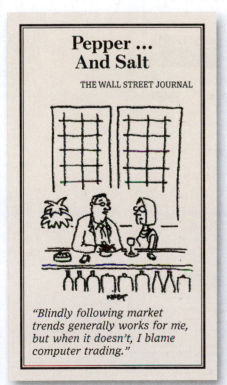

Pepper ... And Salt

THE WALL STREET JOURNAL

"Blindly following market trends generally works for me, but when it doesn't, I blame computer trading."

From *The Wall Street Journal*, permission Cartoon Features Syndicate.

When you make financial investments there is always some degree of risk. Should you invest in Skechers stock, or just keep your money in cash? The *Wall Street Journal* clip in the chapter opener offers some insights about Skechers.

Before we explain the concept of stock, consider the following general investor principles: (1) know your risk tolerance and the risk of the investments you are considering—determine whether you are a low-risk conservative investor or a high-risk speculative investor; (2) know your time frame—how soon you need your money; (3) know the liquidity of the investments you are considering—how easy it is to get your money; (4) know the return you can expect on your money—how much your money should earn; and (5) do not put "all your eggs in one basket"—diversify with a mixture of stocks, bonds, and cash equivalents. It is most important that before you seek financial advice from others, you go to the library and/or the Internet for information. When you do your own research first, you can judge the advice you receive from others.

This chapter introduces you to the major types of investments—stocks, bonds, and mutual funds. These investments indicate the performance of the companies they represent and the economy of the country at home and abroad.

Learning Unit 21–1: Stocks

We begin this unit with an introduction to the basic stock terms. Then we explain the reason why people buy stocks, newspaper stock quotations, dividends on preferred and common stocks, and return on investment.

Introduction to Basic Stock Terms

Companies sell shares of ownership in their company to raise money to finance operations, plan expansion, and so on. These ownership shares are called **stocks.** The buyers of the stock (**stockholders**) receive **stock certificates** verifying the number of shares of stock they own.

The two basic types of stock are **common stock** and **preferred stock.** Common stockholders have voting rights. Preferred stockholders do not have voting rights, but they receive preference over common stockholders in **dividends** (payments from profit) and in the company's assets if the company goes bankrupt. **Cumulative preferred stock** entitles its owners to a specific amount of dividends in 1 year. Should the company fail to pay these dividends, the **dividends in arrears** accumulate. The company pays no dividends to common stockholders until the company brings the preferred dividend payments up to date.

If you own 50 shares of common stock, you are entitled to 50 votes in company elections. Preferred stockholders do not have this right.

Why Buy Stocks?

Some investors own stock because they think the stock will become more valuable, for example, if the company makes more profit, new discoveries, and the like. Other investors own stock to share in the profit distributed by the company in dividends (cash or stock).

For various reasons, investors at different times want to sell their stock or buy more stock. Strikes, inflation, or technological changes may cause some investors to think their stock will decline in value. These investors may decide to sell. Then the law of supply and demand takes over. As more people want to sell, the stock price goes down. Should more people want to buy, the stock price would go up.

How Are Stocks Traded?   Stock exchanges provide an orderly trading place for stock. You can think of these exchanges as an auction place. Only **stockbrokers** and their representatives are allowed to trade on the floor of the exchange. Stockbrokers charge commissions for stock trading—buying and selling stock for investors. As you might expect, in this age of the Internet, stock trades can also be made on the Internet. Electronic trading is growing each day.

© Roberts Publishing Services

How to Read Stock Quotations in the Newspaper's Financial Section[1]

FIGURE 21.1

New York Stock Exchange

Stockholders
↓ elect
board of directors
↓ elect
officers of corporation

We will use Disney stock to learn how to read the stock quotations found in your newspaper. Note the following newspaper listing of Disney stock:

52 WEEKS				YLD				NET
HI	LO	STOCK (SYM)	DIV	%	PE	LAST		CHG
94.50	69.28	Disney (DIS)	1.19	1.3	21	91.49		−.026

The highest price at which Disney stock traded during the past 52 weeks was $94.50 per share. This means that during the year someone was willing to pay $94.50 for a share of stock.

The lowest price at which Disney stock traded during the year was $69.28 per share.

The newspaper lists the company name. The symbol that Disney uses for trading is DIS. Disney paid a dividend of $1.19 per share to stock owners last year. So if you owned 100 shares, you would have received a **cash dividend** of $119 (100 shares × $1.19).

The **stock yield** percent tells stockholders that the dividend per share is returning a rate of 1.3% to investors. This 1.3% is based on the closing price. The calculation is:

$$\frac{\text{Stock}}{\text{yield}} = \frac{\text{Annual dividend per share}}{\text{Today's last price per share}} = \frac{\$1.19}{\$91.49} = 1.3\% \quad \text{(rounded to nearest tenth percent)}$$

The 1.3% return may seem low to people who could earn a better return on their money elsewhere. Remember that if the stock price rises and you sell, your investment may result in a high rate of return.

The Disney stock is selling at $91.49; it is selling at 21 times its **earnings per share (EPS).** Earnings per share are not listed on the stock quote.

$$\begin{aligned} \text{Earnings per share} &= \text{Last price} \div \text{Price-earnings ratio} \\ (\$4.36) &= (\$91.49) \div (21) \end{aligned}$$

The **price-earnings ratio,** or **PE ratio,** measures the relationship between the closing price per share of stock and the annual earnings per share. For Disney we calculate the following price-earnings ratio. (This is not listed in the newspaper.)

Round PE to the nearest whole number.

$$\text{PE ratio} = \frac{\text{Last price per share of stock}}{\text{Annual earnings per share}} = \frac{\$91.49}{\$4.36} = 21$$

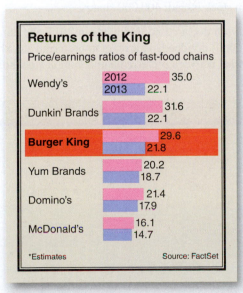

Returns of the King

Price/earnings ratios of fast-food chains

	2012	2013
Wendy's	35.0	22.1
Dunkin' Brands	31.6	22.1
Burger King	29.6	21.8
Yum Brands	20.2	18.7
Domino's	21.4	17.9
McDonald's	16.1	14.7

*Estimates   Source: FactSet

Source: *The Wall Street Journal,* 10/29/12.

Aha!

If the PE ratio column shows ". . . ," this means the company has no earnings. The PE ratio will often vary depending on quality of stock, future expectations, economic conditions, and so on.

Note in the clip "Returns of the King" how different companies have different PE ratios.

The last trade of the day, called the closing price, was at $91.49 per share.

On the *previous day,* the closing price was $91.75 (not given). The result is that the last price is down $.26 from the *previous day.*

An effective long-term strategy for investing in stocks is to continue to invest even when stock prices are falling. As stock prices fall, you purchase more shares with the same amount of money giving you additional future earning potential.

[1]For centuries, stocks were traded and reported in fraction form. In 2001 the New York Stock Exchange and NASDAQ began the conversion to decimals, which is how stocks are reported today.

LO 2

Dividends on Preferred and Common Stocks

If you own stock in a company, the company may pay out dividends. (Not all companies pay dividends.) The amount of the dividend is determined by the net earnings of the company listed in its financial report. The clip from *The Wall Street Journal* shows how Apple has lowered its stock price to make it more attractive to investors.

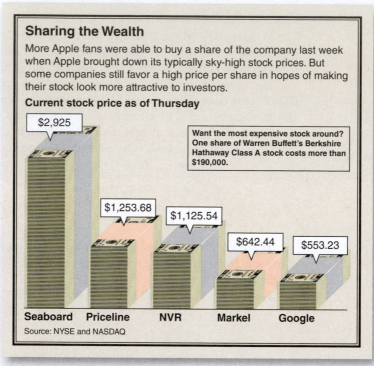

Source: *The Wall Street Journal,* 6/14/14.

Earlier we stated that cumulative preferred stockholders must be paid all past and present dividends before common stockholders can receive any dividends. Following is an example to illustrate the calculation of dividends on preferred and common stocks for 2017 and 2018.

EXAMPLE The stock records of Jason Corporation show the following:

Preferred stock issued: 20,000 shares.

Preferred stock cumulative at $.80 per share.

Common stock issued: 400,000 shares.

In 2017, Jason paid no dividends.

In 2018, Jason paid $512,000 in dividends.

Since Jason declared no dividends in 2017, the company has $16,000 (20,000 shares × $.80 = $16,000) dividends in arrears to preferred stockholders. The dividend of $512,000 in 2018 is divided between preferred and common stockholders as follows:

> Remember that common stockholders do not have the cumulative feature of preferred stockholders.

	2017	2018	
Dividends paid	0	$512,000	
Preferred stockholders*	Paid: 0	Paid for 2017 (20,000 shares × $.80)	$ 16,000
	Owe: Preferred, $16,000 (20,000 shares × $.80)	Paid for 2018	16,000
			$ 32,000
Common stockholders	0	Total dividend	$512,000
		Paid preferred for 2017 and 2018	− 32,000
		To common	$480,000
		$\dfrac{\$480,000}{400,000 \text{ shares}} = \$1.20 \text{ per share}$	

*For a discussion of par value (arbitrary value placed on stock for accounting purposes) and cash and stock dividend distribution, check your accounting text.

Shares are typically traded in groups of 100 called **round lots.** Purchases of fewer than 100 shares of stock are called **odd lots.**

Calculating Return on Investment

Now let's learn how to calculate a return on your investment if you bought a different stock than Disney. Let's assume you decided to buy stock of General Mills given the following:

Bought 200 shares at $39.09.

Sold at end of 1 year 200 shares at $41.10.

1% commission rate on buying and selling stock.

Current $1.21 dividend per share in effect.

Bought		Sold	
200 shares at $39.09	$7,818.00	200 shares at $41.10	$8,220.00
+ Broker's commission		− Broker's commission	
(.01 × $7,818)	+ 78.18	(.01 × $8,220.00)	− 82.20
Total cost	$7,896.18	Total receipt	$8,137.80

Note: A commission is charged on both the buying and selling of stock.

Total receipt	$8,137.80	
Total cost	− 7,896.18	
Net gain	$ 241.62	
Dividends	+ 242.00	(200 shares × $1.21)
Total gain	$ 483.62	

Portion $\to \dfrac{\$483.62}{\$7,896.18} =$ 6.12% rate of return (to nearest hundredth percent)

Base

It's time for another Practice Quiz.

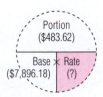

Portion ($483.62)

Base ($7,896.18) × Rate (?)

MONEY tips

Set financial and personal goals. Each goal should be specific, quantifiable, realistic, and given a due date. Review and update each goal annually.

LU 21–1 PRACTICE QUIZ

Complete this **Practice Quiz** to see how you are doing.

1. From the following Texaco stock quotation (**a**) explain the letters, (**b**) estimate the company's earnings per share, and (**c**) show how "YLD %" was calculated.

52 WEEKS			YLD			NET
HI	**LO**	**STOCK (SYM)**	**%**	**PE**	**LAST**	**CHG**
73.90	48.25	Texaco TX	2.5	14	72.25	+0.46
(A)	(B)	(C)	(D)	(E)	(F)	(G)

2. **Given:** 30,000 shares of preferred cumulative stock at $.70 per share; 200,000 shares of common; 2017, no dividend; 2018, $109,000. How much is paid to each class of stock in 2018?

For **extra help** from your authors–Sharon and Jeff–see the videos in Connect.

These videos are also available on YouTube!

✓ Solutions

1. **a.** (A) Highest price traded in last 52 weeks.
   (B) Lowest price traded in past 52 weeks.
   (C) Name of corporation is Texaco (symbol TX).
   (D) Yield for year is 2.5%.
   (E) Texaco stock sells at 14 times its earnings.
   (F) The last price (closing price for the day) is $72.25.
   (G) Stock is up $.46 from closing price yesterday.

   b. EPS = $\dfrac{\$72.25}{14}$ = $5.16 per share

   c. $\dfrac{?}{\$72.25}$ = 2.5% $72.25 × 2.5% = $1.80*

   *Rounding difference

2. **Preferred:** 30,000 × $.70 = $21,000   Arrears 2017
                                    + 21,000   2018
                                 $42,000

        Common: $67,000 ($109,000 − $42,000)

LU 21–1a   EXTRA PRACTICE QUIZ WITH WORKED-OUT SOLUTIONS

Need more practice? Try this **Extra Practice Quiz** (check figures in the Interactive Chapter Organizer). Worked-out Solutions can be found in Appendix B at end of text.

1. From the following Goodyear stock quotation **(a)** explain the letters, **(b)** estimate the company's earnings per share, and **(c)** show how YLD % was calculated.

52 WEEKS		STOCK (SYM)	YLD %	PE	CLOSE	NET CHG
HI	LO					
23.14	3.17	Goodyear GT	.54	16	13.08	+.11
(A)	(B)	(C)	(D)	(E)	(F)	(G)

2. **Given:** 40,000 shares of preferred cumulative stock at $.60 per share; 300,000 shares of common; 2014, no dividend; 2015, $210,000. How much is paid to each class of stock in 2015?

Learning Unit 21–2: Bonds

Have you heard of the Rule of 115? This rule is used as a rough measure to show how quickly an investment will triple in value. To use the rule, divide 115 by the rate of return your money earns. For example, if a bond earns 5% interest, divide 115 by 5. This measure estimates that your money in the bond will triple in 23 years.

This unit begins by explaining the difference between bonds and stocks. Then you will learn how to read bond quotations and calculate bond yields.

When you own stock, you own a share of a company. When you own a bond, you are lending the company money, similar to how banks lend money.

LO 1

Reading Bond Quotations

Bond quotes are stated in percents of the face value of the bond and not in dollars as stock is. Interest is paid semiannually.

Sometimes companies raise money by selling bonds instead of stock. When you buy stock, you become a part owner in the company. To raise money, companies may not want to sell more stock and thus dilute the ownership of their current stock owners, so they sell bonds. **Bonds** represent a promise from the company to pay the face amount to the bond owner at a future date, along with interest payments at a stated rate.

Once a company issues bonds, they are traded as stock is. If a company goes bankrupt, bondholders have the first claim to the assets of the corporation—before stockholders. As with stock, changes in bond prices vary according to supply and demand. Brokers also charge commissions on bond trading. These commissions vary.

LO 2

How to Read the Bond Section of the Newspaper

The bond section of the newspaper shows the bonds that are traded that day. The information given on bonds differs from the information given on stocks. The newspaper states bond prices in *percents of face amount, not in dollar amounts* as stock prices are stated. Also, bonds are usually in denominations of $1,000 (the face amount).

When a bond sells at a price below its face value, the bond is sold at a discount. Why? The interest that the bond pays may not be as high as the current market rate. When this happens, the bond is not as attractive to investors, and it sells for a **discount.** The opposite could, of course, also occur. The bond may sell at a **premium,** which means that the bond sells for more than its face value or the bond interest is higher than the current market rate.

Let's look at this newspaper information given for Aflac bonds:

Bonds	Current yield	Vol.	Close	Net change
Aflac 422	4.02%	214,587	99.50	−1

Note: Bond prices are stated as a percent of face amount.

The name of the company is Aflac. It produces a wide range of insurance coverage. The interest on the bond is 4%. The company pays the interest semiannually. The bond matures (comes due) in 2022. The total interest for the year is $40 (.04 × $1,000). Remember that the face value of the bond is $1,000. Now let's show this with the following formula:

> Yearly interest = Face value of bond × Stated yearly interest rate

$$\$40.00 = \$1,000 \times .04$$

We calculate the 4.02% yield by dividing the total annual interest of the bond by the total cost of the bond. (For our purposes, we will omit the commission cost.) We will calculate more bond yields in a moment.

> $$\frac{\text{Yearly interest}}{\text{Cost of bond at closing}} = \frac{\$40 \ (.04 \times \$1,000)}{\$995 \ (.9950 \times \$1,000)}$$
>
> $= 4.02\%$ This is the same as 99.50%.

Note this bond is selling for more than $1,000 since its interest is very attractive compared to other new offerings.

On this day, $214,587 worth of bonds were traded. Note that we do *not* add two zeros as we did to the sales volume of stock.

The last bond traded on this day was 99.50% of face value, or in dollars, $.9950.

The last trade of the day was down 1% of the face value from the last trade of yesterday. In dollars this is 1% = $10.

$$1\% = .01 \times \$1,000 = \$10$$

Thus, the closing price on this day, 99.50% + 1%, equals yesterday's close of 100.50% ($1,005). Note that *yesterday's close is not listed in today's quotations.*

Remember: Bond prices are quoted as a percent of $1,000 but without the percent sign. A bond quote of 99 means 99% of $1,000, or $990.

Calculating Bond Yields

The Aflac bond (selling at a discount) pays 4% interest when it is yielding investors 4.02%.

> $$\text{Bond yield} = \frac{\text{Total annual interest of bond}}{\text{Total current cost of bond at closing*}}$$

*We assume this to be the buyer's purchase price.

MONEY tips

Spend your money wisely. Cut back on frivolous spending to provide more discretionary income for an emergency fund and retirement savings.

The following example will show us how to calculate **bond yields.**

EXAMPLE   Jim Smith bought 5 bonds of Aflac at the closing price of 99.50 (remember that in dollars 99.50% is $995). Jim's total cost excluding commission is:

$$5 \times \$995 = \$4,975$$

What is Jim's interest?

No matter what Jim pays for the bonds, he will still receive interest of $40 per bond (.04 × $1,000). Jim bought the bonds at $995 each, resulting in a bond yield of 4.02%. Let's calculate Jim's yield to the nearest tenth percent:

(5 bonds × $40 interest per bond per year)

$$\frac{\$200.00}{\$4,975} = 4.02\%$$

Now let's try another Practice Quiz.

LU 21–2   **PRACTICE QUIZ**

Complete this **Practice Quiz** to see how you are doing.

Bonds		Yield	Sales	Close	Net change
Aetna 6.375%	13	6.4	20	100.375	.875

From the above bond quotation, **(1)** calculate the cost of 5 bonds at closing (disregard commissions) and **(2)** check the current yield of 6.4%.

*For **extra help** from your authors—Sharon and Jeff—see the videos in Connect.*

These videos are also available on YouTube!

✓ **Solutions**

1. 100.375% = 1.00375 × $1,000 = $1,003.75 × 5 = $5,018.75

2. 6.375% = .06375 × $1,000 = $63.75 annual interest

$$\frac{\$63.75}{\$1,003.75} = 6.35\% = 6.4\%$$

LU 21–2a | **EXTRA PRACTICE QUIZ WITH WORKED-OUT SOLUTIONS**

Need more practice? Try this Extra Practice Quiz (check figures in the Interactive Chapter Organizer). Worked-out Solutions can be found in Appendix B at end of text.

Bonds		Yield	Sales	Close	Net change
Aetna 7.5	14	7.5%	20	100.25	+.75

From the above bond quotation, **(1)** calculate the cost of 5 bonds at closing (disregard commissions) and **(2)** check the current yield of 7.5%.

Learning Unit 21–3: Mutual Funds

© Steven Senne/AP Images

In recent years, mutual funds have increased dramatically and people in the United States have invested billions in mutual funds. Investors can choose from several fund types—stock funds, bond funds, international funds, balanced (stocks and bonds) funds, and so on. This learning unit tells you why investors choose mutual funds and discusses the net asset value of mutual funds, mutual fund commissions, and how to read a mutual fund quotation. Be sure to read the *Wall Street Journal* clip on window dressing that is found at the end of the unit.

Why Investors Choose Mutual Funds

The main reasons investors choose mutual funds are the following:

1. **Diversification.** When you invest in a mutual fund, you own a small portion of many different companies. This protects you against the poor performance of a single company but not against a sell-off in the market (stock and bond exchanges) or fluctuations in the interest rate.

2. **Professional management.** You are hiring a professional manager to look after your money when you own shares in mutual funds. The success of a particular fund is often due to the person(s) managing the fund.

   Some investors invest in a mutual fund simply because of who the mutual fund manager is.

3. **Liquidity.** Most funds will buy back your fund shares whenever you decide to sell.

4. **Low fund expenses.** Competition forces funds to keep their expenses low to maximize their performance. Because stocks and bonds in a mutual fund represent thousands of shareholders, funds can trade in large blocks, reducing transaction costs.

5. **Access to foreign markets.** Through mutual funds, investors can conveniently and inexpensively invest in foreign markets.

Net Asset Value

Investing in a **mutual fund** means that you buy shares in the fund's portfolio (group of stocks and/or bonds). The value of your mutual fund share is expressed in the share's **net asset value (NAV)**, which is the dollar value of one mutual fund share. You calculate the NAV by subtracting the fund's current liabilities from the current market value of the fund's investments and dividing this by the number of shares outstanding.

$$NAV = \frac{\text{Current market value of fund's investments } - \text{ Current liabilities}}{\text{Number of shares outstanding}}$$

The NAV helps investors track the value of their fund investment. After the market closes on each business day, the fund uses the closing prices of the investments it owns to find the dollar value of one fund share, or NAV. This is the price investors receive if they sell fund shares on that day or pay if they buy fund shares on that day.

Commissions When Buying Mutual Funds

The following table is a quick reference for the cost of buying mutual fund shares. Commissions vary from 0% to $8\frac{1}{2}$% depending on how the mutual fund is classified.

Classification	Commission charge*	Offer price to buy
No-load (NL) fund	No sales charge	NAV (buy directly from investment company)
Low-load (LL) fund	3% or less	NAV + commission % (buy directly from investment company or from a broker)
Load fund	$8\frac{1}{2}$% or less	NAV + commission % (buy from a broker)

*On a front-end load, you pay a commission when you purchase the fund shares, while on a back-end load, you pay when you redeem or sell. In general, if you hold the shares for more than 5 years, you pay no commission charge.

The offer price to buy a share for a low-load or load fund is the NAV plus the commission. Now let's look at how to read a mutual fund quotation.

LO 2

How to Read a Mutual Fund Quotation

We will be studying the American Funds. Cindy Joelson has invested in the Growth Fund with the hope that over the years this will provide her with financial security when she retires. On May 27, Cindy turns to *Barron's* and looks up the American Funds Growth quotation.

The name of the fund is Growth, which has the investment objective of growth securities as set forth in the fund's prospectus (document giving information about the fund). Note that this is only one fund in the American Funds family of funds.

- The $47.15 figure is the NAV plus the sales commission.
- The fund has decreased $.10 from the NAV quotation of the previous day.
- The fund has a 9.7% return this year (January through December). This assumes reinvestments of all distributions. Sales charges are not reflected.

Financial analysts recommend that individual retirement accounts contain some mixture of stocks and bonds. Retirement accounts should be heavily invested in stocks while the investor is young and gradually shift holdings to bonds as retirement approaches. Mutual funds can invest in a variety of securities such as stocks, bonds, money market instruments, real estate, and similar assets. Investors may use a bond fund for income. Consider the following example:

EXAMPLE   Bonnie and Pat Meyer are in their retirement years. They just received $250,000 after taxes from the sale of their vacation home and decided to invest the money in a bond mutual fund. They chose a no-load mutual fund that yields 4.5%. How much will they receive each year? How much would they need to invest if they want to earn $15,000 per year?

Step 1. $I = PRT = \$250,000 \times .045 \times 1 =$ $11,250

Step 2. $P = \dfrac{I}{RT} = \dfrac{\$15,000}{.045 \times 1} =$ $333,333.33

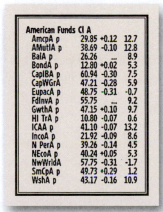

American Funds Cl A

AmcpA p	29.85	+0.12	12.7
AMutlA p	38.69	-0.10	12.8
BalA p	26.26	...	8.9
BondA p	12.80	+0.02	5.3
CapIBA p	60.94	-0.30	7.5
CapWGrA p	47.21	-0.28	5.9
EupacA p	48.75	-0.31	-0.7
FdInvA p	55.75	...	9.2
GwthA p	47.15	+0.10	9.7
HI TrA p	10.80	-0.07	0.6
ICAA p	41.10	-0.07	13.2
IncoA p	21.92	-0.09	8.6
N PerA p	39.26	-0.14	4.5
NEcoA p	40.24	+0.05	5.3
NwWrldA	57.75	-0.31	-1.7
SmCpA p	49.73	+0.29	1.2
WshA p	43.17	-0.16	10.9

Source: *The Wall Street Journal.*

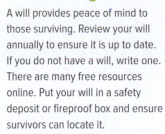

MONEY tips

A will provides peace of mind to those surviving. Review your will annually to ensure it is up to date. If you do not have a will, write one. There are many free resources online. Put your will in a safety deposit or fireproof box and ensure survivors can locate it.

IN TRANSLATION

WINDOW DRESSING

To most people the holiday season means decorations at home and at work, but it also can mean "window dressing" in your mutual fund.

This somewhat disparaging term is used to describe the practice of a mutual fund making cosmetic changes to its portfolio just before the end of each calendar quarter. It's done because funds publish their exact holdings of securities four times a year based on what they own at the end of each quarter.

"The basic concept is that managers are either hiding their mistakes or adding winners to make themselves look a little smarter," says Russ Kinnel, director of manager research at fund researcher Morningstar Inc. in Chicago. "Of course, it doesn't necessarily help performance," he adds.

While most investors focus on a fund's performance more than its portfolio, many investors do pay close attention to funds' holdings—and they don't want to see a fund holding on to a disastrous investment or missing out on a major upward move by a stock. Window dressing helps those investors look more favorably upon the fund manager, Mr. Kinnel says.

Market observers have long suggested that window dressing leads to more stock volatility around the ends of quarters, and a recent study by the Wisconsin School of Business seems to confirm that is a real phenomenon.

"The stocks that rank high on intermediate-term momentum and that are purchased at the end of a quarter experience large positive returns at that time, followed by large negative returns in the next month," says the report, written by David P. Brown, a professor in the school's department of finance, investment and banking.

Or put another way, a high-flying stock may fly even higher near the end of a quarter and then come back to earth the next month.

—Simon Constable

Reprinted by permission of *The Wall Street Journal*, copyright 2014 Dow Jones & Company, Inc. All rights reserved worldwide.

If Bonnie and Pat invest $250,000, they will receive $11,250 in interest each year. If they need to earn $15,000 in interest each year, they must invest an additional $83,333.33: $333,333.33 − $250,000 = $83,333.33.

Now let's check your understanding of this unit with a Practice Quiz.

LU 21–3 PRACTICE QUIZ

Complete this Practice Quiz to see how you are doing.

From the following mutual fund quotation of the Schwab Health Care Growth Fund complete the following:

1. NAV

   _____

2. NAV change

   _____

3. Total return, YTD

   _____

4. You are interested in earning $6,500 each year on a no-load 5% yield mutual fund. How much must you invest?

✓ **Solutions**

1.   18.33

2.   −.11

3.   4.4

4. $$P = \frac{1}{RT} = \frac{\$6,500}{.05 \times 1} = \$130,000$$

```
Schwab Funds:
1000 Inv nr       37.99 -0.06   7.4  74.3
CoreEq n          17.99  0.00   7.1  55.3
DivEqSel n        13.99 -0.06   4.6  58.8
FunUSLgInst nr    10.07 -0.04   6.7 103.1
FunUSSmMdInst nr  10.24 -0.17  10.9 132.8
GNMA Sel n        10.55  0.00   0.2  20.0
HlthCare n        18.33 -0.11   4.4  55.0
Intl Sel nr       15.80 -0.18   8.1  49.4
IntlMstrI n       18.05 -0.18   9.6  84.5
IntlMstr S nr     18.04 -0.17   9.7  85.3
MT AllEq n        12.28 -0.12   8.0  71.2
MT Bal n          15.75 -0.08   4.9  50.5
MT Gro n          17.39 -0.12   6.4  61.1
PremIncInst nr    10.49  0.00   0.7  31.3
S&P Sel n         20.93 -0.03   6.9  72.6
SmCp Sel nr       20.88 -0.46   9.8 107.2
TotBd n            9.61  0.00   0.5  20.8
TSM Sel nr        24.34 -0.08   7.6  77.5
TxFrBd n          11.94  0.00   1.8  23.3
```

Barron's © 2012

LU 21–3a	EXTRA PRACTICE QUIZ WITH WORKED-OUT SOLUTIONS

Need more practice? Try this **Extra Practice Quiz** (check figures in the Interactive Chapter Organizer). Worked-out Solutions can be found in Appendix B at end of text.

From the mutual fund quotation of the Principal Investor High Yield A Fund shown below, complete the following:

1.   NAV

   _____

2.   NAV change

   _____

3.   Total return, YTD

   _____

4.   You are interested in earning $8,000 each year on a no-load 4% yield mutual fund. How much must you invest?

```
Principal Investors:
BdMtgIn        10.79  0.02   1.6  45.2
DivIntlInst     9.55 -0.12   8.0  54.9
EqInclA p      18.71 -0.15   5.0  70.5
FlIncA p       11.59 -0.01   3.4  43.5
GvtHiQltyA     11.32  0.00   0.7  20.2
HighYldA p      7.61  0.00   3.8  66.3
HighYldC t      7.67  0.01   3.8  62.9
HiYld IN       10.50  0.03   3.9  74.7
InfPro IN       8.84  0.03   1.7  32.1
Intl I Inst    10.49 -0.16   9.0  45.1
LgGrIN          8.56  0.03   9.6  65.8
LgIndxI         9.40 -0.01   6.9  72.0
LgValIN         9.92 -0.06   6.6  60.8
LT2010In       11.54 -0.02   4.8  58.9
LT2020 In      11.99 -0.04   6.5  63.9
LT2020J t      11.95 -0.05   6.4  62.0
LT2030In       11.84 -0.06   7.1  67.0
LT2030J t      11.83 -0.06   7.1  64.9
LT2040I        11.99 -0.07   7.7  67.8
LT2050I        11.48 -0.07   8.1  68.6
LTStratI       10.99  0.00   3.2  44.9
MdGrIII Inst   11.30 -0.03  11.2 104.7
MdVaII In      13.50 -0.04   8.4  88.4
MidCpBldA      14.28 -0.05   6.6  93.0
PLgGr2I         8.22 -0.01   8.2  70.4
PreSecI         9.81  0.04   5.1  96.1
PtrLB In       10.07 -0.02   7.1  68.0
PtrLGI In       9.78  0.00  10.1  99.9
PtrLgVal IN    11.06 -0.03   7.9  63.0
PtrLV In       10.40 -0.03   7.0  58.4
SGI In         11.37 -0.17  10.9 121.8
SmCVII IN       9.92 -0.19   9.5  98.5
RealEstSecI    18.52 -0.47   6.1 132.9
SAMBalA p      13.20 -0.05   5.3  56.0
SAMBalC t      13.06 -0.05   5.2  52.6
SAMGrA p       14.09 -0.08   6.3  61.9
SAMGrC t       13.41 -0.09   6.2  58.1
StrGrw A p     15.49 -0.12   7.5  66.0
A p            40.20 -0.33   6.6  70.9
```

Barron's © 2012

INTERACTIVE CHAPTER ORGANIZER

Topic/Procedure/Formula	Examples	You try it*
Stock yield $$\dfrac{\text{Annual dividend per share}}{\text{Today's last price per share}}$$ (Round yield to nearest hundredth percent.)	Annual dividend, $.72 Today's last price, $42.375 $$\dfrac{\$.72}{\$42.375} = 1.70\%$$	**Calculate stock yield to nearest hundredth percent** Annual dividend, $.88 Today's closing price, $53.88
Price-earnings ratio $$PE = \dfrac{\text{Last price per share of stock}}{\text{Annual earnings per share}}$$ (Round answer to nearest whole number.)	From previous example: Last price, $42.375 Annual earnings per share, $4.24 $$\dfrac{\$42.375}{\$4.24} = 9.99 = 10$$	**Calculate PE ratio** From previous example: Closing price, $53.88 Annual earnings per share, $3.70

Dividends with cumulative preferred stock
Cumulative preferred stock is entitled to all dividends in arrears before common stock receives dividend.
	2017 dividend omitted; in 2018, $400,000 in dividends paid out. Preferred is cumulative at $.90 per share; 20,000 shares of preferred issued and 100,000 shares of common issued.
	To preferred:
	  20,000 shares × $.90 = $18,000
	In arrears 2017:
	  20,000 shares × .90 = 18,000
	  Dividend to preferred $36,000
	To common:
	  $364,000 ($400,000 − $36,000)
	$$\dfrac{\$364,000}{100,000 \text{ shares}} = \$3.64 \text{ dividend to common per share}$$
		Calculate dividends to preferred and common stock
		2017, no dividend
		2018, $300,000
		Preferred—$.80 cumulative, 30,000 shares issued
		Common—60,000 shares issued

Cost of a bond Bond prices are stated as a percent of the face value. Bonds selling for less than face value result in bond discounts. Bonds selling for more than face value result in bond premiums.	Bill purchases 5 $1,000, 12% bonds at closing price of $103\frac{1}{4}$. What is his cost (omitting commissions)? $103\frac{1}{4}\% = 103.25\% = 1.0325$ in decimal 1.0325 × $1,000 bond = $1,032.50 per bond 5 bonds × $1,032.50 = $5,162.50	**Calculate cost of bonds** 6 $1,000, 3% bonds at 102.25
Bond yield $$\dfrac{\text{Total annual interest of bond}}{\text{Total current cost of bond at closing}}$$ (Round to nearest tenth percent.)	Calculate bond yield from last example on one bond. $$\dfrac{\overset{(\$1,000 \times .12)}{\$120}}{\$1,032.50} = 11.6\%$$	**Calculate bond yield** 4% bond selling for $1,011.20
Mutual fund $$NAV = \dfrac{\begin{array}{c}\text{Current market value} \\ \text{of fund's investment}\end{array} - \begin{array}{c}\text{Current} \\ \text{liabilities}\end{array}}{\text{Number of shares outstanding}}$$	The NAV of the Scudder Income Bond Fund was $12.84. The NAV change was 0.01. What was the NAV yesterday? $12.83	**Calculate yesterday's NAV** Today—$12.44 Change—.05

KEY TERMS			
	Bond yield Bonds Cash dividend Common stocks Cumulative preferred stock Discount Dividends Dividends in arrears	Earnings per share (EPS) Mutual fund Net asset value (NAV) Odd lot PE ratio Preferred stock Premium Price-earnings ratio	Round lot Stock certificate Stock yield Stockbrokers Stockholders Stocks

Check Figures for Extra Practice Quizzes. (Worked-out Solutions are in Appendix B.)	LU 21–1a	LU 21–2a	LU 21–3a

	1. b. $.82 per share
	   c. $.07/$13.08 = .54%
	2. Pref. $48,000
	   Com. $162,000
		1. $5,012.50
		2. $$\dfrac{\$75}{\$1,002.50} = 7.48\%$$
			1. $7.61
			2. no change
			3. 3.8%
			4. $200,000

*Worked-out solutions are in Appendix B.

Critical Thinking Discussion Questions with Chapter Concept Check

1. Explain how to read a stock quotation. What are some of the red flags of buying stock?

2. What is the difference between odd and round lots? Explain why the commission on odd lots could be quite expensive.

3. Explain how to read a bond quote. What could be a drawback of investing in bonds?

4. Compare and contrast stock yields and bond yields. As a conservative investor, which option might be better? Defend your answer.

5. Explain what NAV means. What is the difference between a load and a no-load fund? How safe are mutual funds?

6. **Chapter Concept Check.** Determine what you would invest in today if you were building a portfolio. Keep in mind your age, marital status, and the financial goals you want to achieve. Use the concepts in this chapter to develop your investment strategy.

Classroom Notes

Check figures for odd-numbered problems in Appendix C.   Name _____ Date _____

DRILL PROBLEMS

Calculate the cost (omit commission) of buying the following shares of stock: *LU 21-1(1)*

21–1. 400 shares of General Mills at $55.80

21–2. 1,200 shares of Apple at $125.50

Calculate the yield of each of the following stocks (rounded to the nearest tenth percent):   *LU 21-1(1)*

Company	Yearly dividend	Closing price per share	Yield
21–3. Boeing	$.68	$64.63	____
21–4. Best Buy	$.07	$9.56	___

Calculate the price-earnings ratio (21-5) and closing price per share (21-6) (to nearest whole number) or stock price as needed: *LU 21-1(1)*

Company	Earnings per share	Closing price per share	Price-earnings ratio
21–5. BellSouth	$3.15	$40.13	____
21–6. American Express	$3.85	_____	26

21–7. Calculate the total cost of buying 400 shares of CVS at $102.90. Assume a 2% commission.   *LU 21-1(1)*

21–8. If in Problem 21–1 the 400 shares of General Mills stock were sold at $50, what would be the loss? Commission is omitted.   *LU 21-1(1)*

21–9. Given: 20,000 shares cumulative preferred stock ($2.25 dividend per share); 40,000 shares common stock. Dividends paid: 2015, $8,000; 2016, 0; and 2017, $160,000. How much will preferred and common stockholders receive each year?   *LU 21-1(2)*

For each of these bonds, calculate the total dollar amount you would pay at the quoted price (disregard commission or any interest that may have accrued):   *LU 21-2(1)*

Company	Bond price	Number of bonds purchased	Dollar amount of purchase price
21–10. Petro	87.75	3	_____
21–11. Wang	114	2	_____

For the following bonds, calculate the total annual interest, total cost, and current yield (to the nearest tenth percent):   *LU 21-2(2)*

	Bond	Number of bonds purchased	Selling price	Total annual interest	Total cost	Current yield
21–12.	Sharn $11\frac{3}{4}$ 12	2	115	_____	_____	_____
21–13.	Wang $6\frac{1}{2}$ 14	4	68.125	_____	_____	_____

21–14.   From the following calculate the net asset values. Round to the nearest cent.   *LU 21-3(1)*

	Current market value of fund investment	Current liabilities	Number of shares outstanding	NAV
a.	$5,550,000	$770,000	600,000	_____
b.	$13,560,000	$780,000	840,000	_____

21–15.   From the following mutual fund quotation, complete the blanks: *LU 21-3(2)*

				TOTAL RETURN		
	Inv. obj.	NAV	NAV chg.	YTD	4 wks.	1 yr.
EuGr	ITL	12.04	−0.06	+8.2	+0.9	+9.6

NAV   _____   NAV change   _____

Total return, 1 year   _____

WORD PROBLEMS

21–16.   Ryan Neal bought 1,200 shares of Ford at $15.98 per share. Assume a commission of 2% of the purchase price. What is the
eXcel   total cost to Ryan?   *LU 21-1(1)*

21–17.   Assume in Problem 21–16 that Ryan sells the stock for $22.25 with the same 2% commission rate. What is the bottom line
eXcel   for Ryan?   *LU 21-1(1)*

21–18.   Jim Corporation pays its cumulative preferred stockholders $1.60 per share. Jim has 30,000 shares of preferred and 75,000
eXcel   shares of common. In 2015, 2016, and 2017, due to slowdowns in the economy, Jim paid no dividends. Now in 2018, the
board of directors decided to pay out $500,000 in dividends. How much of the $500,000 does each class of stock receive
as dividends?   *LU 21-1(2)*

21–19. Maytag Company earns $4.80 per share. Today the stock is trading at $59.25. The company pays an annual dividend of
e**X**cel $1.40. Calculate **(a)** the price-earnings ratio (rounded to the nearest whole number) and **(b)** the yield on the stock (to the nearest tenth percent).   *LU 21-1(1)*

21–20. Jimmy Comfort was interested in pursuing a second career after retiring from the military. He signed up with Twitter to
e**X**cel help network with individuals in his field. Within 1 week, he received an offer from a colleague to join her start-up business in Atlanta, Georgia. Along with his salary, he receives 100 shares of stock each month. If the stock is worth $4.50 a share, what is the value of the 100 shares he receives each month?   *LU 21-1(1, 2)*

21–21. The following bond was quoted in *The Wall Street Journal:*   *LU 21-2(1)*

Bonds	Curr. yld.	Vol.	Close	Net chg.
NJ 4.125 35	3.5	5	96.875	$+1\frac{1}{2}$

Five bonds were purchased yesterday, and 5 bonds were purchased today. How much more did the 5 bonds cost today (in dollars)?

21–22. DailyFinance.com reported one $40 share of Coca-Cola's stock bought in 1919, with dividends reinvested, would be worth $9.8 million today. If the price-earnings ratio was 28.42 at that time, what were the annual earnings per share? Round to the nearest cent.   *LU 21-1(1)*

21–23. Dairy Queen, as part of Warren Buffet's Berkshire Hathaway (BRKA) with 6,400 locations in the USA, gave away free ice cream cones to celebrate its 75th anniversary. If Warren Buffet has a bond bought at 105.25 at $4\frac{3}{4}$ 25, what is the current yield to the nearest percent?   *LU 21-2(2)*

21–24. Abby Sane decided to buy corporate bonds instead of stock. She desired to have the fixed-interest payments. She purchased 5 bonds of Meg Corporation $11\frac{3}{4}$ 09 at 88.25. As the stockbroker for Abby (assume you charge her a $5 commission per bond), please provide her with the following: **(a)** the total cost of the purchase, **(b)** total annual interest to be received, and **(c)** current yield (to nearest tenth percent).   *LU 21-2(1)*

21–25. Mary Blake is considering whether to buy stocks or bonds. She has a good understanding of the pros and cons of both. The
e**X**cel stock she is looking at is trading at $59.25, with an annual dividend of $3.99. Meanwhile, the bond is trading at 96.25, with an annual interest rate of $11\frac{1}{2}\%$. Calculate for Mary her yield (to the nearest tenth percent) for the stock and the bond.   *LU 21-1(1), LU 21-2(1)*

21–26. Wall Street performs a sort of "financial alchemy" enabling individuals to benefit from institutions lending money to them, according to Adam Davidson, cofounder of NPR's "Planet Money." Individuals can invest small amounts of their money in a 401(k), pooling their capital and spreading the risk. If you invested in Fidelity New Millennium, FMILX, one of the "10 Best Rated Funds" by *The Street,* how much would you pay for 80 shares if the 52-week high is $32.26, the 52-week low is $26.38, and the NAV is $31.88?   *LU 21-3(1)*

21–27. Louis Hall read in the paper that Fidelity Growth Fund has an NAV of $16.02. He called Fidelity and asked how the NAV was calculated. Fidelity gave him the following information:

Current market value of fund investment	$8,550,000
Current liabilities	$ 860,000
Number of shares outstanding	480,000

Did Fidelity provide Louis with the correct information?   *LU 21-3(1)*

21–28. Lee Ray bought 130 shares of a mutual fund with an NAV of $13.10. This fund also has a load charge of $8\frac{1}{2}\%$. **(a)** What is the offer price and **(b)** what did Lee pay for his investment?   *LU 21-3(1)*

21–29. Ron and Madeleine Couple received their 2016 Form 1099-DIV (dividends received) in the amount of $1,585. Ron and Madeleine are in the 28% bracket. What would be their tax liability on the dividends received?   *LU 21-1(2)*

CHALLENGE PROBLEMS

21–30. Here's an example of how breakpoint discounts on sales commissions for mutual fund investors work:
Sales charge

> Less than $25,000, 5.75%
> $25,000 to $49,999, 5.50%
> $50,000 to 99,999, 4.75%
> $100,000 to $249,999, 3.75%

Nancy Dolan is interested in the T Rowe Price Mid Cap Fund. Assume the NAV is 19.43. **(a)** What minimum amount of shares must Nancy purchase to have a sales charge of 5.50%? **(b)** What are the minimum shares Nancy must purchase to have a sales charge of 4.75%? **(c)** What are the minimum shares Nancy must purchase to have a sales charge of 3.75%? **(d)** What would be the total purchase price for **(a)**, **(b)**, or **(c)**? Round up to the nearest share even if it is less than 5. *LU 21-3(1)*

21–31. On September 6, Irene Westing purchased one bond of Mick Corporation at 98.50. The bond pays $8\frac{3}{4}$ interest on June 1 and December 1. The stockbroker told Irene that she would have to pay the accrued interest and the market price of the bond and a $6 brokerage fee. What was the total purchase price for Irene? Assume a 360-day year (each month is 30 days) in calculating the accrued interest. (*Hint:* Final cost = Cost of bond + Accrued interest + Brokerage fee. Calculate time for accrued interest.) *LU 21-2(2)*

 SUMMARY PRACTICE TEST

Do you need help? The videos in Connect have step-by-step worked-out solutions. These videos are also available on YouTube!

1. Russell Slater bought 700 shares of Disney stock at $106.50 per share. Assume a commission of 4% of the purchase price. What is the total cost to Russell? *LU 21-1(1)*

2. HM Company earns $2.50 per share. Today, the stock is trading at $18.99. The company pays an annual dividend of $.25. Calculate **(a)** the price-earnings ratio (to the nearest whole number) and **(b)** the yield on the stock (to the nearest tenth percent). *LU 21-1(1)*

3. The stock of Aware is trading at $4.90. The price-earnings ratio is 4 times earnings. Calculate the earnings per share (to the nearest cent) for Aware. *LU 21-1(1)*

4. Tom Fox bought 8 bonds of UXY Company $3\frac{1}{2}$ 09 at 84 and 4 bonds of Foot Company $4\frac{1}{8}$ 10 at 93. Assume the commission on the bonds is $3 per bond. What was the total cost of all the purchases? *LU 21-2(1)*

5. Leah Long bought one bond of Vick Company for 147. The original bond was 8.25 10. Leah wants to know the current yield to the nearest tenth percent. Help Leah with the calculation. *LU 21-2(2)*

6. Cumulative preferred stockholders of Rale Company receive $.80 per share. The company has 70,000 shares outstanding. For the last 9 years, Rale paid no dividends. This year, Rale paid $400,000 in dividends. What is the amount of dividends in arrears that is still owed to preferred stockholders? *LU 21-1(2)*

7. Bill Roundy bought 800 shares of a mutual fund with an NAV of $14.10. This fund has a load charge of 3%. **(a)** What is the offer price and **(b)** what did Bill pay for the investment? *LU 21-3(1)*

SURF TO SAVE

Investments can really pay off! 🔍

PROBLEM 1
Take note!

Go to http://www.treasurydirect.gov/indiv/research/indepth/tnotes/res_tnote_rates.htm. Look up the price and stated interest (coupon) on a 10-year Treasury note. What is the amount of annual interest on a $1,000 face value bond and what is the bond yield? Explain why the bond is selling at a premium or a discount.

Discussion Questions

1. Are these bonds a good investment? Why or why not?

2. What is the advantage to the U.S. government in issuing these Treasury notes?

PROBLEM 2
Social ups and downs

Visit http://finance.yahoo.com and search for Facebook, Inc. (stock symbol FB). Select the "1y" on the stock price graph to bring up the historical price of the stock over the past year. Compare the current price to the price of the stock 1 year ago today. (If either day falls on a weekend, use the preceding Friday.) What percent change in value has the stock had?

Discussion Questions

1. What do you feel contributed to this change in price for this particular stock?

2. Would you feel comfortable purchasing 1,000 shares of this stock at today's price? Why or why not?

PROBLEM 3
DJIA changes over time

Go to http://money.cnn.com/ and investigate the Dow Jones averages for the past 5 years. What was the lowest point value of the Dow? When did that occur? What was the highest point value? When did that occur?

Discussion Questions

1. What do you feel has caused this change to the Dow Jones?

2. Based upon the past 5 years and the performance of the Dow Jones, what do you predict to happen over the next 10 years? Why?

PROBLEM 4
NASDAQ versus NYSE

Go to http://www.nasdaq.com, pick five stocks on the NASDAQ, and then go to word http://www.nyse.com and pick five stocks on the NYSE. Which set of stocks would return a better investment if it continued on the same trend as the present?

Discussion Questions

1. Why would a stock be listed on the NASDAQ versus the NYSE?

2. What characteristics would you look for in a stock before purchasing?

MOBILE APPS ✕

Stock Market HD (Lifelike Apps, Inc.) Tracks stocks during or after market hours from both NASDAQ and NYSE.

Investopedia (Investopedia) Provides financial term definitions to educate investors.

PERSONAL FINANCE

A KIPLINGER APPROACH

By Anne Kates Smith, From *Kiplinger's Personal Finance*, March 10, 2015.

INSIDER INTERVIEW   **JIM STACK**

A Top Strategist Says Trouble Is Looming

A downturn isn't imminent, says Jim Stack, but with the bull market in its seventh year, caution is warranted.

JIM STACK watches Wall Street like a hawk, from a perch 2,200 miles away on the shores of Montana's stunning Whitefish Lake. Stack, publisher of a newsletter called *InvesTech Research* and the president of Stack Financial Management, an investment firm, maintains more than a century's worth of market data that helps him forge a "safety first" strategy. With the bull market having turned 6 on March 9, Stack has turned cautious. In this edited interview, he explains what could make him into a full-fledged bear.

KIPLINGER'S: You've become increasingly nervous about the stock market. Why?
STACK: Every economic recovery and every bull market start out with widespread fears and doubt in the early years. But as the recovery and bull market mature, that doubt dissipates and those fears turn into optimism or even complacency. We're starting to see that today. Remember that, by definition, bull markets peak when optimism is highest.

Is a bear market looming? We don't have those warning flags that appeared back in 2007 before the market top or in the late '90s during the tech bubble. But by historical comparisons, we are most likely in the latter third of this bull market. This is now the fourth-longest bull market in 85 years, and stock prices have tripled from the bottom.

What warning signs are you looking for? Today, you've got a strong dollar and long-term bond yields that were recently near multigenerational lows. Plus, the Federal Reserve has not even announced when it's going to start bringing up short-term interest rates. All three of those factors could change in 2015, providing significant headwinds to this bull market. If we see an unexpected drop in consumer confidence, we will treat it as a warning flag. Finally, we'll be looking for internal technical warning flags from the mar-

ket itself—for example, the breadth of the advance. If fewer and fewer stocks rise, it's a classic warning flag of a deteriorating market.

Are stocks overpriced? It's very difficult to find attractive values, and by some measures, price-earnings multiples are at historical highs. If interest rates are factored into the equation, the market is slightly undervalued. But the dependence on low rates to justify current valuations may make this one of the most interest-rate-sensitive markets ever.

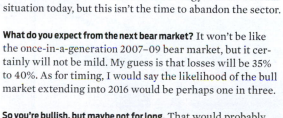

As nervous as you are, you still have a lot of your assets in stocks. We just reduced our allocation to 76%. That's our lowest allocation since the start of the bull market, and down from our peak of 96% in 2009. Why have we reduced our allocation when the economy is hitting on all cylinders? And in the absence of any definitive bear-market warning flags? The answer is simply that you shouldn't have the same investment strategy going into the seventh year of a bull market as you do in the early years.

What's the best strategy now? You can manage risk in two ways: by adjusting your portfolio's allocation to stocks, and by adjusting sector holdings. Technology, health care, industrial and energy stocks typically perform well in the final third of a bull market. Energy is in an unusual situation today, but this isn't the time to abandon the sector.

What do you expect from the next bear market? It won't be like the once-in-a-generation 2007–09 bear market, but it certainly will not be mild. My guess is that losses will be 35% to 40%. As for timing, I would say the likelihood of the bull market extending into 2016 would be perhaps one in three.

So you're bullish, but maybe not for long. That would probably be the best way to call it. I don't try to second-guess the end of a bull market, but at the same time, as a market historian with 40 years in the business, I feel the end is coming. I've just learned to trust that gut feeling. **ANNE KATES SMITH**

TREVON BAKER

BUSINESS MATH ISSUE

In the short run, the stock market always goes up.

1. List the key points of the article and information to support your position.
2. Write a group defense of your position using math calculations to support your view.

CHAPTER 22

Business Statistics

FRAZZ © 2014 Jef Mallett. Dist. By ANDREWS MCMEEL SYNDICATION. Reprinted with permission. All rights reserved.

© Trinette Reed/Blend Images LLC

Cash Flow

A sampling of major metropolitan markets with a high percentage of all-cash home sales.

Market	Median sale price	Percentage of sale that were all cash
Washington-Arlington-Alexandria, D.C.-Va.-Md.-W.Va.	$399,000	15.6%
Denver-Aurora-Lakewood, Colo.	$281,000	18.4%
San Jose-Sunnyvale-Santa Clara, Calif.	$728,000	20.2%
Boston	$405,000	21.8%
Seattle-Bellevue-Everett, Wash.	$383,962	22.5%
Montgomery County-Bucks County-Chester County, Pa.	$295,000	22.9%
Los Angeles-Long Beach-Glendale, Calif.	$460,000	26.0%
San Francisco-Redwood City-South San Francisco, Calif.	$890,000	27.1%
Bridgeport-Stamford-Norwalk, Conn.	$438,475	30.3%
Urban Honolulu, Hawaii	$494,000	31.8%
New York-Jersey City-White Plains, N.V.-N.J.	$400,100	46.5%
Nassau County-Suffolk County, N.Y.	$391,400	51.2

Source: CoreLogic

Source: *The Wall Street Journal*, 10/10/14.

LU 22–1: Mean, Median, and Mode

1. Define and calculate the mean.
2. Explain and calculate a weighted mean.
3. Define and calculate the median.
4. Define and identify the mode.

LU 22–2: Frequency Distributions and Graphs

1. Prepare a frequency distribution.
2. Prepare bar, line, and circle graphs.
3. Calculate price relatives and cost comparisons.

LU 22–3: Measures of Dispersion (Optional)

1. Explain and calculate the range.
2. Define and calculate the standard deviation.
3. Estimate percentage of data by using standard deviations.

VOCABULARY PREVIEW

Here are key terms in this chapter. After completing the chapter, if you know the term, place a checkmark in the box. If you don't know the term, look it up and put the page number where it can be found.

Bar graph ☐ Circle graph ☐ Empirical Rule ☐ Frequency distribution ☐ Index numbers ☐ Line graph ☐ Mean ☐ Measure of dispersion ☐ Median ☐ Mode ☐ Normal distribution ☐ Price relative ☐ Range ☐ Standard deviation ☐ Weighted mean ☐

In this chapter we look at various techniques that analyze and graphically represent business statistics. For example, in the chapter opener clipping we see the median sale price of all-cash home sales in major markets. Learning Unit 22–1 discusses the mean, median, and mode. Learning Unit 22–2 explains how to gather data by using frequency distributions and express these data visually in graphs. Emphasis is placed on whether graphs are indeed giving accurate information. The chapter concludes with an introduction to index numbers—an application of statistics—and an optional learning unit on measures of dispersion.

Learning Unit 22–1: Mean, Median, and Mode

Companies frequently use averages and measurements to guide their business decisions. The mean and median are the two most common averages used to indicate a single value that represents an entire group of numbers. The mode can also be used to describe a set of data.

Mean

The accountant of Bill's Sport Shop told Bill, the owner, that the average daily sales for the week were $150.14. The accountant stressed that $150.14 was an average and did not represent specific daily sales. Bill wanted to know how the accountant arrived at $150.14.

The accountant went on to explain that he used an arithmetic average, or **mean** (a measurement), to arrive at $150.14 (rounded to the nearest hundredth). He showed Bill the following formula:

$$\text{Mean} = \frac{\text{Sum of all values}}{\text{Number of values}}$$

The accountant used the following data:

	Sun.	Mon.	Tues.	Wed.	Thur.	Fri.	Sat.
Sport Shop sales	$400	$100	$68	$115	$120	$68	$180

To compute the mean, the accountant used these data:

$$\text{Mean} = \frac{\$400 + \$100 + \$68 + \$115 + \$120 + \$68 + \$180}{7} = \$150.14$$

LO 2

When values appear more than once, businesses often look for a **weighted mean.** The format for the weighted mean is slightly different from that for the mean. The concept, however, is the same except that you weight each value by how often it occurs (its frequency). Thus, considering the frequency of the occurrence of each value allows a weighting of each day's sales in proper importance. To calculate the weighted mean, use the following formula:

$$\text{Weighted mean} = \frac{\text{Sum of products}}{\text{Sum of frequencies}}$$

Let's change the sales data for Bill's Sport Shop and see how to calculate a weighted mean:

	Sun.	Mon.	Tues.	Wed.	Thur.	Fri.	Sat.
Sport Shop sales	$400	$100	$100	$80	$80	$100	$400

Value	Frequency	Product
$400	2	$ 800
100	3	300
80	2	160
		$1,260

The weighted mean is $\dfrac{\$1,260}{7} = \$180$

Note how we multiply each value by its frequency of occurrence to arrive at the product. Then we divide the sum of the products by the sum of the frequencies.

When you calculate your grade point average (GPA), you are using a weighted average. The following formula is used to calculate GPA:

$$\text{GPA} = \frac{\text{Total points}}{\text{Total credits}}$$

Now let's show how Jill Rivers calculated her GPA to the nearest tenth.

Given   A = 4; B = 3; C = 2; D = 1; F = 0

Courses	Credits attempted	Grade received	Points (Credits × Grade)
Introduction to Computers	4	A	16 (4 × 4)
Psychology	3	B	9 (3 × 3)
English Composition	3	B	9 (3 × 3)
Business Law	3	C	6 (2 × 3)
Business Math	3	B	9 (3 × 3)
	16		49 $\dfrac{49}{16} = 3.1$

When high or low numbers do not significantly affect a list of numbers, the mean is a good indicator of the center of the data. If high or low numbers do have an effect, the median may be a better indicator to use.

LO 3

Median

The **median** is another measurement that indicates the center of the data. An average that has one or more extreme values is not distorted by the median. For example, let's look at the following yearly salaries of the employees of Rusty's Clothing Shop.

Alice Knight	$95,000	Jane Wang	$67,000
Jane Hess	27,000	Bill Joy	40,000
Joel Floyd	32,000		

Note how Alice's salary of $95,000 will distort an average calculated by the mean.

$$\frac{\$95,000 + \$27,000 + \$32,000 + \$67,000 + \$40,000}{5} = \boxed{\$52,200}$$

The $52,200 average salary is considerably more than the salary of three of the employees. So it is not a good representation of the store's average salary. The following *Wall Street Journal* clip "Flattening Out" shows that the median income for men plateaus when they are in their late 40s. How was that conclusion reached? We use the following steps to find the median of a group of numbers.

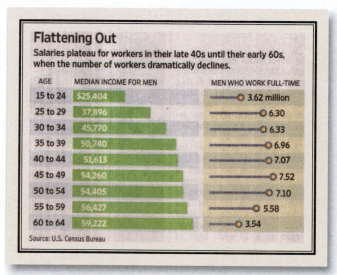

Reprinted by permission of *The Wall Street Journal*, copyright 2011 Dow Jones & Company, Inc. All rights reserved worldwide.

FINDING THE MEDIAN OF A GROUP OF VALUES

Step 1. Orderly arrange values from the smallest to the largest.

Step 2. Find the middle value.

    a. *Odd number of values:* Median is the middle value. You find this by first dividing the total number of numbers by 2. The next-higher number is the median.

    b. *Even number of values:* Median is the average of the two middle values.

For Rusty's Clothing Shop, we find the median as follows:

1. Arrange values from smallest to largest:

    $27,000; $32,000; $40,000 ; $67,000; $95,000

2. Since we have a total number of five values and 5 is an odd number, we divide 5 by 2 to get $2\frac{1}{2}$. The next-higher number is 3, so our median is the third-listed number, $40,000.

If Jane Hess ($27,000) were not on the payroll, we would find the median as follows:

1. Arrange values from smallest to largest:
$32,000; $40,000; $67,000; $95,000

2. Average the two middle values:
$$\frac{\$40,000 + \$67,000}{2} = \$53,500$$

Note that the median results in two salaries below and two salaries above the average. Now we'll look at another measurement tool—the mode.

Mode

 LO 4

The **mode** is a measurement that also records values. In a series of numbers, the value that occurs most often is the mode. If all the values are different, there is no mode. If two or more numbers appear most often, you may have two or more modes. Note that we do not have to arrange the numbers in the lowest-to-highest order, although this could make it easier to find the mode.

EXAMPLE   3, 4, 5, 6, 3, 8, 9, 3, 5, 3

3 is the mode since it is listed 4 times.

Use a bar graph to find the mode if you do not have a list of the data set.

Now let's check your progress with a Practice Quiz.

MONEY tips
Create a list of all your accounts and passwords and ensure a survivor knows where to locate it in the event of death. Keep the list up to date.

LU 22–1   PRACTICE QUIZ

Complete this **Practice Quiz** to see how you are doing.

Barton Company's sales reps sold the following last month:

Sales rep	Sales volume	Sales rep	Sales volume
A	$16,500	C	$12,000
B	15,000	D	48,900

Calculate the mean and the median. Which is the better indicator of the center of the data? Is there a mode?

✓ Solutions

$$\text{Mean} = \frac{\$16,500 + \$15,000 + \$12,000 + \$48,900}{4} = \$23,100$$

$$\text{Median} = \frac{\$15,000 + \$16,500}{2} = \$15,750$$

$12,000, **$15,000, $16,500,** $48,900. Note how we arrange numbers from smallest to highest to calculate median.

For **extra help** from your authors–Sharon and Jeff–see the videos in Connect.

These videos are also available on YouTube!

Median is the better indicator since in calculating the mean, the $48,900 puts the average of $23,100 much too high. There is no mode.

LU 22–1a   EXTRA PRACTICE QUIZ WITH WORKED-OUT SOLUTIONS

Need more practice? Try this **Extra Practice Quiz** (check figures in the Interactive Chapter Organizer). Worked-out Solutions can be found in Appendix B at end of text.

Barton's Company sales reps sold the following last month:

Sales rep	Sales volume	Sales rep	Sales volume
A	$17,000	C	$11,000
B	14,000	D	51,000

Calculate the mean and median. Which is the better indicator of the center of the data? Is there a mode?

Learning Unit 22–2: Frequency Distributions and Graphs

In this unit you will learn how to gather data and illustrate these data. Today, computer software programs can make beautiful color graphics. But how accurate are these graphics? This *Wall Street Journal* clipping gives an example of graphics that did not agree with the numbers beneath them. The clipping reminds all readers to check the numbers illustrated by the graphics. This is an old clip that is still relevant today.

What's Wrong With this Picture? Utility's Glasses Are Never Empty

By Kathleen Deveny
Staff Reporter of The Wall Street Journal
When Les Waas, an investor in Philadelphia Suburban Corp., paged through the company's 1994 annual report, he was impressed by what he saw.

The water utility had used a series of charts to represent its revenues, net income and book value per share, among other results. Each figure was represented by the level of water in a glass. Each chart showed strong growth.

Then Mr. Waas looked a little more carefully. The bars in the chart seemed to indicate far more impressive growth than the numbers beneath them. A chart showing the growth in the number of Philadelphia Suburban's water customers, for ex-

Number of Metered Water Customers (thousands)

ample, seemed to indicate the company's customer base had more than tripled since 1990. But the numbers actually increased only 6.4%.

The reason for the disparity: The charts don't begin at zero. Even an empty glass in the accompanying chart would represent a customer base of 230,000.

Reprinted by permission of *The Wall Street Journal,* copyright 1995 Dow Jones & Company, Inc. All rights reserved worldwide.

LO 1

Collecting raw data and organizing the data is a prerequisite to presenting statistics graphically. Let's illustrate this by looking at the following example.

A computer industry consultant wants to know how much college freshmen are willing to spend to set up a computer in their dormitory rooms. After visiting a local college dorm, the consultant gathered the following data on the amount of money 20 students spent on computers:

Price of computer	Tally	Frequency
$ 1,000	ШТ	5
2,000	I	1
3,000	ШТ	5
4,000	I	1
5,000	II	2
6,000	II	2
7,000	I	1
8,000	I	1
9,000	I	1
10,000	I	1

$1,000 $7,000 $4,000 $1,000 $ 5,000 $1,000 $3,000
5,000 2,000 3,000 3,000 3,000 8,000 9,000
3,000 6,000 6,000 1,000 10,000 1,000

Note that these raw data are not arranged in any order. To make the data more meaningful, the consultant made the **frequency distribution** table. Think of this distribution table as a way to organize a list of numbers to show the patterns that may exist.

As you can see, 25% ($\frac{5}{20} = \frac{1}{4} = 25\%$) of the students spent $1,000 and another 25% spent $3,000. Only four students spent $7,000 or more.

Typically between 5 and 20 classes are used in a frequency distribution for ease in analyzing the data.

Now let's see how we can use bar graphs.

LO 2

Bar Graphs

Bar graphs help readers see the changes that have occurred over a period of time. This is especially true when the same type of data is repeatedly studied.

The following *Wall Street Journal* clipping, "One Hundred Candles," uses bar graphs to show the number of Americans age 100-plus up through 2050.

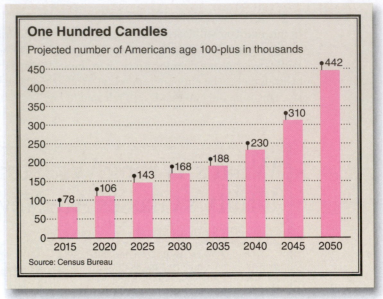

Source: *The Wall Street Journal.*

Let's return to our computer consultant example and make a bar graph of the computer purchases data collected by the consultant. Note that the height of the bar represents the frequency of each purchase. Bar graphs can be vertical or horizontal.

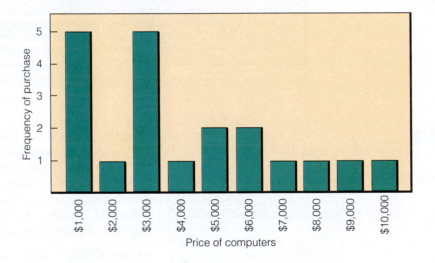

We can simplify this bar graph by grouping the prices of the computers. The grouping, or *intervals,* should be of equal sizes.

A bar graph for the grouped data follows.

Class	Frequency
$1,000–$3,000.99	11
3,001– 5,000.99	3
5,001– 7,000.99	3
7,001– 9,000.99	2
9,001– 11,000.99	1

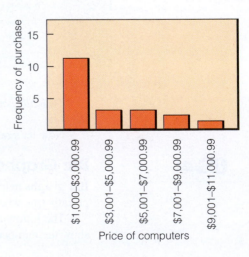

Next, let's see how we can use line graphs.

Line Graphs

A **line graph** shows trends over a period of time. Often separate lines are drawn to show the comparison between two or more trends.

The *Wall Street Journal* clip "Changing Landscape" shows trends up through 2018 of smartphone shipments versus PC shipments.

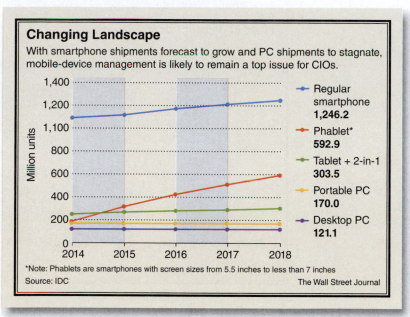

Source: *The Wall Street Journal*, 10/20/14.

We conclude our discussion of graphics with the use of the circle graph.

Circle Graphs

.15 × 360° =   54.0
.11 × 360° =   39.6
.36 × 360° = 129.6
.38 × 360° = 136.8
               360.0

Circle graphs, often called *pie charts,* are especially helpful for showing the relationship of parts to a whole. The entire circle represents 100%, or 360°; the pie-shaped pieces represent the subcategories. Note how the circle graph in the *Wall Street Journal* clipping "Threats From the Net" uses pie charts to show attitudes on cybersecurity.

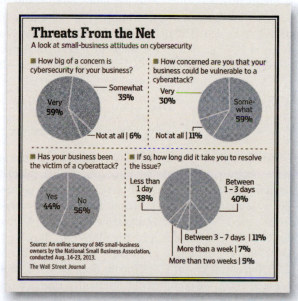

Reprinted by permission of *The Wall Street Journal*, copyright 2014 Dow Jones & Company, Inc. All rights reserved worldwide.

To draw a circle graph (or pie chart), begin by drawing a circle. Then take the percentages and convert each percentage to a decimal. Next multiply each decimal by 360° to get the degrees represented by the percentage. Circle graphs must total 360°. Note the following *Wall Street Journal* clip "An Enduring Challenge" shows the use of a pie chart.

You can use Excel, and many other software programs, to create graphs easily. Try it!

We conclude this unit with a brief discussion of index numbers.

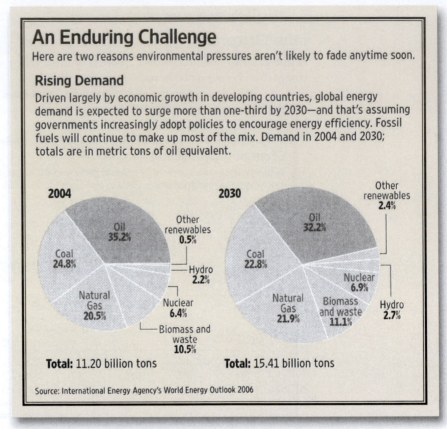

An Enduring Challenge
Here are two reasons environmental pressures aren't likely to fade anytime soon.

Rising Demand
Driven largely by economic growth in developing countries, global energy demand is expected to surge more than one-third by 2030—and that's assuming governments increasingly adopt policies to encourage energy efficiency. Fossil fuels will continue to make up most of the mix. Demand in 2004 and 2030; totals are in metric tons of oil equivalent.

2004
Oil 35.2%
Other renewables 0.5%
Coal 24.8%
Natural Gas 20.5%
Hydro 2.2%
Nuclear 6.4%
Biomass and waste 10.5%
Total: 11.20 billion tons

2030
Other renewables 2.4%
Oil 32.2%
Coal 22.8%
Natural Gas 21.9%
Nuclear 6.9%
Biomass and waste 11.1%
Hydro 2.7%
Total: 15.41 billion tons

Source: International Energy Agency's World Energy Outlook 2006

Reprinted by permission of *The Wall Street Journal,* copyright 2007 Dow Jones & Company, Inc. All rights reserved worldwide.

LO 3

An Application of Statistics: Index Numbers

The financial section of a newspaper often gives different index numbers describing the changes in business. These **index numbers** express the relative changes in a variable compared with some base, which is taken as 100. The changes may be measured from time to time or from place to place. Index numbers function as percents and are calculated like percents.

Frequently, a business will use index numbers to make comparisons of a current price relative to a given year. For example, a calculator may cost $9 today relative to a cost of $75 some 30 years ago. The **price relative** of the calculator is $\frac{\$9}{\$75} \times 100 = 12\%$. The calculator now costs 12% of what it cost some 30 years ago. A price relative, then, is the current price divided by some previous year's price—the base year—multiplied by 100.

$$\text{Price relative} = \frac{\text{Current price}}{\text{Base year's price}} \times 100$$

Index numbers can also be used to estimate current prices at various geographic locations. The frequently quoted Consumer Price Index (CPI), calculated and published monthly by the U.S. Bureau of Labor Statistics, records the price relative percentage cost of many goods and services nationwide compared to a base period. Table 22.1 gives a portion of the CPI that uses 1982–84 as its base period. Note that the table shows, for example, that the price relative for housing in Los Angeles is 139.3% of what it cost in 1982–84. Thus, Los Angeles housing costs amounting to $100.00 in 1982–84 now cost $139.30. So if you built a $90,000 house in 1982–84, it is worth $125,370 today. (Convert 139.3% to the decimal 1.393; multiply $90,000 by 1.393 = $125,370.)

Once again, we complete the unit with a Practice Quiz.

MONEY tips

Review your accounts annually to ensure the correct beneficiary is listed. All too often, the incorrect beneficiary is listed on life insurance policies, retirement accounts, and bank accounts.

TABLE 22.1

Consumer Price Index (in percent)

Expense	Atlanta	Chicago	New York	Los Angeles
Food	131.9	130.3	139.6	130.9
Housing	128.8	131.4	139.3	139.3
Clothing	133.8	124.3	121.8	126.4
Medical care	177.6	163.0	172.4	163.3

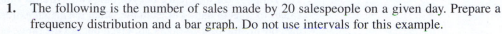

LU 22–2   **PRACTICE QUIZ**

Complete this **Practice Quiz** to see how you are doing.

1. The following is the number of sales made by 20 salespeople on a given day. Prepare a frequency distribution and a bar graph. Do not use intervals for this example.

5	8	9	1	4	4	0	3	2	8
8	9	5	1	9	6	7	5	9	10

2. Assuming the following market shares for diapers 5 years ago, prepare a circle graph:

Pampers	32%	Huggies	24%
Luvs	20%	Others	24%

3. Today a new Explorer costs $30,000. In 1991 the Explorer cost $19,000. What is the price relative? Round to the nearest tenth percent.

*For **extra help** from your authors–Sharon and Jeff–see the videos in Connect.*

These videos are also available on YouTube!

✓ **Solutions**

1.
Number of sales	Tally	Frequency
0	I	1
1	II	2
2	I	1
3	I	1
4	II	2
5	III	3
6	I	1
7	I	1
8	III	3
9	IIII	4
10	I	1

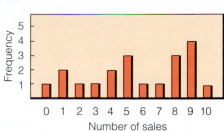

2.

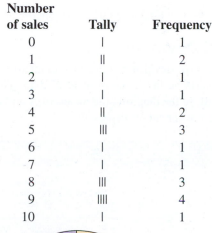

$.32 \times 360° = 115.20°$
$.20 \times 360° = 72.00°$
$.24 \times 360° = 86.40°$
$.24 \times 360° = 86.40°$

3. $\dfrac{\$30,000}{\$19,000} \times 100 = 157.9$

LU 22–2a   **EXTRA PRACTICE QUIZ WITH WORKED-OUT SOLUTIONS**

Need more practice? Try this **Extra Practice Quiz** (check figures in the **Interactive Chapter Organizer**). Worked-out Solutions can be found in Appendix B at end of text.

1. The following is the number of sales made by 20 salespeople on a given day. Prepare a frequency distribution and a bar graph. Do not use intervals for this example.

0	8	9	1	4	4	0	3	2	8
8	9	0	1	9	6	7	0	9	10

2. Assuming the following market shares for diapers 5 years ago, prepare a circle graph.

Pampers	40%	Huggies	25%
Luvs	20%	Others	15%

3. Today a new Explorer costs $35,000. In 1991, the Explorer cost $19,000. What is the price relative? Round to the nearest tenth percent.

Learning Unit 22–3: Measures of Dispersion (Optional)

In Learning Unit 22–1 you learned how companies use the mean, median, and mode to indicate a single value, or number, that represents an entire group of numbers, or data. Often it is valuable to know how the information is scattered (spread or dispersed) within a data set. A **measure of dispersion** is a number that describes how the numbers of a set of data are spread out or dispersed.

This learning unit discusses three measures of dispersion—range, standard deviation, and normal distribution. We begin with the range—the simplest measure of dispersion.

Range

The **range** is the difference between the two extreme values (highest and lowest) in a group of values or a set of data. For example, often the actual extreme values of hourly temperature readings during the past 24 hours are given but not the range or difference between the high and low readings. To find the range in a group of data, subtract the lowest value from the highest value.

> Range = Highest value − Lowest value

Thus, if the high temperature reading during the past 24 hours was 90° and the low temperature reading was 60° the range is 90° − 60°, or 30°. The range is limited in its application because it gives only a general idea of the spread of values in a data set.

EXAMPLE Find the range of the following values: 83.6, 77.3, 69.2, 93.1, 85.4, 71.6.

Range = 93.1 − 69.2 = 23.9

Standard Deviation

Since the **standard deviation** is intended to measure the spread of data around the mean, you must first determine the mean of a set of data. The following diagram shows two sets of data—A and B. In the diagram, the means of A and B are equal. Now look at how the data in these two sets are spread or dispersed.

Data set A	Data set B
x x x x x	x x x x
0 1 2 3 4 5 6 7 8 9 10 11 12 13	0 1 2 3 4 5 6 7 8 9 10 11 12 13
Mean = (1 + 2 + 5 + 10 + 12) ÷ 5 = 6	Mean = (4 + 4 + 5 + 8 + 9) ÷ 5 = 6

Note that although the means of data sets A and B are equal, A is more widely dispersed, which means B will have a smaller standard deviation than A.

A statistics calculator will allow you to calculate the mean, variance, standard deviation, and many more basic and advanced statistics calculations easily.

To find the standard deviation of an ungrouped set of data, use the following steps:

FINDING THE STANDARD DEVIATION

Step 1. Find the mean of the set of data.

Step 2. Subtract the mean from each piece of data to find each deviation.

Step 3. Square each deviation (multiply the deviation by itself).

Step 4. Sum all squared deviations.

Step 5. Divide the sum of the squared deviations by $n - 1$, where n equals the number of pieces of data.

Step 6. Find the square root ($\sqrt{\ }$) of the number obtained in Step 5 (use a calculator). This is the standard deviation. (The square root is a number that when multiplied by itself equals the amount shown inside the square root symbol.)

Two additional points should be made. First, Step 2 sometimes results in negative numbers. Since the sum of the deviations obtained in Step 2 should always be zero, we would not be able to find the average deviation. This is why we square each deviation—to generate positive quantities only. Second, the standard deviation we refer to is used with *sample* sets of data, that is, a collection of data from a population. The population is the *entire* collection of data. When the standard deviation for a population is calculated, the sum of the squared deviations is divided by n instead of by $n - 1$. In all problems that follow, sample sets of data are being examined.

EXAMPLE Calculate the standard deviations for the sample data sets A and B given in the previous diagram. Round the final answer to the nearest tenth. Note that Step 1—find the mean—is given in the diagram.

Standard deviation of data sets A and B: The table on the left uses Steps 2 through 6 to find the standard deviation of data set A, and the table on the right uses Steps 2 through 6 to find the standard deviation of data set B.

Data	Step 2 Data − Mean	Step 3 (Data − Mean)^2
1	1 − 6 = −5	25
2	2 − 6 = −4	16
5	5 − 6 = −1	1
10	10 − 6 = 4	16
12	12 − 6 = 6	36
	Total 0	94 **(Step 4)**

Step 5: Divide by $n - 1$: $\dfrac{94}{5 - 1} = \dfrac{94}{4} = 23.5$

Step 6: The square root of $\sqrt{23.5}$ is 4.8 (rounded).

The standard deviation of data set A is 4.8.

Data	Step 2 Data − Mean	Step 3 (Data − Mean)^2
4	4 − 6 = −2	4
4	4 − 6 = −2	4
5	5 − 6 = −1	1
8	8 − 6 = 2	4
9	9 − 6 = 3	9
	Total 0	22 **(Step 4)**

Step 5: Divide by $n - 1$: $\dfrac{22}{5 - 1} = \dfrac{22}{4} = 5.5$

Step 6: The square root of $\sqrt{5.5}$ is 2.3.

The standard deviation of data set B is 2.3.

As suspected, the standard deviation of data set B is less than that of set A. The standard deviation value reinforces what we see in the diagram.

LO 3

Normal Distribution

One of the most important distributions of data is the **normal distribution.** In a normal distribution, data are spread *symmetrically* about the mean. A graph of such a distribution looks like the bell-shaped curve in Figure 22.1. Many data sets are normally distributed. Examples are the life span of automobile engines, women's heights, and intelligence quotients.

FIGURE 22.1

Standard deviation and the normal distribution

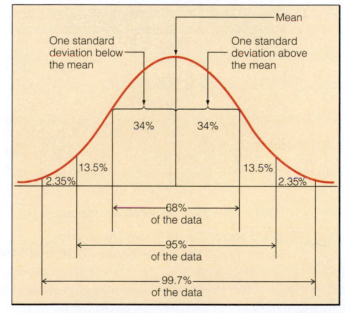

In a normal distribution, the mean, median, and mode are all equal. Additionally, when the data are normally distributed, the **Empirical Rule** (Three Sigma Rule) applies, stating that for a normal distribution, also known as a bell curve, approximately:

* 68% of the observations will fall within ± 1 standard deviation of the mean,

* 95% will fall within ± 2 standard deviations of the mean, and

* 99.7% will fall within ± 3 standard deviations of the mean.

Figure 22.1 above illustrates these facts.

EXAMPLE   Assume that the mean useful life of a particular lightbulb is 2,000 hours and is normally distributed with a standard deviation of 300 hours. Calculate the useful life of the lightbulb with **(a)** one standard deviation of the mean and **(b)** two standard deviations of the mean; also **(c)** calculate the percent of lightbulbs that will last 2,300 hours or longer.

MONEY tips 🌱

Start achieving financial security today! Reduce spending, pay off debt, and start saving. Set small milestones, increasing them as you reach each goal. It's worth the effort and will make tomorrow financially brighter.

a. The useful life of the lightbulb one standard deviation from the mean is one standard deviation above *and* below the mean.

$$2{,}000 \pm 300 = 1{,}700 \text{ and } 2{,}300 \text{ hours}$$

The useful life is somewhere between 1,700 and 2,300 hours.

b. The useful life of the lightbulb within two standard deviations of the mean is within two standard deviations above *and* below the mean.

$$2{,}000 \pm 2(300) = 1{,}400 \text{ and } 2{,}600 \text{ hours}$$

c. Since 50% of the data in a normal distribution lie below the mean and 34% represent the amount of data one standard deviation above the mean, we must calculate the percent of data that lie beyond one standard deviation above the mean.

$$100\% - (50\% + 34\%) = \boxed{16\%}$$

So 16% of the bulbs should last 2,300 hours or longer.

It's time for another Practice Quiz.

LU 22–3 | PRACTICE QUIZ

Complete this Practice Quiz to see how you are doing.

1. Calculate the range for the following data: 58, 13, 17, 26, 5, 41.
2. Calculate the variance and the standard deviation for the following sample set of data: 113, 92, 77, 125, 110, 93, 111. Round answers to the nearest tenth.
3. If the mean tax refund for the year is $3,000 with a $300 standard deviation, what is the refund range within three standard deviations above and below the mean?

For **extra help** from your authors–Sharon and Jeff–see the videos in Connect.

These videos are also available on YouTube!

✓ Solutions

1. $58 - 5 = \boxed{53 \text{ range}}$

2.

Data	Data − Mean	(Data − Mean)^2
113	113 − 103 = 10	100
92	92 − 103 = −11	121
77	77 − 103 = −26	676
125	125 − 103 = 22	484
110	110 − 103 = 7	49
93	93 − 103 = −10	100
111	111 − 103 = 8	64
	Total	1,594

$$1{,}594 \div (7 - 1) = \boxed{265.6666667} \text{ variance}$$

$$\sqrt{265.6666667} = \boxed{16.3} \text{ standard deviation}$$

3. $3,000 +/− ($300 \times 3) = $ Between $2,100 and $3,900

LU 22–3a | EXTRA PRACTICE QUIZ WITH WORKED-OUT SOLUTIONS

Need more practice? Try this Extra Practice Quiz (check figures in the Interactive Chapter Organizer). Worked-out Solutions can be found in Appendix B at end of text.

1. Calculate the range for the following data: 60, 13, 17, 26, 5, 41.
2. Calculate the variance and the standard deviation for the following sample set of data: 120, 88, 77, 125, 110, 93, 111. Round answers to the nearest tenth.
3. If the mean tax refund for the year is $2,000 with a $250 standard deviation, what is the refund range within two standard deviations above and below the mean?

INTERACTIVE CHAPTER ORGANIZER

Topic/Procedure/Formula	Examples	You try it*
Mean $\dfrac{\text{Sum of all values}}{\text{Number of values}}$	Age of team players: 22, 28, 31, 19, 15 $\text{Mean} = \dfrac{22 + 28 + 31 + 19 + 15}{5}$ $= \boxed{23}$	**Calculate mean** 41, 29, 16, 15, 18
Weighted mean $\dfrac{\text{Sum of products}}{\text{Sum of frequencies}}$		**Calculate weighted mean**

Weighted mean example:

	S.	M.	T.	W.	Th.	F.	S.
Sales	$90	$75	$80	$75	$80	$90	$90

Value	Frequency	Product
$90	3	$270
75	2	150
80	2	160
	7	$580

$\text{Mean} = \dfrac{\$580}{7} = \boxed{\$82.86}$

You try it — Calculate weighted mean:

	S.	M.	T.	W.	Th.	Fr.	S.
Sales	80	90	100	80	80	90	90

Topic/Procedure/Formula	Examples	You try it*

Median
1. Arrange values from smallest to largest.
2. Find the middle value.
  a. **Odd number of values:** median is middle value.
  $\left(\dfrac{\text{Total number of numbers}}{2}\right)$
  Next-higher number is median.
  b. **Even number of values:** average of two middle values.
	12, 15, 8, 6, 3
	1. 3 6 8 12 15
	2. $\dfrac{5}{2} = 2.5$
	Median is third number, $\boxed{8}$.
		Calculate median
		14, 16, 9, 7, 4

Mode Value that occurs most often in a set of numbers	6, 6, 8, 5, 6 Mode is 6	**Find mode** 7, 7, 4, 3, 2, 7
Frequency distribution Method of listing numbers or amounts not arranged in any particular way by columns for numbers (amounts), tally, and frequency	Number of sodas consumed in one day: 1, 5, 4, 3, 4, 2, 2, 3, 2, 0	**Prepare frequency distribution** Number of coffees consumed in one day: 1, 4, 5, 8, 2, 2, 3, 0

Frequency distribution example:

Number of sodas	Tally	Frequency
0	I	1
1	I	1
2	III	3
3	II	2
4	II	2
5	I	1

Topic/Procedure/Formula	Examples	You try it*
Bar graphs Height of bar represents frequency. Bar graph used for grouped data. Bar graphs can be vertical or horizontal.	From soda example above: 	**From coffee example above, prepare bar graph**
Line graphs Shows trend. Helps to put numbers in order.	**Sales** 2014 $1,000 2015 2,000 2016 3,000 	**Prepare line graph** **Sales** 2014 $5,000 2015 3,000 2016 2,000

(continues)

INTERACTIVE CHAPTER ORGANIZER

Topic/Procedure/Formula	Examples	You try it*

Circle graphs
Circle = 360°
% × 360° = Degrees of pie to represent percent
Total should = 360°

60% favor diet soda
40% favor sugared soda

Sugared 40%
Diet 60%

.60 × 360° = 216°
.40 × 360° = 144°
360°

Create circle graph
70% coffee drinkers
30% non-coffee-drinkers

Price relative

$$\text{Price relative} = \frac{\text{Current price}}{\text{Base year's price}} \times 100$$

A station wagon's sticker price was $8,799 in 1982. Today it is $14,900.

$$\text{Price relative} = \frac{\$14,900}{\$8,799} \times 100 = 169.3$$

(rounded to nearest tenth percent)

Calculate price relative
Old price, $ 9,000
Today's price,   12,000

Range (optional)
Range = Highest value − Lowest value

Calculate range of the data set consisting of 5, 9, 13, 2, 8
Range = 13 − 2 = 11

Calculate range
6, 8, 14, 2, 9

Standard deviation (optional)
1. Calculate mean.
2. Subtract mean from each piece of data.
3. Square each deviation.
4. Sum squares.
5. Divide sum of squares by $n - 1$, where n = number of pieces of data.
6. Take square root of number obtained in Step 5, to find the standard deviation.

Calculate the standard deviation of this set of data: 7, 2, 5, 3, 3.

1. Mean = $\frac{20}{5} = 4$

2. 7 − 4 = 3
   2 − 4 = −2
   5 − 4 = 1
   3 − 4 = −1
   3 − 4 = −1

3. $(3)^2 = 9$
    $(-2)^2 = 4$
    $(1)^2 = 1$
    $(-1)^2 = 1$
    $(-1)^2 = 1$

4.   16
5. 16 ÷ 4 = 4
6. Standard deviation = 2

Calculate standard deviation
8, 1, 6, 2, 2

KEY TERMS	Bar graph	Line graph	Normal distribution
	Circle graph	Mean	Price relative
	Empirical Rule	Measure of dispersion	Range
	Frequency distribution	Median	Standard deviation
	Index numbers	Mode	Weighted mean

Check Figures for Extra Practice Quizzes. (Worked-out Solutions are in Appendix B.)	LU 22–1a	LU 22–2a	LU 22–3a
	Mean $23,250	1. 9 1111 4	1. Range is 55.
	Median $15,500	2. Pampers 40% 144°	2. Standard deviation is 17.7.
	There is no mode.	3. 184.2%	3. Between $1,500 and $2,500

*Worked-out solutions are in Appendix B.

Critical Thinking Discussion Questions with Chapter Concept Check

1. Explain the mean, median, and mode. Give an example that shows you must be careful when you read statistics in an article.

2. Explain frequency distributions and the types of graphs. Locate a company annual report and explain how the company shows graphs to highlight its performance. Does the company need more or fewer of these visuals? Could price relatives be used?

3. Explain the statement that standard deviations are not accurate.

4. **Chapter Concept Check.** Visit the Apple website. Gather new statistics on the iPad, Apple Watch, and/or iPhone. Use concepts in this chapter for your presentation.

Classroom Notes

END-OF-CHAPTER PROBLEMS

Check figures for odd-numbered problems in Appendix C.   Name _____   Date _____

DRILL PROBLEMS (*Note:* Problems for optional Learning Unit 22–3 follow the Challenge Problem 22–24)

Calculate the mean (to the nearest hundredth):   *LU 22-1(1)*

22–1.   7, 8, 10, 6

22–2.   5, 4, 8, 12, 15

22–3. $55.83, $66.92, $108.93

22–4. $1,001, $68.50, $33.82, $581.95

22–5.   Calculate the grade point average: A = 4, B = 3, C = 2, D = 1, F = 0 (to nearest tenth).   *LU 22-1(2)*

eXcel

Courses	Credits	Grade
Computer Principles	3	B
Business Law	3	C
Logic	3	D
Biology	4	A
Marketing	3	B

22–6.   Find the weighted mean (to the nearest tenth):   *LU 22-1(2)*

Value	Frequency	Product
4	7	
8	3	
2	9	
4	2	

Find the median: *LU 22-1(3)*

22–7.   55, 10, 19, 38, 100, 25

22–8.   95, 103, 98, 62, 31, 15, 82

Find the mode: *LU 22-1(4)*

22–9.   8, 9, 3, 4, 12, 8, 8, 9

22–10.   22, 19, 15, 16, 18, 18, 5, 18

22–11.   Given: Truck cost   2012 $30,000
   Truck cost   2008 $21,000

Calculate the price relative (rounded to the nearest tenth percent).   *LU 22-2(3)*

22–12.   Given the following sales of Lowe Corporation, prepare a line graph (run sales from $5,000 to $20,000).   *LU 22-2(2)*

eXcel

2012	$ 8,000
2013	11,000
2014	13,000
2015	18,000

22–13. Prepare a frequency distribution from the following weekly salaries of teachers at Moore Community College. Use the following intervals: *LU 22-2(1)*

$200–$299.99
$300–$399.99
$400–$499.99
$500–$599.99

$210	$505	$310	$380	$275
290	480	550	490	200
286	410	305	444	368

22–14. Prepare a bar graph from the frequency distribution in Problem 22–13. *LU 22-2(2)*

22–15. How many degrees on a circle graph would each be given from the following? *LU 22-2(2)*

Wear digital watch	42%
Wear traditional watch	51
Wear no watch	7

WORD PROBLEMS

22–16. The first Super Bowl on January 15, 1967, charged $42,000 for a 30-second commercial. Create a line graph for the following Super Bowl 30-second commercial costs: 2007, $2,385,365; 2008, $2,699,963; 2009, $2,999,960; 2010, $2,954,010; 2011, $3,100,000; 2012, $3,500,000; 2013 and 2014, $4,000,000; and 2015, $4,500,000. *LU 22-2(2)*

22–17. The American Kennel Club announced the "Most Popular Dogs in the U.S. for 2015." Labrador retrievers remained number one for the 24th consecutive year. German shepherds came in second followed by Yorkshire terriers, golden retrievers, and beagles. Create a circle graph for Dogs for Life Kennel Club with the following members: 52 labrador retrievers, 33 German shepherds, 22 beagles, 15 golden retrievers, and 10 Yorkshire terriers. *LU 22-2(2)*

22–18. Despite tuition skyrocketing, a college education is still valuable. Recent calculations by the Federal Reserve Bank in San Francisco demonstrate a college degree is worth $800,000 in lifetime earnings compared to the average high school education. If graduates in 2017 earn $40,632, $35,554, $42,192, $33,432, $69,479 and $43,589, what is the standard deviation for this sample? Round to a whole number for each calculation. *LU 22-3(2)*

22–19. Costcotravel.com provided a member with the following information regarding her upcoming travel. Construct a circle graph for the member. *LU 22-2(2)*

Transportation	35%
Hotel	28
Food and entertainment	20
Miscellaneous	17

22–20. Jim Smith, a marketing student, observed how much each customer spent in a local convenience store. Based on the following results, prepare **(a)** a frequency distribution and **(b)** a bar graph. Use intervals of $0–$5.99, $6.00–$11.99, $12.00–$17.99, and $18.00–$23.99. *LU 22-2(2)*

$18.50	$18.24	$ 6.88	$9.95
16.10	3.55	14.10	6.80
12.11	3.82	2.10	
15.88	3.95	5.50	

22–21. Angie's Bakery bakes bagels. Find the weighted mean (to the nearest whole bagel) given the following daily production for June: *LU 22-1(2)*

200	150	200	150	200
150	190	360	360	150
190	190	190	200	150
360	400	400	150	200
400	360	150	400	360
400	400	200	150	150

22–22. The United Nations states the gender pay gap will not close for 70 years. Women across the world earn $0.77 for every $1.00 of what men earn. Construct a bar graph reflecting the following Harvard University study on pay for women based on $1.00 for men: financial specialists, $0.66; physicians, $0.71; aircraft pilots, $0.71; accountants, $0.76; lawyers, $0.82; and nurses, $0.89.   *LU 22-2(2)*

CHALLENGE PROBLEMS

22–23. Listed below are annual revenues for a few travel agencies:

AAA Travel Agency	$86,700,000
Riser Group	63,200,000
Casto Travel	62,900,000
Balboa Travel	36,200,000
Hunter Travel Managers	36,000,000

(a) What would be the mean and the median? **(b)** What is the total revenue percent of each agency? **(c)** Prepare a circle graph depicting the percents.   *LU 22-1(1, 2), LU 22-2(2)*

22–24. The following circle graph is a suggested budget for Ron Rye and his family for a month. Ron would like you to calculate the percent (to the hundredth) for each part of the circle graph along with the appropriate number of degrees.   *LU 22-2(2)*

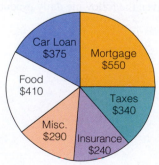

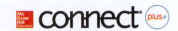
Name _____ Date _____

DRILL PROBLEMS

1. Calculate the range for the following set of data: 117, 98, 133, 52, 114, 35.   *LU 22-3(1)*

Calculate the standard deviation for the following sample sets of data. Round the final answers to the nearest tenth.   *LU 22-3(2)*

2. 83.6, 92.3, 56.5, 43.8, 77.1, 66.7

3. 7, 3, 12, 17, 5, 8, 9, 9, 13, 15, 6, 6, 4, 5

4. 41, 41, 38, 27, 53, 56, 28, 45, 47, 49, 55, 60

WORD PROBLEMS

5. The mean useful life of car batteries is 48 months. They have a standard deviation of 3. If the useful life of batteries is normally distributed, calculate **(a)** the percent of batteries with a useful life of less than 45 months and **(b)** the percent of batteries that will last longer than 54 months.   *LU 22-3(2)*

6. The average weight of a particular box of crackers is 24.5 ounces with a standard deviation of 0.8 ounce. The weights of the boxes are normally distributed. What percent of the boxes **(a)** weigh more than 22.9 ounces and **(b)** weigh less than 23.7 ounces?   *LU 22-3(2)*

7. An examination is normally distributed with a mean score of 77 and a standard deviation of 6. Find the percent of individuals scoring as indicated below.   *LU 22-3(2)*

   a. Between 71 and 83

   b. Between 83 and 65

   c. Above 89

   d. Less than 65

   e. Between 77 and 65

8. Listed below are the sales figures in thousands of dollars for a group of insurance salespeople. Calculate the mean sales figure and the standard deviation. *LU 22-3(1, 2)*

$117	$350	$400	$245	$420
223	275	516	265	135
486	320	285	374	190

9. The time in seconds it takes for 20 individual sewing machines to stitch a border onto a particular garment is listed below. Calculate the mean stitching time and the standard deviation to the nearest hundredth. *LU 22-3(1, 2)*

67	69	64	71	73
58	71	64	62	67
62	57	67	60	65
60	63	72	56	64

 SUMMARY PRACTICE TEST

Do you need help? The videos in Connect have step-by-step worked-out solutions. These videos are also available on YouTube!

1. In July, Lee Realty sold 10 homes at the following prices: $140,000; $166,000; $80,000; $98,000; $185,000; $150,000; $108,000; $114,000; $142,000; and $250,000. Calculate the mean and median. *LU 22-1(1, 3)*

eXcel

2. Lowes counted the number of customers entering the store for a week. The results were 1,100; 950; 1,100; 1,700; 880; 920; and 1,100. What is the mode? *LU 22-1(4)*

3. This semester Hung Lee took four 3-credit courses at Riverside Community College. She received an A in accounting and C's in history, psychology, and algebra. What is her cumulative grade point average (assume A = 4 and C = 2) to the nearest hundredth? *LU 22-1(2)*

4. Pete's Variety Shop reported the following sales for the first 20 days of May. Prepare a frequency distribution for Pete's. *LU 22-2(1)*

$100	$400	$600	$400	$600
100	600	300	500	700
200	600	700	500	200
100	600	100	700	700

5. Leeds Company produced the following number of maps during the first 5 weeks of last year. Prepare a bar graph.
e**X**cel *LU 22-2(2)*

Week	Maps
1	800
2	600
3	400
4	700
5	300

6. Laser Corporation reported record profits of 30%. It stated in the report that the cost of sales was 40% with expenses of 30%. Prepare a circle graph for Laser.   *LU 22-2(2)*

7. Today a new Explorer costs $39,900. In 1990, Explorers cost $24,000. What is the price relative to the nearest tenth percent?   *LU 22-2(3)*

*8. Calculate the standard deviation for the following set of data: 7, 2, 5, 3, 3, 10. Round the final answer to the nearest tenth.   *LU 22-3(2)*

*Optional problem.

SURF TO SAVE

Making sense with numbers 🔍

PROBLEM 1
Average performance

Visit your school's website to access your grades in classes you have completed up to this point. If you have not completed more than five courses, then use grades from your high school courses. Convert your letter grades to their numerical equivalent. Compute the mean and median for your grades.

Discussion Questions

1. What do these numbers tell you about your academic performance thus far?
2. What could you do to improve your grade average?

PROBLEM 2
What GDP "means" to me

Visit https://www.cia.gov/library/publications/the-world-factbook/ and choose a country from The World Factbook. Use the GDP (Gross Domestic Product) purchasing power parity and the population to calculate the mean GDP for this country. If this differs from the per capita GDP listed in The World Factbook, explain why.

Discussion Questions

1. What can GDP per capita tell us about the financial standing of a country?
2. How might a country's GDP influence the decision of foreign companies to do business within that country?

PROBLEM 3
Swinging for the money

Visit http://www.spotrac.com/mlb/rankings/. Calculate the range, mean, median, and mode of the top 10 MLB players' earnings.

Discussion Questions

1. How does the median compare to the highest-paid player?
2. How does the median compare to the lowest-paid player?

PROBLEM 4
Far and wide?

Track the time you spend commuting (driving, walking, bicycling, etc.) to work and/or school for 1 week. Record each trip as a separate time. Once you have recorded all of your commute times, calculate the mean and median for your commutes. Compare your answers with other students and discuss the differences.

Discussion Questions

1. What options are available for you to commute to school and work?
2. Based on your commute time analysis, would these other options increase or decrease your average commute time?

MOBILE APPS ❌

Calculator: Statistics (SaleCalc Software) Calculates basic statistics.

Mean, Median, Mode and Range Quiz Master (King Wong) Quickly calculates the mean, median, mode, and range of a set of numbers.

By Kimberly Lankford, From *Kiplinger's Personal Finance*, December 2013.

INSURANCE»

Make Long-Term Care More Affordable

We help you navigate the maze of choices to get the best deal. **BY KIMBERLY LANKFORD**

THE AVERAGE COST OF A PRIVATE room in a nursing home is now about $248 per day (or about $90,000 per year), and 12 hours a day of home care costs even more, according to the MetLife Mature Market Institute. But for many baby-boomers, it takes more than the threat of financial catastrophe to be prodded into buying a long-term-care insurance policy.

"If people have experience with family members needing care, they sign up immediately," says Ted Sarenski, a CPA and personal financial specialist in Syracuse, N.Y. "But if they don't, they worry that they are throwing their money away."

Sarenski recommends to clients in their fifties that they have some form of long-term-care coverage to protect their retirement savings. Until recently, people who bought policies generally got enough insurance to cover 100% of the cost of care. But insurers boosted their rates after paying more money in claims than they expected. Rates for new policies have shot up—especially for women buying on their own—and it has become a lot more difficult to qualify for coverage if you have health issues.

Sarenski helps his clients calculate how much of their savings they can afford to spend on long-term-care costs and still keep enough money for the other spouse to live on, possibly for decades. Then he recommends buying enough coverage to fill the

gap—usually at least half of the cost of care. Fortunately, insurers are offering new options that shift more risk to you but make policies less costly.

Buy his and her policies. Several major long-term-care insurers have switched from unisex to gender-differentiated pricing. Genworth, the largest long-term-care insurer, announced the change in late 2012, and John Hancock, Transamerica and Mutual of Omaha quickly followed suit.

In many cases, single women—who tend to live longer than men and are more likely to need care—now pay about 50% more than single men, says Claude Thau, a long-term-care insurance consultant in Overland Park, Kan. The rate hikes haven't been approved yet in some states, and a few insurers still offer unisex rates, especially for policies sold through employers.

Most insurers continue to offer discounts for couples of about 30%, says Thau. For example, Genworth's couples policies give women a big break.

For healthy 55-year-olds buying a policy with a three-year benefit period and a $150 daily benefit, plus 5% compound inflation protection, the cost is $2,190 a year for a single man and $2,966 for a single woman. But the price drops to $1,854 each if they buy as a couple.

OWEN DAVEY

BUSINESS MATH ISSUE

When you look at all of the statistics it is evident that long-term care is not worth the premiums.

1. List the key points of the article and information to support your position.
2. Write a group defense of your position using math calculations to support your view.

Learning Unit 1–1:   Reading, Writing, and Rounding Whole Numbers

DRILL PROBLEMS

1. Express the following numbers in verbal form:

a. 7,821 _____

b. 160,501 _____

c. 2,098,767 _____

d. 58,003 _____

e. 50,025,212,015 _____

2. Write in numeric form:

a. Eighty thousand, two hundred eighty-one _____

b. Fifty-eight thousand, three _____

c. Two hundred eighty thousand, five _____

d. Three million, ten _____

e. Sixty-seven thousand, seven hundred sixty _____

3. Round the following numbers:

a. To the nearest ten:

76 _____ 379 _____ 855 _____ 5,981 _____ 206 _____

b. To the nearest hundred:

9,664 _____ 2,074 _____ 888 _____ 271 _____ 75 _____

c. To the nearest thousand:

21,486 _____ 621 _____ 3,504 _____ 9,735 _____

4. Round off each number to the nearest ten, nearest hundred, nearest thousand, and round all the way. (Remember that you are rounding the original number each time.)

	Nearest ten	Nearest hundred	Nearest thousand	Round all the way
a. 4,752	_____	_____	_____	_____
b. 70,351	_____	_____	_____	_____
c. 9,386	_____	_____	_____	_____
d. 4,983	_____	_____	_____	_____
e. 408,119	_____	_____	_____	_____
f. 30,051	_____	_____	_____	_____

5. Name the place position (place value) of the underlined digit.

a. 8,<u>3</u>48 _____

b. <u>9</u>,734 _____

c. 3<u>4</u>7,107 _____

d. 72<u>3</u> _____

e. 28,2<u>0</u>0,000,121 _____

f. 706,359,00<u>5</u> _____

g. 27,5<u>6</u>3,530 _____

A

WORD PROBLEMS

6. Gim Smith was shopping for an Apple computer. He went to three different websites and found the computer he wanted at three different prices. At website A the price was $2,018, at website B the price was $1,985, and at website C the price was $2,030. What is the approximate price Gim will have to pay for the computer? Round to the nearest thousand. (Just one price.)

7. Amy Parker had to write a check at the bookstore when she purchased her books for the new semester. The total cost of the books was $564. How will she write this amount in verbal form on her check?

8. Matt Schaeffer was listening to the news and heard that steel production last week was one million, five hundred eighty-seven thousand tons. Express this amount in numeric form.

9. Jackie Martin is the city clerk and must go to the aldermen's meetings and take notes on what is discussed. At last night's meeting, they were discussing repairs for the public library, which will cost three hundred seventy-five thousand, nine hundred eighty-five dollars. Write this in numeric form as Jackie would.

10. A government survey revealed that 25,963,400 people are employed as office workers. To show the approximate number of office workers, round the number all the way.

11. Bob Donaldson wished to present his top student with a certificate of achievement at the end of the school year in 2016. To make it appear more official, he wanted to write the year in verbal form. How did he write the year?

12. Nancy Morrissey has a problem reading large numbers and determining place value. She asked her brother to name the place value of the 4 in the number 13,542,966. Can you tell Nancy the place value of the 4? What is the place value of the 3?

The 4 is in the _____ place.

The 3 is in the _____ place.

Learning Unit 1-2 :   Adding and Subtracting Whole Numbers

DRILL PROBLEMS

1. Add by totaling each separate column:

	a.	b.	c.	d.	e.	f.	g.	h.
	668	43	493	36	716	535	751	75,730
	338	58	826	76	458	107	378	48,531
		96		43	397	778	135	15,797
				24	139	215	747	
					478	391	368	

2. Estimate by rounding all the way, and then add the actual numbers:

a.		b.		c.	
580		1,470		475	
971		7,631		837	
548		4,383		213	
430				775	
506				432	

d.		e.		f.	
442		2,571		10,928	
609		3,625		9,321	
766		4,091		12,654	
410		928		15,492	
128					

3. Estimate by rounding all the way, and then subtract the actual numbers:

   a.   90
       − 38

   b.   91
       − 33

   c.   68
       − 59

   d.   981
     − 283

   e.   622
     − 328

   f. 1,125
     − 913

4. Subtract and check:

   a.   4,947
     − 4,362

   b.   3,724
     − 2,138

   c. 474,820
     − 85,847

   d. 50,000
     − 21,762

   e. 65,003
     − 24,987

   f. 15,715
     − 3,503

5. In the following sales report, total the rows and the columns, and then check that the grand total is the same both horizontally and vertically.

Salesperson	Region 1	Region 2	Region 3	Total
a. Becker	$ 5,692	$ 7,403	$ 3,591	
b. Edwards	7,652	7,590	3,021	
c. Graff	6,545	6,738	4,545	
d. Jackson	6,937	6,950	4,913	
e. Total				

WORD PROBLEMS

6. June Long owes $8,600 on her car loan for a new Chevy volt, plus interest of $620. How much will it cost her to pay off this loan?

7. Sales at Rich's Convenience Store were $3,587 on Monday, $3,944 on Tuesday, $4,007 on Wednesday, $3,890 on Thursday, and $4,545 on Friday. What were the total sales for the week?

8. Poor's Variety Store sold $5,000 worth of lottery tickets in the first week of August; it sold $289 less in the second week. How much were the lottery ticket sales in the second week of August?

9. A truck weighed 9,550 pounds when it was empty. After being filled with rubbish, it was driven to the dump where it weighed in at 22,347 pounds. How much did the rubbish weigh?

10. Joanne Hoster had $610 in her checking account when she went to the bookstore. Joanne purchased an accounting book for $140, the working papers for $30, and a study guide for $35. After Joanne writes a check for the entire purchase, how much money will remain in her checking account?

11. A used Ford truck is advertised with a base price of $6,986 delivered. However, the window sticker on the truck reads as follows: tinted glass, $210; automatic transmission, $650; power steering, $210; power brakes, $215; safety locks, $95; air conditioning, $1,056. Estimate the total price, including the accessories, by rounding all the way and *then* calculating the exact price.

12. Four different stores are offering the same make and model of a Panasonic Smart television:

Store A	Store B	Store C	Store D
$1,285	$1,380	$1,440	$1,355

Find the difference between the highest price and the lowest price. Check your answer.

13. A Xerox copy machine has a suggested retail price of $1,395. The net price is $649. How much is the discount on the copy machine?

Learning Unit 1-3 :   Multiplying and Dividing Whole Numbers

DRILL PROBLEMS

1. In the following problems, first estimate by rounding all the way, and then work the actual problems and check:

	Actual	Estimate	Check
a.	$\begin{array}{r} 160 \\ \times\ 15 \\ \hline \end{array}$		
b.	$\begin{array}{r} 4{,}216 \\ \times\ 45 \\ \hline \end{array}$		
c.	$\begin{array}{r} 52{,}376 \\ \times\ 309 \\ \hline \end{array}$		
d.	$\begin{array}{r} 3{,}106 \\ \times\ 28 \\ \hline \end{array}$		

2. Multiply; use the shortcut when applicable:

   a.   4,072
         $\times$ 100

   b.   5,100
          $\times$ 40

   c.   76,000
         $\times$ 1,200

   d. 93 $\times$ 100,000

3. Divide by rounding all the way; then do the actual calculation and check showing the remainder as a whole number.

      Actual   **Estimate**   **Check**

   a. $8\overline{)7,709}$

   b. $26\overline{)5,910}$

   c. $151\overline{)3,783}$

   d. $46\overline{)19,550}$

4. Divide by the shortcut method:

   a. $200\overline{)5,400}$

   b. $50\overline{)5,650}$

   c. $1,200\overline{)43,200}$

   d. $17,000\overline{)510,000}$

WORD PROBLEMS

5. Mia Kaminsky sells state lottery tickets in her variety store. If Mia's Variety Store sells 720 lottery tickets per day, how many tickets will be sold in a 7-day period?

6. Arlex Oil Company employs 100 people who are eligible for profit sharing. The financial manager has announced that the profits to be shared amount to $64,000. How much will each employee receive?

7. John Duncan's employer withheld $4,056 in federal taxes from his pay for the year. If equal deductions are made each week, what is John's weekly deduction?

8. Anne Domingoes drives a Volvo that gets 32 miles per gallon of gasoline. How many miles can she travel on 25 gallons of gas?

9. How many 8-inch pieces of yellow ribbon can be cut from a spool of ribbon that contains 6 yards (1 yard = 36 inches)?

10. The number of commercials aired per day on a local television station is 672. How many commercials are aired in 1 year?

11. The computer department at City College purchased 18 computers at a cost of $2,400 each. What was the total price for the computer purchase?

12. Net income for Goodwin's Partnership was $64,500. The five partners share profits and losses equally. What was each partner's share?

13. Ben Krenshaw's supervisor at the construction site told Ben to divide a load of 1,423 bricks into stacks containing 35 bricks each. How many stacks will there be when Ben has finished the job? How many "extra" bricks will there be?

Learning Unit 2-1 :   Types of Fractions and Conversion Procedures

DRILL PROBLEMS

1. Identify the type of fraction—proper, improper, or mixed number:

a. $\dfrac{7}{8}$ 　　　　　　　 b. $\dfrac{31}{29}$ 　　　　　　　 c. $\dfrac{29}{27}$

d. $9\dfrac{3}{11}$ 　　　　　　　 e. $\dfrac{18}{5}$ 　　　　　　　 f. $9\dfrac{1}{8}$

2. Convert to a mixed number:

a. $\dfrac{29}{4}$ 　　　　　　 b. $\dfrac{137}{8}$ 　　　　　　 c. $\dfrac{27}{5}$

d. $\dfrac{29}{9}$ 　　　　　　 e. $\dfrac{71}{8}$ 　　　　　　 f. $\dfrac{43}{6}$

3. Convert the mixed number to an improper fraction:

a. $9\dfrac{1}{5}$ 　　　　　　　 b. $12\dfrac{3}{11}$ 　　　　　　　 c. $4\dfrac{3}{7}$

d. $20\dfrac{4}{9}$ 　　　　　　　 e. $10\dfrac{11}{12}$ 　　　　　　　 f. $17\dfrac{2}{3}$

4. Tell whether the fractions in each pair are equivalent or not:

a. $\dfrac{3}{4}$　$\dfrac{9}{12}$ _____ 　 b. $\dfrac{2}{3}$　$\dfrac{12}{18}$ _____ 　 c. $\dfrac{7}{8}$　$\dfrac{15}{16}$ _____

d. $\dfrac{4}{5}$　$\dfrac{12}{15}$ _____ 　 e. $\dfrac{3}{2}$　$\dfrac{9}{4}$ _____ 　 f. $\dfrac{5}{8}$　$\dfrac{7}{11}$ _____

g. $\dfrac{7}{12}$　$\dfrac{7}{24}$ _____ 　 h. $\dfrac{5}{4}$　$\dfrac{30}{24}$ _____ 　 i. $\dfrac{10}{26}$　$\dfrac{12}{26}$ _____

5. Find the greatest common divisor by the step approach and reduce to lowest terms:

a. $\dfrac{36}{42}$

b. $\dfrac{30}{75}$

c. $\dfrac{74}{148}$

d. $\dfrac{15}{600}$

e. $\dfrac{96}{132}$

f. $\dfrac{84}{154}$

6. Convert to higher terms:

a. $\dfrac{9}{10} = \dfrac{}{70}$

b. $\dfrac{2}{15} = \dfrac{}{30}$

c. $\dfrac{6}{11} = \dfrac{}{132}$

d. $\dfrac{4}{9} = \dfrac{}{36}$

e. $\dfrac{7}{20} = \dfrac{}{100}$

f. $\dfrac{7}{8} = \dfrac{}{560}$

WORD PROBLEMS

7. Ken drove to college in $3\frac{1}{4}$ hours. How many quarter-hours is that? Show your answer as an improper fraction.

8. Mary looked in the refrigerator for a dozen eggs. When she found the box, only 5 eggs were left. What fractional part of the box of eggs was left?

9. At a recent meeting of a local Boosters Club, 17 of the 25 members attending were men. What fraction of those in attendance were men?

10. By weight, water is two parts out of three parts of the human body. What fraction of the body is water?

11. Three out of 5 students who begin college will continue until they receive their degree. Show in fractional form how many out of 100 beginning students will graduate.

12. Tina and her friends came in late to a party and found only $\frac{3}{4}$ of a pizza remaining. In order for everyone to get some pizza, she wanted to divide it into smaller pieces. If she divides the pizza into twelfths, how many pieces will she have? Show your answer in fractional form.

13. Sharon and Spunky noted that it took them 35 minutes to do their exercise routine. What fractional part of an hour is that? Show your answer in lowest terms.

14. Norman and his friend ordered several pizzas, which were all cut into eighths. The group ate 43 pieces of pizza. How many pizzas did they eat? Show your answer as a mixed number.

Learning Unit 2–2 :   Adding and Subtracting Fractions

DRILL PROBLEMS

1. Find the least common denominator (LCD) for each of the following groups of denominators using the prime numbers:

   a. 8, 16, 32   **b.** 9, 15, 20

   c. 12, 15, 32   **d.** 7, 9, 14, 28

2. Add and reduce to lowest terms or change to a mixed number if needed:

   a. $\dfrac{1}{9} + \dfrac{4}{9}$ **b.** $\dfrac{5}{12} + \dfrac{8}{15}$

   c. $\dfrac{7}{8} + \dfrac{5}{12}$ **d.** $7\dfrac{2}{3} + 5\dfrac{1}{4}$

   e. $\dfrac{2}{3} + \dfrac{4}{9} + \dfrac{1}{4}$

3. Subtract and reduce to lowest terms:

a. $\dfrac{5}{9} - \dfrac{2}{9}$

b. $\dfrac{14}{15} - \dfrac{4}{15}$

c. $\dfrac{8}{9} - \dfrac{5}{6}$

d. $\dfrac{7}{12} - \dfrac{9}{16}$

e. $33\dfrac{5}{8} - 27\dfrac{1}{2}$

f. $9 - 2\dfrac{3}{7}$

g. $15\dfrac{1}{3} - 9\dfrac{7}{12}$

h. $92\dfrac{3}{10} - 35\dfrac{7}{15}$

i. $93 - 57\dfrac{5}{12}$

j. $22\dfrac{5}{8} - 17\dfrac{1}{4}$

WORD PROBLEMS

4. Dan Lund took a cross-country trip. He drove $5\frac{3}{8}$ hours on Monday, $6\frac{1}{2}$ hours on Tuesday, $9\frac{3}{4}$ hours on Wednesday, $6\frac{3}{8}$ hours on Thursday, and $10\frac{1}{4}$ hours on Friday. Find the total number of hours Dan drove in the first 5 days of his trip.

5. Sharon Parker bought 20 yards of material to make curtains. She used $4\frac{1}{2}$ yards for one bedroom window, $8\frac{3}{5}$ yards for another bedroom window, and $3\frac{7}{8}$ yards for a hall window. How much material did she have left?

6. Molly Ring visited a local gym and lost $2\frac{1}{4}$ pounds the first weekend and $6\frac{1}{8}$ pounds in week 2. What is Molly's total weight loss?

7. Bill Williams had to drive $46\frac{1}{4}$ miles to work. After driving $28\frac{5}{6}$ miles he noticed he was low on gas and had to decide whether he should stop to fill the gas tank. How many more miles does Bill have to drive to get to work?

8. Albert's Lumber Yard purchased $52\frac{1}{2}$ cords of lumber on Monday and $48\frac{3}{4}$ cords on Tuesday. It sold $21\frac{3}{8}$ cords on Friday. How many cords of lumber remain at Albert's Lumber Yard?

9. At Arlen Oil Company, where Dave Bursett is the service manager, it took $42\frac{1}{3}$ hours to clean five boilers. After a new cleaning tool was purchased, the time for cleaning five boilers was reduced to $37\frac{4}{9}$ hours. How much time was saved?

Learning Unit 2–3 :   Multiplying and Dividing Fractions

DRILL PROBLEMS

1. Multiply; use the cancellation technique:

a. $\dfrac{6}{13} \times \dfrac{26}{12}$

b. $\dfrac{3}{8} \times \dfrac{2}{3}$

c. $\dfrac{5}{7} \times \dfrac{9}{10}$

d. $\dfrac{3}{4} \times \dfrac{9}{13} \times \dfrac{26}{27}$

e. $6\dfrac{2}{5} \times 3\dfrac{1}{8}$

f. $2\dfrac{2}{3} \times 2\dfrac{7}{10}$

g. $45 \times \dfrac{7}{9}$

h. $3\dfrac{1}{9} \times 1\dfrac{2}{7} \times \dfrac{3}{4}$

i. $\dfrac{3}{4} \times \dfrac{7}{9} \times 3\dfrac{1}{3}$

j. $\dfrac{1}{8} \times 6\dfrac{2}{3} \times \dfrac{1}{10}$

2. Multiply; do not use canceling but reduce by finding the greatest common divisor:

   a. $\dfrac{3}{4} \times \dfrac{8}{9}$

   b. $\dfrac{7}{16} \times \dfrac{8}{13}$

3. Multiply or divide as indicated:

   a. $\dfrac{25}{36} \div \dfrac{5}{9}$

   b. $\dfrac{18}{8} \div \dfrac{12}{16}$

   c. $2\dfrac{6}{7} \div 2\dfrac{2}{5}$

   d. $3\dfrac{1}{4} \div 16$

   e. $24 \div 1\dfrac{1}{3}$

   f. $6 \times \dfrac{3}{2}$

   g. $3\dfrac{1}{5} \times 7\dfrac{1}{2}$

   h. $\dfrac{3}{8} \div \dfrac{7}{4}$

   i. $9 \div 3\dfrac{3}{4}$

   j. $\dfrac{11}{24} \times \dfrac{24}{33}$

   k. $\dfrac{12}{14} \div 27$

   l. $\dfrac{3}{5} \times \dfrac{2}{7} \div \dfrac{3}{10}$

WORD PROBLEMS

4. Mary Smith plans to make 12 meatloafs to store in her freezer. Each meatloaf requires $2\frac{1}{4}$ pounds of ground beef. How much ground beef does Mary need?

5. Judy Carter purchased a real estate lot for $24,000. She sold it 2 years later for $1\frac{5}{8}$ times as much as she had paid for it. What was the selling price?

6. Lynn Clarkson saw an ad for a camcorder that cost $980. She knew of a discount store that would sell it to her for a markdown of $\frac{3}{20}$ off the advertised price. How much is the discount she can get?

7. To raise money for their club, the members of the Marketing Club purchased 68 bushels of popcorn to resell. They plan to repackage the popcorn in bags that hold $\frac{2}{21}$ of a bushel each. How many bags of popcorn will they be able to fill?

8. Richard Tracy paid a total of $375 for lumber costing $9\frac{3}{8}$ per foot. How many feet did he purchase?

9. While training for a marathon, Kristin Woods jogged $7\frac{3}{4}$ miles per hour for $2\frac{2}{3}$ hours. How many miles did Kristin jog?

10. On a map, 1 inch represents 240 miles. How many miles are represented by $\frac{3}{8}$ of an inch?

11. In Massachusetts, the governor wants to allot $\frac{1}{6}$ of the total sales tax collections to public education. The total sales tax collected is $2,472,000; how much will go to education?

Learning Unit 3–1 :   Rounding Decimals; Fraction and Decimal Conversions

DRILL PROBLEMS

1. Write in decimal:

  a. Sixty-two hundredths _____

  b. Six tenths _____

  c. Nine hundred fifty-three thousandths _____

  d. Four hundred one thousandths _____

  e. Six hundredths _____

2. Round each decimal to the place indicated:

  a. .8624 to the nearest thousandth _____

  b. .051 to the nearest tenth _____

  c. 8.207 to the nearest hundredth _____

  d. 2.094 to the nearest hundredth _____

  e. .511172 to the nearest ten thousandth _____

3. Name the place position of the underlined digit:

  a. .8$\underline{2}$6 _____

  b. .91$\underline{4}$ _____

  c. 3.1$\underline{1}$69 _____

  d. 53.17$\underline{5}$ _____

  e. 1.017$\underline{4}$ _____

4. Convert to fractions (do not reduce):

   a. .91 _____

   b. .426 _____

   c. 2.516 _____

   d. .62$\frac{1}{2}$ _____

   e. 13.007 _____

   f. 5.03$\frac{1}{4}$ _____

5. Convert to fractions and reduce to lowest terms:

   a. .4

   b. .44

   c. .53

   d. .336

   e. .096

   f. .125

   g. .3125

   h. .008

   i. 2.625

   j. 5.75

   k. 3.375

   l. 9.04

6. Convert the following fractions to decimals and round your answer to the nearest hundredth:

   a. $\frac{1}{8}$

   b. $\frac{7}{16}$

   c. $\frac{2}{3}$

   d. $\frac{3}{4}$

   e. $\frac{9}{16}$

   f. $\frac{5}{6}$

   g. $\frac{7}{9}$

   h. $\frac{38}{79}$

   i. $2\frac{3}{8}$

   j. $9\frac{1}{3}$

   k. $11\frac{19}{50}$

   l. $6\frac{21}{32}$

   m. $4\frac{83}{97}$

   n. $1\frac{2}{5}$

   o. $2\frac{2}{11}$

   p. $13\frac{30}{42}$

WORD PROBLEMS

7. Alan Angel got 2 hits in his first 7 times at bat. What is his average to the nearest thousandths place?

8. Bill Breen earned $1,555, and his employer calculated that Bill's total FICA deduction should be $118.9575. Round this deduction to the nearest cent.

9. At the local college, .566 of the students are men. Convert to a fraction. Do not reduce.

10. The average television set is watched 2,400 hours a year. If there are 8,760 hours in a year, what fractional part of the year is spent watching television? Reduce to lowest terms.

11. On Saturday, the employees at the Empire Fish Company work only $\frac{1}{3}$ of a day. How could this be expressed as a decimal to the nearest thousandth?

12. The North Shore Cinema has 610 seats. At a recent film screening there were 55 vacant seats. Show as a fraction the number of filled seats. Reduce as needed.

13. Michael Sullivan was planning his marketing strategy for a new product his company had produced. He was fascinated to discover that Rhode Island, the smallest state in the United States, was only twenty thousand, five hundred seven ten millionths the size of the largest state, Alaska. Write this number in decimal.

14. Bull Moose Company purchased a new manufacturing plant, located on an acre of land, for a total price of $2,250,000. The accountant determined that $\frac{3}{7}$ of the total price should be allocated as the price of the building. What decimal portion is the price of the building? Round to the nearest thousandth.

Learning Unit 3-2 :   Adding, Subtracting, Multiplying, and Dividing Decimals

DRILL PROBLEMS

1. Rearrange vertically and add:

    a. 7.57 + 6.2 + 13.008 + 4.83   **b.** 1.0625 + 4.0881 + .0775

    c. .903 + .078 + .17 + .1 + .96   **d.** 3.38 + .175 + .0186 + .2

2. Rearrange and subtract:

    a. .96 − .43   **b.** .885 − .069

    c. 11.67 − .935   **d.** 261.2 − 8.08

3. Multiply and round to the nearest tenth:

    a. 13.6 × .02   **b.** 1.73 × .069

    c. 400 × 3.7   **d.** 0.025 × 5.6

4. Divide and round to the nearest hundredth:

    a. 13.869 ÷ .6   **b.** 1.0088 ÷ .14   **c.** 18.7 ÷ 2.16   **d.** 15.64 ÷ .34

5. Complete by the shortcut method:

    a. 6.87 × 1,000   **b.** 927,530 ÷ 100   **c.** 27.2 ÷ 1,000

    d. .21 × 1,000   **e.** 347 × 100   **f.** 347 ÷ 100

    g. .0021 ÷ 10   **h.** 85.44 × 10,000   **i.** 83.298 × 100

    j. 23.0109 ÷ 100

WORD PROBLEMS (Use *Business Math Handbook* Tables as Needed.)

6. Andy Hay noted his Ford Explorer odometer reading of 18,969.4 at the beginning of his vacation. At the end of his vacation the reading was 21,510.4. How many miles did he drive during his vacation?

7. Jeanne Allyn purchased 12.25 yards of ribbon for a craft project. The ribbon cost 37¢ per yard. What was the total cost of the ribbon?

8. Leo Green wanted to find out the gas mileage for his company truck. When he filled the gas tank, he wrote down the odometer reading of 9,650.7. The next time he filled the gas tank the odometer reading was 10,112.2. He looked at the gas pump and saw that he had taken 18.5 gallons of gas. Find the gas mileage per gallon for Leo's truck. Round to the nearest tenth.

9. At Halley's Rent-a-Car, the cost per day to rent a medium-size car is $35.25 plus 37¢ a mile. What would be the charge to rent this car for 1 day if you drove 205.4 miles?

10. A trip to Mexico costs 6,000 pesos. What is this in U.S. dollars? Check your answer.

11. If a commemorative gold coin weighs 7.842 grams, find the number of coins that can be produced from 116 grams of gold. Round to the nearest whole number.

Learning Unit 4–1 : The Checking Account

DRILL PROBLEMS

1. The following is a deposit slip made out by Fred Young of the F. W. Young Company.

   a. How much cash did Young deposit? _____

   b. How many checks did Young deposit? _____

   c. What was the total amount deposited? _____

Fleet Bank Checking Deposit	This deposit is subject to: proof and verification, the Uniform Commercial Code, the collection and availability policy of this bank.		
TO THE ACCOUNT OF	DATE 3/27/16		

DESCRIPTION	DOLLARS	CENTS	ADDITIONAL CHECKS DESCRIPTION	DOLLARS	CENTS
BILLS	415	XX	7.		
COIN	15	64	8.		
LIST CHECKS 1 53-1297	188	44	9.		
2 51-1509	98	37	10.		
3 53-1290	150	06	11.		
4.			12.		
5.			13.		
6.			14.		
SUB TOTAL ITEMS 1-6			SUB TOTAL ITEMS 7-14		
			TOTAL		

   NAME _____ (PLEASE PRINT) PLEASE ENDORSE ALL CHECKS — PLEASE ENTER CLEARLY YOUR ACCOUNT NUMBER

   ⑆521 2000 17⑈

2. Blackstone Company had a balance of $2,173.18 in its checking account. Henry James, Blackstone's accountant, made a deposit that consisted of 2 fifty-dollar bills, 120 ten-dollar bills, 6 five-dollar bills, 14 one-dollar bills, $9.54 in change, plus two checks the company had accepted, one for $16.38 and the other for $102.50. Find the amount of the deposit and the new balance in Blackstone's checking account.

3. Answer the following questions using the illustration:

| No. _113_ | $ 750 00/100 |
| _October 4_ 20 _XX_ |
| To _Neuner Realty_ |
| For _real estate_ |

	DOLLARS	CENTS
BALANCE	1,020	93
AMT. DEPOSITED	2,756	80
TOTAL	3,777	73
AMT. THIS CHECK	750	00
BALANCE FORWARD	3,027	73

Jones Company
22 Aster Road
Salem, MA 01970

No. 113

October 4 20 XX   5-13/110

PAY
TO THE
ORDER
OF   _Neuner Realty Company_ $ 750 00/100

Seven Hundred Fifty and 00/100   DOLLARS

Fleet Bank FLEET BANK OF MASSACHUSETTS,
NATIONAL ASSOCIATION
BOSTON, MASSACHUSETTS   _Kevin Jones_

MEMO   _real estate_

A011000138A   14   0380 113

a. Who is the payee? _____

b. Who is the drawer? _____

c. Who is the drawee? _____

d. What is the bank's identification number _____

e. What is Jones Company's account number? _____

f. What was the balance in the account on September 30? _____

g. For how much did Jones write Check No. 113? _____

h. How much was deposited on October 1? _____

i. How much was left after Check No. 113 was written? _____

4. Write each of the following amounts in verbal form as you would on a check:

a. $40 _____

b. $245.75 _____

c. $3.98 _____

d. $1,205.05 _____

e. $3,013 _____

f. $510.10 _____

Learning Unit 4–2 :   Bank Statement and Reconciliation Process; Trends in Online Banking

WORD PROBLEMS

1. Find the bank balance on January 31.

Date	Checks and payments			Deposits	Balance
January 1					401.17
January 2	108.64				_____
January 5	116.50			432.16	_____
January 6	14.92	150.00	10.00		_____
January 11	12.29			633.89	_____
January 18	108.64	18.60			_____
January 25	43.91	23.77		657.22	_____
January 26	75.00				_____
January 31	6.75 sc				_____

2. Joe Madruga, of Madruga's Taxi Service, received a bank statement for the month of May showing a balance of $932.36. His records show that the bank had not yet recorded two of his deposits, one for $521.50 and the other for $98.46. There are outstanding checks in the amounts of $41.67, $135.18, and $25.30. The statement also shows a service charge of $3.38. The balance in the check register is $1,353.55. Prepare a bank reconciliation for Madruga's as of May 31.

3. In reconciling the checking account for Nasser Enterprises, Beth Accomando found that the bank had collected a $3,000 promissory note on the company's behalf and had charged a $15 collection fee. There was also a service charge of $7.25. What amount should be added/subtracted from the checkbook balance to bring it up to date?

   Add: _____   Deduct: _____

4. In reconciling the checking account for Colonial Cleaners, Steve Papa found that a check for $34.50 had been recorded in the check register as $43.50. The bank returned an NSF check in the amount of $62.55. Interest income of $8.25 was earned and a service charge of $10.32 was assessed. What amount should be added/subtracted from the checkbook balance to bring it up to date?

   Add: _____   Deduct: _____

5. Matthew Stokes was completing the bank reconciliation for Parker's Tool and Die Company. The check register balance was $1,503.67. Matthew found that a $76.00 check had been recorded in the check register as $67.00; that a note for $1,500 had been collected by the bank for Parker's and the collection fee was $12.00; that $15.60 interest was earned on the account; and that an $8.35 service charge had been assessed. What should the check register balance be after Matthew updates it with the bank reconciliation information?

6. Consumers, community activists, and politicians are decrying the new line of accounts because several include a $3 service charge for some customers who use bank tellers for transactions that can be done through an automated teller machine. Bill Wade banks at a local bank that charges this fee. He was having difficulty balancing his checkbook because he did not notice this fee on his bank statement. His bank statement showed a balance of $822.18. Bill's checkbook had a balance of $206.48. Check No. 406 for $116.08 and Check No. 407 for $12.50 were outstanding. A $521 deposit was not on the statement. Bill has his payroll check electronically deposited to his checking account—the payroll check was for $1,015.12. (Bill's payroll checks vary each month.) There are also a $1 service fee and a teller fee of $6. Complete Bill's bank reconciliation.

7. At First National Bank in San Diego, some customers have to pay $25 each year as an ATM card fee. John Levi banks at First National Bank and just received his bank statement showing a balance of $829.25; his checkbook balance is $467.40. The bank statement shows an ATM card fee of $25.00, teller fee of $9.00, interest of $1.80, and John's $880 IRS refund check, which was processed by the IRS and deposited to his account. John has two checks that have not cleared—No. 112 for $620.10 and No. 113 for $206.05. There is also a deposit in transit for $1,312.10. Prepare John's bank reconciliation.

Learning Unit 5–1 :   Solving Equations for the Unknown

DRILL PROBLEMS

1. Write equations for the following situations. Use N for the unknown number. Do not solve the equations.

   a. Three times a number is 180.

   b. A number increased by 13 equals 25.

   c. Seven less than a number is 5.

   d. Fifty-seven decreased by 3 times a number is 21.

   e. Fourteen added to one-third of a number is 18.

   f. Twice the sum of a number and 4 is 32.

   g. Three-fourths of a number is 9.

   h. Two times a number plus 3 times the same number plus 8 is 68.

2. Solve for the unknown number:

   a. $C + 40 = \ 90$

   b. $29 + M = \ 44$

   c. $D - 77 = \ 98$

   d. $7N = 63$

   e. $\dfrac{X}{12} = 11$

   f. $3Q + 4Q + 2Q = 108$

   g. $H + 5H + 3 = \ 57$

   h. $2(N - 3) = \ 62$

   i. $\dfrac{3R}{4} = 27$

   j. $E - 32 = \ 41$

   k. $5(2T - 2) = \ 120$

   l. $12W - 5W = 98$

m. $49 - X = 37$ **n.** $12(V + 2) = 84$ **o.** $7D + 4 = 5D + 14$

p. $7(T - 2) = 2T - 9$

Learning Unit 5–2 :   Solving Word Problems for the Unknown

WORD PROBLEMS

1. A sweater at the Gap was marked down $30. The sale price was $50. What was the original price?

Unknown(s)	Variable(s)	Relationship

2. Goodwin's Corporation found that $\frac{2}{3}$ of its employees were vested in their retirement plan. If 124 employees are vested, what is the total number of employees at Goodwin's?

Unknown(s)	Variable(s)	Relationship

3. Eileen Haskin's utility and telephone bills for the month totaled $180. The utility bill was 3 times as much as the telephone bill. How much was each bill?

Unknown(s)	Variable(s)	Relationship

4. Ryan and his friends went to the golf course to hunt for golf balls. Ryan found 15 more than $\frac{1}{3}$ of the total number of golf balls that were found. How many golf balls were found if Ryan found 75 golf balls?

Unknown(s)	Variable(s)	Relationship

5. Linda Mills and Sherry Somers sold 459 tickets for the Advertising Club's raffle. If Linda sold 8 times as many tickets as Sherry, how many tickets did each one sell?

Unknown(s)	Variable(s)	Relationship

6. Jason Mazzola wanted to buy a suit at Giblee's. Jason did not have enough money with him, so Mr. Giblee told him he would hold the suit if Jason gave him a deposit of $\frac{1}{5}$ of the cost of the suit. Jason agreed and gave Mr. Giblee $79. What was the price of the suit?

Unknown(s)	Variable(s)	Relationship

7. Peter sold watches ($7) and necklaces ($4) at a flea market. Total sales were $300. People bought 3 times as many watches as necklaces. How many of each did Peter sell? What were the total dollar sales of each?

Unknown(s)	Variable(s)	Price	Relationship

8. Peter sold watches ($7) and necklaces ($4) at a flea market. Total sales for 48 watches and necklaces were $300. How many of each did Peter sell? What were the total dollar sales of each?

Unknown(s)	Variable(s)	Price	Relationship

9. A 3,000 piece of direct mailing cost $1,435. Printing cost is $550, about $3\frac{1}{2}$ times the cost of typesetting. How much did the typesetting cost? Round to the nearest cent.

Unknown(s)	Variable(s)	Relationship

10. In 2016, Tony Rigato, owner of MRM, saw an increase in sales to $13.5 million. Rigato states that since 2013, sales have more than tripled. What were his sales in 2013?

Unknown(s)	Variable(s)	Relationship

Learning Unit 6-1 :   Conversions

DRILL PROBLEMS

1. Convert the following to percents; round to the nearest tenth of a percent if needed:

a.	.04	_____ %	**b.**	.729	_____ %	**c.**	.009	_____ %
d.	8.3	_____ %	**e.**	5.26	_____ %	**f.**	6	_____ %
g.	.0105	_____ %	**h.**	.1180	_____ %	**i.**	5.0375	_____ %
j.	.862	_____ %	**k.**	.2615	_____ %	**l.**	.8	_____ %
m.	.025	_____ %	**n.**	.06	_____ %			

2. Convert the following to decimals; do not round:

a.	68%	_____	**b.**	.09%	_____	**c.**	4.7%	_____
d.	9.67%	_____	**e.**	.2%	_____	**f.**	$\frac{1}{4}\%$	_____
g.	.76%	_____	**h.**	110%	_____	**i.**	$12\frac{1}{2}\%$	_____
j.	5%	_____	**k.**	.004%	_____	**l.**	$7\frac{5}{10}\%$	_____
m.	$\frac{3}{4}\%$	_____	**n.**	1%	_____			

3. Convert the following to percents; round to the nearest tenth of a percent if needed:

a.	$\frac{7}{10}$	_____ %	**b.**	$\frac{1}{5}$	_____ %	**c.**	$1\frac{5}{8}$	_____ %
d.	$\frac{2}{7}$	_____ %	**e.**	2	_____ %	**f.**	$\frac{14}{100}$	_____ %
g.	$\frac{1}{6}$	_____ %	**h.**	$\frac{1}{2}$	_____ %	**i.**	$\frac{3}{5}$	_____ %
j.	$\frac{3}{25}$	_____ %	**k.**	$\frac{5}{16}$	_____ %	**l.**	$\frac{11}{50}$	_____ %
m.	$4\frac{3}{4}$	_____ %	**n.**	$\frac{3}{200}$	_____ %			

4. Convert the following to fractions in simplest form:

a.	40%	_____	**b.**	15%	_____	**c.**	50%	_____
d.	75%	_____	**e.**	35%	_____	**f.**	85%	_____
g.	$12\frac{1}{2}\%$	_____	**h.**	$37\frac{1}{2}\%$	_____	**i.**	$33\frac{1}{3}\%$	_____
j.	3%	_____	**k.**	8.5%	_____	**l.**	$5\frac{3}{4}\%$	_____
m.	100%	_____	**n.**	10%	_____			

5. Complete the following table by finding the missing fraction, decimal, or percent equivalent:

	Fraction	Decimal	Percent		Fraction	Decimal	Percent
a.		.25	25%	h.	$\frac{1}{6}$	$.16\overline{6}$	
b.	$\frac{3}{8}$		$37\frac{1}{2}\%$	i.		$.083\overline{3}$	$8\frac{1}{3}\%$
c.	$\frac{1}{2}$	.5		j.	$\frac{1}{9}$		$11\frac{1}{9}\%$
d.	$\frac{2}{3}$		$66\frac{2}{3}\%$	k.		.3125	$31\frac{1}{4}\%$
e.		.4	40%	l.	$\frac{3}{40}$	.075	
f.	$\frac{3}{5}$	.6		m.	$\frac{1}{5}$		20%
g.	$\frac{7}{10}$		70%	n.		1.125	$112\frac{1}{2}\%$

WORD PROBLEMS

6. If in 2016 Mutual of New York reported that 80% of its new sales came from existing clients, what fractional part of its new sales came from existing clients? Reduce to simplest form.

7. Six hundred ninety corporations and design firms competed for the Industrial Design Excellence Award (IDEA). Twenty were selected as the year's best and received gold awards. Show the gold award winners as a fraction; then show what percent of the entrants received gold awards. Round to the nearest tenth of a percent.

8. If in the first half of 2016 stock prices in the Standard & Poor's 500-stock index rose 4.1%, show the increase as a decimal.

9. In the recent banking crisis, many banks were unable to cover their bad loans. Citicorp, the nation's largest real estate lender, was reported as having only enough reserves to cover 39% of its bad loans. What fractional part of its loan losses was covered?

10. Dave Mattera spent his vacation in Las Vegas. He ordered breakfast in his room, and when he went downstairs to the coffee shop, he discovered that the same breakfast was much less expensive. He had paid 1.884 times as much for the breakfast in his room. What was the percent of increase for the breakfast in his room?

11. Putnam Management Company of Boston recently increased its management fee by .09%. What is the increase as a decimal? What is the same increase as a fraction?

12. Joel Black and Karen Whyte formed a partnership and drew up a partnership agreement, with profits and losses to be divided equally after each partner receives a $7\frac{1}{2}\%$ return on his or her capital contribution. Show their return on investment as a decimal and as a fraction. Reduce.

Learning Unit 6-2 :   Application of Percents—Portion Formula

DRILL PROBLEMS

1. Fill in the amount of the base, rate, and portion in each of the following statements:

a. The Logans spend $4,000 a month on food, which is 30% of their monthly income of $20,000.

Base _____   Rate _____   Portion _____

b. Rocky Norman got a $15 discount when he purchased a new camera. This was 20% off the sticker price of $75.

Base _____   Rate _____   Portion _____

c. Mary Burns got a 12% senior citizens discount when she bought a $7.00 movie ticket. She saved $0.84.

Base _____   Rate _____   Portion _____

d. Arthur Bogey received a commission of $13,500 when he sold the Brown's house for $225,000. His commission rate is 6%.

Base _____   Rate _____   Portion _____

e. Leo Davis deposited $5,000 in a certificate of deposit (CD). A year later he received an interest payment of $450, which was a yield of 9%.

Base _____   Rate _____   Portion _____

f. Grace Tremblay is on a diet that allows her to eat 1,600 calories per day. For breakfast she had 600 calories, which is $37\frac{1}{2}$% of her allowance.

Base _____   Rate _____   Portion _____

2. Find the portion; round to the nearest hundredth if necessary:

a. 7% of 74 _____

b. 12% of 205 _____

c. 16% of 630 _____

d. 7.5% of 920 _____

e. 25% of 1,004 _____

f. 10% of 79 _____

g. 103% of 44 _____

h. 30% of 78 _____

i. .2% of 50 _____

j. 1% of 5,622 _____

k. $6\frac{1}{4}$% of 480 _____

l. 150% of 10 _____

m. 100% of 34 _____

n. $\frac{1}{2}$% of 27 _____

3. Find the rate; round to the nearest tenth of a percent as needed:

a. 30 is what percent of 90? _____

b. 6 is what percent of 200? _____

c. 275 is what percent of 1,000? _____

d. .8 is what percent of 44? _____

e. 67 is what percent of 2,010? _____

f. 550 is what percent of 250? _____

g. 13 is what percent of 650? _____

h. $15 is what percent of $455? _____

i. .05 is what percent of 100? _____

j. $6.25 is what percent of $10? _____

4. Find the base; round to the nearest tenth as needed:

a. 63 is 30% of _____

b. 60 is 33% of _____

c. 150 is 25% of _____

d. 47 is 1% of _____

e. $21 is 120% of _____

f. 2.26 is 40% of _____

g. 75 is $12\frac{1}{2}$% of _____

h. 18 is 22.2% of _____

i. $37.50 is 50% of _____

j. 250 is 100% of _____

5. Find the percent of increase or decrease; round to the nearest tenth percent as needed:

	Last year	This year	Amount of change	Percent of change
a.	5,962	4,378	_____	_____
b.	$10,995	$12,250	_____	_____
c.	120,000	140,000	_____	_____
d.	120,000	100,000	_____	_____

WORD PROBLEMS

6. A machine that originally cost $8,000 was sold for $800 at the end of 5 years. What percent of the original cost is the selling price?

7. Joanne Byrne invested $75,000 in a candy shop and is making 12% per year on her investment. How much money per year is she making on her investment?

8. There was a fire in Bill Porper's store that caused 2,780 inventory items to be destroyed. Before the fire, 9,565 inventory items were in the store. What percent of inventory was destroyed? Round to nearest tenth percent.

9. Elyse's Dress Shoppe makes 25% of its sales for cash. If the cash receipts on January 21 were $799, what were the total sales for the day?

10. The YMCA is holding a fund-raiser to collect money for a new gym floor. So far it has collected $7,875, which is 63% of the goal. What is the amount of the goal? How much more money must the YMCA collect?

11. Leslie Tracey purchased her home for $51,500. She sold it last year for $221,200. What percent profit did she make on the sale? Round to nearest tenth percent.

12. Maplewood Park Tool & Die had an annual production of 375,165 units this year. This is 140% of the annual production last year. What was last year's annual production?

Learning Unit 7-1 :   Trade Discounts—Single and Chain*

DRILL PROBLEMS

1. Calculate the trade discount amount for each of the following items:

Item	List price	Trade discount	Trade discount amount
a. iPhone	$ 200	20%	_____
b. Flat-screen TV	$1,200	30%	_____
c. Suit	$ 500	10%	_____
d. Bicycle	$ 800	$12\frac{1}{2}\%$	_____
e. David Yurman bracelet	$ 950	40%	_____

2. Calculate the net price for each of the following items:

Item	List price	Trade discount amount	Net price
a. Home Depot table	$600	$250	_____
b. Bookcase	$525	$129	_____
c. Rocking chair	$480	$95	_____

3. Fill in the missing amount for each of the following items:

Item	List price	Trade discount amount	Net price
a. Sears electric saw	_____	$19	$56.00
b. Electric drill	$90	_____	$68.50
c. Ladder	$56	$15.25	_____

4. For each of the following, find the percent paid (complement of trade discount) and the net price:

List price	Trade discount	Percent paid	Net price
a. $45	15%	_____	_____
b. $195	12.2%	_____	_____
c. $325	50%	_____	_____
d. $120	18%	_____	_____

5. In each of the following examples, find the net price equivalent rate and the single equivalent discount rate:

Chain discount	Net price equivalent rate	Single equivalent discount rate
a. 25/5	_____	_____
b. 15/15	_____	_____
c. 15/10/5	_____	_____
d. 12/12/6	_____	_____

*Freight problems to be shown in LU 7–2 material.

6. In each of the following examples, find the net price and the trade discount:

List price	Chain discount	Net price	Trade discount
a. $5,000	10/10/5	_____	_____
b. $7,500	9/6/3	_____	_____
c. $898	20/7/2	_____	_____
d. $1,500	25/10	_____	_____

7. The list price of a handheld calculator is $19.50, and the trade discount is 18%. Find the trade discount amount.

8. The list price of a silver picture frame is $29.95, and the trade discount is 15%. Find the trade discount amount and the net price.

9. The net price of a set of pots and pans is $65, and the trade discount is 20%. What is the list price?

10. Jennie's Variety Store has the opportunity to purchase candy from three different wholesalers; each of the wholesalers offers a different chain discount. Company A offers 25/5/5, Company B offers 20/10/5, and Company C offers 15/20. Which company should Jennie deal with? *Hint:* Choose the company with the highest single equivalent discount rate.

11. The list price of a television set is $625. Find the net price after a series discount of 30/20/10.

12. Mandy's Accessories Shop purchased 12 purses with a total list price of $726. What was the net price of each purse if the wholesaler offered a chain discount of 25/20?

13. Kransberg Furniture Store purchased a bedroom set for $1,097.25 from Furniture Wholesalers. The list price of the set was $1,995. What trade discount rate did Kransberg receive?

14. Susan Monk teaches second grade and receives a discount at the local art supply store. Recently she paid $47.25 for art supplies after receiving a chain discount of 30/10. What was the regular price of the art supplies?

Learning Unit 7-2 : Cash Discounts, Credit Terms, and Partial Payments

DRILL PROBLEMS

1. Complete the following table:

	Date of invoice	Date goods received	Terms	Last day of discount period	End of credit period
a.	February 8		2/10, n/30		
b.	August 26		2/10, n/30		
c.	October 17		3/10, n/60		
d.	March 11	May 10	3/10, n/30, ROG		
e.	September 14		2/10, EOM		
f.	May 31		2/10, EOM		

2. Calculate the cash discount and the net amount paid.

	Invoice amount	Cash discount rate	Discount amount	Net amount paid
a.	$75	3%		
b.	$1,559	2%		
c.	$546.25	2%		
d.	$9,788.75	1%		

3. Use the complement of the cash discount to calculate the net amount paid. Assume all invoices are paid within the discount period.

	Terms of invoice	Amount of invoice	Complement	Net amount paid
a.	3/10, n/30	$1,400		
b.	3/10, n/30 ROG	$4,500		
c.	2/10, EOM	$375.50		
d.	1/15, n/45	$3,998		

4. Calculate the amount of cash discount and the net amount paid.

	Date of invoice	Terms of invoice	Amount of invoice	Date paid	Cash discount	Amount paid
a.	January 12	2/10, n/30	$5,320	January 22		
b.	May 28	2/10, n/30	$975	June 7		
c.	August 15	2/10, n/30	$7,700	August 26		
d.	March 8	2/10, EOM	$480	April 10		
e.	January 24	3/10, n/60	$1,225	February 3		

5. Complete the following table:

	Total invoice	Freight charges included in invoice total	Date of invoice	Terms of invoice	Date of payment	Cash discount	Amount paid
a.	$852	$12.50	3/19	2/10, n/30	3/29		
b.	$669.57	$15.63	7/28	3/10, EOM	9/10		
c.	$500	$11.50	4/25	2/10, n/60	6/5		
d.	$188	$9.70	1/12	2/10, EOM	2/10		

6. In the following table, assume that all the partial payments were made within the discount period.

Amount of invoice	Terms of invoice	Partial payment	Amount to be credited	Balance outstanding
a. $481.90	2/10, n/30	$90.00	_____	_____
b. $1,000	2/10, EOM	$500.00	_____	_____
c. $782.88	3/10, n/30, ROG	$275.00	_____	_____
d. $318.80	2/15, n/60	$200.00	_____	_____

WORD PROBLEMS

7. Ray Chemical Company received an invoice for $16,500, dated March 14, with terms of 2/10, n/30. If the invoice was paid March 22, what was the amount due?

8. On May 27, Trotter Hardware Store received an invoice for trash barrels purchased for $13,650 with terms of 3/10, EOM; the freight charge, which is included in the price, is $412. What are (a) the last day of the discount period and (b) the amount of the payment due on this date?

9. The Glass Sailboat received an invoice for $930.50 with terms 2/10, n/30 on April 19. On April 29, it sent a payment of $430.50. (a) How much credit will be given on the total due? (b) What is the new balance due?

10. Dallas Ductworks offers cash discounts of 2/10, 1/15, n/30 on all purchases. If an invoice for $544 dated July 18 is paid on August 2, what is the amount due?

11. The list price of a Luminox watch is $299.90 with trade discounts of 10/20 and terms of 3/10, n/30. If a retailer pays the invoice within the discount period, what amount must the retailer pay?

12. The invoice of a sneakers supplier totaled $2,488.50, was dated February 7, and offered terms 2/10, ROG. The shipment of sneakers was received on March 7. What are (a) the last date of the discount period and (b) the amount of the discount that will be lost if the invoice is paid after that date?

13. Starburst Toy Company receives an invoice amounting to $1,152.30 with terms of 2/10, EOM and dated November 6. If a partial payment of $750 is made on December 8, what are (a) the credit given for the partial payment and (b) the balance due on the invoice?

14. Todd's Sporting Goods received an invoice for soccer equipment dated July 26 with terms 3/10, 1/15, n/30 in the amount of $3,225.83, which included shipping charges of $375.50. If this bill is paid on August 5, what amount must be paid?

Learning Unit 8–1 :   Markups Based on Cost (100%)

DRILL PROBLEMS

1. Fill in the missing numbers:

	Cost	Dollar markup	Selling price
a.	$14.80	$4.10	_____
b.	$8.32	_____	$11.04
c.	$25.27	_____	$29.62
d.	_____	$75.00	$165.00
e.	$86.54	$29.77	_____

2. Calculate the markup based on cost; round to the nearest cent.

	Cost	Markup (percent of cost)	Dollar markup
a.	$425.00	30%	_____
b.	$1.52	20%	_____
c.	$9.90	$12\frac{1}{2}$%	_____
d.	$298.10	50%	_____
e.	$74.25	38%	_____
f.	$552.25	100%	_____

3. Calculate the dollar markup and rate of the markup as a percent of cost, rounding percents to nearest tenth percent. Verify your result, which may be slightly off due to rounding.

	Cost	Selling price	Dollar markup	Markup (percent of cost)	Verify
a.	$2.50	$4.50	_____	_____	_____
b.	$12.50	$19.00	_____	_____	_____
c.	$0.97	$1.25	_____	_____	_____
d.	$132.25	$175.00	_____	_____	_____
e.	$65.00	$89.99	_____	_____	_____

4. Calculate the dollar markup and the selling price.

	Cost	Markup (percent of cost)	Dollar markup	Selling price
a.	$2.20	40%	_____	_____
b.	$2.80	16%	_____	_____
c.	$840.00	$12\frac{1}{2}$%	_____	_____
d.	$24.36	30%	_____	_____

5. Calculate the cost, rounding to the nearest cent.

Selling price	Rate of markup based on cost	Cost
a. $1.98	30%	_____
b. $360.00	60%	_____
c. $447.50	20%	_____
d. $1,250.00	100%	_____

6. Find the missing numbers. Round money to the nearest cent and percents to the nearest tenth percent.

Cost	Dollar markup	Percent markup on cost	Selling price
a. $72.00	_____	40%	_____
b. _____	$7.00	_____	$35.00
c. $8.80	$1.10	_____	_____
d. _____	_____	28%	$19.84
e. $175.00	_____	_____	$236.25

WORD PROBLEMS

7. If the cost of a Pottery Barn chair is $499 and the markup rate is 40% of the cost, what are **(a)** the dollar markup and **(b)** the selling price?

8. If Barry's Furniture Store purchased a floor lamp for $120 and plans to add a markup of $90, **(a)** what will the selling price be and **(b)** what is the markup as a percent of cost?

9. If Lesjardin's Jewelry Store is selling a gold bracelet for $349, which includes a markup of 35% on cost, what are **(a)** Lesjardin's cost and **(b)** the amount of the dollar markup?

10. Toll's Variety Store sells an alarm clock for $14.75. The alarm clock cost Toll's $9.90. What is the markup amount as a percent of cost? Round to the nearest whole percent.

11. Swanson's Audio Supply marks up its merchandise by 40% on cost. If the markup on a cassette player is $85, what are **(a)** the cost of the cassette player and **(b)** the selling price?

12. Brown's Department Store is selling a shirt for $55. If the markup is 70% on cost, what is Brown's cost (to the nearest cent)?

13. Ward's Greenhouse purchased tomato flats for $5.75 each. Ward's has decided to use a markup of 42% on cost. Find the selling price.

Learning Unit 8-2 : Markups Based on Selling Price (100%)

DRILL PROBLEMS

1. Calculate the markup based on the selling price.

Selling price	Markup (percent of selling price)	Dollar markup
a. $25.00	40%	_____
b. $230.00	25%	_____
c. $81.00	42.5%	_____
d. $72.88	$37\frac{1}{2}\%$	_____
e. $1.98	$7\frac{1}{2}\%$	_____

2. Calculate the dollar markup and the markup as a percent of selling price (to the nearest tenth percent). Verify your answer, which may be slightly off due to rounding.

Cost	Selling price	Dollar markup	Markup (percent of selling price)	Verify
a. $2.50	$4.25	_____	_____	____
b. $16.00	$24.00	_____	_____	____
c. $45.25	$85.00	_____	_____	____
d. $0.19	$0.25	_____	_____	____
e. $5.50	$8.98	_____	_____	____

3. Given the *cost* and the markup as a percent of *selling price*, calculate the selling price.

Cost	Markup (percent of selling price)	Selling price
a. $5.90	15%	_____
b. $600	32%	_____
c. $15	50%	_____
d. $120	30%	_____
e. $0.29	20%	_____

4. Given the selling price and the percent markup on selling price, calculate the cost.

Cost	Markup (percent of selling price)	Selling price
a. _____	40%	$6.25
b. _____	20%	$16.25
c. _____	19%	$63.89
d. _____	$62\frac{1}{2}\%$	$44.00

5. Calculate the equivalent rate of markup, rounding to the nearest hundredth percent.

Markup on cost	Markup on selling price		Markup on cost	Markup on selling price
a. 40%	_____		**b.** 50%	_____
c. _____	50%		**d.** _____	35%
e. _____	40%			

WORD PROBLEMS

6. Fisher Equipment is selling a Wet/Dry Shop Vac for $49.97. If Fisher's markup is 40% of the selling price, what is the cost of the Shop Vac?

7. Gove Lumber Company purchased a 10-inch table saw for $225 and will mark up the price 35% on the selling price. What will the selling price be?

8. To realize a sufficient gross margin, City Paint and Supply Company marks up its paint 27% on the selling price. If a gallon of Latex Semi-Gloss Enamel has a markup of $4.02, find **(a)** the selling price and **(b)** the cost.

9. A Magnavox 20-inch color TV cost $180 and sells for $297. What is the markup based on the selling price? Round to the nearest hundredth percent.

10. Bargain Furniture sells a five-piece country maple bedroom set for $1,299. The cost of this set is $700. What are **(a)** the markup on the bedroom set, **(b)** the markup percent on cost, and **(c)** the markup percent on the selling price? Round to the nearest hundredth percent.

11. Robert's Department Store marks up its sundries by 28% on the selling price. If a 6.4-ounce tube of toothpaste costs $1.65, what will the selling price be?

12. To be competitive, Tinker Toys must sell the DS software for $89.99. To meet expenses and make a sufficient profit, Tinker Toys must add a markup on the selling price of 23%. What is the maximum amount that Tinker Toys can afford to pay a wholesaler for the DS software?

13. Nicole's Restaurant charges $7.50 for a linguini dinner that costs $2.75 for the ingredients. What rate of markup is earned on the selling price? Round to the nearest hundredth percent.

Learning Unit 8-3 :   Markdowns and Perishables

DRILL PROBLEMS

1. Find the dollar markdown and the sale price.

Original selling price	Markdown percent	Dollar markdown	Sale price
a. $200	40%	_____	_____
b. $2,099.98	25%	_____	_____
c. $729	30%	_____	_____

2. Find the dollar markdown and the markdown percent on original selling price.

Original selling price	Sale price	Dollar markdown	Markdown percent
a. $19.50	$9.75	_____	_____
b. $250	$175	_____	_____
c. $39.95	$29.96	_____	_____

3. Find the original selling price.

Sale price	Markdown percent	Original selling price
a. $328	20%	_____
b. $15.85	15%	_____

4. Calculate the final selling price.

Original selling price	First markdown	Second markdown	Final markup	Final selling price
a. $4.96	25%	8%	5%	_____
b. $130	30%	10%	20%	_____

5. Find the missing amounts.

Number of units	Unit cost	Total cost	Estimated* spoilage	Desired markup (percent of cost)	Total selling price	Selling price per unit
a. 72	$3	_____	12%	50%	_____	_____
b. 50	$0.90	_____	16%	42%	_____	_____

*Round to the nearest whole unit as needed.

WORD PROBLEMS

6. Speedy King is having a 30%-off sale on its box springs and mattresses. A queen-size, back-supporter mattress is priced at $325. What is the sale price of the mattress?

7. Murray and Sons sells a Dell computer for $602.27. It is having a sale, and the computer is marked down to $499.88. What is the percent of the markdown?

8. Coleman's is having a clearance sale. A lamp with an original selling price of $249 is now selling for $198. Find the percent of the markdown. Round to the nearest hundredth percent.

9. Johnny's Sports Shop has advertised markdowns on certain items of 22%. A soccer ball is marked with a sale price of $16.50. What was the original price of the soccer ball?

10. Sam Grillo sells seasonal furnishings. Near the end of the summer a five-piece patio set that was priced $349.99 had not been sold, so he marked it down by 12%. As Labor Day approached, he still had not sold the patio set, so he marked it down an additional 18%. What was the final selling price of the patio set?

11. Calsey's Department Store sells its down comforters for a regular price of $325. During its white sale the comforters were marked down 22%. Then, at the end of the sale, Calsey's held a special promotion and gave a second markdown of 10%. When the sale was over, the remaining comforters were marked up 20%. What was the final selling price of the remaining comforters?

12. The New Howard Bakery wants to make a 60% profit on the cost of its pies. To calculate the price of the pies, it estimated that the usual amount of spoilage is five pies. Calculate the selling price for each pie if the number of pies baked each day is 24 and the cost of the ingredients for each pie is $1.80.

13. Sunshine Bakery bakes 660 loaves of bread each day and estimates that 10% of the bread will go stale before it is sold and thus will have to be discarded. The owner of the bakery wishes to realize a 55% markup on cost on the bread. If the cost to make a loaf of bread is $0.46, what should the owner sell each loaf for?

Learning Unit 8-4 :   Breakeven Analysis

DRILL PROBLEMS

1. Calculate the contribution margin.

	Selling price per unit	Variable cost per unit	Contribution margin
a.	$14.00	$8.00	
b.	$15.99	$4.88	
c.	$18.99	$4.99	
d.	$251.86	$110.00	
e.	$510.99	$310.00	
f.	$1,000.10	$410.00	

2. Calculate the selling price per unit.

	Selling price per unit	Variable cost per unit	Contribution margin
a.		$12.18	$4.10
b.		$19.19	$5.18
c.		$21.00	$13.00
d.		$41.00	$14.88
e.		$128.10	$79.50
f.		$99.99	$60.00

3. Calculate the breakeven point, rounding to the nearest whole unit.

	Breakeven point	Fixed cost	Selling price per unit	Variable cost per unit
a.		$50,000	$4.00	$1.00
b.		$30,000	$6.00	$2.00
c.		$20,000	$9.00	$3.00
d.		$100,000	$12.00	$4.00
e.		$120,000	$14.00	$5.00
f.		$90,000	$26.00	$8.00

WORD PROBLEMS

4. Jones Co. produces bars of candy. Each bar sells for $3.99. The variable cost per unit is $2.85. What is the contribution margin for Jones Co.?

5. Logan Co. produces stuffed animals. It has $40,000 in fixed costs. Logan sells each animal for $19.99 with a $12.10 cost per unit. What is the breakeven point for Logan? Round to the nearest whole number.

6. Ranyo Company produces lawn mowers. It has a breakeven point of 6,000 lawn mowers. If its contribution margin is $150, what is Ranyo's fixed cost?

7. Moore company has $100,000 in fixed costs. Its contribution margin is $4.50. Calculate the breakeven point for Moore to the nearest whole number.

Learning Unit 9–1 :   Calculating Various Types of Employees' Gross Pay

DRILL PROBLEMS

1. Fill in the missing amounts for each of the following employees. Do not round the overtime rate in your calculations and round your final answers to the nearest cent.

Employee	Total hours	Rate per hour	Regular pay	Overtime pay	Gross pay
a. Mel Jones	38	$11.25	_____	_____	_____
b. Casey Guitare	43	$9.00	_____	_____	_____
c. Norma Harris	37	$7.50	_____	_____	_____
d. Ed Jackson	45	$12.25	_____	_____	_____

2. Calculate each employee's gross from the following data. Do not round the overtime rate in your calculation but round your final answers to the nearest cent.

Employee	S	M	Tu	W	Th	F	S	Total hours	Rate per hour	Regular pay	Overtime pay	Gross pay
a. L. Adams	0	8	8	8	8	8	0	_____	$8.10	_____	_____	_____
b. M. Card	0	9	8	9	8	8	4	_____	$11.35	_____	_____	_____
c. P. Kline	2	$7\frac{1}{2}$	$8\frac{1}{4}$	8	$10\frac{3}{4}$	9	2	_____	$10.60	_____	_____	_____
d. J. Mack	0	$9\frac{1}{2}$	$9\frac{3}{4}$	$9\frac{1}{2}$	10	10	4	_____	$9.95	_____	_____	_____

3. Calculate the gross wages of the following production workers.

Employee	Rate per unit	No. of units produced	Gross pay
a. A. Bossie	$0.67	655	_____
b. J. Carson	$0.87\frac{1}{2}$	703	_____

4. Using the given differential scale, calculate the gross wages of the following production workers.

Units produced	Amount per unit
From 1–50	$.55
From 51–100	.65
From 101–200	.72
More than 200	.95

Employee	Units produced	Gross pay
a. F. Burns	190	_____
b. B. English	210	_____
c. E. Jackson	200	_____

5. Calculate the following salespersons' gross wages.
   a. Straight commission:

Employee	Net sales	Commission	Gross pay
M. Salley	$40,000	13%	_____

b. Straight commission with draw:

Employee	Net sales	Commission	Draw	Commission minus draw
G. Gorsbeck	$38,000	12%	$600	_____

c. Variable commission scale:

Up to $25,000	8%
Excess of $25,000 to $40,000	10%
More than $40,000	12%

Employee	Net sales	Gross pay
H. Lloyd	$42,000	_____

d. Salary plus commission:

Employee	Salary	Commission	Quota	Net sales	Gross pay
P. Floyd	$2,500	3%	$400,000	$475,000	_____

WORD PROBLEMS

For all problems with overtime, be sure to round only the final answer.

6. In the first week of December, Dana Robinson worked 52 hours. His regular rate of pay is $11.25 per hour. What was Dana's gross pay for the week?

7. Davis Fisheries pays its workers for each box of fish they pack. Sunny Melanson receives $.30 per box. During the third week of July, Sunny packed 2,410 boxes of fish. What was Sunny's gross pay?

8. Maye George is a real estate broker who receives a straight commission of 6%. What would her commission be for a house that sold for $197,500?

9. Devon Company pays Eileen Haskins a straight commission of $12\frac{1}{2}$% on net sales. In January, Devon gave Eileen a draw of $600. She had net sales that month of $35,570. What was Eileen's commission minus draw?

10. Parker and Company pays Selma Stokes on a variable commission scale. In a month when Selma had net sales of $155,000, what was her gross pay based on the following schedule?

Net sales	Commission rate
Up to $40,000	5%
Excess of $40,000 to $75,000	5.5%
Excess of $75,000 to $100,000	6%
More than $100,000	7%

11. Marsh Furniture Company pays Joshua Charles a monthly salary of $1,900 plus a commission of $2\frac{1}{2}$% on sales over $12,500. Last month, Joshua had net sales of $17,799. What was Joshua's gross pay for the month?

12. Amy McWha works at Lamplighter Bookstore where she earns $7.75 per hour plus a commission of 2% on her weekly sales in excess of $1,500. Last week, Amy worked 39 hours and had total sales of $2,250. What was Amy's gross pay for the week?

Learning Unit 9–2 : Computing Payroll Deductions for Employees' Pay; Employers' Responsibilities

DRILL PROBLEMS

Use tables in the *Business Math Handbook* (assume FICA rates in text).

Employee	Allowances and marital status	Cumulative earnings	Salary per week	Taxable earnings S.S.	Taxable earnings Medicare
1. Pete Small	M—3	$118,000	$2,300	a. _____	b. _____
2. Alice Hall	M—1	$119,000	$1,100	c. _____	d. _____
3. Jean Rose	M—2	$140,000	$2,000	e. _____	f. _____

4. What is the tax for Social Security and Medicare for Pete in Problem 1?

5. Calculate Pete's FIT by the percentage method.

6. What would the employer contribute for this week's payroll for SUTA and FUTA?

WORD PROBLEMS

7. Cynthia Pratt has earned $117,000 thus far this year. This week she earned $3,500. Find her total FICA tax deduction (Social Security and Medicare).

8. If Cynthia (Problem 7) earns $1,050 the following week, what will be her new total FICA tax deduction?

9. Roger Alley, a service dispatcher, has weekly earnings of $750. He claimed four allowances on his W-4 form and is married. Besides his FIT and FICA deductions, he has deductions of $35.16 for medical insurance and $17.25 for union dues. Calculate his net earnings for the third week in February. Use the percentage method.

10. Nicole Mariotte is unmarried and claimed one withholding allowance on her W-4 form. In the second week of February, she earned $707.35. Deductions from her pay included federal withholding, Social Security, Medicare, health insurance for $47.75, and $30.00 for the company meal plan. What is Nicole's net pay for the week? Use the percentage method.

11. Gerald Knowlton had total gross earnings of $118,200 in the last week of November. His earnings for the first week in December were $804.70. His employer uses the percentage method to calculate federal withholding. If Gerald is married, claims two allowances, and has medical insurance of $52.25 deducted each week from his pay, what is his net pay for the week?

Learning Unit 10–1 : Calculation of Simple Interest and Maturity Value

DRILL PROBLEMS

1. Find the simple interest for each of the following loans:

	Principal	Rate	Time	Interest
a.	$12,000	2%	1 year	_____
b.	$3,000	12%	3 years	_____
c.	$18,000	$8\frac{1}{2}\%$	10 months	_____

2. Find the simple interest for each of the following loans; use the exact interest method. Use the days-in-a-year calendar in the text when needed.

	Principal	Rate	Time	Interest
a.	$900	4%	30 days	_____
b.	$4,290	8%	250 days	_____
c.	$1,500	8%	Made March 11 Due July 11	_____

3. Find the simple interest for each of the following loans using the ordinary interest method (Banker's Rule).

	Principal	Rate	Time	Interest
a.	$5,250	$7\frac{1}{2}\%$	120 days	_____
b.	$700	3%	70 days	_____
c.	$2,600	11%	Made on June 15 Due October 17	_____

WORD PROBLEMS

4. On October 17, Gill Iowa borrowed $6,000 at a rate of 4%. She promised to repay the loan in 7 months. What are **(a)** the amount of the simple interest and **(b)** the total amount owed upon maturity?

5. Marjorie Folsom borrowed $5,500 to purchase a computer. The loan was for 9 months at an annual interest rate of $12\frac{1}{2}\%$. What are **(a)** the amount of interest Marjorie must pay and **(b)** the maturity value of the loan?

6. Eric has a loan for $1,200 at an ordinary interest rate of 9.5% for 80 days. Julie has a loan for $1,200 at an exact interest rate of 9.5% for 80 days. Calculate **(a)** the total amount due on Eric's loan and **(b)** the total amount due on Julie's loan.

7. Roger Lee borrowed $5,280 at $13\frac{1}{2}$% on May 24 and agreed to repay the loan on August 24. The lender calculates interest using the exact interest method. How much will Roger be required to pay on August 24?

8. On March 8, Jack Faltin borrowed $10,225 at $9\frac{3}{4}$%. He signed a note agreeing to repay the loan and interest on November 8. If the lender calculates interest using the ordinary interest method, what will Jack's repayment be?

9. Dianne Smith's real estate taxes of $641.49 were due on November 1, 2015. Due to financial difficulties, Dianne was unable to pay her tax bill until January 15, 2016. The penalty for late payment is $13\frac{3}{8}$% ordinary interest. What is the penalty Dianne will have to pay, and what is Dianne's total payment on January 15?

10. On August 8, Rex Eason had a credit card balance of $550, but he was unable to pay his bill. The credit card company charges interest of $18\frac{1}{2}$% annually on late payments. What amount will Rex have to pay if he pays his bill 1 month late?

11. An issue of *Your Money* discussed average consumers who carry a balance of $2,000 on one credit card. If the yearly rate of interest is 18%, how much are consumers paying in interest per year?

12. AFBA Industrial Bank of Colorado Springs, Colorado, charges a credit card interest rate of 11% per year. If you had a credit card debt of $1,500, what would your interest amount be after 3 months?

Learning Unit 10-2 :   Finding Unknown in Simple Interest Formula

DRILL PROBLEMS

1. Find the principal in each of the following. Round to the nearest cent. Assume 360 days. *Calculator hint:* Do denominator calculation first, and do not round; when answer is displayed, save it in memory by pressing [M+]. Now key in the numerator (interest amount), [÷], [MR], [=] for the answer. Be sure to clear memory after each problem by pressing [MR] again so that the M is no longer in the display.

	Rate	Time	Interest	Principal
a.	8%	70 days	$68	_____
b.	11%	90 days	$125	_____
c.	9%	120 days	$103	_____
d.	$8\frac{1}{2}$%	60 days	$150	_____

2. Find the rate in each of the following. Round to the nearest tenth of a percent. Assume 360 days.

Principal	Time	Interest	Rate
a. $7,500	120 days	$350	_____
b. $975	60 days	$25	_____
c. $20,800	220 days	$910	_____
d. $150	30 days	$2.10	_____

3. Find the time (to the nearest day) in each of the following. Assuming ordinary interest, use 360 days.

Principal	Rate	Interest	Time (days)	Time (years) (Round to nearest hundredth)
a. $400	11%	$7.33	_____	_____
b. $7,000	12.5%	$292	_____	_____
c. $1,550	9.2%	$106.95	_____	_____
d. $157,000	10.75%	$6,797.88	_____	_____

4. Complete the following. Assume 360 days for all examples.

Principal	Rate (nearest tenth percent)	Time (nearest day)	Simple interest
a. $345	_____	150 days	$14.38
b. _____	12.5%	90 days	$46.88
c. $750	12.2%	_____	$19.06
d. $20,260	16.7%	110 days	_____

WORD PROBLEMS

Use 360 days.

5. In June, Becky opened a $20,000 bank CD paying 1% interest, but she had to withdraw the money in a few days to cover one child's college tuition. The bank charged her $1,000 in penalties for the withdrawal. What percent of the $20,000 was she charged?

6. Dr. Vaccarro invested his money at $12\frac{1}{2}$% for 175 days and earned interest of $760. How much money did Dr. Vaccarro invest?

7. If you invested $10,000 at 5% interest in a 6-month CD compounding interest daily, you would earn $252.43 in interest. How much would the same $10,000 invested in a bank paying simple interest earn?

8. Thomas Kyrouz opened a savings account and deposited $750 in a bank that was paying 2.5% simple interest. How much were his savings worth in 200 days?

9. Mary Millitello paid the bank $53.90 in interest on a 66-day loan at 9.8%. How much money did Mary borrow? Round to the nearest dollar.

10. If Anthony Lucido deposits $2,400 for 66 days and makes $60.72 in interest, what interest rate is he receiving?

11. Find how long in days David Wong must invest $23,500 of his company's cash at 8.4% in order to earn $652.50 in interest.

Learning Unit 10–3 :   U.S. Rule—Making Partial Note Payments before Due Date

DRILL PROBLEMS

1. A merchant borrowed $3,000 for 320 days at 11% (assume a 360-day year). Use the U.S. Rule to complete the following table:

Payment number	Payment day	Amount paid	Interest to date	Principal payment	Adjusted balance
					$3,000
1	75	$500	_____	_____	_____
2	160	$750	_____	_____	_____
3	220	$1,000	_____	_____	_____
4	320	_____	_____	_____	_____

2. Use the U.S. Rule to solve for total interest costs, balances, and final payments; use ordinary interest.

Given

Principal, $6,000, 5%, 100 days
Partial payments on 30th day, $2,000
　　　　　　　 on 70th day, $1,000

WORD PROBLEMS

3. John Joseph borrowed $10,800 for 1 year at 14%. After 60 days, he paid $2,500 on the note. On the 200th day, he paid an additional $5,000. Use the U.S. Rule and ordinary interest to find the final balance due.

4. Doris Davis borrowed $8,200 on March 5 for 90 days at $8\frac{3}{4}\%$. After 32 days, Doris made a payment on the loan of $2,700. On the 65th day, she made another payment of $2,500. What is her final payment if you use the U.S. Rule with ordinary interest?

5. David Ring borrowed $6,000 on a 13%, 60-day note. After 10 days, David paid $500 on the note. On day 40, David paid $900 on the note. What are the total interest and ending balance due by the U.S. Rule? Use ordinary interest.

Learning Unit 11–1 :   Structure of Promissory Notes; the Simple Discount Note

DRILL PROBLEMS

1. Identify each of the following characteristics of promissory notes with an **I** for simple interest note, a **D** for simple discount note, or a **B** if it is true for both.

   ___ Interest is computed on face value, or what is actually borrowed.   ___ Borrower receives the face value.

   ___ A promissory note for a loan usually less than 1 year.   ___ Paid back by one payment at maturity.

   ___ Borrower receives proceeds = Face value − Bank discount.   ___ Interest computed on maturity value, or what will

   ___ Maturity value = Face value + Interest.   be repaid, and not on actual amount borrowed.

   ___ Maturity value = Face value.

2. Find the bank discount and the proceeds for the following; assume 360 days:

Maturity value	Discount rate	Time (days)	Bank discount	Proceeds
a. $8,000	3%	120	_____	_____
b. $4,550	8.1%	110	_____	_____
c. $19,350	12.7%	55	_____	_____
d. $63,400	10%	90	_____	_____
e. $13,490	7.9%	200	_____	_____
f. $780	$12\frac{1}{2}\%$	65	_____	_____

3. Find the effective rate of interest for each of the loans in Problem 2. Use the answers you calculated in Problem 2 to solve these problems; round to the nearest tenth percent.

Maturity value	Discount rate	Time (days)	Effective rate
a. $7,000	2%	90	_____
b. $4,550	8.1%	110	_____
c. $19,350	12.7%	55	_____
d. $63,400	10%	90	_____
e. $13,490	7.9%	200	_____
f. $780	$12\frac{1}{2}\%$	65	_____

WORD PROBLEMS

Assume 360 days.

4. Kaylee Putty signed an $8,000 note for 140 days at a discount rate of 5%. Find the discount and the proceeds Kaylee received.

5. The Salem Cooperative Bank charges an $8\frac{3}{4}\%$ discount rate. What are the discount and the proceeds for a $16,200 note for 60 days?

6. Bill Jackson is planning to buy a used car. He went to City Credit Union to take out a loan for $6,400 for 300 days. If the credit union charges a discount rate of $11\frac{1}{2}\%$, what will the proceeds of this loan be?

7. Mike Drislane goes to the bank and signs a note for $9,700. The bank charges a 15% discount rate. Find the discount and the proceeds if the loan is for 210 days.

8. Flora Foley plans to have a deck built on the back of her house. She decides to take out a loan at the bank for $14,300. She signs a note promising to pay back the loan in 280 days. If the note was discounted at 9.2%, how much money will Flora receive from the bank?

9. At the end of 280 days, Flora (Problem 8) must pay back the loan. What is the maturity value of the loan?

10. Dave Cassidy signed a $7,855 note at a bank that charges a 14.2% discount rate. If the loan is for 190 days, find **(a)** the proceeds and **(b)** the effective rate charged by the bank (to the nearest tenth percent).

11. How much money must Dave (Problem 10) pay back to the bank?

Learning Unit 11-2 : Discounting an Interest-Bearing Note before Maturity

DRILL PROBLEMS

1. Calculate the maturity value for each of the following promissory notes; use 360 days:

Date of note	Principal of note	Length of note (days)	Interest rate	Maturity value
a. June 9	$5,000	180	3%	_____
b. August 23	$15,990	85	13%	_____
c. December 10	$985	30	11.5%	_____

2. Find the maturity date and the discount period for the following; assume no leap years. *Hint:* See Exact Days-in-a-Year Calendar, Chapter 7.

Date of note	Length of note (days)	Date of discount	Maturity date	Discount period
a. March 11	200	June 28	_____	_____
b. January 22	60	March 2	_____	_____
c. April 19	85	June 6	_____	_____
d. November 17	120	February 15	_____	_____

3. Find the bank discount for each of the following; use 360 days:

Date of note	Principal of note	Length of note	Interest rate	Bank discount rate	Date of discount	Bank discount
a. October 5	$2,475	88 days	11%	9.5%	December 10	_____
b. June 13	$9,055	112 days	15%	16%	August 11	_____
c. March 20	$1,065	75 days	12%	11.5%	May 24	_____

4. Find the proceeds for each of the discounted notes in Problem 3.

a. _____

b. _____

c. _____

WORD PROBLEMS

5. Connors Company received a $4,000, 90-day, 10% note dated April 6 from one of its customers. Connors Company held the note until May 16, when the company discounted it at a bank at a discount rate of 12%. What were the proceeds that Connors Company received?

6. Souza & Sons accepted a 9%, $22,000, 120-day note from one of its customers on July 22. On October 2, the company discounted the note at Cooperative Bank. The discount rate was 12%. What were **(a)** the bank discount and **(b)** the proceeds?

7. The Fargate Store accepted an $8,250, 75-day, 9% note from one of its customers on March 18. Fargate discounted the note at Parkside National Bank at $9\frac{1}{2}$% on March 29. What proceeds did Fargate receive?

8. On November 1, Marjorie's Clothing Store accepted a $5,200, $8\frac{1}{2}$%, 90-day note from Mary Rose in granting her a time extension on her bill. On January 13, Marjorie discounted the note at Seawater Bank, which charged a 10% discount rate. What were the proceeds that Majorie received?

9. On December 3, Duncan's Company accepted a $5,000, 90-day, 12% note from Al Finney in exchange for a $5,000 bill that was past due. On January 29, Duncan discounted the note at The Sidwell Bank at 13.1%. What were the proceeds from the note?

10. On February 26, Sullivan Company accepted a 60-day, 10% note in exchange for a $1,500 past-due bill from Tabot Company. On March 28, Sullivan Company discounted at National Bank the note received from Tabot Company. The bank discount rate was 12%. What are **(a)** the bank discount and **(b)** the proceeds?

11. On June 4, Johnson Company received from Marty Russo a 30-day, 11% note for $720 to settle Russo's debt. On June 17, Johnson discounted the note at Eastern Bank at 15%. What proceeds did Johnson receive?

12. On December 15, Lawlers Company went to the bank and discounted a 10%, 90-day, $14,000 note dated October 21. The bank charged a discount rate of 12%. What were the proceeds of the note?

Learning Unit 12-1 :   Compound Interest (Future Value)—The Big Picture

DRILL PROBLEMS

1. In the following examples, calculate manually the amount at year-end for each of the deposits, assuming that interest is compounded annually. Round to the nearest cent each year.

	Principal	Rate	Number of years	Year 1	Year 2	Year 3	Year 4
a.	$530	4%	2	_____	_____		
b.	$1,980	12%	4	_____	_____	_____	_____

2. In the following examples, calculate the simple interest, the compound interest, and the difference between the two. Round to the nearest cent; do not use tables.

	Principal	Rate	Number of years	Simple interest	Compound interest	Difference
a.	$4,600	10%	2	_____	_____	_____
b.	$18,400	9%	4	_____	_____	_____
c.	$855	$7\frac{1}{5}\%$	3	_____	_____	_____

3. Find the future value and the compound interest using the Future Value of $1 at Compound Interest table or the Compound Daily table. Round to the nearest cent.

	Principal	Investment terms	Future value	Compound interest
a.	$20,000	6 years at 4% compounded annually	_____	_____
b.	$10,000	6 years at 8% compounded quarterly	_____	_____
c.	$8,400	7 years at 12% compounded semiannually	_____	_____
d.	$2,500	15 years at 10% compounded daily	_____	_____
e.	$9,600	5 years at 6% compounded quarterly	_____	_____
f.	$20,000	2 years at 6% compounded monthly	_____	_____

4. Calculate the effective rate (APY) of interest using the Future Value of $1 at Compound Interest table.

Investment terms	Effective rate (annual percentage yield)
a. 12% compounded quarterly	_____
b. 12% compounded semiannually	_____
c. 6% compounded quarterly	_____

WORD PROBLEMS

5. John Mackey deposited $7,000 in his savings account at Salem Savings Bank. If the bank pays 2% interest compounded semi-annually, what will be the balance of his account at the end of 3 years?

6. Pine Valley Savings Bank offers a certificate of deposit at 12% interest compounded quarterly. What is the effective rate (APY) of interest?

7. Jack Billings loaned $6,000 to his brother-in-law Dan, who was opening a new business. Dan promised to repay the loan at the end of 5 years, with interest of 8% compounded semiannually. How much will Dan pay Jack at the end of 5 years?

8. Eileen Hogarty deposits $5,630 in City Bank, which pays 12% interest compounded quarterly. How much money will Eileen have in her account at the end of 7 years?

9. If Kevin Bassage deposits $3,500 in Scarsdale Savings Bank, which pays 8% interest compounded quarterly, what will be in his account at the end of 6 years? How much interest will he have earned at that time?

10. Arlington Trust pays 6% compounded semiannually. How much interest would be earned on $7,200 for 1 year?

11. Paladium Savings Bank pays 9% compounded quarterly. Find the amount and the interest on $3,000 after three quarters. Do not use a table.

12. David Siderski bought an $8,000 bank certificate paying 4% compounded semiannually. How much money did he obtain upon cashing in the certificate 3 years later?

13. An issue of *Your Money* showed that the more frequently the bank compounds your money, the better. Consider a $10,000 investment earning 6% interest in a 5-year certificate of deposit at the following three banks. What would be the interest earned at each bank?
   a. Bank A (simple interest, no compounding)
   b. Bank B (quarterly compounding)
   c. Bank C (daily compounding)

Learning Unit 12-2 : Present Value—The Big Picture

DRILL PROBLEMS

1. Use the *Business Math Handbook* to find the table factor for each of the following:

	Future value	Rate	Number of years	Compounded	Table value
a.	$1.00	2%	5	Annually	_____
b.	$1.00	12%	8	Semiannually	_____
c.	$1.00	6%	10	Quarterly	_____
d.	$1.00	12%	2	Monthly	_____
e.	$1.00	8%	15	Semiannually	_____

2. Use the *Business Math Handbook* to find the table factor and the present value for each of the following:

	Future value	Rate	Number of years	Compounded	Table value	Present value
a.	$1,000	2%	6	Semiannually	_____	_____
b.	$1,000	16%	7	Quarterly	_____	_____
c.	$1,000	8%	7	Quarterly	_____	_____
d.	$1,000	8%	7	Semiannually	_____	_____
e.	$1,000	8%	7	Annually	_____	_____

3. Find the present value and the interest earned for the following:

	Future value	Number of years	Rate	Compounded	Present value	Interest earned
a.	$2,500	6	8%	Annually	_____	_____
b.	$4,600	10	6%	Semiannually	_____	_____
c.	$12,800	8	10%	Semiannually	_____	_____
d.	$28,400	7	8%	Quarterly	_____	_____
e.	$53,050	1	12%	Monthly	_____	_____

4. Find the missing amount (present value or future value) for each of the following:

	Present value	Investment terms	Future value
a.	$3,500	5 years at 8% compounded annually	_____
b.	_____	6 years at 12% compounded semiannually	$9,000
c.	$4,700	9 years at 14% compounded semiannually	_____

WORD PROBLEMS

Solve for future value or present value.

5. Paul Palumbo assumes that he will need to have a new roof put on his house in 4 years. He estimates that the roof will cost him $17,000 at that time. What amount of money should Paul invest today at 2%, compounded semiannually, to be able to pay for the roof?

6. Tilton, a pharmacist, rents his store and has signed a lease that will expire in 3 years. When the lease expires, Tilton wants to buy his own store. He wants to have a down payment of $35,000 at that time. How much money should Tilton invest today at 6%, compounded quarterly, to yield $35,000?

7. Brad Morrissey loans $8,200 to his brother-in-law. He will be repaid at the end of 5 years, with interest at 10% compounded semiannually. Find out how much he will be repaid.

8. The owner of Waverly Sheet Metal Company plans to buy some new machinery in 6 years. He estimates that the machines he wishes to purchase will cost $39,700 at that time. What must he invest today at 8%, compounded semiannually, to have sufficient money to purchase the new machines?

9. Paul Stevens's grandparents want to buy him a car when he graduates from college in 4 years. They feel that they should have $27,000 in the bank at that time. How much should they invest at 12%, compounded quarterly, to reach their goal?

10. Gilda Nardi deposits $5,325 in a bank that pays 12% interest compounded quarterly. Find the amount she will have at the end of 7 years.

11. Mary Wilson wants to buy a new set of golf clubs in 2 years. They will cost $775. How much money should she invest today at 9%, compounded annually, so that she will have enough money to buy the new clubs?

12. Jack Beggs plans to invest $30,000 at 10%, compounded semiannually, for 5 years. What is the future value of the investment?

13. Ron Thrift expects his Honda Pilot will last 3 more years. Ron does not like to finance his purchases. He went to First National Bank to find out how much money he should put in the bank to purchase a $20,300 car in 3 years. The bank's 3-year CD is compounded quarterly with a 4% rate. How much should Ron invest in the CD?

14. The Downers Grove YMCA had a fund-raising campaign to build a swimming pool in 6 years. Members raised $825,000; the pool is estimated to cost $1,230,000. The money will be placed in Downers Grove Bank, which pays daily interest at 6%. Will the YMCA have enough money to pay for the pool in 6 years?

Learning Unit 13–1 : Annuities: Ordinary Annuity and Annuity Due (Find Future Value)

DRILL PROBLEMS

1. Find the value of the following ordinary annuities; calculate manually:

Amount of each annual deposit	Interest rate	Value at end of year 1	Value at end of year 2	Value at end of year 3
a. $1,000	8%	_____	_____	_____
b. $2,500	12%	_____	_____	_____
c. $7,200	10%	_____	_____	_____

2. Use the Ordinary Annuity Table: Compound Sum of an Annuity of $1 to find the value of the following ordinary annuities:

Annuity payment	Payment period	Term of annuity	Interest rate	Value of annuity
a. $650	Semiannually	5 years	6%	_____
b. $3,790	Annually	13 years	12%	_____
c. $500	Quarterly	1 year	8%	_____

3. Find the annuity due (deposits are made at beginning of period) for each of the following using the Ordinary Annuity Table:

Amount of payment	Payment period	Interest rate	Time (years)	Amount of annuity
a. $900	Annually	7%	6	_____
b. $1,200	Annually	11%	4	_____
c. $550	Semiannually	10%	9	_____

4. Find the amount of each annuity:

Amount of payment	Payment period	Interest rate	Time (years)	Type of annuity	Amount of annuity
a. $600	Semiannually	12%	8	Ordinary	_____
b. $600	Semiannually	12%	8	Due	_____
c. $1,100	Annually	9%	7	Ordinary	_____

WORD PROBLEMS

5. At the end of each year for the next 9 years, D'Aldo Company will deposit $25,000 in an ordinary annuity account paying 9% interest compounded annually. Find the value of the annuity at the end of the 9 years.

6. David McCarthy is a professional baseball player who expects to play in the major leagues for 10 years. To save for the future, he will deposit $50,000 at the beginning of each year into an account that pays 11% interest compounded annually. How much will he have in this account at the end of 10 years?

7. Tom and Sue plan to get married. Because they hope to have a large wedding, they are going to deposit $1,000 at the end of each month into an account that pays 24% compounded monthly. How much will they have in this account at the end of 1 year?

8. Chris Dennen deposits $15,000 at the end of each year for 13 years into an account paying 7% interest compounded annually. What is the value of her annuity at the end of 13 years? How much interest will she have earned?

9. Amanda Blinn is 52 years old today and has just opened an IRA. She plans to deposit $500 at the end of each quarter into her account. If Amanda retires on her 62nd birthday, what amount will she have in her account if the account pays 8% interest compounded quarterly?

10. Jerry Davis won the citywide sweepstakes and will receive a check for $2,000 at the beginning of each 6 months for the next 5 years. If Jerry deposits each check in an account that pays 8% compounded semiannually, how much will he have at the end of 5 years?

11. Mary Hynes purchased an ordinary annuity from an investment broker at 8% interest compounded semiannually. If her semiannual deposit is $600, what will be the value of the annuity at the end of 15 years?

Learning Unit 13–2 :   Present Value of an Ordinary Annuity (Find Present Value)

DRILL PROBLEMS

1. Use the Present Value of an Annuity of $1 table to find the amount to be invested today to receive a stream of payments for a given number of years in the future. Show the manual check of your answer. (Check may be a few pennies off due to rounding.)

Amount of expected payments	Payment period	Interest rate	Term of annuity	Present value of annuity
a. $1,500	Yearly	9%	2 years	_____
b. $2,700	Yearly	13%	3 years	_____
c. $2,700	Yearly	6%	3 years	_____

2. Find the present value of the following annuities. Use the Present Value of an Annuity of $1 table.

Amount of each payment	Payment period	Interest rate	Time (years)	Compounded	Present value of annuity
a. $2,000	Year	7%	25	Annually	_____
b. $7,000	Year	11%	12	Annually	_____
c. $850	6 months	12%	5	Semiannually	_____
d. $1,950	6 months	14%	9	Semiannually	_____
e. $500	Quarter	12%	10	Quarterly	_____

WORD PROBLEMS

3. Tom Hanson would like to receive $200 each quarter for the 4 years he is in college. If his bank account pays 8% compounded quarterly, how much must he have in his account when he begins college?

4. Jean Reith has just retired and will receive a $12,500 retirement check every 6 months for the next 20 years. If her employer can invest money at 12% compounded semiannually, what amount must be invested today to make the semiannual payments to Jean?

5. Tom Herrick will pay $4,500 at the end of each year for the next 7 years to pay the balance of his college loans. If Tom can invest his money at 7% compounded annually, how much must he invest today to make the annual payments?

6. Helen Grahan is planning an extended sabbatical for the next 3 years. She would like to invest a lump sum of money at 10% interest so that she can withdraw $6,000 every 6 months while on sabbatical. What is the amount of the lump sum that Helen must invest?

7. Linda Rudd has signed a rental contract for office equipment, agreeing to pay $3,200 at the end of each quarter for the next 5 years. If Linda can invest money at 12% compounded quarterly, find the lump sum she can deposit today to make the payments for the length of the contract.

8. Sam Adams is considering lending his brother John $6,000. John said that he would repay Sam $775 every 6 months for 4 years. If money can be invested at 8%, calculate the equivalent cash value of the offer today. Should Sam go ahead with the loan?

9. The State Lotto Game offers a grand prize of $1,000,000 paid in 20 yearly payments of $50,000. If the state treasurer can invest money at 9% compounded annually, how much must she invest today to make the payments to the grand prize winner?

10. Thomas Martin's uncle has promised him upon graduation a gift of $20,000 in cash or $2,000 every quarter for the next 3 years. If money can be invested at 8%, which offer will Thomas accept? (Thomas is a business major.)

11. Paul Sasso is selling a piece of land. He has received two solid offers. Jason Smith has offered a $60,000 down payment and $50,000 a year for the next 5 years. Kevin Bassage offered $35,000 down and $55,000 a year for the next 5 years. If money can be invested at 7% compounded annually, which offer should Paul accept? (To make the comparison, find the equivalent cash price of each offer.)

12. Abe Hoster decided to retire to Spain in 10 years. What amount should Abe invest today so that he will be able to withdraw $30,000 at the end of each year for 20 years after he retires? Assume he can invest money at 8% interest compounded annually.

Learning Unit 13–3 :   Sinking Funds (Find Periodic Payments)

DRILL PROBLEMS

1. Given the number of years and the interest rate, use the Sinking Fund Table based on $1 to calculate the amount of the periodic payment.

Frequency of payment	Length of time	Interest rate	Future amount	Sinking fund payment
a. Annually	19 years	5%	$125,000	_____
b. Annually	7 years	10%	$205,000	_____
c. Semiannually	10 years	6%	$37,500	_____
d. Quarterly	9 years	12%	$12,750	_____
e. Quarterly	6 years	8%	$25,600	_____

2. Find the amount of each payment into the sinking fund and the amount of interest earned.

	Maturity value	Interest rate	Term (years)	Frequency of payment	Sinking fund payment	Interest earned
a.	$45,500	5%	13	Annually	_____	_____
b.	$8,500	10%	20	Semiannually	_____	_____
c.	$11,000	8%	5	Quarterly	_____	_____
d.	$66,600	12%	$7\frac{1}{2}$	Semiannually	_____	_____

WORD PROBLEMS

3. To finance a new police station, the town of Pine Valley issued bonds totaling $600,000. The town treasurer set up a sinking fund at 8% compounded quarterly in order to redeem the bonds in 7 years. What is the quarterly payment that must be deposited into the fund?

4. Arlex Oil Corporation plans to build a new garage in 6 years. To finance the project, the financial manager established a $250,000 sinking fund at 6% compounded semianually. Find the semiannual payment required for the fund.

5. The City Fisheries Corporation sold $300,000 worth of bonds that must be redeemed in 9 years. The corporation agreed to set up a sinking fund to accumulate the $300,000. Find the amount of the periodic payments made into the fund if payments are made annually and the fund earns 8% compounded annually.

6. Gregory Mines Corporation wishes to purchase a new piece of equipment in 4 years. The estimated price of the equipment is $100,000. If the corporation makes periodic payments into a sinking fund with 12% interest compounded quarterly, find the amount of the periodic payments.

7. The Best Corporation must buy a new piece of machinery in $4\frac{1}{2}$ years that will cost $350,000. If the firm sets up a sinking fund to finance this new machine, what will the quarterly deposits be assuming the fund earns 8% interest compounded quarterly?

8. The Lowest-Price-in-Town Company needs $75,500 in 6 years to pay off a debt. The company makes a decision to set up a sinking fund and make semiannual deposits. What will its payments be if the fund pays 10% interest compounded semiannually?

9. The WIR Company plans to renovate its offices in 5 years. It estimates that the cost will be $235,000. If the company sets up a sinking fund that pays 12% quarterly, what will its quarterly payments be?

Learning Unit 14–1 :   Cost of Installment Buying

DRILL PROBLEMS

1. For the following installment problems, find the amount financed and the finance charge.

	Sale price	Down payment	Number of monthly payments	Monthly payment	Amount financed	Finance charge
a.	$1,500	$300	24	$58	_____	_____
b.	$12,000	$3,000	30	$340	_____	_____
c.	$62,500	$4,700	48	$1,500	_____	_____
d.	$4,975	$620	18	$272	_____	_____
e.	$825	$82.50	12	$67.45	_____	_____

2. For each of the above purchases, find the deferred payment price.

	Sale price	Down payment	Number of monthly payments	Monthly payment	Deferred payment price
a.	$1,500	$300	24	$58	_____
b.	$12,000	$3,000	30	$340	_____
c.	$62,500	$4,700	48	$1,500	_____
d.	$4,975	$620	18	$272	_____
e.	$825	$82.50	12	$67.45	_____

3. Use the Annual Percentage Rate Table per $100 to calculate the estimated APR for each of the previous purchases.

	Sale price	Down payment	Number of monthly payments	Monthly payment	Annual percentage rate
a.	$1,500	$300	24	$58	_____
b.	$12,000	$3,000	30	$340	_____
c.	$62,500	$4,700	48	$1,500	_____
d.	$4,975	$620	18	$272	_____
e.	$825	$82.50	12	$67.45	_____

4. Given the following information, calculate the monthly payment by the loan amortization table.

	Amount financed	Interest rate	Number of months of loan	Monthly payment
a.	$12,000	10%	18	_____
b.	$18,000	11%	36	_____
c.	$25,500	13.50%	54	_____

WORD PROBLEMS

5. Jill Walsh purchases a bedroom set for a cash price of $3,920. The down payment is $392, and the monthly installment payment is $176 for 24 months. Find **(a)** the amount financed, **(b)** the finance charge, and **(c)** the deferred payment price.

6. An automaker promotion loan on a $20,000 automobile and a down payment of 20% are being financed for 48 months. The monthly payments will be $367.74. What will be the APR for this auto loan? Use the table in the *Business Math Handbook*.

7. David Nason purchased a recreational vehicle for $25,000. David went to City Bank to finance the purchase. The bank required that David make a 10% down payment and monthly payments of $571.50 for 4 years. Find **(a)** the amount financed, **(b)** the finance charge, and **(c)** the deferred payment that David paid.

8. Calculate the estimated APR that David (Problem 7) was charged per $100 using the Annual Percentage Rate Table.

9. Young's Motors advertised a new car for $16,720. Young's offered an installment plan of 5% down and 42 monthly payments of $470. What are **(a)** the deferred payment price and **(b)** the estimated APR for this car? Use the table.

10. Angie French bought a used car for $9,000. Angie put down $2,000 and financed the balance at 11.50% for 36 months. What is her monthly payment? Use the loan amortization table.

Learning Unit 14–2 :   Revolving Charge Credit Cards

DRILL PROBLEMS

1. Use the U.S. Rule to calculate the outstanding balance due for each of the following independent situations:

	Monthly payment number	Outstanding balance due	$1\frac{1}{2}\%$ interest payment	Amount of monthly payment	Reduction in balance due	Outstanding balance due
a.	1	$9,000.00	_____	$600	_____	_____
b.	5	$5,625.00	_____	$1,000	_____	_____
c.	4	$926.50	_____	$250	_____	_____
d.	12	$62,391.28	_____	$1,200	_____	_____
e.	8	$3,255.19	_____	$325	_____	_____

2. Complete the missing data for a $6,500 purchase made on credit. The annual interest charge on this revolving charge account is 18%, or $1\frac{1}{2}$% interest on previous month's balance. Use the U.S. Rule.

Monthly payment number	Outstanding balance due	$1\frac{1}{2}$% interest payment	Amount of monthly payment	Reduction in balance due	Outstanding balance due
1	$6,500	_____	$700	_____	_____
2	_____	_____	$700	_____	_____
3	_____	_____	$700	_____	_____

3. Calculate the average billing daily balance for each of the monthly statements for the following revolving credit accounts; assume a 30-day billing cycle:

Billing date	Previous balance	Payment date	Payment amount	Charge date(s)	Charge amount(s)	Average daily balance
a. 4/10	$329	4/25	$35	4/29	$56	_____
b. 6/15	$573	6/25	$60	6/26	$25	
				6/30	$72	_____
c. 9/15	$335.50	9/20	$33.55	9/25	$12.50	
				9/26	$108	_____

4. Find the finance charge for each monthly statement (Problem 3) if the annual percentage rate is 15%.

   a. _____   **b.** _____   **c.** _____

WORD PROBLEMS

5. Niki Marshall is going to buy a new bedroom set at Scottie's Furniture Store, where she has a revolving charge account. The cost of the bedroom set is $5,500. Niki does not plan to charge anything else to her account until she has completely paid for the bedroom set. Scottie's Furniture Store charges an annual percentage rate of 18%, or $1\frac{1}{2}$% per month. Niki plans to pay $1,000 per month until she has paid for the bedroom set. Set up a schedule for Niki to show her outstanding balance at the end of each month after her $1,000 payment and also the amount of her final payment. Use the U.S. Rule.

6. Frances Dollof received her monthly statement from Brown's Department Store. The following is part of the information contained on that statement. Finance charge is calculated on the average daily balance.

Date	Reference	Department	Description	Amount
Dec. 15	5921	359	Petite sportswear	84.98
Dec. 15	9612	432	Footwear	55.99
Dec. 15	2600	126	Women's fragrance	35.18
Dec. 23	6247	61	Ralph Lauren towels	20.99
Dec. 24	0129	998	Payment received—thank you	100.00CR

Previous balance		Annual percentage rate	Billing date
719.04	12/13	18%	JAN 13

Brown's Charge Account Terms
Payment is required in monthly installments upon receipt of monthly statement in accordance with Brown's payment terms.

When my new balance is:	My minimum required payment is:	When my new balance is:	My minimum required payment is:
Up to $20.00	New Balance	$350.01 to $400.00	$40.00
$ 20.01 to $200.00	$20.00	$400.01 to $450.00	$45.00
$200.01 to $250.00	$25.00	$450.01 to $500.00	$50.00
$250.01 to $300.00	$30.00	More than $500.00	$50.00 plus
$300.01 to $350.00	$35.00		$10.00 for each $50.00 (or fraction thereof) of New Balance over $500.00

   a. Calculate the average daily balance for the month.
   b. What is Ms. Dollof's finance charge?
   c. What is the new balance for Ms. Dollof's account?
   d. What is the minimum payment Frances is required to pay according to Brown's payment terms?

7. What is the finance charge for a Brown's customer who has an average daily balance of $3,422.67?

8. What is the minimum payment for a Brown's customer with a new balance of $522.00?

9. What is the minimum payment for a Brown's customer with a new balance of $325.01?

10. What is the new balance for a Brown's customer with a previous balance of $309.35 whose purchases totaled $213.00, given that the customer made a payment of $75.00 and the finance charge was $4.65?

RECAP OF WORD PROBLEMS IN LU 14–1

11. A home equity loan on a $20,000 automobile with a down payment of 20% is being financed for 48 months. The interest is tax deductible. The monthly payments will be $401.97. What is the APR on this loan? Use the table in the *Business Math Handbook*. If the person is in the 28% income tax bracket, what will be the tax savings with this type of a loan?

12. An automobile with a total transaction price of $20,000 with a down payment of 20% is being financed for 48 months. Banks and credit unions require a monthly payment of $400.36. What is the APR for this auto loan? Use the table in the *Business Math Handbook*.

13. Assume you received a $2,000 rebate that brought the price of a car down to $20,000; the financing rate was for 48 months, and your total interest was $3,279. Using the table in the *Business Math Handbook*, what was your APR?

Learning Unit 15–1 :   Types of Mortgages and the Monthly Mortgage Payment

DRILL PROBLEMS

1. Use the table in the *Business Math Handbook* to calculate the monthly payment for principal and interest for the following mortgages:

Price of home	Down payment	Interest rate	Term in years	Monthly payment
a. $200,000	15%	6%	25	_____
b. $200,000	15%	$5\frac{1}{2}\%$	30	_____
c. $450,000	10%	$11\frac{3}{4}\%$	30	_____
d. $450,000	10%	11%	30	_____

2. For each of the mortgages, calculate the amount of interest that will be paid over the life of the loan.

Price of home	Down payment	Interest rate	Term in years	Total interest paid
a. $200,000	15%	$6\frac{1}{2}\%$	25	_____
b. $200,000	15%	$10\frac{1}{2}\%$	30	_____
c. $450,000	10%	$11\frac{3}{4}\%$	30	_____
d. $450,000	10%	11%	30	_____

3. Calculate the increase in the monthly mortgage payments for each of the rate increases in the following mortgages. Then calculate what percent of change the increase represents, rounded to the nearest tenth percent.

Mortgage amount	Term in years	Interest rate	Increase in interest rate	Increase in monthly payment	Percent change
a. $175,000	22	9%	1%	_____	_____
b. $300,000	30	$11\frac{3}{4}\%$	$\frac{3}{4}\%$	_____	_____

4. Calculate the increase in total interest paid for the increase in interest rates in Problem 3.

Mortgage amount	Term in years	Interest rate	Increase in interest rate	Increase in total interest paid
a. $175,000	22	9%	1%	_____
b. $300,000	30	$11\frac{3}{4}\%$	$\frac{3}{4}\%$	_____

WORD PROBLEMS

5. The Counties are planning to purchase a new home that costs $150,000. The bank is charging them 6% interest and requires a 20% down payment. The Counties are planning to take a 25-year mortgage. How much will their monthly payment be for principal and interest?

6. The MacEacherns wish to buy a new house that costs $299,000. The bank requires a 15% down payment and charges $11\frac{1}{2}\%$ interest. If the MacEacherns take out a 15-year mortgage, what will their monthly payment for principal and interest be?

7. Because the monthly payments are so high, the MacEacherns (Problem 6) want to know what the monthly payments would be for (a) a 25-year mortgage and (b) a 30-year mortgage. Calculate these two payments.

8. If the MacEacherns choose a 30-year mortgage instead of a 15-year mortgage, (a) how much money will they "save" monthly and (b) how much more interest will they pay over the life of the loan?

9. If the MacEacherns choose the 25-year mortgage instead of the 30-year mortgage, (a) how much more will they pay monthly and (b) how much less interest will they pay over the life of the loan?

10. Larry and Doris Davis plan to purchase a new home that costs $415,000. The bank that they are dealing with requires a 20% down payment and charges $12\frac{3}{4}\%$. The Davises are planning to take a 25-year mortgage. What will the monthly payment be?

11. How much interest will the Davises (Problem 10) pay over the life of the loan?

Learning Unit 15–2 :   Amortization Schedule—Breaking Down the Monthly Payment

DRILL PROBLEMS

1. In the following, calculate the monthly payment for each mortgage, the portion of the first monthly payment that goes to interest, and the portion of the payment that goes toward the principal.

Amount of mortgage	Interest rate	Term in years	Monthly payment	Portion to interest	Portion to principal
a. $170,000	8%	22	_____	_____	_____
b. $222,000	$11\frac{3}{4}\%$	30	_____	_____	_____
c. $167,000	$10\frac{1}{2}\%$	25	_____	_____	_____
d. $307,000	13%	15	_____	_____	_____
e. $409,500	$12\frac{1}{2}\%$	20	_____	_____	_____

2. Prepare an amortization schedule for the first 3 months of a 25-year, 12% mortgage on $265,000.

Payment number	Monthly payment	Portion to interest	Portion to principal	Balance of loan outstanding
1	_____	_____	_____	_____
2	_____	_____	_____	_____
3	_____	_____	_____	_____

3. Prepare an amortization schedule for the first 4 months of a 30-year, $10\frac{1}{2}$% mortgage on $195,500.

Payment number	Monthly payment	Portion to interest	Portion to principal	Balance of loan outstanding
1	_____	_____	_____	_____
2	_____	_____	_____	_____
3	_____	_____	_____	_____
4	_____	_____	_____	_____

WORD PROBLEMS

4. Jim and Janice Hurst are buying a new home for $235,000. The bank that is financing the home requires a 20% down payment and charges a $13\frac{1}{2}$% interest rate. Janice wants to know (a) what the monthly payment for the principal and interest will be if they take out a 30-year mortgage and (b) how much of the first payment will be for interest on the loan.

5. The Hursts (Problem 4) thought that a lot of their money was going to interest. They asked the banker just how much they would be paying for interest over the life of the loan. Calculate the total amount of interest that the Hursts will pay.

6. The banker told the Hursts (Problem 4) that they could, of course, save on the interest payments if they took out a loan for a shorter period of time. Jim and Janice decided to see if they could afford a 15-year mortgage. Calculate how much more the Hursts would have to pay each month for principal and interest if they took a 15-year mortgage for their loan.

7. The Hursts (Problem 4) thought that they might be able to afford this, but first wanted to see (a) how much of the first payment would go to the principal and (b) how much total interest they would be paying with a 15-year mortgage.

8.

	1980	2016
Cost of median-priced new home	$44,200	$136,600
10% down payment	$4,420	
Fixed-rate, 30-year mortgage		
Interest rate	8.9%	$7\frac{1}{2}$%
Total monthly principal and interest	$316	

Complete the 2016 year.

9. You can't count on your home mortgage lender to keep you from getting in debt over your head. The old standards of allowing 28% of your income for mortgage debt (including taxes and insurance) usually still apply. If your total monthly payment is $1,033, what should be your annual income to buy a home?

10. Assume that a 30-year fixed-rate mortgage for $100,000 was 9% at one date as opposed to 7% the previous year. What is the difference in monthly payments for these 2 years?

11. If you had a $100,000 mortgage with $7\frac{1}{2}\%$ interest for 25 years and wanted a $7\frac{1}{2}\%$ loan for 35 years, what would be the change in monthly payments? How much more would you pay in interest?

Learning Unit 16–1 :   Balance Sheet—Report as of a Particular Date

DRILL PROBLEMS

1. Complete the balance sheet for David Harrison, Attorney, on December 31, 2016 and show that

    Assets = Liabilities + Owner's equity

    Account totals are as follows: accounts receivable, $4,800; office supplies, $375; building (net), $130,000; accounts payable, $1,200; notes payable, $137,200; cash, $2,250; prepaid insurance, $1,050; office equipment (net), $11,250; land, $75,000; capital, $85,900; and salaries payable, $425.

DAVID HARRISON, ATTORNEY
Balance Sheet
December 31, 2016

Assets

Current assets:
  Cash _____
  Accounts receivable _____
  Prepaid insurance _____
  Office supplies _____
    Total current assets _____

Plant and equipment:
  Office equipment (net) _____
  Building (net) _____
  Land _____
    Total plant and equipment _____
Total assets _____

Liabilities

Current liabilities:
  Accounts payable _____
  Salaries payable _____
    Total current liabilities _____

Long-term liabilities:
  Notes payable _____
    Total liabilities _____

Owner's Equity
David Harrison, capital, December 31, 2016 _____

Total liabilities and owner's equity _____

2. Given the amounts in each of the accounts of Fisher-George Electric Corporation, fill in these amounts on the balance sheet for December 31, 2016 to show that

    Assets = Liabilities + Stockholders' equity

    Account totals are as follows: cash, $2,500; merchandise inventory, $1,325; automobiles (net), $9,250; common stock, $10,000; accounts payable, $275; office equipment (net), $5,065; accounts receivable, $300; retained earnings, $6,895; prepaid insurance, $1,075; salaries payable, $175; and mortgage payable, $2,170.

FISHER-GEORGE ELECTRIC CORPORATION
Balance Sheet
December 31, 2016

Assets

Current assets:
  Cash   _____
  Accounts receivable   _____
  Merchandise inventory   _____
  Prepaid insurance   _____
    Total current assets   _____

Plant and equipment:
  Office equipment (net)   _____
  Automobiles (net)   _____
    Total plant and equipment   _____

Total assets   _____

Liabilities

Current liabilities:
  Accounts payable   _____
  Salaries payable   _____
    Total current liabilities   _____

Long-term liabilities:
  Mortgage payable   _____
    Total liabilities   _____

Stockholders' Equity

Common stock   _____
Retained earnings   _____
    Total stockholders' equity   _____

Total liabilities and stockholders' equity   _____

3. Complete a vertical analysis of the following partial balance sheet; round all percents to the nearest hundredth percent.

THREEMAX, INC.
Comparative Balance Sheet Vertical Analysis
At December 31, 2015 and 2016

	2016		2015	
	Amount	Percent	Amount	Percent
Assets				
Cash	$ 8,500	_____	$ 10,200	_____
Accounts receivable (net)	11,750	_____	15,300	_____
Merchandise inventory	55,430	_____	54,370	_____
Store supplies	700	_____	532	_____
Office supplies	650	_____	640	_____
Prepaid insurance	2,450	_____	2,675	_____
Office equipment (net)	12,000	_____	14,300	_____
Store equipment (net)	32,000	_____	31,000	_____
Building (net)	75,400	_____	80,500	_____
Land	200,000	_____	150,000	_____
Total assets	$398,880	_____	$359,517	_____

4. Complete a horizontal analysis of the following partial balance sheet; round all percents to the nearest hundredth percent.

THREEMAX, INC. Comparative Balance Sheet Horizontal Analysis At December 31, 2015 and 2016				
	2015	2016	Change	Percent
Assets				
Cash	$ 8,500	$ 10,200	_____	_____
Accounts receivable (net)	11,750	15,300	_____	_____
Merchandise inventory	55,430	54,370	_____	_____
Store supplies	700	532	_____	_____
Office supplies	650	640	_____	_____
Prepaid insurance	2,450	2,675	_____	_____
Office equipment (net)	12,000	14,300	_____	_____
Store equipment (net)	32,000	31,000	_____	_____
Building (net)	75,400	80,500	_____	_____
Land	200,000	150,000	_____	_____
Total assets	$398,880	$359,517	_____	_____

Learning Unit 16–2 : Income Statement—Report for a Specific Period of Time

DRILL PROBLEMS

1. Complete the income statement for the year ended December 31, 2016, for Foley Realty, doing all the necessary addition. Account totals are as follows: office salaries expense, $15,255; advertising expense, $2,400; rent expense, $18,000; telephone expense, $650; insurance expense, $1,550; office supplies, $980; depreciation expense, office equipment, $990; depreciation expense, automobile, $2,100; sales commissions earned, $98,400; and management fees earned, $1,260.

FOLEY REALTY Income Statement For the Year Ended December 31, 2016	
Revenues:	
Sales commissions earned	_____
Management fees earned	_____
Total revenues	_____
Operating expenses:	
Office salaries expense	_____
Advertising expense	_____
Rent expense	_____
Telephone expense	_____
Insurance expense	_____
Office supplies expense	_____
Depreciation expense, office equipment	_____
Depreciation expense, automobile	_____
Total operating expenses	_____
Net income	_____

2. Complete the income statement for Toll's, Inc., a merchandising concern, doing all the necessary addition and subtraction. Sales were $250,000; sales returns and allowances were $1,400; sales discounts were $2,100; merchandise inventory, December 31, 2015, was $42,000; purchases were $156,000; purchases returns and allowances were $1,100; purchases discounts were $3,000; merchandise inventory, December 31, 2016, was $47,000; selling expenses were $37,000; and general and administrative expenses were $29,000.

TOLL'S, INC. Income Statement For the Year Ended December 31, 2016		
Revenues:		
Sales		_____
Less: Sales return and allowances	_____	
Sales discounts	_____	_____
Net sales		_____
Cost of goods sold:		
Merchandise inventory, December 31, 2015		_____
Purchases	_____	
Less: Purchases returns and allowances	_____	
Purchase discounts	_____ _____	
Cost of net purchases		_____
Goods available for sale		_____
Merchandise inventory, December 31, 2016		_____
Total cost of goods sold		_____
Gross profit from sales		_____
Operating expenses:		
Selling expenses		_____
General and administrative expenses		_____
Total operating expenses		_____
Net income		_____

3. Complete a vertical analysis of the following partial income statement; round all percents to the nearest hundredth percent. Note net sales are 100%.

THREEMAX, INC. Comparative Income Statement Vertical Analysis For Years Ended December 31, 2015 and 2016				
	2016		**2015**	
	Amount	**Percent**	**Amount**	**Percent**
Sales	$795,450		$665,532	
Sales returns and allowances	−6,250		−5,340	
Sales discounts	−6,470		−5,125	
Net sales	$782,730		$655,067	
Cost of goods sold:				
Beginning inventory	$ 75,394		$ 81,083	
Purchases	575,980		467,920	
Purchase discounts	−4,976		−2,290	
Goods available for sale	$646,398		$546,713	
Less ending inventory	−66,254		− 65,712	
Total costs of goods sold	$580,144		$ 481,001	
Gross profit	$202,586		$ 174,066	

4. Complete a horizontal analysis of the following partial income statement. Round all percents to the nearest hundredth percent.

THREEMAX, INC. Comparative Income Statement Horizontal Analysis For Years Ended December 31, 2015 and 2016				
	2016	**2015**	**Change**	**Percent**
Sales	$795,450	$665,532	_____	_____
Sales returns and allowances	−6,250	−5,340	_____	_____
Sales discounts	−6,470	−5,125	_____	_____
Net sales	$782,730	$655,067	_____	_____
Cost of goods sold:				
Beginning inventory	$ 75,394	$ 81,083	_____	_____
Purchases	575,980	467,920	_____	_____
Purchase discounts	−4,976	−2,290	_____	_____
Goods available for sale	$646,398	$546,713	_____	_____
Less ending inventory	−66,254	−65,712	_____	_____
Total cost of goods sold	$580,144	$481,001	_____	_____
Gross profit	$202,586	$174,066	_____	_____

Learning Unit 16–3 :   Trend and Ratio Analysis

DRILL PROBLEMS

1. Express each amount as a percent of the base-year (2014) amount. Round to the nearest tenth percent.

	2017	**2016**	**2015**	**2014**
Sales	$562,791	$560,776	$588,096	$601,982
Percent	_____	_____	_____	_____
Gross profit	$168,837	$196,271	$235,238	$270,891
Percent	_____	_____	_____	_____
Net income	$67,934	$65,927	$56,737	$62,762
Percent	_____	_____	_____	_____

2. If current assets = $42,500 and current liabilities = $56,400, what is the current ratio (to the nearest hundredth)?

3. In Problem 2, if inventory = $20,500 and prepaid expenses = $9,750, what is the quick ratio, or acid test (to the nearest hundredth)?

4. If accounts receivable = $36,720 and net sales = $249,700, what is the average day's collection (to the nearest whole day)?

5. If total liabilities = $243,000 and total assets = $409,870, what is the ratio of total debt to total assets (to the nearest hundredth percent)?

6. If net income = $55,970 and total stockholders' equity = $440,780, what is the return on equity (to the nearest hundredth percent)?

7. If net sales = $900,000 and total assets = $1,090,000, what is the asset turnover (to the nearest hundredth)?

8. In Problem 7, if the net income is $36,600, what is the profit margin on net sales (to the nearest hundredth percent)?

WORD PROBLEMS

9. Calculate trend percentages for the following items using 2015 as the base year. Round to the nearest hundredth percent.

	2018	**2017**	**2016**	**2015**
Sales	$298,000	$280,000	$264,000	$249,250
Cost of goods sold	187,085	175,227	164,687	156,785
Accounts receivable	29,820	28,850	27,300	26,250

10. According to the balance sheet for Ralph's Market, current assets = $165,500 and current liabilities = $70,500. Find the current ratio (to the nearest hundredth).

11. On the balance sheet for Ralph's Market (Problem 10), merchandise inventory = $102,000. Find the quick ratio (acid test).

12. The balance sheet of Moses Contractors shows cash of $5,500, accounts receivable of $64,500, an inventory of $42,500, and current liabilities of $57,500. Find Moses' current ratio and acid test ratio (both to the nearest hundredth).

13. Moses' income statement shows gross sales of $413,000, sales returns of $8,600, and net income of $22,300. Find the profit margin on net sales (to the nearest hundredth percent).

14. Given:

Cash	$ 39,000	Retained earnings	$194,000
Accounts receivable	109,000	Net sales	825,000
Inventory	150,000	Cost of goods sold	528,000
Prepaid expenses	48,000	Operating expenses	209,300
Plant and equipment (net)	487,000	Interest expense	13,500
Accounts payable	46,000	Income taxes	32,400
Other current liabilities	43,000	Net income	41,800
Long-term liabilities	225,000		
Common stock	325,000		

Calculate (to nearest hundredth or hundredth percent as needed):

a. Current ratio. **b.** Quick ratio. **c.** Average day's collection.

d. Total debt to total assets. **e.** Return on equity. **f.** Asset turnover.

g. Profit margin on net sales.

15. The Vale Group lost $18.4 million in profits for the year 2016 as sales dropped to $401 million. Sales in 2015 were $450.6 million. What percent is the decrease in Vale's sales? Round to the nearest hundredth percent.

Learning Unit 17–1 : Concept of Depreciation and the Straight-Line Method

DRILL PROBLEMS

1. Find the annual straight-line rate of depreciation, given the following estimated lives.

Life	Annual rate	Life	Annual rate
a. 25 years	_____	**b.** 4 years	_____
c. 10 years	_____	**d.** 5 years	_____
e. 8 years	_____	**f.** 30 years	_____

2. Find the annual depreciation using the straight-line depreciation method. Round to the nearest whole dollar.

Cost of asset	Residual value	Useful life	Annual depreciation
a. $2,460	$400	4 years	_____
b. $24,300	$2,000	6 years	_____
c. $350,000	$42,500	12 years	_____
d. $17,325	$5,000	5 years	_____
e. $2,550,000	$75,000	30 years	_____

3. Find the annual depreciation and ending book value for the first year using the straight-line depreciation method. Round to the nearest dollar.

Cost	Residual value	Useful life	Annual depreciation	Ending book value
a. $6,700	$600	3 years	_____	_____
b. $11,600	$500	6 years	_____	_____
c. $9,980	–0–	5 years	_____	_____
d. $36,950	$2,500	12 years	_____	_____
e. $101,690	$3,600	27 years	_____	_____

4. Find the first-year depreciation to the nearest dollar for the following assets, which were only owned for part of a year. Round to the nearest whole dollar the annual depreciation for in-between calculations.

Date of purchase	Cost of asset	Residual value	Useful life	First year depreciation
a. April 8	$10,500	$1,200	4 years	_____
b. July 12	$23,900	$3,200	6 years	_____
c. June 19	$8,880	$800	3 years	_____
d. November 2	$125,675	$6,000	17 years	_____
e. May 25	$44,050	–0–	9 years	_____

WORD PROBLEMS

5. North Shore Grinding purchased a lathe for $37,500. This machine has a residual value of $3,000 and an expected useful life of 4 years. Prepare a depreciation schedule for the lathe using the straight-line depreciation method.

6. Colby Wayne paid $7,750 for a photocopy machine with an estimated life of 6 years and a residual value of $900. Prepare a depreciation schedule using the straight-line depreciation method. Round to the nearest whole dollar. (Last year's depreciation may have to be adjusted due to rounding.)

7. The Leo Brothers purchased a machine for $8,400 that has an estimated life of 3 years. At the end of 3 years the machine will have no value. Prepare a depreciation schedule using the straight-line depreciation method for this machine.

8. Fox Realty bought a computer table for $1,700. The estimated useful life of the table is 7 years. The residual value at the end of 7 years is $370. Find (a) the annual rate of depreciation to the nearest hundredth percent, (b) the annual amount of depreciation, and (c) the book value of the table at the end of the *third* year using the straight-line depreciation method.

9. Cashman, Inc., purchased an overhead projector for $560. It has an estimated useful life of 6 years, at which time it will have no remaining value. Find the book value at the end of 5 years using the straight-line depreciation method. Round the annual depreciation to the nearest whole dollar.

10. Shelley Corporation purchased a new machine for $15,000. The estimated life of the machine is 12 years with a residual value of $2,400. Find (a) the annual rate of depreciation by the straight-line method to the nearest hundredth percent, (b) the annual amount of depreciation, (c) the accumulated depreciation at the end of 7 years, and (d) the book value at the end of 9 years.

11. Wolfe Ltd. purchased a supercomputer for $75,000 on July 7, 2013. The computer has an estimated life of 5 years and will have a residual value of $15,000. Find (a) the annual depreciation amount by the straight-line method, (b) the depreciation amount for 2013, (c) the accumulated depreciation at the end of 2014, and (d) the book value at the end of 2015.

Learning Unit 17–2 : Units-of-Production Method

DRILL PROBLEMS

1. Find the depreciation per unit for each of the following assets. Round to three decimal places.

Cost of asset	Residual value	Estimated production	Depreciation per unit
a. $3,500	$800	9,000 units	_____
b. $309,560	$22,000	1,500,000 units	_____
c. $54,890	$6,500	275,000 units	_____

2. Find the annual depreciation expense for each of the assets in Problem 1.

Cost of asset	Residual value	Estimated production	Depreciation per unit	Units produced	Amount of depreciation
a. $3,500	$800	9,000 units	_____	3,000	_____
b. $309,560	$22,000	1,500,000 units	_____	45,500	_____
c. $54,890	$6,500	275,000 units	_____	4,788	_____

3. Find the book value at the end of the first year for each of the assets in Problems 1 and 2.

Cost of asset	Residual value	Estimated production	Depreciation per unit	Units produced	Book value
a. $3,500	$800	9,000 units	_____	3,000	_____
b. $309,560	$22,000	1,500,000 units	_____	45,500	_____
c. $54,890	$6,500	275,000 units	_____	4,788	_____

4. Calculate the accumulated depreciation at the end of year 2 for each of the following machines. Carry out the unit depreciation to three decimal places.

Cost of machine	Residual value	Estimated life	Hours used during year 1	Hours used during year 2	Accumulated depreciation
a. $67,900	$4,300	19,000 hours	5,430	4,856	_____
b. $3,810	$600	33,000 hours	10,500	9,330	_____
c. $25,000	$4,900	80,000 hours	7,000	12,600	_____

WORD PROBLEMS

5. Prepare a depreciation schedule for the following machine: The machine cost $63,400; it has an estimated residual value of $5,300 and expected life of 290,500 units. The units produced were:

Year 1	95,000 units
Year 2	80,000 units
Year 3	50,000 units
Year 4	35,500 units
Year 5	30,000 units

6. Forsmann & Smythe purchased a new machine that cost $46,030. The machine has a residual value of $2,200 and estimated output of 430,000 hours. Prepare a units-of-production depreciation schedule for this machine, rounding the unit depreciation to three decimal places. The hours of use were:

Year 1	90,000 hours
Year 2	150,000 hours
Year 3	105,000 hours
Year 4	90,000 hours

7. Young Electrical Company depreciates its vans using the units-of-production method. The cost of its new van was $24,600, the useful life is 125,000 miles, and the trade-in value is $5,250. What are **(a)** the depreciation expense per mile (to three decimal places) and **(b)** the book value at the end of the first year if it is driven 29,667 miles?

8. Tremblay Manufacturing Company purchased a new machine for $52,000. The machine has an estimated useful life of 185,000 hours and a residual value of $10,000. The machine was used for 51,200 hours the first year. Find **(a)** the depreciation rate per hour, rounded to three decimal places, **(b)** the depreciation expense for the first year, and **(c)** the book value of the machine at the end of the first year.

Learning Unit 17-3 :   Declining-Balance Method

DRILL PROBLEMS

1. Find the declining-balance rate of depreciation, given the following estimated lives.

Life	Declining rate
a. 25 years	_____
b. 10 years	_____
c. 8 years	_____

2. Find the first year depreciation amount for the following assets using the declining-balance depreciation method. Round to the nearest whole dollar.

Cost of asset	Residual value	Useful life	First year depreciation
a. $2,460	$400	4 years	_____
b. $24,300	$2,000	6 years	_____
c. $350,000	$42,500	12 years	_____
d. $17,325	$5,000	5 years	_____
e. $2,550,000	$75,000	30 years	_____

3. Find the depreciation expense and ending book value for the first year, using the declining-balance depreciation method. Round to the nearest dollar.

Cost	Residual value	Useful life	First year depreciation	Ending book value
a. $6,700	$600	3 years	_____	_____
b. $11,600	$500	6 years	_____	_____
c. $9,980	–0–	5 years	_____	_____
d. $36,950	$2,500	12 years	_____	_____
e. $101,690	$3,600	27 years	_____	_____

WORD PROBLEMS

4. North Shore Grinding purchased a lathe for $37,500. This machine has a residual value of $3,000 and an expected useful life of 4 years. Prepare a depreciation schedule for the lathe using the declining-balance depreciation method. Round to the nearest whole dollar.

5. Colby Wayne paid $7,750 for a photocopy machine with an estimated life of 6 years and a residual value of $900. Prepare a depreciation schedule using the declining-balance depreciation method. Round to the nearest whole dollar.

6. The Leo Brothers purchased a machine for $8,400 that has an estimated life of 3 years. At the end of 3 years, the machine will have no value. Prepare a depreciation schedule for this machine. Round to the nearest whole dollar.

7. Fox Realty bought a computer table for $1,700. The estimated useful life of the table is 7 years. The residual value at the end of 7 years is $370. Find **(a)** the declining depreciation rate to the nearest hundredth percent, **(b)** the amount of depreciation at the end of the *third* year, and **(c)** the book value of the table at the end of the *third* year using the declining-balance depreciation method. Round to the nearest whole dollar.

8. Cashman, Inc., purchased an overhead projector for $560. It has an estimated useful life of 6 years, at which time it will have no remaining value. Find the book value at the end of 5 years using the declining-balance depreciation method. Round to the nearest whole dollar.

9. Shelley Corporation purchased a new machine for $15,000. The estimated life of the machine is 12 years with a residual value of $2,400. Find **(a)** the declining-balance depreciation rate as a fraction and as a percent (hundredth percent), **(b)** the amount of depreciation at the end of the first year, **(c)** the accumulated depreciation at the end of 7 years, and **(d)** the book value at the end of 9 years. Round to the nearest dollar.

Learning Unit 17–4 : Modified Accelerated Cost Recovery System (MACRS) with Introduction to ACRS

DRILL PROBLEMS

1. Using the MACRS method of depreciation, find the recovery rate, first-year depreciation expense, and book value of the asset at the end of the first year. Round to the nearest whole dollar.

Cost of asset	Recovery period	Recovery rate	Depreciation expense	End-of-year book value
a. $2,500	3 years	_____	_____	_____
b. $52,980	3 years	_____	_____	_____
c. $4,250	5 years	_____	_____	_____
d. $128,950	10 years	_____	_____	_____
e. $13,775	5 years	_____	_____	_____

2. Find the accumulated depreciation at the end of the second year for each of the following assets. Round to the nearest whole dollar.

Cost of asset	Recovery period	Accumulated depreciation at end of 2nd year using MACRS	Book value at end of 2nd year using MACRS
a. $2,500	3 years	_____	_____
b. $52,980	3 years	_____	_____
c. $4,250	5 years	_____	_____
d. $128,950	10 years	_____	_____
e. $13,775	5 years	_____	_____

WORD PROBLEMS

3. Colby Wayne paid $7,750 for a photocopy machine that is classified as equipment and has a residual value of $900. Prepare a depreciation schedule using the MACRS depreciation method. Round all calculations to the nearest whole dollar.

4. Fox Realty bought a computer table for $1,700. The table is classified as furniture. The residual value at the end of the table's useful life is $370. Using the MACRS depreciation method, find **(a)** the amount of depreciation at the end of the *third* year, **(b)** the total accumulated depreciation at the end of year 3, and **(c)** the book value of the table at the end of the *third* year. Round all calculations to the nearest dollar.

5. Cashman, Inc., purchased an overhead projector for $560. It is classified as office equipment and will have no residual value. Find the book value at the end of 5 years using the MACRS depreciation method. Round to the nearest whole dollar.

6. Shelley Corporation purchased a new machine for $15,000. The machine is comparable to equipment used for two-way exchange of voice and data with a residual value of $2,400. Find **(a)** the amount of depreciation at the end of the first year, **(b)** the accumulated depreciation at the end of 7 years, and **(c)** the book value at the end of 9 years. Round to the nearest dollar.

7.* Wolfe Ltd. purchased a supercomputer for $75,000 at the beginning of 1996. The computer is classified as a 5-year asset and will have a residual value of $15,000. Using MACRS, find **(a)** the depreciation amount for 1996, **(b)** the accumulated depreciation at the end of 1997, **(c)** the book value at the end of 1998, and **(d)** the last year that the asset will be depreciated.

*These problems are placed here for a quick review.

8.* Cummins Engine Company uses a straight-line depreciation method to calculate the cost of an asset of $1,200,000 with a $200,000 residual value and a life expectancy of 15 years. How much would Cummins have for depreciation expense for each of the first 2 years? Round to the nearest dollar for each year.

9. An article in an issue of *Management Accounting* stated that Cummins Engine Company changed its depreciation. The cost of its asset was $1,200,000 with a $200,000 residual value (with a life expectancy of 15 years) and an estimated productive capacity of 864,000 products. Cummins produced 59,000 products this year. What would it write off for depreciation using the units-of-production method?

*These problems are placed here for a quick review.

Learning Unit 18–1 : Assigning Costs to Ending Inventory—Specific Identification; Weighted Average; FIFO; LIFO

DRILL PROBLEMS

1. Given the value of the beginning inventory, purchases for the year, and ending inventory, find the cost of goods available for sale and the cost of goods sold.

	Beginning inventory	Purchases	Ending inventory	Cost of goods available for sale	Cost of goods sold
a.	$1,000	$4,120	$2,100	_____	_____
b.	$52,400	$270,846	$49,700	_____	_____
c.	$205	$48,445	$376	_____	_____
d.	$78,470	$2,788,560	$100,600	_____	_____
e.	$965	$53,799	$2,876	_____	_____

2. Find the missing amounts; then calculate the number of units available for sale and the cost of the goods available for sale.

Date	Category	Quantity	Unit cost	Total cost
January 1	Beginning inventory	1,207	$45	_____
February 7	Purchase	850	$46	_____
April 19	Purchase	700	$47	_____
July 5	Purchase	1,050	$49	_____
November 2	Purchase	450	$52	_____
Goods available for sale		_____		_____

3. Using the *specific identification* method, find the ending inventory and cost of goods sold for the merchandising concern in Problem 2.

Remaining inventory	Unit cost	Total cost
20 units from beginning inventory	_____	_____
35 units from February 7	_____	_____
257 units from July 5	_____	_____
400 units from November 2	_____	_____
Cost of ending inventory		_____
Cost of goods sold		_____

4. Using the *weighted-average* method, find the average cost per unit (to the nearest cent) and the cost of ending inventory.

Units available for sale	Cost of goods available for sale	Units in ending inventory	Weighted-average unit cost	Cost of ending inventory
a. 2,350	$120,320	1,265	_____	_____
b. 7,090	$151,017	1,876	_____	_____
c. 855	$12,790	989	_____	_____
d. 12,964	$125,970	9,542	_____	_____
e. 235,780	$507,398	239,013	_____	_____

5. Use the *FIFO* method of inventory valuation to determine the value of ending inventory, which consists of 40 units, and the cost of goods sold.

Date	Category	Quantity	Unit cost	Total cost
January 1	Beginning inventory	37	$219.00	_____
March 5	Purchases	18	230.60	_____
June 17	Purchases	22	255.70	_____
October 18	Purchases	34	264.00	_____
Goods available for sale		___		_____

Ending inventory = _____   Cost of goods sold = _____

6. Use the *LIFO* method of inventory valuation to determine the value of the ending inventory, which consists of 40 units, and the cost of goods sold.

Date	Category	Quantity	Unit cost	Total cost
January 1	Beginning inventory	37	$219.00	_____
March 5	Purchases	18	230.60	_____
June 17	Purchases	22	255.70	_____
October 18	Purchases	34	264.00	_____
Goods available for sale		___		_____

Ending inventory = _____   Cost of goods sold = _____

WORD PROBLEMS

7. At the beginning of September, Green's of Gloucester had 13 yellow raincoats in stock. These raincoats cost $36.80 each. During the month, Green's purchased 14 raincoats for $37.50 each and 16 raincoats for $38.40 each, and it sold 26 raincoats. Calculate **(a)** the average unit cost rounded to the nearest cent and **(b)** the ending inventory value using the weighted-average method.

8. If Green's of Gloucester (Problem 7) used the FIFO method, what would the value of the ending inventory be?

9. If Green's of Gloucester (Problem 7) used the LIFO method, what would the value of the ending inventory be?

10. Hobby Caterers purchased recycled-paper sketch pads during the year as follows:

January	350 pads for $.27 each
March	400 pads for $.31 each
July	200 pads for $.36 each
October	850 pads for $.26 each
November	400 pads for $.31 each

At the end of the year, the company had 775 of these sketch pads in stock. Find the ending inventory value using **(a)** the weighted-average method (round to the nearest cent), **(b)** the FIFO method, and **(c)** the LIFO method.

11. On March 1, Sandler's Shoe Store had the following sports shoes in stock:

13 pairs running shoes for $33 a pair
22 pairs walking shoes for $29 a pair
35 pairs aerobic shoes for $26 a pair
21 pairs cross-trainers for $52 a pair

During the month Sandler's sold 10 pairs of running shoes, 15 pairs of walking shoes, 28 pairs of aerobic shoes, and 12 pairs of cross-trainers. Use the specific identification method to find **(a)** the cost of the goods available for sale, **(b)** the value of the ending inventory, and **(c)** the cost of goods sold.

Learning Unit 18–2 : Retail Method; Gross Profit Method; Inventory Turnover; Distribution of Overhead

DRILL PROBLEMS

1. Given the following information, calculate **(a)** the goods available for sale at cost and retail, **(b)** the cost ratio (to the nearest thousandth), **(c)** the ending inventory at retail, and **(d)** the cost of the March 31 inventory (to the nearest dollar) by the retail inventory method.

	Cost	Retail
Beginning inventory, March 1	$57,300	$95,500
Purchases during March	$28,400	$48,000
Sales during March		$79,000

2. Given the following information, use the gross profit method to calculate **(a)** the cost of goods available for sale, **(b)** the cost percentage, **(c)** the estimated cost of goods sold, and **(d)** the estimated cost of the inventory as of April 30.

Beginning inventory, April 1	$30,000
Net purchases during April	81,800
Sales during April	98,000
Average gross profit on sales	40%

3. Given the following information, find the average inventory.

Merchandise inventory, January 1, 20XX	$82,000
Merchandise inventory, December 31, 20XX	$88,000

4. Given the following information, find the inventory turnover for the company in Problem 3 to the nearest hundredth.

Cost of goods sold (12/31/XX) $625,000

5. Given the following information, calculate the **(a)** average inventory at retail, **(b)** average inventory at cost, **(c)** inventory turnover at retail, and **(d)** inventory turnover at cost. Round to the nearest hundredth.

	Cost	Retail
Merchandise inventory, January 1	$ 250,000	$ 355,000
Merchandise inventory, December 31	$ 235,000	$ 329,000
Cost of goods sold	$1,525,000	
Sales		$2,001,000

6. Given the floor space for the following departments, find the entire floor space and the percent each department represents.

		Percent of floor space
Department A	15,000 square feet	_____
Department B	25,000 square feet	_____
Department C	10,000 square feet	_____
Total floor space	50,000 square feet	_____

7. If the total overhead for all the departments (Problem 6) is $200,000, how much of the overhead expense should be allocated to each department?

Overhead/department

Department A _____

Department B _____

Department C _____

WORD PROBLEMS

8. During the accounting period, Ward's Greenery sold $290,000 of merchandise at marked retail prices. At the end of the period, the following information was available from Ward's records:

	Cost	Retail
Beginning inventory	$ 53,000	$ 79,000
Net purchases	$204,000	$280,000

Use the retail method to estimate Ward's ending inventory at cost. Round the cost ratio to the nearest thousandth.

9. On January 1, Benny's Retail Mart had a $49,000 inventory at cost. During the first quarter of the year, Benny's made net purchases of $199,900. Benny's records show that during the past several years, the store's gross profit on sales has averaged 35%. If Benny's records show $275,000 in sales for the quarter, estimate the ending inventory for the first quarter, using the gross profit method.

10. On April 4, there was a big fire and the entire inventory of R. W. Wilson Company was destroyed. The company records were salvaged. They showed the following information:

Sales (January 1 through April 4)	$127,000
Merchandise inventory, January 1	16,000
Net purchases	71,250

On January 1, the inventory was priced to sell for $38,000 and additional items bought during the period were priced to sell for $102,000. Using the retail method, calculate the cost of the inventory that was destroyed by the fire. Round the cost ratio to the nearest thousandth.

11. During the past 4 years, the average gross margin on sales for R. W. Wilson Company was 36% of net sales. Using the data in Problem 10 and the gross profit method, calculate the cost of the ending inventory destroyed by fire.

12. Chase Bank has to make a decision on whether to grant a loan to Sally's Furniture Store. The lending officer is interested in how often Sally's inventory turns over. Using selected information from Sally's income statement, calculate the inventory turnover for Sally's Furniture Store (to the nearest hundredth).

Merchandise inventory, January 1	$ 43,000
Merchandise inventory, December 31	55,000
Cost of goods sold	128,000

13. Wanting to know more about a business he was considering buying, Jake Paige studied the business's books. He found that beginning inventory for the previous year was $51,000 at cost and $91,800 at retail, ending inventory was $44,000 at cost and $72,600 at retail, sales were $251,000, and cost of goods sold was $154,000. Using this information, calculate for Jake the inventory turnover at cost and the inventory turnover at retail.

14. Ralph's Retail Outlet has calculated its expenses for the year. Total overhead expenses are $147,000. Ralph's accountant must allocate this overhead to four different departments. Given the following information regarding the floor space occupied by each department, calculate how much overhead expense should be allocated to each department.

Department W	12,000 square feet	Department Y	14,000 square feet
Department X	9,000 square feet	Department Z	7,000 square feet

15. How much overhead would be allocated to each department of Ralph's Retail Outlet (Problem 14) if the basis of allocation were the sales of each department? Sales for each of the departments were:

Department W	$110,000	Department Y	$170,000
Department X	$120,000	Department Z	$100,000

Learning Unit 19-1 : Sales and Excise Taxes

DRILL PROBLEMS

1. Calculate the sales tax and the total amount due for each of the following:

Total sales	Sales tax rate	Sales tax	Total amount due
a. $536	5%	_____	_____
b. $11,980	6%	_____	_____
c. $3,090	$8\frac{1}{4}\%$	_____	_____
d. $17.65	$5\frac{1}{2}\%$	_____	_____
e. $294	7.42%	_____	_____

2. Find the amount of actual sales and amount of sales tax on the following total receipts:

Total receipts	Sales tax rate	Actual sales	Sales tax
a. $27,932.15	5.5%	_____	_____
b. $35,911.53	7%	_____	_____
c. $115,677.06	$6\frac{1}{2}\%$	_____	_____
d. $142.96	$5\frac{1}{4}\%$	_____	_____
e. $5,799.24	4.75%	_____	_____

3. Find the sales tax, excise tax, and total cost for each of the following items:

Retail price	Sales tax, 5.2%	Excise tax, 11%	Total cost
a. $399	_____	_____	_____
b. $22,684	_____	_____	_____
c. $7,703	_____	_____	_____

4. Calculate the amount, subtotal, sales tax, and total amount due of the following:

Quantity	Description	Unit price	Amount
3	Taxable item	$4.30	_____
2	Taxable item	$5.23	_____
4	Taxable item	$1.20	_____
		Subtotal	_____
		5% sales tax	_____
		Total	_____

5. Given the sales tax rate and the amount of the sales tax, calculate the price of the following purchases (before tax was added):

Tax rate	Tax amount	Price of purchase
a. 7%	$71.61	_____
b. $5\frac{1}{2}\%$	$3.22	_____

6. Given the sales tax rate and the total price (including tax), calculate the price of the following purchases (before the tax was added):

Tax rate	Total price	Price of purchase
a. 5%	$340.20	_____
b. 6%	$1,224.30	_____

WORD PROBLEMS

7. In a state with a 4.75% sales tax, what will be the sales tax and the total price of a video game marked $110?

8. Browning's invoice included a sales tax of $38.15. If the sales tax rate is 6%, what was the total cost of the taxable goods on the invoice?

9. David Bowan paid a total of $2,763 for a new computer. If this includes a sales tax of 5.3%, what was the marked price of the computer?

10. After a 5% sales tax and a 12% excise tax, the total cost of a leather jacket was $972. What was the selling price of the jacket?

11. A customer at the RDM Discount Store purchased four tubes of toothpaste priced at $1.88 each, six toothbrushes for $1.69 each, and three bottles of shampoo for $2.39 each. What did the customer have to pay if the sales tax is $5\frac{1}{2}$%?

12. Bill Harrington purchased a mountain bike for $875. Bill had to pay a sales tax of 6% and an excise tax of 11%. What was the total amount Bill had to pay for his mountain bike?

13. Donna DeCoff received a bill for $754 for a new chair she had purchased. The bill included a 6.2% sales tax and a delivery charge of $26. What was the selling price of the chair?

Learning Unit 19-2 :   Property Tax

DRILL PROBLEMS

1. Find the assessed value of the following properties, rounding to the nearest whole dollar:

Market value	Assessment rate	Assessed value	Market value	Assessment rate	Assessed value
a. $195,000	35%	_____	**d.** $2,585,400	65%	_____
b. $1,550,900	50%	_____	**e.** $349,500	85%	_____
c. $75,000	75%	_____			

2. Find the tax rate for each of the following municipalities, rounding to the nearest tenth of a percent:

Budget needed	Total assessed value	Tax rate	Budget needed	Total assessed value	Tax rate
a. $2,594,000	$44,392,000	_____	**d.** $13,540,000	$143,555,500	_____
b. $17,989,000	$221,900,000	_____	**e.** $1,099,000	$12,687,000	_____
c. $6,750,000	$47,635,000	_____			

3. Express each of the following tax rates in all the indicated forms:

By percent	Per $100 of assessed value	Per $1,000 of assessed value	In mills
a. 7.45%	_____	_____	_____
b. _____	$14.24	_____	_____
c. _____	_____	_____	90.8
d. _____	_____	$62.00	_____

4. Calculate the property tax due for each of the following:

Total assessed value	Tax rate	Total property tax due	Total assessed value	Tax rate	Total property tax due
a. $12,900	$6.60 per $100	_____	**e.** $78,900	59 mills	_____
b. $175,400	43 mills	_____	**f.** $225,550	$11.39 per $1,000	_____
c. $320,500	2.7%	_____	**g.** $198,750	$2.63 per $100	_____
d. $2,480,000	$17.85 per $1,000	_____			

WORD PROBLEMS

5. The county of Chelsea approved a budget of $3,450,000, which had to be raised through property taxation. If the total assessed value of properties in the county of Chelsea was $37,923,854, what will the tax rate be? The tax rate is stated per $100 of assessed valuation.

6. Linda Tawse lives in Camden and her home has a market value of $235,000. Property in Camden is assessed at 55% of its market value, and the tax rate for the current year is $64.75 per $1,000. What is the assessed valuation of Linda's home?

7. Using the information in Problem 6, find the amount of property tax that Linda will have to pay.

8. Mary Faye Souza has property with a fair market value of $219,500. Property in Mary Faye's city is assessed at 65% of its market value and the tax rate is $3.64 per $100. How much is Mary Faye's property tax due?

9. Cagney's Greenhouse has a fair market value of $1,880,000. Property is assessed at 35% by the city. The tax rate is 6.4%. What is the property tax due for Cagney's Greenhouse?

10. In Chester County, property is assessed at 40% of its market value, the residential tax rate is $12.30 per $1,000, and the commercial tax rate is $13.85 per $1,000. What is the property tax due on a home that has a market value of $205,000?

11. Using the information in Problem 10, find the property tax due on a grocery store with a market value of $5,875,000.

12. Bob Rose's home is assessed at $195,900. Last year the tax rate was 11.8 mills, and this year the rate was raised to 13.2 mills. How much more will Bob have to pay in taxes this year?

Learning Unit 20–1 :   Life Insurance

DRILL PROBLEMS

1. Use the table in the *Business Math Handbook* to find the annual premium per $1,000 of life insurance and calculate the annual premiums for each policy listed. Assume the insureds are males.

	Face value of policy	Type of insurance	Age at issue	Annual premium per $1,000	Number of $1,000s in face value	Annual premium
a.	$25,000	Straight life	31	_____	_____	_____
b.	$40,500	20-year endowment	40	_____	_____	_____
c.	$200,000	Straight life	44	_____	_____	_____
d.	$62,500	20-payment life	25	_____	_____	_____
e.	$12,250	5-year term	35	_____	_____	_____
f.	$42,500	20-year endowment	42	_____	_____	_____

2. Use Table 20.1 to find the annual premium for each of the following life insurance policies. Assume the insured is a 30-year-old male.

	Face value of policy	Five-year term policy	Straight life policy	Twenty-payment life policy	Twenty-year endowment
a.	$50,000	_____	_____	_____	_____
b.	$1,000,000	_____	_____	_____	_____
c.	$250,000	_____	_____	_____	_____
d.	$72,500	_____	_____	_____	_____

3. Use the table in the *Business Math Handbook* to find the annual premium for each of the following life insurance policies. Assume the insured is a 30-year-old female.

	Face value of policy	Five-year term policy	Straight life policy	Twenty-payment life policy	Twenty-year endowment
a.	$50,000	_____	_____	_____	_____
b.	$1,000,000	_____	_____	_____	_____
c.	$250,000	_____	_____	_____	_____
d.	$72,500	_____	_____	_____	_____

4. Use the table in the *Business Math Handbook* to find the nonforfeiture options for the following policies:

Years policy in force	Type of policy	Face value	Cash value	Amount of paid-up insurance	Extended term
a. 10	Straight life	$25,000	_____	_____	_____
b. 20	20-year endowment	$500,000	_____	_____	_____
c. 5	20-payment life	$2,000,000	_____	_____	_____
d. 15	Straight life	$750,000	_____	_____	_____
e. 5	20-year endowment	$93,500	_____	_____	_____

WORD PROBLEMS

5. If Mr. Davis, aged 39, buys a $90,000 straight-life policy, what is the amount of his annual premium?

6. If Miss Jennie McDonald, age 27, takes out a $65,000 20-year endowment policy, what premium amount will she pay each year?

7. If Gary Thomas decides to cash in his $45,000 20-payment life insurance policy after 15 years, what cash surrender value will he receive?

8. Mary Allyn purchased a $70,000 20-year endowment policy when she was 26 years old. Ten years later, she decided that she could no longer afford the premiums. If Mary decides to convert her policy to paid-up insurance, what amount of paid-up insurance coverage will she have?

9. Peter and Jane Rizzo are both 28 years old and are both planning to take out $50,000 straight-life insurance policies. What is the difference in the annual premiums they will have to pay?

10. Paul Nasser purchased a $125,000 straight-life policy when he was 30 years old. He is now 50 years old. Two months ago, he slipped in the bathtub and injured his back; he will not be able to return to his regular job for several months. Due to a lack of income, he feels that he can no longer continue to pay the premiums on his life insurance policy. If Paul decides to surrender his policy for cash, how much cash will he receive?

11. If Paul Nasser (Problem 10) chooses to convert his policy to paid-up insurance, what will the face value of his new policy be?

Learning Unit 20–2 :   Fire Insurance

DRILL PROBLEMS

1. Use the tables in the *Business Math Handbook* to find the premium for each of the following:

Rating of area	Building class	Building value	Value of contents	Total annual premium
a. 3	A	$80,000	$32,000	_____
b. 2	B	$340,000	$202,000	_____
c. 2	A	$221,700	$190,000	_____
d. 1	B	$96,400	$23,400	_____
e. 3	B	$65,780	$62,000	_____

2. Use the tables in the *Business Math Handbook* to find the short-term premium and the amount of refund due if the insured cancels.

Annual premium	Months of coverage	Short-term premium	Refund due
a. $1,860	3	_____	_____
b. $650	7	_____	_____
c. $1,200	10	_____	_____
d. $341	12	_____	_____
e. $1,051	4	_____	_____

3. Find the amount to be paid for each of the following losses:

	Property value	Coinsurance clause	Insurance required	Insurance carried	Amount of loss	Insurance company pays (indemnity)
a.	$85,000	80%	_____	$70,000	$60,000	_____
b.	$52,000	80%	_____	$45,000	$50,000	_____
c.	$44,000	80%	_____	$33,000	$33,000	_____
d.	$182,000	80%	_____	$127,400	$61,000	_____

WORD PROBLEMS

4. Mary Rose wants to purchase fire insurance for her building, which is rated as Class B; the rating of the area is 2. If her building is worth $225,000 and the contents are worth $70,000, what will her annual premium be?

5. Janet Ambrose owns a Class A building valued at $180,000. The contents of the building are valued at $145,000. The territory rating is 3. What is her annual fire insurance premium?

6. Jack Altshuler owns a building worth $355,500. The contents are worth $120,000. The classification of the building is B, and the rating of the area is 1. What annual premium must Jack pay for his fire insurance?

7. Jay Viola owns a store valued at $460,000. His fire insurance policy (which has an 80% coinsurance clause) has a face value of $345,000. A recent fire resulted in a loss of $125,000. How much will the insurance company pay?

8. The building that is owned by Tally's Garage is valued at $275,000 and is insured for $225,000. The policy has an 80% coinsurance clause. If there is a fire in the building and the damages amount to $220,000, how much of the loss will be paid for by the insurance company?

9. Michael Dannon owns a building worth $420,000. He has a fire insurance policy with a face value of $336,000 (there is an 80% coinsurance clause). There was recently a fire that resulted in a $400,000 loss. How much money will he receive from the insurance company?

10. Rice's Rent-A-Center business is worth $375,000. He has purchased a $250,000 fire insurance policy. The policy has an 80% coinsurance clause. What will Rice's reimbursement be (a) after a $150,000 fire and (b) after a $330,000 fire?

11. If Maria's Pizza Shop is valued at $210,000 and is insured for $147,000 with a policy that contains an 80% coinsurance clause, what settlement is due after a fire that causes (a) $150,000 in damages and (b) $175,000 in damages?

Learning Unit 20–3 : Auto Insurance

DRILL PROBLEMS

1. Calculate the annual premium for compulsory coverage for each of the following.

	Driver classification	Bodily	Property	Total premium
a.	17	_____	_____	_____
b.	20	_____	_____	_____
c.	10	_____	_____	_____

2. Calculate the amount of money the insurance company and the driver should pay for each of the following accidents, assuming the driver carries compulsory insurance only.

Accident and court award	Insurance company pays	Driver pays
a. Driver hit one person and court awarded $15,000.	_____	_____
b. Driver hit one person and court awarded $12,000 for personal injury.	_____	_____
c. Driver hit two people; court awarded first person $9,000 and the second person $12,000.	_____	_____

3. Calculate the additional premium payment for each of the following options.

	Addition to premium
Optional insurance coverage	
a. Bodily injury 50/100/25, driver class 20	_____
b. Bodily injury 25/60/10, driver class 17	_____
c. Collision insurance, driver class 10, age group 3, symbol 5, deductible $100	_____
d. Comprehensive insurance, driver class 10, age group 3, symbol 5, deductible $200	_____
e. Substitute transportation, towing, and labor; driver class 10, age group 3, symbol 5	_____

4. Compute the annual premium for compulsory insurance with optional liability coverage for bodily injury and damage to someone else's property.

Driver classification	Bodily coverage	Premium
a. 17	50/100/25	_____
b. 20	100/300/10	_____
c. 10	25/60/25	_____
d. 18	250/500/50	_____
e. 20	25/50/10	_____

5. Calculate the annual premium for each of the following drivers with the indicated options. All drivers must carry compulsory insurance.

Driver classification	Car age	Car symbol	Bodily injury	Collision	Comprehensive	Transportation and towing	Annual premium
a. 10	2	4	50/100/10	$100 deductible	$300 deductible	Yes	_____
b. 18	3	2	25/60/25	$200 deductible	$200 deductible	Yes	_____

WORD PROBLEMS

6. Ann Centerino's driver classification is 10. She carries only compulsory insurance coverage. What annual insurance premium must she pay?

7. Gary Hines is a class 18 driver. He wants to add optional bodily injury and property damage of 250/500/50 to his compulsory insurance coverage. What will be Gary's total annual premium?

8. Sara Goldberg wants optional bodily injury coverage of 50/100/25 and collision coverage with a deductible of $300 in addition to the compulsory coverage her state requires. Sara is a class 17 driver and has a symbol 4 car that is 2 years old. What annual premium must Sara pay?

9. Karen Babson has just purchased a new car with a symbol of 8. She wants bodily injury and property liability of 500/1,000/100, comprehensive and collision insurance with a $200 deductible, and transportation and towing coverage. If Karen is a class 10 driver, what will be her annual insurance premium? There is no compulsory insurance requirement in her state. Assume age group 1.

10. Craig Haberland is a class 18 driver. He has a 5-year-old car with a symbol of 4. His state requires compulsory insurance coverage. In addition, he wishes to purchase collision and comprehensive coverage with the maximum deductible. He also wants towing insurance. What will Craig's annual insurance premium be?

11. Nancy Poland has an insurance policy with limits of 10/20. If Nancy injures a pedestrian and the judge awards damages of $18,000, **(a)** how much will the insurance company pay and **(b)** how much will Nancy pay?

12. Peter Bell carries insurance with bodily injury limits of 25/60. Peter is in an accident and is charged with injuring four people. The judge awards damages of $10,000 to each of the injured parties. How much will the insurance company pay? How much will Peter pay?

13. Jerry Greeley carries an insurance policy with bodily injury limits of 25/60. Jerry is in an accident and is charged with injuring four people. If the judge awards damages of $20,000 to each of the injured parties, **(a)** how much will the insurance company pay and **(b)** how much will Jerry pay?

14. An issue of *Your Money* reported that the Illinois Department of Insurance gave a typical premium for a brick house in Chicago built in 1950, assuming no policy discounts and a replacement cost estimated at $100,000. With a $100 deductible, the annual premium will be $653. Using the rate in your textbook, with a rating area 3 and class B, what would be the annual premium? (This problem reviews fire insurance.)

15. An issue of *Money* ran a story on cutting car insurance premiums. Raising the car insurance deductible to $500 will cut the collision premium 15%. Theresa Mendex insures her car; her age group is 5 and symbol is 5. What would be her reduction if she changed her policy to a $500 deductible? What would the collision insurance now cost?

16. Robert Stuono lost his life insurance when he was downsized from an investment banking company early this year. So Stuono, age 44, enlisted the help of an independent agent who works with several insurance companies. His goal is $350,000 in term coverage with a level premium for 5 years. What will Robert's annual premium be for term insurance? (This problem reviews life insurance.)

Learning Unit 21–1 :   Stocks

DRILL PROBLEMS

| 52 weeks | | | | | Yld | | Vol | | | | Net |
Hi	Lo	Stocks	SYM	Div	%	PE	100s	High	Low	Close	chg
43.88	25.51	Disney	DIS	.21	.8	49	49633	27.69	26.50	27.69	+0.63

1. From the listed information for Disney, complete the following:
   a. _____ was the highest price at which Disney stock traded during the year.
   b. _____ was the lowest price at which Disney stock traded during the year.
   c. _____ was the amount of the dividend Disney paid to shareholders last year.
   d. _____ is the dividend amount a shareholder with 100 shares would receive.
   e. _____ is the rate of return the stock yielded to its stockholders.
   f. _____ is how many times its earnings per share the stock is selling for.
   g. _____ is the number of shares traded on the day of this stock quote.
   h. _____ is the highest price paid for Disney stock on this day.
   i. _____ is the lowest price paid for Disney stock on this day.
   j. _____ is the change in price from yesterday's closing price.

2. Use the Disney information to show how the yield percent was calculated.

3. What was the price of the last trade of Disney stock yesterday?

WORD PROBLEMS

4. Assume a stockbroker's commission of 2%. What will it cost to purchase 200 shares of Saplent Corporation at $10.75?

5. In Problem 4, the stockbroker's commission for selling stock is the same as that for buying stock. If the customer who purchased 200 shares at $10.75 sells the 200 shares of stock at the end of the year at $18.12, what will be the gain on investment?

6. Holtz Corporation's records show 80,000 shares of preferred stock issued. The preferred dividend is $2 per share, which is cumulative. The records show 750,000 shares of common stock issued. In 2015, no dividends were paid. In 2016, the board of directors declared a dividend of $582,500. What are **(a)** the total amount of dividends paid to preferred stockholders, **(b)** the total amount of dividends paid to common stockholders, and **(c)** the amount of the common dividend per share?

7. Melissa Tucker bought 300 shares of Delta Air Lines stock listed at $61.22 per share. What is the total amount she paid if the stockbroker's commission is 2.5%?

8. A year later, Melissa (Problem 7) sold the stock she had purchased. The market price of the stock at this time was $72.43. Delta Air Lines had paid its shareholders a dividend of $1.20 per share. If the stockbroker's commission to sell stock is 2.5%, what gain did Melissa realize?

9. The board of directors of Parker Electronics, Inc., declared a $539,000 dividend. If the corporation has 70,000 shares of common stock outstanding, what is the dividend per share?

Learning Unit 21-2 :   Bonds

DRILL PROBLEMS

Bond	Current yield	Sales	Close	Net change
IBM $10\frac{1}{4}$ 25	10.0	11	102.5	+.125

1. From the bond listing above complete the following:
   a. _____ is the name of the company.
   b. _____ is the percent of interest paid on the bond.

   c. _____ is the year in which the bond matures.
   d. _____ is the total interest for the year.
   e. _____ was the previous day's closing price on the IBM bond.

2. Show how to calculate the current yield of 10.0% for IBM. (Trade commissions have been omitted.)

3. Use the information for the IBM bonds to calculate **(a)** the amount the last bond traded for on this day and **(b)** the amount the last bond traded for yesterday.

4. What will be the annual interest payment **(a)** to the bondholder assuming he paid $101\frac{3}{4}$ and **(b)** to the bondholder who purchased the bond for $102\frac{1}{2}$?

5. If Terry Gambol purchased three IBM bonds at this day's closing price, **(a)** what will be her total cost excluding commission and **(b)** how much interest will she receive for the year?

6. Calculate the bond yield (to the nearest tenth percent) for each of the following:

	Bond interest rate	Purchase price	Bond yield
a.	7%	97	_____
b.	$9\frac{1}{2}$%	101.625	_____
c.	$13\frac{1}{4}$%	104.25	_____

7. For each of the following, state whether the bond sold at a premium or a discount and give the amount of the premium or discount.

Bond interest rate	Purchase price	Premium or discount
a. 7%	97	_____
b. $9\frac{1}{2}\%$	101.625	_____
c. $13\frac{1}{4}\%$	104.25	_____

WORD PROBLEMS

8. Rob Morrisey purchased a $1,000 bond that was quoted at 102.25 and paying $8\frac{7}{8}\%$ interest. **(a)** How much did Rob pay for the bond? **(b)** What was the premium or discount? **(c)** How much annual interest will he receive?

9. Jackie Anderson purchased a bond that was quoted at 62.50 and paying interest of $10\frac{1}{2}\%$. **(a)** How much did Jackie pay for the bond? **(b)** What was the premium or discount? **(c)** What interest will Jackie receive annually? **(d)** What is the bond's current annual yield (to the nearest tenth percent)?

10. Swartz Company issued bonds totaling $2,000,000 in order to purchase updated equipment. If the bonds pay interest of 11%, what is the total amount of interest the Swartz Company must pay semiannually?

11. The RJR and ACyan companies have both issued bonds that are paying $7\frac{3}{8}\%$ interest. The quoted price of the RJR bond is 94.125, and the quoted price of the ACyan bond is $102\frac{7}{8}$. Find the current annual yield on each (to the nearest tenth percent).

12. Mary Rowe purchased 25 of Chrysler Corporation $8\frac{3}{8}\%$ bonds of 2009. The bonds closed at 93.25. Find **(a)** the total purchase price and **(b)** the amount of the first semiannual interest payment Mary will receive.

13. What is the annual yield (to the nearest hundredth percent) of the bonds Mary Rowe purchased?

14. Mary Rowe purchased a $1,000 bond listed as ARch $10\frac{7}{8}$ 19 for 122.75. What is the annual yield of this bond (to the nearest tenth percent)?

Learning Unit 21–3 :   Mutual Funds

DRILL PROBLEMS

From the following, calculate the NAV. Round to the nearest cent.

	Current market value of fund investments	Current liabilities	Number of shares outstanding	NAV
1.	$6,800,000	$850,000	500,000	_____
2.	$11,425,000	$690,000	810,000	_____
3.	$22,580,000	$1,300,000	1,400,000	_____

Complete the following using this information:

NAV	Net change	Fund name	Inv. obj.	YTD %Ret	Total return 1 Yr R
$23.48	+.14	EuroA	Eu	+37.3	+7.6 E

4. NAV _____

5. NAV change _____

6. Total return year to date _____

7. Return for the last 12 months _____

8. What does an E rating mean? _____

Calculate the commission (load) charge and the offer to buy.

NAV	% commission (load) charge	Dollar amount of commission (load) charge	Offer price
9. $17.00	$8\frac{1}{2}\%$	_____	_____
10. $21.55	6%	_____	_____
11. $14.10	4%	_____	_____

WORD PROBLEMS

12. Paul wanted to know how his Fidelity mutual fund $14.33 NAV in the newspaper was calculated. He called Fidelity, and he received the following information:

Current market value of fund investment	$7,500,000
Current liabilities	$910,000
Number of shares outstanding	460,000

Please calculate the NAV for Paul. Was the NAV in the newspaper correct?

13. Jeff Jones bought 150 shares of Putnam Vista Fund. The NAV of the fund was $9.88. The offer price was $10.49. What did Jeff pay for these 150 shares?

14. Pam Long purchased 300 shares of the no-load Scudder's European Growth Company Fund. The NAV is $12.61. What did Pam pay for the 300 shares?

15. Assume in Problem 14 that 8 years later Pam sells her 300 shares. The NAV at the time of sale was $12.20. What is the amount of her profit or loss on the sale?

16. Financial planner J. Michael Martin recommended that Jim Kelly choose a long-term bond because it gives high income while Kelly waits for better stock market opportunities down the road. The bond Martin recommended matures in 2030 and was originally issued at $8\frac{1}{2}\%$ interest and the current yield is 7.9%. What would be the current selling price for this bond and how would that price appear in the bond quotations?

17.

Bonds		Vol.	Close	Net chg.
Comp USA $9\frac{1}{2}$ 20		70	102.375	−.125
GMA 7 22		5	101.625	−1.25

From the above information, compare the two bonds for:

a. When the bonds expire.
b. The yield of each bond.
c. The current selling price.
d. Whether the bond is selling at a discount or premium.
e. Yesterday's bond close.

Learning Unit 22–1 :   Mean, Median, and Mode

Note: Optional problems for LU 22–3 are found after the Challenge Problems in Chapter 21.

DRILL PROBLEMS

1. Find the mean for the following lists of numbers. Round to the nearest hundredth.
    a. 12, 16, 20, 25, 29   Mean _____
    b. 80, 91, 98, 82, 68, 82, 79, 90   Mean _____
    c. 9.5, 12.3, 10.5, 7.5, 10.1, 18.4, 9.8, 6.2, 11.1, 4.8, 10.6   Mean _____

2. Find the weighted mean for the following. Round to the nearest hundredth.
    a. 4, 4, 6, 8, 8, 13, 4, 6, 8   Weighted mean _____
    b. 82, 85, 87, 82, 82, 90, 87, 63, 100, 85, 87   Weighted mean _____

3. Find the median for the following:
    a. 56, 89, 47, 36, 90, 63, 55, 82, 46, 81   Median _____
    b. 59, 22, 39, 47, 33, 98, 50, 73, 54, 46, 99   Median _____

4. Find the mode for the following:
    24, 35, 49, 35, 52, 35, 52   Mode _____

5. Find the mean, median, and mode for each of the following:
    a. 72, 48, 62, 54, 73, 62, 75, 57, 62, 58, 78
        Mean _____   Median _____   Mode _____
    b. $0.50, $1.19, $0.58, $1.19, $2.83, $1.71, $2.21, $0.58, $1.29, $0.58
        Mean _____   Median _____   Mode _____
    c. $92, $113, $99, $117, $99, $105, $119, $112, $95, $116, $102, $120
        Mean _____   Median _____   Mode _____
    d. 88, 105, 120, 119, 105, 128, 160, 151, 90, 153, 107, 119, 105
        Mean _____   Median _____   Mode _____

WORD PROBLEMS

6. The sales for the year at the 8 Bed and Linen Stores were $1,442,897, $1,556,793, $1,703,767, $1,093,320, $1,443,984, $1,665,308, $1,197,692, and $1,880,443. Find the mean earnings for a Bed and Linen Store for the year.

7. To avoid having an extreme number affect the average, the manager of Bed and Linen Stores (Problem 6) would like you to find the median earnings for the 8 stores.

8. The Bed and Linen Store in Salem sells many different towels. Following are the prices of all the towels that were sold on Wednesday: $7.98, $9.98, $9.98, $11.49, $11.98, $7.98, $12.49, $12.49, $11.49, $9.98, $9.98, $16.00, and $7.98. Find the mean price of a towel.

9. Looking at the towel prices, the Salem manager (Problem 8) decided that he should have calculated a weighted mean. Find the weighted mean price of a towel.

10. The manager of the Salem Bed and Linen Store above would like to find another measure of the central tendency called the *median*. Find the median price for the towels sold.

11. The manager at the Salem Bed and Linen Store would like to know the most popular towel among the group of towels sold on Wednesday. Find the mode for the towel prices for Wednesday.

Learning Unit 22–2 :   Frequency Distributions and Graphs

DRILL PROBLEMS

1. A local dairy distributor wants to know how many containers of yogurt health club members consume in a month. The distributor gathered the following data:

17	17	22	14	26	23	23	15	18	16
18	15	23	18	29	20	24	17	12	15
18	19	18	20	28	21	25	21	26	14
16	18	15	19	27	15	22	19	19	13
20	17	13	24	28	18	28	20	17	16

Construct a frequency distribution table to organize these data.

2. Construct a bar graph for the Problem 1 data. The height of each bar should represent the frequency of each amount consumed.

3. To simplify the amount of data concerning yogurt consumption, construct a relative frequency distribution table. The range will be from 1 to 30 with five class intervals: 1–6, 7–12, 13–18, 19–24, and 25–30.

4. Construct a bar graph for the grouped data.

5. Prepare a pie chart to represent the above data.

WORD PROBLEMS

6. The women's department of a local department store lists its total sales for the year: January, $39,800; February, $22,400; March, $32,500; April, $33,000; May, $30,000; June, $29,200; July, $26,400; August, $24,800; September, $34,000; October, $34,200; November, $38,400; December, $41,100. Draw a line graph to represent the monthly sales of the women's department for the year. The vertical axis should represent the dollar amount of the sales.

7. The following list shows the number of television sets sold in a year by the sales associates at Souza's TV and Appliance Store.

115	125	139	127	142	153	169	126	141
130	137	150	169	157	146	173	168	156
140	146	134	123	142	129	141	122	141

Construct a relative frequency distribution table to represent the data. The range will be from 115 to 174 with intervals of 10.

8. Use the data in the distribution table for Problem 7 to construct a bar graph for the grouped data.

9. Expenses for Flora Foley Real Estate Agency for the month of June were as follows: salaries expense, $2,790; utilities expense, $280; rent expense, $2,000; commissions expense, $4,800; and other expenses, $340. Present these data in a circle graph. (First calculate the percent relationship between each item and the total; then determine the number of degrees that represents each item.)

10. Today a new Jeep costs $25,000. In 1970, the Jeep cost $4,500. What is the price relative? (Round to the nearest tenth percent.)

Worked-Out Solutions to Extra Practice Quizzes and You Try It Problems

Chapter 1

LU 1-1a

1. **a.** Eight thousand, six hundred eighty-two
    b. Fifty-six thousand, two hundred ninety-five
    c. Seven hundred thirty-two billion, three hundred ten million, four hundred forty-four thousand, eight hundred eighty-eight

2. **a.** 43 = 40   **b.** 654 = 700   **c.** 7,328 = 7,000   **d.** 5,980 = 6,000

3. Kellogg's sales and profit:

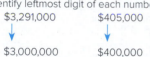

The facts	Solving for?	Steps to take	Key points
Sales: Three million, two hundred ninety-one thousand dollars. *Profit:* Four hundred five thousand dollars.	Sales and profit rounded all the way.	Express each verbal form in numeric form. Identify leftmost digit in each number.	Rounding all the way means only the leftmost digit will remain. All other digits become zeros.

Steps to solving problem

1. Convert verbal to numeric.
    Three million, two hundred ninety-one thousand ⟶ $3,291,000
    Four hundred five thousand ⟶ $ 405,000

2. Identify leftmost digit of each number.
    $3,291,000 $405,000
        ↓   ↓
    $3,000,000 $400,000

LU 1-2a

1.		2.	**Estimate**	**Actual**	3.	$\overset{8\ \ 17717}{9,787}$	**Check**
	10		3,000	3,482		$-5,968$	3,819
	18		7,000	6,981		$\overline{3,819}$	$+5,968$
	19		$+5,000$	5,490			$\overline{9,787}$
	24		$\overline{15,000}$	$\overline{15,953}$			
	$\overline{26,090}$						

4. Jackson Manufacturing Company over- or underestimated sales:

The facts	Solving for?	Steps to take	Key points
Projected 2013 sales: $878,000 *Major clients:* $492,900 *Other clients:* $342,000	How much were sales over- or underestimated?	Total projected sales − Total actual sales = Over- or underestimated sales.	Projected sales (minuend) − Actual sales (subtrahend) = Difference.

Steps to solving problem

1. Calculate total actual sales.

    $492,900
    + 342,000
    $834,900

2. Calculate over- or underestimated sales.

    $878,000
    − 834,900
    $ 43,100 (overestimated)

LU 1-3a

1.
Estimate	Actual	Check

$$
\begin{array}{r} 5,000 \\ \times\ 20 \\ \hline 100,000 \end{array}
$$

$$
\begin{array}{r} 4,938 \\ \times\ 19 \\ \hline 44442 \\ 4938 \\ \hline 93,822 \end{array}
$$

$$
\begin{array}{r} 9 \times 4,938 = \quad 44,442 \\ 10 \times 4,938 = +49,380 \\ \hline 93,822 \end{array}
$$

2. $86 \times 19 = 1,634 + 5$ zeros $= 163,400,000$

3. $86 + 4$ zeros $= 860,000$

4.
Rounding	Actual	Check

$$
\begin{array}{r} 200 \\ 30\overline{)6,000} \\ \underline{6\ 0} \end{array}
$$

$$
\begin{array}{r} 245 \ \ \text{R24} \\ 26\overline{)6,394} \\ \underline{5\ 2} \\ 1\ 19 \\ \underline{1\ 04} \\ 154 \\ \underline{130} \\ 24 \end{array}
$$

$$
\begin{array}{r} 26 \times 245 = 6,370 \\ +\ 24 \\ \hline 6,394 \end{array}
$$

5. Drop 3 zeros $= 3\overline{)99}^{\,33}$

6. General Motors' total cost per year:

	The facts	Solving for?	Steps to take	Key points
BLUEPRINT	Cars produced each workday: 850 Workweek: 5 days Cost per car: $7,000	Total cost per year.	Cars produced per week × 52 = Total cars produced per year. Total cars produced per year × Total cost per car = Total cost per year.	Whenever possible, use multiplication and division shortcuts with zeros. Multiplication can be checked by division

Steps to solving problem

1. Calculate total cars produced per week. $5 \times 850 = 4,250$ cars produced per week

2. Calculate total cars produced per year. $4,250$ cars $\times 52$ weeks $= 221,000$ total cars produced per year

3. Calculate total cost per year. $221,000$ cars $\times \$7,000 = \$1,547,000,000$ (multiply 221×7 and add zeros)

Check $\$1,547,000,000 \div 221,000 = \$7,000$ (drop 3 zeros before dividing)

You Try It

1. 571 → Five hundred seventy-one
7,943 → Seven thousand, nine hundred forty-three

2. 691 = 691 = 690

Identify digit   Less than 5

3. 429,685 → 429,685 → 400,000

Identify digit   Less than 5

4.
$$
\begin{array}{r} {}^{1}\ \ \\ 76 \\ +38 \\ \hline 114 \end{array}
$$

5.
$$
\begin{array}{r} {}^{512} \\ \cancel{6}29 \\ -134 \\ \hline 495 \end{array}
$$

6.
$$
\begin{array}{r} 491 \\ \times\ 28 \\ \hline 3928 \\ 982 \\ \hline 13,748 \end{array}
$$

$13 \times 10 = 130$ (attach 1 zero)
$13 \times 1,000 = 13,000$ (attach 3 zeros)

7.
$$
\begin{array}{r} 5\ \text{R15} \\ 16\overline{)95} \\ \underline{80} \\ 15 \end{array}
$$

$4,000 \div 100 = 40$ (drop 2 zeros)
$4,000 \div 1,000 = 4$ (drop 3 zeros)

Chapter 2

LU 2-1a

1. a. Proper
  b. Improper
  c. Mixed
  d. Improper

2.
$$7\overline{)155}\ \ ^{22\ 1/7}$$
$$\underline{14}$$
$$15$$
$$\underline{14}$$
$$1$$

3. $\dfrac{(9 \times 8) + 7}{9} = \dfrac{79}{9}$

4. a.
$$42\overline{)70}\ ^1 \quad 28\overline{)42}\ ^1 \quad 14\overline{)28}\ ^2$$
$$\underline{42} \qquad\quad \underline{28} \qquad\quad \underline{28}$$
$$28 \qquad\quad 14 \qquad\quad 0$$

14 is greatest common divisor

$$\dfrac{42 \div 14}{70 \div 14} = \dfrac{3}{5}$$

b.
$$96\overline{)182}\ ^1 \quad 86\overline{)96}\ ^1 \quad 10\overline{)86}\ ^8$$
$$\underline{96} \qquad\quad \underline{86} \qquad\quad \underline{80}$$
$$86 \qquad\quad 10 \qquad\quad 6$$

$$6\overline{)10}\ ^1 \quad 4\overline{)6}\ ^1 \quad 2\overline{)4}\ ^2$$
$$\underline{6} \qquad\quad \underline{4} \qquad\quad \underline{4}$$
$$4 \qquad\quad 2 \qquad\quad 0$$

$$\dfrac{96 \div 2}{182 \div 2} = \dfrac{48}{91}$$

5. a. $\dfrac{300}{30} = 10 \times 16 = 160$
    b. $\dfrac{60}{20} \times 3 \times 9 = 27$

LU 2-2a

1.

2⌞10	15	9	4
3⌞ 5	15	9	2
5⌞ 5	5	3	2
1	1	3	2

LCD $= 2 \times 3 \times 5 \times 1 \times 1 \times 3 \times 2 = 180$

2. a. $\dfrac{2}{25} + \dfrac{3}{5} = \dfrac{2}{25} + \dfrac{15}{25} = \dfrac{17}{25}$
$\left(\begin{array}{l} \dfrac{3}{5} = \dfrac{?}{25} \\ 25 \div 5 = 5 \times 3 = 15 \end{array} \right)$

b.
$$\begin{array}{r} 3\frac{3}{8} \\ +6\frac{1}{32} \\ \hline \end{array} \qquad \begin{array}{r} 3\frac{12}{32} \\ +6\frac{1}{32} \\ \hline 9\frac{13}{32} \end{array}$$

$\dfrac{3}{8} = \dfrac{?}{32}$

$32 \div 8 = 4 \times 3 = 12$

3. a.
$$\begin{array}{r} \frac{5}{6} = \frac{5}{6} \\ -\frac{1}{3} = \frac{2}{6} \\ \hline \frac{3}{6} = \frac{1}{2} \end{array}$$

b.
$$\begin{array}{r} 9\frac{1}{8} = 9\frac{4}{32} = 8\frac{36}{32} \\ -3\frac{7}{32} = -3\frac{7}{32} = -3\frac{7}{32} \\ \hline 5\frac{29}{32} \end{array}$$
$\left(\dfrac{32}{32} + \dfrac{4}{32} \right)$

c. Note how we showed the 6 as $5\frac{5}{5}$

$$5\frac{5}{5}$$
$$-1\frac{2}{5}$$
$$\overline{4\frac{3}{5}}$$

4.

$$209\frac{1}{8} \qquad 209\frac{1}{8} \qquad 985\frac{1}{4} \qquad 985\frac{2}{8} \qquad 984\frac{10}{8}$$

$$+382\frac{1}{4} \qquad +382\frac{2}{8} \qquad 591\frac{3}{8} \qquad -591\frac{3}{8} \qquad -591\frac{3}{8}$$

$$\overline{} \qquad \overline{591\frac{3}{8}\ \text{sq. feet}} \qquad \qquad \overline{393\frac{7}{8}\ \text{sq. feet}}$$

LU 2-3a

1. a. $\dfrac{\overset{1}{\cancel{6}}}{8} \times \dfrac{3}{\underset{1}{\cancel{6}}} = \dfrac{3}{8}$ **b.** $\dfrac{\overset{6}{\cancel{42}}}{7} \times \dfrac{1}{\underset{1}{\cancel{7}}} = \dfrac{6}{1} = 6$

2. $\dfrac{13}{117} \times \dfrac{9}{5} = \dfrac{117}{585}$

$$117\overline{)585}$$
$$\underline{585}$$
$$0$$

117 is greatest common divisor

$$\frac{117 \div 117}{585 \div 117} = \frac{1}{5}$$

3. a. $\dfrac{1}{8} \times \dfrac{5}{4} = \dfrac{5}{32}$ **b.** $\dfrac{61}{6} \times \dfrac{7}{6} = \dfrac{427}{36} = 11\dfrac{31}{36}$

4. Total cost of Jill's new home:

	The facts	Solving for?	Steps to take	Key points
BLUEPRINT	*Jill's mobile home:* $10\frac{1}{8}$ as expensive as her brother's. *Brother paid:* $10,000	Total cost of Jill's new home.	$10\frac{1}{8}$ × Total cost of Jill's brother's mobile home = Total cost of Jill's new home.	Canceling is an alternative to reducing.

Steps to solving problem

1. Convert $10\frac{1}{8}$ to a mixed number. $\dfrac{81}{8}$

2. Calculate the total cost of Jill's home. $\dfrac{81}{\underset{1}{\cancel{8}}} \times \overset{1,250}{\cancel{\$10,000}} = \$101,250$

You Try It

1. $\frac{3}{10}$ proper, $\frac{9}{8}$ improper, $1\frac{4}{5}$ mixed

2. $\frac{18}{7} = 2\frac{4}{7}$ $5\frac{1}{7} = \frac{35+1}{7} = \frac{36}{7}$

3. $\frac{16 \div 8}{24 \div 8} = \frac{2}{3}$

4. $\frac{20}{50} = 20\overline{)50}$ ... $\frac{2}{10}$

   $\begin{array}{r} 2 \\ 20\overline{)50} \\ \underline{40} \\ 10 \end{array}$

   $\begin{array}{r} 2 \\ 10\overline{)20} \\ \underline{20} \\ 0 \end{array}$

   10 is greatest common denominator

5. $\frac{16}{31} = \frac{}{310}$

   $310 \div 31 = 10$ $10 \times 16 = 160$

6. $\frac{3}{7} + \frac{2}{7} = \frac{5}{7}$ $\frac{5}{7} - \frac{2}{7} = \frac{3}{7}$

   $\begin{array}{r} \frac{5}{8} = \frac{25}{40} \\ + \frac{3}{40} = \frac{3}{40} \\ \hline \frac{28}{40} = \frac{7}{10} \end{array}$

7. Prime numbers 2, 3, 5, 7, 11, 13, 17

8. $\frac{1}{2} + \frac{1}{4} + \frac{1}{5} = \begin{array}{c} 2\underline{\big/}\,2 \quad 4 \quad 5 \\ 1 \quad 2 \quad 5 \end{array}$

   $2 \times 1 \times 2 \times 5 = 20$ LCD

9. $2\frac{1}{4}$
   $+ 3\frac{3}{4}$
   $\overline{5\frac{4}{4}} = 6$

10. $11\frac{1}{3}$ $10\frac{4}{3}$
    $- 2\frac{2}{3}$ $- 2\frac{2}{3}$
    $\overline{}$ $\overline{8\frac{2}{3}}$

11. $\frac{4}{5} \times \frac{25}{26} = \frac{\overset{2}{\cancel{4}}}{\cancel{5}_{1}} \times \frac{\overset{5}{\cancel{25}}}{\cancel{26}_{13}} = \frac{10}{13}$

12. $2\frac{1}{4} \times 3\frac{1}{4} = \frac{9}{4} \times \frac{13}{4} = \frac{117}{16} = 7\frac{5}{16}$

13. $\frac{1}{8} \div \frac{1}{4} = \frac{1}{\cancel{8}_{2}} \times \frac{\cancel{4}^{1}}{} = \frac{1}{2}$

14. $3\frac{1}{4} \div 1\frac{4}{5} = \frac{13}{4} \div \frac{9}{5} = \frac{13}{4} \times \frac{5}{9} = \frac{65}{36}$

Chapter 3

LU 3–1a

1. .309 (3 places to right of decimal)

2. Hundredths

3. Ten thousandths

4. **a.** .8 (identified digit 8 – digit to right less than 5)   **b.** .844 (identified digit 3 – digit to right greater than 5)

5. **a.** .9 (identified digit 6 – digit to right greater than 5)   **b.** .879 (identified digit 9 – digit to right less than 5)

6. .0008 (4 places)

7. .00016 (5 places)

8. $\frac{938}{1,000}\left(\frac{938}{1+3 \text{ zeros}}\right)$

9. $17\frac{95}{100}$

10. $\frac{325}{10,000}\left(\frac{325}{1+4 \text{ zeros}} \quad \frac{1}{4} \times .01 = .0025 + .03 = .0325\right)$

11. .125 = .13

12. .571 = .57

13. 13.111 = 13.11

LU 3–2a

1. $\begin{array}{r} 16.0000 \\ .8310 \\ 9.8500 \\ 17.8321 \\ \hline 44.5131 \end{array}$

2. $\begin{array}{r} {}^{14}\;{}^{17} \\ 8\;\;\overset{4}{\cancel{5}}\;\overset{7}{\cancel{8}}\;\overset{13}{\cancel{3}}2 \\ 29.\cancel{5}\cancel{8}\cancel{3}2 \\ -\;\;.9980 \\ \hline 28.5852 \end{array}$

3. $\begin{array}{r} 29.64 \\ \times\;18.2 \\ \hline 5928 \\ 23712 \\ 2964 \\ \hline 539.448 = 539.4 \end{array}$

4. $\begin{array}{r} 774.08 = 774.09 \\ 494\overline{)382400.00} \\ \underline{3458} \\ 3660 \\ \underline{3458} \\ 2020 \\ \underline{1976} \\ 4400 \\ \underline{3952} \\ 448 \end{array}$

5. 17.48 = 1,748

6. 8.432 = 8.432

7. .9643 = .9643

8. A: $8.88 ÷ 64 = $.14   B: $7.25 ÷ 50 = $.15   Buy A

9. Avis Rent-A-Car total rental charge:

	The facts	Solving for?	Steps to take	Key points
BLUEPRINT	*Cost per day:* $29.99 22 cents per mile. Drove 709.8 miles. 2-day rental.	Total rental charge.	Total cost for 2 days' rental + Total cost of driving = Total rental charge.	In multiplication, count the number of decimal places. Starting from right to left in the product, insert decimal in appropriate place. Round to nearest cent.

Steps to solving problem

1. Calculate total costs for 2 days' rental. $29.99 × 2 = $59.98

2. Calculate the total cost of driving. $.22 × 709.8 = $156.156 = $156.16

3. Calculate the total rental charge.
$$\begin{array}{r} \$\ 59.98 \\ +\ 156.16 \\ \hline \$216.14 \end{array}$$

10. 7,000 × $.0715 = $500.50

Check $500.50 × 13.9876 = $7000.79 pesos off due to rounding

You Try It

1. .8256 → Ten thousandths place

2. .841 = .8
   ↑↑
   Less than 5

3. $\dfrac{9}{1,000}$ = .009

   $\dfrac{3}{10,000}$ = .0003

4. $\dfrac{1}{7}$ = .142 = .1

5. $5\dfrac{4}{5} = \dfrac{4}{5}$ = .80 + 5 = 5.80

6. .865 $\dfrac{865}{1}$ $\dfrac{865}{1,000}$ (attach 3 zeros)

7.
$$\begin{array}{r} 1.7 \\ 3.0 \\ .8 \\ \hline 5.5 \end{array} \qquad \begin{array}{r} {}^{5\ 10} \\ \cancel{6}.\cancel{0}0 \\ -4.10 \\ \hline 1.90 \end{array}$$

8.   3.49 (2 places)
$$\begin{array}{r} .015\ \text{(3 places)} \\ \hline 1745 \\ 349 \\ \hline .05235 \end{array}$$

9.
$$\begin{array}{r} 1.5 \\ 33\overline{)49.5} \\ 33 \\ \hline 165 \\ 165 \\ \hline 0 \end{array}$$

10.   .46 = .5
$$\begin{array}{r} 3.2\overline{)1.480} \\ 128 \\ \hline 200 \\ 192 \end{array}$$

11. 6.92 × 100 = 692 (move 2 places to right)
   6.92 ÷ 100 = .0692 (move 2 places to left)

Chapter 4

LU 4-1a

1.

LU 4-2a

EARL MILLER			
Bank Reconciliation as of March 8, 2015			
Checkbook balance		**Bank balance**	
Earl's checkbook balance	$1,200.10	Bank balance	$ 300.10
Add:		Add:	
Interest	24.06	Deposit in transit	1,200.50
	$1,224.16		$1,500.60
Deduct:		Deduct:	
Deposited check returned fee	$30.00	Outstanding checks:	
		No. 300	$ 22.88
ATM	15.00 45.00	No. 302	15.90
		No. 303	282.66 321.44
Reconciled balance	$1,179.16	Reconciled balance	$1,179.16

You Try It

Sample

1. Pete Co.   Pay to the order of   Pay to the order
   24-111-9   Reel Bank   of Reel Bank for
                   Pete Co. 24-111-9   deposit only
                                              Pete Co. 24-111-9

Checkbook

Beg. balance		$300
2. *Less*: NSF	$50	
ATM service charge	20	70
Ending balance		$230

Chapter 5

LU 5-1a

1. **a.** $\frac{1}{2}Q - 8 = 16$ **b.** $12(Q + 41) = 1,200$ **c.** $7 - 2Q = 1$

   d. $4Q - 2 = 24$ **e.** $3Q + 3 = 19$ **f.** $2Q - 6 = 5$

2. **a.**
$$B + 14 = 70$$
$$\frac{-14}{B} = \frac{-14}{56}$$

   b.
$$\frac{5D}{5} = \frac{250}{5}$$
$$D = 50$$

   c.
$$\frac{11B}{11} = \frac{121}{11}$$
$$B = 11$$

   d.
$$8\left(\frac{B}{8}\right) = 90(8)$$
$$B = 720$$

   e.
$$\frac{B}{2} + 2 = 250$$
$$\frac{-2 \quad -2}{\frac{B}{2} = 248}$$
$$2\left(\frac{B}{2}\right) = 248(2)$$
$$B = 496$$

   f.
$$3(B - 6) = 18$$
$$3B - 18 = 18$$
$$\frac{+18 \quad +18}{\frac{3B}{3} = \frac{36}{3}}$$
$$B = 12$$

LU 5-2a

1.

	Unknown(s)	Variable(s)	Relationship
BLUEPRINT	Original price	P*	P − $50 = Sale price
			Sale price = $140

*P = Original price.

1. **Mechanical steps**
$$P - \$50 = \$140$$
$$\frac{+ \ 50 \quad + \ 50}{P \quad = \$190}$$

2.

BLUEPRINT	Unknown(s)	Variable(s)	Relationship
	Yearly salary	S^*	$\frac{1}{7}S$ Entertainment = $7,000

*S = Salary.

2. **Mechanical steps**

$$\frac{1}{7}S = \$7,000$$

$$\cancel{7}\left(\frac{S}{\cancel{7}}\right) = \$7,000(7)$$

$$S = \$49,000$$

3.

BLUEPRINT	Unknown(s)	Variable(s)	Relationship
	Micro	$8C^*$	$5C$
	Morse	C	$\underline{-\ C}$ 49 computers

*C = Computers.

3. **Mechanical steps**

$$8C - C = 49$$

$$\frac{-7C}{\cancel{7}} = \frac{49}{7}$$

$$C = 7\ (Morse)$$
$$8C = 56\ (Micro)$$

4.

BLUEPRINT	Unknown(s)	Variable(s)	Relationship
	Stoves sold:		
	Susie	$2S^*$	$2S$
	Cara	S	$\underline{+S}$ 360 stoves

*S = Stoves.

4. **Mechanical steps**

$$2S + S = 360$$

$$\frac{-3S}{\cancel{3}} = \frac{360}{3}$$

$$S = 120\ (Cara)$$
$$2S = 240\ (Susie)$$

5.

BLUEPRINT	Unknown(s)	Variable(s)	Price	Relationship
	Meatball	M	$7	$7M$
	Cheese	$3M$	6	$\underline{+\ 18M}$ $1,800 total sales

5. **Mechanical steps**

$$7M + 18M = 1,800$$

$$\frac{25M}{25} = \frac{1,800}{25}$$

$$M = 72\ \ (meatball)$$
$$3M = 216\ (cheese)$$

Check

$$(72 \times \$7) + (216 \times \$6) = \$1,800$$

$$\$504 + \$1,296 = \$1,800$$

$$\$1,800 = \$1,800$$

6.

BLUEPRINT	Unknown(s)	Variable(s)	Price	Relationship
	Unit sales:			
	Meatball	M^*	$7	$6M$
	Cheese	$288 - M$	6	$\underline{+\ 6(288 - M)}$ $1,800 total sales

*We assign the variable to the most expensive item to make the mechanical steps easier to complete.

6. **Mechanical steps**

$$7M + 6(288 - M) = \$1,800$$
$$7M + 1,728 - 6M = \$1,800$$
$$M + 1,728 = \$1,800$$
$$\underline{-1,728 = -1,728}$$
$$M = 72$$
$$Meatball = 72$$
$$Cheese = 288 - 72 = 216$$

Check

$$72(\$7) + 216\ (\$6) = \$504 + \$1,296$$

$$= \$1,800$$

You Try It

1.
$$E + 15 = \quad 14$$
$$\underline{-15 \quad\ -15}$$
$$E \quad = \quad -1$$

2.
$$B - 40 = \quad 80$$
$$\underline{+40 \quad +40}$$
$$B \quad = \quad 120$$

3.
$$\frac{5C}{\cancel{5}} = 75$$
$$C = 15$$

4.
$$\frac{A}{6} = 60 \quad (\cancel{6})\frac{A}{\cancel{6}} = 6(60)$$
$$A = 360$$

5.
$$\frac{C}{4} + 10 = \quad 17$$
$$\underline{\qquad -10 \quad -10}$$
$$\frac{C}{4} \qquad = \quad 7$$
$$(\cancel{4})\frac{C}{\cancel{4}} \quad = 7(4)$$
$$C \qquad = 28$$

6.
$$7(B - 10) = \quad 35$$
$$7B - 70 = \quad 35$$
$$\underline{+70 \quad +70}$$
$$\frac{7B}{7} \qquad = \frac{105}{7}$$
$$B \qquad = 15$$

7. $5B + 3B = 16$

$$\frac{8B}{8} = \frac{16}{8}$$

$$B = 2$$

Sit. 1. $P - \$53 = \$110$

$$\frac{+53 \quad +53}{P \quad = \$163}$$

Sit. 2. $\frac{1}{7}B = \$6,000$

$$7\left(\frac{B}{7}\right) = 6,000(7)$$

$$B = \$42,000$$

Sit. 3. $9S - S = 640$

$$\frac{8S}{8} = \frac{640}{8}$$

$$S = 80 \qquad 9S = 720$$

Sit. 4. $9S + S = 640$

$$\frac{10S}{10} = \frac{640}{10}$$

$$S = 64 \qquad 9S = 576$$

Sit. 5. $400(3N) + 300N = 15,000$

$$\frac{1,500N}{1,500} = \frac{15,000}{1,500}$$

$$N = 10$$

$$3N = 30$$

Sit. 6. $400S + 300(40 - S) = 15,000$

$$400S + 12,000 - 300S = 15,000$$

$$100S + 12,000 = 15,000$$

$$\frac{-12,000 \quad -12,000}{\frac{100S}{100} = \frac{3,000}{100}}$$

$$S = 30$$

$$40 - S = 10$$

Chapter 6

LU 6-1a

1. $.44.44 = 44.4\%$

2. $.78.2 = 78.2\%$

3. $.00.6 = .6\%$

4. $7.93.333 = 793.3\%$

5. $\frac{1}{5}\% = .20\% = .0020$

6. $7\frac{4}{5}\% = 7.80\% = .0780$

7. $92\% = .92 = .92$

8. $765.8\% = 7.65.8 = 7.658$

9. $\frac{1}{3} = .33.333 = 33.33\%$

10. $\frac{3}{7} = .42.857 = 42.86\%$

11. $17\% = 17 \times \frac{1}{100} = \frac{17}{100}$

12. $82\frac{1}{4}\% = \frac{329}{4} \times \frac{1}{100} = \frac{329}{400}$

13. $150\% = 150 \times \frac{1}{100} = \frac{150}{100} = 1\frac{50}{100} = 1\frac{1}{2}$

14. $\frac{1}{4}\% = \frac{1}{4} \times \frac{1}{100} = \frac{1}{400}$

15. $17\frac{8}{10}\% = \frac{178}{10} \times \frac{1}{100} = \frac{178}{1,000} = \frac{89}{500}$

LU 6-2a

1. $504 = 1,200 \times .42$
    $(P) = (B) \times (R)$

2. $\$560 = \$8,000 \times .07$
    $(P) = (B) \times (R)$

3. $\frac{(P)510}{(B)6,000} = .085 = 8.5\%$

4. $\frac{(P)400}{(B)900} = .444 = 44.4\%$

5. $\frac{(P)30}{(R).60} = 50(B)$

6. $\frac{(P)1,200}{(R).035} = 34,285.7(B)$

7. Percent of Professor Ford's class that did not receive the A grade:

	The facts	Solving for?	Steps to take	Key points
BLUEPRINT	10 As. 25 in class.	Percent that did not receive A.	Identify key elements. *Base:* 25 *Rate:* ? *Portion:* 15(25 − 10). $\text{Rate} = \dfrac{\text{Portion}}{\text{Base}}$	Portion (15) Base × Rate (25) (?) The whole Portion and rate must relate to same piece of base.

Steps to solving problem

1. Set up the formula. $Rate = \dfrac{Portion}{Base}$

2. Calculate the rate. $R = \dfrac{15}{25}$

   $R = 60\%$

8. Abby Biernet's original order:

	The facts	Solving for?	Steps to take	Key points
BLUEPRINT	70% of the order not in. 90 lobsters received.	Total order of lobsters.	Identify key elements. *Base*: ? *Rate*: 30 (100% − 70%) *Portion*: 90. $Base = \dfrac{Portion}{Rate}$	Portion (90) Base × Rate (?) (.30) 90 lobsters represent 30% of the order Portion and rate must relate to same piece of base.

Steps to solving problem

1. Set up the formula. $Base = \dfrac{Portion}{Rate}$

2. Calculate the base. $B = \dfrac{90}{.30}$ ← 90 lobsters are 30% of base

   $B = 300$ lobsters

9. Dunkin' Donuts Company sales for 2014:

	The facts	Solving for?	Steps to take	Key points
BLUEPRINT	*2013*: $400,000 sales. *2014*: Sales up 35% from 2013.	Sales for 2014.	Identify key elements. *Base*: $400,000 *Rate*: 1.35. Old year 100% New year + 35 ___ 135% *Portion*: ? Portion = Base × Rate	2014 sales Portion (?) Base × Rate ($400,000) (1.35) 2013 sales When rate is greater than 100%, portion will be larger than base.

Steps to solving problem

1. Set up the formula.   Portion = Base × Rate

2. Calculate the portion. $P = \$400,000 \times 1.35$
   $P = \$540,000$

10. Percent decrease in Apple Computer price:

	The facts	Solving for?	Steps to take	Key points
BLUEPRINT	Apple Computer was $1,800; now $1,000.	Percent decrease in price.	Identify key elements. *Base*: $1,800 *Rate*: ? *Portion*: $800 ($1,800 − $1,000) Rate = $\dfrac{\text{Portion}}{\text{Base}}$	Difference in price / Portion ($800) / Base × Rate ($1,800) (?) / Original price

Steps to solving problem

1. Set up the formula. $\text{Rate} = \dfrac{\text{Portion}}{\text{Base}}$

2. Calculate the rate. $R = \dfrac{\$800}{\$1,800}$
$R = 44.44\%$

11. Percent increase in Boston Celtics ticket:

	The facts	Solving for?	Steps to take	Key points
BLUEPRINT	$14 ticket (old). $75 ticket (new).	Percent increase in price.	Identify key elements. *Base*: $14 *Rate*: ? *Portion*: $61 ($75 − $14) Rate = $\dfrac{\text{Portion}}{\text{Base}}$	Difference in price / Portion $61 / Base × Rate ($14) (?) / Original price. When portion is greater than base, rate will be greater than 100%.

Steps to solving problem

1. Set up the formula. $\text{Rate} = \dfrac{\text{Portion}}{\text{Base}}$

2. Calculate the rate. $R = \dfrac{\$61}{\$14}$
$R = 435,714 = 435.71\%$

You Try It

1. $.92 = 92\%$
$.009 = .9\%$
$5.46 = 546\%$

2. $\dfrac{2}{9} = 22.222\% = 22.22\%$

3. $78\% = .0078$ (2 places to left)
$96\% = .96$ (2 places to left)
$246\% = 2.46$ (2 places to left)

$7\dfrac{3}{4}\% = 7.75\% = .0775$

$\dfrac{3}{4}\% = .75\% = .0075$

$\dfrac{1}{2}\% = .50\% = .0050$

4. $\dfrac{3}{5} = .60 = 60\%$

5. $74\% \to 74 \times \dfrac{1}{100} = \dfrac{74}{100} = \dfrac{37}{50}$

$\dfrac{1}{5}\% \to \dfrac{1}{5} \times \dfrac{1}{100} = \dfrac{1}{500}$

$121\% \to 121 \times \dfrac{1}{100} = \dfrac{121}{100} = 1\dfrac{21}{100}$

$17\dfrac{1}{5}\% \to \dfrac{86}{5} \times \dfrac{1}{100} = \dfrac{86}{500} = \dfrac{43}{250}$

$17.75\% \to 17\dfrac{3}{4}\% = \dfrac{71}{4} \times \dfrac{1}{100} = \dfrac{71}{400}$

6. Portion ($1,600) = Base ($2,000) × Rate (.80)

7. Rate (25%) = $\dfrac{\text{Portion } (\$500)}{\text{Base } (\$2,000)}$

8. Base ($1,000) = $\dfrac{\text{Portion } (\$200)}{\text{Rate } (.20)}$

9. $\dfrac{\text{Difference in price } (\$100)}{\text{Base (orig. \$500)}} = 20\%$

Chapter 7

LU 7-1a

1. Dining room set trade discount amount and net price:

	The facts	Solving for?	Steps to take	Key points
BLUEPRINT	*List price:* $16,000. *Trade discount rate:* 30%.	Trade discount amount. Net price.	Trade discount amount = List price × Trade discount rate. Net price = List price × Complement of trade discount rate.	Trade discount amount ↗ Portion (?) Base × Rate ($16,000) (.30) ↗ List price · Trade discount rate

Steps to solving problem

1. Calculate the trade discount. $16,000 × .30 = $4,800 Trade discount amount
2. Calculate the net price. $16,000 × .70 = $11,200 (100% − 30% = 70%)

2. Video system list price:

	The facts	Solving for?	Steps to take	Key points
BLUEPRINT	*Net price:* $400. *Trade discount rate:* 20%.	List price.	List price = $\dfrac{\text{Net price}}{\text{Complement of trade discount}}$	Net price ↗ Portion $400 Base × Rate (?) (.80) ↗ List price · 100% −20%

Steps to solving problem

1. Calculate the complement of trade discount.
$$\begin{array}{r} 100\% \\ -\ 20\% \\ \hline 80\% = .80 \end{array}$$

2. Calculate the list price. $\dfrac{\$400}{.80} = \$500$

3. Lamps Outlet's net price and trade discount amount:

	The facts	Solving for?	Steps to take	Key points
BLUEPRINT	*List price:* $14,000. *Chain discount:* 4/8/20.	Net price. Trade discount amount.	Net price = List price × Net price equivalent rate. Trade discount amount = List price × Single equivalent discount rate.	Do not round off net price equivalent rate or single equivalent discount rate.

Steps to solving problem

1. Calculate the complement of each chain discount.
$$\begin{array}{ccc} 100\% & 100\% & 100\% \\ -\ 4 & -\ 8 & -\ 20 \\ \hline 96\% & 92\% & 80\% \end{array}$$

2. Calculate the net price equivalent rate. .96 × .92 × .80 = .70656
3. Calculate the net price. $14,000 × .70656 = $9,891.84
4. Calculate the single equivalent discount rate.
$$\begin{array}{r} 1.00000 \\ -\ .70656 \\ \hline .29344 \end{array}$$

5. Calculate the trade discount amount. $14,000 × .29344 = $4,108.16

LU 7-2a

1. End of discount period: July 8 + 10 days =   July 18
   End of credit period: By Table 7.1, July 8 =   189 days
                                                   +30 days
                                                   ─────────
                                                   219 → search ⟶ Aug. 7

2. End of discount period: June 12 + 10 days = June 22
   End of credit period: By Table 7.1, June 12 =   163 days
                                                    +30 days
                                                    ─────────
                                                    193 → search ⟶ July 12

3. End of discount period: By Table 7.1, May 12 =   132 days
                                                    +30 days
                                                    ─────────
                                                    162 → search ⟶ June 11

   End of credit period: By Table 7.1, May 12 =   132 days
                                                   +60 days
                                                   ─────────
                                                   192 → search ⟶ July 11

4. End of discount period: May 10
   End of credit period: May 10 + 20 = May 30

5. End of discount period: June 10
   End of credit period: June 10 + 20 = June 30

6. Vasko Corporation's cost of equipment:

	The facts	Solving for?	Steps to take	Key points
BLUEPRINT	List price: $9,000. Trade discount rate: 30%. Terms: 2/10 EOM. Invoice date: 6/29 Date paid: 8/9	Cost of equipment.	Net price = List price × Complement of trade discount rate. EOM before 25th: Discount period is 1st 10 days of month that follow sale.	Trade discounts are deducted before cash discounts are taken. Cash discounts are not taken on freight or returns.

Steps to solving problem

1. Calculate the net price. $9,000 × .70 = $6,300   100%
                                                                 − 30%
2. Calculate the discount period.   Until Aug. 10
3. Calculate the cost of office equipment. $6,300 × .98 = $6,174   100%
                                                                     − 2%

7. $\dfrac{\$600}{.98} = \$612.24$ Credited

   $700 − $612.24 = $87.76 Balance outstanding

You Try It

1. $700 × .20 = $140

2. $\begin{array}{l} 1.00 \\ -\ .20 \\ \hline .80 \end{array}$ $700 × .80 = $560

3. Seller will pay the freight

4. $\dfrac{\$240}{.40} = \$600$

   (100% − 60%)

5. $\begin{array}{cc} \$200 & \$188 \\ \times\ .06 & \times\ .08 \\ \hline \$12.00 & \$15.04 \end{array}$

   $\begin{array}{l} \$188.00 \\ -\ 15.04 \\ \hline \$172.96 \end{array}$ .94 × .92 = $\begin{array}{r} .8648 \ \text{NPER} \\ \times\ \$200 \\ \hline \$172.96 \end{array}$

6. .94 × .92 × $2,000 = $1,729.60

7. $\begin{array}{l} 1.0000 \\ -\ .8648 \quad (.94 × .92) \\ \hline .1352 × \$2,000 = \$270.40 \end{array}$

8. $\begin{array}{l} \$2,000 \\ -\quad 80 \quad \text{(Freight and returns)} \\ \hline \$1,920 × .02 = \$38.40 \end{array}$

9. April 12, May 2

10. $\begin{array}{l} \$700 \\ -\ 100 \\ \hline \$600 \quad × .98 = \quad \$588 \\ \qquad\qquad\qquad\quad +\ 100 \\ \qquad\qquad\qquad\ \ \overline{\$688} \end{array}$

11. No discount; pay full $700

12. November 10; November 30

13. $300/.98 = $306.12

Chapter 8

LU 8-1a

1. Irene's dollar markup and percent markup on cost:

	The facts	Solving for?	Steps to take	Key points
BLUEPRINT	*Desk cost:* $800. *Desk selling price:* $1,200.	% \$ C 100% \$ 800 +M 50^2 400^1 = S 150% \$1,200 ^{1}Dollar markup. ^{2}Percent markup on cost.	$\dfrac{\text{Dollar}}{\text{markup}} = \dfrac{\text{Selling}}{\text{price}} - \text{Cost.}$ $\dfrac{\text{Percent}}{\text{markup on cost}} = \dfrac{\text{Dollar markup}}{\text{Cost}}$	Dollar markup Portion $400 Base × Rate $800 (?) Cost

Steps to solving problem

1. Calculate the dollar markup.

$$\text{Dollar markup} = \text{Selling price} - \text{Cost}$$
$$\$400 \quad = \quad \$1,200 \quad - \$800$$

2. Calculate the percent markup on cost.

$$\text{Percent markup on cost} = \dfrac{\text{Dollar markup}}{\text{Cost}}$$
$$= \dfrac{\$400}{\$800} = 50\%$$

Check

$$\text{Selling price} = \text{Cost} + \text{Markup} \quad\text{or}\quad \text{Cost } (B) = \dfrac{\text{Dollar markup } (P)}{\text{Percent markup on cost } (R)}$$

$$\$1,200 = \$800 + .50(\$800) \qquad\qquad = \dfrac{\$400}{.50} = \$800$$

$$\$1,200 = \$800 + \$400$$
$$\$1,200 = \$1,200$$

2. Dollar markup and selling price of doll:

	The facts	Solving for?	Steps to take	Key points
BLUEPRINT	*Doll cost:* $14 each. *Markup on cost:* 38%.	% \$ C 100% \$14.00 +M 38 5.32^1 = S 138% \$19.32^2 ^{1}Dollar markup. ^{2}Selling price.	Dollar markup: $S = C + M$ $S = \text{Cost} \times \left(1 + \dfrac{\text{Percent}}{\text{markup on cost}} \right)$	Selling price Portion (?) Base × Rate ($14) (1.38) Cost 100% +38%

Steps to solving problem

1. Calculate the dollar markup.

$S = C + M$
$S = \$14.00 + .38(\$14.00)$
$S = \$14.00 + \$5.32 \longleftarrow$ Dollar markup

2. Calculate the selling price.

$S = \$19.32$

Check

$$\underset{(P)}{\text{Selling price}} = \underset{(B)}{\text{Cost}} \times \underset{(R)}{(1 + \text{Percent markup on cost})} = \$14.00 \times 1.38 = \$19.32$$

3. Cost and dollar markup:

	The facts	Solving for?	Steps to take	Key points
BLUEPRINT	*Selling price:* $16. *Markup on cost: 42%.*	% $ C 100% $11.27 + M 42 4.73[1] = S 142% $16.00[2] [1]Cost. [2]Dollar markup.	$S = C + M$ or $$\text{Cost} = \frac{\text{Selling price}}{1 + \frac{\text{Percent}}{\text{markup on cost}}}$$ $M = S - C$	 Selling price Portion $16 Base × Rate (?) (1.42) Cost 100% +42%

Steps to solving problem

1. Calculate the cost.

$$S = C + M$$
$$\$16 = C + .42C$$
$$\frac{\$16}{1.42} = \frac{1.42C}{1.42}$$
$$\$11.27 = C$$

2. Calculate the dollar markup.

$$M = S - C$$
$$M = \$16 - \$11.27$$
$$M = \$4.73$$

Check

$$\text{Cost}\ (B) = \frac{\text{Selling price}\ (P)}{1 + \text{Percent markup on cost}\ (R)} \qquad \frac{\$16}{1.42} = \$11.27$$

LU 8-2a

1. Irene's dollar markup and percent markup on selling price:

	The facts	Solving for?	Steps to take	Key points
BLUEPRINT	*Desk cost:* $800. *Desk selling price: $1,200.*	% $ C 66.7% $ 800 + M 33.3[2] 400[1] = S 100% $1,200 [1]Dollar markup. [2]Percent markup on selling price.	$$\frac{\text{Dollar}}{\text{markup}} = \frac{\text{Selling}}{\text{price}} - \text{Cost}$$ $$\frac{\text{Percent}}{\text{markup on}} = \frac{\text{Dollar}}{\text{markup}}$$ $$\frac{}{\text{selling price}} = \frac{}{\text{Selling price}}$$	 Markup Portion $400 Base × Rate $1,200 (?) Selling price

Steps to solving problem

1. Calculate the dollar markup.

$$\text{Dollar markup} = \text{Selling price} - \text{Cost}$$
$$\$400 \quad = \quad \$1,200 \quad - \$800$$

2. Calculate the percent markup on selling price.

$$\frac{\text{Percent markup}}{\text{on selling price}} = \frac{\text{Dollar markup}}{\text{Selling price}}$$

$$= \frac{\$400}{\$1,200} = 33.3\%$$

Check

$$\text{Selling price} = \text{Cost} + \text{Markup} \qquad \text{or} \qquad \text{Selling price}\ (B) = \frac{\text{Dollar markup}\ (P)}{\text{Percent markup on selling price}\ (R)}$$

$$\$1,200 = \$800 + .333(\$1,200)$$

$$\$1,200 = \$800 + \$399.60$$

$$= \frac{\$400}{.333} = \$1,201.20 \text{ (off due to rounding)}$$

$$\$1,200 = \$1,199.60 \text{ (off due to rounding)}$$

2. Selling price of doll and dollar markup:

	The facts	Solving for?	Steps to take	Key points
BLUEPRINT	*Doll cost:* $14 each.		$S = C + M$	Cost
	Markup on selling price: 38%.	% $	or	Portion $14
		C 62% $14.00		
		$+M$ 38 8.58[2]	$S = \dfrac{\text{Cost}}{1 - \substack{\text{Percent markup} \\ \text{on selling price}}}$	Base × Rate (?) (.62)
		$= S$ 100% $22.58[1]		
		[1]Selling price.		Selling price 100%
		[2]Dollar markup.		−38%

Steps to solving problem

1. Calculate the selling price.

$$S = C + M$$
$$S = \$14.00 + .38S$$
$$\underline{-.38S \qquad\qquad -.38S}$$
$$\frac{\cancel{.62}S}{\cancel{.62}} = \frac{\$14.00}{.62}$$
$$S = \$22.58$$

2. Calculate the dollar markup.

$$M = S - C$$
$$\$8.58 = \$22.58 - \$14.00$$

Check

$$\text{Selling price } (B) = \frac{\text{Cost } (P)}{1 - \text{Percent markup on selling price } (R)} = \frac{\$14.00}{.62} = \$22.58$$

3. Dollar markup and cost:

	The facts	Solving for?	Steps to take	Key points
BLUEPRINT	*Selling price: $16.*		$S = C + M$	Cost
	Markup on selling price: 42%.	% $	or	Portion (?)
		C 58% $9.28[2]		
		$+M$ 42 6.72[1]	$\text{Cost} = \text{Selling price} \times$	Base × Rate ($16) (.58)
		$= S$ 100% $16.00	$\left(1 - \substack{\text{Percent markup} \\ \text{on selling price}}\right)$	
		[1]Dollar markup.		Selling price 100%
		[2]Cost.		−42%

Steps to solving problem

1. Calculate the dollar markup.

$$S = C + M$$
$$\$16.00 = C + .42(\$16.00)$$

2. Calculate the cost.

$$\$16.00 = C + \$6.72 \;\leftarrow\; \text{Dollar markup}$$
$$\underline{-6.72 \qquad\qquad -6.72}$$
$$\$9.28 = C$$

Check

$$\underset{(P)}{\text{Cost}} = \underset{(B)}{\text{Selling price}} \times \underset{(R)}{(1 - \text{Percent markup on selling price})} = \$16.00 \times .58 = \$9.28$$

$$(1.00 - .42)$$

4. Cost $= \dfrac{\$5}{\$7} = 71.4\%$ $\dfrac{.417}{1 - .417} = \dfrac{.417}{.583} = 71.5\%$

Selling price $= \dfrac{\$5}{\$12} = 41.7\%$ $\dfrac{.714}{1 + .714} = \dfrac{.714}{1.714} = 41.7\%$ (due to rounding)

LU 8-3a

1.　　$S = C + M$

　　　$S = \$800 + .30S$

　　$\dfrac{-.30S}{}\quad\dfrac{-.30S}{}$

　　$\dfrac{\cancel{.70}S}{\cancel{.70}} = \dfrac{\$800}{.70}$

　　　$S = \$1,142.86$

Check

$$S = \dfrac{\text{Cost}}{1 - \text{Percent markup on selling price}}$$

$$S = \dfrac{\$800}{1 - .30} = \dfrac{\$800}{.70} = \$1,142.86$$

First markdown:　.90 × \$1,142.86 = \$1,028.57 selling price
Second markdown:　.95 × \$1,028.57 = \$977.14
Markup:　1.02 × \$977.14 = \$996.68 final selling price

$$\$1,142.86 - \$996.68 = \dfrac{\$146.18}{\$1,142.86} = 12.79\%$$

2.

The facts	Solving for?	Steps to take	Key points
500 lb. tomatoes at $.16 per pound. *Spoilage:* 10% *Markup cost:* 55%.	Price of tomatoes per pound.	Total cost. Total dollar markup. Total selling price. Spoilage amount $TS = TC + TM$	Markup is based on cost.

Steps in solving problem

1. Calculate the total cost.　　　　　　　　　　$TC = 500$ lb. $\times \$.16 = \$80.00$

2. Calculate the total dollar markup.　　　　　$TS = TC + TM$

　　　　　　　　　　　　　　　　　　　　　　$TS = \$80.00 + .55(\$80.00)$

　　　　　　　　　　　　　　　　　　　　　　$TS = \$80.00 + \$44.00$ ← Total dollar markup

3. Calculate the total selling price.　　　　　$TS = \$124.00$ ← Total selling price

4. Calculate the tomato loss.　　　　　　　　500 lb. $\times .10 = 50$ lb. spoilage

5. Calculate the selling price per pound of tomatoes.　$\dfrac{\$124.00}{450} = \$.28$ per pound (rounded to nearest hundredth)

$(500 - 50)$

LU 8-4a

$\$240 - \$80 = \$160$　　　$\dfrac{\$96,000}{\$160} = 600$ units

You Try It

1. $S = C + M$
   $S = \$400 + \$200$
   $S = \$600$

2. $\dfrac{\$50}{\$200} = 25\%$

   $\dfrac{\$50}{.25} = \$200$

3. $S = C + M$
   $S = \$8 + .10(\$8)$
   $S = \$8 + \$.80$
   $S = \$8.80$

4. $S = C + M$
   $\$200 = C + .60\,C$
   $\dfrac{\$200}{1.60} = \dfrac{\cancel{1.60}C}{\cancel{1.60}}$
   $\$125 = C$

5. $M = S - C$
   $(\$2,500) = (\$4,500) - (\$2,000)$

6. $\dfrac{\$700}{\$2,800} = 25\%$

   $\dfrac{\$700}{.50} = \$1,400$

7. $S = C + M$

$S = \$800 + .40(S)$

$\underline{-.40 \qquad\qquad -.40}$

$\dfrac{.60S}{.60} = \dfrac{\$800}{.60}$

$S = \$1333.33$

8. $S = C + M$

$\$2,000 = C + .70(\$2,000)$

$\$2,000 = C + \$1,400$

$\dfrac{-1,400}{\$600} = \dfrac{-1,400}{C}$

9. $\dfrac{.47}{1 + .47} = \dfrac{.47}{1.47} = 32\%$ rounded

10. $\begin{array}{r} \$50 \\ \times\ .20 \\ \hline \$10 \end{array}$ $\dfrac{\$10}{\$50} = 20\%$

11. $TS = TC + TM$

$TS = \$9 + .30(\$9)$

$TS = \$9 + \$2.7$

$TS = \$11.70$

$\dfrac{\$11.70}{45} = \$.26$

12. $\dfrac{\$70,000}{\$20} = 3,500$ units

Chapter 9

LU 9-1a

1. 40 hours $\times$ \$12.00 = \$480.00

14 hours $\times$ \$18.00 = $\underline{\$252.00}$ (\$12.00 $\times$ 1.5 = \$18.00)

$\qquad\qquad\qquad\qquad$ \$732.00

2. \$210,000 $\times$ .08 = $\begin{array}{r} \$16,800 \\ -\ 4,000 \\ \hline \$12,800 \end{array}$

3. Gross pay = \$1,200 + (\$3,000 $\times$ .01) + (\$8,000 $\times$ .03) + (\$20,000 $\times$ .05) + (\$20,000 $\times$ .08)

$\qquad\qquad$ = \$1,200 + $\qquad$ \$30 $\qquad$ + $\qquad$ \$240 $\qquad$ + $\qquad$ \$1,000 $\qquad$ + $\qquad$ \$1,600

$\qquad\qquad$ = \$4,070

LU 9-2a

1. **Social Security** $\qquad\qquad\qquad\qquad$ **Medicare**

$\qquad$ \$118,500 $\qquad\qquad\qquad\qquad$ \$10,000 $\times$ .0145 = \$145.00

$\qquad$ $\underline{-\ 118,000}$

$\qquad$ \$ $\quad$ 500 $\times$ .602 = \$31

FIT

Percentage method: $\qquad$ \$10,000.00

\$333.30 $\times$ 1 = $\qquad\quad$ $\underline{-\ \$333.30}$ (Table 9.1)

$\qquad\qquad\qquad\qquad$ \$ 9,666.70

$\qquad\qquad\qquad\qquad$ \$7,754 to \$15,967 $\longrightarrow$ \$1,540 plus 28% of excess over \$7,754 (Table 9.2)

$\qquad$ \$9,666.70 $\qquad\qquad$ \$1,540.00

$\qquad$ $\underline{-\ 7,754.00}$ $\qquad\qquad$ $\underline{+\ \ 535.56}$ (\$1,912.70 $\times$ .28)

$\qquad$ \$1,912.70 $\qquad\qquad$ \$2,075.56

2. 13 weeks $\times$ \$200 = \$ 2,600

13 weeks $\times$ \$800 = $\quad$ 10,400 (\$10,400 − \$7,000) $\quad$ \$3,400 $\;\rbrace$

13 weeks $\times$ \$950 = $\underline{\quad 12,350}$ (\$12,350 − \$7,000) $\longrightarrow$ $\underline{\quad 5,350}$ $\;\Big\rbrace$ exempt wages (not taxed for

$\qquad\qquad\qquad\qquad$ \$25,350 $\qquad\qquad\qquad\qquad\longrightarrow$ \$8,750 $\;\Big\rbrace$ FUTA or SUTA)

\$25,350 − \$8,750 = \$16,600 taxable wages

SUTA = .051 $\times$ \$16,600 = \$846.60

FUTA = .006 $\times$ \$16,600 = \$99.60

Note: FUTA remains at .006 whether SUTA rate is higher or lower than standard.

You Try It

1. 38 hrs × $9.25 = $351.50

2. **Reg $ Overtime $**
(40 × $7) + (3 × $10.50)
$280 + $31.50 = $311.50 gross pay

3. 2,250 × $.79 = $1,777.50

4. 600 × $.79 = $474
300 × $.88 = +264
$738

5. $175,000 × .07 = $12,286.96

6. $6,000 × .05 = $300
$2,000 × .09 = 180
$4,000 × .12 = 480
$960

7. $600 + ($6,000 × .04)
$600 + 240 = $840

8. Gross $490.00
Less: FIT   24.81 $490.00
       SS   30.38   − 76.90
       Med.   7.11 $413.10
             $427.70   −165.00
                          $248.10 × .10 = $24.81

9. Social Security = $118,500 × .062 = $7,347
Medicare = $150,000 × .0145 = $2,175

10. $1,400.00   ($76.90 × 3)
      230.70 $35.50 + .15($649.30)
    1,169.30 $35.50 + $97.40
    − 520.00 $132.90 FIT
    $ 649.30

11. FUTA $200 × .006 = $1.20
SUTA $200 × .054 = $10.80

Chapter 10

LU 10-1a

1. $16,000 × .03 × $\frac{8}{12}$ = $320

2. $15,000 × .06 × 6 = $5,400

3. $50,000 × .07 × $\frac{18}{12}$ = $5,250

4. August 14 → 226 $20,000 × .07 × $\frac{100}{365}$ = $383.56
   May 6 → − 126
           100   MV = $20,000 + $383.56 = $20,383.56

5. $20,000 × .07 × $\frac{100}{360}$ = $388.89   MV = $20,000 + $388.89 = $20,388.89

LU 10-2a

1. $\dfrac{\$9,000}{.04 \times \frac{90}{360}} = \dfrac{\$9,000}{.01} = \$900,000$ $P = \dfrac{I}{R \times T}$

2. $\dfrac{\$280}{\$6,000 \times \frac{180}{360}} = \dfrac{\$280}{\$3,000} = 9.33\%$ $R = \dfrac{I}{P \times T}$

3. $\dfrac{\$190}{\$900 \times .06} = \dfrac{\$190}{\$54} = 3.52 \times 360 = 1,267$ days $T = \dfrac{I}{P \times R}$

LU 10-3a

$4,000 × .04 × $\frac{15}{360}$ = $6.67 $2,000.00 $3,306.67
                                          −   9.19   −1,990.81
                                          $1,990.81 $1,315.86

$700.00 $4,000.00
− 6.67   − 693.33 $1,315.86 × .04 × $\frac{20}{360}$ = $2.92
$693.33 $3,306.67

                          $ 2.92
$3,306.67 × .04 × $\frac{25}{360}$ = $9.19   +1,315.86
                                      $1,318.78

You Try It

1. $\$4,000 \times .03 \times \dfrac{18}{12} = \$180$

2. $\$3,000 \times .04 \times \dfrac{45}{365} = \$14.79$
   $\begin{array}{rr} \text{Feb 22} & 53 \\ \text{Jan 8} & -8 \\ \hline & 45 \end{array}$

3. $\$3,000 \times .04 \times \dfrac{45}{360} = \$15.00$

4. $\$2,000 \times .04 \times \dfrac{90}{360} = \$20$

5. $\dfrac{\$20}{.04 \times \dfrac{90}{360}} = \$2,000$

6. $\dfrac{\$20}{\$2,000 \times \dfrac{90}{360}} = 4\%$

7. $\dfrac{20}{\$2,000 \times .04} = .25 \times 360 = 90$ days

8. $\$4,000 \times .04 \times \dfrac{30}{360} = \$13.33$

   $\begin{array}{r} \$400.00 \\ -\quad 13.33 \\ \hline \$386.67 \end{array}$

   $\$4,000 - 386.67 = \$3,613.33$

   $\$3,613.33 \times .04 \times \dfrac{40}{360} = \$16.06$

   $\$300 - \$16.06 = \$283.94$
   $\$3,613.33 - \$283.94 = \$3,329.39$

   $\$3,329.39 \times .04 \times \dfrac{20}{360} = \$7.40$

   $\$3,329.39 + \$7.40 = \$3,336.79$
   Total interest $= \$13.33 + \$16.06 + \$7.40 = \$36.79$

Chapter 11

LU 11-1a

1. **a.** Maturity value = Face value = $14,000

   b. Bank discount $= MV \times$ Bank discount rate $\times$ Time

   $$= \$14,000 \times .045 \times \frac{60}{360}$$

   $$= \$105$$

   c. Proceeds $= MV -$ Bank discount

   $$= \$14,000 - \$105$$

   $$= \$13,895$$

   d. Effective rate $= \dfrac{\text{Interest}}{\text{Proceeds} \times \text{Time}}$

   $$= \frac{\$105}{\$13,895 \times \dfrac{60}{360}}$$

   $$= 4.53\%$$

2. $\$10,000 \times .04 \times \dfrac{13}{52} = \$100$ interest
   $\dfrac{\$100}{\$9,900 \times \dfrac{13}{52}} = 4.04\%$

LU 11-2a

1. **a.** $I = \$40,000 \times .05 \times \dfrac{170}{360} = \$944.44$

   $MV = \$40,000 + \$944.44 = \$40,944.44$

   b. Discount period $= 170 - 61 = 109$ days.

   $\begin{array}{lr} \text{April} & 30 \\ & -10 \\ \hline & 20 \\ \text{May} & +31 \\ \hline & 51 \\ \text{June} & +10 \\ \hline & 61 \end{array}$

   or by table:
   $\begin{array}{lr} \text{June 8} & 161 \\ \text{April 8} & -100 \\ \hline & 61 \end{array}$

   c. Bank discount $= \$40,944.44 \times .02 \times \dfrac{109}{360} = \$247.94$

   d. Proceeds $= \$40,944.44 - \$247.94 = \$40,696.50$

You Try It

1. $4,000 \times .02 \times \dfrac{30}{360} = \$6.67$

   $\begin{array}{r} \$4,000.00 \\ -6.67 \\ \hline \$3,993.33 \text{ Proceeds} \end{array}$

2. $15,000 \times .04 \times \dfrac{40}{360} = \$66.67$

   $\begin{array}{r} \$15,000.00 \\ -66.67 \end{array}$ $\dfrac{\$66.67}{\$14,933.33 \times \dfrac{40}{360}} = 4.02\%$

3. $\begin{array}{r} \text{Dec 15} \quad 349 \\ \text{Nov 5} \quad -309 \\ \hline 40 \text{ days} \end{array}$ $\$2,000 \times .03 \times \dfrac{60}{360} = \$10$

   $MV = \$2,010$ (Left to go)

   $\$2,010 \times .05 \times \dfrac{20}{360} = \$5.58$

   $\$2,010 - \$5.58 = \$2,004.42 \text{ Proceeds}$

Chapter 12

LU 12-1a

1. **a.** $4 \,(4 \times 1)$ **b.** $\$541.21$ **c.** $\$41.27 \,(\$541.27 - \$500)$

   $\$500 \times 1.02 = \$510 \times 1.02 = \$520.20 \times 1.02 = \$530.60 \times 1.02 = \$541.21$

2. $\$500 \times 1.0824 \,(4 \text{ periods at } 2\%) = \$541.20$

3. 16 periods, 2%, $\$7,000 \times 1.3728 = \$9,609.60$

4. 4 periods, $1\frac{1}{2}\%$

   $\begin{array}{r} \$8,000 \times 1.0614 = \quad \$8,491.20 \\ -\ 8,000.00 \\ \hline \$\ \ 491.20 \end{array}$ $\dfrac{\$491.20}{\$8,000} = 6.14\%$

5. $\$1,800 \times 1.3498 = \$2,429.64$

LU 12-2a

1. 14 periods (7 years × 2) $2\frac{1}{2}\%\,(5\% \div 2)$ .7077 $\$6,369.30\,(\$9,000 \times .7077)$

2. 20 periods (20 years × 1) $4\%\,(4\% \div 1)$ .4564 $\$9,128\,(\$20,000 \times .4564)$

3. 6 years × 4 = 24 periods $\dfrac{8\%}{4} = 2\%$ $.6217 \times \$40,000 = \$24,868$

4. 4 × 4 years = 16 periods $\dfrac{4\%}{4} = 1\%$ $.8528 \times \$28,000 = \$23,878.40$

You Try It

1. $\begin{array}{r} \$200 \\ \times\ 1.04 \\ \hline \$208 \end{array}$ $\begin{array}{r} \$\ \ 208 \\ \times\ \ \ 1.04 \\ \hline \$216.32 \end{array}$

2. $\$4,000 \times 1.4258 \,(3\% \ 12 \text{ periods})$
   $= \$5,703.20$

3. Table 1.0609 (3% 2 periods)

   6.09%

   $\begin{array}{r} \$4,000 \times 1.0609 = \quad \$4,243.60 \\ -\ 4,000.00 \\ \hline \$\ \ 243.60 \end{array}$

   $\dfrac{\$243.60}{\$4,000.00} = 6.09\%$

4. Table .7880 (1.5% 16 periods)

   $\begin{array}{r} \times\ \$6,000 \\ \hline \$4,728 \end{array}$

Chapter 13

LU 13-1a

1. **a.** **Step 1.** Periods = 4 years × 2 = 8
   $\qquad\qquad 4\% \div 2 = 2\%$

   b. Periods = 4 years × 2 **Step 1**
   $\qquad\qquad\quad = 8 + 1 = 9$
   $\qquad 4\% \div 2 = 2\%$

   Step 2. Factor = 8.5829
   Step 3. $\$5,000 \times 8.5829 = \$42,914.50$

   Factor = 9.7546 **Step 2**
   $\$5,000 \times 9.7546 = \quad \$48,773$ **Step 3**
   $-1 \text{ payment} \qquad\quad -\ 5,000$ **Step 4**
   $\qquad\qquad\qquad\qquad \$43,773$

2. Step 1. 6 years $\times$ 2 = 12 + 1 = 13 Periods $\dfrac{6\%}{2} = 3\%$

     Step 2. Table factor, 15.6178
     Step 3. $2,500 $\times$ 15.6178 = $39,044.50
     Step 4.
$$\begin{array}{r} -\ 2,500.00 \\ \hline \$36,544.50 \end{array}$$

LU 13-2a

1. Step 1. Periods = 5 years $\times$ 2 = 10; Rate = 5% $\div$ 2 = $2\frac{1}{2}\%$
     Step 2. Factor, 8.7521
     Step 3. $20,000 $\times$ 8.7521 = $175,042

2. Step 1. Periods = 10; Rate = 4%
     Step 2. Factor, 8.1109
     Step 3. $15,000 $\times$ 8.1109 = $121,663.50

3. Step 1. Calculate present value of annuity; 30 periods, 3%

            $80,000 $\times$ 19.6004 = $1,568,032

     Step 2. Find the present value of $1,568,032 $\times$ .8626 = $1,352,584.40

LU 13-3a

20 years $\times$ 2 = 40 Per. $\dfrac{6\%}{2} = 3\%$ $120,000 $\times$ .0133 = $1,596

Check

$1,596 $\times$ 75.4012 = $120,340

You Try It

1.
$$\begin{array}{r} 4.4399 \ \text{(7\% 4 periods)} \\ \times\quad 6,000 \\ \hline \$26,639.40 \end{array}$$

2. $6,000 $\times$ 5.7507 =
$$\begin{array}{r} \$34,504.20 \ \text{(7\% 5 periods)} \\ -\quad 6000.00 \\ \hline \$28,504.20 \end{array}$$

3.
$$\begin{array}{r} 5.2421 \ \text{(4\% 6 periods)} \\ \times\ \$20,000 \\ \hline \$104,842 \end{array}$$

4.
$$\begin{array}{r} .0302 \ \text{(5\% 20 periods)} \\ \times\ \$400,000 \\ \hline \$\ 12,080 \end{array}$$

Chapter 14

LU 14-1a

1. a. $13,999 − $1,480 = $12,519

   b. $17,700 ($295 $\times$ 60) − $12,519 = $5,181

   c. $17,700 ($295 $\times$ 60) + $1,480 = $19,180

   d. $\dfrac{\$5,181}{\$12,519} \times \$100 = \$41.39$; between 14.50% and 14.75%

   e. $\dfrac{\$5,181 + \$12,519}{60} = \$295$

2. $\dfrac{\$8,000}{\$1,000} = 8 \times \$20.28 = \$162.24$ (8%, 60 months)

LU 14-2a

1.

Month	Balance due	Interest	Monthly payment	Reduction in balance	Balance outstanding
1	$300	$3.75 (.0125 $\times$ $300)	$20	$16.25 ($20 − $3.75)	$283.75
2	$283.75	$3.55 (.0125 $\times$ $283.75)	$20	$16.45	$267.30

2. Average daily balance calculated as follows:

No. of days of current balance	Current balance	Extension
3	$400	$1,200
7	300 ($400 − $100)	2,100
5	360 ($300 + $60)	1,800
5	340 ($360 − $20)	1,700
11	540 ($340 + $200)	5,940

31 − 20 (3 + 7 + 5 + 5)

Average daily balance = $\dfrac{\$12{,}740}{31}$ = $410.97

Finance charge = $410.97 × 2% = $8.22

You Try It

1. $5,400 amount financed
  −   100
  $5,300

2.
$129.99 × 60 = $\begin{array}{r}\$7{,}799.40 \\ -\ 5{,}300.00 \\ \hline \$2{,}499.40 \text{ FC}\end{array}$

3. $7,799.40 + $100 = $7,899.40

4. $\dfrac{\$2{,}499.40}{\$5{,}300.00}$ × $100 = 47.16 (between 16.25% and 16.50%)

5. $\dfrac{\$2{,}499.40 + \$5{,}300}{60}$ = $129.99

$\dfrac{\$5{,}300}{1{,}000}$ = 5.3 × 24.32 = $128.9

(off due to using 16% instead of using between 16.25% and 16.50%)

6. $5,000 × .035 = $175
  $275 − $175   = $100
  $5,000 − $100 = $4,900

7. 12 days × $200 = $2,400
  4 days × $120 [$200 − $80] = $480
  14 days × $180 [$120 + $60] = $2,520
  Total = $5,400
  $5,400/30 = $180 daily balance
  Finance charge = $180 × 2.5% = $4.50

Chapter 15

LU 15-1a

1. $180,000 − $54,000 = $126,000

$\dfrac{\$126{,}000}{\$1{,}000}$ = 126 × 6.66 = $839.16

$176,097.60 = $302,097.60 − $126,000

($839.16 × 360)   30 years × 12 payments per year

2. 5% = $676.62 monthly payment
      (126 × $5.37)

Total interest cost $117,583.20 = ($676.62 × 360) − $126,000
Savings $58,514.40 = $176,097.60 − $117,583.20

LU 15-2a

$70,000 mortgage; monthly payment of $466.20 (70 × $6.66)

Payment number	Principal (current)	Interest	Principal reduction	Balance of principal
		PORTION TO—		
1	$70,000	$408.33	$57.87	$69,942.13
		$70{,}000 × .07 × \dfrac{1}{12}$	($466.20 − $408.33)	($70,000 − $57.87)
2	$69,942.13	$69{,}942.13 × .07 × \dfrac{1}{12}$	($466.20 − $408.00)	($69,942.13 − $58.20)
		$408	$58.20	$69,883.93

You Try It

1. $\dfrac{\$70,000}{\$1,000} = 70 \times \$4.50 = \$315$

2. 30 years = $\begin{array}{r} 360 \text{ payments} \\ \times \$ \quad 315 \\ \hline \$113,400 - \$70,000 = \$43,400 \text{ interest} \end{array}$

3.
Payment	Interest	Principal reduction	Balance
1	$204.17	$110.83	$69,889.17
	$\left(\$70,000 \times .035 \times \dfrac{1}{12} = \$204.17\right)$	($315 − $204.17)	($70,000 − $110.83)
2	$203.84	$111.16	$69,778.01
	$\left(\$69,889.17 \times .035 \times \dfrac{1}{12}\right)$	($315 − $203.84)	($69,889.17 − $111.16)

Chapter 16

LU 16-1a

		2014	2013
1. a.	Cash	$\dfrac{\$38,000}{\$180,000} = 21.11\%$	$\dfrac{\$35,000}{\$140,000} = 25.00\%$
b.	Accounts receivable	$\dfrac{\$19,000}{\$180,000} = 10.56\%$	$\dfrac{\$18,000}{\$140,000} = 12.86\%$
c.	Merchandise inventory	$\dfrac{\$16,000}{\$180,000} = 8.89\%$	$\dfrac{\$11,000}{\$140,000} = 7.86\%$
d.	Prepaid expenses	$\dfrac{\$20,000}{\$180,000} = 11.11\%$	$\dfrac{\$16,000}{\$140,000} = 11.43\%$

2. $\begin{array}{r} \$16,000 \\ -\ 11,000 \\ \hline \$\ 5,000 \end{array}$ Percent $= \dfrac{\$5,000}{\$11,000} = 45.45\%$

LU 16-2a

1. a. $36,000 − $2,800 = $33,200
   (Gross sales − Sales returns and allowances)

   b. $5,900 + $6,800 − $5,200 = $7,500
   (Beginning inventory + Net purchases − Ending inventory)

   c. $33,200 − $7,500 = $25,700
   (Net sales − Cost of merchandise sold)

   d. $25,700 − $8,100 = $17,600
   (Gross profit from sales − Operating expenses)

LU 16-3a

	2015	2014	2013	2012
1. Sales	36%	86%	71%	100%
	$\left(\dfrac{\$25,000}{\$70,000}\right)$	$\left(\dfrac{\$60,000}{\$70,000}\right)$	$\left(\dfrac{\$50,000}{\$70,000}\right)$	

2. a. $\dfrac{CA}{CL} = \dfrac{\$14,000}{\$9,000} = 1.6$

   b. $\dfrac{CA - Inv.}{CL} = \dfrac{\$14,000 - \$3,900}{\$9,000} = 1.12$

   c. $\dfrac{AR}{\left(\dfrac{\text{Net sales}}{360}\right)} = \dfrac{\$5,500}{\left(\dfrac{\$36,500}{360}\right)} = 54.2 \text{ days}$

   d. $\dfrac{NI}{\text{Net sales}} = \dfrac{\$8,000}{\$36,500} = 21.92\%$

You Try It

1.
$$\begin{array}{rr} \$\ 400 & 40\% \\ +\ 600 & 60\% \\ \hline \$1{,}000 & 100\% \end{array}$$

2.

	2017	2016	Change	%
Cash	$8,000	$2,000	$6,000	300%

$\dfrac{\$6{,}000}{\$2{,}000}$

3. $400 − $20 − $5 = $375   net sales

4. $50 + $200 − $20 = $230

5. $400 − $250 = $150   gross profit

6. $210 − $180 = $30   net income

7.

2016	2015	2014
1,200	800	1,000
120%	80%	100%

$\left(\dfrac{1{,}200}{1{,}000}\right)\quad \dfrac{200}{1{,}000}$

8. $\dfrac{\$40{,}000}{\$160{,}000} = .25$

9. $\dfrac{\$40{,}000 - \$2{,}000 - \$3{,}000}{\$160{,}000} = \dfrac{\$35{,}000}{\$160{,}000} = .22$

10. $\dfrac{\$4{,}000}{\left(\dfrac{\$60{,}000}{360}\right)} = 24$ days

11. $\dfrac{\$180{,}000}{\$70{,}000} = 257.14$

12. $\dfrac{\$16{,}000}{-\$110{,}000} = -14.55\%$

13. $\dfrac{\$60{,}000}{70{,}000} = .86$

14. $\dfrac{\$16{,}000}{\$60{,}000} = .27$

Chapter 17

LU 17-1a

1.

End of year	Cost of truck	Depreciation expense for year	Accumulated depreciation at end of year	Book value at end of year (Cost − Accumulated depreciation)
1	$20,000	$6,000	$ 6,000	$14,000 ($20,000 − $6,000)
2	20,000	6,000	12,000	8,000
3	20,000	6,000	18,000	2,000

2. $\dfrac{\$20{,}000 - \$2{,}000}{3} = \$6{,}000 \times \dfrac{11}{12} = \$5{,}500$

LU 17-2a

1. $\dfrac{\$30{,}000 - \$2{,}000}{56{,}000} = \$.50$

End of year	Cost of machine	Units produced	Depreciation expense for year	Accumulated depreciation at end of year	Book value at end of year (Cost − Accumulated depreciation)
2012	$30,000	1,000	$500 ($1,000 × $.50)	$ 500	$29,500
2013	30,000	6,000	3,000	3,500	26,500
2014	30,000	4,000	2,000	5,500	24,500
2015	30,000	2,000	1,000	6,500	23,500
2016	30,000	2,500	1,250	7,750	22,250

LU 17-3a

End of year	Cost of machine	Accumulated depreciation at beginning of year	Book value at beginning of year (Cost − Accumulated depreciation)	Depreciation (Book value at beginning of year × Rate)	Accumulated depreciation at end of year	Book value at end of year (Cost − Accumulated depreciation)
1	$31,000	$ -0-	$31,000	$12,400	$12,400	$18,600
2	31,000	12,400	18,600	7,440	19,840	11,160
3	31,000	19,840	11,160	4,464	24,304	*6,696

*An additional $5,696 could have been taken to reach residual value.

LU 17-4a

1. $90,000 × .1920 = $17,280

2. $900,000 × .05 = $45,000

You Try It

1. $\dfrac{\$50,000 - \$10,000}{4} = \dfrac{\$40,000}{4} = \$10,000$ per year

2. $\dfrac{\$4,000 - \$500}{700} = \dfrac{\$3,500}{700} = \$5$ depreciation per unit

   $150 × \$5 = \$750$

3.

Year	Cost	Depreciation expense	Book value at end of year
1	$40,000	$20,000 ($40,000 × .50)	$20,000
2	$20,000	$10,000 = ($20,000 × .50)	$10,000

4. .20 × $7,000 = $1,400 depreciation expense

Chapter 18

LU 18-1a

1. **a.** 58 units of ending inventory × $4.76 = $276.08 Cost of ending inventory

   b. $\underset{\text{available for sale}}{\text{Cost of goods}} - \underset{\text{inventory}}{\text{Cost of ending}} = \underset{\text{goods sold}}{\text{Cost of}}$

   $$\$810 \quad - \quad \$276.08 \quad = \quad \$533.92$$

2. **a.** 50 units from November 1 purchased at $7 $350
   8 units from April 1 purchased at $5   + 40
   58 units $390 Cost of ending inventory

   b. $\underset{\text{available for sale}}{\text{Cost of goods}} - \underset{\text{inventory}}{\text{Cost of ending}} = \underset{\text{goods sold}}{\text{Cost of}}$

   $$\$810 \quad - \quad \$390 \quad = \quad \$420$$

3. **a.** 20 units from January 1 purchased at $4 $ 80
   38 units from March 1 purchased at $3   + 114
   58 units $194 Cost of ending inventory

   b. $\underset{\text{available for sale}}{\text{Cost of goods}} - \underset{\text{inventory}}{\text{Cost of ending}} = \underset{\text{goods sold}}{\text{Cost of}}$

   $$\$810 \quad - \quad \$194 \quad = \quad \$616$$

LU 18-2a

		Cost	Retail
1.	Beginning inventory	$ 19,000	$ 60,000
	Net purchases during the month	265,000	392,000
	Cost of goods available for sale	$284,000	$452,000
	Less net sales for the month		375,000
	Ending inventory at retail		$ 77,000
	Cost ratio ($284,000 ÷ $452,000)		62.8%
	Ending inventory at cost (.628 × $77,000)		$ 48,356

2. Goods available for sale

	Cost	Retail
Beginning inventory, January 1, 2017		$ 30,000
Net purchases		8,000
Cost of goods available for sale		$ 38,000
Less estimated cost of goods sold:		
Net sales at retail	$ 16,000	
Cost percentage (100% − 30%)	.70	
Estimated cost of goods sold		$ 11,200
Estimated ending inventory, January 31, 2017		$ 26,800

3. Inventory turnover at cost $= \dfrac{\text{Cost of goods sold}}{\text{Average inventory at cost}} = \dfrac{\$76,500}{\$11,200} = 6.83$

Inventory turnover at retail $= \dfrac{\text{Net sales}}{\text{Average inventory at retail}} = \dfrac{\$129,500}{\$21,800} = 5.94$

4.

		Ratio			
Department A	10,000	$\dfrac{10,000}{60,000}$	= .17 × $60,000 =	$10,200	
Department B	$\dfrac{50,000}{60,000}$	$\dfrac{50,000}{60,000}$	= .83 × $60,000 =	49,800	
				$60,000	

You Try It

1. 4 × 9 = 36
    3 × 10 = 30
        66 total cost
    1 × $9 = $9
    1 × $10 = $10
        $19
    $66 − 19 = $47 Cost of goods sold

2. $\dfrac{89}{15}$ = $5.93 unit cost

    4 × $5.93 = $23.72

3. FIFO   4 × $7 = $28

4. LIFO   4 × $5 = $20

5.

	Cost	Retail
Cost of goods available for sale	$88,000	$117,000
		− 90,000
Net sales		$ 27,000

Cost ratio: $\dfrac{\$88,000}{\$117,000}$ = 75%
.75 × $27,000 = $20,250

6.

Cost of goods available for sale		$42,000
Net sales at retail	$20,000	
	× .25	
COGS at retail		5,000
Ending inventory		$37,000

7. $\dfrac{\$90,000}{\left(\dfrac{\$40,000 + \$60,000}{2}\right)} = \dfrac{\$90,000}{\$50,000} = 1.8$

8. Total sq. ft. for dept. 10,000
    .40 to Dept A $30,000 × .40 = $12,000
    .60 to Dept B   30,000 × .60 = 18,000

Chapter 19

LU 19-1a

Shampoo	$ 5.90
Laundry detergent	4.10
	$10.00 × .07 = $.70

LU 19-2a

1.   .40 × $150,000 = $60,000

2. $\dfrac{\$159,000}{\$1,680,000}$ = .0946 per dollar

3.   **a.** .09.46 = 9.46%

     b. .09.46 × 100 = $9.46

     c. .094.6 × 1,000 = $94.60

     d. $\dfrac{.0946}{.001}$ = 94.6 mills (or .0946 × 1,000)

4.   .0946 × $60,000   = $5,676
     $9.46 × 600   = $5,676
     $94.60 × 60   = $5,676
     94.60 × .001 × $60,000 = $5,676

You Try It

1. $62.80 − $5.02 = $57.78
             × .06
           $3.47 sales tax

2. $6,000 + $30 + $60 = $6,090

3. $200,000 × .40 = $80,000 assessed value

4. $\dfrac{\$700,000}{\$8,400,000}$ = .0833

5. 1. 8.3%   2. $8.33
     3. $83   4. $\dfrac{.0833}{.001}$ = 83.3 = 83 mills

6. 1. 9.5% × $40,000 = $3,800
    2. $\dfrac{\$40,000}{\$100}$ = 400 × $9.50 = $3,800
    3. $\dfrac{\$40,000}{\$1,000}$ = 40 × $95 = $3,800
    4. $\dfrac{\$.0950}{.001}$ = 95 × .001 × $40,000 = $3,800

Chapter 20

LU 20-1a

1. $\dfrac{\$70,000}{\$1,000}$ = 70 × $2.67 = $186.90 No cash value in term insurance

2. $\dfrac{\$95,000}{\$1,000}$ = 95 × $7.75* = $736.25

    Option 1: Cash value   95 × $29 = $2,755
    Option 2: Paid up   95 × $86 = $8,170
    Option 3: Extended term   9 years 91 days
    *For females we subtract 3 years.

LU 20-2a

1. $\dfrac{\$80,000}{100}$ = 800 × $.41 = $328 $\dfrac{\$20,000}{100}$ = 200 × $.50 = $\dfrac{\$100}{\$428}$ ← total premium

2. $428 × .74 = $316.72 $428 − $316.72 = $111.28

3. $\dfrac{\$140,000}{\$200,000}$ = $\dfrac{7}{10}$ × $50,000 = $35,000

    (.80 × $250,000) $170,000 never more than face value

LU 20-3a

1. **Compulsory**

Bodily	$ 98	(Table 20.5)
Property	160	(Table 20.5)
Options		
Bodily	146	(Table 20.6)
Property	164	(Table 20.7)
Collision	174 ($154 + $20)	(Table 20.8)
Comprehensive	71 ($67 + $4)	(Table 20.9)
Towing	4	(Table 20.10)
Total annual premium	$817	

2. **Insurance**   **Carl**
   $7,981 $0 Property damage
   $6,454 $0 Passenger 1
   $4,239 $0 Passenger 2
   $25,000 $250 Passenger 3
   $11,620 $500 Deductible
   $55,294 $750

You Try It

1. 1. $\dfrac{\$90,000}{\$1,000} = 90 \times \$2.44 = \$219.60$

   2. $\dfrac{\$90,000}{\$1,000} = 90 \times \$11.84 = \$1,065.60$

   3. $\dfrac{\$90,000}{\$1,000} = 90 \times \$15.60 = \$1,404.00$

   4. $\dfrac{\$90,000}{\$1,000} = 90 \times \$27.64 = \$2,487.60$

2. Option 1: $\dfrac{\$60,000}{\$1,000} = 60 \times \$265 = \$15,900$

   Option 2: $60 \times \$550 = \$33,000$

   Option 3: 21 yr 300 days

3. $\dfrac{\$80,000}{\$100} = 800 \times \$.61 = \$488$

   $\dfrac{\$20,000}{\$100} = 200 \times \$.65 = \underline{\$130}$

   Total $\underline{\$618}$

4. $600 \times \$.44 = \$264$
   Refund $\$600 - \$264 = \$336$

5. $\$600 \times \dfrac{1}{3} = \$200$

   $\$600 - \$200 = \$400$

6. $\dfrac{\$40,000}{\$60,000} \times \$9,000 = \$6,000$

7. 10/20/5 $184 ($55 + $129)
   Bodily   94
   Property   132
   Collision   196
   Comprehensive   178
   Total premium $\underline{\$784}$

Chapter 21

LU 21-1a

1. a. (A) Highest price traded in last 52 weeks.
     (B) Lowest price traded in past 52 weeks.
     (C) Name of corporation is Good Year (symbol GT).
     (D) Yield for year is .54%.
     (E) Good Year stock sells at 16 times its earnings.
     (F) The last price (closing price for the day) is $13.08.
     (G) Stock is up $.11 from closing price yesterday.

   b. EPS $= \dfrac{\$13.08}{16} = \$.82$ per share   c. $\dfrac{\$.07}{\$13.08} = .54\%$

2. Preferred: $40,000 \times \$.60 = \$24,000$ Arrears 2014
                           $+ 24,000$ 2015
                           $\$48,000$
   Common: $162,000 ($210,000 - $48,000)

LU 21-2a

1. $100.25\% \times \$1,000 = \$1,002.50 \times 5 = \$5,012.50$

2. $7\frac{1}{2}\% = .075 \times \$1,000 = \$75$ annual interest $\dfrac{\$75.00}{\$1,002.50} = 7.48\%$

LU 21-3a

1. 7.61   2. 0.00   3. 3.8%   4. $P = \dfrac{1}{RT} \quad \dfrac{\$8,000}{.04 \times 1} = \$200,000$

You Try It

1. $\dfrac{\$.88}{\$53.88} = 1.63\%$

2. $\dfrac{\$53.88}{\$3.70} = 14.56 = 15$

3. $30,000 \times \$.80 = 24,000$
   $\dfrac{30,000 \times \$.80 = 24,000}{48,000 \text{ to preferred}}$

$$\begin{array}{r} \$300,000 \\ -\ \ 48,000 \\ \hline \$252,000 \div 60,000 = \$4.20 \text{ to common} \end{array}$$

4. $\$1,022.25 \times 6 = \$6,133.50$

5. $\dfrac{\$40}{1,011.20} = 3.96\%$

6. $\$12.44 + \$.05 = \$12.49$

Chapter 22

LU 22-1a

$$\text{Mean} = \frac{\$17,000 + \$14,000 + \$11,000 + \$51,000}{4} = \$23,250$$

$$\text{Median} = \frac{\$14,000 + \$17,000}{2} = \$15,500 \qquad \$11,000, \boxed{\$14,000, \$17,000,}\ \$51,000.$$

Note how we arrange numbers from smallest to highest to calculate median.

Median is the better indicator since in calculating the mean, the $51,000 puts the average of $23,250 much too high. There is no mode.

LU 22-2a

1.

Number of sales	Tally	Frequency
0	IIII	4
1	II	2
2	I	1
3	I	1
4	II	2
5		0
6	I	1
7	I	1
8	III	3
9	IIII	4
10	I	1

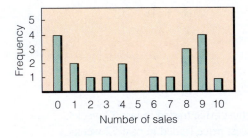

2.

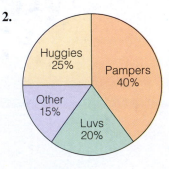

$.40 \times 360° = 144°$
$.20 \times 360° = 72°$
$.25 \times 360° = 90°$
$.15 \times 360° = 54°$

3. $\dfrac{\$35,000}{\$19,000} \times 100 = 184.21$

LU 22-3a

1. 60 − 5 = 55 range

2. | Data | Data − Mean | (Data − Mean)² |
    |------|-------------|----------------|
    | 120 | 120 − 103 = 17 | 289 |
    | 88 | 88 − 103 = −15 | 225 |
    | 77 | 77 − 103 = −26 | 676 |
    | 125 | 125 − 103 = 22 | 484 |
    | 110 | 110 − 103 = 7 | 49 |
    | 93 | 93 − 103 = −10 | 100 |
    | 111 | 111 − 103 = 8 | 64 |
    | | | Total   1,887 |

    1,887 × (7 − 1) = 314.5

    $\sqrt{314.5}$ = 17.7 standard deviation

3. Mean = $2,000 Standard deviation = $250

    $2,000 +/− ($250 × 2) = $1,500 − $2,500 range

You Try It

1. $\dfrac{41 + 29 + 16 + 15 + 18}{5} = 23.8$

2. | Value | Frequency | Product |
    |-------|-----------|---------|
    | 80 | 2 | 160 |
    | 90 | 3 | 270 |
    | 100 | 1 | 100 |
    | | 6 | 690 |

    Mean = $\dfrac{690}{6}$ = 115

3. 4 7 ⑨ 14 16

4. | Coffees consumed | Tally | Frequency |
    |------------------|-------|-----------|
    | 0 | I | 1 |
    | 1 | I | 1 |
    | 2 | II | 2 |
    | 3 | I | 1 |
    | 4 | I | 1 |
    | 5 | I | 1 |
    | 6 | | 0 |
    | 7 | | 0 |
    | 8 | I | 1 |

5.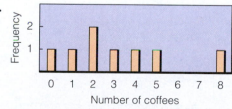

6.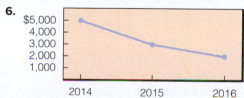

7. Coffee 70%   Non-coffee 30%

    .70 × 360° = 252°
    .30 × 360° = 108°

8. 7

9. $\dfrac{\$12,000}{\$9,000}$ × 100 = 133.3

10. Range = 14 − 2 = 12

11. 1. Mean = $\dfrac{19}{5}$ = 3.8

    2. 8 − 3.8 = 4.2
        1 − 3.8 = −2.8
        6 − 3.8 = 2.2
        2 − 3.8 = −1.8
        2 − 3.8 = −1.8

    3. (4.2)² = 17.64
        (−2.8)² = 7.84
        (2.2)² = 4.84
        (−1.8)² = 3.24
        (−1.8)² = 3.24

    4.   36.8

    5. 36.8 ÷ 4 = 9.2

    6. Standard deviation = 3.03

Check Figures

Odd-Numbered Drill and Word Problems for End-of-Chapter Problems.

Challenge Problems (all).

Summary Practice Tests (all).

Cumulative Reviews (all).

Odd-Numbered Additional Assignments by Learning Unit from Appendix A.

Check Figures to Drill and Word Problems (Odds), Challenge Problems, Summary Practice Tests, and Cumulative Reviews

Chapter 1

End-of-Chapter Problems

1–1. 82
1–3. 154
1–5. 13,580
1–7. 113,690
1–9. 38
1–11. 3,600
1–13. 1,074
1–15. 31,110
1–17. 340,531
1–19. 126,000
1–21. 90
1–23. 86 R4
1–25. 405
1–27. 1,616
1–29. 24,876
1–31. 17,989; 18,000
1–33. 80
1–35. 133
1–37. 216
1–39. 19 R21
1–41. 7,690; 6,990
1–43. 70,470; 72,000
1–45. 700
1–47. $27,738
1–49. $240; $200; $1,200; $1,080
1–51. $2,436; $3,056; $620 more
1–53. 905,600
1–55. 1,080
1–57. a. $4,569
　　　 b. $4,200
　　　 c. $369
1–59. 15 euros
1–61. $1,872,000
1–63. $4,815; $250,380
1–65. $64,180
1–67. 200,000; 10,400,000
1–69. $1,486
1–71. Average $33; no concern
1–73. $40 per sq yard

1–75. $7,680 difference between drugstore and bakery
1–76. $12,000 difference

Summary Practice Test

1. 7,017,243
2. Nine million, six hundred twenty-two thousand, three hundred sixty-four
3. a. 70
　　b. 900
　　c. 8,000
　　d. 10,000
4. 17,000; 17,692
5. 8,100,000; 8,011,758
6. 829,412,000
7. 379 R19
8. 100
9. $95
10. $500; no
11. $1,000

Chapter 2

End-of-Chapter Problems

2–1. Proper
2–3. Improper
2–5. $61\frac{2}{5}$
2–7. $\frac{59}{3}$
2–9. $\frac{11}{13}$
2–11. 60 (2 × 2 × 3 × 5)
2–13. 96 (2 × 2 × 2 × 2 × 2 × 3)
2–15. $\frac{13}{21}$
2–17. $15\frac{5}{12}$
2–19. $\frac{5}{6}$
2–21. $7\frac{4}{9}$

2–23. $\frac{5}{16}$
2–25. $\frac{3}{25}$
2–27. $\frac{1}{3}$
2–29. $\frac{7}{18}$
2–31. $215,658
2–33. 4 million
2–35. $35\frac{1}{4}$ hours
2–37. $10\frac{3}{4}$ hours
2–39. $6\frac{1}{2}$ gallons
2–41. $875
2–43. $\frac{23}{36}$
2–45. 10 specialists
2–47. $3\frac{3}{4}$ lbs apple; $8\frac{1}{8}$ cups flour; $\frac{5}{8}$ cup marg.; $5\frac{15}{16}$ cups sugar; 5 teaspoons cin.
2–49. 400 people
2–51. 275 gloves
2–53. $450
2–55. $45\frac{3}{16}$
2–57. $62,500,000; $37,500,000
2–59. $\frac{3}{8}$
2–61. $2\frac{3}{5}$ hours
2–63. $8\frac{31}{48}$ feet; Yes
2–64. a. 400 homes　**b.** $320,000
　　c. 3,000 people　**d.** 2,500 people
　　e. $112.50　**f.** $8,800,000

Summary Practice Test

1. Mixed number
2. Proper
3. Improper
4. $18\frac{1}{9}$
5. $\frac{65}{8}$
6. $9; \frac{7}{10}$
7. 64
8. 24 (2 × 2 × 3 × 2 × 1 × 1 × 1)
9. $6\frac{17}{20}$
10. $\frac{1}{4}$
11. $6\frac{2}{21}$
12. $\frac{1}{14}$
13. $3\frac{5}{6}$ hours
14. 7,840 rolls
15. a. 60,000 veggie
    b. 30,000 regular
16. $39\frac{1}{2}$ hours
17. $26

Chapter 3

End-of-Chapter Problems

3–1. Hundredths
3–3. .7; .74; .739
3–5. 5.8; 5.83; 5.831
3–7. 6.6; 6.56; 6.556
3–9. $4,822.78
3–11. .08
3–13. .06
3–15. .91
3–17. 16.61
3–19. $\frac{71}{100}$
3–21. $\frac{125}{10,000}$
3–23. $\frac{825}{1,000}$
3–25. $\frac{7,065}{10,000}$
3–27. $28\frac{48}{100}$
3–29. .005
3–31. .0085
3–33. 818.1279
3–35. 3.4
3–37. 2.32
3–39. 1.2; 1.26791
3–41. 4; 4.0425
3–43. 24,526.67
3–45. 161.29

3–47. 6,824.15
3–49. .04
3–51. .63
3–53. 2.585
3–55. .0086
3–57. 486
3–59. 3.950
3–61. 7,913.2
3–63. .583
3–65. $19.57
3–67. $1.40
3–69. $119.47
3–71. $29.00
3–73. 128,982,699.866
3–75. $423.16
3–77. $105.08
3–79. $25,000.16
3–81. 9.8
3–83. $1.58; $3,713
3–85. $6,465.60
3–86. Yes, $16,200
3–87. $560.45

Summary Practice Test

1. 767.849
2. .7
3. .07
4. .007
5. $\frac{9}{10}$
6. $6\frac{97}{100}$
7. $\frac{685}{1,000}$
8. .29
9. .13
10. 4.57
11. .08
12. 390.2702
13. 9.2
14. 118.67
15. 34,684.01
16. 62,940
17. 832,224,982.1
18. $24.56
19. $936.30
20. $385.40
21. A. $.12; B $.15
22. $436.45
23. $3.45

Cumulative Review 1, 2, 3

1. $216
2. $200,000
3. $50,560,000
4. $25.50
5. $225,000
6. $750
7. $369.56
8. $130,000,000
9. $63.64

Chapter 4

End-of-Chapter Problems

4–1. $4,720.33
4–3. $4,705.33
4–5. $753
4–7. $540.82
4–9. $577.95
4–11. $998.86
4–13. $1,530
4–14. $1,862.13
4–15. $3,061.67

Summary Practice Test

1. End Bal. $15,649.12
2. $8,730
3. $1,282.70
4. $10,968.50

Chapter 5

End-of-Chapter Problems

5–1. $X = 230$
5–3. $Q = 300$
5–5. $Y = 15$
5–7. $Y = 12$
5–9. $P = 25$
5–11. Fred 25; Lee 35
5–13. Josh, 16; Jessica, 240
5–15. 50 shorts; 200 T-shirts
5–17. $B = 70$
5–19. $N = 63$
5–21. $Y = 7$
5–23. $P = 610.99
5–25. Pete = 90; Bill = 450
5–27. 48 boxes pens; 240 batteries
5–29. $A = 135$
5–31. $M = 60$
5–33. 211 Boston; 253 Colorado Springs
5–35. $W = 129$
5–37. Shift 1: 3,360; shift 2: 2,240
5–39. 22 boxes of hammers
      18 boxes of wrenches
5–41. 135,797 lenders
5–42. a. 2.5
      b. 15 miles
      c. 6 hours
5–43. $B = 4$

Summary Practice Test

1. $541.90
2. $84,000
3. Sears 70; Best Buy 560
4. Abby 200; Jill 1,000
5. 13 dishes; 78 pots
6. Pasta 300; 1,300 pizzas

Chapter 6

End-of-Chapter Problems

6–1. 96%
6–3. 40%

6–5. 356.1%
6–7. .04
6–9. .643
6–11. 1.19
6–13. 8.3%
6–15. 87.5%
6–17. $\dfrac{1}{25}$
6–19. $\dfrac{19}{60}$
6–21. $\dfrac{27}{400}$
6–23. 10.5
6–25. 102.5
6–27. 156.6
6–29. 114.88
6–31. 16.2
6–33. 141.67
6–35. 10,000
6–37. 17,777.78
6–39. 108.2%
6–41. 110%
6–43. 400%
6–45. 59.40
6–47. 1,100
6–49. 40%
6–51. +20%
6–53. 80%
6–55. $10,000
6–57. $640 per month
6–59. 677.78%
6–61. 6%
6–63. .2%
6–65. Yes, $15,480
6–67. 900
6–69. $742,500
6–71. $220,000
6–73. 33.3%
6–75. 61.1%
6–77. $39,063.83
6–79. $138.89
6–81. $1,900
6–83. $102.50
6–85. 3.7%
6–87. $2,571
6–89. $41,176
6–91. 40%
6–93. 585,000
6–94. a. 68%
   b. 125%
   c. $749,028
   d. $20
   e. 7 people
6–95. $55,429

Summary Practice Test
1. 92.1%
2. 40%
3. 1,588%
4. 800%
5. .42

6. .0798
7. 4.0
8. .0025
9. 16.7%
10. 33.3%
11. $\dfrac{31}{160}$
12. $\dfrac{31}{500}$
13. $540,000
14. $2,330,000
15. 75%
16. 2.67%
17. $382.61
18. $639
19. $150,000

Chapter 7

End-of-Chapter Problems
7–1. .9603; .0397; $31.72; $767.28
7–3. .893079; .106921; $28.76; $240.24
7–5. $369.70; $80.30
7–7. $1,392.59; $457.41
7–9. June 28; July 18
7–11. June 15; July 5
7–13. July 10; July 30
7–15. $138; $6,862
7–17. $2; $198
7–19. $408.16; $291.84
7–21. $59.80; $239.20
7–23. .648; .352; $54.56; $100.44
7–25. $576.06; $48.94
7–27. $5,100; $5,250
7–29. $5,850
7–31. $1,357.03
7–33. $8,173.20
7–35. $8,333.33; $11,666.67
7–37. $99.99
7–39. $489.90; $711.10
7–41. $4,658.97
7–43. $1,083.46; $116.54
7–45. $5,008.45
7–47. $781.80 paid
7–48. a. $1,500
   b. 8.34%
   c. $164.95
   d. $16,330.05
   e. $1,664.95
7–49. $4,794.99

Summary Practice Test
1. $332.50
2. $211.11
3. $819.89; $79.11
4. a. Nov. 14; Dec. 4
   b. March 20; April 9
   c. June 10; June 30
   d. Jan. 10; Jan. 30
5. $15; $285

6. $7,120
7. A: 20.9% B: 20.95%
8. $1,938.78; $6,061.22
9. $7,076.35

Chapter 8

End-of-Chapter Problems
8–1. $90; $690
8–3. $4,285.71
8–5. $6.90; 45.70%
8–7. $450; $550
8–9. $110.83
8–11. $34.20; 69.8%
8–13. 11%
8–15. $3,830.40; $1,169.60; 23.39%
8–17. 16,250; $4.00
8–19. $166.67
8–21. $14.29
8–23. $600; $262.50
8–25. $84
8–27. 42.86%
8–29. $3.56
8–31. 20,000
8–33. $44; 56%
8–35. $195
8–37. $.59
8–39. $2.31
8–41. 12,000
8–42. $266
8–43. $94.98; $20.36; loss

Summary Practice Test
1. $126
2. 30.26%
3. $482.76; $217.24
4. $79; 37.97%
5. $133.33
6. $292.50
7. 27.27%
8. $160
9. 25.9%
10. $1.15
11. 11,500

Cumulative Review 6, 7, 8
1. 650,000
2. $296.35
3. $133
4. $2,562.14
5. $48.75
6. $259.26
7. $1.96; $1.89

Chapter 9

End-of-Chapter Problems
9–1. 39; $310.05
9–3. $12.00; $452
9–5. $1,680
9–7. $60
9–9. $13,000
9–11. $4,500

9–13. $11,900; $6,900; $138; $388
9–15. $378.20; $101.50
9–17. $174.23; $99.20; $23.20; $1,303.37
9–19. $752.60; $85.20
9–21. $1,298.02
9–23. $2,635.56
9–25. $825
9–27. $1,089.72
9–29. $357; $42
9–31. $1,082.82
9–32. **a.** $280
   b. $196.91
   c. $36.47
9–33. $1,653.60, $193.13 understated; $52

Summary Practice Test
   1. 49; $428
   2. $794
   3. $24,700
   4. $465; $290
   5. $258.45
   6. $798 SUTA; $84 FUTA;
      no tax in quarter 2

Chapter 10

End-of-Chapter Problems
10–1. $497.25; $8,927.25
10–3. $1,012.50; $21,012.50
10–5. $28.23; $613.23
10–7. $20.38; $1,020.38
10–9. $73.78; $1,273.78
10–11. $1,904.76
10–13. $4,390.61 balance due
10–15. $618.75; $15,618.75
10–17. $2,377.70; Save $1.08
10–19. 4.7 years
10–21. $21,596.11
10–23. $714.87; $44.87
10–25. 266 days
10–27. $2,608.65
10–29. $18,666.85
10–31. 12.37%
10–33. 15 days
10–35. 5.6%
10–36. **a.** $1,000
   b. 8%
   c. $280; $1,400
10–37. $7.82; $275.33

Summary Practice Test
   1. $27.23; $2,038.11
   2. $86,400
   3. $14,901.25
   4. $14,888.90
   5. $32,516
   6. $191.09; $10,191.09

Chapter 11

End-of-Chapter Problems
11–1. $56.08; $4,193.92
11–3. 25 days

11–5. $51,451.39; 57; $733.18; $50,718.21
11–7. 4.04%
11–9. $7,566.67; 6.9%
11–11. $8,937
11–13. $5,309.80
11–15. $5,133.33; 56; $71.87; $5,061.46
11–17. $4,836.44
11–19. **a.** $90.13
   b. $177.50
   c. 3.64%
   d. 3.61%
11–20. $2,127.66; 9.57%

Summary Practice Test
   1. $160,000
   2. $302.22; $16,697.98; $17,000; 4.1%
   3. $61,132.87
   4. $71,264.84
   5. $57,462.50; 7.6%
   6. 5.58%

Chapter 12

End-of-Chapter Problems
12–1. 4; 2%; $1,353.04; $103.04
12–3. $15,450; $450
12–5. 12.55%
12–7. 16; $1\frac{1}{2}$%; .7880; $4,728
12–9. 28; 3%; .4371; $7,692.96
12–11. $17,600.72
12–13. $64,188
12–15. Mystic $4,775, Four Rivers $3,728
12–17. $25,734.40
12–19. $12,698
12–21. $3,636.92
12–23. $37,644
12–25. Yes, $17,908 (compounding)
      or $8,376 (p. v.)
12–27. $3,739.20
12–29. $19,727.25
12–31. $105,878.50
12–32. $689,125; $34,125 Bank B

Summary Practice Test
   1. $48,760
   2. $31,160
   3. $133,123.12
   4. No, $26,898 (compounding)
      or $22,308 (p. v.)
   5. 6.14%
   6. $46,137
   7. $187,470
   8. $28,916.10

Chapter 13

End-of-Chapter Problems
13–1. $51,587.55
13–3. $53,135.10
13–5. $3,118.59

13–7. End of first year $2,405.71
13–9. $1,410
13–11. $3,397.20
13–13. $137,286; $1,721,313
13–15. $38,841.30
13–17. $900,655
13–19. $8,160
13–21. $13,838.25
13–23. Annuity $12,219.11 or
      $12,219.93
13–25. $3,625.60
13–27. $111,013.29
13–29. $404,313.97
13–30. $199.29
13–31. $120,747.09

Summary Practice Test
   1. $100,952.82
   2. $33,914.88 or $33,913.57
   3. $108,722.40
   4. $2,120
   5. $2,054
   6. $264,915.20
   7. $83,304.59
   8. $237,501.36
   9. $473,811.99
   10. $713,776.37

Cumulative Review 10, 11, 12, 13
   1. Annuity $2,058.62 or $2,058.59
   2. $5,118.70
   3. $116,963.02
   4. $3,113.92
   5. $5,797.92
   6. $18,465.20
   7. $29,632.35
   8. $55,251

Chapter 14

End-of-Chapter Problems
14–1. Finance charge $7,180
14–3. Finance charge $1,279.76;
      12.75%–13%
14–5. $119.39; $119.37
14–7. $2,741; $41.12
14–9. $1,400
14–11. **a.** $4,050 **b.** $1,656 **c.** $5,756
   d. $40.89, falls between 14.25%
      and 14.50%
   e. $95.10
14–13. $1,245; $18.68; $1,318.68
14–15. $940.36
14–17. Peg is correct
14–18. 15.48%

Summary Practice Test
   1. $26,500; $4,100
   2. $52.66
   3. 4.25% to 4.5%
   4. $6,005.30
   5. $400; $8

Chapter 15

End-of-Chapter Problems

15–1. $651.30
15–3. $894.60
15–5. $118,796
15–7. $1,423.80; $179,326.20
15–9. $73,696
15–11. $636.16; $117,017.60
15–13. Payment 3, $119,857.38
15–15. $57,921.60
15–17. $87.50
15–18. $793.50
15–19. a. $92,495.50
    b. $1,690.15
    c. $415,954

Summary Practice Test

  1. $1,020; $850; $169,830
  2. $499.84; $91,942.40
  3. a. $434.97; $75,589.20
    b. $460.08; $84,628.80
    c. $486; $93,960
    d. $512.73; $103,582.80
  4. $5.71; $1,027.80
  5. $251,676

Chapter 16

End-of-Chapter Problems

16–1. Total assets $74,000
16–3. Inventory −16.67%; mortgage note +13.79%
16–5. Net sales 13.62%; Net earnings 2013 47.92%
16–7. Depreciation $100; + 16.67%
16–9. 1.43; 1.79
16–11. .20; .23
16–13. .06; .08
16–15. 13.57%
16–17. 87.74%; 34.43%; .13; 55.47%
16–19. 2016 68% sales
16–21. $9,447 net worth
16–22. $3,470; 6.8%; $431; .8%
16–23. 3.5; 2.3

Summary Practice Test

  1. a. $161,000
    b. $21,000
    c. $140,000
    d. $84,000
  2. Acc. rec. 15.15%; 24.67%
  3. Cash $11,000; 137.50%
  4. 2018; 74%
  5. Total assets $175,000
  6. a. .70 **b.** .50 **c.** 45 days
    d. 1.05 **e.** .25

Chapter 17

End-of-Chapter Problems

17–1. Book value (end of year) $29,600
17–3. Book value (end of year) $23,000
17–5. Book value (end of year) $16,400
17–7. Book value (end of year) $9,800
17–9. Book value (end of year) $15,000
17–11. Book value (end of year) $5,400
17–13. $2,240
17–15. $18,000
17–17. $22,560
17–19. $15,000
17–21. $6,000; $18,000
17–23. $6,760 below
17–25. $83,667
17–27. a. $87,750   **b.** $11.40
    c. $21,489   **d.** 4 years
17–28. $13,320; $1.11

Summary Practice Test

  1. Book value end of year 2: $10,800
  2. $1,713.60
  3. Acc. dep., $4,000; $8,000; $12,000; $16,000; $20,000
  4. $1,500
  5. $12,600

Chapter 18

End-of-Chapter Problems

18–1. $7,180; $22,635
18–3. $543; $932
18–5. $10
18–7. $36
18–9. $72
18–11. $140.80
18–13. $147.75; $345.60
18–15. $188.65; $304.70
18–17. 3.56; 3.25
18–19. .75; $67,500
18–21. $10,550; $24,645
18–23. $45,000
18–25. $55,120
18–27. $38,150
18–29. $13,499.50
18–30. $1,900

Summary Practice Test

  1. a. 31 **b.** $66.87; $93.30; $80.29
  2. $40,000
  3. 1.10
  4. $109,275
  5. $97,960

Chapter 19

End-of-Chapter Problems

19–1. $870
19–3. $83,018.87
19–5. $39,000
19–7. $.0233
19–9. 6.99%; $6.99; $69.90; 69.90
19–11. $4,462.50
19–13. $16,985.05
19–15. $112.92
19–17. $577,300
19–19. $6,940
19–21. $64,000
19–23. $8,176.35
19–25. $23,065 more in Minn.
19–26. $3,665
19–27. $979

Summary Practice Test

  1. $284.76; $14.24
  2. $4,710
  3. $146,000
  4. 5.1 mills
  5. $1,237.50
  6. $18,141.20

Chapter 20

End-of-Chapter Problems

20–1. $1,184
20–3. $138.75
20–5. $53,000
20–7. 21 years, 300 days
20–9. $518; $182
20–11. $16,500
20–13. $1,067
20–15. $208 vs $240
20–17. $801 No cash value
20–19. $118,750
20–21. $1,100
20–23. $373.67
20–25. $22,900; $10,700
20–27. $24,000; $16,300
20–29. $7,512.64; $1,942.00; $787.89
20–30. $176.00

Summary Practice Test

  1. $1,993.50; $28,530
  2. $2,616.60; $55,650; $115,500; 21 years 300 days
  3. $234,375; $450,000
  4. $990; $326.70
  5. $1,755
  6. Insurance company pays $31,600; Roger pays $10,000

Chapter 21

End-of-Chapter Problems

21–1. $22,320
21–3. 1.1%
21–5. 13
21–7. $41,983.20
21–9. 2015   preferred $8,000
    2016   0
    2017   preferred $127,000
         common $33,000
21–11. $2,280
21–13. $260; $2,725; 9.5%
21–15. $12.04; −$.06; 9.6%
21–17. Gain $6,606.48

21–19. 12; 2.4%
21–21. $4,843.75; $75
21–23. 4.5%
21–25. Stock 6.7%; bond 11.9%
21–27. Yes, $16.02
21–29. $443.80
21–30. a. 1,287 shares
    b. 2,574 shares
    c. 5,147 shares
    d. $26,381.76 for (a);
        $52,388.43 for (b);
        $103,756.44 for (c)
21–31. $1,014.33

Summary Practice Test
    1. $77,532
    2. 8; 1.3%
    3. $1.23
    4. $10,476
    5. 5.6%
    6. $160,000
    7. $14.52; $11,616

Chapter 22

End-of-Chapter Problems
22–1. 7.75
22–3. $77.23
22–5. 2.7
22–7. 31.5

22–9. 8
22–11. 142.9
22–13. $200–$299.99 卌
22–15. Traditional watch 183.6°
22–17.

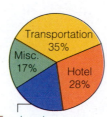

Golden retriever 11%
Yorkshire terrier 8%
Labrador retriever 39%
Beagle 17%
German shepherd 25%

22–19. Transportation 126°

Hotel 100.8°
Food 72°
Miscellaneous 61.2°

Transportation 35%
Misc. 17%
Hotel 28%
Food and entertainment 20%

22–21. 250

22–23. a. 57,000,000 mean
        62,900,000 median
    b. AAA = 30.42%
        Riser = 22.18%
        Casto = 22.07%
        Balbon = 12.70%
        Hunter = 12.63%
    c. 109.51°, 79.85°, 79.45°, 45.72°,
        45.47°
22–24. 24.94%; 15.42%; 10.88%; 13.15%;
    18.59%; 17.01%
    89.78°, 55.51°, 39.17°, 47.34°,
    66.92°, 61.24°

Optional Assignment
    1. 98
    3. 4.3
    5. 16%; 2.5%
    7. 68%; 81.5%; 2.5%; 2.5%; 47.5%
    9. 5.02

Summary Practice Test
    1. $143,300; $141,000
    2. 1,100
    3. 2.50
    4. 100; 卌; 4
    5. Bar 1 on horizontal axis goes up
        to 800 on vertical axis
    6. Profits 108°
        Cost of sales 144°
        Expense 108°
    7. 166.3%
    8. 3.0 standard deviation

Check Figures (Odds) to Additional Assignments by Learning Unit from Appendix A

LU 1–1

1. a. Seven thousand, eight hundred
    twenty-one
  d. Fifty-eight thousand, three
3. a. 80; 380; 860; 5,980; 210
  c. 21,000; 1,000; 4,000; 10,000
5. a. Hundreds place
  c. Ten thousands place
  e. Billions place
7. Five hundred sixty-five
9. $375,985
11. Two thousand, four

LU 1–2

1. a. 1,006
  c. 1,319
  d. 179
3. a. Estimated 50; 52
  c. Estimated 10; 9
5. $71,577
7. $19,973
9. 12,797 lbs
11. Estimated $9,400; $9,422
13. $746 discount

LU 1–3

1. a. Estimated 4,000; actual 2,400

  c. Estimated 15,000,000;
    actual 16,184,184
3. a. Estimated 1,000; actual 963 R5
  c. Estimated 20; actual 25 R8
5. 5,040
7. $78
9. 27
11. $43,200
13. 40 stacks and 23 "extra" bricks

LU 2–1

1. a. Proper
  b. Improper
  c. Improper
  d. Mixed number
  e. Improper
  f. Mixed number
3. a. $\frac{46}{5}$ **c.** $\frac{31}{7}$ **f.** $\frac{53}{3}$
5. a. 6; $\frac{6}{7}$ **b.** 15; $\frac{2}{5}$ **e.** 12; $\frac{8}{11}$
7. $\frac{13}{4}$
9. $\frac{17}{25}$
11. $\frac{60}{100}$

13. $\frac{7}{12}$

LU 2–2

1. a. 32 **b.** 180 **c.** 480 **d.** 252
3. a. $\frac{1}{3}$ **b.** $\frac{2}{3}$ **e.** $6\frac{1}{8}$ **h.** $56\frac{5}{6}$
5. $3\frac{1}{40}$ yards
7. $17\frac{5}{12}$ miles
9. $4\frac{8}{9}$ hours

LU 2–3

1. a. 1 **b.** $\frac{1}{4}$ **g.** 35 **i.** $1\frac{17}{18}$
3. a. $1\frac{1}{4}$ **b.** 3 **g.** 24 **l.** $\frac{4}{7}$
5. $39,000
7. 714
9. $20\frac{2}{3}$ miles
11. $412,000

LU 3–1

1. a. .62 **b.** .6 **c.** .953
  d. .401 **e.** .06

3. a. Hundredths place
   d. Thousandths place

5. a. $\dfrac{2}{5}$ **b.** $\dfrac{11}{25}$

   g. $\dfrac{5}{16}$ **l.** $9\dfrac{1}{25}$

7. .286

9. $\dfrac{566}{1,000}$

11. .333

13. .0020507

LU 3–2

1. a. 31.608 **b.** 5.2281 **d.** 3.7736
3. a. .3 **b.** .1 **c.** 1,480.0 **d.** .1
5. a. 6,870 **c.** .0272
   e. 34,700 **i.** 8,329.8
7. $4.53
9. $111.25
11. 15

LU 4–1

1. a. $430.64 **b.** 3 **c.** $867.51
3. a. Neuner Realty Co.
   b. Kevin Jones
   h. $2,756.80

LU 4–2

1. $1,435.42
3. Add $3,000; deduct $22.25
5. $2,989.92
7. $1,315.20

LU 5–1

1. a. $3N = 180$ **e.** $14 + \dfrac{N}{3} = 18$

   h. $2N + 3N + 8 = 68$

LU 5–2

1. $80
3. $45 telephone; $135 utility
5. 51 tickets—Sherry;
   408 tickets—Linda
7. 12 necklaces ($48);
   36 watches ($252)
9. $157.14

LU 6–1

1. a. 4% **b.** 72.9% **i.** 503.8% **l.** 80%
3. a. 70% **c.** 162.5%
   h. 50% **n.** 1.5%
5. a. $\dfrac{1}{4}$ **b.** .375 **c.** 50%

   d. .66$\overline{6}$ **n.** $1\dfrac{1}{8}$

7. 2.9%

9. $\dfrac{39}{100}$

11. $\dfrac{9}{10,000}$

LU 6–2

1. a. $20,000; 30%; $4,000
   c. $7.00; 12%; $.84
3. a. 33.3% **b.** 3% **c.** 27.5%
5. a. −1,584; −26.6%
   d. −20,000; −16.7%
7. $9,000
9. $3,196
11. 329.5%

LU 7–1

1. a. $40 **b.** $360 **c.** $50
   d. $100 **e.** $380
3. a. $75 **b.** $21.50; $40.75
5. a. .7125; .2875 **b.** .7225; .2775
7. $3.51
9. $81.25
11. $315
13. 45%

LU 7–2

1. a. February 18; March 10
   d. May 20; June 9
   e. October 10; October 30
3. a. .97; $1,358
   c. .98; $367.99
5. a. $16.79; $835.21
7. $16,170
9. a. $439.29 **b.** $491.21
11. $209.45
13. a. $765.31 **b.** $386.99

LU 8–1

1. a. $18.90 **b.** $2.72
   c. $4.35 **d.** $90 **e.** $116.31
3. a. $2; 80% **b.** $6.50; 52%
   c. $.28; 28.9%
5. a. $1.52 **b.** $225
   c. $372.92 **d.** $625
7. a. $199.60 **b.** $698.60
9. a. $258.52 **b.** $90.48
11. a. $212.50 **b.** $297.50
13. $8.17

LU 8–2

1. a. $10.00 **b.** $57.50
   c. $34.43 **d.** $27.33 **e.** $.15
3. a. $6.94 **b.** $882.35 **c.** $30
   d. $171.43 **e.** $0.36
5. a. 28.57% **b.** 33.33% **d.** 53.85%
7. $346.15
9. 39.39%
11. $2.29
13. 63.33%

LU 8–3

1. a. $80; $120
   b. $525; $1,574.98
3. a. $410 **b.** $18.65

5. a. $216; $324; $5.14
   b. $45; $63.90; $1.52
7. 17%
9. $21.15
11. $273.78
13. $.79

LU 8–4

1. a. $6.00 **b.** $11.11
3. a. 16,667 **b.** 7,500
5. 5,070
7. 22,222

LU 9–1

1. a. $427.50; 0; $427.50
   b. $360; $40.50; $400.50
3. a. $438.85 **b.** $615.13
5. a. $5,200 **b.** $3,960
   c. $3,740 **d.** $4,750
7. $723.00
9. $3,846.25
11. $2,032.48

LU 9–2

1. a. $500; $2,300
3. $0; $2,000
5. $314.23
7. $143.75
9. $595.97
11. $667.04

LU 10–1

1. a. $240 **b.** $1,080 **c.** $1,275
3. a. $131.25 **b.** $4.08 **c.** $98.51
5. a. $515.63 **b.** $6,015.63
7. a. $5,459.66
9. $659.36
11. $360

LU 10–2

1. a. $4,371.44 **b.** $4,545.45
   c. $3,433.33
3. a. 60; .17 **b.** 120; .33
   c. 270; .75 **d.** 145; .40
5. 5%
7. $250
9. $3,000
11. 119 days

LU 10–3

1. a. $2,568.75; $1,885.47; $920.04; $0
3. $4,267.59
5. $4,715.30; $115.30

LU 11–1

1. I; B; D; I; D; I; B; D
3. a. 2%
   c. 13%
5. $15,963.75

7. $848.75; $8,851.25
9. $14,300
11. $7,855

LU 11–2

1. a. $5,075.00
  b. $16,480.80
  c. $994.44
3. a. $14.76
  b. $223.25
  c. $3.49
5. $4,031.67
7. $8,262.74
9. $5,088.16
11. $721.45

LU 12–1

1. a. $573.25 year 2
  b. $3,115.57 year 4
3. a. $25,306; $5,306
  b. $16,084; $6,084
5. $7,430.50
7. $8,881.20
9. $2,129.40
11. $3,207.09; $207.09
13. $3,000; $3,469; $3,498

LU 12–2

1. a. .9804   **b.** .3936   **c.** .5513
3. a. $1,575.50; $924.50
  b. $2,547.02; $2,052.98
5. $14,509.50
7. $13,356.98
9. $16,826.40
11. $652.32
13. $18,014.22

LU 13–1

1. a. $1,000; $2,080; $3,246.40
3. a. $6,888.60   **b.** $6,273.36
5. $325,525
7. $13,412
9. $30,200.85
11. $33,650.94

LU 13–2

1. a. $2,638.65   **b.** $6,375.24; $7,217.10
3. $2,715.54
5. $24,251.85
7. $47,608
9. $456,425
11. Accept Jason $265,010

LU 13–3

1. a. $4,087.50   **b.** $21,607
  c. $1,395   **d.** $201.45
  e. $842.24
3. $16,200
5. $24,030

7. $16,345
9. $8,742

LU 14–1

1. a. $1,200; $192
  b. $9,000; $1,200
3. a. 14.75%   **b.** 10%
  c. 11.25%
5. a. $3,528   **b.** $696
  c. $4,616
7. a. $22,500   **b.** $4,932
  c. $29,932
9. a. $20,576   **b.** 12.75%

LU 14–2

1. a. $465; $8,535
  b. $915.62; $4,709.38
3. a. $332.03   **b.** $584.83
  c. $384.28
5. Final payment $784.39
7. $51.34
9. $35
11. $922.48
13. 7.50% to 7.75%

LU 15–1

1. a. $1,096.50   **b.** $965.60;
  $4,090.50; $3,859.65
3. a. $117.25, 7.7%
  b. $174, 5.7%
5. $774
7. $2,584.71; $2,518.63
9. a. $66.08   **b.** $131,293.80
11. $773,560

LU 15–2

1. a. $1,371.90; $1,133.33; $238.57
3. #4 balance outstanding $195,183.05
5. $587,612.80
7. $327.12; $251,581.60
9. $44,271.43
11. $61,800

LU 16–1

1. Total assets $224,725
3. Merch. inventory 13.90%; 15.12%

LU 16–2

1. Net income $57,765
3. Purchases 73.59%; 71.43%

LU 16–3

1. Sales 2017, 93.5%; 2016, 93.2%
3. .22
5. 59.29%
7. .83
9. COGS 119.33%; 111.76%;
  105.04%

11. .90
13. 5.51%
15. 11.01%

LU 17–1

1. a. 4%   **b.** 25%   **c.** 10%
  d. 20%
3. a. $2,033; $4,667
  b. $1,850; $9,750
5. $8,625 depreciation per year
7. $2,800 depreciation per year
9. $95
11. a. $12,000   **b.** $6,000
  c. $18,000   **d.** $45,000

LU 17–2

1. a. $.300   **b.** $.192   **c.** $.176
3. a. $.300, $2,600
  b. $.192, $300,824
5. $5,300 book value end of year 5
7. a. $.155   **b.** $20,001.61

LU 17–3

1. a. 8%   **b.** 20%   **c.** 25%
3. a. $4,467; $2,233
  b. $3,867; $7,733
5. $121, year 6
7. a. 28.57%   **b.** $248   **c.** $619
9. a. 16.67%   **b.** $2,500
  c. $10,814   **d.** $2,907

LU 17–4

1. a. 33%; $825; $1,675
3. Depreciation year 8, $346
5. $125
7. a. $15,000   **b.** $39,000
  c. $21,600   **d.** 2001
9. $68,440

LU 18–1

1. a. $5,120; $3,020
  b. $323,246; $273,546
3. $35,903; $165,262
5. $10,510.20; $16,345
7. $37.62; $639.54
9. $628.40
11. $3,069; $952; $2,117

LU 18–2

1. a. $85,700; $143,500; .597;
  $64,500; $38,507
3. $85,000
5. $342,000; $242,500; 5.85; 6.29
7. $60,000; $100,000; $40,000
9. $70,150
11. $5,970
13. 3.24; 3.05
15. $32,340; $35,280; $49,980;
  $29,400

LU 19–1

1. **a.** $26.80; $562.80
   b. $718.80; $12,698.80
3. **a.** $20.75; $43.89; $463.64
5. Total is **(a)** $1,023; **(b)** $58.55
7. $5.23; $115.23
9. $2,623.93
11. $26.20
13. $685.50

LU 19–2

1. **a.** $68,250   **b.** $775,450
3. **a.** $7.45; $74.50; 74.50
5. $9.10
7. $8,368.94
9. $42,112
11. $32,547.50

LU 20–1

1. **a.** $9.27; 25; $231.75
3. **a.** $93.00; $387.50; $535.00; $916.50
5. $1,242.90
7. $14,265
9. $47.50 more
11. $68,750

LU 20–2

1. **a.** $488   **b.** $2,912
3. **a.** $68,000; $60,000
   b. $41,600; $45,000
5. $1,463
7. $117,187.50

9. $336,000
11. **a.** $131,250   **b.** $147,000

LU 20–3

1. **a.** $98; $160; $258
3. **a.** $312   **b.** $233   **c.** $181
   d. $59; $20
5. **a.** $647   **b.** $706
7. $601
9. $781
11. $10,000; $8,000
13. $60,000; $20,000
15. $19.50; $110.50

LU 21–1

1. **a.** $43.88   **f.** 49
3. $27.06
5. $1,358.52 gain
7. $18,825.15
9. $7.70

LU 21–2

1. **a.** IBM   **b.** $10\frac{1}{4}$ **c.** 2025

   d. $102.50   **e.** 102.375
3. **a.** $1,025
   b. $1,023.75
5. **a.** $3,075
   b. $307.50
7. **a.** $30 discount
   b. $16.25 premium
   c. $42.50 premium
9. **a.** $625   **b.** $375 discount
   c. $105   **d.** 16.8%

11. 7.8%; 7.2%
13. 8.98%

LU 21–3

1. $11.90
3. $15.20
5. +$.14
7. 7.6%
9. $1.45; $18.45
11. $.56; $14.66
13. $1,573.50
15. $123 loss
17. **a.** 2020; 2022
    b. 9.3% Comp USA; 6.9% GMA
    c. $1,023.75 Comp USA
       $1,016.25 GMA
    d. Both at premium
    e. $1,025 Comp USA; $1,028.75 GMA

LU 22–1

1. **a.** 20.4   **b.** 83.75   **c.** 10.07
3. **a.** 59.5   **b.** 50
5. **a.** 63.7; 62; 62
7. $1,500,388.50
9. $10.75
11. $9.98

LU 22–2

1. 18: ⅢⅠ 7
3. 25–30: ⅢⅠ 8
5. 7.2°
7. 145–154: ⅢⅠ 4
9. 98.4°; 9.9°; 70.5°; 169.2°; 11.9°

Classroom Notes

Classroom Notes

Classroom Notes

Classroom Notes

Classroom Notes

Classroom Notes

Metric System

John Sullivan: Angie, I drove into the gas station last night to fill the tank up. Did I get upset! The pumps were not in gallons but in liters. This country (U.S.) going to metric is sure making it confusing.

Angie Smith: Don't get upset. Let me first explain the key units of measure in metric, and then I'll show you a convenient table I keep in my purse to convert metric to U.S. (also called customary system), and U.S. to metric. Let's go on.

The metric system is really a decimal system in which each unit of measure is exactly 10 times as large as the previous unit. In a moment, we will see how this aids in conversions. First, look at the middle column (Units) of this to see the basic units of measure:

U.S.	Thousands	Hundreds	Tens	Units	Tenths	Hundredths	Thousandths
Metric	Kilo-	Hecto-	Deka-	Gram	Deci-	Centi-	Milli-
	1,000	100	10	Meter	.1	.01	.001
				Liter			
				1			

- Weight: Gram (think of it as $\frac{1}{30}$ of an ounce).
- Length: Meter (think of it for now as a little more than a yard).
- Volume: Liter (a little more than a quart).

To aid you in looking at this, think of a decimeter, a centimeter, or a millimeter as being "shorter" (smaller) than a meter, whereas a dekameter, hectometer, and kilometer are "larger" than a meter. For example:

1 centimeter $= \frac{1}{100}$ of a meter; or 100 centimeters equals 1 meter.

1 millimeter $= \frac{1}{1,000}$ meter; or 1,000 millimeters equals 1 meter.

1 hectometer $= 100$ meters.

1 kilometer $= 1,000$ meters.

Remember we could have used the same setup for grams or liters. Note the summary here.

Length	Volume	Mass
1 meter:	1 liter:	1 gram:
= 10 decimeters	= 10 deciliters	= 10 decigrams
= 100 centimeters	= 100 centiliters	= 100 centigrams
= 1,000 millimeters	= 1,000 milliliters	= 1,000 milligrams
= .1 dekameter	= .1 dekaliter	= .1 dekagram
= .01 hectometer	= .01 hectoliter	= .01 hectogram
= .001 kilometer	= .001 kiloliter	= .001 kilogram

Practice these conversions and check solutions.

1	PRACTICE QUIZ

Convert the following:

1. 7.2 meters to centimeters
2. .89 meter to millimeters
3. 64 centimeters to meters
4. 350 grams to kilograms
5. 7.4 liters to centiliters
6. 2,500 milligrams to grams

✓ Solutions

1. 7.2 meters = 7.2 × 100 = 720 centimeters (remember, 1 meter = 100 centimeters)
2. .89 meter = .89 × 1,000 = 890 millimeters (remember, 1 meter = 1,000 millimeters)
3. 64 centimeters = 64/100 = .64 meters (remember, 1 meter = 100 centimeters)
4. 350 grams = $\dfrac{350}{1,000}$ = .35 kilogram (remember 1 kilogram = 1,000 grams)
5. 7.4 liters = 7.4 × 100 = 740 centiliters (remember, 1 liter = 100 centiliters)
6. 2,500 milligrams = $\dfrac{2,500}{1,000}$ = 2.5 grams (remember, 1 gram = 1,000 milligrams)

Angie: Look at the table of conversions and I'll show you how easy it is. Note how we can convert liters to gallons. Using the conversion from metric to U.S. (liters to gallons), we see that you multiply numbers of liters by .26, so for 37.95 liters we get 37.95 × .26 = 9.84 gallons.

Common conversion factors for U.S./metric					
A. To convert from U.S. to	**Metric**	**Multiply by**	**B. To convert from metric to**	**U.S.**	**Multiply by**
Length:			*Length:*		
Inches (in)	Meters (m)	.025	Meters (m)	Inches (in)	39.37
Feet (ft)	Meters (m)	.31	Meters (m)	Feet (ft)	3.28
Yards (yd)	Meters (m)	.91	Meters (m)	Yards (yd)	1.1
Miles	Kilometers (km)	1.6	Kilometers (km)	Miles	.62
Weight:			*Weight:*		
Ounces (oz)	Grams (g)	28	Grams (g)	Ounces (oz)	.035
Pounds (lb)	Grams (g)	454	Grams (g)	Pounds (lb)	.0022
Pounds (lb)	Kilograms (kg)	.45	Kilograms (kg)	Pounds (lb)	2.2
Volume or capacity:			*Volume or capacity:*		
Pints	Liters (L)	.47	Liters (L)	Pints	2.1
Quarts	Liters (L)	.95	Liters (L)	Quarts	1.06
Gallons (gal)	Liters (L)	3.8	Liters (L)	Gallons	.26

John: How would I convert 6 miles to kilometers?

Angie: Take the number of miles times 1.6; thus 6 miles × 1.6 = 9.6 kilometers.

John: If I weigh 120 pounds, what is my weight in kilograms?

Angie: 120 times .45 (use the conversion table) equals 54 kilograms.

John: OK. Last night, when I bought 16.6 liters of gas, I really bought 4.3 gallons (16.6 liters times .26).

2 **PRACTICE QUIZ**

Convert the following:

1. 10 meters to yards
2. 110 quarts to liters
3. 78 kilometers to miles
4. 52 yards to meters
5. 82 meters to inches
6. 292 miles to kilometers

✓ Solutions

1. 10 meters $\times$ 1.1 = 11   yards
2. 110 quarts $\times$ .95 = 104.5 liters
3. 78 kilometers $\times$ .62 = 48.36 miles
4. 52 yards $\times$ .91 = 47.32 meters
5. 82 meters $\times$ 39.37 = 3,228.34 inches
6. 292 miles $\times$ 1.6 = 467.20 kilometers

Appendix D: Problems

DRILL PROBLEMS

Convert:

1. 65 centimeters to meters

2. 7.85 meters to centimeters

3. 44 centiliters to liters

4. 1,500 grams to kilograms

5. 842 millimeters to meters

6. 9.4 kilograms to grams

7. .854 kilogram to grams

8. 5.9 meters to millimeters

9. 8.91 kilograms to grams

10. 2.3 meters to millimeters

Convert, rounding to the nearest tenth:

11. 50.9 kilograms to pounds

12. 8.9 pounds to grams

13. 395 kilometers to miles

14. 33 yards to meters

15. 13.9 pounds to grams

16. 594 miles to kilometers

17. 4.9 feet to meters

18. 9.9 feet to meters

19. 100 yards to meters

20. 40.9 kilograms to pounds

21. 895 miles to kilometers

22. 1,000 grams to pounds

23. 79.1 meters to yards

24. 12 liters to quarts

25. 2.92 meters to feet

26. 5 liters to gallons

27. 8.7 meters to feet

28. 8 gallons to liters

29. 1,600 grams to pounds

30. 310 meters to yards

WORD PROBLEM

31. A metric ton is 39.4 bushels of corn. The Russians bought 450,000 metric tons of U.S. corn, valued at $58 million, for delivery after September 30. Convert the number of bushels purchased from metric tons to bushels of corn.

Glossary/Index

Note: Page numbers followed by n indicate material found in footnotes.

CONNECT WITH SMARTBOOK® WORKS

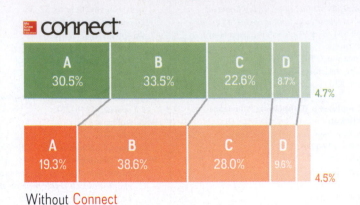

More C students earn B's

*Study: 690 students / 6 institutions

Without Connect

Over 20%
more students
pass the class
with Connect

*A&P Research Study

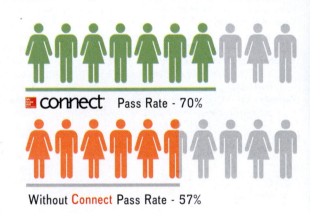

Connect Pass Rate - 70%

Without Connect Pass Rate - 57%

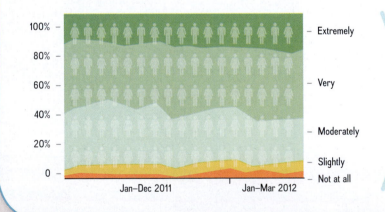

100% — Extremely

80%

60% — Very

40%

20% — Moderately

0 — Slightly
— Not at all

Jan–Dec 2011   Jan–Mar 2012

More than 60%
of all students agreed
Connect was a
very or extremely
helpful learning tool

*Based on 750,000 student survey response

> AVAILABLE ON-THE-G

http://bitly.com/TryConnect

> Shop and Sign In